THE CAMBRIDGE HISTORY OF SOUTH AFRICA

VOLUME 2

1885–1994

This book surveys South African history from the discovery of gold in the Witwatersrand in the late nineteenth century to the first democratic elections in 1994. Written by many of the leading historians of the country, it pulls together four decades of scholarship to present a detailed overview of South Africa during the twentieth century. It covers political, economic, social, and intellectual developments and their interconnections in a clear and objective manner. This book, the second of two volumes, represents an important reassessment of all the major historical events, developments, and records of South Africa and will be an important new tool for students and professors of African history worldwide, as well as the basis for further development and research.

Robert Ross received a Ph.D. from the University of Cambridge in 1974 and has worked since then at Leiden University, the Netherlands. He has written seven books, including *A Concise History of South Africa* and *Status and Respectability in the Cape Colony: A Tragedy of Manners*, both published by Cambridge University Press in 1999.

Anne Kelk Mager has worked at the University of Cape Town since receiving a Ph.D. in 1995. *Gender and the Making of a South African Bantustan: A Social History of the Ciskei, 1945–1959*, her first book, was published in 1999; her second book, *Beer, Sociability and Masculinity in South Africa*, was published in 2010.

Bill Nasson was educated at the Universities of Hull, York, and Cambridge. After spending many years at the University of Cape Town, he now works at the University of Stellenbosch. His most recent book is *The War for South Africa: The Anglo-Boer War, 1899–1902* (2010). He is an editor of the *International Encyclopaedia of the First World War*.

In Memory of Stan Trapido

THE CAMBRIDGE HISTORY OF

SOUTH AFRICA

VOLUME 2

1885–1994

Edited by

ROBERT ROSS

Leiden University, Netherlands

ANNE KELK MAGER

University of Cape Town, South Africa

BILL NASSON

University of Stellenbosch, South Africa

CAMBRIDGE
UNIVERSITY PRESS

CAMBRIDGE
UNIVERSITY PRESS

University Printing House, Cambridge CB2 8BS, United Kingdom

One Liberty Plaza, 20th Floor, New York, NY 10006, USA

477 Williamstown Road, Port Melbourne, VIC 3207, Australia

4843/24, 2nd Floor, Ansari Road, Daryaganj, Delhi - 110002, India

79 Anson Road, #06-04/06, Singapore 079906

Cambridge University Press is part of the University of Cambridge.

It furthers the University's mission by disseminating knowledge in the pursuit of
education, learning and research at the highest international levels of excellence.

www.cambridge.org
Information on this title: www.cambridge.org/9780521869836

First published 2011

A catalogue record for this publication is available from the British Library

Library of Congress Cataloging in Publication data
(Revised for Volume 2)
Main entry under title:
The Cambridge history of South Africa / edited by Carolyn
Hamilton, Bernard Mbenga, Robert Ross.
    p. cm.
Includes bibliographical references and index.
ISBN 978-0-521-51794-2 (hardback)
1. South Africa – History.   I. Hamilton, Carolyn.   II. Mbenga, Bernard.
III. Ross, Robert, 1949 July 26–   IV. Title: History of South Africa.
DT1787.C36   2009
968–dc22   2009028976

ISBN 978-0-521-86983-6 Hardback

CONTENTS

Contributors   *page* vii

Acknowledgments   ix

Note on References   xi

Introduction   1
ROBERT ROSS, ANNE KELK MAGER, AND BILL NASSON

1   South Africa and South Africans: Nationality, Belonging,
     Citizenship   17
     SAUL DUBOW

2   Imperialism, Settler Identities, and Colonial Capitalism: The
     Hundred-Year Origins of the 1899 South African War   66
     STANLEY TRAPIDO

3   Class, Culture, and Consciousness in South Africa,
     1880–1899   102
     SHULA MARKS

4   War and Union, 1899–1910   157
     SHULA MARKS

5   South Africa: The Union Years, 1910–1948 – Political and
     Economic Foundations   211
     BILL FREUND

6   South African Society and Culture, 1910–1948   254
     PHILIP BONNER

7   The Apartheid Project, 1948–1970   319
     DEBORAH POSEL

8   Popular Responses to Apartheid: 1948–c. 1975   369
     ANNE KELK MAGER AND MAANDA MULAUDZI

9 Resistance and Reform, 1973–1994   409
   TOM LODGE

10 The Evolution of the South African Population in the
   Twentieth Century   492
   CHARLES SIMKINS

11 The Economy and Poverty in the Twentieth Century   518
   NICOLI NATTRASS AND JEREMY SEEKINGS

12 Modernity, Culture, and Nation   573
   TLHALO RADITLHALO

13 Environment, Heritage, Resistance, and Health: Newer
   Historiographical Directions   600
   ALBERT GRUNDLINGH, CHRISTOPHER SAUNDERS, SANDRA
   SWART AND HOWARD PHILLIPS

   Statistical Appendix   625
   Bibliography   651
   Index   697

CONTRIBUTORS

PHILIP BONNER
Department of History
University of the Witwatersrand
Johannesburg, South Africa

SAUL DUBOW
Department of History
University of Sussex
Falmer, Brighton, UK

BILL FREUND
University of KwaZulu-Natal
Durban, South Africa

ALBERT GRUNDLINGH
Department of History
University of Stellenbosch
Stellenbosch, South Africa

TOM LODGE
Department of Politics and Public
    Administration
University of Limerick
Limerick, Ireland

ANNE KELK MAGER
Department of Historical Studies
University of Cape Town
Rondebosch, South Africa

SHULA MARKS
Department of History
School of Oriental and African
    Studies
London, England, UK

MAANDA MULAUDZI
Department of Historical Studies
University of Cape Town
Rondebosch, South Africa

BILL NASSON
Department of History
University of Stellenbosch
Stellenbosch, South Africa

NICOLI NATTRASS
Department of Economics
University of Cape Town
Rondebosch, South Africa

HOWARD PHILLIPS
Department of Historical Studies
University of Cape Town
Rondebosch, South Africa

DEBORAH POSEL
Department of Sociology
University of Cape Town
Rondebosch, South Africa

TLHALO RADITLHALO
Department of Language and
 Literature
University of South Africa
Pretoria, South Africa

ROBERT ROSS
Talen en Culturen van Afrika
Leiden, Netherlands

CHRISTOPHER SAUNDERS
Department of History
University of Cape Town
Rondebosch, South Africa

JEREMY SEEKINGS
Department of Sociology
University of Cape Town
Rondebosch, South Africa

CHARLES SIMKINS
School of Economics and Business
 Science
University of the Witwatersrand
Johannesburg, South Africa

SANDRA SWART
Department of History
University of Stellenbosch
Stellenbosch, South Africa

STANLEY TRAPIDO (1933–2008)

ACKNOWLEDGMENTS

The second chapter of this book was written by Stanley Trapido as the last work of his academic life. We would therefore like to dedicate this volume to his memory and to thank Ian Phimister for recovering Stan's work from his computer and turning the many drafts into the chapter that is included here.

In addition to the support of our own institutions and Cambridge University Press, we specifically thank the National Research Foundation of South Africa for the funding of a workshop in Cape Town, at which drafts of some of these chapters were discussed. The comments of the various contributors to the two volumes, at this workshop and on other occasions, also, we hope, strengthened the work, and for this we are very grateful.

NOTE ON REFERENCES

In principle, authors have restricted the footnote references in their articles to those works from which they cite directly. The Bibliography thus contains not only those works but also a select list of the other books and articles on which the chapters are based. These can be considered an initial introduction to the relevant literature on the subject.

INTRODUCTION

ROBERT ROSS, ANNE KELK MAGER, AND BILL NASSON

Going back more than a century, it is the tradition of Cambridge Histories to provide synthetic and authoritative surveys of the history of various parts of the world. Their primary concern is to produce broad essays that cover a given field of history at any given point and that serve as a starting point for those who need to gain access to the established historical scholarship on a given country or field of inquiry. This volume in the history of South Africa seeks to maintain this approach. It represents a culmination of several decades of scholarship on the history of South Africa in the twentieth century, above all, that produced by so-called radical or revisionist historians and their successors since about 1970. In this period, South Africa and its past turned from being an international historiographical backwater into what was, at least temporarily, one of the most dynamic and innovative fields of African historical scholarship. That said, producing a synthesis of the present kind has offered particular scholarly challenges. In this introduction, we try to examine what those challenges represent and how this volume attempts to meet them, if not necessarily to resolve them.

As the second volume of this Cambridge series, we begin at the moment when the colonial conquest of South Africa was more or less completed and when the discovery of immense supplies of gold on the Witwatersrand in what was then the South African Republic, or Transvaal, lifted the agrarian economy of the region into a new industrial phase. Both events had enormous ramifications throughout the region that was to become the Union and later Republic of South Africa and neighbouring countries. We end in 1994, with the transition to majority rule democracy, after which the rules of political and social life changed dramatically.[1] The mid-1990s was also, largely coincidentally, the moment just before the devastating

---

[1] The final chapter of this volume does survey the historical scene post-1994 but only peripherally discusses broader political, social and economic developments.

HIV/AIDS epidemic began to have a huge impact on mortality in South Africa.[2]

It goes almost without saying that this has in no way amounted to a simple or uniform history. South Africa has been cursed throughout its existence as a unit with an enormous level of internal diversity. Famously, or notoriously, it has a level of income inequality that today is rivalled only by that of Brazil. Its inhabitants speak eleven official languages and a number of others not recognised as such by the post-1994 constitution. For a long time, its own government refused to recognise its unity and to deny the vast majority of the population any claim on common citizenship within their own country. Politically, economically and socially, South Africa remains a country united in and by its exceptional diversity.

That heterogeneity has been reflected in the history that has been written about South Africa. What this volume attempts to do is to recognise and to reflect the immense variety of, and the contradictions inherent in, South African society. To be authoritative, as any Cambridge History should be, we have to be catholic in our approaches. Within certain limits, South African history should be inclusive – both in its range of subjects and in its treatment of them – in a way in which most of its proponents have had difficulty in doing. For the country's political divisions were, and have largely remained, reflected in the divisions in its historical profession. In being mindful of this, we are consciously setting ourselves against various historical approaches that propound 'master narratives' for the South African past and, implicitly, for its future.

Over the years, like prison sentences, a number of these narratives have run successively or concurrently through South African history. Each, in its own way, has reflected the political stance of those who have developed it and has naturally also been influenced by the sociology of the historical profession. In this respect, it is hardly surprising that the initial thrusts of South African historiography were defined in the context of white politics. In the first instance, therefore, the country's history since the 1880s was written in terms of the development of its constitution and on the place of South Africa as a new dominion in the British Empire. Matters such as the unification of the country and the terms of the franchise and the law were of consuming interest. It is by no means incidental that the previous *Cambridge History of South Africa* appeared as volume 8 of the *Cambridge History of the British Empire*.[3] This was, after all, the high point of the

---

[2] John Iliffe, *The African AIDS epidemic: a history* (Oxford: James Currey; Athens: Ohio University Press; Cape Town: Double Storey, 2006).

[3] Eric Walker (ed.), *Cambridge history of the British empire*, vol. 8, *South Africa, Rhodesia and the protectorates* (Cambridge: Cambridge University Press, 1936).

liberal imperialist vision of South African history. It was a line of enquiry that probably reached its final moment with the early work of Leonard Thompson, although there have been a few attempts since then to incorporate South Africa into projects driven in the first instance by a concern for imperial history.[4]

The reaction to a historiographically dominant liberal imperialism came from two sides. One was, of course, Afrikaner nationalist historiography. Both in Stellenbosch in the Western Cape and in the Transvaal, particularly at the influential University of Pretoria, this came to be the presiding vision of the increasingly assertive Afrikaans-medium universities. Emerging Afrikaner nationalist historiography was particularly concerned with preindustrial matters, with the Cape colonial origins of an Afrikaner *volk*, with the Great Trek, and with the history of the Afrikaner republics. At the same time, it also had a close relationship with later Afrikaner politics and chronicled many of its organisational changes and adaptations, as could be seen, for instance, in the production of successive biographies of party leaders. The context of such nationalist writing was, it should be noted, at least as cosmopolitan as the country's Anglophone histories. But here the connections were to Germany and the Netherlands, rather than to Britain, and those were to atrophy (though never to disappear entirely) in the hardening years of apartheid.

The second development out of empire constitutionalism was a more full-blown English liberal historiography, concerned much less with the development of political institutions than with the historical potential for the establishment of a common and all-inclusive society in South Africa. This vision was first enunciated in the 1930s, by W. M. Macmillan, H. M. Robertson and C. W. de Kiewiet most notably,[5] primarily in opposition to segregationist ideas. These scholars began to bring issues such as the development of migrant labour and the growth of poverty into the orbit of historical enquiry, and to contrast economic integration with social and political segregation. As a consistent indictment of what it saw as the political and social injustice and economic irrationality of segregation and apartheid, in a general sense, liberal historical writing may

---

[4] Examples include John Darwin, *The empire project: the rise and fall of the British world system, 1830–1970* (Cambridge: Cambridge University Press, 2009); James Belich, *Replenishing the earth: the settler revolution and the rise of the Anglo-world, 1783–1939* (Oxford: Oxford University Press, 2009).

[5] Notably W. M. Macmillan, *Complex South Africa: an economic footnote to history* (London: Faber and Faber, 1930); H. M. Robertson, '150 years of economic contact between black and white', *South African Journal of Economics* 2 (1934), 381–425; 3 (1935), 3–25; C. W. de Kiewiet, *A history of South Africa: social and economic* (Oxford: Oxford University Press, 1941).

be seen as something of a manifesto for a multiracial capitalist society built on individual rights. Major representative studies of liberal history in general, whether coauthored, such as the *Oxford History of South Africa*, or in the work of individual writers, such as Leonard Thompson's *History of South Africa*, all argue for the ideal of an integrated, market-order South Africa.[6]

Equally, in attempting to come to terms with the social consequences of landlessness, industrialisation and urbanisation, liberal scholarship pressed more than one perspective. Whereas in the interpretations of some earlier semihistorical writers such as Hobart Houghton in his 1964 *The South African Economy*, a liberal free market was the implicit future solvent of South Africa's historical tragedy,[7] later historically influenced work on social inequality and poverty associated with bodies such as the Study Project on Christianity in an Apartheid Society (SPROCAS) and the Southern Africa Labour and Development Research Unit (SALDRU), identified with a more interventionist, social-democratic outlook on the country. Naturally, however soft or hard its centre, liberal writings remained an essentially oppositional historiography except for brief periods, even though it became dominant intellectually, at least in the English-medium university world.

That intellectual predominance in fact, remained the case through much of the apartheid period, at least until the outbreak of the most vehement of the debates in South African historiography – that known as the clash between the liberals and the radicals, or Marxists, from the later 1960s onward. This was an argument over historical analysis in which there were very significant differences between the various participants, both on the structure of South African history and society and on their political consequences. Yet what is remarkable, at least in retrospect, was the level of common ground between the opposing scholarly camps in this debate. Thus, both liberals and radicals accepted that the main historical process of the country was its economic integration and that over the previous century this had largely been completed. In other words, for both doctrinaire Marxists and doctrinaire liberals, in opposing and attempting to halt this integration, apartheid was a quixotic attempt to defy the trends of history. The real issue of contention, though, was whether capitalism profited from apartheid. On the one hand, there were those who argued vigorously that

---

[6] Monica Wilson and Leonard Thompson (eds.), *Oxford history of South Africa*, 2 vols. (Oxford: Oxford University Press, 1968, 1971); Leonard Thompson, *A history of South Africa* (New Haven, CT: Yale University Press, 1990).

[7] D. Hobart Houghton, *The South African economy*, 4th ed. (London: Oxford University Press, 1976).

apartheid was hindering the full development of capitalism and retarding economic growth, and consequently that the ending of apartheid would remove the brakes on what they saw as healthy competition in a colour-blind market. On the other hand, there were those, overwhelmingly Marxists, for whom apartheid was supporting South Africa's particular version of capitalism, and that conversely capitalism was benefiting from apartheid, so that the collapse of apartheid would in turn bring on the development of some form of socialist society.

Earlier, a more popular kind of radical historiography had already begun to emerge in the 1950s in the context of a rapidly changing political landscape. Beginning with the African National Congress–led Defiance Campaign in 1952, opposition to apartheid intensified as the Communist Party drew closer to the newly invigorated and radicalised ANC and trade union activity became more militant. A handful of activist intellectuals, following Eddie Roux's 1948 *Time Longer Than Rope*,[8] provided interpretations of South African history that drew on fundamental Marxist notions of class exploitation and oppression and offered a view of history as a progression away from capitalism toward a more egalitarian society. Almost two decades later, Mary Benson's history of African nationalism in South Africa, *The African Patriots*, written and published from political exile, contributed another chapter to the story of national history as that of a struggle against oppression.[9]

From the late 1970s, then virtually twenty years after the banning of the major African political organisations and the exodus of most of their leaders, institutional histories and activist biographies, located in, and contributing to, an ascending mood of resistance to apartheid, expanded the genre of struggle history. Benson's biography of ANC leader Nelson Mandela, Francis Meli's history of the ANC, and even Ken Luckhardt and Brenda Wall's commissioned 1980 book on the South African Congress of Trade Unions provided important, if circumscribed, accounts of the main liberation movement.[10] Alongside such works, Baruch Hirson's writings offered a critical, but no less partisan, account of the formal struggle against apartheid. Also to the left were the histories of segregation and the

---

[8] Edward Roux, *Time longer than rope: a history of the black man's struggle for freedom in South Africa* (London: Gollancz, 1948).

[9] Mary Benson, *The African patriots, the story of the African National Congress of South Africa* (London: Faber and Faber, 1963).

[10] Mary Benson, *Nelson Mandela* (London: Panaf, 1980); Francis Meli, *South Africa belongs to us: a history of the ANC* (London: James Currey, 1989); Ken Luckhardt and Brenda Wall, *Organize or starve! The history of the South African Congress of Trade Unions* (London: Lawrence and Wishart, 1980).

colour bar crafted by intellectuals linked to the Unity Movement and its noncollaborationist political tradition.[11]

As embedded accounts, these histories were selective, often partisan and stilted and, to various degrees, ideologically driven. Most were profoundly limited, even homogenised, by the secretive, caucus-based politics of the three-way alliance among the exiled ANC, the Communist Party and the South African Congress of Trade Unions and the political imperative to maintain a version of unity in the liberation movement.

Though officially proscribed, exile-based histories were bolstered from inside the country by a slew of university Marxist postgraduate theses on aspects of trade union activity, women's organisation and local community political struggles, many of them doing the rounds as photocopied texts in the study groups that sprang up among activists, across the divides. Of possibly more lasting significance was the clutch of activist autobiographies, written by men and women who had been imprisoned, had taken up arms or who had fled the country. Also 'speaking from below', black (auto)biographical and fictional writers sought to challenge oppression, to provide political role models and to celebrate lives sacrificed in the service of liberation. Many of these authors avoided complexity and adopted instrumentalist notions of social engagement. Others, however, avoided submitting to political self-censorship. The autobiographical accounts of Emma Mashanini, Ellen Kuzwayo and Ann Marie Wolpe, for example, sought to demonstrate how the personal interfaced with the political, laying bare the turbulence and ambiguities of lives lived in the antiapartheid struggle.[12]

Unsurprisingly, Marxist political ways of knowing extended particularly to the labour movement where, from 1974, the *South African Labour Bulletin* provided a forum for thrashing out strategies and contributing to the notion of worker consciousness. Driven by powerful trade union leaders intent on forging a strategy most likely to lead to the victory of the working class, debate was often so heated and acrimonious that one journalist memorably likened the task of writing about trade union politics to scuba diving in a shark tank.[13] Although this public airing of views may have contributed to an uncompromising discussion of labour prospects for trade

---

[11] Notably *Yours for the union: class and community struggles in South Africa, 1930–1947* (London: Zed, 1989) and *A history of the left in South Africa: writings of Baruch Hirson* (London: Tauris, 2005).

[12] Ellen Kuzwayo, *Call me woman* (London: Women's Press, 1985); Emma Mashinini, *Strikes have followed me all my life: a South African autobiography* (New York: Routledge, 1991); Ann Marie Wolpe, *The long way home* (London: Virago, 1994).

[13] See Martin Plaut, 'Debates in a shark tank – the politics of South Africa's non-racial trade unions', *African Affairs* 91 (1992), 389–403n1.

unions, it did not encourage the first chronicler of the Congress of South African Trade Unions to adopt a more reflective approach to writing the institution's history. Nor, it seems, was the legacy of debate detachable from its acrimonious tone. The history of the rifts and controversies in the labour movement and their effect on South African politics remains a challenge for labour historians. Moreover, labour history itself undoubtedly needs to move beyond the confines of studying organised labour movements and to pay more attention to questions such as the development of the labour process, whether in mining, industry, agriculture, or in the service sector – for the historical experience of labour encompasses far more than its organisational or unionised form.

One perspective that separates Marxist approaches from earlier liberal histories is the understanding of power as racial and class oppression and their conscious engagement with the meaning of *nonracial* in the struggle to overthrow apartheid. Yet, being fragile and contested, the idea of nonracialism was far from static. Thus, the notion was germane to the Communist Party and to the ANC-aligned trade unions that insisted on organising workers across apartheid colour lines. Equally, it was unacceptable to those unions and political organisations that believed that black workers were primary and had special needs. Moreover, for the ANC, nonracialism was wielded strategically, less a principle and often little more than a rhetorical expression as the movement drew in activists from the Black Consciousness Movement at the same time as it held on to its Communist Party allies. Eventually, the postapartheid constitution and its preamble provided a symbolic moment of triumph for the ideal of nonracialism, an idea that surely contributed to the creation of a South African 'miracle' whose history remains still only partly written. In that respect, one part of that notion of peaceful and consensual transition from an oppressive apartheid era of human rights abuse and the confiscation of rightful ownership of, or access to, resources, has been documented through probing investigations by the Truth and Reconciliation Commission and the Land Claims Commission.

In a not-always-easy articulation with explicit Marxism was what has come to be known in South African historiography as radical history. Here, much of the important early debate took place outside of South Africa, particularly in the seminars organised in London by Shula Marks and around Stanley Trapido in Oxford. More broadly, both in the United Kingdom and among some of those South Africanists trained and working in the United States, the influence of work on tropical Africa was, for a rare moment, of considerable importance. There were also extensions from Britain (more so than from the United States) into such bodies as the History Workshop at the University of the Witwatersrand in Johannesburg. The intellectual connections between Europe and South Africa have always been closer than might be imagined, just as the space for intellectual debate in the country was never closed off, as in some fully totalitarian regime. Radical history has been, for the most part, synonymous with social history or certainly that form in which the politics has been left in. Like other varieties of left-wing South African historiography, it was shaped by the usual daunting analytical challenges posed by the character of South African society. The terrain that came to be traversed by radical writings was dominated by brooding themes, notably, the complicated intersections of racial and class structures and consciousness, the nature of South African political economy and the shape of its capitalist order, the role played by the dominated black majority in the shaping of that system and the intrusive and authoritarian inclinations of the state. As already noted, the explicitly Marxist materialist scholarship of the 1970s tended to focus more on theoretically chunky questions such as the role of capital and the state or the reproduction of cheap migrant labour, drawing explicitly on classically Marxian concepts and terminology, such as the hegemony of capitalism as a system of social relations between the dominant and the dominated.

By contrast, radical history as social history evolved as a distinctive and different kind of interpretative strand. Granted, these studies were generally written in a Marxist ambience of class formation, consciousness and conflict. Yet the analytical lens adopted by the new social histories came to be that of a more mildly *marxisant* or no more than a notionally materialist approach to understanding of circumstances of South Africa's urban and rural past. If it is treated as a roughly coherent body of work, three further features can be seen as distinguishing the culture of social history. Although many of those who crafted it were doing so as critically engaged and oppositional intellectuals, their writings may have been activist but were rarely partisan, in the sense of providing an intellectual gloss to the struggles of this or that component of the liberation struggle. Second, although the concerns of this brand of radical history certainly responded to, and were shaped by, the pull of influential social, economic and political developments, such as the labour struggles of the earlier 1970s, it preserved and sustained an independent momentum and range of its own. Therefore, it is certainly true enough that the fact that urban black townships were crackling into flame over rent, transport and other municipal grievances by the end of the 1970s inspired some scholars to investigate housing crises and squatter struggles in the 1940s. Yet it is equally true that, at the same time, other social historians were continuing to write away on poor white woodcutters or African football or Indian hawkers.

Radical social history therefore displayed a broad common agenda. If its historical topics ran from pass law struggles to the popular cinema, these were not competing but complementary interests. In this respect, one significant lasting contribution of social history to South African historiography has been to make it more like the historiographies of other societies, developed or otherwise, as they had come to be written. For the past social experience of South Africans has, in some ways, mirrored those of people elsewhere, in which work and leisure have been connected and have found an important place alongside politics in the formation of consciousness and identity.

A further important element to be considered is the way in which some social history approaches came to be influenced by a new generation of feminist scholars, whose subversive perspective criticised conventional South African histories of all types – nationalist, liberal, Marxist – for having been almost exclusively concerned with the doings of men, be they white or black.[14] In this view, by inserting the history of female experience, and giving it due weight, not only could underlying inequalities and tensions between the sexes be defined and explained, so also could the oppressive roots of male domination be exposed. Thus, masculine rhetoric about shared struggles for emancipation from racial oppression could be undercut powerfully by the competing blade of gender analysis. Although some work on the experience of labouring life in factories and on farms or on the growth of unionisation incorporated women, what feminist historians brought to this historiography was an analytical focus that argued that, though women as workers were one thing, women as women were another.

These social history approaches reflected a wide range of currents, from studies of struggling peasant communities that embodied a streak of cultural Africanism to urban 'workerist' analyses of shop-floor organisation and culture, but what held them all together was an underlying preoccupation with human agency as the lever with which to prise open history from below. Drawing on the radical historical revisionism associated with the British History Workshop at Ruskin College, Oxford, and inspired especially by what might best be termed the non-Marxist materialism of the eminent British social historian E. P. Thompson, human agency and its encounter with other oppressive social forces became the core analytical lubricant of these new ways of understanding. The investigative focus fell on the small change of everyday friction, conflict and accommodation among a dense patchwork of classes, groups and communities. For radical social history, this was the ground across which the peculiar pattern of class, culture and ideology in South Africa was being determined.

---

[14] The most important early texts were Belinda Bozzoli, 'Marxism, feminism and South African studies', *Journal of Southern African Studies* 9 (1982), 99, 131–72; Cherryl Walker, *Women and resistance in South Africa* (London: Onyx, 1982).

In this framework, scholars working from both documentary and oral sources set out to provide a depiction of the making of South Africa's disfigured world. Thus, the creation of household and community forms was shaped not only by the wants of industrial capitalists and urban planners but also by the needy exertions of working-class and other urban inhabitants. The long development of South Africa's system of labour migration could be understood properly if it were explored not simply as the manipulative imposition of capitalists but also as something to which rural migrants themselves had been contributing. Equally, the landscape of capitalism in large parts of the countryside had been created not through capitalising commercial farmers having had it all their own way, but through the modifying contributions of resisting labour tenants and sharecroppers.

Unpacking the meanings of consciousness in both urban and rural settings also became a key analytical theme, with scholars exploring their intricate connections with class, community and ethnicity to reveal the experiences and struggles of ordinary people in striving to make something for themselves in a world of oppressively structured reality. Here, numerous social historians, following the lead set in particular by Charles van Onselen in his essays on the early Witwatersrand,[15] analysed townships and other sites of community life as a web of classes, paying particular attention to the notion of class-based cultures, exhibited by a string of testimonies, oral biographies and recorded memories of past cultural pursuits. Cumulatively, this all suggested the construction of a robust and largely warmhearted notion of a social history of 'the people', but one in which straightforward national and racial expressions were likely to be superseded by competing identities resting on class and cultural sensibilities.

For quite some time in historical scholarship, it was the class rather than the cultural sensibilities that prevailed as a mode of explanation, and for several reasons. In part, the so-called cultural turn was slow to reach South African historiography.[16] Thus, the perspectives being fashioned by scholars whose background was in literary studies were barely acknowledged.[17]

---

[15] Charles van Onselen, *Studies in the social and economic history of the Witwatersrand, 1886–1914*, 2 vols. (Johannesburg: Ravan Press, 1982).

[16] The main exception to this was Patrick Harries, *Work, culture, and identity: migrant laborers in Mozambique and South Africa, c. 1860–1910* (Portsmouth, NH: Heinemann; London: James Currey; Johannesburg: Witwatersrand University Press, 1994).

[17] Isabel Hofmeyr, *'We spend our years as a tale that is told': oral historical narrative in a South African chiefdom* (Portsmouth NH: Heinemann; London: James Currey; Johannesburg: Witwatersrand University Press, 1993); Elizabeth Gunner, 'Power house, prison house: an oral genre and its use in Isaiah Shembe's Nazareth Baptist Church', *Journal of Southern African Studies* 14 (1987–1988), 204–27; Tim Couzens, *The new African: a study of the life and work of H. I. E. Dhlomo* (Johannesburg: Ravan Press, 1985).

Moreover, before the early 1990s, oppositional politics was still too heavily Marxist in orientation. To these could be added two more intellectual impediments. The shift of South Africanist anthropology away from what used to be its disciplinary core – kinship, political structures and, to a lesser extent, witchcraft – decreased the fertility of exchanges in the sphere of historical anthropology. Furthermore, for most of the historians in question, knowledge of South African languages other than English (and to a limited degree, Afrikaans) was either nonexistent or too meagre for the full import of cultural statements in, for instance, Sesotho or isiZulu, to be appreciated.

In that equation, radical history's explanatory categories of living experience through the local cleavages of social class, gender, generation, religion, ethnicity and the like could be seen by critics as sealing out both older Africanism as well as the narrower and more exclusive associational perspectives of newer Black Consciousness literature. Indeed, as some of the historians in that mould sought to reconcile their intellectual curiosities and progressive political inclinations through the cultivation of new public audiences and the popularisation of history, their critical approach toward a racialised South African history was perhaps edging them, almost imperceptibly, in an ironic direction. There lay the traditional narrative of liberalism, soft on capitalism but hard on racism and itching to usher in a common society bound by class rather than race.

Equally significant, politically inspired popular history did not end with the arrival of the new constitution. Although concern with the past has remained driven by the need to prefigure the future, a newer generation of popular writing is increasingly reframed as Africanist and is defined by a search for 'authentic' responses to the mounting disappointments of post-apartheid liberation – the failure of national leaders to deal with the HIV/AIDS epidemic, rampant crime, gender-based violence, the failure of social services and corrupt political and business leadership.

At the same time, the new ruling establishment was finding its most congenial or digestible forms of history writing both in simplistic Africanist writings and by sponsoring work on the history of the 'struggle'. The obvious danger in these stark works is that they present a contemporary history that turns on the dichotomies between those who were on the right side and those who were not. What is reflected thereby is at once an unnecessarily Manichaean view of recent South African history, and one that moreover ignores the manifold trends in South African society that were only tangentially connected to the political conflicts of the later years of apartheid.

This volume represents the expression of some four decades of scholarship on South Africa's history through the long twentieth century. That period of historical production was, as this introduction has already noted, one in which the history of South Africa became a vibrant and innovative field of international historical scholarship. Not coincidentally, the same decades saw a major transformation in the political dispensation of South Africa, and at least the halting beginnings of a transformation in its economic and social relationships. The long existence of white minority rule, summarised as the apartheid state, had always given a clear focus to South African political and intellectual life. History, then, was inevitably informed by politics, and to some extent was even a surrogate for it. To adapt Clausewitz's classic dictum on war, South African history has always been the continuation of politics by other means, and this has been reflected in the ways in which its debates have been conducted. Accordingly, the contributions to this book reflect in various ways an engagement with the politics of opposition to apartheid, and sometimes also the desire, akin to that of the pathologist, to understand it after its formal demise.

It is, however, no less important to stress that there was generally an obvious distance between the academic world, at least in the field of history, and that of politics. Something of the nature of that engagement is to be seen in the fact that all the contributors to the present volume (and most of those to its companion first volume) are South Africans, either by birth and/or by long residence. It is instructive to reflect on the fact that, were similar volumes to be attempted for almost any other country in Africa, this would not, mutatis mutandis, be the case.[18] This nationality is both an example of the country's proverbial exceptionalism in the continent, but it also brings with it the danger of insularity, against which we have attempted to guard. At the same time, for reasons that we hope this volume can explain, its South African scholars are disproportionately white. The entry of Africans into the historical profession has been, and continues to be, slow, as a result of both pre-1994 restrictions and of post-1994 market opportunities, with significant consequences for the way in which South African history has been written.

That said, there have been many strengths in the practice of South African history. The temporary ascendancy of a heavily structuralist Marxism had the beneficial effect, even if in reaction, of increasing the basic empiricism of the historiography – eventually forcing even Marxist theorists to confront the challenging results of archival and other research.[19] The riches of South Africa's oral history and of its archival record have been exploited both widely and imaginatively. Whatever their identity, historians have

---

[18] The guild of South African historians does include a number of Americans, a significant proportion of whom are black, but the latter fact has had little effect on their historical production.

[19] Postmodernists are slowly meeting the same fate.

generally felt the need to give prominence to African stories, and not, for instance, to accept that colonially created archives can have nothing of value to say about the reality of African life. The result has been a historiography that broadly has a very sharp appreciation of locality. Indeed, much of the best South African history over the past decades has been closely grounded in place and in time, focusing on specific struggles to acquire livelihoods, dignity or political rights. It would be invidious to mention specific examples here, but they are to be found in studies of all the provinces of the modern country.[20]

Equally, given the nature of this book, emphasis has to fall on what the broader patterns amounted to, more than on the local or discrete manifestations. The period covered, 1886–1994, forms a unit because of its white domination. This was based essentially on what has been called 'the uneasy union of "gold and maize"', or, at the very least, of a multitude of white factions linked in some ways to mining, industry and agriculture.[21] The mineral revolution was set off by the discovery, first of diamonds around Kimberley and then, crucially, of gold on the Witwatersrand. It spawned massive derivatives in terms of urbanisation, industrialisation and the creation of a physical infrastructure, of roads and railways and for the provision of the services that such an economy required.

This occurred in the context of settler control of the mass of South African land, in continuation of the colonial conquest of the nineteenth century, which indeed, was completed only after the opening of the diamond and gold mines. It also entailed the steadily increasing attempt at control over the black population, and indeed over potentially dissident whites. This was to be achieved through the potential and actual use of force and by the establishment of political relationships of mutual dependency between the state and African client groups. In turn, that required the imposition of a state-determined classification of the population, both to assign everyone to a controllable position in society and to maintain the political purchase of the state's African intermediaries. This taxonomic urge behind control went back to the period of segregation, before the Second World War and, indeed, further into the nineteenth century, and it would later reach its apogee under apartheid. However, the politics associated with this project failed to deliver the acquiescence of the great majority of the South African population. The result was an increasing recourse to coercion and to displays of outright force. It was in the end the cost and the failure of that assertion

---

[20] The bibliographies of the various chapters in this book include references to them.

[21] Stanley Trapido, 'Africa in a comparative study of industrialization', *Journal of Development Studies* 7:3 (1971), 309–20.

of control that led to the great political changes in South Africa during the last decade of the twentieth century.

Once the period under investigation is seen as a unit, as it must be, then the historical continuities at the level of the state between segregation and its predecessors on the one hand, and apartheid on the other hand, become most evident. For the politics and economics that lay behind those continuities permeated the whole of society. This, perhaps more than anything else, and expressed in many different ways, is what holds the history of South Africa in the twentieth century together and thus forms the spine of this book. It will be for future historians to investigate the continuities between the apartheid era and South Africa since 1994, which undoubtedly far exceed the 'legacies' of apartheid that are, as yet, the main subjects of exploration.

At the same time, such an uneasy cohabitation, and its constituent parts, had to be serviced. It was in that provisioning that the great majority of South Africans acquired their livelihoods, either directly or at one or two removes. In so doing, they continually moved around the country, following opportunities and escaping those places where there was nothing to be gained. As part of this search, they created new identities for themselves. These bore witness to extensive African initiatives in constrained circumstances, both politically and in a variety of other ways. Inevitably, a collision with the formal rules of society led to innumerable new sets of human meanings. In particular, religion, primarily the changing and highly diverse interpretations of Christianity, has provided spaces for dealing with the burdensome weight of white rule.

Here, account needs to be taken of the African women's prayer groups known as *manyanos*, the continuing power of the historic Western churches – Anglican, Methodist, Catholic and Dutch Reformed – and of the great movements of Isaiah Shembe's amaNazaretha or the Lekganyanes' Zion Christian Church. Along with the literally thousands of small churches, many with multiple congregations, set up by a host of prophets and itinerant charismatic preachers, these have dominated the lives of masses of South Africans to a degree that would be difficult to trace without a resort to culturalist understandings. Likewise, there have been multiple, and not easily depicted, responses to the differential treatment by the state of men and women. Because gender was one of the major elements of state classification, women have responded along tracks different from those of men. This sometimes created clashes, not just between women and the state but also with their own menfolk. Yet at the same time, what accompanied this was the positive creation both of African female identities and of remarkable degrees of female initiatives in a wide range of spheres.

A deeper investigation of these histories might well entail that the conceptual apparatus of South African history be substantially expanded. In general, for reasons that relate to the extreme inequality of South African society over the past century, historians and other social scientists have found most inspiration in those social theorists whose work has been primarily dominated by the investigation of social and economic stratification and its consequences. Marx has been the most obvious of these, but there is also a strong Weberian undercurrent in much South African sociology.[22] This means that some classic themes of Western sociology, notably the transition from gemeinschaft to gesellschaft, or from mechanical to organic solidarity, are scarcely represented in South African historiography, and thus in this book. It would be possible to write a social history of South Africa around such transitions, thus with major attention to shifts in local relations of authority, in kinship, in the sexual division of labour and so forth. How apposite the evolutionary schemes of Tönnies and Durkheim may be for South African society is of course a matter for debate, but it is significant that this debate has not happened.[23]

Finally, it is as well to reflect on the vexed question of South African exceptionalism. How does South Africa fit into the continent? In many ways, of course, South Africa has never been an exceptional place. It shares its deep linguistic and much of its social structures with, certainly, the regions immediately to its north and, arguably, with much of the rest of the continent. Granted, South African cultural expression is particular, but arguably no more so than that of any other African country. Moreover, South Africa was much less of an exception in the continent and in the world in 1920, say, than it was to have become in 1970. It was the accidents of geology and, to some extent, of the length and depth of its colonial history that had made it richer and far more industrially complex than the rest of the continent. In its ruling ethos, however, it was a colonial society like most others. The large point about South Africa is that as a colonial society

[22] Jeremy Seekings, 'The rise and fall of the Weberian analysis of class in South Africa between 1949 and the early 1970s', *Journal of Southern African Studies*, 35 (2009), 865–81.

[23] The works that come closest to developing such perspectives are indeed those in which questions of African female initiative come to the fore. See, e.g., Belinda Bozzoli, *Women of Phokeng: consciousness, life strategy, and migrancy in South Africa, 1900–1983* (Portsmouth NH: Heinemann; London: James Currey; Johannesburg: Witwatersrand University Press, 1991); Anne Kelk Mager, *Gender and the making of a South African Bantustan: a social history of the Ciskei, 1945–1959* (Portsmouth, NH: Heinemann; Oxford: James Currey; Cape Town: David Philip, 1999); Rebekah Lee, *African women and apartheid: migration and settlement in South Africa* (London: I. B. Tauris, 2009).

it lasted for much longer than elsewhere. As such, therefore, it is precisely in the continuities between colonial rule, segregation and apartheid, in that spinal relationship between the mining and the industrial economy, in the domination of land and the scale of state control, that South Africa came to differ. It is in these factors, and their equivalents, that South Africa came to diverge after the independence of most of the rest of the continent between 1957 and 1968.

After 1994, as the bases of that exceptionalism diminish steadily, there is a new set of stories that are currently unfolding. But in closing we must stress once again that it will be for other, later generations of historians to bring these alive and to explain them as being rooted in the past, and not just that of the twentieth century, but in one that may be much older.

SOUTH AFRICA AND SOUTH AFRICANS:
NATIONALITY, BELONGING, CITIZENSHIP

SAUL DUBOW

I

Over the past two decades, many South African historians, like their peers elsewhere in the world, have been absorbed in analysing problems associated with nationalism, race, and identity formation. Questions about the process of national imagining have transformed our understanding of nationalism and ethnic identity, especially in relation to Africans and Afrikaners. Yet the larger categories of 'South Africa' (as a nation-state) and 'South Africans' (its constitutive peoples) have largely been taken for granted or else addressed only in passing. Given the stress on nation building in contemporary South Africa, as well as growing sensitivity around issues of citizenship, race, belonging, and entitlement, there is a palpable need to explore such questions historically.

One of the few scholars to have addressed the problem directly in recent years observes that, '[i]n the political catechism of the New South Africa, the primary enquiry remains the National Question. What is the post-apartheid nation? Who belongs or is excluded, and on what basis?'[1] The problem has implications for the present, not least with respect to policies like black empowerment or hostile attitudes toward immigrants from elsewhere in Africa (the so-called *makwerekwere*). Although questions of inclusion in, and exclusion from, the South African nation or nation-state lie at the core of many of South African society's central debates, they have not always been expressed as such. This chapter therefore takes a step back from the existing emphasis on problems of collective identity to ask a deceptively simple prior set of questions: how was South Africa conceived

---

[1] Colin Bundy, 'New nation. New history? Constructing the past in post-apartheid South Africa', in Stolten (ed.), *History making and present day politics*, p. 73.

and imagined, how did ideas about South Africans and South African societies develop and change, and how has the South African 'problem' been defined over time?

Before becoming a political entity in 1910, South Africa was little more than a figurative expression. The term *South Africa* was current from as early as the 1830s, but until the beginning of the twentieth century, it referred principally to a region extending northward from the Cape Peninsula to the Zambezi. Only the constituent elements of the subcontinent – African territories and societies, British colonies and Boer republics – had any definite meaning, and even then the makeup and boundaries of those states and societies were vague. Indicative of this state of indeterminacy is the fact that G. M. Theal's single-volume book *South Africa*, published in the Story of the Nations series in 1894, had to be augmented by an explanatory subtitle: 'The Cape Colony, Natal, Orange Free State, South African Republic and All the Other Territories South of the Zambesi'.[2] Where the epithet *South Africa* was in use – as for example, to describe late-nineteenth-century political movements like the South African Native Congress, the South African League, or journals and newspapers like *De Zuid Afrikaan* – this was a question of aspiration, a claim on citizenship rights, or else an effort to promote forms of political or ethnic affiliation.

The decade of the 1870s proved a defining period with respect to the conceptualisation of South Africa. Within just ten years of the start of diamond mining at Kimberley, the Cape was granted responsible government; Lord Carnarvon's ambitious scheme of South African political confederation was floated; decisive wars of colonial conquest were conducted against the Pedi, Xhosa, Sotho, and Zulu kingdoms; and the imperial government first annexed and then lost control of the South African Republic. These tumultuous events acted to bring South Africa into focus as never before, within the region as well as without.

From a metropolitan British perspective, the subcontinent languished in relative oblivion until the 1870s. J. H. Davidson remarks that the term *South Africa* was so unfamiliar in England, and ignorance of the Cape so marked, that the *Illustrated London News* preferred to speak in the plural of the 'Cape colonies'.[3] The sudden interest displayed by British journals and newspapers in South Africa was therefore noted with bemused satisfaction by Cape colonial newspapers; it duly prompted them to conceive of the country in broader terms. Tellingly, a detailed index of the Cape Town English-language press lists only two entries under the subject 'South

---

[2] London: T. Fisher Unwin, 1894.
[3] Introduction by J. H. Davidson to new edition of Anthony Trollope's *South Africa* (Cape Town: Balkema, 1973), p. 1.

Africa' for 1871 as against more than forty for the year 1876. Yet the meaning of *South Africa* remained inchoate, and the term continued to be used in a manner akin to the contemporary phrase 'southern Africa'.

II

The mutual process of imagining South Africa in the last quarter of the nineteenth century may usefully be seen in terms of a developing imperial and colonial dialogue that saw outside observers engage in discussion with locally based commentators and intellectuals. A small group of travellers and visitors to South Africa during the 1870s, spurred by growing metropolitan curiosity toward a neglected part of the imperial chain, helped to initiate this dialogue and to frame the country's defining problems.[4] Of these, the most important were the celebrated English historian James Anthony Froude, who toured South Africa in 1874 and 1875, and the novelist and traveller Anthony Trollope, who visited in 1877. Both were important Victorian public moralists whose views helped to crystallise thinking on and about the country.

Froude arrived as the emissary of the Colonial Secretary, Carnarvon. Charged with assessing and preparing local opinion for confederation, Froude aroused suspicion, and his progress through the country was closely observed. A Tory radical and independent-minded student of Carlyle, Froude was an early proponent of the idea of a Greater Britain, which would soon coalesce into the 'new imperialism'. But unlike other exponents of this creed, Froude became greatly enamoured of the Dutch settlers, whom he likened to the vigorous and conservative-minded patriarchal Protestant 'peasant proprietary' of Tudor England. In his view, 'The Dutch alone are attached to the soil, and unless we change our ways the Dutch must be the ruling race there'.[5] Froude commended the firm native policies of the Boer republics and, conversely, deplored the inconsistency of the British. An intriguing but overlooked dimension of his writings is the manner in which his favourable opinion of ordinary Boers was absorbed into the gestating Afrikaner nationalist movement.[6] Froude's impolitic intervention

---

[4] Other treatments of South Africa by recent British visitors include Henry Rider Haggard, *Cetywayo and his white neighbours; or remarks on recent events in Zululand, Natal, and the Transvaal* (London: Trubner, 1882), and R. M. Ballantyne, *Settler and the savage; a tale of peace and war in South Africa* (London: Nisbet, 1877).

[5] J. A. Froude, 'Leaves from a South African journal', in *Short studies on great subjects* (London: Longmans, 1898), vol. 3, p. 505.

[6] Note the prominence with which Froude's views appear in S. J. du Toit's *Die geskiedenis van ons land in die taal van ons volk* (Cape Town: Smuts and Hofmeyr, 1877), chap. 17, 'What Froude said of the Boers'.

in complex colonial problems was counterproductive so far as promoting Carnarvon's confederation plans were concerned, but the debates that ensued served to clarify the competing political, strategic, and jurisdictional forces associated with the concept of a unitary South Africa dominion in the British empire, as well as to draw attention to the centrality of the 'native question'.

Another leading intellectual who helped to shape views on South Africa at this time was the writer Anthony Trollope, who arrived in Cape Town in 1877 and published his two-volume work *South Africa* a few months later. Trollope's book went through four editions in its first year of publication, and it soon became a standard work of reference for editorialists, parliamentarians, and polemicists. Local responses to Trollope's presence were initially tinged by apprehension, for the memory of Froude's visit was still keen in the public mind. But the book was graciously received in the main, not least because it could easily be considered a validation of colonial achievement. As a reviewer observed in *Cape Monthly Magazine*, 'It is only when active and energetic travellers come amongst us, and in a few weeks rattle gaily through the length and breadth of the land, and find their way up to Natal and the Transvaal, Free State and the Diamond-fields, that we wake up to the true magnitude and importance of our possessions.'[7]

Trollope's work was filled with memorable aphorisms and sharp insights. Like Froude, he emphasised the singular importance of the native question. Trollope was quick to appreciate the importance of the diamond fields for South Africa's future development. He considered that industrial work rhythms would do far more to 'civilise' Africans than any amount of missionary enterprise. His dislike of humanitarians and philanthropists was equalled only by his disapproval of those who insisted that Africans should be ruled by a 'rod of iron'. Famously, he proclaimed, 'South Africa is a country of black men, – and not of white men. It has been so; it is so; and it will continue to be so. In this respect it is altogether unlike Australia, unlike the Canadas, and unlike New Zealand.' The point of this observation was not to deny that 'the white man has to be master and the black man servant'; on the contrary, Trollope endorsed the idea of white supremacy – while cautioning that 'that ascendancy should not be too complete'.[8] He was in fact pointing to South Africa's exceptional colonial status and warning that, in contrast to other British colonies of settlement, the indigenous races of South Africa enjoyed overwhelming numerical superiority and were not likely to die out in the face of colonisation. For many nineteenth-century writers (though

---

[7] *Cape Monthly Magazine*, 16 (Jan. 1878), 'New Books', 61.
[8] Trollope, *South Africa*, pp. 39, 454–5, 456–7.

not necessarily for Trollope) this demographic – and eugenic – reality was one of the country's most distinctive and troubling features.

The discovery of South Africa by Froude and Trollope was paralleled by the initiatives of locally based intellectuals who likewise sought to make sense of the country, its history, and its peoples. In the field of history, important examples include G. M. Theal's *Compendium of South African History and Geography*,[9] John Noble's *South Africa: Past and Present*,[10] A. Wilmot and J. C. Chase's *History of the Cape Colony*,[11] A. Wilmot's *History of the Zulu War* (1880), S. J. du Toit's *Die Geskiedenis van ons Land in the Taal van ons Volk*, and F. R. Statham's *Blacks, Boers and British: A Three-Cornered Problem*.[12] This cluster of books, all published within a decade of one another, represent a definitive departure from the familiar genre of almanac-like compendia aimed principally at prospective immigrants, in which brief historical digests were mixed randomly with statistical information, geographical description, and economic and social data.

Considered as a body of literature, we see the emergence at this time of a distinctive and competing use of historical narrative and interpretation to define, survey, and explain the South African predicament. Noble and Theal, as well as Wilmot and Chase, attempt to narrate a continuous story starting with the period of first European settlement. S. J. du Toit, who began his account with Bartolomeu Dias and concluded with a vision of a United States of Africa, recounted a narrative of Afrikaner heroism and English duplicity. His history marked an important step in the construction of a providential view of Afrikaner history with events like the Great Trek and the Slagtersnek rebellion accorded the status of foundation myths. The interpretations and intentions of these texts may have differed significantly from one another, but in all cases, the history of discovery and the discovery of history were used to inscribe European settlers as a permanent fixture of the African continent. In this sense, their authors were all laying claims to a colonial or settler identity.

Theal's work is rightly viewed as a justification for and legitimation of settler colonialism, yet he was by no means ignorant of or uninterested in narrating the histories of indigenous South African peoples. Indeed, his ability to master, by means of narrative, the history of conquered as well as conquerors, made him all the more effective as an authoritative exponent of settler nationalism. But his preeminence as South Africa's first and most influential colonial historian should not occlude the work of other contemporaries who advanced different interpretations.

---

[9] Lovedale: Lovedale Institution Press, 1873. [10] London: Longmans, 1877.
[11] Cape Town: Juta, 1869. [12] London: Macmillan, 1881.

John Noble's *History*, wherein the story of European colonisation is narrated from the times of Portuguese and Dutch settlement, gave voice to the liberal constitutionalism and colonial nationalism of the Western Cape. His focus is therefore on achievements such as freedom of the press, the success of local anticonvict agitation, and the acquisition of responsible government. By contrast, Wilmot and Chase's *History of the Cape Colony* presents a decidedly pro-settler chronicle of complaint as seen from the viewpoint of Eastern Cape separatists. African agency is represented by Wilmot and Chase rather more fully than in Noble's account, but only for the purpose of documenting, in considerable detail, a story of continuous depredations and unprovoked aggression by Africans, abetted by the wilful deceptions of missionaries and philanthropists, and compounded by neglect and ignorance on the part of most Cape Town–based colonial governors. Wilmot's later works focus more fully on South Africa as a totality, its pro-imperial, loyalist, and anti-black rhetoric emerging ever more stridently.

Strongly opposed to this expression of settler triumphalism is the anti-imperial and procolonial viewpoint of the maverick British journalist F. R. Statham, editor of the *Natal Witness*, in 1877. Statham's horror at the annexation of the Transvaal was powerfully reinforced by his opposition to High Commissioner Bartle Frere's belligerence against the Zulu. He duly joined Bishop Colenso in supporting the Zulu cause. Statham's *Blacks, Boers and British* (whose title is noteworthy for the fact that it singles out Africans for first mention) is an eloquent polemic that berates the advent of jingo imperialism, personified by Frere, for sharpening conflict and inducing instability in South Africa. He urges his readers to place their faith in the 'Dutch' or the 'Africanders' – a loose-weave term embracing leading members of the Afrikaner Bond, Anglophone colonial liberals, and moderate republicans such as his friend F. W. Reitz. In Statham's view, the country could solve its 'three-cornered problem' only if colonists were afforded the space to resolve their own difficulties without external interference.[13]

Statham's crystallisation of the South African predicament bears comparison with High Commissioner Hercules Robinson's perceptive identification, in his parting speech of 1889, of the major competing influences in South Africa as 'Colonialism, [Boer] Republicanism, and Imperialism'. Robinson's sympathies with Irish home rule and his experience in Australia and New Zealand had helped to sensitise him to local opinion, and he came to identify with the colonial nationalist viewpoint in South Africa, namely with the primacy of colonial institutions and the Cape constitution. Having previously been a supporter of imperial intervention in Bechuanaland, he

---

[13] Statham, *Blacks, Boers and British*, p. 259.

predicted that imperialism was 'a diminishing quantity, there being now no permanent place in South Africa for Imperial control on a large scale'.[14] In this respect, Robinson was wrong, as the Jameson Raid was shortly to prove. But Cape colonial nationalism was indeed a vibrant tradition; it survived manipulation by Rhodes and, in the years following the South African War, reemerged in the form of white 'South Africanism'.

III

Although the variants of settler or colonial nationalist histories of the late nineteenth century foregrounded whites, the presence of blacks could not be ignored. The centrality of the native question with respect to national integration had been apparent since George Grey's efforts in the 1850s to promote colonial federation in South Africa. Carnarvon's confederation strategy in the 1870s hinged on a collective colonial solution to the linked problems of labour supply and collective white security. From midcentury, researches on vernacular language and grammar were conducted by missionaries and administrators such as J. W. Appleyard, J. E. Casalis, Henry Callaway, Theophilus Hahn, and F. W. Kolbe. In less than a half century following Moffat's translation of the New Testament in 1840, the entire Bible was available in the major languages of isiXhosa, Sesotho, Setswana, and isiZulu. Along with biblical translations, missionaries were engaged in the production of grammars, the codification of dialects, the collection of folklore, and the recording of local social customs. Such activities all formed part of the process by which evangelists laid claim to 'their people'. They were also, by extension, the means by which groups of people came to be constituted as discrete collectivities.

The basis on which this demarcation took place (a process that ultimately contributed to the emergence of modern 'tribal' or ethnic units) was significantly shaped by the assumptions that intellectuals, imbued with the spirit of European romantic nationalism, brought to their ethnographic labours. This was largely, though not entirely, a one-way process. Tiyo Soga, the first African to be ordained into an established Christian church, and whose literary achievements include translating Bunyan's *Pilgrim's Progress* into isiXhosa, was a notable but unusual example of a cultural broker equipped to mediate between the colonial and African intelligentsia in the 1850s and 1860s. Soga spoke of the 'destiny' of Africans in the context of South Africa at the time and articulated an incipient sense of a pan-African identity in ways that bear comparison with West African contemporaries like James

---

[14] Vindex (F. Verschoyle), *Cecil Rhodes: his political life and speeches, 1881–1900* (London: Bell, 1900), p. xxxi.

Africanus Horton and Edward Wilmot Blyden. Such sentiments were to have important resonances into the twentieth century.

Along with linguistic and ethnographic research, developments in the fields of geology and earth history were of great importance to the development of ideas about African peoples and to the way in which white settlers gradually positioned themselves as authorities on, and custodians of, the country. The nativist inclinations of South Africa's early white intellectuals also helped to provide the categories and empirical ammunition that subsequently helped to define the country's native question. The single most important contributor to the understanding and conceptualisation of South Africa's indigenous societies in the mid-nineteenth century was the German immigrant Wilhelm Bleek, whose pioneering research into African languages and mythology from the 1850s was motivated by a belief that the study of comparative grammars might disclose the origins and evolution of mankind. Bleek's groundbreaking *Comparative Grammar of South African Languages* provided a robust methodological basis for linguistic research in South Africa and established the first working classification of the country's indigenous peoples:[15] it was Bleek who coined the term *Bantu* to describe the Nguni-speaking linguistic community. In so doing, he introduced a core analytical term that has remained in use ever since.

Bleek also made a signal contribution to the establishment of the field that later became known as African studies – a form of enquiry that implied a clear distinction between knowledgeable citizens and their ethnographic subjects, though it did not preclude the possibility that subjects might in time themselves become citizens. Bleek's patron, Governor Sir George Grey, understood well that the ordering of knowledge was integral to the creation of colonial order. As well as being one of the most active proponents of the civilising mission in his day, Grey was a supporter of colonial intellectual institutions like the South African Library and Museum. His midcentury vision of a future, confederal South Africa, radiating out from an expanding Cape, conjoined growing knowledge of the country with an extension of colonial power and influence.

In this, as well as in his enthusiasm for confederation, Grey's ambitions were echoed by Frere. An accomplished linguist and geographer who prided himself on his robust evangelical liberalism as much as on his imperialism, the ambitious new high commissioner took an active role in encouraging the creation in 1877 of the South African Philosophical Society, assuming its presidency in 1878. Frere's choice of topic for his inaugural address to the prestigious new scientific body was 'The Native Races of South Africa'. It stands as an important and early example of applied ethnography.

[15] London: Trübner, 1862–1869.

Frere used the occasion to discuss the relationship of scientific ideas to imperial expansion. He drew on a fast-growing corpus of local ethnological and linguistic work and attempted a rudimentary classification of the 'yellow', 'black', and 'brown' races of South Africa, reminding his audience that such divisions had a 'social' (i.e., applied) as well as a scientific purpose. Echoing Trollope's concerns about black demographic predominance, and drawing on the ethnographic researches of Bleek and G. W. Stow, Frere's tone of scholarly indulgence toward the customs and beliefs of Bushmen and Hottentots (whose demise he regarded as inevitable) changed register when he moved on to deal with the 'indestructible' Bantu-speaking Africans. Their future, he hinted darkly, would have to be decided by 'legislative and other means'. Knowledge of these races and efforts to assess their capacity for 'improvement' raised practical issues of immediate concern. Not least, Africans should be 'subdued and converted to habits of useful labour and civilization' and thereby made into 'the subject races of an Imperial mistress, races strong to labour and capable of development into worthy integral sections of population in vast and growing empires'.[16] Citizenship, in other words, was not a right: it would have to be earned by individuals who could show that they were conforming to the norms and precepts of the Victorian moral economy.

Answers to key questions about African societies – who they were, how they should be governed, their ability to attain civilisation, whether they would diminish and die out in the face of colonialism, how they evolved, and so on – had practical implications as Frere, and Governor Grey before him, well understood. Yet knowledge of indigenous peoples was not generated merely to satisfy immediate instrumental needs by establishing the coordinates of social and physical control. Nor did such knowledge predetermine the nature of that control. Intellectual curiosity was stimulated as well by the impulse to achieve cognitive mastery over the subcontinent. Scientific and intellectual developments played an important part in the process of familiarisation, acquaintance, and control that British colonialism sought to achieve. Questions about the collective 'other' were thus simultaneously questions about the collective self; in particular, they referred to European understandings of their own place in history, their status in respect of other peoples, and their own national destiny. Such questions were closely associated with efforts to develop a collective sense of colonial national identity. Over time, and in conjunction with racialised accounts of successive waves of racial migrations from north and south, they helped to nurture a sense of acquired indigeneity on the part of white South African settlers.

[16] Sir B. Frere, 'Native races of South Africa', *Transactions of the South African Philosophical Society* 1, no. 2 (1877–1888), xxii, xxiii, xxiv.

Until the mid-1870s, the ideological implications of the rapidly burgeoning interest in African societies and peoples remained fluid. Bleek's
studiedly ambiguous view on evolution and the racial status of the Bushmen
is a case in point. The evolutionist ideas that would give such impetus to
the development of scientific racism would take time to be widely accepted.
Resistance to evolutionist thought was prompted not only by the authority
of the Bible but also by a growing awareness that if earth history extended
well beyond the limits of scriptural interpretation, the human imprint in
southern Africa (e.g., stone tools, shell middens) might extend back into
deep time – with troubling implications for questions of land ownership
and possession. By the final decades of the nineteenth century, however, a
broad swath of colonial opinion was prepared to correlate human evolutionary development with racial taxonomies to assert the inherent inferiority
of blacks, Bushmen, and Hottentots in particular. Dutch-speaking 'Boers'
were by no means exempt from the casual aspersions of social Darwinist
thinking. They were frequently charged with having undergone a process
of cultural, if not actually biological, degeneration as a consequence of their
isolated existence in a depleting environment.

The racialisation of knowledge in the last quarter of the nineteenth century is well illustrated by the uses made of the rich ethnographic legacy left
by George Stow, whose appreciation of rock art, coupled with his understanding of the geological record, led him to suggest that Bushmen were
the oldest or most 'ancient' South African inhabitants. Stow regarded Bushmen as the 'true aborigines' of the country, having been its 'sole proprietors'
until their displacement as a result of 'the Intrusion of the Stronger Races':
Hottentots came next, followed by 'savage' Bantu-speaking Africans and,
ultimately, Dutch and English settlers. Bushmen, Stow supposed, must
have moved southward down the African continent at 'some immensely
remote period'.[17] Human populations were rendered by Stow's vivid use of
broad snakelike arrows on a large colour sketch map purporting to show the
'main lines of migration' of the races inhabiting southern Africa, including
the 'European intruders'. The prospective book was dedicated to Bartle
Frere, who had offered help with its publication, but Stow died in 1882,
before completing his massive, rambling manuscript.

Stow's work was intended in part as a defence of the Bushmen, whose
artistic talents and humanity he much admired. In private correspondence
with Lucy Lloyd, he spoke of wishing to do 'away with a few of the old
cherished ideas; and place the Bushmen in rather a higher scale of original

---

[17] G. W. Stow, *The native races of South Africa: a history of the intrusion of the Hottentots and
Bantu into the hunting grounds of the Bushmen, the aborigines of the country* (London: Swan
Sonnenschein, 1905), pp. ix, 7–8, 14.

land-owners than has been previously conceded to them'. Yet he remained viscerally anti-African.[18] It seems that Stow felt able to treat his Bushmen painters admiringly (just like Frere in his 1878 address) because they no longer posed a physical threat to colonists. Moreover, their historical presence served to undermine any claim that the destructively warlike Nguni-speaking Africans might have had to first-nation status. The logic of this argument suggested that, in much the same way that the Bantu had displaced the Khoesan, so they were in turn overtaken by white settlers, the most recent bearers of superior civilisation.

This is the underlying message of Stow's *Native Races of South Africa*, which eventually appeared in print in 1905 after extensive editing by the historian George Theal, who did more than any other single writer to document, chronicle, and legitimise the presence of white settlers in South Africa. Theal gave form and focus to Stow's race-migration thesis. Moreover, departing from his own earlier sensitivity to precolonial African history and colonial dispossession, he sought to rank the cultural and physical capacities of races according to a linear scale of superiority by narrating, in teleological fashion, the history of human habitation in South Africa in terms of the survival of the fittest. The racist, settler-nationalist imprint of Theal's voluminous works (e.g., in his *History of South Africa*[19] and his *Yellow and Dark-Skinned People of Africa South of the Zambesi*[20]) was to have an enormous influence on historical and public understanding for at least fifty years.

IV

In addition to prompting intellectual curiosity about the constituent peoples of southern Africa, and their relationships to one another, growing imperial intervention evoked a more assertive political response by subjects of the Crown who also aspired to colonial citizenship. This impulse stretched back to the early decades of the nineteenth century, when Thomas Pringle and John Fairbairn challenged the gubernatorial authority of Somerset by seeking to exercise their rights to publish without restriction. In 1824 they pronounced in the *South African Commercial Advertiser*, 'Whatever we are, whether born in the Northern or Southern hemisphere, in England, in Holland, or in Africa, if we have made Africa our home, and feel a common interest in the prosperity of the Colony, we are all African.'[21]

---

[18] Stow to Lloyd, 19 February 1880, Stow papers, MSB, 472, letter 24, National Library of South African, Cape Town.
[19] London: Swan Sonnenschein, 1892–1919.   [20] London: Swan Sonnenschein, 1910.
[21] *South African Commercial Advertiser*, 17 March 1824.

Two decades later, in 1848, a remarkable coalition of Dutch- and English-speaking colonists combined in an anticonvict transportation association. This organisation initiated a public boycott of the colonial government, which fed into growing calls for self-government. The *Cape Town Mail* asserted that the struggle had 'created a people in South Africa,' while Fairbairn's *Commercial Advertiser* argued that, by their resistance, 'the people of the Cape of Good Hope have shown to the world what it is that constitutes a state.'[22]

With the acquisition of representative government in 1853, followed by responsible government in 1872, a colonial state with a developing political system was maturing at the Cape. The Boer republics of the Transvaal and the Orange Free State were also enjoying a considerable measure of autonomy from imperial interference. But moves by the imperial power to achieve confederation threatened that autonomy and caused politicians to reconsider their affiliations. When campaigning for parliament in 1874, the leading liberal defender of the Cape parliament and its constitutional traditions, Saul Solomon, declared himself an 'Afrikander' who gloried in being an Englishman while at the same time wishing to remain under the jurisdiction of the British crown. The following year, his liberal counterpart John X. Merriman (who likewise took a strong line against imperial intervention in colonial politics and publicly castigated Froude's interference in South African affairs) asserted that he was himself a 'Colonist first, then an Englishman'.[23]

It was out of the confrontation between imperialism and colonial nationalism, prompted by the Cape's acquisition of responsible government, that competing conceptions of South African affinity emerged. J. T. Eustace, an opponent of responsible government, claimed in 1872 that he was 'as good an Africander or South African' as anyone else in the House. He was reproached by James Buchanan, who chose to speak as a 'South African colonist born and bred', and noted that Eustace kept referring to his own side as 'We Englishmen'. In the first documented use of the term, Buchanan criticised Eustace for 'still [being] in a state of transition to South Africanism'.[24]

Bold actions such as the annexation of the Transkeian territories, of the Transvaal, of Griqualand West, and of Basutoland and Bechuanaland, gave the 'imperial factor' new and in many ways unprecedented salience. The use

---

[22] Cited in A. F. Hattersley, *The convict crisis and the growth of unity*, p. 80.

[23] E. Drus, 'The political career of Saul Solomon: Member of the Cape Legislative Assembly from 1854 to 1883', unpublished M.A. thesis, University of Cape Town (1939), p. 11; P. Lewsen, *John X. Merriman: Paradoxical South African statesman* (Cape Town: Donker, 1982), pp. 56–7.

[24] *Cape Argus*, 25 May 1872.

of the nebulous office of the high commissioner of South Africa was a source of great frustration to colonists like Solomon, who observed in 1872 that he did not understand the powers it conferred (unlike the governor of the Cape, whose function was self-explanatory). It was also resented by Natalians, who deplored the fact that High Commissioner Wodehouse had wielded 'a "concealed sceptre" with "occult and undefined powers"' that exceeded even the usual restraints on kings.[25] Growing imperial ambitions engendered reactive forms of colonial self-assertion in the two most important regions of the country: an adamant reassertion of colonial nationalism in the Cape and an invigorated republicanism in the Transvaal after 1878.

Ethnically based and incipiently pan–South African nationalist forces – Afrikaner as well as African – were coalescing in embryonic form at this time. The first explicitly political organisation to represent Africans, the Imbumba Yama Nyama, was formed at Port Elizabeth in 1882 to fight for 'national rights'. Its name recalled the words of the early-nineteenth-century visionary and Christian convert Ntsikana, who had advised Africans to achieve 'unity that binds everyone together'. Modelled on and partly inspired by the Afrikaner Bond, members of the Imbumba regarded their body as truly 'Afrikaner', by contrast with the organisation representing the Boers. The Imbumba was dedicated to protecting the rights of all Africans in South Africa, and it sought to overcome denominational, ethnic, and regional divisions. In practice, however, it was restricted to one or two centres in the Eastern Cape.

The objectives of African and Afrikaner nationalisms were incompatible, and they differed in method, scale, and belief systems. Yet it is nevertheless worth noting that both drew support from farming and religious organisations; both were shaped by their respective constituency's varied experiences of political incorporation in, as well as marginalisation from, the centres of power; and both found outlets in journalism and in cultural and language movements. Another common factor is that the nationalisms represented by the Bond and the Imbumba were significantly inflected by the influence of Cape colonial nationalism, itself a complex, unstable, and fluid local political tradition that found common purpose in its opposition to imperialism and its pride in local achievements.

Cape colonial nationalism was allied, on the one hand, to the 'true patriotism' of the Bond in the form of the improbable but effective Rhodes-Hofmeyr alliance; on the other hand, it interacted, through the medium

---

[25] J. Benyon, '"Intermediate" imperialism and the test of empire: Milner's "excentric" High Commission in South Africa', in Lowry (ed.), *The South African War reappraised*, pp. 89–90.

of Cape liberalism, with the modernising ambitions of the Cape mission-educated African elite who, in turn, did so much to incubate modern African nationalism. The complexities and fissile qualities of these proto-nationalisms cannot be underestimated, and they remain underresearched in key areas. In the case of African nationalism, linguistic, ethnic, and regional differences had to be negotiated, as did tensions between town and country, modernisers and traditionalists, Christians and non-Christians. As far as Afrikaner nationalism was concerned, allegiances had to be forged between the politically moderate and incipiently anglophile Afrikaner Bond, based in the Cape, and conservative republicans in the Orange Free State and the Transvaal. The antimodernist Dutch religious 'revival' of the 1860s and 70s and the linguistic revolution heralded by the first language movement of the 1880s together provided vital ideological momentum.

The British annexation of the Transvaal in 1877 and the ensuing war of retrocession in 1880–1881 did much to facilitate the emergence of an Afrikaner nationalism that was pan–South African in scope, though the process was far more fragmented than many conventional accounts admit. In 1872, for example, the newly elected president of the Transvaal was able to look forward to a future South Africa that was prosperous and free, 'a great country, when all nationalities shall disappear, and the words English and Dutch become obsolete, and like Americans or Canadians, we shall be more proud to call ourselves Africanders than either English or Dutch.'[26] In similar vein, the 1879 programme of principles for the Afrikaner Bond, articulated by S. J. du Toit, stated its political ambitions in a broadly inclusive manner such that the term *Afrikaner* incorporated all those who were genuinely committed to the interests of a 'United South Africa'.

Until, and sometimes even after the 1895 Jameson Raid, which caused enduring damage to Anglo-Dutch relations, many political leaders antic-ipated the possibility of a common identity that would permit loyalty to the empire to coexist with Afrikaner and English colonial patriotisms. This expression of Afrikaner nationalism did not necessarily entail a rejection of British authority; nor did it imply a commitment to republicanism. Thus, Afrikaner Bondsmen did not seek ethnic exclusivity. They were wholly committed to a vision 'in which Cape Afrikaner ethnicity, white Cape colo-nialism, pan-Afrikaner solidarity, and British imperialism lived side by side, not without tension, but on the whole quite happily.'[27]

---

[26] *Standard and Mail*, 24 September 1872 (editorial).

[27] M. Tamarkin, 'The Cape Afrikaners and the British empire from the Jameson Raid to the South African War', in Lowry (ed.), *The South African War reappraised*, p. 136; H. Giliomee, *The Afrikaners: biography of a people* (Cape Town: Tafelberg, 2003), p. 227.

English-speaking politicians who abhorred imperialist ascendancy and felt betrayed by Rhodes for abusing Cape colonial nationalism in the service of wider imperial designs on southern Africa also continued to resist the bifurcation of complex affiliations and loyalties – albeit in tones that were out of keeping with the demand for making simple choices. In language that recalled Merriman and Solomon before him, W. P. Schreiner, soon to become premier of the Cape, informed the House of Commons in 1897: 'I am South African first, but I think I am English after that.'[28]

Failure to achieve confederation did not signal the end of the idea of a unitary South Africa in the closing years of the nineteenth century. On the contrary, it opened up the prospect by encouraging competing local visions of a future unified state, shaped by forces such as Cape expansionism, Boer republicanism, Afrikaner ethnic nationalism, and a reinvigorated British imperialism. Under pressure on several fronts, African leaders were less able to respond with a viable vision of the future. Representatives of the Cape African elite, A. K. Soga and John Tengo Jabavu for instance, sought alliances with liberalism and with imperialism, in part out of moral conviction but also in the hope of securing future benefits or rewards. This, and the need to protect the Cape franchise, militated against alliances with their compatriots to the north, whose constitutional position was far weaker, and impeded the emergence of a broadly based African nationalist sentiment until after the South African War.

Conversely, widespread expectation of imminent 'race conflict' amongst whites (personified by the standoff between Milner and Kruger) encouraged many non-Africans to reflect on the nature of a future South Africa. Amongst those who grappled with the prospects for future South African unity, a fascinating and dissonant voice was provided by the feminist novelist and activist Olive Schreiner. Tortured by the march of events and desperate to avert war, Schreiner strove to imagine a future South African nation in which all could play a part. Her sense of despair, coupled with her idiosyncratic absorption of social Darwinist nostrums, meant that she could predict a positive outcome for the country only by making a virtue of racial necessity and expounding the merits of unity in diversity. She anticipated modern 'rainbow national' ideology by a century when she wrote in *Thoughts on South Africa*:

there is a subtle but a very real bond, which unites all South Africans, and differentiates us from all other peoples in this world. *This bond is our mixture of races itself.* It is this which divides South Africans from all other peoples in the world, and

---

[28] *Second Report from the Select Committee on British South Africa* (HMSO, 1897), questions 4134, 4175; N. G. Garson, 'English-speaking South Africans and the British connection, 1820–1961', in de Villiers (ed.), *English-speaking South Africa today*, p. 28.

makes us one.... The only form of organization which can be healthily or naturally assumed by us is one which takes cognizance of this universal condition.[29]

Olive Schreiner was more aware than most of the increasing racialisation of the colour question in the 1890s. This process meant that conventional distinctions between 'civilised' and 'uncivilised' Africans were becoming increasingly blurred, even anachronistic, as whites found common cause on the need to exclude all Africans from political power and sought to foreclose on the liberal promise that colour should not of itself constitute a bar to full membership of society. In his capacity as prime minister of the Cape, Rhodes introduced important protosegregationist legislation, such as the 1894 Glen Grey Act, which presumed the need to solve the native question in a more systematic fashion. This measure, presented by Rhodes as nothing less than a 'Native Bill for Africa',[30] was in part designed to satisfy the requirements of an increasingly integrated economy based on infinite supplies of cheap labour. Yet it was also freighted with political symbolism, as Rhodes well understood: a decisive native policy that was broadly attractive to whites would facilitate the creation of a unified white nation capable of expanding throughout the subcontinent and beyond.

By the late nineteenth century, commentators and politicians routinely identified the native question as the country's real unanswered problem, yet its salience was occluded by the growing crisis in white politics. The impulse to defer the issue to the future was always tempting, as exemplified by the career of Jan Smuts, whose overwhelming sense of racial anxiety was tempered by a lifelong tendency to temporise when presented with hard political decisions relating to race policy. Even the widely travelled liberal historian and jurist James Bryce, an astute observer of the South African predicament and an advocate of racial tolerance, found it hard to conceive of the 'colour problem' as a pressing political issue in the 1890s. Nevertheless, like Trollope, Bryce was acutely aware in his 1890s *Impressions of South Africa* of the numerical preponderance of blacks and could imagine a distant time – say, one or two centuries hence – when Africans might progress sufficiently to pose a real political challenge to a white-dominated polity.

V

The experience of the South African War did more than anything to clarify the basis on which South African nationhood would develop in the twentieth century. Viewed as a cathartic civil war involving all the inhabitants of the country, the conflagration bears the distinction of being South Africa's

---

[29] Olive Schreiner, *Thoughts on South Africa* (London: Unwin, 1923), p. 61.
[30] Vindex, *Cecil Rhodes*, p. 390.

first national political event. A conflict that was ostensibly about the extent of imperial economic and political control over the subcontinent, it has to be seen also as a war for South Africa fought by people who were to become South Africans. Crucially, it established the parameters for the emergence of a modern unitary state and cleared the terrain on which South African citizenship would be contested during and after the reconstruction era that followed.

In the political space created by the partial retreat of imperialism, but not yet filled by the emergence of full-fledged nationalisms, the ideology of white South Africanism began to unfold on broader terrain. Reconfigured and radiating out from Cape colonial nationalism, South Africanism was animated by a powerful spirit of reconciliation that sought to assuage bitterness and to construct a common white identity within a spatially integrated but racially separated nation-state. South Africanism was a composite ideology that placed a premium on accommodating aspects of imperial and national sentiment and loyalty. It drew on the experience of Anglo-Afrikaner cooperation in the period before the Jameson Raid; it was actively supported by Anglophone intellectuals and Milnerite sympathisers who recognised that imperialist ascendancy could not be sustained indefinitely; it gained credence from the statesmanship of Louis Botha and Jan Smuts, who swiftly recognised the rewards and opportunities that reconciliation could bring.

In 1905 J. H. Meiring Beck, a prominent member of the Cape delegation to the 1909 National Convention and a Union senator, delivered a lecture titled 'South Africanism'. The challenge for those guiding the destiny of the British Commonwealth, he declared, was 'not how to banish for ever the phantom of a South African Nation, but how, by fostering the national spirit, to drive it into grooves sympathetic to common interests rather than into grooves out of harmony with those interests'. Inverting the established eugenic trope, which insisted on a fundamental distinction between Boers and Britons, the medically trained Beck maintained in neo-Lamarckian fashion that environmental and evolutionary forces were acting together on the different 'human elements' of the country to create a vigorous 'South African type'. Whereas the tendency in Europe was 'towards physical deterioration', the opposite was the case in South Africa. Beck's appeal was clearly directed to English and Dutch speakers, but he ended by reminding his audience that they also had responsibilities to 'our Native population', who were the 'oldest Africanders in the land'. Only by recognising our duties toward them would whites 'be able to make good our own title to our national birthright'.[31]

[31] W. C. Scully, *Sir J. H. Meiring Beck: a memoir* (Cape Town: Maskew Miller, n.d.), pp. 94, 96, 99, 106.

The Selborne Memorandum of 1907, a defining manifesto of the 'closer union' movement, declared similarly that both white nationalities shared 'Teutonic' origins and that 'the fusion between them is merely a matter of time'.[32] This sentiment represents a marked change from the Colonial Office memorandum drafted by Selborne a decade earlier that reflected on 'racial rivalries' in the following terms: 'Dutch and English; English and Dutch. Most curiously though sprung from the same stock, the two races do not amalgamate. It shows what a lot of Celtic and Norman blood must be infused in us'.[33]

Postwar reappraisals of the underlying racial affinities between white South Africans were intended to lay the theoretical ground for the achievement of a 'white man's country'. But unlike Olive Schreiner or Meiring Beck (both of whom left open the possibility that nonwhites might be included in the national body politic), the trend in the politics of union was determinedly in the opposite direction. As Lionel Curtis, who had a close hand in the drafting of the 1907 Selborne Memorandum, and who did much to direct the closer union movement, observed: 'The fact is we have all been moving steadily from the Cape idea of mixing up white, brown and black and developing the different grades of colour strictly on the lines of European civilisation, to the very opposite conception of encouraging as far as possible the black man to separate from the white and to develop a civilisation, as he is beginning to do in Basutoland, on his own lines'.[34]

The inclusive white nation that was practically realised at Union in 1910 was predicated on the exclusion of Africans, coloureds (those of slave, Khoesan, and mixed-race descent), and Indians as full citizens of the new nation-state. In spheres of law and administration, South African citizenship was largely defined negatively and tangentially, that is, in relation to attempts to control, register, and naturalise immigrants, as well as in the process of classifying the population within strict racial hierarchies. In the period before Union and up to 1937 (when a more precise definition of 'Union nationality' was eventually arrived at in law), definitions of citizenship were significantly shaped by the imperative to restrict the mobility and immigration of 'Asiatics' – Indians in particular. The question of South African Indian citizenship, greatly compounded by the growing

---

[32] Lord Selborne, 'A review of the present mutual relations of the British South African colonies', memorandum prepared at the request of the Government of Cape Colony, 1 January 1907, reprinted in Newton, *Select documents relating to the unification of South Africa*, vol. 2, pp. 54–5.

[33] Cited in R. Robinson and J. Gallagher, *Africa and the Victorians: The official mind of imperialism* (New York: William Blackwood, 1961), p. 435.

[34] Curtis to Duncan, 26 November 1907, Patrick Duncan papers, BC 294, C23.3.8, University of Cape Town.

sovereignty of India itself, was a continuing political problem that blew up spectacularly at the first session of the UN General Assembly in 1946. By contrast, the status of Africans ('Union' natives as well as 'extra-Union' or 'alien natives') was not yet subject to sustained international criticism.

Africans were of course subjected to unprecedented ideological and political scrutiny from the beginning of the twentieth century. Discussions about their moral and intellectual status; their capacity to absorb European civilisation; and, indeed, the desirability of their being encouraged to do so, acquired urgency and focus in constituting the native question as a unitary problem requiring a national solution. This was the clear message of the landmark 1903–1905 South African Native Affairs Commission, whose terms of reference explicitly stated the need for comprehensive agreement on 'affairs relating to the Natives and Native administration' in light of 'the coming Federation of South African Colonies'.[35]

The concept of segregation, which had entered general political discourse, was duly presented as the appropriate answer: proponents of segregation assumed that the interests of blacks and whites were fundamentally at variance, and they rationalised the need for political and social separation, either by reference to immutable racial differences or else on the theoretically more flexible grounds of cultural relativism. Considerable intellectual and political energy was expended to render Africans perpetual political minors by removing their vestigial citizenship and franchise rights. Naturally suited to a 'tribal' existence, Africans were deemed best left to develop 'along their own lines' in specially delimited rural 'native reserves' – subject, of course, to their availability for labour on white-owned farms and industries. The elaborate system of labour migration that emerged to satisfy such needs depended on, and helped to give practical reinforcement to, the notion of tribalism. Yet the ideas and experiences that labour migrants took with them served to undermine such notions and, in time, provided the material basis for the emergence of a proletarian-based nationalist consciousness.

It also became increasingly clear after 1910 that the hard-won and jealously guarded privileges won by several generations of modernising African peasants, artisans, teachers, churchmen, clerks, and traders were imperilled. Neither the established African elite in the Eastern Cape nor the Christian *amakholwa* in Natal could depend on retaining their particular rights and privileges. The growing tendency of the South African state to treat Africans as a single collective 'tribal' entity helped to break down regional, ethnic, and class barriers. The economic threat to the status of middling Africans, coupled with measures to standardise the operation of the migrant

---

[35] South African Native Affairs Commission, *Report 1903–1905* (Cd.2399, 1905).

labour system and extend the pass laws, had an unintended consequence in respect of black solidarity: by flattening regional and social differences, opportunities for wider social and political networks to develop were inadvertently created. African leaders thus became ever more persuaded of the need to surmount historical divides and to develop a more coordinated response to white power.

This opportunity was grasped at the 1909 South African Native Convention, which had been called specially to oppose the framework of Union and included a broad coalition of African opinion. The inaugural meeting of the South African Native National Congress (SANNC) in 1912 marked the emergence of the first truly national black political party in the country, dedicated to overcoming inter-African ethnic divisions and to securing citizenship and voting rights on a nonracial basis. The name chosen to depict the new organisation aptly reflected the SANNC's national ambitions and status. But it also hinted at the African elite's defensiveness and sense of marginality, for in common with potential political allies like the (coloured) African People's Organisation and the Natal Indian Congress, the SANNC defined itself as a special interest organisation by using the term *native* – in striking contrast, say, to Botha's South African Party or Hertzog's rival National Party, neither of which felt obliged to signal the colour or ethnic nature of their constituencies or claims. The antiapartheid activist and Indian Congress leader, Ismail Meer reflects on this problem of nomenclature thus:

> One of the things that bothered us in the 1930s was what we South Africans should be called. Africa was not popular; the ANC was founded as the Native, not African Congress. I recall A. W. G. Champion taking umbrage at one of our meetings when I introduced him as an African. He corrected me emphatically, proudly declaring, 'I am not an African, I am a native of this country', as if he was being deprived of his claim to the country as its indigenous inhabitant. The African People's Organisation, the APO alone, laid claim to African; as did its leader, Dr Abdurahman, who, though Indian in origin and perceived as Coloured, referred to himself as African.[36]

Although the formative history of African nationalism has been well researched, the question of how Africans saw themselves as South Africans or, indeed, how they viewed white claimants to that status, has scarcely been addressed. Important clues lie embedded in the literary output of Africans writing in the segregationist era. Sol Plaatje's great polemic and social commentary, *Native Life in South Africa*, is an obvious point of departure,

[36] Ismail Meer, *A fortunate man* (Cape Town: Zebra, 2002), p. 38.

not only in view of Plaatje's eminence as political activist and man of let-ters but also in virtue of the book's title, which situates the predicament of black victims of segregation in a national context (even though the Orange Free State is the major focus of attention). The author's insistence that the terms *South African* and *white* not be regarded as coterminous is borne out by the book's famous opening sentence, which declares that, on the day of the passage of the 1913 Land Act, 'the South African native found himself, not actually a slave, but a pariah in the land of his birth'. This message is further reinforced by Plaatje's early use of the term *black South Africans*, his self-description in the prologue as a 'South African native workingman', and his questioning of the right of the journal *South Africa* to proclaim views about the country without reference to any African voice or opinion.[37]

Plaatje's Tswana compatriot and associate Silas Modiri Molema was another pioneering writer who set out to explain the predicament of blacks in segregationist South Africa to an external audience, in this case by way of an anthropological and historical survey. Molema's *Bantu – Past and Present*,[38] written while he was a medical student in Glasgow, is presented in part as a personal account to underline its authenticity. Yet Molema's abid-ing confidence in human progress and his disavowal of racism sit uneasily with much of the book's content, which remains heavily reliant on the racial typologies that framed so much of the standard anthropological and historical literature of the day. As in Plaatje's writing, such ambivalences are heightened by structural tensions: in particular, the burden imposed by the author's attempt to be both an authentic indigenous witness and an objective interpreter, and the challenge of finding a suitable literary register for the book's intended 'foreign' audience of British sympathisers, such that passion does not compromise persuasiveness and reasonableness does not give way to rancour.

These tensions, not to say contradictions, are displayed even more strik-ingly in D. D. T. Jabavu's collection of essays *The Black Problem*, whose title is itself capable of multiple readings. As the leading representative of lib-eral, educated African opinion, Jabavu found himself squeezed between the rising tide of postwar black radicalism on the one hand and an increasingly repressive state on the other hand. He still supposed that his membership in the Christian liberal elite equipped him uniquely to act in the role of interlocutor. Thus, in *The Black Problem*, Jabavu presumes not only to

---

[37] S. T. Plaatje, *Native life in South Africa, before and since the European war and the Boer rebellion* (London: P. S. King, 1916), prologue and chap. 1.
[38] S. M. Molema, *The Bantu: past and present* (Edinburgh: Green, 1920).

'provide a serious and comprehensive explication of the Native question' for the benefit of whites but also to 'advise his fellow countrymen' on the basis of his intimate knowledge of their problems, their 'racial and social characteristics', and their strengths and weaknesses.[39]

The uneasy and frequently defensive response of Africans to proposed segregationist legislation – whereby promises of land were held out in compensation for the loss of putative franchise rights – is also borne out in the case of the prominent interwar African spokesman Selope Thema. Writing about 'the race problem' in 1922, Thema stressed that racial 'intermixture' was undesirable, and he advanced a two-pronged claim for citizenship, founded first on autochthonous status and second on the rights accruing to British subjects: 'While we do not wish to encroach upon the society of the whites, nevertheless we claim our rights of citizenship first as the aboriginals of this country, and second as British subjects'.[40]

The genres of literary narrative and historical chronicle also provide valuable insights into Africans' fractured sense of collective self and national identity at this time. Works devoted to the subject of Shaka written in English and in vernacular languages by Thomas Mofolo (1925), John Dube (1932), Rolfes Dhlomo (1936) and B. W. Vilakazi fit into this category; here, too, the result is 'profoundly ambiguous'.[41]

Magema Fuze's *The Black People and Whence They Came*, first published in Zulu as *Abantu Abamnyama Lapa Bavela Ngakona* (1922), illustrates especially well the equivocal negotiation of boundaries and cultural worlds that characterises such works. Fuze, who has aptly been characterised as a 'native informant' turned *kholwa* intellectual, speaks simultaneously in the voices of Zulu oral tribal chronicler and literate historian-ethnographer. He retains affiliations to the world of the Christian mission as well as the sphere of tradition and custom; and although his primary focus of his interest is on Zulu history, there are strong suggestions of his desire to cultivate a wider sense of pan-African identity and unity. Fuze's statement that Nguni speakers 'sprang from a common source, and there is no doubt that we were one in ancient times' provides an implicitly nationalist twist to standard colonial genealogies – the Hamitic myth in particular – of Bantu southward migration from the Horn of Africa. The point of this reworked 'narrative

[39] D. D. T. Jabavu, *The black problem* (Lovedale: Lovedale Press, 1920), preface.

[40] Selope Thema, 'The race problem' (1922), in Karis and Carter (eds.), *From protest to challenge*, vol. 1, p. 214, doc. 41a. Thema and Jabavu were supporters of the common franchise, yet they were both accused of being prepared to concede this matter of principle in the process of bargaining that led up to the passage of the 1936 segregationist legislation.

[41] C. Hamilton, *Terrific majesty: The powers of Shaka Zulu and the limits of historical invention* (Cambridge, MA: Harvard University Press, 1998), p. 20.

of origins' is the manner in which Fuze 'understood "the black people's" origins in continental and not ethnic or local terms'.[42]

Mofolo's *Shaka* (1925) is similarly suggestive of an Afrocentric perspective. Its opening sentence represents South Africa as 'a large headland situated between two oceans',[43] and it proceeds to describe the different black nations that inhabit the subcontinent. Although reminiscent of colonial accounts that commonly mix geographical with ethnographic descriptions, the effect is subtly different and subversive of colonial accounts that conventionally portray the Cape Peninsula as the colonial bridgehead into Africa. In this unusual way, Mofolo locates South Africa as a southern extension of the African landmass.

VI

If ambiguity and complex subjectivity characterise the work of African writers such as these – Petros Lamula's pioneering 1924 study of African history, *UZulukaMalandela*, provides another striking example – a contrary tendency is evident on the part of white observers and self-appointed experts who strove, from the early years of the century, to pronounce on the native question with increasing technical precision and scientific detachment. The lead given here by the 1905 Report of the South African Native Affairs Commission (the SANAC report) has already been noted. Other contemporaneous attempts to frame and solve the native question resulted from discussions associated with opinion formers in the Fortnightly Club and the Native Affairs Society in Johannesburg.

Interventions by scholars and academics were stimulated by a presentation given by the Cambridge ethnologist Alfred Haddon to the 1905 joint meeting of the British and South African Associations for the Advancement of Science. Haddon, who did much to promote anthropology in the service of colonial administration, used the occasion to survey the state of ethnological work in South Africa. He called for state assistance to research, in systematic fashion, many of the important intellectual questions that remained unanswered. At the same conference, and on the urging of the author of the SANAC report, the well-connected accountant and incipient liberal philanthropist Howard Pim publicly outlined an overall scheme of

---

[42] M. Fuze, *The black people and whence they came*, trans. H. C. Lugg, ed. A. T. Cope (Pietermaritzburg: Killie Campbell Africana Library, 1979), pp. vi, 1: 'Our forebears tell us that all we black people originally came from the north'; H. Mokoena, 'The making of a *kholwa* intellectual: a discursive biography of Magema Magwaza Fuze', unpublished D.Phil. thesis, University of Cape Town (2005), p. 9.

[43] T. Mofolo, *Shaka*, trans. D. P. Kunene (London: Heinemann, 1981), p. 1.

racial segregation. Its impact on later political developments was considerable. The quest for theoretical and applied anthropological knowledge was
by then closely interlinked, and a close dialogue between segregation and
anthropology was henceforth established. It was in large part as a result of
this ongoing exchange that the new sociological concept of South African
society – or, more especially, societies – emerged.

Anthropology was as yet unprofessionalised, and it lacked firm institutional foundations. But anthropologically minded investigations of the
condition of Africans and the future relationship between whites and blacks
were gaining currency. Dudley Kidd's trilogy, *The Essential Kafir*,[44] *Savage
Childhood*,[45] and *Kafir Socialism and the Dawn of Individualism*,[46] exemplifies
aspects of the transition from traveller 'manners and customs' depictions
of African societies toward an altogether tougher and more prescriptive
treatment of the native question. Drawing on popular stereotypes as well
as fashionable new eugenic theories, Kidd outlined the exotic customs and
beliefs of Africans in a tone of indulgent jocularity pitched for a popular
as well as a specialist audience. Kidd emphasised the irrational nature of
African 'mentality', dwelling on Africans' reliance on magic and belief in
sorcery, so as to make the point that they were inherently unsuited to the
spirit of democratic individualism characteristic of Western civilisation.

In striking contrast to Kidd's underlying tone of ridicule and derision is
the detailed study of the Tsonga people conducted by the Swiss missionary
and naturalist Henri-Alexandre Junod. Like Kidd, Junod was influenced
by theories of natural selection; he, too, viewed the tribe as an organic unit
with its own inner mental life. Yet Junod's evolutionism was rooted in a
humane Christian universalism. Thus, in describing their encounter with
the powerful disaggregating forces of industrialism, Junod manifested a
remarkable empathy toward the Tsonga people. His classic work, *Life
of a South African Tribe*,[47] may be said to mark the inauguration of the
ethnographic 'tribal' monograph in South Africa; it serves as a bridge
between older ethnological and modern anthropological approaches.

For A. R. Radcliffe-Brown, one of the founding figures of social anthropology, Junod's work exemplified the inadequacies of what he called con-
jectural history and speculative ethnology (terms that may have had the
effect of stifling or discrediting vernacular research conducted by members
of the interwar African intelligentsia and by white amateur investigators
alike). What was required instead was a comparative 'science of man' based
on firm sociological principles. Thus, shortly after taking the country's
first chair of social anthropology at the University of Cape Town in 1921,

---

[44] London: Adam and Charles Black, 1904.   [45] London: Adam and Charles Black, 1906.
[46] London: Adam and Charles Black, 1908.   [47] London: Macmillan, 1912–1913.

Radcliffe-Brown began to develop the core concepts of structural function-alism. This theory, owing much to the positivism of Comte and Durkheim, conceived of societies as integrated systems, the elements of which (culture, ritual, values, kinship, and so on) worked in concert to reinforce one another, thereby serving to promote group solidarity and social stability. Radcliffe-Brown's counterpart, Bronislaw Malinowski, provided a vital counterpoint to structural-functionalist theory with his emphasis on rigorous participant observation and fieldwork research.

The new discipline of social anthropology encouraged respect for African societies by imputing rational motives and meanings to practices that casual observers, like Dudley Kidd, had been inclined to dismiss as evidence of innate barbarism. Relativist understandings of culture dissuaded anthropologists from drawing societal comparisons based on the supposed universality and superiority of European 'civilisation' and downplayed or displaced altogether evolutionist assumptions based on the primacy of biological race. For the first generation of anthropologists trained in the traditions of structural functionalism, the idea of culture contact presumed that African societies were dynamic entities. The implication was that attempts to freeze Africans into static or distinct tribes were contrived and unsustainable. Therein lay the basis of a potentially powerful liberal critique of segregation, but it was often left implicit – and therefore conveniently overlooked by policy makers who were attracted instead by the notion that African societies were static units capable of being manipulated to suit the objectives of white governance.

The liberal message was in any case undermined by the natural disposition of functional anthropologists to develop specialist knowledge about particular tribal groups and to stress variation and difference over similarity and commonality – a tendency that was enthusiastically adopted by conservative anthropologists for whom segregation and, later, tribally based apartheid, was a distinctly desirable outcome. Those who advocated segregation as a moderate compromise between the supposed alternatives of assimilation and outright repression proved adept at turning anthropological ideas to their advantage. In the hands of politicians like George Heaton Nicholls or Jan Smuts, cultural relativist notions could be deployed alongside (or as an alternative to) theories of innate biological superiority to legitimate racial separation and paternalist notions of trusteeship. Conceptions of tribe, accounts of customary law, and efforts to counterpose African 'tradition' to European 'modernity' were likewise utilised to sustain the idea that essential differences between black and white South Africans ought to be entrenched socially and politically. The terms of this new discourse also suggested that the old nineteenth-century distinction between 'civilised' and 'barbarous' Africans was outmoded.

The intellectual attack on social anthropology was led by the historian W. M. Macmillan, whose major conceptual contribution to the understanding of South Africa was his insight that the country could only be understood as an economic and social unity. In developing this concept of South Africa as a single structural entity, Macmillan lambasted anthropology's 'paralysing conservatism' and fixation on 'decaying cultures',[48] a criticism that seems unfair in the case of writers like Schapera, Hunter, or Hellman but was clearly applicable to segregationist-inclined social reformers like C. T. Loram or Rheinallt Jones. Practical-minded thinkers such as these were dazzled by the promise of social anthropology as an applied science in the 1920s and 1930s. Schapera was disposed instead to study the 'changing native'. This was not, however, the consensus view in the developing interwar field of African studies, which absorbed older traditions of linguistic research as well as the strong imprint of race typology associated particularly with the growing vogue for physical anthropology.

Notably, Schapera's own edited volume *Bantu-Speaking Tribes of South Africa* (1937) began with the chapter 'Racial Origins' by the celebrated anatomist and palaeoanthropologist Raymond Dart. It included a contribution by the Native Affairs Department ethnologist N. J. van Warmelo that categorised Bantu speakers into primary groups – Nguni, Shangaan-Thonga, Sotho, Venda, and Lemba – along with tribal subcategories. For liberal anthropologists who insisted that Africans were not all identical, such divisions may have made good sense, but in the apartheid era, when Van Warmelo laboured unstintingly for the Department of Native Affairs (or Bantu Administration), the designations were used as the rationale for the political balkanisation of African societies into bounded tribes and, subsequently, 'homelands' or 'Bantustans'. Thus, whatever one's view about the intentions and consequences of their research – and in spite of calls by social anthropologists for greater awareness and understanding of African problems – the growing bifurcation of South African society into black and white was not seriously challenged by their work; indeed, it may be that social anthropologists unwittingly contributed to this process by virtue of their professional impulse to preserve the study of particular African groups as their own special intellectual domain.

VII

The interwar fiction that the native question somehow existed at a remove from national politics was given endorsement by segregationist demands to strip Africans of their political rights and status as citizens. Even as

[48] W. M. Macmillan, *My South African years* (Cape Town: David Philip 1975), p. 215.

Hertzog's clutch of 'Native Bills' came to dominate his legislative agenda, the major white political parties regularly upbraided one another for treating segregation as a 'political football'. Until well into the 1920s, if not the 1930s, it was assumed that *race* referred to tensions between Englishmen and Afrikaners (the latter term now exclusively associated with white descendants of Boers rather than the much more embracing nineteenth-century term *Africander*).

Efforts to excise the African presence from national politics were given practical reinforcement by the Native Affairs Department, which strove to achieve sole charge over Africans and regarded the governance of blacks as essentially a technical and administrative exercise, albeit mitigated by paternalist empathy born of long familiarity. Sarah Gertrude Millin captured this duality well in *The South Africans* (1926), which was conceived of as a reprise to Trollope and rendered in comparable aphoristic style. Millin sketches the country's races and ethnic groups – 'Boers', 'English', 'Jews', 'Asiatics', and 'Half-Castes' – in one section and relegates 'The Kaffir' to another.[49] To Trollope's question of whether South Africa was to be a land of white or of black men, Millin could not provide a definite answer. Instead, she portrayed blacks as a menacing, subterranean presence, largely invisible to whites but nonetheless exerting a palpable influence on all key aspects of national life. In his more even-handed way, J. H. Hofmeyr similarly remarked on the 'fear that perhaps after all Anthony Trollope may have been right' when he spoke of South Africa as a country of black men.[50]

Africans' shadowy, dangerous presence is borne out in much contemporary historiography. Although blacks figured in historical accounts of the nineteenth century (principally as a foil to the story of conquest and pacification), interwar historians largely failed to grasp the idea of black, coloured, or Indian political agency, whether expressed through individuals or by means of collective organisation. For example, Eric Walker's standard *History of South Africa*[51] makes virtually no mention of any late-nineteenth-century or twentieth-century political figure or organisation that was not white (Gandhi is the sole exception); J. S. Marais's brief coverage of the same period in his *The Cape Coloured People, 1652–1937*[52] relegates Dr Abdurahman to two footnotes; and, for all its appreciation of the underlying unity of South African society, De Kiewiet's elegantly conceived social and economic *History of South Africa: Social and Economic*[53] treats blacks as

---

[49] S. G. Millin, *The South Africans* (London: Constable, 1926).

[50] J. H. Hofmeyr, 'Introduction', in Brookes et al. (eds.), *Coming of age*, pp. 1–2.

[51] London: Longmans, Green, 1928.   [52] London: Longmans, 1939.

[53] Oxford: Oxford University Press, 1941.

an abstraction. The same is largely true of Macmillan's writings. It goes almost without saying that blacks are virtually entirely absent from early Afrikaner nationalist historiography, whose major themes in the 1920s and 1930s concentrate on the Trek, the political and constitutional history of the Boer republics, and the experience of the two Anglo-Boer wars. If Africans feature at all, it is as warlike tribes, cattle thieves, and obstacles to civilisation. The contrast with black efforts at self-definition and self-projection is striking, an exemplar being T. D. Mweli Skota's *African Yearly Register*, which is presented tellingly as a 'national biographical dictionary'.[54]

Closer readings of individual texts by recognised white scholars are required to make the argument with more subtlety, but the general point that blacks intrude into national politics only as a generalised problem or menace is difficult to refute. Seen in this context, Edward Roux's singular study of black resistance, *Time Longer Than Rope*, seems all the more remarkable. In his foreword, Roux argues that, despite the considerable literature on 'the so-called "Native problem" up to now there has been no general account of the political history of the black man in South Africa, the battles he has waged, the organisations he has built and the personalities that have taken part in the struggle'. Roux went on to observe, 'The phrase "South African" almost always implies "white South African"', a point made even more forcibly some twenty years later by an American visitor who observed: 'It is only by swallowing hard, either apologetically or defiantly, that most whites can bring themselves to refer to their black fellow-citizens as South Africans'.[55] The Afrikaans language distinguished between *volk* (nation) and *bevolking* (those who formed part of the South African population but were not included in the political community); when applied to whites, the concept of *volk* precluded English speakers or those with divided South African loyalties.

African responses to their political effacement and denial of citizenship took different forms. It has already been noted that, for those who projected the privileges and freedoms of the nineteenth-century Cape onto a common South African future, the hope of inclusion in the body politic on the basis of common humanity and individual citizenship was increasingly remote after 1910. The failure of the African elite to reverse segregationist measures in the 1920s and 1930s damaged the political credibility of their leaders, whose standing was further eroded by activists with a more radical

---

[54] T. D. Mweli Skota (ed.), *The African yearly register: being an illustrated national biographical dictionary (who's who) of black folks in Africa* (Johannesburg: [Esson, 1930]).

[55] Roux, *Time longer than rope*, pp. 7, 16; Douglas Brown, *Against the world: attitudes of white South Africans* (London: Collins, 1966), p. 80.

and populist social agenda. A different response was to opt out of the idea of a unitary, inclusive South Africa and to stress instead a common African or black identity. This reaction had roots in the rise of independent African churches during the second half of the nineteenth century. It was exemplified by the separatist 'Ethiopian' movement and epitomised by the rapid growth of the African Methodist Episcopal Church. It rejected white paternalism and traditional missionary views of incremental progress, emphasising instead the virtues of self-reliance, autonomy, and racial unity. Often expressed in the notion of Africa for the Africans, such ideas were not always easily contained in the civic and political boundaries of South Africa and, indeed, were often incommensurable with liberal notions of gradual self-improvement or prototypical nationalist forms of organisation. They were pan-African in scope and often looked elsewhere, black America in particular, for inspiration and guidance. In the political ferment of the 1920s, the impact of Garveyism and the emergence of populist racial movements, led by charismatic leaders like Wellington Butelezi, tended to seek deliverance or freedom from, rather than inclusion in, a white-dominated state.

A less pronounced variant of Africanism focused more closely on national politics, stressing the need for unity in opposing white supremacy. Amongst the most prominent proponents of this tendency were the African National Congress (ANC) presidents John Dube and Pixley ka Isaka Seme. The central themes were expressed in Seme's 1911 call for a 'Native Union' and in his 1906 statement 'The Regeneration of Africa', which sounded a lyrical note of race pride and looked forward to the emergence of a uniquely African civilisation. Although held in check by more pragmatic and con-stitutionally oriented liberal approaches, this form of prophetic cultural nationalism later reemerged in the Africanism of the Youth League; one of its chief exponents, Anton Lembede, was directly influenced by Seme. In the intervening decades, Africanism coexisted with, and sometimes rein-forced, other forms of social radicalism, including the rural populism of the Industrial and Commercial Workers Union (ICU) in the 1920s and Josiah Gumede's presidency of the ANC (1927–1930). Gumede's dual sympa-thies to Garveyism and communism found an echo in the 1928 decision of the Communist Party of South Africa to adopt the slogan of the 'Native Republic' – a formulation that, however painful and problematic to those associated with its elaboration, signalled an awareness that South Africa's destiny would henceforth be shaped by the needs and claims of its major-ity black population. Before this controversial decision, even communists presumed that the coming revolution would be led by white workers. Amongst the many paradoxes of the 1922 Rand Revolt was the fact that white militants rarely regarded working black miners as scabs: 'Africans were simply not admitted to the community of labour to which the white strikers belonged'.[56]

The constraints on developing a black sense of South Africanism during the interwar years were heightened by the episodic nature of black resistance to the segregationist state, by the quiescence of black opposition in the 1930s in comparison with the ferment of the preceding decade, and by the failure of movements and organisations like the ICU or ANC to develop a coherent and stable national presence. Outward demonstrations of class consciousness, such as the strikes that occurred on the Witwatersrand in the aftermath of the First World War, suggested the potential for concerted black opposition to white capitalist power. But they remained the exception rather than the rule.

Expressions of ethnic particularism, regionalism, and factionalism were in any case at least as characteristic of the period as expressions of pan-South African nationalism. True enough, in 1923 J. T. Gumede declared that, whereas he used 'to pride himself before to be called "Zulu"', after becoming a 'man of the world' he 'discovered there is no Zulu, Xosa, Mosotho or Coloured but [only] "Africans"'.[57] But this should be read as a statement of self-discovery and aspiration rather than a reflection of widely shared assumptions. Ethnic nationalist loyalties were neither secondary to nor easily subsumed into a broader nationalist consciousness, even when this was stated as an explicit objective.

VIII

The leading ANC intellectual Z. K. Matthews once described how, at Fort Hare in the early postwar era:

> The consensus was that the makers of the world did not count us as a nation or as part of any nation. We used to argue over the meaning of the word nation itself. We were of different chiefdoms and languages. We lived in South Africa, but we were not regarded as part of the South African nation. Indeed, when white leaders spoke of the 'nation' of South Africa, they meant only the white nation. When they gave their population figures of the nation, they gave only the number of Europeans.[58]

It is self-evident that the African intelligentsia of the early twentieth century were fervently engaged in discussions about their identity, status,

[56] J. Krikler, *White rising: The 1922 insurrection and racial killing in South Africa* (Manchester: Manchester University Press, 2005), p. 133.

[57] Gumede, cited in La Hausse de Lalouvière, *Restless identities*, p. 88.

[58] Z. K. Matthews, cited in B. M. Magubane, 'Whose memory – whose history? The illusion of liberal and radical historical debates', in Stolten (ed.), *History making*, p. 275.

and place in South Africa. But when did they begin to see themselves first and foremost as South Africans? This difficult question is perhaps unanswerable, but it is nonetheless worth putting. Although there are clearly identifiable expressions of a pan–South African identity from the late nineteenth century, it was the lived experience of the two world wars that proved momentous in this regard, as in so many others. The First World War had helped to unleash a wave of African nationalist thinking and activism, but new ideas failed to flourish as segregation was imposed from the late 1920s in deteriorating economic circumstances.

In the 1940s, a revived urban-based African literary and political intelligentsia rose to prominence. During this era, the rhetoric of African nationalism began to focus fully on the illegitimacy – rather than the unfairness – of white power and on the necessity of replacing minority with majority rule. In conjunction with rights-based rather than rights-conditional approaches to citizenship, such thinking signalled a major change in expectations and entitlement. Thus, whereas African nationalist leaders had routinely petitioned the Queen or King in their capacity as subjects ('we humbly submit') until after the First World War, the Second World War put an end to such discourse. The emergence of mass-based politics, a growing international discourse of democratic rights and freedoms, and a developing anticolonial sentiment in Africa and Asia all helped to entrench the idea that to be an African was, ipso facto, to be a South African citizen.

Along with new ideas about democracy, words like *welfare* and *citizenship* became defining terms in the 1940s. The expanded meaning and popular force of citizenship contrast with earlier uses. For mid-nineteenth-century Africans in the Cape, qualification for the nonracial common franchise had been a crucial test, as well as a telling symbol, of citizenship. For white colonial nationalists, similarly, the acquisition of responsible and then representative government secured their claims to be citizen-subjects of a maturing British colony dedicated to progress and improvement. In the mid-1870s, there was extensive discussion in the Cape linking African citizenship rights and gun ownership to colonial loyalty. It was proposed, for example, that those amaMfengu issued with 'certificates of citizenship' should be obliged to enrol in the burgher (or citizen) militia force. Writing in the *Christian Express* in 1891, the Lovedale teacher Andrew Smith looked back at this institution as a unique establishment wherein 'the foundation is laid for the true relationship between Europeans and Africans, who must find out how to live together as citizens in the same country.'[59]

---

[59] Cited in R. H. W. Shepherd, *Lovedale South Africa: The story of a century, 1841–1941* (Lovedale: Lovedale Press, [1941]), p. 99.

The language of citizenship was also to the fore in the lead-up to the South African War when President Kruger's reluctance to grant full political rights to Uitlanders featured as a key, if contrived, reason for imperial intervention. Associations between citizenship, the right to bear arms, and republicanism were again highlighted in the Union Defence Act of 1912. This measure, which represented a key stage in realising the newly unified South African state, entailed the demobilisation of the Boer commando system (still a potent symbol of republican statehood and masculine values) and its replacement by the so-called Active Citizen Force, comprising white conscripts and volunteers and designed to supplement the nucleus of a standing army. The new military arrangement underlined the loss of republican citizenship – for many Boer ex-combatants it became a source of intense resentment.

In the post-Union era, questions of citizenship and belonging bore significantly on the emerging South African nation-state. Protracted debates around the language, 'status', and flag acts – all matters of intense controversy in interwar intrawhite politics – illustrate the challenge of reconciling a resurgent Afrikaner nationalism in the constitutional framework of the emerging Commonwealth. In the first three decades of the century, white labour activism was emboldened by the conviction that race conferred rights to minimum 'civilised' standards of pay. This activism was in turn sustained by the assumption that subjects of the British empire, including its overseas working class, were entitled to special rights and privileges by virtue of being fellow colonial citizens of the white dominions.

During the interwar years, ideas of citizenship were worked out externally through negotiations around national sovereignty and the relationship of the dominions to the empire. Internally, citizenship was addressed via the exclusionary politics of segregation and, in particular, through the medium of immigration policies. Hertzog's segregationist legislation was predicated on the exclusion of Africans, both on an individual and a collective basis, from common citizenship. Coloured identity presented an ontological minefield, not only because of the inherent difficulties the state faced in defining the category 'coloured' but also because the coloured elite, and their representatives in the African People's Organisation, 'embraced nonracial values as a matter of principle' even if they were forced for pragmatic reasons to mobilise on a racial basis.[60] Although coloureds were condemned to second-class citizenship, their South Africanness was tacitly accepted by Hertzog and his followers, who had long sought to co-opt them politically and who could never quite forget, or deny, that many were, in matters of

---

[60] M. Adhikari, *Not white enough, not black enough: racial identity in the South African coloured community* (Cape Town: Double Storey, 2005), p. 72.

culture and descent, 'brown Afrikaners'. Indicative of their intermediate racial and social status, Hertzog, in his Coloured Persons Rights Bill of 1926, proposed to grant those included in this category a degree of constitutional protection: he claimed, disingenuously, that the bill would, for the first time, establish 'unequivocally the principle of political equality' between 'Europeans' and 'coloureds'. (There was a stark contrast here with Indians, who were conspicuously ignored.[61])

At the same time, D. F. Malan, who had assiduously courted the coloured vote in the Cape over the previous decade, assured 'Malays' that they too 'formed one of the oldest elements of the South African nation' – apparently to differentiate them from 'Asiatics', who were discriminated against at least as much on account of their alien status as their colour.[62] Immigrant Eastern European Jews shared the alien label with Indians. However, their growing presence cast a shadow on the whiteness of Europeans. The 1930 Immigration Quota Act, launched by Malan on a rising tide of popular anti-Semitism, prompted fresh reflections on the constitution of the white South African nation and the meaning of civilisation. One newspaper reminded its readers that, because 'the Dutch and English were the real pioneers, it was they who had "a right to say whom they would have as fellow citizens"'.[63]

The defeat of fascism and the fervent communal efforts on the part of local Jewish organisations to absorb and underline the loyalty of new immigrants ultimately served to stabilise and secure Jewish membership of the white nation. On the other side of the racial spectrum, efforts from within the Indian community, spurred by diplomatic pressure from the newly independent state of India, sought to clarify the citizenship status of Indians. By the 1940s, Indians were consciously asserting their rights and aspirations through membership of organisations such as the Colonial Born South African Indian Association. Radical Indian leaders pressed their claims to common citizenship through increasing involvement in Congress and Alliance politics. Thus, the 1947 Doctors' Pact signed by ANC president A. B. Xuma, along with G. M. Naicker and Y. M. Dadoo, spoke of the urgent need for cooperation between the non-European peoples

---

[61] G. Lewis, *Between the wire and the wall: a history of 'Coloured' politics* (Cape Town: David Philip, 1987), pp. 136–8; J. C. Smuts, *Memorandum on government natives and coloured bills* (Pretoria: South African Party, 1926), pp. 13, 16.

[62] Cited in Shamil Jeppie, 'Re-classifications: Coloured, Malay, Muslim', in Erasmus (ed.), *Coloured by history, shaped by place*, pp. 85, 95; also J. Klaaren, 'Migrating to citizenship: mobility, law, and nationality in South Africa, 1897–1937', unpublished Ph.D. thesis, Yale University (2004), pp. 40, 55.

[63] Cited in M. Shain, *The roots of antisemitism in South Africa* (Johannesburg: Witwatersrand University Press, 1994), pp. 4, 137–9.

so as to attain basic human rights and full citizenship for all sections of the South African population.

During the Second World War, basic civil and political dimensions of citizenship, as illustrated herein, were augmented by new ideas of social citizenship, a concept foreshadowed in Britain's Beveridge Report and formalised at the end of the decade in T. H. Marshall's classic essay 'Citizenship and Social Class'. It was the 'radical moment' of the 1940s that gave rise to the idea of '[b]road-based social citizenship' in South Africa.[64] Notions of social citizenship were implicit in the extension of welfare benefits to black as well as white South Africans on a universal basis, albeit within the framework of a differential racially coded system. Measures to extend social and medical provision were in large measure a response to the expectations and demands of a rapidly urbanising black society. Greater recognition of social and economic interdependence from the late 1930s also prompted moves to recognise the permanency of blacks in towns and cities. However, whether concessions made in the name of 'a fundamentally different notion of urban citizenship'[65] conferred political rights – or were a substitute for such rights – depended on one's view of race and democracy in postwar society.

By the 1940s, the reinvigorated African National Congress was not prepared to tolerate concessions in the sphere of welfare as a substitute for civic or political rights: inspired by the worldwide democratic fight against fascism, young ANC intellectuals increasingly demanded citizenship as an entitlement rooted in South African nationality, birth, and belonging. No longer could citizenship be proffered by the colonial state as a reward for demonstrable cultural assimilation to standards of 'civilisation', as had been the case in the nineteenth century, nor could it be traded for land and trusteeship, as was the case in the segregationist compact of the 1930s.

In the case of white politics, citizenship became integrally linked to the expansive South Africanism of Smuts and Hofmeyr, a movement or sentiment that reached its apogee as English and Afrikaner volunteers joined battle in the fight against fascism. Wartime conditions proved conducive to extensive schemes of social welfare and scientific planning, and the role of the state as an agent of positive change was thereby considerably enhanced. Vigorous publications with a strong South Africanist flavour, like *The Democrat*, *Trek*, and *The Forum*, provided new avenues for liberal

---

[64] J. Seekings, 'Visions, hopes and views about the future: the radical moment of South African welfare reform', in Dubow and Jeeves (eds.), *South Africa's 1940s*, p. 50.

[65] D. Posel, 'The case for a welfare state: poverty and the politics of the urban African family in the 1930s and 40s', in Dubow and Jeeves (eds.), *South Africa's 1940s*, pp. 74, 78.

and radical thought. The extensive programme of army education devised by E. G. Malherbe, R. F. A. Hoernlé, and Leo and Nell Marquard, exposed many receptive soldiers to liberal-democratic ideas and prompted them to reflect on South African society in novel ways. Education in principles of citizenship was an important aspect of this programme, although Malherbe clearly favoured a more restrictive and conservative approach to citizenship and social justice than did the Marquards. Leo Marquard's radical thinking at this time was essayed in *The Black Man's Burden* (published under the pseudonym John Burger – that is, John Citizen).[66] It mixed historical with contemporary analysis to produce a powerful indictment of racial and capitalist exploitation. For Marquard, hope for the future lay in the emergence of a strong nonracial working-class movement.

The forward-looking, inclusive vision of South Africa advanced by Marquard and others on the liberal left was not, however, deeply rooted in the white electorate. In 1941 G. H. Calpin, a conservative English-speaking journalist, wrote the best-selling book titled *There Are No South Africans*, in which he lamented the lack of any shared national sentiment and dismissed spurious attempts to cultivate a common South Africanism. Divisions between English and Afrikaners meant that there were 'two flags, two languages, two policies towards the Native, two ideas of economic advance. . . . ' Far from bringing the country together, participation in the war was causing the 'two streams' of national life' to 'diverge to polar limits'.[67] Consumed by the absence of a common white identity, Calpin had nothing whatsoever to say about black South Africans, for whom the war had a transforming effect, socially, politically, and intellectually.

Like most of his fellow white South Africans, Calpin did not register the emergence in the 1940s of a newly confident and assertive generation of urban-based black intellectuals. Their leading representatives pressed for inclusion in South African society, not as a privilege, but as a right. In the paintings of George Pemba and Gerard Sekoto, in the proletarian *marabi* music of the streets and shebeens, or the more sophisticated American-influenced swing rhythms of big bands such as the Jazz Maniacs, township life acquired vibrant and tumultuous cultural forms that embraced modernity and progress even while drawing on older African motifs and traditions. Middle-class African educators attempted, not always successfully, to steer this exuberant creativity into 'a model African National Culture' suitable 'for all classes of African townsmen'.[68]

[66] London: Gollancz, 1943.

[67] G. H. Calpin, *There are no South Africans* (London: Nelson, 1941), pp. 25, 32.

[68] D. B. Coplan, *In township tonight: South Africa's black city music and theatre* (Johannesburg: Ravan Press, 1985), pp. 132, 138.

The gradualism and deferential attitudes of mission-educated Africans and the paternalism of well-meaning white liberals were dismissed with amused disdain by the writer Herbert Dhlomo, who proclaimed the emergence of the progressive and forward-looking 'New African' (a term inviting comparison with the Howard University philosopher Alain Locke's identification of a 'new spirit . . . awake in the masses' in his 1925 essay 'Enter the New Negro'). To the journalist Jordan Ngubane, writing in 1941, Dhlomo's writing moved 'beyond tribalism and tutelage to a "truly national spirit" which affirmed that "it will be the African himself who shall rise to fight to reach his goal".' His poems were, Ngubane felt, "an encouragement to fight with greater confidence to become a citizen of the country of [our] birth".[69]

The African National Congress reemerged during the war years as the leading force in black oppositional politics, its character newly reshaped by a growing mass base and an infusion of trade union, communist, and Africanist ideas. In documents such as Africans' Claims in South Africa and the Atlantic Charter from the Standpoint of Africans (adopted as official ANC policy in 1943), the rhetoric of democratic rights, citizenship, and national self-determination is conspicuously present. Africans' Claims included a bill of rights that began by demanding, as a matter of urgency, the granting of 'full citizenship rights such as are enjoyed by all Europeans in South Africa'.[70] As well as being the ANC's most ambitious and clear statement of African political aspirations and rights to date, it is also notable for the way it universalised the meaning of freedom set out in the Atlantic Charter (rather against the wishes of Churchill, whose substitution of the phrase 'all the men in all the lands' for 'all peoples' in the Atlantic Charter proved a hostage to democratic fortune). Long-standing transatlantic links were reaffirmed with African Americans by A. B. Xuma, who forged a political alliance with the pan-Africanist-inclined Council on African Affairs led by Paul Robeson and Max Yergan. This radical organisation looked to support the transatlantic African diaspora and 'international anti-colonialism'. It was with the support of the Council on African Affairs that Xuma petitioned the newly created United Nations to challenge Smuts's racial policies.

With even greater insistence and in tones of conspicuous racial pride, the African National Congress Youth League and its leading intellectuals, Anton Lembede and Peter Mda, proclaimed the philosophy of Africanism. Whereas earlier emanations of Africanist ideas frequently countenanced

---

[69] N. Visser and T. Couzens (eds.), introduction to *H. I. E. Dhlomo, Collected works* (Johannesburg: Ravan Press, 1985), p. xiv.

[70] Karis and Carter (eds.), *From protest to challenge*, vol. 3, p. 217, doc. 29.

avoidance of white authority (and flourished in the countryside, where white authority was dispersed and separatist dreams could take hold), the Africanism of the 1940s was overwhelmingly urban in orientation and addressed directly the institutions of state. It focused on the need for African unity, was fulsome in its rejection of 'tribalism', and had as its primary objective the removal of white domination and the attainment of full citizenship under African leadership. As if in answer to Trollope and Millin, Lembede made the blunt assertion, '*Africa is a blackman's country*'.[71]

Variants of socialist and Marxist analysis provided intellectual ballast for the Africanist-inspired radicalism of the Youth League and sought to explain South African history by reference to colonial dispossession, social class, and economic exploitation. The Communist Party benefited from a large increase in its membership during the 1940s and served as an important source of radical ideas; so, too, did the small Western Cape–based and Trotskyite-influenced Non-European Unity Movement (est. 1943), whose leadership was drawn predominantly from coloured teachers and intellectuals. Unity Movement activists associated with the Anti-CAD (Anti-Coloured Affairs Department) campaign of 1943 expressed 'our right to be full citizens of South Africa' and reminded supporters that we 'have always fought against any political move or legislation which wanted to treat us as "special" creatures who need "special" political, economic, educational and social institutions'.[72]

The pamphlets and newspaper articles generated by Unity Movement intellectuals were in theory addressed to the black working class, but they were typically written in an arcane, didactic style suitable only for an audience of converts and activists. Efforts were, however, made to write instructional material utilising a wide-ranging historical approach that sought to subvert standard interpretations of the South African past. These included two pseudonymous works published in the same year as the 1952 Van Riebeeck tercentenary: Mnguni's (Hosea Jaffe's) *Three Hundred Years: A History of South Africa*[73] and Nosipho Majeke's (Dora Taylor's) *The Role of the Missionaries in Conquest*.[74] Both works emerged under the aegis of the Unity Movement and aimed to analyse South African history from the perspective

---

[71] A. M. Lembede, 'Policy of the Congress Youth League' *Inkundla ya Bantu* (May 1946), cited in Karis and Carter (eds.), *From protest to challenge*, vol. 2, p. 317.

[72] A. Drew (ed.), *South Africa's radical tradition: A documentary history*. vol. 2, 1943–1964 (Cape Town: Mayibuye, 1996), pt. 1, doc. 2. Anti-C[oloured] A[ffairs] D[epartment] refers to government proposals in 1943 to establish a special government department to deal with matters affecting 'coloured' people.

[73] Landsdowne: New Era Fellowship, 1952.

[74] Johannesburg: Society of Young Africa, 1952.

of the indigenous peoples' experience of colonial conquest and ideological subjection. The Communist Party's perspective on the South African past, and its own contribution to the struggle, was articulated by Lionel Forman in a pamphlet and in episodic essay form in the Party journal *New Age*.

IX

These examples of politically engaged history can be seen as forerunners of the *marxisant* popular history approach that flourished in South African liberal universities from the mid-1970s, but they remained almost unknown and unread beyond narrow circles of political activists before their rediscovery by left-wing academic historians. Until the publication of Jack and Ray Simons's *Class and Colour in South Africa* in 1969 – a landmark work that combined original scholarly research with Communist Party discipline – only Leo Marquard's *Black Man's Burden* and Eddie Roux's *Time Longer Than Rope* were available to a broader audience, notwithstanding government banning orders, which meant that Roux's and the Simons's texts could be read only clandestinely. The ephemeral writings and intense debates of Unity Movement and communist intellectuals during the 1950s (whose participants also included Kenny Jordaan, Ben Kies, A. C. Jordan, Thomas Ngwenya, Michael Harmel, Ruth First, and Joe Matthews) were important in raising theoretical questions such as the nature of capitalist exploitation, the relationship between race and class, and approaches to the perennial 'national question'. In so doing, the essence of the South African problem was being thoroughly reconceived, not just in historical terms but politically as well.

Communist debate on the national question and the concept of the national democratic revolution was a recondite activity laden with references to Stalinist theory, yet it had palpable practical implications. Marxist ideology invariably struggled to comprehend colonial nationalist and ethnic sentiments in its conceptual framework; racism presented even greater difficulties. If the left chose to finesse or avoid this issue, the right was not so deterred. Bonds of nation and race were real enough in South Africa, and the apartheid state duly devoted more and more energy during the 1950s to their manipulation.

Meanwhile, South Africa's changing constitutional position in the Commonwealth prompted rethinking of citizenship. An act of primary legislation in 1949 gave legal meaning to South African citizenship for the first time. Before this date, the relevant categories were 'British subjects' or 'Union nationals', and the latter category bore few substantive rights. To be a British subject was thus to be a citizen not only of South Africa but of the Commonwealth as well. Unlike the case in other former dominions,

South African citizens henceforth ceased to be British subjects. Blacks were not actually deprived of citizenship in 1949, but the legislation nonetheless marked a step in the process of making citizenship exclusive and race dependent. This was clearly signalled in the 1950 Population Registration Act, which gave statutory recognition to mechanisms of racial classification. The 1951 Bantu Authorities Act set in train a pattern of 'retribalisation' that, in the words of the 1959 Promotion of Bantu Self-Government Act, sought to divide Africans into 'separate national units on the basis of language and culture'.[75] From the constitutional point of view, separate development 'became a process of denationalisation in which the citizenship of black South Africans was recreated as foreign citizenship regardless of the individual's place of birth or preference'.[76] The prospect of a South Africa so exclusive that blacks were not merely second-class citizens but not citizens at all, was for many a genuine possibility. It was a vision that exemplified the apartheid state at its most hubristic.

The Verwoerdian government's growing insistence on ethnic or tribal subdivisions represented a significant reformulation of long-established distinctions between 'westernised' or 'detribalised' city-based Africans on the one hand and tribal traditionalists on the other hand. Official use of the term *Bantu* in preference to *natives* dates from this period, indicating efforts to clothe apartheid policies in the enabling language of an Afrikanerised *volks* anthropology. One option for opponents of apartheid was to deny the existence of racial and ethnic groupings – often signalled by a refusal to deal in its linguistic coinage. But this strategy of principled nonracialism, favoured by many liberals as well as by Marxists, failed to take account of practical identity politics. For the ANC, the problem was all the more acute because the increasingly assertive 'Africanist' constituency in its ranks remained deeply suspicious of the participation of non-Africans in Congress affairs.

At the historic Congress of the People in 1955, the ANC was confirmed as first among equals within a liberation movement structured as a parallel organisational alliance, comprising interest groups (trade unionists and women) and peoples (African, coloured, Indian, and white). The revolutionary tone of the Freedom Charter signalled a departure from the wartime aspirations of the ANC, where 'the figure of the black as an equal human being and as a citizen' emerged to the fore. Increasingly, the communist-authorised theory of 'national democratic revolution' came to be expressed in tones of vernacular populism: the people, the masses, workers, peasants,

---

[75] Promotion of Bantu Self-Government Act, No.46 of 1959.

[76] H. Klug, *Constituting democracy: law, globalism and South Africa's political reconstruction* (Cambridge: Cambridge University Press, 2000), pp. 40–1.

and so on. Strikingly, every constituent organisation at the Congress of the People bore the name *South African* in its title, thereby reinforcing the idea that the Congress movement's goal was a unitary state in which 'national' and 'cultural' differences would be accorded recognition, celebrated even, so long as this did not jeopardise the achievement of a common or supra–South African nationality. This was made clear by Congress's strong disdain for 'tribalism'. It was powerfully reiterated by the Freedom Charter's declaration that 'South Africa belongs to all who live in it, Black and White' and the promise that 'all national groups shall have equal rights'.

Notably, there is only one passing mention of 'citizenship' in this landmark document that conceives of democracy in the radical idiom of popular sovereignty and collective 'will' rather than through the discourse of bourgeois or liberal constitutionalism or civil rights. Notwithstanding the charter's revolutionary tone, it was evident to some that the multiracial configuration of the Congress movement mirrored the officially sanctioned racial categories of the apartheid state in uncomfortable ways. The 'four nation' makeup of Congress was thus attacked by proponents of nonracialism, such as the Unity Movement, as well as by members of the ANC Youth League and pan-Africanists who resented the formal equivalence of African and non-African groupings.

The downgrading of individual citizenship rights in the Freedom Charter was paralleled by Christian-national apartheid discourse, which was ontologically founded on recognition of ethnic groups rather than individual citizens. But whereas charterism was inclusive in respect of South African nationhood, Afrikaner nationalism was manifestly exclusive. In the first decades of the century, Afrikaner nationalist demands focussed on the need to establish ethnic and cultural parity with white English speakers. By the 1940s, however, republicanism had become central to Afrikaner nationalist aspirations, and the emphasis of nationalist politics shifted decisively to capture and control of the state by the *volk*. In other words, an ethnic minority sought to secure its future by assuming majority status. Verwoerd's declaration of a republic in 1961 gave substance to Afrikaner nationalists' growing assumption 'that only they were truly South Africans'.[77] Although Verwoerd made soothing overtures to English speakers after leading South Africa out of the British Commonwealth (this was arguably the high point of his political career), there could be no doubting that Afrikaners saw the themselves as South Africans in a primary, indissoluble sense. It was their natural homeland or 'fatherland'.

Tellingly, the adjectival term *English-speaking South African* came increasingly into vogue. Afrikaner nationalists delighted in goading the English

---

[77] Giliomee, *The Afrikaners*, p. 399.

into declaring their loyalties in the language of exclusive dualism: to England or to South Africa. In the decade after 1948, English speakers expressed shock at their sudden exclusion from political power and cavilled at what they considered their second-class citizenship.[78] The historian Arthur Keppel-Jones observed at the time, 'From the Nationalist point of view there is much to be said for using *Afrikaner* in one case and *Engelssprekende* in the other, as implying that one has a nationality and the other only a language.'[79] Yet other English speakers adjusted to the new regime and took comfort in their marginalised, minority status. For one thing, it seemed to excuse them from complicity in the more odious aspects of apartheid. Moreover, English-speaking South Africans were notable for being the only group in the category-obsessed apartheid state who largely avoided being defined in ethnic or national terms. The universality of the English language and the presumed universality of British culture and institutions facilitated this claim.

The uneasy similarity in the discourse of government and the liberation movement around issues like groups and peoples can also be seen as a reflection of the growing acceptance of the politics of multiracialism. The term seems to have been first used by the liberal philosopher Alfred Hoernlé in 1939 to define the South African condition; however, it was only a decade later that it came into vogue. One source of its reintroduction was the shift from empire to commonwealth: in debates around federation in the Rhodesias, for example, multiracialism was recommended as a means of reconciling settler political interests with those of the indigenous majority. In 1950s South Africa, multiracialism came to be closely associated with moderate Christian and liberal bridge-building initiatives. Albert Luthuli envisaged the Congress of the People as the embodiment of 'our multiracial nation', much to the disquiet of Youth Leaguers and Africanist spokespeople like Potlake Leballo and Josias Madzunya. Tensions with the pan-Africanists were reaching a critical point when, in December 1958, Luthuli pointedly endorsed the idea of a multiracial society eleven times in his presidential speech to the ANC.[80] For its part, the white liberal Progressive Party, formed in 1959, made a great deal of the idea that multiracialism was an undeniable reality that the government could ill afford to ignore.

With backing like this, it is hardly surprising that apartheid ideologues disparaged multiracialism as a left-liberal concept that wrongly presumed

---

[78] Ibid., p. 492.

[79] A. Keppel-Jones, *Friends or foes?* (Pietermaritzburg: Shuter and Shooter, [1949]), p. 81.

[80] G. Pillay, *Voices of liberation*, vol. 1, *Albert Lutuli* (Pretoria: HSRC, 1993), p. 7; A. Luthuli, 'The Christian and political issues', in *The Christian citizen in a multi-racial society*, www.anc.org.za/ancdocs/speeches/1950s/lutuli58.html.

different groups could coexist peacefully in a single political framework. In their view, only total separation between black and white – coupled with a recognition that the 'Bantu' were a heterogeneous collection of different 'ethnic groups', each of whom should enjoy a measure of 'self-determination' – would suffice. The bristling rejection of multiracialism by apartheid intellectuals like Werner Eiselen nonetheless concealed tacit acceptance of its underlying assumptions. Thus, when the overweening plans of apartheid's engineers began to falter in the 1970s, apartheid would itself be reinterpreted in terms of multiracial or multinational partnership. Later, still, the idea would reemerge in the more fluid and inclusive language of the 'rainbow nation', pioneered by Archbishop Desmond Tutu and given secular political authority by Nelson Mandela.

Another term for multiracialism was *ethnic pluralism*, a term enjoying the advantage of a more distinguished academic lineage. The concept was initially developed by J. S. Furnivall to examine how communities in Dutch colonial Southeast Asia, divided along lines of language, culture, and religion, coexisted uneasily in a common political entity and a shared economic system. It was elaborated further by the Caribbean anthropologist M. G. Smith in the 1960s, acquiring a specifically South African dimension through the writings of Leo Kuper and Pierre van den Berghe. Pluralism's slippery character facilitated its entrance into debates bearing on the nature of South African society. From the 1970s, it was deployed in theoretical discussions about the relationship of race, culture, and ethnicity; in considerations of group interaction and identity; and in the context of reformist attempts to devise alternative constitutional arrangements capable of taking some account of the need for power sharing between racial groups.

The idea of group-based power sharing was adopted enthusiastically by liberal conservatives advocating consociational models of governance in the 1970s and 1980s. But it was strongly rejected by those who insisted on the idea of a unitary South Africa embracing common citizenship and who therefore refused to countenance notions of divided sovereignty or minority privileges. Even so, beyond liberal circles of the legal profession and the opposition Progressive Federal Party, little interest was displayed at this time in the need for a Bill of Rights guaranteeing substantive freedoms and liberties for all South African citizens. The government remained actively hostile to 'humanist' or liberal emphasis on individual rights until the mid-1980s.

During the transition to majority rule in the 1990s, the government's desperate invocation of multiple 'group rights' was countered by the ANC's proprietorial claim to represent 'the people' – always conceived of in the singular as if to signal African primacy and indivisibility. However, as this political argument proceeded, the ANC made increasing recourse to the language of citizenship and human rights thinking, having previously relied on the populist Freedom Charter as the guarantor of constitutional rights. The formation of the United Democratic Front in 1983 and the reassertion of the Congress tradition that accompanied it, revived interest in the thirty-year-old Freedom Charter. Debates about the meaning of the historical document focused on whether it was a blueprint for socialism or an endorsement of bourgeois democracy. Strikingly, there was little if any discussion on the left at this time about the constitutional and legal implications of 'the people' – beyond the presumption that nonracism should be a cardinal principle. The post-1989 global shift toward human rights discourse became especially evident during the political bargaining at the Convention for a Democratic South Africa (CODESA) negotiations and debates around the principles of a new constitution. Here, the ANC counterposed its own commitment to a democratic order based on the participation of individual citizens with the government's last-ditch attempts to guarantee minority 'group rights'.

The preamble to the 1994 (interim) South African Constitution recalls the Freedom Charter in its opening phrase, 'We, the people of South Africa', but immediately goes on to state the entitlement of all South Africans to common citizenship.[81] An advanced bill of rights professing itself the 'cornerstone of democracy in South Africa' lies at the heart of the new constitutional dispensation. Notably, this dispensation necessitated the repeal of the 1970 Bantu Homelands Citizenship Act, which in the era of high apartheid, amounted to 'mandatory denationalization' of black South Africans: in the notorious dystopia formulated by Minister Connie Mulder, minister of plural relations in 1978, it implied there would ultimately 'not be one Black man with South African citizenship'.[82]

X

From the 1960s, a new generation of liberal historians invested complexity and time-depth to the idea of South Africa as a multiracial or plural society. Africanists, as they styled themselves, stressed themes of interaction and mutual dependence among the 'peoples' of southern Africa, and they placed special emphasis on instances of African agency and initiative. The defining statement of liberal Africanism was the two-volume *Oxford History of South Africa*, edited by the anthropologist Monica Wilson and

---

[81] Cf. preamble to the Constitution, adopted by the Constitutional Assembly, on 8 May 1996. See also 1994 ANC national election manifesto, which begins with the declaration, 'On 27 April, for the first time in our history, all of us will stand tall and proud as equal citizens in our common home', www.anc.org.za/ancdocs/policy/manifesto.html.

[82] J. Dugard, *Human rights and the South African legal order* (Princeton, NJ: Princeton University Press, 1987), p. 95.

the historian Leonard Thompson. Its opening words declared: 'This work derives from our belief that the central theme of South African history is interaction between peoples of diverse origins, languages, technologies, ideologies, and social systems, meeting on South African soil.'[83]

To this ringing statement, in which there is little if any sense of South African nationality, the editors added a qualification: 'It is peculiarly difficult to write the history of a society which has become as rigidly stratified as South African society. Recent histories of South Africa illustrate the difficulties.' The works cited to prove their point included recent reissues of Eric Walker's *History of South Africa* and the South African volume of the *Cambridge History of the British Empire*, both of which were first published in the mid-1930s. An even better example appeared in the same year in English translation: *500 Years: A History of South Africa*, edited by C. F. J. Muller. [84] This product of Afrikaner nationalist historiography was everything the *Oxford History* was not. It began by recounting the 'activities and experiences of the White man in South Africa' from the era of Portuguese colonisation and took no account whatsoever of precolonial African history (a theme much stressed by Wilson and Thompson). Blacks were so marginal to the story recounted in *500 Years* that their chief appearance was in the form of an appendix by a little-known anthropologist titled 'The Natives of South Africa' (along with the addendum 'South African Monetary Systems'). Muller's relegation of blacks to the fringes of history mirrored contemporaneous legislative provisions to strip most Africans of their South African citizenship.

It is a measure of the division that existed between English liberals and Afrikaner nationalists at this time that the Wilson-Thompson and Muller histories occupied separate intellectual spheres, neither of which felt the need to take more than passing account of each other. Indeed, the real challenge to the *Oxford History* came nearer to home from a new generation of scholars, strongly influenced by historical materialist analysis, including Shula Marks, Stanley Trapido, and Martin Legassick. For these so-called revisionists, the conceptual assumptions of the *Oxford History* – in particular, its lack of attention to structural economic determinants – were a fatal weakness. As the liberal-radical historiographical debate gathered momentum, in an environment of intense and sometimes acrimonious disagreement, argument centred on the importance or otherwise of social class to the formation of South Africa's past and the making of its future.

The 'Societies of Southern Africa' seminar at the University of London, inaugurated in 1969 (the same year in which volume 1 of the *Oxford*

---

[83] Wilson and Thompson (eds.), *A history of South Africa*, vol. 1, preface.
[84] Pretoria: Academica, 1969.

History and the English translation of Muller's *500 Years* was published) provided a key forum for the production and dissemination of radical history. This innovative seminar had a political as well as an intellectual agenda, and in its early years, many of its participants launched powerful attacks on liberal presuppositions. Viewed in retrospect, however, the paradigmatic differences in approach that apparently divided liberals and radicals occluded underlying similarities in approach. It is worth observing, for example, that the name of the London seminar could equally have been adopted by Wilson and Thompson. Many (though by no means all) revisionists shared with liberal Africanists a concern with precolonial African history, a sensitivity to anthropological approaches, and an engagement with a wider Africanist scholarship. Both groups were, moreover, indebted to the earlier insights of Macmillan and De Kiewiet, and both viewed South Africa as a zone of interaction and conflict among different peoples, all of whom by implication had a legitimate claim on common citizenship.

A further similarity between liberal Africanist and radical historians lay in their determination to avoid apartheid-imposed labels and tribal categories. This often manifested itself in punctilious efforts to produce correct African orthographies; it soon became a convention to preface monographs with a critical note on racial terminology and nomenclature. Important as such emendations undoubtedly were for the world of academic scholarship, their impact was, necessarily, limited. Indeed, a wider-ranging and politically ambitious challenge to apartheid habits of mind and linguistic conventions was arising at the same time, though from a very different direction. This was expressed by intellectuals of the Black Consciousness Movement whose thinking was sharply opposed to that of liberal Africanists and Marxists alike.

Intellectuals associated with the Black Consciousness Movement rejected racial categorisations that divided the 'oppressed', arguing instead for a common black identity encompassing the shared experience of Africans, coloureds, and Indians. In denouncing the studied nonracialism of liberals, which was often interpreted as supercilious or patronising, they argued that white South Africans, regardless of political outlook or sympathies, were all beneficiaries of the apartheid system. The Black Consciousness Movement was indebted to the earlier Africanism of Lembede and Mda in key respects, but its objectives were broader and more radical. True liberation required a transformation in black self-image. The word *black* was therefore infused with powerful new resonance; it became a synonym for the oppressed as well as a byword for freedom. By embracing Africa as a whole and by rejecting extraneous 'European' influences, black-consciousness ideology laid claim to a sense of national identity and self-realisation that transcended the country's borders and extended the idea of liberation beyond the realms of tangible political power.

The Black Consciousness Movement's determination to confront white supremacy by challenging the hegemony of colonial linguistic construc-tions was signalled by its frequent usage of *Azania* in preference to *South Africa*. Terms bearing negative connotations such as *nonwhite* or *non-European* were dismissed with contempt. By contrast, 'blackness' became invested with positive spiritual and moral qualities and was divested of its bio-physical connotations. Steve Biko's courtroom exchange in the 1976 South African Students' Organisation/Black People's Convention trial, when he mocked the anomalous character of his judge-inquisitor's 'whiteness', is a telling example of this strategy of linguistic inversion and destabilisation. The rebuff delivered to white liberals in 1969 when Biko's organisation denounced the hypocrisy of the National Union of South African Students was another sharp reminder – this time directed to an ostensibly sym-pathetic political constituency – that the very status of whites as South Africans was problematic. It underlined the message that blacks had to be the agents of their own liberation and that white sympathisers should aspire only to play a supportive part in the struggle for freedom; hence the iconic black-consciousness slogan enunciated by Barney Pityana in 1971: 'Black man, you are on your own'.

The effect of black consciousness on young white South Africans who sought to identify with the liberation movement was immediate and pro-found, in some cases traumatic: no longer could whites presume to speak on behalf of others or take their South Africanness for granted. Leaders in the National Union of South African Students duly began to consider the problem of 'whiteness'. Rick Turner's influential *Eye of the Needle* (1972), published just before the Durban strike wave, was an especially important intervention, both because of its perspicacious understanding of the his-torical moment and by virtue of its fundamental challenge to underlying white South African assumptions and self-perceptions. In the post-1976 era, the onus was increasingly on white sympathisers to prove themselves white Africans, to eschew European cultural dominance, and to engage in a process of personal and institutional Africanisation. At the same time, the ideology of nonracism emerged as a powerful unifying force, embraced by the United Democratic Front in the 1980s and underpinned by many, albeit not all, black trade unions.

Nonracial and inclusive Africanisation, pressed especially by left-wing student activists and intellectuals, was at first influential only on the mar-gins. It gained momentum through the crisis years of the 1980s through advocacy by pressure groups like the National Union of South African

Students and the campus-based End Conscription Campaign. This organisation maintained that white soldiers on the borders and in the townships were not fighting foreign communists and agitators, as the government insisted, but were instead being drafted into a civil war against their black South African fellow citizens. As the solidity of the apartheid state began to collapse, more and more white opinion formers became cognisant of this reality. Yet it was probably only after the unbanning of the ANC and the Communist Party in 1990 that the opening line of the 1955 Freedom Charter – 'South Africa belongs to all who live in it, black and white' – can be said to have imprinted itself in the consciousness of most South Africans. Defenders of white supremacy, who would previously have regarded this statement as subversive, hurried to embrace it as a protection that should not be lightly spurned.

In the 'new' South Africa, whose coming was so often referred to as a 'miracle', the apartheid vision of a 'land of contrasts' effortlessly yielded to the ANC's slogan 'One Nation, Many Cultures'. This transformation has become visibly apparent in dress, style, food, and in the way the country projects itself as an attractive destination for foreign tourists keen to experience effervescent multiculturalism in an agreeably exotic location. Conversely, the government soon became concerned with protecting the country's borders from immigrants and refugees from elsewhere in Africa. Archbishop Tutu's compelling metaphor of the 'rainbow nation', nowhere performed more poignantly than when Nelson Mandela donned captain Francois Pienaar's jersey in the 1995 Rugby World Cup, came to symbolise reconciliation and newfound freedom. These principles were given official endorsement through the Truth and Reconciliation Commission (TRC), which reported in 1998. Under Archbishop Tutu's leadership, the TRC strove to create a sense of cathartic South Africanness based on restorative justice, shared humanity (*ubuntu*), and collective moral redemption. A secondary but no less important function of the TRC was to legitimate the nation-building project by infusing the fragile new dispensation with a living culture of human rights founded on the rule of law.

The politics of reconciliation were, however, only momentarily bonding, and they were soon given a different angle by Mandela's deputy and successor, Thabo Mbeki, who increasingly took the view that reconciliation should not be read as moral equivalence with respect to those who fought for, and those who opposed, apartheid. Nor should reconciliation obstruct redress. Mbeki's adoption of the idea of the African Renaissance was one means to achieve societal and attitudinal transformation. In his 1996 'I Am an African' speech, delivered on the occasion of the adoption of the new constitution, Mbeki was elegiac in his evocation of a common

South African identity 'born of the peoples of the continent of Africa'. He disavowed a sense of Africanness 'defined by our race, colour, gender or historical origins'.[85] Yet it is not clear from a close reading of this speech whether all Africans are constituted as being equally African – or, indeed, South African.

Increasingly, Mbeki's African Renaissance was harnessed to race-based historical entitlement. Programmes of black economic empowerment stressed the need for practical economic redress, at least with respect to the newly privileged political elite (the formation in 1993 of the African Renaissance Holdings company was an early example). For the African poor who were not visible beneficiaries of the new dispensation, rights brokered through struggle and conferred by South African citizenship were a precious political resource: citizenship became the basis of social claims on the South African state, ranging from pensions and welfare provision to housing, electricity, and clean water. The inability or unwillingness of the state to satisfy such demands, coupled with a perception that 'foreigners' and refugees from the rest of the African continent were taking unfair advantage of economic opportunities, gave rise to widespread anti-immigrant sentiment from the mid-1990s, which was to deteriorate into xenophobic violence in the early years of the twenty-first century. This was a clear repudiation of the view espoused in the Freedom Charter (and confirmed by the South African Constitution's human rights provisions) that 'South Africa belongs to all who live in it'.

XI

Over the course of more than a century of modern South African history, from the 1870s to the present, a great deal has changed with respect to thinking about the country and its peoples. Awareness of South Africa as an imagined unity dates from the beginnings of this period; but the achievement of a unitary state inhabited by a community of citizens enjoying common legal rights took more than a century to realise. The process is still incomplete and rather more fragile than politicians of a variety of stripes would wish to acknowledge. Does the claim to Africanness take precedence over that of South Africanness? Is the national community coterminous with those who struggled against or suffered under apartheid? Does it extend to members of neighbouring states who did so much to

---

[85] www.anc.org.za/ancdocs/history/mbeki/1996/sp960508.html. It is unclear what Mbeki meant when he said, 'At times, and in fear, I have wondered whether I should concede equal citizenship of our country to the leopard and the lion, the elephant and the springbok, the hyena, the black mamba and the pestilential mosquito'.

support the anti-apartheid struggle? Is it possible, in the words of two recent commentators, 'to facilitate historical social justice while building a single national identity'?[86]

In one postapartheid history of the country, the author observes, 'even if the essential unity of South Africa and the identity of South Africans are beyond dispute, there remains the question of what is, and what is not, South Africa. Who are, and who are not, South Africans[?]' Another comparable historical introduction turns around the idea of 'a state without a nation'.[87] Arguably, such questions would have been more familiar to observers of the first new South Africa in 1910 than they were to subsequent generations of professional historians, for whom the unit of analysis – South Africa – has been rather less problematic. At that time, the Afrikaner nationalist poet C. J. Langenhoven, who later wrote the words of the country's first national anthem, 'Die Stem', was unfashionably sceptical about the '"roseate hue of enthusiasm" that flourished in "the first flush of the dawn of our Union"'. He warned:

It is true, no doubt, that the racial bitterness of the past has been buried; but since neither of the two races has been buried, it is equally true that racialism is not dead but sleepeth. That this must be so is abundantly taught us by the history of our own past.[88]

Central to the argument of this chapter is that there is nothing self-evident about South Africa or South Africans and that the struggle for South Africa has always been, and in many ways continues to be, a struggle to become South African.

[86] A. Habib and K. Bentley (eds.), *Racial redress and citizenship in South Africa* (Pretoria: HSRC, 2008), p. 14.

[87] R. Ross, *A concise history of South Africa* (Cambridge: Cambridge University Press, 1999), p. 3; W. Beinart, *Twentieth century South Africa* (Oxford: Oxford University Press, 1994).

[88] C. J. Langenhoven, 'The problem of the dual language in South Africa', *State* (March 1910), 403.

2

IMPERIALISM, SETTLER IDENTITIES, AND COLONIAL CAPITALISM: THE HUNDRED-YEAR ORIGINS OF THE 1899 SOUTH AFRICAN WAR

STANLEY TRAPIDO

The South African War of 1899–1902 was the culmination – if not an inevitable one – of a hundred years of British domination of the region. That domination began with the seizure of the Cape of Good Hope from the Dutch in 1795, beginning an economic and ideological as well as political hegemony. Britain's presence in South Africa followed from strategic assumptions born of its need to defend Indian Ocean interests. Strategic considerations meant that the British, like the Dutch before them, had to provision the Indian Ocean's naval and mercantile fleets. Settler expansion into more and more distant hinterlands – to secure ecological zones where crops or stock could be raised – not only had to be allowed but also had to be furthered with imperial troops. The impact of British rule in South Africa, with Downing Street's power and Whitehall's administration, was willy-nilly, turning social structures in the Cape, and beyond, into a series of new and changing collaborations, alliances, oppositions and identities. Expansion required conquering African territories and, thereafter, the distribution of African land and labour. This was a process that mostly favoured British merchants and traders at the expense of Dutch Afrikaner settlers in the interior. Eventually, local ethnic and regional groupings were provoked into a new assertiveness and began to acquire objectives of their own. In this way, subimperialisms emerged. Then, in the last third of the century, the region was further transformed by the discovery of diamonds and, thereafter, gold. Out of these latter discoveries came a powerful and confident mining capitalism embedded in South Africa but linked to the world's major financial centre, which was the City of London. Determining how these transformations took place and how interactions among the imperial state, settler ambitions and capitalist enclaves eventually erupted into war is the major purpose of this chapter. The analysis and the narrative that trace these developments have a well-known and considerable, if contentious, literature. It stretches from the contemporary observers of empire and imperialism to the analysts and the analysis operating before and after the South African War. The first section of what follows examines the many forces shaping the political economy of southern Africa in the period up to the mid-1890s. Section II concentrates on the tumultuous years between circa 1895 and 1899, from the moment when the discovery of 'deep levels' of gold underneath the first Rand caused the pace of events to quicken throughout the region.

I

The Cape Colony

European colonisation of the Cape – the Dutch between 1652 and 1795, the British occupation beginning in the nineteenth century – was secured to further Britain's strategic-cum-mercantile preoccupations in India and East Asia. Those strategic objectives led the colonising power to hold not only the region's coastline and safe harbours but also to secure inland agricultural lands. To reduce costs, they found collaborators who would help secure their primary purpose, guarding the Cape against the designs of other European powers. Although indigenous Khoe peoples were employed in military roles, Britain chose its own settlers, and the inaccurately named Cape Dutch, as its principal collaborators. In practice, however, British settlers immediately became a strategic liability in that they required additional military intervention to ensure their security. But in addition to the military support that Britain gave its settlers, it bestowed on them economic, political and ideological power. Settlers, old and new, building on this authority, rapidly acquired additional aspirations of their own, and several settler identities, associated with separate economic and partisan objectives, emerged. These settlers came to be known as Afrikaners – either Dutch or British – each with interests of his or her own and varying degrees of antagonism to the imperial power.

Dutch Afrikaner society in the Western Cape, settled since the mid-seventeenth century, included prosperous landowners and an urban population of administrators, lawyers, and other professionals, as well as merchants, Reformed Church clergy and newspaper editors. Also encapsulated in this wider society was a population drawn in part from freed and manu-mitted slaves, some of whom were craftspeople, as well as petty traders and labouring poor of various ethnic origins. Those nearest the rising harbour-cum-town were involved in the cultivation of arable land, the wealthiest among them being slave owners and landowners. Landowners enclosed tenants and servants to establish settled existences. Property and wealth defined these stratified communities and gave rise to administrative and church-focused villages such as Stellenbosch and Paarl. Credit was rooted in the community, and the worst effects of economic cycles of depression and expansion were contained by ensuring that landed property did not pass to outsiders. This was a moral economy that underpinned the commercial and social activities of Dutch Afrikaner society.

British Occupation and Settler Economics

As the British occupation began, the Dutch-speaking elite of Cape Town was on the verge of a cultural transformation. They created a theatre, together with historical, intellectual and linguistic associations that sought to advance a new colonial Dutch identity. These activities, combined with an agitation for self-rule, kindled a Cape Dutch nationalism in the 1830s, although that was not a name that stemmed from that identity. At first, the west's affluent Dutch Afrikaners, styled a gentry by some, seemed to be developing an anti-British identity, but by the 1840s, they began to develop a pragmatic loyalty to the British regime, which was to last for most of the nineteenth century. Beyond the arable western lands were districts made up mostly of impoverished pastoralists, although those with connections to the monopolists and traders of Cape Town acquired a degree of prosperity. By the end of the eighteenth century, these several populations had developed diverging identities and patois in separate parts of the settlement.

The arrival of the British saw the establishment not only of an imperial administrative-cum-military caste attached to Britain but also of a merchant circle that was gradually developing local roots and interests. This was followed by the fostering of additional settler communities, which evolved their own social and political identities. British settlers not only obeyed the laws of the market but also attached themselves to imperial strategic objectives, although they quickly sought to ensure that those helped to foster their own material well-being. The initial strategic imperatives of British policy makers might have confined the occupation of the Cape to such coastal havens as the subcontinent offered. Those policy makers had, however, to recognise – as their Dutch counterparts had done before them – that the region's ecology required that cattle be reared at a considerable distance from the colony's only major town and harbour, Cabo, turned into Cape Town. At the same time, we should not underestimate the economic importance of the colony's provisioning role. The early-nineteenth-century Cape may not have exported tropical crops to Europe as other colonies were doing, but its exports were consumed on board ship without ever needing to be off-loaded.

An eastward and a northern movement of colonists was condoned and even encouraged, and colonial settlement was propelled further and further inland. This was so much so that one of the earliest decisions taken by the new imperial authorities in 1819 was to introduce four thousand British settlers into territory seized from Xhosa occupants. The British newcomers were meant to defend the region against recently dispossessed Khoesan and Xhosa clans in an eastern district known for its pasturage. It was called the Zuurveld by Dutch Afrikaners and then Albany by the latest (British) occupiers. The latter settlers were supposed to act as a first line of defence against African polities, but they were also seen as a means of assimilating old colonists into a British political culture.

In the 1820s and 1830s, two related ideological quests nourished and sustained that British culture in its colonial setting. The first of these emerged from the evangelical movement, which announced that 'providence' was 'marking out' Britain to be the 'great mother of Empires'. Britons had displaced the original inhabitants of the land, but that was God's will. The second great ideological venture was, inevitably, the antislavery movement. British settlers in Cape Town and Albany held public dinners to celebrate the abolition of slavery in the British Empire. They were not only doing God's work; they must have brought discomfort to Dutch Afrikaners, the only legal slave owners in South Africa. British settlers were forbidden slaves from the beginning of their settlement. In that context, it has been claimed that British employers supported the abolition of the other serfdom that controlled the lives of Cape Khoesan because it freed workers for equally harsh wage labour, for which they sought a remorseless vagrancy law.[1]

Settlers could, of course, come by the territory they occupied only by plundering the land and the cattle of the people whom they conquered. There were some who saw that such despoliation must lead to bitter resistance. For a moment, in the mid-1830s, Andries Stockenström, the Cape-born Lieutenant Governor, and the evangelical 'Saints' in the British parliament, recognised the vicious circle that was created by conquest and resistance. They set about persuading the British government to reverse aspects of its Cape frontier policy. As a result, some land was returned to the Xhosa, and diplomatic negotiations replaced retribution. But the majority of Albany's settlers vehemently opposed such changes, and the British army's officer corps, and a part of the colonial administration, sabotaged efforts at liberal transformation. Policy reverted to its earlier course, and the circle of despoliation, retaliation and counterretaliation continued.

---

[1] S. Newton King, 'The labour market of the Cape Colony, 1807–1828', in Marks and Atmore (eds.), *Economy and society in pre-industrial South Africa*, pp. 171–207.

As the pillaged and the plundered tried to defend themselves, they became the murderers and the destroyers. The victims had become the source of their own victimhood, and this became a central feature of settler ideology. For the rest of the century, most of Albany's settlers concurred in Britain's frontier policy, strategic and economic, both proclaiming that they were serving the others' interests.

The Dutch Afrikaners

By contrast, in the 1830s and 1840s, in the eastern and northern districts of the colony, a far less affluent class of Dutch Afrikaner notables, sustained by their moral economy, presided over communities of landless and impoverished clients. British rule, their leaders concluded, could not alleviate their land shortage or allow them to control their labour. They could hope to prosper only by breaking away from imperial control. These notables reinforced other dissatisfactions among their dependents, intensifying an urge among them to break completely with British rule. Those leading this break came to seek not only a political but also a mercantile and diplomatic independence from Britain. The Colonial Office allowed internal independence to two such Dutch Afrikaner settler groups – the Oranje Vrystaat (OVS) and the Zuid-Afrikaansche Republiek (ZAR) – but almost immediately it regretted this decision. Thereafter, external connections, whether diplomatic or commercial, were prevented because they were seen as a threat to Britain's purpose and presence in South Africa. It also became British policy to prevent the Dutch Afrikaner polities from gaining access to economic activities that would generate fiscal resources and allow them to challenge British power. This undoubtedly lay behind the exclusion of both the ZAR and the OVS from oversight of the diamond fields in the 1870s. The effect of this action was to inhibit the economic growth of the ZAR, but not without spurring its leadership to make a number of attempts to break out of this imperial grip. From the earliest beginnings of these Afrikaner states, therefore, attempts were made to acquire outlets to the sea and to build either a substantial wagon road or, from the 1870s, a railway that would connect the ZAR to the sea.

But it was not only the imperial government whose actions inhibited the economic well-being of the citizens, the burghers, of the ZAR. The intrusion into the ZAR and OVS of British merchants, traders and even peddlers rapidly led to them dominating the economy of these fledgling Dutch Afrikaner states. These traders were directly linked to the commercial houses of the Cape and Natal and had access to credit and information, which played a considerable part in restricting the growth of an

Afrikaner trading class. So great was this coastal-merchant domination that the villages and towns of the republican states were largely English-speaking enclaves. Moreover, absentee land speculators from Britain and the two British colonies rapidly bought up sizable tracts of land in the two republics. And this was despite statutory attempts by the ZAR to prohibit the presence of foreign traders and landowners in its state.

Whilst some citizens of the ZAR employed land consigned to them to raise crops and used its water for their stock, much of the land claimed by the state was occupied by African inhabitants. Often, those with titles to land could not enforce occupation, and at best, they might be able to claim rent from their 'farms'. There was, however, a speculative market, and those holding rights to land were able to sell holdings at a profit in the belief that minerals or other resources might increase the value of their property. The products of the hunt were another source of income, and increasingly those with land title refused to allow outsiders, even burghers, to hunt on their property. Increasingly, impoverishment was associated with the presence of land speculators, and they were identified with English speakers.

British hegemony in South Africa was not, of course, universally to the disadvantage of Dutch Afrikaners. The Cape's economy grew briskly and many of the colony's Dutch Afrikaners prospered under British rule. The vast increase in British commercial and naval – Asia-bound – ocean traffic added substantially to the colonial provisioning trade. But Cape agriculture began to expand beyond that trade, however successful it might be. At midcentury, the entrepreneurial activities of its merchants began to bind the colony to the metropolitan economy. This was so even when its merchant houses were not British in origin. The appeal of the manufacturers or traders of Liverpool or Glasgow made them identify with Britain's ever-growing economic and political power. By the 1840s, recently established merchants began to build a trading infrastructure for a new South African pastoral industry, wool farming. The Cape's landowning capitalists, encouraged by the Jewish German brothers Mosenthal, completed the conversion from fat-tailed mutton sheep into the far more profitable wool-bearing breeds. In 1839 and 1840, the brothers Joseph and Adolph Mosenthal arrived in Cape Town from Germany, initially as clerks to a Frankfurt-am-Main firm. They soon set themselves up as general merchants in their own right and, seeing the need for marketing facilities for the colony's primary products – wool, hides and skins and ostrich feathers – established a succession of trading posts at district centres throughout the colony. Port Elizabeth became the focus of their activities, and as early as 1856, they had opened offices in London.

The prosperity of the Mosenthals paralleled the growth of the colony's trade. Between 1822 and 1855, Cape wool exported to Britain grew from 20,000 pounds valued at £2,000 to 15 million pounds valued at £643,000. It exceeded £1 million by 1860 and £2 million by 1866. There was, however, also another conversion taking place, as significant as the move from fat-tail to Merino sheep or Angora goats that the firm brought to the colony. With their major market in Britain, some of the second generation of Mosenthals began to associate themselves with a British loyalism that led them to London's West End and the country house in the Home Counties. Such a route was to be taken by others of continental European origin as their economic activities brought them closer and closer to the wool merchants of Bradford as well as to the financial markets of the City of London. By the 1870s, one branch of the Mosenthal family became involved in a new enterprise, diamonds. This was to lead Harry Mosenthal into a partnership with the likes of Rhodes, the Beits and Julius Wernher, of whom we will see more in due course. The Cape was generating its own class of 'millionaires'.

The ZAR, by contrast, was descending into further and further impoverishment and economic backwardness. With a limit on land and on labour, Dutch Afrikaners turned to coercing African peoples living in the regions they were attempting to occupy.[2] Such compulsion strained relationships between the ZAR and the contiguous African societies and ultimately led to an unsuccessful war with the Pedi state. Unsurprisingly, the imperial authorities were alarmed by the disruptive effects of this Dutch Afrikaner behaviour, and it was to become a justification for British intervention in the ZAR. Moreover, it was not only the inhabitants of societies adjacent to the ZAR that suffered from such raiding. It also became a practice for officials of the ZAR to waylay Africans moving between their homes in distant polities and the plantations of the Natal colony and the diamond fields of the territory that became known as Griqualand West. Such behaviour brought the ZAR into conflict with colonial merchants, plantation owners, mining prospectors and the imperial and colonial governments because it drastically diminished the labour available to them. African clansmen from independent polities complied with their role as workers – partly because decisions were mostly made for them by superiors and rulers – and they were travelling from all over the subcontinent to work on the diamond fields. A similar outcome awaited those who moved through Mozambique and the Zulu polity, thus placing further obstacles to labour reaching the British colonies.

---

[2] S. Trapido, 'Reflections on land, office and wealth in the South African Republic, 1850–1900', in Marks and Atmore (eds.), *Economy and society*, pp. 350–68.

Colonial Policy and Diamond Economics

This interference with the sources of mining and plantation labour was to transform the behaviour of British policy makers concerned with South Africa. Between 1850 and 1870, Britain limited itself to reacting to the specific actions of the Afrikaner republics. If these disturbed Britain's Indian Ocean strategy or destabilised southern Africa's interior, then they were likely to be forced to restore the status quo. But no new policy was created. Then, in the mid-1870s, that procedure changed and the Colonial Office in London and its South African assistants began to devise a strategy that would initiate proceedings and anticipate events. In part this was the result of the growing importance to Britain of the South African economy. The Indian Ocean provisioning trade played some role in that increased importance, but as we have noted, Cape agriculture had begun to expand independently of that trade. At that moment came the discovery of diamonds in the region that was to become Griqualand West and the new mining centre that took its name from a Colonial Secretary, Lord Kimberley. What followed was Britain's determination to ensure that the fiscal potential of the diamond fields would not facilitate the efforts of the Dutch Afrikaner states to break free of the imperial grip.

The imperial annexation of diamond fields was far from welcomed by the immigrant and settler-prospector population who flocked to Kimberley. These were the diggers, mainly British or colonial hopefuls but also including Europeans and Americans in their number. They had come to the fields in what would be the vain hope that they would restore fortunes that the new structures of world capitalism were in the process of denying them. This ragbag of humanity would have preferred the less effective control of the Dutch Afrikaner states. In particular, they favoured the indifferent administrative capacity of the republican states, with their inherent opposition to African diggers. However, if the diamond output was to be sustained as a profitable enterprise, the production and sale of gems needed to be controlled. But this required a degree of cooperation for which the initially anarchic social relations of the diamond fields did not allow. Instead, the racism of white diggers, traders, entrepreneurs and the vast array of those living by their wits turned on African and coloured prospectors and workers. The latter group was accused of supplying diamonds illegally to unauthorised dealers.

Hostility to African and coloured prospectors led the white diamond fields' population to form populist mobs that attacked the source of their anger, and they attempted to coerce the colony's Lieutenant-Governor, Richard Southey, into denying digger's licences to African and coloured men. The social unrest that followed led the imperial authorities to send a

military detachment to the diamond fields to make it plain that ultimate
British authority could not be challenged. Still, Southey, who had supported
a nonracial prospecting class, was recalled, and the right to prospect was
withdrawn from African and coloured men. White diggers, workers and the
traders counted his removal as a triumph, but it was to be a Pyrrhic victory.[3]
For the new administration altered the rules determining the number of
claims, or diggings, that individual prospectors could hold.

The resulting structure of ownership was determined by parallel geological and financial considerations. Geology determined that the search
and excavation of diamonds could not be continued by the existing exploration of discrete, single claims. Not only did prospectors spread into one
another's ground, but irresolvable problems were created as the walls of
diggings began to collapse into one another, threatening life and limb. If
the search for diamonds was not to be limited to scratching the surface,
underground mining would have to take place. Not only would mining
boundaries have to far exceed the single claim but also shafts would have to
be sunk, tunnels excavated, waste disposed of, flooding prevented and all
the other tasks associated with mining at depth undertaken. It followed,
therefore, that if the structure of ownership had to take note of the geological features of the fields, these were also going to impose particular financial
characteristics on diamond mining.

New economic organisations had to be brought into being. To be effective, these had to be consolidated, requiring the most successful of the
diggers, as well as their financial collaborators – usually diamond buyers,
increasingly with City of London connections – to combine in acquiring
substantial numbers of claims. Financial as well as engineering skills had,
therefore, to be united, and they had to be merged with managerial and
administrative capacities. This returns us to the earliest problem associated
with the search for diamonds. Diamonds were so easily unearthed that
mining them could not be left to supply and demand. Abundance meant
that a 'true' market price would hardly make mining profitable. Large-scale
excavators and vendors of diamonds set out, therefore, to create an artificial
scarcity.

From the outset of the rush, attempts were made to limit the sale and
purchase of diamonds to a small and exclusive coterie. At first, this was
barely successful. Transactions outside this group were made illegal but
were nevertheless widespread. Illegal sales were initiated by both immigrant diggers and African labourers alike. The former group was inhibited

---

[3] R. Turrell, 'Kimberley: labour and compounds, 1871–1888', in Marks and Rathbone,
Industrialisation and social change in South Africa, pp. 45–76.

by the imprisonment that followed a conviction for participating in illegal transactions. Attempts were made to search white miners, but their resistance prevented employers from imposing such intimate and personal examinations. African miners, already subjected to imprisonment, were in addition placed in closed compounds to prevent them from becoming unsanctioned vendors. In addition to inhibiting illegal diamond sales, the closed compounds limited the capacity of African workers to challenge their employers. White workers, with experience of political participation and trade union membership, were less restrained than their African counterparts, but they were constantly undermined by the mine owners' economic and political rule of Kimberley town. Every aspect of the mine workers' lives was controlled by their employer so that the ability to resist mine owners' regulation was increasingly whittled away. Moreover, between mining conditions that imposed the consolidation of diamond claims and marketing circumstances that determined diamond sales, the industry evolved from chaotic individual holdings to joint stock companies to a cartel, known as the De Beers Company.

The Cape government sanctioned this cartel in 1889. The Cape Colony had succeeded the imperial government in administering the diamond fields in 1880. As Cape rule came into operation on the diamond fields, it began, increasingly, to be influenced, and then dominated, by a prime agent in the diamonds saga, Cecil Rhodes. Rhodes was only the most visible of a new class of mining capitalists who were to overshadow the South African economic and political landscape for the following half century and longer. Nevertheless, he was unique in the way in which he combined his economic, ideological and political roles. In the decade after 1880, he played a significant but local role in the politics of the diamond fields and its contingent territories. Because these extended into Bechuanaland and beyond, into Central Africa, he began securing this region for the joint hegemony of his capitalist conferees and his imperialist allies. All the while he was developing a naive but astonishing ideology of empire, creating a unique role for what he called the English race. As we shall see, however, Rhodes was above all a pragmatist and an opportunist, transferring his allegiances from imperial to settler interests and back again. He, and his diamond fields' colleagues even more so, moved from Kimberley to the new stage that was to become Johannesburg and then to London and then to the colonial world once more. Meanwhile, with the ability of Kimberley workers – white and black – to organise and bargain for better conditions largely overwhelmed, the greater part of the white working class sought every opportunity to break away from the diamond cartel's influence. Many mine workers who deserted Kimberley made their way to the new mining districts of Lydenburg, Barberton and above all the Witwatersrand. The migrants took with them a deep mistrust of both centralised capitalism and imperial and colonial power.

Events on the diamond fields created radically new classes and new identities, and these were to transform the dynamics of economy and society and polity in South Africa. But even where the influence of the diamond fields was excluded, as in the case of the ZAR, there were consequences and repercussions. The endless poverty of the ZAR, and its frustration at being excluded from the diamond fields, was accompanied by the constant efforts of its notables to break out of that poverty. Above all, they made incessant efforts to search for what was their great chimera; they wanted a port of their own to which they would construct an all-weather road from their landlocked republic to the ocean. In the 1860s, the ZAR's president, M. W. Pretorius, attempted to annex half the east coast of southern Africa as well as to acquire the legendary Tati gold fields. He succeeded in mobilising the hostility of Natal's merchants and intensifying the antipathy of the British government, but he achieved nothing else. And he was outwitted by British agents when he attempted to claim the diamond fields for the ZAR. The search began, therefore, among Dutch Afrikaner notables, for a different kind of leader whose experience and understanding of the outside world might enable him to deal not only with settler societies and the imperial power but also with leading politicians and bankers in continental Europe.

ZAR Politics and Policy

The first choice of the ZAR's notables was J. H. Brand, the president of the OVS and scion of a progressive Cape Dutch Afrikaner family. The ZAR's leadership wanted Brand to establish a federal union between the two republics, but he was unwilling to take on that dual post. Instead, he recommended Thomas François Burgers – a Cape Dutch Reformed (Nederduits Gereformeerde Kerk; NGK) minister and member of a leading Graaff-Reinet family – as president of the ZAR. Burgers had been taught in English at his Graaff-Reinet school in the 1850s. He then studied at the University of Utrecht, where he came under the influence of a liberal theologian. Burgers came away rejecting a literal interpretation of the Scriptures, doubting the resurrection and original sin, and becoming convinced of the perfectibility of human nature. He returned to the Cape to become the NGK minister at Hanover in the Karoo in 1859, but his liberal theology led him into conflict with his congregation and the Cape Synod. In 1862, Burgers was found guilty of heresy.

Burgers was thus an improbable presidential candidate to find favour among a population largely committed to the literal interpretation of the

Old Testament as well as with a complete conviction in the doctrine of the resurrection. Although Burgers had the support of some clergy, most were opposed to him, as were such notables as the acting President D. J. Erasmus and Commandant General S. J. P. Kruger, the latter a leading landowner and a key figure in the most fundamentalist wing of the Reformed Church, the so-called Doppers. This circle nominated William Robinson, the son of an 1820 settler, as their candidate, but factional politics played an essential part in his defeat and Burgers's election. The view that the presidency should go to a candidate who could be described as learned was of considerable importance to the unofficial electoral college of the ZAR. Burgers, in accepting the nomination that would allow him to run for office, asserted that he would awaken:

the patriotism of the nation as a whole to its great destiny, and to attain for the South African Republic an honourable place among the States of South Africa to enable her to play an important role in the union of the South African people and to enter into an honourable Federation or federal relationship with the Sister Republic whose interests are identical to those of the Transvaal.

Once he was elected, Burgers set about expounding a radical economic, political and even ideological programme intended to modernise the ZAR.[4] Early on, he proposed that the ZAR should raise capital in Europe with which to build a rail link to Delagoa Bay. This was a scheme with deep political as well as economic objectives, and he feared that the British would try to purchase or annex the Bay to frustrate the ZAR's objectives. He therefore entered into negotiations with the OVS to begin mobilising an international opposition to Britain. His modernising design, he also recognised, would need a cadre of educated non-British and Dutch-speaking administrators, and it was he who began the pivotal process of recruiting men from the Netherlands to serve the ZAR's state. In similar fashion, he also began to create an educational system, not only by establishing the Republic's first secondary school but also by again turning to the Netherlands to recruit instructors. In 1873 – to advance his modernising ambition – he launched the first newspaper in the ZAR, the *De Volksstem*. He also recognised that if the economy was to make headway, it was necessary to transform the state's currency by underwriting its value. Burgers, therefore, negotiated a bank loan by borrowing £60,000 from the Cape Commercial Bank. Moreover, under his aegis, the first South African coins were minted from gold extracted from the recently opened diggings at Lydenburg. In addition, the five hundred English-speaking prospectors at the diggings were brought

---

[4] C. W. de Kiewiet, *The imperial factor in South Africa: a study in politics and economics* (London: Cass, 1965), pp. 94–5.

into the ZAR's political system by granting them two Volksraad seats. Unfortunately, his ambitious economic and constitutional objectives took him away from the everyday factional politics of his adopted state, thus making him vulnerable to their conspiracies. Ultimately, however, what was to undo Burgers was the ZAR's relationship with the Pedi state. In the clash between the two polities, Burgers was deserted by his militia and had to retreat in disarray. At this point, the imperial power chose to intervene. But this was the occasion rather than the cause of the intervention.

Shepstone and the Annexation of the ZAR

The annexation of the ZAR had long been proposed as the solution to the problems it created and was favoured by both Natal's merchants and its colonial administrators. The historian C. W. de Kiewiet observed that, as early as 1866, the *Natal Mercury* reported, 'We have got into the way of looking upon the vast states of the interior, as being almost part of ourselves. They rank amongst the mainstays of our prosperity.'[5] Equally, interference with its labour supplies (and its trade) had repeatedly moved Natal officials to urge that the republic be annexed by Britain. Others could find philanthropic and magnanimous motives for wanting to extend British power. Such an extension, wrote Natal's Lieutenant Governor R. W. Keate, would ensure 'the advancement of civilization, enlightenment and good government in this part of the world.'[6] Moreover, from the mid-1860s, colonial secretaries and high commissioners also began to claim, in private, that South Africa would be better governed under a British-dominated state. As High Commissioner Wodehouse asserted, Britain must be the 'paramount power' in South Africa.[7] For the following ten years, however, it was neither appropriate nor propitious for federation to become explicit imperial policy. That moment came in 1876, when the political economy and an array of imperial developments, cabinet and parliamentary opportunities and opportunisms, as well as settler interests and ambitions, combined to allow federalism to be acknowledged as Britain's design for South Africa.

---

[5] *Natal Mercury*, 24 October 1866, cited in de Kiewiet, *British colonial policy and the South African republics, 1848–1872*, p. 258.

[6] 'Copy of a despatch from Lieutenant Governor Keate to His Grace the Duke of Buckingham and Chandos', in Cape of Good Hope and Natal, *Despatches from the governor of the Cape of Good Hope and the lieut. governor of Natal, on the subject of the recognition of Moshesh, chief of the Basutos, and of his tribe, as British subjects* [command paper 4140] (London: HMSO, 1869), p. 124.

[7] De Kiewiet, *British colonial policy*, p. 161.

The Natal government created the occasion that brought federalism to life when it sent Theophilus Shepstone to London to counter claims that its militia had been guilty of atrocities in the colony. Shepstone took advantage of his ready access to the Colonial Secretary to put forward a proposal that would advance long-held ambitions. This was the overthrow of Dutch Afrikaner rule in the ZAR to promote a grand economic project that would have an unimpaired labour supply. Shepstone was best able to advocate this proposal because he combined being a diplomatic agent with the role of continental labour recruiter. In addition, he and his family had their own commercial interests in imposing British rule in the interior of the continent. Lord Carnarvon, the Colonial Secretary, with his own designs already formulated, listened with interest to Shepstone's views on the obstacles that the ZAR placed in the way of economic growth in South Africa. Britain's strategic interest entailed the establishment of 'a great South African Dominion' that would help 'advance . . . civilization in Africa and the general interests of the Empire.'[8] This view coincided with, and may have been driven by, the desire in particular of Natal to ensure the labour supply of the whole region. Shepstone's additional warning, made on the basis of information collected by his agents, that there was a strong possibility that the independent African kingdoms were planning their own confederation to wage war against the settler societies, would also have encouraged British interference in the affairs of those states. Carnarvon found that all this information conveniently suited his own purpose, and Shepstone was at last given permission to annex the Afrikaner republic. Finally he had found a Colonial Secretary who was willing to advance a federal blueprint drawn up to his own specifications.[9]

Shepstone returned to South Africa with his commission from Carnarvon to annex the ZAR. He assembled a staff of twelve, which included a representative of the Standard Bank, and together with twenty-five mounted police, he eventually rode into Pretoria.[10] He immediately declared that the purpose of his visit to President Burgers was to promulgate Britain's annexation of the ZAR. To begin with, he sought to persuade the president and various factions in the republic to agree to annexation. Shepstone found

---

[8] R. L. Cope, 'Strategic and socio-economic explanations for Carnarvon's South African confederation policy', *History in Africa* 13 (1986), 11, 16. De Kiewiet, *The imperial factor*, p. 113.

[9] C. F. Goodfellow, *Great Britain and South African federation, 1870–1881* (Cape Town: Oxford University Press, 1966), p. 70; Cope, 'Carnarvon's South African confederation policy', 13–34. N. A. Etherington, 'Labour supply and the genesis of South African Confederation in the 1870s', *Journal of African History* 20 (1979), 235–53.

[10] De Kiewiet, *The imperial factor*, p. 113.

virtually no support for his proposal, but nor was there an organised opposition. He parlayed for four months before he decided to act without local backing and then had a proclamation read that announced that the ZAR, which would henceforth be known as the Transvaal, was to be a British colony. Shepstone had assured Carnarvon that the Afrikaner state would readily submit to British rule, and to begin with, it looked as if he might not be altogether wrong.

The ZAR was in disarray. Taxes were not being collected, and the Bapedi had defeated the president's forces, largely because his men had deserted him. Because Shepstone put it about that the Zulu army was massing on the ZAR's border intent on invading the Afrikaner republic, and there was anxiety about Pedi intentions, there was some relief that Britain would provide protection if such an attack took place. Shepstone promised financial support for the bankrupt state, and some looked on, waiting to see what he would dispense. Little was forthcoming, but circumstances changed as the British army took on the Bapedi and then the amaZulu and ultimately defeated both African states. Ironically, this may have freed those who resented the British takeover of the ZAR and allowed them to grow bolder because African adversaries no longer threatened them. Gradually, Burgers was abandoned by the majority of Transvaalers, and a triumvirate, consisting of S. J. P. Kruger, E. J. P. Jorissen and Piet Joubert, emerged to lead them. Under their aegis, a series of mass meetings were called. There were four of these, one in 1878, two in 1879 and the last in 1880.

The ZAR's Return to Independence and the Transvaal British

Yet the leadership was circumspect. Four years had passed since Shepstone's arrival in the Afrikaner republic, and although there had been much in the way of petitions and deputations, there was as yet no outright resistance to British annexation. The triumvirate was reluctant to challenge the British head-on. The most important of the Afrikaner leaders was Kruger, who saw the dangers of rallying supporters into an immediate and direct confrontation with the British state. Rather, he and his fellows sought to temper their supporters, seeking to persuade the Colonial Secretary that there was no popular endorsement for British rule. Moreover, Gladstone and the Liberal Party let it be known that they were opposed to the annexation. When the Liberals defeated the Conservatives in the 1880 election, Kruger and his followers assumed that their independence would be restored. But Gladstone then claimed that what had been done could not be undone, although he offered Dutch Afrikaners self-government in a British-dominated federation. The triumvirate would not accept Gladstone's compromise, and as they began to rally their supporters, events overtook them. Kruger could see that, whilst there were those who wanted immediate action, there were equally some who were hesitant and against precipitous action. Kruger, the adroit political leader, was determined to keep the two wings of the population united in the face of the old opponent. Then circumstance determined the course of events.

In November 1880, Shepstone's permissive administration was replaced by that of the more financially disciplinarian Sir Owen Lanyon.[11] He insisted that burghers had to pay taxes or have their property seized. The court sheriffs of Potchefstroom, therefore, chose to seize the property of a defaulter. A wagon was expropriated to meet a tax bill of £28 and 10s. In response, an armed posse of Afrikaners, led by a burgher named Piet Cronje, seized the wagon and returned it to its owner. Cronje had forced the hand of the triumvirate. The meeting scheduled for Paardekraal on the 10 December 1880 took the decision to restore the republic four years after it had been annexed. The old executive council was restored, as was the 1877 legislature, the Volksraad; the flag of the ZAR – the Vierkleur – was hoisted above them.[12] Independence was proclaimed, and the small British garrisons in the English-speaking towns were all besieged. At the same time, the main military force under Joubert was sent to the Natal border to prevent the British army from relieving the towns. The story of the disastrous campaign fought by the British army is well known. The effect of the annexation and its overthrow was to create a Dutch Afrikaner confidence and a nationalism in the ZAR that had not been there before. This was to affect the politics of South Africa up to and beyond the war of 1899–1902.[13]

But it was not only the Dutch Afrikaners whose identity had changed because of the annexation and the recession. The British Afrikaners, whose trading and commercial activities had brought them to the ZAR, were also to suffer the consequences of Britain's bungled annexation and the recession. The harassment of 'friendly neighbours' meant that some British settlers felt it necessary to flee the once more independent ZAR. But whether they stayed or withdrew, self-styled Transvaal Loyalists came to portray themselves as having been abandoned to the mercies of a vengeful Boer state and society by a perfidious and ungrateful imperial government. In the following decade, the Transvaal British, when they sought to advance their political rights, did so by first announcing themselves as republicans, albeit 'true' republicans. This probably allowed them to distance themselves – and their wish for reform – from the accusation that their call for political

---

[11] Ibid., pp. 241–2.   [12] Ibid., p. 274.
[13] Robinson and Gallagher, *Africa and the Victorians*, p. 72.

rights was merely a cloak for once more inviting British intervention. Nor should this conceal from us the growing belief among British settlers in the ZAR that they would be better off without having to owe allegiance to an untrustworthy imperial state that would always put its own interest above theirs. British republicanism emerged in the ZAR's newly established mining town of Barberton, the site of an 1886 gold discovery. From among Barberton's population of prospectors, traders and speculators were some who had moved on from Kimberley. From their number, a small group of political activists emerged to found the Transvaal Republican Union. The organisation they created modelled itself, its members said, on the Cape's Afrikaner Bond, and the purpose of their strategy was to place themselves beyond Dutch Afrikaner and imperial power. Their programme was signalled by a local newspaper, the *Barberton Herald*, and their methods of achieving their ends emerged in the rowdy demonstration that greeted the visit to the town of Paul Kruger, president of the ZAR, in 1887. For Kruger these were ominous events, yet for those who felt the impact of the British annexation, Kruger was not necessarily the enemy.[14]

Kruger's Economic Policy

If gold mining at Barberton hinted at new opportunities (and turbulence), discoveries on the Witwatersrand offered a far greater set of possibilities. But none could have anticipated the change in fortune that would come to those who shared the aspirations of Paul Kruger. Kruger was the latest of the presidents of the ZAR to attempt the break from the economic and diplomatic straitjacket that a succession of British proconsuls had imposed on the Afrikaner republic. After his election in 1883, he announced what contemporary parlance would call a development strategy. He proposed erecting local monopolies to encourage the creation of manufactured goods and, using the language of the eighteenth-century Dutch East India Company, he called these *konsessies*, concessions. The concessions, he proposed would lead to 'the development of the resources of the country'.[15] The country needed, he said, to reduce imports and increase exports. Local raw materials such as wool, hides, fruits and grains should be processed locally

---

[14] These Barberton British were not, in any event, the first British republicans of the middle years of Victoria's reign. It should be noted that the South African expression of the British political movement had far more to do with colonial hostility to imperial rule than to a rejection of a hereditary monarchy. There would, however, have been a rejection of the class hierarchy with which it was associated.

[15] C. T. Gordon, *The growth of Boer opposition to Kruger, 1890–1895* (Cape Town: Oxford University Press, 1970), p. 36.

and could be sold more cheaply than expensively priced foreign manufactures. Ambitiously, Kruger hoped that factories would be erected to manufacture gunpowder and ammunition, sugar and strong drink.

Kruger found a fellow enthusiast for economic development through manufacturing. Alois Hugo Nellmapius, a Hungarian-born but Dutch-trained civil engineer, came to the Afrikaner state in 1874, and his skills allowed for the building of the first substantial road from the eastern ZAR into Mozambique. Kruger was much impressed by Nellmapius's vision and energy, and together the two men embarked on the ZAR's first industrial project outside Pretoria, on the latter's Hatherley farm, which they called Het Eerste Fabrieken (HEF). Although it was to be known primarily for the distillation of liquor, HEF also included a glass works and a cooperage, and it began an elementary smelting works. The partnership of Lewis and Marks replaced Nellmapius during the decade, and their firm was to provide Kruger with the engineering and entrepreneurial skills, and sometimes the capital, for his ventures.[16] However, even if the activities of the HEF may have been encouraging to Kruger, it was hardly likely to set the ZAR free of Britain's economic grip. It was the massive Witwatersrand gold discovery of 1887 that increased the long-term prospects of the ZAR's capacity to become an economic actor, and it made two major attempts to turn the newfound wealth to its advantage in a spectacular, if not highly successful, way. The Kruger government's economic policy was best known for its dynamite monopoly and the railway franchise it gave the German-Dutch Company to build a rail link between Delagoa Bay and Pretoria. Yet there were many other monopolies or sought-after monopolies, and there were hundreds of concessions that became mere speculative licences.

If these monopolies had the immediate impact that Kruger intended for them, explaining his political economy would be a simple matter. But they did not. The holders of the dynamite concession did not go about manufacturing their product in the ZAR, but for more than a decade they imported its ingredients from Europe and sold it at grossly exorbitant prices to the increasing irritation of the mining industry because, they claimed, the excessive returns threatened the profits of their mining ventures. Kruger was resolute in his defence of the dynamite concession in spite of criticisms from significant parts of his 'own' Afrikaner population, who saw it as holding up economic growth and being the result of corrupt practices.

Similarly, his railway policy was extremely unpopular, not only to the mining industry but also to various sections of the burgher population. Such was the hostility to these aspects of his policy that he came close

[16] I. R. Smith, *The origins of the South African War, 1899–1902* (London: Longman, 1996), p. 53.

to losing the 1893 election to Piet Joubert. The policies were seen as the result of corruption, which, on occasion, they were. They were also seen to result in gross inefficiency and provoked difficulties for Kruger at every point on the political compass. The British government, the Chamber of Mines and the self-styled progressive Afrikaners all attacked him for his concessions policy. Yet he stubbornly persisted with them. Why? Did the owners of the concessions buy his support? The dynamite concessionaires undoubtedly bought influence, but there is no evidence that Kruger was personally corrupt, although some in his entourage, such as his son-in-law, may have been. But the policies persisted for reasons that extend beyond the simple need for patronage.

If there were Dutch Afrikaner critics of Kruger, then those who stood outside of those circles could hardly contain themselves. The mining industry and the Colonial Office, for overlapping reasons, saw Kruger as denying good government, encouraging corrupt practices and holding up economic growth. Kruger and the political philosophy that was said to emanate from him, Krugerism, extolled an antimodernist social and economic order. Whether we report the political observations of Lionel Phillips or the historical claims of Percy Fitzpatrick, the propaganda of the *Times* newspaper, the sociological observations of the Fabian Society or of George Bernard Shaw, or even the sympathetic assertions of Olive Schreiner, we get the same picture of the *kommandant* of a medieval oligarchy.[17] Kruger was hemmed in by the 'hurrying tide of civilization', which left him and his following 'rooted in the "seventeenth century"'. All this led Lionel Phillips to give currency to the myth that 'Kruger seems to think that too many people and too much capital is coming in here and that this must be checked!!' If Kruger's perception prevailed, it would mean 'our interests might be affected frightfully by oppressive legislation or political complications'. Above all, Lionel Phillips contended, Kruger was 'untractable and oblivious to all argument'.[18]

II

The concept of modernisation and the modernising state are deeply embedded in the ideology, politics and class structures of particular societies. Indeed, as we have seen, Kruger and his circle had long sought to break

---

[17] L. Phillips, *All that glittered: selected correspondence of Lionel Phillips, 1890–1924* (Cape Town: Oxford University Press, 1977), pp. 83–5; L. Phillips, *Some reminiscences* (London: Hutchinson, 1924), pp. 68, 136–9; P. Fitzpatrick, *The Transvaal from within: a private record of public affairs* (London: Heinemann, 1900).

[18] Phillips to Beit, LA 670, Johannesburg, 16 June 1894, in *All that glittered*, p. 78.

out of Britain's economic and political grip in an attempt to lay the foundations of a modern society. And modern historians such as J. S. Marais, H. J. Simons and R. E. Simons and Charles van Onselen have all attested to the modernising achievements of the ZAR's notables with a diametrically different vision of the modern to that held by imperial proconsuls, their political masters in London and their sometime allies, the Randlords.[19] Kruger and his associates sought both to enhance the economic standing of their own Dutch Afrikaner notables and to extend the welfare of their increasingly landless poor. In his 1898 inauguration speech to his legislature, the Volksraad, Kruger sought to widen his appeal to those who were buffeted by economic depression, the result of capitalist cycles and the speculative chicanery of mine owners, stock jobbers and banks calling in mortgages. He also held out a hand to the white miners. The latter, he claimed, had been deceived about the cost of living on the Witwatersrand, faced poverty created by the limits of existing wages and were forced to work in dangerous and unpleasant conditions. And those miners lived with the fear that the Randlords would create a Kimberley-like monopoly that would reduce wages and undermine their political and social conditions by creating again a company town. For their part, the mine owners denied that this was one of their objectives, but this belief always coloured the relationship between Randlords and mine workers.

The Randlords wanted to reduce the wages of the white mine workers to ensure the profitability of their mines. The wages of the European and colonial mine workers were, however, only a part of a much larger problem faced by the mine owners. As the mining economy of the Witwatersrand grew more complex, the owners found themselves confronted by a set of administrative, economic and social problems over which they only had limited control. On the diamond fields, the owners had direct charge over the relevant institutions, or their relationship with the officers of the state meant that solutions were quickly found with relatively minimal costs. The magnates became political actors and achieved a very nearly complete control of the state in Griqualand West. Ensuring the same degree of control over the ZAR was far more difficult. By 1894 to 1895, the major Randlords, Rhodes included, came to believe that the policies of the Afrikaner state threatened to reduce profitability significantly. This was not only because of its effect on white wages but also because its administrative and social policies added significantly to mining costs. Rhodes and his Randlord colleagues, encouraged in 1894 by the High Commissioner, Lord Loch (who was, however, acting beyond his brief), began creating an insurrectionary coterie set on transforming the ZAR's state.

Although they had the tacit support of the imperial government, which intended to step in once their rebellion was successful, tactical considerations made the capitalist rebels distance themselves from the suggestion that their insurrection was intended to achieve British colonial rule. In part, this was to neutralise the anti-imperialists emerging among Kruger's adversaries, that is, the so-called progressive Afrikaners, American mining engineers and others. Partly, too, it was because revealing proimperialist sympathies would have alienated sections of the white working class. Confusion about the insurrection's aims may have contributed to its overall failure early in 1896. At the same time, the Colonial Office became increasingly anxious of a cosmopolitanism, or a British republicanism, threatening imperial power. Both, moreover, were seen to threaten British interests to an even greater extent than the Kruger state was thought to be doing.

Thereafter, the imperial authorities determined on reasserting direct British supremacy in South Africa, while at the same time there were avowals of loyalty from the British settlers of the Eastern Cape and from the Cape Dutch. The new High Commissioner, Alfred Milner, appointed in 1897, was determined to force a definition of allegiance on these Cape loyalists that was bound to disconcert them. Milner's timing was not without interest. In part, it was nothing more than a signal to British South Africans that he was about to strengthen resistance to any challenge to imperial supremacy in southern Africa. By rejecting Cape Dutch declarations of loyalty as little more than deceit, he was announcing that the imperial power had acquired a new determination and could be depended on in any conflict with Afrikaner power. Nevertheless, denying the validity of Afrikaner loyalty ran the risk of alienating the colonial Dutch while leaving British interests no better off than they had been to begin with. All the while, counterbalancing this attempt to summon a British nationalism – *jingoism* was the contemporary term – was the republicanism of the ZAR as well as that voiced by the alienated British among the miners of the Witwatersrand. Both republicanisms were seen as defying British political supremacy, but they were also challenges to the economic power of mining capitalists.

To recapitulate, for the most part, British administrators in South Africa always saw economic independence as closely connected to political independence, and wherever they could, they attempted to hinder the emergence of economic autonomy. However, British trader-merchants, whose own movements paralleled Afrikaner migrations into the interior, had sufficient commercial and financial strength to overwhelm would-be competitors without needing to call on direct assistance from the imperial state. Under these circumstances, newly evolving and sometimes competing ethnic alliances were brought together in nineteenth-century South Africa. Although some of the alliances challenged British rule, loyalists were just as likely to emerge, as were anti-imperialists, and, by the 1880s, loyalists could very well be Afrikaners, whereas anti-imperialists were sometimes ethnically British. And as the various movements of loyalists and anti-imperialists were emerging, corresponding mining capitalists and white workers were also arriving on the South African stage. Such movements materialised first in the newly uncovered diamond fields of the 1870s and then in the gold fields of the 1880s and 1890s – and with those movements came new class antagonisms and newly intensified nationalist perceptions.

The Origins of the South African War: Old and New Explanations

Out of these several complex processes have come conflicting portrayals of the origins of the South African War. There is the account, provided by J. C. Smuts and others, of the hundred-year-long assault by Britain on an essential Afrikaner essence, famously depicted as *A Century of Wrong*.[20] Then, by contrast, there is the imperial representation of a Britain defending its empire against a republican Afrikaner polity bent on opposing British institutions of liberty and progress. Out of these representations came alternative depictions of the route to war. In the first explication of the war's origins, we see ruthless economic processes and imperial acquisitiveness at work, which are ultimately frustrated by the rise of an Afrikaner spirit of resistance. In the second, the war's origins are understood almost entirely in political and ideological terms, and its context is given no significance whatever.

This second view ultimately revolves around establishing liability, in British circles, for the outbreak of war. There is therefore a concern with discovering which particular politicians or high administrators were most responsible for decisions that ultimately can be said to have led to the war. This historiography is dismissive of an earlier body of work that held that gold lay at the heart of the crisis that resulted in war.[21] It argues that

---

[20] F. W. Reitz, *Een eeuw van onrecht* (Dordrecht: Morks and Gueuze, 1899) was probably written by J. C. Smuts and J. de V. Roos. Smith, *Origins of the South African War*, p. 427.

[21] In this regard, Mawby is particularly critical of Marks and Trapido's essay 'Lord Milner and the South African state', in M. Twaddle (ed.), *Imperialism, the state and the third world* (London: British Academic Press, 1992), pp. 80–94. See A. A. Mawby, *Goldmining and politics: Johannesburg, 1900–1907*, vol. 1, *The origins of the Old South Africa* (Lewiston, NY: Edwin Mellen Press, 2000), pp. 63, n181 and 184, n646.

the British state wanted nothing more than 'good government'. Thereby it underplays or ignores the role of the magnates both in financing and disseminating opposition to Kruger, and in making reforms politically impossible. Yet in 1898 and 1899, the major mining magnates were recipients of a stream of intelligence reports that sought to establish that the ZAR was incapable of being reformed, and they sent these on to the Colonial Office. The government of the ZAR was said to be riddled with corruption and inefficiency – a state of affairs that came to be known as Krugerism in reference to the republic's president. But in this interpretation, Krugerism is allowed to be no more than a shibboleth for a dishonest and wasteful patronage system, built on a semifeudal edifice, as its contemporary opponents, such as Percy Fitzpatrick, were asserting.[22] However, neither group was above buying political and administrative favours. Nor, we must assume, could corruption and inefficiency be sufficient to challenge imperial and mining interests. Moreover, and paradoxically, mining companies were not always enthusiastic about administrative changes and improvements that the Kruger government was showing itself willing to make. Thus, although in 1897 and 1898 Kruger had brought reform-minded officeholders into his government, those were not always enthusiastically received by either British administrators or by mining capitalists.[23]

What of that mineral at the heart of the matter, gold? Its production, its exchange and ultimately its economic function set it aside from other minerals and gave it unique importance. Although the costs of mining gold on the Witwatersrand were, it was claimed, abnormally high, producers could not raise the price of their commodity. For that reason, profits were dependent on mine owners' cutting of expenditures to an exceptional extent. Because they could not restrict the price of machinery and other stores, mine managers needed to control the price of foodstuffs, transport, and above all labour. Within the cost structure in which they were working, they needed to reduce the price they were paying for African labour. Another way to cut labour costs would have been to reduce the wage bill for the far more expensive European and white settler workers. Although they were far fewer in number than their African counterparts, they were able to command much higher wages because initially they were more skilled and had a greater capacity to defend their interests. But for as long as the mining capitalists needed the white workers as political allies against the Kruger republic, they were going to find it difficult to challenge white workers' pay or jobs. This dilemma brought them up against Kruger's patronage networks, as Kruger needed to ensure welfare for an increasing number of

[22] Fitzpatrick, *The Transvaal from within*, pp. 75, 115, 213–28.
[23] Van Onselen, *New Babylon*, pp. 12–17.

Afrikaners who were being reduced to landlessness and poverty – some of whom were, potentially, part of the white urban working class. In this way, the long-term implications of Krugerism were easily as important to its adversaries as corruption and inefficiency.

The final question to be asked revolves around gold, its role as the major medium of exchange and the effect, if any, that this had on the making of British government attitudes and policy toward the ZAR. Gold, as we know, was central to the world's trading system, then dominated by the financial and mercantile institutions of the City of London. As world trade grew in the second half of the nineteenth century, so the amount of gold required to underpin it increased enormously. The discovery of gold on the Witwatersrand, which became the world's largest producer in little more than a decade, was a tremendous fillip to international trade. This was particularly so because, at much the same time, production in other major gold fields was declining. We must, therefore, ask why it was that neither the Bank of England nor the City of London expressed public or private disquiet that a diplomatic crisis, or worse, a war, was brewing between Britain and the world's leading gold producer, the ZAR. Successive Chancellors of the Exchequer had made it clear that they recognised the importance of gold to the Bank of England. The Treasury may not, in the years before the South African War, have formulated an economic doctrine to allow it to theorise about the role of gold in the British economy, but its practice left it in no doubt that gold was absolutely central to the financial system. As the Liberal Chancellor, Sir William Harcourt, observed in 1894 when being exasperated by a supporter of bimetallism:

I desire London to remain what it is, the Metropolis of the Commerce of the World to which all nations resort to settle their business. This I believe and I think all those who have practical knowledge of the money market (with the striking exception of yourself) believe to be owing to the soundness of our monetary system, London being the only place where you can always get gold. It is for that reason that all the exchange business of the world is done in London.[24]

Mining capitalism generated two parallel industrial working classes, one originally unskilled and drawn from the indigenous population, the other migrant and largely drawn from Britain and its settler empire. Initially, both populations were involved in a mass search for diamonds. In the process, some diggers, mostly holding some financial resources, began to accumulate claims. From their number emerged an entrepreneurial class, whereas the majority of diggers became labourers. In this descent into

---

[24] Cited in David Kynaston, *The city of London.* vol. 2, *Golden years, 1890–1914* (London: Pimlico Press, 1995), pp. 72–3.

the proletariat, the immigrant white diggers, in an attempt to stave off the prospect, used the state's power to help themselves to exclude African diggers from the role of independent claim holders. Yet both African and European diggers were reduced to proletarians, although white workers – some with mining skills, political rights and a knowledge of syndicalism – clung precariously, and with less and less success, to higher wages and greater social privileges. African workers were reduced to ever-lower wages and were held for the duration of their contracts in prisonlike compounds. Meanwhile, capitalists and their European financiers, aided by the colonial legal system, were consolidating their holdings of diamond-bearing ground until they were able to create an enormously rich cartel. As for the remaining number of white workers on the diamond fields, many of them saw their predicament as the result of capitalism and British colonialism. Although the majority of them were British, or British colonials, this experience left them with a greater sympathy for republicanism.

As noted earlier, a similar republicanism had emerged among British settlers in the Afrikaner state annexed by Britain in the late 1870s. This annexation had been part of a scheme to create a South African federation, and initially the settlers were reluctant to see a process of British appropriation succeed. Once the annexation had become a fait accompli, however, British settlers were won over to accept their obligation to the imperial state. But when Britain changed its policy, abandoning the annexation and thereby leaving its own subjects compromised and at the mercy of a hostile Afrikaner society that by then regarded them with suspicion, 'old-British settlers' became mistrustful of all Britain's intentions. Although some of them aligned themselves to reform movements in the ZAR, they invariably asserted that they sought merely to reform the Republic's existing institutions and vigorously opposed proposals to bring the state under imperial control.

Mining Capital and the Jameson Raid

The discovery of gold on the Witwatersrand in 1886 led the British government to regret its earlier decision to withdraw from direct control of the ZAR, and it was soon to assert a doctrine of suzerainty as fact. Witwatersrand gold mines were giving Britain an increasingly important economic stake in the republic, but alarmingly, the wealth generated by the mines was evidently strengthening the ZAR's capacity to negotiate with, and to distance itself from, the imperial power. Yet British perceptions of this Afrikaner threat took a most paradoxical form. It became widely believed in Colonial Office circles that Britain's hold on the territory was threatened, not so much by Dutch Afrikaners, as the Boers were called, but by British

Afrikaners and their cosmopolitan allies. At first glance, the most tangible example of this cosmopolitanism was perceptible in the National Union, an organisation committed to achieving political and economic reforms in the ZAR but that wished to maintain the republican system of government. It was largely supported by the middle classes, if only because trade unionists saw the organisation as an agent of the capitalists. *Cosmopolitan* was a euphemism for non-British capitalist mine owners, but despite the British government's suspicion of them, these capitalists looked to London for much of their financial support and for most of their political backing.

The mine owners varied in the size and scale of their operations. By far, the largest of them were now held in the Wernher, Beit and Eckstein (WB&E) group. Wernher and Beit had made their fortunes on the diamond fields. By the end of the 1890s, they held two-fifths of the mining property on the Witwatersrand and produced half the country's gold. Two other mining houses, Rand Mines, with Cecil Rhodes as its managing director, and the property held by George Farrar, were responsible for half again of the gold sold abroad. By 1894, the mines of these groups were not only about to become the major sources of deep-level gold; the same companies were to remain as the major outcrop mines – a point that can dispose of the argument that it was the distinction between deep level and outcrop mining that generated a major structural division in the gold mining companies.

Rand Mines, WB&E, and Farrar were loud in their complaints about the ZAR, whose tariffs and monopolies were, they claimed, making profitable mining very difficult. Witwatersrand gold mines, we know, had specific problems created by the combination of a very low internationally set price of gold, along with the proportion of gold in the Witwatersrand seams, which again, was low, for all that it was consistent. In addition, the gold ore had to be excavated from ever-deeper levels. The ZAR state was said to be ill informed on the industry's difficulties and unrealistic about the amount of revenue that it could expect to extract from the industry. The workings of patronage and the need for armaments drove the ZAR's fiscal policy, and from this, the mine owners could see no escape. However, once it appeared that a new and major uncertainty about costs might emerge, when leading republican politicians proposed that the state take over an essential patent to a vital metallurgical process that would have added significantly to mine owners' expenditure', some mining houses had their anxieties about the Boer state greatly increased. All these factors exacerbated the economic malaise from which the Witwatersrand was suffering. Coinciding with this, and intensifying it, was a restlessness among the immigrant or Uitlander population in the ZAR, a restlessness detected by the visiting British High Commissioner in South Africa, Sir Henry Loch, and one that his attention seemed likely to aggravate. With Lionel Phillips, chair of the recently formed Chamber of Mines, the High Commissioner raised the question of how long a Johannesburg rising, fuelled by this unrest, could hold out. The issue was for how long until a British military force could arrive to intervene on its behalf.

Phillips, who was a director of the WB&E group and head of its Intelligence Department, had already begun to contemplate the possibility of such a Johannesburg uprising as a way of achieving reforms for the mining industry, even before his meeting with the British High Commissioner. Significantly, while discussing the possibility with some of his fellow Johannesburg capitalists and senior managers, Phillips was urged to involve Cecil Rhodes in the conspiracy. Although Rhodes largely left management of Rand Mines to others, he was very much a key actor in southern Africa. As Prime Minister of the Cape Colony, chair of the De Beers diamond cartel and chair of the British South Africa Company, he had access to arms and ammunition, troops, the Colonial Office and other influential circles in London. Rhodes's motives – like those of Phillips and Alfred Beit, the senior figure in WB&E – were to ensure the profitability and safety of his investments in the ZAR. As was reported by Percy Fitzpatrick, a leading publicist and one of the conspirators, Rhodes wanted to 'obtain an amelioration of the conditions such as he was entitled to claim as representing an enormous amount of capital invested in the Transvaal'. Both Beit and Rhodes, Fitzpatrick went on to observe:

may be regarded as the chiefs to whom the ultimate decision as to whether it was necessary, from the capitalistic point of view, to resort to extreme measures was . . . left. Each of these gentlemen controls in person and through his business associates many millions of money invested in the Transvaal; each of them was, of course, a heavy sufferer under the existing conditions affecting the mining industry, and each as a businessman must have been desirous of reform in the administration.[25]

Rhodes might have been essential to the logistics of a coup d'état, but he was ultimately incapable of understanding the coup's political needs. The conspiratorial plan, as it evolved, was for an uprising to take place in Johannesburg and for troops to come to the assistance of the would-be rebels.

The troops would be stationed on territory ceded to the British South Africa Company by the Colonial Secretary, Joseph Chamberlain. Chamberlain, whose political life had begun in the Liberal Party, with him as an advocate of social welfare, had broken with that party over imperialism.

[25] Fitzpatrick, *The Transvaal from within*, p. 97.

Then in the Conservative government, he saw empire as an important buttress to Britain's domestic policy. Almost his first action as minister, his clandestine support for the capitalists' conspiracy, was to lead to considerable embarrassment for his new party. Additionally, he was to impose a policy on the conspirators that had the unintended consequence of ensuring that their plot came to nothing. Rhodes, in acquiring resources from the Colonial Secretary, had sealed its fate by acceding to Chamberlain's demand that the Johannesburg conspiracy be undertaken to raise the Union Jack over the ZAR.

In Johannesburg, the plot disintegrated, probably because the majority of Johannesburg conspirators were hostile to the possibility of an imperial takeover and were committed to the idea of a reformed republican system of government. Thus, for example, a week before the rising was to take place, Fitzpatrick had told a public meeting that he would not, in any way, undermine republican government. He and the other reformers knew that they must include 'progressive' Afrikaners and American mine managers in their number if they were to succeed. The Johannesburg conspirators' attempts to postpone the coup and the raid failed, because Rhodes's associate and lieutenant, Leander Starr Jameson, probably with the former's support, cut the telegraph wires, so preventing the receipt of countermanding orders. Jameson and his troops were surrounded and detained by an Afrikaner militia and eventually handed over to the British government. They were then tried for breach of their military oath forbidding them to wage war against a friendly government, and they received nominal sentences.

The collapse of the conspiracy greatly strengthened the ZAR, diplomatically, militarily and psychologically. It was able to take advantage of its opponent's embarrassment, welcoming the support it received from continental European powers, and it embarked on a programme of rearmament. Simultaneously, however, the British government began reformulating policy in light of this strengthening challenge to its preeminence in the region. That reformulation had begun within days of the collapse of the raid. But it was not Chamberlain – part hero and part embarrassment to the British government – who led the way here. Rather, it was Arthur Balfour, leader of the House of Commons and nephew of the Prime Minister, Lord Salisbury who announced that the 'Transvaal is independent as regards internal, but not external, relations'.[26] Moreover, to give body to this formulation, William Waldegrave Palmer, otherwise Lord Selborne, Chamberlain's undersecretary, and Salisbury's son-in-law, drew up a memorandum in which he laid

---

[26] A. Porter, 'Lord Salisbury, Mr. Chamberlain and South Africa, 1895–1899', *Journal of Imperial and Commonwealth History* 1:1 (1972), 5.

out the likely prospective changes in the ZAR and the dangers that those
would contribute to British objectives.

The Selborne Memorandum

Salisbury was wary of Chamberlain, who had compromised the government
over the raid, and it was convenient for him to use Selborne to keep him
informed of his Colonial Secretary's activities. For his part, Chamberlain
often left Selborne 'to make the Colonial Office's case privately to the Prime
Minister', if only because the domestic arrangements of the latter two men
meant that they lived under the same country-house roof for much of the
year. This allowed Selborne, the go-between, to become the effective policy
maker on South African matters, although we must assume that his doing
so was sanctioned by Salisbury. Selborne took advantage – or was allowed
to take advantage – of being left to deal with South African issues and
officials on a daily basis.[27]

Possibly the most important policy formulation that followed from this
collective view of the threat to British supremacy in South Africa, came soon
after the Jameson Raid when Selborne drew up the well-known, if much
less understood, memorandum. As Ian Phimister has explained, Selborne's
Memorandum in effect asserted that 'Dutch' power in South Africa was only
a secondary obstacle to British imperial hegemony.[28] The primary obstacle was likely to be the 'cosmopolitan' threat. Selborne's Memorandum,
addressed to the Prime Minister and to the Colonial Secretary, argued:

The worst thing that could happen to us and to South Africa, would be for the
English whether in the Transvaal or in the Queen's dominions to come definitely to
the conclusion that the imperial government had no sympathy for their aspirations
and to decide that the imperial connection was a barrier to their legitimate hopes.[29]

This, Selborne thought, would be worse than the emergence of a South
Africa–wide Afrikaner unity, for, he wrote, 'the next worse thing for us
would be to unite all the Dutch in South Africa in determined hostility
to British rule and the British flag'.[30] Selborne was convinced that the
Transvaal was 'the richest spot on earth' and that its British inhabitants
would inevitably come to be dominant within it. Above all, what worried

---

[27] Robinson and Gallagher, *Africa and the Victorians*, p. 432.

[28] I. Phimister, 'Empire, imperialism and the partition of Africa', in Akita (ed.), *Gentlemanly
capitalism, imperialism and global history*, pp. 75–6.

[29] G. D. Boyce (ed.), *The crisis of British power: the imperial and naval papers of the Second Earl
of Selborne, 1895–1910* (London: Historians' Press, 1990), pp. vii, 438 (hereafter: *Selborne
Papers*), draft memorandum by Lord Selborne, January [1896].

[30] *Selborne Papers*, draft memorandum by Lord Selborne, January [1896].

him was the prospect of a sizable immigration of mostly British settlers, who would make their way to the ZAR and, in consequence, change the political configuration of that state:

Just think what would be the result of 10 or of 20 years of an immigration maintained at one fifth or even one tenth of [the present] rate! Therefore, according to all the experience of history, this country so powerful in its future wealth and population must be a British Republic if it is not a British Colony; and I cannot myself see room for doubt but that a British Republic of such great wealth and of so large a population situated at the geographical centre of political South Africa would assuredly attract to itself all British Colonies in South Africa.[31]

This would mean that the British population of the Transvaal would necessarily settle the destiny of southern Africa and create a federal South Africa. But there were two distinct routes to such a federation. Either it could become a United States of Southern Africa flying a republican flag, or it could follow the Canadian model owing economic and political allegiances to Britain as the Dominion of Southern Africa. However, he also made it clear that the route British settlers in the Transvaal would take would not be entirely in their own hands. The extent to which the imperial government intervened, and the effectiveness of its policy, would determine whether South Africa was to have a new Canada or a new United States.[32]

Without Rhodes's involvement, the real risk of an insurrection in Johannesburg was that it might lead to the creation of a new United States, in the process of forcing through reforms in the gold mining districts of the ZAR while retaining its republican form. The leading Johannesburg conspirators, all of them major figures in the mining industry, agreed that they should not transform the existing state into a British colony and that it should remain an independent republic. All conspirators believed that Afrikaners would not resist determined opposition.

In the months immediately after the raid, Chamberlain, acting on his own initiative, appeared to be trying to reverse the results of the failed coup. At first he toyed with the idea of acquiring a municipal government for Johannesburg. This was to be preferred to independence because it would still leave the Uitlanders dependent on the British government. He also tried to cajole Kruger into coming to London, where he hoped to browbeat the President into making certain concessions. Then, in November 1896, he attempted to persuade the cabinet that a show of force against the ZAR would be desirable, but the government, with other international

---

[31] *Selborne Papers*, Selborne to Marquis of Salisbury, 30 March 1896.
[32] Robinson and Gallagher, *Africa and the Victorians*, pp. 410–61.

problems to deal with, refused to send reinforcements to South Africa.[33]
Early in 1897, an undeterred Chamberlain sent an indiscrete, supposedly
hypothetical question to Lionel Phillips, asking him about the possibility
and the likely effect of shutting down the Johannesburg mines. 'It has been
represented to me,' he wrote to Lionel Phillips, 'that the mining magnates
of Johannesburg could, if they chose, bring matters to a satisfactory issue by
closing the mines, and that in this case the Transvaal Government would
be obliged to make concessions in order to secure their revenues'.[34]

A number of international complications made it difficult for Britain to
act against the ZAR at that particular moment. Thus, on several occasions,
British officials in South Africa were to restrain themselves, or their over-
enthusiastic local imperialists, when Britain's other commitments made
it impossible to support an agitation within the ZAR.[35] In an apparent
attempt to be helpful to the Colonial Office, but one that must be seen
as another form of lobbying, WB&E shared information and intelligence
with both the British agent in Pretoria, Connyngham Greene, and with
Whitehall.

A year after the raid, some of the gold producers began again to protest
against state measures that were seen as inhibiting the growth of the mining industry. To meet these complaints, the ZAR established the Industrial Commission. The government was persuaded that such a commission
would show that the industry's complaints were unfounded. All but one
of the commissioners initially appointed lacked the technical expertise to
undertake the inquiry, and they therefore accepted the help offered by the
mining houses. Five experts, drawn from the chamber as well as from the
association, were asked to join the panel, and they soon became its leading
members.

Their report's nonnegotiable demands included the cancellation and
expropriation of the state's dynamite monopoly, an end to its control over
railway tariffs, control of the movement of African labour, prohibition of
alcohol sales to Africans and the eradication of the illegal gold trade. The
administration and the enforcement of these demands were to be in the
hands of a local board. It was to have a police force independent of the ZAR
state and placed under mining-house control. The demands not only questioned the sovereignty of the state but also threatened key groups within it
with the loss of a major part of their patronage. In short, it was beyond the

---

[33] E. Drus, 'Select documents from the Chamberlain Papers concerning Anglo-Transvaal
relations, 1896–1899', *Bulletin of the Institute of Historical Research* 27 (1954), 164.

[34] Drus, 'Select documents', p. 165 (Chamberlain to L. Phillips, 1 January 1897).

[35] BA to HC, 24 March 1898, BA 18, 175, Transvaal Archive Depot, Pretoria; Milner to B.
Synge, Morija, Basutoland, 20 April 1898, Milner papers, MS Milner dep. 17, Bodleian
Library, Oxford; C. Headlam (ed.), *The Milner papers* (Toronto: Cassell, 1933), pp. 227–9.

capacity of the existing ZAR government to implement the recommendations. When the government duly declined to implement the commission's recommendations, it aroused hostility from alliance entrepreneurs. German and French firms protested to the ZAR government over its failure to put into effect the recommendations.

Percy Fitzpatrick of WB&E also sought to influence Alfred Milner, the incoming High Commissioner, knowing full well that there was no constitutional way of achieving his demands. Milner, in endorsing the demands, announced, 'There is only one possible settlement – war! It has got to come'. They must resolve 'the status of the Courts, the native policy, the franchise, redistribution of seats, language, customs, Railways, Court of Appeal, etc., settled once and forever, so that we may have peace to follow our business and an end to all the South African turmoil and unrest'.[36]

By this point, Milner was all set to take on the ZAR. Yet when he first arrived in South Africa, he did not allow himself to be hurried into revealing his strategy. He waited, instead, for the ZAR to hold its presidential election before deciding on his course. Once that election showed that Kruger was not to be challenged, let alone defeated, by the progressives, he embarked on his own course to determine the future of South Africa. Whether or not he was convinced by Selborne's breakdown of the forces at work in South Africa, he determined to bring about a new set of parameters around which he expected subjects of the Crown would regroup.

But no sooner had Milner committed himself to a policy that had to result in a direct confrontation with the ZAR – and he had let Chamberlain know that this was so – that he was reminded by the Colonial Secretary that Britain's immediate foreign policy left no room for such a conflict. He would have to bide his time. 'If it had not been for all our troubles elsewhere, I should not have striven . . . for a peaceful issue', Milner wrote. He went on, 'The Boer Government is too great a curse to all South Africa to be allowed to exist, if we were not too busy to afford the considerable war which alone can pull it down'.[37]

If Milner was having to restrain himself because the British government was elsewhere engaged, Fitzpatrick and the Randlords had similarly to avoid a crucial part of the long-term policy of the mining industry when they were addressing the Industrial Commission. The issue was that of white wages. As Fitzpatrick confided to Wernher, when the former was being examined by the commission, 'white wages was the most difficult

[36] JPF to Beit, 4 March 1898, Fitzpatrick papers, National English Literary Museum (NELM), Grahamstown.
[37] Milner to Synge, 20 April 1898, MS Milner dep. 17.

question to handle in evidence'. They could find a way to reduce the wages of white workers, 'but it should not be the subject of public discussion or of concerted action'. To have allowed white wages to be discussed openly would have been calamitous. 'Few things would be more disastrous to us or more acceptable to the Government, than a split between the white labourers and employers at the present juncture'.[38] John Hobson noted the importance to the mining industry of the white workers' wages bill. The saving, he noted, 'to be effected out of white wages is greater than out of black, for the aggregate of the wages paid to white miners has hitherto been larger than that paid to black, though the numbers of the latter are eight times as large'. Hobson could see the mine owners' predicament. If the alliance of white workers and capitalists was achieved and maintained, then the costs of production must remain high. If white wages could be cut, then that alliance would collapse. 'White wages have not been reduced in the past, because the Outlanders desired to work together for political salvation, and any attack upon the white labourers pay would have caused a split in the ranks. However, when new conditions prevail, white wages must come down'.[39]

By the start of 1899, there was a new mood in the air. Britain had, for the time being, settled its differences with Germany, France and the United States and was free to act in South Africa if it chose to do so. Both the government of the ZAR and its protagonists in South Africa reassessed their positions. Leading figures in the Kruger government set out to offer the Randlords a set of financial and commercial compromises in return for a political settlement. The ZAR would provide the mining houses with tax concessions and allow them to control the *bewaarplaatsen*. This was land originally granted to the mining companies for storage and surface work only but that now lay above the gold reefs as they plunged to the great depths where mining's future lay. More than any other mining group, WB&E based its future well-being on the assumption that it would ultimately be able to acquire the *bewaarplaatsen*. Until that moment, the state threatened to give them to its clients, but now it was prepared to offer them to the Randlords in return for a settlement that would have them disavow the South African League (SAL), end the anti-Boer tone of the *Star* and accept the continuation of the dynamite monopoly. It also offered to grant the Uitlanders the right to vote after five years' residence in the ZAR. They were to urge Britain to concede the republic's right to treat coloured and Indians as it saw fit.

[38] JPF to J. Wernher, 1 May 1897, Fitzpatrick papers, NELM, Grahamstown.
[39] J. A. Hobson, *The war in South Africa: its causes and effects* (London: Nisbet, 1900), p. 240.

If implemented, this would have gone a considerable way toward meeting the economic demands of the mining houses. At any rate, this set of proposals, which came to be known as the Great Deal, could have been seen as the basis for negotiations. Fitzpatrick, though, was wary of the offer, partly because the ZAR would not and could not deliver what it was offering. But more than this, if the ZAR did produce the settlement it was offering, the mining houses would not achieve the kind of domination they wanted. Fitzpatrick informed his London directors of the ZAR's offer and expressed his continuing distrust. Wernher and Beit agreed with him and organised the support of the major mining houses in London.

The Republic offered the Randlords a new compromise. In addition to the *bewaarplaatsen*, it would resolve the franchise question. In return, the mining industry was to provide the ZAR with a loan, suppress the hostile press, disavow the SAL and Uitlander opposition and oppose the British government's criticism of the ZAR's treatment of Indians. In effect, the proposals were an attempt to divide the capitalists, the SAL and the Uitlanders from one another and from British influence. Once again, Fitzpatrick accepted the tactical necessity of examining the ZAR's offer while ensuring that the mine owners were persuaded to look beyond their immediate interests.

The WB&E directors believed that the outcome of economic negotiations should be to the mine owners' advantage, but not bought at the price of alienating the SAL and the Uitlanders. This was a circle that could never be squared. The franchise on offer from the ZAR government would still have left considerable numbers of Uitlanders without the vote, and, worse, without citizenship for the qualifying period. The London representatives of three major mining houses, Consolidated Gold Fields, WB&E and Goerz and Company, welcomed the concessions being offered on the *bewaarplaatsen* but were unwilling to detach this from the franchise settlement.

Eckstein, Wernher and Beit were, however, alarmed by the prevarications they had encountered in separate visits to the Colonial Office in March 1899. When Wernher spoke to Chamberlain and Selborne on 8 and 9 March, he was surprised that they recommended a municipality for Johannesburg. When Wernher raised the question of the franchise for the Uitlanders, Selborne evaded the query, cautioning that it 'was going at once to the point of most resistance'.[40] Once again the major capitalists were concerned at the prevarication of the leading actors in the Colonial Office. Eckstein told the British vice agent in Johannesburg that, unless Britain acted decisively

---

[40] Minute by Selborne and Chamberlain, 8–9 March 1899, CO 417/259; Marais, *The fall of Kruger's republic*, pp. 251–2.

against the ZAR, he would not risk all by rejecting the latter's terms; he would 'go to Pretoria and make peace with the SAR [ZAR]'.[41]

By the spring and summer of 1899, relations between Britain and the South African Republic had begun to deteriorate dangerously, but the City of London conveyed no particular anxiety. On the contrary, the war, when it came, was extremely popular among members of the British financial community. And although that popularity stemmed in part from the end of uncertainty and in part from the jingoism that late-Victorian nationalism had spawned, it also stemmed from the assumed interests of the financial communities. To begin with, it was widely believed that the intense pressure put on the government of the ZAR was likely to succeed without Britain's need of recourse to war. Equally, when war came, there was considerable confidence – although not among those few who were closest to the conflict – that Britain would soon force the Afrikaner republic into submission. Had the Bank of England and the City of London thought that their interests were being endangered by the political and diplomatic policy of the government, these influential spheres of interest would have let their anxieties be known. Whatever doubts remained were in any event swept aside by the final rush to war. Determined to get its blow in first, the ZAR, together with the OVS, issued an ultimatum in October 1899 demanding the recall of British troops on their way to South Africa and the withdrawal of existing forces from republican borders. Having provoked the ultimatum, Britain 'naturally ignored it',[42] and within days, the first Boer columns were streaming into Natal and the Cape.

Conclusions

This chapter has attempted to advance an interpretation of the causes of the South African War, which integrates context with agency. By emphasising the struggle's long- and short-term contexts, it has tried to give meaning to the responsibility for war so assiduously sought by generations of liberal historians. In so doing, this analysis has stressed the pivotal role of the Selborne Memorandum as well as the key part played by Percy Fitzpatrick in overcoming the inertia and caution characteristic of much mining-house behaviour. It was Fitzpatrick who helped to set the stage on which Milner acted. Overall, the conclusions suggested here have also attempted to avoid

---

[41] Her Majesty's Agent Pretoria to High Commissioner, summary of letter from Vice Consul, Johannesburg, 19 April 1899, MS Milner dep. 208, P81, pp. 408–409.

[42] D. Judd and K. Surridge, *The Boer War* (London: John Murray, 2002), p. 50.

the polarised positions taken up in so many accounts of the causes of the war. Rather than having to choose between a political and strategic set of explanations on the one hand and the economic determinism of gold and gold mining's imperatives on the other hand, this approach has argued for the convergence of both, particularly in the decisive period between 1895 and 1899.

3

CLASS, CULTURE, AND CONSCIOUSNESS IN SOUTH AFRICA, 1880–1899

SHULA MARKS

The mineral discoveries that launched its industrial revolution between the late 1860s and the end of the 1890s were crucial in the shaping of modern South Africa and the peculiarities of its social order. Within that period, the years between 1880 and 1899 were both violent and formative. Framed by wars of conquest at their beginning and by the outbreak of the South African War of 1899–1902 at their end, at the heart of those years lay the mineral discoveries of the 1860s–1880s, first diamonds in Griqualand West in 1868 and then alluvial gold in the eastern Transvaal in the early 1870s, followed by gold on the Witwatersrand in 1886. All over southern Africa, mining led to a dramatic increase in economic activity and to renewed imperial intervention in its affairs. For the first time, the region received large flows of immigrants and capital investment from abroad. New towns, railways, roads and harbours were built, and new urban markets opened up for locally produced food and manufactured goods. The earlier movement of African migrants in search of work in colonial labour markets was greatly accelerated. And as the demand for African land and labour spiralled, conflict was heightened as white farmers tightened their grip on rent and labour tenants on their land and encroached on African lands beyond the colonial and republican borders.

Important as the mineral discoveries were in the industrialisation and urbanisation of South Africa, in the late nineteenth century, the majority of South Africans, black and white, still earned their living on the land, though under rapidly changing circumstances. Land values shot up as commercial farming developed and eager speculators bought up large tracts in the hope of further mineral discoveries. At the same time, settler agricultural enterprise benefited from the availability of credit and improvements in transport. Indeed, in these years, '[m]ore capital was probably invested into the pastoral farms of the Karoo and Eastern Cape than in the diamond mines of Kimberley', and even after 1880 when it was overtaken by diamonds as the colony's most significant export, wool remained the Cape's most important agricultural export.[1] The coincidence in this period of 'climatic and pestilential calamities' with rapid social and political change, especially in the 1890s, added to the turmoil.[2]

Farming interests dominated also in local settler politics. In the Cape, where more scientific farming practices advanced rapidly with the establishment of the Department of Agriculture toward the end of the nineteenth century, struggles over agricultural policy between a 'progressive', largely English-speaking modernising elite and poorer, more conservative sheep farmers fractured colonial politics. From the mid-1880s, legislation introducing the compulsory dipping of sheep to curb infection gave rise to what was probably the most widespread popular agitation among Afrikaners in the nineteenth-century Cape Colony. This agitation threatened to split the party representing Afrikaner farmers' interests, the Afrikaner Bond, and to end that organisation's support for the Rhodes ministry. The struggle also fostered a new sense of ethnic solidarity among the hitherto-isolated sheep farmers of the northern Cape.

If in the Cape white landowners continued to determine the character of the state, this was also true of the Afrikaner republics, where the vast majority of burghers were farmers and determined policy to the end of the century – to the increasing dissatisfaction of mine magnates in the Transvaal who competed with Boers for labour and had relatively little control over the state. Natal was something of an exception: there, a combination of sugar planters, absentee landlords and mercantile interests dominated the policies of the colonial government until the 1880s and supported the continuance of the African 'homestead' economy. By the late 1880s, however, it was clear that economic development rested on settler agriculture, although 'urban, mercantile and mining interests continued to dominate official policy' until 1898, when white farming interests gained ascendancy.[3]

Central to the development of the modern South African state was both the mailed fist of force and the velvet glove of 'bureaucratic modernity'.[4] Together, these forged its economy, formed its institutions and helped

---

[1] William Beinart, *The rise of conservation in South Africa: settlers, livestock, and the environment, 1770–1950* (Oxford: Oxford University Press, 2003), pp. xviii–xix.

[2] Pule Phoofolo, 'Epidemics and revolution: the rinderpest epidemic in late nineteenth-century southern Africa', *Past and Present* 138 (February 1993), 131.

[3] John Lambert, *Betrayed trust: Africans and the state in colonial Natal* (Scottsville: University of Natal Press, 1995), p. 99.

[4] Clifton Crais, *The politics of evil: magic, state power and the political imagination in South Africa* (Cambridge: Cambridge University Press, 2002), p. 69.

to fashion the ideology of all its inhabitants. Renewed imperial military intervention and administrative mapping and counting challenged and often transformed older loyalties, politicised culture, transformed gender relations and gendered the state in different ways and reshaped the struggle for power in the region. At the same time, there was a profound ambiguity at the heart of these attempts at re-forming African society in the interests of the colonial political economy. That was how to draw Africans into its labour and consumer markets while maintaining those elements of African society essential to the maintenance of law and order.

An important part of this new dispensation was established by enquiries into 'native laws and customs', which were designed to assist in the administration of conquered and annexed African peoples. There were two strategic moves in this direction. One was Natal's 1878 Code of Native Law, which was applied in Zululand from 1887, and the other the Cape Colony's wide-ranging 1883 Commission on Native Laws and Customs. This was designed to compile a code of criminal and civil law on marriage and succession, on land tenure and on the introduction of local self-government to assist the newly established administration in the recently annexed African polities of British Kaffraria and the Transkeian Territories. Both the evolving Natal Code and the commission report were based on evidence provided by African men (mainly chiefs, in the case of the code, but including Christian men by the 1880s), Christian missionaries and 'native' administrators. Both were deeply patriarchal statements, which appropriated and transformed African notions of patriarchy.

Gender, sexuality and marriage, property and land tenure, succession and inheritance, as well as civil and criminal law were fundamental in these codifications. Nor was this accidental: gender and generational relations were at the heart of the kinship ties that structured African society and were increasingly under pressure with the weakening of the African homestead and of chiefly authority by settler colonialism. Although African women were crucially constructed within these discourses of the colonial state, they did not participate in the debate, except slightly later in church circles. Indeed, in the final analysis, their portrayal as perpetual minors was the outcome of debates between men of unequal power and position, by 'an accommodation of patriarchs'.[5] Accordingly, by the turn of the century, African 'customary law' bore little resemblance to the reality of women's lives, especially of those Christian women who had access to education and who were beginning to move into urban areas in small numbers.

---

[5] Jeff Guy, 'An accommodation of patriarchs: Theophilus Shepstone and the foundations of the system of native administration in Natal', paper presented at the Conference on Masculinities in Southern Africa, University of Natal, Durban (July 1997).

By then, intense social, economic and political transformations had led to the emergence of new forms of culture and consciousness, partly reflected in new notions of race, gender and class, as new subjects and new forms of subjectivity were crafted and recrafted. Yet change was always uneven. New ideas and subjectivities coexisted with, or were grafted onto, older patterns of behaviour and mores. Thus, in the Cape, where modernity came earlier than elsewhere and struck deeper roots in refashioning society, well into this period farm labourers were still woken by the clanging of the old slave bell, and 'the critical punctuations of working hours were [occasioned] by the rations of . . . wine which were given four times a day as well as by the breaks for meals'.[6] Everywhere, colonial and colonised subjects were actively engaged in complex cultural choices, although some had more 'choice' than others. In the 'world the mine-owners made', British workers no less than Africans and Afrikaners appropriated and subverted aspects of bourgeois Anglophone culture, and created new, multistranded identities. Workers, peasants and farmers, as well as the growing numbers of professionals and entrepreneurs, experienced themselves simultaneously as male or female, rich or poor, white or black, English or Afrikaner or Zulu or Xhosa or Sotho or Tswana. Yet there were also those who – albeit usually only fleetingly – considered themselves South African. For many, religion provided yet another powerful source of personal identity that, like gender and class, was experienced and expressed as part of a palimpsest of identities mutually constituted in contexts of shifting social and power relations. Inevitably, in the face of the rapid social changes and insecurities of the times, patriarchs, whether white or black, were increasingly anxious to police overlapping moral, ethnic and gender boundaries. New forms of identity were also increasingly imagined and consciously reconfigured for nationalist purposes, and the notion of a wider, unified 'South Africa' gained ground among all sections of the population. Paradoxically, ethnic identities were also strengthened as people moved into new urban spaces and encountered unpredictable and often dangerous circumstances.

Thus, in 1883 the Mfengu court interpreter Joseph Moss, perhaps the most prominent, certainly the wealthiest, African in Kimberley at the time, exhorted the newly formed Africander League, consisting 'principally of Coloured men': 'We are Africans. . . . We are not like Englishmen, who return to their own land. You are not here for a certain period to make money alone and then return to England to make yourselves great men. You are born here, your interest is here, Africa is of very great materiality

---

[6] Pam Scully, *The bouquet of freedom: social and economic relations in Stellenbosch, c.1870–1900* (Cape Town: University of Cape Town, 1990), p. 81.

to you.'[7] His words, an echo of the contemporaneous rise of Afrikaner nationalism in the Cape, were themselves to be echoed over the years by many another nationalist, black and white.

It was not only the boundaries of identity that were refashioned in these years; the intensified imperial intervention in South Africa that followed on the mineral discoveries also redefined its political boundaries. Far from resolving the conflicts in the region, the attempts by Lord Carnarvon to confederate the South African territories exacerbated existing tensions. Confederation was crucially dependent on the Cape Colony. Jealous of its recently won sovereignty, however, and reluctant to face the costs of confederation, the Cape government refused participation on Carnarvon's terms. His attempts at persuading the Boer republics to his scheme were equally inept and ineffective, and in the end, it was the failure of the South African Republic (Zuid-Afrikaanse Republiek, ZAR) to subdue the Pedi kingdom in 1876 that provided the Secretary of State with an excuse to annex the bankrupt Boer state. Far from securing confederation, however, the Transvaal annexation was the prelude to the disintegration of Carnarvon's project in a welter of wars and uprisings, as the expansionist Governor of the Cape Colony and British High Commissioner in South Africa, Sir Bartle Frere, continued to pursue a merger after Carnarvon's departure.

For Frere, the conquest of the amaZulu was essential to confederation and to peace, civilisation and the security of white enterprise, convinced as he was that the Zulu king, Cetshwayo, was forging a pan-African conspiracy to drive out whites. That, however, was little more than a fantasy, promoted by Natal's Secretary for Native Affairs, Theophilus Shepstone. Nevertheless, the late 1870s and early 1880s did see unprecedented African resistance to colonial expansion across a vast swathe of territory. Although the Anglo-Zulu War was the costliest and best known of the engagements, these were the years in which most remaining African polities in southeast Africa, including the still-powerful Sotho, Gcaleka and Pedi kingdoms, were finally conquered and subordinated to settler society and incorporated into a world dominated by British capital and imperial institutions. The after-effects reverberated through the 1880s in civil wars, filibustering and the piecemeal acquisition of territory by the British and the Boers in the form of protectorates, High Commission territories and, on occasion, annexations, which were subsequently incorporated by the Cape and Natal.

---

[7] R. Turrell, *Capital and labour on the Kimberley diamond fields, 1871–90* (Cambridge: Cambridge University Press, 1987), p. 199, citing *Daily Independent*, 13 December 1883.

The Anglo-Zulu War of 1879 was followed by the disastrous defeat of the British by republican commandos at the Battle of Majuba, which in 1881 ended the First Anglo-Transvaal War. That brought any hope of a confederation of the South African territories to an abrupt halt. The imperial push was foiled as much by the divergent interests and imperatives of the South African congeries of settler states and the resistance of African kingdoms, as by the reluctance of the British Liberal Party for further embroilment in southern Africa. Yet the genie could not be replaced in the bottle quite so easily. The wars that had begun in the late 1870s, and especially the conquest of the two most powerful African polities, the Zulu and the Pedi, tilted the balance of power between independent African kingdoms and white settlers all over the region. As a result of the British withdrawal after Majuba, the early 1880s saw an uneasy and untidy continuation of the political, institutional and social diversity that had characterised the region since the expansion of white settlement from the Cape in the third decade of the century. The business of confederation remained unfinished, but the need for it was, if anything, growing.

The discovery of gold on the Witwatersrand intensified the requirement of an overarching state, capable of overcoming frontier disputes (through abolishing internal boundaries), addressing the needs of capital for stability (by strengthening state institutions and the 'rule of law') and answering the demand of the burgeoning economy for a cheap and controlled labour supply (by transforming independent Africans into 'native' wage labourers). Its absence exacerbated the separatist tendencies of the colonial states, Boer republics and African chiefdoms, all facing the demands posed by more forceful imperial intervention and accelerated capitalist development.

The changing international context was also important. By the 1880s, British imperial intervention in southern Africa was intersecting with the accelerated European scramble for Africa, and London's anxieties about its world dominance as Germany and the United States began to overtake its economic supremacy and undermine its naval superiority. The loss of British control over Delagoa Bay to the Portuguese as a result of the Macmahon Award in 1875 further heightened imperial apprehensions. Challenged in West Africa by the French, in southern Africa the British found themselves facing their greatest threat from German expansion. In 1884 Bismarck declared a protectorate over South-West Africa, and German vessels were sighted on the southeast African coast. Fear of an alliance between an expansionist Germany and an increasingly assertive Transvaal Republic, especially after the discovery of gold, troubled the Colonial Office and undoubtedly fuelled British determination to remain in control of their 'natural sphere' in the region. It would contribute to bringing on Britain's most costly war of the nineteenth century.

As in the earlier Cape Colony and Ciskei, for the most part it was naked force that opened the way to the imposition of colonial rule elsewhere, although the northern Tswana on the fringes of white settlement achieved the status of a British protectorate at the behest of their chiefs. For the amaZulu, a manifestly unacceptable British ultimatum had led at the beginning of 1879 to a bitter and bloody struggle, as Shepstone and Frere had determined on the destruction of the kingdom in the interests of confederation. Still, by the time the first phase of the armed conflict ended with the Battle of Ulundi in 1879, the hostility of the British public to a war that had come to be seen as 'not only bloody and expensive but as unjust and unnecessary as well' made an outright Zululand annexation 'politically impossible'.[8]

The peace settlement that resulted was a recipe for disaster. With the king exiled, the country was divided among thirteen chiefs, who were instructed to dismantle the regimental system and to 'allow and encourage all men . . . to work on Natal or the Transvaal . . . for themselves or for hire'.[9] Most of the appointed chiefs were hostile to the Zulu royal family, yet were placed in authority over its supporters, many of them powerful chiefs in their own right, and struggles soon broke out between those loyal to the ancien régime and those benefiting from the new. By 1882, the British government had agreed to the return of Cetshwayo in the hope that he would be able to restore order. The policy was fatally undermined, however, by the king's restoration to only a fraction of his realm and by the determination of local Natal officials to destroy the power of the royal house. The true destruction of Zululand followed: shortly after Cetshwayo's return, the country erupted once again in bitter civil war, and in July 1883, at the second Battle of Ulundi, almost all the king's most important councillors were killed. A fugitive Cetshwayo died the following year, leaving as heir his young son Dinuzulu.

In 1886, Dinuzulu appealed for help from the Boers against his father's old foe, Zibhebhu, chief of the amaNdwandwe, who had been a key figure in the destruction of Cetshwayo's supporters during the civil war and who was widely regarded as responsible for his death. However, Boer assistance merely compounded Dinuzulu's problems: his enemies were routed, but the Boers claimed a third of Zululand as their reward. When this threatened imperial control of the coastlands, the British, alarmed also by a German presence off St Lucia Bay, intervened and annexed Amatongaland along the coast. Nevertheless, the Boers retained most of the rest until after the South African War, when what had become the New Republic (the districts

---

[8] R. L. Cope, *The ploughshare of war: the origins of the Anglo-Zulu War of 1879* (Pietermar-itzburg: University of Natal Press, 1999), p. 251.
[9] Ibid., p. 254.

of Vryheid, Utrecht and Wakkerstroom) was incorporated into Natal. In 1887, Dinuzulu was tried for treason and exiled to St Helena, and Britain declared what was left of the Zulu kingdom a Crown colony, transferring it to the colony of Natal in 1897, four years after the colonists had been granted self-government. By then, the power, if not the authority, of the monarchy had been destroyed, and the relative self-sufficiency of African life in Zululand had been fatally undermined. Within five years, the Natal government had appointed the Delimitation Commission, which opened up a further third of the territory's best lands to white settlers, planters and stock farmers, who had long seen it as their hinterland.

This conquest was followed by the defeat of the powerful Pedi kingdom, regarded by the imperial authorities, then in control in the Transvaal, as an equal 'obstacle to colonial control[,] . . . a potent symbol of the possibility of continued African resistance to colonial claims to the land and demands for labour and tax'.[10] By the late 1870s, there was little room remaining for independent African or Boer polities in the new imperial dispensation. Although President Burgers's attack on the Pedi in 1876 had ended in stalemate and an uneasy peace had ensued after imperial annexation of the Transvaal, none of the issues that had precipitated the 1876 conflict had been resolved. In 1878, war erupted once more and continued intermittently until Sir Garnet Wolseley overcame the kingdom in November 1879 with a combination of British troops and Swazi warriors, who had long contested Pedi hegemony in the eastern and northern Transvaal. About a thousand Bapedi were killed, including Sekhukhune's son and heir. The king himself was captured and taken to Pretoria. Although Sekhukhune was allowed by the Boers to return to his kingdom in 1881, he found his rule contested by his brother and rival, Mampuru, who had assisted the amaSwazi and British in the war. In 1882, Sekhukhune was assassinated by Mampuru's supporters, whereas Mampuru himself was captured and hanged just more than a year later by the Boers. The once-powerful Pedi kingdom that 'had held the amaZulu, the amaSwazi, the Boers and the British at bay and had provided a haven in a dangerous and turbulent world' had been reduced to 'fragments of its old domain', its people subjected to 'new rulers demanding taxes', new 'landlords claiming rents' on their lands, which had been 'converted, virtually overnight, into crown land, land company farms, mission lands, and, increasingly privately owned farms'.[11]

[10] Peter Delius, *The land belongs to us: the Pedi polity, the Boers and the British in the nineteenth century Transvaal* (Johannesburg: Ravan Press, 1983; Berkeley: University of California Press, 1984), p. 1.

[11] Peter Delius, *A lion amongst the cattle; reconstruction and resistance in the Northern Transvaal* (Johannesburg: Ravan Press, 1996; Portsmouth, NH: Heinemann; Oxford: James Currey, 1996), pp. 1, 10.

Ironically, imperial victories against the Republic's most formidable African neighbours opened the way for the Boers' successful uprising against British rule in 1880–1881. Within months of the ignominious and bloody defeat of British troops at Majuba in February 1881, the British had withdrawn with the signing of the Convention of Pretoria, despite the outrage of Transvaal English loyalists and the apprehension of numerous African chiefs who feared Boer dominion. The convention 'conceded the substance of Transvaal independence while appearing to retain ultimate imperial control' through the use of the 'nebulous term', *suzerainty*, which restricted the Republic's right to sign treaties with foreign powers and gestured vaguely toward the protection of African rights.[12] The Transvaalers, under their new president, Paul Kruger, chafed at the first restriction and paid scant attention to the second.

Carnarvon's aggressive policies aroused a tide of pan-Afrikaner emotion in both the Orange Free State and the Cape Colony, and in their confrontation with the British, the Transvalers turned to their kin for help. Thus, in 1880, the leaders of republican opposition, P. J. Joubert and Paul Kruger, shortly to become commandant general and president of the restored Republic, respectively, visited the Cape to rally support among the colony's Afrikaners. 'We are, after all, *one* nation, *one* blood, *one* bone and *one* flesh. Our interests are your interests, even as the Bible says, our God is your God, and our people are your people', Joubert exhorted them.[13]

This sense of unity was to prove short-lived, however. In the midst of the upsurge, S. J. du Toit, who had founded the Afrikaner Bond in the Cape in 1879 with a broadly based nationalist programme, attempted to establish the Bond in the Orange Free State and the Transvaal but enjoyed little enduring success. Its objective – a united South Africa under its own flag but still defended by the imperial navy – was far from the aspirations of the majority of Boers, especially in the republics. There, the material and social base for Afrikaner nationalism and the institutional nexus for pan–South African Afrikanerism were still largely lacking. Outside of the Cape, an indigenous Afrikaner bourgeoisie was virtually nonexistent except for a small group of landowners who were accumulating wealth through trade and land speculation, and for much of the nineteenth century, there was little by way of a local intelligentsia with an interest in fostering a wider national consciousness.

---

[12] John Laband, *The Transvaal rebellion: the First Boer War, 1880–1* (Harlow, U.K.: Longman-Pearson, 2005), p. 222.

[13] Cited in F. A. van Jaarveld, *The awakening of Afrikaner nationalism, 1868–1881* (Cape Town: Human and Rousseau, 1961), p. 170, citing *De Volkstem*, 29 June 1880.

In the Cape, especially, Afrikaner mobilisation in defence of their 'oppressed brothers' proved remarkably ephemeral. There, within the Bond, under the leadership of J. H. Hofmeyr, whose own farmers' organisation, the Afrikaansche Beskermings Vereeniging had merged with – and effectively taken over – Du Toit's movement, anti-imperialism was always ambivalent, and economic interests had very rapidly replaced any sense of ethnic identity with the Transvaal. The wealthier farmers who dominated in Hofmeyr's Bond were not hostile to the imperial connection. It brought access to metropolitan markets and credit as well as the continued deployment of British troops against independent African societies in the subcontinent, and they were also not enthused by the cultural and linguistic nationalism of Du Toit's movement. Although the Bond retained some adherence to the notion of a unified South Africa, propertied Afrikaners were largely unsympathetic to pan–South African nationalist claims, not least because they feared they would have to bear its financial and military consequences. Indeed, in 1886, even a customs union with the northern republics was rejected on the grounds that it might harm local farming interests. It was left to Rhodes, by this time a member of the Cape parliament, one of the richest men in South Africa and increasingly in control of the diamond fields, to argue the case for cooperation.

The Bond was soon to regret its parochialism. In that year, gold was discovered on the Witwatersrand, and the Republic then no longer needed the support of the Cape. Increasingly, its alliances were with Mozambique, and its harbour at Delagoa Bay, and with the predominantly English-speaking colony of Natal, and its port of Durban, whereas the Orange Free State was also drawn into the orbit of its gold-rich northern neighbour. By that time, Kruger had acquired a profound suspicion of Cape Afrikaners, with their uncertain loyalties. Thus, when in 1889 the Republic attempted to secure an independent outlet to the sea through the annexation of Swaziland, this was opposed by some of the stalwarts of the Afrikaner Bond.

As the Transvaal's mineral wealth transformed the local balance of power and, in the second half of the 1880s, began to challenge the Cape's regional political and economic dominance, competition for capital, agricultural markets and labour led to new tensions between Afrikaners in the different South African states, and among Afrikaners within each of them. Nothing could have been further from reality than the spectre that haunted official minds in Whitehall of a pan-Afrikaner conspiracy that with 'English South African' assistance was seeking to overturn British hegemony in the region.

Still, despite Britain's withdrawal from Pretoria, the short annexation marked a 'crucial turning point in the history of the Transvaal',[14] which emerged from the imperial interregnum dramatically strengthened. At the centre of the new state was the entrenchment of private property in land and the 'free' movement of labour. Finances and administration were also greatly improved. The Land Commission appointed in terms of the Convention set aside limited reserves for African communal occupation under their chiefs, although all Africans were subject to taxation and ZAR state impositions. By the turn of the century, these reserves constituted less than 10 per cent of the land in the Republic – for considerably more than half the population. As elsewhere, they were rapidly overcrowded and impoverished.

With its increased control over the African population, the restored Republic had little difficulty in maintaining its hold over the defeated Pedi state. Its military ruthlessness was revealed in 1883, when General Piet Joubert mounted a massive campaign against the Ndzundza amaNdebele in the eastern Transvaal after they refused to pay newly imposed taxes. Starved, their mountain caves blasted, the survivors were 'apprenticed' and their lands distributed to white farmers. In the western Transvaal, the Rolong and Kora, erstwhile Boer allies in the early 1880s, fared no better: they found themselves forced into meagre reserves or 'apprenticed' to white farmers who had claimed their lands. Although the Venda and Lovedu chiefdoms of the northern Transvaal were only conquered finally on the eve of the South African War, black resistance in the Republic had effectively been broken by the mid- to late 1880s.

Moreover, although the Pretoria Convention prohibited the Republic's expansion beyond its frontiers, the early 1880s also saw continued Boer incursions into the lands of the southern Tswana beyond its western flank, taking advantage, as in Zululand, of internecine conflicts. Here, by the late 1870s, Tswana and Griqua chiefdoms were competing with each other and with expanding Afrikaner farmers as the new market for food and fuel at Kimberley intensified the struggle over the region's fragile land and water resources. In the area north of the Orange, chiefdoms were destabilised, and civil wars wracked many communities as land-hungry Boers, profiteering, mainly British concessionaires, 'freebooting' mercenaries and colonial officials latched on to and manipulated the social fault lines in unravelling chiefdoms. From 1878, southern Tswana chiefs and the London Missionary Society missionary the Reverend John Mackenzie appealed for help from the imperial authorities against Boer incursions, but to no avail. In the early 1880s, ostensibly at the invitation of contending local chiefs, Afrikaner mercenaries established the little republics of Stellaland and Goshen to the

---

[14] Delius, *The land belongs to us*, p. 146.

north of Griqualand West, straddling the missionary and merchant route to the interior. Backed by land speculators in the South African Republic and Cape Colony, they were also supported by Kruger's government, eager to test the resolve of the British government and to gain additional land.

At the Cape, an amalgam of mercantile, missionary and mining interests, spearheaded by Rhodes, urged action on a reluctant Cape government. Bechuanaland represented a source of labour, food and fuel for the mines, whereas the tiny republics threatened those sources and blocked trade, mineral prospecting and spiritual endeavour to the north. By the mid-1880s, a reluctant British government was persuaded to act, as by then the geopolitical situation had been transformed by German intervention. In 1884, Bismarck annexed the whole of what became South-West Africa apart from Walvis Bay, which had been annexed by Britain in 1878 and had been transferred to the Cape. Despite efforts to secure Cape interests in an area long regarded as its commercial hinterland, Germany had acquired its first colony in Africa. Its presence along the Atlantic coast led to fears that the German colony and South African Republic would act jointly to block the road to the north. Bechuanaland was no longer insignificant to British interests. At the end of 1884, the imperial government forced Kruger to withdraw his support of the Goshen Republic, and in 1885, a British protectorate was proclaimed over the region; the territory south of the Molopo River was annexed as the Crown colony of British Bechuanaland and incorporated into the Cape Colony ten years later.

For Kruger, expansion to the east and an independent outlet to the sea were even more important goals, and in 1884, he tried in vain to get British consent to the annexation of Swaziland that blocked his way. As we have seen already, Cape opposition foiled his endeavour to annex the kingdom in 1889. In 1890, when the British agreed to his expansion there in exchange for the withdrawal of Transvaal Boers from Rhodes's newly acquired territory of Rhodesia, the Volksraad vetoed the deal as its participation in the Cape customs union was part of the price. Finally, at the end of 1894, Britain consented to the establishment of a Transvaal protectorate over the territory, despite strenuous Swazi opposition. This lasted until after the South African War when the territory was placed temporarily under the Transvaal Crown Colony. In 1907, when the Transvaal received self-government, Swaziland, drastically reduced by the authorities' decision to sanction the loss of two-thirds of its land to concessionaires, joined Basutoland and Bechuanaland as a British protectorate.

South of the Orange River, too, few African societies escaped the turmoil of these years unscathed as the attention of the newly self-governing Cape was drawn eastward. Initially, at least ostensibly in the interests of maintaining peace in the always-sensitive frontier zone, the Cape despatched 'agents' to a number of chiefdoms east of the Kei River. Yet by the second half of the decade, this policy was beginning to fall apart, as tensions between chiefdoms, and between white and black, were exacerbated by fearful and prolonged drought.

In August 1877, a wedding party scuffle between the Gcaleka and long-resented Mfengu loyalists, who had been resettled by the government on Gcaleka and Ngqika lands as a reward for their military and police services, led to the ninth and final Frontier War against the amaXhosa. It turned into a bloody and merciless affair that left both branches of the amaXhosa utterly defeated. Thousands of men were taken as forced labour to the Western Cape, whereas women and children were expelled across the Kei into Gcaleka territory, further crowding the lands on which so many amaXhosa and amaMfengu had been relocated over the years of frontier warfare. Having witnessed at close hand the penalties for defiance, in the following months remaining Transkeian chiefdoms were 'persuaded' to ask for Cape protection.

However, despite this defeat and initial Xhosa compliance, resistance to the encroachment of Cape Colony rule soon resurfaced. Frere's proclamation of magisterial control over the entire region from the Kei to the borders of Natal, with the exception of Pondoland, and the passing in the Cape parliament of the ironically titled Peace Preservation Act, which aimed at taking from Africans the guns they had earned on the mines, ensured that turbulence on the frontiers of white settlement would continue unabated. As Walter Stanford, chief magistrate of the Transkei, wrote to his Them-buland counterpart in the middle of 1879, Frere's policies in the Eastern Cape had 'destroyed the confidence in us of every tribe from the Kei to Natal and afforded such an opportunity as I believe has never been before for the Natives to unite in a war of races'.[15] Although there is no evidence of there having been a united African front, his words were in many ways prescient.

In that year, a new conflict had begun in Basutoland, where a series of confrontations between a vindictive and tactless magistrate and the aged chief Moorosi of the Baphuthi in the Quthing District had culminated in rebellion. Despite their inability to suppress the Phuti uprising, the Cape government, with singular ineptitude, chose this moment to double the hut tax in Basutoland, confiscate Sotho land and insist on disarmament. By the middle of 1880, the colony was faced with the far more serious and costly Gun War, which spread across the whole of Basutoland and led to widespread looting of traders' stores. Conflict ended only in 1883.

---

[15] Cited in Crais, *The power of evil*, p. 95.

The conflagration soon spread across the Transkeian territories to the East Griqua and then the amaMpondomise. A coda to the Ninth Frontier War, it was a last futile attempt by these groups to regain their independence from an increasingly invasive and subversive Cape Colony. Colonial rule was ever more resented as magistrates proceeded with unprecedented thoroughness to map the land and create new boundaries, depose chiefs, count people and control movement; bring subjects before unfamiliar courts; and collect their hut tax. The deposition of chiefs and outlawing of witchcraft accusations were seen as particularly insidious, rendering Africans feeling defenceless in a perilous and unpredictable world.

Although rebellion in the Transkei was suppressed within six months, by 1883, once again in the midst of economic depression and drought, the Cape government was no longer in expansionist mode. Frere's plans to settle whites in the already-overcrowded Transkei were aborted, and faced with widespread rebellion, ministers had to confess to failure in 'efforts to restore order and good government' in Basutoland and the Transkeian territories. Cape politicians were only too willing to hand 'all the native dependencies of the Colony, including Basutoland, Fingoland, Tembuland, East Griqualand and [Port] St John's' back to the imperial government. In the event, the British agreed to resume control over Basutoland but declined to take on the Transkeian territories, despite the Cape's assurance that together they 'would form a tolerably homogeneous and self-supporting territory with a sea-board, independent of the Colony proper'.[16]

Everywhere, the critical issue for chiefs in this era of imperial and colonial encroachment was how to maintain control while fending off increasing demands from colonial authorities and remaining responsive to the expectations of their followers. Their responses were both varied and complex, for which the terms resistance and accommodation are inadequate. For most, these were subtly interwoven, as chiefs manoeuvred within increasingly narrow constraints and their subjects sought to make sense of their experience of conquest through the prism of their former loyalties and cosmologies, including, crucially, a belief in witchcraft as a protection against evil.

The failure of armed resistance by the powerful amaZulu and Bapedi, and the ferocious Ninth Frontier War and its aftermath, signalled the futility of further armed resistance. Some peoples, like the northern Batswana, the Basotho and the amaSwazi, were able to evade the full brunt of white domination through their resistance and diplomatic skill, but in the final

---

[16]'Summary of Memorandum, JXM to Derby, 29 May 1883', in Phyllis Lewsen (ed.), *Selections from the correspondence of John X. Merriman, 1870–1890* (Cape Town: Van Riebeeck Society, 1960), pp. 125 (sec. 27) and 126 (sec. 38).

analysis, the success of this strategy had depended on the strength of changing and changeable imperial and settler imperatives – economic, political and strategic. The petitions to the Crown of chiefs in the Transvaal who watched with dismay its reversion to Boer rule had little possibility of success once the British government decided to withdraw. Others, like the Swazi, Mpondo and Griqua chiefs, tried to protect their position and their people through the expansion of trade, using tariffs to fund their polities, or through the granting of concessions and the development of mining and transport, strategies not too different from those adopted by President Kruger in the restored South African Republic. But in none of these cases did the policies provide more than a breathing space.

Outright collaboration also availed its practitioners little in the new harsher environment of the 1880s. Former imperial allies like the amaSwazi in the Transvaal, the Emigrant abaThembu and the amaMfengu in the Cape Colony, and the *amaKholwa* (Christian believers) of Natal who had fought on the colonial side in the wars of the 1870s and early 1880s found themselves facing intensified settler designs on their lands and labour and exclusion from colonial produce markets. Yet despite the scale of defeats neither imperial, colonial nor republican authorities could still impose their will uncontested on newly conquered territories. Granted, despite frequently fierce African resistance, by the mid-1890s, colonial authority was far more firmly established across the whole region south of the Zambezi, and the political boundaries between black and white and the contours of the future Union of South Africa and the British Protectorates had become largely defined. They were to endure through much of the twentieth century. Nevertheless, for the most part, recently annexed lands of the Transkei, Zululand and Sekhukhuneland and lands in the Bechuanaland and Basutoland protectorates became reserves. There, Africans remained on communally-owned land under their own chiefs, a recognition by colonial and white administrators of potential resistance to any further expropriation.

Moreover, despite the intensified pressure of these years and the far-greater powers of the settler states, magistrates had to come to terms with African notions of appropriate authority, and even to borrow African political symbols and idioms. Much also happened beyond their immediate gaze or comprehension. Through the 1880s, magistrates in the Transkei ruled with a light hand, only too aware of the danger of further rebellion. Even the Glen Grey Act, designated by Rhodes 'a Native Bill for Africa', a measure passed by the most powerful of the colonial states at the height of its authority, was implemented only partly as Africans squatted on the commonage intended for individual tenure, and the labour tax it imposed proved uncollectable.

For the *amaKholwa*, the wars of the 1870s and early 1880s marked a key political moment. In many parts of South Africa, but especially in the Cape Colony and Natal, they were faced with a critical test of their loyalties. Although many of the older divisions between believers and unbelievers remained, colonists could no longer count on unconditional *kholwa* support. Disillusioned with earlier imperial promises of equality and liberation signalled in its slave emancipation and the Cape's nonracial franchise, itself under attack in the 1880s, they recognised the need for new strategies of opposition to colonial rule and turned to alternative forms of resistance. As we will see, it was in the 1880s that large numbers of Cape and Natal Africans sought redemption in independent churches and adopted new forms of political opposition. Earlier converts sought the meaning of these events in letters to one another and to sympathetic missionary figures like Natal's Bishop Colenso, as well as to sympathisers in London. To fight with the pen rather than the sword became their leitmotif. Nor is it any coincidence that the years of military defeat inaugurated the real beginnings of numerical growth in mission churches and an increase in the numbers of schools and in school attendance all over the region.

In the last two decades of the nineteenth century, most whites and blacks continued to live on the land in a variety of social relationships, with land and rural production remaining at the heart of politics. In many parts of the countryside, already being transformed as a result of the early mineral discoveries, change was spurred further by the concatenation of wars with the presence of British garrisons, and their demand for food, fodder and transport, from which many white farmers profited. So did a few black peasants, for whom 'forced involvement in the cash economy' as a result of war and the imposition of taxes could elicit a more 'positive response to whatever economic opportunities were available'; wartime 'loyalty' could also bring economic rewards in the form of openings in government service or land, often confiscated from resisters.[17] The newcomers augmented the small class of more prosperous peasants that had already begun to emerge in the 1860s and 1870s.

For the most part, however, conquest of the most powerful African polities had led to the loss of lives and livelihoods, and considerable tracts of land were forfeited to colonists or collaborators. In areas of conflict, the capture of vast quantities of cattle and sheep, destruction of crops and burning of corn stores and huts – the archetypal mode of colonial warfare – left people destitute and desperate. In the short term, at least,

---

[17] Colin Bundy, *The rise and fall of the South African peasantry* (London: Heinemann, 1979), p. 48.

the availability of work in the colonial economy helped to prevent the total destitution of African communities; in the longer term, spells of waged work even in the most remote rural areas sucked families into a dependence on the burgeoning capitalist economy. These processes accelerated sharply with the discovery of gold; the enormously increased demand for labour in the 1880s; and the drought, locusts and, especially, the devastating epizootic of rinderpest that ravaged cattle herds in the 1890s.

Nevertheless, as in the protectorates of Bechuanaland and Basutoland, after the wars, the remaining lands in the Transkei, Zululand and Sekhukhuneland were reserved solely for African occupation. Land continued to be communally held, and the household remained the unit of production. Colonial administrators acknowledged the potential of resistance to any further widespread expropriation. For similar reasons, chiefly rule was sanctioned, if also manipulated, in an attempt to ensure complicit rulers on the model of earlier Cape and Natal colonial reserves. These also provided a prototype for the small reserves set aside in the Transvaal and Orange Free State. Well into the following century, inhabitants of the reserves could not easily be dislodged from either their remaining lands or their political allegiances. Meanwhile, by 1880, 'the entrenchment and deepening of labour migrancy, the diminishing ability of the majority of people to produce sufficient food for subsistence; the intensification of state control and constraints in everyday life; [and] the limited, but increasing spread of Christianity'[18] had already frayed the fabric of life in the Ciskei and parts of Natal. In the region that became known as the Transkeian Territories and in the remaining reserves, similar political and economic pressures followed conquest in the last decades of the nineteenth and the early twentieth century, albeit with significant local variation. And the changes were accompanied by shifts in ideology and consciousness as people attempted to come to terms with the meaning of their changed circumstances.

Outside reserves and recently proclaimed protectorates, land was owned by white farmers, land companies and speculators, and by a small but significant number of richer African peasants who had secured individual tenure in the Cape and Natal. Although the majority of white producers and a considerable number of black peasants were already dependent on the market, everywhere there were considerable disparities in wealth, status and outlook, and this was reflected in black and white, as well as in

---

[18] William Beinart and Colin Bundy, *Hidden struggles in rural South Africa: politics and popular movements in the Transkei and Eastern Cape, 1890–1930* (London: James Currey; Berkeley: University of California Press; Johannesburg: Ravan Press, 1987), p. 2. Beinart and Bundy are referring specifically to the Transkeian Territories, but the processes were similar everywhere.

republican and colonial, politics. Class, race and ethnicity created divisions both between white and black farmers and within each group. These fault lines correlated largely but imperfectly with the other apparent cleavage that characterised much of political debate in settler and to some extent African societies in the last years of the century: that between a largely (but not wholly) Anglophone elite who embraced technology and scientific authority in the interest of economic modernisation and those who believed that the elite's progressive ideology both undervalued a hard-won knowledge born of experience and threatened their way of life. The polemic did little to illuminate the complex alignments that, in large measure, were shaped by different interests, interpretations, experiences and understandings of modernity.

That cleavage was exposed most spectacularly in the fierce debate that dominated Cape politics between 1884 and 1896 over the government's anti-scab legislation, but it was evidenced also in the Cape Town conflict between the largely English-speaking elite, who advocated public health measures and sanitary reform, and those poorer Afrikaners and Cape Malays who resisted these. Although the divisions were portrayed by the elite as a conflict between progressives and conservatives (or in the case of Cape Town's municipal politics, more graphically as between the Clean Party and the Dirty Party), they often served to underline an assumed ethnic divide. This was between 'enlightened' Englishmen for whom progress was 'an important marker of their ethnocultural identity'[19] and essential to their continued prosperity, and Afrikaners who were shackled by darkness and superstition. Yet this was to oversimplify greatly. In the Cape and to some extent in the Orange Free State, the Afrikaner elite was often as imbued with progressive enlightenment ideas as its Anglophone counterpart, whereas its opponents were often both pragmatic and selective in adapting to social and economic change, in the light of their different interests, interpretations, experiences and understandings of modernity.

Nowhere was this polemic about 'backward Boers' still mired in the seventeenth century and 'progressive Englishmen' stronger than in imperial portrayals of the South Africa Republic and its president in the years before and after the South African War. Still, it is clear that the policies of the much-maligned Paul Kruger toward the mining industry, far from being 'antediluvian', were, in the final analysis, determined by the immediate interests of his rural constituents. Moreover, at least in the early years of

---

[19] Mordechai Tamarkin, *Volk and flock: ecology, culture, identity and politics among Cape Afrikaner sheep farmers in the late nineteenth century* (Pretoria: UNISA Press, 2009), p. 34.

his presidency, he was well attuned to the ways in which engagement with entrepreneurs from outside could benefit the Republic.

Nor was the contest over progress confined to Englishmen and Afrikaners. African communities were equally divided in their encounters with modernity, and for not dissimilar reasons. Indeed, 'science as a prerequisite for rural development was appreciated as much by the progressives in the Transkei as it was in Cape Town.'[20] In Natal, too, mission-educated Africans shared much of the progressive ethos of their Anglophone neighbours and were as concerned about the spread of animal disease and soil erosion as settler farmers, whereas the 'traditionalist' majority, and especially their chiefs, were only too aware of the threat to their world concealed in the promises and premises of progress.

In the Western Cape, wine and wheat remained the most important agricultural crops, whereas in the more arid Cape midlands and Eastern Cape, pastoralism was critical: in the period covered by this chapter, wool, ostrich feathers, mohair, hides and skins together brought in almost as much revenue as the diamonds that had overtaken wool as the colony's major export by 1880. In the southern Orange Free State, wool and other pastoral products continued to form the basis of the economy, with Cape merchant houses responsible for their export. At the same time, arable farming expanded everywhere in response to demand from Kimberley and the Rand, although it was Basutoland that became 'the granary of South Africa' until its peasants were undercut by grain imported from the United States in the closing years of the century. Natal's small settler economy also expanded dramatically in these years; sugar remained its most important export, but dairy, meat, maize and wattle production were all stimulated by the mineral discoveries and consequent demographic increase and new market for food. As in the Cape in the 1870s, and in Natal in the 1880s and 1890s, the state promoted agrarian expansion by underwriting the development of an infrastructure of roads and railways and harbour expansion. Although in the 1870s and 1880s settler farmers found it difficult to compete with African peasants in the production of food, the tide turned against the latter in the following decade.

The mineral discoveries and the associated rise of a property market and in agricultural produce had driven the price of land well beyond the means of poorer Afrikaners. Everywhere, the availability of new markets and the increase in the value of land provided an incentive for richer white farmers to intensify their agricultural production, and behind them, they had the support of the state. Increasingly, poorer white farmers without the capital

---

[20] Karen Brown, 'Progressivism, agriculture and conservation in the Cape Colony, c. 1902–1908', unpublished D.Phil. thesis, Oxford University (2002), p. v.

to modernise either lost their land to their wealthier kinsmen or to new speculators in land and mining futures. Class divisions had always existed among the trekkers; with the capitalisation of agriculture they became increasingly accentuated. Landless whites known as bywoners (squatters) who had been able to live on the farms of their richer kinsmen ever since the Great Trek now found themselves evicted in favour of more efficient – and more controllable – black labour. Many drifted into towns, where they were ineluctably transformed into unskilled and often jobless workers, becoming an allegedly unemployable class of poor whites. In evidence as early as the 1880s in the republics, if not before in the Cape Colony, this process was greatly accelerated by the environmental disasters of the 1890s and by Britain's scorched-earth policy during the South African War.

At the same time, African squatters and tenants living on white-owned lands also came under pressure, as absentee landlords and land companies sold their valuable land to new owners with less interest in the rents tenants could pay or the share of the crop they could produce. Although many of the richer farmers, with land to spare, continued to value tenancy and sharecropping arrangements, the cry against the evils of 'kaffir farming' became increasingly strident, especially from poorer farmers with little land or capital and less labour. Complaints about labour shortage were nothing new, and much of the clamour was more about the lack of cheap, controllable labour. Nevertheless, the opening of the Rand mines with their insatiable demand for cheap labour, and the ability of African peasants to produce for colonial markets on their own account, or to make their way to better-paid work in mining, construction and transport, aggravated what was perceived as a crisis in labour relations on white farms and resulted in a barrage of legislation. Despite the clamour, however, the laws had little effect in the face of opposition from the better off.

The majority of peasants lived on white-owned lands in exchange for rent, labour or a share of their crop – usually between a third and a half. Known as squatters and sharecroppers, they formed a large and 'historically important and economically significant proportion of the peasantry'.[21] In the Transvaal, for example, where only 10 per cent of the land was set aside for African occupation, some two-thirds of the black population was living as farm rent or labour tenants or sharecroppers, with the rest inhabiting Crown lands. In the Orange Free State, all but some 17,000 who lived on the two tiny reserves of Witzieshoek and Thaba 'Nchu had perforce to live on white farms: more than 195,000 people in the early twentieth century. In Natal (excluding Zululand), too, some two-thirds of the African population lived on white-owned lands.

[21] Bundy, *Rise and fall*, p. 8.

Everywhere, farm labourers with no access to land 'were the least privileged and most depressed of the black population'.[22] On the wine and
wheat farms of the Western Cape, the majority were landless, coloured
wage labourers. Bound to farmers by tied accommodation, debt peonage
and alcohol dependence induced by the so-called tot system of payment in
wine, they worked side by side with migrant Mozambican contract workers
and local labourers who were paid by the day, week or month. As competition for labour increased, even wheat farmers and railway contractors gave
alcohol as part of the wage. By that time, the contradiction between a farming sector that was becoming increasingly mechanised and capitalised and
a befuddled workforce had become increasingly stark, especially as a growing number of more aspirant coloured labourers made their way to urban
areas of the Cape and the Transvaal. Whereas more than three-quarters of
coloureds in the Greater Cape Town region were classified as agricultural
labourers in the 1860s, by the mid-1900s, they constituted less than a fifth
of the total workforce. At the same time, despite a spate of laws in the Cape
Colony (as in the rest of South Africa) prohibiting the sale of alcohol to
Africans, the interests of the producers of poor-quality wine ensured that
Africans employed by whites were excluded from the ban, and the state
neither limited the sale of wine to coloureds nor abolished the tot system.

In Natal, indentured Indians worked on the sugar and wattle plantations,
as did a number of migrant workers from Mozambique and the Eastern
Cape. A high death rate called for investigation by the Protector of Indians
who had been appointed at the insistence of the government of India to
ensure the welfare of Indian labourers. By the late 1880s, he had relatively
little authority, however, as employers were favoured by local courts and
the police. Initially, as their indentures expired, however, a majority of 'free'
Indians who remained in Natal became peasants or small-scale farmers. A
few even became successful landowners. Although their 'peasant experience
reached its apogee in the late nineteenth and early twentieth centuries', by
1910, most local Indians were nevertheless 'essentially proletarianised'.[23]
Although elsewhere, the number of African farm labourers without any
access to land remained low, everywhere their wages were minimal and
living conditions abysmal. Whether white, African, Indian or coloured,
working conditions were poor, and there was little welfare provision by
either employers or the state.

[22] Tim Keegan, *Facing the storm: portraits of black lives in rural South Africa* (Cape Town:
David Philip, 1988), p. 46.
[23] Bill Freund, *Insiders and outsiders: the Indian working class of Durban, 1910–1990*
(Portsmouth, NH: Heinemann; Pietermaritzburg: University of Natal Press; London:
James Currey, 1995), p. xiv.

By and large, after the boom of the early 1880s, the late 1880s and 1890s were years of impoverishment for the African peasantry, as reserves became increasingly overcrowded with those evicted from white farms. Where colonialism had penetrated most deeply, and poverty had already eaten into the fabric of society, recovery from the most recent spate of wars was most difficult. In those areas, perhaps especially in the Ciskei and in some parts of Natal, land was already in short supply and peasants were in the throes of proletarianisation. However, the processes were uneven, and side by side with increasingly acute poverty were pockets of wealthier peasant farmers, especially in the Eastern Cape and Natal. They had been able to take advantage of the boom conditions of the 1870s and early 1880s, and even to purchase additional land, adopt new farming methods and use money earned on the mines to invest in seed, fertiliser and ploughs. For the most part, they were drawn from among Christian converts – most notably the amaMfengu in the Eastern Cape and the *amaKholwa* on the Methodist and American Mission Board stations in Natal. Many of these wealthier farmers 'drained and irrigated their lands, used fertilizers and practised crop rotation: these were techniques which demanded capital, and which rewarded the practitioners with increased profits'.[24] The most successful were those able to supplement agriculture with earnings from lucrative wagon building and transport riding (which lasted until they were preempted by the construction of railways) or some form of government service, a source of income dependent on access to education, literacy and language proficiency. As land became scarcer and more expensive, some rented land to poorer African tenants and labour tenants or purchased tracts of land in syndicate. A number of wealthier African families, especially on the mission reserves of Natal, had moved into commercial farming on a considerable scale.

If much of this entrepreneurial response came from the Cape and Natal Christian converts, even the so-called Oorlams (descendants of 'apprenticed' labour) in the Transvaal and Sotho-Tswana in the Orange Free State, who could not purchase land but had productive access to white-owned farms, could achieve considerable prosperity. As this suggests, by the 1880s independent *kholwa* producers had been joined by Africans living on communally owned land and by some peasants who continued to live communally under chiefs on white-owned or Crown land. Successful sharecropping, particularly in the Orange Free State and southern Transvaal, continued into the second decade of the twentieth century and, indeed, gained a new lease of life after the South African War, when many indigent farmers returned to

[24] Bundy, *Rise and fall*, p. 186.

their lands and found they were dependent not only on the crops produced by sharecropping families but also on their ploughs and oxen.

Land shortage was at its most acute in Natal, where the African population had increased threefold between the late 1840s and the late 1870s. There, the reserves – some 2.5 million acres – which had been set aside between 1846 and 1864 for sole African occupation, were already overcrowded by the late 1870s. More than half the African peasantry paid rents or labour dues to absentee landlords, who controlled 5 million of the 6 million acres allocated to white interests. The new railway from Durban to Pietermaritzburg and the enlarged British garrison in Natal as a result of the Anglo-Zulu War and the first Anglo-Boer War brought a new prosperity to farming, accelerating the rise in land values and leading to the eviction of African tenants. The sale of land around Durban and Pietermaritzburg for market gardening to small-scale white farmers, many of them new settlers, and to Indians whose indentures had expired, also led to the eviction of peasants. So-called faction fights in the 1890s were an early warning of mounting friction over land, and chiefs began to demand a title to their lands with some – most notably Chief Mqawe – even purchasing land for their following, emulating the example of the *kholwa* community at Edendale who had 'spearheaded the acquisition by blacks of freehold in Natal' as early as midcentury.[25] So serious was the situation that, fearful of unrest, the Executive Council tried put a break on some of the most egregious evictions and, in 1882, allowed Africans to bid for Crown land that had recently been opened up for sale. Overall, however, by the beginning of the following decade, it was apparent that the sale of Crown lands had done little to alleviate African land shortage; many had been forced to surrender their lands, and very few had become large landowners. Less than twenty years later, land impoverishment was to fuel the last armed uprising in the colony, the so-called Bhambatha, or poll-tax, rebellion of 1906.

It was, however, Kimberley that was the crucible of South Africa's industrial revolution, built on the expropriation of its original inhabitants, the bitterness of the ousted republics and the unrealisable expectations of thousands of overoptimistic prospectors. The site of South Africa's first industrial insurrection over racial claims within two decades of the first discoveries, Kimberley was also the site of the world's first diamond monopoly, as the De Beers Company bought out its competitors. Here, in the maelstrom of a brash mining town in which fortune was fickle and tempers raw, the relationship between race and class was first fought out in an industrial and urban setting, and new class, racial and ethnic identities were forged. It was

---

[25] Lambert, *Betrayed trust*, pp. 73–4.

here that a new racial hierarchy evolved in which whites came to own the mines and machinery and to serve as overseers and skilled workers while supposedly unskilled black men laboured for a fraction of the pay. It was here, too, that the nexus of institutions that came to characterise labour relations in South Africa – the systematisation of male migrant labour, the introduction of closed compounds and the unprecedented use of the law to control workers – was brought into being and the contours of its industrial environment were first discernible. Its racial, gendered and class characteristics are equally significant.

There were three phases in the development of Kimberley, each of which had significance for the nature of these relationships and each of which shaped consciousness in different ways. The first was the day of the individual digger and claim holder, which culminated in the Black Flag rebellion of 1875. The second phase witnessed the rapid formation of joint stock companies and the introduction of new technology to resolve problems in mining. A collapse in the European demand for diamonds and the need to secure additional control heightened the demand by mine owners for increased greater productivity and increased surveillance over workers and led to a series of strikes in 1883–1884. The first of these phases was a victory for the mine workers, the second for the mine owners. Finally, in the third phase, from the mid-1880s, the diamond fields were monopolised by Rhodes's De Beers Company. This was accompanied by the establishment of closed compounds for African labour and of the 'model' suburb of Kenilworth for the rigidly segregated white skilled workers, overseers and managers.

With the incorporation of Griqualand West into the Cape Colony in 1880, the mine magnates gained increasing influence over the colonial state and its legislative procedures, and an earlier liberal hegemony was contested by a more powerful alliance of interests. Whereas the old merchant class at the Cape was prepared to concede representation, property rights and equality before the law to black peasant producers and customers, white farmers and mine magnates were not. What distinguished this new industrial coterie of mine magnates from the thousands of earlier claim holders was a modicum of capital, social networks, a capacity for hard work and a certain amount of luck. Some, like their most successful entrepreneur and political leader, Rhodes, had an entrée to the British upper-middle-class, 'gentlemanly' circle on the diggings. Access to Anglo-German financial circles and the great centres of the European diamond trade could be equally important. By the 1880s, many of the early capitalists had moved beyond the confines of Kimberley and were in the throes of making themselves into an entrepreneurial class, with pan–southern African ambitions. Rhodes was both the archetype and a key creator of their new Anglophone–South African colonial identity. At the same time, he sealed their sometimes uneasy alliance with Afrikaner farmers when, in 1890, he became Prime Minister of the Cape with the support of the Bond.

The country's new entrepreneurs believed in their civilising mission that would transform the allegedly backward and lazy 'native' through the moral discipline of labour. It was a creed they shared with some missionaries and imperialists and would have much in common with later notions of trusteeship and separate development. It was also, however, a discourse used to justify ruthless exploitation, the denial of citizenship rights to Africans, harsh discipline and authoritarian control.

Mine owners, it should be said, had no great enthusiasm for the extension of political rights to any of their workforce, whether white or black. As the magnates increasingly gained sway over Kimberley, the random violence of individual diggers gave way to more systematic and institutionalised control over labour. The ambition of the mine owners to constrain white workers was limited, however, by the organisational experience of expatriate white workers, existing franchise arrangements at the Cape and the alliance between white workers and local traders and merchants, as well as by the entrepreneurs' own well-honed racial assumptions. They were to be far more successful in eliminating the rights of, and using the law against, conquered African migrant workers. With the growth of the diamond-mining monopoly, the tenuous liberalism of the earlier British administration in Griqualand West gave way to a far harsher regime in which Africans' bargaining power was systematically undermined.

By the 1880s, as the larger mining companies determined to reduce wages and introduced stringent searching against diamond theft, a struggle erupted between capital and labour. At first, the mine magnates were unable to impose their will. During the wars of the late 1870s and early 1880s, there was a shortage of labour as Africans responded to the call of their chiefs and left the mines to fight. This shortage, together with a surplus of white labour resulting from a South Africa–wide economic depression from 1882, modified the traditional racial division of labour: whites were employed as unskilled labourers, and for a brief period, the wage gap between black and white workers narrowed. In the event, the merchant case for the employment of more white workers – who, they believed, would provide them with a more substantial market – was defeated by the mine magnates, who argued that the increased costs could not be compensated for by the increased productivity or reliability of white workers.

Under these circumstances, many white workers used race to defend their position. It was no coincidence that the Engine-Drivers and Artisans Union, which was founded in 1883, excluded Africans from membership and received its most enthusiastic support from poorer mines where wage and skill differentials between white and black were under greatest threat.

In 1884, its members protested that bodily searching 'would "lower" white workers to the "level" of the black labourer' and objected to being treated like a 'nigger' or a 'Kaffir'.[26] Although this was not yet the full-blown ideology of 'white labourism' that permeated the British Empire in the years before the First World War and has been traced to the influence of Australian and Cornish miners on the Rand, it was a powerful premonition of the future.

Changes in the racial division of labour were insufficient to solve the problems of the mining industry, however, and mine owners sought to reduce costs more directly through further wage reduction and by increasing the surveillance of all workers. At the same time, amalgamations, another slump on European diamond markets in the early 1880s and inordinately high mortality rates from disease and accidents increased the insecurity of all mine workers. In these conditions, white and black workers joined in major strike action in 1883 and again in 1884.

For capitalists, this association of black and white raised the spectre of unified working-class action. Rhodes, for one, believed, 'It was not a contest between whites, but what he hoped never to see in this colony again, white men supported by natives in a struggle against whites.'[27] Any such alliance, however, was tenuous, fatally undermined by the anxiety of white miners that they would be unable to control striking African workers and by their fear of black competition. We should thus not mistake this combined action for a unified nonracial working-class consciousness. Despite their collaboration, a great gulf separated black and white workers.

Unfortunately, we can only guess at black motives for participating in the strikes. Were they equally hostile to body searches, angered by their subordination on the mines, imbued with a sense of worker solidarity – or intimidated? Whatever the answer, within a couple of years, after the conquest of the remaining independent African societies by colonial and British troops, and the incorporation of Griqualand West into the Cape Colony, the position of white and black workers on the mines was to be very different. The possibility of creating working-class solidarity was rendered even more difficult.

Central to consolidating and perpetuating labour differences was the success of the mining companies – first the Compagnie Française and then Rhodes's De Beers – in establishing closed compounds for black workers. It was of fundamental importance for the future of southern Africa that

---

[26] William H. Worger, *South Africa's city of diamonds: mine workers and monopoly capitalism, 1867–95* (New Haven, CT: Yale University Press; Johannesburg: Ravan Press, 1987), p. 174.

[27] Turrell, *Capital and labour*, p. 143.

white workers were able to resist being housed in compounds, although this was being seriously discussed by mine magnates in the early 1880s. White workers were vigorously supported by Kimberley's merchants, who feared that closed compounds would threaten their livelihood, although they couched their opposition in terms of free trade and protecting native interests. In the end, a compromise was struck. In relation to African workers, merchants were satisfied by promises that they would be able to provision the compounds; partly through their intervention, however, skilled white and coloured workers escaped similar confinement. White workers were as carefully, if somewhat more congenially, controlled in the white working-class suburb of Kenilworth, effectively tied to the company and isolated from the African workers.

By this time, only a small proportion of the white workforce remained in Kimberley, and not all lived in Kenilworth; many of the erstwhile overseers had been made expendable by the monopolisation of the industry and its changed technology, the establishment and expansion of closed compounds and the introduction of a new system of subcontracting and piecework. After 1888, the marginal mines that survived the recession of the early 1880s were shut down, and many of their workers were dismissed. The reduction in the number of colonial miners, most of them overseers, was dramatic.

Although the opening up of the Witwatersrand provided employment for many of the redundant white diamond miners, in the 1890s, there were still large numbers of poverty-stricken white workers in Griqualand West, some of them attempting to eke out a living in the old alluvial diggings on the Vaal River or in debris washing around the mines in Kimberley. Then, with a new excavation, hundreds of former claim holders and workers attempted to create a public digging. Rhodes swiftly outmanoeuvred them, however, by ensuring that De Beers acquired the new mine. Not surprisingly, the political atmosphere was charged. One 'Americus', writing to the *Daily Independent*, attacked the 'De Beers Monopoly' as 'the South African contribution to the modern system of aggregating huge capital and creating Trusts and Monopolies'; 'this heartless combination of capital' he continued, exacerbated 'the struggle between capital and labour', which would 'eventually lead to revolution'.[28]

For a brief moment, a radical anger reigned in Kimberley. A second rush on the mine was followed by the refounding of the Diggers' Association and the establishment of a secret society modelled on the American Knights of Labour. Despite the appointment of a select committee (which Rhodes carefully stacked in his favour), hostility to De Beers culminated in the

---

[28] *Daily Independent*, 24 February, 15 April 1891, cited in Worger, *Kimberley*, p. 276.

dynamiting of the company's head office in July 1893. White worker hostility to De Beers was combined with bitter denunciation of Indian, Chinese and other cheap labour. By 1894, when black workers struck, they were put down with the assistance of white workers. As hostility to capital and to cheap black labour deepened, the ideology of white labourism was to be reproduced and intensified in the 1890s when embittered diamond miners were joined on the gold fields by white workers from across the empire who brought similar understandings of class and race to the labour movement on the Rand.

For all its longer-term utility, migrant labour and the compound system were not simply decided on and imposed by De Beers of its own volition; nor were workers ever as fully controlled as an earlier literature has contended. Migrancy had often been adopted as a strategy by Africans in search of economic betterment long before the coming of colonial rule and the mineral revolution. Indeed, the new industrialists, epitomised by Rhodes, might well have preferred the stability offered by some form of indentured servitude, if not outright slavery as practised in the Brazilian mining industry. Clearly, by the last third of the nineteenth century, this was no longer possible in the British Empire. The closed compound emerged to address the contradictions of migrancy on the diamond fields and the increasingly shrill demand from employers for control over illicit diamond dealing at a time of falling profits. In closed compounds, Africans could be subordinated to the disciplines of industrial teamwork and controlled by the rhythms of clock and machine. Compounds limited the possibilities of united worker action, prevented desertion and diamond smuggling and very substantially reduced the costs of reproducing the labour force. Workers were literally incarcerated for the months of their contract; at its termination, they were detained further, naked and under guard, to ensure that they had not swallowed any diamonds. The closed compound was thus a crucial link in the chain of laws and institutions that were to shackle the African working class for the following century.

Although initial attempts by mine owners to lower wages and to increase the surveillance of workers had met with resistance, from the mid-1880s, magnates found it increasingly possible to control African labour and impose the closed compound more widely. Mining amalgamation under the single ownership of De Beers and the growing political power of Rhodes greatly assisted the process. Kimberley Central and De Beers mines provided the foundation, and by the end of the decade, there were seventeen closed compounds. This marked a complete transformation in the position of Africans by the mid-1880s in comparison to the 1870s.

This transformation can be understood only against the wider sociopolitical changes of the period and the spate of colonial wars between 1877 and 1884. As they lost their independence, Africans found themselves disarmed and taxed, and although at first many migrants were able to pay their taxes by increasing their agricultural production, in the long run, the vast majority of young men were forced into wage labour. Company amalgamations, the introduction of new technology and a generous supply of convict labour further weakened the position of workers as the numbers needed on the diamond fields were drastically reduced and earlier labour shortages gave way to a surplus.

What can be called the incarceration of the working class of Kimberley was, moreover, accompanied by its criminalisation as mine magnates used the new machinery of the colonial state to tighten control over their labourers through a multiplicity of pass laws, Masters and Servants legislation and registration. Thereafter, by combining a level of surveillance with the prospect of higher wages than anywhere else in South Africa, and a degree of 'racial paternalism', the diamond mines found the requisite quota of black workers. The earlier bargaining power of Kimberley's migrant workers was, if not entirely at an end, at least greatly curtailed.

Nor were employers the only ones to applaud the introduction of closed compounds. For missionaries, the clean, well-lit compounds seemed a welcome alternative to the squalor and vice of shantytowns: they were 'spaces in which tribesmen could be instilled with notions of discipline, frugality, sobriety, cleanliness and other virtues, while being protected from the evils of industrialism'.[29] The diamond fields (and later the Witwatersrand) rapidly became key centres of missionary endeavour. As migrants became incorporated, African evangelists, many of whom had themselves first come into contact with 'the Word' in the mines, played a major role in the spread of Christianity across the subcontinent.

It is less clear what workers themselves thought of the compounds. What is apparent, however, is that even in these confined spaces, they were able to create a more humane habitat. It is not so much the much-vaunted official swimming pool in the De Beers compound that impresses. It is more the extraordinary inventiveness and resilience of men who found possibilities inside these spaces for a social life; for running eating houses, barber shops and tailoring establishments; and for staging a variety of entertainments. Moreover, Africans were able to use the self-image of the manager as 'the great White Chief' to establish a more familiar pattern of authority and to use it to extract concessions that made everyday life more tolerable, and to appropriate and interpret the signs and symbols of missionaries in their own ways and for their own purposes. Some mission-educated Africans

[29] Harries, *Work, culture and identity*, p. 72.

helped migrants to maintain their rural links with wives and families by acting as scribes, a way of earning a living for the literate and of providing a vital social service.

If later experience in urban centres is anything to go by, migrants on the diamond fields would also have discovered both a sharper sense of ethnic consciousness as they sought solidarity in kin-based associations and, on occasion, wider racial and class identities. Unfortunately, however, here too detailed evidence is frustratingly sparse. What records do reveal is the highly developed stereotype of a hierarchy of African ethnicities that settlers brought with them to the mines and that was rapidly adopted by newcomers rather than the ways in which Africans themselves identified and interacted.

Some of those observations may have been based on what Africans themselves reported, and much of it seems repetitive and clichéd. By the early 1870s, diggers were convinced that the Basotho and the amaZulu were inveterate enemies, yet we cannot be sure to whom exactly these terms referred or whether the enmity was more than ephemeral. The simultaneous desertion of large numbers of Africans from the diamond fields to fight in the wars of the late 1870s and 1880s suggests an unsurprising level of organisation and a continuation of earlier political loyalties, yet those are equally difficult to delineate in detail. At the same time, the rumours of a pan–South African black conspiracy in 1879 and of joint working-class action on the mines suggest that there was also evidence of black, and even of black-white, 'combination'. And, certainly, as we will see, among the *amaKholwa* in Kimberley and in other urban centres that grew up in the last third of the nineteenth century, there were also intimations of pan-African feeling – between Africans and 'coloureds' as well as between different groups of 'Africans'.

On the diamond mines themselves, the creation of closed compounds nipped much of this in the bud. Not only were black workers divided from white far more rigorously than before; mine owners could divide their workers into 'tribal' units and arrange for their despatch home at the end of their contracts. Furthermore, ethnic divisions could be manipulated when trouble threatened. Even missionaries, who were allowed to preach and teach in the compounds, were carefully chosen for their message of industry, honesty and sobriety. The vernacular Bibles they handed out may have served further to emphasise ethnic boundaries. The end result was a far greater degree of ethnic encapsulation than was possible in more fluid urban locations.

These processes of industrialisation and social change were greatly accelerated when extensive seams of deep-level gold were discovered on the Witwatersrand. Although alluvial gold had been worked in the eastern Transvaal from the 1870s, their riches proved ephemeral. Despite the scepticism of some, like Rhodes, who had burnt their fingers in earlier mine speculation, by the late 1890s, the Rand mines were producing between a fifth and a quarter of the world's supply of gold, and within ten years, around one hundred thousand Africans were making their way to the 'Egoli' annually.

New markets for agricultural produce, the demand for more efficient transport and a host of ancillary industries all sprang up in the wake of the gold discoveries. Skilled white miners flocked to the Rand from the hard-rock mining frontiers of the world. As in Kimberley, there was an incessant and well-nigh insatiable demand for cheap and controllable black labour, and within three years of the sinking of the first mine shaft, the handful of Rand mining houses had come together to form the Chamber of Mines to promote the interests of the industry as a whole. Given the cost of extracting deep-level gold, the international ceiling on the gold price and its own long-term commitment to mining even the lowest grade of ore, the most important imperative from the outset was to push down the cost of labour, especially black labour. To achieve this, the Chamber established its own centralised recruiting apparatus, the Rand Native Labour Association in 1897, the forerunner of the Witwatersrand Native Labour Association founded three years later, in the hope of eliminating the myriad independent recruiters who were driving up competition, costs and desertion rates; this was only fully achieved with 'massive and persistent', if at times 'equivocal', assistance from the South African state by the 1920s.[30]

Ideally, the industry would have liked to reduce the cost of all labour. Yet in its early days, skilled expatriate miners could only be attracted to the Witwatersrand, with its extremely high cost of living and inordinately dangerous working conditions, by the prospect of high wages. Fully aware that skills could be learnt and that owners had every incentive to find less expensive substitutes, white miners, mostly British born, quickly organised to protect their position. Thus, the first mine workers' union on the Rand, the Witwatersrand Mine Employees and Mechanics Union, was formed in 1892 to protest 'against the attempt of the Chamber of Mines to flood these fields with labour by means of cheap emigration' from Britain.[31] But they perceived African miners working under them as the greatest danger. Kimberley had already shown that, where magnates dominated the

---

[30] Alan H. Jeeves, *Migrant labour in SA's mining economy: the struggle for the gold mines' labour supply, 1890–1920* (Kingston: McGill-Queen's University Press; Johannesburg: Witwatersrand University Press, 1985), pp. 4–13, 17.

[31] Simons and Simons, *Class and colour*, p. 53.

state, the compound system, labour migrancy and pass laws ensured that black labour was both cheaper and more easily controlled than its white counterpart and that capital had every incentive to substitute it for white. At the union's first meeting, its secretary 'warned that the Chamber meant to cut wages by bringing out miners with wives clinging around their necks.... "If any wages had to be reduced" he appealed, "let the wages of black labour be cut down"'.[32]

Initially, the shortage of labour gave black miners a degree of bargaining power, and wages were high through the mid-1890s. However, the combination of the conquest of the Gaza kingdom in Mozambique in 1895 and the outbreak of the rinderpest epizootic the following year forced large numbers of men from rural areas onto colonial labour markets. Between 1896 and the later importation of indentured labour from China, the majority of workers on the Rand were from Mozambique. Unlike in Kimberley, however, the class forces on the Rand did not permit the total incarceration of the black workforce.

In the early years of the mining industry, black workers both in Kimberley and on the Rand also had a degree of discretion over when, where and how they worked, and management was at times forced into negotiations and compromise. Even so, working conditions were a compound of accidents and commonplace violence, poor food and disastrously unhealthy working and living conditions. Although health conditions improved in Kimberley with the introduction of compounds, on the Rand rates of illness, injury and death were inordinately high. Still, if an earlier generation of revisionist scholars writing in the heyday of apartheid saw black migrants as both powerless and rightless victims, criminalised and controlled by a grid of labour repressive laws and institutions, we then have a far more nuanced picture of the world created by mine workers. In Kimberley and on the Rand, the basis of that lay in the deep rural roots of migrant culture and in the patterns of organisation, social networks, and forms of identity that they created on the mines. Even on the gold fields, where industrialisation was at its most disruptive, the notion that the Randlords totally controlled every aspect of a worker's life can no longer be sustained. The terms of adaptation, however, also had their costs.

For the first ten years, Rand mine wages had – for mine magnates – an uncomfortable habit of rising in times of relative plenty when peasants still had a choice over when and where they worked. In the second half of the 1890s, however, a series of disasters of 'biblical proportions' hit

---

[32] *The Star*, 20 August 1892, cited in Simons and Simons, *Class and colour*, p. 53. I discuss the gold mines in greater detail herein.

African societies and substantially reduced the bargaining power of labour migrants. For many Africans, the natural disasters made migrancy a matter of survival. The sequence began with severe locust attacks between 1894 and 1896 that stripped the land of crops; they were followed in 1896 by wheat blight and the worst drought in living memory. Even more devastating was the arrival from East Africa of rinderpest, a viral panzootic that 'changed the fauna of Africa'.[33]

Within a couple of years of its first appearance across the Zambezi at the beginning of 1896, it had destroyed some 2.5 million head of cattle in South Africa, as well as vast numbers of wild ruminants. Carried with speed along the network of ox-wagon routes crisscrossing the subcontinent, rinderpest spread swiftly south of the Limpopo in March, reaching the Orange River by September. The river and a policed barbed wire cordon introduced by a belatedly concerned Cape Colony led to a temporary lull, but by the middle of 1897, the epizootic had penetrated Basutoland, Natal and Swaziland; by the end of the year, no region was free of the scourge. One missionary, the Reverend François Coillard, wrote of oxen dropping dead in their yokes: 'hundreds of carcasses lay here and there on the roadside or piled up in the fields.'[34] Although white farmers also suffered badly, for most African families, rinderpest was catastrophic: they lost almost all of their animals. Although Africans had been drawn into the money economy in many ways by the late nineteenth century, wealth was still accumulated in cattle: their loss was, quite simply, the equivalent of the great Wall Street Crash of 1929. Cattle were essential for transport and ploughing and provided food, fertiliser and fuel. But they were not only a crucial economic resource. Above all, they were central to the reproduction of the social and political order. The panzootic thus led to the further unravelling of kinship and homestead relationships, as elders could no longer provide their juniors with cattle for *lobola* (bridewealth), and starving families became totally dependent on the meagre wages earned by young migrants. In area after area, young men were unable to marry and achieve adult status. For many, the meat of dead animals was their only resource, and magistrates remarked on the fatalism of people who took refuge in drinking, dancing and debauchery. More seriously, malnutrition, if not outright starvation, was rife, lowering resistance to infectious disease and causing death among the vulnerable.

---

[33] Gordon R. Scott, 'The murrain now known as rinderpest', *Newsletter of the Tropical Agriculture Association* 20:4 (2000), 14–16, at http://post.queensu.ca/~forsdyke/rindpsto.htm.

[34] F. Coillard, *On the threshold of Central Africa* (London: Hodder and Stoughton, 1897), p. 626, cited in Phoofolo, 'Epidemics and revolutions', p. 125. This section relies heavily on this article and his 'Face to face with famine: the Basotho and the rinderpest, 1897–1899', *JSAS* 29:2 (2003), 503–27.

The wider political impact was also profound. In the absence of a cure, colonial authorities adopted draconian measures to curb the movement of cattle, shooting both infected beasts and those suspected of infection. Initial attempts to discover a vaccine were unsuccessful, and African farmers were not alone in thinking that inoculation was simply another way of killing their cattle.

As a result, when a more effective vaccine was found, African farmers – like many an Afrikaner – were slow to adopt it. All over the region there were rumours of African restlessness and potential uprisings – which became an actuality in British Bechuanaland, which had been recently annexed by the Cape – when infected cattle strayed out of the Taungs Reserve and were shot.

White settlers found the way open to acquire more African land, now free of its cattle: as the Chief Native Affairs Commissioner in Zululand noted in 1900, the destruction of African cattle gave the colony a 'most favourable opportunity' for delimiting lands in Zululand.[35] As crucially for employers, their persistent problem of labour shortage could at last be solved, as increasing numbers of Africans were forced to seek work beyond their homesteads. For the Chamber of Mines, the combination of rinderpest, drought and the defeat of Gungunyane in Mozambique could not have been more fortuitous. At the end of 1896, the Chamber exploited the opportunity to lower African wages by 30 per cent and to increase the length of the workday.

As we have seen, the conquest of the remaining African polities of southern Africa was in large measure a consequence of the mineral discoveries. At the same time, it was the loss of African land and the rapid transformation of potential warriors and peasants into workers that made possible the profitable exploitation of minerals, and indeed the wider transformation of the South African economy. We should remember, however, that the black, urban working class was both more ethnically varied than the migrant labour force and had greater chronological depth than the mining industry. African, Indian and coloured male and female workers had all occupied distinct niches in colonial and republican labour markets long before mining, and many resisted labour on the mines well into the twentieth century, despite the strenuous efforts of the Chamber of Mines and its recruiters.

From the mid-nineteenth century, small groups of African wage earners had been making their way to the towns and villages of the Cape and Natal, some from as far afield as the northern Transvaal and Mozambique.

---

[35] Phoofolo, 'Epidemics and revolutions', pp. 135–137, citing the 'Report of the Chamber of Mines' in the *South African Mining Journal and Financial News*, 7 (November 1996).

A few were even beginning to put down more permanent roots. Although the oldest coloured working class in the Western Cape had long emerged out of Khoesan dispossession and slavery, Cape Town's economic expansion between 1891 and 1902 – a delayed response to the discovery of gold – brought an influx of new workers into the labour market. Skilled workers were imported from Britain and Australia, bringing with them some experience of craft unionism and 'the desire to protect privilege' especially among those with scarcer skills, although in the 1890s there were 'examples . . . of inclusion and co-operation between white and coloured artisan'.[36] Poorer white and coloured women began to enter the city's factories and workshops in preference to domestic work, and an organised migrant labour system brought cheap unskilled labourers to the docks from the Eastern Cape after a successful strike by coloured workers had led to a rise in wages. In the early 1900s, African migrants constituted almost half of Cape Town's lowest paid unskilled workforce, labouring mainly in the docks, in construction and on the railways. In general, workers, other than white artisans, remained unorganised, and strikes were rare until the following decade, although worker protest especially in the docks and in domestic labour was widespread. Poor pay, squalid conditions and unfair treatment led workers to boycott jobs, desert harsh employers and deliberately commit acts of minor sabotage at the workplace.

In Natal, many of the first Africans in town were several thousand *togt*, or daily workers, in domestic employ, who were paid more and had more choice of employment than in the case of monthly paid workers. Others were independent workers, many of them modifying their traditional craft skills to meet the needs of the colonial labour market. Thus, for forty years after 1850, an association of African washermen, or *amawasha*, as they were known in isiZulu, established a monopoly over a trade in which they could deploy the known skills of artisans who specialised in hide or skin dressing: this was yet another form of translation. Displaced by Indian dhobis and commercial laundries in the 1890s, many then made their way to the Rand, where they served the domestic need of thousands of single white miners for clean clothes.

By the 1880s, an African's wage-earning trajectory may well have taken him (and wage earners were mostly, though not only, male in this period) into and then out of migrancy to the roads, railways and harbours of industrialising South Africa or to the mines, then back to the countryside or, increasingly, into other more lucrative forms of urban employment.

---

[36] Vivian Bickford-Smith, 'Protest, organisation and ethnicity among Cape Town workers, 1891–1902', in E. van Heyningen (ed.), *Studies in the history of Cape Town* (Cape Town: University of Cape Town Press, 1994), vol. 7, pp. 92, 99.

Although there were a few African women in towns in the last two decades of the nineteenth century, most came as the wives and daughters of the more settled African intelligentsia – preachers and teachers, alongside a small scattering of journalists and artisans.

For Indians and coloureds, the movement was no less complex. An indentured worker uprooted from the economic vicissitudes but cultural certainties of life in India would probably find himself (and more rarely herself) on a labour-intensive Natal sugar or wattle plantation. By the 1880s, after they had completed their first term of indenture, many remained on the land as peasants and small-scale farmers and found their way to the outskirts of Durban; others sought work on the railways or the coal mines, which expanded in response to demand from the Rand. Increasingly, the majority of those who did not return to India were proletarianised, especially after the imposition in 1895 of a £3 tax on indentured Indians, and its subsequent extension to their children, which made it more difficult for them to acquire land. The handful of Indians who had become large landowners, rentiers and merchants were largely of free 'passenger' immigrant origin, almost exclusively so in the case of those who came directly from India to the Cape Colony.

Poorly paid coloured workers, too, were increasingly making their way to more varied payment in the interlocked colonial economies of southern Africa from the 1880s, swelling the proletariat in the burgeoning mining towns and port cities of the subcontinent. Many were able to bring artisan skills learnt on the farms to the urban workplace. They, too, were forging new cultural and religious patterns, as their 'values, practices and beliefs' came up against the dissonances of imperialism's racialised modernity. If the experience of urbanisation frequently sharpened ethnic identities, in these years, the lines between ethnic groups and even between 'coloured' and 'African' were as frequently blurred.

Much of the new historiography of South Africa in the 1970s and 1980s was devoted to the mining industry and its role in creating many of the institutions of twentieth-century South Africa. The strategic importance of mining in shaping South Africa's political economy, the political, social and cultural, as well as the economic and numerical importance of migrant labour to the mines, makes the discovery of minerals a key point of departure. It was central, too, to the transformation of agriculture, which remained the occupation of the majority of South Africa's population, whether black or white, until well into the twentieth century. Yet social relations forged in the countryside critically informed the culture and consciousness of the majority of black South Africans and Afrikaners at least as powerfully as social relations on the mines. Indeed, the formative experience of the

compounds in Kimberley and on the Rand was far from universal. Moreover, older notions of a black working class consisting largely of migrant
mine workers have to be inflected in a host of different ways. Nor does
work on the mines or on the land (or a combination of the two) exhaust
the possibilities. For the majority of South Africa's coloured and Indian
workers, the forces shaping their consciousness were very different.

Most Indian indentured and ex-indentured workers were drawn from
southern India; the remainder came from the north. The majority were
Hindu, belonging to a variety of castes, although some 12 per cent were
Muslim and 2 per cent Christian. Yet during the journey to Natal, new
bonds were forged while 'the breakdown of caste, language, religion and
religious differences accelerated on plantations where Indian workers did
the same work at the same rate, irrespective of religious status or taboos.'[37]
Harsh working conditions, a shared sense of cultural 'otherness' in relation
to Natal's African population and white settlers, and the social segregation
of colonial society contributed to 'a loose sense of community' and the birth
of a shared sense of South African Indian identity by 1910, albeit one that
was fragile and easily fractured.[38]

The convergence of language was another marker: although northerners
developed a South African Hindi vernacular, English served increasingly as
the lingua franca not only for the educated elite but also among the largely
Gujarati traders, Hindi speakers and the Tamil and Telegu speakers of
south India. The establishment of shrines, madrasahs and mosques, as well
as cemeteries and orphanages, by the wealthier merchants who followed in
their wake from the 1870s, reinvigorated Islamic culture among indentured
Muslims and their offspring. There were also numerous Hindu associations,
and religious identification remained strong.

Indian merchants had long traded on the East African littoral. With the
resumption of indentures to Natal in 1874, they made their way to South
Africa as 'passengers', paying their own passage, to cater to Indian workers.
Mostly Gujarati Muslims, some were Hindu, and there was a sprinkling of
Christians from southern India, who often came via Mauritius. Although
a handful were men of real wealth who established businesses in both the
Transvaal and Natal, most were small-scale hawkers or agents of larger firms
who spread into rural areas, where they traded with and supplied credit

---

[37] G. Vahed, 'Uprooting and rerooting: culture, religion and community among indentured
Muslim migrants in colonial Natal, 1860–1911', *South African Historical Journal* 45
(November 2001), 191–222.

[38] Parvathi Raman, 'Being an Indian communist the South African way: the influence of
Indians in the South African Communist Party, 1934–1952', unpublished Ph.D. thesis,
University of London (2002), p. 56.

to an increasing African clientele. By the mid-1880s, however, whites in both the Transvaal and the Orange Free State responded to their presence with discriminatory laws that required their registration and prevented their acquisition of landed property or citizenship rights. By the early 1890s, the handful of Indian merchants in the Orange Free State had been expelled, whereas in the Transvaal there were frequent calls from the Volksraad to prohibit Indian immigration. Nor did Natal's draft constitution providing for colonial self-government contain safeguards for their interests. It was in this context that the more privileged merchants and traders, professionals and white-collar workers, Muslim and Hindu, formed the Indian Committee to defend their interests, and it was at their behest that Mohandas K. Gandhi, then a struggling lawyer in Delhi, arrived in Natal in 1893.

Although planters and big employers continued to support the use of indentured labour, Natal's mostly British settlers were more ambivalent. As increasing numbers of Indians established themselves in the colony, they felt threatened by competition from Indian traders, market gardeners and skilled workers. The granting of self-government to the colony in 1893 was swiftly followed by a spate of anti-Indian measures. In the face of a barrage of impending legislation, Gandhi founded the Natal Indian Congress in 1894, largely to defend the interests of the merchants who were to dominate its proceedings. Nevertheless, 'western educated white collar workers . . . were members of Congress from very early days'.[39] There was more than enough for Gandhi to do: in 1895, the government imposed an annual tax of £3 on all nonindentured boys older than sixteen and girls older than thirteen, a sum that could swallow up a family's annual income. Thousands were forced to renew their indentures or return to India. In 1896, the vote was denied to all those who came from countries without parliamentary institutions – a formula that was intended, but failed, to mask its anti-Indian intent. At the same time, licensing policy was used to hamper Indian trade and steps were taken to curb further immigration.

The intensity of white working-class and commercial animosity against Indian competition was dramatically displayed in 1897, when Gandhi landed with two shiploads of passenger Indians, to be confronted by a rowdy but well-organised mob, acting with the support of members of government. The mob apparently believed that he was deliberately importing indentured skilled workers into Natal. This episode 'left a permanent imprint on the character of Natal. . . . [T]he Indian population was to some extent stabilised, but the intensity of the feeling stirred up by the white

---

[39] Maureen Swan, *Gandhi: the South African experience* (Johannesburg: Ravan Press, 1985), pp. 38–57; the quotation is on p. 53.

inhabitants, mainly in Durban where the disturbance took place, produced a fixity of hostility to Indians.'[40]

If the relationship between whites and Indians was largely hostile, it is more difficult to interpret the limited evidence for African-Indian interaction in this period. Manifestly, there were points of both interaction and of friction, as they competed over work, land and commerce. The majority of passenger Indians, both in Natal and in the Transvaal, probably shared the sentiments of those who complained to the Viceroy in 1884 that they were 'treated like Kafirs, who are barbarians, and are only being brought within the pale of civilisation, whereas the Indians are known to have been a civilised nation from the earliest times.'[41] Gandhi himself was to echo such sentiments both publicly and privately on many an occasion.

The fact that around Durban, and subsequently other towns, Africans were tenants and customers of Indian landowners and shopkeepers may have increased rather than diminished tensions (and certainly did so later) on the African side, especially as urban Indians tended to congregate together, in the customary practice of new migrants. It may have been that the most intimate relationships were forged where Indians and Africans worked side by side, whether on plantations or in the burgeoning working-class suburbs of Kimberley and Johannesburg, although the evidence is sparse. In rural Natal, it seems, 'Indians often became fluent Zulu speakers and very occasionally sex and marriage took place across a cultural divide'. For the most part, however, even in the countryside, Indians retained their strong sense of Indianness and 'were rarely if ever assimilated into African social structure'.[42]

In the Western Cape, too, the black working class was subject to intense racism and white demands for increased control. There, for many downtrodden coloured farm workers, the mineral revolution opened up new possibilities in the towns, and in the surge of road, rail and harbour construction. A litany of complaints followed from farmers, who demanded ever more stringent punishment for 'deserting' labourers and extraeconomic measures to secure labour at the cost and under the conditions of their choosing. Nevertheless, by the 1900s, the status quo ante had been restored, not least because the natural disasters of the 1890s swelled rural

---

[40] Mabel Palmer, *The history of the Indians in Natal*, Natal Regional Survey vol. 10 (Cape Town: Oxford University Press, 1957), p. 63.

[41] Surendra Bhana and Bridglal Pachai (eds.), *A documentary history of Indian South Africans* (Cape Town: David Philip, 1984), p. 10: Pillay and others petition the viceroy of India 14 July 1884.

[42] Freund, *Insiders and outsiders*, p. 38. For relations in rural Natal at a slightly later date, see Meer, *A fortunate man*, pp. 6–7.

labour markets. Although some Africans joined compatriots from as far away as Mozambique in Cape Town, others found work on Western Cape farms alongside a depleted coloured proletariat.

Apart from Indians, commitment to life in town was most evident among coloureds and African Christians with skills and education. In Natal by 1880, there was hardly a black Christian without some experience in wage labour; and the major mission societies 'all had substantial town congregations composed mostly of men who drifted in and out of the developing urban proletariat'.[43] In towns, new communities of aspirant artisans and professionals sprang up, many of whom had been educated on the missions and who were able to find new opportunities for those with the all-important skill of literacy and a knowledge of English and Dutch; they still had some degree of independence in labour markets. Indeed, some used capital from their rural activities to establish businesses.

Among these communities, rather different forms of identity were to be forged, shaped by their Christian universalism, their literacy and their acceptance of imperial notions of progress, and sharpened by their encounters with growing white racism, Afrikaner ethnic nationalism and, slightly later, the influences of black America. In Natal, the colonial attack on Langalibalele in 1873, the invasion of the Zulu kingdom in 1879, the travails of the Zulu monarch, Cetshwayo and the exile of his son, Dinuzulu, to St Helena thereafter all left in their trail hundreds of letters and petitions between Zululand, Natal, London, Robben Island and St Helena as a network of letter writers 'commented, reflected upon and articulated their views on social, political, intellectual and economic situations in the colony'.[44]

Elsewhere, too, articulate, settled, westernised black families had emerged by the 1870s. In Port Elizabeth, for example, the largest and most prosperous of the Eastern Cape towns but by no means an exception, Africans established cricket clubs, benefit societies and temperance organisations. The latter, affiliated to the International Order of True Templars, were particularly important for Christian converts throughout South Africa, who saw only too vividly the destructive impact of liquor on society; many African and coloured political activists of the time, like Cape Town's early white feminists, were ardent prohibitionists.

[43] Norman Etherington, *Preachers, peasants and politics in southeast Africa, 1835–1880. African Christian communities in Natal, Pondoland and Zululand* (London: Royal Historical Society, 1978), p. 126.

[44] Cyrius Vukile Khumalo, 'Epistolary networks and the politics of cultural production in KwaZulu-Natal, 1860–1910', unpublished Ph.D. thesis, University of Michigan (2004), pp. 17, 19.

By the 1890s, the Port Elizabeth black community boasted sufficient black-owned businesses to warrant the formation of the African and American Working Men's Union, which assisted in the development of black economic enterprise and espoused an explicitly Africanist programme. Its shares were advertised as far afield as Basutoland, Bechuanaland and Natal, and it inspired similar initiatives across the region. As late as 1910, the union was still in existence, running a store, employing its own staff and holding shareholders' meetings. Its formation was explicitly political and was closely associated with political mobilisation. As in so much else, the Eastern Cape was formative in the creation of these new, ethnically mixed, urban communities. With the mineral discoveries, however, many of the most ambitious and aspirant were drawn first to the burgeoning city of diamonds, slightly later to the Witwatersrand. By the 1890s, Kimberley was home to a vigorous black – African and coloured – aspirant petty bourgeoisie and independent artisanry, an emergent class of black teachers, interpreters, clerks, ministers of religion, tradespeople and others, many of them drawn from the smaller towns of the Eastern Cape. Poised 'between a largely unskilled proletariat on the one hand and a propertied bourgeoisie on the other',[45] their lives were perhaps epitomised by Solomon Plaatje, an author and newspaper editor, whose translations of Shakespeare into Setswana and of Tswana proverbs into English illustrated vividly his role as a transcultural interpreter. The Mafeking administration's secretary and interpreter during the South African War, he was to become the first secretary of the South African Native National Congress in 1912.

All of them Christian, Kimberley's black inhabitants were as remarkable for the diversity of their origins as for their rich social life, with its all-male social associations and sporting societies – the South Africans Improvement Association, the Come Again Lawn Tennis Club, the Duke of Wellington's Cricket Club and the John Bull Debating Society. For the black urban elite, a range of occupational, recreational and religious organisations all demonstrated their capacity to become respectable Victorian gentlemen. The one social arena in which women played some role was in its many musical performances, as music was almost the group's defining characteristic. It is thus no coincidence that much of the music of contemporary black South Africa had its roots in the interwoven traditions of Orpheus McAdoo's Virginia Jubilee Singers, who visited Kimberley in the 1890s, the carnival songs of Cape Town, and the Christian hymnody being adapted at this time by the African composer John Knox Bokwe.

[45] Brian Willan, 'An African in Kimberley', in S. Marks and R. Rathbone (eds.), *Industrialisation and social change: African class formation, culture and consciousness, 1870–1930* (London: Longman, 1982), p. 238.

Paradoxically, however, Kimberley, which gave educated Africans and coloureds their greatest opportunity, was also the harbinger of their marginalisation. If industrialisation meant the formation of class, it also represented, then as now, its deformation. The path into the middle class was neither linear nor ever onward, as the black elite soon experienced a devaluation of their skills in the face of the insatiable appetite of the mines and farms for cheap unskilled labour. It was also in Kimberley that many of the characteristic features of segregation were developed and exported to other urban communities seeking ways of maintaining 'social order in a society undergoing rapid urbanisation, immigration and industrialisation.'[46]

Thus, for many of those who had responded most enthusiastically to the new order, the last decades of the nineteenth century were to see a subversion of the optimistic missionary faith in 'progress' and 'improvement' and belief in the liberal, ostensibly colour-blind institutions of the Cape Colony, the most notable of which was its nonracial franchise. Thus, although some were to find expanding opportunities in burgeoning towns, this was also a period that saw the consolidation of settler society and heightened racial hostility, from which even missionaries were not immune.

Racially discriminatory practices had been part of South African social life long before the mineral revolution, with the de facto segregation of many social activities and institutions in colonies and republics. Most notably, black people (along with women of whatever hue) were denied full citizenship by being excluded from the franchise everywhere except in the Cape Colony. There, there was still a 'colour-blind' property-based franchise for adult males, whereas in the republics there existed an explicit barrier to equality in church or state.

In the late nineteenth century, the racial practices were reshaped and powerfully strengthened by being systematically linked to a range of laws and institutions developed in Kimberley and the Rand and, in the Cape, by the rise of the Afrikaner Bond as the main political mouthpiece of Cape Dutch farming interests, and by the grant of responsible government to Natal in 1893. On the mines, as we have seen, the nexus of laws and institutions established by the mine magnates and the impact of labour registration effectively segregated black from white workers and reinforced racial stereotypes that overseas workers brought with them. We have also seen how the accelerated establishment of rural reserves and the increasing recognition of chiefly authority and customary law came to form building blocks for the migrant labour system and, in turn, to bolster and justify

---

[46] Vivian Bickford-Smith, *Ethnic pride and racial prejudice in Victorian Cape Town* (Cambridge: Cambridge University Press, 1995), p. 8, who is referring specifically to Cape Town, where there had been a rather more permeable colour line before the mineral revolution.

segregated institutions. Granted, 'segregationist ideology' was 'relatively undeveloped as a *systematic* political doctrine'[47] before 1914, with the word *segregation* itself seemingly only coming into use in the first years of the twentieth century, deriving from the American South. But racist thinking – and more specifically belief in the superiority of white (especially English) men (and to a lesser extent of English women) – was deeply embedded in the settler worldview, as well as in the ideology of the 'imperial working class' that came to South Africa in the last third of the nineteenth century. This was true even in the Western Cape, where in the mid-Victorian years, there had been a greater degree of social mobility and a more 'permeable colour line' than in the rest of the country.

Cape 'liberalism' was always a minority creed, however, and a rather frail one at that. From the 1880s, it is clear that even this limited tradition was being increasingly challenged in myriad institutional and political spaces, as city fathers and colonial politicians witnessed with alarm the huge influx of black and white migrant workers into the colony's towns and were influenced by the dominant discourse of Social Darwinism, on the one hand, and by the strains of rapid social transformation – dramatic demographic increase, the influx of new immigrants and unruly urbanisation – on the other hand. Urban squalor and disease were metaphorically equated with coloureds and Africans, a source of danger to be housed in segregated spaces, whereas urban sanitation and public health were elevated to touchstones of progress in political discourse.

Social Darwinism, in particular, eroded an earlier liberal faith in the educability of all humans and therefore their capacity for redemption. By the late nineteenth century, many of the most Westernised and assimilated Africans and coloureds began to find the foundations of their world shaken, their dreams of incorporation into a common colonial society betrayed. Their experience over the following ten years was to intensify their disillusion.

It was in that context that, from the 1880s, educated Africans in the Cape and Natal sought to protect their position through a host of new initiatives, including the establishment of Western-type political organisations to defend African interests, the creation of African newspapers and the founding of independent African churches by some of South Africa's most respected African pastors. The diaspora of the black intelligentsia of the Eastern Cape to Kimberley and Johannesburg, but also their dispersal as missionaries to distant rural chiefdoms, carried these political and

---

[47] Saul Dubow, *Racial segregation and the origins of apartheid in South Africa, 1919–1936* (Basingstoke, U.K.: Macmillan, in association with St Antony's College, Oxford: 1989), p. 3, my italics.

religious innovations with them. This in part accounts for the tenacity of the elite belief in the old ideals of imperial liberalism, which had long disappeared, even from the Cape. This diaspora was also to strengthen greatly the 'revolutionary idea that all Africans were one people' despite 'tribal' differences – an 'idea propagated by missionaries',[48] but also fostered by town life and in mine compounds.

The first western-type, explicitly political black organisation, the Imbumba Yama Nyama, was established in Port Elizabeth in 1882. Modelled partly on the Bond, the main impetus behind the founding of Imbumba was the continuous conquest of Xhosa-speaking peoples and their incorporation into the Cape. In its colonial order, their limited franchise access meant that Africans, like Afrikaners, were encouraged to mobilise ethnic and racial identities in new ways in the period. Despite their moderate constitutionalism, the aim of the new generation was to fight for African rights in what they saw as an increasingly hostile colonial world through ensuring the registration of those eligible to vote in Cape elections and mobilising African voters behind sympathetic candidates at election time. Although Imbumba's geographical reach was as limited as its temporal survival was short, it was to be replaced by successive organisations with similar class constituencies and constitutional briefs. The organisation's most articulate and sophisticated spokesperson was the newspaper editor John Tengo Jabavu, who dominated Eastern Cape politics for the following three decades, using first the mission paper *Isigidimi* and later his own *Imvo Zabantsundu* to express African grievances and to urge Africans to vote, especially in marginal constituencies. The launch of the independent *Imvo* was a major development in the political history of South Africa and signalled a broader political, professional and economic mobilisation by African 'modernisers' in the Eastern Cape. It was crucial in fostering a wider sense of 'imagined community' and political unity for the educated elite, as was evidenced in the widespread and organised opposition aroused by the Parliamentary Registration Act of 1887, which threatened to disenfranchise African voters.

These developments were accompanied by a new sense of self-sufficiency in the church, as educated Africans expressed their bitterness against the paternalism and racism of European missionaries. The Wesleyan minister Nehemiah Tile, who established his Thembu Church in 1884, is generally regarded as having been the first to break away. This was at a time of widespread Thembu popular protest against the failure of government to stem settler encroachment on their lands. In fact, Johannes Dinkwanyane, brother of the Pedi paramount Sekhukhune, has the prior claim. Although

---

[48] Etherington, *Preachers, peasants and politics*, p. 172.

he only formed his Lutheran Bapedi Church in 1889, he had already asserted his independence of the Berlin Mission Society when he proclaimed himself and his followers to be subjects of the Pedi paramount in 1873. At his new settlement, Dinkwanyane not only 'mounted a challenge to the authority of the Berlin mission'[49] but also challenged the legitimacy of the Transvaal state. In Natal, the first independent church was established in 1890, when Mbiana Ngidi, after years of tension with the American Mission Board, finally broke with white missionaries to found his own Zulu Mbiana Congregational Church because they refused him permission to relocate to the newly annexed Zululand. The colony soon became the site of numerous independent churches, despite the efforts of the Natal government to exclude them.

The interweaving of religious independence and recognition of chiefly authority reflected a new mood among African Christians in the last decades of the nineteenth century. Unlike the independent Zionist church leaders, who were to follow, these early pioneers of independency were fired by a more explicit political project and were drawn largely from the same social stratum as the leaders of overtly political associations. Many were already respected churchmen in mission denominations, with years of devoted evangelising behind them. Independency arose when other opportunities for African Christians were being whittled away, their hopes of equality in the church disappointed, their participation in a more inclusive society dashed. Apart from the Catholics, no denomination was immune. Over the ensuing years Methodists, Lutherans and Congregationalists, Anglicans and Presbyterians, were all to experience schism.

Of these, the most unsettling for missionaries was the 'defection' of the highly respected Free Church of Scotland pastor at Lovedale, Pambani J. Mzimba, who took with him his entire congregation when he left the church in 1899. It was, however, the establishment of Mangena M. Mokone's significantly named Ethiopian Church in 1896 – so called from the biblical phrase 'And Ethiopia shall stretch out its hands to God' but also inspired by the defeat of the invading Italians at Adowa in that year – which was to cause the greatest challenge to white mission Christianity. Through a chain of apparently unconnected and bizarre circumstances, the visit of McAdoo's Jubilee Singers to Kimberley also led to the affiliation of Mokone's church on the Rand with the well-established African Methodist Episcopal Church (AMEC) in the United States. This, in turn, was to have dramatic consequences for the relationship between black South Africans and African Americans at a critical moment in the development of a nascent black South African politics and culture. Thereafter, 'for much

[49] Delius, *The land belongs to us*, p. 176.

of the twentieth century black America would remain a symbol of urbanity and sophistication among black South Africans, especially [but not only] in cities'.[50]

With their protonationalist vision of black unity, their provision of educational resources and their emphasis on black independence, the AMEC attracted thousands of African and coloured adherents all over southern Africa. By 1899, it was estimated to have had some eleven thousand members, and by 1910, this had risen to forty thousand, to the consternation of administrators and missionaries everywhere; at the turn of the century, the threat of what was somewhat loosely termed *Ethiopianism* was as potent as the later fear of Communism in the 1920s and 1930s. The class constituency of independent churches went beyond that of most of the early nationalist political organisations and was regionally inflected. For example, in the Western Cape, and especially in cosmopolitan Cape Town, with its heterogeneous black population, the AMEC brought together coloured and African adherents. It is no coincidence that the founder of the first viable black political organisation in Cape Town, the African Political (later People's) Organisation (APO), was William Collins, commercial traveller and lay preacher for the AMEC, who 'urged the formation of an organisation to unite "the coloured races of South Africa"'; [51] among its important adherents were the Trinidad-born, London-trained barrister and pan-Africanist Henry Sylvester Williams and the Ghanaian newspaper editor F. Z. S. Peregrino, both of whom also appear to have had close contact with the AMEC. They urged the coloured elite 'to organise on the grounds of [its] shared "blackness"' and to seek 'black unity': Peregrino, for example, denounced 'Coloureds who felt superior to Africans, and declared the term "so-called Colored" a "vague, meaningless and indefinite appellation"'.[52] The ambiguities of the terminology and ambivalences of coloured identity were to shape their politics through the twentieth century. By 1910, the APO was estimated to have attracted twenty thousand mainly coloured adherents.

In the Orange Free State, the AMEC and subsequent political organisations found a ready constituency in little towns, where it was the very considerable class of 'aspirant petty bourgeoisie' that was most responsive to their call. Enterprising and industrious, from a heady mix of ethnic backgrounds and with some education, these men and women had moved into small towns and villages in response to the rural disasters of the 1890s and the later devastation of the South African War. They were soon to find themselves battling against a host of bureaucratic obstacles barring their

[50] James Campbell, *Songs of Zion: The African Methodist Episcopal Church in the USA and South Africa* (New York: Oxford University Press, 1995), p. 131.
[51] Lewis, *Between the wire and the wall*, p. 1.   [52] Ibid., pp. 17–18.

way to the very 'progress' and 'improvement' that were their hallmark. Yet there as elsewhere, the 'Ethiopian message' was as potent in the rural as in the urban areas: sharecroppers and labour tenants on white-owned farms turned to the AMEC after the South African War as landowners attempted to restore their ruined farms and to reassert control over labourers who had found some respite during the years of turmoil.

In the Eastern Cape, too, the American connection brought a new voice of racial populism to the more sedate milieu of liberal politics. There, Jabavu's political domination was shaken by his support for white parliamentary allies, the Cape liberals who came to support the Bond as a result of the Jameson Raid and the South African War. This had a profound effect on Eastern Cape loyalties, strengthening the hand of Jabavu's opponents in the South African Native Congress, or Ingqungqutela, which had been founded in 1891 but had until then been struggling to find its voice. In 1897, with Rhodes's assistance, it established a rival newspaper, *Izwi Labantu*. Differences over the raid and the war were intensified by other ideological differences, as Jabavu and his followers opposed separatists in the church while Congress leaders identified strongly with their independence. Most Cape religious separatist leaders participated in Congress activities, and James Dwane, the newly appointed general (and short-lived) superintendent of the AMEC in South Africa, chaired its Queenstown conference in 1898.

Even in the more remote reserves of the rural Transkei where 'proletarianisation seeped rather than swept through communities' and 'people clung tenaciously to their rural identities and rural resources', these ideas found adherents. As the Cape colonial state's priorities shifted from support for a progressive class of peasant farmers to the regular supply of migrant labour, many families found they had little choice but to send their sons to the mines. In such communities, 'radical separatist Christianity and Africanist thought took hold and expanded' as their leaders 'sought to bridge the gap with traditionalists through populist politics and the use of a common language of protest'.[53]

If, in the 1880s and 1890s, black South Africans were beginning to find a wider African identity, all over South Africa whites became far more starkly divided along ethnolinguistic lines after the attempted incursion into the South African Republic by Rhodes's lieutenant Leander Starr Jameson at the end of 1895. In the Orange Free State, the raid destroyed long-standing friendships and aroused intense pro-Kruger and anti-British sentiments

---

[53] Beinart and Bundy, *Hidden struggles*, pp. 3, 11.

among the populace. According to J. B. M. Hertzog, the Amsterdam-educated lawyer and High Court judge, this moment helped to create his nationalist consciousness, as it did for many of his countrymen. The Cape-born, Cambridge-educated Jan Christiaan Smuts, who had ardently admired Rhodes and was then Pretoria's state attorney, believed that, as a consequence of the raid, 'Afrikanerdom throughout South Africa finds itself now at the most critical moment of its existence. Now or never the foundation of a comprehensive nationalism must be laid.... [L]et us lay the corner stone of a truly united South Africa on the foundation of a pure and comprehensive national feeling'.[54] Whereas before the raid, this 'comprehensive national feeling' had embraced English-speaking South Africans, Smuts turned to his fellow Afrikaners in the republics, declaring that their history showed that blood was thicker than water. In the South African Republic, even those members of the elite who had been critical of Kruger's policies rallied behind him, whereas the president in turn felt that he could rely on now more nationally minded Cape Afrikaners to staff his civil service. Whereas in 1893 he had only just managed to win the presidential elections, in 1898, Kruger was able to claim a very substantial victory.

At the same time, English speakers across South Africa (and in Britain itself) adopted an increasingly jingoistic rhetoric, mobilised by a chauvinist press and by political associations like the South African League, 'an ultra-imperialist, anti-Bond organisation' founded by English-speaking loyalists in the wake of the Jameson Raid.[55] At times, even Chamberlain found it politic to rein in their populist bombast. In this largely manufactured wave of loyalist emotion, Lord Selborne's fears that British republicans might have been tempted to declare a United States of Africa outside the empire would appear to have been comprehensively outflanked.

In the Transvaal, the South African League drew its constituency from Johannesburg's nascent business and professional class, men who were beginning to put down roots and to think of it as home. They included mine managers, engineers, wholesalers and building contractors, solicitors and businessmen, doctors, journalists, ministers and teachers who came from similar backgrounds and shared the same visions, attended the same functions and joined the same clubs. Psychologically incapable of taking a backseat to the Boers, whom they considered inadequate to the task of

---

[54] *Ons Land*, 12 March 1896 cited in W. K. Hancock and Jean van der Poel, *Selections from the Smuts Papers*. vol. 1, *June 1886–May 1902* (Cambridge: Cambridge University Press, 1962), pp. 105–6.

[55] Mordechai Tamarkin, *Cecil Rhodes and the Cape Afrikaners: the imperial colossus and the colonial parish pump* (London: Frank Cass, 1996), p. 258.

managing a modern city and industry, they were men who were trained to take command and who expected to be heard.[56] Imbued with notions of progress by temperament and upbringing, most shared the views of a Milner or a Fitzpatrick that there were two implacably opposed systems functioning in southern Africa. One was a medieval Boer race oligarchy, and the other the 'modern industrial state' of the British. Much of the empire and loyalist rhetoric was couched in terms of these oppositions, which went back to the beginnings of British rule at the Cape, between progress and backwardness, science and superstition, development and stagnation. By the last decades of the century, these dualisms were powerfully reinforced by a new European scientific racism drawing on Darwinian notions of the survival of the fittest. So pervasive were these tropes that, on the eve of war, even Olive Schreiner, the early South African feminist and socialist, could write, ostensibly in their defence and in an anti-imperialist pamphlet, that 'the Boer' was a 'seventeenth century fossil, cut off from the benefits of the European enlightenment for two hundred years by their backward language.' For Schreiner, as for many Dutch-speaking Afrikaners, the taal would inevitably be swept away, and a new, unified white South African people, speaking English and with bourgeois Victorian values, would emerge.[57]

Like Olive Schreiner herself, at this moment of ethnolinguistic polarisation, a small number of leading Cape politicians were affronted by the virulent jingoism that emerged after the Raid and were increasingly disillusioned with imperial intervention in South Africa. They came to see in the Bond a useful counterpoise. These included some of the more liberally minded English-speaking Cape politicians, such as John X. Merriman, Richard Solomon and Olive's brother W. P. Schreiner, who had in the past all expressed their opposition to the Bond's policies toward Africans. With J. W. Sauer, the Afrikaner liberal independent who joined them, this group was dependent on African support in the parliamentary elections of 1898 and 1904. Schreiner (in 1898) and Merriman (in 1908) were both to become Prime Ministers of the Cape with Afrikaner support; both felt their isolation at a time when 'the machinations of evil men' as Merriman put it,

---

[56] D. Cammack, *The Rand at war, 1899–1902: the Witwatersrand and the Anglo-Boer War* (London: James Currey; Berkeley: University of California Press; Pietermaritzburg: University of Natal Press, 1990), p. 9.

[57] Paula M. Krebs, 'Interpreting South Africa to Britain: Olive Schreiner, Boers, and Africans', unpublished paper presented to the Seminar on the Societies of Southern Africa, Institute of Commonwealth Studies, London, 1995. See also her *Gender, race, and the writing of Empire: public discourse and the Boer War*, Cambridge: Cambridge University Press, 1999, pp. 115–22.

had divided South Africans into 'two camps'.[58] It is perhaps here that one should seek the origins of both the sense of white South Africanism of the postwar years and the remnants of Cape liberalism.

The civil rights of British subjects, black as well as white, and the protection of African peoples in the subcontinent played as important a role in anti-republican propaganda as it had in humanitarian crusades earlier in the century. Pretoria's refusal to grant the franchise to Uitlanders and the wrongs suffered by Her Majesty's coloured and Indian subjects in the Transvaal provided Whitehall with a powerful means of mobilising domestic public opinion. Important as these issues may have been in rousing the British public, however, they were of little concern to most Uitlanders. Although mine magnates of whatever origin wanted an end to current insecurity and recognised that only British rule could bring the kind of state and infrastructure they needed, most had little interest in the franchise. Many professional and middle-class Uitlanders had, as yet, no intention of making permanent homes on the Rand. Few, if any, evinced much interest in the rights of Her Majesty's coloured and Indian subjects in the Transvaal.

Nor did working-class Uitlanders necessarily all share the concerns of Milner or the South African League. Almost all had come on their own, with strong ties to the families they had left behind, many of whom were dependent on remittances from South Africa. Few thought they would have a long-term future on the Rand; and the death toll from miners' phthisis lent a chilling reality to their forebodings. Moreover, national and cultural identities were infused by the class and racial consciousness of 'white labourism', in which hostility to capitalist exploitation and racism 'were inextricably intermingled.'[59] By drawing on the then well-established sense of identity fostered initially by Eastern Cape settlers, proimperialists like Rhodes and Fitzpatrick, as well as imperial officials, subsumed 'employers, employees, trades union organisers, producers, consumers and suppliers . . . in the blanket description "South African British"'.[60] Yet British settlers had diverse origins, whose primary allegiance was often still to their English, Irish, Welsh, Cornish or Scottish roots, and there was sometimes tension among them. By the end of the nineteenth century, the Scots had a well-defined presence in South Africa, with Caledonian societies, the celebration

---

[58] J. X. Merriman to T. P. Theron, Britstown, 27 February 1900, in Lewsen (ed.), *Selections from the Merriman correspondence*, vol. 3, p. 158.

[59] Jonathan Hyslop, 'The imperial working class makes itself "White": white labourism in Britain, Australia and SA before the First World War', *Journal of Historical Sociology* 12:4 (December 1999), 398.

[60] The quotation is from Donald Denoon, *The grand illusion: the failure of imperial policy in the Transvaal colony during the period of reconstruction, 1900–1905* (London: Longman, 1973), p. 5, who poses the question as to whether they really constituted a community.

of grand days on the Scottish calendar and Highland games, and Scottish regiments with kilts and bagpipes. Although other smaller 'British' ethnicities were far less prominent and less well organised during the 1890s, a small but conspicuous cluster of Irish nationalists established themselves in the Johannesburg-Pretoria area; included in their number were Arthur Griffith and John MacBride, both of whom were to distinguish themselves later in the fight for Irish independence. Cornishmen, who brought their mining skills first to Kimberley and then to the Rand, also established myriad local associations and societies that maintained close links with their homeland.

In due course, they were joined by Australians and North Americans, as well as by a sprinkling of European Jews and Germans, equally anxious to be absorbed into the 'progressive' Anglophone elite of an increasingly cosmopolitan Johannesburg. Some, like Irish republicans, were anti-imperial – as Lord Selborne had recognised in his 1896 Memorandum, which predicted a future United States of South Africa outside of the British Empire if action were not taken to preempt it. Whatever its meaning and ambiguity, the category of 'South African British' did not include black or Indian South Africans, whether or not they were British subjects or indeed English speaking. There certainly were English-speaking settlers in the Cape Colony who believed with Dr Darley-Hartley that, 'if the Colony were not a British colony the natives would be treated little better than dogs', and who, like Darley-Hartley himself, considered themselves 'friends of the natives'. The group included such obvious figures as Rose Innes, Merriman and Solomon, who sought and generally received African votes at election time and who could be counted on to oppose more extreme anti-African measures in Parliament. However, they had little support in the wider English-speaking community, even in the Cape: when Darley-Hartley and his associate Arthur Fuller proposed that the Loyal Colonial League in the Cape form 'native branches' on condition that there was a white man on the executive, they 'got nearly hanged, drawn and quartered because of the heresy'.[61]

Ironically, divisions among Cape whites gave rise for the first time to clear-cut political parties in the 1898 election, which lent the colony's black voters increased political leverage as both the Progressives (as the Loyal Colonial League renamed itself for electoral purposes) and the Bond

---

[61] This draws heavily on Mabelle F. Bitensky, 'The South African League British Imperialist Organisation in South Africa, 1896–1899', unpublished M.A. thesis, University of the Witwatersrand (1950); the quotations from W. H. Darley-Hartley are from his account, 'The beginnings of the South African League being some personal reminiscences,' a pamphlet based on extracts from articles in the *New Era*, May–August 1904, cited in ibid., p. 130.

canvassed their support. In 1904, for example, the Fort Beaufort branch of the Afrikaner Bond decided to invite Jabavu to stand as its candidate in the forthcoming elections. The Bond's bid for the African vote was undoubtedly strengthened by its alliance with 'Cape liberals'. The Rhodes-Bond alliance had been constructed in part on their mutual interest in 'govern[ing] the native as a subject race';[62] when that alliance dissolved, there was briefly a modest opportunity for blacks to influence parliamentary politics. This remained true until the Cape's nonracial franchise was devalued by the construction of the new white alliance that led to the Act of Union in 1910. Beyond the Cape, even fewer English speakers were in favour of enfranchising black people. In Natal, which removed Indians from the voters' roll in 1896, only six Africans had managed to qualify for the franchise under the colony's highly restrictive regulations by 1910, and opposition to the Cape's more liberal provisions would lead many to oppose Union. In the South African Republic, if not all Uitlanders were convinced of their own need for the vote, even fewer showed any enthusiasm for taking up the cudgels on behalf of coloureds, Indians or Africans. There, the vast majority of Uitlanders were united in their opposition to political rights for blacks. In 1897, Milner wrote to the Liberal politician Henry Asquith, who had urged the need to restore good relations between 'Dutch and English' and 'secure for the Natives . . . adequate and sufficient protection against oppression and wrong'. 'The whole *crux* of the S. African position,' he declared, was that 'you might indeed unite Dutch and English by protecting the black man but you would unite them against yourself and your policy of protection.'[63] In the event, Milner would prove less concerned with either of Asquith's objectives than with securing British dominance in South Africa.

On his arrival in 1897, the high commissioner may have hoped to accomplish his ambitions without the use of force. His attitude was, however, transformed by Kruger's 1898 electoral victory: he accepted that British supremacy could not be attained 'through radical political reform in the Transvaal' and began to push 'for a head-on collision with Kruger'.[64] The deeper political, economic and strategic reasons for war, as well as the immediate events leading up to it, are dealt with elsewhere in this volume, and its course is documented in the next chapter. A crucial moment in

---

[62] Robert I. Rotberg, *The founder: Cecil Rhodes and the pursuit of power* (New York: Oxford University Press, 1988), p. 225.

[63] Milner to H. H. Asquith, 18 Nov. 1897, in C. Headlam (ed.), *The Milner papers: South Africa, 1897–1899* (Toronto: Cassell, 1931–1933), pp. 177–8, italics in original.

[64] Tamarkin, 'The Cape Afrikaners and the British empire', in D. Lowry (ed.), *The South African War reappraised*, p. 124.

the run-up to hostilities came in May 1899, when a last-ditch attempt to prevent war was sabotaged by Milner's deliberate intransigence over the Uitlander franchise. As Kruger bitterly remarked, it was not the franchise but his state that Britain wanted. Five months later, the Transvaal issued its ultimatum to the British government: withdraw all troops or face its forces combined with those of its republican ally, the Orange Free State. On 9 October 1899, war erupted. Its outcome would prove the anvil on which the modern South African state would be forged.

FURTHER READING

Beinart, William, *The rise of conservation in South Africa: settlers, livestock, and the environment, 1770–1950*, Oxford: Oxford University Press, 2003

Beinart, William and Colin Bundy, *Hidden struggles in rural South Africa: politics and popular movements in the Transkei and Eastern Cape, 1890–1930*, London: James Currey; Berkeley: University of California Press; Johannesburg: Ravan Press, 1987

Bhana, Surendra and Bridglal Pachai (eds.), *A documentary history of Indian South Africans*, Cape Town: David Philip, 1984

Bickford-Smith, Vivien, *Ethnic pride and racial prejudice in Victorian Cape Town*, Cambridge: Cambridge University Press, 1995

Brown, Karen. 'Progressivism, agriculture and conservation in the Cape Colony, c. 1902–1908', unpublished D.Phil. thesis, Oxford University (2002)

Bundy, Colin, *The rise and fall of the South African peasantry*, London: Heinemann, 1979

Cammack, Diana, *The Rand at war, 1899–1902: the Witwatersrand and the Anglo-Boer War*, London: James Currey; Berkeley: University of California Press; Pietermaritzburg: University of Natal Press, 1990

Campbell, James T., *Songs of Zion: the African Methodist Episcopal Church in the USA and South Africa*, New York: Oxford University Press, 1995

Cope, Richard L., *Ploughshare of war: the origins of the Anglo-Zulu War of 1879*, Pietermaritzburg: University of Natal Press, 1999

Crais, Clifton, *The politics of evil: magic, state power and the political imagination in South Africa*, Cambridge: Cambridge University Press, 2002

Delius, Peter, *The land belongs to us: the Pedi polity, the Boers and the British in the nineteenth century Transvaal*, Johannesburg: Ravan Press, 1983; Berkeley: University of California Press, 1984

Delius, Peter, *A lion amongst the cattle: reconstruction and resistance in the Northern Transvaal*, Johannesburg: Ravan Press; Portsmouth, NH: Heinemann; Oxford: James Currey, 1996

Dubow, Saul, *Racial segregation and the origins of apartheid in South Africa, 1919–1936*, Basingstoke, U.K.: Macmillan, in association with St Antony's College, Oxford, 1989

Erlank, Natasha, 'Gendering ethnicity: African men and the 1883 Commission on Native Law and Custom', *Journal of Southern African Studies* 29:3 (December 2003), 937–53

Etherington, Norman, *Preachers, peasants and politics in southeast Africa 1835–1880: African Christian communities in Natal, Pondoland and Zululand*, London: Royal Historical Society, 1978

Freund, Bill, *Insiders and outsiders: the Indian working class of Durban, 1910–1990*, Portsmouth, NH: Heinemann; Pietermaritzburg: University of Natal Press; London: James Currey, 1995

Guy, Jeff, 'An accommodation of patriarchs: Theophilus Shepstone and the foundations of the system of native administration in Natal', unpublished paper presented at the Conference on Masculinities in Southern Africa, University of Natal, Durban, July 1997

Hancock, W. K. and Jean van der Poel (eds.), *Selections from the Smuts Papers*, vol. 1, *June 1886–May 1902*, Cambridge: Cambridge University Press, 1962

Harries, Patrick, *Work, culture and identity: migrant labourers in Mozambique and South Africa, c. 1860–1910*, Portsmouth, NH: Heinemann; Johannesburg: Witwatersrand University Press; London: James Currey, 1994

Headlam, Cecil (ed.), *The Milner papers. South Africa*, vol. 1, *1897–1899*. London, Toronto: Cassell, 1931

Hyslop, Jonathan, 'The imperial working class makes itself "White": white labourism in Britain, Australia and SA before the First World War', *Journal of Historical Sociology* 12:4 (December 1999), 398–421

Hyslop, Jonathan, *The notorious syndicalist: J. T. Bain, a Scottish rebel in colonial South Africa*, Johannesburg: Jacana, 2004

Jeeves, Alan H., *Migrant labour in South Africa's mining economy: the struggle for the gold mines' labour supply, 1890–1920*, Kingston: McGill-Queen's University Press; Johannesburg: Witwatersrand University Press, 1985

Keegan, Tim, *Facing the storm: portraits of black lives in rural South Africa*, Cape Town: David Philip, 1988

Khumalo, Cyrius Vukile, 'Epistolary networks and the politics of cultural production in KwaZulu-Natal, 1860–1910', unpublished Ph.D. thesis, University of Michigan (2004)

Krebs, Paula M., *Gender, race, and the writing of Empire: public discourse and the Boer War*, Cambridge: Cambridge University Press, 1999

Laband, John, *The Transvaal Rebellion: the First Boer War, 1880–1*, Harlow, U.K.: Longman-Pearson, 2005

Lambert, John, *Betrayed trust: Africans and the state in colonial Natal*, Scottsville: University of Natal Press, 1995

Lewis, Gavin, *Between the wire and the wall: a history of South African 'Coloured' politics*, Cape Town: David Philip; New York: St Martin's Press, 1987

Lewsen, Phyllis (ed.), *Selections from the correspondence of John X. Merriman. vol. 1, 1870–1890*, Cape Town: Van Riebeeck Society, 1960

Marks, Shula and Richard Rathbone (eds.), *Industrialisation and social change in South Africa: African class formation, culture and consciousness, 1870–1930*, London: Longman, 1982

Meer, Ismail, *A fortunate man*, Cape Town: Zebra Press, 2002

Odendaal, André, 'African political mobilisation in the Eastern Cape, 1880–1910', unpublished D.Phil. thesis, University of Cambridge (1983)

Palmer, Mabel, *The history of the Indians in Natal*, Natal Regional Survey vol. 10, Cape Town: Oxford University Press, 1957

Phoofolo, Pule, 'Epidemics and revolution: the rinderpest epidemic in late nineteenth-century southern Africa', *Past and Present* 138 (February 1993), 112–43

Phoofolo, Pule, 'Face to face with famine: the Basotho and the rinderpest, 1897–1899', *Journal of Southern African Studies* 29:2 (2003), 503–27

Rotberg, Robert I., *The founder: Cecil Rhodes and the pursuit of power*, New York: Oxford University Press, 1988

Scully, Pam, *The bouquet of freedom: social and economic relations in Stellenbosch, c1870–1900*, Cape Town: University of Cape Town, 1990

Simons, H. J. and R. E. Alexander, *Class and colour in South Africa, 1850–1950*, Harmondsworth, U.K.: Penguin Books, 1969

Swan, Maureen, *Gandhi: the South African experience*, Johannesburg: Ravan Press, 1985

Tamarkin, Mordechai, *Cecil Rhodes and the Cape Afrikaners: the imperial colossus and the colonial parish pump*, London: Frank Cass, 1996

Tamarkin, Mordechai, *Volk and flock: ecology, culture, identity and politics among Cape Afrikaner sheep farmers in the late nineteenth century*, Pretoria: University of South Africa Press, 2009

Turrell, Robert, *Capital and labour on the Kimberley diamond fields, 1871–90*, Cambridge: Cambridge University Press, 1987

Vahed, Goolam, 'Uprooting and rerooting: culture, religion and community among indentured Muslim migrants in colonial Natal, 1860–1911', *South African Historical Journal* 45 (November 2001), 191–222

Van Jaarsveld, F. A., *The awakening of Afrikaner nationalism, 1868–1881*, Cape Town: Human and Rousseau, 1961

Worger, William H., *South Africa's city of diamonds: mine workers and monopoly capitalism, 1867–95*, New Haven, CT: Yale University Press; Johannesburg: Ravan Press, 1987

4

WAR AND UNION, 1899–1910

SHULA MARKS

The conflict that broke out on 10 October 1899, with the expiry of President Kruger's ultimatum to the British government, was South Africa's 'Great War', as important to the shaping of modern South Africa as was the American Civil War in the history of the United States. South African union, on the imperial agenda since the failure of confederation in the 1870s, was born in its ashes, as whites on both sides joined hands to shore up white supremacy against the background of rumours of revolt by restive Africans. If, at one level, it was a war about colonial self-determination – however limited – at another, it was also a war for the survival of a settler society, and about the credibility and international reputation of the British Empire, raising major moral issues of global importance. As the 'biggest ever "small war" of late Victorian "new Imperialism", the 1899–1902 conflagration has a recognised significance in world history', not least because of the way it touched the fin de siècle European and American imagination.[1]

Contrary to most British expectations that the empire would achieve a swift victory, hostilities lasted for nearly three years and had a devastating effect on the countryside for another two. Initially, Britain was ill prepared for the possibility of a lengthy and challenging campaign, and began reinforcing its modest coastal garrison only on the outbreak of war. It was this breathing space that the Transvaal State Attorney, Jan Smuts, sought to exploit at the outset with a strategic plan for a rapid two-front offensive that would thrust south and east of the Zuid Afrikaansche Republiek (ZAR) to block any British advance on its lengthy and poorly defended borders. Having sealed its military alliance with the Orange Free State, Pretoria declared war ahead of London, with the intention of catching the enemy on the back foot. Gambling on that early advantage, republican commanders

[1] Bill Nasson, *The South African War, 1899–1902* (London: Arnold, 1999), author's preface, p. xi.

hoped for a short war in which a wounded enemy might be obliged to come to a negotiated peace that would preserve internal independence. Some leaders also pinned their hopes on diplomatic pressure on Britain to accept an early peace deal from continental European governments sympathetic to the republican position. The bleak alternative, perceived by Smuts, was a lengthy conflict in which the republicans would be ground down into submission.

Initially, the war did indeed seem to be going the way of the Republics. In the closing months of 1899, invading republican forces plunged into Britain's coastal colonies, inflicting heavy and humiliating defeats in battles with badly organised and poorly led enemy troops and going on to encircle and to lay siege to the Cape and Natal towns of Mafeking, Kimberley and Ladysmith. The victorious outcome of these early battle engagements at places like Modder River, Stormberg, Magersfontein and Colenso was a consequence of the republicans' tactical advantages in the field, especially in marksmanship, superior long-range weaponry, skill in exploiting terrain and exceptional mounted mobility.

The failure to retain and to extend the crucial opening military advantage lay in the indecisiveness or failure of strategy. Republican generalship soon succumbed to a defensive war of position based on besieging British garrison positions in what turned into demoralising and futile occupation operations. Not only did this stop commando forces from campaigning to their established strengths of manoeuvrability and speed. It gave their imperial adversary breathing space, thus handing over a great deal of the initiative in organisation and planning, and allowing the British time to recover and to ship in massive reinforcements for an invading counteroffensive against the Transvaal and the Orange Free State. Determined to turn the tide, by early 1900, British command had amassed an imperial field force of more than 180,000 troops, an invading army whose size was already virtually that of the combined white citizenry of the Republics.

Waging a methodical and increasingly ruthless campaign, Britain's new chief commander, Field Marshal Lord Roberts, with Lord Kitchener as his chief of staff, forced republican opponents back into their territories. After the crushing blows of defeat in the Battle of Paardeberg in February 1900 and the enemy occupation of Pretoria in June of that year, the tactical basis of the republican war effort changed. Giving up on the impossible objective of trying to halt the British advance, commando forces switched to irregular tactics and launched running attacks on their enemy's columns and supply lines. British commanders responded to the guerrilla tactics by adopting and intensifying a scorched-earth policy and rounding up civilians

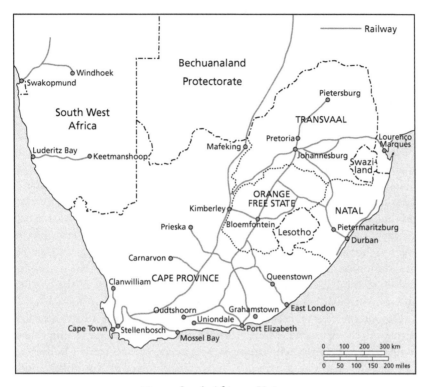

MAP 1. South Africa at Union.

into internment or concentration camps. These soon became notorious, as insanitary conditions, poor rations and overcrowding led to major epidemics and fearsome mortality. By the end of the war, more than 28,000 of a total of 118,000 white inmates had died of disease, the vast majority of the victims being women and young children.

As a percentage of the total Afrikaner population of the Transvaal and Orange Free State, the number of civilian fatalities was devastating. Thousands of displaced Africans, too, were rounded up and put into segregated internment camps, many of which also served as labour depots for the British army. Recent estimates suggest that African camp mortality may have been even greater than that of the Boers, although proportionately it naturally had less of an impact on a much larger total population. At the same time, it should perhaps be noted that the British army itself was little better at looking after the health of its own men than it was at safeguarding that of civilians in the camps: close to two-thirds of its wartime losses were from disease and illness rather than in action. Severe mortality in concentration camps and the scorched-earth policy led Sir Henry Campbell-Bannerman, leader of the British Liberal Party, itself deeply torn over the war, to condemn Britain's 'methods of barbarism' in South Africa. Those methods of barbarism were to shape Afrikaner identities in complex and contradictory ways and to provide nationalists, both then and later, with a powerful metaphor for the suffering of their people.

The shift in nomenclature in recent decades from the Boer War or Anglo-Boer War to the South African War is a significant pointer to important changes in our understanding of the meaning of the conflict. Quite simply, it is no longer possible to conceive of it traditionally as a 'white man's' war. Indeed, it was neither white nor the gentleman's war of Victorian mythology. For, as in other rural colonial wars of the later nineteenth century, the invading British carried destruction into the heart of the enemy's homestead; everywhere burnt crops, incinerated huts and looted or slaughtered cattle accompanied their advance. Inevitably, the waging of war on so total a scale had a profound impact on the course of the conflict and, in particular, on gendered responses to it.

One of the most striking features of the war was the bitter hostility displayed by Afrikaner women toward the British forces sacking their homes and scorching their farmlands. Kitchener, who succeeded Roberts as Commander-in-Chief of Britain's expeditionary forces in November 1900, was not alone in viewing them as a 'bad and dangerous lot'. The same destructiveness of imperial conquest would also lead many of their husbands, sons and brothers to desert the front to protect their 'male patrimony' in the rear, following the first major republican defeat at the Battle of Paardeberg in February 1900.

As commandos 'peeled away', so women 'took the lead in facing British aggression'. In this respect, the coming of war 'altered gender power relations' between men and women in Afrikaner society. As demoralised and disheartened male combatants left the front line, placing the need for farm and families before the defence of the state, many militant women came to espouse an explicitly nationalist and republican rhetoric. Tales circulated of men who had left fighting for the security of their domestic domain being prodded back into action with injunctions to 'go and fight. I can get another husband, but not another Free State'. At the same time, the destructiveness of British tactics may also have contributed to keeping combatants in the field. The spreading of scorched earth and the multiplying of concentration camps gave men few options, for 'the homeless could not flee home'. Laying waste to the countryside increasingly eroded 'the rural base of patriarchy', transforming deserting patriarchs into 'a *volk* of *broeders'*, imbued with 'greater nationalist consciousness, greater discipline, greater lust for revenge'.[2]

Female activism in these fraught years was not restricted to strengthening male combat resolve or to providing kin with essential food, shelter and intelligence. Women's own wartime narratives also testify to their resilience in the face of atrocity and immense suffering, 'their flight from dangerous situations, their resistance against camp authorities, their persistence in the struggle for physical and mental survival in the camps – and their actual participation in the fighting.'[3] Nonetheless, whatever the tenacity of women and the determination of men who stuck it out in the field, they could not prevail in the face of overwhelmingly superior enemy power. By 1902, it was clear that the destruction of farms, the chilling death rates among women and children in camps, increasingly tight British control of the countryside through a string of blockhouses and barbed wire, and the large resources of the imperial army had ground Afrikaner republicans down to a perilously low level. Inevitably, their leadership was forced to sue for peace. Even so, this was undertaken only after considerable heart-searching. Although a diehard minority, especially from the devastated Orange Free State, wished to continue fighting, the majority, under the Transvaal generalship of Louis Botha and Jan Smuts, recognised that they would have to sacrifice republican independence if the Afrikaner people were to survive.

Behind that strategic political recognition lay a harsh military reality. However tough the commitment of commandos still left in the field, they were perilously close to being on their last legs. Dwindling fighting numbers had been a headache throughout the conflict. Generals were uncomfortably aware of the desertion rate of their burghers once the British had broken through initial republican resistance. Within nine months of the outbreak of war, almost fourteen thousand commandos had surrendered, representing some 40 per cent of those initially mobilised and 26 per cent of those liable for service. To make matters worse, a considerable number had joined the British army as enlisted collaborators, so that by the end of hostilities, the number of Boers serving the imperial military amounted to almost a third of the Boer army left in the field. In encouraging the formation of units of 'joiners' (as they were contemptuously termed by commando diehards) like the Transvaal National Scouts, British army

[2] All the quotations in this paragraph are from Helen Bradford, 'Gentlemen and Boers: Afrikaner nationalism, gender and colonial warfare', in Cuthbertson, Grundlingh, and Suttie (eds.), *Writing a wider war*, pp. 47, 48, 50, 51, 55, 56.

[3] Christina Landman, *The piety of Afrikaner women* (Pretoria: University of South Africa Press, 1994), p. 78.

intelligence understood well how it would corrode the political unity of the republican war effort.

At the same time, Boer commandos faced difficulties with their African followers and collaborators. Servants or other dependents who had been commandeered into assisting republican forces through provisioning and as largely noncombatant auxiliaries – *agterryers* – and who had constituted around a quarter of total Boer manpower in the first phase of the war, also deserted in large numbers after the collapse of conventional warfare. If by the end of hostilities Botha and the other leaders feared 'that if conditions did not change there would shortly be more Afrikaners fighting against the republican cause than for it',[4] they perhaps also faced something even more threatening. This was the fact that there were by that time 50 per cent more armed Africans fighting with the British than there were Boers left on commando.

As alarming for the generals was their loss of control over the countryside. Africans not only rendered large areas of the western, northern and eastern Transvaal 'inaccessible to the Boer commandos', thus cramping their mobility.[5] Armed by the British, the Bakgatla had actually pushed back the frontiers of white settlement in the Pilansberg, thus avenging themselves on decades of Boer oppression. Encouraged by the British, Africans also looted Boer livestock on a massive scale, while beyond the reach of the imperial forces, Africans and coloureds took the opportunity of the so-called white man's war to wage their own struggle against Boer landowners and overlords by robbing farms and raiding their cattle. As a result, in large tracts of the Transvaal, many combatants returned from fighting to find their livestock gone and their farms occupied by African peasants, who were reasserting older rights to the land in the expectation of retaining them after completion of the British conquest. In the northern Cape, too, proletarianised coloured workers confronted invading commandos threatening to deprive them of their tenuous but tenaciously held status and liberties. In the Colony's 'farms, missions, mines, homesteads, artisan villages and offices, blacks entered the war with their own distinctive aspirations, resentments, and social visions.' Some even took their erstwhile masters to court, denouncing them as treasonous rebels. Indeed, all over South Africa, 'customary relations of hierarchy and obedience' were subverted, leaving not merely Afrikaners but also rural colonists more generally

---

[4] Albert Grundlingh, 'Collaborators in Boer society', in Warwick (ed.), *The South African War*, p. 27.
[5] Fransjohan Pretorius, 'Boer attitudes to Africans in wartime', in Lowry (ed.), *The South African War reappraised*, p. 106.

shaken and apprehensive about the impact of the conflict on 'the African mind'.[6]

Yet, arguably, the war's impact on the 'white mind' was more important. Nowhere can this be seen more vividly than in the emotionally charged letter Smuts wrote to the British pro-Boer journalist W. T. Stead in January 1902. It is difficult in a short extract to capture Smuts's almost hysterical outburst. For thirty passionate pages, he pronounced on how shocking it was 'to employ armed barbarians under white officers in a war between two white Christian peoples'. For Smuts, the involvement by Britain, of the 'coloured races' in a dispute between whites, thus allowing them to 'become the arbiter in disputes between . . . [them] and in the long run the predominating factor or "casting vote" in South Africa', portended 'an eventual débâcle of society' in which the white population would 'have to bow before a Native constabulary and soldiery'. This 'Frankenstein Monster', he asserted, was far worse than 'the utter desolation of South Africa and the unprecedented sufferings of the whole Boer people in field and prison camps', and 'would soon cause South Africa to relapse into barbarism.'[7]

Early in 1901, the governments of the two Republics considered and rejected a peace proposal from Lord Kitchener, because its terms meant the end of Boer independence. Significantly, the second of the ten points brought by the republicans to the Middelburg talks was that they should be permitted to retain their rifles 'for protection against the natives'.[8] A year later, the situation had deteriorated further. Everywhere there were rumours of an impending uprising of Africans, who had acquired a considerable quantity of firearms during the conflict. When, in April 1902, in response to republican overtures, the British offered revised proposals that still insisted on British annexation, South African Republic and Orange Free State leaders were forced to consider them. After prolonged and agonised debate at a meeting of commando representatives, the Peace of Vereeniging was concluded at the end of May. A revenge Zulu attack on a commando encampment at Holkrantz earlier that month was decisive in bringing on peace. The Commander-in-Chief of the Transvaal army, Louis Botha, termed it 'the foullest deed of the war'.[9] It helped to make a general surrender all but inevitable.

[6] Bill Nasson, *Abraham Esau's War: a black South African war in the Cape, 1899–1902* (Cambridge: Cambridge University Press, 1991), p. 10.

[7] Smuts to W. T. Stead, 4 January 1902, in Hancock and van der Poel (eds.), *Selections from the Smuts Papers*, vol. 1, pp. 482, 486, 494–6.

[8] Headlam (ed.), *Milner papers*, vol. 2, p. 209 (editor's comment).

[9] CO 179/229/3538, Botha to Actg High Commissioner, Sub. Encl. in 1, desp. 4, 6 Jan 1904.

By May 1902, as we have seen, large parts of the Transvaal had been reclaimed by Africans, most of whom had been dispossessed in living memory. Landowners returning to their ravaged farms now found large numbers of labour tenants refusing to work or to pay rent. According to one local official, as late as September 1903, there were complaints 'all over the country' that 'the natives . . . were disposed to be very disrespectful to the farmers and were very disinclined to work for them'.[10] Some went further than 'disrespect' and, armed with firearms acquired in wartime, forcibly prevented the farmers from returning to their lands. In this respect, 'The wartime expropriation of the Boer landlord class, and the role played in this by the rural underclasses, had turned the Transvaal rural world upside down.'[11] In effect, 'an undeclared civil war' or, perhaps more accurately, 'an agrarian class war', accompanied the South African War and its aftermath, as black peasants struggled for land and liberty in the countryside.[12] But the odds were against them. Faced by threats to white masters and their property, the imperial authorities took swift action. Within a remarkably short time, the former enemies had joined hands to shore up the supremacy of white men and to defend white property rights in the face of what amounted to a widespread black jacquerie in the Transvaal.

At one level, it is true that the Vereeniging peace talks brought the war to an end 'with a truce rather than a victory' and resolved neither political nor racial conflict in South Africa.[13] What it did do was to end military hostilities and extinguish republican independence. At the same time, the treaty also disillusioned those Africans who had pinned their hopes of a more inclusive social order in a British South Africa. Although probably only a few realised it at the time, imperial acceptance of the formulation of clause 8 of the treaty, which excluded any consideration of a franchise for Africans until after the grant of self-government to the new colonies, was

---

[10] Jeremy Krikler, *Revolution from above, rebellion from below: the agrarian Transvaal at the turn of the century* (Oxford: Clarendon University Press, 1993), p. 27, citing SNA vol. 169, Griffith to Sec. NA, 18 September 1903.

[11] Ibid., p. 29.

[12] John Higginson, 'Upending the century of wrong: the American South: agrarian elites, collective violence, and the transformation of state power in the American South and South Africa, 1865–1914', *Social Identities* 4:3 (1998), 400, sees it as a 'civil war'; Krikler, *Revolution from above*, p. 32, argues that in the Transvaal the South African War was accompanied by an 'agrarian class war', albeit one in which there was little if any manifestation of 'class consciousness' (pp. 33–6).

[13] John Darwin, 'Afterword,' in Omissi and Thompson (eds.), *The impact of the South African War*, p. 291.

effectively to exclude African people from citizenship for more than ninety years.

At another level, however, it can be argued that the imperial conquest of South Africa achieved what it had set out to do: this was British control over what Lord Selborne at the Colonial Office described as 'the richest spot on earth', in the face of the challenges posed by German and American competitors, 'cosmopolitan interests' that would have been prepared to settle for reform within the Republic, and potential British supporters of an independent Anglophone Republic outside of the empire.[14] The conquest of the Republics created the framework for the construction of a new social and political order sought by the British and, to a large extent, by mining capital in the 1890s. Under empire, white supremacy was assured, property rights secured, mining costs considerably reduced and black labour increasingly controlled.

With the capture of Johannesburg and Pretoria at the end of May 1900, the centre of gravity in South African politics had already shifted definitively from the Cape to the Transvaal. Initially, the British appointed a military governor, Colin Mackenzie, who took as his main advisers several of the men who had played a major role in fomenting the agitation against the Kruger regime, many with close associations with the mining industry and many intent on implementing 'their [own] long sought-after goals'.[15]

Mackenzie's immediate task was to restore law and order and to deal with those many Uitlanders who wished to return to their homes and businesses on the Witwatersrand. Given the difficulties of wartime conditions, the British authorities were concerned both to restrict their numbers and to prevent 'foreigners' from reestablishing themselves in Johannesburg. Within a few days, a policy of deportations was adopted that aimed at ridding the new colony of the 'disaffected', 'foreigners' and 'undesirables' – usually those terms were synonymous and generally meant 'destitute foreigners, especially East European and Russian Jews', stigmatised as Peruvians and held responsible for the illicit sale of alcohol to Africans and 'the seamier side of Johannesburg's nightlife' in the 1890s.[16] Moreover, in the second half of 1900, pro-Boers, striking railway workers, and various and alleged plotters against the military were sent to the coast, whereas hundreds of poor 'foreigners' were deported to Europe, on extremely dubious

---

[14] Selborne to the Marquess of Salisbury, 30 March 1899, in Boyce (ed.), *The crisis of British power*, p. 34.
[15] Cammack, *The Rand at war*, p. 135.   [16] Ibid., p.158.

legal grounds. From the Cape, Milner demurred, concerned with potential European diplomatic repercussions. Indeed, complaints and claims for
compensation – some 1,600 of them – soon did arrive at the Foreign Office,
which was forced to set up the Compensations Commission in 1901 and to
pay damages to deportees' governments.

More broadly, Milner was suspicious of military rule. Wanting to maintain control over the longer-term reconstruction of the new colonies, he
despatched his private secretary, George Fiddes, to Pretoria as his representative. Fiddes was soon at loggerheads with the Uitlanders around
Mackenzie, not so much because they differed in their long-term goals –
whether those were deporting 'undesirables' or Anglicising Johannesburg
commerce – but because he and Milner had come to deplore 'their timing,
their methods and, on occasions, their personalities and behaviour'.[17] This
was evident in the self-interested way in which the Uitlanders attempted
to transfer the capital of the Transvaal to Johannesburg. Although Milner
was by no means hostile to the Uitlander and mining elite, and came to
rely on them himself, he and Fiddes managed to put paid to that notion,
aware that it would preempt a decision that they felt could only be made
in the wider context of reconstruction.

Although Uitlander dominance lasted only three or four months before
Milner regained the upper hand, Mackenzie's scheming advisers 'had gone
a long way towards Anglicising the Rand's commerce, fostering industrial
development, protecting the sanctity of private property and public morality, and creating a new society devoid of paupers, Jews and foreigners. These
few months of Uitlander rule in the winter of 1900 were to leave a lasting
mark on Johannesburg's "clean slate"'.[18]

With Mackenzie's clique gone, Milner appointed his own acolytes – a
handful of young Oxford Balliol men, dubbed his 'kindergarten' – to assist
in the 'reconstruction' of the former Republics, by establishing an efficient
bureaucracy, setting up municipal and local government, addressing the
most obvious prewar grievances of the mining houses and restoring order
in the countryside. Of these, it was perhaps Lionel Curtis who most left
his mark on Johannesburg and more broadly on South Africa. Despite
the strong opposition of the industry, he insisted that mining properties
should fall within the municipal boundaries of Johannesburg, thus ensuring
that they contribute to the city's coffers and become subject to the town
council's bylaws and regulations. With Milner's assistance and the backing
of Fitzpatrick as President of the Chamber of Mines, he overcame objections

[17] Ibid., p. 159.   [18] Ibid., p. 160.

from mine magnates by making owners, not occupiers, liable to tax and agreeing that land, not buildings, be assessed.

For all his compromise with the industry, however, Curtis, imbued with Victorian Christian socialist ideals and urban reformist ambitions, was, if anything, hostile to the mines, conducting 'a crusade . . . against magnate wealth and power' and 'the machinations of unscrupulous land corporations and liquor lords', which he felt needed to be 'curbed by responsible municipal authorities'. For him, Johannesburg was 'a new Jerusalem' in which to implement the ideas of contemporary British urban reformers. Indeed, a hostile press accused the town council under his guidance of 'exceeding the municipal socialism of Glasgow or Birmingham'.[19] At the same time, this was wholly compatible with his support for the removal of Africans and Indians (but not 'poor whites') from central Johannesburg to locations on the urban fringe, on the grounds that they constituted a health hazard, a familiar segregationist justification in South African towns at the turn of the century.

Between 1903 and 1906, Curtis held the position of Assistant Colonial Secretary with specific responsibility for urban affairs. Like the rest of the kindergarten, he saw 'local government as the means of regenerating the Transvaal', and in that position in effect established the administrative framework for its governance.[20] Naturally, Curtis's kindergarten vision was limited to white inhabitants, and his views rarely rose above the racial prejudices and stereotypes of his day; these, too, shaped his approach to urban and rural governance in the new Transvaal colony, perhaps most significantly in relation to the position of Indians.

That Curtis was obliged to compromise with the Rand mining interest was hardly a coincidence. Central to Milner's postwar plans was the swift restoration of the industry; as 'South Africa's one substantial, taxable asset',[21] the mines were crucial to his plans, as they have been to every Transvaal and South African government from the 1890s. Although the High Commissioner's motives are a matter of some controversy between those who argue that gold and especially its conditions of production were of the essence, and those who stress Milner's purely political ambitions, the two were inextricably linked, if also at times in apparent conflict. As their more astute spokespeople recognised, the mining companies needed a strong state to prevent them from setting their own short-term interests against the long-term interests of the industry. For the magnates,

---

[19] Deborah Lavin: *From empire to international commonwealth: a biography of Lionel Curtis* (New York: Clarendon Press, 1995), p. 50.

[20] Ibid., p. 52. [21] Jeeves, *Migrant labour*, p. 10.

getting the mines running again was particularly urgent. Production and profits had declined as a result of the war, most of their labour had left the mines and their own investment in a number of low-grade mines during the boom of the mid-1890s made further capital investment an urgent necessity.

Nowhere was the state's action more important than in addressing the issue of mine labour in the aftermath of the war, and it is clear that Milner saw no contradiction between the labour demands of the mines and his professed humanitarianism: for, as he saw it, 'the greatest benefit that could be bestowed upon [the African population]... would be to teach them habits of regular and skilled labour.... [T]he more natives that are engaged in mining and other industrial pursuits the better for them and for the country'.[22] Even before the war was over, the railway and dynamite monopolies were eliminated, and the pass laws 'as bearing on the supply of Native labour' were 'being gone into thoroughly';[23] by the end of 1901, Milner had issued proclamations revising and strengthening the old republican pass and liquor laws. An efficient Native Affairs Department was established under Sir Godfrey Lagden as Secretary, a corps of experienced Native Commissioners was appointed and a military police force, the South African Constabulary, was organised. They were to be crucial if the old republican legislation was to be efficiently deployed, order was to be restored to the countryside and labour mobilised for the mines.

As South African High Commissioner and now Governor of the Transvaal, Milner also renegotiated Kruger's 1897 agreement (or modus vivendi) with the Portuguese authorities that gave the Transvaal access to Mozambican labour in exchange for lowering the territory's railway tariffs to the disadvantage of the Cape and Natal. This would not be the last time that the labour needs of the mines were to override other colonial interests.

However, none of these measures was sufficient to resolve the serious, if still exaggerated, mine labour shortage. Whereas on the eve of the war some one hundred thousand Africans had been employed there, relatively few remained at its end. It took time for widespread recruiting to get off the ground in Mozambique, and for a variety of reasons, black South Africans were reluctant to return to the Rand. Some had earned money and cattle from the British army and were engaged in restoring their homesteads. Others found that, before drought and the postwar depression

---

[22] Milner to Chamberlain, 6 December 1901, in Headlam (ed.), *Milner papers*, vol. 2, pp. 307–8.

[23] Milner to Chamberlain, 23 May 1900, and Milner to Chamberlain, 6 December 1901, in Headlam (ed.), *Milner papers*, vol. 2, pp. 145 and 308.

set in, in 1903–1904, there were far better wages to be earned in repairing war-damaged roads and railways and on harbours. Somewhat bizarrely, the mine owners took the opportunity of the British occupation to introduce stringent new working conditions and to slash wages to 30s a week (down from the 52s to which they had been lowered in 1897), apparently in the belief that Africans were simple target workers who came to the mines to satisfy their immediate needs. In fact, all the evidence suggests that Africans were well aware of wage rates and conditions in different sectors of the economy and were unsurprisingly reluctant to take on employment in the poorly paid and dangerous mining environment if there were alternative options.

For mine owners, anxious for new investment and to restore wartime losses, and for Milner, equally concerned to raise reconstruction revenue for the Transvaal, the labour shortage was a major blow. Conditions were all the more serious because, from the end of 1902, the postwar flurry of speculation and rapid expansion led to rising costs and falling or stagnant output, with a falling rate of profit creating a crisis of profitability that lasted until at least 1910. In addition, the problems of a generally low and declining grade of ore, and a fixed and increasingly unfavourable selling price, were aggravated by the geological nature of Witwatersrand reefs and the constraints these imposed on mechanisation. All this meant that, although the South African mining industry was 'colossally wealthy', it 'could be wealthy only on condition that it jealously watched every penny of its expenditure'.[24]

Given the sensitivities of the domestic British public and the widespread disaffection of the black population in the Transvaal, the new native commissioners could not employ the strong-arm tactics that had been characteristic of prewar expedients to force out African labour. Thus, the mining industry's solution to its crisis then, and later, was to search out ever-cheaper sources of unskilled labour. In this, it was aided and abetted by the imperial authorities. At the beginning of the twentieth century, the impoverished masses of war-torn imperial China seemed to provide an answer. By early 1903, the Chamber of Mines had convinced Milner of its dire labour shortage and of the critical importance of importing Chinese indentured labour. A commission, appointed ostensibly to enquire into the labour shortage, in practice to sanction the importation of Chinese indentured workers, accepted the Chamber's projected shortage of 365,000 men in 1908 and rejected any idea of employing unskilled white labour, as recommended in

some quarters. With this backing, Milner was able to persuade the imperial authorities to sign the necessary treaty with China, and in 1904, the
first batch of Chinese workers arrived in Durban. Between 1904 and 1907,
when the decision was taken to repatriate them, some sixty thousand Chinese workers were contracted to work on the mines, under the most severe
conditions. As we shall see, whether or not he realised it, the decision to
import Chinese labour was to jeopardise what have conventionally been
seen as Milner's political objectives.

The use of indentured Chinese labour caused a furore in both South Africa
and Britain. White workers feared being undercut by Chinese labour, and
the settler population disliked the thought of further racial 'swamping'; in
Britain, meanwhile, the Liberal opposition contrived to combine a rhetoric
against the threat of a 'yellow peril' with moral outrage against 'Chinese
slavery'. Faced with this outcry, the British administration defended its
action by insisting that the mines improve compounds and food for indentured labourers and that they provide some minimal health care. Given the
cost of moving a huge new workforce over thousands of miles of ocean to
wholly unfamiliar living conditions, mining self-interest dictated the provision of health facilities at embarkation ports and during voyages, for high
recruiting costs meant that labourers had to be kept healthy if possible.

The involvement of the imperial state in the recruiting process also
led to the imposition of minimum health standards on those mines wishing to employ Chinese labour. The Coloured Labour Importation Ordinance of 1904, which regulated the scheme, obliged mines that wanted
contingents of Chinese labour to provide for the medical examination of
workers at ports and to provide suitable accommodation, adequate food
and hospital facilities to take care of the sick and injured. The diet of
indentured labourers was carefully controlled, with food for each Chinese
miner costing the industry more than twice as much as that for an African
worker.

Milner's successor, Lord Selborne, was equally anxious to see improvements in the compounds, as well as in diet and health conditions more
generally. As did Milner, he understood clearly that it was frequently necessary for the state to take measures on behalf of an industry most of whose
magnates were 'too short-sighted to recognize as conducive to long-term
prosperity'.[25] High mortality rates, whether of Chinese or of African miners, were a case in point. Apart from any humanitarian considerations (and
Selborne was always aware of a hostile Liberal government in the wings),

---

[25] David R. Torrance: *The strange death of the Liberal empire: Lord Selborne in South Africa*
(Liverpool: University of Liverpool Press; Montreal: McGill University Press, 1996),
p. 190.

unless something was done to reduce the incidence of accidents and disease, labour wastage would prevent a resolution of the urgent needs of the industry for workers. Accordingly, shortly after his arrival, Selborne recognised that the health of the miners could no longer be left solely to the benevolence of the Chamber of Mines and that it was essential that the state have 'full statutory powers to enforce a proper standard of accommodation, health and treatment'. For the most part, however, Selborne's regulatory prescriptions, like those of Milner, remained a dead letter.[26]

Imperial attempts at welfare were invariably tempered by considerations of profit. Although the return home of crippled workers may have been bad for recruiters, crippling the industry had to be avoided at all costs. In any case, general managers bitterly resented any interference with the 'internal management of natives on the mines', which they feared would 'lead, possibly, to upsetting discipline and undermining [their] authority'.[27] Thus, almost every change suggested met with resistance. Equally, the British administration was not exactly overinsistent. Despite Lagden's personal outrage at mine mortality rates, and Milner's own emphasis on the mindful treatment of labour, the Native Affairs Department 'treated the mines with great leniency', leading one scholar to conclude that 'Lagden and his officials answered rather to the Chamber and the [Witwatersrand Native Labour Association] WNLA than to their superiors in government.'[28]

The consequences for miners' health can be described only as catastrophic. The huge influx of white single male migrants from the mining frontiers of the world, coupled with an even greater migration of hundreds of thousands of their black counterparts from as far afield as Nyasaland, Northern Rhodesia and Mozambique, provided a fertile terrain for the exchange of pathogens. Predictably, respiratory diseases – tuberculosis and pneumonia – were rife. Above all, however, it was the 'deadly dust' that took men's lives, although this was not initially recognised in black workers who remained on the mines for relatively short periods.

What raised the levels of dust dramatically were new technologies that were crucial to making the exploitation of deep-level mines possible. In combination, steam-driven engines, the widespread application of machine drilling and the large-scale introduction of cheap dynamite made the mining of hitherto-inaccessible levels of ore possible. At the same time,

---

[26] Bodleian Library, Oxford, Selborne Ms. Box 57 ff 3–4: Selborne to Sir Arthur Lawley, Lieut. Gov. of the Transvaal. 8 June 1905.

[27] Memo for L. Reyersbach from Mine Managers, 31 May 1906, BRA Box 782 44/III, Rand Mines Archives.

[28] Jeeves, *Migrant labour*, pp. 59, 49.

however, it raised a great deal of dust in confined spaces. This created dense concentrations of fine silica particles, which adversely affected the lungs of all underground workers. When added to an arduous work regime, tremendous temperature fluctuations both below and above ground, overcrowded and filthy barracks and poor nutrition, the mix was lethal.

Initially, the burden of ill health was borne by white as well as black workers. The impact of 'miners' phthisis', or silicosis, on the lungs of white miners led to inordinately high death rates, with miners dying from the 'white death' within four or five years of commencing work on the Rand, where the working life of a white miner was on average twenty-eight years less than that of the white male population as a whole. The militancy of white labour and the explosion of strikes in this early-twentieth-century period need to be understood in the context of so exceptionally hazardous a work environment. By the outbreak of World War I, however, white workers had begun, through their political muscle, trade union organisation and strike action to improve their wages and living conditions and to win a degree of protection and compensation from the industry.

In a very real way, however, improvements for white miners were bought at the expense of black workers. Over time, the changing proportion of white miners 'both relative to black miners and absolutely meant that the costs of compensation measures could be effectively controlled'. It also meant that the 'major burden of phthisis could be passed on to the black work force'.[29] For the successive waves of African migrants from the subcontinent drawn to the mines by rural impoverishment and the absence of alternative economic opportunities, such improvements as there were came far more slowly and were more meagre, and their infectious diseases were carried back into the countryside. Tuberculosis, pneumonia and silicosis took a fearful toll, whereas in the early years scurvy and typhoid were testimony to appalling living conditions in the compounds. Indeed, the death rate from respiratory disease among so-called tropical labour outraged even the new Union government, which in 1913 banned the importation of labour from north of latitude 22° south.

From the outset of his administration, the restoration of the social hierarchy of rural society and an end to the turbulence in the countryside were equally crucial to Milner's goals. This was essential if 'the right kind of Englishmen' were to be attracted to rural South Africa in the interests of securing their demographic dominance in the subcontinent and the dissemination of more

---

[29] Gillian Burke and Peter Richardson, 'The profits of death: a comparative study of miners' phthisis in Cornwall and the Transvaal, 1876–1918', *Journal of Southern African Studies* 4:2 (April 1978), 169.

efficient farming practices in the Transvaal and Orange River Colony. Nor was this unconnected to labour issues: with restiveness in the countryside, recruiting was difficult, whereas a more efficient agriculture would do much to reduce the cost of labour. It was also necessary, however, to reconcile the Boer population to imperial rule. Returning farmers were granted generous compensation and practical assistance through the establishment of the special Repatriation Department, and British immigrants with capital were promised subsidised land and labour. For any of this to succeed, Africans, who had acquired a formidable number of guns during the war, had to be disarmed. Instructed to act circumspectly but with the backing of an omnipresent army, newly appointed native commissioners were able to carry this out with remarkable little African resistance. In part, the conciliatory approach of the administration, the compensation paid and the permission given to strategically placed chiefs and headmen to retain their weapons had their effect. Perhaps no less persuasive were recently displayed British power and severe penalties for noncompliance. As a peasant leader in the Pietersburg District put it succinctly, the command to disarm should be obeyed, because they had 'all quite recently seen the might of the Government giving the order'.[30]

Where possible, the administration tried to use concessions rather than force in resettling Boers on the land and in persuading tenants to render labour, pay rent or return looted cattle. Still, where diplomacy would not work, the South African Constabulary was used to restore property and class relations in the countryside; it was frequently assisted by Boers themselves, who were as swiftly rearmed as Africans were disarmed. By refurbishing and implementing the Republic's pass laws, as well as its masters and servants and antisquatting legislation, native commissioners ensured that by early 1903 taxes were being collected, returning Boers expeditiously resettled on disputed lands, African tenancies reestablished and labourers forthcoming. The authority of the landlords was further bolstered by a propaganda offensive intended to dispel any notion that Boers had been displaced from the land in their favour. As the Lydenburg native commissioner informed the Pedi, 'the land belongs to the Boers as before the war. You must understand that the land is still the property of the Boers'.[31] Not surprisingly, the Pedi, and many other rural communities

---

[30] Krikler, *Revolution from above*, pp. 53–5, citing SNA, vol. 47, NA 1299/02, Wheelwright to Sec. NA, 10 January 1903.
[31] SNA vol. 67 NA 2336/02, SNA to Actg Pte Sec. to Lieut-Gov., 25 October 1902; SNA vol. 47, NA 1569/02, Minutes of meeting at 'Sekukuni's', 5 September 1902, encl. Hogge to SNA 17 September 1902, both cited in Krikler, *Revolution from above*, pp. 42–3.

similarly addressed, nonetheless continued to believe that the land belonged to them.

Given British worries that an independent-minded British population on the Rand could not be wholly relied on to identify its interests with those of the empire, the postwar years also saw intense ideological, political and cultural activity in which a new 'white South African patriotism' was created by local interests aided and abetted by Selborne, and by members of his coterie still in South Africa. As in its Dominions' counterparts, this patriotism was a contradictory brew of colonial nationalism and notions of imperial service; the full extent of its achievement was to be fully revealed in 1914, when, despite an Afrikaner uprising, the Boer generals, Smuts and Botha, led South Africa into war on the British side. A natural corollary of the creation of a new 'white nation' was the exclusion of blacks from the body politic: it is no coincidence that those years saw a renewed debate about racial identity and the nature of white supremacy.

At the same time, the appointment of the South African Native Affairs Commission in 1903 to provide a blueprint for a unified 'native policy' was a further indication of the centrality of the issue to the construction of a new South African state and a white South African identity. The commission signalled the end of the era of 'native wars' and a realignment of the 'native policy' of the different British colonial states. Rejecting overt coercion or forced labour, it recommended a series of policies that were subsequently to be elaborated by the South African state under the general rubric of segregation. Its proponents viewed this as an alternative to what they saw as the dangerously assimilationist model of the Cape and the potentially unstable repressive regimes of the Afrikaner Republics. Segregation was to be the cement of the new white South Africa.

Thus, the Commission contributed directly to the articulation of a far more systematic ideology of territorial and institutional segregation (a new word that crept into official discourse around this time from the United States). Initially the creation of disparate and contradictory interests, and constantly reshaped by the contest between them, the new socioeconomic and political dispensation nonetheless lasted for the best part of the twentieth century. The 'self-governing white Community' underpinned by black labour envisaged by Cecil Rhodes and Alfred Milner now became a possibility. In less than a decade after the war, the new Union of South Africa had been constituted out of the former republics and colonies south of the Limpopo.

Within a remarkably brief period, then, there had been what seemed to many observers a striking reconciliation of the white 'races', but in this they may have overlooked Afrikaner women, who, according to the British Labour politician Ramsay Macdonald, 'had forgotten nothing and forgiven nothing'.[32] The swift settlement between Briton and Boer was partly a product of the tremendous white insecurities unleashed by the war. In the end, the republicans had been forced to make peace in large measure because they could not command support in the countryside. Whatever the hostility between Briton and Boer, they were, in Smuts' words, 'two white Christian peoples' surrounded by 'barbarians' who had to be kept in their place.[33]

White reconciliation and the unification of the country were thus forged in the face of the fear of Africans brought on by the war. If Britain's postwar High Commissioners were less fearful, they, too, were convinced of the need for a unified South Africa based on white supremacy. As Milner put it, 'The white man must rule, because he is elevated by many, many steps above the black man; steps which it will take the latter centuries to climb, and it is quite possible that the vast bulk of the black population may never be able to climb at all.'[34] And he set about giving effect to these precepts.

The reconstruction of agriculture and mining was part of a far wider-ranging reconstruction of the state, which in turn was to reshape the nature of political affiliation and the construction of national identities. In control over the former Republics as well as the Cape and Natal, British authorities held unprecedented power to intervene in South African society and to shape its future. Nevertheless, there were limits to this power. These derived not only from the rumbling discontent of the defeated Boers but also from the dissatisfactions of the Anglophone population. Thus, within months of the war, Milner found himself confronted by Uitlanders demanding a direct voice in the running of the new colony. As impatient of Milner's autocracy as they had been of Kruger's, they were vociferous in their criticisms of the new administration.

Yet, whatever their aspirations for control, there was little unity among the returning Uitlanders. Even their nomenclature poses problem. For the most part, English speakers called themselves 'British', whatever their origin; indeed, even non-British, South African–born English speakers referred to the British Isles as 'home'. Nevertheless, as Milner himself was to reflect ruefully toward the end of his period of office:

[I]t would require some very potent and exceptional influence to unite the non-Dutch population in support of anything. Differing widely to begin with

[32] J. Ramsay Macdonald, 'What I saw in South Africa, Sept and Oct 1902', p. 24, cited in H. Bradford, 'Regendering Afrikanerdom: Afrikanerdom, the 1899–1902 Anglo-Boer War', in Blom, Hagerman and Hall (eds.), *Gendered nations*, p. 219.

[33] See *supra* note 7.

[34] Headlam (ed.), *Milner papers*, vol. 2, Milner in his 'Watchtower speech' to the Johannesburg Municipal Congress, 18 May 1903, p. 467.

in origin and traditions – home-born British, South African British, and British from other Colonies, together with a large admixture of naturalized foreigners – they are further split up by numerous cross-divisions arising from business rivalry, from class antagonism, or from local jealousies. Mining interests versus commercial interest, Capital versus Labour, Pretoria versus Johannesburg, Town versus Country, each of these antagonisms and others which might be enumerated, tend to divide the Europeans of more recent advent and would make co-operation between them, except in the actual presence of some grave catastrophe threatening them all, almost inconceivably difficult.[35]

All these tensions came to a head in late 1903 over the Chinese labour issue. The policy managed simultaneously to unite the Afrikaner opposition and to fracture Milner's potential proimperial English-speaking alliance, by evoking profound and widespread anticapitalist sentiment even in the metropole, where opposition to 'Chinese slavery' was suffused by racist rhetoric. The policy thus united liberals and Bondsmen like J. X. Merriman, J. W. Sauer, F. S. Malan and the African supporters of John Tengo Jabavu in the Cape, with English-speaking workers and Afrikaner farmers in the Transvaal and the opposition Liberal Party and the labour movement in Britain in common hostility to the power of the Rand mine magnates. As a result, when politics revived among Afrikaners in the Transvaal with the party formation of Het Volk, opposition to Chinese labour gave it an anticapitalist thrust, which enabled Smuts and Botha to appeal to both their 'natural' Afrikaner constituency and to English-speakers' opposition to Milner.

The decision to bring Chinese workers to the Rand had ramifications beyond those already considered. Not the least of those was the vast extension and institutionalisation of the 'colour bar', which reserved work defined as skilled for whites and relegated 'unskilled' work to others. The policy was rationalised vigorously in terms of maintaining white supremacy, and it had a profound impact on both class formation and class consciousness. In preventing Africans from acquiring skilled employment, and by opting for Chinese labour, the Transvaal government also signalled that white men would not be employed as unskilled labourers alongside blacks, notwithstanding the high rate of white unemployment on the Rand at the time and Milner's desire to swamp Afrikaners demographically. He may have wanted South Africa to be a 'white man's country' – but neither he nor the mine owners were prepared to see the growth of large numbers of unskilled, nonsupervisory white workers on the Rand. Apart from being considered too costly, the international white working class unfortunately had notions

---

[35] CO 291/74 Milner to Colonial Secretary, 5 December 1904, cited in Le May, *British supremacy in South Africa, 1899–1907*, p. 169.

of rights and, even more unfortunately, experience of trade union organisation. Kruger's enlistment of white workers to the republican cause in 1897 was an uncomfortable reminder that radical – if racist – white workers might even rally to a reassertion of republicanism under a modernising leadership.

For Milner, these apprehensions were reinforced by racial and eugenic assumptions. Given the composition of the population, he wanted to see immigration to the Transvaal of 'colonists of the best class' – that is, 'a selected British population'. Only thus could imperial supremacy be assured. Although immigration to the industrial centres needed no encouragement, Milner hoped that British settlers could be attracted to the countryside, where he wanted them to dilute the 'wholly Dutch, agriculturally unprogressive' populace.[36] Despite imperial efforts, however, agricultural settlement was largely a failure. No more than 1,200 settlers were established on the land as a result of these schemes, well more than half of them in the Orange River Colony. Too few to act as a leaven in the Highveld countryside, they were also too few to provide a conservative buffer against the volatility of Johannesburg's English-speaking politics.

Nevertheless, this was a period in which notions of scientific agriculture were being disseminated by new departments of agriculture, and nowhere more notably than in the Cape during Jameson's Progressive Party ministry between 1904 and 1908. Despite the suspicion with which the architect of the Jameson Raid was regarded, Jameson's recognition of the need to modernise Cape agriculture, and the extraordinarily ambitious and wide-ranging programme he launched to achieve this, was supported by the opposition South African Party under John X. Merriman. Modernization also resonated with educated Africans in the Transkei, who shared this progressive scientific agenda and sent their sons to new agricultural training institutions. To some extent, agrarian reform served to defuse postwar communal tensions. But its supporters were not to be found among poorer farmers – whether white or black, English-speaking or Bondsmen – who lacked the capital, access to good land and access to water to profit from the new developments.

The emergence in 1904 of new political organisations among Transvaal English speakers reflected an intensification of the debate about the constitutional future of the colony. In an increasingly tense political climate, exacerbated by the collapse of the postwar boom, British South Africans demanded greater representation based on the principle of equal constituencies delimited according to the number of white adult male voters and not on the total white population, a measure designed to favour the British

[36] Milner to Chamberlain, 25 January 1902, in Headlam (ed.), *Milner papers*, vol. 2, p. 283.

population, which consisted largely of adult males. White women were not considered worthy of enfranchisement.

Despite the electoral advantage it would have conferred, and the significant wartime role of Afrikaner women, Afrikaner leaders were equally loath to demand any extension of the vote to women: the franchise remained the domain of men, whatever their political persuasion. The politicisation of many Afrikaner women during the recent conflict may have 'engendered' Afrikaner nationalism in the ex-republics, but most women now expressed this nationalism through forms of ethnic philanthropy, in home and church, rather than in explicitly political terms. In the Cape Colony from the 1890s and in Natal after 1902, small groups of feminists, inspired by British suffragettes, had begun to organise, but their voices were inaudible in discussions around the Transvaal franchise. Although white women were ineluctably part of the nation, they would still be represented by men.

English-speaking workers, many of them organised in trade unions, also favoured immediate self-government with an adult white male suffrage to reduce the power of mine magnates. If South Africa was to be a white man's country, labour leaders argued, this could be achieved only through a white labour policy; a white labour policy was therefore in the interests of the entire white 'community', women as well as men. As we have already seen, in the 1890s white workers (especially miners) who felt threatened by policies that weakened their bargaining position were hostile to the importation of cheaper contract workers of any kind. Predictably, it was in relation to large numbers of Chinese and especially African labourers that white workers felt most vulnerable and most hostile. Although the majority of unorganised white workers came reluctantly to accept indentured Chinese as the only alternative to the loss of their jobs, organised labour continued to see the policy as a direct threat, despite the stiff contract restrictions placed on the Chinese and their compulsory repatriation.

In the long run, African workers posed a more enduring threat. This was particularly true for those industrial workers whose training occurred at the workplace and who were unable to defend themselves behind apprenticeship and craft barriers. In response to what they saw as the unfair advantage possessed by cheap labour, trade union leaders demanded a job colour bar that would exclude 'coloured' labour from what was defined as skilled and better-paid work, and they deployed a variety of arguments to justify it. Under Kruger, they had had little success except to reserve to themselves the use of dynamite for blasting. However, to defuse the white working class outcry over Chinese labour, the Transvaal British authorities introduced a far more extensive job colour bar, which remained intact for Africans even after Chinese repatriation.

In addition, labour leaders were among the first to advocate the total territorial separation of Africans as a way of protecting their constituency. James Riley, President of the Witwatersrand Trades and Labour Council in 1907, presented an early version before the Mining Industry Commission of 1908. 'If this country is to be a white man's country and a home in a British colony for white people,' he asserted,

then we must take seriously . . . our attitude to the coloured question. . . . [W]ith respect to the Indian coolie and the Chinese I would absolutely exclude them altogether. . . . The Kaffir is a permanent factor here, and we cannot exterminate him. . . . [H]e should be located on territories set apart according to their different races . . . and let them come up to our civilised standard in their own particular territories. As soon as they wish to leave that and come into ours, then they must come up to both our standard of living and pay as ourselves, so that they shall not compete unjustly with the white workers.[37]

Wilfred Wybergh, onetime mining engineer, advocate of the use of exclusively white labour on the mines and soon-to-be founder of the South African Labour Party, put it even more bluntly:

[T]hose who are haunted by the military danger have failed to perceive that the struggle has already been transferred from the battlefield to the workshop and the mine. That is where the question of racial supremacy will be decided, and it avails little to secure ourselves from the spectre of an armed Kafir nation if we welcome within our gates a host armed with pick, shovel and plough.[38]

Although in Cape Town small socialist societies and even some trade unions that had formed at the turn of the century clung to a more consistently nonracial position, by 1910, the territorial separation of Africans was part of the political manifesto of the newly formed South African Labour Party. This soon became the common currency of all South Africa's mainstream white political parties, but in 1910, the Labour Party had by far the most explicitly segregationist programme of any of the parties fighting the national election. In its defence, labour leaders played on an older, profoundly British, antislavery tradition, which had been evoked in the recent anti-Chinese labour agitation. Moreover, a fusion of militant labour and racist visions was common to the political platform of the imperial working class, whether in South Africa, Britain or Australia.

---

[37] TG2, *Mining Industries Commission*, pt IV, 1426, q. 20477, Evidence of J. Riley, cited in Elaine Katz, *A trade union aristocracy: a history of white workers in the Transvaal and the General Strike of 1913* (Johannesburg: African Studies Institute, 1976), pp. 64–5.
[38] 'Native Policy: Assimilation or segregation', *State* 1:3 (March 1909), 455–464.

Confronting what they saw as a constant threat from capital from above and from African 'slave labour' from below, in the immediate postwar years, English-speaking white workers in the Transvaal were ready to accept overtures from Afrikaner generals with their anticapitalist rhetoric and their 'understanding of the native', despite their ambivalence about the role of landless Afrikaners as potential competitors in the labour market. In 1904, faced with widespread discontent in the Transvaal, the High Commissioner and the Colonial Office began to explore alternative constitutional proposals, and by March 1905, the British government had agreed to a new constitution. Although this proved far too little to satisfy those demanding immediate responsible government, publication of the proposals served to mobilise the Afrikaner and trade unionist opposition. By early 1905, leading Afrikaner generals had organised a new political party, Het Volk (the People) as the standard bearer of their resistance to British policies in the Transvaal.

If the constitution of Colonial Secretary Lord Lyttelton provided the immediate spur to action, the formation of Het Volk was also the outcome of a prolonged process of regrouping among defeated Afrikaners. Immediately after the war, a delegation of generals had gone to Europe, where their position as spokespeople was confirmed first by former President Kruger, in exile in the Netherlands, and then, de facto, by the British government. Intent on regaining some degree of political initiative, the Transvaal's ex-generals used republican funds to secure all but one of the Dutch-language newspapers, exploited their old commando networks to mobilise support and lost no time in putting themselves forward as spokesmen of the *volk*.

Het Volk became the vehicle for bringing together a wide spectrum of Afrikaner society behind the demand for self-government. Its counterpart in the Orange River Colony was the Oranje Unie (the Orange Union) established between 1904 and 1906. In addition to fighting for self-government, the new party 'portrayed itself as non-racial [i.e., between British and Afrikaner whites] and non-partisan, promising job-creating programmes and labour colonies for "poor whites"'.[39] This strategy had the advantage of bringing support from a white working class as much opposed to Chinese labour as to the limitations of the Lyttelton proposals.

In the face of the almost-unanimous demand for self-government, and the Liberal Party victory in the British elections at the end of 1905, the constitutional proposals were scrapped by Selborne. In 1906, the Transvaal was granted fully self-governing institutions, as was the Orange River

---

[39] J. Bottomley, 'The Orange Free State and the Rebellion of 1914: the influence of industrialisation, poverty and poor whiteism', in Morrell (ed.), *White but poor*, p. 30.

Colony a year later. In both territories, Afrikaner parties won the ensuing elections, and their generals then held the political initiative. Representing the old – and to some extent the new – landed notables, they had access to the patronage and loyalty that made them the potential restorers of social order. They were supported by their wartime subordinates: an intelligentsia of clergy, teachers, lawyers, law agents, writers and journalists, and a group of women who began to reconstitute the *volk* through new welfare and philanthropic institutions.

The generals had established their authority remarkably quickly. Yet this was no easy task, for in the early years of the century, Afrikaners were fratricidally divided. The war and its settlement were not an automatic forcing ground for Afrikaner nationalism, as is often held, although they served as such in retrospect. These events may have fostered nationalist, or at least anti-British, sentiment, but they also fomented divisions on the Republican side. The negotiating generals at Vereeniging were prompted, as we have seen, by the stark realisation that the very survival of the *volk* was at stake. Only slightly less drastically, they also realised that the war had come close to destroying any shared sense of Afrikaner community and their own moral authority.

As so often, the need to create a new 'imagined' community arose at the moment of greatest external challenge and internal disintegration. The task was particularly critical in the Transvaal, where there was a large and influential English-speaking population that Afrikaner leaders believed they could not afford to alienate. However, the need to restore Afrikaner morale and cohesion was also delicate in the Orange River Colony. Its population may have been more ethnically homogeneous, but it was equally stratified by class, gender and generational divisions. It is true that Afrikaner leaders there had no need to reconcile a potentially powerful Uitlander opposition, yet they faced at least as difficult a task in re-creating a sense of Afrikaner unity. This meant drawing in poor whites, 'protected burghers' – a phrase that included both collaborators and those who were seen to have surrendered too easily in return for British protection – and some of the English-speakers who had dominated urban commercial and educational life in the former Republic.

Furthermore, during the war itself, as has been noted, a large minority of Afrikaners in the British-occupied Orange Free State and South African Republic had deserted or collaborated with the imperial authorities. To later nationalists, they were the 'joiners', dismissed in one vivid if contemptuous phrase as *"n klompie verraaier bywoner"*.[40] In reality, individual motives for

---

[40] S. Pauw, *Beroepsarbeid van die Afrikaner in die stad* (Stellenbosch: Pro Ecclesia, 1946), p. 67.

surrender had been varied. Thus, 'many wealthy farmers, officers and middle class men' had been among the first to abandon the cause, and 'generational differences' and 'differences in relationships to women' may even have been 'more significant than class' in distinguishing between *hendsoppers*, who had surrendered early on, and diehard *bittereinders*, who had held out to the end.[41] Nonetheless, for many poorer burghers, the possibility of securing work as British auxiliaries, on the railways or in construction, had been sufficient inducement to lay down arms. Many of these were indeed landless bywoners, squatters who had already been displaced from the farms of accumulating farmers or who had become marginal to rural production by the late nineteenth century. Their numbers had been swelled earlier by the natural disasters of the 1890s – by the mid-1890s there were already some six thousand landless Afrikaners along the Rand. Kitchener's scorched-earth policy had added significantly to their number.

The war thus both exposed and aggravated the dangerous cleavages that had already emerged in Dutch-Afrikaner society with the rise of capitalist agriculture and land speculation. The processes of dispossession seriously damaged the ties that had bound bywoners and the poor to landowners and the clergy, and that had sustained the social hierarchy of prewar republican society. After the war, yet another flood of indigent, unskilled and barely literate whites flocked to new industrial centres. There, they faced competition from organised, skilled white expatriate labour as well as from equally poor, unskilled and illiterate black workers who still had some access to subsistence cultivation in rural areas. Nor was 'poor whiteism' confined to the former Republics. In the Cape, too, observers noted with concern the growth of a dispossessed white rural underclass, exacerbated by the subdivision of land under the Roman Dutch inheritance system. Unemployed and, to some extent, unemployable, poor whites came to be seen as a major problem of social control for government and as a volatile constituency for political mobilisation, whether by Afrikaner nationalists or English-speaking socialists. Over time, the former were to be more successful in attracting their loyalty than the latter, yet it was not a foregone conclusion that the nationalists would win.

If the dispossessed poor and the new proletariat were to be captured for the nationalist cause, the social networks so essential to their mobilisation would have to be repaired and replaced. The need to police moral and ethnic boundaries was acutely felt, especially as numbers of young, single women were also moving into town in search of a livelihood, either because their entire families were displaced from the land or because the labour of young

---

[41] Bradford, 'Gentlemen and Boers', in Cuthbertson et al., *Writing a wider war*, p. 47.

men was more valued in a reduced Afrikaner homestead. Such women also had few skills, with many forced to make their living in domestic labour or sexual services.

As elsewhere in the world, middle-class women were crucial to the ethnic task of rescuing their *volk*. Already by the late nineteenth century, at a time when thousands of Uitlanders were arriving in the Transvaal, Afrikaner women were being caught up in the movement to construct national icons. And, as noted, that republican consciousness was heightened by the circumstances of the war.[42] At Naauwpoort on 16 December 1900, the annual Day of the Covenant, Smuts was among the first to link the wartime suffering of women and children to their suffering and heroism during the Great Trek. Parallels between the trek and the war were also re-created emotively in the popular imagination in the early twentieth century through the work of the prolific populariser of the Great Trek, Gustav Preller. There was, in Preller as in other male authors, an ambiguity, however: women were heroic through suffering, not through their own agency. Yet the recent reality was rather different: many Afrikaner women had been caught up in war not simply as victims but as assertive participants in their own right.

Women's agency in war was transient, however. For men, and indeed for many women themselves, peace meant a return to a more 'natural' gendered order. In early-twentieth-century Transvaal as in late-nineteenth-century Cape Colony, philanthropy provided a legitimate public space for female agency both during and after hostilities. The suffering of women and children in camps had aroused a powerful female charitable response. In wartime, middle-class Afrikaner women were prominent in voluntary teaching, nursing and welfare work in the camps, and thereafter they became prominent in church-related philanthropic activities. It would be misleading, however, to see these acts as apolitical, given the manner in which racially circumscribed philanthropic enterprise, such as that of the Afrikaanse Christelike Vroue Vereniging (Afrikaans Christian Women's Society) became bound up with early Afrikaner nationalism.

New welfare organisations were established by women of independent means or of some social standing; they were frequently the wives of prominent men, giving them access to necessary patronage. Thus, shortly after the war, Afrikaner women in Pretoria established the Zuid-Afrikaansche Zustersvereniging (South African Union of Sisters) to care for war orphans and a *reddingshuis* (Rescue Home) as a sanctuary for 'young unmarried mothers and girls in need of care who were leading an immoral life because

---

[42] Ibid.

they could not find employment'.[43] A proposal that they should enter domestic service fell on stony ground, although Emily Hobhouse's scheme to train destitute Boer women to spin and weave was somewhat more successful. Part of the same mobilisation of Afrikaner women to rescue the *volk* lay behind the founding of the Bond van Afrikaanse Moeders (Union of Afrikaner mothers) and its attempts to provide maternity care for poor rural women, especially in rural areas, through the training of midwives and the establishment of maternity homes.

Although these, like the wider-ranging Afrikaans Christian Women's Society, were explicitly Afrikaner initiatives, the South African Women's Federation, or Vroue Federasie, was founded in 1904–1905 to encourage reconciliation between English-speaking and Afrikaner 'races' by Annie Botha and Johanna Preller, both wives of leading members of Het Volk, and by Georgina Solomon, widow of Saul Solomon, a renowned Cape liberal, and campaigner for African and women's rights in South Africa and Britain. Here, too, the object was to provide relief for those rendered destitute by the war. By and large, however, the joint efforts were to prove ephemeral.

For the new nationalist intelligentsia, male and female, there was a special urgency in educating women as 'mothers of the nation', and this politicised many of their philanthropic initiatives. With the 'disintegration' of the *volk* being closely connected to the decay of the family, attempts to establish orphanages for Afrikaner children, to 'rescue fallen Afrikaner women', and later to train qualified Afrikaner midwives to work in rural areas and establish maternity clinics had an ethnic and political as well as a simple humanitarian purpose.[44]

Given their central role in socialising youth, women were made a special target by male as well as female cultural nationalists in the ensuing years. Nor was the importance of socialising the next generation lost on Milner. Without a bridgehead into the family, he turned to schooling in the hope of capturing it from what he saw as the bigotry of Krugerism. As early as 1900, with the war still raging, the High Commissioner had already begun to enunciate a new language and education policy for the conquered territories.

Early in 1901, he appointed a leading educationist, E. B. Sargant, to South Africa to restructure education in both ex-republics and to undertake

---

[43] Thariza van Rensburg (ed.), *Camp diary of Henrietta Armstrong: experiences of a Boer nurse in the Irene Concentration Camp, 6 April–11 October 1901* (Pretoria: Human Sciences Research Council, 1980) p. 18.

[44] Marijke du Toit, '"Dangerous motherhood": maternity care and engendered construction of Afrikaner identity, 1904–1939', in Fildes, Marks and Marland (eds.), *Women and children first*, p. 210.

the Anglicisation of children in camps with imported English teachers. Unusually, Sargant himself had rather more sympathy for Afrikaans than most of his English-speaking contemporaries and advised teachers to learn the language of their pupils. Yet he also insisted on their pro-imperial credentials, and he used Victorian public schools as his educational model. Although parents retained the right to have their children given religious instruction in Dutch, this amounted to no more than fifteen minutes a day. Furthermore, although schooling was free, it was not compulsory, and regular attendance by children was minimal.

Whatever the response to schools, as with his settlement scheme and Chinese labour, Milner's education and language policy served to heighten the antagonism of the politically conscious Afrikaner elite to British rule. In both colonies, there was a nationalist reaction and Afrikaner leaders, whether ex-generals or Dutch Reformed Church clergymen, were prompted to fight back. By 1903, they were attempting to establish their own Christian-national schools. Still, parents seem to have been no more enthusiastic about the private schools than they were about state education, and in the Transvaal, the movement soon faded. Even in the Orange River Colony, by 1904, political leaders had signed a concordat with the administration, agreeing to close down private schools in exchange for minor concessions to Dutch in the state schools.

It was nevertheless in the Orange Free State that the politics of language was to be most furiously contested after the granting of responsible government. James Barry Munnik Hertzog, a Boer general and founder of Oranje Unie, emerged as its leading protagonist; for him, language was central to Afrikaner identity. Regarded by imperial officials and most English speakers as an irresponsible firebrand, his vision was nonetheless of a white South African nation composed of two groups, each with its own language, culture and identity. However, without equality between the two, he believed white unity would be impossible.

It was as a propagator of Dutch – and later Afrikaans – that Hertzog most distinguished himself from the nationalism of Botha, Smuts and Het Volk in the late 1900s. Yet, in many ways, Hertzog's notions of the appropriate relationship of English and Dutch were at one with those of the redoubtable Onze Jan in the Cape Colony, who had throughout his long political career advocated the equality of Dutch and English; he had founded the Taalbond in 1890 to simplify and thus popularise Dutch in the face of widespread Anglicisation and in the contest with the first Afrikaans language movement.

In the Cape Colony, too, debates about language that had characterised early nationalist stirrings revived among Afrikaners in postwar years. Here, too, the conflict had been a traumatic experience. By the late nineteenth century, Cape Afrikaners had been able to accommodate an ethnic Afrikaner identity within the overarching framework of the British Empire. Such accommodation was rudely shattered by the polarising effects of the Jameson Raid and by Milner's demands for unconditional loyalty in the 1890s. The events of the war had further divided loyalties as republican armies invaded the Cape and demanded local support: as colonial rebel support, it was given at the risk of execution and of inflaming further an already-angry coloured proletariat in the countryside.

At the same time, the language struggle in the Cape also intensified as the right to use Dutch in the civil service and courts was undermined during and immediately after the war. In 1904, the Progressive Party won the Cape elections, largely as a result of the disenfranchisement of rebels. The recrudescence of jingoism and triumphalism that the Progressives' victory reflected served to intimidate the Afrikaner population and entrench their fear of using their language in public. Partly in response to this situation, the Taalbond was revived in the Cape, but ironically, it encountered new opponents, especially in the Transvaal, where a new intelligentsia was emerging that saw the reconstruction and recognition of Afrikaans, rather than the simplification of Dutch, as central to the task of redeeming 'the people'.

The language issue was thus not merely about the contest between English and Dutch; it was further bedevilled by divisions between supporters of Dutch and Afrikaans. In a world in which English was the language of the workplace and where English education paved the way to state employment, and where an increasingly unfamiliar Dutch remained the language of the church, the question of the vernacular was central to the dilemma of journalists, writers, teachers and clerics. Indeed, it was critical if they were to mobilise a new constituency.

The language issue had concerned some of the Afrikaner intelligentsia as early as the 1870s as an aspect of early nationalism. A decade later, the subject of an appropriate education for Afrikaner girls was arousing nationalist passions in the Republics. Thus, in 1892, A. D. W. Wolmarans, chair of the South African Republic Volksraad, was arguing that 'experience had taught him that if a girl spoke half a dozen words of English correctly she despised her nationality. Their morality', he continued, 'would be ruined by giving their daughters higher education. An Afrikaner girl did not require arithmetic and book-keeping. These sciences might be necessary for English girls, who sometimes served in shops; but they would ruin the morality of their race by teaching their girls these things.'[45] In the Orange

---

[45] *The Press* (Pretoria), 30 May 1892, cited in Gordon, *The growth of Boer opposition*, p. 12.

Free State, too, an observer was appalled that in the Dutch Reformed Church Huguenot School, where future mothers of the country were being educated, everything was in English. Whatever the situation before the war, during and immediately after it, Afrikaner women were at the forefront in assertively using their mother tongue.

Nonetheless, in the absence of an acceptable form of Afrikaans and the difficulties of Dutch, even during the war some republicans wrote telegrams, letters and despatches in English. At the same time, despite the preparedness of Cape Afrikaner intellectuals to participate in the wider culture opened up by English, its dominance also called forth a forceful nationalist response. Members of the intelligentsia came to demand the systematic revision of the vernacular to create a standardised respectable Afrikaans, purged of its lower-class and 'coloured' associations and capable of holding its own against the massive English influence. If, as was frequently argued, Afrikaans was not a literary language, it was up to intellectuals to transform that. In 1905, the Taalgenootskap (Language Society) was formed in the Transvaal to further the cause of the Afrikaans language. From there it spread to the Cape, where it was received with enthusiasm by some of the founders of the original Genootskap van Regte Afrikaners, who established an Afrikaanse Taalvereeniging (Afrikaans language society) the following year. In 1908, D. F. Malan, then chair of the Taalvereeniging, urged the unification of the two organisations to provide 'a bulwark against . . . anglicisation'. He believed that 'a healthy national feeling can only be rooted in ethnic [*volks*] art and science, ethnic customs and character, ethnic language and ethnic religion, and, not least, in ethnic literature'.[46] Thus, the regeneration of language, culture and nation were intimately connected.

A literature tailored specifically to Afrikaner women was also brought into being – increasingly by female as well as male authors – which emphasised the dangers of urban life (in particular from non-Afrikaner males) to young girls making their way to town from the countryside. Through this literature, the early-twentieth-century ideal of femininity and motherhood was given a specifically Afrikaner content. According to this ideal, women should give themselves selflessly, not only to their families but also to the *volk*. The home, so they were urged, should become the incubator in which the new Afrikaner spirit could be nurtured.

For Botha and his closest associate, Smuts, language issues were of secondary importance, given the centrality of the gold-mining industry and

---

[46] Cited in T. Dunbar Moodie, *The rise of Afrikanerdom: power, apartheid and the Afrikaner civil religion*, p. 47.

the need to win over a substantial number of Uitlanders. Having secured the position of Dutch in primary school, they were willing to accept its subordinate status in secondary education. In 1906, securing an electoral pact with English-speaking supporters of 'responsible government' and overcoming their mistrust overrode most other considerations. To achieve this, Het Volk, under the Botha-Smuts leadership, pragmatically accepted the primacy of the English language in the Transvaal. This should not be surprising. Even before the war, Smuts had shared in the vision of a unified white South Africa, promulgated by the Bond and by Rhodes. Although this notion of a white South African nationalism was stalled in the impassioned atmosphere after the Jameson Raid, in the war that followed, Smuts was, as we have seen, horrified by what he foresaw as the consequences of white civil war and the British arming of Africans. That lent a special urgency to ending hostilities in a spirit of conciliation.

The presence of the British army, African disarmament, the systematisation of 'native administration' and the arrival of Chinese workers may have seemed to have resolved problems of security and labour in the ex-republics – at least temporarily. However, the outbreak of a poll-tax rebellion in Natal in February 1906, which was put down with great brutality by colonial troops, cast a long shadow over the whole of South Africa and prompted Smuts to return once more to the 'black menace'. In April 1906, Smuts wrote that the controversial handling of the disturbances illustrated the dangers 'of leaving large questions affecting the future of all South Africa to be dealt with by a small colony like Natal, where there is neither the largeness of vision nor the wholesome check of a strong opposition and influential leaders.'[47] The position of a small white population in a black continent was clearly a major part of the mental landscape of English- and Afrikaans-speaking South Africans alike, and the uprising hastened the unification movement, partly shaped the form that unification took and profoundly affected the nature of white identity.

Quite apart from fear of black uprisings, in the aftermath of the war, there were other pressing reasons for advocating reconciliation. Smuts soon found an ally in his advocacy of reconciliation in the veteran Cape politician John X. Merriman, who saw in an Anglo-Afrikaner alliance a way of thwarting future imperial intervention in South Africa. In May 1904, Smuts wrote to Merriman, who was then in the throes of founding the Cape Liberal Association, for advice on 'a programme of principles' for Het Volk that would 'avoid racial issues' and appeal not only to Afrikaners but also to

[47] Smuts to Merriman, 3 April 1906, in Hancock and van der Poel (eds.), *Smuts papers*, vol. 2, p. 253, no. 294.

'every fair-minded Englishman' throughout South Africa. Hoping for a future Liberal victory in Britain, Smuts was already beginning to think in more concrete terms of moving 'in the direction of Federation'.[48]

Smuts's vision of reconciliation and a broader white 'South African patriotism' powerfully reinforced and complemented his recognition that, in the Transvaal, political power depended on dividing the English-speaking parties and securing a degree of British–South African support. Indeed, as the 1907 election results were declared, he confided in Merriman that he was 'exceedingly anxious not to have a pure Het Volk Ministry. On our policy on racial peace we carried many English constituencies with us, and I think we shall continue that policy night and day'.[49] Thus, despite his party's majority, Botha gave ministerial places to the English-speaking National Party and was even prepared to woo mine magnates in the pursuit of power, despite Het Volk's courting of the white labour movement in the run-up to the elections.

As Smuts remarked to Wernher in 1906, when again attempting to dissuade the mine magnates from backing the English-speaking Progressive Party, 'it would be much more to our [i.e., the mining] interest to go more with the Boers, the conservative element in the country' as the interests of the mine owners were 'in so many ways identical with [those of] the Boers as large property-holders'.[50] Well aware of the centrality of mining to the colony, ministers were soon discussing the day-to-day problems of the industry with magnates on a friendly basis. Smuts not only intervened in a labour dispute in the Chamber of Mines that could have destroyed WNLA; a couple of years later, ministers negotiated a revision of Milner's modus vivendi with Mozambique over transport concessions and access to labour. Yet more emphatic was Het Volk's attitude to a strike by English-speaking miners in 1907 over an attempt by one mine's management to increase the number of Africans working drills under white supervision. The strikers were swiftly dismissed as Smuts called out imperial troops to break up picket lines and to protect the largely unskilled Afrikaner scabs, who were workers taking on the role of supervisors. As the miners' union surmised, probably correctly, the owners were hoping to cut costs by retrenching skilled white workers. Indeed, after labour's defeat, the number of white miners was reduced and the cost of rock drilling was cut.

What the outcome of the strike made clear, both to mine owners and to a perspicacious African witness, H. L. Phooko, representing the Transvaal

[48] Ibid., Smuts to Merriman, 30 May 1904, pp. 170–1.
[49] Ibid., Smuts to Merriman, 25 February 1907, p. 337.
[50] J. Wernher to Fitzpatrick, 6 February 1906, in Duminy and Guest (eds.), *Fitzpatrick*, pp. 420–1.

Native Congress to the Mining Commission of 1907, was the capacity of African and Chinese workers to keep the mines running on their own. This marked a key moment in the history of Afrikaner workers on the mines and in changing work practices on the Rand. It was also highly ironic. In the view of Lionel Phillips, Johannesburg director of Werner Beit and Eckstein, 'the whole world is really getting topsy-turvy. A Boer government calling out the British troops to keep English miners in order while the Dutch men are replacing them in the mines'.[51]

This new coalescence of interest between the Het Volk government and the mining industry was also manifest in the drive toward closer union, which dominated politics in the years from 1907 to 1910. Behind his courtship of the mine magnates lay Smuts's belief that their power would be tempered in a more broadly based state in which imperial power was denied a directing role. It was doubtless also born of his recognition of the importance of mining to South Africa's economy. Not for nothing has it been concluded that before Union, 'no government did more for the mines than Louis Botha's Het Volk administration in the Transvaal'.[52]

The economic advantages of 'closer union' in the interest of stability and development had, of course, long been evident. From the mid-nineteenth century, empire builders like Sir George Grey in the 1850s and Carnarvon in the 1870s had advocated some form of federation. Their mantle had been adopted by Rhodes, who was a champion of a united South Africa in the 1890s. By 1899, Rhodes had even more grandiose notions of unifying all the British colonies in Africa. Milner, too, thought that 'all South Africa should be *one Dominion* with a common government dealing with Customs, Railways and Defence, perhaps also with Native policy'.[53] Selborne was as convinced of the need for closer union, and his support was to be vital for that cause.

Even before the war was over, with much of the region already under imperial control, prominent British South Africans were discussing the possibilities of a unified state in which their interests would dominate, with Milner considering the moment opportune for the incorporation of Southern Rhodesia, then under British South Africa Company rule. Although he had not achieved this objective by the time of his departure from South Africa, and felt that his policies had failed on several fronts, his more

---

[51] Philips to Wernher, 3 June 1907, in Phillips, *All that glittered*, p. 179.

[52] Jeeves, *Migrant labour*, p. 14.

[53] Milner to Fitzpatrick, 28 November 1899, in Headlam (ed.), *Milner papers*, vol. 2, pp. 35–6.

conciliatory successor, Selborne, and the kindergarten were fully engaged in furthering closer union. In this, they were encouraged by the movement for union between Natal and the Transvaal, by support of federation in Ons Land and by its advocacy from leading members of Het Volk. By October 1906, Curtis, working for the High Commissioner, had drafted a memorandum on the subject that was, with some significant amendments, adopted by Selborne and circulated under his name. This powerful polemic, intended to advance the cause of federation, was circulated to the colonial governments early in 1907. Anxious to allay suspicions of 'imperial interference', Curtis persuaded the leading Bondsman, F. S. Malan, to act as intermediary, and in July 1907, Malan tabled the Selborne Memorandum in the Cape parliament.

Thereafter, events moved swiftly, spurred on by the victories of Afrikaner parties in the Transvaal, Orange Free State and Cape Colony in 1907–1908. Self-government with Afrikaner governments in power in the conquered territories threatened even that measure of centralisation achieved by Milner as the Transvaal withdrew from the Customs Union. Both for the kindergarten and for the farther-sighted capitalists who had long advocated the rationalisation of labour supplies, railway policy and customs and tariffs in the interests of economic development, the dangers of 'Transvaal isolationism' had to be prevented. As the Selborne Memorandum put it, the 'evil effects' of disunity were 'crippling the power of government to remove obstacles from the path of enterprise'.[54] By this time, the High Commissioner had enlisted the support of many of the leading mine magnates. As he assured Lionel Phillips, 'if you had a united South Africa, you would probably have a satisfactory solution of the labour question and the Home Government would not dare to interfere'.[55] He and a number of others were enthusiastic supporters of some form of unification or federation in South Africa for economic reasons. His diplomatic role in negotiations with governors and leading politicians in the different colonies and with the Colonial Secretary in London was equally important.

From the beginning of 1907, more flexible kindergarten members recognised the need to approach Botha and Smuts in the hopes of working together for some form of closer union. Initially, they were rebuffed. Once Afrikaner parties were in control in three of the four provinces, however, Het Volk leadership came to realise there were advantages to collaborating with political opponents and the kindergarten over union, whatever their residual suspicions of imperial motives. The kindergarten embarked on the

[54] Lord Selborne, 'Memorandum', 7 January 1907, in Newton (ed.), *Select documents*, vol. 2, p. 143.
[55] Phillips to Wernher, 28 January 1907, in Phillips, *All that glittered*, p. 173.

much broader strategy of providing expertise and resources for the closer union movement. This included researching and writing *The Government of South Africa*, a comparative study of the four colonial governments as basis for a future union, and mobilising popular support through the establishment of Closer Union Societies. These had local branches throughout South African with bipartisan Afrikaner-British support and financial assistance from the mine magnate Abe Bailey. By October 1908, when a national convention met in Durban to discuss a South Africa–wide constitution, the Transvaal delegation included members of both Het Volk and the Progressive Party, who had a carefully agreed-on position on the nature of the union they required. On most matters, the composite Transvaal view prevailed. By and large, where there were conflicts of interest between the Cape and the Transvaal, Smuts and Merriman had taken care to negotiate a shared position beforehand. The only exception – over the location of a new capital – was to prove one of the most vigorously contested issues before the convention. Its resolution was particularly important in swinging opinion in the Cape in favour of unification. Federation, Natal's preference, was given short shrift.

The draft constitution that emerged out of the deliberations of the convention and some subsequent amendments recommended in the colonial parliaments were given legal force by British Parliament. The Act of Union in 1909 provided for a sovereign, central, bicameral legislature, based on a first-past-the-post constituency model, but with considerable weighting in favour of rural areas. Although the Cape delegates urged a nonracial franchise for the future Union, this was fiercely opposed by those delegates who wanted a total colour bar. A compromise, already agreed to between Smuts and Merriman before the convention, led to acceptance of existing colonial arrangements. This left the Cape's nonracial but qualified male franchise in the Cape intact, whereas in the Transvaal and Orange Free State, all adult white males were enfranchised, as they were in Natal. There, the half dozen Africans who had managed to achieve the highly restrictive qualifications needed for enfranchisement retained their vote. In the Cape, coloured and African voters also lost their notional right to stand for parliament. Although the black franchise could be changed only by a two-thirds majority of both houses of parliament sitting together, it was seriously diluted in the wider political arena, and the effective role Africans had been able to play in a number of Cape electoral districts in the 1890s and 1900s was ended.

The Bond's view that the parliamentary majority deciding on the franchise 'ought to include a majority of the voting representatives of the Cape Colony' and that Cape experience had 'not proved the necessity of the introduction of colour restrictions in respect of the membership of parliament' was disregarded.[56] So was Natal's proposal to introduce white female suffrage. Although its prime minister was supported by petitions signed by more than 3,700 people, these were more than matched by a counterpetition signed by more than 7,000 women and the opposition of the majority of the 'fathers of the people' present at the convention. Clearly, the message of the female suffrage movement, which had originated in the Cape in the 1890s among the small number of white professional women and activists in the Women's Christian Temperance Union, received scant support.

Although discussions around union did lead to a wider debate about the franchise and the formation of a Women's Enfranchisement League, with Olive Schreiner as one of its vice presidents, the league made little headway in the face of postwar 'suspicion and distrust' between English-speaking and Afrikaner women. The colour bar in the draft constitution that led to Schreiner's resignation from the League, along with a handful of like-minded Cape women, was equally divisive. It would take a further twenty years for white women to be enfranchised, and more than eighty before any black people entered parliament.

If the constitution established the boundaries of citizenship, excluding the vast majority of black men and all women, the geopolitical boundaries of the state remained to be settled. There were those who wished for the immediate incorporation of the High Commission Territories of Basutoland, Swaziland and Bechuanaland, imperial-controlled enclaves that were resented by more ardent colonial nationalists. But a combination of African resistance, British humanitarian opposition and perhaps strategic considerations led to imperial caution over the incorporation of the territories. In the event, a schedule to the act setting out the conditions for the ultimate transfer of the territories served to ignite South Africa's demands for incorporation over the years – and to frustrate them. Southern Rhodesia was also regarded by many as legitimately part of the 'white man's country', including by observers at the national convention, although its status under the British South Africa Company precluded its becoming part of the new Union. When, in 1923, the company's charter lapsed, Southern Rhodesians decided by referendum to remain outside the Union. The pipe dream of expansionists like Smuts of a white dominion stretching to Lake Tanganyika and beyond remained precisely that.

In the Cape and the ex-republics, the new Union constitution probably had the backing of the majority of the white population. Natal's support for federation rather than union, born of a visceral dislike of the Cape non-racial franchise and dread of being swamped by Afrikaners, was ultimately

---

[56] T. R. H. Davenport, *The Afrikaner Bond: the history of a South African political party, 1880–1911* (Cape Town: Oxford University Press, 1966), p. 279.

outweighed by even greater fear of the Zulu. With powerful economic incentives to come in rather than stay out, and a vigorous referendum campaign – and a good deal of politicking managed by the kindergarten – that colony also voted overwhelming to join the Union.

Yet state making, even when approved by the electorate, was not the same thing as nation building, as the bitter dispute over the location of the new Union capital revealed, an issue resolved only when each of the former capitals was allowed a role. The contrivance of a constitution needed to be bolstered by the construction of a community. Perhaps stung by an assertion in *The Times* (of London) at the time of the National Convention that 'South African nationalism did not exist' and prompted by the thought that 'a handful of leaders may fashion a state but they cannot create a nation',[57] the kindergarten followed the convention with the launch of a new journal, the *State*. Published initially in both Dutch and English, its explicit object was to create a white South African national identity; it had funding once again from Bailey – and from Selborne. The *State* devoted itself to the ideological construction of both the nation and nationalism.

One need not take at face value the importance that members of the kindergarten and their admirers attributed to their role in bringing about union. As recent historians of the period have stressed, their contribution was more limited; they were most successful when they were working with the colonial tide. Nevertheless, neither should their role be underestimated. They – especially Lionel Curtis – were crucial in facilitating union, in finding the funds for propaganda work, in undertaking comparative constitutional research and in providing the mechanisms for its ultimate realisation. Both the Closer Union Association, which Curtis forged out of twenty-two local societies, and the *State* were important in preparing for union through forging a new sense of common white nationalism, especially for British South Africans, who had to be reeled in if union were to be successful. Undoubtedly, the conscious creation of a 'white South Africanism' was 'a crucial dimension in the process of cultural and political rapprochement which secured white supremacy in South Africa and helped redefine South Africa's rule in the empire'.[58]

In the process of creating the new nation, however, older, more imprecise notions of incorporation were thrust aside. The mine magnates, Milner's kindergarten (including some with liberal scruples), English-speaking workers, northern Afrikaners and white Natalians rested secure that the

---

[57] Wybergh, 'Native Policy: Assimilation or segregation', citing *The Times*, 4 June 1909.

[58] S. Dubow, 'Colonial nationalism, the Milner Kindergarten and the rise of "South Africanism", 1902–1910', *History Workshop Journal* 43 (1997), 55.

new constitution would exclude Africans and coloureds from the body politic. For them, segregation was to be the cement of the Union.

In the Cape, however, there remained another minority tradition, and there were those among the white elite who were less certain about the wisdom of the new dispensation. Increasingly embattled and discomfited, their tone was almost painfully apologetic and ambiguous. Writing to the conservative Coloured Peoples' Vigilance Committee, which had thanked him for the Bond's defence of the Cape franchise in the debate on the Union constitution, the older statesman Jan Hofmeyr captured the subconscious racism of early-twentieth-century Cape liberalism well:

I, however, hardly deserve *their* particular thanks, for . . . I did not think of their interests exclusively, but quite as much of those of my white fellow-South Africans. With a European population of only a million at the Southern extremity of a continent occupied by some two hundred millions, mostly barbarians and semi-barbarians, I cannot help feeling, whatever my own prejudices of colour and race may be, that the political and social security of white South Africa would be none the worse for retaining the goodwill of the five millions of coloured and aboriginal inhabitants, with whom we live interspersed and for reconciling them with our political institutions.

When the political Union of all British South Africa shall have been fully established . . . it would be a bad day for the new Commonwealth if, in addition to protecting our Northern frontiers against the teeming millions of Darkest Africa, we had to be continually on our guard against a malcontented coloured and native population in our midst, outnumbering us by five or six to one.[59]

For the moment, at least, Hofmeyr's ambiguous discourse carried the Afrikaner Bond.

For the black intelligentsia, exclusion from citizenship in the new Union proved a particularly bitter, if not totally unexpected, disappointment, a spur to concerted intercolonial protest, and even to the first faltering steps toward an alliance of Africans, coloureds and Indians. If the wars of conquest in the late 1870s and 1880s had first shaken the confidence of the African elite in the promises of empire, the settlement after the South African War, which disarmed African chiefdoms, tightened the control of the colonial states over African life and excluded educated Africans from any prospect of common citizenship, jolted them further. Much imperial propaganda before and during the 1899–1902 war had been concerned with the political rights of British subjects, and educated Africans, Indians and coloureds all over South Africa believed that with British victory at

---

[59] J. H. Hofmeyr in collaboration with F. W. Reitz, *The life of Jan Hendrik Hofmeyr (Onze Jan)* (Cape Town: van de Sandt de Villiers, 1913) p. 629.

the very least discrimination against them would cease and the limited nonracial franchise that existed at the Cape would be extended to the new Crown colonies.

Whatever Britain's rhetoric about black rights before and during the war, the Treaty of Vereeniging had made it clear that London had little intention of disturbing the existing relationship between white 'masters' and black 'servants', or of extending the Cape franchise northward. Despite their essentially moderate and pro-British stance, small black organisations, many of them influenced by Cape traditions of parliamentary politics, were almost invariably rebuffed. In the Transvaal, in particular, the post-1902 period defined yet another moment in the progressive disillusion of the black intelligentsia. There, Africans soon found that there was little except increased efficiency to distinguish British from Boer repression and discrim-ination. Expectations of a Cape franchise entitlement were quickly dashed. In practice, Cape liberalism may always have been something of a myth, but its surviving 'tradition' set the standard for black 'modernisers' in the rest of the country. In the view of one historian, 'the roots of much of twentieth century South African politics are here, in African Christians' bitterness at a world that preached progress and incorporation while practising restriction and exclusion'.[60] Ironically, in their language of universalism, moreover, the missionaries had provided their converts with a measuring stick for their own performance.

By the beginning of the century, the small vigilance associations, con-gresses and educational bodies that had been formed everywhere by the coloured and African intelligentsia had begun to establish colonywide organisations and newspapers. Mission conferences, vernacular and other newspapers, epistolary networks and the fact that all southern African terri-tories were under British control meant that black leaders were increasingly aware of one another and of developments across the region. They were all to be spurred into increased activity by the failure of the imperial authorities to live up to their wartime promises.

Their own sense of a wider South Africanism, though sharpened, was not new. The mobility of Africans in the last third of the nineteenth century meant that political, cultural and religious ideas circulated widely across the subcontinent, both orally and in constant letter writing by the intelligentsia. As early as 1891, the Cape-based Ingqugqutela had called itself the South African Native Congress (SANC) in English and claimed to speak on behalf of all Africans in South Africa. By 1902, three representatives of the Transvaal – including the redoubtable Charlotte Manye – attended the SANC's annual conference, and the Congress also

[60] Campbell, *Songs of Zion*, p. 115.

helped to draw up petitions addressed to the British authorities in the Transvaal and Orange River colonies. In 1903, SANC members assisted in the establishment of the Transvaal Native Congress, which swiftly became the leading African organisation in that colony. An abortive attempt in 1904 to establish the pan–South African Native Press Association was only one of the numerous contacts in this decade. And although this may have been stillborn, the newspapers helped to unify African opinion in response to the 1903–1905 South African Native Affairs Commission, the Bhambatha rebellion and approaching unification.

Political and religious contact and independency were accompanied by assertions of educational independence. This is hardly surprising: education had long been promoted by missionaries as the key to the future, and teachers were the first and largest African professional group. Yet their pay and conditions remained woefully inadequate. The Native Educational Association was the earliest African voluntary association in the Eastern Cape, and it took on a formal political role until the late 1880s and the emergence of formally political organisations. In the Cape and elsewhere, teachers were frequently the most politicised members of their community. As such, they were anything but immune to wider ideological currents of the time, sharing, for instance, black aspirations to be free of missionary paternalism. Here, too, the American Methodist Episcopal Church (AMEC) and African American experience added to the ferment.

By the turn of the century, dozens of black South Africans were studying in the United States, following earlier pioneers like Mavuma Nembula, who qualified as a medical doctor in Chicago in 1891; John Dube, who studied in America between 1887 and 1891 under the auspices of the American Board of Missions; and Charlotte Manye (later Maxexe), they were the first of many black South African students to be supported by the AMEC. On their return, both Manye and John Dube established their own educational institutions and became leading political figures. The AMEC was also an important sponsor of independent school initiatives, which were often backed by the SANC. In addition, among a number of African chiefs, aware of changing times, there was a growing interest in the spread of a Western education, other than that offered by white missionaries. In Thembuland, for example, Paramount Chief Dalindyebo himself invited Charlotte Manye and her husband Marshall Maxeke, to set up an AMEC school in Tembuland; more remarkably, perhaps, Dalindyebo also asked Manye to participate in his councils.

These independent educational initiatives culminated in the SANC's ambitious Queen Victoria Memorial scheme to establish an institution for African higher education in South Africa. In the event, this was overtaken by the Inter-State Native College, launched by the South African Native Affairs Commission in a bid to preempt such a demonstration of African educational independence. Promoted enthusiastically by Jabavu, its paid travelling secretary, the Inter-State College gained widespread support not only from the educated elite in the Eastern Cape but also from across southern Africa. It was finally launched as the University College of Fort Hare in 1916. Although its own independent scheme had not borne fruit, the SANC was making its mark. Its focus on religious and educational independence, its assertive Africanism and its intercolonial outreach (especially in the run-up to Union) were to make the Congress the most important precursor of the South African Native National Congress (later the African National Congress) founded shortly after Union.

Although plans for a Queen Victoria Memorial suggest that Great Britain and its monarch still retained some of their iconic status in the Cape Colony (and Natal) after the war, black American experience increasingly presented an alternative vision, both to aspirant modernisers and to millennial dreamers, with their far more anarchic visions. Beyond the AMEC and the Ethiopian churches were myriad other independent churches whose members drew little distinction between politics and a religion of redemption. It was in the unsettled years after the war, too, that Zionist or 'spirit' churches with their distinctive forms of adult baptism and foot washing and their apocalyptic and faith-healing beliefs emerged from the unlikely 1903 contact between a Dutch Reformed Church missionary, J. L. le Roux, and Reverend Alexander Dowie's Chicago-based Christian Catholic Church in Zion. Four years later, Pentecostalism, characterised by speaking in tongues, also entered South Africa from Los Angeles, to seduce le Roux and many of his acolytes. Though still embryonic in this period, 'flamboyant' Zionist and Pentecostal sects with their 'lusty songs and ingenious uniforms' were rapidly to 'eclipse' older forms of mission Christianity in rural South Africa in the twentieth century.[61]

Within and beyond them, there was, furthermore, an even more vulnerable section of the African population. These were individuals who survived in a kind of no-man's-land and everyman's land between the older elite of chiefs and headmen, and the new elite of teachers and preachers, lawyers and clerks, nurses and social workers on the one hand, and migrant workers on mines and railways, farms and municipal services, on the other. They made up the host of 'in-between people', excommunicants and apostates; displaced minor chiefs and indigenous healers; prophets and visionaries; entertainers and confidence tricksters; gangsters and shebeen queens; and

---

[61] Jean Comaroff, *Body of power, spirit of resistance: the culture and history of a South African people* (Chicago: University of Chicago Press, 1985) p. 167.

the aspirant and desperate of all ranks and fortunes, who lived vividly expressive lives.

'Ethiopianism' was expressed in a host of millennial dreams and fantasies like those of the 'lunatic' who 'got up in Durban outside the gardens, sprang up on the palisade there and cried that he was the Lord Jesus Christ and that he came there to lead the Natives into their own kingdom and to take possession of the land which was a black man's land', or the African who informed a member of the Natal Legislative Assembly that in two years' time he would own a store on the main street in Durban and 'that a white man would work for him'.[62] Close up, this was a world of 'diverse voices and complex subjectivities, ... kaleidoscopic incoherences and ... fragmentary realities'.[63] These were the people who often concerned colonial officials most because they seemed beyond categorisation and control; they are also most difficult for the historian to picture and present. Still, what can be suggested is that these modes of human self-representation were 'linked not to the breakdown of tradition nor to an emerging or incomplete modernity but to a specific political-economic and social conjuncture within which people improvise motivated and durable strategies of self-construction and self- presentation'.[64]

Whatever the exact nature of the relationships among them, the war itself, intense postwar disillusion, the growing influence of independent churches and 'the broader traffic with black America which the church facilitated' all contributed to a radical ferment in black politics in the post-war decade, which had been less marked in the prewar politics of the African elite.[65] Generationally, many younger Africans came to reject older notions of incorporation and looked to the more militant message of 'Ethiopians' and of the even more millenarian messages that spread dramatically in the years leading up to Union. For their part, some whites were not unaware of this ferment. As the writer and later public administrator and politician Violet Markham observed in 1904:

A strange leaven is at present working among the educated Kaffirs throughout the country, a leaven to which the affairs of the Ethiopian Church bear emphatic testimony.... A new ideal is taking possession of the black man's mind. 'Africa for the Africans'.... The aim of the latter-day educated native is freedom... in

---

[62] Shula Marks, *Reluctant rebellion: the 1906–8 disturbances in Natal* (Oxford: Clarendon Press, 1970), pp. 65–6, citing Natal Legislative Assembly, *Debates*, vol. 34, speech by W. McLarty, MLA on the Mission Reserves Bill, 21 July 1903.

[63] Jean Comaroff and John Comaroff (eds.), *Modernity and its malcontents: ritual and power in postcolonial Africa* (Chicago: University of Chicago Press, 1993), p. viii.

[64] James Ferguson, *Expectations of modernity: myths and meanings of urban life on the Zambian Copperbelt* (Berkeley: University of California Press, 1999), p. 230.

[65] Campbell, Songs of Zion, p.150.

all matters political and social. This spirit is manifesting itself by a series of new movements, generally connected with religion. . . . The result has been the creation of much discontent and restlessness throughout the country.[66]

Even in Natal, where the AMEC was proscribed, something of its message seems to have filtered through, although it is difficult to winnow the wheat from the chaff of colonial rumour. James Stuart, for example, assistant magistrate in Durban, Zulu linguist and interlocutor of African oral tradition, regarded the AMEC as 'the harbinger of general revolution among the native population in South Africa . . . [with] its supreme and persistent ideal . . . nothing less than a reclamation and recovery not merely of South Africa but *Africa*.'[67] There, even American Board missionaries were regarded with suspicion by colonial authorities, whereas the colony's foremost African personality, the American-educated Reverend John Dube, by that time a newspaper editor and principal of the Ohlange Industrial School that he had founded, was regarded as 'a pronounced Ethiopian' who ought to be watched.[68]

Colonial fears were substantiated when, in February 1906, two white police officers were killed in a skirmish near Richmond by armed Africans who were members of Mzimba's Presbyterian Church of Africa. Local settler anxieties had been heightened by insecurities following on the South African War, and rumours that Dinuzulu, the son and heir of the last Zulu king, who had been allowed to return from exile in 1898 after Zululand had been handed over to Natal, was planning an uprising to reestablish the monarchy. Far more potent than Ethiopianism or the attempts by Dinuzulu to reassert royal authority, however, was the imposition of an ill-advised poll tax on an increasingly landless; impoverished and sorely pressed people; the overhasty declaration of martial law and aggressive colonial army action, which served to push angry and desperate men into rebellion.

Thus, the promulgation at the end of 1905 of a new one-pound poll tax on all unmarried males older than eighteen generated alarming reports that Africans were about to rebel and were 'doctoring' themselves for war. In many areas, Africans were killing their white animals and destroying tools of European manufacture, allegedly at the behest of Dinuzulu, in preparation for a widespread uprising. Magistrates attempting to collect the tax before it was legally enforceable met with defiance. Early in February 1906, martial

---

[66] Violet Markham, *The new era in South Africa* (London: Smith, Elder, 1904), p. 177.

[67] Stuart to SNA, Johannesburg, 22 June 1904, press copy of the paper 'The Ethiopian Movement', compiled and partly written by Stuart. Italics in original. Stuart Papers, Killie Campbell Library, Durban.

[68] Gov. to Sec State, 30 May 1906, CO 179/235/22645, cited in Marks, *Reluctant rebellion*, p. 74.

law was declared, and for several weeks the Natal militia marched through the colony, burning crops and kraals, looting cattle and deposing chiefs of communities reported to be defiant or restless. At the end of the following month, twelve of those involved in the Richmond affray with the police were executed.

These activities met with no opposition until the second week of April, when the recently deposed Chief Bhambatha of the amaZondi in the Weenen division kidnapped an uncle who had been appointed in his stead and then fired on the magistrate sent to investigate. Thereafter, Bhambatha fled into the mountainous Nkhandla forests on the southern boundary of Zululand, where he began to build up an army of resistance. In these forests, Bhambatha, joined by a number of prominent chiefs, conducted guerrilla warfare against colonial forces for nearly a month, making use of Dinuzulu's name and the royal war cry and war badge as his authority. As heir to the Zulu monarchy and interlocutor to the ancestors, Dinuzulu was the embodiment of their lost autonomy and fractured sense of unity. By early June, however, this resistance was ended when Natal militia slaughtered Bhambatha and many of his followers in the Mome Gorge.

This seemed to bring the uprising to an end, but a week later, resistance flared up again in the thickly populated Maphumulo District. Here, defiance of the poll tax had been followed by the humiliation and deposition of powerful chiefs, punitive raids and brutal floggings. An attack on a wagon convoy later in June brought out increasing numbers of white volunteers eager to enlist for action. Maphumulo impis were swiftly dispersed and run down by enlarged Natal Field Forces, and by mid-July all active resistance was over, although 'mopping up' operations continued and martial law was only lifted in September. Unrest continued to simmer through 1907. In the absence of a general amnesty, fugitives fled into Zululand and were rumoured to be about to start another rebellion. Trials of 'rebels', the breaking up and relocation of 'rebellious' 'tribes' and the replacement of their chiefs by unpopular collaborators perpetuated the turmoil and festering feuds in the territory. At the end of 1907, the government arrested Dinuzulu, an old suspect. Found guilty of high treason charges in 1908, after serving part of his Natal prison term, he died in exile in the Transvaal 1913.

The Bhambatha rebellion, or the *impi yamakhanda* (the war of the heads, that is, of the poll tax) as Africans described it, had much of the flavour of a self-fulfilling prophecy. It also had 'a profoundly religious character', as Africans turned to ritual to propitiate their ancestors and to invite supernatural intervention.[69] However one characterises it, the results were

---

[69] Jeff Guy, *The Maphumulo uprising: war, law and ritual in the Zulu Rebellion* (Scottsville: University of Natal Press, 2005), p. 5.

disastrous. Almost four thousand Africans were killed and tens of thousands rendered homeless; white casualties were trifling. In the aftermath of the rebellion, the pace of proletarianisation quickened as destitute people, driven from the land, were forced to seek employment on white farms, mines and industries. Fortuitously for the mine owners, it brought a new army of workers to the Rand as the Chinese departed.

For the African elite across South Africa, the implacable crushing of the rebellion confirmed those who had long advocated the pen against the sword. For them, the counterpart to the Bhambatha rebellion were the new political associations that emerged in the 1900s to struggle for African rights. Yet Natal's brutal suppression and the treatment of Dinuzulu also fuelled the radicalism of the political elite. This was in turn given further momentum by the growing political unification movement, itself at least in part a response to the uprising. Educated blacks throughout the region viewed these exclusionary deliberations with alarm, given that even the slender Cape voting right seemed to be under fire. Publication of the Selborne Memorandum galvanised both the South African Native Congress and the leading coloured organisation, the African Political (later People's) Organisation (APO), which had been founded in 1903, into setting out their demands. At its 1907 Queenstown conference, the SANC called for a federal constitution that would at least have enshrined the rights of Cape black voters, objected to the proposed colour bar in parliament and warned against the inclusion of the High Commission territories and protectorates in Union before Africans there had equal rights. Their first two demands were rejected by the convention discussing Union. If the third succeeded, it was because of imperial objectives rather than any responsiveness to local black views.

The SANC's Queenstown Conference was notable for the presence for the first time of representatives of the APO in joint black agitation in the run-up to Union. If that was unprecedented and equally unavailing, it was also explicable. Despite imperial promises, coloureds and Indians in the former Republics found their situation after the war no better than it had been before. Bitterly disappointed by the terms of the 1902 peace treaty, they quickly found that the British authorities, like their Boer predecessors, were determined to restore the discriminatory status quo ante.

Even in the Cape, coloureds found that there was no postwar new deal. If anything, for some, their situation deteriorated as authorities used the urban outbreak of bubonic plague as an excuse for removing the African population to a new location on the outskirts of town and imposed stringent control measures on even 'respectable' coloureds in the name of disease prevention. The creeping segregation of public institutions, especially schools, already evident in the 1880s and 1890s, was accelerated, and the plague outbreak intensified moves to segregate Africans residentially. At the same time, during the postwar depression that hit the Colony between 1903 and 1908, coloured artisans and semiskilled workers found themselves squeezed by the influx of Africans from below and their exclusion from white unions from above. This all 'provided a fertile field for political organisers'.[70]

For coloureds as for Africans, the advent of the Liberal government in Britain in 1905, the granting of responsible government to the Transvaal and Orange River Colony, and the thrust toward Union produced a spurt of political activity as organisations pushed for a more inclusive new dispensation. From 1905, Dr Abdullah Abdurahman, now leader of the APO, battled for the extension of the Cape franchise, exhausting 'every conceivable tactic', including joint action with African organisations. In 1909, publication of the draft constitution by the National Convention led to a historic black national convention in Bloemfontein. This assembly resolved on despatching a delegation to London to lay their constitutional objections before the British government and to form a new umbrella organisation. A delegation to Britain was the most concerted action ever, yet it proved no more successful than previous efforts, despite its inclusion not only of leading members of the South African Native Convention but also of W. P. Schreiner, former Cape Prime Minister, Abdurahman of the APO, and J. T. Jabavu on behalf of the Imbumba. Nevertheless, the initiatives drew educated Africans and coloureds together in a pan–South African endeavour and led directly to the formation in 1912 of the first national African nationalist organisation, the South African Native National Congress, later the African National Congress.

It may have been evidence of increased African and coloured unity that prompted Selborne to advocate recognition of the rights of 'respectable' coloured men on the eve of the 1908 national convention. As he wrote to Smuts:

It seems to me sheer folly to classify them with Natives, and by treating them as natives to force them away from their natural allegiance to the whites and into making common cause with the Natives. If they are so forced in the time of trouble they will furnish exactly those leaders which the Natives could not furnish themselves.[71]

However racialised, Selborne's view may in turn have stiffened liberals in their fight for special safeguards for the Cape's nonracial franchise, although it did not sway ruling politicians in the other colonies. Nor did it prevent

---

[70] Lewis, *Between the wire and the wall*, p. 17.
[71] Torrance, *The strange death of the Liberal empire*, p. 121.

Cape liberals from allowing the introduction of a parliamentary colour bar. Unsurprisingly, for APO and SANC leadership, the draft Act of Union was an act of betrayal by Cape National Convention delegates and by the imperial government, which was in the end prepared to sacrifice black rights to its overriding goal of a unified South Africa.

As Selborne's words suggest, coloureds were often ambivalent over their identity and identification, and there was certainly no unanimity within the APO over coloured-African cooperation. Abdurahman veered between defending purely coloured rights and playing a major role in common political protest action, even as his rivals, Peregrino and Tobin, had more inclusive definitions of coloured identity, stressing the need for coloured-African unity more consistently. Thus, in 1906, Abdurahman argued that clause 8 of the Vereeniging Treaty referred to Africans and not coloureds, declaring again in 1910 that the APO was a Coloured organisation, which should 'concentrate on the rights and duties of the Coloured people of SA, as distinguished from the native races'.[72] In a society in which rights and privilege depended increasingly on whiteness, the aspiration of all coloured organisations was for integration into white society, not its radical subversion. At the same time, as coloureds in the Cape experienced an intensification of segregation, a more radical APO rhetoric that rejected older patterns of hierarchy and deference was to attract an increasing number of members.

If an emerging common coloured identity was a defensive elite's response to growing discrimination, among both Transvaal and Natal Indians, these years saw the similar growth of a common sense of identity and a more assertive political purposefulness. In Natal, the emergence of a new generation of colonial-born Indians and their pressing tax and other grievances had led, by the middle of the decade, to the emergence of a new and more radical form of politics than that espoused by the merchant elite and the Natal Indian Congress (NIC); the latter which had seen most of its campaigns defeated before the end of the South African War. Indeed, in 1901, Gandhi returned to India, convinced that the NIC was dead.

By 1903, he was back in South Africa at the invitation of the Congress, which hoped that he would influence imperial policy in the newly annexed republics to address Indian disabilities, particularly given their loyal services to Britain's war effort. That, in turn, it was hoped, would improve the discriminatory situation in Natal. The early outlook was not hopeful. Before the end of the war, the British administration in the Transvaal had begun moving Indians into locations for both residential and trading purposes, thus enforcing republican legislation to which the imperial government had actually been opposed since the 1880s and advocating further

---

[72] Adhikari, *Not white enough*, p. 173.

restriction of Indian immigration into the Transvaal. Thus, in 1904, all Transvaal Indians had to be registered.

The approaching grant of responsible government further intensified Indian burdens. Given the kindergarten view that 'the white consensus against Indians [is]... a "national question upon which the Government, the Legislature, and the people are absolutely united... a glorious opportunity of getting everyone together"', the Colonial Office was persuaded to agree to proposals that existing businesses be protected in exchange for an immigration restriction act.[73] It was in the complex but ineffectual politics of compromise and constitutional protest in the Transvaal between 1903 and 1906 that Gandhi began to formulate his moral philosophy and techniques of nonviolent resistance.

The decisive catalyst, however, was the requirement that all Indians legally in the Transvaal be fingerprinted. The response was a meeting of three thousand Indians 'who rose to their feet to repeat... that they would go to jail rather than submit themselves to registration under the new ordinance'.[74] This was the beginning of a lengthy campaign that lasted until 1914, and led Gandhi into honing his political and moral philosophy of satyagraha, addressing a far wider set of issues and mobilising a far wider constituency than before.

Over the following three years, hundreds of Transvaal Indians resisted the registration law and were jailed, and thousands attended meetings and rallies. In the protests they were joined by some Chinese traders who, like the passenger Indians, had made their way to the Cape and Transvaal in the second half of the nineteenth century, and who for a brief moment also resisted 'the plethora of discriminatory acts introduced [against them] in the Transvaal'.[75] Gandhi himself became involved in direct confrontation with Smuts and was imprisoned three times. Although the British government disallowed the discriminatory legislation in 1906, with responsible government in the Transvaal the registration act was reintroduced by Smuts. Despite renewed protest, in the end, the movement failed, hampered by insufficient funding and internal disorganisation. By February 1909, almost all Transvaal Asians had been registered, and Gandhi's own authority was under question.

There were relatively few meeting points at this stage between Gandhi and the desperately impoverished indentured and ex-indentured Indian labourers of Natal or the poorer Indians of the Transvaal. Contact was equally slight with the young white-collar workers and professionals who

[73] Lavin, *Lionel Curtis*, p. 61, citing Curtis to Mrs Curtis, 28 April [1907], MSS Curtis 142.
[74] Swan, *Gandhi*, p. 120.
[75] Karen L Harris, 'A history of the Chinese in South Africa to 1912', unpublished Ph.D. thesis, University of South Africa (1998), p. xxi.

formed the Natal Indian Patriotic Union in 1907 to address the grievances of the Indian underclasses: the indentured labour system, the burdensome tax on ex-indentured workers and their families, the barriers to civil service occupations, and the Dealers' Licences Act. Although their political movement was again short lived, sabotaged by Hindu revivalism, their demands were to reemerge after Union in the Colonial Born Indian Association, the passive resistance campaign and the wildfire strikes of 1913–1914. Importantly, too, this was the first time that colonial-born Indians asserted their rights as South African Indians. As the vice president Lazarus Gabriel put it in September 1908:

I am proud to stand before this audience, and to own that I am a descendant of an immigrant Indian who shed his life blood for the welfare of this Colony – we have made this our home, and as Colonial Born Indians we have an inherent right to remain in this Colony and enjoy all the rights and privileges of a properly constituted British Colonist.[76]

If during these years there was little in common between the Natal Indian Congress or the British Indian Association and the mass of Indians, this was no less true of the relationship between the African Political Organisation and the coloured proletariat, or that between the native congresses and vigilance associations and the majority of African peasants and workers. For that matter, too, links among African, Indian and coloured leaders were mostly equally tenuous and ephemeral. Nevertheless, as they found their efforts at incorporation rejected, middle-class leaders were on occasion radicalised and driven to speak on behalf of all blacks, if only to increase their claim on their constituency and credibility. Yet the racial hierarchy of the colonial order both encouraged and ensured division as Indians and coloureds and the African elite sought equal citizenship as 'civilised' men but found themselves equally firmly excluded. There were liberal voices like those of Schreiner and even Hofmeyr in the Cape, Harriette Colenso in Natal and the socialist Keir Hardie in Britain who warned against the colour bar at the time of Union. But their voices went unheard. South Africa's twentieth-century history would be dominated in large measure by that failure.

FURTHER READING

Adhikari, Mohamed, *Not white enough, not black enough: racial identity in the South African coloured community*, Athens: Ohio University Press; Cape Town: Double Storey, 2005

[76] Cited in Swan, *Gandhi*, p. 197, from the *African Chronicle*, 12 September 1908.

Boyce, D. George (ed.), *The crisis of British power: the imperial and naval papers of the second Earl of Selborne, 1895–1910*, London: Historians' Press, 1990

Bradford, Helen, 'Regendering Afrikanerdom: Afrikanerdom: the 1899–1902 Anglo-Boer War', in Blom, Hagerman and Hall (eds.), *Gendered nations*, pp. 207–25

Brown, Karen, 'Progressivism, agriculture and conservation in the Cape Colony, c. 1902–1908', unpublished Ph.D. thesis, Oxford University (2002)

Burke, Gillian and Peter Richardson, 'The profits of death: a comparative study of miners' phthisis in Cornwall and the Transvaal, 1876–1918', *Journal of Southern African Studies* 4:2 (April 1978), 147–71

Cammack, Diana, *The Rand at war, 1899–1902: the Witwatersrand and the Anglo-Boer War*, London: James Currey; Berkeley: University of California Press; Pietermaritzburg: University of Natal Press, 1990

Campbell, James T., *Songs of Zion: the AMEC in the USA and South Africa*, New York: Oxford University Press, 1995

Comaroff, Jean, *Body of power, spirit of resistance: the culture and history of a South African people*, Chicago: University of Chicago Press, 1985

Comaroff, Jean and John Comaroff (eds.), *Modernity and its malcontents: ritual and power in postcolonial Africa*, Chicago: University of Chicago Press, 1993

Cuthbertson, Greg, Albert Grundlingh and Mary-Lynn Suttie (eds.), *Writing a wider war: rethinking gender, race, and identity in the South African War, 1899–1902*, Athens: Ohio University Press; Cape Town: David Philip, 2002

Denoon, Donald, *A grand illusion: the failure of imperial policy in the Transvaal Colony during the period of reconstruction, 1900–1905*, Harlow, U.K.: Longman, 1973

Dubow, Saul, 'Colonial nationalism, the Milner Kindergarten and the rise of "South Africanism", 1902–1910', *History Workshop Journal* 43 (1997), 53–86

Duminy A. H. and W. R. Guest (eds.), *Fitzpatrick: South African politician – selected papers, 1888–1906*, Johannesburg: McGraw-Hill, 1976

Du Toit, Marijke, '"Dangerous motherhood": *maternity care and engendered construction of Afrikaner identity, 1904–1939*' in Fildes, Marks and Marland (eds.), *Women and children first*, pp. 203–29

Du Toit, Marijke, 'The domesticity of Afrikaner nationalism: *Volksmoeders* and the ACVV, 1904–1929', *Journal of Southern African Studies* 29:1 (March 2003), 155–76

Fraser, Maryna and Alan Jeeves (eds.), *All that glittered: selected correspondence of Lionel Phillips, 1890–1924*, Cape Town: Oxford University Press, 1977

Giliomee, Hermann, *The Afrikaners: biography of a people*, London: Hurst and Company, 2003

Gordon, C. T., *The growth of Boer opposition to Kruger, 1890–1895*, Cape Town: Oxford University Press, 1970

Grundlingh, A. M., *Die 'Hensoppers' en 'Joiners': die rasional en verskinsel van verraad*, Pretoria: HAUM, 1979

Guy, Jeff, *The Maphumulo uprising: war, law and ritual in the Zulu Rebellion*, Scottsville: University of Natal Press, 2005

Hancock, W. K., *Smuts*, vol. 1, *The sanguine years, 1870–1919*, Cambridge: Cambridge University Press, 1968

Hancock W. K. and Jean Van Der Poel (eds.), *Selections from the Smuts Papers*, vol. 2, *June 1902-May 1910*, Cambridge: Cambridge University Press, 1966

Harris, Karen L., 'A history of the Chinese in South Africa to 1912', unpublished PhD thesis, University of South Africa (1998)

Headlam, Cecil (ed.), *Milner papers (South Africa)*, vol. 2, *1899–1905*, London: Cassell, 1933

Hofmeyr, Isabel, *'We spend our years as a tale that is told': oral historical narrative in a South African chiefdom*, Portsmouth, NH: Heinemann; Johannesburg: Witwatersrand University Press; London: James Currey, 1994

Hofmeyr, J. H., in collaboration with F. W. Reitz, *The life of Jan Hendrik Hofmeyr (Onze Jan)*, Cape Town: van de Sandt de Villiers, 1913

Hyslop, Jonathan, 'The imperial working class makes itself "White": white labourism in Britain, Australia and SA before the First World War', *Journal of Historical Sociology* 12:4 (December 1999), 398–421

Jeeves, A. H., *Migrant labour in South Africa's mining economy: the struggle for the gold mines' labour supply, 1890–1920*, Kingston, Ontario: McGill-Queen's University Press; Johannesburg: Witwatersrand University Press, 1985

Katz, Elaine, *A trade union aristocracy: a history of white workers in the Transvaal and the General Strike of 1913*, Johannesburg: African Studies Institute, 1976

Katz, Elaine, *The white death: silicosis on the Witwatersrand gold mines, 1886–1910*, Johannesburg: Witwatersrand University Press, 1994

Krikler, Jeremy, *Revolution from above, rebellion from below: the agrarian Transvaal at the turn of the century*, Oxford: Clarendon University Press, 1993

La Hausse de Lalouvière, Paul, *Restless identities: signatures of nationalism, Zulu ethnicity and history in the lives of Petros Lamula (c. 1881–1948) and Lymon Maling (1889–c.1936)*, Pietermaritzburg: Natal University Press, 2000

Landman, C., *The piety of Afrikaner women*, Pretoria: Unisa Press, 1994

Lavin, Deborah, *From empire to international commonwealth: a biography of Lionel Curtis*, New York: Clarendon Press, 1995

Lewis, Gavin, *Between the wire and the wall: a history of South African 'Coloured' politics*, Cape Town: David Philip, 1987

Lewsen, Phyllis, *John X. Merriman: paradoxical South African statesman*, New Haven, CT: Yale University Press, 1982

Lewsen, Phyllis (ed.), *Selections from the correspondence of Merriman papers*. Vols. 3 and 4, *1899–1905* and *1905–1924*, Cape Town: Van Riebeeck Society, 1966 and 1969

Lowry, Donal (ed.), *The South African War reappraised*, Manchester, U.K.: Manchester University Press; New York: St Martin's Press, 2000

Markham, Violet, *The new era in South Africa: with an examination of the Chinese labour question*, London: Smith Elder, 1904

Marks, Shula, *Reluctant rebellion: the 1906–8 disturbances in Natal*, Oxford: Clarendon Press, 1970

Marks, Shula and Richard Rathbone (eds.), *Industrialisation and social change in South Africa*, London: Longmans, 1982

Marks, Shula and Stanley Trapido, 'Lord Milner and the South African state', *History Workshop*, 8 (Autumn 1979), 50–80

Marks, Shula and Stanley Trapido (eds.), *The politics of race, class and nationalism*, Harlow, U.K.: Longman, 1987

Mokoena, Hlonipha, 'The making of a *kholwa* intellectual: a discursive biography of Magema Magwaza Fuze', unpublished D.Phil. thesis, University of Cape Town (2005)

Moodie, T. Dunbar, *The rise of Afrikanerdom: power, apartheid and the Afrikaner civil religion*, Berkeley: University of California Press, 1975

Morrell, Robert (ed.), *White but poor: essays on the history of poor whites in southern Africa, 1880–1940*, Pretoria: University of South Africa, 1992

Nasson, Bill, *Abraham Esau's War: a black South African war in the Cape, 1899–1902*, Cambridge: Cambridge University Press, 1991

Nasson, Bill, *The South African War, 1899–1910*, London: Arnold, 1999

Newton, A. P. (ed.), *Select documents relating to the unification of South Africa*, vol. 2, London: Longmans, Green, 1968

Odendaal, Andre, *Vukani Bantu! The beginnings of black protest politics in South Africa to 1912*, Cape Town: David Philip, 1984

Omissi, D. and A. Thompson (eds.), *The impact of the South African War*, Basingstoke, U.K.: Palgrave Macmillan, 2002

Packard, Randall M., *White plague, black labor: tuberculosis and the political economy of health and disease in South Africa*, Berkeley: University of California Press, 1989

Pauw, S., *Beroepsarbeid van die Afrikaner in die stad*, Stellenbosch: Pro Ecclesia, 1946

Steyn, J. C., *Tuiste in eie taal: die behoud en bestaan van Afrikaans*, Cape Town, Tafelberg, 1980

Swan, Maureen, *Gandhi: the South African experience*, Johannesburg: Ravan Press, 1985

Thompson, Leonard M., *The unification of South Africa*, Oxford: Clarendon Press, 1960

Torrance, David R., *The strange death of the Liberal empire: Lord Selborne in South Africa*, Liverpool: University of Liverpool Press; Montreal: McGill University Press, 1996

Van Onselen, Charles, *Studies in the social and economic history of the Witwatersrand*, vol. 2, *New Nineveh*, Johannesburg: Ravan Press, 1982

Van Rensburg, Thariza (ed.), *Camp diary of Henrietta Armstrong: experiences of a Boer nurse in the Irene Concentration Camp, 6 April–11 October 1901*, Pretoria: Human Sciences Research Council, 1980

Walker, Cherryl, *Women and gender in southern Africa to 1945*, Cape Town: David Philip; London: James Currey, 1990

Walton, E. H., *The inner history of the National Convention of South Africa*, Cape Town: Maskew Miller, 1912; Westport, CT: Negro Universities Press, 1970

Warwick, Peter (ed.), *The South African War: the Anglo-Boer War, 1899–1902*, Harlow, U.K.: Longmans, 1980

5

SOUTH AFRICA: THE UNION YEARS, 1910–1948 – POLITICAL AND ECONOMIC FOUNDATIONS

BILL FREUND

INTRODUCTION

The Union of South Africa came into being with the opening of Parliament in November 1910, following a lengthy period of negotiation between the four self-governing British colonies in southern Africa. The Union closely resembled an independent country, and it would evolve, as would the other British dominions, further in that direction. This chapter considers that what ensued after 1910 was an attempt, an attempt that ultimately failed, to establish a hegemonic order in South Africa. By *hegemony*, what is meant is not merely dominance, not merely state control, but pervasive and internalised dominance that flows through nationally based and structured institutions and civil society. In other words, the goal was the construction of a society based on shared assumptions and mediated conflicts contained in a legal and political order that could endure.

Several major factors threatened this dominance from the outset. The economic development of southern Africa in the previous generation had been explosive but also extremely uneven. The potential for a prosperous growing Union of South Africa rested on the great gold resources of the Witwatersrand that had been exploited over a generation, but the gold mines both made massive organisational and economic requirements of other sectors of the economy and stood in stark contrast to what had in general been a slow-growing and impoverished section of the world. In 1910, urban infrastructure was limited, agriculture was generally technologically backward and unproductive and secondary industry was only at a modest level of development. How could one harness mineral wealth to build a more generalised prosperity? One challenge the Union faced was the establishment of a regulated system for capitalist development that would integrate a regional economy and give a boost to some of its many backward sectors. Over the period covered, there was hesitant but growing confidence in the ability of the national state to play this regulatory role.

A peculiar feature of the Union was its failure to integrate politically what economic geographers would certainly already have considered the natural socioeconomic terrain on which it stood. The British continued to administer the three High Commission Territories of Basutoland (entirely surrounded by the Union), Swaziland (surrounded by the Union apart from a border with Mozambique) and Bechuanaland. The natural port for the Witwatersrand, Lourenço Marques (now Maputo), remained part of the oddly shaped Portuguese colony of Mozambique. North of the Limpopo, the British colony of Southern Rhodesia, administered by the British South Africa Company, determined to remain separate from South Africa in a plebiscite in 1922 when the company charter ran out. South Africa tried to annex German South-West Africa directly after conquest in 1915, but it had to administer the territory in trust for the League of Nations after the conclusion of the First World War and was never able to incorporate what later become the republic of Namibia either. Therefore, a changing system of interrelationships had to be devised to deal with South Africa's weaker and economically dependent neighbours in the region.

At the time of Union, South African capitalism was also seriously threatened from below by militant white workers. The core of these workers were British immigrants, often single, male itinerants attracted to the Rand and to other South African cities by high wages but confronting high expenses, the vagaries of the industry, murderous work conditions and the threat of likely death from miners' phthisis. The confrontation between workers and bosses would intensify to reach its climax with the Rand Revolt of 1922.

Simultaneously, the creation of a social and political order in South Africa depended on regulating relations between the long-established white population speaking the Afrikaans language and the growing immigrant white population. The South African War had crushed the national aspirations of the Boer republics, but defeat had only intensified the spread of Afrikaner national feeling with the goal of dominance throughout the territories of the new Union. In several key respects, this conflict of Boer versus Briton had also a strong class dimension. The so-called poor-white problem derived from the increasing proletarianisation of Boers unable to make a living on the land, a phenomenon that began to be noticeable before the South African War but that grew enormously in the years before and after Union. Many unskilled Afrikaner men themselves became miners, and the Rand Revolt had reverberations from their militant traditions as much or more as from trade unionism or socialist ideas. Struggle gave way increasingly to a policy of institutional and social incorporation of a white working class that was becoming predominantly Afrikaner. In 1910, Afrikaners were only a slight majority among adult male voters in South Africa, but the Afrikaner majority would gradually rise through this period. The rise of an Afrikaner capitalist class, gradually more integrated into a national business elite, would also be a significant process that parallelled changes in the relation of the white working class to the state. This combination of class and ethnicity in the white South African population would have seemed like the big political issue to the men who forged the Union in 1910 and their successors throughout the period. For there was close to unanimity among them that the white race deserved to rule South Africa, that hegemony was about white dominance, 'a white man's country'. This racial mind-set had powerful international underpinnings and was especially resonant with the values of other British settler societies, for instance Australia and the United States, moderated as it might be in colonies where white settlers were only a small minority of the population. The Union of South Africa occupied, in demographic terms, an intermediate position. It had a very substantial white population, but the large majority of its residents were blacks, the descendants of the conquered people of southern Africa. Indeed, the immigrant Indians and their descendants, together with the coloured population of heterogeneous origins, themselves constituted very large minorities, further problematising the racial assumptions of the Union founding fathers. So long as the British imperium held sway, some effort to balance white supremacy with incorporation of individuals into a colour-blind society had been part of the political weave in its southern African colonies, but after 1910, there was a consistent movement toward creating a political and social order systematically based on racial segregation. *Segregation* was copied as a term largely from the United States, where the Southern states enshrined it, but it took on its own dimensions as an ideology in the South African context. A key element was the persistence of native locations on the land, territories where black Africans were to be administered according to their own customs by their own chiefs in such a way as to harmonise with the needs of the white masters of the country, who would themselves operate in the confines of a democratic, elected government. This system of bifurcated sovereignty, as Mahmood Mamdani has termed it, was more of a model for other African colonies than a mere American-style system of separate racial institutions.[1] The evolution after 1910 of a system 'for administering the Natives' by white South Africans is probably the best-studied and analysed aspect of the available scholarly literature on this period.

The black majority, and indeed the coloured and Indian minorities as well, did not simply settle for the gradual tying up of their hopes and aspirations into this larger system of control imposed on them. There was

---

[1] Mahmood Mamdani, *Citizen and subject: contemporary Africa and the late colonialism* (Kampala: Fountain, David Philip and James Currey, 1996), pt. 1.

little opportunity for revolt or revolution. However, during the Union period, phases of considerable militancy took place, with urban and rural resistance to state action. This sometimes played a role not in changing the course of state policy but in making aspects of that policy ineffective. It also greatly enhanced the possibility of political organisation to people of colour. During this period, organisation remained sporadic and halting.

A POLITICAL OVERVIEW

During the thirty-eight years covered by this chapter, only three prime ministers headed the government of the Union, and all three were veteran generals of the South African War. The first, General Louis Botha, came from the part of northern Natal that had previously belonged to the Zuid-Afrikaansche Republiek (ZAR). He died less than a decade into the Union in August 1919, being replaced by Jan Christiaan Smuts, a native of the Cape, who had become State Attorney in the ZAR under Kruger after studying law in Britain. Smuts was the most many-sided and significant political figure in the world of white politics through this period; he spent much of the First World War years in Britain as part of the British war cabinet.

Initially, after the creation of the Union, the South African Party ruled with virtually no opposition. However, there were important breakaways in the form of the proimperial Unionist Party in 1912 and the Afrikaner-led National Party in 1913. In the cities, many English-speaking men supported the Labour Party, which had never been incorporated into the Botha-Smuts government. The most formidable antagonist to the ruling party was the National Party, and its dominant figure was the Free Stater James Barrie Munnik Hertzog. Although partly of British extraction, Hertzog was already known as a committed nationalist with a stronger position than Botha or Smuts. And more intense nationalist feeling yet bubbled under the surface. In 1914, inspired by the possibility of a German alliance, still other nationalist figures with a South African War past, notably Generals Jacobus de la Rey and Christiaan Beyers, mounted resistance to the impending attack on the Germans in South-West Africa in the so-called Rebellie. This was successfully repressed by state force with the last rebels surrendering early in 1915.

Intense labour conflicts marked the prewar and postwar years and helped to weaken the government. In 1920, Smuts was barely reelected with the support of the Unionist Party. He succeeded in incorporating the Unionists into a South African Party under his leadership and, in 1921, secured a more stable majority. In 1924, he was defeated and replaced by a coalition of the

Nationalist and Labour parties headed by Hertzog. Hertzog's reputation has survived far less well than that of Smuts. He was in phases a very skilful politician, but his inconsistencies and pettiness have lived on in memory. Nevertheless, he was prime minister for a slightly longer period of time than both of Smuts's terms put together.

The 1924 government is generally known as the Pact government. It was really the large gains by the National Party that had marked its entry into power, although Labour was a significant junior partner, particularly in the early years. Certainly, it represented those whites who felt excluded or marginalised by the Smuts regime. In general, common wisdom is that the Pact was anxious to distance itself from Britain, more committed to the construction of a national economy, more sympathetic to the promotion of culture associated with the Afrikaans language and harsher on South Africans of colour. The 1929 election certainly was remembered as the *swart gevaar* (black threat) election because of the extent to which the National Party rounded on the opposition as soft on concessions to blacks. In this election, Labour ceased to be a major factor, and the National Party won an outright majority of the votes.

However, with the onset of the Great Depression, the popularity of the government fell. Losing a key by-election in the Rand constituency of Germiston in 1932, its days were numbered. Political manoeuvres focussed on dumping the gold standard to which the South African pound was tied, with a key government politician, Tielman Roos, as the main actor. In the end, Smuts agreed to form a coalition government with Hertzog, who remained prime minister until 1939. The old National Party and the South African Party came together to form the United Party. However, just as in the first years of the Union, the stronger British and Afrikaner minded did not long stay in the fold. Although Smuts was always able to prevail largely against the Dominion Party (and Labour henceforth remained fairly limited in its appeal), a more dangerous (in the long term) opponent appeared in the form of Daniel François Malan's Purified National Party, which regrouped, mainly in the Cape at first, in 1934. Yet the ministry, presiding over an unprecedented period of prosperity, was fairly easily returned to power in 1938. The Fusion government of Hertzog and Smuts is of at least as much importance as a shaper of politics and creator of institutions as its predecessor, the Pact. It came to an end as a result of the outbreak of the Second World War. Hertzog was opposed to supporting the British position, preferring neutrality vis-à-vis Nazi Germany, and a split with Smuts led to Smuts's formation of the new government. The Governor-General refused to call, as Hertzog asked, for a new election, and thus South Africa entered the war as a British ally.

Smuts was again prime minister between 1939 and 1948, a period that covered the tumultuous Second World War years. There was massive hostility to the regime by Afrikaner nationalists attracted to radical solutions in the uncertain international environment; however, there was no repetition of the 1914 rebellion. This period is perhaps the hardest to characterise, marked as it was by a mixture of conservatism and reform. At times the government appeared to consider going beyond the boundaries of the main lines that had been followed for a generation by South African politics on race, but that appearance was probably more deceptive than real. Together with the Fusion period, it marked a very important phase in terms of the industrialisation of South Africa and the creation of critical national institutions. Certainly, Smuts had increasingly to consider that the black majority and its representatives were deeply discontented with the settlement that whites had imposed on them in the legislation of the day and were finding a broad range of fronts on which resistance became manifest.

As we will also see, with Hertzog out of the government, a very complex reshuffling of the deck was set up in Afrikaner nationalist politics. The 1943 election, the so-called Khaki Election, was a last resounding victory for Smuts but, in the Nationalist camp, Malan was clearly the dominant figure. After the war, the National Party improved its position in by-elections. Nonetheless, most commentators were astonished when, despite a United Party popular majority, Malan won a sufficient number of parliamentary seats so as to be able to form a government in alliance with the small Afrikaner Party in May 1948. The constitution weighted rural seats heavily, and the United Party vote was overwhelmingly concentrated in the cities. Intense as were the party political conflicts of the time, it is probably fairly clear from this outline that there was much continuity through the period. Leadership overlapped and issues emerged in repetitive debates, leading to the formulation of policies that either had very wide support or were disputed intensely in the detail. The assumptions underlying white dominance and segregation were never shaken in official circles.

MATERIAL FACTORS

The most remarkable fact at the onset of this period about material conditions in the new Union of South Africa was their extreme unevenness. In the previous generation, the gold-mining industry of the Witwatersrand had risen from nothing to become the world's major source of gold. The implications for South Africa could not have been greater. Johannesburg became within a generation the largest city in the southern half of the continent, not merely in the country. A large transport infrastructure, based on the rail network, was created and largely in place by 1910.

South Africa attracted regional migrants on a massive scale to work in the mines and other economic activities indirectly brought into motion while international immigrants on an unprecedented scale arrived from Europe and elsewhere. There were some two hundred thousand workers in the gold-mining industry by 1910. Technologically, mining was certainly the most advanced sector of the economy. However, perhaps its key feature lay in its dependence on unfree forms of labour. These forms were more systematised and applied to other sectors of the economy during this period to an unprecedented extent, replacing older forms less appropriate to an industrial era.

However, at the same time, other sectors of the economy were in great contrast with mining. Agriculture remained very backward by comparison, although certain modern sectors began to emerge. Industry, as we will see, grew very quickly but from extremely modest beginnings. Attacking the problem of unevenness and creating a national economy that was more balanced was the obvious task of the new state. Its success before 1948 was considerable but far from complete. This section introduces the reader to general conditions unfolding through the period.

A survey of economic conditions must start with the population itself. The census of 1911 estimated its numbers at 5,972,757. By 1946, that figure had nearly doubled to 11,415,925. The racial percentages in the population altered very little during this period. Whites continued throughout to number approximately 21 per cent of the total. It was estimated that less than 10 per cent of the white population increase was due to immigration.[2] There were fewer foreign-born whites in South Africa in 1946 than in 1911, although the number of migrants thereafter and before 1948 grew very fast. Immigration from India was virtually cut off at the start of this period; whether the figures are accurate for African migration, substantial but again not the main source of population increase, must be uncertain.

In one important sense, the population did change considerably: it became very much more urban. Table 1 shows figures for the population of the Witwatersrand cities, including Johannesburg, in 1921 and 1951 together with the five largest urban populations elsewhere.

Thus, this total rose from 18 per cent to 30 per cent over thirty years. By 1951, in fact, the census would estimate the urban population as more than 40 per cent of the total. Whites had been tabulated as just beyond the 50 per cent mark at the onset of Union and well more than 75 per cent by 1951. However, the black population in the same years had also increased its urban

[2] J. C. du Plessis, *Economic fluctuations in South Africa, 1910–49* (Stellenbosch: Bureau for Economic Research, University of Stellenbosch, 1950), p. 36.

TABLE 1. *Urban population*

	1921	1951
1. Witwatersrand	537,707	1,670,242
2. Cape Town	220,562	547,648
3. Durban	168,743	479,974
4. Pretoria	74,347	285,379
5. Port Elizabeth	52,753	188,957
Total	1,054,112	3,172,200

percentage from 12.6 per cent to 27.2 per cent between 1911 and 1951, and the Indian and coloured minorities had become predominantly urban. Where the urban black population had once consisted of long-established urban communities together with large new groups of black men hired as miners and resident in compounds, the number of black women in towns rose markedly and many miners used their growing knowledge of the labour market to shift to other types of urban employment. This was a very significant shift and one that worked to the benefit of the Transvaal. The Cape Province especially bore less demographic weight in the Union by 1948 than in 1911.

If diamond mining continued to have an importance (and a diamond rush attracting farmers and poor whites especially to the southwestern Transvaal was a feature of the 1920s) and new mining enterprises in minerals such as coal were of local significance, throughout this period, gold mining remained of overwhelming importance in terms of employment, investment and earnings. Nonetheless, it would be a mistake to see this as simply a history of continuity. The great discoveries of the years after 1886 on the central and eastern Rand were beginning to be less profitable and require far more labour per yield by the time of Union, and this continued to be the case thereafter. Cost constraints were a major factor in the pressure that the mining industry put on labour to adjust to lower numbers of highly paid white workers, pressure that engendered intense industrial conflict as we will see, in the first dozen years of Union. As a result of these struggles, however, the industry was able to secure a more disciplined and controlled labour force, divided as capitalists generally desired between white and black. At their nadir after 1920, half the gold-mining companies in South Africa were losing money. After the defeat of the Rand Revolt in 1922, the mines were able to resume production on a far more profitable basis. The size of the white labour force was reduced, and especially the number of less skilled whites working underground. The technical innovation of the jackhammer drill was critical in enabling the reordering of underground production. Simultaneously, black wages were reduced, the recruiting system made more economical and many aspects of the controls system improved. Nonetheless, the development of gold mining was constrained in the 1920s by the fixed price of gold, which limited profits considerably, if providing stability in the economy.

The 1920s were a period of moderate economic growth that ended with the onset of the Great Depression in 1929. Much of the natural resource–based economy of South Africa went into a nose dive, with drastic falls in prices for the second and third biggest exports, wool and diamonds. Industrial production fell considerably. Gold mining, however, continued to be profitable, moderating the impact of the Depression. Nonetheless a key date in the history of the gold mines was 1933, when the South African state authorised the South African pound to float independent of the value of gold, which as a result rose by more than 50 per cent over the currency; by this time it had become a demand of the Chamber of Mines itself. This essentially brought about boom-time conditions that lifted South Africa out of the Depression quickly and dramatically. It made possible the exploitation of the far eastern and then the far western Rand, which had already been the source of 80 per cent of industry profits and 85 per cent of dividends by 1929. The key firm that developed this area was Anglo American, formed in 1917, and its presiding genius, a German Jewish immigrant named Ernest Oppenheimer (died 1957). Although both Anglicised and an Anglophile, Oppenheimer was noticeably more rooted in South Africa and the South African economy than his Randlord predecessors. With his successful interventions in the diamond industry through the gradual purchase of De Beers following the bargain purchase of seized German assets after the First World War, and the creation of something like a world diamond monopoly, this orientation to South Africa and the emergence of a business giant based in the country were cemented (despite the continued necessity to raise capital overseas, supplementing the diamond industry in this regard). Oppenheimer's Anglo American would also prove the driving force in the opening of new goldfields discovered on the eve of the Second World War in the northern Orange Free State. Their technically difficult opening after the war would bring in a new era of gold-mining wealth in South Africa starting from the very end of this period. On the eve of the Second World War, the black labour force in gold mining topped four hundred thousand, although it was to decline in the 1940s again.

Hungry as the mines were for labour, by the late 1930s, they were again hiring unprecedented numbers of whites in supervisory and skilled jobs. From 1932, they had secured permission to establish recruiting for 'tropicals', workers from north of the $22°$ south latitude who had been seen as potential lung disease sufferers from the conditions of the Witwatersrand

and excluded in 1913. Malawi (then known as Nyasaland Protectorate) and Mozambique became more important in the 1940s especially, and the Eastern Cape somewhat less important, as sources of mine labour, and the overall number of mine workers grew to new record numbers. Control was a factor as important as numbers. The 1920s were the golden age of black miners finding their own way to the mines. This allowed for more independence perhaps for some workers, but it also represented the power of the labour touts active especially on the frontiers of South Africa. In the 1930s, this tended to give way to structured recruitment with its purposeful withholding of wages until the end of contracts, rewards for colonial governments that favoured the Witwatersrand Native Labour Association (WNLA) recruitment network and so on. Throughout, the mine managers learned to perfect their capacity to control, military style, tens of thousands of male workers of whom only the small white minority were unionised. These lessons were adapted, moreover, by employers in other sectors of the economy.

If mining was the dynamic sector of the South African economy throughout this period, agriculture was the poor relation. The great majority of rural South Africans were African peasants whose access to land was structured in accordance with the modified traditional system that prevailed on the rural 'locations' of South Africa. Far from seeking to raise their productivity, the South African state actively sought to restrict their opportunities by virtue of the view that they 'competed' with white farmers. They did in fact do so in the sense that white farmers depended on specific, dependent and usually very exploitative relationships with black tenants on their own land. They needed a black tenantry that was extremely dependent, lacking in independent resources and with only a minimum of autonomy so as to allow for flexibility. In 1913, the most important piece of early Union legislation, the Land Act, tried to block black sharecropping on white farms to benefit those whites who wanted a more vulnerable labour force. The act also made it impossible for blacks to continue purchasing land in areas designated for white ownership as they had been doing, particularly in Natal and parts of the Transvaal. Although scheduled to grow somewhat with the release of state land, less than 7 per cent of the countryside was designated for black ownership.

There was pressure, notably from the mining industry, to preserve this land, so as to block the formation of a black proletariat and force many young men to work for the mines while enabling them to return to the land for periods of rest as well, as when they were too old to work. At the same time, a section of white farmers were very anxious to see this labour directed their way and preserved from large employers with whom they could not compete. These struggles, which were waged throughout the period and bore both on the history of 'Native legislation' and on the actual cut and thrust of politics in South Africa, represented a low road for South African agriculture that could at most benefit the poorest and least efficient of employers. According to the most serious student of agricultural production in the African Reserves, Charles Simkins, the overall picture was one of stagnation. By 1910, the dependence on migrant labour for obtaining cash was already heavy. He suggests that self-sufficiency in food averaged no more than 45 per cent for households. This figure did not really systematically increase or decrease until after 1948. By 1936, 54 per cent of the population was 'absent' from the reserves, presumably largely earning a living on the mines, in towns and elsewhere.

Through most of this period, the economic weaknesses of 'white' agriculture were manifest and multifold. In 1910, the major agricultural exports were ostrich feathers and the old Cape staple of wool, mostly products of the drier parts of the country and employing relatively few workers. By the 1920s, the feather market had collapsed and wool was in the doldrums. Agriculture grew as a sector only after the mining-led recovery from 1933. It did so led by the activities of specialised farmers in various sectors that began to become more significant. A relatively large amount of attention has gone to the potato farmers of the South-Central Transvaal. These capitalists were uninterested in the strictures and demands of the smaller farmers. They used large armies of recruited labour not unlike the mines, were quick to employ foreigners from the poor surrounding territories to the Union and later experimented on a significant scale with state-supplied prison labour. To some extent, contracts to supply mine workers were a major stimulus for the bigger farmers. A marker of the advance of capitalist agriculture and its links with industry was tractorisation. Tractors increased in number from 231 in 1918 to 20,292 in 1946.

By contrast with agriculture, manufacturing grew very rapidly almost throughout the period, although the big period of growth was once again in the boom years of the middle and late 1930s and then the phase of the Second World War and after. It was growth from very small beginnings, with the First World War representing a significant fillip. There were essentially two sources of industrial growth in this early phase. First were the direct needs of the mining industry, which would itself generate a need, for example, for chemical products as well as major energy resources. The second lay in the actual consumer demand of the rapidly increasing urban population, which had depended almost entirely on imports. On this basis, for instance, a small garment industry using imported raw materials took off around the time of the First World War. From the Rand, it later spread, largely to take advantage of cheaper labour, to Durban and Cape Town. The textile industry was slower to develop. It began with the insight by

TABLE 2. *Industrial growth*

	Number of factories	Worth of machinery	Number of workers	Worth of output
1915–1916	3,638	8,413	88,844	35,699
1929–1930	6,472	17,010	141,616	78,425
1938–1939	8,614	26,103	236,123	140,587
1948–1949	12,060	88,801	473,873	531,195

Note: Sums in this table measured in thousands of pounds.

blanket salesmen that blankets could perhaps be manufactured locally with South African wool or cotton. In fact, although local raw materials never became important in the industry, a blanket manufacture did take off in the interwar years. Food processing was the other obvious possibility for local manufacturers to take up. The industries began to receive more attention from the state from the time of the First World War, and especially during and after the Pact period, but this factor, which undoubtedly played a very large part in further developing and integrating South African industry, is considered separately in the final part of this chapter. Industry proved a meagre source of export income for South Africa, although what it did export found markets in southern and central Africa, but it was significant as a magnet for investment and impressive as a source of employment. The state's dream that industry could in particular provide good jobs for white men would only partly come true. Whites formed only about 40 per cent of the industrial workforce in the first census of 1915–1916. Thirty years later, however, they still provided almost one-third of the much larger total number of workers. Only gradually, moreover, did manufacturers begin to conceptualise their market as the whole national population (Table 2). In the 1940s, the growing value of production in terms of output and capital investment became far more marked.

Some final comments need to be made on the continued colonial nature of the South African economy. In the 1920s, Britain supplied South Africa with more than 50 per cent of its imports.[3] Despite some diversification, the major purchaser of South African goods and the major source of its imports remained Britain, which continued to have an enormous influence on the South African economy. The two dominant private banks, Standard and Barclays (which had absorbed the National Bank of South Africa in 1926), were closely linked to London finance. As late as 1948, they controlled 93.4 per cent of the demand deposits and 86.7 per cent of loans and discounts

[3] Russell Ally, *Gold and empire: the Bank of England and South Africa's gold producers* (Johannesburg: Witwatersrand University Press, 1994), p. 71.

TABLE 3. *Economic sectors*

	Agriculture	Mining	Industry
1912	£23 1m	£36 0m	£8 9m
1920	£51 0	£51 9	£26 0
1928	£53 0	£50 3	£35 8
1933	£30 6	£56 4	£32 0
1939	£50 8	£81 5	£69 7
1945	£81 9	£95 9	£132 7
1948	£138 7	£86 0	£182 0

offered in the country. London was the great source of mining investment and the home of most of the foreign companies that were beginning to manufacture in South Africa in the 1930s and 1940s. The struggle to create a more national economy was an important part of the economic history of this period, but only partially successful before 1948.

In 1948, the unevenness of the South African economy was still very apparent, even though the modernisation of agriculture was well under way, and the emergence of manufacturing was rapidly proceeding. Table 3 shows figures for the total annual income of agriculture, mining and industry in the period.

Agriculture's poor performance through the disastrous Depression years of the early 1930s was manifest. Recovery in the 1930s was very modest. Real expansion waited for the war years and, subsequently, when world commodity prices were excellent. Mining by comparison held its own in the earlier phases, albeit through a perilous history, to rebound to new levels in the boom of the 1930s. However, in the last years of the period, it declined in capacity to generate income, awaiting new discoveries. Industry was the great source of expansion. Even the Depression years affected industry far less than agriculture. Much less important than either mining or farming in 1910, industry became the biggest generator of income after the Second World War, although, unlike either, it would also remain a net importer of capital through to the end of the century.

With the rapid increase in manufacturing investment, the ratio of black wages to white wages rose from 22.7 per cent to 28.9 per cent from 1940 to 1946, but by that time, the ratio was on its way down again, falling back to 26.0 per cent in 1950. What the conventional observers of the time took for granted, the poverty, the low skill level and lack of economic possibility for the black majority, and indeed the nearly four-fifths of the population who were not white, created the basis for a very cheap labour force to be exploited in relatively primitive kinds of labour processes, but they would in time represent a brake to a farther-reaching form of development for the country. But this was understood by only a few. At the end of this period, a local observer, at the beginning of the golden era of development economics, when growth rate measurement began to seem very important, could compare the growth rate of the South African economy favourably with that of Britain, the United States, Australia or Canada for the period under investigation. This easily led to the view that the golden land of South Africa had found, or was finding, a useful regulatory and structural formula for success in the postwar world.

THE CLASS STRUGGLE

In the first phase of Union, the most obvious threat to an emergent hegemony lay in intense struggles between white workers, particularly mine workers on the Rand, and their bosses. Botha and Smuts were essentially seen as allies of the latter, whereas the Pact government specifically put itself forward as the champion of the little man, whose place needed to be secured in the new South Africa, primarily constructed by the mining magnates with the aid of a cooperative state. From the time of the Kimberley diamond discoveries and through the conflict over the fate of the Transvaal, there was an important digger factor. Immigrant miners from Britain, joined by South Africans, struggled to find a living on the mines, first as independent miners and/or small merchants and businessmen and then, increasingly, as workers. The immigrants themselves in part can be viewed as belonging to a travelling army of single men crossing the oceans from Europe to its colonies and in between those colonies, trying to reap the rewards of the massive natural resources the high tide of imperialism was taking in.

Given that wages were high for miners (in 1920, white miners earned twice as much as the same number of white workers in manufacturing in South Africa), what accounts for the militancy, the intensity of conflicts, these workers engaged in? First, many of them were independent of family ties but forced to disgorge much of their wage in high expenses. Until the eve of the First World War, imported commodities and a housing crisis made Johannesburg in particular an expensive city in which to live. Second, the mining industry had unpredictable ups and downs in which men could be suddenly thrown out of employment or have their wages lowered substantially. Third, workplace conditions in mining were in some respects unusually harsh. Through the 1910s, men died in huge numbers of miners' phthisis from the dust that accrued in their lungs in the deep mines, whereas the accident rate for injury and death was also extremely elevated. Feelings also ran very high about issues such as the length of the workweek.

However, the white miners also operated in a structurally insecure position. Some had genuine, difficult-to-acquire skills, but many were skilled only in the sense of instinct tempered by experience and socialisation. As the gold-mining industry persisted, such an instinct was increasingly being acquired by South African natives, white and black. During the phase of radical confrontation, increasingly, the British immigrant miner, whose numerical decline was hastened by injury and disease, was being replaced by proletarianised Afrikaners. The proportion of Afrikaners among white workers is disputed, ranging between 50 per cent and 75 per cent in different accounts. This was therefore one dimension of the situation; capitalism working its way through agrarian society turned some farmers into successful businesspeople, especially those with state assistance, but a larger number were pushed to the wall and forced to look for employment outside the traditional rural milieu. This lay at the heart of what was called the poor-white problem through this period. However, although it was possible for miners to imagine the incorporation of *boere* into their ranks – for instance, from the point of view of organising trade unions – they could not conceive of incorporating black miners as well. This was an excellent example of a bounded working class with absolutely no concept of solidarity that extended beyond certain lines. The heart of the structural insecurity lay in this conjuncture: the very real possibility that mine owners would replace some or all of their white workforce with far cheaper black labour. Only to a very limited extent did the mine workers hold exclusive right to jobs by statutory means; in general, they had to rely on custom and racial solidarity.

It was this conjuncture that promoted intensive strikes in 1913 and 1914 and then led to the Rand Revolt of 1922, when the mine owners effectively won a decisive victory against the workers. During these momentous events, one major attack, and numerous minor attacks, were launched against black victims, few of them directly involved in the conflict or working on the mines at all. This was concomitant with the broad and typical fears of white workers of the time at what they understood to be a threat to a racially defined standard of living. The goal of the mine magnates was not to eliminate whites as a workforce. What they wanted was a balance between black and white that would maximise profits and minimise conflict and disorder; that is what hegemony meant to them. The ratio of white to black on the mines rose quickly from about 1:8 to about 1:10, with fewer and fewer white workers underground, barring supervisors and particular skilled slots. The yawning white-black wage gap, perhaps 15:1 in 1921 was restored to its 1910 levels of 10:1 or 11:1, a level that would remain fairly intact through the 1940s.

Notoriously, the fledgling South African Communist Party supported the Rand Revolt, but it played a minor role in its operation. By contrast, the militancy of the strike owed much of its feeling and character to the commando traditions familiar to Afrikaner workers. Potentially, the possibility that Afrikaners would rally to the call of revolt rather than serve peacefully in the army to preserve law and order was extremely threatening to the Union government. Half of those arrested by the state in 1922 were Afrikaners. It is hard not to connect the bitter defeat of the Rand Revolt with the successful electoral campaign of the National and Labour parties, which came together to form the Pact, although the urban vote was not very critical to its success.

This left the Pact government that came to power, fuelled in part by the feeling that the Smuts government represented a narrow big-business element, with the task of balancing between the resentments of its voters and the need to sustain capitalism as the mine owners saw it. As Hertzog wrote, 'I have no feeling of antagonism against Capital.... I heartily wish every citizen of the Union was a capitalist'.[4] His government in 1926 promulgated the Mines and Works Amendment Act, which intensified the colour bar, especially as it was later amended in such a way as capital could accept, one foundation stone in a growing consensus about class and colour in the Union of South Africa. The mine workers' continued strength at the workplace began to rest largely on the goodwill of management. Their union was weak and corrupt with official recognition only from 1937, and eventually Afrikaner nationalists were able successfully to seize control of it. Even before the Pact came in, the Smuts government had moved to create a new balance of power, notably through the passage of the Industrial Conciliation Act of 1924. The new legislation laid the groundwork for massive intervention by the state in the case of industrial disputes. Pact legislation added the Wage Act of 1925, which allowed for minimum wages and state intervention in situations when workers were unorganised. Henceforth, labour organisation, and the position of white workers, changed dramatically to one that relied either on skills and education or directly on the intervention of a racist state acting as patron. The structures created by the state overshadowed trade union power in constructing hegemony.

This did not, however, resolve what was called in the interwar years the poor-white problem, a state of mind whose social realities are covered elsewhere by Bonner in depth. Although the Pact government occupied

---

[4] Cited in Frederick Johnstone, *Class, race and gold: a study of class relations and racial discrimination in South Africa* (London: Routledge and Kegan Paul, 1976), p. 164.

its mind with this problem, the Carnegie Commission report defining it came out only at the end of its tenure in 1932. As has been mentioned, poverty among whites took on serious dimensions in this period. On the one hand, ideologues were concerned with the question of racial mixing and a 'falling away' from 'white standards'. Perhaps one-quarter of Afrikaners were destitute in the 1920s.[5] Poor white people, whether in Cape Town, on the dry veld of Namaqualand or in the Knysna forests, tended to merge imperceptibly with the darker skinned. This could potentially happen in the intense atmosphere of the mining and industrial towns that had sprung up as well. More prosaically, Afrikaner nationalists had to worry about keeping this population loyal to the advancing Afrikaner cause in the new urban context. In the cities, the Dutch Reformed Church and the schools played a part in social uplift. On the land, the 1912 Land Settlement Act aimed at resettling *boere* on farms, a policy that had constantly to be measured against the cruel vagaries of the market. The church was equally involved in extensive agricultural and forestry settlement schemes intended to keep some poor whites effectively on the land. Rural and other schemes for helping poor whites tended to founder on the requirements of respectability and business standards that were imposed in the contradictory Pact outlook toward capitalism. Thus, the Precious Stones Act of 1927 was intended to assist the many poor people who went to the far southwestern Transvaal with the hopes of finding wealth in the new diamond diggings by regulating mine conditions. In fact, its provisos tended instead to disadvantage the poorest workers and independent diggers. However, the Pact government came to recognise that the main possibilities for its poor white clients lay in wage labour.

The state itself had, since before Union, hired poor white labourers for construction and other purposes. Under the Pact government, this policy – known as the civilised labour policy – was advanced much further at the cost of Indian and African workers. (Coloureds, normally paid less, were often included in these schemes, as they were not infrequently National Party voters). Between 1924 and 1933, the proportion of whites among unskilled workers on the railways, the most significant state employer of such labour, rose from 9.5 per cent to 39.3 per cent. Here state patronage worked at its crudest. Yet it is noticeable that even on the railways there was a growing reluctance, especially by the 1940s, to take on white labour at much higher rates than black labour for low-skill jobs; relations between the unskilled and the more skilled (and at first primarily English-speaking) workers were not good. In the 1930s, the state began to employ unskilled white workers

---

[5] H. Giliomee, 'The Afrikaner economic advance', in Adam and Giliomee, *Ethnic power mobilized*, p. 150.

in the new South African Iron and Steel Industrial Corporation (ISCOR) plant; this too was unpopular with management, in theory committed to white uplift, which quickly moved to start making more use of black labour. In 1934, the largest ISCOR plant regretfully dropped its civilised labour policy as uneconomical for the time being. Despite the legislation put into place under both Smuts and Hertzog, it proved much harder to accommodate whites with few skills but much higher pay expectations than blacks in the private sector.

Three factors were finally most critical in bringing the poor-white problem down to modest levels: first, the great prosperity that began after 1933 with expansion of the labour market; second, the support for white farmers that reduced the risk of being thrown off the land; and third, and probably most vitally, because the future of the poor whites did lie in the city, the growing state-supported diffusion of numeracy, literacy and vocational skills through the urban-born population. White workers were not always as malleable as intellectuals hoped, but in the second half of the period covered in this chapter, they ceased to be a class that held dangerous potential for their governors. Not only were they being 'incorporated' into the world of white South Africa; they were being 'incorporated' in part on their own terms. Between 1939 and 1948, the Afrikaner percentage of whites among managers increased from 8 per cent to 15 per cent, among clerical employees from 19 per cent to 32 per cent, among teachers from 49 per cent to 61 per cent, among fitters from 8 per cent to 21 per cent and among carpenters from 31 per cent to 46 per cent, measured against white males as a whole. This ethnic count masks only a little a fairly rapid process of white social promotion in general, as non-Afrikaners were certainly not being pushed out of these occupations in absolute numbers during boom times. Finally, the Pact government began the gradual process of erecting a modest social net for white South Africans. Old-age pensions, a cornerstone of the safety net, were introduced in 1928.

There was a shift thereby from the 1920s; revolt from below within the white population ceased to feature in the fears of the South African bourgeoisie. The Labour Party was thereafter confined to a small share of the electorate, largely on the Reef, and held no appeal to Afrikaners. Nor did it retain much of its early radicalism. The year of Pact victory saw the emergence of the South African Trade and Labour Congress, which was to contain a variety of opinions and organising strategies during its existence through this period. Many white workers were organised in craft unions, the strongest of which were those that maintained a hold on particular work skills. The more flexible and intelligent sectors among them were able to institute policies that incorporated and organised outsiders (unskilled workers, Afrikaners, women and children and above all workers of colour) on terms that favoured the senior skilled workers but sometimes benefited all workers.

The best-researched example is that of the Garment Workers Union. As the clothing industry expanded during and after the First World War on the Rand, it attracted many young Afrikaner women, who were frequently the first in their families to obtain gainful employment in the cities. Later, many married railway workers became dependent on state patronage through the civilised labour policy. Faced with the challenge of industrial expansion and a new category of workers, female and Afrikaans speaking, a socialist organiser named Solly Sachs, who kept some independence from the Communist Party, proved successful at moulding the women into a committed union. The union survived a serious defeat at the hands of employers during industrial conflicts in 1932 at the height of the Depression. Sachs conducted a long struggle to retain the allegiance of Afrikaners against the bitter antagonism of Afrikaner Nationalists who wished to see Afrikaner women organised on ethnic lines. This struggle was a crusade for him to keep workers as committed workers, out of the hands of ethnic patrons who would destroy working-class politics.

The very successes of the union led garment manufacturers to relocate in Durban and Cape Town, where reliance was heavily on coloured and Indian workers. In Cape Town, the garment workers unionised, but along paternalist lines dependent on the determinations of the Wage Board. Even in Johannesburg, coloured women increasingly came into the trade during the Second World War. Sachs had to try to keep in line white women with deeply racist prejudices so that they would accept coworkers of colour for the sake of preserving the union. This was successfully done in large part through the activities of close associates, such as Anna Scheepers, whom Sachs had found among the ranks of the Afrikaner women workers. But it was essential for the union to accept separate racially defined locals and to allow for social segregation on the factory floor (use of washrooms) to placate white sensibilities. The balance between patronage, interracial cooperation and racial segregation was a very delicate one. In 1943, Sachs ran for Parliament as an independent labour candidate, hoping his workers would bring him to office. Here he failed totally; as voters, his women largely chose to go with their men who were frequently railway workers owing their jobs to the civilised labour policy of the government. They had little interest in a wider vision of South African politics that would subvert the hegemonic racial norm. Finally, and after Sachs himself was forced into British exile, the union gradually lost the union battle as well in the sense that more and more of the growing industry was found in the coastal cities, where other, more conservative trade union structures (as well as lower wages) captured coloured and Indian workers. The Labour Party was beginning at this period to rethink its strong commitment to racial segregation, but with that came a subsidence into terminal decline. The process of incorporation had taken effect. The white working class was no longer a dangerous class fraction. Its special interests were partially attended to in a more prosperous South Africa, and it no longer lay outside the hegemonic consensus that governed the Union.

AFRIKANER NATIONALISM

At one level, the promotion of Afrikaner nationalism meant sharpening the definition of Afrikaner identity through the adoption of national symbols, notably the increasing legal use of the Afrikaans language (Pact-promoted Language Act of 1925). In 1910, although there were many experiments with written Afrikaans, educated Afrikaners such as Smuts had been educated in and wrote Dutch much as Netherlanders did. Under Union, the Afrikaans language acquired an official and defining status. During the Pact period, the South African flag was also deliberately modified following a long controversy so as to incorporate symbolically the two trekker republics. Second, although usually taken for granted, it ought to be mentioned that Afrikaner nationalism operated almost entirely within the rubric of the white South African citizenship that predominated as Union policy. There was little or no attempt by whites to include Afrikaans speakers who were visibly not white into the fold of the *volk*, even though, through the 1920s, coloureds of this description were not unimportant as voters to be won for the National Party. The white electorate, with its gradually increasing Afrikaner majority, was the field of battle that had to be won, as it constituted the only legitimate basis for the polity.

As the last section has already made clear, there was an important class dimension to Afrikaner politics, which in many respects parallelled the nationalist politics of many smaller ethnic groups in contemporary Europe, many of whom also 'competed' with old ruling-class elements, dynamic commercial minorities or rival nationalists with a potential base among peasants and workers. Afrikaner nationalists, whose discourse was at first firmly based in the countryside, were extremely concerned with keeping or acquiring a hold on the support of poor Afrikaners and, notably, the growing number found in towns, in urban neighbourhoods such as Johannesburg's Fordsburg, the vortex of the 1922 general strike. In the 1930s, for instance, a very public effort was made, associated especially with the activities of Hertzog's son, Albert, a genuine critic of capitalism, to create trade unions loyal to the Nationalist tradition. On this basis, the corrupt and ineffective Mine Workers' Union was eventually won over in 1948. However, there were not many other successes. The railway workers' union, the Spoorbond, was able to organise only the least skilled grades, a minority of white trade unionists on the railways. The metal workers' union, while conservative on racial and other matters, was never entirely in the Nationalist camp. Albert Hertzog's efforts were probably far more successful if measured by the voting record of Afrikaner workers, the large majority of whom in time would come around to the National Party in one or other of its manifestations. Strikes in 1947 aimed at blocking dilution in the building trades marked the racial insecurity of this class, and there was good reason to believe that the National Party of D. F. Malan would take a harsher line on race than the Smuts government.

However, it is also clear that the National Party was always a party pre-eminently of small businesspeople and professionals (with strong support from its women's associations). Although anxious for most of its history to woo workers, it was never a workers' party, and its dominant discourse reflected closely the anxieties and ambitions of the upwardly mobile. Promoting the interests of the Afrikaner business elite was absolutely fundamental to the National Party. Much of this elite gathered in the Western Cape, stood behind the creation of the Nasionale Pers and *Die Burger* in 1914 and were involved in founding Suid-Afrikaanse Nasionale Trust Maatskappy (SANTAM) and Suid-Afrikaanse Nasionale Lewens Assuransie Maatskappy (SANLAM), as Afrikaner insurance companies, in 1918, meant to appeal especially to capitalist farmers. By contrast, the Afrikaner Broederbond was founded in the same year by a small gathering of police officers, railway clerks and clergy in the Transvaal.[6] In 1929, it generated in turn the organisation of a broad cultural organisation, the Federasie van Afrikaanse Kultuurvereenigings (FAK), which brought it to a much wider public, especially among civil servants, teachers, clergy and other professional men. Its importance grew in the context of the political split between Hertzog and Malan, which left political Nationalists divided for a critical decade.

From here, the Bond also tended to reorient itself toward constructing economic power (founding of Volkskas as a savings bank for the northern provinces, 1935; convening of the first Ekonomiese Volkskongres, 1939; creation of the Afrikaanse Handelsinstituut, 1941). From a focus in the 1930s on trying to mobilise the savings of the majority of Afrikaners, there was toward the end of this period a growing shift toward the construction of effective, viable business enterprises dominated by Afrikaners. Thus, the Reddingsdaadbond monies, created in 1939 through the mobilisation

---

[6] D. O'Meara, *Volkskapitalisme: class, capital and ideology in the development of Afrikaner Nationalism, 1934–48* (Cambridge: Cambridge University Press, 1983), p. 60.

of Afrikaner savings, went not, as was initially proposed, to assist poor whites but overwhelmingly to assist capital-poor Afrikaner businesses.[7] Between 1938–1939 and 1948–1949, Afrikaner-identified credit associations increased their capital from £27 million to £74 million. This was a significant, though given the impact of inflation, not enormous, gain. Enthused Professor L. J. du Plessis:

[T]he finance company will stand in the forefront of the forthcoming struggle of the Afrikaner to find his legitimate share in the commerce and industry of our country. It will mesh together the farmer, the investor, the consumer and the employee on the one side, and the retailer, wholesaler, manufacturer and credit establishment on the other.[8]

By contrast, few Afrikaners enjoyed much success in industry, let alone mining, apart from some ventures closely aligned to agriculture. However, many Afrikaner merchants began to prosper in this period.

Much of the support enjoyed by D. F. Malan's rebels after 1934 came from the Cape party. To a large extent, other Afrikaners stayed loyal to Hertzog, but with his removal from power in 1939, they were in a sense homeless. This was one reason many, and notably young intellectuals, turned to extraparliamentary organisations, such as the very large and initially successful Ossewabrandwag. These organisations were strongly influenced by German fascism, which promised to overturn the world order created at the Versailles Treaty of 1919. Nazi prestige certainly influenced a rejection of parliamentary politics in favour of paramilitary mobilisation and a proposed corporate order that could take over in South Africa in conjunction with a German victory in Europe. Nazi racism found a sympathetic chord in South Africa, although no particular shift was proposed with regard to black-white policies. Mobilisation against Jewish immigration to South Africa from Germany in 1936, Jews by then forming 4 per cent of the white population, was, however, a key moment in the radicalisation of Afrikaner nationalism. It led to the passage of the Aliens Act of 1937, which virtually blocked further such immigration. At least at a cultural and social level, Nazism provided some inspiration to many Afrikaners toward a shift in the character of capitalist hegemony in South Africa; it gave them hope too that the British preeminence in cultural and economic life could be substantially reduced.

Malan (unlike Hertzog, who flirted with the radical Nationalists before his death in 1942), though showing some sympathy in this direction, shrewdly kept a foot and most of his balance in the parliamentary camp.

---

[7] It was abolished in 1946 having enjoyed very little success.
[8] Cited in O'Meara, *Volkskapitalisme*, p. 112.

An increasingly elderly dominie, radicalism of any sort was foreign to his nature. Despite street clashes with anti-Nazi supporters, attacks on Jews and Jewish property from time to time and some attempts at wartime sabotage, pro-German Afrikaner Nationalists failed to mount anything that could be called a rebellion; indeed, they failed to keep large numbers of Afrikaners from enlisting in the armed forces. The Ossewabrandwag, founded in 1939 in the Orange Free State, was immensely successful at first in bringing together enthusiastic members after the successful Voortrekker centenary celebrations. However, it fragmented and tended to fade as it moved to define a clear programme after 1941. With German strength waning in Europe, there was nowhere for the Nuwe Orde, Ossewabrandwag men, the Greyshirts and others to go – except back to the parliamentary party organised by Malan. There was no sharp line of distinction between the constitutional Nationalists and the radical right; they blended into one another ideologically, although personal antagonisms sometimes marred their relations. The Broederbond, which operated effectively on a national basis, played a major role in bringing the feuding elements together again. Following the war, the support base of the Purified National Party grew very rapidly in the Transvaal especially, given the declining willingness of the Smuts government to support poorer farmers or to answer white urban insecurities in a period of rapid black population growth on the Witwatersrand. The Malan government that came to power in 1948, though absorbing some of the most determined and talented of the radicals and their energies, had more in common by far with the pre-purified Nationalists of the Pact days. These radicals in turn, men such as Eric Louw and Nico Diederichs, were sufficiently opportunistic to be perfectly prepared to drop their antiparliamentarism and anti-Semitism, certainly for public, and increasingly for private, consumption. At the same time, and despite considerable continuities, Afrikaner nationalism certainly to outsiders appeared to be a culturally and sociologically distinct force generating its own problematic and operating outside the norms of conventional white parliamentary politics as its opponents conceived of them.

THE CONSTRUCTION OF SEGREGATION

'I hope you will agree that no injustice is done when different grazing is given to sheep from that given to cattle'.[9]

---

[9] Prime Minister Hertzog addressing the Native Conference, Pretoria, December 1925, in W. K. Hancock, *Smuts: the fields of force, 1919–50* (Cambridge: Cambridge University Press, 1968), p. 211.

There was little fundamental dispute among white politicians or the white general public that a basic justification for the new Union in 1910 would be its capacity to pursue the systematic development of 'native policy' along the lines of racial segregation, native policy that could in some ways extend to the Indian and coloured minorities. Outside the conventional consensus, the radical Afrikaner Nationalists and Labour, at its most left wing in its earliest days, simply urged a more rapid and ruthless application of policy, if anything. Among whites, only a tiny, numerically insignificant fringe differed from the consensus. Thus, the 'liberal' mainstay, Jan Hofmeyr, deputy prime minister in Smuts's last years, believed that his task was 'making South Africa safe for European civilisation without paying the price of dishonour to the highest ideals of that civilisation'.[10] However, this fringe included influential and eloquent intellectuals who wrote increasingly about South Africa's 'race problem', often in studies that cast a large influence as much internationally as well as nationally. Moreover, the Second World War and the thrust of international ideas thereafter certainly increased the diffusion of critical ideas at the very end of this period. For instance, a few white leaders in the established churches, often themselves immigrants to South Africa, began to lay the foundations of a religious critique of the South African racial system through the Campaign for Right and Justice toward the close of the Second World War. However, the consensus essentially held, and segregation remained the most fundamental hallmark of the hegemonic temper of the entire period.

Nonetheless, there were lengthy debates and discussions along highly politicised lines over the construction of segregation until the passage of the so-called Native Bills in 1936–1937. One reason for this was the influence of particular interest groups that competed with one another, eager to push segregation a bit further one way or another. Thus the Botha-Smuts Unionist government tended to allow too many loopholes in its preliminary segregationist legislation to please the more rigid and ideologically minded Hertzogites. By contrast, under the Pact, guarantees about the rights of Africans in the reserves tended to become vague to please farmers who believed their interests were threatened by any African economic independence at all and thus wanted to minimise those rights. This kind of lobby was less influential under Fusion and thereafter. There is a bewildering repetitiveness to some of the legislation of the day. A major reason lay in the lack of means on the ground actually to enforce the clear-cut segregationist ideas as laid out neatly in legislation. Thus, anxious

---

[10] Cited in A. Paton, *South African tragedy: the life and times of Jan Hofmeyr* (New York: Charles Scribner's Sons, 1965), p. 127, a view from 1930 that he never disavowed.

whites returned to the fray again and again, affirming segregationist policy while adding new detail.

A particular problem in the segregationist thrust lay in the growing importance of black urbanisation. As early as 1912, an urban segregation bill was put forward under Botha. Yet the final decade of the period covered witnessed the rapidest advance of black people into the cities, thus posing the biggest challenge to segregation laws. On the urban and labour frontiers, there was therefore a constant reconstruction and reconsideration of legislation that did not amount to much from the point of view of change of principle but often had quite significant ramifications as applied on the ground.

The chief elements in segregationist legislation lay in the following:

- Exclusive use of most land area in South Africa for whites alone, with movement toward a racial partition of the countryside on terms favourable to white security and white economic needs
- Movement toward the creation of some kind of suitable self-government for 'natives' on lines that did not threaten whites in the areas where they lived
- Exclusion of blacks from the right to vote and participate in the white-dominated political system
- Stemming from this, attempts to regulate the basis on which blacks could reside in 'white' South Africa, where they were useful to the economy
- Attempts to regulate the conditions under which black people worked in the South African economy, some of which have already been noted in the case of the all-important gold mines
- Finally, and most fitfully, regulation of the rights of coloured and Indian people in South Africa so as to fit in with this general pattern

Although the terminology of segregation was borrowed from the model of the American South, these elements were all partially or entirely different from those applying there. At the same time, laws, often local in character, covering social behaviour with close U.S. parallels (Mixed Marriage Act, 1937) have received far less attention from scholars but were passed in tune with the general picture. Throughout this period, the Native Affairs Department was manned by old-fashioned paternalists who administered African notables respectfully. Neither prestigious nor well financed, they were nonetheless the key operators in the empire of law and order that 'bifurcated sovereignty' represented in rural South Africa. Gradually an urban variant of 'native' officialdom also built up.

It is possible, despite this broad outline of consensus, to distinguish perspectives and periods in a way that is analytically useful. For the National and Labour parties, the Botha and Smuts governments before 1924 were somewhat too generous in their conception of segregation. Thus, the Beaumont Commission of 1916 was attacked as overly generous for wishing to add some 8 million morgen of land to the reserves, increasing their total area to some 13 per cent of the national territory. The Godley Commission of 1919 on urban areas, though envisioning a system of thorough controls over blacks in urban areas, assumed that black urbanisation was in South Africa to stay and favoured exempting educated black people from the pass laws. The Godley Commission and the tougher, more racist Stallard Commission were both important sources in the creation of the Natives (Urban Areas) act of 1923 (amended and tightened in 1930). This act is usually taken as the charter for racial segregation in the cities and towns of South Africa. It envisioned the 'proclamation' of areas for the use of exclusive race groups, the systematic use of influx controls to govern the numbers of black people in the cities and the use of special budgets to govern state expenditure on black urban dwellers. In fact, the so-called Durban system, whereby black people were forced to drink only at special municipal beer halls as a source of municipal revenue, was being widely applied by the 1920s as a model in this system.

The 1923 act was very important in laying out segregationist intentions in a zone of potentially intense conflict. However, it was not seriously applied at first. Pass laws at that time, and indeed for most of the period, were intended to control and order blacks in the cities, not to exclude them where their presence had potential benefit to the economy. The proclamation of segregated areas came slowly and needed to be taken up by individual municipalities, which had considerable autonomy in how they applied policy. The construction of housing for African families on segregated lines, for instance, hardly advanced in the 1920s and acquired only a modest momentum in the biggest cities in the 1930s.

The most infamous legislative innovation of the new Union government, however, was certainly the Land Act of 1913. Its position in the segregationist canon was absolutely fundamental. Perhaps no quote from this period by a black intellectual is remembered as much as that of the journalist Sol Plaatje: 'Awakening on Friday morning, June 20th, 1913, the South African Native found himself, not actually a slave, but a pariah in the land of his birth.'[11] A key and enduring feature of the act lay in its withdrawal of the right of blacks to purchase land in areas proclaimed as white. Less than 7 per cent of the land area of South Africa was unaffected by this act, although in fact the amount of land that would be allowed

[11] Cited in Colin Tatz, *Shadow and substance in South Africa: a study of land and franchise policies affecting Africans* (Pietermaritzburg: University of Natal Press, 1962).

as the black share was 'reserved' – left for further dickering and debate. Land purchase by blacks had become a significant feature in the Transvaal and Natal particularly, often with the assistance of missionary churches or through the activity of companies of individuals. This practice had to stop except, for a time, in the Cape. The act also banned sharecropping, which rested on the basis of some kind of sense of black rights on land owned by whites. Although this worked in the interest of the more dynamic white farmers who were desirous of undermining the status of black sharecroppers, poorer whites actually relied on them in many areas to produce most of the farm crop and did not benefit from the act. It was later followed by other legislation (1937) aimed at reducing or eliminating tenancy and the rights of tenants, thus turning white farmers into capitalists with the rights of other employers. Although this legislation, often actually counterproductive to the practical needs of the farmers, was not easily enforced systematically, it did lead to hardship and reduced power on the land for many African agriculturalists from the start. Keegan has suggested that reducing the potential social status of black tenants, making it clear who depended on whom, was itself a prime reason for the bill.

Shortly after the Pact government assumed power, Hertzog announced the outlines of his views on segregation in a speech at Smithfield in the Orange Free State (1925). This in turn led to the proposal of the four so-called Native Bills. Debates over them dominated the parliamentary sessions of the middle 1920s. The Unionists under Smuts refused to agree to the bills in the form Hertzog desired, thereby postponing their effective promulgation. Hertzog wished to take away from Cape Africans their right to vote along with the general population, offering in turn various other potential racially defined systems of representation. To do this required a two-thirds majority, which effectively gave Smuts veto power, and, during this period, he stood behind the Cape African vote, a survival of presegregationist thinking with all its limitations. It has been suggested that what concerned the opposition was not in fact the black voting rights (although, of course, they were able to profit from their retention politically). Rather, they were worried about the weakness of Hertzog's commitment to creating plausible reserve territory where some kind of African self-sufficiency could be maintained. This was their assessment of his Natives Land Act Amendment Bill of 1927.

By the mid-1920s, the chiefs were no longer a source of tension or worry to white South Africa. The Natal elite, symbolised by Senator Heaton Nicholls and the sugar magnate William Campbell, were cultivating the Zulu monarchy, via the first Inkatha movement, as a prop for conservative, paternalist, precapitalist labour and social relations. In 1927, the power of chiefs was sustained in theory by the Native Administration Act. This was consequently followed in the Transkei by the creation of the United Transkeian Territories General Council in 1931. In this important area, where no equivalent to the Zulu monarchy existed, the council, or *bunga*, was supposed to reflect the paternalist authority of legitimate chiefs, with power over domestic and property rights. However, throughout the period of Fusion and the United Party government, this system developed only slowly and locally. In one of his bills, Hertzog advocated giving representation in Parliament to blacks elected by chiefs. But this was never put into effect, although they had considerable weight in the voting system that was introduced in 1936. It would be only under a National Party government converted to the importance of the reserves as the counterweight to African nationalism that this element would take off on the national and systematic basis already envisioned by the early Union period.

In general, the Fusion period confirmed and refined the segregationist initiatives of the Pact government. Nicholls, together with Colonel C. F. Stallard, the defender of the prerogatives of white labour and white city dwellers, were key figures in defining the transitional legislation that would be acceptable under the Fusion ministry. In 1930, parliament granted the vote to white women in the Women's Enfranchisement Act. The Women's Enfranchisement Association, which had roots back before the turn of the century, had been prepared to accept its racist strictures (thus denying the vote to coloured women where coloured men did continue to vote, a late shift in policy by Hertzog). Olive Schreiner, South Africa's most remarkable feminist, had in fact left the association for that reason. Shortly after, the white male franchise was made comprehensive, further enlarging the white vote. In consequence, the black male vote in the Cape became of little importance. This, together with a growing willingness by Hertzog to accept something like the terms of the Beaumont Commission, brought Smuts around to agreement with him, and this was what made the Native Bills, those key elements of interwar segregation, possible.[12] In the end, no more than eleven members of Parliament were prepared to vote in defence of the old nonracial franchise in the Cape.

In return for closing down the Cape African franchise, blacks received two principal sops: first, they were able to vote for a limited number of whites representing their interests in the House of Assembly and the Senate. Second, the state created the Native Representatives Council (NRC) with purely consultative powers. The basis on which individuals were elected to these bodies was very complicated, a mix of direct and indirect suffrage practice. The latter was always the intention of reform; the former was

---

[12] Marian Lacey, *Working for Boroko: origins of a coercive labour system in South Africa* (Johannesburg: Ravan Press, 1981), p. 294.

actually introduced late in the day to win over some supporters of the old Cape franchise. This was the essence of the Representation of Natives Act of 1936. In reflection, this bargain was not entirely a negative one, given the extraordinary constraints under which the remaining black franchise was being exercised. The whites representing blacks were increasingly radical individuals who brought a voice never before heard to South African Parliament, especially after 1948. The NRC was able also to give expression at least to black beliefs and perspectives. However, these structures were hardly capable of providing blacks with any real power in the Union. Their very existence, moreover, was such as to form a barrier to progress toward citizenship in an open society. For the time being, the coloured right to vote remained as it was (existing black names on the voters' rolls in the Cape could also remain), and the virtually total exclusion of Indians, in accordance with the pre-Union systems in Natal and the Transvaal, where most lived, also was sustained.

A land settlement offering the black majority only perhaps 13 per cent of South Africa's land area was hardly generous, but this arrangement, never entirely put into full operation in its existence, was at least offering more, especially in the inland provinces, than the somewhat vague guarantees Hertzog had held in mind in the 1920s. This was the essence of the Native Trust and Land Act of 1936. At the same time, chapter 4 was intended to police limits on the numbers and rights of tenants on white-owned land. This provision continued to be difficult to enforce throughout the preapartheid period. In this sense, the influence of Smuts was toward greater, if more generous, segregation.

A final category of important legislation structuring the segregationist system, aligned in effect to the urban policies, lay in the ongoing shifts in rules on the rights of black labour. Before Union, the official rights of black workers belonged in large part to a precapitalist world with the profusion of masters and servants laws that prescribed punishments for contract breaking. Controls were enforced through the pass regime, which allowed officials power over the movement and residence of all African men (women were not, however, covered). This system was qualified and refined only in the interwar years. Trade unions were not permitted to include black men in their bargaining arrangements; effectively, black men had no legal right to organise. Nor could they strike legally. The Wage Act was potentially available to allow the state to regulate conditions and allow, for instance, for the pressures of inflation. The reality did include unauthorised trade union organisation and real strikes, especially in the 1940s, and that reality did engender considerable worry for the state, but it did not lead, before 1948, to substantial chinks in the segregationist state formulae.

On the land, although the state's capacity to enforce legislation was limited, things were worse. The rights of black workers were severely circumscribed. A strong feature of Hertzog's National Party was the importance of white farmers and their success as a lobbying group. The Pact government substantially raised black poll taxation, tightened up provision of the Master and Servants laws and paved the ground for the massive use of convict labour for private purposes. The Native Service Contract Act, passed in its waning days of government at the low ebb of agricultural prosperity in 1932, aimed to force black employees to stay on the farm for long, unequally constructed contract periods and, in particular, to control the movement of their dependent women and children. This really defined a legal forced labour regime on the land. In reality, the potential for self-organisation was much lower, and the situation on the ground considerably worse, than in the urban context.

But it was the cities that worried the United Party government of 1939–1948. This was a period of rapid urban growth, with rapid economic growth, and the lack of real provision according to the 1923 act became an ever more serious issue. At the height of the war years, for instance, the pass laws were held in abeyance largely because they were almost unenforceable. Black workers in secondary industry were able to organise in trade unions fairly extensively. It was in the urban forum that some experts began to question the feasibility of segregation itself. Nonetheless, when in a famous speech in 1942, Smuts suggested that 'segregation had fallen on evil days', he was hardly planning to abolish it. Instead, he sought to modernise and improve on it. The Smuts government entertained considerable thought of reform; for instance, the Smit Commission of 1942 proposed abolishing the pass system entirely, improving wages and allocating money to health and housing improvements for black urban dwellers. Voices in the government certainly sought the legalisation of black trade unions. By 1938 the Fusion Minister of Labour, Harry Lawrence, had envisioned creating some kind of system of governance for segregated black unions with the involvement of the Native Affairs Department. Recognition was granted in a grudging and halting way in the proposed Industrial Conciliation (Natives) Bill of 1947. The Fagan Commission, whose recommendations were the guiding light of the Smuts government at its close, rested on the assumption that large-scale urbanisation of black South Africans was an irreversible social phenomenon. By contrast, the Sauer Commission, proposed by the National Party, still held out the possibility of territorial segregation that would eventually encompass the cities.

Both commissions, however, maintained the view that the state would need to support the construction of segregated townships in the cities for black residents on an unprecedented basis in the short term. Moreover, these plans were in line with those that had been developed over the previous decade by municipal authorities, including those in the supposedly most liberal cities. In each of these cities, new housing construction was linked to the idea of physical segregation by race (and, informally, by class), the separation of residence and business premises and the establishment on an economic basis of a greatly expanded public housing commitment. Social uplift programmes restricted to whites were themselves critical in the deepening racial lines of exclusion in towns, as Parnell has argued.[13] The Slums Act of 1934 had already pointed in this direction, mixing modern, internationally normative urban planning initiatives with the imperatives of segregation. In Johannesburg, Port Elizabeth, Durban and Cape Town (a more equivocal case), at least, municipal authorities had prefigured the post-1948 destruction of multipurpose, multiracial neighbourhoods that had sprung up over the decades and were often identified as the source of crime and potential political disorder.

In effect, the Union government faced a growing urban crisis in the form of rapidly expanding housing, health and educational needs and swelling costs that could no longer be postponed or put off without the character of the cities changing in basic ways. The nature of the Smuts government in this regard, however, was to temporise. On the one hand, there was no way that white voters would dream of supporting a fundamental break with the segregationist system that had been forged since 1910. To this Smuts was also committed. On the other hand, there was a willingness to temper the system through qualification and, to a lesser extent, negotiation but also a genuine belief that material conditions could be substantially improved for black South Africans without any real extension of political rights.

Smuts was a Keynesian and a strong believer in directed development. The wartime Social and Economic Planning Commission of 1942 was the starter motor for a range of broad reforms. In the social sphere, and specifically with regard to reform that crossed the racial divide, there were some important elements in this period. School feeding (1943), the pension system (1944) and the disability system (1946) were extended (albeit on a discriminatory basis) to all races. Smuts's Minister of Health favoured a general socialised health system benefiting the entire population.[14] Although this was rejected as extravagant, urban health problems did begin to be addressed, compared to the earlier tradition of laissez-faire mixed with racial segregation. Smuts's deputy Hofmeyr helped sponsor the law that allowed for general funding to be used to pay for African education.

---

[13] Susan Parnell, 'Creating racial privilege: the origins of South African public health and planning legislation', *Journal of Southern African Studies* 19 (1993), 471–88.

[14] Gluckman Commission, 1942–44.

Neither Smuts nor even the more equivocal Hofmeyr (who, in any event, Smuts did not appear to envision as his successor) were prepared to move toward creating a politically more inclusive society allowing for any black empowerment. Politically, they stood by the compromise of 1936 entirely, if not always comfortably. The government was involved through the 1940s with the particular issue of Indian participation in the political system. In Durban, where most Indians lived, the war years were marked by white racist panic over so-called Indian penetration, whereby Indians were purported to be furtively buying into supposedly white areas of the city. The Pegging Act of 1943 was intended to prevent this process from getting any further. Smuts's master plan, devised after the Second World War, was to extend these limitations in return for minor Indian parliamentary representation, paralleling the basic vision with regard to Africans (Asiatic Land Tenure and Indian Representation Bill, 1946). At the same time, the policy of trying to repatriate ethnic Indians to India, on the verge of independence, was retained. This plan hardly pleased many Indians; at the same time, it was too pragmatic and generous to appeal to the main thrust of white opinion. The modest attempts to reform Indian representation, with parallel efforts regarding coloured people, had the effect of mobilising and radicalising Indian and coloured opinion. It proved very difficult to find representative Indian and coloured notables prepared to serve in the consultative institutions advocated in the reforms.

By 1946, moreover, the Native Representatives Council (NRC), which had attracted the participation of many African dignitaries, reached a point of frustration as to begin a process of formal boycott. This 'liberal' sop of the Fusion deal thus was perilously close to collapse, as no successful compromise to bring the NRC back into session was devised by the time of Smuts's fall. According to Roth, NRC elections moved steadily in the direction of rejecting liberals and toward supporting more radical candidates.[15] Nor did the National Party opposition believe in reviving it.

During the renewed Smuts years, debates, political conflict, government commissions and legislation all revealed the contradictions of the late segregation period. However, there was no potential, so long as the United Party remained in power, of any real break in the wall of segregation as the basic hegemonic idea governing the Union of South Africa. Racial segregation was, beyond stabilising a capitalist economy, the principal hegemonic project of all its regimes.

---

[15] M. Roth, 'Domination by consent: elections under the Representation of Natives Act 1937–40', in Lodge (ed.), *Resistance and ideology*, pp. 144–67.

RELATIONS IN THE REGION AND THE WORLD

If the establishment of the Union of South Africa could be said to have initiated a hegemonic project critically involving the state, something must be said about that aspect of it that bound the Union to the wider world and established a place for it. Here we can certainly observe considerable differences in the conventional political spectrum. On the Afrikaner Nationalist side, the main issue was the achievement of full independence from Britain. Some Nationalists put more emphasis on the side of an Afrikaner hegemony in South Africa, but many, and notably Hertzog, were as much or more concerned with the international ramifications. Through the 1920s Hertzog stood for the widest possible autonomy in the Commonwealth, culminating in the Statute of Westminster in 1931, which he assumed to be a declaration of independence. At best, Commonwealth membership for him was a practically advisable necessity. The desirability of hovering in the British defensive shield in the 1930s was balanced against the interest in Germany as a potential counterweight to British economic and political influence. For Hertzog, the South African declaration of war in 1939 was a betrayal of this gradual struggle for independence. The Allied war victory would stifle the republican thrust, but it would finally triumph fifteen years later under Nationalist auspices.

By contrast, Smuts accepted wholeheartedly by 1910 the objective of working in the context of the British Empire and, after the First World War, the League of Nations. He was in his way a South African nationalist, but he saw this road as the desirable one; Germany (and its presence in southern Africa in particular) was almost always a menacing object to him. Rhodes's vision of South Africa as the basis of an African commonwealth was dear to his heart and important to his own interpretation of South African manifest destiny: 'The Union is going to be for the African continent what the United States has become for the American continent.' At the minimum level, it was a question of completing South Africa's irregular northern boundaries in a form more logical to the political economy of the region. The grander vision, as propounded in a letter to British Colonial Secretary L. S. Amery, was 'a great white Africa'.

Smuts and Botha brought South Africa into the First World War to realise these goals in large part. The early war years were filled with secret negotiations to partition or gobble up Mozambique. Although the South African government hoped that this strategically desirable move could be accomplished by buying out the Portuguese, it did not reckon with the stubborn desire of Portugal to remain a colonial power, a desire that brought the Portuguese into the war on the Allied side as an insurance policy. As a result, the northeastern frontier of South Africa would remain unaltered, and attempts in the 1920s for a virtual takeover of the Mozambican ports by South Africa also failed. The 1928 convention confirmed Portuguese rights, permitting large-scale South African labour recruitment in Mozambique in return for continuing the deferred payment system for the labourers. Portugal's sovereign rights over the all-important transport nexus remained intact as well.

In the northwest, Smuts was more successful. The South Africans forced German troops in South-West Africa to surrender and, after the war, acquired a League mandate over the territory. Its acquisition was desirable in a number of ways. Apart from eliminating the presence of a great power from South Africa's vicinity, it allowed for the present of cheap land to hundreds of poor, largely Afrikaner, white farmers. Indeed by the 1920s, Afrikaners formed the majority of the white population in the territory. The rich diamond fields were acquired by Oppenheimer interests cheaply after a forced sale. South-West Africa was administered in fact as though it would ultimately become the fifth province of South Africa, although that would never happen. The Second World War settlement transferred the territory to the United Nations, with continued South African social and economic penetration under the trusteeship system.

This was to prove South Africa's only territorial success of the Union period. Smuts's dream of absorbing at least the British colonies of southern and central Africa, to a large extent shared at first by imperial authorities in London, was never to be. All South African regimes aspired to control the so-called High Commission territories, which were joined to South Africa by a customs union. Swaziland, much desired by the old South African Republic, was a particular object of acquisitive interest. In the case of the other two territories, the intention would have been to assimilate them into the segregation structure being built up for the Union as a whole. The original Union promulgation half promised this expansion to South Africa. In practise, however, British reluctance to force the territories into the Union persisted and strengthened. For the most part, this was directly the result of doubts about the potential dominance of Afrikaner nationalism. However, obtaining the goodwill of the principal chiefs operating under British rule was a factor as well. Only the Swazi king Sobhuza ever (and in his case, only to a limited extent) even considered annexation as a bargain, despite some financial incentives. In the 1930s, the question of African consent began to be raised more consistently. It is notable that, when queried in the 1940s, African National Congress representatives strongly opposed incorporation of the High Commission territories into the South African system. The British government began to conceive of itself and the Union as having distinct and perhaps incompatible 'native policies'. Indeed, Hertzog, with the passage of the Native Bills, largely lost interest in the territories apart from Swaziland.

In the early years of Union, there was also a serious question of expansion north of the Limpopo into the Rhodesias. Here again, British reluctance tended to grow, especially when the Unionist party was not in the harness, although in fact Afrikaner nationalists saw Rhodesia as ineffably British and themselves strongly opposed this expansion drive of Smuts and his allies. When the British South Africa Company approached the end of its charter, the British gave the white settlers of Southern Rhodesia their choice, and the majority opted late in 1922, in the wake of the Rand Revolt, for Crown colony status and against Union. Not long after, South African customs policies were adjusted to reflect recognition of the permanence of the Limpopo frontier. The future Zimbabwe (and Zambia) would become important customers and economic partners for South Africa but, in part and in phases, rivals and competitors as well.

With the passage of time, Smuts was forced to accept the failure of his territorial ambitions. Except for South-West Africa, the frontier would stay where it was in 1910. However, in the Second World War years and after, he shifted toward looking at the possibility of closer economic relations within Africa that would harmonise with the rapid industrialisation of South Africa. At least the Union would lie at the economic heart of a modernising Africa. This was a potent vision so long as the African nationalist moment had not yet dawned. It ties into the final section of this chapter, which seeks to survey one final element of the hegemonic project, the emergence of South Africa as a developmental state.

Despite the Unionist and South African Party policies of working in the British Commonwealth context, the 'sovereign independence' sought by Hertzog, involving the emergence of an autonomous South African diplomatic and military presence in the world, did emerge by fits and starts through this period. Part of the reason lay in gradual British decline, part in the implications of the economic development of South Africa in coordination with the Union state.

SOUTH AFRICA AS A DEVELOPMENTAL STATE

Previous sections have all considered the creation of hegemony as a means of integrating fundamental elements of state policy during this period. This is not to say, of course, that hegemony was simply created by an integrative state. Undoubtedly, the cultural element and the racial element that belonged to the discourse of hegemony stemmed equally from strong forces that existed in civil society at many levels. The state's role was, however, particularly important in a defining or regulatory sense and in teasing out problems that existed from the social contradictions that ensued. From the perspective of the formation of a racial order and the narrower sense of forming a state in which Afrikaans as a language and Afrikaner political traditions could be dominant, the hegemonic project of the Union period proved doomed in the end. It sat on the base of too narrow a section of the population. Segregation had too little to offer people of colour to attract them; in fact, it was a source of alienation, opposition and the intermittent emergence of counterhegemonic activity.

It is possible, however, to argue that in other spheres, the Union represented an attempt at nation building where continuities are still manifest. This is perhaps most obvious during the era of Smuts's second premiership where social policies began to include, albeit on a segregated basis, the entire population of the country. There was some recognition, fuelled by world trends, that the overall development of South African capitalism required more inclusive arrangements. However, this phase was brief and relatively superficial in the broader political discourse of white hegemony. This kind of contradiction would remain at play after 1948 and become more acute in the reform period of apartheid.

In the economic sphere, the Pact government and even its Unionist predecessor were eager to intervene to establish national economic policy that would respond to our starting dilemma, the extreme unevenness of development in South Africa after the mineral revolution. Some authors have tended to assimilate this subject into the general growth of the economy or to exaggerate state intervention as the sole cause of this growth; there is hopefully some virtue therefore in focusing on state intervention in this section, separate from the general analysis of the economy summarised early in this chapter.

In this period, there is considerably continuity. Nevertheless, some distinctions can be made. The Pact government was politically bound to the less well-off section of the white population; in reality, it was never really prepared to challenge the prerogatives of business but, within limits, it did try to assist small farmers and promote 'civilised labour'. By contrast, under Fusion and particularly after 1939, there was a growing willingness to serve the dictates of big business effectively. At the same time, the boom in gold in the 1930s allowed the state far more possibilities through revenue. Already by 1930, some 13 per cent of direct revenue came from mining activities, and there were considerable indirect revenue sources as well. Moodie estimates that by the end of the decade, one-third of government revenues were derived from gold mining.[16] After 1933, state budgets were again in surplus, and taxes on the gold mines were raised. As we have seen, Hertzog, though conciliatory toward English-speaking South Africans, was anxious for South Africa to move as far as possible outside the

---

[16] T. Dunbar Moodie, 'The South African state and labour conflict in the 1940s', *International Journal of African Historical Studies* 21 (1988), 25.

British imperial sphere. By contrast, Smuts certainly envisioned the South African system developing with, and to a marked degree, in that sphere. Oscillation leading toward the achievement of a stable balance marked the interwar decades.

A significant development even before the Pact came to office was the emergence of the South African Reserve Bank in charge of the issuance of South African currency in 1921, the first central bank in any of the British dominions. Before this time, South Africa was financially entirely integrated with the British banking world. During the war, all its gold (far and away the main national export) was sold at a fixed price to the Bank of England. The pressures to bring about a South African central bank were in fact very practical. Much of this currency needed to be paid in gold to mine workers and could not conveniently be produced in Britain without constant importations. As a result, South Africa began to refine and mint its own currency. In the post–First World War years, moreover, gold as measured in sterling resulted in a substantial premium at the cost of the banks, required to operate according to the fixed rate, thus causing massive smuggling of gold and a crisis in balance of payments. The demands for local credit were such as to force the British banks to want more financial independence for South Africa themselves. Once gold began to be sold directly to the Reserve Bank in 1925, the bank was able to begin to have a significant influence on the South African economy. However, it continued to work closely with the Bank of England, and its significance was all the more marked because conservative advisers put the Pact government off the more radical idea of a South African national bank. Indeed, in the 1920s, South African dependence on Britain as its export market increased again very substantially to reach almost 80 per cent in 1933.

Yet Hertzog retained the dream of building a national economy on the basis of an independent gold standard and stubbornly refused after the onset of the Depression to go off the gold standard, despite the advice of South African business. It was only when Smuts proved willing to support such a shift that Hertzog's position weakened, and the decision to go off gold was made at the end of 1932, precipitating Fusion and bringing about the boom conditions with the price of gold moving dramatically up. This was of signal importance in the construction of an economically independent, postimperial South Africa, but it operated half by accident and as part of a general movement of fits and starts.

Railway rates were systematically manipulated from the time of the First World War to encourage South African manufacturers. The Pact government's interventions in the economy included the institution of tariffs intended to protect local industry and reduce industrial imports (Customs Tariff and Excise Duties Amendment Act, 1925). The tariffs had a stimulating effect but were probably not quite so fundamental in the emergence of industrial plant as is sometimes assumed. Their institution flew in the face of imperially orientated free-trade ideologues with links to the universities and commerce and took place only after the forging of complex alliances of different economic sectors and considerable struggle.

Even before, the state had launched into the creation of state enterprise. Under the directorship of H. J. van der Bijl, Smuts had authorised the Electricity Act, which led to the formation of the Electricity Supply Commission (ESCOM) in 1923. Van der Bijl saw its primary function as 'the promotion of private enterprise throughout South Africa by a process of industrialisation built on a foundation of cheap electricity' managed by the state rather than by private monopoly. Electric power became a major justification for the expansion of South Africa's massive coal reserves. However, after the Second World War, ESCOM took over the Victoria Falls and Transvaal Power Company, which supplied electricity to the mines. The success of ESCOM was marked by the spectacular opening of ESCOM House in downtown Johannesburg in 1937, often described as South Africa's first skyscraper.

It was the Pact government, however, that founded the Iron and Steel Corporation (ISCOR) against the fears of the mining interest of an over-priced and inferior state product. Van der Bijl, also entrusted with its management, developed it on lines intended to complement rather than stifle existing economic interests. By 1936, given state protection and after two years of operation, ISCOR was profitable. More important, the energy and metal industries were critical in the rapid industrialisation that was taking place during the 1930s and then at the time of the Second World War. Beyond this, in 1935, the National Roads Act was introduced to move toward creating a tarmac grid for South Africa. The South African Broadcasting Corporation was created shortly afterward. Further efforts were marked by the formation of the Industrial Development Corporation in 1939. The creation of the Ministry of Economic Development and the formation of the Council for Scientific and Industrial Research were important markers in this regard during the war years. The United Party government under Smuts was particularly committed to developmentalism. Indeed, Smuts's own standing as an intellectual and his scientific interests gave him a particular weight here in contrast to his marked reluctance to challenge 'traditional' race norms.

When the war ended, emphasis was laid on the financing of a textile industry that would be located on the edge of reserves, where cheap black labour could be found – policy, indeed, that is usually associated with the extremes of apartheid ideology a generation later. By that point, state industrial thinking had come to the verge of realising the importance of black labour and black consumption, but it was deeply committed, as much under Smuts as his successors, to harmonising this with the social requirements of segregation and white domination. Steering industry in certain ways was as important as the actual economic stimulus supplied.

State intervention was also of growing importance in the weakest sector of the economy, agriculture. Already in 1912, the National Land and Agricultural Bank was founded as a means of helping white farmers who were unwelcome to the commercial banks. Nonetheless, it proved mainly to help the more affluent farmers. Yet much of the state's role in agriculture through the 1920s remained geared toward solving the poor-white problem. Under the Fusion government, by contrast, agricultural organisation with a prime role for the leading capitalist producers advanced substantially. Interventions of the Pact period seemed retrospectively rather timid. At first, there was considerable focus on relief as state revenues expanded. The Marketing Act of 1937 structured the creation of compulsory buying boards aimed at stabilising and raising farm prices, several of which had already come into being. Marketing boards such as the Meat Industry Board were organised to monopolise purchases from farmers who in turn set up cooperatives in most key agricultural sectors (Cooperative Societies Act, 1939). The cooperative movement was already a generation old but it had been ineffective in its early manifestations. The Sugar Act of 1936 created a national system of production quotas to stabilise prices and tried to harmonise the interests of smaller and bigger producers while leaving Indians and Africans with little. However, although farmers competed with mining interests for labour, their needs were to some extent complementary: the mines were massive consumers of beef and maize. Thus, the labour regulations developed in this period, as well as other measures aimed at farming, were not only a manifestation of the impulse to segregate and control black workers; they were also concerned to regulate this mix of competition and interdependence.

Irrigation schemes and dam construction were undertaken, often on the basis of the employment of poor whites. State subsidisation of agriculture reached £15 million in 1939 and continued to expand. In 1946, the Soil Conservation Act (preceded by the Forest and Veld Conservation Act of 1941) aimed for the first time at dealing with environmental degradation and made possible punitive measures against poor farmers who violated good practice as it was defined. Successful farmers were able to benefit as well from cheap foreign labour being deflected their way. The Foreign Farm Labour Scheme of 1944–1948 was intended to make sure that some of the migrant labour from north of the border was passed on to farmers. It was the outcome of an informal compact between the Native Affairs

Department and the South African Agricultural Union. So long as state aid to agriculture was dominated by the dream of poor white uplift on the land, its impact economically was limited. Once, as under Fusion and even more afterward, it put its emphasis on building up the big farmers as capitalists, it became an important element in strengthening the weak sister of the economy.

It is likely that the dominant economic reality in the reserves was one of stagnation at low levels of production. However, a concomitant of segregationist thinking was concern about the reserves' inability to feed African producers and their families and the consequences of that situation. In the Fusion period and after, the outlines of strategy for restructuring black living and farming arrangements, usually called betterment, were being mooted but not really put into force before 1948. Only the first couple of districts in the Eastern Cape were beginning to be 'planned' by the time of the National Party's election victory.

Through trial and error, with dramatic phases of rhetorical hyperbole and soberer ones of forging solid linkages with the actual plans of South African capitalists, the state moved toward a symbiotic developmental relation in which it was playing an ever-greater interventionist role in the economy. This needs to be considered alongside the social imperatives and political manoeuvres of the day in the construction of the hegemonic project of Union, and it is probably this side that has to some degree remained relatively intact to the present. The postapartheid government in 1994 had to reckon with the trees filling the landscape that had been nurtured on South African soil during this period. By contrast, the political and social hegemony, on the construction of which so much labour had also gone in the Union period up to 1948, has been challenged and ultimately destroyed with still uncertain consequences.

FURTHER READING

Alexander, Peter, *Workers, war and the origins of apartheid, 1939–48*, Oxford: James Currey, 2007

Ally, Russell, *Gold and empire: the Bank of England and South Africa's gold producers*, Johannesburg: Witwatersrand University Press, 1994

Beinart, William and Colin Bundy, *Hidden struggles in rural South Africa: politics and popular movements in the Transkei and Eastern Cape, 1890–1930*, Johannesburg: Ravan Press, 1987

Berger, Iris, *Threads of solidarity: women in South African industry*, London: James Currey, 1982

Bhana, Surendra, *Gandhi's legacy: the Natal Indian Congress, 1894–1994*, Pietermaritzburg: University of Natal Press, 1997

Bonner, Philip, 'The Transvaal Native Congress, 1917–20: the radicalization of the black petty bourgeoisie on the Rand', in Marks and Rathbone (eds.), *Industrialisation and social change*, pp. 270–313

Bonner, Phillip, P. Delius and D. Posel (eds.), *Apartheid's genesis, 1935–62*, Johannesburg: Ravan Press and Witwatersrand University Press, 1993

Bozzoli, Belinda, *The political nature of a ruling class*, London: Routledge, 1981

Bozzoli, Belinda (ed.), *Town and countryside in the Transvaal*, Johannesburg: Ravan Press, 1983

Bradford, Helen, *A taste of freedom: the ICU in rural South Africa, 1924–30*, New Haven, CT: Yale University Press, 1987

Christie, Renfrew, *Electricity, industry and class in South Africa*, London: Macmillan, 1984

Clark, Nancy, *Manufacturing apartheid: state corporations in South Africa*, New Haven, CT: Yale University Press, 1994

Coleman, F. L. (ed.), *Economic history of South Africa*, Pretoria: Hollandsch Afrikaansche Uitgevers MaatschappijM, 1983

Cope, Nicholas, *To bind a nation: Solomon ka Dinizulu and Zulu nationalism, 1913–33*, Pietermaritzburg: University of Natal Press, 1993

Crush, Jonathan, Alan Jeeves and David Yudelman, *South Africa's labor empire: a history of black migrancy to the gold mines*, Boulder, CO: Westview; Cape Town: David Philip, 1991

De Kock, Gerhard, *History of the South African Reserve Bank, 1920–52*, Pretoria: Van Schaik, 1954

Drew, Alison, *South Africa's radical tradition: a documentary history*, vol. 1, 1907–50, Cape Town: Buchu, Mayibuye and University of Cape Town Press, 1996

Duncan, David, *The mills of God: the state and African labour in South Africa, 1918–48*, Johannesburg: Witwatersrand University Press, 1995

Du Plessis, J. C., *Economic fluctuations in South Africa, 1919–49*, Stellenbosch: Bureau for Economic Research, University of Stellenbosch, 1950

Evans, Ivan, *Bureaucracy and race: native administration in South Africa*, Berkeley: University of California Press, 1997

Freund, Bill, 'The social character of secondary industry in South Africa, 1915–45', in A. Mabin (ed.), *Organisation and social change*, pp. 78–119

Furlong, Patrick, *Between crown and swastika: the impact of the radical right on the Afrikaner Nationalist movement in the Fascist era*, Johannesburg: Witwatersrand University Press, 1991

Gelb, Stephen, 'The origins of the South African Reserve Bank,' in A. Mabin (ed.), *Organisation and economic change*, pp. 48–77

Giliomee, Hermann, 'The Afrikaner economic advance,' in Adam and Giliomee, *Ethnic power mobilized*, pp. 145–76

Guest, Bill and John Sellers, (eds.), *Receded tides of empire: aspects of the social and economic history of Natal and Zululand since 1910*, Pietermaritzburg: University of Natal Press, 1994

Hancock, W. K., *Smuts: the fields of force, 1919–50*, Cambridge: Cambridge University Press, 1968

Hindson, Doug, *Pass controls and the urban African proletariat*, Johannesburg: Ravan Press, 1987

Hirson, Baruch, *Yours for the union: class, community and struggle in South Africa*, London: Zed, 1989

Innes, Duncan, *Anglo: Anglo American and the rise of modern South Africa*, Johannesburg: Ravan Press, 1984

Jeeves, Alan, *Migrant labour in South Africa's mining economy: the struggle for the gold mines' labour supply, 1890–1920*, Johannesburg: Witwatersrand University Press, 1985

Jones, Stuart and Andre Muller, *The South African economy, 1910–90*, London: Macmillan, 1992

Katzenellenbogen, Simon, *South Africa and southern Mozambique: labour, railways and trade in the making of a relationship*, Manchester, U.K.: Manchester University Press, 1982

Keegan, Timothy, 'The making of the rural economy: from 1850 to the present,' in Konczaki, Parpart and Shaw (eds.), *Studies in the economic history of Southern Africa*, vol. 2, pp. 36–63

Krikler, Jeremy, *The Rand Revolt: the 1922 insurrection and racial killing in South Africa*, Johannesburg: Jonathan Ball, 2005

Lacey, Marian, *Working for Boroko: origins of a coercive labour system in South Africa*, Johannesburg: Ravan Press, 1981

Lewis, Gavin, *Between the wire and the wall: a history of South African 'coloured' politics*, Cape Town: David Philip, 1987

Lewis, Jon, *Industrialisation and trade union organisation in South Africa, 1924–55: the rise and fall of the South African Trades and Labour Council*, Cambridge: Cambridge University Press, 1984

Marks, Shula, 'Afterword: worlds of impossibilities,' in Dubow and Jeeves (eds.), *South Africa's 1940s*, pp. 267–82

Marks, Shula, *The ambiguities of dependence in South Africa: class, nationalism and the state in twentieth-century Natal*, Johannesburg: Ravan Press, 1986

Maylam, Paul, *A history of the African people of South Africa: from the early Iron Age to the 1970s*, London: Croom Helm, 1986

Moodie, T. Dunbar, *The rise of Afrikanerdom: power, apartheid and the Afrikaner civil religion*, Berkeley: University of California Press, 1975

Moodie, T. Dunbar, 'The South African state and labour conflict in the 1940s', *International Journal of African Historical Studies* 21 (1988), 21–61

Morrell, Robert, (ed.), *White but poor*, Pretoria: UNISA Press, 1992

O'Meara, Dan, *Volkskapitalisme: class, capital and ideology in the development of Afrikaner Nationalism, 1934–48*, Cambridge: Cambridge University Press, 1983

Parnell, Susan, 'Creating racial privilege: the origins of South African public health and planning legislation', *Journal of Southern African Studies* 19 (1993), 471–88

Paton, Alan, *South African tragedy: the life and times of Jan Hofmeyr*, Boston: Charles Scribner's Sons, 1965

Robinson, Jennifer, *The power of apartheid: state, power and space in South African cities*, Oxford: Butterworth-Heinemann, 1996

Roth, Mirjana, 'Domination by consent: elections under the Representation of Natives Act, 1937–48,' in Lodge (ed.), *Resistance and ideology*, pp. 144–67

Stein, Mark, 'Max Gordon and African trade unionism on the Witwatersrand, 1935–40,' in Webster (ed.), *Essays in Southern African labour history*, pp. 143–60

Swan, Maureen, *Gandhi: the South African experience*, Johannesburg: Ravan Press, 1985

Thompson, P. S., *Natalians first: separatism in South Africa, 1909–61*, Johannesburg: Southern, 1990

Trapido, Stanley, 'Putting a plough to the ground: a history of tenant production on the Vereeniging Estates, 1896–1920', in Beinart et al., *Putting a plough to the ground*, pp. 336–72

Western, John, *Outcast Cape Town*, Minneapolis: University of Minnesota Press, 1981

Yudelman, David, *The emergence of modern South Africa: state, capital and the incorporation of organized labor on the South African gold fields*, Westport, CT: Greenwood Press, 1983

6

SOUTH AFRICAN SOCIETY AND CULTURE, 1910–1948

PHILIP BONNER

The Act of Union of 1910 provided the keystone to the edifice of white supremacy. It consolidated efforts that had been under way through the period of reconstruction, and more particularly responsible government (1907–1910), to reestablish white colonial hegemony after the shocks it had sustained during the South African War by putting an end to debilitating interstate competition over railways, labour and a variety of other issues. It provided a basis on which this could be systematically extended through the policy of segregation. Union facilitated the prosecution of two complementary and closely related programmes – the upliftment of poor whites and the subjugation of Africans. These two themes – poor whites and poor blacks – are generally treated separately from each other and have their own segregated historiographies, yet they are intimately related and constantly refract off each other. An attempt is made in this chapter to discuss them together.

Two acts in particular enabled the containment and subjugation of blacks. The first was the Native Labour Regulation Act of 1911; the second, the Natives' Land Act of 1913. They were intimately connected and complemented by colour bars in the main spheres of employment, and they underwrote white supremacy and a measure of white prosperity up to 1948. The continued profitability of mining low-grade, deep-level ores depended on depressing the average wages of African workers on the mines to about 50 per cent of its previous level. The Native Labour Regulation Act (NLRA) provided solutions to the mine owners' problems, once the use of indentured Chinese labour had been forbidden, by enacting a comprehensive grid of regulations aimed at undercutting the bargaining power of African labour and at eliminating or restricting most forms of informal redress. By binding together the mining companies to observe the same rules of operation it institutionalised migrant labour from the perspective of the employers and the state; it constituted the mining industry's equivalent of the Act of Union. A prime effect and intention of the Act was to subject

African mine workers much more comprehensively than before, to the Pass Laws and Masters' and Servants' Acts. Deserting workers – previously 15 per cent per annum had deserted – could be traced to their rural homes, often in another South African province, gaoled for their crimes and then returned to the mines from which they had absconded to complete their contracts. Following Union and the passage of the act, employers became prepared to collaborate on a variety of other issues. As desertion rates plummeted (to 1.83 per cent in 1912), mine owners could contemplate imposing other measures to depress African miners' wages and to hold them steady at ultracheap levels. In 1912, the Chamber of Mines formed the Native Recruiting Corporation to control all labour recruiting in South Africa. The Witwatersrand Native Labour Association (WNLA) managed recruiting in Mozambique and colonies north of the Limpopo River, and competitive recruiting was thus eliminated. From 1912, the maximum average system capped African wage rates in gold mines across the Rand to two shillings and threepence a shift, the non-observation of which was met with a hefty fine. Again, wage competition was suppressed so as to allow the maximum profit to be earned by working the low-grade as well as the higher-grade ores.

Faced with this comprehensive mesh of laws whose reach stretched to the farthest corners of the newly formed Union of South Africa, African mine workers found most of their former routes of escaping, evading or softening their working conditions closed off. Mine recruitment, moreover, steadily mounted. Between 1912 and 1914, for example, Transkeians flooded to the mines. There then followed an extended period of labour unrest, beginning when thirteen thousand African mine workers struck work partly inspired by the example of the white workers' strike of the same time, and partly in protest at the maximum average system, the loafer ticket, contracts and the absence of upward mobility. Wage grievances continued to rankle, particularly after prices rose steeply from 1917 as a result of the economic exigencies prevailing during the First World War. A rash of boycotts and strikes spread across the African working population of the Rand, mining and non-mining, culminating in the massive strike of February 1920, in which seventy-one thousand workers of most ethnic groups (especially East Coasters and North Sotho) took part, with more than thirty thousand coming out over six consecutive days.

The strike was broken by a combination of wage increases and harsh police repression, as the government made use of the full panoply of provisions of the 1911 NLRA. The spirit of agitation that it had expressed, however, subsided only as price levels dropped in 1921. No major strike of African workers would again grip the industry until 1946, but the 1920 strike was a profoundly formative moment. Dunbar Moodie has described

how a 'moral economy of the mines' regulated relations between workers and managers from the 1920s.[1] This moral economy, breach of which
would lead to more or less acceptable resistance, seems to have been tacitly
negotiated in the aftermath of strike. Formal resistance, driven by inflation, followed the suppression of most informal ways of evasion, resistance
or improvement. This was suppressed, but all were conscious that a new
order had to be set in place.

This moral economy was not fashioned simply on the mines. A variety of
migrant cultures infused and underpinned this world of migrant behaviour
and manners. They were forged as much in the rural homestead as in the
mine compound or underground. Their central commitment was to the
perpetuation of the rural homestead, through channelling mine wages into
its sustenance and conservation. Although these migrant cultures were
recursively modified by the experience of the mines, they were nevertheless
inculcated in the first instance by socialisation administered in the rural
villages, above all in the rite of passage of initiation. Migrant societies
that fashioned their own migrant cultures were thus as responsible as the
framers of the 1911 NLRA for forging and sustaining these particular
sets of practices and values. They were set in place at the moment of the
shift from discretionary to institutionalised migrant labour, probably first
among the Shangane and the Bapedi, who were in the vanguard of the 1920
mine workers' strike, but also, for example, in the Transkei between 1912
and 1914.

TERRITORIAL SEGREGATION

The second major act determining the place that Africans would hold in
the political economy of South Africa, and their status vis-à-vis whites, was
the Natives' Land Act of 1913. The act can and has been interpreted as
creating the framework for segregation and hence as one of the first fruits
of Union. That it did, but it fell well short of imposing a common 'native
policy' for South Africa. It was principally framed to cater to the interests
of white farmers in the Orange Free State (OFS) and the Transvaal. Its
two principal thrusts were to outlaw sharecropping or farming by Africans
on white farms and to prohibit Africans from buying land outside their
existing reserve areas, which amounted to a paltry 7.7 per cent of the land
surface of Union. Yet sharecropping was immediately outlawed only in the
OFS. A stay of execution was built into the bill in the Transvaal and Natal,
where a ban would have damaged the interests of huge mine-owned land

[1] T. D. Moodie, *Going for gold: men, mines and migration* (Berkeley: University of California
Press, 1994), pp. 84–98.

companies and many poor white farmers, respectively. Similarly, the land purchase provision affected really only the Transvaal. The Cape Province was excluded entirely from the provisions of the act, which infringed on the Cape African franchise. The OFS had long prohibited land purchase by Africans, who had managed to secure ownership of a scant 156,000 acres of the province's land. Despite the gallant efforts of land agents like J. T. Gumede, Natal Africans had lost as much as they repurchased after the South African War, being squeezed out by the racialised operation of market forces well before the act was passed.

The squatter clauses in the act are more easily explained than are those banning land purchase by Africans. Ever since the end of the 1899–1902 war, increasing sharecropping had caused political tension in the OFS. At the end of hostilities, many black former sharecroppers and tenants flooded back into the OFS from neighbouring Basutoland in particular, recolonising land long lost in earlier wars with the Boers. In contrast to such relatively well-heeled returnees, Boer farmers had been uniformly impoverished. Postwar drought compounded their problems. As a result, the traditional Boer economy of pastoralism for large-scale landowners and small-scale subsistence production for lesser farmers and bywoners was shattered. In its place, dependence on marketed arable production grew markedly. Because few at that point owned more than one or two span of oxen, black farmers found themselves in a position 'to take advantage of white impoverishment and dependence on an unprecedented scale'. Landowners as a result were doubly keen after the war to welcome back any black tenants possessing stock and equipment with which to plough and sow, especially as stock was needed only for a brief period in early summer for such use. Tenants therefore had much greater economic leverage in striking tenancy agreements than before the war. They either cultivated entirely independently or in partnership with white landlords. Many bywoners were as a result squeezed out of arable land by more productive black tenants and slipped inexorably into the ranks of poor whites. Sharecroppers were not only better off than whites but were 'as good or better farmers than some white men'.[2]

The provisions of the Land Act that outlawed sharecropping thus derived from the OFS farming interest. In addition, land purchases by Africans were another deep-seated, though less repeatedly articulated, fear among parts of the white farming community, above all in the Transvaal. Purchases of land were admittedly few, though increasing since Union, but this should be seen against a longer trajectory and in context. A full

[2] T. J. Keegan, *Rural transformations in industrializing South Africa: the southern highveld to 1914* (Johannesburg: Ravan Press, 1986), pp. 90–1.

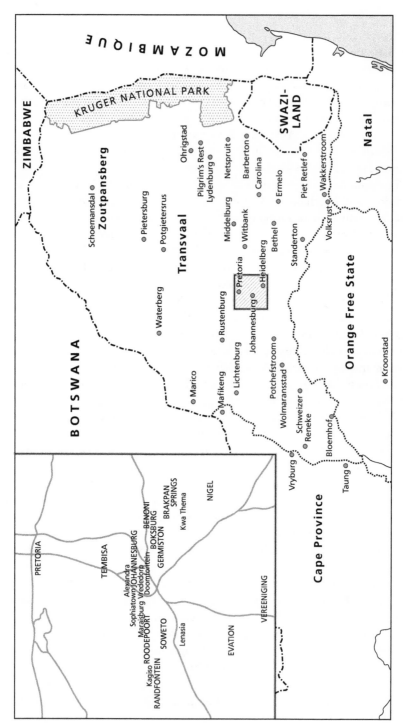

MAP 2. The Transvaal

one-fifth of the Transvaal was in the possession of land companies and mostly occupied by rent-paying African tenants. Moreover, buying back of land had been taking place, initially through missionary nominees, as far back as the 1860s. In the Rustenburg, Pilanesberg and Pretoria districts and in the Northern Transvaal, huge tracts of land had come into African possession, and more was on its way. The final schedule accompanying the act enumerated African freehold farms in Zoutpansberg, Waterberg, Middelburg, Lydenburg, Marico, Lichtenburg, Rustenburg, Wakkerstroom, Pretoria and Potchefstroom. It was members of Parliament from those areas who in fact put the Land Act on the political agenda in January 1913. Five months later, after an astonishingly short period of gestation and discussion (it was published only on 5 May), the bill passed into law, reserving 7.7 per cent of South Africa's land for African occupation (though promising a commission to allocate more) and banning sharecropping in the single province of the OFS.

POOR WHITES, IMPROVING BLACKS

One of the consequences of sharecropping with African tenants in the postwar years was the gradual elimination of the white bywoners. This proceeded fast as land prices rose, as farmers' heirs subdivided the land of their fathers, as the white rural population increased and as capitalist farming, especially including fencing, grew more prevalent. Poor white bywoners searched out new options for survival in the arid northwestern Cape and Western Transvaal, thereby accelerating environmental deterioration, as well as the impact of drought, in the malarial reaches of the Northern Transvaal and in isolated forest zones in the Cape. By the 1920s, rising land prices combined with drought, which struck the Cape every seven years, on average, eliminated the possibility of whites and coloureds finding cheaper land in the *trekvelden* of the northern and northwestern Cape – the area stretching from Clanwilliam in the west to Hopetown in the north. As a result, the 1910s and 1920s also witnessed a steady migration to the port cities along the coast, which hosted steadily growing poor white populations. The white population of Cape Town, for example, increased by 30 per cent (one hundred thousand) between 1911 and 1921, most arriving from neighbouring country districts after the savage droughts of the late 1910s. Many others followed the railways to Uitenhage and Port Elizabeth. The term *poor-white problem*, which first entered political vocabulary in the 1890s Cape, was recognised and feared all over the new Union by 1910.

The very notion of the poor-white problem could have arisen, as the Carnegie Commission remarked in 1931, only in a multiracial situation.[3] Interest focused on the issue because the white community feared that the situation could lead to the destruction of white rule in South Africa. Poor whites were contrasted with those blacks who were rising in the social ladder; the damage that this was inflicting on white domination and white prestige made it an absolute priority for politicians to rehabilitate poor whites and reincorporate them in the white nation. The first-generation social engineer white supremacists recognised that short-term solutions had to be employed, including poor white road-relief work, agricultural settlements, forestry projects and railway employment. Policy makers however saw education as the long-term solution that would bridge the gap between rural poverty and the labour aristocracy.

Recurrent recessions in 1896, 1897, 1902–1903, 1906–1908, 1916, 1919, 1920–1924, 1926–1927, 1930–1932, and 1939 intensified white indigency and social distress, all adding urgency to a mounting sense of desperation. The droughts of 1916 and 1919 were particularly savage, driving tens of thousands of poor whites to small rural towns and city slums, and prompting the formation of the Drought Distress Commission of 1920, whose findings painted a dismal scenario for the future. As a result of the depredations of white farmers, the country was thought to be drying up. 'The simple unadorned truth', the report concluded, 'is sufficiently terrifying without the assistance of rhetoric. *The logical outcome of it all is "The Great South African Desert", uninhabitable by man.*'[4] The message was clear and was regularly repeated, notably in the final report on the census of 1921, which was to have major repercussions on public perceptions, public debate and public policy. Here, graphically, the widening trajectories of white and black population plotted the route to Armageddon. Education was increasingly seen as insufficient to guarantee entry into skilled employment. Planners increasingly recognised that many school leavers did not possess marketable skills, and even where they did, there were not enough jobs to absorb them. They and the government as a whole therefore both encouraged and took advantage of wartime industrialisation, above all for the additional white jobs it could offer, and initiated the Apprenticeship and Vocational Guidance system to train and direct white youths into these jobs. In 1916, the first Juvenile Affairs Boards were set up. In the later years of the war, an apprenticeship system was also initiated, and in 1921, both were formalised by the passage of the Apprenticeship Act. From that point on, the towns and secondary industry assumed a new importance in the life

---

[3] Cited in D. Berger, 'White poverty and government policy in South Africa, 1892–1934', unpublished Ph.D. thesis, Temple University (1982), p. 13.

[4] U.G. 29 '22 *Interim report of the Drought Investigating Commission April 1922*, Cape Town, p. 2.

of South Africa and in official thinking that they would never subsequently lose.

TOWNS

In the years around Union, many Afrikaners began to stream into towns that had previously been seen as foreign. For them, the cities offered an economic and social safety net from the vicissitudes of an often-harsh rural life. There, Afrikaners mingled with foreigners, who dominated their economic and social life. The danger of this for Afrikaner leaders was that it would lead to Anglicisation. Colonial towns were also places where races integrated, sometimes on almost-equal terms. They were accordingly viewed as sites of potential racial pollution. Fear of the evil ambience of the towns thus evoked the final racial phobia of white and especially Afrikaner society – miscegenation – to join its two companions, numerical 'swamping' and the economic and social slippage of poor whites.

Destitute and other whites were drawn to the towns by varieties of relief, by jobs and by informal and sometimes illegal income earning opportunities – the latter often involving some transactions with blacks. Up until 1908, poor whiteism was viewed as a rural phenomenon, and not much attention was paid to the towns. The combination of rural distress and economic recession culminating in 1906–1908, however, saw a refocusing of attention in this direction as poor whites flooded the cities, and the city slums became identified as the central source of moral and racial degeneration. The Dutch Reformed Church (DRC) synods reported 'a remarkable interracial contact brought about through depressed conditions' and warned that, unless the moral decline of the people was arrested, many Afrikaners would sink below the level of 'the natives'.[5]

Most of the major and many of the lesser towns of South Africa began to spawn teeming slum communities in the years before and after Union. The Witwatersrand was the fastest-growing urban area and thus offered the greatest opportunities to the poor. In Johannesburg, a whole zone of the city took on the character of mixed-race slums in which poor whites and members of countless racial and ethnic groups took refuge, embracing Ferreirastown, Fordsburg, Marshallstown and Vrededorp. In Cape Town, too, Salt River and Woodstock assumed the same role, whereas Port Elizabeth's inner-city slums were home to 30,000 residents of all races by the Second World War. By 1917, 39,021 of the Union's white population were classified as 'extremely poor' and another 67,497 as poor, the greatest

---

[5] I. Hexham, *The irony of apartheid: the struggle for national independence of Afrikaner Calvinism against British imperialism* (New York: Mellen Press, 1981), p. 71.

concentration of whom were to be found in the Transvaal and the Witwatersrand. And in 1920, an astonishing 48 per cent of the total white
population, of whom Afrikaners constituted a sizable minority, lived in
South Africa's towns. The towns had become the hub around which South
African society turned.

The spectre of racial degeneration stalked the streets in the decade of
Union, where boys between the ages of eight and fourteen roamed in cross-
racial packs. Of Johannesburg's unemployed Afrikaner population, 10 per
cent were estimated to be involved in the selling of illicit liquor to Africans
in the first decade of Union. Poor white, slum women were depicted as
lascivious and debased, easily breaking the colour line in sex. In 1911,
Jacob de Villiers Roos, the secretary of justice and prisons, introduced the
Prisons and Reformatories Act, the key aim of which was to save children
from the corrupting effect of city life. Crime was viewed as 'a sort of
moral illness', especially in children. The prime object of the reformatory
and industrial school provided for in the new legislation was teaching 'the
habits of discipline' to attain moral reform. In a speech that explicitly linked
poor whites to poor blacks, Roos explained that, 'the white man's burden
in South Africa was to control blacks and uplift whites'.[6] The slums were
'social sores', and a key index of degeneration was infection with venereal
disease. In 1917, it was asserted that 30 per cent of the Witwatersrand's
whites were infected with syphilis, a claim that subsequently turned out to
be simply the product of hysteria and overheated imagination. A panoply
of relief schemes, irrigation works, land-settlement schemes, railway and
road development and maintenance schemes had been set in place to 'save'
or rehabilitate poor whites well before the end of the Pact administration.
By 1922, for example, government relief works of various kinds provided
jobs for thirteen thousand poor whites.

One core objective of government policy was to curb the supposed
wanderlust spirit of the former bywoner, or trekboer, seen as the bane of
government efforts to stabilise white society and buttress white supremacy.
After the war, many marginal trekboers in the Cape and southern Free State
sought new opportunities in arid peripheral areas in the Northern Cape
and Western Transvaal. Others tried to survive – and even accumulate
a little – by prospecting on diamond diggings, by occasional spells of
transport riding, where this was possible, and by hunting and cutting
wood in the Eastern Cape, in the Limpopo Valley and in the Potgietersrus
region (where they were known as pap-and-game farmers). From the early
twentieth century at least, this unstable segment of the population added

---

[6] K. J. Jochelson, *The colour of disease: syphilis and racism in South Africa* (New York: Palgrave,
in association with St Antony's College, 2001), p. 54.

the towns to their repertoire of movement. Researchers for the Carnegie Commission, for example, found many of their informants in small country towns. Others headed for the larger cities such as on the Witwatersrand, in Port Elizabeth and Cape Town. Many continued to harbour a nostalgia for the land (though not necessarily for the precarious existence of full-time farming). A common aspiration among Afrikaner mine workers at least to the 1930s was to invest their savings in smallholdings, which from 1919 surrounded the main towns. These, it seems probable, they viewed as spaces of freedom – much like African migrant labourers from the reserves – free of the constant surveillance and irksome restrictions of resettlement colonies, and where a whole variety of core necessities of life – such as lodgings and food – were free to be drawn from the gift of nature's bounty, not bought for a price on a market. Others were perpetually on the move and were distrusted by the elite. One Lands Department official distinguished between two classes of poor whites, 'the fixed bywoner' and 'the semi-townsman, transport rider and diamond digger who outwit the government'. 'The poor white who has tasted town life', another noted, 'gave a great deal of trouble'.[7]

Poor whites, both respectable and unrespectable, were not only unstable but also a politically volatile class, especially in the first two decades of the twentieth century. Many joined the South African Labour Party in the years leading up to the First World War, before being disillusioned by its shift away from bread-and-butter issues and toward an English jingoist orientation at the outbreak of the First World War. Poor whites made up the principal constituents of the 1914 rebels, and General de Wet is said to have characterised many of his supporters not as 'gentlemen' but as 'slum-dwellers', who looted whenever they got the chance.[8]

THE WHITE WORKING CLASS

The white working class, or white waged workers, was neither a stable group nor particularly English speaking. Just before the turning point of the 1913 general strike, mining still held by far the largest section of waged labour on the Witwatersrand, employing 24,107 white workers, as compared to the next largest sector, the railways, which employed 3,721 men. An approximately similar overall number (25,000) found work in a scatter of small heterogeneous industrial concerns. The railways were already mopping up numbers of unemployed poor whites and had assumed

[7] R. Morrell, 'The poor whites of Middelburg Transvaal, 1912–1930: resistance, accommodation and class struggle,' in Morrell (ed.), *White but poor*, pp. 7–9, 14.
[8] Ibid., p. 14.

at least a partly Afrikaner complexion. The mines, by contrast, were viewed then and later as dominated by English-speaking and stable family-based workers. In reality, they were manned increasingly by Afrikaners. These were able to make their 'silent and unobtrusive' entry on the mines because of the mine owners' efforts at job fragmentation, which broke down skilled 'all round' jobs, which had been dominated by the English, into their semiskilled components, which were relatively quickly mastered by new Afrikaner arrivals, and to the mortality inflicted by the dust-imparted lung disease, silicosis, which opened up large areas of employment to local-born miners. By 1910, the average life expectancy of white miners was twenty-nine years.

The new bywoner workers laboured mainly underground, where they themselves became victims of the deadly lung disease. By 1914, they probably accounted for 50 per cent of the white underground labour force. They were predominantly single, while their foreign-born fellows, if they were married, usually had their wives living overseas. Although the mines provided married quarters for 3,617 of their employees, the bulk of the accommodation they offered took the form of barracks, two men to a room, for single men, which housed well over half of the white miners. A significant sector of this labour force was astonishingly unstable. Between January and June 1911, labour turnover stood at an average of 13.3 per cent a month, partly due to management autocracy. Of 22,815 white employees in the mines in 1912, 20,172 were subject to 24-hours notice. Sacking at short notice was standard practice. Bywoner habits and mentalities contributed to that pattern. Some farmers deliberately sent sons to the mines so that they could jointly retain a foothold in the land; most dreamt of returning to the self-sufficient, independent life of the countryside and geared their efforts toward that end. In the mines, the worlds of the bywoner poor white, the semiskilled Afrikaner worker and, to a lesser extent the skilled, unionised English-speaking artisan overlapped. These porous and shifting boundaries made the mines increasingly volatile places. Mine owners' reliance on racial and ethnic hierarchies of power and occupation to obstruct combination among their employees was imperceptibly weakened by changes in work arrangements underground.

The English-speaking artisans continued to dominate skilled positions and positions aboveground, and a pattern of language-based residential, suburban segregation gradually evolved. Nevertheless, much intermarriage between the Rand's English- and Afrikaans-speaking populations occurred during the first two decades of the twentieth century, not least because of the relative scarcity of single English-speaking women. Moreover, although suburbs like Brixton gradually acquired an Afrikaans-speaking identity, they continued to house many English-speaking residents. English-speaking and Afrikaans-speaking miners moreover shared common workplace grievances, notably miners' phthisis, the arbitrary and autocratic behaviour of managements and the threat of displacement by cheaper African labour. Deskilling also represented a major threat. In 1907, the Chamber of Mines employed 2,234 white miners to supervise 1,890 African-operated drilling machines. By 1913, 2,000 white miners were supervising well more than double that number of machines (4,481), while white gangers were being rapidly replaced by African boss boys. Semiskilled Afrikaner workers were most directly threatened by these developments, but skilled artisans also feared that they were just one or two steps away from the same fate.[9]

A watershed was reached in all of these areas in May 1913, when a general strike was mounted by the Rand's mine workers that shook the newly formed state to its foundations. It was triggered by autocratic and arbitrary management on the New Kleinfontein mine in Benoni, which had earned a reputation for being 'a hotbed of labour'.[10] More miners signed up there to the Miners' Union than at any other single mine. The arrival of a new manager and the enforced departure of fifty employees clearly underscored the insecurity of employment of practically all white miners on the mines, management's deep aversion to unions, its determination both not to offer them any recognition and the wish to reimpose management autocracy. These were problems shared by all miners on the Rand. With the added instigation of militant, socialist white union leaders like James Bain, and management intransigence, the strike soon spread to other neighbouring mines until a general strike was called on 4 July 1913. Ultimately, nineteen thousand miners on all the Rand mines came out on strike.

Both the mine managements and the state were unprepared to meet a challenge of this kind. For some weeks, the government dithered. Once the strike became general, the state found it did not possess the resources to restore law and order. The number of police was inadequate, and the defence force, only just created in 1912, was in the process of reorganisation. After a mass meeting in Benoni on 29 June that degenerated into violence, the government secured permission to use three thousand imperial troops still remaining in South Africa, and they were rushed to the Rand. Even those were not enough. On 4 July, a mass meeting in Johannesburg's

[9] U.G. 51, *1913 Report of the Smallholdings Commission Transvaal*, Cape Town, 1913, pp. 11–28.

[10] Elaine Katz, *A trade union aristocracy: a history of white workers in the Transvaal and the General Strike of 1913* (Johannesburg: African Studies Institute, 1976), p. 382.

market square was called, and then turned violent. Indecisive to the last, Jan Smuts finally banned the meeting. Twenty-one civilians were killed and 166 police injured over the following two days. Rioters thronged the streets of central Johannesburg on the evening of 4 July. The offices of the promagnate *Star* newspaper and Park Station were burnt down. Rioting and looting became widespread. After consultation with the Chamber of Mines, Smuts and Prime Minister Louis Botha met with the strike committee in an effort to broker a truce. For the government and the mines, this was a moment of profound humiliation. Persistent rumours thereafter claimed that the two generals had been forced to negotiate with the Federation's leaders at revolver point. Smuts denied the allegation but subsequently acknowledged that it had been 'one of the hardest things' in his life to place his signature on a document together with that of Federation leader James Bain.[11] The terms of the truce that was reached were full reinstatement, compensation for the victims of rioting and strikebreakers, no victimisation and the submission to the government of a list of grievances by the trade unions. Yudelman believes that with this the union leaders 'missed the clear opportunity to seize control of the state'.[12]

A second major strike, this time among railway workers, flared up in January 1914 and soon developed into another general strike. However, ever since the humiliation of July 1913, the government had prepared to react ruthlessly and decisively. Railway workers had numerous workplace grievances that had been the subject of several enquiries in the course of preceding years. In 1914, however, the main issue was yet another recession and the spectre of unemployment. In late 1913, the railway administration announced its intention to retrench six hundred railway workers. The railways union responded by calling a strike. The strike was scheduled for two days later, 8 January, and was undertaken without even the most basic preparations. It had no strike committee, no funds and no organisation. An equally ill-prepared federation called a general strike in very uneven sympathy on 14 January. This was the moment that the government had been eagerly awaiting. Before the strike Smuts had brought ten thousand troops to the Rand. On 14 January, martial law was declared, and press censorship was imposed. On 15 January, hundreds were arrested (under sedition clauses) in Benoni, and the whole of the Pretoria strike committee was detained while discussing the strike with the city's mayor. On the same day, the Johannesburg Trades Hall was besieged

[11] Ibid., p. 461.

[12] D. Yudelman, *The emergence of modern South Africa: state, capital, and the incorporation of organized labour on the South African gold fields, 1902–1939* (Westport, CT: Greenwood, 1983), p. 100.

and all Federation executives were arrested. From 14 January, martial law regulations forbade picketing; any effort to induce workers to strike; any interference, direct or indirect, with employees or relatives of employees of railways, power stations and related facilities, even the use of 'objectionable epithets'; material assistance of any kind to strikers; and the sale of red flags and of alcohol. Finally, Smuts illegally deported nine foreign-born strike leaders, including Poutsma and Bain. Without leadership, unable to communicate and deprived of the use of strike tactics, the strike rapidly collapsed.[13]

One new ingredient in the strikes of 1913 and 1914 was the spirit of industrial unionism and direct action. By 1913, job fragmentation and the large-scale entry of Afrikaner miners into mine work had rendered craft unionism among the general run of miners obsolete. In recognition of this change, the Transvaal Miners' Association 'accepted its transition from an artisan union to an industrial union by allowing white miners to receive blasting certificates (their "licence" to work) after only nine months' training'.[14] One fruit of this change was the strikes of 1913 and 1914 led by direct action industrial union advocates like Bill Andrews and James Bain.

Once the First World War was joined in August 1914, the terms of engagement between government and labour quickly changed. After initial vacillation, the South African Labour Party (SALP) and the bulk of the trades unions backed what leftist critics called the imperialist war. Because the continued production of gold was central to the success of the war effort, the government made every endeavour to prevent the resumption of class war between the Chamber of Mines and the miners' trades unions, an exercise in which the SALP gladly connived. An exodus of skilled British artisan miners from 1915 (an estimated 25 per cent of the workforce) also changed the face of industry. The mines found themselves chronically short of skilled white labour, which provided extra negotiating leverage to the mining unions. One high-profile incident that took place in January 1917 attested to the strength of the swing. Then, white underground workers at Van Ryn Deep embarked on a spontaneous, unofficial strike in protest at the employment of black labour in semiskilled positions. In this instance, white waste packers were being replaced by black recruits at a wage of 5s as opposed to 15s per day, but as investigations of the strike showed, the same general grievance was shared by white workers in a number of mines. The broad contours of the 1922 rebellion were coming into view. Nearly 2,500 Afrikaners, mostly from the Free State, had recently secured jobs on the mines of the East Rand in place of workers who had left for the European

---

[13] Ibid., pp. 109–11.   [14] Ibid., p. 128.

front. They felt especially threatened by the gathering trend of recruiting Africans into semiskilled jobs and took the lead in the strike. The veil of invisibility hanging over Afrikaner workers had finally lifted.

The concentration of growing numbers of Afrikaner workers in underground work injected a new current of militancy into the mine workers and their union. Their role was most conspicuous at the grass roots. There, works committees of shaft and shop stewards were formed that contested managerial authority and decisions by such tactics as lightning strikes and go-slows. Numbers of absentee shifts had rocketed, and the more moderate central leadership of the Union struggled to retain authority over local branches. It was such considerations that had induced the chamber to take the hitherto utterly unacceptable steps of recognising the South African Industrial Federation (SAIF), institutionalising the Board of Reference system that oversaw arbitration and later accepting a status quo agreement (in 1918) that prohibited any new semiskilled jobs being opened to blacks. As the secretary of mines grimly warned his minister, a distinct possibility existed of 'a third rebellion, starting on industrial lines instead of having its origin in the country districts'.[15]

The mining industry was temporarily shielded from the full impact of the extra costs associated with these developments by the rising international price of gold during and immediately after the First World War. After reaching a record level in February 1920, the premium fell steadily during 1921. All of the low-grade mines, which constituted the majority of the industry, teetered on the brink of insolvency. The source of the problem as identified by the Chamber of Mines was white labour, whose costs were 60 per cent higher than in 1914 (a result of the cost of living increases to offset inflation) and whose trade unionist practices in a variety of ways restricted the full exploitation of African labour.

After protracted negotiations and some union concessions, the chamber decided at the end of 1921 that the time had come 'to face them'. On 8 December, it demanded a reduction of wages for the highest-paid white workers, the abolition of the status quo agreement, and the retrenchment of two thousand semiskilled white workers whose jobs would be allocated to lower-paid African labour. Throughout the ensuing discussions, the Chamber insisted that it had no intention of displacing skilled labour – the target was thus semiskilled Afrikaners. On 10 January 1922, white workers on the gold mines, the power stations and the engineering shops came out on strike.

The strike that was summoned on 10 January lasted for a remarkable eight weeks. During that period, it underwent several changes of

---

[15] Johnstone, *Class, race and gold*, p. 116.

personality that confound both liberal and Marxist interpretations. Twenty-two thousand white miners struck work, along with workers from one or two ancillary industries. Strike committees were set up across the Rand. Their representatives sat on an augmented SAIF executive strike committee. Although the Chamber of Mines remained obdurate and at times provocative, the government adopted a posture of relative neutrality and made several efforts to broker an agreement between the parties to the dispute. At the very opening of the strike, it nevertheless despatched a large force of South African Mounted Rifles from other centres in the Transvaal to the Rand. Fears about the potential role of such a force, and the need to create bodies that would prevent scabbing or strikebreaking led to the formation of a unique institution of the strike – the commando – about two weeks into the strike. These represented a formidable defensive and coercive force, without whose existence the slide into outright rebellion would have been totally unthinkable. Strike commandos sprang up all across the Reef – Johannesburg alone probably had ten commandos, their membership ranging from one hundred in Fordsburg to a massive one thousand in Langlaagte. The East Rand had many, Germiston being the hub of at least six.

The strike commandos derived as much from ex–South African soldiers' experiences on the front in the First World War as from republican yearnings. The ex-combatants inflected military idiom, significantly different from a traditional strike organisation. Among them, Afrikaner miners comprised the principal component. A large percentage of those tried in military tribunals after the rebellion, for instance, gave their place of origin as the Orange Free State. But theirs was a different kind of nationalism from that of the 1914 rebels, and they desired an entirely different kind of republic in which class consciousness and socialism were central. Radical elements in their ranks, such as the Lancastrian Percy Fisher, became major figures. In the later stages of the war, Afrikaner miners had spurned the advice of the republican faction and joined the Mine Workers' Union (MWU). Fisher was elected MWU general secretary in 1921, no doubt by some of their votes, only to be unseated on constitutional grounds by the trades union hierarchy. Once the strike started, he grew steadily in stature as one of the most popular strike and commando leaders, until he took his own life when its Fordsburg headquarters were stormed.

Although the strikers' programme was disfigured by its racial agenda – most notoriously, the slogan 'Workers of the World Unite for a White South Africa' – it did not for the most part seek out racial targets. Tens of thousands of African miners continued to toil underground in the course of the strike but were rarely viewed as enemies of the striking miners. For the first six weeks of the strike, which were surprisingly disciplined and peaceful, it was white miner scabs and white management who were targeted, not Africans. Only on 7–8 March were African communities targeted, in grisly episodes in which forty-four people were killed. However, few of these were African miners, and the reasons for the attack lay in factors outside of the strike.

The denouement of the strike followed shortly after the racial killings. A month earlier Smuts had openly sided with the mine owners and urged the miners to return to work. Later in February, the government stepped up the pressure. Police violently dispersed a commando in Boksburg, killing three strikers and injuring others. With this a crossroads was reached. The Chamber of Mines contemptuously rejected a SAIF request for a roundtable conference. As some strikers trickled back, a meeting of the joint executives of the striking unions deliberated over what to do (even the possibility of calling off the strike). A mass meeting of workers outside the Trades Hall forced them to take the decision to call a general strike. This was very patchily heeded. Both sides drew up battle lines. On the morning of 10 March, commandos attacked police across the length and breadth of the Witwatersrand. The strike had entered the final phase: an attempted revolution had begun.

Over the following few days, the strike was crushed by artillery, machine guns, aeroplanes and tanks. By 14 March, the rising was put down at a cost of between 150–220 people killed, 500–600 wounded, 5,000 arrested, and 18 sentenced to death, of whom four were hanged. The chamber moved on to its own offensive. Wages of white workers were reduced by 25–50 per cent, two paid holidays were abolished, white underground work was reorganised and intensified, about one thousand jobs previously held by whites were eliminated, and two thousand white workers were displaced from the mines. The white miners had been routed, with semiskilled Afrikaners paying the highest price. Defeated and fractured, the white working class would never attain this zenith of unity again.

AFRIKANER ETHNICITY AND THE WHITE NATION

Experiences and representations of the war, as well as reactions to it, also helped swell and give shape to two other currents of white South African identity and belonging; Afrikaner nationalism and the doctrine of a broad white South Africanism. These would stand in an often tense and always uneasy relationship to one another until after the Second World War. Smuts handsomely won a general election on the ticket of white South Africanism in 1921, and it remained a potent political force until after the Second World War. Seventy-five thousand white South Africans enlisted and fought in the First World War. Their gallantry in European engagements such as that at Delville Wood left an indelible impression on the South African public imagination. Experiences and images of the war cemented and underwrote a common white South African patriotism, a more popularly accessible counterpart to the achievements of white South African science that Smuts also deployed to underwrite a common white South African identity, as a loyal, if junior, member of the white Commonwealth of nations in which Great Britain stood at the centre. Its most obvious constituent elements included sport, notably rugby and cricket. The designation 'Springbok' likewise evoked another dimension of a common white South African consciousness that came into its own fully only between the wars. National game parks were another. Smuts had long advocated the proclamation of national parks in which wild fauna and flora would be preserved. Only in 1926 was the National Parks Act passed, and the Kruger Park was named and proclaimed. All the national newspapers at the time welcomed the formation of a national park. They stressed the common heritage and values that wildlife represented, reflected on how these could strengthen national unity and spoke of the international recognition and prestige that this would garner as well. In this respect, national parks appear to have been connected with a certain stage in the country's cultural evolution, serving to weld together different groups within it. In that search for common ground, whites totally excluded blacks.[16]

As against this, hostility to South Africa's participation in the First World War, and especially its invasion of German South-West Africa, for the first time consolidated Afrikaner nationalism as a political force. This was manifested in the Afrikaner rebellion of October 1914 and a few years later in the National Party victory in alliance with the SALP in the 'Poor White' election of 1924, in which it capitalised on Smuts's brutal repression of the 1922 strike and his seeming incapacity to make a serious dent in the problem of poor whites. Hitherto, the political climate immediately pre- and certainly post-Union had not been conducive to the articulation of any kind of Boer Republicanism. A 'saved history' was nurtured, made up of 'two cycles of suffering and death' (the Great Trek and the South African War), in which the sufferings of women and children in the South African War was the central theme. This found expression in the remarkable explosion of Afrikaans lyric poetry penned by Jan Celliers, Totius and Louis Leipoldt in the decade following the war. A second language movement also sought to preserve national identity by securing recognition for Afrikaans as a national language. Under the leadership of Gustav Preller and his *Volkstem* newspaper in the Transvaal, it

[16] J. Carruthers, *The Kruger National Park: a social and political history* (Pietermaritzburg: University of Natal Press, 1995), pp. 48, 61.

attempted to standardise a middle-class variant of Afrikaans and purge it of coloured and English interpellations. However, the whole issue of Afrikaans had to await Union before it could make a significant advance. It served, then, as a kind of nationalist surrogate and was particularly sustained by the many Afrikaner women's organisations, who took as their constituency poor and vulnerable Afrikaner women at a moment when poverty was becoming increasingly 'ethnicised'.[17] For the first years after Union, this was to prove an uphill battle, particularly as elite Afrikaners often used English at home. Eventually, though it was precisely the educated women, often the wives of dominies, teachers and academics, who led the women's movement while their husbands were the men most active in the construction of an Afrikaner nationalism, which no longer looked for the reconstruction of the old republics. This nationalism had to struggle for political support.

If the language movement was in some senses a proxy for Afrikaner nationalism, the two did not automatically or immediately coincide. For instance, provincial loyalties and antipathies remained deep. Even the 1914 Afrikaner rebellion of De Wet and De la Rey was inspired by a narrow vision of republican restoration, while the core appeal of the Nationalist delegation led by Hertzog to the postwar Paris peace talks in 1919 was for a restoration of the old republics. Their failure spelled the end of old-style republicanism and the real beginning of the civil religion of pan-Afrikanerism. Meanwhile, poor whites' political allegiances were fluid and fickle. Many Afrikaners and poor whites were drawn into the orbit of the South African Labour Party before its lapse into a jingoistic English nationalism in the early months of the war. Even in the midst of the war, Afrikaner miners on the Rand spurned the appeals of the republicans by deciding to join the Mine Workers' Union, while their activities in the strike betrayed an entirely different brand of republicanism to that propagated by the Hertzogite group.

It was not only political parties that sought to capture or sway this volatile constituency. Across the Witwatersrand and the Transvaal, apostolic religious sects, including the early Zionists, attracted growing numbers of Afrikaners, especially women. Pentecostalist churches, dating from this period, dotted the Witwatersrand, and the 1914 rebellion in the Western Transvaal took on the character of a millenarian movement under the inspiration of the visions of Niklaas van Rensburg. Finally, a quasi-millennial socialism-republicanism infused many rebels in 1922. In these episodes,

---

[17] I. Hofmeyr, 'Building a nation from words: Afrikaans language, literature and identity, 1902–1924', in Marks and Trapido (eds.), *The politics of race, class and nationalism*, p. 106; see also M. du Toit, 'Women, welfare and the nurturing of Afrikaner nationalism: a social history of the Afrikaans Christelike Vroue Vereeniging, c 1879–1936', unpublished Ph.D. thesis, University of Cape Town (1996).

poor whites asserted their generally recognised agency, thus creating a distinct brand of radical rural populism. The bulk of those espousing this brand of agrarian utopianism eked out livelihoods from incomes drawn from temporary wage work in the platteland on government relief works or from speculative ventures such as diamond digging or farming – 'a mass of wanderers' as the newspaper the *Star* described them in 1926.[18] This small-*r* republicanism had two main components: a nostalgia for an idyllic and unstratified rural past and a deep-seated sense of Afrikaner racial superiority to blacks. This sense of superiority was, however, shot through with ambiguity and contradiction. Points of association and convergence between rural whites and rural blacks had always been present and continued to be. Members of isolated rural Afrikaner homesteads often resorted to the services of African traditional doctors when laid low by ailments or disease, whereas the physical plan of Free State farmsteads, in which an extended homestead of African servants and labourers was attached to the back of the farmer's house, attests to the physical proximity between the races.[19] Again, the presence of an intermediary acculturated Afrikaans-speaking Oorlams class in the farming areas and small towns must also have facilitated a measure of social and cultural exchange.

As the economic distance between sections of the two races closed, however, after the South African War, a heightened sense of racial competition bred a more visceral racism among a large swath of poor whites. Many platteland Afrikaners had always entertained the contradictory belief that the African presence represented a potential threat to the existence of the Afrikaner people; hence their covenant with God in 1838. However, it was not until Union or after, that Totius, C. J. Langenhoven and D. F. Malherbe were to push back the national sacred history of the Afrikaner from its origins in the suffering of the South African War to the epic of the Great Trek and Dingane's murder of Retief. This change coincided with the growing visibility of the 'problem' of poor whites and with small farmers desperately attempting to halt their downward economic spiral by imposing an ever-tightening squeeze on their black tenants, thereby setting the scene for the rise of the rural Industrial and Commercial Workers' Union (ICU). These developments gave rise to two related fears; first, that some blacks might surpass poor whites in economic achievement; second, that rural blacks might mount a peasant insurgency – a much more immediate preoccupation than a red revolt of poorly paid proletarians. Between

[18] *Star*, 17 May 1926; T. Clynick, 'Afrikaner political mobilisation in the Western Transvaal, 1920–1930', unpublished Ph.D. thesis, Queens University (1996), pp. 8, 30.

[19] My thanks to David Coplan for this insight.

them they generated repeated 'black peril' scares, including several panicky retreats into the laager, in the Western and Eastern Transvaal. The filming of Preller's film *Die Voortrekkers* outside Germiston in 1916, in which the battle of Blood River was reenacted and at which Boer commandos hired as extras lost their heads and fired a fusillade of live and blank ammunition into three thousand East Rand Proprietary Mine black workers, can be viewed in one sense as an absurd throwback to racial aberration.[20] It nevertheless chimed with popular rural racial paranoia current at the time.

The depths of white paranoia about white slippage, black upliftment and an imagined loss of black respect for whites can be gauged by the insistence in the decades on either side of Union that Africans, in the former republics at least, submit to an unwritten quasi-sumptuary code of dress and behaviour. Veteran African political leaders frequently reflected in the 1920s and 1930s on how whites had formerly made them doff their hats when their paths crossed and had prohibited them from walking on pavements or travelling in second-class railway carriages, and reacted violently against the adoption of 'civilised' behaviour by blacks, be it through stylish dress or even smoking a cigarette, which would often result in the hapless smoker having the cigarette smashed down his throat. These indeed triggered some of the early campaigns and legal actions of the Transvaal wing of the African National Congress.

The rise of white racism thus accompanied the economic decline of poor whites. Many dispossessed poor whites, moreover, ended up in or spent periods of time in the towns. Here, they often gravitated toward multiracial slums, where they lived in close social proximity, even intimacy, with Africans, coloureds and other races. This closing of the social and economic distance between races had two utterly contradictory effects. It fostered the development of a multiracial culture, and it cultivated the most vicious forms of racial prejudice and race hysteria. Both were clearly visible in the early 1920s. The year 1920 both witnessed the birth of the distinctive culture of *marabi* in Johannesburg, which is explored later in this chapter, and the 1920 Vrededorp riots in which poor whites attacked poor blacks living alongside them in a multiracial suburb. The year 1920 also witnessed the Port Elizabeth race riots, and during the 1922 strike, a brief racial pogrom broke out, when mobs of white strikers and their supporters attacked blacks – not in mine compounds but in the multiracial living areas of West-Central Johannesburg (notably Ferreirastown).

---

[20] I. Hofmeyr, 'Popularising history – the case of Gustav Prellar', *Journal of African History* 29:3 (1988), p. 522.

RECONFIGURING THE RESERVES

The 1913 Land Act stands in many respects as a truly foundational piece of legislation because it set in place both a framework for racial territorial segregation and the bedrock of a cheap migrant-labour system. A central feature or commitment of segregation was to conserve traditional structures and customs in the African reserves. Yet this was in many respects a fiction or myth. The patterns and structures of African rural life had been irrevocably transformed by conquest and dispossession, and all that remained was a surface similarity with the past. As a policy, segregation was also devoid of clear and unambiguous content, beyond the injunction that, as far as possible, the races should be kept apart. Different traditions of native administration coexisted in the different provinces and even in different regions, shaped both by the nature of each initial encounter between the African societies concerned and the expanding colonial frontier and by the varying structures and characters of the respective precolonial African societies themselves. In consequence, local voices and practices filled in the silences and gaps in the empty vessel of segregation, so that life in the segregated reserves was bewilderingly diverse. Even in the twenty-six districts of the Transkei, there was so much variation as to render it difficult to extract any generalisation.

Nevertheless, some broader patterns or traditions are discernable beyond the chaos. The best known of these are the Transkei model of direct personal administration by white magistrates, sidelining chiefs and using appointed headmen, and the system of indirect rule through chiefs granted civil jurisdiction, which prevailed in Zululand and Natal. A much more diffuse Transvaal model ruled through chiefs and not headmen but was then reworked in each locality through the whims and idiosyncrasies of individual sub–native commissioners. The Orange Free State's one tiny reserve area had no tradition at all and was left largely to administer itself.

Two other common features united all three broad (if internally fractured) modes of administration. The first was that all models worked in some way or another through African social structures and political networks, either direct rule working through headmen or indirect rule working through more substantial chiefs. The second was the systematic discouragement of peasant agriculture by South Africa's 'native administrators' which ensured the absence of other ways to accumulate. Therefore, the authority of chiefs and headmen in South Africa rested solely on their ability to allocate land (especially when not closely monitored by magistrates or sub–native commissioners, constrained by the one-man-one-plot principle) and the adjudication of civil disputes. In the Transkeian districts, even the latter was constrained, but in the rest of the African Reserves in South Africa, the dispensing of customary law provided the principal armature chiefly authority. The functioning of customary law was again highly variable in the different reserve areas of post-Union South Africa. In the Transkei, magistrates reserved most of it for themselves, totally denying criminal and civilian jurisdiction to chiefs and strictly limiting civil jurisdiction to headmen. In sharp contrast to the rest of the country, customary law was codified in Natal, and chiefs enjoyed civil and later some criminal jurisdiction. Transvaal fell somewhere in between. The powers of chiefs were consciously kept in check at least until the mid-1920s, but a number of senior chiefs were accorded civil jurisdiction. Once more in this area, the intention and the practice diverged. The heads of *dikzaro* and *dikzosama* at the bottom of the rung of the traditional hierarchy (headmen elsewhere) were simply disregarded, but they continued to allocate land and ran their own courts notwithstanding. Chiefs' courts, moreover, in practice settled both criminal and civil cases in direct contravention of the letter of the law.

Customary law permeated all aspects of rural African life. It operated largely unseen, unless appeals were made to magistrates and to higher appeal courts (the latter formed in 1925). It regulated the core institutions of African Reserve life. Its courts and court officers settled disputes over marriage, divorce, bridewealth, land, family, property and inheritance. In addition, as administration began to fear the subversive influence of chiefs less and instead began to worry over the weakening of chiefly structures and chiefly discipline, especially with regard to women and youths, they put previous policy into reverse and began the difficult task of revitalising tribal institutions. Eventually, impelled by widespread popular militancy, spearheaded by the Industrial and Commercial Workers' Union, the extraordinarily far-reaching Native Administration Act of 1927 was passed. This decisively separated white and African administration besides endowing the Governor-General (for this, read 'Secretary for Native Affairs'), the Department of Native Affairs and chiefs with sweeping and arbitrary new power. It also brought a uniformity into 'native administration' that Union had promised. The act extended the operation of customary law to the whole of the country, conferred on chiefs and headmen the rights to administer it, decreed that *lobola* was consistent with the principles of natural justice and instituted the segregated systems of Native Commissioners' Courts and Native Divorce Courts across the country. In more arbitrary register, it extended to the whole of the country government by proclamation under the Governor-General as Supreme Chief (the Shaka fallacy), thus placing officers outside the separation of powers. This simultaneously reinforced chiefly powers, thereby tilting sharply toward the Natal tribal model, and bringing all Africans in the reserves under tight state control by retribalising them.

One express intention of the 1927 act was to reinforce patriarchal as well as chiefly power. A matter of growing concern to all categories of white society in the 1920s was the steady haemorrhage of young black rural men, but especially rural women, to the towns. The act confirmed and entrenched the already-common practice of consigning women to the status of perpetual minors, enjoying negligible legal rights and unable to represent themselves, other than through a male relative, in a court of law. By generalising the operation of customary law, women were also denied rights in property in land. Upon a husband's death, moreover, male heirs secured their father's inheritance, and widows received none. Aggrieved wives were also refused the right to sue unaided (by male relatives) for divorce. Finally, those African women married under Roman Dutch law were denied even the circumscribed right, enjoyed by white women married in the same fashion, to a share of inheritance in terms of the principle of community of property.

The status of African women in the reserves had been imperceptibly changing and declining well before the act of 1927. One consequence of applying a one-man-one-plot regime in a context of growing land shortage was that polygamous men could not assign to each wife her own plot of land to farm. As a result, rates of polygamy plunged to 14 per cent of the African adult male population in 1921, perhaps one-third of the figure fifty years earlier.[21] The exact distribution of polygamous households almost certainly varied according to the constraints exercised by shortages of land, and oral testimonies from various areas recall large herds, multiple wives and substantial allotments of land well into the 1940s. Areas with an extreme shortage of land and increasingly costly cattle, notably in the Ciskei and Basutoland, saw a steady unravelling of stable family life, with even monogamous marriage becoming rarer and postponed. Abduction and elopement became more common. Increasing numbers of women remained single or were abandoned and together with widows were denied access to inheritance, becoming valued (by men) more for their sexuality than their fertility. Only where, as in Phokeng, women had acquired skills marketable in the white economy could they exploit migrancy to form their own households and, both in town and in the reserve, constitute a segment of the respectable working class, sharply contrasting with the 'unrespectables' from Basutoland and the Ciskei, who were shortly to overwhelm the urban areas. Thus, the availability of land; its corollary, migrancy; and, more generally, the relationship of rural society to the towns framed the nature of rural society. True migrant men generally encapsulated themselves in

[21] H. J. Simons, *African women: their legal status in South Africa* (London: C. Hurst and Co., 1968), p. 78.

home-boy networks in the towns, but the urban experience did not fail to leave its imprint on these men and, by extension, on rural society as a whole.

A major part of this process entailed the significant and sometimes radical transformation of rural youth cultures, youth sexuality and sexual socialisation. In Natal and the Transvaal, youth gangs, known as *amalaita*, encapsulated young men (many yet to be initiated) from the urban environment, and particularly urban women, and preserved links with home. Such youth cultures and practices were reimported into the countryside, fanning adult fears about an increasingly uncontrolled youth. In the context of dramatic socioeconomic changes that followed the First World War, 'ferocious armed conflicts' as well as *ingoma* dancing began to replace *umgangela* stick fights as farm labourers, young migrants in Johannesburg and dockworkers in Durban began to redefine groups' alliances, oppositions and conflicts in the countryside, expressed in dances such as *umqongo, indlanu, ingadla* and *inkondlo* wedding dances. In Mpondoland in the late 1920s and 1930s, homestead heads, headmen and chiefs began to lament a loss of control over youths, especially the youngest of all who found work on Natal's sugar fields.[22] One of the most conspicuous of these were the Isitoshozi gangs that grew up in the mine compounds of the Rand in the late 1920s and embarked on a reign of terror against other migrant miners inside and outside their walls. The Isitoshozi gangs were led by experienced migrant workers – *amarumshe* (old-timers) and boss boys, who operated the gangs for two broad purposes – to sustain control over homosexuality in the compounds by regularly inviting young Mpondo boys into Isitoshozi ranks and to rob and often murder fellow migrant workers. Although the older leaders of the Isitoshozi had minimal direct impact on the countryside (with which they mostly had cut links), their younger homosexual *rikot-shana* (wives) undoubtedly did. Beer-drinking groups in the countryside borrowed the hierarchical form of organisation associated with the gangs. A new kind of youth association, the *indlavini*, composed of *imirantiya* (those who wandered about), who partly embraced an urban lifestyle as a result of their exposure to schooling and their experiences of migrants, also emerged. Gradually, greater violence, both sexual and otherwise, began to characterise *indlavini* youth culture.

The impression of the towns was thus increasingly visible as Christianity acted as a further solvent of rural society. In the Ciskei and Transkei, the key divide was between the 'red' traditionalist and 'school' (Christian). The former can be interpreted as a way of preserving the integrity of migrant

---

[22] W. Beinart, *The political economy of Pondoland, 1860–1930* (Cambridge: Cambridge University Press, 1982), pp. 146, 157.

societies. The latter, with its stigmatisation of *hlobonga* or *ukumetsha* (non-penetrative thigh sex), contributed to an initial increase in premarital pregnancy, but increasingly a decline in parental control and the effectiveness of youth peer group surveillance spread this much more widely. Finally, independence from parental authority conferred by migrant earnings, along with the new values infused in young male migrants by a violent urban world, inclined returning migrants to resort to sexual violence toward women.

Much of the stuff of local politics was conducted in the arena of the customary courts. Disputes centred on the purchase of land, administrative intervention in subsistence agricultural activities and chiefly succession. In the latter, the conflict was often exacerbated by the efforts of provincial native administrations to break down the larger precolonial political units of paramountcies and chiefdoms into their constituent parts. Sekhukhune III in the Pedi heartland, Solomon in Zululand and the Mpondo rulers ceaselessly attempted to acquire recognition as paramount chiefs. In the 1910s and 1920s, the paramounts of both Eastern and Western Pondoland managed to claw some of their authority back as local magistrates began to recognise reluctantly that a strong paramount, if cooperative, was crucial to maintaining secure local political control.

In Zululand, Solomon was confronted by a rival heir to the succession and, after the 1920 Native Administration Act, by the prospect of a local council further supplanting his authority. As in Pondoland, a major goal of Solomon's strategy was to reserve for himself the position of intermediary. He succeeded in one limited respect in elbowing aside his brother, and chief rival, for the succession. Beyond that he also made significant progress by blocking the establishment of a government council and elevating an alternative – Inkatha – into a similar space. Solomon's strategy was to unite the Zulu nation in two directions. First, he attempted to bridge divisions extending back to the Zulu civil war of the 1880s by seeking reconciliation with the Mandlakazi faction under Chief Bokwe and with the collaborator Buthelezi chiefdom, which formerly furnished Zulu prime ministers. Second, he sealed a pact – through Inkatha – with the conservative Natal politicians under J. L. Dube and W. F. Bhulose. In this, he was aided by an upsurge of popular resistance to cattle levies and dipping that swept through the towns and white rural areas of Natal, alarming planters, politicians, Zulu tribal and Zulu *kholwa* elite alike. Planters and some local Native Affairs officials suddenly saw the attraction of a strong collaborative paramountcy. However, not grasping that this was his moment of opportunity, an increasingly inebriated Solomon squandered it by insulting the administration at a Governor-General's *indaba* and by a momentary but utterly indiscrete flirtation with Champion's ICU.

Some reserves, notably Zululand and the Transkei, were close to self-sufficient in subsistence terms in the mid-1920s; others depended on grain imports and all were tightly enmeshed into the migrant labour system. In 1911, roughly 25 per cent of men between the ages of fifteen and forty-five were absent from their Pondoland homesteads, a figure that rose to 45 per cent by 1946. In Zululand, at around the same time, 86 per cent of the adult male population was absent at any one time on migrant labour contracts. All, too, suffered from a series of natural disasters from which they had repeatedly to recover, such as lengthy visitations of East Coast fever around the time of Union, which wiped out up to 75 per cent of cattle. In the 1910s and 1930s, the coastal areas of Zululand were afflicted by epidemics of malaria. In October 1918, Spanish flu ravaged much of South Africa, wreaking particular havoc in the Ciskei and Transkei, where the mortality rate rose as high as one hundred deaths per one thousand people. Finally, drought struck repeatedly and harshly over these years, notably in 1912, 1916, 1919, 1926–1928 and 1930–1933. Between June and November 1931, for example, two hundred thousand cattle died in Zululand alone.

African societies across South Africa felt themselves powerless to withstand these visitations. Many took recourse in religious or supernatural explanations. Those sections of the Ciskeian and Transkeian peasantry most disrupted by colonialism were especially receptive to such appeals. Late in 1918, for example, Nontetha Nkwenkwe began preaching and prophesying as a direct result of the October influenza episode. This she interpreted as the punishment of God for not obeying his laws and as a clear signal that the day of judgement was coming. Nontetha was not specifically anti-white and urged her followers to stop blaming whites when things went wrong. Her central messages were unity and moral self-control and the ending of various traditional practices (like dances). Her doctrine was non-violent and passive but implicitly critical of the authority of chiefs. When her followers were gaoled for refusing chiefs' orders, some began to incorporate into their belief system and dreams the idea that black Americans were coming to release them. Nontetha herself was consigned to psychiatric hospitals, where she spent the rest of her life.

The minor theme of black Americans can be traced back to the growing Garveyite influence in South Africa over the course of the rest of the decade. Most spectacularly, in 1919, Enoch Mgijima, a prophet of the independent church called the Israelites, began warning his followers of an impending millennium and instructed them to congregate at his local village near Queenstown. From there they refused to move, bolstered by the belief in the support of black America arriving in aeroplanes to help them. A force of eight hundred police was sent to evict them and, on 24 May 1921, attacked them with rifles and machine guns. In the ensuing massacre, nearly two hundred Israelites died. In the mid-1920s, the theme of black American liberators and the impending millennium was elaborated still further by the Zulu Garveyite Wellington Buthelezi. Wellington attracted widespread support in several parts of the Transkei that were reeling under the impact of drought and trying to absorb yet another increase in tax. He preached that black Americans would arrive by aeroplane and would release balls of burning charcoal on Europeans and nonsubscribing Africans. The most oppressive of white impositions would be abolished, notably taxes and dipping, but some of their benefits would be retained. Factories would be established in the Transkei, and clothing would be distributed to the people. Believers were to paint their huts black and kill their pigs (a recurrent motif in Transkeian ideologies). Buthelezi's movement was directly subversive of authority. It challenged chiefs, headmen, missions and mission schools, and it held a great appeal for Transkeian women, who were exceptionally prominent in all Transkei political and other protest in this period. It was, as Beinart and Bundy note, vigorously suppressed by the state. Elsewhere, notably in the north, the association of women with witchcraft and the naming of witches became much more common.[23]

The passage of the Land Act ensured that land would be the central issue in African politics for the following thirty years. Between the 1910s and 1930, huge amounts of resources and energy were expended on trying to repurchase land. In the Transvaal and parts of Natal, it became the central issue of black rural life, as African chiefdoms exploited a loophole in the act. Transvaal Province, however, was where tribally identifying Africans were most in need of land. Their plight was recognised by the Beaumont Commission of 1918, which recommended the allocation of five times more land in the Transvaal to African-ownership than in any other province. Likewise, the 1926 Native Land and Trust Act allocated 4,753,922 morgen of land to Transvaal Africans out of a national total of 6,729,853 morgen. Because of white opposition, little of that allocated was purchased by the state for African occupation. Therefore, it was left to Africans themselves to band together to purchase land. This they did on a formidable scale in the Transvaal (though not anywhere else). Between 1896 and 1938, for example, the Koena chief August Mokgatle alone bought nine farms in his own name in the district of Rustenburg. By 1913, the Kgatla in Pilansberg had bought thirty-six farms. Just about every other chiefdom in the Transvaal, from Rustenburg in the Southwest to Venda in the North, followed suit. In the Pretoria Hammanskraal district, for example, fifty thousand morgen of land were purchased by Africans,

---

[23] P. Delius, 'Witches and missionaries in nineteenth century Transvaal', *Journal of Southern African Studies* 27:3 (2001), pp. 441–2.

mostly in the first three decades of the twentieth century. The scale of this accomplishment can be fully apprehended only when one is reminded that the largest official location (i.e., reserve) in the Transvaal at the time was 120,000 morgen in extent.[24]

The buying back of land was most effectively accomplished by the larger and better-endowed chiefdoms, but it was also engaged in by smaller chiefdoms and syndicates with no distinct tribal identity. Among each of these the question of access to land dominated political thinking. Levies on members or tribesmen to accomplish their purpose became one of the principal sources and sites of rural conflict in the old Transvaal, as virtually every chiefdom ran heavily into debt. Many subsections, in addition to groups of migrants, contested such allocations and refused to pay. Conflict mounted during near constant drought conditions in the late 1920s to mid-1930s. In general, though, when disputes reached the Native Commissioners' Courts, these backed the chief.

The increase in African landholding did not prevent a partially imaginary, and certainly contrived, belief among officials in the threatening ecological collapse of the reserves, above all through soil erosion. This formed the justification for the Native Trust and Land Act of 1936, which allowed state intervention to induce the 'betterment' and rehabilitation of the land. The act was first applied in the Northern Transvaal, engendering much opposition.

RECLAIMING THE RESERVES

In 1932, the Native Economic Commission proposed restoring the unproven[25] but supposed failing productivity of the reserves through 'a comprehensive re-organisation of rural society, which would include significant reductions of stock, the fencing of lands, concentrated settlements, improved seed and the expansion of agricultural education'.[26] In 1936, as part of the package of Hertzog bills, the Native Trust and Land Act was passed, which introduced betterment and rehabilitation in areas controlled

---

[24] G. N. Simpson, 'Peasants and politics in the Western Transvaal', unpublished M.A. thesis, University of the Witwatersrand (1986), p. 128; B. K. Mbenga, 'The Bakgatla-Baga-Kgafela in the Pilansberg district of the Western Transvaal from 1899–1931', unpublished Ph.D. thesis, University of South Africa (1996), p. 263.

[25] H. Wolpe, 'Capitalism and cheap labour: power in South Africa from segregation to apartheid', *Economy and Society* 1 (1972); C. E. W. Simpkins, 'Agricultural production in the African Reserves of South Africa, 1918–1969', *Journal of Southern African Studies* 7:2 (1981), 256–83.

[26] P. Delius and S. Schirmer, 'Soil conservation in a racially ordered society: South Africa, 1930–1970, *Journal of Southern African Studies* 26:4 (2000), 721.

by the Trust. The act made its major impression in the Transvaal. The vast bulk of land added to the Trust's holdings was in the Transvaal, much of it in the northern and eastern regions, where huge tracts were locked up in land company holdings and inhabited by Africans. These were the first to feel the effects of the Trust's policies of betterment and rehabilitation. In Pietersburg alone, 224,294 morgen embracing 319 farms on which lived a population of 10,000 Africans, was purchased by the Trust between 1937 and 1938. At first the inhabitants had to pay less than the rental that the land companies had formerly charged, and the transition to Trust control proceeded smoothly. In 1940, however, the first signs of unhappiness and opposition surfaced, around issues of chiefly power, the size of tenants' plots, stock limitation and tree felling. Under the instigation of local activists – Matthews Molepo in Pietersburg and Communist Party leader Alpheus Malivhe in Zoutpansberg – resistance exploded in 1942 and 1943. In Pietersburg, the high peak but also the turning point of resistance was October 1943, when between 1,500 and 2,000 armed resisters took to the bush. Much intensified repression, the effective closure of loopholes in the regulations, and a large number of successful prosecutions, deportations and the defections of headmen and chiefs caused the resistance to collapse. Thereafter, the Trust successfully enforced its designs.

FARM LABOUR

Between 1918 and 1928, the number of white-owned farms in South Africa rose by 23 per cent, and the number of owner-occupied farms increased to 67 per cent of the total. In the first three decades of the century, the average acreages of farms declined by 66 per cent. At the same time, the steadily rising price of land burdened farmers with heavy mortgages, whereas from 1925, their capacity to repay them was sabotaged by declining agricultural prices. Through large areas of the Orange Free State, the Transvaal and Natal, labour tenancy became the dominant tenurial relationship, although both sharecropping and wage labour were employed in parts of the southwestern Transvaal and Eastern Transvaal. Under labour tenancy, Africans enjoyed less access to land and were under the command of the white landowner. In the Orange Free State in the thirty years after Union, pasturage allowed to labour tenants was reduced by 40–50 per cent and their numbers of stock were sharply curtailed. At the same time, more land was brought into cultivation directly by white farmers as new varieties of plough were introduced.

At the beginning of the 1930s, the conditions of labour tenants went into even steeper decline, first as a result of the Great Depression, which witnessed the gross value of agricultural production decline from £61,848,000 in 1919 to £37,425,000 in 1933. Different commodities enjoyed different fortunes in this broadly depressed environment. Maize fared better than wool but considerably worse than wheat. Second, the onset of drought in 1932 killed off thousands of stock and brought agricultural activity in many districts to a halt. Starvation was rife. Many white farmers abandoned their lands to seek relief in neighbouring small towns, leaving their black labour tenants to survive as they might. Those who remained laid-off labour tenants in their thousands, finding themselves unable even to furnish food in kind, let alone a cash wage. The 1932–1934 drought shook rural society to its foundations, loosening bonds of servitude and dependence. Young black men had to be sent out to work to raise much-needed cash for often-indebted homesteads. As the decade wore on, they became more inclined not to remit money home and to overstay their time in the towns, 'because they get no wages on the farm and they see their parents have no stock and they have nothing to look forward to [themselves]'.[27] This produced a constant state of tension and struggle in the labour tenant households.

Once the drought broke late in 1933, farmers immediately sought to recoup their losses by increasing their output and placing intensified demands on their tenants. 'A crisis of control' consequently gripped labour tenancy in the 1930s. Young men bolted the farms in ever increasing numbers. As Chief Gebennewini told the Natives Economic Commission, 'Our children have become like wild cats. You can no more catch a wild cat than a flash of lightning. It disappears and runs away from you, and so do our children nowadays'.[28] One panic measure that was enacted to meet this crisis in 1932 was the Native Service Contract Act. This allowed the homestead head to enter into a legally binding labour contract on behalf of his sons as well as tightened pass controls on the sons and daughters of labour tenants, any breach of which could be punished by flogging.[29] Though unenforceable, this law attempted both to capture labour for white farms and to maintain the authority of the heads of labour tenant households.

Conditions varied widely on white farms, but many labour tenants, quite possibly the majority, nurtured a sense of racial injustice and oppression. Labour tenants' agricultural production diminished, and they were frequently in debt to their master or his merchant. The £1 poll tax on each African male older than the age of eighteen again often forced them to place themselves into debt to the farmer. Debt bondage radically restricted labour

[27] T. V. McClendon, *Genders and generations apart: labor tenants and customary law in segregation-era South Africa, 1920s to 1940s* (Cape Town: David Philip, 2002), p. 169.
[28] Ibid., p. 134.
[29] Ibid., pp. 91–2.

tenant freedom of movement. A near-universal grievance among labour tenants was the farmer's refusal to draw up a written contract of employment. Farmers exploited the freedom this gave them to partly immobilise their labour. Labour tenants complained that their 90–180 days annual labour requirement was no longer rendered continuously but spread right through the year, and farmers could insist that their tenant work for a meagre cash wage after his contract had expired. Any objection by the tenant to this demand was liable to lead to his being charged with breach of contract, in which instances rural magistrates invariably sided with the farmer.

Although the lynchings of rural America were conspicuously absent from twentieth-century South Africa, racial violence was routine. African newspapers periodically erupted in outrage at the shootings of African teenagers by farmers who claimed that they had mistaken them for wild game (usually baboons). Labour tenants around Bloemfontein complained about severe assaults for alleged breach of contract, those around Ventersdorp about harsh treatment and thrashing and those around Wakkerstroom about 'unprovoked harsh treatment'. The district surgeon of the modest sized district of Wepener dealt with nine hundred cases of farmers' assaults on labour tenants in a year. Elsewhere, the alter ego of slavery, paternalism, involving some measure of quasi-kinship between farmer patriarch and labour tenant families, clearly helped stabilise relationships of structured inequality as in the southwestern Transvaal. The prevalence of sharecropping and the weak penetration of the market economy in this area partly accounted for its purchase and persistence. In more market-dominated areas and at times of intergenerational tension and economic stress, however, the paternalistic ethic was attenuated and an ideology of *baaskap* evolved increasingly in its place.

Mounting shortages of labour on white farms and a rising crescendo of farmer protest that had prompted the appointment of the Native Farm Labour Committee resulted in the inscription of chapter 4 into the Native Land and Trust Act of 1936, which was smuggled in to allow the restriction and regulation of labour tenancy on white farms. Where implemented, in the Lydenburg District, this set in train a protracted struggle by labour tenants and their representatives, who bluntly and virtually unanimously refused to register and embarked on an exodus from the area. White farmer organisations and the Native Affairs Department found themselves bare of legal instruments with which to respond and soon deferred and eventually let drop the implementation of chapter 4. The entire episode was perceived by government departments and neighbouring districts as a humiliating fiasco, not to be risked again anywhere else. White farmer grievance nevertheless persisted and contributed to the Afrikaner Nationalist electoral victory in 1948.

URBANISATION

The mounting pressures on livelihoods in the countryside together with the periodic onslaught of drought had two main effects on rural populations; first, heightened incidences of poverty, malnutrition and disease, above all for Africans, and second a drift to the towns. This occurred most dramatically among rural whites: by 1936, 65 per cent of the white population was described as 'urban'. This move, however, was by no means a one-way or uncomplicated process. White farmers went to extreme lengths to cling on to their lands. In the drought-ridden 1930s, for example, the number of small white farms and of white smallholdings surrounding the main towns multiplied considerably. In a not entirely dissimilar way, Indian ex-indentured labourers, once released from the sugar plantations of Natal, moved in large numbers to smallholdings around Durban, where they practised market gardening and subletting to Africans before being unevenly drawn into the expanding secondary industrial sector in and around the city.

Among Africans counted in the 1936 census – the first to be undertaken since 1922 – 17 per cent were recorded as urban, twice as many as fifteen years earlier. Much, however, remained undisclosed by these broad, bland census categories. The key question is how far 'the mere physical change of abode' entailed urbanisation, or rather a more fundamental change in social universe and patterns of behaviour.[30] By the stricter definition, few Africans in the interwar towns of South Africa would have been considered urban. The great majority were rural born, rurally rooted and intended to return to rural areas. Former labour tenants, conversely, were among the most likely to gravitate decisively to the urban. Thus, counter-intuitively, the urban dwellers of the sleepy Free State dorps extending to the much grander Bloemfontein were the most settled urban populations in the Union, raising families, building solid dwellings with municipal loans and growing steadily in numbers. Equally, or almost as urbanised, were all population groups in Port Elizabeth and Uitenhage. The area acted as a sump for poor whites from Port Elizabeth's Afrikaans-speaking rural hinterland and poor coloureds squeezed off farms and missions. They flocked to the secondary industries and to Uitenhage's railway marshalling yards. Of all South Africa's major industrial centres, Port Elizabeth boasted the highest percentage of white labour. Both white and coloured groups had an even ratio of men to women, a figure unheard of in other towns in South Africa. So did the town's African residents. Certainly, the erection

---

[30] P. Mayer, *Townsmen or tribesmen: conservatism and the process of urbanization in a South African city* (Cape Town: Oxford University Press, 1971), pp. 2–5.

of housing schemes in New Brighton in the late 1920s and 1930s implied recognition of the permanency of the African population. On the other hand, it is also apparent that, as elsewhere, inner-city slum clearances, the sanitation syndrome and black-peril scares were responsible for the first phase of the building of New Brighton, eight kilometres outside of the centre of a city that ranked as one of the most segregated towns in the Union. This was in contrast to the freehold township of Korsten. Until the construction of McNamee Village to house its African population in late 1937 and a bubonic plague scare that flared in 1938, Korsten was probably the most racially mixed urban area in South Africa, its population of 23,758 being made up of 5,138 whites, 5,082 coloureds, 362 Asians and 12,456 Africans. These, moreover, were overwhelmingly settled in families. Later, under the swamping impact of wartime immigration, Korsten's African population would again explode, and shack communities also mushroomed throughout the periurban area.

Durban shared with Port Elizabeth one marked similarity, in the shape of the presence of an intermediate and different stratum of the black population – in this case, Indians. The majority, once they had escaped the fetters of indenture, took up market gardening on the outskirts of Durban, where the second generation, from the 1920s, began to enter Durban's factories in large numbers. The same family would typically rent land, often no more than two acres, on which they would market garden, hawk their products in the town and despatch their sons to engage in industrial work. This was the murky world of the periurban, housing an Indian population of fifty thousand or more. Its greatest spread and concentration were in the Mayville and Cato Manor area, where market gardening was slowly overtaken by shack renting to Africans, particularly during the Second World War. By this time, a majority of its residents had shifted into industrial and service work in the urban areas.

In another sense, however, Durban lay at the opposite end of the urban residential spectrum to Port Elizabeth. Durban was home to the 'Durban system' of African urban administration whose aim was to ensure that Africans working in the towns be as impermanent and migratory as possible. At its core was the municipal monopolisation of the production and sale of sorghum beer to African inhabitants, which came into effect in 1909, and which generated gigantic revenues, which were used to house and control the city's population of single male migrant *togt* (daily paid) workers. In this way, the coercive influx control provisions of the existing *togt* system could be extended and refined. Even so, only about a third of Durban's African population could be housed in municipal accommodation. The rest lived in private barracks, in domestic servants' quarters in white suburban backyards and as rent-paying tenants in white backyards, and in premises owned by Indian rack renters in the town. Private accommodation increased as manufacturing boomed in 1917–1918, in common with the Rand and other coastal ports. Many of the new arrivals were African women, who in many instances built shacks on the properties of Indian market gardeners, which were home to married households or households 'in family circumstances'. Women who were shut out from other forms of employment, including domestic service, brewed illicit beer, thus at least partly puncturing the Durban system. The municipality and government responded between 1929 and 1932 with a vigorous campaign of repression of illicit beer brewing and 'squatting', which triggered a militant two-year campaign against the beer hall, the fiercest, largest-scale and most protracted resistance to municipal control seen in any urban area.[31]

The trajectory of Cape Town's urbanisation was dictated by the character of its rural hinterland and by the character of its industry. Drought and depression in the farms of Cape Town's hinterland forced both poor white Afrikaners and poor coloureds from labouring families to move into Cape Town in search of subsistence and shelter. The main avenues of employment were in food and drink, clothing, building and light engineering. These sectors first began to register significant growth during the First World War. Their workforce was made up preponderantly of poor whites (Afrikaners constituted more than 50 per cent of the white labour force in 1936). Africans accounted for only 4 per cent of Cape Town's workers in 1916, a figure that grew only modestly over the following two decades (reaching 14 per cent by the mid-1920s), and African migration was largely discouraged. No decent housing was available for families in the Ndabeni location to which Cape Town's black population was forced to move in 1901 (characteristically because of a bubonic plague scare), and many Africans resided in inner-city slums. These were cleared in 1927 when the first 'bachelor' section of the new location of Langa was opened, although African families were allowed to remain. In August 1926, when the provisions of the Natives' (Urban Areas) Act were applied to Cape Town, ten thousand African workers registered.

Further brakes on African immigration were other distinctive features of Cape Town's labour market in the interwar years. The combination of civilised labour and light industry meant that local industry favoured whites and women, particularly coloured women over coloured men, especially in the garment and food and drink sectors. Coloured men, by contrast, were squeezed out of significant sectors of the industrial labour force by being

---

[31] P. La Hausse, 'The struggle for the city: alcohol, the Ematsheni and popular culture in Durban, 1902–1936', unpublished M.A. thesis, University of Cape Town (1984), pp. 52–7.

excluded from apprenticeships. Both they and white males appear to have been among those hardest hit by the depression in the 1930s, from which Cape Town pulled out much more slowly than the Rand.

Slum clearance, which punctuated the 1920s and 1930s, and the inadequacy and expense of location accommodation in Ndabeni and Langa (alongside the low availability and remuneration of jobs) inhibited and in a sense redirected the process of African urbanisation in Cape Town. Here, again, we encounter the world of the periurban. Both coloureds and Africans, but especially coloureds, had erected shacks on the Cape Flats from the turn of the twentieth century, and shack settlements developed up to and during the Second World War. Much like Durban, therefore, residential and other shackles shaped the process of African urbanisation, impeding it and then displacing it into the twilight periurban zone. This left a powerful imprint on African communities in both areas, helping to shape a hybrid self-sufficient culture and injecting a capacity and will to resist that would erupt in the late 1950s and 1960s in the Cato Manor riots and lengthy March 1960 stay-away at Langa and Nyanga.[32]

East London in some senses represents a case all on its own, as a deliberately and self-consciously nonindustrial town. Its council centring all its energies in promoting tourism, and imports, not import substitution, dominated the town's economy until the mid-1930s. The export – but deliberately not the processing – of wool was the dominant sector of the economy, and the town was the premier wool port of southern Africa from 1904 until the 1930s Depression, when it was displaced from this position by Port Elizabeth. It had few poor whites and fewer white women workers. All this added up to a distinctive kind of town. East London actively discouraged the permanent urbanisation of its black population up until after the Second World War, when a clear shift in gears occurred from tourism to industry. Nevertheless, reflecting the pressure of drought and farm evictions in its immediate hinterland, the town's black population swelled significantly in the 1920s and early 1930s, even though it remained for the most part immigrant and casual. Intimate and ongoing connections of the town's African community between countryside and town prevailed, in part as a result of its proximity to the reserves. In a survey conducted just after the Second World War, it was reported that 'adult native males' were probably 'the least urbanised group', 70 per cent being seasonal, regular or casual migrants. The same report described two groups of the town's urban African population as 'permanent' – the 'educated' and the 'illegitimate group of

[32] V. Bickford-Smith, E. van Heyningen and N. Worden, *Cape Town in the twentieth century* (Cape Town: David Philip, 1999).

women and children'. It likewise identified one thousand urbanised, compared with five thousand non-urbanised families.[33]

As elsewhere, African women were more likely to settle permanently,
brewing liquor and renting property. Household heads were permitted to
build their own tin and wood shacks on plots that they leased in the location. Increasingly, women gained control of these stands. As the population
increased, the new migrants were accommodated by householders continually adding new rooms without furnishing additional rental payments to
the council. The poverty-stricken, rack-rented slums were not much of a
place in which to become 'town rooted' for the majority of the population,
who stubbornly and perhaps unavoidably retained rural roots.

The pattern of urbanisation on the Rand has shared certain characteristics
with Port Elizabeth, Cape Town and East London, but in some respects, it
stands entirely on its own. This has largely been due to the legacy of gold.
The rise of the gold-mining industry is commonly seen as initiating the
process of urbanisation on the Rand, and in a broad sense that is true. The
mining industry almost immediately spawned a service and small-scale
engineering and jobbing sector that employed whites, Africans, Indians
and coloureds on a longer-term basis than was typical on the mines. This
induced a growing number to set down roots and raise families on the Rand.
In contrast to the other urban centres just reviewed, the Witwatersrand
was also host to modestly sized coloured and Indian populations, which
created a much more bipolar racial world than elsewhere. However, the
Witwatersrand drew to it far and away the most heterogeneous white and
African populations of any urban area in South Africa. It was this as much
as anything else that made it South Africa's premier urban centre.

White urbanisation was premised on the presence of white women, and
ultimately white wives. From early on, most white women on the Rand
were Afrikaans speakers, some of whom married English-speaking men.
White women considerably outnumbered white men as permanent residents in the larger cities, emphatically so on the Rand, and the imbalance
was substantially higher among the Afrikaans-speaking section of the population. The 1926 census, for example, recorded 58,133 Afrikaner men
and 64,057 women. Again, the 1931 census of urban areas noted a ratio
of white women to white men of 505:495 in urban areas, compared with a
rural ratio of 531:459.[34]

---

[33] G. Minkley, 'Border dialogues: race, class and space in the industrialisation of East
London, c 1902–1963', unpublished Ph.D. thesis, University of Cape Town (1994),
p. 242.

[34] M. L. Lange, 'The making of the white working class: class experience and class identity in
Johannesburg, 1890–1922', unpublished Ph.D. thesis, University of the Witwatersrand
(1998), p. 186.

The growing exodus of both white men and white women from the rural areas to the Rand was driven by a combination of rural distress and urban opportunity. The 1916 drought, for example, uprooted thousands of white bywoners from the land, of whom 4,220 descended on Johannesburg in search of employment and succour.[35] In 1917, of the 106,518 poor whites recorded countrywide, the greatest concentration were to be found on the Rand. Across the span of the interwar period, an estimated nineteen thousand to twenty thousand whites poured into the city annually. In 1921, the figures published for poor whites nationally stood at 120,000. By 1933, this had risen to an estimated three hundred thousand, a large proportion of which sought relief in Johannesburg and the Rand. The white rural population registered a corresponding decline, dropping from 51.7 per cent of the total white population in 1920 to 41.8 per cent in 1927 to 38.7 per cent in 1931.

Industrial expansion and the growth of employment opportunities more generally on the Rand offered some hope of relief. The numbers of white workers employed nationally in secondary industry rose from 66,000 in 1911 to 88,844 in 1915 and 124,702 in 1919–1921. From 1925, the expansion of industry centred on the Rand continued at an even faster rate, in response to protective tariffs that were imposed by the Pact government to aid selected secondary industries, particularly in the food, drink, tobacco, clothing and textiles, books and printing and leatherware sectors. White women were the principal beneficiaries of the civilised labour policies adopted by the Pact government in 1924 to protect white labour. It was thought that they needed only to support themselves (and not a family, like white men) and so could be paid at a rate that was governed by considerations similar to black (migrant) men. The number of women employed in industrial jobs accordingly trebled between 1927 and 1936, and the number employed as shop assistants doubled. By 1924, 48 per cent of the industrial work force was made up of women, rising to 73 per cent in 1935. This did not happen to the exclusion of men, whose employment continued to increase. Overall, moreover, white men secured more new jobs than anyone else in this period, with white women second and black men not far short of them. During the depression years, however, the bias toward white women was accentuated. Subsequently, in the industrial boom of the late 1930s, men of all races fared better.

Afrikaner families came to town to take advantage of their children's (and especially their daughters') wage-earning opportunities. Many single, rural Afrikaner women took this course because poverty at home drove them there to support themselves (15 per cent in one survey) or to support their

---

[35] Macmillan, *Complex South Africa*, pp. 57–8.

dependents. They were generally housed and fed abysmally, and they were often seen as promiscuous. From the late 1910s and especially the 1920s, a moral panic began to take hold on the Rand about white Afrikaner women's prostitution, promiscuity, racial mixing in the slums and factory work. Arduous factory work (along with breadline wages) was claimed to be weakening Afrikaner women's physical and moral powers, thus leading to sexual immorality. The urban 'problem' also now presented itself as essentially one of housing, with houses mostly rented and sublet, in the latter instance often to Africans.

Clearing Africans out of slums and rehabilitating poor whites through subsidised and supervised public housing schemes such as Jan Hofmeyr Estate in Brixton, and the ex-slum lands of Bertrams, became key priorities of the council and white politics. This was achieved through the passage of the Slums Act in 1934, through reduced rates of interest on government loans to councils for subeconomic housing and by shifting the bulk of the financial loss arising from these loans to the central government. Only at that point did it become possible to clear and rehabilitate the slums.

A disproportionate percentage of the earliest African migrants to the urban precincts of Johannesburg (as opposed to the mines on which they abutted) were well-educated professionals and artisans drawn from the mission stations and mission reserves of the Eastern Cape and Natal – in other words, South Africa's equivalent of the 'talented tenth'. They moved in response both to the new opportunities that were opening up for mission-educated men in the towns in clerical work and the ministry and to their accelerating exclusion from artisanal work in the countryside and small towns. Many were drawn to the American Methodist Episcopal Church.

The number of industrial establishments along the Witwatersrand as a whole, most of which were located in Johannesburg, more than doubled from 862 to 1,763, with the nonmining African working population swelling from 67,111 in 1918 to 92,569 in May 1920. The essentially service-oriented character of the city, however, remained etched on the occupational distribution of its working African population, 50 per cent of whom were employed in domestic service in 1920, 23 per cent in commerce, 18 per cent in industries and 9 per cent in municipal service. Municipal workers, like mine workers, were accommodated in single-sex compounds in which they were insulated, and insulated themselves, from white and black urban society. Domestic servants, who generally lived in rooms in the backyards of white households, were mainly drawn from the ranks of teenage boys or young males from the Northern Transvaal or Natal.

A substantial section of African workers in other categories of employment also lived in bachelor quarters on their employers' premises or in the central slum areas of Johannesburg, 32,231 being housed in this way in 1923. Further bursts of industrial expansion took place on the Witwatersand in the mid- to late-1920s following protectionist legislation, again in the mid- to late-1930s following South Africa's abandonment of the gold standard and in the early 1940s after its entry into the Second World War. During this period, the Witwatersrand's non-mining African population doubled. On their journey to the Rand, many labour tenants stopped off in a small rural town first. For Free Staters who eventually ended up in Germiston's Dukathole location, Vrede seems to have been a favourite staging post, although Ficksburg, Heilbron, Bloemfontein and Heidelburg served the same function. Men generally made the initial foray by themselves. Thereafter, wives or other female relatives joined them. Absconding wives naturally travelled by themselves or with female friends. Thus, across the 1930s to the 1950s, only a fraction of the urban population was actually born in the towns and was hence unequivocally urban. Most, indeed, returned to their rural homes within a few years, often after working as domestic servants. Relatively few worked in industry, and only a tiny percentage in semiskilled work.

MALNUTRITION AND DISEASE

Accompanying this drift to the towns was another transition. Reserve populations were growing, but reserve agriculture maintained its aggregate productivity levels, drought periods aside. Subsistence agriculture survived largely because the excess population was siphoned off into longer and longer stints of migrant labour, on occasion settling permanently into the town, and through an intensifying exploitation of the land. Survival, however, came at a price. The drift of adult male labour to the towns entailed a reorganisation of the reserves' division of labour. More and more of the burden of subsistence cultivation fell on women, to the detriment of the growing and gathering of vegetables or relishes. The steady accumulation of cattle meant intensifying demands on the labour of youthful male herders. At the same time, the economic stratification of the population grew, especially in respect to holdings of stock. A significant slice of reserve society was getting poorer. This led inexorably to increasingly impoverished diets for many and the disturbing phenomenon of mass malnutrition.

Similar developments could be discerned on white farms. As agriculture flourished and more and more land was brought into production, more tenant labour was needed. At the same time, reduced access to land for labour tenants along with no extra earnings in cash or kind produced both an increasing resort to migrant labour among the sons and daughters of labour tenants and a massive nutritional deficit. Nevertheless, in contrast to much of the rest of the continent, South Africa's African population grew throughout the century. Starvation was precluded by improved transportation networks, which allowed the easy and quick movement of food to famine-stricken areas, thereby heading off outright starvation, and the pervasive spread of migrant labour, which provided the wherewithal for that food to be bought, even though straightforward famine relief was exceptional in South Africa. The result of this, though, was both widespread chronic malnutrition and the spread of enervating or partly disabling afflictions such as tuberculosis, venereal diseases and malaria. These were all quintessentially industrial ailments. In short, the South African pattern was heightened and pervasive morbidity rather than rising levels of mortality. This was the hidden cost of South Africa's migrant-labour system.[36] The labour and political struggles of the Second World War and thereafter need to be read and understood against that gloomy backdrop.[37]

BLACK PROTEST AND POLITICS, 1921–1937

The prime site of large-scale African resistance during and just after the First World War was the Rand. Following the African mine workers' strike and the Vrededorp riot of February 1920, however, the scale and tempo of African political contestation abruptly subsided. Part of this was due to a drawing back from the brink on the part of the Transvaal Native Congress's radical political leadership. They appear to have been shaken by the violence that they had unleashed, and became receptive to the West African educationalist J. E. G. Aggrey, who toured South Africa advocating racial conciliation and injected new life into one of the main vehicles for racial dialogue and political moderation, the Joint Council movement. The mass base of the radically inclined section of Congress was at the same time suddenly shrinking as recession hit. Finally, the display of brute force and naked power of the government when it massacred followers of the Israelite sect movement at Bulhoek and participants in the Bondelswarts rebellion in South-West Africa had a profoundly sobering effect on African political leadership throughout South Africa. On the Rand, government repression of the 1922 rebellion left an even deeper and more lasting impression. From that point, Congress's leadership and the ordinary black population of the Rand in general both became more defensive. Among the latter something akin to a cultural reincarnation seems to have occurred. The tumultuous

---

[36] D. Wylie, *Starving on a full stomach: hunger and the triumph of cultural racism in modern South Africa* (Charlottesville: University Press of Virginia, 2001), pp. 85–8, 106, 130, 143, 205–7, 209 (for quote).

[37] H. Wolpe, 'Capitalism and cheap labour'.

events on the streets and in the locations on the Rand between 1918 and 1920 helped to forge a new inward-looking and defensive urban culture, known in the slum yards of Johannesburg as *marabi*, and equally strongly present in the ramshackle municipal locations of the East and West Rand and even in distant Kroonstad.

Marabi took shape as the slums spread and their population doubled. In their perimeters, a new urban culture took shape. Taking its name from a style of music and dance, *marabi* centred on the brewing of liquor for sale to local residents, visiting mine workers and domestics, impermanent relationships between liquor-brewing women and wage-earning men, colloquially referred to as *vat-en-sit* and various redistributive social institutions such as the *stokvel* and *mahodisane* groups. The main public concern of *marabi*'s practitioners was to deflect official attempts at removal, regulation and control.[38] This it achieved with comparative ease. Once official attempts at clearing the slums had been legally pre-empted in 1925, the main threat to the slum dwellers' existence was police raiding for liquor. To combat this, a variety of ingenious measures were devised, such as quick-brewing concoctions, early-warning systems and the burying of liquor in caverns underground. These inner-city sanctums as a result provided their residents with a considerable measure of individual social and economic space around which they erected a variety of informal social but rarely formal political defences. Slumyard society was politically passive and neutral, representing highly unpromising material for either national or local political organisations.

In the locations municipalities provided serviced plots or stands, on which stand holders could erect their own wood and tin structures, sometimes aided by loans or low-cost building materials furnished by the municipal authorities. This opened up a number of opportunities for blacks within the structure of urban control, thus softening the harsh regimen of urban life. In theory, stand holders were permitted to reside in the location so long as they then paid their rent and observed the location regulations. In practice, the ambiguous status of stand holders who were at once lessors of the property and owners of the house meant that they might be fined or otherwise penalised for misdemeanours but rarely expelled. Stand holders exploited this space to effect a number of tacit understandings and to assert de facto rights. Widows, along with other women who had been abandoned or divorced, were allowed to hold on to stands, most central and local government thinking notwithstanding. Men who possessed stand owners' permits also seem to have been able to secure daily labourer's passes

[38] E. Koch, '"Without visible means of subsistence": slumyard culture in Johannesburg, 1918–1940', in Bozzoli (ed.), *Town and countryside in the Transvaal*, pp. 151–75.

with relative ease, with the much greater measure of personal latitude and economic independence that this allowed. They could also permit workers and their families to lodge on stand holders' plots, sometimes in rooms in their houses, more often in separate shacks. Stand holders thus acquired an economic edge to match their comparatively more secure residential status.

The net result of these conditions and circumstances was that black urban politics on the Rand remained relatively passive and inert for most of the 1920s, the Industrial and Commercial Union (ICU) period included. By contrast, in the Orange Free State and the Cape, urban protest politics in the first half of the 1920s were much more decisively coloured by the presence of the ICU, led by Clements Kadalie, which emerged out of a slew of strikes and protest activities in most of these provinces' urban centres in 1919–1920. Two of the more notable features of the ICU's constitution and strategy were commitments to recruit and to fight for improvements in the conditions of farmworkers and women, along with the inclusion of coloured workers. The explicit inclusion of both groups in the Union's prospectus of action was of massive potential significance. Women were assuming an increasingly prominent role in grassroots protest. It was a deliberate provocation by women beer brewers in Bloemfontein for example that led to a one-day stay-away by the town's twenty-three thousand black residents in 1925, which in turn degenerated into a riot. Equally, a large proportion of the ICU's membership was coloured, though overwhelmingly urban in composition and confined to the Cape and the Orange Free State. Despite the ICU's recognition of the potential significance of women and labour tenants on the farms, however, it was overwhelmingly urban in composition and orientation in its early years, as well as geographically confined to the Cape and the Free State.

If the ICU was the most significant political organisation in the Cape until 1924, it did not stand alone. Also present and intermittently active in the area were the African National Congress (ANC) and the African People's Organisation (APO). Walshe describes the Cape Province Congress of the ANC as 'insular'. Cocooned by the qualified franchise that Africans enjoyed in the province and by its exemption from the Land Act of 1913, the Cape held aloof or as Walshe puts it 'interested . . . but not wholeheartedly committed' to the ANC nationally or to any other national political organisation.[39] In the early 1920s, both the Western Cape and Griqualand West unilaterally seceded from the wider region, the former led by the flamboyant 'Professor' James Thaele, who returned from the United States in 1923, where he had studied for a B.A. degree, cresting a wave of

[39] P. Walshe, *The rise of African nationalism in South Africa: the African National Congress, 1912–1952* (Berkeley: University of California Press, 1971), pp. 223–54.

Garveyite fervour in 1923. Thaele matched Kadalie in unbridled egoism. This impelled him for a time in a radical direction, and then, when challenged by rivals more radical than he, into unprincipled opportunism. Thaele who formed his own independent Western Cape Congress on his return in 1923, was initially close to the ICU. When Kadalie left Cape Town in 1924 and moved the ICU's headquarters to Johannesburg the following year, the Cape ICU repudiated the authority of the ICU headquarters, and Thaele's Western Cape African Congress moved into the vacuum that was left by Kadalie's departure from the region. Thaele's Congress then flourished, promoting demonstrations (up to one thousand strong in Cape Town) and passive resistance rather than the respectful representation of the parent organisation. It gathered an even larger proportion of its membership from Cape coloureds, and in many branches, coloureds formed the large majority.[40] A second competitor was the African People's Organisation, led by Dr. Abdullah Abdurahman, which never admitted African members and sought a more privileged status for coloureds. Its concern was mainly with the needs of the coloured elite. Paradoxically, the APO actively courted cooperation with African organisations and rejected segregation with fiery radical rhetoric. When the ICU's headquarters moved north, the APO went into its own protracted decline. This started in 1923–1924, as Hertzog sought to woo coloured voters by offering them an extension of economic opportunities and political rights as a separate ethnic group, provided they foreswore all aspirations toward social equality with Afrikaners. This broke the consensus among the mainly urban coloured elites, and the APO never fully recovered.

The ICU remained confined to the Cape and the Orange Free State until the end of 1923. Then, at its annual conference in December 1923, the Union launched its first national organising campaign. A fledgling branch was established on the Witwatersrand by Bloemfontein members early in 1924. A branch in Durban followed in July 1925. Initially, the ICU retained much of its original character as an urban organisation with a membership of predominantly 'urban and detribalised' Africans. However, on the Rand, its broadly industrial approach failed, and from mid-1925, it focused on recruiting educated men. It was an opportune moment. The educated self-employed craftsman or trader, the independent educated African farmer and white-collar employees of the state or private ventures were remorselessly squeezed downward into the ranks of the proletariat. Laws or market forces limited the availability of land accessible to Africans. Crafts like cobbling that had previously absorbed significant numbers of mission-educated blacks were undermined by capitalist advances. Above

---

[40] Ibid., pp. 224–5.

all, the 'civilised labour' policies instituted by the Pact government in 1924 aimed at displacing blacks and replacing them with whites in all the more attractive niches of employment. This left teaching and preaching as virtually the only avenues of white-collar employment open to educated Africans. Both were poorly remunerated and, in the case of Ethiopian churches, insecure. Throughout the 1920s, the great bulk of teachers irregularly received pay of between £2 and £5 a month. This made an ICU's Branch Secretary pay (before other emoluments) of £4 a month highly attractive. Perhaps, unsurprisingly, the majority of ICU branch secretaries had formerly held employment as teachers, whereas a number had a prior incarnation as Ethiopian preachers. The core of ICU support on the Rand were those oscillating between wage and self-employment. They provided a basis on which, despite a failing and often peculating organisation, the ICU could survive as a significant force there for five years. In this, its single most potent resource was language. ICU speakers used public oratory to rouse passions, to voice outrage, to stir indignation, to inspire confidence, to register a flat collective refusal, to kindle hope and to predict a better future. Words were weapons for leaders of the ICU and were employed with extreme facility, verve and effect.

Starting in Durban, Natal was probably the most successful theatre of operations of the ICU, building on a distinct regional political tradition, with its own distinctive polarities ranging from John L. Dube on the one side to J. T. Gumede and A. Lamula on the other. Natal ANC leader John L. Dube's engagement in a segregationist debate after the passage of the 1913 Land Act had led to his views being at least partly misunderstood in the higher reaches of South African Native National Congress politics and caused his ousting and replacement by the Transvaaler S. M. Magkatho in 1917. This expulsion pressed Dube to mobilise his own constituency and prompted a further realignment on his part (and that of his section of Congress) toward the Zulu royal family and accommodationist politics. It was shortly out of such ingredients and currents that the first Inkatha movement was formed in 1924.

Inkatha was the brainchild of the Reverend Samuel Simelane, a clergyman based at the royal homestead of Mahashini. Its initial formation represented an attempt by *amakholwa* to create a framework for cooperation between them and the Zulu chiefly establishment to exploit the 1920 act, which would also have the additional and perhaps overriding advantage of forming the basis of a powerful cooperative organisation. It can be seen as an inward-looking regional alliance that was to be distinguished from other rival initiatives to mobilise Zulu ethnicity, developed by Alfred Lamula and the Pietermaritzburg-based and subsequent ANC President J. T. Gumede, among others. Both were inspired by a cooperative vision (which pervaded

African politics in the 1920s and 1930s) that they presented as the only way to address popular landlessness and to cope with dispossession. From 1921 at least, Lamula began preaching a programme of racial renewal and redemption espousing 'a pan Africanist nationalism sourced in Zulu history and ethnic consciousness'.[41] Lamula's Durban and Gumede's Pieter-maritzburg offered a more congenial home to the ICU than probably any other urban centre. When Kadalie made his first visit there in July 1924, he in fact stayed at Lamula's home, where they discussed a vision of trade unionism based on business enterprise and economic nationalism. In the immediate aftermath of this, J. T. Gumede founded the Self Help Labour Union and Organisation of Non-European Races of South Africa. In many senses, in fact, the Gumede-Lamula wing of the Natal Native Congress (renamed the Natal African Congress in 1926) anticipated the populist politics of the ICU. Once George Champion took over the local branch of the ICU (formed in July 1925), the two organisations worked closely together. Champion's highly successful legal challenges to the dipping of new arrivals in Durban, and to the curfew, registration and pass byelaws took place on the back of Lamula's Congress. The kernel of an alternative political culture that this represented, however, became fully mobilised only in 1929–1930.

Between late 1926 and the end of 1927, the ICU greatly increased the size, range and intensity of its activities. Barring its considerable impact in the Lichtenburg diamond diggings, its sudden expansion of scale and profile was centred in a stretch of white countryside extending from the southern Natal midlands through to the eastern and southeastern districts of the Transvaal. Some years earlier, the districts of Volksrust, Wakker-stroom and Standerton at the northern apex of this stretch had been the scene of a particularly intense agitation led by Chief Mandlesilo Nkosi of Daggaskraal in support of cash wages for labour tenants. This led in many cases to labour tenants giving notice or refusing to work and to farmers combining together in local associations in an effort to suppress labour ten-ant action. When alleged strikers were being prosecuted in Standerton in 1923 a gathering of between six hundred and one thousand mounted labour tenants convened to protest against the action. Similar though less organ-ised movements occurred in the Western and Northern Transvaal. Through much of 1920 and 1921, S. M. Makgatho, president of the SANNC, and his lieutenants crisscrossed the Transvaal, addressing meetings in Standerton, Nylstroom, Pietersburg, Phokeng and a variety of other rural locations, focusing attention on land questions, notably, farming on the half, passes

---

[41] P. La Hausse de Lalouvière, *Restless identities: signatures of nationalism, Zulu ethnicity and history in the lives of Petros Lamula (c.1881–1948) and Lymon Maling (1889–c.1936)* (Pietermaritzburg: University of Natal Press, 2000), p. 102.

and evictions. It was on this foundation that the ICU built its Transvaal membership, being conservatively estimated at twenty-seven thousand in 1927.

An equal number bought the ICU's signature red membership cards in Natal, where their grievances had not yet found formal political expression. These areas were the scene of the most rapid agricultural transformation in South Africa. Simultaneous dispossessions, evictions and the raising of labour obligations drove labour tenants into the ICU. The millennial message and style of many ICU leaders encouraged dreams of redemption, freedom and the return of the land. Besides this, ICU rural recruits were also attracted by more practical rewards. The preferred mode of struggle adopted by the organisation in the countryside was to take up cases against landowners in the courts. This was massively expensive and ultimately self-defeating, but it was one of the few sources of leverage to which ICU leaders in the countryside had access. After significant favourable Supreme Court rulings were made over evictions in Natal (especially regarding notice and the reaping of crops), the ICU's Natal membership began to soar. The ICU's fortunes were more chequered in the rest of rural South Africa, although a mainly rural membership probably leaped to between one hundred thousand and two hundred thousand by the end of 1927. Generally, it found itself unable to win the support of chiefs and hence to penetrate the reserves (millennial moments in Pondoland being the exception). A number of Swazi chiefs joined along with their followers in the Eastern Transvaal, but this was precisely because they had been dispossessed and lived on white farms. Zululand's Chief-King Solomon, by contrast, along with his Natal *kholwa* allies, was acutely suspicious of the ICU, and Solomon was even induced to denounce it by white sugar barons in August 1927.

The rural ICU collapsed in 1927–1928 as a result of its manifest strategic and organisational shortcomings, its repeated reverses and failure to deliver to members who had joined, and Kadalie's own adoption of a more muted, circumscribed and constitutionalist unionism following a lengthy visit to sympathizers and trade unionists in Europe. This quickly resulted in demoralisation, recrimination and charges of corruption, which in turn led to a number of splits and secessions in the union. Kadalie himself was expelled from the parent body in 1928 at the instigation of his imported Scottish trade union adviser William Ballinger, and he then proceeded to form the Independent ICU, which soldiered on the Rand until 1931 before rooting itself firmly in the new headquarters chosen by Kadalie in East London. For the rest of the 1930s, labour tenants in the white countryside licked their wounds or decamped to the cities, and virtually every avenue of rural resistance was closed down.

Despite the fracturing of the ICU into several competing provincial branches, a second, if foreshortened, period of black worker militancy ensued in the towns and in their immediate vicinity. On the Rand, a rejuvenated Communist Party of South Africa (CPSA) succeeded in making momentary but significant inroads into the black working class in the late 1920s via the small-town mobilisation against lodger permits and liquor raiding in places like Potchefstroom, Vereeniging and Germiston and the formation of African trade unions on the Rand. Complementary to the CPSA's new burst of activism was J. T. Gumede's elevation to the leadership of the ANC and his conversion to communism, both of which occurred in 1927. Gumede's politics had been moving in a more radical direction since 1923. The Hertzog bills of 1926 and the Balfour Declaration a year later which were seen by the black political leadership as a disavowal of responsibility by Britain for South Africa's 'disenfranchised masses' reinforced this trend.[42] After two trips to Europe, including one to Russia, Gumede began to flirt openly with the CPSA. In consequence, he deeply offended the more conservative sections of Congress, above all its chiefly component. At the ANC's Annual Congress in April 1929 (which thirty-six chiefs attended), resolutions for Congress to affiliate to the CPSA were rejected, as were 'revolutionary methods'. This signalled Gumede's marginalisation from the core and mainstream of the ANC. In August of that year, he added insult to injury by allowing himself to be elected president of the CPSA's new united front in the form of the League of African Rights (LAR), which was soon to spearhead one of the more radical political challenges of the decade.

A significant part of the power mobilised by the LAR was provided by the CPSA-backed South African Federation of Native Trade Unions. Formed in 1928, the federation had capitalised on a new phase of industrial prosperity and growth following the passage of the Tariffs Act of 1925. Important changes in the volume and structure of employment accompanied this burst of economic expansion. Employment in manufacturing in the Transvaal increased by a massive 25 per cent, most of which was centred on the Rand, in such industries as baking, laundry and dry cleaning, clothing and furniture and mattress making. The African unions were able to register substantial wage increases in 1928–1929, but they shortly began to weaken as a result of the loss of a number of strikes and internal political dissension.

The CPSA pursued a different tack, mobilising support under the banner of the League of African Rights. A core appeal of the league programme was its campaign against passes, which came to a head on Dingaan's Day (16 December) in 1929. Perhaps the most conspicuous feature of this

---

[42] *Die Burger*, 4 January 1927.

protest was the alliance temporarily forged between Gumede's wing of the ANC, the CPSA and Kadalie's Independent ICU. Among them, they mobilised a column of membership five thousand to nine thousand strong to protest against passes. This was the biggest demonstration of Johannesburg's African population to be undertaken for many years and was staged with a minimum of preparation. Between January and April 1930, attempts were made to capitalise on this success, and all energies were directed toward organising a general strike and mass pass burning to take place on 1 May 1930, but this proved a dismal failure. A key misjudgement appears to have been the attempt to persuade workers whose jobs were already extremely vulnerable to down tools. Further demonstrations failed. Gumede was then ousted from the presidency of the ANC by the conservative Pixley Seme, and not a single communist was elected to his executive. The same purge was carried out shortly afterward in the Transvaal, and the Transvaal wing of Congress thereafter withdrew from the LAR, which it then vigorously opposed. The CPSA was likewise riven by divisions through much of 1930, which led to its ditching of the LAR as well.

Durban gave expression to the largest and most sustained burst of militancy to be seen in this period in any of South Africa's towns. This erupted in its periurban areas, where a massive unregulated population had gathered by the early 1920s. Police had made an abortive effort to regain control of the area in 1926, when they deported hundreds of African women whom they deemed responsible for the illicit brewing of beer. This had prompted Lamula's and Champion's initial efforts to challenge the council by laws in the courts. That attracted a mass membership to the ICU, but Champion and Lamula, because of the legal nature of their challenge, were unable to translate this into mass action. The stalemate was broken in March 1929, when the central government authorised the Durban municipality to erect a beer hall in Sydenham. At this point, the patience of the diverse segments of the periurban areas, suffering from declining wages and the travails in the countryside, snapped. A thousand-strong picket, led by Ma Dhlamini, the ICU Women's Auxiliary League leader, closed down the beer hall. *Amalaita* groups of young men provided militias to the union. Secret meetings were held by them and others in Tusi's dance hall to organise the boycott, prompting Hamilton Msomi to celebrate Champion as 'king of the *amalaitas*'. An extraordinarily hybrid syncretic culture became distilled around this time, exemplified by a march led by a brass band that was followed by Africans in Highland costume bearing Union Jacks and flags decorated with the hammer and sickle. Violence reached its peak in midyear, when J. T. Gumede addressed a meeting of six thousand organised by the ICU *yase Natal* to sustain support for the beer-hall boycott. Vicious clashes with Borough Police broke out the following day, at which point two thousand white vigilantes besieged the ICU hall. Six thousand of Durban's African residents marched on the hall to relieve those trapped inside. In the ensuing clash, 120 people were injured, 6 fatally.[43] A later pass-burning demonstration on Dingaan's Day, 16 December, under the leadership of Johannes Nkosi, was violently broken up by police, who assassinated Nkosi in the process, turning him into the CPSA's first black political martyr. Thereafter, with the Depression enveloping Durban and other urban centres, repression reached new heights, and organised resistance collapsed.

The third example of this relatively unremarked insurgent spirit of the age arose in the rural towns of the Western Cape. As on the Rand, it was led by the CPSA, which had recruited several key local militants in the persons of John Gomas, Elliot Ntonjeni and Bransby Ndobe into its ranks. The initial base of the operations that the CPSA undertook with Western Cape ANC leader James Thaele was Worcester, which was being swamped by coloured farm workers fleeing the effects of recession and the grip of drought. They survived by, among other things, brewing illicit liquor – prompting police raids and a surge of resistance led by the communist militants. In 1930, they set up branches in all the small Western Cape towns and promoted the doctrine of noncooperation with whites and adherence to separatist churches. Such militancy contrasted with the conspicuous moderation of other Western Cape black organisations at the time. On May Day in 1930, Ntonjeni and others led a mass demonstration through the streets of Worcester. This proceeded without incident but was followed by another meeting on 5 May, which in turn prompted a clash with police and sparked the Parker Street riots in which a crowd attacked the police, who shot back and both sides suffered serious casualties, including five deaths. At this point, Thaele disassociated himself from the militants and, in September 1930, persuaded the executive of the Western Cape ANC to expel all members of the CPSA. Ntonjeni and Ndobe responded by forming the Independent ANC in November 1930. Expounding the policy and slogan of a 'Black Republic', they mounted a series of rural strikes, which elicited more repression, and the exile of their leaders to Port Elizabeth. The new body finally collapsed in much the same way as the LAR on the Rand when the CPSA Bolshevised, executed an abrupt turn to the left and purged many of its most active members.

If African politics spoke with many voices in the 1920s, at a national level at least, it fell totally mute in the 1930s. The ascent to the ANC

[43] P. La Hausse de Lalouvière, 'The message of the warriors. The ICU, the labouring poor and the making of popular culture in Durban, 1925–30', in Bonner et al. (eds.), *Holding their ground: class, locality and culture in 19th and 20th century South Africa*, pp. 23–40.

Presidency by Pixley ka Izaka Seme in a sense symbolised the politics of the decade. The moment he took the helm of the organisation in April 1930 he steered it unerringly into the doldrums where it languished until 1937. Even the passage of Hertzog's native bills did little to spur him or the ANC into action. His primary objective, as it had been earlier in the decade, was to fend off and neutralise alternative political organisations (in this case, the All Africa Convention), which had arisen to meet the prevailing challenges, rather than take decisive action to confront the problem that had brought those organisations into being. Even when Seme was replaced as President in 1937 (when he appeared, to visiting black American academic Ralph Bunche's derision and amazement in 'frock coat and white spats, a stove pipe hat, morning pants'),[44] Congress continued to languish, and it was not until A. B. Xuma took over the leadership of the organisation in 1940 that it began to revive.

More activity was evident in the orbit of provincial politics, but every province was split either two or three ways, which ushered in what has been described as 'years of anguished impotence for the ANC.'[45] Equally, the ICU imploded. Even in Natal, its three factions were increasingly preoccupied with cultural activities, such as *ngoma* dancing, dance halls and sport. The CPSA was, if anything, even more bankrupt of leadership, strategy and ideas, as Comintern instructions led to the near disintegration of the party.

One reason for the multiple failure of black national political organisations and for the broader failure of the black political imagination in the 1930s lay in the combined ravages of depression and drought. Even the politically conscious reached for nothing more ambitious than a simple means of survival. The scale of the disaster with which black South Africans in particular were confronted seems to have numbed political thinking and drained political initiative. Instead, various forms of self-help and its linked institution, the cooperative, became attractive. Specifically, they satisfied a growing desire of many black intellectuals to retain a link with, and in some senses effect a return to, the land, through the urban marketing of rural produce. The cooperative also served to bridge the divide between black proletariat and black elite (black proletarians should buy from the black elite) while simultaneously affording the elite the means of maintaining their distance. Preaching the need for 'self help and a more effective mobilisation of our economic forces for that purpose', J. T. Jabavu stressed

[44] R. J. Bunche, *An African American in South Africa: the travel notes of Ralph J Bunche, 28 September 1937–1 January 1938* (Johannesburg: Witwatersrand University Press, 1992).
[45] Walshe, *African nationalism*.

the need for Africans to 'concentrate on law, medicine, progressive farming, business and commerce.'[46]

Disillusion with urban civilisation led the elite to look to the reserves as the sites and motors of progress of African civilisation and of an African renaissance. A large part of the political energies of the revamped old autochthonous black elite in the Transvaal was devoted to such enterprises, in the largest buyback of land to be seen anywhere in the country. Here, migrant earnings were the key – earnings that might be used ultimately to escape the migrant life. Chiefs were central to such initiatives, but the eyes of the local black urban elite were likewise often equally fixed on this chimerical idea of black rural economic independence. Many, if not most, of the major black political leaders of this period doubled as land agents, searching out plots or purchasable land. These included Seme, Dube, Kadalie, Gumede, Makgatho and no doubt many other less prominent figures. Clearly, in much the same way as the influence of the urban seeped into virtually every pore of black rural life, so the countryside insinuated itself into the fabric of black urban living while the seductive image of the rural suffused the mental landscape of the black urban world.

The continued pull of the countryside left a further mark on black political life – the resurrection, redefinition and remobilisation of ethnic identities, notably in KwaZulu-Natal but also in many places elsewhere. Splits between Sotho and Ndebele (i.e., Xhosa and Zulu) interlopers divided the Transvaal Congress. In Port Elizabeth, the New Brighton Advisory Board was likewise split during the interwar period between Xhosa and Mfengu factions, while in Cape Town the politics of African ethnicity was more influential and pervasive than that of African nationalism. In each of these centres, as elsewhere in Africa, competition for urban jobs and urban resources like housing lay at the root of such ethnic mobilisation, competition that was massively amplified by the onset of economic depression in 1930. At the same time, and in the same way as in much of the rest of the continent, such ethnic identities were massively reworked and recrafted within and to suit the urban context.

The urban areas were also the site of much other cultural, social and political re-energising and reworking in this superficially 'dormant' decade. Overwhelmingly, politics in this period was conducted at and confined to the level of the local. The reasons again lie primarily in a devastating combination of depression and drought that traumatised South African society in the first half of the 1930s. Local struggles developed, in Benoni, Germiston and many other places, largely in resistance to invasive municipal policing and attacks on illegal brewing. Elsewhere, state intervention seemed

[46] Ibid., p. 146.

less intrusive, for example in Port Elizabeth, where the pass laws were not imposed and the domestic brewing of beer was allowed and forms of accommodation developed, particularly as periurban settlements expanded around Cape Town and Durban. In many places, women came to dominate the ownership of location stands. They defended themselves with vigour but were absent from formal politics, as in Germiston, maintaining their position through semi-spontaneous riots in reaction to police raids.

The Urban Areas Act of 1923 and invasive location policing were less extensively disposed in other urban areas of the Union, thus producing even less active forums of local politics. Bloemfontein and the smaller Orange Free State towns in general reveal a picture similar to that of New Brighton, Port Elizabeth. During the recession and drought, populations swelled, but a combination of domestic brewing, the system of patronage and low levels of municipal interference reduced politics wholly to the level of the mundane and the local. East London and Pretoria reveal different patterns that, nevertheless, yielded the same overall effect. Much of Pretoria's population lived in the township of Marabastad, where subletting and illicit brewing flourished, and women constituted the largest part of the urban population. Here, the absence of an aggressively segregationist or controlling municipal policy kept African politics localised and restrained. In East London, massive subletting and relatively uncontained brewing of liquor confirmed its character, first noted in the 1920s, as 'a place for widows'. By the 1940s, their numbers were augmented by 'runaway girls'. The male population meanwhile continued to be overwhelmingly migrant, conservative and politically passive and disengaged. As long as the more tenaciously urban location women were not excessively intruded on by the authorities (which began to happen between 1938 and 1940), their concerns remained domestic and parochial. Their space of freedom and relative contentment lay in the houses and shacks that they rented out. By 1940, municipal sources claimed every street in the location was 'controlled by women', and that an extraordinary 60–70 per cent of shack houses were owned by them.[47] This left an indelible imprint on local political culture that would not be politically disturbed until the late 1940s.

CULTURAL TRANSFORMATIONS

A kaleidoscope of cultural transformations and reconstructions occurred during this period, above all among those confronted by the twin blights of conquest and dispossession. The interwar period witnessed much intellectual work being invested in the reworking of identities, as both African

[47] Minkley, 'Border dialogues', pp. 248–9.

and Afrikaner intellectuals grappled with the acute social and ideological dislocations that followed in the wake of rapid urbanisation. African intellectuals, such as the Dhlomo brothers and Lamula, ransacked written and oral versions of oral transitions to refashion ethnic identities through histories, drama, liturgy and prose. Afrikaner intellectuals did much the same, because the problems that the Afrikaners confronted differed little from those of the Africans.

After 1925, a flood of Afrikaner immigration to the cities transformed the social profile of the Afrikaner community. Afrikaner intellectuals universally lamented the changes, believing that a total crisis was threatening the foundations of the Afrikaner value system. Afrikaner literature steeped itself in a misty and ultimately unconstructive nostalgia, its principal genre between the wars being the *plaas roman* that celebrated rural probity and rural life and that excoriated the corrupting influence of the town. For church leaders and academics, the cities were identified as the sites of the twin threats of pluralisation (other white values, identities and languages) and equalisation (with blacks). This required, as Professor J. F. Burger wrote in 1930, that Afrikaner leaders would have to 'teach Afrikaners to retain their souls in the cities where they have settled: in the midst of foreign elements [they must be taught] to remain Afrikaners in heart and soul'.[48] To accomplish this task, a new cultural body was summoned into being late in 1929, the Federasie van Afrikaner Kultuurorganisasies (FAK). It was largely through the Federation's activities that the Christian-national interpretation of Afrikaner-saved history became the most widely accepted version of civil theology. Leading Afrikaner literary figures like N. P. van Wyk Louw began engaging with the issue of bridging town and country. This was finally achieved, almost by accident, by the Ossewatrek – commemorating the centenary of the Great Trek. This set out from Cape Town in 1938 to reenact the Great Trek and elicited a phenomenal response from grassroots Afrikaners, penetrating the popular imagination to make the reconnections. As the ox wagons passed through small rural towns, streets were renamed – most notably to the ubiquitous Voortrekker Street – 'Die Stem' was elevated to the status of virtually a national anthem and the *braaivleis* became fashionable among city people. One hundred thousand people attended its concluding ceremony in Pretoria when the foundation stone of the Voortrekker Monument was laid. Former clergyman and then leader of the Purified National Party D. F. Malan put the changed sentiment into words and reconfigured the cultural landscape in the most skilful and influential speech of his career at the Blood River Centennial celebrations held at Blood River on 16 December 1938. There,

---

[48] Moodie, *Afrikanerdom*, p. 133.

he developed the theme of the Second Great Trek, which set the urban migration of the Afrikaner firmly in the context of civil religion. A century after the first Trek, Afrikaners had set out on a Second Great Trek to a new frontier, which was the city, where Afrikaners confronted a new Blood River. Here, Afrikaners, 'defenceless on the open plain of equalization', perished daily on a new battleground, the labour market. This was a ringing call to arms. The urban problem had been extensively publicised before by Afrikaner politicians, but never previously 'had an analysis of Afrikaner urban poverty been so skillfully blended with so many of the racial and ethnic themes of the civil faith'.[49]

Afrikaner politics attempted to bridge the gap between the elite and the poor whites and thus reduce the perceived threat of slippage into the category of coloured. Among the coloureds, in contrast, there was a profound difference in worldview and in the experience of the coloured elite and the coloured working class, and the various cultural and social mechanisms that enabled each group to construct its own versions of being coloured – coloured fraternal lodges, coloured churches for the elite and in various resource- and hardship-sharing mechanisms for the poor. For the elite, the attempt at assimilation into the white community meant that 'respectability and shame' were the key defining terms of middle-class coloured experience in the Western Cape. However, these were much less prominent features of the personality and consciousness of the majority of working-class coloureds, both there and elsewhere in the country. Certainly, if the experience of the Witwatersrand and the Malay Location in particular is anything to go by, willing acceptance of social integration with Africans (and Indians) and a relatively open and harmonious co-existence seem to have been more the norm, all fusing into 'a mixed mass of humanity', as one East Rand black resident put it, conspicuous neither for its respectability nor its shame.

South Africa's Indian community was even more splintered than that of coloureds, its commonness sundered along lines of class, caste, region of origin and language. However, a sense of Indianness did develop, partly grounded in mutual interpenetration across caste, class and language lines and intense spatial concentration, as was the case in and around Durban; partly on the patronage and credit extended by traders to ex-indentured South Indians, but most of all through the development of a common colonial-born Indian identity among ex-indentured labourers, which took organisational expression in such bodies as the Colonial Born and Settler Indian Association (1911). This common identity that distilled among the

[49] Ibid., p. 198–201.

more successful offspring of indentures (often nurtured in Indian schools) permitted this group to link downward toward the underclasses, whose leaders likewise began to articulate a similar identity. Further cementing this sometimes somewhat elusive sense of commonality was the Gandhian legacy of satyagraha, which implied cross-class solidarity in the Indian community and a transnational identification with Indian nationalism, socialism and its liberation struggle. Of all South African Indian leaders, Yusuf Dadoo most clearly exemplified how the construction of Indianness, in this sense, went hand in hand with a sense of South African belonging. It was he, too, who translated it in the Transvaal into coherent political organisation from 1939. The Transvaal Indian Congress (TIC) had hitherto been dominated by Indian-trader interests, for whom the notion of a South African Indian community still remained at the level of rhetoric. Dadoo's position triumphed politically in the elections to the TIC executive in December 1945. In Natal it achieved a similar success under Dr G. M. Naicker, a South African Indian leader. Between them, these two would spearhead a new alliance with African Nationalist organisations, which would transform the face of resistance politics and further reshape identities over the following two decades.

Among the most important African reactions to social change was con-version to Christianity, followed by secessions from the mainline mission churches in the form of Ethiopian groups and the reworking of the Christian gospel in an indigenous African idiom, in the form of syncretist Zionist sects. Ethiopian secessions took place largely in response to the entrench-ment of racist practices and ideas in the mission churches in the 1880s along with the discountenancing of African ordinations, and they grew increasingly common in the 1890s. The Zionist movement was intro-duced into South Africa from the United States in the late 1890s. Among its distinguishing features were triune immersion (baptism in the name of the Trinity) and divine healing. Such churches were prime examples of African cultural reconfiguration, blending Christian practices with a variety of African practices and beliefs (e.g., witchcraft, ancestor worship, polygamy). Isaiah Shembe's Nazarite church in many ways illustrates this point. Shembe was baptised into a Zionist group in Witsieshoek (in the Free State) in 1906. In 1911, he founded his Church of Nazareth on the outskirts of Durban. The proliferation of Zionist churches in this period, of which Shembe's was but one, has been seen partly as a response to poverty and dispossession. One of their prime preoccupations was to gain access to land. Shembe achieved this in one of the few areas on the outskirts of Durban when Africans could purchase freehold land. Shembe's church, like other churches of its kind, was profoundly syncretistic, exhibited for example in a new kind of ritual dress developed by its creator, combining

Zulu regalia with white colonial uniforms called *ama-scotch* and a hybrid religious dance choreography. Shembe's church emerged as a mechanism for 'restoring, reconstructing, social ideological and cultural life'. His hymns and sermons appeal to God to '[r]emember us in our outcast place . . . the rump land that is Zululand'. 'Wake up, wake up you African . . . our land is broken into pieces'.[50] Likewise, the musical genre of *thula ndlavini*, for example, which derived from Xhosa melodies and that emerged in the late 1920s and was recorded by Caluza in 1930, centres on the collapse of traditional value systems under the constraints of urban living, one song 'Izhiwane Elihle' (Hope Does Not Kill) blaming alcoholism among slum dwellers for the breakup of family ties.[51]

The Zionist proclivities of many African immigrants to the town were not shared by Africans alone. In 1906, early preachers, notably P. L. le Roux, were reinforced by a group of Pentecostal missionaries from Indianapolis, in the United States. South Africa's Pentecost was inaugurated in Doornfontein's (Johannesburg) Zion chapel. This was marked by ecstatic phenomena such as glossolalia, 'holy laughter', shakings and prostrations under the power of the Holy Spirit and public confessions of sin, and divine healing. The movement then quickly spread to the western suburbs of Vrededorp and Newlands, and then into the Orange River Colony. What was particularly striking about its composition at this time was its multiracial character, its practices having a particular appeal to destitute, urbanising, unemployed Afrikaners who were among the prime casualties of the 1906–1908 depression. The Pentecostal churches soon introduced segregationist practices and segregated structures. Substantial conversions among Afrikaners persisted, however, showing in part that the malaise they experienced was similar to that proletarianising of African migrants. From their initial urban base, the Pentecostal churches achieved huge conversions in the Free State, Basutoland and the southeastern Transvaal, where they left a massive imprint on a successive generation of Zionist churches. Here, again, the link between town and country is clear.

Despite that, mainstream churches commanded the loyalty of the majority of both black and white South Africans and were outpaced only by African Initiated Churches later in the century, largely as a result of urban migration. Among Afrikaners, the Dutch Reformed Church quickly reclaimed ground lost in the early part of the century. By 1910, occasional flirtations with Pentecostalism aside, the vast majority of Afrikaners in the Free State and Transvaal were steady members of DRC congregations,

---

[50] L. Gunner, *The man of heaven and the beautiful one* (Leiden: Brill, 2002), pp. 8, 29–31.
[51] V. Erlman, 'But hope does not kill: black popular music in Durban', in Maylam and Edwards (eds.), *The people's city*, pp. 73–7, 90.

again probably as a result of the massive dislocations of the South African War. They clove to a more conservative Calvinist version of the Protestant faith, in contrast to the Cape, where an evangelical current held sway, characterised by individual religious experience, the virtues of modernity, diligence, sobriety and a somewhat mystical piety. The latter's ideological ascendancy was dramatically overturned by the ousting of J. du Plessis from the Theology Faculty at Stellenbosch in 1930. There, the northern tradition finally triumphed, repudiating among other things du Plessis's acceptance of Darwin's conception of evolution. Thereafter, the Nederduits Gereformeerde Kerk (NGK) appointed only pseudo-Kuyperian nationalists to seminaries and to universities, so by the mid-1930s, the NGK was the intellectual bastion of resistance against modernisation. At the missionary conference of 1935, the burden of emphasis on man, the individual, shifted to man as part of a collective organic unit, and the search began to provide a theological basis for apartheid (the term was coined in that year) in a neo-Calvinist framework. Meanwhile, the leadership of most English-speaking churches was moving in the opposite direction, leading the Anglican bishops in 1930 to ask for full citizenship in South Africa of all, irrespective of colour.

MUSIC

Music among the black populations of South Africa's towns helped both middle-class and working-class Africans to cope with the dehumanisation of the South African system. Most of the leading South African black politicians of the 1910s and 1920s, for example, were musicians, composing and performing in their own right, including John Dube, J. S. Letanka, Moses Mphahlele, and S. M. Makgatho. Indeed, for the mission-educated African elite, whose economic circumstances were being ever more straitened, the embracing of particular styles of music, which developed in relationship to African American traditions, became a key social marker to create social distance between themselves and the black urban working class. Choir performances, provincial and national eisteddfods, and a constant stream of concerts in which jazz performances featured steadily more prominently contributed to this goal. Their exemplar, in many respects, was the American Methodist Episcopal Church, which was introduced into South Africa by Charlotte Maxeke after visiting the United States in the early 1890s as part of a musical troupe, where she attended Wellington's Wilberforce Institution. African American ideas of self-advancement in black independent churches along with African American musical styles, such as African American minstrelsy, which was introduced to South Africa by Orpheus McAdoo and his Jubilee singers, had a massive impact on South Africa's black mission-educated elite and went some way to restoring racial confidence. Two decades later, when ragtime was added to the mix, it made, as writer R. R. R. Dhlomo observed, 'many feel proud of being black'.[52] This African American cultural infusion also gave rise, so Erlmann argues, to two genres of stage performance – musical comedy and drama. At this point, a distinct ironical and critical school of black humour made its public, though little remarked, debut – opening up a space for cultural resistance as well as intracommunal criticism.

Meanwhile, in the inner-city slums and packed municipal locations of the Rand, an entirely new and utterly distinctive African musical tradition of *marabi* was being formed. There, in the 1920s, 'musicians assimilated elements from every available performance tradition into a single African musical style called *marabi*'. In a sense, *marabi* stood for, or constituted, a whole way of life: simultaneously a musical style, a form of dance, a neighbourhood gathering and category of people. The musicians that constructed this musical form displayed an interesting marginality standing on the edges of traditional society, being termed *abaqhafi* by Vilakazi (cultural driftwood), and like the Xhosa *abathakati*, neither traditional nor Christian and school educated. They were, in Coplan's telling terms, urban but not Western. Among the early contributors to *marabi* were Cape coloured musicians, known in Johannesburg as *die oorlamse mense van Vrededorp*. To this was added the Xhosa melodies of *thula n'divile* (the colloquial name by which Johannesburg's Western Native Township also went). Assimilating elements from virtually every South African musical tradition, *marabi* created a unique nonethnic, non-Western, polyglot, urban South African musical style.

SPORT

Alongside church and music, sport was the most important social activity in any black community in South Africa and of most of its other racial or ethnic communities throughout the twentieth century. Three developments in particular prompted this explosion of sporting engagement and prowess: urbanisation, bourgeoisification and the near-throttling grip of racial discrimination.

Sport arrived in South Africa via three main routes: the British imperial administration, the army and private schools. Two team sports enjoyed social and ideological preeminence by the beginning of the period with which this chapter is concerned – cricket and rugby. Cricket was the British imperial game par excellence, and it largely excluded Afrikaners

---

[52] Ibid., p. 95.

until the 1950s. Elite mission-educated Africans were more eager to make the effort. Mission institutions, especially those concentrated in the Eastern Cape, promoted games that they saw as instilling the values of sporting behaviour, teamwork and civilisation. African students enthusiastically adopted the sports, convinced, at least for a time, that this would gain recognition for their civilised status and distinguish them clearly from the mass of tribal and noneducated Africans.

Rugby enjoyed a slightly broader reach, appealing to Afrikaners to a much greater extent than did cricket. None of the existing studies of rugby convincingly explain exactly why. For a time in the early twentieth century, rugby seems to have partly bridged the yawning ethnic divides between Briton and Boer. In 1906, the first South African national team toured Britain, during which the combination of the Springbok emblem and their glittering record of wins seems to have drawn Boers and Britons more closely together. For white South Africa in general, the mostly exclusive pursuit of 'civilised' sports became an important affirmation of its superior status and played a major role in constructing relatively invisible networks and rituals of social cohesion, which were often able to cross the widening class divides.

In general, rugby and other sports became symbols and activities uniting the white middle class, particularly following the increasing upward mobility of Afrikaners and the related proliferation of Afrikaner tertiary educational institutions, which provided an expanded pool of potential rugby players from a burgeoning Afrikaner middle class to engage in organised sport. It also divided them off from the soccer-playing white working class, Africans and Indians.

Soccer was the first major sport to break the class (and to some extent the racial) divide, in part because of its proletarian origins and associations in Britain and their importation into South Africa by a newly forming white working class. Certainly well before the First World War soccer was widely played among white workers in Durban and on the Rand, and in the interwar years, it was of a sufficiently high standard to allow for the export of a steady stream of players to play in the English first division before 1939. Again, it was soccer that was played, rather than any other sport, by working-class Afrikaner children in South Africa's cities in the 1920s and 1930s. Black soccer never really took off in South Africa until after the First World War, although football matches in both the major cities and the small towns were played by the higher ranks of blue-collar workers on an informal basis much earlier. Certainly, the scale of African football expanded enormously in the 1920s and 1930s. In Durban, for example, the number of clubs registered rose from seven in 1917 to twenty-six in 1931 and forty-seven in 1935. On the Witwatersrand, similarly, the number of teams affiliated to the Johannesburg Bantu Football Association climbed from 39 in 1930 to 103 in 1935, and those affiliated with the Johannesburg African Football Association leaped from 50 to 84 in the three years between 1933 and 1935. The physical closeness and the intimacy of the sport to its players and supporters were intense. On match days, spectators crowded on the touchlines. Neighbourhoods identified intensely with local teams. Soccer was one of the few autonomous places where African men could win public esteem for their prowess and be popularly acclaimed. As a result, a specific black soccer aesthetic could develop.

Beyond this, though, there were attempts at social control through sport. For Afrikaner nationalists, among the cultural symbols that were elevated and burnished in the 1920s and 1930s were *boeremusiek*, *volkspele*, and above all rugby. Unacceptable, and suppressed, was dog racing. Equally, municipalities tried to harness and control soccer as a form of urban social control, but African politicians were also likely to sponsor football teams as part of their campaigning. At the other end of the social scale, around 1950, township gangsters adopted or appropriated their own sides. Such teams it was prudent not to beat.

WAR

The Second World War caused a seismic shift in South African society. The expansion of the manufacturing sector and the steady rise of both white and black immigration to the towns had been in process since the economy entered a cycle of recovery around 1935. These movements accelerated rapidly one year after South Africa joined the Allied cause. The so-called poor-white problem virtually ceased to exist, although a substantial slice of this was displaced by the recruitment of indigent whites into the armed services in the first two years of the war. At the same time, African workers, and over time their families, flooded into towns throughout the Union. Overall, the black urban population grew by 500,000 to 1,689,000 in the course of the war. In Port Elizabeth, for instance, slum areas and periurban shack lands mushroomed, and the freehold township of Korsten, which had been cleared of its African population in the late 1930s, was swamped by an irresistible new influx.

This abrupt and dramatic surge to the towns was matched by the massive and intractable social problems it brought in its wake. Services for the new migrants were virtually nonexistent. The government made some moves toward a recognition of African urbanisation and a cutback of segregationist measures, notably the enforcement of the pass laws, but quickly retreated. In part, this was a result of Allied victories and the impending general election. It was also in response to a series of strikes, first on the Rand in December 1942 and then a more momentous series of multiracial strikes in the confectionary industry and more momentarily in the OK Bazaars – in which white women and black men participated – the former joining Indian and African men in Durban. Between them they were the biggest challenge to state authority in twenty-two years. Both waves of strikes were triggered by a steep rise in inflation.

UNIONS AND POLITICS

The only sector of the black political world that made its presence felt in this period and made a serious attempt to occupy the new political space that was opening up was the black trade union movement. This had been revived both on the Witwatersrand and around Durban in the second half of the 1930s. In November 1941, the two main trade union groups on the Witwatersrand merged to form the Council of Non-European Trade Unions (CNETU). At that point, black trade union membership had reached a figure of more than forty thousand. In the following years, membership would grow considerably. The unions also managed to force up real wages through a number of successful strikes. However, the gains were neither solid nor durable. By 1950, membership had collapsed. The reasons were multiple. First, even by 1944, the vast majority of urban African workers remained transitory or migrant. Labour turnover was massive. It was thus extremely difficult for even the most diligent and exemplary trade union organiser to consolidate union organisation. Second, and related, only a tiny percentage of African workers were semiskilled. Their small number appreciably reduced their bargaining power. Third, in the 1940s, virtually no effort was made to implant organisation in the factories and plants via shop-steward committees or to contest power relations on the factory floor with respect to managerial prerogatives, dismissals and discipline. They were simply interested in wages and organisational props like the closed shop. Fourth, CNETU itself was riven with political divisions over the extent to which strike action should be encouraged during the war, and it split decisively in May 1944. Finally, a certain amount of self-delusion and wishful thinking can be detected among trade unionists of the time.

Each of these factors helps explain the decline of CNETU and organised unionism from their high point in 1943–1944. A final shattering blow was delivered, however, by the violent crushing of the black mine workers' strike involving 65,500 miners on the Witwatersrand and affecting twenty-one mines in August 1946. The African Mine-Workers Union, which led the strike, boasted a membership of thirty thousand strong at its peak (again in 1944) and was the biggest affiliate in CNETU. The CNETU's failure to organise a general sympathy strike in support of the miners' strike – indeed, to make a showing of any kind – revealed its deep inner fissures and flaws and lack of self-belief. It never recovered from the ignominy of this devastating failure. In addition, it decisively accelerated a trend toward urbanisation among South African–born miners, who had been drifting from the mines into industry since the early 1940s. The failure of the strike and the brutality with which it was suppressed left many black miners deeply embittered and aggrieved.

The extraordinarily high labour turnover was one facet of the staggering fluidity and fragmentation of the wider process of black urbanisation in these years. Among the social consequences of this unfolding pattern was that, for most of the 1940s, new and unstable communities often remained parochial, sectional, introverted and individual. State officials found great difficulty in comprehending, let alone controlling, this diverse urban mass. Equally, the political leadership of the main resistance organisations of the day, the ANC and CPSA, proved inept and bereft of comprehension.

In every province, the ANC was plagued by splits until the late 1940s, as it was written off on all sides as insipid and ineffectual. On the Witwatersrand, the ANC was directionless. The provincial body remained split, requiring several interventions from the national Secretary-General, A. B. Xuma, and played no role whatsoever in those key social movements of the mid-1940s, the Alexandra Bus Boycott of 1943–1944 and the squatter movement of 1944–1946. Although the CPSA was considerably more active on the Rand, and played a leading role in many location struggles and trade union campaigns, it too failed to understand many of the key dynamics that informed the dramatic urbanisation of the time, and it resolutely refused to work with some of the pivotal contemporary local political leaders, such as James Sofazonke Mpanza in Orlando (or for that matter, Phungula, the equally influential and flamboyant and semiproletarian dockworker leader in Durban). Nevertheless, in a somewhat impoverished political environment, the CPSA regularly took the lead. It won considerable support, for example, for its seminal and sustained involvement in the antipass campaign in 1944. It was also instrumental in radicalising both the Natal and the Transvaal Indian congresses around renewed efforts at urban residential segregation, which began to be implemented from the late 1930s, thereby laying the foundation for multiracial politics, and it was in many respects better supported than the contemporary Transvaal ANC. Indeed, it took the Treason Trial that followed the collapse of the 1946 black mine workers' strike, in which fifty-two CPSA members were arrested, to set the Party back. The CPSA never fully recovered.

Such shortcomings left huge swaths of the political terrain open to parochial, charismatic and generally a-party political local leaders, to fill and exploit through cooperatives, squatter camps, churches and a variety of other sectional organisations. They did this with great panache and effect, demonstrating the scale of opportunity that remained available for political parties. Two of the most important acts of such local collective self-assertion that left a major impression on political configurations were, as just noted, the Alexandra bus boycott of 1943–1943 and the Johannesburg squatter movement of 1944–1946. The bus boycott, in particular, was utterly seminal. It provided an alternative model for political action, as well as the stimulant that led to the formation of the ANC's Youth League, and it began the tactic of the stay-away, a key weapon for the ANC for the following decade and a half. The second movement of similar implications or proportions was Mpanza's Shantytown squatter movement, which he piloted on to vacant land in Orlando West in April 1944. Again, the core demand was to be recognised as urban. Again, the ANC and CPSA held aloof. Again, the Johannesburg City Council was implacably opposed to conceding to the squatter demands and to providing temporary housing for squatters, and it engaged in endless twists and turns to avoid giving in to the unthinkable but inevitable. Again, the government refused to admit the issue, closing its eyes and sitting on its hands. Again, finally and decisively, a local social movement seized the initiative and exploited an opening, finally forcing recognition of the claim to be urban and, in so doing, creating a new topography of political struggle. These in many ways were the key turning points of the 1940s, opening the way to the crushing retaliation of apartheid.

FURTHER READING

Alegi, P., *Laduma: soccer politics and society in South Africa*, Pietermaritzburg: University of KwaZulu-Natal Press, 2002

Alexander, P., *Workers war, and the origins of apartheid: labour and politics in South Africa, 1939–1948*, Oxford: James Currey; Athens: Ohio University Press, 2000

Baines, G. F., 'New Brighton, Port Elizabeth, c.1903–1955: a history of an urban African community', unpublished Ph.D. thesis, University of Cape Town (1994)

Berger, D., 'White poverty and government policy in South Africa, 1892–1934', unpublished Ph.D. thesis, Temple University (1982)

Berger, I., *Threads of solidarity: women in South African industry, 1900–1980*, Bloomington: Indiana University Press; London: James Currey, 1992

Bickford-Smith, V., E. van Heyningen and N. Worden, *Cape Town in the twentieth century*, Cape Town: David Philip, 1999

Bonner, P., D. Posel and P. Delius (eds.), *Apartheid's genesis, 1935–1962*, Johannesburg: Ravan Press, 1993

Bradford, H., *A taste of freedom: the ICU in rural South Africa, 1924–1930*, Johannesburg: Ravan Press, 1987

Campbell, J. T., *Songs of Zion: the African Methodist Episcopal Church in the United States and South Africa*, Chapel Hill: University of North Carolina Press, 1998

Chanock, M., *The making of South African legal culture, 1902–1936: fear, favour and prejudice*, Cambridge: Cambridge University Press, 2001

Delius, P., *A lion amongst the cattle*, Portsmouth, NH: Heinemann, 1996

Dubow, S., *Racial segregation and the origins of apartheid in South Africa, 1919–1936*, Basingstoke, U.K.: Palgrave Macmillan, 1989

Evans, I., *Bureaucracy and race: native administration in South Africa*, Berkeley: University of California Press, 1996

Feinburg, H. M., 'The Natives Land Act of 1913 in South Africa: politics, race and segregation in the early 20th century', *International Journal of African Historical Studies* 26:1 (1993), 65–109

Johnstone, F. A., *Class, race and gold: a study of class relations and racial discrimination in South Africa*, Lanham, MD: University Press of America, 1976

Krikler, J., *The Rand revolt*, Johannesburg: Jonathan Ball, 2005

Lewis, G., *Between the wire and the wall*, Cape Town: David Philip, 1987

Moodie, T. D., *The rise of Afrikanerdom: power, apartheid and the Afrikaner civil religion*, Berkeley: University of California Press, 1975

Parnell, S. M., 'Johannesburg slums and racial segregation in South African cities, 1910–1937', unpublished Ph.D. thesis, University of the Witwatersrand (1993)

7

THE APARTHEID PROJECT, 1948–1970

DEBORAH POSEL

The idea of apartheid has long had an international currency that goes well beyond its national historical reference. *Apartheid* originated as a label for the system of institutionalised racism and racial social engineering inaugurated by the National Party after its election victory in 1948. But the term has since been appropriated as a global signifier of racialised separation, inhumanity and exploitation. International cross-references have the virtue of prompting a more global reading of apartheid as one among many projects of racialised discrimination and subjugation. The historiography of apartheid has tended to be rather more insular and inward looking in the past, particularly in the thick of the anti-apartheid struggle, when the specificities of the South African experience dominated both the analytical and the political agenda of debate. Yet there is also the obvious risk of caricature, essentialising and dehistoricising a system of rule that was more internally fractious and fractured, historically fluid and complex, than the formulaic reductions can possibly render. The symbolic condensation of apartheid as the global signifier of racism risks conferring an apparent – and misleading – transparency on the system of apartheid, as if comprehensible simply as the extremity of racism. This renders its historical unevenness and complexity irrelevant and/or uninteresting.

Indeed, the international précis of apartheid as the apogee of racism tends to reiterate and reinforce long-standing national myths about apartheid, as if it had been a single, coherent, monolithic project. The apartheid regime dominated South African society from 1948 to the early 1990s, but its durability should not be mistaken as a sign of internal stability or coherence. The terms of apartheid rule were never uncontested; the project was never implemented exactly according to plan. Even at the zenith of apartheid in the late 1960s, a blustering dogmatism and ideological certitude were always accompanied by a radical provisionality, manifest in attempts to redefine, rethink and reposition the apartheid regime, in response to shifting global political fields, as much as the fluidity of the internal milieu.

The dogged pursuit of rigid racial boundaries also created sites of porosity, producing a mobile and sometimes unruly dialectic of racial proximity and distance. The commitment to white political supremacy – and with that, the political exclusion of the black majority – never wavered, yet its conditions remained tenuous, as the apartheid project contained enduring sites of contradiction and tension, and with that, lingering ambivalence and some strategic fluidity.

Moreover, the development of apartheid cannot be read teleologically, as if having been wholly foretold in the thinking and policies of its original architects and practitioners. Apartheid evolved through three distinct phases, marked by successive efforts to manage its internal contradictions and the effects of external pressures. The version of apartheid that informs its iconic global rendition is largely the apartheid of the 1960s, the second phase, which was a far more ambitious and unyielding phase of apartheid than the first rendition during the 1950s, when a somewhat more pragmatic and cautious approach to racial social and economic engineering was taken. (The third phase, which began in the mid-1970s, is not covered in this chapter.) Yet even at the peak of grand apartheid, its protagonists were divided, often torn – the full hubris of their project subverted by the weight of social, economic and political realities that resisted the malleability presumed by apartheid's architects. This is not to say, however, that the imprints of apartheid were not deep, nor that the regime did not notch up formidable successes that seared the national landscape – many of which have blighted the efforts to democratise and 'reconcile' in the postapartheid era.

This chapter has three primary purposes: to draw attention to the singular aspects of apartheid along with the more generically modern and/or colonial facets of the project; to identify the historical conditions (nationally and internationally) that made apartheid possible; and to locate the mix of vision and blunder, principle and pragmatism, that marked the apartheid project during its first two phases. Throughout this discussion, an analysis of apartheid statecraft occupies a central place. I understand 'the state' as an institutional matrix that posits and performs an ideological and operational unity, in historically varying ways and with varying degrees of efficacy. Intrinsic to the work of 'the state' is a discourse about its own institutional parameters, modes of power, conditions of legitimacy and terms of rule – that is, statecraft. Perhaps the most fundamental assumption of the apartheid project – and the decisive condition of its possibility – was the characteristically modern presumption that societies were thoroughly malleable in the hands of suitably powerful states. In the twentieth century, this discourse of the state as the primary author of the social fabric was expressed more specifically in the enthusiasm for wide-ranging and ambitious projects of social engineering (be it in the case of Stalinism, the American New Deal or what James Scott sees as the high modernism of postcolonial African 'development',[1] for example.) Apartheid was born, then, of the appropriation of globally current enthusiasms for a big interventionist state yoked, in the South African case, to an ideologically distinctive vision of racial order and nationalist advance. This produced fantasies of an omnipotent and omniscient state that exceeded the realities of social, economic and political life. These shortcomings reveal both internally contradictory dynamics, 'the result of irreconcilable imperatives and disparate logics of power' and the limits of a state ill-equipped for the grandiosity of its ambitions.

This chapter is primarily thematic rather than narrative, giving my reading of apartheid's principal defining features with respect to the aspirations of the project, the techniques of power that it deployed, and their primary effects. Because the goal is to distill and interpret the lineaments of the apartheid project, the chapter provides few of the details of political processes or the agency of key political figures. Even thematically, the discussion is highly selective. The dominant focus is on the most prominent issues that the apartheid state sought to manage – with a particular interest in conflicting and contradictory elements of the project – which means in turn that there is relatively little discussion of interests, races, ethnicities, class dynamics, geographical regions and issues that were not centre stage.

The chapter is divided into four parts. The first summarises the central imperatives that enabled and constrained the apartheid project throughout the 1950s and 1960s. The second considers the genealogy of the apartheid project, by identifying its principal conditions of possibility, locally and more globally. The third part identifies key constitutive elements of the apartheid project, and the fourth reviews the impact and limits of the central exercise in social and economic engineering.

APARTHEID'S PRIMARY IMPERATIVES

The champions of apartheid presented their cause as first and foremost the preservation of white racial political supremacy, as an essential requisite for perpetuating the supposed superiority of white 'civilisation'. Yet as had been the case during the segregationism of preceding decades, the apartheid project was an attempt to sustain white political supremacy in ways that simultaneously promoted the cause of white economic prosperity.

[1] J. Scott, *Seeing like a state: how certain schemes to improve the human condition have failed* (New Haven, CT: Yale University Press, 1999).

Interventions to buttress the white racist regime, and the attendant political divisions and contestations, were therefore inseparable from efforts to sustain and regulate practices of capital accumulation and economic growth, along with the class interests and conflicts associated with those.

How to reconcile these dual imperatives rapidly became a site of controversy and conflict in the Afrikaner nationalist alliance that brought the National Party to power – a marker, in turn, of the competing class interests undergirding this alliance. The critically divisive issue concerned the place of black labour in a 'white South Africa' – more specifically, whether the continued reliance on black labour was a necessary precondition for continued white prosperity, or whether that dependency had to be forfeited because it would lead inexorably to unmanageable black disaffection, and ultimately black enfranchisement. The purist version of apartheid advocated total segregation – including the withdrawal of black labour from the white economy – as the only reliable bulwark against black majority rule. The competing practical version, endorsed by powerful Afrikaner capitalist interests, was more pragmatic, recognising the economic necessity of black labour and the need to reconcile that with the imperative of white minority rule by equipping a suitably powerful state with appropriate techniques of control. The contention between purist and practical versions of apartheid never altogether receded, but only a small minority of Afrikaner nationalists lobbied for a politics of economic sacrifice. Most looked to apartheid as a system that would guarantee their access to an abundance of cheap black labour, kept in check by rigorous and wide-ranging methods of state control.

Apartheid, therefore, was never an exterminationist project – unlike other systematically racialised regimes such as the Nazi state. On the contrary, one of the abiding imperatives of apartheid was to keep (most) black people alive, albeit under conditions of perpetual servitude and submission, so as to keep the structures of white supremacy intact. This did not exclude – indeed, it was inextricable from – tactics of violence and brutalisation. Racialised terms of access to health services – worst for black people in rural areas – also created conditions of neglect and disinterest for the most vulnerable and marginal, whose lives counted for little. But in the main, black life remained the condition of white prosperity, and the apartheid project proliferated myriad laws, regulations and proscriptions designed to sustain and regulate the conditions of black life accordingly.

Black life was also, of course, the single greatest threat to white supremacy. It was a danger rooted in the ineradicable fact of an overwhelming black majority in the country. In 1946, blacks accounted for around 79 per cent of a population of 11.5 million; by 1970, the proportion had grown to 89 per cent.[2] Bold and brazen assertions of white supremacy were therefore always simultaneously fearful and insecure. The spectre of the black mass was also the spectre of violent revenge, unleashed in proportion to the desired harshness of white rule. So it was unsurprising that the 1948 election that brought the National Party to power was dominated by the iconography of *die swart gevaar* (the black menace): a sprawling black mass – disaffected, restless and increasingly militant – threatening to swamp the white minority and contaminate its racial 'purity'. That this remained the abiding image of blackness in the white polity throughout the apartheid years, underscores the persistence of white fear of the black mob – a dread of incipient insurgency – as one of the primary drivers of apartheid ambitions.

At the nub of the apartheid project, then, was a particular politics of population: a project of social and economic engineering preoccupied with trying to reconfigure spatial ratios of blacks to whites and regulate the conditions of their association. In Foucault's terms, this was apartheid's central and defining biopolitics: focusing the exercise of power on the regulation of large units of population, designating spaces for authorised residence, pathways of authorised migration, channels of authorised employment and the terms of political and communal organisation. These regulatory practices would target the population at large, constituted in racial terms: whites, coloureds, Indians and Natives (or Bantu) would all find their conditions of residence, employment, migration, political association, communal life, leisure and intimacy governed by the terms of apartheid policy. But given the numerical preponderance of the black population, it was they – and Africans in particular – who bore the brunt of the harshest and most brutalising biopolitics. The practitioners of apartheid made increasingly aggressive – if unevenly effective – efforts to contain the numbers of African people living and working in proximity to whites, proscribe the conditions of their everyday lives and loves, and relegate as many as possible to spaces of political and geographical remoteness.

Soon after the National Party's narrow election victory in 1948, with D. F. Malan at its helm, it became clear that the economically more pragmatic version of apartheid would prevail. This meant that the apartheid project took shape around a foundational contradiction. As the most powerful engines of economic expansion were concentrated in the urban areas, the suction of vast numbers of black workers into urban employment simultaneously created the conditions that most seriously threatened the future of white supremacy. South Africa's trajectory of capitalist development had rendered the vitality of its primary and secondary industries, as well as its agricultural sector, heavily dependent on black labour

[2] See Chapter 10, in this volume.

(most of it African), the price of which had been driven downward by the political and ideological imposition of racial hierarchies of skill and reward. Although the demand for more skilled labour was on the rise, in ways that would set employers' interests increasingly at odds with the political imaginary of economic processes, white economic prosperity had become profoundly dependent on continued access to abundant supplies of cheap labour (with historically changing degrees of skill, albeit remaining cheap in comparison with their white counterparts). Yet with economic expansion concentrated in the cities, the resultant growth in the size of black urban settlements – largely poor, overcrowded and poorly serviced – nourished the seeds of black political malcontent and its threat to the political status quo.

By the 1940s, the acceleration of industrial growth stimulated by South Africa's war effort had burst the boundaries of segregationist controls, with sprawling squatter settlements overflowing the confines of municipally controlled African townships. The decade had also seen a growing sense of political solidarity between disaffected African, Indian and coloured communities, and their rising expectations of political entitlements beyond the meagre offerings of the wartime government. The apartheid project promised more rigorous controls over black peoples' access to housing and work in the cities, as well as over the conditions of political mobilisation. But large urban concentrations of black people, earning relatively low wages and confined to spaces of relative deprivation and overcrowding, were understood to reproduce possibilities for a unifying consciousness of shared racial grievances, thus increasing the risks of mass uprisings and strikes. In contrast, if living conditions in the cities improved substantially – a function of higher wages and greater public investment in township infrastructures and services – it would be significantly more difficult for state institutions to contain the size of the black urban presence and curb the stream of black migrants fleeing rural poverty. Apartheid's *demographic conundrum* meant, therefore, that the project of coupling white prosperity and white supremacy was inherently tenuous.

The determination to buttress a regime of white political supremacy on the back of a racially exploitative economic regime was not unique to apartheid. Its segregationist predecessors had done likewise; and other settler colonial regimes – such as in nearby Rhodesia and Kenya – had had similar objectives. Apartheid, however, was also an ethnic nationalism, that sought to position white Afrikaners at the helm of the new state and its mission. The preceding decades had seen the advance of Afrikaner nationalism, dedicated to the economic, political and cultural advancement of the white Afrikaner *volk*.

There were several elements of the Afrikaner nationalist version of rule, which informed the ways in which the apartheid project was imagined and enacted and that contributed to its ideological and political distinctiveness. The first was an avowedly Christian theology of power, which had its roots in the epic of the Great Trek, as 'formal proof of God's election of the Afrikaner people and His special destiny for them'.[3] In this sense, the apartheid project was pervaded by the neo-Fichtean idealisation of a divinely inspired Afrikaner nation as the political vanguard of the white race. Thus, although steeped in the values of instrumental rationality and scientific planning that shaped secular logics of rule elsewhere, apartheid was also informed by an avowedly sacred imaginary of power, captured in the idea of Christian nationalism. This idea, which had predated the inception of apartheid, also harboured an intrinsically patriarchal notion of power. Women, following God's will, were destined to serve and follow their men, even if heroically and dynamically. Nor were Afrikaner women passive or meek in the elaboration of this view. As Marijke du Toit has argued, Afrikaner women contributed actively to the idea of the archetypal *volksmoeder* (mother of the nation) as a figure of feisty political loyalty as much as of deference to male authority.[4] The nation would be headed by a male leader – the father of the nation – answerable first and foremost to God. And the mission to which God had assigned him was twofold.

The first was the task of preserving and advancing the divine logic of racial difference. Because blacks and whites were born different in accordance with God's plan, racial integration was a sacrilege. The abiding imperative of Christian nationalism, therefore, was to promote racial – and unequal – separate development. An integral component of this task was to reinforce and embolden the boundaries of race, so as to prevent the 'impurity' that came from racial 'mixing'. For National Party supporters, by 1948, the country's racial geography had become too porous for comfort. In the aftermath of accelerating urban migration during the Second World War, urban slums and shantytowns had proliferated, inhabited by a mix of races. And many black townships situated close to white residential areas had swollen, with residents living in overcrowded and deprived conditions. These edgy proximities fanned fears of rampant miscegenation.

Anxieties about miscegenation were particularly acute on behalf of poor whites, a large proportion of whom were Afrikaans-speaking. They were

[3] Moodie, *The rise of Afrikanerdom: power, apartheid and the Afrikaner civil religion* (Berkeley: University of California Press; Johannesburg: Witwatersrand University Press, 1975), p. 3.

[4] M. du Toit, 'The domesticity of Afrikaner nationalism: *volksmoeder* and the ACVV, 1904–1929', *Journal of Southern African Studies* 29:1 (2003), 155, 176.

considered most at risk of racial mixing, living close to the poor of other races. This was also thought to lead to the possibility of cross-racial political solidarity, mobilised by the Communist Party of South Africa – support for which had grown considerably during the war years as urban living conditions deteriorated. The apartheid project offered the promise of an unyielding and ubiquitous racial order that would guarantee and redeem the whiteness of the poor.

The second element of the *volk*'s Christian mission was to establish the economic, political and cultural ascendancy of white Afrikaners in the country, and finally to shed the yoke of British authority. Following Union in 1910, South Africa had become a British dominion, with full independence in matters of domestic policy but with its control over foreign policy more ambiguous. Once elected to power in 1948, the National Party would set about redefining the country's relationship to Britain. In 1951, British citizenship was abolished; as of 1957, 'God Save the Queen' was no longer a national anthem and the Union Jack no longer a national flag, and the Royal Navy was ousted from its base in Simonstown. This culminated in the withdrawal from the British Commonwealth and creation of an independent republic in 1961.

The Broederbond (a secret Afrikaner nationalist organisation dedicated to the promotion of Afrikaner interests) had already established an institutional presence and influence in the country by 1948. It had spearheaded the launch of the Economic Movement in 1934, to advance the economic prospects of Afrikaners, through preferential employment, trading and other economic transactions within the *volk*. The Broederbond had also asserted its powers in other organs of Afrikaner nationalism, such as the South African Bureau of Racial Affairs (SABRA) and the Federasie van Afrikaanse Kultuurverenigings (FAK). With the National Party's accession to power, the activities of the Broederbond could find platforms and champions in the state itself, as part of the Christian-nationalist advance. Enlarging and invigorating the state, filling key positions with influential National Party supporters, the Bond would thus become a vehicle of Afrikaner nationalist ambitions as much as an exercise in racial domination.

From this standpoint, apartheid was a project of white Afrikaner patronage, and its key instrument would be the institutions of state. A strategy of colonising the public service with white Afrikaners, under the rubric of apartheid, had dual ambitions: first, to create relationships of debt and dependency within the *volk*, by offering sheltered employment to those demonstrably loyal to the apartheid cause; and second, to evict from state bureaucracies those with dissenting political positions and interests, largely English-speakers supportive of the United Party (the National Party's principal parliamentary opposition).

Apartheid's dual drivers – as a project of white supremacy and of Afrikaner nationalism – produced an abiding ambiguity in the definition of the nation: as white and as (white) Afrikaans. From the outset, the exponents of apartheid simultaneously appealed to the particular interests of the white Afrikaner *volk* and looked for support and legitimacy from the white population at large in advancing the cause of white supremacy. The political management of this ambiguity – the changing terms on which apartheid's ambitions on behalf of both Afrikaners and whites were defined – affected the evolution and impact of the apartheid project. And the terms of this admixture shifted over time.

On the eve of the 1948 election, Afrikaans speakers constituted 57 per cent of South Africa's white population. There were many factors that explained the National Party's surprising victory that year – including a series of weaknesses and ineptitudes in the opposition party, the relative weighting of rural constituencies where support for the National Party was strongest and the tactical skill of an election campaign buoyed by white fears of *die swart gevaar*. However, the voters who brought the National Party to power were all Afrikaans speaking. It is likely, therefore, that its narrowly Afrikaner nationalist platform was a critical component of the National Party's initial electoral success. This remained the case throughout the 1950s: according to Newell Stultz, 'given the limitations of their appeal for non-Afrikaners, Afrikaner nationalists were thus faced with the necessity of winning and holding the allegiance of approximately 85 per cent of all Afrikaners, if Afrikaner nationalists were to rule. They had therefore to stress the importance of Afrikaner group identity and solidarity. . . . [T]he fact of being an Afrikaner was elevated to supreme importance.'[5] Simultaneously, the fact that electoral support for the National Party was so narrowly constituted also played an important role in an initially more cautious and pragmatic approach to the project of apartheid social engineering, particularly with respect to the controversial issue of economic integration.

The consolidation and escalation of the apartheid project, however, depended critically on the National Party's capacity to extend its appeal to whites more generally. Mobilising both whiteness and Afrikaansness as bases of its support and legitimacy, the advance of apartheid was marked – and in key ways, enabled – by the growing numbers of English-speaking whites voting for the National Party. The National Party did not achieve a majority of the electoral vote (as opposed to parliamentary seats) until 1960, when a public (white) referendum on the country becoming a republic received 52.3 per cent of the total vote. The National Party then proceeded

[5] N. Stultz, 'The politics of security: South Africa under Verwoerd, 1961–6', *Journal of Modern African Studies* 7:1 (1969), 8.

to win the 1961 election with a majority of votes, as well as seats, for the first time. This was a significant milestone in the political fortunes of the party and in the strength of its grip on the reins of power – a vital factor in explaining the shift to a more aggressive, authoritarian phase of policy making after 1961. That the size of the National Party's electoral majority continued to increase through the decade signalled the extent to which English-speaking voters endorsed the ideological and political shifts. And this was reflected, too, in discursive and strategic reorientations embracing the support and contribution of English-speaking whites far more than in the preceding decade. In 1961, the state initiated a programme to encourage the immigration of whites to the new republic – having previously suspended the postwar immigration programme initiated by then prime minister Jan Smuts, on the grounds that it would 'submerge the Afrikaner'. In the election of 1966, for the first time, six National Party candidates were English speaking. By the time apartheid social engineering reached its zenith in the late 1960s, then, it had become a more inclusively white project. The imagery and special claims of the Afrikaner *volk* were never abandoned, however. Indeed, during the 1960s, preferential employment for Afrikaners in the public service and private sector reached its peak, and the Broederbond the height of its power.

As the power of the apartheid state and the scope of its ambitions expanded, then, so the ideological and political tensions between narrowly Afrikaans, and more inclusively white, renditions of the nation intensified. One of the consequences was a deepening conflict between so-called *verligte* (more pragmatic) and *verkrampte* (more conservative) factions that culminated in the 1969 breakaway of the most right-wing faction of the National Party as the Herstigte Nasionale Party, a party that reasserted a more emphatically ethnic definition of political allegiance.

THE GENEALOGY OF APARTHEID

The apartheid project was a distinctively ambitious and durable, yet fallible and tenuous, project of racialised social and economic engineering. It derived, in the first place, from the perceived need for radical overhaul of the instruments of segregationist domination, itself deeply conditioned by a long-standing colonial imprint. The longevity of colonial bureaucracies in South Africa, and an already elaborate framework of surveillance (initially inaugurated by the mining companies), made a project as ambitious as apartheid possible. Yet by the late 1940s, the well-established systems of regulation had established a degree of state control over the movements and activities of its subject population that was episodic at best; and the resultant overcrowding and unruliness in the black urban townships had produced a pervasive white fear that the segregationist system was teetering. Thus, on the eve of the 1948 election, contending parties agreed that a different form of state – bigger, more centralised, with a wider and more systematic bureaucratic reach, better informed and more 'scientific' in its efforts to plan – had become necessary. It was a consensus enabled and shaped by the foundations already set down by a long history of racialised rule, and its articulation with the enterprise of accumulation and industrialisation.

A second condition of the apartheid project was spatial. The extent of the country's territory offered enough space to enable an ambitious project of racial separatism on a large scale, for which the 1913 Land Act and the 1923 Natives (Urban Areas) Act provided an existing framework of spatial regulation. Apartheid social engineering appropriated and refashioned those racialised geographies. During the first phase of apartheid in the 1950s, the ideology of temporary sojourn (the idea, bequeathed from segregationist regimes, that African people resided in cities only so long as they ministered to white needs) was tempered by a pragmatic acceptance of urbanised Africans as having de facto residential rights to remain in white urban areas. Ironically, the early apartheid project thus oversaw the authorised creation of a settled, urbanised African population with little connection to the reserves or rural areas, an outcome that the second phase of policy making, during the 1960s, would attempt to unsettle. From 1948, a geography of separation was maintained nevertheless, in the creation of racially defined and regulated townships, set some way away from white areas separated by buffer zones.

As apartheid entered its second phase after 1961, the principle of temporary sojourn was more aggressively applied, manifest, inter alia, in the removal of hundreds of thousands of Africans deemed 'surplus' to the labour requirements of white areas to barren resettlement zones far from white sight and concern. From the early 1960s, the former reserves began to be refashioned into self-governing Bantustans, and later, as independent homelands, on an ethnic basis. But self-government never displaced the relationships of economic dependency that tied African peoples' prospects to the white industrial heartland.

The geographies of distance and proximity were fundamental to the apartheid project of racial regulation, co-producing racially distinct spaces of community, schooling, friendship and mutuality, along with sites of routinised interracial contact and dependency, be it in the factories, on the mines or in white homes employing domestic workers. For the most part, apartheid institutionalised the intimacy of strangers, and the uncertainty, ignorance, fear, threat and temptation associated with it. But the everyday racial crossings also opened (dangerous and vulnerable) spaces for political allegiances, solidarity and friendships that would ultimately contribute critically to the regime's demise.

A third enabling condition of apartheid was its discourse of statecraft, which drew on the then-international orthodoxy about the desirability of big, powerful states as drivers of large-scale social and economic change. From the outset, the apartheid project was animated by a hankering for rigorous and uncompromising social, economic and political order, which entailed a process of institutional refashioning within the state: centralising policy making and coordinating disparate institutions of state in the pursuit of common objectives; moving beyond long-standing norms of administrative decentralisation in both rural and urban areas; enlarging existing bureaucracies and creating new ones, in line with more ambitious visions of the reach of the state. This new infrastructure of rule depended, in turn, on a rethinking of the idea and powers of the state. In this respect, apartheid's dual imperatives were well served by the faith in ambitious agendas of state-led social engineering that had gained ground in many other parts of the world. Indeed, it was this confidence in the possibility and legitimacy – indeed, the necessity – of large-scale national planning, driven by an appropriately interventionist state, that made the apartheid project intelligible.

Alongside these shifts in statecraft, the twentieth century also saw related changes in international thinking about economic processes and their relationship to politics. Timothy Mitchell has argued that the idea of the national economy was a twentieth-century invention, brought into being through the collapse of an imperial economic order and the ensuing national 'framing of an economy'.[6] Particularly with the influence of John Maynard Keynes, the economic sphere came to be thought of as 'something that could be managed and made to grow'.[7] This notion of a national economy subject to scientific scrutiny and effective political regulation was discursively fundamental to the apartheid aspiration of regulating and refashioning economic processes in line with a politically defined tempo and trajectory of economic development.

Yet the underlying distinction between political and economic spheres would also render that interventionism liable to critique as excessive interference in capitalist market processes. Indeed, this remained one of the enduring sites of contestation throughout the apartheid era, within and beyond state institutions, as officials, employers and workers collided over the degree to which political reconfigurations of labour supply and demand could ever be effective or legitimate.

A further genealogical strand that informed apartheid statecraft was the specific case for a welfare state. Welfarism was predicated on the recognition

---

[6] T. Mitchell, *Rule of experts: Egypt, techno-politics, modernity* (Los Angeles: University of California Press, 2002), p. 6.
[7] Ibid., p. 104.

that the national economy needed careful managing; that it could not be left to its own devices without incurring unfair hardships in the lives of the poor, to the detriment of social and political stability; and that such management could be effectively and judiciously undertaken through the offices of the state. In South Africa, welfarist interventions dating back to the 1930s had called for the moral uplift of the poor across the racial divide while maintaining white privilege; in practice, the primary beneficiaries had been poor white recipients of economic aid. The National Party produced a farther-reaching programme of white welfarism than the previous regime, partly as a strategy of political patronage to buy support, but also in recognition of far higher orders of state responsibility toward the fate of the white poor. Moral rehabilitation became integral to the racial redemption of poor whites. In its dealings with the black population, the apartheid project was far less beneficent, showing less concern for economic hardship or moral malaise in black communities.[8] Yet the apartheid state did accept higher orders of responsibility for the provision of mass housing and mass education, including in black areas – even if in the interests of better control rather than amelioration or upliftment. Thus the 1950s saw the accelerated construction of township housing, along with the expansion of black access to primary education. The apartheid project also absorbed the welfarist redefinition of regulatory boundaries between public and private, so that questions of marriage, sexuality and juvenile delinquency became sites of intensive policy making (see 'The Regulation of Family, Gender and Sexuality').

DEFINING FEATURES OF THE APARTHEID PROJECT

The Ubiquity of Race

Although the regulation of race was long-standing in modern Western and colonial states, the apartheid state went further in adopting an explicit principle of systematic, legalised racial separatism and exclusion. The institutionalisation of racism and racial discrimination permeated every facet of everyday life – from the most public through to the most intimate – in the name of a particular ideology of white supremacy and racial purity. Its ideologues represented apartheid as a divinely sanctioned crusade to protect the purity of the white race, resisting the 'temptation of assimilation' and subverting the prospect of white 'civilisation' being 'submerged in the Black heathendom of Africa'.[9] This was not an instance of racism

---

[8] Posel, 'The case for a welfare state', in Dubow and Jeeves (eds.), *South Africa's 1940s*, pp. 64–86.

[9] D. F. Malan writing to John Piersma, 1954, cited in D. Hirson, *White scars: on reading and rites of passage* (Johannesburg: Jacana, 2006), p. 77.

in the name of political hygiene, as had been the case in Nazi Germany. If Nazi discourse had rendered Jews as contaminants to be eliminated, apartheid's racism was predicated on a recognition of the fundamental economic interdependency of the races. It was exactly because blacks and whites were economically entangled that it became imperative to regulate race by means of robustly impermeable boundaries, so as to preserve racial 'purity' and the racial hierarchies that underpinned white power and privilege.

The most fraught racial boundary – because it was the most ambiguous – was the dividing line between whites and coloureds: people of 'mixed' race, deemed by whites to be a residual and unsettling grouping, neither 'white' nor 'native'. The dread of miscegenation emerged in the midst of a history of racial intermingling, particularly among the poor. Many white South Africans – Afrikaners in particular – had a somewhat mixed ancestry. It was reflected, inter alia, in the Afrikaans language, a hybrid of Dutch and the Cape slave patois. This history of a porosity of boundaries, born of cultural and sexual mixing, contributed another animus to the intense anxiety and fear attached to apartheid's racial project. As dissident Afrikaner writer Breyten Breytenbach put it, '[W]e are a bastard people with a bastard language . . . and like all bastards – uncertain of their identity – we began to adhere to the concept of purity. That is apartheid. Apartheid is the law of the bastard'.[10] The obsession with racial purity was a symptom, then, of the historical pervasiveness of its absence.

Early parliamentary debates about racial classification illustrated the extent to which white Afrikaners feared the prospect of a racial 'throwback' – a birth in the family that would betray a racial transgression, the sign of a past that resisted erasure and that contaminated claims to whiteness in the present. Preserving white racial purity included a quest for a secure, immobile racial classification as white, and all the privilege that went with it. Apartheid's comprehensive racialisation of experience, and the system of racial classification that underpinned it, were attempts to fix, demarcate and order racial identity, where otherwise there might have been uncertainty and ambiguity. No longer would it be possible for educated and/or affluent coloureds to 'pass' for white. People became either white, once and for all, or coloured, similarly rigidly and irrevocably. A similar fixity pertained to the categorisation of 'natives' who, like whites, were deemed a 'pure' race but lower down in the hierarchy of civilisation.

Contrary to popular renditions, the bureaucratic politics of race under apartheid was driven not merely by a putative biology of race but by a version of race as an expressly social judgement of relative socio-economic

---

[10] B. Breytenbach, *A season in paradise* (London: Jonathan Cape, 1980), p. 156.

standing and cultural accomplishment, closely linked to readings of bodily difference. As the Minister of the Interior put it, the test of race was 'the judgment of society – conventions which had grown up during the hundreds of years we have been here. . . . The intention of the legislature was . . . that the classification of a person should be made according to the views held by members of that community'.[11] The reasons were logistic as much as political. An exercise in mass racial classification was envisaged, the scale of which would have been unthinkable had objective 'scientific' evidence been necessary for each and every classification. Rather, the exercise of apartheid invoked a version of race that was far more explicitly culturalist, in a way that read cultural meanings into bodily features, according to the supposed racial common sense of white South Africans.[12] In contradistinction to other racist regimes that defined race in terms of ancestry (as in the American South) or in combination with other biological markers (as in Nazism), the apartheid project invoked race as the bodily marker of cultural and 'civilisational' difference, the evidence for which was the ordinary experience of difference in everyday life rather than any scientific test of ancestry or physiology. Ordinary white people – without any particular expertise or training – were considered appropriate judges of another's race, purely on the basis of their everyday experiences: did the person act, and look, like one widely 'known' to be a member of one race rather than another? A combination of bodily appearance and social judgement ('general acceptance') was therefore deemed relevant in determining a person's race, but the latter was the decisive factor. Thus, the Population Registration Act of 1950, which gave a working legal definition of the country's races, characterised 'a white person [as] one who in appearance is, or who is generally accepted as, as white person, but does not include a person who, although in appearance obviously a white person, is generally accepted as a coloured person.'[13]

From this perspective, superior races were obviously and self-evidently superior in their degree of 'civilisation', expressed in both cultural and bodily ways. To the extent that black people were deemed less advanced than whites, their skin colour, other physiological features (e.g., tight curly

---

[11] Union of South Africa, *House of Assembly Debates*, 17 March 1967, cols. 3172, 3183.

[12] D. Posel, 'Race as common sense', *African Studies Review* 44:2 (2001), 87–114; S. Dubow, *Illicit Union: scientific racism in modern South Africa* (Johannesburg: Witwatersrand University Press, 1997).

[13] Population Registration Act, no. 30 of 1950, section 1 (xv). A 'native' was defined as 'a person who is in fact or is generally accepted as a member of any aboriginal race or tribe of Africa' (section 1 (x)) and a 'coloured person' as 'a person who is not a white person or a native' (section 1 (iii)). Subsequent amendments to this law differentiated a fourth racial category, of Asians.

hair) and deportment became markers of cultural inferiority, expressed in ways of life, social standing and levels of education. In circular fashion, bodily differences were in turn taken as evidence of the cultural and status hierarchies that informed the ways that the racialised body was read.

Racial 'purity' was also read as a sign of cultural integrity. Apartheid ideologues were more suspicious of racial 'crossbreeds' than authentically or 'purely' black people, who – if inferior to whites – nevertheless had a way of life that was distinctively their own. So educated, Westernised Africans, seeking to 'mimic' the ways of white civilisation, were racially far more threatening than their tribalised counterparts who spurned the trappings of Western living. Hence the ongoing valorisation of tribal authenticity, which went hand in hand with the politics of separate development.

Apartheid social engineering gave bureaucratic fixity to notions of race that articulated and reproduced hierarchies of status, opportunity and power, read off and onto peoples' bodies. There was no attempt to deny the extent to which racial classification was an interpretative judgement about social standing and personal worth. And this was an enterprise deliberately allocated to whites, as the grouping whose social realities would confirm commonsense representations of white superiority. Indeed, one of the key drivers of the racial classification system was precisely to institutionalise lived experiences of race on the part of those who were socially accepted as whites – and whose racial judgements would therefore reiterate and confirm the racial hierarchy of which they were part.

Apartheid thus reiterated notions of race that had a longer history in South African society. What distinguished the apartheid project from the segregationism that preceded it was the effort to harness well-established versions of racial common sense to the most ambitious project of racial bureaucratisation and normalisation yet undertaken – nationally and internationally. Across the population at large, every facet of experience would be subject to racial categorisation and surveillance, predicated on the allegedly self-evident fact of white civilisation and the desirability of a way of life that preserved white supremacy.

The Regulation of Family, Gender and Sexuality

One of the earliest manifestations of the newfound obsession with racial difference was in the regulation of family, gender and sexuality. Drawing on the then-dominant discourse of modern statecraft, which allocated the state the responsibility, as much as the prerogative, to extend the reach of its regulatory powers into the sphere of family life; the apartheid state proceeded from the assumption that appropriate controls over the domestic sphere were critical to the causes of white political supremacy and economic prosperity, along with the advancement of the *volk*. In the first instance, all families had to be exemplars and vectors of racial purity. Two of the very first apartheid laws – the Immorality Act of 1949 (amending the earlier law of 1921) and the Mixed Marriages Act of 1950 – were primarily concerned with prohibiting sex and marriage between whites and blacks. Symbolically, the figure of the black man as would-be rapist was deeply entrenched in the imagery of *die swart gevaar*. The purpose of this legislation, then, was to anchor the defence of racial purity and moral discipline firmly in the politics of intimacy, with the state at the front line of the battle. The laws were crafted in tandem with the Group Areas Act of 1950, which authorised the creation of racially homogeneous residential areas, and the 1950 Prevention of Illegal Squatting Act, which outlawed settlement outside of officially designated – and therefore racially demarcated – living spaces. In the aggregate, these were measures to nail down racial separatism as the bedrock of family life, on the one hand, and to locate family life firmly and irrevocably in the purview of state authority, on the other hand.

The concern with domestic life was farther reaching too, including many strategies of what Foucault would call biopower: regulatory regimes designed to produce disciplined, economically productive and law-abiding subjects – particularly in white communities, and perhaps most markedly in efforts to rehabilitate poor whites to take their place in a 'modernising' society and workforce. Family life also thus became the focus of increasingly prolific analyses, surveys and official commentaries, with the Dutch Reformed Church (as the moral custodian of the informal Afrikaner Nationalist alliance) and the South African Bureau of Racial Affairs (one of the think tanks contributing to intra-Afrikaner thought and debate about apartheid) playing prominent roles. Central anxieties included the declining fertility of the white population, alongside high fertility rates in black communities; teenage pregnancies; the influence of 'immoral' youth subcultures (e.g. Beatles music, long hair and sexual experimentation); and the instability of marriage – particularly in black communities.

From the outset, the norms and values of Christian nationalism informed the rendition of the problems and the recommended solutions. Resolutely patriarchal, and critical of the moral laxity of the 'liberal' ways proliferating elsewhere in the West, apartheid officialdom authored a regime of moral authoritarianism. It peaked during the late 1960s, in tandem with the ideological broadsides against 'communism', encompassing any aspect of anti-Christian politics and ways of life. Strict media censorship restricted the circulation of images and text deemed immoral; the introduction of television was delayed by fears that this would contaminate the nation's morality with decadent and/or subversive programmes from abroad.

Apartheid's Economic Engineering

The apartheid project produced one of the most unequal societies in the world. This was not entirely a consequence of coherent and seamless planning. Nor was it an unintended outcome; on the contrary, the degree of deliberate economic engineering, with the goal of racialising access to resources, property and wealth, within the rubric of a capitalist economy, was one of the striking singularities of the apartheid project. The imperatives of racial purity, white power and the advance of the Afrikaner *volk* were understood to be inseparable from multifaceted strategies of economic engineering – including efforts to direct economic growth, refigure labour markets and manipulate class formation by regulating access to income, opportunities for accumulation, education, skill and training. When the National Party ascended to power, the country already had an economy shaped by the contours of race. The apartheid project substantially deepened the economic imprints of race, hardening racial boundaries on the possibilities of accumulation, access to skills and economic advancement. Indeed, the idea of race was explicitly regarded as a currency of economic opportunity and reward, as much as the measure of social standing, respectability and moral worth. Being black under apartheid was a sign of economic subordination, along with political subjugation – an idea captured by some Marxist scholars through the notion of racial capitalism.

A boldly interventionist state, confident of its powers to refashion markets according to political desiderata, was the key means by which the National Party sought to manage apartheid's foundational contradiction. Its preconditions were not merely ideological. Globally, this was a period of postwar prosperity, in which South Africa partook. Exports grew, along with foreign investment, creating favourable economic and political conditions for the costly work of large-scale economic regulation. The critical site of intervention was in the cities and towns, where the effects of the foundational contradiction were most intense. The persistent challenge was to regulate access to African labour in the urban areas in line with white economic needs, so as to promote industrial and commercial expansion but in ways that simultaneously minimised the rate of the growth of the black urban presence to what was economically necessary. Hence the advent of an urban labour preference policy at the heart of apartheid's economic engineering during its first phase in the 1950s. White employers were required to exhaust resident urban African labour supplies before importing any additional African labour into the area. In the Western Cape, specifically, the Coloured Labour Preference Policy reinforced this. Both policies were designed to keep the rate at which the urban African population grew as low as possible.

Underlying these policies were a series of assumptions about the nature and workings of labour markets, as well as the regulatory powers of the state – assumptions that took the postwar international conventional wisdom about the political malleability of markets to an ambitious, if deluded, extreme. The plan was to bring employers and work seekers together by bureaucratic fiat, with state officials deciding which work seekers to allocate to designated workplaces. Moreover, by applying the principle of urban labour preference, the state would ensure that this match occurred by draining existing urban labour supplies before additional labour was permitted to enter the urban area from outside. A national system of labour bureaux, intended to monitor, register and channel work seekers to employers, was created forthwith.

In the early 1950s, acknowledging the reality of large numbers of 'detribalised' Africans living in the cities on a de facto permanent basis, the apartheid regime had taken the pragmatic view that it would be impossible to dismantle these communities. The challenge was rather to prevent them from growing substantially bigger, at the same time as ensuring that urban employers' first port of call would be those already urbanised rather than migrants entering the cities from outlying areas. The basis of the first phase of apartheid economic engineering was thus an ideological and administrative distinction between urbanised Africans (de facto permanent city dwellers) and work-seeking migrants (who retained a permanent base in a rural area). This distinction was written into the law,[14] and became the basis of so-called section 10(1) rights[15] – the 'residential right' to remain in an urban area, with or without employment, 'for the foreseeable future'.[16] Hendrik Verwoerd, Minister of Native Affairs at the time and already the chief architect of apartheid, also conceded that residential rights were in recognition that urbanised Africans were entitled to 'certain guarantees,

---

[14] 1952 Native Laws Amendment Act.
[15] Section 10 of the Native Laws Amendment Act created three categories of people who qualified for what became known as 'section 10 rights': in terms of section 10(1)(a) of the law, African people who had been born and continuously resident in an urban area for ten years or more; in terms of 10(1)(b), Africans who had been working and continuously resident in an urban area for fifteen years or more; and 10(1)(c) recognised the dependents on those qualifying under 10(1)(a) and (b) as entitled to the same residential rights. The terms of the law applied equally to adult men and women; in practice, the resistance to applying the law to women was sufficiently intense to induce a more cautious approach. It was only in the early 1960s that African women were fully subsumed within the scope of the labour and influx control legislation.
[16] Secretary for Native Affairs, 'Draft regulations for the establishment, management and control of Native Labour Bureaux', 1951, cited in D. Posel, *The making of apartheid, 1948–1961* (Oxford: Clarendon Press, 1971 and 1997), p. 78.

security and stability.'[17] Most notably, their right to live in a city was not conditional on their being employed there. Yet the distinction between urbanised and tribalised Africans that the urban labour preference policy presupposed also rendered it internally contradictory: urbanised Africans, who had earned the residential right to live in the city, thus had legitimate grounds on which to refuse offers of employment and to resist efforts on the part of labour bureaux to 'channel' them into jobs ahead of migrant work seekers. Ironically, this de facto permanence was enhanced through the extended provision of urban township housing, as part of the aspiration to urban 'order'. Many erstwhile shantytowns were removed and their legal inhabitants rehoused in formal township structures in a bid to widen the ambit of effective state control. Its unintended consequence, however, was to increase the numbers of legal African city dwellers with an official residential foothold in 'white' South Africa.

One of the other major contradictions of the first phase of apartheid economic engineering occurred on the rural policy-making end. Regulating agricultural production in rural African communities constituted the other side of managing the urbanisation problem: clearly, efforts to stem the urban African tide would also depend on measures to reduce the population flow at its source. Africans outside the cities were largely concentrated in two sorts of rural locations: either in the reserves or on white-owned farms. The reserves had been initially defined and demarcated by the 1913 Land Act. By the 1940s, they were sites of worsening poverty, born of agricultural decline and overcrowding – one of the major drivers of the urban migrations of the postwar years, which the apartheid state sought to contain. The Tomlinson Commission – appointed to reconsider policy toward the reserves – found that, by 1951, only a small sector of the peasantry had escaped extreme poverty, calculating that 13 per cent of the population of the reserves generated around 46 per cent of their income.[18] The Commission recommended a far-reaching and expensive programme of economic rehabilitation and development in the reserves. But these were rejected; instead, the government offered a modest injection of cash, in the name of agricultural betterment. Irrigation schemes were introduced in some areas, soil conservation measures in others; but the overall effect was desultory, and the dearth of industrial or mining development in the reserves increased the economic pressure on ailing agricultural production. Communal land tenure was retained – with strong support from rural Africans. Rather than a serious effort at boosting the sustainability of the

---

[17] Native Affairs Department, 'Progress report . . . for 1950', cited in Posel, *Making of apartheid*, p. 79.

[18] Union of South Africa, *Summary of the Report of the Commission for the Socio-Economic Development of the Bantu Areas within the Union of South Africa* (Pretoria: Government Printer, UG 61/1955), p. 98.

reserves, the intention of apartheid's planners was to sustain relations of economic dependency so as to reproduce reservoirs of migrant labour to service the needs of white employers. Therefore, the pressures to migrate townward simply intensified as the 1950s wore on.

Conditions for Africans living on the farms also deteriorated. This was partly a consequence of the trend for agricultural production to mechanise, which diminished the demand for African farm labour. The number of tractors in use on South African farms rocketed from around 20,000 in 1946 to almost 120,000 by 1960. White farmers – who had complained repeatedly during the 1940s of labour shortages – lamented the 'surplus' population inhabiting their lands and put pressure on the state to remove them. The result was a two-pronged assault, on the institutions of share-cropping and labour tenancy – both mainstays of rural African families for many decades in the past. Sharecropping had already been deemed illegal, and the apartheid state now made determined efforts to eradicate it. Similarly, large numbers of African labour tenants were driven off white-owned lands to the reserves – thereby further worsening the population pressure on farming lands in these areas. Indeed, during the 1950s, the population of the reserves soared, largely as a consequence of the assault on labour tenancy.

Other facets of apartheid economic engineering were expressly designed to redeem and then entrench white economic privilege. The policy of job reservation was introduced in the mid-1950s with the purpose of reserving designated categories of work for whites. This intervention signalled the power of white working-class interests in the Afrikaner Nationalist alliance. As a consequence, by the end of the 1950s, African workers were barred from skilled work in many sectors, and all black workers (Africans, Indians and coloureds) were prohibited from being in positions of authority over white workers.

Job reservation went hand in hand with the policy of Bantu education – one of the abiding centrepieces of apartheid legislation. Prior to 1948, African education had been primarily the preserve of mission schools. With a relatively small reach (in the region of five thousand schools), these schools were deemed by Verwoerd, along with the influential Secretary of Native Affairs W. Eiselen to have provided an inappropriately Western, liberal education aimed at an African elite – an education that, in Verwoerd's words, 'drew [the African] away from his own community and misled him by showing him the green pastures of European society in which he was not allowed to graze.'[19] Afrikaner nationalists had long been deeply suspicious – and fearful – of the political and ideological powers of the mission-educated

---

[19] Senate Debates, 7 June 1954, cited in J. Pampallis, *Foundation of the new South Africa* (Cape Town: Maskew Miller Longman, 1971), p. 184.

elite, who dominated the leadership of the African National Congress and other political opposition movements. By contrast, Verwoerd and Eiselen envisaged a new system of mass education, the explicit aim of which was to educate far larger numbers of African children, but with a ceiling placed on their level of knowledge and skill. As Verwoerd put it, '[W]hat is the use of teaching the Bantu child mathematics when it cannot use it in practice? That is quite absurd. Education must train people in accordance with their opportunities in life, according to the situation in which they live.'[20]

In terms of the Bantu Education Act of 1953, all educational institutions were to be racially segregated. And in the case of schools, central government was authorised to exercise direct control over the appointment of teachers and the content of the curriculum. The law also saw to the dramatic expansion of access to schooling among African children. If a cynical diminution of the quality of education in African schools, Bantu education also oversaw a substantial increase in the quantity of schooling, with a vast increase in school enrolments, particularly in primary schools. This would turn out to be one of the more explosive contradictions of the apartheid project, leading directly to the 1976 Soweto uprisings (and thereby to the beginning of apartheid's political undoing). Bantu education produced large numbers of school-goers with mounting grievances about the inferiority of their education. Their racial segregation and concentration became both the locus of their complaint and the vehicle of their collective mobilisation.

Escalation of political protest in the late 1950s provided the immediate trigger for the shift from the first to the second phase of apartheid, brought on by the dawning realisation in policy-making circles, from the mid-1950s, of the contradictions inherent in the logic of 'practical' apartheid. The internal incoherence in the urban labour preference policy was well known and widely discussed in national policy-making circles and among local native administrators, who named the idea of residential rights for urbanised Africans as the root of the problem. By the end of the decade, it was similarly clear that the labour bureaux system was failing to produce the desired degree of state control over the allocation and distribution of African labour to white employers. Employers and work seekers alike simply flouted the rules and made their own arrangements. Urban administrators were confronted with growing labour 'surpluses' in the cities – people either unwilling or unable to find formal employment – at the same time that the urban African population was continuing to expand. Indeed, by the end of the first phase of apartheid (in the late 1950s), efforts to curb African urbanisation had largely failed. The urban African population grew by 49.5 per cent between 1950 and 1960 (from 2,559,200 to 3,825,500),

[20] Ibid.

notwithstanding the plethora of controls over urban migration and residence.

To some extent, the urban African population had been better housed, with lower rates of informal squatting. But overall, the decade had seen rising levels of disaffection, again concentrated in the cities. Pass laws – the main instruments of the desired urbanisation control – were the source of intense opposition and had triggered the most politically destabilising protests of the decade, catapulting the apartheid regime into international notoriety. The apartheid project was not seriously at risk; but by the late 1950s, a decade of largely black defiance had reinstated the spectre of mass black opposition, *die swart gevaar*.

In response to the protests, and buoyed by the National Party's electoral successes in the late 1950s, the apartheid government inaugurated an ideological and strategic shift linked to new strategies of economic and social engineering, albeit once again in the midst of controversy and division in the Afrikaner nationalist alliance. It rejected the earlier notion of detribalisation on the grounds of an allegedly irrevocable and primordial 'tribalism' that characterised the African psyche. In consequence, all Africans were believed to be culturally and spiritually anchored in an ethnic 'homeland', whether or not they had ever set foot in the place. Apartheid's planners then inaugurated another shift, in advocating the allocation of 'self-government' to these homelands (a renaming and political configuration of the erstwhile African Reserves). One of the early renditions of apartheid had been as a means of racial 'separate development' – but conceptualised largely in spatial terms. By the late 1950s, the notion of separate development was redefined within a new ideological discourse of multinationalism and ethnic self-determination, and in 1959, the Promotion of Bantu Self-Government Act was passed. As Verwoerd told Parliament in 1961, this policy represented a departure from the regime's original intentions; 'it is not what we wanted to see', he said.[21] Partly defensive – an attempt to deflect mounting international criticism of the denial of political rights to blacks by invoking the globally ascendant discourse of political self-determination – the new homeland strategy was also an offensive move in the effort to re-engineer the country's economic architecture.

By negating the notion of African detribalisation and advocating homeland self-government, the architects of apartheid authorised and legitimised the new strategic imperative of undermining any African claims to a permanent place in the cities. Its immediate instrument was a sustained legal assault on the scope and terms of section 10(1) residential rights, in a bid to redefine the settled African urban population as a mere labour supply, temporarily settled with no security of urban residence other than by way

[21] Union of South Africa, *House of Assembly Debates*, 1961, vol. 107, col. 4191.

of an officially authorised contract of employment. The effort to scrap the provision in law was persistently unsuccessful, but a series of more indirect legal and administrative measures succeeded in chipping away at some of the security that urbanised Africans had enjoyed during apartheid's first phase.

Destabilising the notion of residential rights was linked, in turn, to a new policy of population removals, to deal far more aggressively with the problem of urban population growth. During the first phase of apartheid, population removals were enacted under the auspices of the Group Areas Act of 1950, which designated residential areas for racially homogeneous occupation and was applied in tandem with the Elimination of Squatting Act of 1951. Black people living in urban areas designated for whites were then forcibly removed to other parts of the city. As the racial schema of the Population Registration Act was constituted, it created the grid into which all apartheid regulation and surveillance were fitted. Its repetition across all sites of experience meant that the ideas of race and racial difference, and more particularly, the four racial groups designated by apartheid, became facts of life in South Africa, elements of social common sense, even among many of those who vehemently opposed the ideology and policies of apartheid. In the 1950s, racially homogeneous residential areas – or 'group areas', to use the official parlance – were created, along with the gradual eradication of informal squatter settlements. In many instances, this involved forced removals of communities located in the allegedly wrong place, or with histories of racial mixing – such as the removal of Sophiatown in Johannesburg during the late 1950s and District Six in Cape Town. Black inhabitants were sorted into racial groups and reassigned accommodation in coloured, Indian or African townships, all subject to the jurisdiction of local authorities. So the remapping and reconfiguration of black communities were simultaneously a reorganisation of the parameters of urban governance, steadily eliminating residential zones beyond the control of the authorities. During apartheid's second phase, removals were used to excise large chunks of the urban African population altogether, dumping people in areas designated as outside the boundaries of 'white' South Africa and subject to the authority of a self-governing homeland. This was also a way of diminishing the apartheid state's responsibility for the welfare of those people once they had been removed to a supposedly distinct political authority. Then, any African person deemed 'surplus' to the (white) labour requirements of the area was deemed liable for removal to one of the Bantustans. By the end of the 1960s, around 3.5 million people had been forcibly removed from 'white' areas of South Africa.

Partly in an effort to create employment for the people thus relocated and partly in the hope of making the homelands economically viable, a policy of industrial decentralisation was introduced. A further assumption was that taking industries to the urban peripheries would thereby diminish the demand for African labour in the urban heartlands, thus allowing for a reduction in urban migration. Simultaneously, an attempt was made to impose labour quotas limiting the employment of black workers in the remaining urban industries and businesses.

The 1960s also saw a newly aggressive effort to manipulate patterns of class formation in the country, focusing in particular on the fortunes and location of the emerging African middle class. Uncomfortable with the proximity and political profile of the urban elite, the apartheid state rapidly withdrew the (modest) privileges accorded before 1948. Thus, all Africans in the cities were uniformly subject to the indignities and harassment of the pass laws, irrespective of their social standing or class – a source of intense grievance. During the 1950s, the allocation of residential rights had protected the economic foothold of the middle class in the cities, which continued to grow in income and social standing. From the early 1960s, however, self-employed Africans – a substantial chunk of the urban African middle class – were designated as surplus to the labour requirements of the cities, and therefore liable for removal to one of the homelands, where supposedly their skills and business acumen would benefit their own people.

Apartheid as a Modernising Project

The apartheid project was, throughout, an explicitly modernising one. The concept of modernity – which following Fred Cooper, I use to refer to a discourse of power, shaping the aspirations, norms and expectations of rule – has two defining elements. The first is its version of the passage of time, as a narrative of progress from that which was not modern ('tradition'), with clear markers along a linear route of social, economic and political advancement. The second is a more spatial situating, a self-conscious positioning within the wider world. Modernity, after all, has been a globalising cause, exporting originally Western notions of rule across other parts of the world. And the claim to being modern involves a certain kind of worldliness: a recognition of, and aspiration to, linkages with other similarly modern regimes and societies. From that vantage point, the project of modernity was evident in South African governance from the time of Union in 1910. The advent of apartheid in 1948 gave a fillip to this way of thinking about power, in line with the new global enthusiasm for more aggressively 'orderly' and centrally planned modes of regulation and social engineering. And in this respect, discourses of power were closely aligned with those elsewhere in the West, where the notion of a modern state foregrounded the prerogative and responsibility for ambitious national planning. Indeed, South Africa's reference point, and political standard, was always Western – even at the height of the country's international isolation as a racist pariah state. The idea of proper planning became integral to the discourse of power here, as in colonial states elsewhere. Indeed, the aspiration to 'create order from chaos'[22] became one of the mantras of apartheid policy making. The advance of apartheid was therefore closely associated with the professionalisation of administration. This was especially formative in the case of 'urban native administration', which produced a growing cohort of men who prided themselves on their specialised expertise. During the 1950s and 1960s, these bureaucrats working in cities had formative degrees of discretionary power to implement central government policy.

Much of their discretionary power was eroded, however, with the shift to apartheid's second phase, which produced an increasingly aggressive onslaught on the autonomy and expertise of urban native administrators who were considered too 'liberal' in their practice – typically English speakers – and therefore politically untrustworthy. During the 1960s, then, at the very moment that the remit of state bureaucracies was expanding dramatically, they were purged of experience and expertise; increasingly ambitious efforts at control were entrusted to unqualified and overstretched officials. This was one of the sources of the crippling shortages of bureaucratic capacity that went hand in hand with the expansions of apartheid's ambitions during the 1960s (see 'Evaluating the Efficacy of the Apartheid Project').

Yet the realities of limited bureaucratic capacity did not deter the determination to 'modernise', linked to the escalating hubris of the apartheid planning enterprise. As the ambitions of apartheid's planners expanded, so too did their aspirations to knowledge. In 1965, a new national ministry – the Department of Planning – was created, to coordinate, stimulate and accelerate the activity of national planning, in tandem with labyrinthine systems of measurement. Indeed, by the late 1960s, devotion to the idea of informed planning had stimulated a veritable avalanche of measurement, notably in respect of what was then termed Bantu Affairs. The aspiration was to a horizontally layered, vertically integrated system of quantitative information gathering, with local authorities compiling masses of local data, more composite pictures being produced at the district and regional level, and the central Department of Bantu Affairs synthesising and collating all of these measurements with panoptic completeness.[23] With the central Department a huge and labyrinthine bureaucracy with many

---

[22] Quoted in South African Bureau of Racial Affairs (SABRA) *Newsletter* (October 1954), 7.

[23] D. Posel, 'A mania for measurement: statistics and statecraft in the transition to apartheid', in Dubow (ed.), *Science and society in southern Africa*, p. 129.

divisions and subdivisions, its own routine statistical enterprise included monthly counts of the number of work seekers' permits issued on a national basis; the number of service contracts registered (showing the area of origin of each of the registered workers); the numbers of registered vacancies in urban areas, homelands and on farms; annual counts of the number of Africans seeking assistance from special 'aid centres'; the compilation of an 'occupational register . . . in respect of each national unit . . . containing certain particulars of each of the Bantu concerned'; the creation of a separate database of 'existing and anticipated employment opportunities in the homelands for Bantu with advanced qualifications'; and the list goes on and on. However, at no stage was there an effective operational connection between the assemblage of statistics and the daily business of the labour bureaux or in the regulation of African employment more generally. Indeed, the apartheid obsession with measurement was more significant as a symptom of the deluded limits of its modernising aspirations than as a descriptor of governmental practice.

Yet for all the ineptitude and inefficiency, apartheid's modernist dementia remained a powerful facet of apartheid statecraft. If the efforts at planning and surveillance never wholly matched the intentions of the planners, their failures were never total either. At any point in time, city dwellers, workers, or employers were not in a position to gauge or predict what would succeed and what would fail. But they would have experienced the institutions of state as ever on the lookout, ever in the throes of an ambitious planning exercise: a performance of power that gave some substance to an ideology of planning and surveillance. This, in turn, would have had some impact on the ways apartheid's subjects oriented themselves in relation to state officials and state policy: never able to disregard it altogether, in case they did come into the vision of a competent official, in case theirs was one of the instances of non-compliance that did register in the arcane bureaucratic mind.

The Interconnectedness of Law and Violence

Although the sociological canon on modernity has emphasised its rational-legal dimensions, recent literature, inspired by Foucault's later works, points to the ubiquity of violence in modern regimes 'behind, or rather in the neighbourhood of, the official rationality and rule of law to which the modern state is committed.'[24] In the case of the apartheid state – as with other repressive states – the recourse to violence was both secret and widely known: an open secret, on the understanding that the instability of white supremacy necessitated coercive tactics that, for the most part,

[24] V. Das et al. (eds.), *Violence and subjectivity* (Berkeley: University of California Press, 2000), p. 6.

should remain discreet, albeit with sometimes intermittent, sometimes more frequent, flashes of state brutality – a reassurance for the regime's supporters and a threat for those who opposed it. So even if state violence was never official, its effects were palpable. Apartheid produced a milieu of 'social danger'[25] that moulded the practice of domination.

The simultaneity of law and violence is crucial to understanding how apartheid worked. Apartheid was never a totalitarian project. The making of apartheid was thoroughly bound up with the workings of a (racially distorted) version of parliamentary democracy. The ideologues and practitioners of the project went to great lengths to invoke the law as their principal instrument and to route the practice of apartheid through legal democratic channels. It was neither wholly tokenistic nor simply ideologically expedient: within the limits of a racially delimited parliamentary democracy, the apartheid system worked through the conduits of legal prescription and proscription, along with bureaucratic regulation and surveillance. From the outset, it was constituted within the rubric of a parliamentary democracy – albeit with racially defined exclusions and limits, with the vote denied to Africans, coloureds and Indians. Around fifty thousand coloured voters were removed from the common voters' roll in the Cape. Democratic institutions were manipulated; the powers of an independent judiciary were fettered; Parliament was increasingly sidelined, as power was centralised within sites of executive authority. A battery of repressive legislation limiting and then banning militant political opposition ensued. Beginning with the 1950 Suppression of Communism Act, this legislative armoury included restrictions on trade union organisation, the banning of the African National Congress and the Pan African Congress in 1960, and then the suspension of habeas corpus, recourse to detention without trial, and the banning of individuals deemed subversive. Yet law remained the primary instrument of apartheid rule, and the idea of a (racialised) democratically regulated legal process was central to apartheid's modus operandi.

At the same time, techniques of arbitrary intimidation and brutalisation were thoroughly insinuated into the texture of everyday life, particularly for black people. An authoritarian political culture marked the practice of apartheid and accompanied the apartheid version of parliamentary democracy. The prerogative to command acquiescence, if not active consent, was integral to apartheid statecraft. Its manifestations were multiple, as much from the regime of stringent censorship, accompanied by heavy doses of proapartheid propaganda that spewed through the media, as in the palpable muscularity with which the apartheid order was policed.

As the severity of apartheid intensified, so too did the penalties for disobedience. By the late 1960s, state officials had at their disposal an arsenal

---

[25] Ibid., p. 2.

of laws and regulations allowing for anyone suspected of any 'communistic' inclinations (very loosely defined, to cover any form of antiapartheid protest) to be arrested and detained without trial. And for those who preferred to stay on the right side of the law, apartheid propaganda suffused the society with a sense of endemic threat and menace. At first, its source was the ominous black mass that had overwhelmed the cities; by the 1960s, the story of immanent and ubiquitous danger had extended to include 'terrorists' and 'communists' lurking in every nook and cranny, endangering the lives of innocent civilians. On both counts, the only protection for the 'civilised' was purported to lie with a strong state that did not flinch from ruthless counterattack, where necessary. The police were thus regarded as an arm of government, mandated to enforce its authority, rather than as a relatively independent agency charged to protect the populace.

If the milieu of fear and suspicion gave some popular credence to a forceful state, the everyday routines of apartheid social engineering necessitated it. The sheer volume – indeed the ubiquity – of legal regulation fostered apartheid's endemic violence. For an African person, all the minutiae of everyday life – where and with whom they lived, worked, had sex, travelled, shopped, walked or sat down, what they owned and consumed – were governed either by the issue of appropriate permits or passes or by public prohibitions and proscriptions. So encounters with police, charged with enforcing the racial boundaries that animated these regimes of surveillance, were inevitable, and breaches of the myriad regulations were legion. The advent of apartheid saw a substantial increase in the number of prosecutions in court, with possession of sorghum beer and pass-law offences topping the list. And the collisions with police were ignited by force – to the extent that gratuitous violence became a feature of apartheid policing, with mounting numbers of reports of torture.

From the early 1950s, it was already apparent that 'the police controlled the boundaries between the races with a level of systematic inhumanity which was not known before, and the legal and political constraints which moderated police conduct in the past were lifted.'[26] As apartheid advanced, so too did the scope and intensity of the violence. By the 1960s, the repressive arsenal of the apartheid state had expanded, with the promulgation of anti-terrorist legislation and the concomitant increase in the size and powers of both the military and the police. The task of policing white supremacy spread across a wider range of institutions, from the South African Police (its size and budget boosted) through to the Reserve Police (established in 1961) and eventually the Bureau of State Security (created in 1969), with closer working links between the police and the army.

[26] John Brewer, *Black and blue: policing in South Africa* (Oxford: Clarendon Press, 1994), p. 222.

If apartheid proliferated higher orders of coercive regulation and surveillance in some spheres, it was also marked by remarkable disinterest and
incapacity in others. For black South Africans, racial borders were stringently policed – evident, for example, in the escalating rates of prosecution
for pass law infringements. Yet far less attention was paid to ordinary crime,
particularly in black residential areas – to the extent that the rampant crim-
inality, gangsterism and vigilante violence in townships were almost wholly
disregarded. By the late 1960s, public pressure forced something of a shift,
and greater efforts were made to police township crime. But in the main,
townships and informal settlements with populations of many hundreds of
thousands had ridiculously small resident police forces – a symptom of the
disinterest within the state in attending to the problems of assault, murder,
sexual violence and child abuse that were known to be the product of a
brutalised life.

Apartheid's violence, then, lay as much in the violence of everyday life
as the coerciveness of the state; indeed, in the articulation of the two.
Hence one of the abiding paradoxes of the apartheid project: it produced
an intensely regulated society, with high degrees of racial and political
surveillance, yet this coexisted with large zones of utter lawlessness that
licensed exceptionally high levels of everyday violence. Arguably, the fact
that the white residential areas were marked by high levels of 'law and
order' while the black townships remained unruly, crime-ridden and violent became ideological confirmation of apartheid's racist hierarchy – as
if demonstrating the place of black people at lower levels of 'civilisation'.
The figure of the unscrupulously violent black criminal kept white fears of
black menace alive, which sustained support for the rigid racial segregation
that the apartheid state promised to sustain.

The Politics of Ethnicity

For all its racial distortions, the salience of the legal-democratic rubric
would have critically important implications for the management of
apartheid's foundational contradiction. Despite being the single greatest
threat to white political supremacy, black political ambitions could nevertheless not be dismissed as wholly illegitimate – only as misplaced within
the ambit of the 'white' polity. The political exclusion of blacks would
require careful political and ideological work, in ways that fitted with
the pretensions of a national democratic ethos. Institutionally, this was
realised through the establishment, under the Separate Representation of
Voters Act (1956), of the South African Indian Council in 1963 and the
Coloured Representative Council a year later, with first elections for the
latter in 1969 and for the former in 1974. As regards Africans, apartheid's

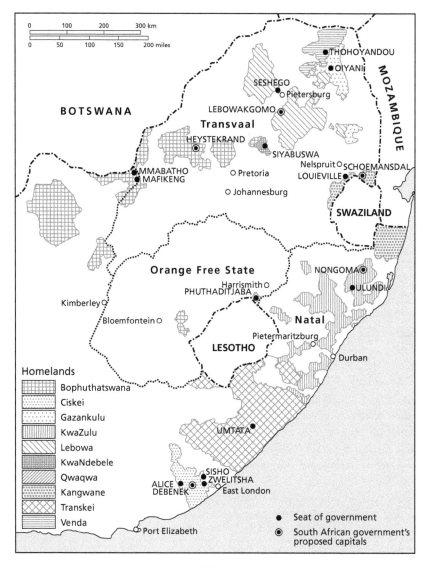

Homelands

▦	Bophuthatswana
░	Ciskei
⋯	Gazankulu
▥	KwaZulu
╱	Lebowa
▓	KwaNdebele
▨	Qwaqwa
▒	Kangwane
▩	Transkei
▤	Venda

● Seat of government
◉ South African government's proposed capitals

MAP 3

architects looked to the ideology of separate development and the institu-tion of the chieftaincy, linked to a long history of indirect rule, as the basis of attempts to resolve the problem of African political representation.

The meaning of separate development changed as apartheid evolved. During the 1950s, its primary locus was the strengthening and further bureaucratisation of the chieftaincy, by way of the 1951 Bantu Authorities

Act. This was coupled with assaults on the authority of oppositional chiefs and the invention of claims to chiefly authority on the part of those deemed more pliable, if popularly illegitimate. By the late 1950s, as waves of decolonisation were breaking over other parts of Africa and in the midst of mounting international opposition to apartheid's racism, the apartheid regime tackled the problem of African political representation anew. The long-standing idea of distinct African Reserves was reworked, as the basis of two successive versions of the idea of territorially demarcated, ethnically defined African polities. From the early 1960s, this took the form of self-governing ethnic homelands, and then, by the early 1970s, the notion of ethnically distinct, independent homelands.

Central – and distinctive – to the 'grand' apartheid project of the 1960s, therefore, was the attempt to produce distinct, and putatively legitimate, African polities that excised the African majority from the ambit of the country's white parliamentary democracy, and that inhibited the prospects of a wider black political mobilisation. This was to be done on an ethnic basis. The African majority was disaggregated into a series of discrete ethnic groups, each allocated its own territory and (supposed) powers of self-government. These were the amaXhosa, divided between the Transkei and Ciskei, the amaZulu in KwaZulu, the South Basotho in Qwaqwa, the North Basotho in Lebowa, the Vhavenda in Venda, the amaNdebele in KwaNdebele, the amaSwati in Kangwane and the Vatsonga in Gazankulu. This variant of indirect rule promised self-government to those who identified with chiefly norms and ambitions, and provided an antidote to the more modernist political notions and expectations embraced by urban educated elites, typically at the vanguard of African nationalist movements and causes. Separate development was therefore a strategy of reinvigorating, refashioning and rewarding 'traditional' African notions of authority and political culture – indeed, reinventing, bureaucratising and disciplining tradition as part of the wider project of creating political 'order' – at the same time as fragmenting African peoples into discrete ethnic components.

In the early 1950s, the apartheid state had taken the first step toward ethnic governance in urban areas, through a policy of so-called ethnic grouping in townships. Township planners and municipal officials were instructed to settle families in ethnically homogeneous zones, linked to schools with corresponding mediums of instruction. In practice, some administrators were more zealous than others in implementing this policy – the obvious complication of which was the urban commonplace of ethnically mixed marriages. With the shift to the second phase of apartheid (as discussed in the previous section), more concerted measures at ethnic governance were instituted, in line with the ideological repudiation of the notion of detribalisation and the determination to 'stimulate . . . the yearning [of the]

Bantu citydweller... for his homeland'.[27] Homeland chiefs were requested to appoint 'urban representatives' who were employed to 'link' ethnic communities in homelands and townships. Chiefs' representatives were charged with conveying information from one setting to the other, and with acting as cultural and political proxies for the chief. In the main, however, the men were ill educated and out of their depth in the hurly-burly of township politics, and the system was a rather spectacular failure.

The more serious effort at the politicisation of ethnicity came through the bureaucratisation of hierarchies of chiefly authority in homeland governments, particularly in the 1970s. Self-government attempted to establish higher and more durable orders of control, based on more overtly clientelist modes of politics than had been the case during segregationism. Not only would chiefs become salaried officials in the employ of the state; self-governing, and later, independent homelands, became protected sites for the enrichment and advancement of their local elites, as rewards for acquiescence in and collaboration with the system of separate development. At the same time, greater orders of power were conferred on the rulers and homelands than had been considered tenable or desirable during the earlier eras of indirect rule.

Yet clientelism as a mode of rule never escapes what John Lonsdale has termed the 'paradox of rule: power could not be exercised without giving some of it away'.[28] Efforts to resuscitate chiefly authority depended, by their very nature, on a compromise: consent from chiefs was conditional on meaningful retention of at least some of their traditional powers as chiefs. A careful calculus was required. If too little power was given away, the chief – as the state's client – would have been perceived by his people as a mere stooge, which would have diminished his usefulness as an agent of the state. In contrast, giving away a significant modicum of power created the risk of an unruly client who proved too independent and assertive for the likes of the apartheid state. This dilemma proved intractable. The apartheid state was never prepared to risk the prospect of an unpliable client, to the extent that the majority of homeland leaders were widely perceived as puppets of the apartheid regime. The enduring problem of African political representation, therefore, was never effectively resolved. Still, the extent to which clientelist strategies succeeded in creating African elites with a vested interest in separate development, and the legacies thereof for the postapartheid era, should not be underestimated and remain an area meriting further research.

---

[27] Deputy Minister of Bantu Affairs, Blaar Coetzee, cited in Posel, *Making of apartheid*, p. 233.

[28] Cited in B. Berman, 'Structure and process in bureaucratic states', *Development and Change* 15:2 (1984), 182.

EVALUATING THE EFFICACY OF THE APARTHEID PROJECT

The overall impact of the apartheid project was somewhat fluid, changing over time; it was also mixed, even at the zenith of 'grand' apartheid in the late 1960s – as much a consequence of the unintended consequences of state policies as of the failures to implement policies according to the aspirations of their architects. The final section of this chapter reviews the extent to which the problems of population that animated the apartheid project were effectively solved and the impact thereof.

Remaking the State

The apartheid project positioned the state at its apex, as the author and agent of a wide-ranging exercise in social change. Clearly, the operationalisation of the project depended fundamentally on the capacities and efficacy of the re-forming state. These, in turn, were subject to two central dynamics: the reconfiguration of the balance of power between central state departments and local bureaucracies, and the changing racial and ethnic composition of state institutions at large. By 1948, the major parties contesting the election had produced similar diagnoses of the failings of the decentral-isation of power within the segregationist state; likewise, they shared an enthusiasm for the prospects of a modernising of state, in pursuit of a more orderly society. In the case of the National Party, the critique of the segregationist state was infused too, with an abiding mistrust of 'liberal' local authorities, vested with too much discretion in the implementation of central government policies. After the National Party's accession to power, the metropolitan city councils of Johannesburg, Cape Town and Durban were still dominated by the English-speaking supporters of the opposition United Party. So, the attempt to shift the balance of power from the local to central state was also an indirect strategy of counteracting the dominance of the United Party in local government. Predictably, the primary locus of contention was the regulation of race, and particularly in its articulation with local economies and the dynamics of local class interests, through the auspices of municipal Non-European Affairs departments, accountable to elected city or town councils.

In its first phase, the implementation of apartheid remained largely in the hands of municipal officials, and subject to the oversight and mediating power of elected local authorities. Because the apartheid state was not yet sufficiently strong or assertive to wrest this power, the result was a highly uneven operationalisation of national policy. The workings of the labour bureaux were a typical case in point. Staffed by municipal officials, these bodies were tasked with implementing the urban labour preference policy that lay at the heart of the effort to reengineer urban labour markets. In some towns, where the National Party dominated the local authority and where the labour bureaux officials were Afrikaner loyalists, efforts were made to adhere to the text of national policy. But in the main, the policy remained inert. This was partly a consequence of its mismatch with the realities of employment; preferring less sophisticated migrant workers to their allegedly excessively choosy urban counterparts, many employers simply ignored the labour bureaux, and officials were either unwilling or unable to deter them. But the failure of the urban labour preference policy was also a product of the reluctance of most labour bureaux officials to apply it. In the face of strong opposition from employers and work seekers alike, most officials deferred to local class interests and powers.

The tardiness in applying pass laws to African women testified similarly to the early discretionary powers of local authorities. Although some nationalist diehards were particularly vindictive and hard-line toward African women, most preferred a more conciliatory approach, in the interests of less volatile relations with township communities. In the midst of a decade of politically turbulent township politics, many local authorities opted tactically for a less provocative approach, so that by 1956, most of the large urban local authorities had chosen not to apply the influx control laws to African women.

The predilection of local authorities to undermine or defer the implementation of national policies should not be overstated. But nor should the significance of local powers of discretion be understated. As supporters of the opposition United Party, some local authorities were overt critics of apartheid policies – albeit supporters of the principles of racial separatism – and could use their limited spheres of operation to sabotage or blunt the application of national policy. Their opposition was countered, in turn, by the increasingly discerning oversight of central state officials. Indeed, it was in response to the palpable effects of the critical manoeuvrings of local authorities that the second phase of apartheid inaugurated a sustained attack on their powers, and forced a more uniform and stricter application of the terms of national policy. This attack would not bear fruit fully, however, until the early 1970s, with the creation of administration boards to usurp the application of influx control and labour bureaux regulations from local authorities altogether.

The state's visions of power grew bolder and more expansive as the electoral grip of the National Party strengthened, which in turn allowed for more aggressive solutions to its foundational contradiction. Unsurprisingly, then, one of the most obvious features of the apartheid state throughout the period under discussion was its unremitting and extraordinary growth. On the eve of the National Party's election, there were twenty-six government departments; by 1970, this had increased to forty-one. In 1950, a total of 110,000 people of all races occupied permanent positions in the public service; by 1967, this had risen to 212,788 – an increase of 48 per cent in seventeen years. Many thousands of state officials, however, were temporary appointees. According to one set of measures, a total staff establishment in the public service of around 280,000 in 1950 shot up to 549,865 by 1970 – an extraordinary increase of 96 per cent in twenty years.[29] Yet the growth in the bureaucratic bulk of the state went hand in hand with diminishing capacity. Paradoxically, the staff establishment of state bureaucracies continued to expand in the midst of worsening shortages of personnel, particularly at more senior levels. By 1968, many government departments were up to 60 per cent understaffed.

The root of the problem was the 'Afrikanerisation' of the civil service, depleting it of its English-speaking appointees inherited from the previous regime and then repopulating it with Afrikaans speakers loyal to the National Party's cause.[30] A matriculation (school-leaving) certificate was required for civil servants appointed to permanent positions at middle and senior levels. In the 1950s, however, the National Party's affirmative action policy was pursued more aggressively than the pace at which Afrikaner matriculation rates increased, thus producing a shrinking supply of recruits. By the 1960s, the shortage was further exacerbated by the country's unprecedented economic growth, which gave all white work seekers far more lucrative job opportunities in the private sector – a factor that also accounted for accelerating rates of resignation from the civil service.

The staff shortages were worsened, too, by racialised job reservation: giving white people preferential access to all jobs ahead of any black competitors. The effects of this policy on the project of refashioning the state were profoundly ironic: intent on protecting privileged spheres of work for whites, the apartheid state created its own labour-shortage problem. Job reservation policies prevented the state from training black people in sufficiently large numbers to supply state bureaucracies with the scale and level of skill required to operationalise its apartheid project. Even so, given the enormity of the staff shortages, it was impossible not to recruit an increasingly black workforce – to the point that, by 1970, black civil servants outnumbered their white counterparts by 22 per cent. They remained excluded from the more senior positions, however, where vacancy rates were woefully high. The resultant dearth of top-end skill, coupled with the ballooning of bureaucracy in lower ranks, prompted one of the opposition

---

[29] D. Posel, 'Whiteness and power in the South African civil service: paradoxes of the apartheid state', *Journal of Southern African Studies* 25:4 (1999), 104.

[30] By 1959, of more than forty government departments and subdepartments, only six had English-speaking heads. Posel, 'Whiteness and power', 105.

members of Parliament to liken the apartheid state to 'a dinosaur with a massive body and small brain':[31] an apt characterisation of a state that had refashioned itself into a sprawling and unwieldy – if uneven – instrument of regulation and surveillance but with little of the lithe intelligence required to respond strategically and creatively to an increasingly complex operational milieu.

Racial Governance

Apartheid South Africa was unique in promulgating legislation that defined racial difference and specified mechanisms whereby those differences would be established, authorised and operationalised. Between 1950 and 1966, more than 12 million racial classifications had been entered on the national population register: the database intended, ultimately, to record the race of each and every citizen. Following the promulgation of the Population Registration Act, the first exercise in mass racial classification was harnessed to the national population census of 1951, with census takers assuming the role of racial classifiers. After that, the powers of racial classification were allocated to all officials of the Department of Native (later Bantu) Affairs and then – in 1969 – to all white public servants. Guided loosely by the racial definitions supplied by the legislation, these officials made decisions that would then dominate the lives of the individuals concerned at all times and in every facet of their experience.

From the outset, the racial classification process exhibited the culturalist logic of the apartheid notion of race enshrined in the law, which in turn determined the manner and level of official qualification required for the job. If race was as much a matter of 'general acceptance' as bodily appearance, then racial classifiers needed no special expertise, or any particular training, to undertake the task of classification. On the contrary, given that the exercise was intended to fix and entrench the country's existing racial hierarchy, the only necessary qualification for the job was the experience of white superiority: it was the white classifiers' ordinary everyday experience of racial difference that was expected to inform their judgements. This remained deliberately vague, in the interests of a swift process of classification unencumbered by rigorous criteria or standards of evidence. The enabling legislation provided no manual for the task; there were no clear criteria for reading the markers of race in the body, or for evaluating a person's social standing, reputation or way of life. The classification process, therefore, became as heterogeneous as the officials undertaking it, with some finding definitive signs of race in the texture of hair or the

[31] Ibid., 111.

colour of fingernails and others placing overriding emphasis on a person's clothing, modes of leisure or home language.

As a consequence, some individuals found themselves with an official racial classification at odds with their subjective sense of their race and/or the verdict on the race of other family members. The impact was devastating, as the apartheid project made racial homogeneity a compulsory condition of family and community life. Husbands or wives redefined as members of different races were forced to separate and live in different areas; families were also forcibly ruptured when children were classified differently from their parents. Literally overnight, such people found themselves disbarred from living in the houses and areas where they had lived up to that point, their children excluded from the schools that they had been attending, their positions of employment suddenly in question, and with instant liability for a new set of racially specific levies and taxes.

The Population Registration Act did authorise the creation of the Race Classification Appeal Boards, to consider appeals from people who objected to their racial classification. By 31 March 1964, 3,940 appeals had been lodged, of which 2,823 succeeded.[32] So the large majority of appeals were successful. But the more remarkable feature of these statistics is the fact that the number of appeals represents a tiny proportion of the many millions of classifications undertaken. To some extent, this may have derived from ignorance of the appeal procedure or a reluctance or inability to proceed with it. But this is unlikely to provide a full explanation for the fact that the large majority of people who were classified accepted that classification. Arguably, appeals might also have been forestalled by the extent to which the state's racial classifiers ratified peoples' subjective sense of their race. This is not to presume an exact fit between bureaucratic and lived versions of race – rather, that the official typology of racial difference was sufficiently institutionalised and normalised for racial classifiers, armed with a notion of race explicitly sensitised to existing hierarchies of class, cultural styles and patterns of prejudice, to have produced classifications that resonated sufficiently closely with those produced socially. In other words, to a significant extent, the national population register confirmed what had become a commonsense experience of the fact and substance of racial differentiation.

A spate of early apartheid laws was applied to impose racial boundaries into all everyday experiences of work, leisure, schooling, worship and community. These included so-called petty apartheid measures, such as the Reservation of Separate Amenities Act of 1953, which imposed racial separation in all public amenities, public buildings and on public transport. As the apartheid project moved into the second phase, the deployment of racial difference became increasingly obsessive, and often in respect of

[32] Posel, 'Race as common sense', 107.

relative trivia – as in an instruction from the Minister of Education to the South African Bird Watchers' Society to banish all 'non-white' members; or in the requirement that 'glasses for white and non-whites were to be washed separately and kept apart . . . [using] separate cloths for drying the glasses'.[33]

Yet the nature of racial separatism – even at its zenith – should not be overstated. Even at the peak of this kind of separatist dementia, the fundamental motor of race in South Africa remained dialectical, driven by the necessary interdependence of mutually antagonistic dynamics. As much as the racial architecture of apartheid set people apart in racially defined enclaves of power and experience, it simultaneously and necessarily also pulled them together, in workplaces, public spaces and homes. This produced a more nuanced and complex interpersonal racial dynamic than blunt conceptualisations of racial segregation can capture. The most obvious aspect of apartheid's hybrid of racial distance and racial proximity was the case of those who actively pursued illicit friendships, relationships, business partnerships, and political alliances across racial boundaries. Here the most prominent were the people exposed and prosecuted under the Immorality Act and/or Mixed Marriages Act, for cross-racial sex and marriage.

The institution of domestic service was another instance of greater complexity and porosity in the practice of race, in producing unexpected companionships, mutual dependencies, even intimacies, in tandem with unambiguously hierarchical, often authoritarian power relations. The degradations of domestic service endured by black domestic workers who were poorly paid and housed, with arduous working hours and who were often sexually abused, are well known. They make the relationships of black domestic workers to white children in their care all the more paradoxical and complex. We need to know more about the workings of race in settings such as these – where white parents, including ardent exponents of apartheid discourse and dogma about racial purity, superiority and so on, entrusted their children to the care of black women, who, in another discursive space, were rendered as vessels of contamination, vectors of lust.

Regulating the Domestic Sphere

In attempting to refashion the domestic sphere, the impact of the state's moral conservatism was mixed. One of the more effective interventions was in the resolution of the so-called poor white problem, including the moral and cultural 'rehabilitation' of once marginal families. Yet these and

---

[33] Reported in the *Cape Times*, 21 October 1960, cited in B. McLennan, *Apartheid: the lighter side* (Cape Town: Chameleon Press, 1990), p. 30.

wider-ranging efforts to bolster family life as the nation's moral bastion and bulwark did not deter rising rates of divorce. In white communities, by the 1960s, one in five marriages ended in divorce. And within a judgemental officialdom, rates of teenage pregnancy, particularly in coloured and African communities, were deemed unacceptably high. Yet it was the efforts to regulate the terrain of African family life in the cities that brought apartheid's uncertainties and contradictions in the regulation of gender most acutely into focus. Political concern about the precariousness of African marriage (particularly in the cities) and its deleterious effect on communal order and economic productivity was long standing. After 1948, nationalist ideologues and politicians continued in similarly vitriolic vein, lamenting the corrosive effects of 'detribalisation' on marriage and patriarchy in African communities. The Dutch Reformed Church went so far as to identify 'Bantu marriage' as 'one of the most important social problems in South Africa today'[34] and urged the state to intervene.

In the apartheid regime, some remedial steps seemed obvious: subject African women to the full brunt of influx control legislation, which would inhibit their access to the cities independently of their husbands, make an officially recognised marriage a condition of access to urban housing ('one man, one wife, one house', as an influential urban administrator put it) and create a register of African customary unions to prevent couples faking a customary marriage as a pretext for securing a house. Yet all proved unexpectedly complicated for the regime. The 1952 Native Laws Amendment Act authorised the extension of influx control legislation to African women, but the vehemence of popular protest against the measure deterred administrators, many of whom chose not to apply the law. When African men protested the state's incursions into their patriarchal authority over the lives of women, white officialdom – as self-appointed custodians of African patriarchy – found it difficult (at least ideologically) to dissent. Paradoxically, therefore, throughout the 1950s, African women enjoyed greater freedom of movement than men, which contributed in no small measure to the continuing acceleration of urban African population growth during this decade. It was only in the early 1960s, with the ideological and administrative hardening of apartheid's second phase, that strict instructions from the highest echelons of government imposed the full gamut of influx control regulation on African women.

With their powers of influx control thus diminished, administrators were all the more set on using access to municipal housing as an instrument for controlling the urban African family. The regulation of township housing occupied a central place in wider-ranging efforts to 'stabilise' townships

---

[34] *Cape Argus*, 27 September 1955, 'Bantu marriages are most important social problem'.

as sites of 'orderly' and economically productive family life. But the inter-ventions were impaled on the horns of a contradiction in the tenets of state policy. After 1948, there was mounting pressure, particularly from urban administrators, to create an official register of customary marriages. But with strong opposition to this prospect from chiefs who regarded it as an illegitimate incursion on their chiefly powers, and with the apartheid regime keen to cultivate clientelist relations of power with chiefs, all efforts toward this end were stillborn. Proof of marriage remained, however, the condition of access to township housing. State officials administering the regulations therefore became complicit with the ongoing proliferation of 'house marriages' (opportunistic unions between men and women intent on gaining and retaining an urban foothold), in some instances, becoming bureaucratic matchmakers themselves.[35]

Although some did endure, many house marriages collapsed as rapidly as they had been engineered; some of those that lingered were typically inse-cure, fractious and violent. More generally, whatever the apartheid rhetoric of the sanctity of family life, the combination of a migrant labour system that eroded the integrity of the rural extended family and the relentless assault on the conditions of urban settlement corroded family ties and the obligations traditionally attached to them. Grinding urban poverty, over-crowding and widespread unemployment exacerbated the problem mat-ters. Yet the persistence of patriarchal values, as much in African com-munities as in state institutions, condoned violent and other assaults on the growing economic independence of African women that accompanied the attrition of marriage. The assaults on the institution of the African family, aggravated by the indifference of apartheid policing (discussed pre-viously) is one of the more tenacious and brutal legacies of the apartheid project.

Implementing Economic and Social Engineering

Apartheid's political arithmetic – as demographer J. L. Sadie put it – remained a central concern. In its most basic formulation – as the problem of the overwhelming black majority – it was an insoluble problem. Indeed, as apartheid advanced, the black population grew at a proportionately greater rate than the white population, having higher fertility rates (although there is some evidence that African fertility rates began to drop by the late 1960s, if not earlier). Concerted efforts were made to reconfigure the country's racial topography; and here, the effects of apartheid were

---

[35] D. Posel, 'Marriage at the drop of a hat: housing and partnership in South Africa's urban African townships', *History Workshop* 61 (2006), 57–76.

more mixed. With the application of the Group Areas Act, the notion of a black majority was spatially (and therefore experientially) fragmented into disparate numbers of coloureds, Indians and Africans, concentrated in racially distinct residential areas. The administrative emphasis fell, then, on trying to reduce the numbers of blacks living in close proximity to whites, in the main, in the urban areas. Once again, the plethora of interventions largely failed to achieve the desired result. The urban African population never ceased to grow; but the implementation of apartheid measures slowed its rate of growth. Around 2.2 million in 1951, it grew to 3.4 million in 1960 (an increase of around 58 per cent), and then to 4.4 million in 1970 (an increase of around 28 per cent).[36]

Embedded in these measures were two equally profound effects. First, notwithstanding the aggression of apartheid prohibitions and proscriptions on migration, urban Africans became increasingly settled by the 1970s. Underlining apartheid's abiding internal contradictions, the implementation of other apartheid policies contributed directly to this outcome. In a bid to transform sites of African settlement in the cities into orderly spaces subject to copious regulation, apartheid's practitioners adopted the global postwar enthusiasm for urban planning, incorporating the idea of hierarchies of class and status into notions of orderly and distinct neighbourhoods. This articulated comfortably with apartheid thinking. With a typically modernist interest in stabilising resident communities in well-planned neighbourhoods, the apartheid state accelerated the pace of housing construction in the townships. Even if meagre in comparison to the white suburbs, the township construction drive of the 1950s, along with the expanded provision of township schooling, created the infrastructure of a population that would put down its roots in the city. During the second phase, the diminishing rate of urban growth during the 1960s illustrated another dynamic at work. This phase of apartheid ushered in a new strategy of population removals, on a far larger scale than had been implemented – or even imagined – during the 1950s. By the end of the 1960s, around 3.5 million people had been forcibly removed from 'white' areas of South Africa.[37] These population removals have become iconic of 'grand' apartheid, a signifier of a state flexing its coercive muscle with relatively little impediment.

Many of the more chaotic and contradictory elements of the workings of apartheid marked official efforts at economic engineering. In the

---

[36] J. Seekings and N. Nattrass, *Class, race and inequality in South Africa* (New Haven, CT: Yale University Press 2005), p. 102.
[37] L. Platzky and C. Walker, *The surplus people: forced removals in South Africa* (Johannesburg: Ravan Press, 1985).

aggregate, during the 1950s and 1960s, the country enjoyed sustained economic growth. This expansion was most dramatic in the industrial and service sectors. For example, 'between 1960 and 1970, real manufacturing output expanded at . . . 8.6 per cent per year, investment expanded at 12.3 per cent per year and real net operating surplus at 5.2 per cent per year'.[38] The two decades saw rising standards of living, if accompanied by deepening inequality. Although this initially seems confirmation of – and a direct consequence of – apartheid's original intentions, the picture of South Africa's thriving economy changes when contextualised globally, particularly in comparison to other developing countries, in relation to which South African growth rates look a lot less impressive.[39] Apartheid's economic record was marked by a mix of costs and benefits, associated with internal contradictions within the project.

One of the shackles on economic growth – particularly during the 1960s, as rates of industrial mechanization rose – was a deepening shortage of skills. This was a problem of the apartheid system's own making: the aggregate effect of job reservation and protection for whites and deliberately diminished education for blacks. Another contradictory, and growth-inhibiting, effect of the apartheid labour regime was the truncated development of domestic consumer markets. Wage rates were racially pegged, which meant that the large majority of the economically active population was concentrated at the bottom end of the income pile. Although standards of living did rise across the board, racial ceilings on earnings set limits on domestic consumption. This was partly offset by the profitability consequent on low wages, but it became one of the costs associated with a growth path generated by heavy reliance on cheap labour.

There were other bottlenecks and distortions, too, associated with the everyday realities of employment, particularly in the case of African workers in the cities. The efforts of labour bureaux to channel African work seekers into the jobs that state officials wanted them to take were somewhat more effective in the 1960s – having failed during the 1950s – with the general tightening up of mechanisms of administrative control. But their effect was to distort employment patterns rather than to fashion a labour market in accordance with the logic of a state-contrived plan. Officials themselves complained about the perverse consequences of the labour bureaux system, including their inability to transfer surpluses of labour in one administrative zone to others experiencing shortages – a consequence of the provisions of section 10 of the Urban Areas Act.

---

[38] Seekings and Nattrass, *Class, race and inequality*, p. 143.

[39] T. Moll, 'Did the apartheid economy "fail"?', *Journal of Southern African Studies* 17:2 (1991), 275.

Section 10(1) residential rights continued to subvert bureaucratic efforts to streamline employment, and officials were continuously vexed by what they called the job choosiness of urbanised workers. In a labour regime that kept wages low and inhibited the acquisition of skills and upward mobility, urbanised workers tended to chop and change jobs repeatedly – particularly in times of economic expansion. And enforced breaks in the employment contracts of migrant workers with little guarantee of the same workers returning on a regular basis – a consequence of the tightening of influx control during the 1960s – created disincentives for employers to undertake on-the-job skills training.

Particularly at the lower end of the skills spectrum, which accounted for the bulk of the workforce, the apartheid labour regime failed to produce 'modern' workers: workers whose work ethics were shaped by aspirations to rise up the social and economic ladder, stay the course, save and improve their skills. In a milieu that set cast-iron ceilings on black aspirations, low levels of skill and inferior education created a different calculus of interests and priorities for work seekers, contributing to what employers experienced as a problem of diminished labour productivity.

The abiding and linear effect of apartheid economic engineering was a pattern of deepening economic inequality that replicated the system's hierarchy of race. At the top, apartheid brought unprecedented prosperity to the white population, albeit with internal inequalities of class and status. As beneficiaries of ethnic patronage in the public service, and job reservation in the private sector, the white Afrikaner population became substantially more stratified, with more entrepreneurs and the ranks of the middle classes expanding. These changing patterns of class and status within white Afrikanerdom contributed substantially to the political realignments of the 1960s that saw growing rapprochement between English and Afrikaans supporters of apartheid and strengthened the state's grip on power. The pleasures of consumerism became one of the fruits of apartheid for whites and increasingly the basis of an identity and sense of self that straddled ethnic divisions.[40] By the late 1960s, the provision of improved pensions and other social welfare grants, in tandem with preferential employment policies, had largely erased the problem of poor whiteism that had exercised the minds of apartheid's ideologues, intent on redeeming white respectability and racial purity at the bottom of the socioeconomic ladder. The white population was not without poverty, however, with the poorest households typically containing pensioners or single mothers.

[40] J. Hyslop, 'Why did apartheid supporters capitulate? "Whiteness", class and consumerism in urban South Africa, 1985–1995', *Society in Transition* 31:1 (2000), 36–44.

More modestly rising incomes, coupled with growing inequality, marked the economic profile of Indians and coloureds. With fewer barriers on employment opportunities than Africans, most coloured and Indian workers were able to increase their earnings with the economic expansion of the 1960s. In the Western Cape, the Coloured Labour Preference policy, introduced in 1956, put coloured workers ahead of Africans in the job queue. Employment in semiskilled, artisanal and professional occupations grew, including for women, many of whom shifted from domestic service into factory work. By contrast, coloured families in rural communities found themselves under deepening economic pressure as the mechanisation of farming made growing numbers of farmworkers redundant. And forced removals, in terms of the Group Areas Act, created intense economic hardship by demolishing economic networks and communal support systems.

In Indian group areas too, with long histories of internal stratification by class, religion, language, ethnicity and religion, the economic impact of apartheid exacerbated inequalities. There was a notable increase in the size of the middle class. Family incomes benefited from the rising rates of female employment. Improving levels of education and commerce led to growth in the numbers and status of Indian professionals and businessmen. In Durban, where a sizable proportion of Indian businesspeople were concentrated, successful entrepreneurs were able to purchase land in the city centre and develop it commercially, as whites moved to the suburbs. But Indian communities too suffered the hardships of removals under the Group Areas Act, which compounded the rigours of poverty in more marginal families.[41]

The intensification of poverty was worst, however, among Africans, who bore the brunt of the immiserating effects of apartheid economic engineering. In rural areas, unemployment levels were high, the African peasantry having been largely eradicated. A lack of serious investment in the reserves (later homelands) turned them into sites of bleak desperation for their poorest, landless inhabitants. At the same time, pockets of industrial and commercial development fostered the creation of local African elites, the beneficiaries of the apartheid state's patronage.

In the cities too, African townships became increasingly stratified. The apartheid project had delivered a varied repertoire to inhibit class mobility, aspiration and social standing in the townships, ranging from the cynical diminution of skill and education, restrictions on the accumulation of capital and development of entrepreneurship, through to the abolition of the privileges of class and status (e.g., pass law exemptions) associated with

---

[41] K. Hart and V. Padayachee, 'Indian business in South Africa after apartheid: new and old trajectories', *Comparative Studies in Society and History* 42:2 (2000), 683–712.

the segregationist regime. Under apartheid, the full gamut of racial legislation was applied uniformly to all Africans, irrespective of class or social
standing – a source of abiding grievance within urban elites. Particularly in
larger townships close to the cities, however, communal life had long been
powerfully structured by hierarchies of class and status; and the economic
growth of the apartheid period, coupled with the expansion of primary and
secondary schooling in the townships, enhanced such stratification. The
overall effect was to produce both (tenuous) upward mobility and mounting disaffection. In the end, the attempt to restructure privilege and status
in ethnic and 'tribal' terms succeeded to some extent in the homelands
but failed in the cities. Many of those who played a leading role in the
political protests of the 1970s and 1980s came from mean middle-class
backgrounds.

Reforming Power

Despite the tenuousness of apartheid, the regime's hold on political power
was remarkably durable, persisting for more than four decades – itself one
of the distinguishing features of the project. Part of apartheid's tenacity
had to do with the efficacy of its systematic racialisation of experience,
its spatial separation of disparate worlds of everyday life, its capricious
and brutalising violence, and its suppression of organised political and
worker resistance. But it was also a consequence of the representations and
performances of stateness. If the representation of apartheid as a unified
and linear grand plan, and the project of a rational, integrated and well-
functioning state, did not match the uneven and contradictory realities of
its rule, it nevertheless had significant consequences as a discourse, and the
practices of power associated with it. The discourse informed how power
was performed, in spite of the failures to achieve intended outcomes. In
practice, the state's purported panoptic vision was fractured and partial.
But for the subjects of apartheid, these lapses of political insight and
bureaucratic surveillance were inscrutable: it was impossible to decipher
how much was and wasn't known. And with the state performing as if it
could see all, these uncertainties were less potent than the aura, or sensation,
of being routinely monitored.

The notorious system of pass laws illustrated this performative dynamic
well. By law, all Africans were required to carry a 'reference book' (a *dompas*,
as colloquially named) at all times, which authorised their presence in an
officially proclaimed urban area and stipulated the conditions under which
they could remain. Any state official could demand at any time to see these
documents, to verify whether the person was legally or illegally in the
place in which he or she happened to be at that time. The thousands of
people arrested for failing to produce a *dompas* or for being endorsed out of

the area as an illegal are legendary in popular memories of the apartheid years. Even so, it was possible to dodge the police. Leading bureaucrats could see too that the attempts to police the pass laws were to some extent a futile exercise. Many people 'endorsed out' of an urban area simply slipped back in again or ignored the order altogether. Thousands of pass books were forged, deluding the eye of the state by turning 'illegals' into 'legals'. Authentic pass books were lost, to create a reprieve for the bearer to apply legitimately for a new one, by which time he or she had slipped back into the anonymous urban mass. So, from the standpoint of the aspirations of the influx control policy and the dictates of its urban labour preference principle, the powers of state officials to police the presence of Africans in urban areas were seriously inadequate and the rate of illegal urbanisation remained high. Yet the sight of police vans rounding up groups of people on the streets, the regular public witnessing of policemen commanding Africans to produce their passes along with township talk about early-morning police raids, all attested to performances of power that created abiding insecurity, necessitating constant vigilance and improvisation in the practice of everyday life.

CONCLUSION

Apartheid was built and consolidated during the two decades of what Hart and Padayachee call state capitalism[42] – good times for projects of large-scale national planning with big states at their helm; when citizenries across the world had high expectations of the capacities and prerogatives of states to solve social, political and economic problems across the gamut of experience. This was also a period, globally, of economic prosperity, triggered by postwar reconstruction efforts and leading into the economic boom period of the 1960s. Very different kinds of regimes emerged, with starkly contrasting ethical projects. In much of the West and in some parts of the developing world, popular confidence in a 'problem-solving' state was harnessed to a democratic cause – such as in Sweden's inclusive welfarism and in the (initially) optimistic programmes of national self-determination and development in postcolonial Africa. South Africa bucked this trend, in mandating its state to advance the cause of white minority rule.

The first two phases of apartheid, from 1948 through to the early 1970s, took the apartheid project through from its pragmatic, sometimes uncertain, beginnings to the zenith of racial social and economic engineering, in the late 1960s. Yet even at its peak, the project was fallible. By the mid-1970s, the hubris of 'grand' apartheid would give way to a third phase

---

[42] Hart and Padayachee, 'Indian business'.

marked by a commitment to 'reform'. A combination of resurgent political activism and economic pressures would bring apartheid's foundational contradiction to the political forefront once again, and a 'reformist' solution would be sought that would return in some ways to the more pragmatic principles and precepts of the first phase.

The analysis in this chapter has emphasised the abiding unevenness of apartheid rule: as simultaneously strong and weak, rigid and plastic, effective and ineffectual. Perhaps this is an unremarkable conclusion to reach, probably true of all regimes with overreaching ambitions. Yet it is also often the case that such regimes do not readily collapse, and their tenacious durability warrants explanation. The apartheid state endured for nearly four decades, notwithstanding an abiding insecurity.

The key to making sense of this mix of fragility and robustness is to recognise the interactive effects of 'successes' and 'failures'. As Ian Kershaw puts it, '[I]t is, of course, easy to exaggerate the "ordered" character of any modern governmental system', all of which generate 'conflicting and sometimes outrightly contradictory spheres of authority', sometimes to a 'chaotic' degree. 'The question is, what significance can be attached to this "chaos"?'[43] In the case of apartheid, a blend of order and chaos marked the project from the outset. The amalgam changed as the project advanced. By the late 1960s, it was simultaneously more orderly and more chaotic – testimony to the centrality of the performative dimensions of power alongside the more instrumental and ideologically explicit aspects, in the midst of an abiding inability to manage effectively the problems of population that animated the project from the start.

FURTHER READING

Abrams, P., 'Notes on the difficulty of studying the state', *Journal of Historical Sociology* 1:1 (1988), 58–89

Bekker, S. and R. Humphreys, *From control to confusion: the changing role of Administration Boards in South Africa*, Pietermaritzburg: Shuter and Shooter, 1985

Bonner, P., P. Delius and D. Posel (eds.), *Apartheid's genesis, 1935–1962*, Johannesburg: Ravan Press and Witwatersrand University Press, 1993

Brandel-Syrier, M., *Reeftown elite: a study of social mobility in a modern African community on the Reef*, London: Routledge and Kegan Paul, 1971

Burman, S. and P. Van Der Spuy, 'The illegitimate and the illegal in a South African city: the effects of apartheid on births out of wedlock', *Journal of Social History* 29 (1996), 613–36

---

[43] Ian Kershaw, *The Nazi dictatorship: problems and perspectives of interpretation* (London: Edward Arnold, 1991), p. 71.

Cooper, F., *Colonialism in question: theory, knowledge and history*, Berkeley: University of California Press, 2005

Crankshaw, O., *Race, class and the division of labour under apartheid*, London: Routledge, 1997

Delius, P., *A lion amongst the cattle: reconstruction and resistance in the Northern Transvaal*, Oxford: James Currey, 1997

Deutsch, J.-G., P. Probst and H. Schmidt (eds.), *African modernities*, Oxford: Greenwood Press, 2002

Dubow, S., *Illicit union: scientific racism in modern South Africa*, Johannesburg: Witwatersrand University Press, 1997

Dubow, S. and A. Jeeves (eds.), *South Africa's 1940s: worlds of possibilities*, Cape Town: Double Storey, 2005

Dyzenhaus, D., *Truth, reconciliation and the apartheid legal order*, Cape Town: Juta, 1998

Elder, G., *Hostels, sexuality and the apartheid legacy*, Athens: Ohio University Press, 2003

Evans, I., *Bureaucracy and race: native administration in South Africa*, Berkeley: University of California Press, 1997

Foucault, M., *Society must be defended*, London: Penguin, 2004

Giliomee, H., *The Afrikaners: biography of a people*, Cape Town: Tafelberg; Charlottesville: University of Virginia Press, 2003

Goldin, I., *Making race: the politics and economics of coloured identity in South Africa*, Cape Town: Maskew Millar Longman, 1987

Horrell, M., *Legislation and race relations*, Johannesburg: South African Institute of Race Relations, 1971

Hyslop, J., *The classroom struggle: policy and resistance in South Africa, 1940–1990*, Pietermaritzburg: University of Natal Press, 1999

Jones, S., '"To come together for progress": modernisation and nation-building in South Africa's Bantustan periphery', *Journal of Southern African Studies* 25:4 (1999), 579–605

Kallaway, P. (ed.), *The history of education under apartheid, 1948–1994*, New York: Peter Lang Publishing, 2002

Kopytoff, I. (ed.), *The African frontier: the reproduction of traditional African societies*, Bloomington: Indiana University Press, 1987

Kuper, L., *An African bourgeoisie*, New Haven, CT: Yale University Press, 1965

Kynoch, G., *We are fighting the world: a history of the MaRashea gangs in South Africa, 1947–1999*, Athens: Ohio University Press; Pietermaritzburg: University of Kwa-Zulu Natal Press, 2005

Lazar, J., 'Conformity and conflict: Afrikaner Nationalist politics, 1948–1961', unpublished D.Phil. thesis, Oxford University (1987)

Lekgoathi, S. P., 'Ethnicity and identity: struggle and contestation in the making of the Northern Transvaal Ndebele, c.1860–2005', unpublished Ph.D. thesis, University of Minnesota (2006)

Mabin, A., 'Comprehensive segregation: the origins of the Group Areas Act and its planning apparatuses', *Journal of Southern African Studies* 18:2 (1992), 405–29

Mager, A., *Gender and the making of a South African Bantustan*, Oxford: James Currey, 1999

Mazower, M., *Dark continent: Europe's twentieth century*, New York: Vintage Books, 2003

Modisane, B., *Blame me on history*, Cape Town: Donker, 1986 (originally published 1963)

Nieftagodien, N., 'The implementation of urban apartheid on the East Rand, 1948–1973: the role of local government and local resistance', unpublished Ph.D. thesis, University of the Witwatersrand (2001)

Norval, A., *Deconstructing apartheid discourse*, London: Verso, 1996

O'Meara, D., *Forty lost years: the apartheid state and the politics of the National Party, 1948–1994*, Johannesburg: Ravan Press; Athens: Ohio University Press, 1996

Parnell, S. and A. Mabin, 'Rethinking urban South Africa', *Journal of Southern African Studies* 21:1 (1995), 39–61

Pelzer, A. N. (ed.), *Verwoerd speaks: speeches, 1948–1966*, Johannesburg: APB Publishers, 1966

Posel, D., *The making of apartheid, 1948–1961*, Oxford: Clarendon Press, 1991 and 1997

Robinson, J., *The power of apartheid: state, power and space in South African cities*, Oxford: Butterworth-Heinemann, 1996

Sadie, J., 'The political arithmetic of the South African population', *Journal of Racial Affairs* 1:4 (1950), 3–8

Sanders, J., *Apartheid's friends: the rise and fall of the South African Secret Services*, London: John Murray, 2006

Simons, H. J., *African women: their legal status in South Africa*, London: C. Hurst and Company, 1968

Wilkins, I. and H. Strydom, *The super-Afrikaners*, London: Corgi Books, 1980

8

POPULAR RESPONSES TO APARTHEID: 1948–C. 1975

ANNE KELK MAGER AND MAANDA MULAUDZI

How did the people most affected by apartheid respond to the implementation of government measures between 1949 and the early 1970s? What informed people's opposition, silences and acquiescence at different moments across the country? In seeking to provide an answer to these questions, this chapter constructs an archive. It begins by mapping out a decade of mass protest against the first wave of apartheid laws. Then it goes some way toward explaining the quiescence that followed the banning of African nationalist organisations in 1960 and understanding the burden of coping with the intensified apartheid controls that followed. Thereafter, it identifies some of the ambivalence in responses to the various stages of Bantustan (homeland self-government) creation in the 1960s and charts the emergence of the Black Consciousness Movement in the early 1970s.

Much of the scholarship on the first two decades of apartheid rule was produced in the wake of a revival of radical social history in the late 1970s. Animated by the resurgence of activism among black students, radical scholars looked to Africanist and Marxist perspectives, and to some extent to feminism, to make sense of everyday life under apartheid, to map the contours of resistance to apartheid rule and to examine political pathways forged through collective action. Following on the premise that African agency demonstrated the ineffectiveness of the apartheid system and a desire to be free of domination, those scholars sought to understand the ways in which race, class and gender inflected experience and shaped the consciousness of social agents.

Their work interrogated nationalism, questioned the nature of power and probed the relationship between elites and poor communities. Although it undoubtedly helped to shift South African historiography in new directions, this scholarship has also come to be seen as having limitations and weaknesses. In light of the culturalist and literary turn in the social sciences, history from below has been criticised for its preoccupation with class and for its failure to explore the significance of symbolic and other cultural practices in the making of social meanings. In particular, it has come under question for failing to draw on the insights of anthropology and linguistics, which might have led to deeper excavations of the ways in which people interpreted experiences through locally produced systems of knowledge.[1] Critics have also pointed to a failure on the part of this scholarship to historicise the narrative conventions that framed its approaches and to the absence of reflexivity on the part of its overwhelmingly white producers. Nonetheless, while acknowledging the validity of such historiographical criticism, the narrative set out in this chapter draws on the force of the social history tradition rather than on expanding its critiques. For the recognised strength of this scholarship lies in the extent to which it was able to talk back to apartheid, to read against the grain of the colonial archive and to amplify African voices. In the first instance, the context of those voices is urban.

Thus, African responses to apartheid need to be understood in the context of increasing urbanisation from the mid-1940s. In 1946, South Africa's urban African population was 1.7 million. By 1951, this figure had risen to more than 2 million. At the same time, the official housing shortage was approximately 250,000. By the mid-1950s, more than 100,000 people were living on the fringes of Johannesburg. Many of those who had moved to the cities dreamed of returning to their rural lives after a period of work. As a survey conducted in East London in 1950 showed, almost 85 per cent of the 66,000 African residents originated in the countryside and considered themselves temporary sojourners in town.

The flow of people to the cities occurred faster than the ability (and political will) of their urban administrations to provide housing, sanitation, health and education facilities. When township houses and backyard shacks became overcrowded, newcomers constructed makeshift structures of corrugated iron, sacks and cardboard on vacant land. Families struggled to achieve stability in the face of unemployment, undisciplined adolescent children, unfaithful spouses, crime and material hardship. Shack dwellers demanding a place to live and the right to remain in town were repeatedly drawn into confrontations with local councils. Distanced from the urban

---

[1] See, e.g., Patrick Harries, 'Histories old and new', *South African Historical Journal* 30:1 (May 1994), 121–34; Hofmeyr, *'We spend our years'*; Charles van Onselen, 'The reconstruction of a rural life from oral testimony: critical notes on the methodology employed in the study of a black South African sharecropper', *Journal of Peasant Studies* 20:3 (1993), 494–516; Gary Minkley and Ciraj Rassool, 'Orality, memory, and social history in South Africa', in Nuttall and Coetzee (eds.), *Negotiating the past*, pp. 89–99; Desiree Lewis, 'Black women and biography in South Africa', in Yousaf (ed.), *Apartheid narratives*, pp. 163–89.

elite who dominated the vigilance associations in the townships, they developed a distinctive brand of popular politics that cohered around charismatic leaders. By controlling access to key resources such as water, self-appointed big men could foster insecurity and dependence and extract loyalty by offering a degree of protection. These charismatic leaders cast themselves as Old Testament prophetic characters, negotiated with municipal authorities for recognition and basic services, collected funds to maintain their own status, took care of the bereaved and needy and engaged in various entrepreneurial trading activities. Leadership styles and the character of politics varied across communities and between individuals. James 'Sofasonke' (we all die together) Mpanza, leader of a Johannesburg shantytown, established a cooperative buying club for the purchase of basic foodstuffs and building materials. At the same time, he sought to control hawking and home brewing by imposing heavy licences. Often inward in orientation, the politics of informal settlements has been described by Philip Bonner as deeply sectional as well as parochial and divisive. Few of its leaders avoided the temptation of exploiting their followers, and they acquired a reputation for extortion and clientelism.

Areas of potential friction in urban relations were also liable to turn violent. Thus, shack dwellers at Cato Manor farm (also known as Mkhumbane) on the outskirts of Durban became caught up in interracial rioting in 1949. Conflict was sparked when a young African employee was assaulted by an Indian shopkeeper in the city centre. Angry Africans reacted by looting Indian property in town. Escalating violence over a weekend left 123 people dead. Much of the action took place at Cato Manor, where tens of thousands of Africans lived in makeshift dwellings and depended on Indian shopkeepers, bus operators, landlords and shebeeners (purveyors of illicit liquor) for goods and services. African resentment of the entrepreneurial power of the Indian-owned businesses, which constituted a strong element of the local economy, was fuelled by frustration with economic contraction as the Second World War came to an end. It was exacerbated by a desperate need for space in the city. In 1946, the Indian population of Natal numbered two hundred thousand and Indians owned approximately 13 per cent of Durban's land value (some ten thousand acres).

This interracial violence was a blow to the African and Indian intelligentsia, which just two years earlier had brought the Natal Indian Congress (NIC) and the Transvaal Indian Congress into an alliance with the African National Congress (ANC). The move toward an alliance was precipitated by the NIC's passive resistance campaign against the Asiatic Land Tenure and Indian Representation Act, which saw 1,710 arrested. As Surendra Bhana notes, this move represented a major shift in the politics of the NIC, which had, since its inception in 1894, revolved around Indian identity.

Determined to protect their working relationship in the aftermath of the disturbances, the NIC and ANC established a joint coordinating council to build positive relations between Indians and Africans.

The Cato Manor episode also exacerbated internal tensions between the leaders of the ANC and its younger members who believed that the leadership had little understanding of popular politics. Toward the end of the year, young militant Africanists in the ANC formed the Youth League and urged Dr A. B. Xuma, the ANC president, to adopt a more radical African nationalism based on the principle of Africa for the Africans. Xuma's unwillingness to comply lost him the support of the youth wing at the annual congress, at which the Youth League backed Dr James Sebe Moroka as candidate for president. A physician, landowner, businessman and Barolong chief, Moroka was quick to call for protest in the months that followed the announcement of the Suppression of Communism Act, the Population Registration Act and the Group Areas Act (1950).

Supported by a national membership of roughly seven thousand at the beginning of 1952, the ANC devised a campaign of passive resistance to unjust laws. Organised by a joint planning council of the ANC, the South African Indian Congress (SAIC), which was an amalgam of the Natal and Transvaal Indian Congresses, and the Franchise Action Committee (FRAC), the Defiance Campaign was the most sustained and successful national campaign the alliance was to mount in the 1950s. Under the slogan 'No bail, no defence, no fine', selected 'volunteers' clad in khaki uniforms and displaying the insignia of African nationalism – black, green and gold lapel ribbons – came forward to defy apartheid legislation, opting to fill the jails rather than pay fines. At its peak in September 1952, 2,500 carefully deployed resisters had been arrested in twenty-four cities and towns. By the end of the campaign, that number had reached more than eight thousand. Though weak in Durban, where the NIC had conducted a similar campaign in 1946, in other parts of the country, it took on a mood of intense political fervour. Links between urban and rural activity were strongest in the Eastern Cape. Across the southern districts of the Ciskei, migrant workers, cattle owners and landless women came to hear speakers denounce cattle culling and land-use regulations as unjust laws. Political foment gripped the townships of Port Elizabeth (eBayi) and East London (iMonti), where police clashed with crowds of angry black people who went on the rampage, burning municipal buildings. Appalled by this outburst of violence, the ANC leadership called off the Defiance Campaign, concluding that political rhetoric had drawn new arrivals to the city into a sophisticated urban politics of which they had little or no experience. Along with Moroka, the ANC president, Nelson Mandela and Walter Sisulu of the Youth League were among those charged with fomenting revolt. Although Mandela and

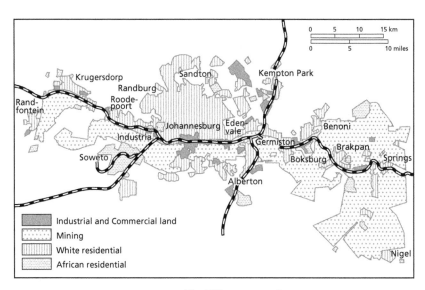

MAP 4. The Witwatersrand

Sisulu were among those convicted of statutory communism, Moroka alienated the militant youths by pleading for mitigation and friendship with
Afrikaners. Meanwhile, local authorities in East London and Port Elizabeth
increased surveillance under the pass laws and influx control regulations,
and they enforced urban apartheid through the Group Areas (1950) and
Separate Amenities (1953) acts.

As the pass laws were extended and controls on the movement of people
intensified, protest became more widespread. Revised influx control laws,
enshrined in the Natives Urban Areas Act, the Natives (Abolition and
Coordination of Documents) Act and the Native Laws Amendment Act
(1952), were designed to divide urban workers from migrants. The purpose
of this differentiation into urban and migrant, Doug Hindson argues, was
to enable a limited number of permanent urban workers to serve industry
in a relatively skilled capacity, whereas migrants would be confined to
unskilled work. The revised legislation also enabled the state to remove
those deemed to be economically inactive – women, children, the aged and
the unemployed and those living in shack settlements – from the cities.

Control was to be achieved through the issue of uniform reference books
to all African men and women between the ages of fifteen and sixty-five.
Africans who were unemployed or seeking work were required to register
with a labour bureau. These regulations effectively criminalised the African
population. Convictions under the pass laws increased from 232,000 in
1951 to 414,000 in 1959 and 694,000 in 1967. Offenders were most often

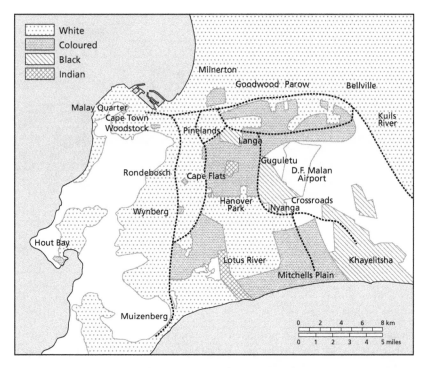

White
Coloured
Black
Indian

Milnerton

Goodwood Parow   Bellville

Malay Quarter
Cape Town   Kuils
Woodstock   River
                    Pinelands
                              Langa

                                    Guguletu
Rondebosch   Cape Flats   D.F. Malan
                                      Airport

                    Hanover   Crossroads
Wynberg   Park   Nyanga

Hout Bay

                    Lotus River   Khayelitsha
                         Mitchells Plain

Muizenberg
                              0   2   4   6   8 km

                              0 1   2   3   4 5 miles

MAP 5. Group Areas in Greater Cape Town

convicted for not carrying documentation or for being in town longer than seventy-two hours, the time permitted for work seekers.

From 1952, section 10 of the Natives (Urban Areas Amendment Act) prevented African women and men from residing in town permanently. Only those Africans who had been born in town, had worked there continuously for fifteen years or for a single employer for ten years or who were the dependent of someone who qualified for residential rights were permitted to take up permanent urban residence. Because a three-day work seeker permit was difficult to obtain, the pass laws made signing up with a mine recruitment agency far less trouble than finding industrial employment in town.

In the early 1960s, more than three hundred thousand African miners lived in single-sex hostels in mining compounds on the Witwatersrand. Between 1946 and 1969, wages increased a mere 6 per cent. Everyday life in the compounds and on the mines suggests that ethnic identities were more loosely defined, often contingent and contextual and invariably slipping away from apartheid categorisations. Individual miners identified themselves in ethnic terms in accordance with how many home friends

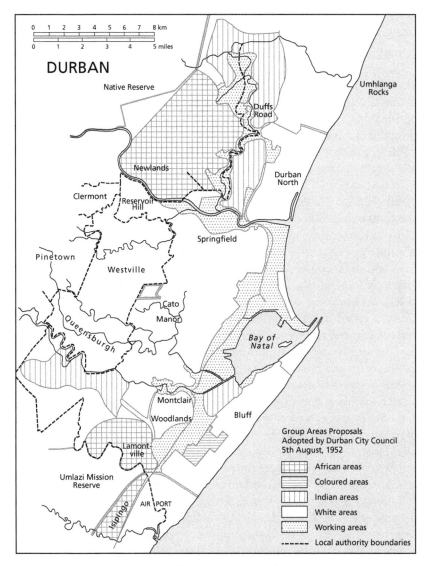

MAP 6. Group Areas in Durban

happened to end up on one mine, how far language constructed identity over rival groups (e.g., the Xhosa-speaking Bomvana and Mpondo) on a particular mine, the period of time spent on that mine and the type of work in which men engaged. Fictive kin might be fostered if circumstances necessitated it. Life in a mine compound was tough. Compound beer halls supplied grain beer, a sloppy mixture of maize grits and sorghum stripped of the nutritional content of home-brewed beer, encouraging a culture of heavy drinking. Outside the compounds, miners could find solace in shebeens (a term introduced by immigrant Irish police in the nineteenth century for illicit drinking houses), where they could obtain anything from spirits to adulterated concoctions spiked with battery acid. Although many 'homeboy' networks helped miners to avoid falling into the wasteful habit of excessive drinking, they were unable to prevent the increasing presence of drink as a marker of masculine and ethnic identities, and as part of the meaning of mine work itself.

Mining compounds were also sites for the construction of new, contextually specific sexualities. Longer and more frequent labour contracts meant increased separation from families. Both casual sex and more stable relationships might be established with women outside of the compound. In the compound, mine 'marriages' might be arranged between senior men and young recruits, offering stability and security and allowing for the possibility of relations of mutual dependence and affection, subject to set rules and the condition of impermanence. Those relationships, born of the system of migrant labour and single-sex compounds, often began with the older man imposing himself on the younger. Over time, the relationships became settled and stable. In return for sexual and other domestic services such as laundry, the young 'wife' would receive a part of the miner's pay. As Dunbar Moodie explains, mine marriages were confined to the mining environment and modelled on heterosexual relations.

Although trade union activity on the mines was effectively crushed when a strike by black miners was suppressed in 1946, industrial workers continued to organise in the face of legislation that circumscribed the meaning of industrial employment for Africans and intensified racial divisions in the workplace. Colour-bar legislation was extended through the 1951 Building Workers Act, which prohibited Africans from taking work outside of designated African areas (the homelands and townships), and the 1956 Industrial Conciliation Act extended job reservation to all types of work, denying any form of skilled or even semiskilled work to Africans. This tying together of job and race in the industrial economy created a highly segmented labour force in which occupation was paired with ethnicity in ways that complicated worker organisation. Segmentation was most pronounced in Durban, where Indian workers occupied skilled jobs, and in Cape Town, where most artisans were coloured. In such places, African workers were largely confined to manual labour. Industrialists in Durban also began to replace unionised Indian workers with nonunionised Africans, compounding the difficulties of nonracial organisation in a highly segmented labour market. In the Cape, the apartheid state structured racial divisions through the Coloured Labour Preference policy, mooted in Parliament in 1952 and stringently applied by the end of the decade.

The 1953 Bantu Labour (Settlement of Disputes) Act prohibited strikes by Africans and set up a racially separate state structure for dealing with African labour disputes. Legal status was granted only to workplace committees under the control of the central Bantu labour board and Bantu labour officers. It also prevented pay deduction facilities for trade union subscriptions. The biggest blow to African workers came in 1956 with the passage of the Industrial Conciliation Act, which removed Africans from the definition of *employee*. The amendment defined employee as 'any person (other than a native)', thereby prohibiting Africans from organising or joining labour unions. The legislation also blocked nonracial labour unity. Faced with the new laws, established nonracial unions responded in different ways. Three unions – the Textile Workers Industrial Union, the Food and Canning Workers Union and the Laundering Cleaning and Dyeing Workers Union – created new African unions alongside the registered union but continued to operate as a single entity. As a registered union, the Food and Canning Workers Union could represent coloured workers but not Africans. Compelled by their separate legal status, African workers formed the African Food and Canning Workers Union. Meetings were held together and decisions taken jointly as the union sought to avoid racialising its work, but organisers struggled to overcome the continuing dominance of the more skilled coloured workers and to collect subscriptions from those members barred from deduction arrangements by their legal status as nonworkers. At the same time, because African workers came under the purview of the Native Affairs Department (NAD) rather than the Industrial Conciliation Act, they were subject to acute forms of harassment that extended beyond the workplace. The case of the African Textile Workers Industrial Union provides a glimpse into this complexity. When a textile worker was prosecuted for absenteeism under the Master and Servants Act, the union took the matter to court. When the judge ruled in its favour, the NAD banished the worker from the area. In another instance, the NAD barred an African Textile Workers Industrial Union organiser from entering the township of Zwelitsha, where workers at the local textile plant resided.

Gender also created divisions in the workplace and in the labour movement. The position of women varied according to the division of labour in the industry and the extent to which job reservation was applied. Coloured and African women constituted a high proportion of workers in the fish, fruit and vegetable canning factories of the Western Cape. Most African women in the industry were employed as seasonal workers, rendering their position in the labour force precarious and their union membership insecure. Driven by the commitment of Ray Alexander, the Food and Canning Workers Union advocated gender equality in the workplace and successfully recruited large numbers of seasonal workers to its ranks. In contrast, the number of women in the textile unions remained small as influx control and job reservation prevented African women from entering the textile industry. Still, the number of women joining trade unions increased after the nonracial labour movement took up the campaign against passes for women.

The nonracial trade union movement was the backbone of the African National Congress and its allies. Significantly, many Communist Party cadres moved into Congress organisations and the trade unions after the Suppression of Communism Act in 1950. Their intervention infused the African nationalist and labour movements with energy, political training and leadership. Furthermore, the formation of the South African Congress of Trade Unions (SACTU) in 1955 strengthened the ties between nonracial trade unions and brought them closer to the nationalist politics of the African National Congress. The SACTU pursued a strategy of political trade unionism, harnessing workers' demands for improved wages and working conditions to the political cause of African nationalism.

The idea of nonracialism, the significance of the working class in opposing apartheid and the demonstration of unity across colour lines were increasingly promoted by the ANC and its allies as a counter to the apartheid state's insistence that racial apartheid was in the interests of black and white. But the idea of a progressive nonracialism remained fragile, and its adoption as policy was cautious and limited. A strong Africanism dominated some ANC branches that expressed unhappiness over working with white activists. In others, rancour occurred when the interests of the elite clashed with those of the working class and their communist supporters.

In an attempt to strengthen commitment to the idea of nonracialism in the wake of the Defiance Campaign, the ANC worked with its allies – the South African Indian Congress (SAIC), the South African Coloured People's Organisation (SACPO), the white South African Congress of Democrats and the nonracial SACTU to prepare for a national congress. This so-called Congress of the People was held at Kliptown near Johannesburg on 26 June 1955, its purpose to affirm a common guiding vision for the Congress movement. In the preceding months, committees were sent out to the branches of the organisations that made up the Congress Alliance to collect responses to the question, 'How would you set about making South Africa a happy place for all who live in it?' The outcome of this consultation was the Freedom Charter. Beginning with the principle that 'South Africa belongs to all who live in it', the charter set out a vision of democratic government encompassing social security and a commitment to human rights in a postapartheid society. It was described by Nelson Mandela, leader of the ANC's Youth League at the time, as a revolutionary document, because its implementation implied the overhauling of the economic and social system of the country.

But the Freedom Charter did not prevent tensions between the alliance and other political organizations, nor did it stem growing political ferment in its own ranks. First, significant political organizations remained outside of the alliance. The moderate white Liberal Party, on the one hand, and the left-wing, Cape-based Non European Unity Movement (NEUM), remained outside the ANC umbrella. Second, the Alliance did not have a clear strategy for women's emancipation. When Minister of Native Affairs Hendrik Verwoerd announced that passes would be issued to African women from 1956, the ANC appeared to be at a loss as to what to do. On the surface, African women appeared to be in a weak position, both politically and socially. In addition to apartheid controls, they were also subject to the patriarchal impositions of customary law and the men who implemented it – chiefs, headmen, fathers, husbands, brothers and (in the case of widows) elder sons. For several decades, however, these controls had failed to prevent women from moving to the cities, where they joined their men, found work and made new lives. Without the sanction of African men or customary law, women's position in the cities was precarious, their position in the family in a state of flux. Yet in assuming new responsibilities and duties, they were also able to exercise greater independence of action and judgement.

Such migrant women most often sought work as live-in domestic workers, connected to other females in similar circumstances through loose networks. Separated from the controlling influence of men and mothers-in-law, many developed a sense of themselves as 'modern' women as Noni Jabavu observed, making their way in a complex world with little from the past to draw on. Many women found support in Christian women's prayer meetings – the Methodist *manyano* (gathering) and the Congregationalist American Board *isililo* (wailing) – which provided a space for women in the cities to come together to preach, sing hymns and lead prayers, and so share the burdens of everyday life. The church saw these meetings as a vector for transmission of church values, including those of feminine domesticity and motherhood. African women held on to this new primacy and meaning in motherhood, as it enabled them to achieve dignity in the absence of men and to acknowledge the pain and suffering that came with motherhood. The form of women's church meetings, characterised by weeping, confessions and outpourings of repentance, held strong ritual qualities that resonated with the oral cultural role of African women, as Deborah Gaitskell noted. In summary, women's prayer meetings offered women an opportunity to take the lead, to pray and to preach. The friendships formed substituted for kin and enabled women to celebrate themselves as doers rather than as silent listeners.

Women also formed revolving credit associations so that they might cope better with the financial demands of living in the city and pay for the costs of funerals. These thrift clubs, *itimiti* or *stokvels*, allowed women to pool their savings and gave each member a turn to receive a payout. *Stokvel* associations also provided turns for members to host parties at which individuals paid to attend and bought food and drink. A good hostess could make substantial profits from a *stokvel* party. Many women also belonged to burial societies, which were usually restricted to small, cohesive groups of women from the same rural background or who shared similar cultural roots.

Like their town-born counterparts, new urban residents faced the risk of disappointments, unwanted pregnancies and single motherhood. In the late 1950s, 40–60 per cent of births in the cities were estimated to be illegitimate. By the early 1960s, African urban communities displayed a distinct shift toward matrifocalism as relationships between mother and child displaced dominance by fathers. Between 10 and 20 per cent of urban households in African townships in 1960–1961 acknowledged that fathers were often absent and that the role of the father had become peripheral. Domestic relations were often difficult and painful, both for adults and for children. There was no dominant family form, however. Families were varied and complex, ranging from male-headed multigenerational households to mother-children extended households. Few families found a comfortable fit in the two-roomed subeconomic housing preferred by most municipalities. Despite the high degree of organisational flexibility that characterised households, many still held on to the ideal of the male-dominated, patrilineal family. These views, like much of everyday life, were influenced by economic circumstances, social customs (including Christianity), relations of affection, marriage and divorce, as well as influx control and access to housing. Many couples struggled to maintain stable, long-term relationships of mutual support, and some women entered into risky marriages with men who had urban residential rights to qualify for housing. In their later years, many women who had worked in town returned to the rural areas to escape monthly rental payments and, as Belinda Bozzoli put it, to 'hold on to dignity, community and hope'.[2]

Women were also attracted to politics, joining local residents' associations, trade unions, the Communist Party and the ANC Women's League. In the run-up to the Congress of the People, women involved in Congress alliance organisations formed the Federation of South African Women

[2] Belinda Bozzoli with Mmantho Nkotsoe, *Women of Phokeng: consciousness, life strategy, and migrancy in South Africa, 1900–1983* (Johannesburg: Ravan Press, 1991), p. 204.

(FSAW). In a bid to bring women together under one umbrella, the FSAW drew up the Women's Charter, setting out a vision of women's emancipation as inextricably linked to national liberation. As an organisation committed to social change for women, the FSAW's first challenge came in 1956, when the Minister of Native Affairs announced that the pass laws would be extended to women. Its response was to plan a mass demonstration of protest outside the Union buildings in Pretoria. Warned by their legal counsel that the march might be illegal, the leaders, Lilian Ngoyi and Helen Joseph, sent out word that the buses had been cancelled and that each woman would have to carry her own letter to present to the minister to avoid 'common purpose'. The subsequent protest was a powerful symbolic moment and a spectacular piece of political theatre. On 9 August 1956, twenty thousand African women made their way to Pretoria and marched down the cement path between the manicured gardens to the government buildings. Popular accounts of the event declare that the minister had 'fled', leaving the protestors to deposit their letters in great piles at his door. After singing, 'Wena Strydom, wa tint' abafazi wa tint' imbokoto. Uzakufa' (Strydom, you have struck the women, you have struck a rock, you will be crushed), the women walked away from the Union buildings.

Female political militancy and initiative indirectly challenged male dominance and unsettled the gender order both in the home and in the arena of African nationalist politics. The FSAW leader Ngoyi berated the timidity of the all-male ANC and hinted that there was tension over the degree of autonomy enjoyed by the women's federation. Women arrested during the antipass campaign complained that their men bailed them out of jail to come home and cook. More directly, the FSAW's campaign encouraged the spread of antipass protest across the country. Hundreds of women in dozens of localities were drawn into petitioning and protesting throughout the next two years. However, the NAD ignored these efforts, dispatched mobile vans and began issuing passes to rural women. By 1962, 3.6 million passes had been issued to African women.

In the homelands, women's livelihoods were dependent on marriage and the family's place in rural social hierarchies. For many, access to land was a critical resource. Land was desperately scarce in all the homelands and dire in places like the Ciskei, where 30 per cent of households were landless by the end of the 1940s. Many women had little chance of obtaining arable land, and in most instances, the plots allowed by the NAD were too small for a single household's livelihood. Rather than augment the amount of land, the NAD presented betterment schemes and land rehabilitation as strategies for shoring up ailing reserve economies. In practice, such measures undermined the security of families by enforcing stock reduction to fit the carrying capacity of land that was often overgrazed and eroded. A handful of NAD officials understood that these technical interventions were deeply invasive and destructive of African cultural values and lifestyles, but they pressed ahead regardless. Subsistence farmers perceived livestock reduction as an attack on customary social relations held in place by transactions involving cattle, sheep and goats.

By separating residential and grazing land, the enforced closer settlement of betterment schemes also disturbed social organisation, and NAD interventions sparked internal friction in many communities as social relations became fractious and support networks fragile. But there were also numerous instances of resistance to NAD interventions from Witzieshoek on the Basutoland border (1946–1950) to the Peddie district in the southern Ciskei, Mpondoland (1957–1960) and Tembuland (mid-1950s) in the east and northeast to Zululand. In some instances, headmen and chiefs led their followers in opposition to betterment and rehabilitation. In others, headmen and chiefs who cooperated with the NAD found themselves isolated from their communities. In some areas, opposition to NAD interventions was led by returning migrant workers who infused rural resistance with some elements of wider nationalist politics. Contestation and modes of organisation varied. In Sekhukhuneland, rural politics was led by the migrant workers' organisations; in Glen Grey, resistance was heavily influenced by the All-African Convention (AAC) and the noncollaborationist ideology of the NEUM, whereas in Peddie, the ANC Youth League and Chief Msutu worked closely together. Those who opposed NAD interventions in these areas cut fences, trampled unwanted construction works, evaded stock inoculation and refused to move into closer settlements. In the drought-stricken areas of the Ciskei where draught animals were weak, women and children dragged cattle and ploughs up and down the hills, crossing the contour to conserve the strength of humans and animals. They also attacked those who collaborated with the NAD. When they were charged with obstruction, they engaged sympathetic legal representatives such as I. B. Tabata and W. M. Tsotsi, of the All-African Convention, who appealed to the courts for justice, although legal victories were rare. Litigation more often brought fines and imprisonment and drained resources and energy from communities. As the communities weakened, NAD officials began to implement government policy.

Yet such implementation could encounter prolonged resistance. Here, the rebellion of migrant workers in Witzieshoek in the northern Orange Free State is a particularly powerful story. Beginning in the mid-1940s, the Witzieshoek rebellion culminated in violent skirmishes, mass arrests and a lengthy trial in 1950. The story has been told in several ways with leading personalities configured anew in each account, but the essence is as follows. Comprising fifty thousand acres of mountainous territory on the border of Basutoland, the Witzieshoek Reserve was home to fourteen thousand inhabitants, two-thirds of whom earned their living from migrant labour. A Betterment Areas proclamation in 1940 set the carrying capacity of the reserve at 12 500 units. In the late 1940s, migrants based in Johannesburg became concerned that betterment officials were fencing grazing camps and counting stock in the reserve, and they revived the Witzieshoek Vigilance Association. Under the leadership of subchief Paulus Mopeli, the association urged cattle owners to ignore culling orders. The Witzieshoek community became bitterly polarised in the ensuing struggles against NAD and the South African Native Trust. Cattle belonging to the paramount chief were seized and removed from the sale pens by militants. A period of intense conflict culminated in those opposed to the NAD – many of them migrant workers who had had some exposure to African nationalist and Communist Party ideas in town – demanding that hearings for a government inquiry into the sentiments of the community be held in public. When they defied a ban on political meetings, the police moved in, gave the crowd ten minutes to disperse and then opened fire. Fourteen men were shot dead and scores wounded. The crowd retaliated, killing two policemen and wounding sixteen others. The deaths and the mass arrests that followed were a blow to Paulus Mopeli and his followers, whose resources were further depleted by a lengthy trial. By the time the trial was concluded, divisions in the community showed no sign of healing, but opposition to betterment had been broken and the NAD moved in.

Elsewhere, as opportunities for advancement became increasingly limited and more tightly circumscribed, the African elite struggled to maintain a grip on the path to upward mobility. Opportunities for entrepreneurship were shrinking as African businesses were removed from white town centres, and only a handful of small dealerships were permitted in the townships. By the 1960s, business licences were issued almost exclusively in the homelands. A tiny handful of mission-educated men became medical doctors, and nursing provided a modest avenue of advancement for women. Teaching was one of the few avenues open for Africans to attain some degree of upward mobility and approximation of middle-class life. The Bantu Education Act of 1953 set out the principle that education for African people was to be restricted to basic literacy, sufficient for labouring work and no more. Primary schooling on the basis of this rudimentary syllabus was to be made widely available, and aspirations to remain at school beyond this level curtailed. The idea of Bantu education threw educators, students and parents into turmoil, bringing conflict between those who would resist its measures and those who sought to avoid upheaval and disruption in schools or confrontation with the state. Professor D. D. T. Jabavu, chair of the All-African Convention and scholar of African languages at Fort

Hare, condemned the Bantu Education Act for racialising education, for systematically stripping the content and value of mission-based black education and for downgrading the black teaching profession. Bantu education closed off the possibilities of black advancement and reduced African intellectuals to the status of interpreters and administrators of *herrenvolk* (white supremacist) knowledge, he declared.

In militant reaction, the Cape African Teachers' Association (CATA) exhorted teachers to refuse to 'operate the machinery of Bantu education'. However, some CATA members disagreed with this strategy and urged teachers to 'fight from within' rather than adopt the boycott tactic of the coloured-dominated Teachers' League of South Africa (TLSA), which did little to engage directly with African schooling realities. Such internal wrangling led to the demise of CATA and its journal, the *Vision*, and to some teachers breaking away to form the Cape African Teachers' Union (CATU). Meanwhile, the ANC branch in Port Elizabeth took a lead in boycotting Bantu education and for a short period ran 'cultural clubs' for students outside of the formal system. In this initiative they were supported by the Cape African Parents' Association, led by Reverend James Calata. In postschool education, politically motivated students at the University of Fort Hare had the option of joining the AAC-affiliated Sons of Young Africa (SOYA) or the Fort Hare branch of the ANC Youth League. When the Separate Universities bill was mooted, three hundred Fort Hare students marched through the streets of nearby Alice carrying placards and distributing pamphlets. In 1957, the Fort Hare branch of the ANC Youth League encouraged trainee nurses at Victoria Hospital to oppose the Nursing Amendment Act for its racist curriculum and separate register of nurses. Like the Bantu Education Act, the Nursing Amendment Act struck a blow at the African middle class and the aspirations of young black people. Nurses across the country protested against the demeaning of the nursing profession set out in the act and condemned its restrictions on the possibilities for African women's upward mobility.

Protest fell on deaf ears. Africans experienced a massive restructuring of the school system after 1954. Pupil and teacher training syllabi were altered to cut down the academic content. Conditions of service were changed to exclude males from primary teaching and to allow underqualified female teachers with a minimal standard-six attainment level, plus two years of teacher training, to enter the classroom. The medium of instruction at primary level was conducted in the vernacular, but that at secondary school was split between English and Afrikaans. Bantu education was designed to provide mass, basic education devoid of critical thinking. In the homelands, the administration and funding of higher primary and secondary schools were devolved to local school boards and tribal authorities. State subsidies declined by more than half between 1955 and 1962. In many schools, classroom and staff shortages necessitated morning and afternoon sessions, known as the platoon system. As a consequence of the changes, the number of African children attending school expanded from 1 million in 1955 to 2 million ten years later. As the number of pupils rose, so did the pupil-teacher ratio, increasing from 46:1 in 1955 to 57:1 in 1961. Yet many children still had no access to schooling at all. In 1970, 34.8 per cent of economically active Africans resident in urban areas and 63.4 per cent in rural areas had no formal education. Less than 1 per cent had a degree or diploma. Nonetheless, as increasing numbers of teachers themselves emerged as products of Bantu education, criticism of the system subsided.

Spatial separation was achieved through the Population Registration and Group Areas Acts (1950). Over the following three decades, in the cities of Durban and Cape Town alone, more than six hundred thousand people of colour were removed and resettled. In Durban, 120,000 Africans were forcibly removed from Cato Manor and about 80,000 Indians were forced to move from their homes. Hostels housing African migrants were relocated to designated townships. Local protest, often led by the ANC, the Indian congresses and the South African Coloured People's Organisation (SACPO), in conjunction with local organisations, had little effect. Indian traders were removed from the centre of Pretoria and other major cities; established inner-city communities like Sophiatown in Johannesburg, Korsten in Port Elizabeth and District Six in Cape Town were ripped apart by forced removals in the late 1950s and 1960s. As with earlier inner-city clearance, public health was used as justification for racial social engineering and control. These city areas had also long been notoriously difficult to regulate and to police, as most residents derived their incomes from informal activities such as rent collection, tailoring, beer brewing, hawking, taxi driving, entertainment and theft. Their livelihoods were destroyed by the obliteration of the inner-city suburbs. Those who were moved included individual African intellectuals, Indian traders, coloured factory workers, others from poor and marginalised groups (e.g., Jews and immigrants from Europe – in the 1950s and 1960s), unemployed men and women and organised gangs.

In the Cape, opposition to the Group Areas Act was sometimes linked to protest against the removal of coloured inhabitants from the common voters roll. Coloured people remained eligible to vote on the basis of a qualified franchise; more than forty-nine thousand of the population of approximately 1 million had voting rights in 1950. Among those electorally eligible were property owners, educated professionals, artisans and better-paid workers. In 1951, the Franchise Action Committee (FRAC) was formed to oppose looming coloured disenfranchisement. The FRAC became the South African Coloured People's Organisation (SACPO) in 1953, changing its name to the South African Coloured People's Congress (CPC) in 1959. Building on the mobilisation started by FRAC, in May 1954, SACPO organised a general strike in opposition to the Separate Representation Act, the Group Areas Act, the Racial Classification Act and the Separate Amenities Act. In the rural Western Cape, Worcester reported 100 per cent observance of the strike, whereas Paarl claimed full support at two large textile plants. In Cape Town, workers at forty-seven of the seventy-nine factories came out on strike, with 95 per cent of coloured-owned shops closing for the day. For more than five years, tens of thousands of liberal-minded white ex-servicemen and other concerned war veterans banded together in the Torch Commando to engage in public protest against government action on the coloured franchise, staging torchlight processions to Parliament. Although mobilisation around such issues did not spread much beyond the Cape, it had a powerful politicising effect in larger rural towns like Worcester and Paarl and in parts of Cape Town where large numbers of workers were mobilised. In Western Cape resistance politics, a strategy of mass action provided an alternative to the inflexible boycott approach of the NEUM, an organisation dominated by teachers and intellectuals.

In Natal, prospects of new separatist legislation generated another kind of response. Initially, the expectation that the vast majority of Indians would be affected by the Group Areas Act produced panic. But the state's promise of new middle-class neighbourhoods for Indians softened the blow, and poorer residents looked forward to the prospect of better housing. According to Bill Freund, many working-class Indians welcomed the chance to move away from rack-renting landlords into the subeconomic sections of Merebank and Chatsworth, ignoring the plight of banana growers who would lose their land. Attempts by local ratepayers organisations and the NIC to create awareness of the political significance of group areas failed to mobilise Indian people.

On the Witwatersrand, 54,000 Africans, 3,000 coloureds, 1,500 Indians and 686 Chinese in Sophiatown, Martindale and Newclare were removed through the policy of 'black spot' clearance. Although the vast majority of these people lived in overcrowded rented accommodation owned by absentee landlords, Sophiatown was renowned less for its poverty and squalor than for its cosmopolitan character. Its culture of *marabi* dance and jazz clubs, larger-than-life shebeen queens, American-style gangs and streetwise youngsters was popularised by *Drum* magazine writers. But even their contemporary chronicles displayed signs of ambivalence that have been largely erased in later, nostalgic accounts of Sophiatown's history. Bloke Modisane, for example, moderated his celebration of Sophiatown's cultural vibrancy by lamenting the all-embracing culture of violence – a 'kind of lingua franca', as he put it – imposed by law-bucking *tsotsis*. For the intellectual elite and the tiny handful of African property owners – no more than 829 – the threat of removal signalled an attack on the achievements of the African middle class. Resisting the removal of Sophiatown quickly translated into the principle of defending African freehold tenure. Local ANC activists urged gangsters to stop gambling, chasing women and going to the cinema and persuaded them to distribute antiremovals pamphlets. Plans for a stay-at-home were cut short when the government banned all public meetings and brought forward the date of the removals. Protest was left to the efforts of outspoken individuals such as Trevor Huddleston, Sophiatown's defiant Anglican priest. Ultimately, Sophiatown residents were relocated to Soweto, an amalgam of the South Western Townships.

In the Eastern Cape, the local authorities used influx control regulations in tandem with the Group Areas Act to clear Korsten, a rack-rented village of five thousand families on the outskirts of Port Elizabeth. Here, the poor lived in shelters made from packing cases discarded by motor-car manufacturers. African residents had their documents inspected by labour bureau officials. A few with permanent urban status were accommodated in the newly constructed township of KwaZakele; the 'Hosannas', or Korsten basket makers, were deported to Botswana, and those whose documents were not in order were sent to the homelands.

By the end of 1970, approximately 111,580 families country wide had been disqualified in terms of the Group Areas Act: 59 per cent were African, 39 per cent Indian and coloured and 2 per cent white. Many individuals and families lived in an unsettled state of anxiety as they waited to be relocated, a process that sometimes took several years. In the ensuing decade, more people were forcibly removed under the Black (Urban Areas) Consolidation Act (Act 25 of 1945, as amended), the Group Areas Act, the Prevention of Illegal Squatting Act (Act 52 of 1951), the Blacks Resettlement Act (Act 19 of 1954) and the Black Land Act (Act 27 of 1913).

The erosion of residence rights was accompanied by pressures on living standards. In the late 1950s, several mass boycotts occurred around the escalating cost of living in the cities. For many working-class communities, the cost of travel posed a significant strain on households. In January 1957, the Transvaal's Public Utility Transport Corporation (PUTCO) increased bus fares by 25 per cent. Commuters responded by refusing to ride to and from work. Guided by the Alexandria People's Transport Committee and rallying to the slogan 'Azikwelwa!' (We will not ride!), which echoed the struggles of the American civil rights movement, an estimated seventy thousand people boycotted PUTCO buses for three months while commuters in the Eastern Cape engaged in a sympathy boycott of the local bus service. After two months, PUTCO suspended all services and began negotiations, but a settlement was delayed by political wrangling between Africanists and the ANC leadership in the boycott committee. After talks, the parties agreed that employer contributions to the Native Services Levy Act would subsidise the bus service.

The Alexandria bus boycott spurred SACTU to launch a campaign for a national minimum wage. In February 1957, SACTU launched the '£1-a-day campaign' under the slogan 'Asinamali, sifun'imali' (We have no money, we demand money). Workers pointed out that the government's calculation of the cost of living bore no relation to their wages, many of which were below the poverty line. £1-a-day committees were formed in the main industrial centres, where they also served as recruitment centres for SACTU. Pamphlets set out workers' grievances and called for the removal of pass laws and group areas, an end to apartheid in nursing and the abolition of Bantu education. They also demanded freedom of expression, association and worship.

The boycott strategy was also used by urban consumers to support rural workers. In 1959, *New Age*, a Congress Alliance paper, exposed the appalling conditions on potato farms in the Bethal district of the Transvaal, where convicts, young children and adults worked side by side digging potatoes with their hands. The newspaper called on consumers not to buy or eat potatoes. For months, *New Age* journalists kept the public informed of conditions on the farms.

In an increasingly restive atmosphere by the end of the 1950s, the ANC leadership claimed it had become a mass popular organisation. Chief Albert Luthuli, ANC president, declared in 1959 that it was 'no longer the organisation of chiefs and nobles' but of 'ordinary people'. Which sectors of the ordinary people Chief Luthuli meant is not clear. Certainly, women's political protests in 1959 came as a shock to the ANC. Their local uprisings began in Cato Manor, the congested and volatile Durban shack settlement, following a raid on beer brewing. As illegal immigrants to the city, the women had little chance of being rehoused; they would be forced to carry passes and would be sent back to the Zululand Reserve (soon to become the KwaZulu homeland). A police raid on beer brewing was simultaneously a blow to livelihood and a sign that the authorities were moving in on them. Braving a police attack, some two thousand women stormed a nearby municipal beer hall and launched a boycott of beer halls. Although the event has received much attention, Iain Edwards has criticised what he sees as a tendency to romanticise the uprising rather than to explore the ambiguities of gendered social and political relations.

In the ensuing weeks, around twenty thousand women in rural Natal protested against restrictions on brewing, the imposition of beer halls and pass laws – regulations that infringed on their livelihoods – and stoned the 'pass vans' that traversed the country issuing reference books. In these areas, women supported their men's refusal to take domestic animals to the dipping tanks where they would be counted. Three-quarters of the dipping tanks in the Zululand Reserve were destroyed in this wave of protest. Again, the ANC was taken by surprise. Moses Mabhida, a leader of the ANC in Natal, commented that his organisation had been unaware of the extent of the women's political awareness and organisational ability, a weakness he attributed to conservative 'African attitudes'.

In the meantime, anxious to give the more conservative elements of the rural population a stake in the apartheid system, government pressed ahead with plans to consolidate the homelands. The fist step was to remove existing African political representation outside of the homelands by disbanding the Native Representative Council on which white representatives, elected by a small number of Africans who qualified for this limited franchise, served. The passing of the NRC went quietly as few among the intellectual elite regarded white representatives as the legitimate voice of African opinion. The second step for the nationalist government was to achieve tighter ethnic separation under the Bantu Authorities Act (1951) through which a three-tiered system of tribal, regional and territorial administrations was established in each of the ten separate ethnic 'homelands'. The Bantu Authorities Act augmented the powers of the chiefs and headmen. In some instances, the act necessitated creating chiefs and tribal affiliations where none existed or where their authority had collapsed. The Promotion of Bantu Self-Government Act (1959) completed the legislative framework for the balkanisation of the country by creating separate ethnic territorial authorities. *Self-government* meant that all Africans would be required to become citizens of one or other homeland. The status of Africans in South Africa would be as 'foreigners', with no protection in law. Critics of this system referred to the independent homelands as Bantustans.

In the Transkei and Ciskei, many Africans baulked at the centralised control of Bantu Authorities who were to replace the partly elected advisory *bunga* councils. Opponents objected to the government appointing headmen and other officials; they were furious that chiefs and other traditional leaders would be compelled to implement government policy regardless of the wishes of the people. In many other homelands, people perceived the Bantu Authorities Act as a violation of the principle *kgoshi ke kgoshi ka batho*, 'a chief is a chief by the people.' If chiefs were required to implement rehabilitation measures and other unpopular laws, how could the leaders make common cause with their people against the government? In the run-up to the appointment of Bantu Authorities, banishment was applied repeatedly to its opponents to make way for government-approved 'traditional leaders'. Many were regarded with disdain as puppets of the authorities. The banishment of the Bahurutse chief in the Zeerust district and his replacement with a deeply unpopular government supporter was one such instance.

The story of Bahurutse resistance reveals the depth of hostility to the Bantustan system in the northeast of the country. It begins with women's opposition to passes. In 1957, the chief of the Bahurutse in the Hurutshe Reserve near Zeerust was instructed by the native commissioner to inform women that they were to take out passes. Chief Abram Moiloa duly made the announcement at a *kgotla* in Dinokana village but gave no further guidance. A mere seventy-six women, most of them teachers and government employees, took passes, but more than four thousand Hurutshe women stayed away. The Bantu Affairs Department's (BAD) response was to dismiss the chief and banish him from the reserve. Moiloa had fallen foul of the BAD because he had declined to sign the Bantu Authorities Act and had refused to persuade the African landowners of two farms, Braklaagte and Leeuwfontein, to give up their land and move into the reserve. The BAD's heavy-handed treatment of the chief propelled the Bahurutshe into action.

Initially, reserve inhabitants simply refused to cooperate, but BAD reprisals heightened antagonism and led to confrontation. The BAD prevented women without passes from drawing pensions, marrying or being admitted to health facilities. Bahurutshe women working on the Witwatersrand hired special buses to take them home to Dinokana so that they might assess the situation. The men followed. How many migrants undertook this journey is not clear. Official accounts implied that large numbers of ANC agitators accompanied the returning migrants. Although there is evidence of some Congress symbolism and rhetoric in the protestors' discourse, such as the women of Dinokana referring to themselves as a Congress village, it is more likely that the escalating conflict itself politicised the women. The NEUM also had some influence among local leaders, as did the Anglican priest at Zeerust, Charles Hooper, who provided supplies for the resistance movement and in 1960 published an acclaimed account of the episode, *Brief Authority*.

Conflict accelerated rapidly when a police mobile column arrived in Lefurutshe and imposed a regime of mass arrests, beatings and harassment. The effect was to further polarise the already sharply divided community and to shift the focus from the women's antipass struggle to the issue of Bantu Authorities. Moiloa supporters withdrew their children from the school and boycotted the local stores where the police positioned themselves. They attacked the chiefs who collaborated, waylaid their bodyguards and destroyed their property. The bus service was suspended and the school and post office were closed down as repression intensified. The police prevented all outsiders from entering the area and prohibited all meetings. By early 1958, agriculture had collapsed and two thousand opponents of Bantu Authorities fled across the border into neighbouring Botswana. Those who remained were rounded up and issued with passes. Collaborative chiefs were officially appointed under the Bantu Authorities Act, with Lucas Mangope as their head. For those like Mangope who were willing to participate in apartheid's invented lineages, Bantu Authorities offered much. Their position as Bantustan administrators afforded unprecedented power, prestige and opportunities for accumulation.

Organisation of the Sekhukhuneland rebellion in the Pedi homeland in the northeast, as Peter Delius has shown, demonstrated the deep involvement of migrant workers drawing on their organisational experience on the Rand. Nearly all Pedi migrants joined burial societies which provided mutual support and a means of saving for funeral costs for men from the same home district. But not all Pedi migrants took part in urban politics and it was those with some primary school education who tended to make contact with trade unions and political movements. Those men preferred to avoid mine labour and sought work in manufacturing, in the service sector or as hawkers and tailors. Many of them attended night schools. From among this cohort were drawn the leaders of community organisations in the Sekhukhuneland Reserve, such as the Zoutpansberg Cultural Association. Some of the organisations were also associated with the Zoutpansberg Balemi (Ploughman's) Organisation beyond the Reserve. In the mid-1950s, when the BAD began to implement rehabilitation measures on land abutting the reserve, these migrant workers initiated Sebatakgomo (a traditional Pedi call to arms). A political organisation, Sebatakgomo was closely linked to the ANC and SACP. It was not opposed to the chieftaincy but insisted that Bantu Authorities had turned the chieftainship into a puppet body by banishing the paramount chief and replacing him with a man of their choice. A secret organisation, Khuduthamaga (Red and White Tortoise), linked to Sebatakgomo was deployed to reconstruct the chieftainship 'by the people' and so to prevent its corruption by Bantu Authorities. In 1958, agitation against Bantu Authorities erupted into violent confrontation, sparked by the police firing on a crowd and killing two people. A wave of attacks and reprisals left nine dead, scores wounded and three hundred arrested. The BAD capitulated and allowed the banished paramount to return. When he died seven years later, his wife took over as regent for their minor son. By the 1960s, she had come round to the view that the only way to save the paramountcy was to submit to Bantu Authorities. In 1968, a tribal authority was established in Sekhukhuneland, and the number of chiefs was expanded. Where there had been just three chiefs in 1955, there were fifty-four in 1970. The Sekhukhuneland revolt,

Delius suggests, contributed to the ANC's decision to launch uMhonto weSizwe (Spear of the Nation, the ANC's armed wing) in 1961, in which Flag Boshielo, Elias Mathope Motsoaledi, John Nkadimeng, Peter Nchabeleng, Nelson Diale, Martin Ramokgadi and John Phala, leading men from Sekhukhuneland, became leaders.

Militancy in eastern Pondoland in 1960 was also sparked by the imposition of Bantu Authorities and by internal conflict over the chieftaincy. Encompassing half a million people, Pondoland was divided into eastern and western zones. Differences in their political trajectories in the mid-twentieth century were due in part to the leadership styles of their chiefs. Chief Poto of western Pondoland walked the tightrope between obeying the government and pleasing his people. Chief Botha Sigcau of eastern Pondoland, in contrast, took little heed of popular opposition to taxation, betterment and rehabilitation regulations. Opposition was particularly intense around Lusikisiki, Flagstaff and Bizana. Sigcau was not a hereditary chief and stood to gain power and resources through the Bantu Authorities system. Opponents of Bantu Authorities directed their anger at Sigcau's councillors, attacking and torching their homes. Some were killed. One of the sources of this militant action was a group known as the Makhulu Span (Big Team), an organisation of unruly youths with criminal tendencies. In Bizana, an organisation known as Congo, led by subheadmen, many of whom had experience as migrant workers, came to direct much of the opposition to Bantu Authorities, betterment and rehabilitation. Some of the Congo leaders were associated with the ANC. Others formed a group known as Intaba (hill committee), led by Solomon Madikizela, a moderate Methodist evangelist and peasant. The ANC, AAC and the NEUM, through I. B. Tabata, also influenced the politics of Intaba. Concerned primarily with drawing in large numbers of supporters, Congo coordinated boycotts against trading stores and labour recruiting agencies and set up an alternative administrative system beyond the purview of Botha Sigcau.

For nine months after Sigcau's installation as chief, his opponents prevented the Bantu Authority from functioning. Thousands of Mpondo refused to pay taxes or to allow government census enumerators to operate. Congo developed an alternative political zone, collecting taxes, allocating land, conducting popular courts and speaking against Bantu Authorities. Many of the movement's followers were young men of working age kept home by a slump in the Natal sugar industry. Working with churchwomen, they sought to harness the energies of unruly youth in the area. Politics, sorcery and violence commingled as the conflict raged on. With no possibility of ending the deadlock internally, some of the leaders prepared a memorandum and collected funds to send a representative to address the United Nations. In November 1960, the government declared a local state of emergency. The police and army moved into eastern Pondoland and gunned down eleven men at a mass meeting. Mass arrests followed and the Pondoland rebellion was brought to an end. Twenty-two men, including chiefs, councillors, bodyguards and alleged informers, were killed in the course of the Mpondo revolt.

Further up the coast in Zululand, a very different politics was being played out. There, in what was to become KwaZulu, Mangosutho Buthelezi, a young Fort Hare graduate who had worked for the Department of Native Affairs for two years, was installed as acting chief in March 1953, pending government approval. Buthulezi's single-minded pursuit of the chiefdom was probably linked to the possibility of becoming prime minister to the Zulu king, his cousin and direct descendant of Shaka, from whom he claimed maternal descent. Buthelezi was officially installed as chief in September 1957, after carefully avoiding any participation in the antipass campaigns or protests against Bantu Authorities instigated by lesser Zulu chiefs. He was known to be eager to accept self-government but more cautious than the Zulu king in showing this eagerness. In 1965, the Mahlabatini tribal area where Buthelezi resided was granted a tribal authority; a year later, 107 such tribal authorities were created for Zululand. Opposition was not quelled, however, and violent resistance delayed the implementation of further tribal authorities until 1970, when the Zululand Territorial Authority was established. Despite his occasional outbursts against the apartheid regime, the government endorsed Buthelezi's position of chief executive officer. In 1972, the KwaZulu Legislative Assembly replaced the territorial authority, assigning legislative and administrative powers to the Bantustan administration.

It remains a moot point whether Buthelezi believed that cooperating with the government best served his people or his own ambitions. He and the Zulu people were undoubtedly materially dependent on the apartheid regime, and his acceptance of state policy and support from large corporations may have provided some benefits. Gerhard Mare and Georgina Hamilton have suggested that Buthelezi benefited politically from the Bantustan system that he used to limit the power of the king, whereas Black Consciousness critics described him as a stooge 'contributing towards the fragmentation of black resistance by encouraging false ethnic consciousness among our people'.[3] By using Bantu Authorities to recast the meaning of tradition and to enhance his own authority, Buthulezi also prevented the royalist lobby from securing an executive king. In 1975, he revived Inkatha yaKwaZulu, a cultural organisation that would serve the 'Zulu nation'.

[3] Mosibudi Mangena, *On your own: evolution of Black Consciousness in South Africa/Azania* (Johannesburg: Skotaville, 1989) p. 53.

As a vehicle for mobilising ethnic nationalism over the following twenty years, Inkatha reinforced Buthelezi's version of Zulu 'tradition', further alienating the king. Inkatha also served to undermine the nonracial nationalism advanced by the ANC.

In the Transkei and Ciskei, dismantling the colonial advisory councils, or *bunga* system, was a prerequisite for constructing Bantu Authorities. Elected *bunga* councillors in the Ciskei responded with dismay at the 'return to tribalism' that Bantu Authorities brought and the 'confusion' that this sowed among people of heterogeneous origins. Closing down the Ciskei *bunga* and finding chiefs to place in charge of people accustomed to elected representatives meant silencing the voices of respected, educated men and riding roughshod over the wishes of ordinary people. Thus, Chief Archibald Sandile, leader of the Ngqika branch of the Rharhabe Xhosa and a reputedly heavy drinker, was made paramount chief of the Ciskei. The process by which he was installed revealed the ingenuity of the Department of Bantu Affairs. Government officials effected a 'tribal separation' between the Xhosa of the Ciskei and the Transkei to create Xhosa paramount chiefs in two territories. They drew up elaborate and costly plans for the installation of Chief Velile Sandile as paramount and for the establishment of a Ciskeian territorial authority. Although three thousand people turned out to enjoy a feast of seventeen head of cattle and one thousand gallons of beer provided by the BAD, Govan Mbeki, intellectual leader of the ANC in the region, declared that the power of Bantu Authorities was a sham.

Lungisile Ntsebeza has described how resistance to rehabilitation in the Xhalanga district was complicated by tensions between conservative, or 'red' (from the custom of daubing with ochre), members of the community and educated, self-consciously modern 'school' people. Bantu Authorities dashed the hopes of those who believed in freehold land but provided satisfaction for those who wanted to shore up chiefly control. Here, the NEUM and AAC worked with local vigilance associations, women's *zenzele* (self-help) clubs, parents' associations, farmers' associations, the Glen Grey Voters' Association (a forum for discussing *bunga* affairs), local branches of the Cape African Teachers' Association and the National Council of African Women (which opposed Bantu Authorities). Influenced by the politics of boycott, Glen Grey residents implemented a strategy of 'noncollaboration', which exasperated officials of the Department of Bantu Development. But after 1956, the tight shield of noncollaboration began to crack. Voters' associations collapsed after the *bunga* councils were closed. Then, George Matanzima, regional chief of the Emigrant Thembu, broke with his radical associates in the AAC and NEUM. He accepted Bantu Authorities and was promoted to the head of the Transkeian Territorial Assembly. In 1958, the district of Glen Grey was transferred from the Ciskei to the Transkei administration, bringing it under Matanzima's control.

Opposition to Bantu Authorities in the Transkei was articulated by Chief Sabata Dalindyebo, paramount of the Tembu, who sent his advisers to Pretoria to present a memorandum to the BAD minister. But his representatives were arrested and sent home. When Transkei was accorded the status of self-rule in 1963, Chief Kaizer Matanzima was elevated to president. As a Bantustan leader, Matanzima 'persecuted and humiliated' his opponents, reputedly deploying spies to rout them out and giving credence to the rumour that 'KD' was everywhere but invisible. Ntsebeza describes Kaizer Matanzima as 'an extreme example of how customary power was used as a coercive administrative arm of the apartheid regime.'[4]

For the conservative rural elite, accepting Bantu Authorities and embarking on the path to homeland self-governance held out the possibility of at least some power, access to resources and control over cultural affairs. Clearly, the prospect of running a substantial administration presented opportunities for a new lifestyle. As Colin Murray puts it, in the eastern Orange Free State, 'the institutional structures of the chieftainship, the Tribal Authority and the emergent "republic" of Bophutatswana formed the public stage upon which many of the Baralong elite made their careers'.[5] Those among the professional elite who preferred business to Bantustan politics were also able to accumulate considerable resources. Even the ANC stalwart Dr. Moroka, for example, used the income from his medical practice to buy several farms near Thaba Nchu. In many areas, expedient leaders deployed oral tradition to legitimate their political aspirations, reinforcing the apartheid government's invented ethnicities, genealogies and chieftaincies and ensuring a stake in the Bantustan system.

In the cities no less than in the countryside, the relentless crushing of all opposition to the implementation of apartheid began to take its toll. By the end of the 1950s, the ANC was being torn apart by ideological conflict. Strife between Africanists and nonracialists reached new heights, particularly in the Orlando branch in the Transvaal. There, the Africanist faction was opposed to the ANC's alliance with white Communists, Indians and coloureds, arguing instead for a radical Pan-Africanist vision and the implementation of the Youth League's programme of action. Others, like Nelson Mandela, were satisfied with the impact of militancy on

---

[4] Lungisile Ntsebeza, *Democracy compromised: chiefs and the politics of the land in South Africa* (Leiden: Brill, 2005), p. 216.

[5] Colin Murray, *Black mountain: land, class and power in the eastern Orange Free State, 1880s–1990s* (Johannesburg: Witwatersrand University Press for the International African Institute, 1992), pp. 188–9.

the Congress Alliance. Blocked by loyalists in the ANC, the Africanists seceded and formed the Pan Africanist Congress (PAC), electing their ideological leader, Robert Mangaliso Sobukwe, as president. Keen to launch itself through a well-organised antipass campaign, PAC activists arranged an open-air protest meeting in Sharpeville on 21 March 1960. As the meeting broke up, groups of people walked toward the police station to hand in their reference books, and others lit fires to burn them. The police opened fire on the dispersing crowd, killing 69 and wounding 180, including 31 women and 19 children. News of the Sharpeville shooting spread immediately across the international media.

Sharpeville was a watershed, for the events that followed the shootings irrevocably changed the character of African nationalist resistance. On 8 April 1960, the ANC, PAC and CPC were banned, and a state of emergency was declared. Hundreds of people were detained and held without trial. The ANC and the PAC went underground, shifting strategy from civil disobedience to armed struggle. Some in the ANC leadership, including Nelson Mandela and Walter Sisulu, were arrested, charged with treason and imprisoned on Robben Island; others went into exile and prepared for armed struggle through their respective military wings – the ANC's uMkhonto weSizwe (Spear of the Nation) and the PAC's Poqo (Pure and/or Alone). Although the NEUM was not banned, it split into two, with one faction forming the African People's Democratic Union of South Africa (APDUSA). For its part, the ANC encouraged leaders of the Congress movement to go into exile and join uMkhonto weSizwe. The exodus that followed left civil society bereft of political leadership and weakened opposition to apartheid.

In 1962, Poqo influence entered Tembuland through young migrant workers whose politicisation at the hands of the PAC occurred in the Cape Town township of Langa. Poqo operatives were sent to organise underground cells whose mission was to remove the collaborating head of Bantu Authorities, Kaiser Matanzima. Poqo men carried out several failed assassination attempts on Matanzima's life and planned a final onslaught on his palace for Christmas Day 1962. But the police got wind of the scheme. They searched the train carrying migrant workers home on 12 December and after a brief skirmish, apprehended several men carrying *pangas* (knives). In the ensuing months, local headmen were provided with police support to raid homesteads and to hunt down suspected militants. Poqo cadres fought back, killed a headman, released his bodyguards and family and then waited to be arrested. Their fearlessness was widely attributed not to political commitment but to faith in their herbalists' protective medicine.

With the obstacles to homeland self-government now cleared, Pretoria passed the National States Citizenship Act (1970), which required every

African to hold permanent residence in a homeland and to take out citizenship there. A year later, the National States Constitution Act (1971) simplified the homeland self-government regulatory regime. Within a few years, eight homelands had been accorded self-government. In the short term, survival in the Bantustans depended on the ability to accommodate to the new dispensation and to utilise available routes to resources. Overcrowding and overgrazing made agriculture unsustainable in many homelands, and residents became increasingly dependent on direct employment in, or the trickle down from, Bantustan bureaucracies.

Through the 1960s, tens of thousands of Africans were relocated to the Bantustans through the process of consolidating white farmland. Some hung on to their independence, livestock and family life as they wandered about the countryside. Few lasted as long as Kas Maine, a sharecropper on the Transvaal highveld who negotiated tenancy arrangements with at least ten landlords between 1948 and 1975, as Charles van Onselen has so graphically illustrated. The processes of dispossession, removal and adjustment to new places, people and politics were all consuming. Between 1960 and 1970, the population of the homelands increased from 33,486 to 594,420. At the same time, 290,000 homeland residents commuted to South Africa every day, departing for work in the early hours of the morning and arriving home late at night. Everyday life in a divided society required enormous resilience.

Social stratification intensified in the homelands through the 1960s. Educated men and women found employment in their administrations or worked as professional doctors, nurses and teachers. Poor roads and transport made travel difficult, and small rural businesses sprang up to provide basic necessities for those who went shopping on foot. Prospects for most young men and women were bleak, and the possibility of establishing themselves as adults able to maintain a household were increasingly difficult. Countless cases of domestic violence in the courts revealed the pressures of diminishing resources on generations and genders; they also suggest that the customary law courts were repeatedly unable to provide a satisfactory remedy in civil disputes. Fixed in law by British colonial authorities, customs had been rendered rigid and incapable of responding to the changing conditions of people and the ways in which apartheid circumscribed options.

Gender relations were increasingly uncontained and individual men and women struggled to hold onto respectable notions of personhood. Women left the homelands to search for work or for husbands who had absconded. Many of those who remained depended on payment in kind from occasional work parties. Some fathers refused to help with initial *lobola* payments, and some young men did not send their wages home; at the same time, chiefs and headmen complained of the difficulties of constraining youngsters who bought their own beer. What it meant to be a man or a woman was changing rapidly, constructed anew in contexts unfamiliar to an older generation. Rural youth organisations drew on urban experiences as well as deep cultural beliefs about the making of masculinity. Delayed circumcision, often a result of parental absence and the declining prospect of establishing a viable rural homestead, meant that large numbers of young people might be whiling away the hours in a rural location. In the Transkei and Ciskei, young people formed new-styled organisations along quasi-militarist lines and adopted more secretive sexual relationships. At the same time, young men engaged in public displays of stick fighting and met their girls at *imitshotsho* dances. When play turned violent or young women were assaulted, young men were charged in the apartheid courts. However, rural communities believed that the circumcision ritual and *isiko* (proper custom), rather than the courts, would teach young men to behave more moderately. For older men and women, ritual beer drinking continued to serve as an important site for the affirmation of social values. Beer drinking promoted mutual assistance and good neighbourliness; it was also a means of reining in resources, seeking the blessing of the ancestors and constructing an agrarian livelihood in the context of increasing urbanisation.

Away in the cities, the apartheid regime speeded up the enforcement of urban racial separation. Accordingly, the Bantu Laws Amendment Act (1963) increased the state's grip on influx control. New dormitory townships were established on the outskirts of all the major cities such as KwaMashu and Umlazi near Durban, Gugulethu and Nyanga East in Cape Town, Motherwell near Port Elizabeth and Mdantsane near East London. Older townships, like Soweto, which was established in 1936, were expanded. Those resettled in these new spaces grappled with the challenges of making communities out of strangers. By 1966, 87,500 houses and 133 schools had been constructed in the suburban sprawl of Soweto. Jobs in the manufacturing sector doubled in the 1960s and the number of wage earners per family increased from 1.2 to 2.2 between 1956 and 1968. Industrial wages also improved slightly as economic growth edged past 9 per cent per annum. Informal work opportunities also increased. Stratification among residents became increasingly complex. Although many urban residents lived in poverty and tens of thousands of residents defaulted on rent payments, for many others, life in this dormitory town was preferable to living in shacks that barely kept out the elements.

The paths available for African respectability in the cities were limited and the number of middle-class people was small. Only 2.5 per cent of the houses in Mdantsane near East London deviated from the standard housing units to cater to this group. Most of the 16,663 houses constructed there between 1963 and 1976 were single-storey, four-roomed dwellings with cement floors, unplastered walls, no ceilings and outside sanitation. Still, a few houses had electricity, and a handful had tiled bathrooms and wall-to-wall carpeting. Class respectability was supported by an increase in the number of semiskilled workers, drivers, clerks and police officers and an increasing number of professional women. Thomas Nyquist suggests that both the middle class and the business elite, the *abaphakamileyo* or 'well-to-do', guarded their own advancement carefully and distanced themselves from the less fortunate. Their leisure activities kept them indoors, where they listened to the radio and read (more than 60 per cent of Soweto residents could read in the mid-1960s and the *Golden City Post* boasted a circulation of two hundred thousand). When they went out, it was to church, selected sporting events or for social visiting. Ellen Kuzwayo has shown how a few women found respectability through voluntary community work, pouring energy into making communities out of large, characterless townships.

At the same time, the relatively well-to-do and the young who had jobs in the cities developed a good eye for consumer goods. Cramped and unimaginative housing boxes were turned into homes by house-proud women who made extensive use of hire-purchase arrangements. Retail stores, like Ackermans and OK Bazaars, which sold everything from furniture and household goods to baby's clothing, and Ellerines, which sold furniture, offered lay-by facilities and later, credit, to African shoppers. Several incomes were needed to sustain repayments, and many saw their lounge suites, fridges and stoves repossessed as they struggled to meet the weekly or monthly instalments. Among the more successful, studio photographs became markers of status. Sophisticated, commodified lifestyles were celebrated in magazines like *Drum* and *Zonk*, whose pages were filled with stories of romance, the high life of beauty pageants, ballroom dances and fancy weddings. These magazines also promoted skin-lightening creams. Young women dressed in fashionable clothing and competed in beauty contests often sponsored by liquor producers. Men, too, dressed up, and those who could afford motor cars were viewed with envy. The shebeener Pegge Senne was dubbed 'Bel-Air' after the model of car he drove. Consumption and trendy urban lifestyles enabled young people to construct new ways of imagining modernity and of performing masculinities and femininities.

The 1950s were South Africa's jazz age. Although the best-known jazz bands were the inner-city bands of Johannesburg, the Manhattan Brothers of Pimville and the Jazz Maniacs of Sophiatown, every township had its band, each with its unique brand of creative virtuosity and devoted following. Bands played for *stokvel* parties in the townships, jive dances and inner-city clubs. David Coplan explains that at late-night jamming sessions, these musicians turned American jazz into distinctive African styles such as *mbaqanga*. Many of them produced popular recordings: the Alexandra All Star Band's *Baby Come Duze* and Spokes Mashiyane's saxophone recordings, among many others, were popular across the racial divide. The female vocalist Miriam Makeba started out as lead singer for the Manhattan Brothers and later formed her own quartet, the Skylarks, which included Mummy Girl Nketle, Letta Mbulu, Abigail Kubheka and Mary Rabotapi. Local recording studios such as Troubador supported this indigenisation of American jazz, and *Drum* magazine journalists promoted it. But the life of a musician became increasingly difficult as the inner city was bulldozed, communities were scattered and the music industry subjected to censorship. Anger and frustration took its toll.

A more strongly Africanist sentiment characterised the new wave of jazz in the 1960s. The alto saxophonist Kippie Moeketsi and the pianist Dollar Brand (Abdullah Ibrahim) in the Jazz Epistles together with Chris McGregor's Blue Notes produced innovative jazz sounds. Philip Thabane, who grew up in Pretoria's Mamelodi township, founded the Molombo Jazz Men. *Molombo* (the Venda word for the spirit world) evoked the expressionist, multivalent African sound produced by Thabane's jazzmen. Beyond the jazz scene, Joseph Shabalala formed the Ladysmith Black Mambazo, the name suggesting a celebration of black power (*mambazo* means "axe" in isiZulu), derived from spiritual beauty rather than politics. The group's musical style drew on migrant workers' singing in choirs of twelve members with a lead singer, two voices for high parts and the majority singing the base. The style was known as *cothozamfana* (walk steadily, boys) or *isicathamiya* (walk steadily on tiptoe). Under Shabalala's leadership, Ladysmith Black Mambazo won popularity and numerous prizes at *isicathamiya* choir concerts in the 1960s.

The African recording industry slowed to a halt. The South African Broadcasting Corporation imposed strict censorship, and Radio Bantu concentrated on church and traditional music with a smattering of light African American jazz and commercial *mbaqanqa*. The songs of Miriam Makeba and Letta Mbulu were not played over the air, and access to their recordings was limited. Castle lager began sponsoring the Castle jazz festival from 1961, but the initiative could not stem the flood of musicians leaving the country. It was left to the Ladysmith Black Mambazo, whose lyrics celebrated rural life and spirituality, and figures like Gibson Kente and Molefe Phetoe, known for entertaining rather than politicising their audiences, to keep township music and musical theatre alive.

Although they could not replicate the jazz dens, new venues emerged in the townships when the prohibition on African consumption of 'European liquor' was lifted in 1961. As it became easier for township shebeeners to buy spirits and bottled beer, they could attract a more affluent clientele.

The number of shebeeners also increased. Because all informal trading in white cities had been banned, backyard furniture manufacturers closed down and two thousand coffee-cart vendors were purged from the streets of Johannesburg in the 1950s, illicit liquor trading in the townships was one of the few avenues for entrepreneurship. Demand was driven partly by consumers' desire to avoid government beer halls and to seek out *espotini* (drinking places) for more convivial sociable interaction. Selection of the appropriate spot was critical for establishing status. Even the stylish Ama-pantsula youths of Soweto – known to spend more on clothes than drink – took their girls to the shebeen. Well-known shebeeners such as Godfrey Moloi, Ray Morolong and Cooksie Senne attested to the lucrative character of shebeening in the 1960s.

Equally, respectable township residents and shebeeners alike feared the increasing presence of street gangs in the new townships. For their members, *bo-tsotsi* was a question of style, a means of asserting one's identity through belonging to a group. Gangs adhered to a particular dress code, spoke *tsotsi* argot, robbed commuters on the suburban trains and generally behaved in the manner of streetwise tricksters. They spent their days watching American cowboy films, offending respectable society and way-laying women. They taunted rival gangs and scorned their age mates who went to school. Although still relatively small in number in the 1960s, *bo-tsotsi* were a conspicuous element of life in townships from Soweto to Duncan Village in East London. They generated anxiety for parents concerned that youngsters might 'go to the bad' and become violent criminals. The MaRashea gangs of Newclare South on the East Rand, associated with Basotho mine workers, were particularly notorious.

Unsurprisingly, much township leisure time was taken up by sport, especially soccer, which developed as a mass spectator sport in Soweto in the 1960s. Orlando Pirates and Moroka Swallows were firm club favourites by 1960 when Pirates and other clubs formed a nonracial South African Soccer League (SASL) to distance themselves from the Johannesburg City Council and to carve out a space for leisure as an autonomous activity, free from official control. However, maintaining an independent stance became increasingly difficult to sustain, as SASL was dependent on the municipal authorities for access to playing fields. Peter Alegi describes an occasion in April 1963 when fifteen thousand soccer fans were locked out of the Natalspruit Indian Sports Grounds. Undeterred, they jumped over the corrugated iron fence. When they saw that the goalposts had been removed, they ran over to a nearby playing ground, 'borrowed' a set of goalposts and lifted them over the fence into the Natalspruit grounds. A jubilant and rowdy crowd then watched Alexandria Real Fighters defeat Transvaal United and Moroka Swallows beat Blackpool United. Although

SASL secured modest sponsorship from the United Tobacco Company, it was local supporters who kept the clubs alive. Fund-raising parties, dances, barbecues and women's beauty pageants brought in small sums of money and provided a space for the forging of a culture of sociability among the fans of local soccer, with its rough style of play. By the mid-1960s, big matches were attracting crowds of between 30,000 and 45,000 spectators. Intense rivalry was by no means confined to the field, and Soweto homes were often painted in the colours of their favourite team. As stories of the stylish play of Soweto soccer stars spread beyond the township, they created an aura of glamour for prominent clubs. So, although SASL folded in 1966, the clubs continued to grow.

Soccer evolved along different lines in the Western Cape, as the Separate Amenities Act prevented African and coloured players from sharing facilities. There, a Cape Federation Professional League emerged while the National Professional Soccer League (NPSL) developed on the Witwatersrand in the late 1960s. Several Natal teams, such as the African Wanderers, the Amazulu and the Lamontville Golden Arrows – and one or two teams from the Orange Free State – were represented in the NPSL. Along with other sports like cricket, soccer in the Cape also came under the influence of the NEUM's noncollaborationist tradition, and from 1973, the strictures of the South African Council of Sport (SACOS), whose slogan, 'No Normal Sport in an Abnormal Society', helped to ensure the isolation of South Africa from the world sporting community. In contrast to Cape Town and Johannesburg, townships in the Eastern Cape developed a culture of rugby playing, despite the paucity of resources. Over the following two decades, team sports and their players also came under the influence of one or other of the antiapartheid political traditions – the antiracism of the NEUM, Black Consciousness or the nonracialism of the Congress movement.

As could sport, religious activity could provide a space away from the relentless controls of apartheid for displaced and disoriented people to reinvent identities and find support. African Pentecostal churches developed from splinters of the established denominations of English, German and Dutch Reformed churches and became increasingly popular through the 1960s. In both urban and rural areas, independent African churches, numbering almost three thousand by the late 1960s, attracted increasingly large numbers of poor people anxious to make sense of the disorder of their lives.

As an African expression of Christianity, the Zionist churches formulated views on a relationship between Ancestors and the Holy Spirit. The largest of these initiatives, the charismatic Zionist Christian Church (ZCC), emerging in the late 1940s, promoted adult baptism and divine healing as mass rituals. Materially, the Zionist church also served as a mode of survival by providing voluntary careers for thousands of lay preachers and by becoming a reference point for millions of followers throughout the apartheid era. Jean Comaroff has argued that resistance rather than separatism was its principal characteristic. In Comaroff's view, the ZCC resisted doctrine – that is, the restrictions of meaning and practice set out by the formal Catholic and Protestant doctrines – and provided a space for the articulation of an alternative cultural identity. Therefore, leaders and their followers could improvise new meanings that drew from, and related to, their lives. For all this, the resistance of Pentecostalism was still symbolic and cultural rather than political in its thrust. Indeed, the ZCC remained outwardly compliant and even supportive of the apartheid regime.

Adherents hoped that faith and the rituals of prayer would alleviate the frustrations and stresses that resulted from the increasingly complexity of everyday life. In the view of Bloke Modisane, a writer and journalist, who had grown up in a shebeen, Pentecostal gatherings were 'invariably attended by histrionics, the congregation sang happy songs to a rhythmic chant of hand clapping, and as the spirit moved them they went into epileptic fits, into howling shrieks which would have seemed more appropriate in a sanatorium for the bewildered; they stood in athletic trances or collapsed in the aisles possessed with fainting spells.'[6]

In contrast to this emotion letting were the restrained efforts of African clergy like Reverend James Calata, who sought to establish an African branch within the established church. Calata was part of the educated elite, an African nationalist who served on the executive committee of the African National Congress in the 1950s, but unlike most of the elite, he identified with the poor and oppressed, wore threadbare clothes and encouraged his family to become politically active. Calata devoted a great deal of energy to the Saint Ntsikana Memorial Association. Believing that the calling of Ntsikana demonstrated the acceptance of African people into the Christian fold, he preached the story of Ntsikana's conversion across the Eastern Cape. But rather than breaking away from the Anglican order, Calata proposed the formation of an African church within the Church of England. His efforts were frustrated, however, by an Anglican establishment that remained suspicious of his Africanism and by fellow African clergy who were distrustful of his ambition.[7]

At the same time as its setup of the Bantustan machinery, the apartheid regime established an administrative system that offered coloureds and Indians some measure of political control over their own affairs 'within the

---

[6] Bloke Modisane, *Blame me on history* (Cape Town: Donker, 1986), p. 188.
[7] See Mandy Goedhals, 'African nationalism and indigenous Christianity: a study in the life of James Calata, (1895–1983)', *Journal of Religion in Africa* 33:1 (February 2003), 63–82.

confines of a common fatherland shared with the Whites'.[8] In this provision, the National Indian Council (later the South African Indian Council) consisted entirely of appointed officials and remained a purely advisory body. But the Coloured Persons Representative Council allowed for elected representation, perhaps because some National Party members, including P. W. Botha, appointed Minister of Community Development and Coloured Affairs in 1961, accepted coloured people as part of a Western culture. Of the 802,500 eligible coloured voters, some 637,936 registered prior to the first segregated council elections in 1969. With the ANC-aligned CPC banned and the noncollaborationist NEUM having foundered organisationally, there was some possibility that leaders who collaborated with apartheid and who called for a coloured homeland or advocated a homeland for the Griqua would become the voice of the coloured people. But a participatory alternative was offered when the educationist Dr Richard van der Ross founded the antiapartheid Labour Party in 1966. Supported mostly by urban middle-income voters younger than the age of forty-five in the Western Cape, Eastern Cape and Natal, the Labour Party won the first elections for the CPRC. But, influenced by the legacy of the NEUM's noncollaborationist tradition, overall voter turnout was low, particularly among middle-class professionals, who boycotted the polls. The Labour Party's Van der Ross soon gave up institutional politics to head the new University College of the Western Cape, an ethnic institution established for coloured students in 1960, to be joined, ten years later, by the University College of Durban Westville for Indians.

Beyond the sphere of racially separatist electioneering politics, the NEUM-inspired Teachers' League continued to condemn discriminatory measures in education, such as the 1963 Coloured Persons Education Act, which placed education under the Department of Coloured Affairs. Cape Town leaders of the Teachers' League such as Livingstone High School's acting principal R. O. Dudley and others at politicised urban schools, like Harold Cressy, Trafalgar and South Peninsula High, generated a strong anticollaborationist discourse and critique of Christian-National Education. These teachers and their students lived through removals under the Group Areas Act and repeated political bannings. When he was served with a banning order, Richard Dudley assured the police officer, '[W]hen we take over this country, we'll give you chaps decent jobs so that you don't have to hunt down human beings'.[9] At the same time, NEUM intellectuals continued to grapple with the colour issue and the question of

[8] South Africa, *South Africa 1984: official year book of the Republic of South Africa* (Johannesburg: Chris van Rensburg Publications, 1984), p. 210.
[9] Alan Wieder, *Teacher and comrade: Richard Dudley and the fight for democracy in South Africa* (Albany: State University of New York Press, 2008), p. 91.

liberation. Mohamed Adhikari observes that the term *coloured* was always set in inverted commas and was invariably preceded by *so-called* in publications of the NEUM and the TLSA. Nonetheless, the TLSA conceded ruefully that what it called the 'myth of Colouredism' influenced political thinking both inside and outside the organisation.[10]

By the mid-1960s, the new ideology of Black Consciousness was emerging. Born of an acute sense of the experience of African people under apartheid and a desire to bring together all oppressed people of colour, it was inspired by the civil rights movement in the United States, and by African American political thought and liberation theology. In the language of Black Consciousness, young black intellectuals expressed their frustration with Bantu education, the state's location of tertiary institutions in the Bantustans and the curriculum's strictures on intellectual development. In 1968, black student leaders cut loose from the National Union of South African Students (NUSAS), a white-dominated English liberal student organisation, to address the particular situation of black students and the problems on black campuses. These activists, among them Steve Biko, a medical student, established the South African Students' Organisation (SASO) at universities and teacher-training colleges and the South African Students' Movement (SASM) in the schools. Black community programmes (BCPs) sought to empower black people through development projects such as literacy training, health clinics and home-industries cooperatives. Supported financially by the South African Council of Churches and the Christian Institute, BCP projects aimed to generate 'self-reliance'. In the cities, Black Consciousness activists formed the Black Allied Workers' Union (BAWU) and the Black Workers' Project (BWP). Neither of these organisations gained a strong footing among workers, however. Some Black Consciousness leaders combined social activism with business. In 1970, Dr Nthatho Motlana, a medical doctor and a founder of BCPs, started Phaphama Africa (Wake up, Africa!) Commercial Enterprises, which produced uniforms for school children, nurses and the police. Short of capital and poorly managed, the enterprise soon folded.

The significance of Black Consciousness lay in its development of a political discourse that focused on the individual, the community and the need for economic development; it was less an African nationalist ideology than a language of healing and pride associated with community programmes for economic and social uplift. Black Consciousness hinged on the importance of self-respect, dignity and self-worth; its programmes were aimed at overcoming passivity. Student publications such as *Black Viewpoint* and *Black Perspectives* printed the work of black poets and fiction writers as well

---

[10] Adhikari, *Not white enough*, p. 134.

as philosophers, psychologists and theologians. Poetry encouraged self-expression and intellectual creativity and allowed for the exploration of the psychological and emotional issues of identity, pain and anger. Writers such as Es'kia Mphahlele and the poets Lefifi Tladi and Nkwenkwe Nkomo influenced a later generation, including Njabulo Ndebele, Mongane Serote and Miriam Tlali, whose works of drama, poetry and fiction were inspired by Black Consciousness. In 1977, the organisations that formed the Black Consciousness movement were banned, and Steve Biko, its preeminent leader, was killed in detention. But by this time, Black Consciousness ideology had influenced the thinking of a generation of young black South Africans.

CONCLUSION

This chapter maps the contours of the social history of the first two decades of life under apartheid. Drawing on an established literature, the narrative of the 1950s tends to follow the stories of key moments, each with more or less radical male and female leaders, militant or cautious followers, ambivalent and tragic outcomes and stories that rely at least partly on the romance of a united and collective resistance that would serve the antiapartheid movement to the early 1990s. But this narrative is unsettled to some extent by the undercurrents of political wrangling and the vicissitudes of oppositional activity that surfaced throughout the 1950s. It is more substantially disrupted by tales of acquiescence and complicity, power and corruption in the 1960s. The binary between resistance and collaboration collapsed as old and new elites entered Bantustan bureaucracies, and separate institutions were established for the affairs of coloureds and Indians in the 1960s and 1970s.

As a synthesis of work produced largely in the apartheid era, this account of people's responses is necessarily incomplete and fragmentary, as there are vast gaps in our knowledge. We still know relatively little about the inner workings of the Bantustan administrations, about the elites that served them and about the daily lives of people who lived under them. We have only a tiny glimpse of how women and men understood marriage, coped with domestic violence and made sense of changing experiences of childhood and parenting in the Bantustans and in dormitory towns. Stories of everyday life in exile and in the political underground and of the interplay between individuals and political groups remain submerged under still dominant political narratives. Also largely submerged are the other daily life stories of how people sought to negotiate a tolerable existence inside the cracks of apartheid society, living and letting live both within and across the colour line. These issues will no doubt be taken up in different ways by a new generation of historians less encumbered by their own memories of apartheid, by fear of its consequences or by a desire to contribute to bringing about its demise.

FURTHER READING

General

Bonner, P., P. Delius and D. Posel (eds.), *Apartheid's genesis, 1935–1962*, Johannesburg: Ravan Press, 1993

Comaroff, J. *Body of power, spirit of resistance: the culture and history of a South African people*, Chicago: University of Chicago Press, 1985

Comaroff, Jean and John Comaroff, *Of revelation and revolution*, vol. 2, *The dialectics of modernity on a South African frontier*, Chicago: University of Chicago Press, 1997

Coplan, D., *In township tonight: South Africa's black city music and theatre*, London: Longman, 1985

Delius, P., *A lion amongst the cattle: reconstruction and resistance in the Northern Transvaal*, Portsmouth, NH: Heinemann, 1996

Elphick, R. and R. Davenport (eds.), *Christianity in South Africa: a political, social and cultural history*, Oxford: James Currey, 1997

Hofmeyr, I., *'We spend our years as a tale that is told': oral historical narrative in a South African chiefdom*, Portsmouth NH, Heinemann; London: James Currey; Johannesburg: Witwatersrand University Press, 1994

Hooper, C., *Brief authority*, London: Collins, 1960

Kynoch, G., *We are fighting the world: a history of the MaRashea gangs in South Africa, 1947–1999*, Athens: Ohio University Press, 2005

Longmore, L., *The dispossessed: a study of sex-life of Bantu women in urban areas in and around Johannesburg*, London: Cape, 1959

Mager, A. K., *Gender and the making of a South African Bantustan: a social history of the Ciskei, 1945–1959*, Portsmouth NH: Heinemann; Oxford: James Currey; Cape Town: David Philip, 1999

Mangena, M., *On your own: evolution of Black Consciousness in South Africa/Azania*, Johannesburg: Skotaville, 1989

Mare, G. and G. Hamilton, *An appetite for power: Buthelezi's Inkatha and the politics of 'loyal resistance'*, Johannesburg: Ravan Press, 1987

Marks, S., *Divided sisterhood: race, class and gender in the South African nursing profession*, Basingstoke, U.K.: Macmillan, 1994

Mayer, P. and I. Mayer, *Townsmen or tribesmen: conservatism and the process of urbanization in a South African city*, Cape Town: Oxford University Press, 1971

Maylam, P. and I. Edwards (eds.), *The people's city: African life in twentieth-century Durban*, Pietermaritzburg: University of Natal Press; Portsmouth, NH: Heinemann, 1996

Moodie, T. Dunbar, with Vivienne Ndatshe, *Going for gold: men, mines and migration*, Johannesburg: Witwatersrand University Press, 1994

Murray, C., *Black mountain: land, class and power in the eastern Orange Free State: 1880s–1980s*, Edinburgh: Edinburgh University Press, 1992

Pauw, B. A., *The second generation*, Cape Town: Oxford University Press, 1963

Pityana, B., M. Mpumlwana and L. Wilson (eds.), *Bounds of possibility: the legacy of Steve Biko and Black Consciousness*, Cape Town: David Philip, 1991

Reader, D. H., *The black man's portion*, Cape Town: Oxford University Press, 1961

Vail, L. (ed.), *The creation of tribalism in southern Africa*, London: James Currey, 1989

Van Onselen, C., *The seed is mine: the life of Kas Maine, a South African sharecropper, 1894–1985*, Cape Town: David Philip, 1996

Walker, C., *Women and resistance in South Africa*, London: Onyx Press, 1982

Biographies and Life Histories

Bozzoli, B. with Mmantho Nkotsoe, *Women of Phokeng: consciousness, life strategy, and migrancy in South Africa, 1900–1983*, Johannesburg: Ravan Press, 1991

Duka, N., *From shanty town to forest: life histories from the revolution, South Africa, ANC 1*, Richmond: LSM Information Centre, 1974

Jabavu, N., *The ochre people: scenes from a South African life*, London: John Murray, 1963

Keegan, T., *Facing the storm: portraits of black lives in rural South Africa*, Cape Town: David Philip, 1988

Kiloh, M. and A. Sibeko (Zola Zembe), *A fighting union: an oral history of the South African Railways and Harbour Workers' Union, 1936–1998*, Johannesburg: Ravan Press, 2000

Kuzwayo, E., *Call me woman*, Johannesburg: Ravan Press, 1996

Maimane A., *Hate no more*, Cape Town: Kwela Books, 2000

Modisane, Bloke, *Blame me on history*, Cape Town: Donker, 1986 (originally published 1963)

Moloi, Godfrey, *My life: the godfather of Soweto*, Johannesburg: Jonathan Ball, 1991

Mphahele, E., *Down Second Avenue*, London: Faber and Faber, 1959

Ndebele, J., 'I hid my love in a sewage', in Couzens and Patel (eds.), *The return of the Amasi bird*, pp. 213–14

Ntantala, P., *A life's mosaic*, Cape Town: David Philip and Mayibuye Centre, University of the Western Cape, 1988

Rive, Richard, *'Buckingham Palace', District Six*, Cape Town: David Philip, 1986

Sibeko, A. (Zola Zembe), with J. Leeson, *Freedom in our lifetime*, Durban: Indicator Press, 1996

Wieder, Alan, *Teacher and comrade: Richard Dudley and the fight for democracy in South Africa*, Albany: State University of New York Press, 2008

9

RESISTANCE AND REFORM, 1973–1994

TOM LODGE

Between 1973 and 1994, a succession of protests and rebellions transfigured South African political life. These eruptions assumed different forms and supplied different leaders and followers within different groups, but increasingly they converged strategically. Together, they embodied a challenge to authority without precedent in its scale, its resilience and in its depth of organisation. Early stages of this resistance engendered significant shifts in government policies. These policy shifts themselves in turn both facilitated and provoked fresh waves of revolt. Whilst opening up new opportunities for organised resistance, a combination of liberal reforms and militarised repression succeeded in containing or at least defining limits to popular insurgency. The relative success of these state policies helps to explain why the political settlement of 1994 left intact much of the structure of an extremely inequitable society.

This chapter focuses on two decades of rebellion between 1973 and 1994. Militant working-class strike action in 1973 incubated new efforts to construct labour organisation. Within a decade, South Africa's trade unions had significantly altered the balance of power between government and opposition. Meanwhile, the expansion of higher and secondary education created a new literate constituency for nationalist revival. The Black Consciousness Movement led this revival initially, but in 1976–1977, nationalist politics acquired a huge following in an insurrectionary movement animated by the preoccupations of a mutinous generation of schoolchildren.

State reforms responded to the revolts of the mid-1970s. Reformist public policy included efforts to institutionalise and, in so doing, to define the scope of industrial action and to expand the provision of education. The introduction of consociational political arrangements for Indians and coloureds as well as the reorganisation of local government for Africans living in the main cities prompted a second major insurrectionary revolt. This time leadership was embodied in the United Democratic Front (UDF), its top echelons including an imposing pantheon of political notables, including veterans associated with the African National Congress's (ANC) uMkhonto weSizwe. uMkhonto weSizwe itself provided a crucial focus of insurgency, as its campaign of armed propaganda helped to inspire the UDF's popular following and to engender an increasingly costly programme of counterinsurgency. By the end of the 1980s, however, the costs of conflict had become increasingly evident to leaders in government and to their opponents, whereas the end of the Cold War supplied new incentives for negotiation. In its conclusion, this chapter explores the processes that led to South Africa's constitutional settlement, the chronological point at which the present volume ends.

The ten years that followed the authorities' suppression of black organisations in the aftermath of Sharpeville represented a decade of sharp social changes. Partly as a consequence of a doubling of foreign direct investment between 1960 and 1972, through the 1960s, the South African economy grew by more than 5 per cent a year, much of that growth concentrated in manufacturing in which black, mainly African, employment rose by 75 per cent between 1958 and 1968. In industry, Africans increasingly undertook relatively skilled work, moving into the foundries and onto the assembly lines, a development acknowledged by the state's successive relaxations of job reservation and the efforts to direct new industry to border areas around the homelands. In the Durban textile industry, for example, 90 per cent of the workforce was African by 1973, with only 10 per cent being unskilled – nearly half were trained machine operators, factory clerks or needle setters.

Eleven million of 15 million Africans in 1970 lived in the homelands, to whose administrations all Africans, irrespective of their residence, were assigned as citizens in that year. But although the government halted the growth of the African share of the population within the official boundaries of the major cities, urbanisation was simply displaced to huge dormitory towns near the historical urban centres: KwaMashu outside Durban, Mdantsane near East London and Mabopane and Garankua, within daily commuting distance of Pretoria. In the centres, industrial workers lived in massive state housing schemes, hostels for single workers, and in houses for families from which, as sociologists noted at the time, they were increasingly likely to send their children to school and to use public services, however meagre.

Economic growth did not bring much prosperity to most black South Africans: their per capita income increased by only 23 per cent through the decade, a period in which inequality between blacks and whites became even more accentuated. However, the cultural changes that accompanied urbanisation and industrialisation – by 1968, 750,000 Africans were reading daily newspapers, and African radio ownership had doubled between

1966 and 1968 – encouraged new awareness of injustice and prepared a fresh constituency for revolt. Growth also expanded an African middle class – teachers, professionals, shopkeepers, civil servants, clerks and so forth: between 1960 and 1970, this group grew from 144,000 to 264,000 nationwide and trebled its size in Soweto.

THE WORKERS' REBELLION

In Durban, on 9 January 1973, several hours before daybreak, workers employed at the Coronation Brick and Tile Works arose early. They walked out of their compound quietly to gather at a nearby football stadium. Workers from other depots owned by the same firm arrived at intervals. By dawn, those present numbered two thousand. That day and the next they refused to go to work. In between their singing they chanted 'Usuthu', the old war cry from the Bambatha rebellion. When the managers arrived, they shouted their demand for more money to raise their minimum daily wage to more than double the present rate.

The Coronation strikers were back at work after two days. The Zulu king, Goodwill Zwelethini, visited the compound on 10 January and persuaded the strikers to bargain with management. One week later, the workers accepted their employer's offer of a 20 per cent increase to the minimum wage of R20.

This was the beginning of a strike movement that in the following two months would spread across Durban, affecting more than a quarter of the local African industrial workforce, drawing into its ranks more than sixty thousand workers. Each of the 160 or so strikes featured a common repertoire of activity: mass meetings on or near the factory premises; processions through the streets of the city; the collective presentation of demands to management and the refusal to appoint representatives; and the maintenance of a strong presence of strikers outside the factory gates for the duration of each protest.

After 10 January, following stoppages at a transport depot in the Durban docks and at a tea-packing firm, the strike movement accelerated, drawing in dozens of other enterprises during the subsequent two weeks. Two weeks later, six thousand workers stepped away from their machines at the Frame Textile Works in New Germany, and in the following few days, they were joined by others at all the other Frame factories in the city. Over February the rolling strike quickened its pace before slowing down in March. About 160 enterprises closed down for at least a day or two during the strikes, including engineering works, textile factories, transport firms, clothing factories and cement works. Most strikes lasted about three days each; a few were longer. Strikers won wage increases in 118 of the protests. The movement prompted similar actions by workers at an East London textile plant on 19 January and among Johannesburg's African bus drivers a week later.

The Durban strike movement represented the first really large-scale industrial rebellion since the 1946 African mine workers' strike. Fewer than ten thousand workers participated in strikes in any year during the 1950s, which up to the 1970s was the most sustained period of African labour unrest. In 1973, the strike ended in victory, not in defeat. It signalled a new consciousness and confidence among African workers.

What were the causes of this unprecedented event? African workers were affected by rising inflation – price hikes in basic foodstuffs were especially sharp in 1972, a reflection of deeper structural problems in the South African economy that were beginning to slow down its growth. In the first three years of the 1970s, food prices rose by 50 per cent. Increases in the cost of living may have affected Durban workers especially adversely. Although employment was still rising, it was not expanding quickly enough to absorb fresh entrants to the labour market. Contract workers with rural families would have had to share their wages with growing numbers of dependents and unemployment was especially severe in the KwaZulu homeland. Wages in the cotton factories in Natal were also especially poor because new enterprises there had tried to undercut their competitors elsewhere. Textile workers were also relatively skilled: difficult to replace quickly with scab labour. Durban was a comparatively new centre of the textile industry, and its workforce was comparatively young. Friedman suggests that in Durban pass laws may have worked to the advantage of the local workforce: the periurban townships where many of the workers lived were in fact within the KwaZulu homeland, and these were therefore people without permanent city (Section 10) rights, yet who lived within easy commuting distance of the factories.

The strike was not the outcome of systematic organisation – even the police conceded that they could find no evidence of 'agitators'. On the other hand, the first strikers may have been influenced by the activities of a University of Natal National Union of Students Wages Commission, which distributed its newsletters outside compounds through 1972. White students from the commission joined the Frame textile workers' march. In 1972, the Wage Board had investigated brick workers' wages and King Goodwill Zwelethini had spoken about the board's activities when visiting Coronation late that year: in January, the workers may have been expecting an increase. It is conceivable that workers may also have been inspired by a successful strike by Ovambo contract labour in Namibia at the end of 1971, though this was not mentioned by participants who spoke to researchers in the wake of the strike. Surveys conducted in 1976 revealed the existence of an informal leadership grouping in Durban factories with previous experience of organisational repression, which included some who had once been members of ANC-aligned affiliates of the South African Congress of Trade Unions.[1] More recent research confirms that former SACTU organisers emerging from prison began to reconstruct a clandestine organisation in Durban in 1972.[2]

The strike's spread was facilitated by the geographical concentration of the movement, but the attentive treatment it received in newspapers may also have helped, as Durban's English-language press probably had around fifty thousand African readers. Police restraint also encouraged the strikers; indeed, some white police officers demonstrated evident sympathy, an attitude that was quite widespread across Durban's white communities. The strike both consolidated and reflected a perception among workers that in acting collectively they could exploit their power. As the strike progressed, this certainty would have proliferated, but even before then, surveys among Durban workers demonstrated the presence by 1971 of a significant militant minority predisposed to engage in collective action.

Such propensities were a consequence of the increasingly significant contribution of African workers to the manufacturing economy as semiskilled workers, a development that began in the mid-1950s and accelerated through the following decade as ownership and production became increasingly centralised. Although the overall size of the manufacturing sector nearly doubled, the proportion of black workers in it increased from 70 per cent in 1960 to 80 per cent in 1970. In the following decade, from 1970 to 1980, Africans in manufacturing would more than double, from 308,000 to 780,000. By 1970, half of South Africa's exports were manufactures. Skill shortages prompted the first official erosion of job reservation in 1972: Africans began to be employed as train marshallers (or shunters) that year and also entered the lowest grade of previously reserved occupations in the steel and engineering industry. As the Afrikaner share of business ownership increased, policy makers became more receptive to the pragmatic objections to industrial apartheid. The strikers and more generally the labour organisations that began to be constructed in the wake of their pioneering insurgency both benefitted from a more receptive political climate, a reflection of broader socioeconomic changes. After the international abandonment of a fixed gold price in 1972, South Africa could well afford

---

[1] Eddie Webster, 'A profile of unregistered trade unions in Durban', *South African Labour Bulletin* 4:8 (January–February 1979), p. 5.
[2] Jabulani Sithole and Sifiso Ndlovu, 'The revival of the labour movement,' in South African Democracy Education Trust, *The road to democracy in South Africa*, pp. 214–20.

wage rises. Moreover as wages and the African manufacturing workforce rose, African consumers constituted an increasingly important market for local factories. The 'lesson' of the Durban strikes, the Prime Minister noted, was that employers should begin to view their workers 'as human beings with souls'. In effect, narrowing the racial wage gap was then official policy. As we have seen, police had held back from arresting strikers, a surprising instance of restraint that was probably officially sanctioned – this was in sharp contrast to the treatment meted out to demonstrating mine workers near Johannesburg, twelve of whom were killed in a confrontation with police in September 1973.

In most sectors, though, in the aftermath of the strikes, initially employers remained deeply opposed to African trade unions. A new labour law established liaison committees that would represent workers and employers in each enterprise and that would make recommendations about working conditions. Within three years, more than three thousand such committees were in existence, providing to thousands of workers important leadership experience at the shop-floor level. In the absence of such liaison committees, workers could elect their own works committees to negotiate with employers. In a very limited technical way, the government also relaxed legal restrictions on African strikes.

Both employers' and official attitudes to black trade unionism would shift sharply in the subsequent six years, though. The shift would be a consequence of two developments. One was the relative success of trade union organisation itself in capturing the allegiance of African workers, and the other was the expansion of external political pressure on the local affiliates of multinational corporations. Against a background of continuing strikes, legally unrecognised African trade unions began to proliferate: there were about twenty-five in existence in 1975, with a membership of seventy-five thousand, most of them established in the previous three years, and expanding despite a succession of banning orders imposed on their organisers. In an accompanying development, the Trades Union Congress of South Africa (TUCSA) sponsored a group of 'parallel' and comparatively unassertive African unions. The small Black Allied Workers' Union (BAWU), an outpost of the Black Consciousness Movement, was 'organised on a communal rather than a factory basis' and, from its inception in 1972, was subjected to fierce repression by the authorities. Meanwhile, from 1970, the Johannesburg-based Urban Training Project (UTP) began working with relatively amenable employers (mainly in the retail sector) to form factory-based trade unions that would be initially characterised by professionalised leadership and an emphasis on benefit functions, all the while eschewing worker militancy. The UTP would benefit from foreign funding, principally from the International Confederation of Free Trade

Unions and the British Trades Union Congress (TUC), both sponsors that discouraged any political affiliation. The ten unions it helped to create were organisationally robust, though, and the UTP's training workshops helped to instil a strong predisposition among rank-and-file workers to hold their leaders accountable. Meanwhile, the Trade Union Advisory and Coordinating Council (TUACC) in Natal and the Council of Industrial Workers in the Transvaal began building factory organisation by encouraging workers to achieve recognition from managers through their own mobilisation – using strikes if necessary – under the leadership of council-trained shop stewards. Both the UTP and the TUACC differed from the BAWU as well as from the earlier generations of black trade unions by their eschewal of formal links with political organizations and their stress on piecemeal factory-by-factory organisation; this was a reflection of the fact that by the 1970s African workers predominated on the assembly lines in many enterprises. The South African Textile Workers Industrial Union secured the first recognition agreement obtained through this approach with a British-owned firm in Durban in 1974. This organisation, as with others in the TUACC-sponsored grouping, featured former members of the National Union of South African Students-Students' Representative Council (NUSAS-SRC) Wages Commission in its early leadership, and white ex–university student activists continued to make a conspicuous contribution to the leadership of the 'unregistered' trade union movement through the rest of the decade and even thereafter.

Tactical differences between this generation of trade union leaders would subsequently develop into ideological fissures, especially over the issue of political affiliation, but such disagreements may have been less important among rank-and-file members as well as those working at the shop-steward level. Petrus Tom, a key middle-level leader during the 1980s in the Metal and Allied Workers Union (MAWU), one of the bodies that emerged in the TUACC grouping, joined both ANC- and Pan-Africanist Congress–linked trade unions in Vereeniging during the 1950s. He organised on behalf of a TUCSA parallel body in 1970. In 1974, he was elected to his works' Liaison Committee. From 1974, Tom was active as an organiser on behalf of the Urban Training Project, before joining MAWU. His case illuminates the complicated genealogy of the new South African trade union movement. Local leadership of the new unions quite often included an older generation of ex–SACTU militants such as Petrus Tom. His consequent moral stature among workers prompted his election to the official liaison committee: in his factory, rather than deflecting the impetus to build a trade union organisation, as was the official intention, the existence of the liaison committee facilitated the organisation of a union branch after his election.

THE SCHOOLCHILDREN'S MOVEMENT

In mid-1976, factory-based protest would be eclipsed by a quite different rebellion, one in which the participants would represent a much more direct challenge to the state's authority. On 16 June 1976, a protest march by schoolchildren would open what would become South Africa's most massive insurrectionary movement to that date. Its scale and intensity were the consequences of profound cultural changes experienced by black South Africans in the previous ten years.

These changes affected urban people most sharply. By 1970, African town dwellers were increasingly likely to have been urban born: surveys and census statistics indicate that adult Africans who had lived in Johannesburg for thirty years represented 60 per cent of the local population in 1967, twice the proportion of five years earlier. City and rural dwellers were much more likely to be literate than a decade previously – two-thirds of African adult city dwellers could read in 1970. More and more African children were attending high school: in Soweto in 1975, three of every four households accommodated secondary schoolchildren. As Craig Charney notes, increasingly literacy and high school enrolment were becoming normal among working-class people, in contrast to the 1950s, when among Africans these attributes were confined to a social elite. Overall, African school enrolment expanded from 1.5 million in 1960 to 3.7 million in 1970. Working-class Africans were increasingly newspaper readers, more than 1.1 million in 1975: that year in Soweto, three of four adult male residents read a daily newspaper, mostly favouring the tabloid *World*, which enjoyed a sixfold increase in readership between 1962 and 1975. With government replacing churches as the chief agency of African education, the geographic location of the African elite shifted from the Eastern Cape to the Transvaal. As the town-born generation grew and became educated, African membership of mainstream Christian churches expanded rapidly: for the Anglicans, Catholics and Methodists, African congregations began to outnumber whites, and African ministers began to move up the church hierarchies. A leisure industry emerged in the 1960s directed at black working-class consumers, focused on football, foreign derived rock and local *mbaqanga* music, and theatre, and helping to fashion new identities and values that were distinctively different from older and more discrete forms.

These changes ensured that political activity would evoke a much wider popular response than hitherto. Fieldwork among urbanised Africans conducted by Philip Mayer in 1971 uncovered evidence of a new pride and a fresh social confidence, his informants telling him that they 'were made of strong stuff', that they were people who were 'surviving under the worst suppression'. One respondent claimed he had 'proved my black power, which is in fact internal'. Another noted, 'I do not feel inferior whatever insults I am confronted with. I am keeping my black pride and don't react with violence'. Such sentiments contrast very sharply with the 'cultural shame' discernable to Mayer a generation earlier, when middle-class Soweto residents often appeared to believe that 'Europeans' were 'superior to us in all fields' and 'close imitation' of 'the Western style' was required 'for us to become truly civilised'. In a context in which people lacked confidence, politics had been through much of the 1960s dominated by the vertical relations of patronage, in which 'big men' supplied protection and benefits in return for support. In such circumstances, clientelism could supply a surprisingly substantial popular base for homeland centred political organisations. By the early 1970s, though, in the wider public domain created by literacy and urbanity, there was room for a different kind of politics in which ideology and camaraderie would, to an extent, replace deferential personalised loyalties directed at patrimonial leaders.

It is this setting that helps us to understand the expanding influence of the Black Consciousness Movement after its foundation as the South African Students Organisation (SASO) in 1969. To be sure, Black Consciousness remained organisationally frail with very restricted formal membership. The Black People's Convention established in 1972 could muster a modest forty-two branches a couple of years later, whereas SASO's newsletter circulated among four thousand subscribers. To become a social movement, though, Black Consciousness did not need legions of disciplined activists. Teachers, priests and journalists spread its messages. These were the graduates from the universities, colleges and seminaries in which the movement incubated. Seminaries were especially important, and the twenty local chapters of the University Christian Movement with three thousand members, mainly black by 1968, were probably the most influential agencies of Black Consciousness (BC) during the early 1970s.

For this new community, 'blackness' was a state of being that represented the reversion of oppression. Being black was not narrowly a matter of race; indeed, the new movement's founders were self-conscious in their refusal to accept any assumptions about the innate characteristics attributed to race. All the oppressed groups – Africans, Indians, coloured – could become black. Becoming black was a process that involved creating a new identity, an identity that might draw on older precolonial memories – though few BC thinkers showed much interest in history – but that would mainly be the product of challenges to, and inversions of, the dominant white values and norms in an oppressive society. To a degree, BC writers drew on *negritude* sources of inspiration – Leopold Senghor and Aime Cesaire, particularly. Julius Nyerere's Ujamaa principles supplied another source of

textual authority, especially in the BC efforts to establish producer cooperatives. But it was the American Black Power movement that impressed
most deeply, particularly in its emphasis on the need for a separatist black
politics, isolated from the enervating influences of white liberals. For Steve
Biko and other principals in the movement, mass activism would be the
outcome of a systematic process of cultural transformation, a shift in consciousness. This could be promoted by organisations that attempted to alter
the beliefs that structured ordinary day-to-day life through cultural activity, welfare and educational projects. South African Black Consciousness
writers borrowed most freely from their American contemporaries. Stokely
Carmichael's dictum 'before a group can enter the open society it must first
close ranks' was almost replicated in the SASO manifesto declaration that
before 'black people should join the open society, they should close ranks'.[3]

By 1972, Black Consciousness organisation began to embrace schoolchildren. The first branches of an African Students Movement grew out of
youth clubs at three schools in Orlando and Diepkloof in 1968. As with
SASO, the University Christian Movement was a key agency in the establishment of the new organisation. In 1972, a name change to the South
African Students Movement (SASM) signalled its embrace of Black Consciousness. Acknowledged as part of the BC family by the annual *Black
Review*, SASM branches began to proliferate beyond Soweto drawing on
the resources and networks of allied formations. The SASM's programmes
regularly featured speakers from the wider movement, and as with the older
organisations, its activities emphasised leadership training, the fostering
of a politically advanced intelligentsia. In contrast to SASO and Black
Peoples Congress, though, from 1974, certain SASM groups also began
organising in a conspiratorial cellular fashion, prompted to do so by ANC
'elders', former activists from the 1950s and ex–Robben Island prisoners.
In 1976, a trial in King Williamstown brought together SASM members
with an ex-prisoner, accused of inciting and encouraging each other to
undergo military training. Within the Soweto leadership there was a group
self-consciously aligned with the ANC as well as people who maintained a
Black Consciousness adherency. In Soweto, SASM networks also overlapped
with a reviving Pan-Africanist Congress (PAC) underground. Despite such
confluences external groups were unable to exercise direct influence over
SASM decision making. By then, SASM was well established across the
schools of the Eastern Cape and also enjoyed a following in the smaller
towns of the Free State and the Transvaal as well as in the main centres. As
Black Consciousness ideas percolated downward, they lost much of their

---

[3] Themba Sono, *Reflections on the origins of Black Consciousness in South Africa* (Pretoria:
Human Sciences Research Council, 1993), p. 103.

subtlety. Although the movement's leaders were careful to avoid racist phraseology, their teenage followers were less fastidious, as exemplified by the 1976 Soweto students who described their clenched-fist salute as crushing whites in their palms. Encouraging such self-confidence were external events that suggested a new vulnerability in authority. The black press reported extensively on South Africa's military reversals in Angola after the failure to prevent the entrenchment of a Soviet-backed *Movimento Popular de Libertação de Angola* (MPLA) in Luanda, asking its readers rhetorically if they would fight for South Africa in the event of an invasion from Angola. In Soweto in 1975, Philip Mayer's informants during his anthropological fieldwork expressed a generalised belief that affairs were turning in their favour, as Frelimo's achievement in Mozambique implied that theirs could not be far behind.

Deteriorating classroom conditions facilitated the spread of political organisation among teenagers. African secondary school enrolment nearly trebled between 1970 and 1975, from 122,489 to 318,568, a rate of increase that was mainly a consequence of children staying in school longer. This growth resulted in an expansion of class sizes, particularly in urban secondary schools and especially in Soweto. The African teaching workforce also expanded in this period, but only by about 75 per cent. Administrative changes in the educational system, notably the lowering of the entry threshold into secondary school and the abandonment of the primary school standard-six class, ensured that junior secondary school classes were very congested indeed: in January 1976, 257,505 children registered in form 1, for which normally there was only provision for 38,000 pupils: increasingly demoralised teachers had to take the classes in shifts. To add to their difficulties, that year a new Deputy Minister of Education, Dr Andries Treurnicht, a hardline apartheid ideologue, began implementing what had been official policy since 1956: the use of Afrikaans for maths and social studies, geography and history. Treurnicht's appointment was a gamble for the National Party leaders, who hoped that his accession to office might placate the mutinous *verkrampte* party faction that he headed.

Initial resistance to the measure came from elected school boards, two of whose members were dismissed in February. That month, an Afrikaans teacher was stabbed in Pimville, and a crowd stoned police attempting to arrest the youth they suspected as the culprit. In March 1976, schoolchildren began boycotting classes in which Afrikaans was in use in several Soweto schools. In April, SASM branches began to adopt the boycott; by mid-May, 1,600 students were boycotting classes. On 8 June, two police officers attempted to arrest the SASM secretary at his school, but they were beaten off.

The students' protest was received with considerable sympathy outside school – after all, it was initially the parents' boards that had first protested against the measure. In any case, parents and adults in Soweto had their own reasons for anger. From 1968, no additional thirty-year leasehold family housing was built and a more general slowdown in housing construction in the main urban centres (in favour of building housing in towns located in homelands) caused acute overcrowding: housing waiting lists in Soweto doubled between 1973 and 1976. In 1973, the assumption of control over township administration by twenty-two central government–controlled administration boards resulted in the loss of municipal cross subsidies – historically quite substantial in the case of Johannesburg – and in additional costs for residents, higher rents and 'lodgers fees' for adult nonfamily members living in family housing. As the boards spent less on street lighting and road maintenance, even customarily compliant Urban Bantu Councillors spoke in public about the general deterioration in services. Discontent arising from the deterioration in local government was accentuated by economic hardship; in Soweto in 1975, the cost of living rose by 10 per cent and unemployment doubled in the same year.

Resentment arising from such conditions may not have engendered rebellion, though, had not the schoolchildren taken the initiative. On 13 June 1976, representatives of several high school SASM branches formed the Soweto Students Representative Council (SSRC). The SSRC immediately began planning a demonstration against the enforcement of instruction in Afrikaans. On 16 June, fifteen thousand children began marching toward Orlando West Junior School, the epicentre of the rebellion, where the headmaster himself had rejected the directive to teach in Afrikaans. A hastily summoned police detachment failed to disperse the marchers with tear gas and fired into the procession, killing two. The children retreated and dispersed. By midday, much of Soweto was in a state of insurrection. In different districts, youths erected barricades, stoned cars, burned down official buildings and killed two white men. The rioting intensified when police baton-charged homecoming crowds of commuters. As the Truth and Reconciliation Commission would note twenty years later, police 'lack of capacity was reflected in their tendency to use maximum force'.[4] This predisposition was given formal cabinet sanction subsequently when ministers agreed that, to break the schoolchildren's movement, even harsher action was required, with deadly consequences.

In the following week, the revolt spread, animating pupils in Krugersdorp, Thembisa, the East Rand and Pretoria and evoking demonstrations

---

[4] Truth and Reconciliation Commission of South Africa, *Report*, vol. 2 (Cape Town: Juta, 1998), p. 175.

of sympathy on several university campuses. Minister Treurnicht closed down the schools on 18 June, and before reopening them on 26 July, the authorities rescinded the Afrikaans-teaching edict. During this interval, the first ANC leaflets appeared and a group of Soweto notables, including Winnie Mandela, formed the Black Parents' Association (BPA). Until its members were detained, the BPA played a significant auxiliary role in the rebellion, arranging legal help, medical treatment and funerals, but leadership remained in the hands of the SSRC. Acknowledging that the schools' closure had divorced the SSRC from its constituency, SSRC leaders announced that children should return to school. In the week following 26 July, arsonists damaged fifty schools in the Transvaal. On 2 August, police raided the schools in search of SSRC leaders. Once again, the schools emptied, and this time the children would stay out for the rest of the year.

Communicating with their following through leaflets, word of mouth, and – crucially – through sympathetic reportage in the black press, the SSRC leaders presided over a second, broader phase of revolt. The Council's call for a stay-at-home by Johannesburg's workers on 4 August achieved a 60 per cent abstention, partly attributable to coercive picketing at transport terminals. On that same day, police gunfire halted a student march on the Johannesburg police headquarters: three teenagers were left dead. On 5 August, similar cycles of student protest and violent police retribution in Cape Town, Port Elizabeth and East London transformed the protest into a national rebellion. The SSRC called two further stay-at-homes during August and September. The first of these, on 23 August, featured clashes between students and the migrant worker residents of Mzimhlope hostel, the latter incited by the police but motivated primarily by resentment of the behaviour of teenage picketers. A more conciliatory approach by SSRC leaders the following month ensured the hostel workers' full participation in the third stay-away, on 13–15 September.

A third and more introspective phase of the rebellion in the latter months of the year was constituted by SSRC-led campaigns against shebeens, alcohol purchases and Christmas celebrations. During October, an urban guerrilla group exploded homemade devices at Jabulani police station and the Pelikan Nite Club (whose proprietor was ignoring the SSRC's ban on alcohol). Through much of early 1977, the SSRC continued to disrupt classes on a major scale. Two hundred thousand pupils were still boycotting schools in September 1977, and nearly five hundred teachers in just Soweto were reported to have resigned. By the closing months of the year, though the rebellion was receding, leaving in its wake at least 575 dead and 2,389 wounded, mainly from police shooting. During the revolt, the police arrested nearly six thousand suspected participants. Demographic analysis of the casualty statistics suggests that participation in the rebellion expanded swiftly, drawing in especially unemployed school leavers in their early twenties.

In 1977, protests and violence spread to many smaller towns, affecting two hundred locations – almost every significant concentration of the African population outside Natal. School protests did occur there, especially around Durban through July to September, but on the whole, events were small scale and more dispersed than elsewhere. Historians have yet to provide a completely persuasive explanation for the region's relative quiescence. In Natal, SASM never succeeded in establishing branches, partly, its leaders suggested, because of the presence in many schools of the Inkatha Youth Brigade. Yet the Brigade was set up only in 1976, and it apparently failed to develop a strong presence in schools. Nonetheless, the Brigade may still have attracted potential classroom leaders at that time. Modelled on Malawi's Young Pioneers, it employed modishly radical rhetoric, and certain of its leaders were ready at this early stage to express criticism of what they called Chief Buthelezi's collaborative and reactionary tendencies. Chief Buthelezi himself did claim credit for Inkatha in keeping unrest out of KwaZulu schools, as by 1977, it had established about a hundred branches in townships around Durban and Pietermaritzburg. Police restraint may also have been a factor in restricting rebellion in Natal. Police reacted to the schoolchildren's demonstrations in Durban more calmly than elsewhere, largely holding their fire. Furthermore, most African schools in Natal were not subjected to the Afrikaans ruling because they were administered through the KwaZulu homeland administration, an exemption that was decisive in keeping them out of the first stages of the revolt. Another consideration in curtailing the scope of protest was that the number of secondary students and their proportional significance were much smaller than in the Eastern Cape and in the Transvaal. A final standard explanation is that parents enjoyed more authority with their children in Natal than elsewhere because the political stature of elders was much higher as a consequence of the strike movement. This seems unlikely, but it is true that patrimonial politics was to succeed in reinforcing elder authority to a considerably greater degree in Natal than elsewhere in the following two decades.

Continuing assertion and strengthening awareness of their generational identity by so-called youth leadership was one important consequence of the revolt. During the rebellion, youngsters often spoke contemptuously about the political predispositions of their elders. A speech made in Cape Town to a parents' meeting is illustrative:

I want to say something to our parents. I must tell you the reasons we did not want to involve you. First of all you want to be leaders. You like to [be] Mrs So-and-so, Chairman of this or Head of that. We don't have leaders. Secondly you are liars.

You rather say something is fine than open your mouths to complain. Thirdly you are cowards.[5]

The revolt accelerated the erosion of elder authority, a process that was a consequence of teenagers often becoming better educated than their parents and an effect of their growing up in a more urbanised cultural context in which patriarchal forms of socialisation no longer functioned effectively. Eyewitness testimony suggests that the effect of the revolt itself made the shift in attitudes to authority much more obvious:

Before '76 most school-going children were controlled. OK, even if they had drinking sessions, or whatever, they did try and hide it from their parents. '76 brought a new breed of school going kids. You find that now immediately after '76 children would not be bothered being seen in their school uniforms in shebeens. They were more open and defiant and more politically aware than the pre-76 era.[6]

About seven thousand teenagers and young men and women left their homes to cross South Africa's borders as refugees, many of them to join the exile community maintained by the African National Congress, in the process substantially rejuvenating its following.

Shifts in political attitudes that resulted from the rebellion affected older generations as well. Opinion polls indicated sharply increasing levels of impatience among black South Africans, as well as more generalised optimism that political freedom would be achieved in their own lifetimes, whereas among whites, they recorded growing propensities in favour of black enfranchisement and the removing of job reservation, as well as restrictions on interracial marriages. Shifts in white morale were also evident in a doubling of the rate of emigration and in capital outflows between 1976 and 1979, although both trends were reversed in a short economic revival at the end of the decade. Increases in white emigration were partly prompted by the doubling of the period of military national service, from one to two years, introduced in 1977. By the beginning of 1978, budget allocations for defence expenditure were nearly three times their level in 1975.

There were other indications that government shared more generalised perceptions of a system in crisis. These were signalled in a series of reformist measures, including the appointment in 1977 of the Wiehahn Commission to address labour relations. In 1979, Professor Wiehahn reported, recommending the legal recognition and registration of black trade unions, as well as the abolition of statutory job reservation. Meanwhile, the Riekert

---

[5] Carol Herder, *The diary of Maria Tholo* (Johannesburg: Ravan Press, 1980), p. 85.

[6] Jeremy Seekings, *Heroes and villains: youth politics in the 1980s* (Johannesburg: Ravan Press, 1993), pp. 30–1.

Commission explored ways of modifying the influx control system, ultimately to recommend a more efficient exclusion of rural migrants from
urban labour markets while enhancing the rights of 'Section 10' Africans as
permanent urbanites. In 1978, as a transitional measure in anticipation of
the Riekert proposals, the government introduced ninety-nine-year leasehold for African householders in the major cities. With the accession of
P. W. Botha to the premiership in 1978, a shift in government leadership
reflected a deeper realignment of power and influence in the state, especially
in favour of the military establishment over which Botha had presided as
Minister of Defence from 1966.

Meanwhile, the social dynamics that had helped to cause the rebellion
in 1976 became more powerful. Between 1975 and 1980, the number of
African schoolchildren completing their secondary education trebled, an
achievement that was repeated by 1984, a rate of matriculation that generated a ballooning of the numbers of relatively well-educated unemployed
school leavers. Against this background, a fresh generation of African, and
more generally black, notables began to accumulate national influence as
political leaders. Both the Black Parents' Association and the (Soweto)
Committee of Ten, with their overlapping membership, signalled the
reassertion of political claims by the middle-class professional elite who
had predominated politically among Africans until the ANC's suppression.
The Committee of Ten was established in reaction to the resignation in mid-
1977 of the Urban Bantu Council after the SSRC organised a succession of
angry meetings to protest against rent increases imposed by the West Rand
Administration Board. At the behest of the Soweto branch of the Black
People's Convention, a meeting was held in June at the offices of the *World*
to elect a popularly responsive civic organisation. The Committee was led
by Dr Ntatho Motlana, once a keen ANC Youth League organiser. For its
other members, the Committee drew on ex-SASO adherents, the Black
Parents' Association and the Teachers' Action Committee. It drew up an
ambitious blueprint for a fully empowered local authority in a new Soweto,
where economic prosperity would partly be the consequence of freehold
land ownership. Such proposals were hardly radical in their implications,
and indeed, the posture that Committee leaders would adopt as 'apostles of
the people' could be frankly elitist. Motlana informed journalists that the
task of leaders was to guide and lead the broad mass of labourers, to move
ahead of their thinking and not just to reflect it.

In 1977, though, the authorities viewed any independent black political
leadership as threatening. The Committee was detained, and the government closed down the *World* and prohibited the seventeen main Black
Consciousness organisations. In September, a month before this crackdown,
security police arrested and fatally assaulted Steve Biko. Biko had just

succeeded in restoring a unified sense of purpose among Black Conscious-ness Movement (BCM) factions that had become divided ideologically. From early 1976, BCM adherents had disagreed with one another about the merits of a new approach proposed by the SASO president, Diliza Mji. He had suggested in an address at SASO's General Student Council that the movement needed to look at its struggle not only in terms of colour but also in terms of class, as apartheid was part of a larger exploitative capitalist system.

Biko's death and the wider government repression that followed it, together with widening philosophical rifts in Black Consciousness, created fresh space for new leaders and different organizations. That the authorities would, in the years that followed the 1977 bans, permit the revival of black political assertion needs more analysis than historians of this era have yet undertaken. Although P. W. Botha's administration is often depicted as exceptionally repressive, in contrast to its predecessors, it was also relatively tolerant of even heavily politicised associational life. There were very few bannings after 1978, individual or organisational. As Nadine Gordimer noted in 1980, a new setting had been created as a consequence of an official politics that combined 'brutality with tolerance'.[7] Certainly, in response to insurrection the government would employ coercion and terror on a scale historically unmatched. Yet simultaneously, it would relax traditional political restraints.

Liberalisation was first of all a pragmatic response to new conditions. Curtailing black organisation, especially after the growth of factory-based trade unionism, would have been a much more ambitious project than the organisational suppression of the early 1960s represented. Second, strategic doctrines proposed by the military emphasised the need for the authorities to win ideological battles: soldiers told cabinet members repeatedly that they would have to find a basis on which all of South Africa's inhabitants would feel involved and part of the country. By itself, repression was insuf-ficient, and in any case would have required high levels of investment to reimpose the disciplined public order of the 1960s. Moreover, as we will see, for even the limited reforms that the Botha administration hoped would extend regime support beyond white South Africans to work, a more open political environment was needed. It is also possible that, in contrast to ear-lier governments, Botha's colleagues were less absolutely morally certain; by the late 1970s, Afrikaner intellectuals were becoming openly critical of apartheid and dissent was growing in the Dutch Reformed Church (DRC) hierarchy as well. Finally, the government's willingness toward the end of

---

[7] Ronald Suresh Roberts, *No cold kitchen: a biography of Nadine Gordimer* (Johannesburg: STE Publishers, 2006).

the 1970s to at least consider the option of according trade union rights
to black workers, in the hope of channelling black militancy into an institutionalised system of labour relations, may have represented the first step
in a more discriminating and subtle strategic alternation of repression and
reform. Significantly, no trade unions, not even the Black Consciousness–
aligned Black Allied Workers' Union, were prohibited in October
1977.

Thus, the standard-bearer of Black Consciousness, the Azanian People's
Organization (AZAPO), however impeded by the detention of office bearers, remained unbanned. Within the following six years, though, Black
Consciousness as a social movement would be eclipsed in another way.
Increasingly, personalities and associations signalling their commitment to
the historical 'Charterism' associated with memories of the ANC's achievements in the 1950s would shape popular political behaviour. There were
several reasons for this shift. It is possible that the ANC's association with
a liberal, nonracial tradition in antiapartheid politics may have resonated
with values of older generations that, even after the Soweto uprising, continued in public opinion polls to support a shared political future that would
involve a compromise with white interests. Despite its radicalisation in
exile, the ANC's historical association with a racially conciliatory political
tradition probably helped it to remain a beneficiary of such public predispositions. Conversely, the reappearance of the ANC as an active agency
in South African internal politics also reflected its success in recruiting
refugees from the exodus during the uprising and its resumption in 1977
of urban guerrilla warfare. Prison contacts between the older generation
of ANC leaders and Black Consciousness Movement activists imprisoned
between 1975 and 1977 after convictions under the Terrorism Act also
helped to extend the older organisation's influence, for on Robben Island,
especially the newer inmates encountered a well-organised and receptive
ANC convict community. Meanwhile, the new legal domains of organisational activity, in the community, in the workplace and in the classroom
each encouraged for different reasons a restoration of the ANC's moral
authority. Externally derived resources on an unprecedented scale helped to
expand the scope of these activities.

THE ANC'S INTERNAL RECONSTRUCTION

The ANC's revival of its organisation inside South Africa began several
years before the Soweto uprising. In May 1971, the ANC Revolutionary
Council's meeting in Lusaka reviewed a report on 'internal reconstruction'
in the Cape Province. In the Transkei, in Pondoland and in Matatiele
near the Lesotho border, the ANC's 'main contacts' had by the end of the

previous year indicated 'that they [were] ready to receive men'. In or around Cape Town, 'we have three contacts who are working independently of each other', but conditions were inauspicious for infiltrating trained cadres into Cape Town because 'the locations' (i.e., the townships) were 'under constant surveillance'. In the Eastern Cape, 'we have not managed to have solid contacts in the area. We are still trying to be in contact with it'. The political climate in the Eastern Cape was favourable for establishing such contacts, the report's author reasoned. One such promising indication was 'growing unrest in secondary and high schools caused by increasing fascist repression'. The report then referred to a list of prestigious Eastern Cape African boarding schools. 'This youth' at these institutions and elsewhere, the report predicted, 'will be the backbone of the armed struggle, hence they deserve constant guidance and attention.'[8]

This sort of evidence confirms that, by the turn of the decade, the ANC's clandestine networks inside South Africa were very rudimentary. The report cited here suggests that the Transkei was the region in which the ANC's organisation was relatively advanced in comparison to elsewhere, but even there, clandestine activism was still very limited. To strategists, consolidating the organisation's Transkeian networks made good sense. At this stage, the ANC's strategic predispositions were still heavily influenced by Cuban *foco* theory, in which externally infiltrated rural guerrilla insurgencies create the political conditions essential for the popular revolutionary mobilisation and the all-out war that will eventually result in the conquest of power. The ANC's 'Strategy and Tactics' adopted at its meeting in Morogoro in 1969 foresaw 'that the main physical environment of such a struggle in the initial period' would be 'outside the enemy strongholds in the cities, in the vast stretches of the countryside'. In truth, since the suppression of the movement in the early 1960s, the ANC's strongest areas of active support remained in the cities. Of particular note was a group in which Winnie Mandela played a leading role, assembling a clandestine cellular organisation in Soweto that recruited more than a hundred mostly young members and that set up corresponding groups in Alexandra, the East Rand, Port Elizabeth, King Williamstown and Umtata. Most of the key figures involved had been arrested in 1969, as police had monitored Mandela's activities from the inception of the conspiracy. Significantly, the Soweto network had no contact with any of the propagandists who were sent from London by the SACP into the country during this period. The 1969 arrests mostly immobilised the ANC revival that Winnie Mandela had attempted

[8] African National Congress, *Internal reconstruction, Document 1, Report on the Cape, May 1971*, documents submitted to the Revolutionary Council Meeting in Lusaka, July 1971, Oliver Tambo Papers, File B8, 7.3.25.3, University of Fort Hare.

to foster, but ex-prisoners were active in the early 1970s in reestablishing ANC groups elsewhere and in making contact with younger people: for example, middle-aged 'stalwarts' in Natal inspired members of the Kwa Mashu Youth Organisation to constitute themselves as 'an underground unit of the ANC that would undertake propaganda activity'. Meanwhile, in southwestern Natal, Johannes Phungula, an ANC rural organiser from the 1950s, established an ANC network among labour tenants.

In 1974, Chris Hani, a veteran of the ANC's Rhodesian guerrilla campaigning, arrived in Lesotho, where he was to remain for the following seven years. He visited South Africa on several occasions from 1974 onward to establish arrangements for military recruitment in the main centres in the Eastern Cape. In 1975, ANC officials in Swaziland began meeting visiting SASO organisers, and in that year, its Swazi-based recruiting operations began despatching prospective trainees to the Soviet Union. Two of them, Mosima 'Tokyo' Sexwale and Naledi Tsiki, had returned to Soweto in the second half of 1976, in time to conduct weapons-handling demonstrations with members of the SSRC. Sexwale's and Tsiki's first political experiences had been as SASM members, and their recruitment by Joe Gqabi in early 1976 represented a crucial moment in the ANC's reestablishment of its political authority among younger dissidents. Meanwhile, the Robben Island veteran Joe Gqabi and Elliot Shabangu, a former member of Winnie Mandela's group, established an ANC cell among members of the SSRC with the objective of exercising a degree of restraint over the students.

The ANC's efforts to influence the revolt were sporadic, reflecting the organization's limited presence. It may have made some impact in its cosponsorship with the SSRC of a stay-at-home strike on 23 August. Barrell's estimate is that in 1976, the ANC's political 'underground' totalled fifty three- to five-person units, located mainly in the bigger towns. However, the ANC was much better organised across Africa than its rivals, and it was able to accommodate most of the exodus of youngsters across South Africa's borders. Between 1976 and 1977, between four thousand and ten thousand (estimates vary) of the refugees joined the ANC. At the beginning of 1977, uMkhonto weSizwe (MK) established a regional operational 'machinery' headed by Siphiwe Nyanda in Swaziland for directing sabotage attacks in Transvaal towns. The first armed operations were mounted under Sexwale's direction when a locally recruited group blew up a railway line outside Pietersburg. Despite this promising beginning, rural guerrilla insurgency remained exceptional. Urban guerrilla operations began prematurely on 13 June 1977, after a confrontation between three recently returned uMkhonto trainees and a private security guard in Johannesburg. In subsequent shootings, two elderly warehouse attendants died. Police captured two of the insurgents. The man responsible for the killing was assaulted so badly he could not stand trial. His comrade, Solomon Mahlangu, was hanged. More effective operations that year were represented by a series of explosions damaging railway lines. In 1978, Mac Maharaj, recently released from Robben Island, took up an appointment as Secretary for Internal Reconstruction and Development, with the task of managing the construction of a political underground, separate from military operations, with the key objective of expanding ANC influence over legal mass organizations. A Maseru-based unit of the Internal Political Reconstruction Committee played an especially important role in helping to direct the construction of student, youth and community organisations in the Eastern Cape. In particular, in this region the Congress of South African Students (COSAS) would function as a virtual ANC surrogate.

The ANC's success in reconstructing its political following inside South Africa was to be more a consequence of the effectiveness of its 'armed propaganda' than a function of its internal organisational coordination. After all, until the 1990s, most of its leaders and most of its disciplined following would remain in exile. Outside South Africa, by 1980, the movement had constructed a formidable bureaucracy administering a community of followers scattered across twenty-five countries. The external ANC maintained an army, from 1976 based principally in Angola; it ran farms and workshops in Zambia and Tanzania, it exercised judicial authority over its members and it received quasi-diplomatic acknowledgement from many governments and several international agencies. A National Executive Committee presided over by Oliver Tambo exercised authority over these undertakings. Senior leadership drew first of all on Tambo's generation, populist-nationalists from the 1950s, a mixture of elite professionals such as Tambo himself, an urbane lawyer who had shared an attorneys' partnership with Nelson Mandela, and working-class militants from the trade union movement, many of them communists. By 1980, the two groups were joined by 'first wave' uMkhonto weSizwe veterans from the campaigns of the 1960s, younger men whose key initial political experience was in clandestine organization: of these, Chris Hani was an outstanding example. Finally, in leadership, there were the diplomats and administrators in their forties and fifties, some with very little internal political or military experience, constituting a technocratic echelon. Thabo Mbeki best typified this group, a second-generation representative of a famous ANC family, groomed for leadership early on after his graduation from Sussex University and by 1978 managing Oliver Tambo's office.

Mbeki, though, was exceptional in winning a place at a British university. Many of the ANC's university graduates in the exile community would obtain their diplomas and certificates at East European and Soviet institutions, including Communist Party schools: by 1990, for example, there were at least one hundred ANC students in various fields earning academic and vocational qualifications in East Germany. Around two hundred ANC members obtained degrees at Soviet universities, and around the same number attended shorter courses at the International Lenin School. Not surprisingly, among this younger generation of exiles especially, the Communist Party was extremely influential, important especially in shaping the ANC's strategic ideas.

What were these ideas? In the ANC, members of the South African Communist Party understood themselves to be engaged in a struggle for national democracy, itself a key stage in the advance to a fully socialist society. In the terminology of the international communist movement as it was developed by the early 1950s, *national democracy* referred to a state, 'neither capitalist nor socialist', in which a formerly anticolonial and even anti-imperial bourgeoisie could prosper and, in so doing, expand the industrial base and the size of the working class. However, South Africa was not a typical colonial formation. Under the conditions of 'colonialism as a special type', an African bourgeoisie would remain nascent. Hence, in the 1950s, leading Communist Party theorists perceived the ANC as a transitional movement, sociologically, led by men and women increasingly influenced by working-class struggle. Because the ANC represented an 'advanced progressive anti-imperialist tendency', national liberation – or the achievement of national democracy – could include a substantive 'economic content', including nationalisation of monopoly industry and the redistribution of land. In such a scenario, nationalist and working-class struggle could fuse. This vision remained a source of inspiration through most of the 1980s for many among the ANC's intellectual following. For example, a commemorative volume on the Freedom Charter published inside South Africa in 1986 was able to reassure its readers that, in the course of an ANC transition to national democracy, it would cater to and even protect the interests of small traders and small farmers, provided that they did not threaten to become big capitalists. From this perspective, national liberation represented a profound systemic alteration of a kind that could follow only a revolutionary rupture. This was an argument that received significant academic support at the time, as a new generation of South African 'revisionist' Marxist scholars maintained that the repression that accompanied early stages of capital accumulation remained indispensable for the operations of industrial enterprises and commercial farming.[9] The aim of guerrilla warfare, therefore, was seizure of power so that systemic reforms

---

[9] See especially Martin Legassick, 'South Africa: capital accumulation and violence', *Economy and Society* 3 (1974), 253–91.

could follow and not be resisted. For the ANC's strategic thinkers, how to achieve that objective became clearer in 1979.

The insurrectionary events in Soweto between 1976 and 1977 called into question the ANC's assumption that armed struggle was needed to 'detonate' political upsurge. In the uprising's aftermath, it was quite evident that there were fresh prospects for legal and semilegal activities, the kinds of activities that had seemed impossible in the mid-1960s. In October 1978, Oliver Tambo and other members of the ANC's Revolutionary Council visited Vietnam. On their return to Lusaka, Joe Slovo presented to the National Executive a review of lessons from the visit. Vietnamese national liberation, Slovo maintained, pointed to the primacy of a political struggle in which the general population could participate. For such purposes, new legal associational life needed encouragement. Hitherto, the ANC's activities inside South Africa had been overly militaristic. The organisation should correct this tendency and build a political base. Armed struggle should help to construct or rather inspire this base, which in turn would provide an organizational platform for a wider people's war. In 1979, the Politico-Military Commission spelled out the strategic implications of these lessons. For the time being, the ANC should encourage mass mobilisation, helping to create a broad national front from existing organisations to promote the widest kinds of unified political struggle around particular issues, including local grievances, a struggle that in certain respects would recall the ostensibly reformist Congress Alliance tradition of the 1950s while also exploiting the Jacobin mood of the townships.

An ANC political underground would recruit the most able activists from the mass organizations and supply direction and purpose to the front organisations. In this phase, military operations, by implication, primarily urban centred, would nurture through 'armed propaganda' the growth of the ANC's political base – at this stage, 'the armed struggle' would be 'secondary'. Armed propaganda would achieve two objectives: supporting and inspiring political activity, and 'keeping alive the perspective of peoples' revolutionary violence as the ultimate weapon for the seizure of power'. Once constructed, then, the base 'would service eventual decisive revolutionary struggle', but until then, the politics that the ANC would promote would not be tightly controlled from above.[10] Given their own organisational limitations, ANC principals acknowledged that their new popular following would have to function with considerable autonomy as well as a beneficial creativity.

[10] Quotations are from the ANC's 'Green Book' (August 1979), reproduced in Thomas Karis and Gail Gerhart, *From protest to challenge*, vol. 5, *Nadir and resurgence, 1964–1979* (Bloomington: Indiana University Press, 1997), pp. 721–3.

Certainly, ANC strategic conceptions of this kind exercised a key influence in subsequent events through the 1980s, but even in the ANC's disciplined community by no means every key actor would be guided by the directives emerging from the 1978–1979 strategic review. To begin with, not all ANC leaders shared the Communist Party's understanding of the quasi-socialist content of national democracy. To cite an especially important exception, Nelson Mandela in the 1950s envisaged a fully fledged, nonracial bourgeois democracy, and that was a position he retained in prison. As we will see, his views were to become increasingly significant through the 1980s. Also, with respect to the Communist Party, it is questionable how intellectually united a community it embodied and the degree to which it could exercise a dominant influence even in the confined community of ANC exiles. To be sure, the Party could count among its membership most of the ANC's national executive. It seems likely, though, contrary to hostile views of its role in the ANC leadership, that the party did not function as a caucus, even in those vicinities in which its members were concentrated. Indeed, many were entirely absorbed by their ANC responsibilities.

Ray Simons's minutes of her SACP unit's meetings in Lusaka supply eloquent testimony of the limitations that party members themselves perceived about the SACP's role. For example, in March 1980, the unit listened to a report on the ANC community in Botswana. There, the party's presence 'was not felt', and political education in the region was confined to a small select group. At a meeting several months later, it was noted that 'a problem that most comrades seem to have is to find time for their party work as well as their ANC work.'[11] Neither the SACP nor the ANC were ideological monoliths, and within the broader movement, there were going to be sharp tactical and even more profound strategic disagreements. Additionally, partly because of bureaucratic rivalries in the exile hierarchy, the ANC's internal political structures remained poorly developed, and the military emphasis in the activities directly instigated by its external leadership continued. Accordingly, with the weakness of the ANC's internal political structures as popular associational life proliferated, while its leaders often acknowledged the organisation's political authority, they developed their own strategic agenda and disagreed among themselves over long-term goals.

In the exile movement, though, at the beginning of the 1980s, there was a widely shared strategic understanding. The ANC was engaged in a revolutionary struggle in which, in the long term, a protracted people's war would bring about 'seizure of power'. For the time being, though

---

[11] SACP unit meetings, Lusaka, minutes, 1980, Simons Collection, University of Cape Town Libraries.

there needed to be a more preparatory politically oriented phase. How the seizure might eventually take place was never described clearly in official ANC documents, although an interview with a senior ANC personality in *Sechaba* referred to an 'armed insurrection – a culmination of guerrilla warfare' as 'the classic method of making revolution', citing both the Iranian and Bolshevik revolutions as suggestive alternative precedents for a South African insurrectionary change of regime.[12] Still, the extent to which all members of the leadership group really believed that this ultimate objective would be realised – or even wanted it to be achieved – is questionable. When senior officials encountered sympathetic North Americans and Western Europeans, they often used a liberal language that contrasted rather sharply with the uncompromising and absolutist phraseology that characterised the organisation's internal strategic propositions. For example, the American researcher Steve Davis was told by one 'top ANC veteran' in Tanzania that, before the arrival of the 1976 activists, 'we were tolerant, non-violent, convinced we could reason with whites'. The older generation remained 'committed only to a controlled armed struggle' and was fearful of younger militants' vision of a wider kind of insurgency: 'This is our fear: the whole-scale burning of the country. We want to avoid that. We are not mad. It's easy to destroy, much harder to rebuild'. Although such leaders valued the ANC's reputation for relative 'responsibility and restraint', these professions may well have been deliberately misleading.[13] At the same time, it is equally possible that the sentiments were not simply prompted by tactical considerations but also expressed deeply held moral concerns that were suppressed in the formal discourses of political debate, discourses that were shaped by a particular internal logic. In the ANC's rank and file, however, the belief in ultimate victory as a consequence of military predominance was quite general.

It was evident, for example, in a 1984 diary kept by an uMkhonto guerrilla commander operating in KwaZulu Natal, which provides a rare contemporary testimony of the perceptions of strategic purpose shared by active combatants. In this document, the objective of trying to establish a local military training program was to 'produce warrior guerrillas', a phrase that deliberately evoked regional martial traditions. In doing so, they had to overcome considerable scepticism among local residents with respect 'to our capability to beat the Boers in real combat'. Would the guerrillas depart, exposing their local supporters to retribution of the South African Defence Force (SADF)?

---

[12] Interview, *Sechaba* (May 1985).
[13] Stephen Davis, *Apartheid's rebels: inside South Africa's hidden war* (New Haven, CT: Yale University Press, 1987), pp. 60–1.

'No,' we answered, we'll better die here than leaving them in the lurch. Really people are expecting much from us. It is up to us to prove our worth. To enhance the confidence people are already having to erase the doubts in their minds about the invincibility of the white man and the SADF and support fully the course to overthrow oppression of the Boers as spearheaded by the ANC. But is MK capable? Their full participation will be determined by our first 50 operations. We will better die here rather than retreat for the sake of the people we are working with now – it is up to us to demonstrate our capability to fight more than the Boers and win the war. We must not leave them whatever the enemy offensive might be. People want a practical man. If need be they must see our dead bodies. They must bury them.[14]

This group was especially ambitious in its aims. More generally, uMkhonto weSizwe activities between 1977 and 1984 more or less corresponded with the first phase of armed propaganda represented in the 1978 Strategic Review. As noted already, guerrillas trained in Angola began to carry out the first attacks in mid-1977. Up to the end of 1979, much of the armed activity was located in African townships in the main urban centres. The primary targets were grenade assaults on security forces; the sabotage of railway links between the townships and city centres; and bombings of administrative buildings, police stations and similar targets. Gun battles with the police were also reported in the northeastern border regions, the consequence of police interception of returning guerrillas or of MK ambushes to divert attention away from the main routes of returning insurgents. After 1980, the guerrilla campaign broadened and became more conspicuous. Operations were directed at targets chosen for their psychological impact on the general population, and not just for those groups most likely to support the ANC, and they occurred more frequently outside the townships, in the commercial and administrative cores of cities. Guerrillas also selected targets that would demonstrate connections between their own activities and popular struggles. For instance, an ambitious attack on Soekmekaar police station in 1980 was intended to demonstrate solidarity with a local struggle to resist removals. On the whole, the campaign was concentrated in the Johannesburg-Pretoria area and in Durban, though by 1982, uMkhonto activities had spread to smaller rural centres in Natal and the Transvaal, and a few attacks had taken place in the main towns of the Eastern and Western Cape. The successful rocket attack on the Sasolburg synthetic fuel refinery in June 1980 and the bombing of the Koeberg nuclear power station in December 1982 represented uMkhonto operations at their most elaborate and dramatic.

---

[14] *State v Wilfred Mapumula*, Estcourt Circuit Court, October–December 1955, Exhibit BB, typescript, pp. 16–22, Tom Lodge papers, University of the Witwatersrand.

Occasional operational sophistication notwithstanding, this remained an embryonic war. Up to the end of 1982, reported attacks numbered fewer than two hundred. The majority of these incidents were acts of sabotage. Railway lines, power cables, electrical substations and other state-owned industrial facilities, official administrative buildings, courts and township municipal offices were favoured targets. But guerrillas also assassinated police officers, former state witnesses in security trials and suspected informers. Seventeen police and military posts were also attacked. Compared to the bloodshed in civil unrest during this period, the guerrillas inflicted a small number of casualties. By the end of 1982, their grenades, limpet mines and guns had been responsible for the deaths of fifteen policemen and sixteen civilians. The ANC regarded four of the civilians as collaborators and the others as accidental victims of the conflict. The ANC deaths totalled seventy, including the victims of South African army raids on ANC buildings in Maputo and Maseru. Trials of guerrillas often revealed elementary lapses in security procedures. For example, in South Africa's neighbouring states, where it had sanctuary, the ANC conducted its radio communications in clear, uncoded English. During this period, command structures remained outside South Africa. The guerrilla campaign depended on complex preparations and elaborate logistical support, and uMkhonto recruits received specialised training for specific functions. A clear division of roles between units characterised field operations with such units, each in separated parallel communication with command structures to enhance their security. Higher-profile attacks were preceded by intelligence sorties, complicated transport arrangements for personnel and equipment, and sometimes even the purchase of operational bases. By 1982, guerrilla units were spending up to a year in the field, each responsible for a number of operations. But the scale remained limited. At any one time, the number of fighters actively deployed inside South Africa would not have exceeded five hundred.

The campaign's conduct reflected the nature of the training the insurgents received in the Angolan camps. This had two dimensions. First, military and technical skills were taught to a degree of sophistication well in excess of the requirements of ANC operations inside South Africa, presumably in anticipation of the more ambitious, later undertakings. For example, in some of the advanced courses, recruits were taught to operate field guns, an accomplishment of little utility in guerrilla campaigning. The ANC units did, however, fight alongside Angolan forces against *União Nacional para a Independência Total de Angola* (UNITA) in a more conventional form of warfare, a commitment that was unpopular and that engendered a harshly suppressed mutiny in Angolan camps in 1984. Second, recruits received political instruction, consisting of ANC history, ANC ideology, the basics of Marxist political economy and the application of policy to practice in the field. For instance, cadres were warned of the dangers of 'militarism' – the isolation of military from political activity – and were encouraged to stick to specific guidelines in selecting targets for attack. The ANC leaders opposed indiscriminate terrorism, and in general, up to 1984, the basic intention of uMkhonto's activity was not intended to represent a serious military challenge but to enhance the ANC's popular status and win for it a loose mass following that later could be converted into more disciplined, organised support.

This effort was decisive, for in the preceding decade, the ANC's political authority was by no means uncontested. The PAC's clandestine networks in the Transkei, around Krugersdorp and in Cape Town were probably comparable in extent to the ANC's during the early 1970s with, once again, ex–Robben Islanders playing a leading role in resurrecting the organisation in South Africa. By 1975, leaders of the internal network were in contact with their exile comrades and ready to begin despatching recruits for Libyan training. Police found the internal movement relatively easy to penetrate, though, perhaps partly because of the way it was reconstituted around fairly high-profile, first-generation leaders all under surveillance. This group's close linkages with the Black People's Convention also rendered it vulnerable to police repression. But it was the conflicts in the external PAC community that ensured that the movement's revival inside South Africa would fail to consolidate. In 1978, the PAC was ready to despatch trained guerrillas back home, and in Operation Curtain Raiser, a group of around twenty trained men based itself in the Transkei for more than a year before arrest, although they do not seem to have undertaken any military operations. The external PAC failed to follow up this relatively successful endeavour mainly because of the paralysis induced by leadership feuding between Templeton Ntantala and Potlake Leballo, feuding that had both ethnoregional and ideological dimensions. Exasperated authorities in Swaziland and Botswana closed down PAC offices, and the Tanzanians deployed their own army to suppress an Azanian People Liberation Army (APLA) mutiny, arresting five hundred. As the PAC's later secretary-general Thami ka Plaatjie notes at the end of his analysis of this period, 'the PAC thus entered the 1980s a moribund organization'.[15]

By the end of 1983, then, the formation of the United Democratic Front (UDF), an assembly that incorporated into its iconography and hierarchy symbols and personalities associated with the ANC tradition, suggested that uMkhonto's armed propaganda had succeeded in its essential objective. Equally, although this development may have been in conformity with

---

[15] Thami ka Plaatjie, 'The PAC in exile,' in South Africa Democracy Education Trust, *The road to democracy*, Vol I. p. 746.

the ANC's strategic intentions, the UDF's formation was the outcome of several quite mutually independent organisational developments. These were certainly influenced by the ANC's clandestine internal presence, but they were also the product of quite distinct trajectories in South African politics. It is to these that we now turn.

THE UNITED DEMOCRATIC FRONT

Ostensibly, it was a succession of government reforms that prompted what was to become the most pervasive and widely supported movement in the history of South African extraparliamentary politics. In 1979, the Industrial Conciliation Amendment Act conferred legal status on black trade unions, with further legislation in 1981 excising most racial references in the law on collective bargaining. In the more favourable climate created by the act, between 1979 and 1982, trade union membership grew from 750,000 to more than 1 million, to include about 10 per cent of the African workforce. In 1982, the Black Local Authorities Act also conceded new powers and responsibilities for what had hitherto been advisory elected township councils. Two further pieces of legislation, the so-called Koornhof Bills – the Orderly Movement and Settlement of Black Persons Bill and the Black Community Development Bill – were drafted in 1982. The Orderly Movement Bill tightened up influx control and threatened to deny any further conferment of section 10 urban residential rights. An immediate policy implication of the proposed legislation would be 'repatriation' of illegal African urban residents, one hundred thousand of whom, for example, were believed to be living in Cape Town. For legal residents, however, the state would offer ninety-nine-year leasehold and would again start building family housing under the Black Community Development Bill, aimed at converting the administration boards into development boards to channel revenue derived from levies on employers to the new Black Local Authorities. Finally, the 1983 Constitution Act would replace the existing exclusively white House of Assembly and Senate with a 'tricameral' legislature in which coloured voters would be represented in the House of Representatives and Indians in the House of Delegates. In place of the Senate, each chamber would elect a multiracial advisory president's council.

The UDF was established to oppose the Koornhof Bills, the new Black Local Authorities and the tricameral parliament. In January 1983, two separate appeals called for the formation of a front. On 8 January, in his customary statement on the ANC's anniversary of its foundation, Oliver Tambo announced 1983 as 'the Year of United Action'. All democratic forces, Tambo urged, should merge 'into one front for national liberation'. Two weeks later, at a congress summoned by the Anti–South African Indian

Council Committee, the Reverend Allen Boesak, president of the World Alliance of Reformed Churches, delivered the keynote address. He advocated a 'politics of refusal' in which mobilisation against the government's constitutional measures assume the form of a 'united front'. 'There is no reason,' Boesak continued, 'why churches, civic associations, trade unions, student organizations should not unite on this issue, pool our resources, inform the people of the fraud which is about to be perpetrated in their name, and on the day of the election expose these plans for what they are.'

Interviewed ten years later, Boesak claimed he had been unaware of Tambo's earlier reference to a front. It is likely, though, that others present were better informed. Boesak had been primed with the suggestion that he might include a reference to the front by Cas Saloojee, a leader of efforts to oppose Group Areas Act removals.[16] The meeting endorsed Boesak's proposal, and at the same time, the Transvaal Anti-South African Indian Council announced that it would reconstitute itself as the Transvaal Indian Congress, a partner in the Congress Alliance of the 1950s. A Natal Indian Congress reassembled shortly thereafter. Eight months later, the United Democratic Front was launched officially in Cape Town. One thousand five hundred delegates representing 565 organisations were in attendance; of those, 313 were from youth groups,[17] and 82 represented civic associations. The next-largest grouping was student bodies, forty-seven organisations. Then and later, the UDF's following was predominantly youthful. The front existed, Reverend Frank Chikane told those present, 'for the sole purpose of opposing the reform proposals and the Koornhof Bills'. All UDF affiliates would be represented in the leadership structures, and the new body would make its decisions consensually. Programmes would vary according to context:

The main organizational focus of the UDF campaign [must be] at the local and regional levels. Organizations affiliated to the UDF will run campaigns around certain aspects of the new Constitution that affect their membership in a direct way. This is to ensure that the UDF does not simply become a political protest group, but is able to build and strengthen non-racial democratic organizations as an alternative to apartheid itself.[18]

[16] Jeremy Seekings, *The UDF: a history of the United Democratic Front* (Cape Town: David Philip, 2000), p. 45.

[17] Of these, 235 were branches of the ephemeral and short-lived Western Cape Inter Church Youth; see Ineke van Kessel, *Beyond our wildest dreams: the United Democratic Front and the transformation of South Africa* (Charlottesville: University of Virginia Press, 2000), p. 17.

[18] United Democratic Front, *National launch* (Cape Town: University of Cape Town Students' Representative Council, 1983).

A 'two-level struggle' would require followers first to 'organize around immediate local issues at the first level' in struggles that would later coalesce 'to challenge broader problems on the second level'. In fact, initial activities were high-profile electoral boycotts. Between August and November 1983, the UDF sponsored an unevenly organised offensive against the elections for the new Black Local Authorities, in the most animated centres using open air meetings, extensive door-to-door visits and the distribution of half a million leaflets. Leaders perceived low electoral turnouts as evidence of success, although they later conceded that in many townships the UDF was still very shaky. A more elaborate and extended campaign was directed at persuading coloured and Indian voters to abstain in the parliamentary elections of August 1984. Here, activities included a programme of public events, including rock concerts, as well as a door-to-door 'signature blitz', mainly in Indian and coloured neighbourhoods, in which residents would be asked to endorse a declaration opposing the constitution. In fact, the decision to mount electoral boycotts was not unanimous. Several Indian Congress leaders favoured participation in favour of a no vote in a constitutional referendum that the government initially planned for coloured and Indian voters. Advocates of participation in the referendum cited Gandhi, Lenin and even Gramsci as their textual authorities, but even so, they failed to persuade the UDF's African leadership. During this first phase of campaigning, the UDF's performance deliberately evoked the mass politics of the 1950s: songs, slogans and speeches extolled Nelson Mandela and other ANC heroes. The Natal Indian Congress's Mewa Ramgobin's address calling for Mandela's release was typical:

These ideals, the passion to realise these ideals, which are enshrined in the Freedom Charter, continue to keep our leaders in jail. Rivonia for us will remain a milestone in the history of South Africa. Generations to come will wonder whether such men as Mandela, Sisulu and Mbeki in fact walked this earth, in fact were prepared to give up their lives for the ideals they believed in.[19]

The UDF appeared to represent the revival of a long-established South African populist tradition in which large and excited gatherings, powerful oratory and charismatic leaders functioned as effective substitutes for systematically structured organisations and carefully calculated programmes. As with the mass campaigns of the 1940s and 1950s, leadership was multiracial, or rather 'nonracial' in the language preferred by activists in the 1980s, although outside Cape Town, Durban and Pietermaritzburg, as

---

[19] *State v Mewa Ramgobin*, Pietermaritzberg, 1984, schedule A in respect of accused no. 1, indictment: transcript of speeches, p. 83, Tom Lodge papers, University of the Witwatersrand.

in the 1950s, supporters were mainly African. Elderly veterans from the 1950s Congress Alliance were also conspicuous among the three presidents and the panel of patrons that the new body nominated. Furthermore, the UDF's own signature campaign recalled the million-signature campaign that followed the drawing up of the Freedom Charter in 1955. Even the body's structure was nothing new. Similarly heterodox federations claiming millions of followers had been popular in the 1940s.

But appearances were deceptive. Although the UDF's style seemed to echo the ANC tactical repertoire of thirty years earlier, the movement was significantly different. The UDF was a federation in which authority and initiative were dispersed, rather than a disciplined centralised force, and its leaders allowed local affiliates to exercise tactical initiative. As Seekings notes, the UDF's main importance was symbolic and inspirational, helping 'to shape and reshape the collective identities of followers . . . helping to construct a sense of "we"'.[20] Especially in the early stages of its history, national leadership was unprepared to give direction when this was required by its local supporters, particularly when these were based in African townships, as leaders were preoccupied with opposing the parliamentary arrangements for Indians and coloureds. Hence, with respect to its African base, in the following two years, local activists would determine and in so doing radicalise the UDF's political programme. They would also draw their tactical repertoire and their emblematic iconography from other sources, particularly the symbolism of the ANC exiles, in which 'the UDF was sometimes incorporated as a symbol in this, but as a subordinate symbol'.[21] The comrades' *toyi-toyi* dance was an especially striking instance of this, imported into the townships from the ANC training camps, where it had been borrowed from Zimbawe African People's Union's goose-stepping parade drill.

At dawn on 3 September 1984, by coincidence the day on which the new tricameral parliament opened its doors,[22] young people on picket lines halted buses from entering the townships around Vereeniging. The picketers represented the Vaal Civic Organisation (VCO), a body with influence in the townships around the city. This civic association had already demonstrated its effectiveness by securing the reinstatement of evicted

[20] Seekings, *The UDF*, p. 22.   [21] Ibid., pp. 22–3.

[22] At least one account suggests that the opening of the tricameral parliament was the decisive provocation in triggering the riots in the Vaal townships on 3 September; see Martin Murray, *South Africa: time of agony, time of destiny: the upsurge of popular protest* (London: Verso, 1987), p. 248. This seems unlikely, though. There is no evidence that participants were influenced by the public ceremonies in Cape Town. A published account of the uprising by a Sebokeng resident, Johannes Rantete, refers to only local preoccupations.

schoolchildren and by mounting successful protest against rent-arrears evictions. The VCO was directing its opposition at recent high rent increases. It could count on a rising tide of public anger, for only 14 per cent of registered voters had participated in the Lekoa Council's election in 1983. Undaunted, after their installation, the council's new leaders had reallocated the spoils of office, awarding most new liquor licences to councillors, twelve of them members of the mayor's own extended family. Venal, self-serving behaviour by councillors might have been unexceptional ten years earlier, but in the emerging new moral economy of public life, what had passed as the customary entitlements of patronage were perceived as offensive.

The VCO's public meetings agreed to a two-day strike and accompanying school boycotts in a campaign for 'affordable' rents. Very soon, most of the shops and public buildings in Sebokeng and Sharpeville had been burned down. The deputy mayor Kuzwayo Dlamini was dead, killed in Sharpeville, by members of an enraged crowd. Thirty more members of the Lekoa Council would die during the following week. This insurrection spread to Soweto on 17 September, Springs on 14 October, and it became national with its extension to the townships of the Eastern Cape in November. By then, its impact had extended beyond the townships. On 5 November, in the Transvaal a two-day stay-away was called by a committee representing the Soweto Youth Congress, the Release Mandela Committee, the Municipal and General Workers Union, a UDF affiliate and the non-UDF-affiliated Federation of South African Workers: in all, 1 million workers participated, including most migrant worker hostel dwellers in the East Rand. Six weeks earlier, seven thousand soldiers had been used in support of a police pass raid in Sebokeng, and by October, the use of SADF personnel as police auxiliaries was general, their first deployment in quelling civil unrest since 1960. This was a significant indication of the scope of the challenge to the state's authority that the uprising embodied. For the following two years, the UDF presided over a rebellion without historical precedent. How was the revolt organised and sustained?

Established initially as a hierarchical network of committees, the UDF's federal structure of regional committees drew together representatives of different organisations. These bodies could affiliate to the UDF, yet retain their separate identity as trade unions, civic bodies, youth clubs, religious communities or cultural associations. In theory, they could be ideologically as well as functionally diverse, united only in their opposition to the government's new political arrangements. At its peak, the UDF claimed the adherence of about seven hundred affiliates, grouped in ten regional clusters embracing every major concentration of population in the country. Its impact across regions varied. The UDF was especially strong in the cities of the Eastern Cape, in Johannesburg, the Vaal, parts of Pretoria, in the

West Rand and in the coloured suburbs of Cape Town. It was weaker in the townships of the East Rand, a centre for the new trade union movement, and was organised only superficially in African townships around Durban and Pietermaritzburg.

Organisationally, the UDF was both more complicated and simpler than the depiction suggested in the preceding paragraph. Many of its affiliates were formed after its formation, with the principal intention of bringing specific constituencies into its embrace, including noncharterist groups. People could not join the organisation as individuals, for at its inception, the UDF was not intended to compete with existing organisations. In practice, in many though not all African townships, the UDF functioned as an ideologically homogeneous mass movement, with individuals being popularly perceived as, and understanding themselves to be, simultaneously UDF and ANC supporters. Despite the initial functional diversity of the UDF, in practice, in most localities a basic triumvirate emerged that supplied its most active following: a civic or a community organisation, a women's group and a 'youth congress'. In the main urban centres of the revolt, the civic association, often led by trade union shop stewards, was probably the most significant agency of rebellion, although not all civics formally affiliated to the UDF. Women's groups were particularly central in African popular political life around Cape Town. In many townships, these bodies would be supplemented by branches of the Congress of South African Students (COSAS), the classroom-based body that had replaced SASO in 1979 but that from its inception had announced its 'Charterist' alignment. Quite frequently, too, there would also be a sympathetic cluster of trade unionists. The UDF's affiliation also included a new and militant teachers' association, the National Education Union of South Africa. It was an important agency in establishing footholds for the organisation in more rural vicinities, especially in the Lebowa homeland, picking up support from younger teachers responding to sharply deteriorating working conditions.[23]

As already noted, the most energetic local components of the UDF tended to be youthful classroom militants and youth congress members, many of the latter of whom were unemployed recent school leavers. Notwithstanding the tactical and ideological ambiguities that characterised the phraseology of its socially eclectic leadership, at its main urban and rural base of working-class Africans and unemployed school leavers, UDF affiliation usually required acknowledgement of the ANC's claims to

[23] Ngoanamadima Johannes Sello Mathabatha, *The struggle over education in the Northern Transvaal: the case of Catholic mission schools* (Amsterdam: Rozenburg Publishers, 2005), pp. 79–82.

political primacy, admiration for the armed struggle, messianic socialism and almost-millennial expectations of revolutionary change. This was the culture of the comrades, the tens of thousands of teenagers and young men and women who carried the movement through its most assertive and influential phases: the overthrow of black township government from September 1984; the assassination and expulsions of perceived collaborators (municipal officials, black police officers and informers); the rent and consumer boycotts; the efforts to develop street-based networks of neighbourhood organisation; and the institution of 'People's Power', programmes directed at substituting state agencies in education, justice and civic administration.

The UDF's explosive energy was partly attributable to structural developments, embodied by the combined forces of inflation and unemployment generated by a recession that had gripped the national economy from 1982. Eighty per cent of black eighteen- to twenty-six-year-olds were unemployed in 1986, and inflation was accelerating at a faster rate then ever experienced in South African history. The economic downturn fatefully coincided and conflicted with the government's efforts to introduce devices to legitimise its authority among black South Africans to a greater extent. Demography and a further massive expansion of the secondary schooling system (African high school enrolment doubled between 1980 and 1984) added an additional destabilising ingredient. Under the pressures generated by expansion, the effectiveness of schooling diminished sharply as the matriculation pass rate fell from 76 per cent to 48 per cent between 1978 and 1982.

The UDF's strength depended not so much on sophisticated leadership and coordinated organizational structures but on the vitality of its township-based affiliates, many of which had emerged in the aftermath of the 1977 uprising. The proliferation of civic associations in the late 1970s and early 1980s reflected deepening grievances concerning housing, an increasing shortage of urban accommodation and rising rents, the latter a consequence of determination by indebted township administrations to balance their books through rent increases. Indeed, as the UDF's most assertive local affiliates, civic associations often identified the key issues around which the most significant popular rebellion would cohere. For example, in early 1984, rent rises in African townships were ignored by a national UDF leadership preoccupied with opposing Indian and coloured elections. In the event, the decision to oppose them in the Transvaal was a civic initiative.

The burgeoning trade union movement had often supplied organisational models to the civics. Classroom rebellion and swiftly expanding youth unemployment constantly added fresh legions to the disaffected generation of highly politicised teenagers. Externally derived flows of financial

resources, mainly from Dutch churches and Swedish trade unions, provided
the support needed to maintain full-time political organisers; to underwrite
community newspapers; to pay for posters, publicity and T-shirts; and to
equip the movement with a common vocabulary, a corporate identity and
a collective iconography that gave it a shared sense of purpose. In this
respect, the mainly white National Union of South African Students and its
press played a critical role in supplying information and, more important,
ideas. South African English-language university campuses, both black
and predominantly white, the latter with significant bodies of black students within their communities, played a major role in the transmission of
local applications of Marxist theory. Naturally, the doctrinal mixture could
vary between centres. Student ideologues at the University of the North
took their marching orders from the orthodox 'national democratic' Marxism Leninism filtered through the ANC's *Sechaba* and the SACP's *African
Communist*. In comparison, the University of the Western Cape students
engaged in the production of the *Grassroots* newspaper were influenced by a
wider range of inspiration including the British 'new left'; Latin American
comunicación popular; Lenin's vision of a newspaper as the key to promoting
a working-class socialist consciousness; and even, perhaps, local strains of
Trotskyite polemics. The UDF's vigorous early growth also reflected the
state's fresh willingness to tolerate mass-based structured opposition as one
of the corollaries of its new effort to create institutions of legitimation.
Between 1977 and 1983, not only did a nationalist culture of political
assertion blossom. As the authors of the ANC's 1978 strategic review had
hoped, this culture was informed by a rediscovery of Congress traditions and
inspired by the martial theatre of uMkhonto weSizwe's armed propaganda.

It was a political culture that was extremely pervasive, functioning especially for young people as a framework of moral reference. For them, it
substituted for the eroded stature of parental authority and the declining
force of church and school as agencies of restraint and discipline. Indeed,
this discourse of resistance could often assume the form of a religious
liturgy, demonstrating its capacity to condition almost every facet of social
life in the community. This account, drawn from a description of a 1983
commemoration of the Soweto uprising, is illustrative:

The Regina Mundi Catholic Church service was held not only to mourn the victims
of 1976, but also the three hanged ANC men. Emotions ran high as speaker
after speaker urged more than 5000 people who packed the church to rededicate
themselves to the cause of total liberation. The highlight of the service was when
the entire crowd stood and repeated the Freedom Charter after Tiego Moseneke,
president of the Black Students Society at the University of the Witwatersrand.[24]

[24] Anon, 'Jhb gets into gear on UDF', *SASPU Focus* (June 1983), 5.

Notwithstanding the almost-sacred textual authority attributed here to the charter, the celebrants at such assemblies were disinclined to defer to older leaders. In one protest song, there is an implicit argument that victory will be achieved mainly through the efforts of the youths, that one day, they will tell the older generation how they, the young lions, fought and triumphed:

> Those who are against us,
> We shall reckon with them,
> The day we take our land back,
> Their names are written down.
> When there's a roll call of our heroes,
> I wonder if my name will be on that roll,
> I wonder what it will be like,
> When we sit down with Tambo,
> And tell him about the fall of the Boers.[25]

Of course, although loyalty to or sympathy for the ANC was a given in UDF ideology, what the ANC represented and how its programme could be interpreted varied considerably according to constituency. In the UDF's leadership echelons, not just formal elected office bearers but also the intelligentsia who predominated in so much of its public discourse, there were discernable tendencies toward the right, the centre and the left. In the right-wing camp could be located many of the older generation of 'spokesmen politicians', the churchmen, social notables and professionals whose forums such as the Committee of Ten had compensated for the absence of organised opposition in the later 1970s. In the centre were people whose predispositions favoured the ANC-SACP view of the revolution as 'national democratic' with a tactically submerged long-term socialist objective. Within this group, the Natal Indian Congress exercised an especially weighty influence. To the left were those whose prime concern was that the working class exercise its own leadership in any political alliance, as within UDF leadership its voice was muted. Nonetheless, an explicit commitment to a rough-and-ready Marxist vision of socialism was very common at the base of the movement, especially in centres of trade union strength. The sentiments expressed by Comrade Bongani, from the Tumahole Youth Congress, reflected this vision:

Question: Would you like to see socialism in this country?
Answer: Yes, because it's going to do away with capitalism.
Question: What do you understand by socialism?

[25] Shaun Johnson, 'Youth in the politics of resistance', in *South Africa*, p. 113.

Answer: It is a system of private ownership by certain individuals who own the means of production. My parents, from Monday to Friday, can make a production of R1,000, but he or she is going to get, say R50. So our parents are being exploited so that certain individuals can get rich. That's why I prefer socialism, because the working class will control production.[26]

It was the twenty-year-old Comrade Bongani, and graduates of school boycotts, street battles, and factory dismissals, who were to supply the UDF with much of its vitality. As well as utopian socialism, these activists brought into the movement a generational consciousness, an antiauthoritarian iconoclasm and a susceptibility for brutal violence, each quite unprecedented features in the culture of black South African political organisations. From March 1985, the violence included 'necklacing', the burning to death with petrol-filled tyres of supposed informers and other renegades, a sadistic purification of the community. Throughout the duration of the 1984–1986 township uprising, the UDF was increasingly pulled along courses determined by the most energetic, militant and volatile of its constituencies.

When SADF soldiers moved into the townships in the wake of the September 1984 rebellion, the UDF became a movement galvanised by local initiatives, with civics and youth congresses organising a remarkable series of consumer boycotts to try to compel white city councils and businesspeople to negotiate on their behalf for the withdrawal of troops, the release from detention of local leaders and the redressing of local grievances. The negotiations were undertaken as local initiatives and were sometimes criticised as reformist in ANC polemics, but modest local victories considerably enhanced the popular moral credentials of civic leaders. In a partial State of Emergency between July 1985 and February 1986, the police detained eight thousand people. In reaction, surviving local leaders called afresh for consumer boycotts and formed street committees that could evade emergency restrictions on mass meetings. In the eight months of this emergency, six hundred people were killed as a consequence of political conflict, about the same number as in the preceding comparable period. By early 1986, conservative opponents of the government were claiming that the UDF and the ANC were in command in twenty-seven townships in the Eastern Cape, in Kagiso on the West Rand and in seven centres in the East Rand. The authorities' failure to contain resistance; the increasing incidence of armed confrontations between the occupation forces and increasingly militarised 'comrades', sometimes trained and equipped as uMkhonto auxiliaries; and the succession of local victories won through

---

[26] 'Talking to a comrade', *Financial Mail* (31 October 1986), 53.

consumer boycotts all served to stimulate a euphoric conviction concerning the state's vulnerability and the imminence of national liberation. Motivated mainly by the pragmatic need to regulate the disorder resulting from the collapse of township administration and the absence of routine policing, but inspired also by an almost apocalyptic expectancy, civics and youth movements began to construct an alternative institutional framework of 'People's Power'.

In particular, local UDF affiliates assumed judicial functions in their efforts to cope with the consequence of a vacuum of authority. 'People's Courts', though, were often inspired by an egalitarian and redemptive conception of their social mission. 'The people's court is not simply a bourgeois court taking place in a back room in a ghetto', insisted a pamphlet circulated in Atteridgeville in Pretoria. 'Unlike the present legal system, it should not be biased in favour of the powerful and must not be a means whereby the interests of the powerful are ensured at the expense of the oppressed'.[27] The courts' main aim, in the view of a Mamelodi activist, was rehabilitation, reeducating the wrongdoers to improve them.[28] In several recorded instances, courts fell short of such exalted ideals, providing summary tribunals in which harsh retribution could be imposed on both political opponents and the socially marginalised. In Kagiso near Krugersdorp, the Residents' Organisation sanctioned the Disciplinary Committee composed initially of young men but later of older 'fathers'; this routinely flogged children brought before it for stealing or assault. The language employed by UDF officials and ideologues to explain the workings of these agencies was significant, despite these shortcomings in practice, because of the aspirations it expressed, for it reflected a more generalised conception of participatory democracy. People's Power was not liberal democracy, as one publication affiliated to the Cape Town UDF noted: 'Democracy means, in the first instance, the ability of the broad working masses to participate in and to control all dimensions of their lives. This for us, is the essence of democracy, not some liberal, pluralistic, debating society notion of a thousand schools contending'.[29]

An eclectic range of models of what were perceived to be democratic practice were cited admiringly in UDF-aligned publications. In Libya, for example, 'the country is governed in a very unusual way with street committees, area committees, etc. up to national people's committees', the Islamic theologian, Faried Essack informed readers of *Grassroots* after his visit to

---

[27] Raymond Suttner, 'Popular justice in South Africa', paper delivered at Sociology Department seminar, University of the Witwatersrand, 5 May 1986, pp. 10–11.

[28] Anonymous, 'Ya, the community is the main source of power' (Interviews), *Isizwe* (March 1986), 40–1.

[29] Anonymous, 'Sowing confusion', *New Era* (Cape Town) (March 1986), 38.

North Africa. In Mozambique, 'all workers together plan the production for the factory . . . work is no longer my burden, it is my joy'.[30] External ANC commentators also appeared to share the view that what was in creation inside South Africa in 1985–1986 was 'a new type of governability – a people's government – at an embryonic stage', a modern version of the Paris Commune.[31] A constant refrain in UDF speeches and statements was that democracy should be the politics of popular participation, that leaders were merely the bearers of the popular mandate and that as delegates they were accountable directly to the organisation's membership (a notion borrowed from recent South African trade union experience with its strong emphasis on shop-steward accountability). Hence, officials in UDF affiliates expressed antipathy toward the concept of an elitist leaders' constitutional conference of the kind that had produced Zimbabwe's constitution. In this vein, leaders could advise and inspire, but they could not prescribe. During the Soweto consumer boycott, for example, trade unionists on the boycott committee objected to youths stoning the wholesalers' trucks that were replenishing township shops that were allowed by the boycotters to remain open. Regional UDF leaders were reluctant to rein them in: 'It is not our duty to tell them not to stone or burn the trucks. We can only tell them why'.[32] National democracy called for the construction of a radically egalitarian social order that reflected popular consensus. 'Our structures must become organs of people's power . . . ordinary people [must] increasingly take part in all the decisions. Few people making all the decisions must end'.[33] In reality, however, the UDF did not always function according to such prescriptions. But though strategic decisions may not always have been sanctioned at mass meetings, the movement's energy and potency were partly a consequence of the room it allowed for the exercise of lower echelon initiatives.

This was especially evident in Sekhukhuneland in the Lebowa homeland, where for two years the UDF succeeded in attracting mass support, the only rural region in which it developed a sustained organisational presence. Here, to a greater degree than anywhere else, it was a youth movement in which the main actors were high school students and recent school leavers and in which the mobilisation of its following both reflected and accentuated intragenerational tensions. The conditions that helped to explain such tensions included a rapid demographic change in which, as a consequence of resettlement and very high birth rates, the population's age structure was

---

[30] Van Kessel, *Beyond our wildest dreams*, pp. 275–6.
[31] Mzala, 'Building people's power', *Sechaba* (September 1986).
[32] Anonymous, 'Tactical differences', *Work in Progress* (October 1985), 23.
[33] Anonymous, 'UDF message', *Grassroots* (Cape Town) (February 1986).

altering in favour of the young. In 1980, 56 per cent of the local resident population was younger than twenty, a proportion that increased to 72 per cent five years later partly as a consequence of the exodus of adult males seeking work. Meanwhile, a regional economic crisis manifested itself in the widespread closure of shops and other business. Also, booming secondary school enrolment had ensured that, by 1986, more than three-quarters of fifteen- to nineteen-year-olds were at school.

These developments were probably paralleled in other rural vicinities. What was different in Lebowa was the presence of modern political organisation. This included a surviving ANC presence from the 1960s, maintained by veterans of the Sebatakgomo, an initiative by SACP activists to build opposition to Bantu Authorities through the agency of urban-based migrant workers associations. In the late 1970s, local ANC activists received encouragement as operatives recruited and trained two uMkhonto units that, before their capture, destroyed a length of railway line near Pietersburg. Moreover, ANC organisation in the vicinity continued in one of the few rural locations in which the exiles succeeded in establishing the 'Area Politico-Military Committee' in 1985. Another nucleus of underground ANC leadership was based on the campus of the University of the North. Here, the university students and sympathetic staff provided printing facilities and intellectual inspiration to Sekhukhune 'comrades'. Lutheran church pastors also helped to distribute externally donated resources. School students despatched from unruly Soweto by their anxious parents in the hope that their offspring might benefit from the more sedate Lebowa boarding schools supplied another channel of urban political influence: COSAS branches began to proliferate. The backbone of the movement was to be the Youth Congresses, which brought together schoolchildren and high school graduates and that supplanted COSAS, widely understood by local activists to be 'a thing from town'. As the Sekhukhuneland Youth Organisation knitted village youth formations together, in their wake, other constituents of UDF associational life began to appear as fledgling civics and women's groups.

Generally, workers in this region (identified by youth activists not by their class affiliation but rather as 'parents') remained on the sidelines of the movement – and in certain locations were increasingly alienated from it. For in Sekhukhuneland, the UDF's formations were ranged against all kinds of authority, not just the apartheid state or its local proxies. Thus, although the Congresses organised consumer boycotts, mass meetings and denunciations of participation in homeland structures, their activities represented a much more comprehensive challenging of authority – for the village congresses both built on and subverted existing forms of socialisation, drawing on the customary recruitment of youngsters into age regiments but repudiating the initiation rituals and other functions that had helped to constitute family structure, communal cohesion and patrimonial order as the 'tribal customs' of an older generation of socially backward illiterates.

People's courts usurped the adjudication functions customarily performed by elders' councils, assuming control over such matters as family disputes and divorce, a perceived social evil that the youthful tribunals forbade. In 1986, Congress activists announced a campaign to make soldiers, closing down clinics that dispensed contraceptives and abducting young women from their homes to produce more babies. In April, thirty-two witch burnings in two villages represented the climax of this challenge, a particularly brutal bucolic version of the purification represented by necklacing. There, youngsters assumed the powers of village hierarchies and medical specialists, *ngakas*, in identifying the perpetrators of witchcraft and in determining their cruel punishment, dismissing elders' pleas for more moderate measures. The harshness of the penalties they imposed was unusual but not unprecedented. In the region in the previous decade, ritual killings had become more frequent, reflecting, according to one account, 'radical disruption' in the relationship between sacred and political authority, a consequence of the deteriorating status of traditional sources of authority, both secular and sacred. In Lebowa during the 1970s, the number of chiefs had multiplied and the levies and other obligations they imposed on villages had proliferated as their moral stature diminished. In Sekhukhuneland in 1986, the victims were elderly women and those most active in their condemnation were fifteen-year-olds, recent recruits to the movement. Those killed included *dingaka*, punished for their failure to supply the comrades with protective medicine against police bullets. More prosaically, the killings may also have been prompted by social resentment of pensioners as the main recipients of income in the villages as well as by unusual climatic conditions, drought and accompanying lightning strikes. That the victims were women may not have been accidental, for the changing demography of the region had conferred new power on female heads of households, a development that conflicted with the expectations of young men in a patriarchal culture. In the wake of the witch burnings, several hundred youths were arrested, and in May, SADF units occupied most of the villages affected by Sekhukhuneland Youth Organisation activity. Although the UDF region continued to claim a range of affiliate structures, with many of the activists and leadership under detention, its rebellion was effectively curtailed.

In the rebellion's urban centres, the sociology and political affiliation of activist participation were more complicated and could extend well beyond the boundaries of formal affiliation. Three civic organisations competed for the allegiance of the 150,000 inhabitants of Alexandra, the crowded freehold slum on Johannesburg's northern outskirts. First, there was the

UDF-affiliated Alexandra Civic Association, formed in 1985 from the former leaders of the Commuters Association, a body that had led a previous bus boycott. The Alexandra Residents' Association (ARA) offered an alternative political accommodation. The ARA's origins lay in the activities of a youthful study group that published between 1982 and 1983 the newsletter *Izwi Lase Township*. One of the members, Jabu Radebe, was a Metal and Allied Workers' Union (MAWU) official who in 1984 was appointed as the East Rand's MAWU organiser. People in the *Izwi* group attended early meetings of the Alexandra Youth Congress (AYCO) but broke with this body, objecting to its uncritical 'charterist' allegiance, as well as AYCO's initial willingness to incorporate into its support base the Liaison Committee's Youth Council. *Izwi* and the Alexandra Residents' Association (ARA) both were heavily critical of what they perceived as a protobourgeois or 'populist' orientation in the UDF that they maintained was reproduced in both the Alexandra Civic Association and the Youth Congress. Finally, there was the Alexandra Action Committee (AAC) established in early 1985. The twenty-two-member committee was chaired by another MAWU organiser, Moses Mayekiso, and though in theory a front organisation for different associations, in practice the AAC controlled a hierarchy of elected neighbourhood committees functioning for each backyard (twenty families), each block (six yards) and each street (seven blocks). The AAC's principals administered a people's court that claimed success in the course of 1986 in significantly reducing the usually high level of violent crime. Although the AAC was not affiliated to the UDF, its adherents often belonged to the UDF-linked Alexandra Youth Congress. Its leaders attributed the density of community organization over which the committee presided to the exceptionally high proportion of its working population who were unionised, especially in MAWU. This characteristic notwithstanding, the AAC's leadership was looked at askance by the 'workerist' adherents of the tiny ARA because of the AAC's willingness to cooperate with the small businesspeople whom the ARA perceived to be grouped in the UDF-linked civic.

A more subtle explanation for the pervasiveness of the AAC's activist culture is sociological. Belinda Bozzoli argues that in oppressively confined communities such as Alexandra, even in everyday life, 'there is a complex, socially constructed interface between the illicit and the legal' in which 'local urban borders' nurtured a particular kind of culture that would be especially receptive or hospitable to rebellious ideas and activities.[34] An obvious example of this was the way in which the gridlike pattern of township layout designed to promote control could be adapted to requirements of revolutionary order. More generally, Bozzoli suggests that the popular

---

[34] Belinda Bozzoli, 'The taming of the illicit: bounded rebellion in South Africa, 1986', *Comparative Studies in Society and History* 46:2 (2004), 326–8.

democracy based on spatial representation constructed by activists represented a 'modest, local' utopia, the limits and design of which were a
reflection of the 'secluded realm' of the township.

It was the AAC that became the most prominent leadership group representing the township during a prolonged 1986 conflict between residents
and the police. In April, Moses Mayekiso announced that his organisation
had assumed authority in Alexandra, and that its yard, street and block
committees as well as the AAC's people's courts were 'parts of the broader
liberation struggle'. Mayekiso, though, was not an uncritical disciple of
the ANC. A strong advocate of trade unions remaining independent of any
political organisations, he dismissively referred to the Freedom Charter as a
capitalist document. The AAC stood for 'political self rule and control' and
for 'socialism and mass democracy', he insisted.[35] Yet in the network over
which it maintained its leadership, many of the activists were members of
the Youth Congress whose aspirations were focused on a future in which
the ANC would prevail. After a sequence of attacks on local police officers'
houses that prompted a police withdrawal from the township, in March
1986, Youth Congress members believed that they were now in a position
to exercise the first part of the Freedom Charter, namely, that the People
shall govern. Public expressions of loyalty to the ANC were abundant on
such occasions as massively attended funerals, helping to strengthen convictions in the exile movement that conditions were ready for an escalation
of the people's war. But as the complicated constitution of associational
life in Alexandra demonstrated, this was not a popular movement easily
susceptible to central discipline, or one subject to a single vision of a future
political order. Indeed, as a rebellion, it was generationally as well as ideologically divided, as numerous adults had developed a feeling that the local
revolution had gone out of control.

The conspicuous contribution of trade unionists to the leadership of the
rebellion in the Alexandra was not unusual, and in the UDF's affiliated formations, the influence of unionists was often decisive. Labour politics itself
was complex, and for many trade unionists, the ANC's strategic directives
were not necessarily authoritative. The organisations that had developed in
the wake of the Wiehahn reforms were grouped into three clusters divided
both by tactical and by more deeply ideological considerations. In 1979,
the TUACC unions formed the Federation of South African Trade Unions
(FOSATU). For the following seven years, FOSATU affiliates were united in
their support for organisation on a nonracial basis (most obviously evident
in the presence of whites in their hierarchies), willingness to register under

---

[35] Charles Carter, 'Community and conflict: the Alexandra rebellion of 1986', *Journal of
Southern African Studies* 18:1 (March 1992), 135.

the provisions of the new industrial legislation and a mode of operation that continued to emphasise democratically accountable leadership and tight factory-floor organisation in which shop stewards supplied decisive leadership. Later, with the emergence of the UDF, FOSATU unions held back from linking themselves through affiliation, arguing that to do so might risk drawing workers' organisations into political actions in which working-class interests might be sacrificed.

The history of SACTU, the ANC's trade union affiliate in the 1950s and early 1960s, was illustrative of such dangers, FOSATU organisers maintained. Joining the UDF's regional committees would reduce unions to the same status as student groups and local civic groups, participants in decision-making bodies in which trade unionists would be a minority. A second group disagreed with this view. This group included the Food and Canning Workers' Union (FCWU), a surviving SACTU affiliate and organisationally reinvigorated in the late 1970s. This second cluster also embraced a number of unions that argued that, in a South African context in which workers had no democratic rights, workers' organisations should take up a wider range of issues than simply workplace concerns; they should acknowledge that workers were members of wider communities. These unions included the South African Allied Workers' Union (SAAWU), formed initially in April 1979 as a breakaway from the Black Conscious Black Allied Workers' Union. Unlike the FOSATU affiliates, SAAWU recruited across a range of industrial undertakings through mass meetings. In 1980 and 1981, the Food and Canning Workers and SAAWU pioneered the use of consumer boycotts in support of workers' struggles for recognition and acceptance of their union at the Fatti's and Moni's pasta factory in Cape Town and at the Rowntrees confectionary enterprise in East London, respectively. In both cases, success supplied a powerful tactical justification for unions involving themselves in 'community' affairs. This group of unions rejected registration, maintaining that compliance with the government's requirements for legal recognition conceded too much control to officials. In this cluster there were disagreements, however, between the more orthodox, professionally organised, single-industry organisations such as FCWU and the general workers' groups such as SAAWU, especially over the ways in which leadership should function; the sectoral unions shared with FOSATU a preoccupation with maintaining internal democracy by viewing leaders as elected delegates, circumscribed by the terms of their mandate. Shortly after its formation, SAAWU adopted the ANC's Freedom Charter, and in 1983 and 1984, the FCWU, SAAWU and a number of other similar general workers' unions joined the UDF. Finally, there was a third trade union alignment. This was constituted by often loosely organised general workers' bodies as well as the Council of Unions of South

Africa (CUSA) grouping, under the leadership of officials linked to Black Consciousness organisations and excluding on the basis of principle whites from their organisations.

In the early 1980s, the issues that had separated FOSATU from the 'community' unions became less contentious. By 1982, the government had capitulated to labour demands that the authorities should rescind their initial policy to limit collective bargaining rights to African workers with urban residential rights. Consumer boycotts, including the threat of such a protest in support of a FOSATU affiliate–led strike at the Colgate-Palmolive factory helped to underline the benefit of unions soliciting community support. In 1981–1982 on the East Rand, FOSATU 'shop stewards' councils' were established in African townships. Their original purpose was to serve as forums in which experienced union organisers could help to extend union activity, bringing together people from different factories to facilitate the recognition of common concerns. These concerns extended beyond narrow plant-based grievances, including the particular preoccupations of migrant workers. For example, during 1983, the councils led struggles of several squatter communities to resist the authorities' efforts to demolish their shacks. The unionists' main constituency was migrant workers, and many of these lived in shacks with their families, illegal fugitives from a devastating drought gripping the countryside. Rising militancy – the incidence of strikes increased by 200 per cent between 1982 and 1983 alone – also made it clear that registration had not rendered African unions docile.

By the end of 1984, there was increasing evidence that trade unions had a unique capacity for mobilising disciplined nationally coordinated political protest. This had been evident first in 1982, when trade unions from all three groups called out workers for a brief stoppage after the death in police custody of Neil Aggett, Transvaal organiser of the FCWU. Affiliates of FOSATU played a leading role in the arrangements for the two-day November 1984 stay-away in protest at the military occupation of the Vaal townships, for one authoritative commentator, 'a decisive break with [the] economism' that had characterised the impetus of FOSATU affiliate activity.[36] In December 1985, the formation of the Congress of South African Trade Unions brought the UDF unions and the more politically independent FOSATU affiliates together in a single federation, representing around half a million workers, in which all senior officials recognised the inseparability of shop-floor struggles from the broader political struggle. The affiliation of COSATU also included the new National Union of

---

[36] Eddie Webster, 'The rise of social-movement unionism: the two faces of the black trade union movement in South Africa', in Frankel, Pines and Swilling (eds.), *State resistance and change in South Africa*.

Mineworkers, established originally in the CUSA fold. Although COSATU itself remained outside the UDF, its officials acknowledged the ANC's senior status in the liberation struggle, and at its 1987 conference, it adopted the Freedom Charter as a guiding document.

The embrace by COSATU of liberation politics was premised on an understanding that any political alliances in which it participated would enable workers to 'play a leading role in the struggle against exploitation and oppression'. According to its 1987 resolutions, in any interaction with other components of 'a united front alliance', COSATU should 'promote the leading role of the working class'. Thus, ostensible recognition of the ANC's political seniority did not imply complete agreement with its strategic orientation. For instance, it is most unlikely that trade union officials would have perceived their own organisations or the political movement in which they so often assumed local leadership roles as merely 'platforms' to service the more ambitious kinds of military operations that would become the prevalent mode of struggle in a people's war. Granted, the encounter between the ANC and COSATU representatives in 1986 signalled a public shift in the exiles' previously sceptical and sometimes hostile attitude to the independent trade union movement. Yet in COSATU, tensions continued to be evident between so-called workerist and populist tendencies. By the mid-1980s, workerists were generally willing to sanction political alliances, but they still perceived as a priority the expansion of shop-floor organisation, and they also believed that unions should participate only in those community struggles in which their influence would be decisive.

Populists characterised the workerists as reformist and neglectful of underprivileged groups including women, farmworkers and the unemployed. Populist unions tended to recruit in townships, not factories, and this inevitably brought them into conflict with authorities, especially in those urban centres situated in the borders of homelands; understandably, therefore, they were readier for political confrontation and less inclined to perceive class-related distinctions between industrial and political insurgency. The populist position was echoed and endorsed in polemics published in *Isizwe: The Nation*, a UDF journal that emphasised in its content representations of SACP strategic orthodoxies. *Isizwe* authors attributed the influence of workerism to the role played in the establishment of the new trade unions by 'young intellectuals, many (but not all) white, coming from the universities' and shaped by an 'academic marxism' that was 'very European in character.'[37] Be that as it may, workerist sentiment was evident in

---

[37] 'Errors of workerism', *Isizwe: The Nation: Journal of the United Democratic Front* 1:3 (November 1986), 15. See also the perception of workerism as a syndicalist movement in L. N. Mahlalela, 'Workerism and economism', *African Communist* 104 (1986), 25–32.

reservations about supporting the UDF and ANC advocacy of sanctions and disinvestment. In 1986, for example, the National Allied and Auto Workers Union, a former FOSATU affiliate, called out its members in protest against General Motors' plans to sell off its South African subsidiary. More generally, COSATU's independence was indicated by its particular stand on the Freedom Charter; by representing the charter as a 'minimum set of demands', trade unionists were suggesting that liberation might extend beyond the charter's goals. Moreover, in its assertion that 'the struggle for national liberation and the struggle against capitalist exploitation' were 'complementary to each other', COSATU was signalling its rejection of a sequential or 'stages' theory of revolutionary change, a critical premise in less sophisticated ANC-SACP understandings of 'national democracy'.

By mid-1986, national democracy, however understood, must have appeared a more distant prospect than it had appeared to the UDF's activist following one year previously. In Alexandra, Sekhukhuneland and elsewhere, the second state of emergency imposed in June 1986 ended the rebellion's most Jacobin phase. Much fiercer press restrictions, a record deployment of soldiers, and twenty-five thousand detentions affected even the most junior layers of leadership, driving the movement off the streets and into semiclandestinity. Still, support for the movement continued to be manifest in a widespread rent boycott. Whistle-blowing teams of comrades and youth congress cadres in Soweto were still capable through all of 1987 of marshalling demonstrations of mass support for evicted tenants. Soweto may have been exceptional though, because of its size, and the concentration in its boundaries of experienced and sophisticated organisers. The Soweto Youth Congress, for example, possessed a parallel 'shadow' leadership hierarchy of people who did not hold elected office and hence were less vulnerable to state harassment. Many of the shadow leaders were ex–Robben Island prisoners, several with experience of clandestine structures. Therefore, despite the embargo on public meetings, despite house-to-house searches, extensive patrolling by police and soldiers, the removal and sometimes torture of key local activists and the presence of a secret military bureaucracy, the UDF's substructure survived intact in Soweto. But its activities had to be discreet and conspiratorial. In contrast with the movement at its peak, politics receded to becoming the activity of committed enthusiasts.

Even before its effective prohibition under a new emergency regulation on 24 February 1988, the UDF as a national body had for more than a year undertaken very little active campaigning. A series of national committees was formed to tighten into functional formations the loose national networks of youth congresses, civic associations and women's groups. The UDF adopted as its own programme the Freedom Charter, giving the movement a more formal ideological coherence. Efforts were also made to launch two centrally directed campaigns, a programme of 'United Action Against Apartheid' and the 'Unban the ANC' drive, the latter mounted primarily through expensive mainstream press advertisements, funded by a commercial bank loan. Neither campaign progressed beyond its opening salvo, for after June 1986, it was virtually impossible to legally mobilise large numbers of people. But why should the UDF hierarchy have confined itself to what was legally permissible? Historically, in other settings, strong organisations had led huge programmes of civil disobedience against ruthless administrations. The UDF's strength, though, was of a particular kind. It expressed a popular mood and reflected an entrenched political culture. Much of its driving force came from its affiliates. Its structure was decentralised and ill suited to the task of coordination. It was also more externally dependent than its leaders cared to admit. When the government cut off the flow of foreign funds in October 1986, it deprived central UDF offices of the resources that had supported full-time activists, paid for publicity, supplied photocopiers and bought and maintained vehicles. Emergency restrictions on newspaper reportage of the UDF and township politics more generally deprived local officials of vital channels of communication; although UDF spokespeople were critically dismissive of the 'commercial press', they had often received sympathetic coverage in liberal English-language newspapers. As a national organisation, the UDF was a thin skein of committees attempting to supply strategic direction to a conglomeration of sometimes assertively independent local political networks of varying character and effectiveness. It proved much easier to immobilise than its progenitors anticipated.

In retreat during the course of 1987, the activities of surviving UDF principals began to emphasise the construction of social alliances in efforts to attract business support in the 'Friends of the UDF'. Classical united front propositions began to replace the egalitarian anticapitalism that had welled up from local activist discourses in the movement's earlier phase. An obliquely expressed and never publicly acknowledged debate began in UDF circles over the tactical merits of the boycott. The possibility that UDF affiliates might have sponsored a Sinn Féin style of participation in the parliamentary or municipal elections may have been one of the considerations influencing the draconian restrictions the government imposed on the UDF in March 1988. By then, though, despite the proliferation and elaboration of its organisational structures, the UDF had lost much of its vitality. In the coerced acquiescent space that it vacated, soldiers and civil servants sought to deflect popular political aspirations with tarred roads, upgraded and privatised housing, water-borne sanitation and a resuscitated politics of patronage. All too often, the latter could be accompanied by state-sponsored terror undertaken by the vigilante gangs commanded by returning councillors, a particular feature of the second state of emergency. Through 1988, a combination of these agencies succeeded in driving off the streets the movement that the UDF had inspired.

In the trials of the activists and leaders associated with these events, prosecutors tried to prove that they were participants in a conspiracy directed by the ANC. Such perceptions have found their reflection in academic history. From this perspective, the 'new revolutionary strategy and realignment toward the ANC were important factors behind the formation of the UDF', and its establishment represented an achievement of 'both the ANC's objective and the Leninist/Gramscian united front.'[38] Such claims are partly true. The ANC did call for the organisation of a front to create the political base it needed before it could launch a people's war. It is also quite probable that its leaders' understanding of the political sociology of such formations was shaped by classical Marxist precedents. Equally, the ANC's original conception of a front was of a much more politically eclectic body than the UDF, one that would incorporate political communities outside the Charterist camp.

The degree to which the UDF's principals were conscious participants in a revolutionary strategy varied sharply and, as we have seen, different groups mobilised during the course of the rebellion were animated by their own preoccupations. Neither Allan Boesak, the movement's most prominent 'patron', nor Popo Molefe, its general secretary, believed that the ANC's vision of a revolutionary capture of power was plausible. Especially in the relatively more conservative coloured and Indian communities, UDF leaders used a politically restrained, rights-based political vocabulary, emphasising the UDF's significance as 'the last mass non-violent effort' to induce the government to concede change peacefully. Such language would have reflected tactical circumspection, but it could also have reflected the preferences of particular UDF leaders. As we have seen, trade unions varied in their degree of commitment to participating in political struggles and in the extent to which they deferred to the ANC's strategic perspectives. Even groups that acknowledged the ANC's political authority determined their own programmes, choosing their own enemies.

In its more senior echelons, too, the UDF was politically complicated. An internal ANC report written from inside South Africa in 1986 detailed 'problems of a subjective nature', arising from 'different, opposing groupings' in its leadership. Some of the groupings comprised senior personalities who considered themselves members of an ANC 'internal leadership',

---

[38] Greg Houston, *The national liberation struggle in South Africa: a case study of the United Democratic Front, 1983–1987* (Aldershot, U.K.: Ashgate Publishing, 1999), pp. 62–3.

dating back to the later 1970s – these comprised 'old stalwarts, former BCM activists and other operatives from student and other circles'. Between 1980 and 1982, these networks played a key role in a series of initiatives that helped to entrench and revive the ANC's popularity, including the 1980 Release Mandela Campaign, commemoration of the Freedom Charter, and COSAS-led school boycotts. During this period, these groupings became increasingly fragmented and remained outside any 'system ensuring proper command and control', even after the establishment in the early 1980s of underground politico-military committees in the Transvaal and Natal, disciplined ANC structures coordinated through external lines of communication with 'Forward Areas' in Swaziland and Botswana.

Three of these 'internal leadership' factions were discussed in the report. The so-called Cabal comprised mainly of key people in the Natal and Transvaal Indian Congress but also with supporters in Soweto, in sections of the Johannesburg 'white left' and among the membership of the Wits Black Students Society, had become increasingly influential in the UDF. Members tended to 'underplay armed struggle and undermine the importance of underground work'. Individuals in the Cabal appeared to favour 'an autonomous internal ANC'. In general, the Cabal paid insufficient attention to the working class. Their 'reformism' was a reflection of a 'lack of grassroots organization and (their social) composition'. Members of this group had in fact been in touch with Mac Maharaj since the mid-1970s. Constituted mainly of ex-students from the University of Durban–Westville, they had played a critical role in the revival of the Natal Indian Congress as an assertive protest movement. Members of this group included Pravin Gordhan and Yunus Mahomed, both of whom belonged to the SACP's clandestine network as well as that of the ANC.[39] A second identified faction comprised a former group of white student activists, including the ex-National Union of South African Students (NUSAS) president Auret van Heerden. As members of the Community Resource Information Centre (CRIC), this group played a major role in producing and publishing propaganda circulated in UDF structures. The CRIC members favoured a 'public socialist' analysis of 'racial capitalism',[40] and they were critical of the

---

[39] Seekings, *The UDF*, p. 33.

[40] As noted earlier, more left-wing versions of national democracy were also premised on the argument that South African capitalism depended on apartheid's restrictions and was probably not susceptible to significant reform. The difference with the advocates of the CRIC position was essentially tactical: the SACP believed that public advocacy of socialism would alienate substantial sections of the ANC's support in the African population. As the members of the ANC's Politico-Military Strategy Commission noted in 1979, no one among them 'had any doubts about the ultimate need to continue our revolution towards a socialist order; the issue was posed only in relation to the tactical

SACP's conception of South Africa representing a 'Colonialism of a Special Type'. They were also critical of more politically moderate sections of the UDF leadership. At the same time, though, CRIC personalities perceived the ANC's external leadership as 'irrelevant and out of touch'. Finally, a third faction was embodied in the mainly African township-based Release Mandela Committee. The RMC's leaders included such veteran ANC notables as Winnie Mandela and Oscar Mpetha, as well as more recent recruits to the Charterist camp from Black Consciousness such as Curtis Nkondo and Aubrey Mokoena. The RMC spokespeople were publicly critical of the mainly Indian Cabal, emphasising the need for 'African' organisations to play a more decisive role in the UDF. The report subsequently included a discussion of comparable difficulties within the UDF and the ANC's following in the Eastern Cape.[41]

Such documentation needs to be interpreted cautiously. It was written from the point of view of a trained and disciplined ANC 'cadre', and the quarrelsome picture it projects may have been exaggerated. Members of the Cabal, CRIC or the RMC may have had very different perceptions of their positions and of their relationships with one another. On the other hand, the conclusions about the extent of the underground ANC's influence over the UDF are probably authoritative. 'There is no central Congress Organization"', the report observed, 'which would be the core of the UDF etc.' 'Our briefings have not been decisive', it continued:

Most of the leadership of the mass democratic movement considers itself Congress but they do not belong to movement structures to which they can account and be given collective assistance. Our discussions with the leadership of the mass democratic movement tend to be suggestive; we do not assert our positions clearly and unambiguously.

In fact, the UDF functioned in much the fashion that was forecast in the ANC strategic review, with a significant degree of autonomy from its own networks. As Seekings observes, although most UDF leaders 'saw themselves as subordinate to the ANC in exile', they understood their role as 'subordinate in the sense more of a subordinate partner than of a subordinate in a straightforwardly hierarchical command structure.'[42] The ANC strategists were well aware of the complexity of the UDF, but they were encouraged by the willingness of its constituents to acknowledge

considerations of the present stage of our struggle' (Karis and Gerhart, *From protest to challenge*, vol. 5, p. 724).

[41] Typed document with handwritten title 'Nkukheli' and handwritten corrections dated 1986, evidently written at the end of that year by a member of the ANC Politico-Military Committee. I am grateful to Gail Gerhart for showing me this document.

[42] Seekings, *The UDF*, p. 292.

the ANC's authority. In the townships, ANC strategic thinkers noted, there were emerging 'organs of self government' that had the potential to develop both as sources of 'alternate power' and as 'organs of insurrection'. 'Uprisings' had 'become a permanent feature of our struggle.'[43] For certain observers in the ANC's exile community, such structures not only would help to promote 'peoples war and insurrection' but also were 'clearly destined to be the embryos of our future democratic state'.[44]

PEOPLE'S WAR

After the outbreak of localised rebellions in 1984, it was clearly time to take guerrilla operations to a more ambitious stage. This view prevailed at the ANC's 'Third Consultative Conference,'[45] held in Kabwe, Zambia, in June 1985, at a time when, for ANC leaders, 'the balance of forces' appeared 'to have shifted radically in our favour'. Here, the ANC made public its intention of moving to a People's War that would conclude in the 'seizure of power'. Essentially, this meant the expansion of the social base of guerrilla operations through the distribution of simple weaponry, along with the organisation of brief instruction sessions on its usage. People's war required bringing under uMkhonto leadership the youthful militants who had already turned the townships into combative arenas. In the phraseology used at the conference, 'the risen masses' would be turned 'into organised groups of combatants' under an externally trained 'officer corps'. Guerrillas needed to become less dependent on external lines of communication: 'the stress should be on training inside the country', and uMkhonto should also 'strive to get our weapons from inside the country'. In an 'intensified confrontation', armed operations would shift 'from the black ghettos into the white areas'. Hereafter, while 'strik[ing] at enemy personnel' would remain a priority, it would, however, become more difficult for the ANC to maintain a distinction between 'soft' and 'hard' targets. Armed struggle should also spread to rural areas where previously 'we had not paid enough attention'. Here, ANC cadres should work 'to revive areas with traditions of resistance and revolt', and in particular, insurgency should be directed at removing white 'soldier farmers' from border areas.[46]

---

[43] 'Political Report of the National Executive Committee,' in African National Congress, *Documentation of the Second National Consultative Conference*, p. 18.

[44] Mzala, 'Building people's power'.

[45] At the time the ANC referred to this meeting as its second such conference. During its exile, three consultative conferences were held, in Lobatsi in 1962, in Morogoro in 1969 and in Kabwe in 1985.

[46] Quotations in this paragraph are from African National Congress, *Documentation of the Second Consultative Conference*, pp. 10–12, 18, and 44; African National Congress, National

Following the conference, uMkhonto stepped up operations using the Botswana National Highway as its main infiltration route.[47] Eighty or so attacks were recorded in the second half of 1985, contributing to an annual record of 136 attacks, and in 1986, guerrillas struck 228 times, almost daily toward the middle of the year. Many of the operations were simple, with hand-grenade attacks accounting for one-third. Almost 160 guerrillas were killed or captured, representing one-third of uMkhonto losses since 1977. The escalation of attacks probably reflected wider weapon distribution. At the beginning of 1987, for example, 'comrades' protecting rent boycotters often possessed side arms, evidence that guerrillas were indeed training and equipping local 'mass combat units'. This may help to explain the growing incidence of attacks on targets such as shopping arcades that inevitably inflicted civilian casualties. Not all such instances of terrorism could be blamed on lapses resulting from loose discipline and perfunctory training of local auxiliaries. A car bomb detonated in July 1988 outside Johannesburg's main rugby stadium just after the match, killing several of the emerging spectators. A carefully planned operation, it occurred shortly after uMkhonto's new chief of staff had said in an interview that future operations would disrupt white civilians' sense of security, their guarantee of a 'sweet life'. The government's incapacity to protect whites from political violence would then become obvious. Steve Tshwete, uMkhonto's political commissar, speaking at the same time, echoed Hani's sentiments: 'A war must be a war in South Africa'.[48]

Not all of their associates shared Hani's and Tshwete's bellicosity. A land-mine offensive initiated in the Northern Transvaal border region in November 1985 was abandoned a year later, as too frequently the victims had been labourers and children rather than the militarised 'soldier farmers' the ANC believed inhabited the area. In this vicinity, ANC guerrillas enjoyed no success in recruiting people locally, nor could they depend on local networks of political support.[49] In October 1988, the ANC released a statement forswearing attacks on civilians. UMkhonto operations continued, though, the number of attacks nearing three hundred in 1989. But

Consultative Conference, June 1985, Report, Main Decisions and Recommendations of the Second National Consultative Conference, p. 6.

[47] Ronnie Kasrils, *Armed and dangerous: from undercover struggle to freedom* (Johannesburg: Jonathan Ball, 1998), p. 279.

[48] Transcript of an unpublished interview by John Battersby with Chris Hani and Steve Tshwete, Lusaka, 3 June 1988.

[49] The uMkhonto guerrillas did not speak the local language, and they worked in isolation; police were alerted to their presence by local informants. See *State v Mncube MZ and Nondula, ME*, Messina, 1988, Lodge Collection, E25 A3104, Historical Papers, Cullen Library, University of the Witwatersrand.

these continued mainly to be the work of externally trained insurgents; generalising the scope of participation beyond their ranks proved much more difficult than had been anticipated at Kabwe. At their peak, uMkhonto's activities scarcely represented a serious threat to South African security.[50] Indeed, in October 1986, the ANC circulated to its national command centres a soberly critical assessment of its military activities. 'Despite all our efforts', it argued, 'we have not come anywhere near the achievement of the objectives we set ourselves'. The ANC structures inside South Africa remained weak and unable to supply reliable support for uMkhonto units, which still operated largely in isolation from 'mass combat groups'. The document expressed anxieties over attacks on shops as well as the casualties inflicted by land mines. These it called 'political setbacks'.[51] The ANC had had to dismantle its organisation and withdraw its people from Mozambique, Lesotho and Botswana; meanwhile, inside South Africa, its organisational shortcomings prevented it from exploiting pockets of 'revolutionary preparedness'. In brief, the declaration of the advent of people's war in 1985 had been premature. Detentions had depleted the ranks of the comrades whom uMkhonto commanders hoped to enlist. South African police continued to anticipate with precision the arrival of trained guerrillas from across the border, an indication of their success in infiltrating uMkhonto command structures.[52] In the field, the average survival period for guerrillas was six months, according to an uMkhonto officer's own estimate.[53] Meanwhile, South African threats and actual 'destabilization' of neighbouring countries made it increasingly difficult for the ANC to maintain supplies and reinforcements. In April 1989, the ANC was compelled to move its guerrilla-training facilities back to Tanzania from Angola, a consequence of the Namibia-Angola peace accord. Although certain uMkhonto commanders remained ebullient,[54] by this time, it was obvious to most ANC

---

[50] For comparative assessment of the threat represented by political violence in South Africa in the late 1980s, see Jeffrey Herbst, 'Prospects for revolution in South Africa', *Political Science Quarterly* 103:4 (Winter 1988–1989), 674–6.

[51] '1987: What is to be done?', document distributed by the ANC Politico-Military Council to regional command centres, October 1986. Later released to South African journalists by the South African authorities at a press conference.

[52] Ellis and Sechaba, *Comrades against apartheid*, pp. 168–9.

[53] Howard Barrell, *MK: the ANC's armed struggle* (Johannesburg: Penguin, 1990), p. 60.

[54] Ronnie Kasrils, director of military intelligence, was convinced that uMkhonto could have considerably expanded its operations during the 1990s, although he conceded that prospects of victory remained constrained by failure to 'link with our rural people' (Kasrils, *Armed and dangerous*, pp. 265–6, 288). Kasrils maintains that, from 1987, ANC sympathisers in the police and army had supplied sufficient information to enable uMkhonto's intelligence to supply field units with accurate and comprehensive information about enemy deployments in their areas.

leaders that, in Alfred Nzo's words, the ANC did 'not have the capacity to intensify the armed struggle in any meaningful way.'[55] This was despite the relative success of Operation Vula, a plan implemented from 1988 to infiltrate senior ANC leaders inside South Africa and with the help of Dutch anti-apartheid allies to extend 'the infrastructure for a people's war', including local military training and new facilities for importing and storing arms.[56]

From 1986, ANC spokespeople began to refer more frequently to the prospect of a negotiated accession to power. At Kabwe, the national executive's report referred dismissively to 'a fair amount of speculation about the ANC and the Pretoria regime getting together to negotiate a settlement'. Equally, the report continued, the ANC should not 'be seen to be rejecting a negotiated settlement in principle', for such a position would rule out the possibility of attracting support 'among our white compatriots.'[57] In September 1985, a meeting between ANC leaders and leading South African businessmen in Zambia represented an encouraging signal that powerful interests inside South Africa were willing to contemplate a change of regime. There, Thabo Mbeki explained the ANC's nationalisation policies to the South African visitors: monopoly capital, including the press, would be under public control, but 'beyond that private capital would exist'. Even so, nationalisation might be on the Zambian model, with a 51 per cent state holding, leaving plenty of room for big companies. In a more uncompromising vein, Mbeki added that, from the ANC's perspective, 'an intensification of the armed struggle was necessary and that it was inevitable that civilians would be accidental victims'.[58] But despite the no-nonsense tone Mbeki adopted in speaking to the businesspeople, within a few months, ANC references to negotiations were implying a very different form of political transition to a 'capture of power'. This latter procedure was interpreted at Kabwe as 'mass action involving revolutionary force, such as land occupation, factory occupation, people's control of the township in the face of constituted authority' and a major uMkhonto 'combat presence' sustained by 'the availability of minimum armouries of weapons'.[59] By

---

[55] Quoted in the *New York Times*, 9 February 1990. By mistake, Nzo was quoting from an internal National Executive Committee document at a press conference.

[56] Padraig O'Malley, *Shades of difference: Mac Maharaj and the struggle for South Africa* (New York: Viking, 2007), p. 244. See also Conny Braam, *Operation Vula* (Bellvue: Jacana, 2004).

[57] 'Political Report of the National Executive Committee', African National Congress, *Documentation of the Second Consultative Conference*, p. 36.

[58] Notes of a meeting at Mfuwe Game Lodge, 13 September 1985.

[59] African National Congress, *Commission on Strategy and Tactics: National Consultative Conference*, June 1985, p. 16.

January 1986, a senior ANC leader was telling the London *Observer* that the objective of the 'offensive' was 'breaking up the power structure'. 'We are not talking of overthrowing the government', he conceded, 'but [of] turning so many people against it that it would be forced to do what Ian Smith had to do.'[60]

With the proliferation of contacts between the ANC and representatives of different interest groups within South African civil society, the likelihood of such a scenario was becoming more and more plausible. Acting on his own initiative, Nelson Mandela initiated an increasingly ambitious schedule of talks with members of the government, beginning with an encounter with the Minister of Justice, 'Kobie' Coetsee, in January 1986. The first contact between the external leadership and South African officials had taken place a couple of months previously, when Kobus Jordaan, an emissary from the Department of Constitutional Affairs, visited Lusaka. This was an initiative by the minister, Chris Heunis, undertaken without Botha's approval, and it led to his subsequent political sidelining.[61] In mid-1986, ANC leaders offered a qualified endorsement of a negotiating framework developed by the British Commonwealth's Eminent Person's Group. By 1988, the Director of the National Intelligence Service, Neil Barnard, was imposing his managerial authority on a range of contacts with the ANC, including communications both with Mandela and with Thabo Mbeki's office in Lusaka.[62] The first official meetings between the ANC and the British and American governments in 1986 and 1987 and the – albeit reluctant – embracing of sanctions by American policy makers, a response to public pressure generated by the campus-based divestment campaign and by African American notables, similarly encouraged perceptions that negotiations represented a viable route to national democracy.

Of course, there remained reservations about such an option, especially among more socially radical sections of the exile community. An SACP politburo document warned about the consequences of 'the revolutionary forces' being drawn 'into negotiation before they are strong enough to impose their basic objectives'. The ANC should 'resist any confusion' between its goal of 'national democratic revolution' and 'the classical constituents of a bourgeois democratic revolution'. From this perspective, the main significance of meetings between the ANC and South African businesspeople or officials was the extent to which they served 'to weaken the

---

[60] *London Observer*, 2 March 1986.

[61] Jan Heunis, *The inner circle: reflections on the last days of white rule* (Johannesburg: Jonathan Ball, 2007), p. 66.

[62] Richard Rosenthal, *Mission improbable: a piece of the South African story* (Cape Town: David Philip, 1998), pp. 228–9.

cohesion of the enemy.'[63] This was a view that maintained as the strategic objective a 'seizure of power' to precede the establishment of a protosocialist national democracy. But by 1988, more qualified expectations about a postapartheid political order were beginning to prevail. A set of constitutional guidelines and economic principles published by the ANC certainly suggested a substantially reorganised political system but a polity that would retain existing laws and personnel. Furthermore, economic prescriptions omitted any specific commitments to nationalisation. Several months earlier, the ANC's national executive had released a statement 'reaffirming' the ANC's commitment to a negotiated transition, accepting 'that a new constitution could include an entrenched bill of rights to safeguard the individual.'[64]

The ANC's hesitant embrace of liberal democracy represented a return to a liberal strand in its own early intellectual formation. Elevated to the status of official policy were the conciliatory convictions about whites eventually becoming reasonable that were evident in the interactions between ANC spokespeople and Western visitors even when the movement's official language was at its most militant. Significantly, a major theme of an authorised 1988 history of the ANC was 'that there is no historical justification for an artificial demarcation between the ANC of today and the early ANC.'[65] That position notwithstanding, there was a considerable disparity between the insurrectionary kinds of strategic goals spelled out at the Kabwe Conference in 1985 and the vision of a negotiated liberation of the ANC's Harare Declaration of 1989. As it was a comparable shift in state strategy that helped to induce the ANC's redefinition of its plans, it is to the sequestered domains of South African officials that we now must turn.

PRETORIA'S PRAETORIANS

From 1979 through most of the 1980s, commentaries on South African public policy often referred to the predominance of a doctrine of total national strategy. As the best guarantor of 'orderly government', the military needed to become more involved in policy making, the architects of this strategy maintained.[66] Official advocacy of this doctrine was widely

---

[63] South African Communist Party, Politburo discussion document on negotiations, circulated May 1986 and referred out in the South African Parliament by P. W. Botha, 12 June 1986. The full text of the document was circulated to journalists.

[64] Statement of the National Executive Committee of the African National Congress on the question of Negotiations, 9 October 1987.

[65] Meli, *South Africa belongs to us*, p. ix.

[66] Deon Geldenhuys, *The diplomacy of isolation: South African foreign policy making* (Johannesburg: Macmillan, 1984), pp. 140–1.

believed to signify the emergence of a new political order, one in which the state and its decision-making processes had become 'dominated by the military', in which soldiers had gained power through a 'constitutional military coup d'etat', and in which 'very few aspects of civilian life' had not become 'dominated by military and security considerations.'[67] This argument that the state had become militarised had three separate but related elements. Its first contention was that the military particularly, and a broader 'security establishment' more generally, had by the 1980s become ascendant. Second, the thesis was buttressed by the proposal that the scale of defence expenditure and arms procurement had put the South African economy on a substantial war footing. Third, exponents of the militarisation view suggested that, at least with respect to white South Africans, soldiers had acquired a very considerable moral and ideological influence.[68]

The institutionalisation of military dominance was ascribed to the emergence in 1979 of the State Security Council (SSC) as a policy-making body. First created in 1972 as a committee to coordinate the activities of different security agencies, the SSC was not intended to develop any executive purposes. In any case, in its early existence it met very occasionally. During John Vorster's premiership, the police enjoyed much greater political influence than the army and were, moreover, primarily responsible for counterinsurgency. P. W. Botha's election as Prime Minister changed this. During his tenure as Minister of Defence, Botha had implemented a reorganisation of command structures, with the emphasis on technocratic efficiency and hierarchical centralisation. He viewed himself as a reformer, committed to Afrikaner survival but willing to reconsider as 'outdated political principles', policies that an earlier generation of political leaders had understood as inviolable precepts.[69]

At senior staff levels within the SADF, the writings of the French strategist of the Algerian war, André Beaufre, became increasingly influential. Beaufre viewed war in the modern age as an inevitably totalising process in which the military and nonmilitary realms are interdependent and in which the key struggles concern the shaping of public opinion. States faced with 'total onslaughts' need to align 'military policy with political policy, with foreign policy, financial policy, economic policy and production.'[70] Beaufre's

---

[67] Quotations from the introduction to Phyllis Johnson and David Martin (eds.), *Frontline southern Africa: destructive engagement* (New York: Four Walls, Eight Windows, 1988).

[68] For the most authoritative analyses of militarisation, see Philip H. Frankel, *Pretoria's Praetorians: civil-military relations in South Africa* (Cambridge: Cambridge University Press, 1984); Kenneth Grundy, *The militarization of South African politics* (Bloomington: Indiana University Press, 1986).

[69] O'Meara, *Forty lost years*, p. 257.

[70] Frankel, *Pretoria's Praetorians*, pp. 47–8.

stress on the political and even psychological dimensions of national security inspired the germination during the late 1960s in the SADF command of 'total onslaught' thinking. Botha brought to the premiership the SADF's managerial principles and its strategic philosophy. With its staff enlarged considerably, SSC meetings were scheduled frequently and regularly, taking place just before cabinet meetings to enable the council to set the agenda for these.

The SSC itself was composed of certain cabinet ministers and the heads of various government departments, with a secretariat drawn from the various security agencies. With the installation in 1979 of the National Security Management System (NSMS), the SSC acquired the power to develop discreetly a national network of committees, regional Joint Management Committees and Joint Management Centres. With its establishment beginning in 1983,[71] this quasi-secret bureaucracy reached its most developed form after the imposition of the second state of emergency in 1986. It represented, in effect, a hidden 'parallel' administration behind the facade of ministries and departments that were responsible to Parliament. The SSC and the NSMS were answerable only to the Office of the State President, the executive authority enacted in the 1983 constitution. Through this office, the council had access to huge amounts of funding and the authority to embrace a wide range of government functions. Its thirteen interdepartmental committees addressed particular concerns of manpower, transport, security forces, civil defence, through to culture and political affairs.

The military's new influence was attributed to the role it played in this structure, particularly in the secretariat and in the Joint Management Centres (JMCs), most of which were chaired and heavily composed of army officers. The presence of military and other security officials on the SSC itself together with the ministers of defence and of law and order (police) accorded to security officials a direct voice in policy making, constituting a unified faction within the council and a predominant influence. The army's power in the NSMS was also strengthened by two other factors, the backing it enjoyed from the prime minister and later the state president between 1978 and 1988, and second, its own institutional capabilities that equipped it with a much wider range of skills and resources than any other department of state for executing policy.[72]

---

[71] Chris Alden, *Apartheid's last stand: the rise and fall of the South African security state* (Basingstoke, U.K.: Macmillan, 1996), p. 94.

[72] For description of the NSMS, see Annette Seegers, 'Extending the security network to the local level', in Heymans and Totemeyer (eds.), *Government by the people?*, pp. 119–39; Mark Swilling and Mark Phillips, 'The emergency state; its power and limits,' in Moss and Obery (eds.), *South African Review* 5, pp. 68–90.

Definite evidence of the military's dominant role in policy making is elusive. Army support for the Renamo insurgency in Mozambique after 1980 and its ever-increasing commitments to supporting UNITA in Angola, as well as South African military support for other more minor rebellions against governments in the region, are usually cited as evidence of military influence over foreign policy. As some of the more sophisticated treatments of militarisation have pointed out,[73] the deployment of the army or of its surrogate forces across South African borders may have furthered the purposes of a broad array of interests within and outside the South African state. There were several key instances, though, both in South African regional relations and in its domestic polices, that appeared to confirm the SADF's political entrenchment.

The most frequently cited of these was the continued support by the SADF's Military Intelligence Department for the *Resistência Nacional Moçambicana* (better known as Renamo or the MNR). This was in contravention of the provisions of the 1984 Nkomati Accord, the agreement in which the South African and Mozambican governments agreed to cease allowing Renamo and uMkhonto to use facilities in their respective territories. The agreement was disliked by General Van der Westhuizen of Military Intelligence, from 1985 the chair of the SSC Secretariat. In documents captured at the Renamo headquarters in Sofala province in 1986, Van der Westhuizen was on record as telling Renamo commanders in February 1984, 'We, the military, will continue to give the MNR support without the consent of our politicians.'[74] The documents also testified to later meetings in Mozambique between the Renamo leaders and other key SADF generals and a junior government minister. In the SSC, however, security representatives had apparently not opposed the Accord during its negotiations. It is possible that the soldiers believed that the Mozambicans would violate the agreement anyway. Businesspeople were keen on the prospect of opening up Mozambican trading and investment, and their perceived priorities certainly affected the conduct of the South African negotiators. The subsequent unravelling of the Accord as a consequence of the SADF's maintenance of Renamo supply lines suggested that, from late 1984, the view of the security representatives on the Council once again prevailed, although it is also the case that the onset of economic recession contributed to a decline in business interest in Mozambique. The diplomatic gains

---

[73] See, e.g., Reginald Green and Carol Thompson, 'Political economies in conflict: SADCC, South Africa and sanctions', in Johnson and Martin, *Frontline southern Africa*, pp. 339–86.

[74] Phyllis Johnson and David Martin. 'Mozambique: victims of apartheid,' in Johnson and Martin, *Frontline southern Africa*, p. 32. Shortly after the signing of the accord, P. W. Botha told foreign affairs officials that he had just sanctioned a final weapons delivery to Renamo at the request of General Malan (Heunis, *The inner circle*, p. 45).

represented by Nkomati were in any event wiped out with the beginning of the Vaal uprising. Even so, SADF logistical support for Renamo up to the end of 1988, evidently the consequence of decisions at the highest level of command, can hardly have been welcomed by Foreign Affairs officials who had to contend with disapproval from U.S. State Department representatives (notwithstanding Central Intelligence Agency complicity in supplying Renamo).[75] Meanwhile, SADF generals were heavily critical of Foreign Minister Pik Botha's commitment to the undertakings that South Africa signed in the 1984 accord. In the view of the SADF chief, General Constand Viljoen, Botha was a 'traitor' and a 'Soviet nark.'[76]

Another key instance in the militarisation of foreign policy was perceived in the mounting of air and commando raids on ANC facilities in Botswana, Zimbabwe and Zambia on 19 May 1986, just after the time when the Commonwealth-sponsored Eminent Persons' Group seemed to be on the brink of securing agreement between South African government and ANC representatives on a 'negotiating concept'. These raids were a significant element in persuading Republicans in the U.S. Congress to support sanctions legislation, and they also drew uncharacteristically sharp condemnation from the Reagan administration. The raids were mounted, it was suggested, because the SSC 'had decided the state was militarily self sufficient ... and sanctions busting networks could be relied upon for import and export networks as well as technology transfers'.[77] In fact, the attacks seem to have been P. W. Botha's personal initiative, taken after consultations with select cabinet ministers including the Foreign Minister, but excluding Chris Heunis, Minister for Constitutional Affairs, who was engaged in discussions with the Commonwealth Mission as the raids were taking place.

With the activation of the NSMS after the June 1986 State of Emergency, the evidence for the SADF's impact on domestic political processes appeared very compelling. During the first year of the emergency, thirty-nine thousand soldiers were used in townships. The largely security force–staffed mini-JMCs supplied the essential organisational network for coordinating an ambitious programme that combined political repression with public works. Soldiers cordoned off township sectors and established roadblocks to prevent the movement of those political activists who had escaped arrest

---

[75] Pauline Baker, *The United States and South Africa: the Reagan years*, South Africa Update Series (New York: Ford Foundation and Foreign Policy Association, 1989), p. 57. The *New York Times*, 10 September 1990, contained a letter on the editorial page suggesting that the CIA helped to obtain Saudi Arabian support for Renamo.

[76] O'Meara, *Forty lost years*, p. 333.

[77] Ivor Sarakinsky, 'The state of the state and the state of resistance', *Work in Progress* 52 (March 1988), 49.

and detention. With the accomplishment of a regimented quiescence, the mini-JMCs set to work building roads, installing sewage systems, digging storm drains, repairing schools and erecting clinics. Their less publicised activities included the compilation and distribution of propaganda and disinformation, the reconstruction of informer networks, the sponsorship or revival of socially conservative voluntary associations, the recruitment of new municipal police forces and the encouragement of strong-arm squads ('vigilantes') to protect and restore the position of the councillor trader class, whose members had been the principal targets in the 1984–1986 insurrection.

This last sphere of JMC activities was a particularly striking transposition to the domestic arena of some of the regional dimensions of SADF activity, but in fact, all the main features of the JMC programme were inspired by a scheme of 'winning hearts and minds' developed by army strategists in Namibia. The official agenda of 'upliftment' was premised on the belief that the chief causes of civil unrest were material rather than political and that all but a small minority of the population was chiefly concerned with an improvement of their living conditions and social prospects. From this perspective, effective counterinsurgency depended on removing the agencies of political agitation and intimidation and making townships more sanitary and comfortable. Thus, the repeal of influx control in 1986 would have represented a major palliative measure and was viewed by officials as the 'final burying of apartheid' – as the white paper that preceded the reform noted, 'the Government has accepted the permanence of Black (African) people in the RSA'.[78] However, P. W. Botha remained obdurate on the issue of retaining the spatial segregation stipulated in Group Areas, though from 1986, authorities began to tolerate the development of 'open' racially mixed neighbourhoods.

'Upliftment', though, represented a reversal of a previous emphasis in government policy that sought to legitimise state authority among black South Africans through opening up limited avenues of political representation. Up to 1986, the prevalent police view had been that the UDF could be contained better through manipulation than suppression. Certain government departments, notably Constitutional Affairs and Development, were prepared to sanction the local-level negotiations between officials and civic associations during the 1985 consumer boycott. From June 1986, though, JMC strategy, it was made known through a leak to the press, was to countenance no negotiations with any representatives of the extraparliamentary opposition.[79]

---

[78] David Welsh, *The rise and fall of apartheid* (Johannesburg: Jonathan Ball, 2009).
[79] Mark Swilling, 'The politics of negotiation', *Work in Progress* 50 (October 1987), 18.

On the whole, early analysts of a militarised South African state tended to discern a broad strategic consistency in government policy between 1978 and 1988 and were dismissive of the significance of reports of tensions and disagreements between different departments of state.[80] Up to 1982, the most important divisions appeared to be opposition to reform from *verkrampte* apartheid supporters led by Andries Treurnicht, who resigned from the cabinet and the National Party in February 1982. In fact, though, at least in its domestic policies, the government's objectives were subject to quite sharp shifts, and P. W. Botha's ministerial appointments included assertive independent personalities even after Treurnicht's departure. Their effects could be felt. The reformist element of 'Total Strategy' required the relaxation of existing restrictions and controls on popular political organisations, and as we have noted, these developed a depth of organization and a scale of following that were without precedent. Similarly, the state's efforts to curb the radicalism of black trade unions, through the registration procedures and collective bargaining mechanisms of the 1979 industrial relations legislation, necessitated conceding to black labour considerable power.

In other ways, too, the first half of the 1980s witnessed an expansion of freedoms and a reduction in the scale of government interference. Thus it was that a cultural renaissance in black townships could find expression in a proliferation of artistic performances, books, journals and newspapers; that critical social theory and revisionist history blossomed at universities; and that the range of censorship was progressively reduced. This blossoming of a civil society in and around African urban communities surely reflects a political order that was a long way from being militarised. It also suggests that those state agencies that sought to influence and incorporate this society rather than suppress it were profoundly at odds with the generals whose social outlook found expression in 'upliftment' programmes. In this context, the reported disagreements between the 'securocrats' and the technocrat civil servants and politicians who predominated in the powerful Department of Constitutional Affairs before they were sidelined after 1986 indicated a much more unstable balance of forces between different bureaucratic factions than is depicted in the view of the state as militarised.

From that perspective, even its critics portrayed the National Security Management System as a smooth and managerially effective apparatus. But such perceptions were misleading. Notwithstanding the expenditure of R4 billion in two years on township 'upgrading',[81] the securocrats signally

---

[80] See, e.g., Joseph Hanlon, *Beggar your neighbours: apartheid power in southern Africa* (London: James Currey, 1986), p. 49.

[81] 'Whamming the radicals', *Weekly Mail* (20 May 1988).

failed in their objective of winning hearts and minds, as became evident with the very low polls in the October 1988 Black Local Authority elections. Of course, they may have drawn encouragement from the fact that the polls were held at all, and in a relatively orderly atmosphere in which 247 out of 260 African councils were able to hold elections. Meanwhile, nearly 45 per cent of registered coloured voters elected local authorities. Even so, in general, the government failed 'to make progress on the political side' in black townships, as its own members later admitted.[82] Some of their efforts to restore legitimate authority were hampered by the indiscipline of the conscript soldiers themselves, who in their everyday behaviour in the townships began to invite unfavourable comparisons with the South African Police.[83]

Furthermore, a significant proportion of the funding was diverted into venal projects.[84] It is also true that certain government departments, even after June 1986, continued to hold meetings with township activists.[85] The sponsorship of vigilante organisations and 'traditionalist' political movements such as Inkatha, though in the short term devastatingly effective in combating activists, could become a double-edged tactic, for the 'privatisation' of repressive forces through the use of such surrogates allowed black conservatives to activate their own political agendas. Domestic destabilisation was inherently risky; state-sanctioned terror might easily outweigh the supposed inducements of upliftment. In other words, the 'parallel state' represented by the post-1986 activation of the NSMS may have been rather less formidable than is projected in the representations of militarisation. It was also far from ideologically monolithic, with its internal tensions between advocates of socioeconomic reforms and those generals who favoured heavier degrees of repression. There were probably deeper political disagreements in the military command structure as well: in 1989, three recently retired senior officers, including General Wally Black, former Director of General Operations, stood for election as Democratic Party parliamentary candidates.

---

[82] The former deputy minister of law and order Roelf Meyer interviewed in 1990 and quoted in Alden, *Apartheid's last stand*, p. 233.

[83] Michael Evans and Mark Phillips, 'Intensifying civil war: the role of the South African Defence Force', in Frankel, Pines and Swilling (eds.), *State, resistance and change*, p. 131.

[84] Kit Katzen, 'Mysteries and unanswered questions in the CCB trial', *Star* (22 September 1990); Sam Sole, 'Top team to reopen probe into arms project's missing millions', *Sunday Independent* (19 May 1996).

[85] On negotiations during 1987 and 1988 between the Department of Development Aid and residents' associations in the Eastern Cape, see Franz Kruger, 'Flirting with the residents' committees', *Work in Progress* 54 (June 1988).

The economic and fiscal indications of militarisation were rather less obvious than the institutional symptoms of the army's political power. Between 1977 and 1984, budgetary allocations to defence remained roughly uniform, even when security expenses included in other government departments are taken into account.[86] It is true that from 1987, with a 30 per cent increase over the previous year, the growth of the military budget began to outpace the 15 per cent rate of inflation significantly. In 1989, security expenditure was officially calculated at 14 per cent of the budget. On the pattern of previous years, hidden expenditures may have raised that proportion to 25 per cent. Yet even so, defence expenditure totalled half the funds taken up by social services. Expressed as a proportion of gross domestic product, defence expenditure at 4 per cent in 1984 did not represent an unusually heavy burden on an economy of South Africa's comparable level of development. Estimates of the size of the standing army fluctuated through the decade from 80,000 to 140,00, but even the larger figure would not have equalled a very heavy demand on manpower available to the economy. In short, the revenues and personnel deployed in defence, though substantial and expanding very quickly towards the end of the decade, do not in themselves seem to be very telling indications of militarisation.[87]

Of course, there are other pointers to a garrison economy, such as the fact that South Africa through the 1960s and 1970s developed a major arms industry. The Armscor parastatal in 1982 itself employed twenty-nine thousand workers and contracted out work for another seventy-six thousand. Contracts aside, the shared concerns between the defence establishment and businesspeople were expressed institutionally in 1973 with the establishment of the Defence Advisory Council and subsequently other bodies bringing together officials and industrialists. But the economy still remained far from militarised. Armscor's labour needs, including the work contracted out, represented about a tenth of the manpower employed in manufacturing. And businesspeople did not share the strategic perceptions of the security officials. Although in 1986 SSC principals could remain sanguine about the continuing possibility of obtaining advanced technology, private-sector researchers were suggesting that an immediate threat posed

---

[86] Rand expenditure increased (see Abdul Minty, 'South Africa's military build-up,' in Johnson and Martin [eds.], *Frontline southern Africa*, pp. 239–40), but proportionately the budgetary allocation to defence and defence expenditure as a proportion of gross national product declined slightly between 1977 and 1984 (Frankel, *Pretoria's Praetorians*, pp. 77–8).

[87] Jeffery Herbst, 'Political and economic implications of South Africa's militarization', *Jerusalem Journal of International Relations* 8:1 (1986), 45–7.

by sanctions and disinvestment was a widening technological gulf between South African industry and its foreign competitors.

What of the broader sociological effects of the army's expanding weight in the political economy? To be sure, a martial patriotism was an important element in the white school curriculum, within state-controlled and – to an extent – privately owned media and in the civic etiquette promoted both by the government and by voluntary associations active in the white community. Many white schoolchildren periodically attended week-long 'veldt schools', where under canvas tents they absorbed a programme based around 'love of that which is one's own, raising and lowering the flag, anti-communism, a love of our own fauna and flora and community singing'. Newspapers and other media cultivated a cheery communal folksiness around the institution of national service (two years for most white male school leavers until its reduction in 1989). Motorists were exhorted to 'give your country a lift' by picking up a 'troopie' at 'Ride Safe' signs, whereas Radio Springbok jingles celebrated the conscript whose 'hair is short, his shoulders broad and strong, more than just a number he's a man's man', so 'pick him up, take him with'. 'Armed forces shoot with Canon cameras' boasted a bumper sticker, and Mobil Oil proclaimed its wish that 'all servicemen' would enjoy 'a safe and happy training', thanking them 'for their outstanding services to our country'.[88]

The ideas and assumptions contained in such declarations may have reflected widely held perceptions and beliefs among white South Africans, but they are an insufficient indication of a society morally or psychologically prepared for war. Tellingly, in the final battles for Angola during 1988, a key factor influencing the decision to withdraw was the authorities' unwillingness to risk three figure casualties among white conscripts. Although such losses were easily sustainable in military terms, they represented a politically unacceptable level of sacrifice. The demoralizing effects of such a rate of mortality might have been mitigated had whites shared a united awareness of social and moral purpose. During the 1980s, however, evidence of such a unifying ideology was strikingly absent. Quite apart from the existence of a lively and well-organised anticonscription movement, a growing evasion rate suggests that significant numbers were reluctant to join their compatriots on the border.[89] Nor was white disaffection confined to evasion of call-up obligations. Opinion polls through the 1980s testified

---

[88] Julie Frederikse, *South Africa: a different kind of war* (Johannesburg: Ravan Press, 1986), pp. 67–72.

[89] For estimations of the extent of white resistance to conscription, see Laurie Nathan, 'Resistance to militarisation: three years of the End Conscription Campaign', in Moss and Obery, *South African Review 4*, p. 105.

to an enlarging popular sentiment predisposed to negotiations and political and social conciliation.[90] Mainstream English-speaking churches – Anglican, Methodist and Roman Catholic – all adopted positions strongly critical of war and the military, a consequence partly of the rise in their hierarchies of black priests but also a reflection of the views of their suburban congregations as well. Even in the Afrikaner cultural establishment, discordant voices became increasingly conspicuous. As Hermann Giliomee has noted, 'very few of the most outstanding [Afrikaner] academics, writers and poets still identified with the NP and apartheid'. More popular and socially resonant examples of Afrikaner disaffection included Johannes Kerkorrel's Voëlvry ballads and the alienated *grensliteratuur* published by national service veterans from the Angolan war.

Explanations for the state's militarisation emphasised a voluntaristic or idiosyncratic political dynamic. P. W. Botha's own experience in directing the modernisation of the South African army found continuing expression in his evident dependence on military advice in 1985. Then, he refused to acknowledge the depth and extent of the township revolt, rejecting the alarming reports produced by the police and by national intelligence, and believing instead the more reassuring analysis given to him by the military. If the soldiers' capacity to determine policy was mainly the consequence of the authoritarian inclinations of a powerful executive president, then the sources of military power would have been quite fragile. Hence, the more ambitious analyses of militarisation suggest that the praetorian state reflected broader developments in the economy and in society. From this perspective, the SADF's activities in the region were understood to be critical in the maintenance of South Africa's economic hegemony. Yet again, there is little evidence that businesspeople shared such perceptions, and indeed, South African trade and transport officials on occasions complained about the effects of sub-continental destabilisation.

In their identification of the beneficiaries of the state's policies, analyses of militarisation reflected more general academic treatments of the South African state. Those of the 1970s and 1980s tended to view the state in an instrumentalist way, drawing on two models of behaviour. Either the state and its policies reflected conflicts and tensions between segments of the dominant classes, or the state possessed a magisterial capacity to rise above the shortsighted quarrels between different economic interests and to make decisions that in the long term would secure the systemic interests

[90] On increasing white public support through the 1980s for the ending of social segregation and for negotiating with the ANC, see poll evidence documented in Andre du Pisani, *What do we think? A survey of white opinion on foreign policy issues* (Braamfontein: South African Institute of International Affairs, 1990), pp. 23–31.

of capital in general. It is, however, probably more helpful to interpreting the state during the 1980s if we draw on the insights of Theda Skocpol and her colleagues in their comparative work on states as autonomous agencies in shaping social processes. Skocpol suggests that politically decisive state structures inclined to assert their authority independently of the main socioeconomic interests are especially likely to occur in contexts in which there exist 'collectivities of state officials' who are neither recruited from nor in any other way intimately connected to the economically dominant classes.[91] Separate channels of socialisation for the state's functionaries, the development of its own information networks and the growth of administrative centralisation are additional factors serving to increase the propensity of such states to act autonomously in disregard of the interests of capitalist groups.

The South African apartheid state fits this generalised model quite well. Until the 1970s, ethnic divisions in the white population tended to reinforce the social and political separation of business and the civil service, though afterward a new Afrikaner bourgeoisie was increasingly likely to identify a common interest with other South African businesspeople in dismantling the more restrictive policies associated with early apartheid. More general social change among Afrikaners would also have weakened support for policies such as job reservation, whose main beneficiaries were white blue-collar workers. By 1980, nearly two-thirds of the Afrikaner labour force worked in white-collar positions. Despite these changes, the National Party's parliamentary representation tended to continue to be drawn from its traditional occupational groupings: farming, the law, education and the priesthood – with the few businesspeople in the party coming from small family enterprises. Certainly, Afrikaner politicians acquired business interests after accession to high public office, but in many cases, these took the form of land speculation and agricultural investments; connections with predominantly industrial corporations were still quite unusual. The roles played by the Universities of Pretoria and Stellenbosch as the main institutions in training public servants helped to strengthen the corporate identity of state officials and to accentuate the effects of a technocratic ideology among them. More important than anything else, the sheer weight of the state itself, the legacy of its central contribution to the construction of an industrial economy, employing in one capacity or another nearly a

[91] Theda Skocpol, 'Bringing the state back in: strategies of analysis in current research', in Peter Evans, Dietrich Rueschemeyer and Theda Skocpol (eds.), *Bringing the state back in*, p. 15. For a critical view of the application of Skocpol's and other state-centric analyses to this period, see O'Meara, *Forty lost years*, pp. 431–40.

million people, including about a quarter of the economically active white population, explains its social assertiveness.

The extent to which the state became more militarised between 1978 and 1988 reflected an administrative dynamic not a class imperative. The efforts to reorganise civil society embodied in the post-1979 reforms required a loosening of the traditional mechanisms of intervention and control; a bureaucratic reflex to this process was the strengthening of the state's repressive functions. Still, military influence in the state's decision-making bodies did not represent a militarised political order. South Africa was not a war economy, and white South Africans were disinclined to support a garrison state. Within the state, even the army's influence was contested, and soldiers were not the only voices on the State Security Council. The Foreign Affairs Department, for example, had its own representation and could bypass the SSC Secretariat to present its own proposals. The National Intelligence Service also retained autonomy and influence and was, by 1988, with P. W. Botha's consent, conducting secret talks with Nelson Mandela and Thabo Mbeki.[92] Senior officials were probably also affected by rifts in Afrikaner nationalist politics after the early 1980s. Jan Heunis, then a senior civil servant in the President's office, refers in his memoir to a reformist group in the cabinet constituted by his father, Chris Heunis (Constitutional Affairs); Pik Botha and the Minister of Finance, Barend du Plessis; and a 'hardline' conservative faction led by Louis le Grange (Law and Order), Magnus Malan and F. W. de Klerk.[93] The state's internal divisiveness as well as its increasing fiscal frailty both contributed to the abandonment of military strategic doctrines at the end of the 1980s.

The withdrawal of South African soldiers from Angola in 1988 followed by the agreement by Pretoria to cease supplying and reinforcing UNITA in return for the removal of ANC bases from Angola heralded a sharp turnabout in South African government strategy. Pulling the soldiers back from the region and prompting a series of dramatic internal policy reversals was a growing official perception of crisis generated by a mixture of military failures and financial difficulties. Arguably, the precipitating event was the reluctance of the (considerably outnumbered) SADF to inflict a decisive defeat on the Angolan and Cuban forces concentrated in the town of Cuito Cuanavale after repulsing an Angolan offensive directed at the capture of UNITA's headquarters in Jamba. The positional warfare that developed in the first six months around Cuito demonstrated new vulnerabilities in the South African Air Force. South African pilots, confronted by Angolan

---

[92] Alden, *Apartheid's last stand*, pp. 266–7. For disagreements between the National Intelligence Service and the police and army, see Giliomee, *The Afrikaners*, p. 624.

[93] Heunis, *The inner circle*, p. 123.

antiaircraft batteries, radar systems and MiG-23 fighters, could no longer offer their army effective air cover. With Cuban troops closing in on the Namibian border and the evident disinclination of the U.S. administration to in any way discourage their advance, the likely costs of sustaining an army presence in Angola seemed unsupportable.[94] In the calculations of the generals and the politicians, the numbers of white casualties were already unacceptably high, and the risks inherent in attempting to transfer the burden of sacrifice to black soldiers were dramatised in late 1987 with the mutiny of a battalion of the South West African Territorial Force. Then there was the financial burden. Arms procurements during 1989, largely related to the renovation of the air force, totalled R5.8 billion, more than half the defence budget.

The impact of Angolan military setbacks was compounded by the political failure of township upliftment. The implementation of sanctions by formerly friendly governments as well as the Republic's exclusion from financial markets also appeared much more immediately alarming than the increasingly untenable vision of a Soviet-sponsored revolutionary tide enveloping the subcontinent, the major threat identified in total onslaught doctrine. In any case, by 1987, the shifts and subtleties in Soviet perceptions of political realities in the subcontinent were being extensively reported in South Africa. In fact, from the 1984 Nkomati Accord, the tight limits to the resources that the Soviet Union was willing to commit to the defence and development of its allies in the region were quite apparent.

South African total external debt in mid-1989 stood at US$21 billion. Against that backdrop, the urgency of rescheduling 1990–1991 repayments was probably one of the most pressing inducements favouring the appearance of negotiations on the government's agenda. At the beginning of the decade, South African belief that armed excursions into Mozambique and Angola enjoyed the tacit approval of the U.S. administration had been a significant factor encouraging the use of the army or its proxies as an instrument to ensure regional compliance. By 1988, though, South African officials were being told that their government's complicity in the carnage inflicted on Mozambique by Renamo would render inevitable the prospect of Western sanctions. In any case, with the implementation of sanctions,

[94] An authoritative overview of the considerations informing the SADF's withdrawal from Angola is Chester Crocker's *High noon in southern Africa: making peace in a rough neighborhood*, (Johannesburg: Jonathan Ball, 1992), pp. 358–72. Crocker's account suggests that the importance of Cuito Cuanavale was exaggerated by Pretoria's opponents and that the SADF's success in defending UNITA against the earlier Soviet-backed offensive was more decisive, for it convinced the Soviet Union that it should withdraw from the region. See also Frederick van Zyl Slabbert, *The other side of history* (Johannesburg: Jonathan Ball, 2006), p. 38.

the regional economy acquired fresh importance. In 1988, trade between South Africa and its neighbours expanded by US$300 million, two-thirds of the decline in South African–U.S. trade. In a context in which, partly because of the pressures engendered by destabilisation and partly in spite of them, economic linkages between the region and South Africa were beginning to multiply, the disruption of the 'Frontline' economies made less sense. In this setting, the army's political importance diminished. More generally, as O'Meara has noted, at all times, the South African state's freedom of manoeuvre was subject to the limitations represented by 'structural' conditions, which became increasingly restrictive during the 1980s as South African access to international capital markets became curtailed. This was acknowledged at the time: there is an abundance of commentary from South African officials and financiers confirming the damage inflicted by financial sanctions, although it is possible that the total external divestment may have been exceeded by domestic capita flight: between 1980 and 1985, direct investment abroad doubled. Understandably, supporters of the British and North American antiapartheid movements view their own influence among shareholders in the United Kingdom and the United States as decisive in bringing about these measures.[95]

By 1989, the government was in severe financial trouble. Twelve per cent of its expenditure in 1987 and 14 per cent in 1988 were simply directed at debt repayment. In 1989, increased budgets for the military and for education, the two single largest items in the government's projected expenditure, and a general 21 per cent increase in the overall total were to be funded by raising taxation. By 1989, individual, mainly white, taxpayers were supplying 60 per cent of government revenue. Spending increases contrasted with falling growth rates – in the first three months of 1989, economic growth fell to 1.5 per cent. South Africa's gold and foreign exchange reserves were actually worth less than its short-term debts.

Finally, with the replacement of P. W. Botha first as leader of the National Party and later as President by F. W. de Klerk, political organisation resurfaced as an institutional force in state decision making. De Klerk's previous cabinet appointments identified him with none of the especially powerful civil service bureaucracies, as had been the case with his three predecessors; instead, his influence and support were chiefly consequences of the positions he had held in the Transvaal National Party, which he had led from 1982. In that capacity, he became increasingly preoccupied with defending the party against electoral threats from the right, gaining favour with P. W. Botha at the expense of Pik Botha and Chris Heunis, relatively

---

[95] Roger Fieldhouse, *Anti-apartheid: a history of the movement in Britain* (London: Merlin Press, 2005).

adventurous advocates of political change. By temperament and inclination more cautious than his predecessor, de Klerk was nevertheless willing in 1989 to opt for an electoral strategy of identifying the Party with what its strategists perceived to be significant reformist predispositions in white political sentiment. After his accession to the presidency, the State Security Council stopped meeting every fortnight and later de Klerk announced that the council would be relegated to its earlier advisory functions. On 2 February 1990, F. W. de Klerk opened Parliament with a speech he had written out by hand, for which he had consulted only his closest advisers. The government would legalise all prohibited organisations, he announced. Political prisoners not guilty of violence would be freed. The authorities would release Nelson Mandela without conditions. Nine days later Mandela walked out of prison, hand in hand with his wife.

TRANSITION

Over the following four years, South Africans would negotiate a political settlement that would establish a constitutional liberal democracy. To many observers, their achievement appeared a miraculous reversal of an inevitable trajectory toward a full-scale civil war. Only the most schematic explanation of the success of this democratic transition can be offered here. At least five considerations facilitated the settlement. First, elite perceptions of threats and opportunities changed in important ways. Second, during the course of the 1980s, the issues in the conflict altered. Third, by the time negotiations began, South Africans had already acquired the leadership, skills and experience needed to conduct them successfully. Fourth, the continuation of political violence after 1990 helped to induce willingness to compromise in the two main protagonists, the government and the ANC. Finally, settlement was easier because public access to conflict resources was generally subject to centralised leadership control.

Changes in the perceptions of the principal adversaries in the conflicts described in this chapter were very important in prompting the opening of negotiations between the government and the ANC. An especially significant consideration for F. W. de Klerk was the fall of the Berlin Wall, which effectively ended any further prospect of Soviet support for the ANC's armed insurgency. He believed that without its Eastern European allies, a domesticated ANC would be a much weaker opponent.[96] He also knew that the exiles were under increasing pressure from African governments to

---

[96] See Adrian Guelke, *Rethinking the rise and fall of apartheid* (Basingstoke, U.K.: Macmillan, 2005), pp. 162–3. See also Frederick van Zyl Slabbert's report of a conversation with de Klerk in 1990, in Slabbert, *The other side of history*, p. 28.

settle with Pretoria. De Klerk could be confident that a dramatic gesture of liberalisation would probably win him strengthened diplomatic support from conservative administrations in London and Washington, the kind of support that had helped to broker a pragmatic liberal regime in Namibia. He was encouraged that he would enjoy such support by the warm receptions he encountered in London, Washington, Lusaka and Maputo, all of which helped to convince him that 'a window had suddenly opened'. For its part, the ANC's willingness to suspend hostilities and participate in a 'pacted' transition was partly a consequence of its leadership's recognition of a 'military stalemate' in 1989. It would have also derived encouragement from the South West African People's Organisation's constitutional accession to power in Namibia. The history of the previous decade had represented evidence of the breadth of its public support. De Klerk, in contrast, believed that he might reach a settlement without conceding majority rule through a consociational dispensation, through building coalitions with black conservatives and by recruiting black supporters for the National Party itself.

By 1990, most South Africans shared a common understanding of their nationhood. Through various incremental reforms, by the end of the 1980s, government policy had moved closer and closer to acceptance of black South Africans as citizens. The emphatic nonracialism of both the UDF and the ANC also helped to diminish the salience of identity issues in politics. During the 1980s, among an increasingly affluent middle-class white population, the appeal of racially defensive Afrikaner nationalism receded as both government and the National Party attempted to project broader notions of political community. As early as the mid-1970s, opinion polling indicated that anxiety about the future of the Afrikaans language was near the bottom of a list of concerns, much less important than materialistic preoccupations.[97] In P. W. Botha's rhetoric, the South Africa to be defended against 'total onslaught' was increasingly a multiracial 'Christian civilisation' rather than an Afrikaner nation.[98] Opinion polls indicated that whites were increasingly predisposed to share public goods during a period in which they themselves were less and less likely to use public services. The paradoxical combination in government policy of tolerance and repression may have encouraged a growth in white support for liberal conceptions of rights. In particular, the Dutch Reformed Church's rejection of apartheid in 1986 affected white political beliefs decisively. The church's reversal of its earlier doctrine was in reaction to its expulsion from the World Alliance of Reformed Churches and subsequent condemnations by coloured ministers of the Sendingkerk of its role in supplying apartheid with its moral

---

[97] Giliomee, *The Afrikaners*, p. 607.   [98] O'Meara, *Forty lost years*, p. 265.

foundations. All these developments helped to build public support within the white community for democratisation, as did rising anxieties about the effects of sanctions.

'Pacted' transitions require strong political leadership. In 1990, too, this was available. In Nelson Mandela, the ANC had a leader of messianic stature who was able to draw on a battery of skilful negotiators, many of them trained in industrial collective bargaining arenas. Participants in the negotiations that began formally in 1992 had already developed an understanding of the views of their adversaries. The informal encounters between South African officials and members of the ANC and UDF that had proliferated within and outside South Africa between 1985 and 1990 had helped, through 'non-binding' communications, to foster new relationships. By 1992, the main protagonists were willing to abandon intransigent or 'positional' approaches. As important in the ultimate success of their encounters was that they commanded formidable organisational resources. The ANC's establishment of itself between 1990 and 1994 as a mass political organisation inside South Africa was especially important in its ability to mobilise and to exercise discipline over its mass following. The Mass Democratic Movement's revival of organised mass protest in the 1989 'defiance campaign' also helped to reconstitute the 'charterist' movement's urban following. Moreover, COSATU, a partner with the UDF in the Mass Democratic Movement, had been relatively unaffected by the militarised suppression of township organisation and trade unionists played a prominent role in the ANC's reconstruction, exercising a decisive influence on its policies. In the countryside, the ANC assembled its support rather differently, drawing on the patrimonial networks that had historically sustained political life in the ethnic homelands. From 1987, the UDF-aligned Congress of Traditional Leaders had sought to draw disaffected homeland notables into the charterist camp, a response to events in KwaNdebele, where members of the royal house had sought the UDF's support in their effort to resist independence.

Still, violent political conflict continued to claim increasing numbers of victims after 2 February 1990. Between the beginning of the Vaal uprising and de Klerk's unbanning of the ANC in 1990, about five thousand people had been killed. Of those, about four thousand were casualties of armed conflict between Inkatha supporters and activists loyal to the UDF and the ANC. Between 1990 and the end of 1994, another sixteen thousand people died, again mainly victims of Inkatha-ANC hostilities. The bloodshed continued, though on a diminishing scale for about two years after the 1994 election. Certainly, this was a conflict to which covert police and military agencies contributed as agent provocateurs and, for the most part, as Inkatha allies, but supporters of the two organisations undertook most of the killing. The PAC's Azanian People's Liberation Army (APLA) also contributed to the violence after 1990 from bases it established in the Transkei. Declaring 1993 to be the 'Year of the Great Storm', 142 APLA operations killed sixty-one people, thirty-two of them farmers and farmworkers. The APLA's activities were evidently the responsibility of a chain of command and informed by a sense of political purpose. The PAC leaders were quite unabashed in their belief 'that what has not been won on the battlefield will never be won at the negotiating table'.[99]

The extent to which the Inkatha-UDF violence was shaped by a central strategic vision remains contentious. At the time of the UDF's formation, Chief Buthelezi adopted a tone of 'cautious welcome'. Subsequently, attacks by Inkatha supporters on students at the University of Zululand and on civic activists protesting against the administrative takeover by the KwaZulu authorities of Durban townships prompted UDF leaders to denounce the chief as a traitor and a collaborator. From 1984, local Inkatha principals would 'mobilise' their branches to oppose protest directed at what were Inkatha-controlled institutions: schools, councils and police stations. Inkatha leaders maintained that the movement and its leaders were key targets in an ANC campaign to render South Africa ungovernable. Supporters of the UDF and ANC insisted that Inkatha was the instigator of most of the violence, acting in complicity with secret military organisations, the latter a 'third force' that by its own activities accelerated the momentum of the conflict. The 1988 Trust Feed Massacre was an especially notorious instance of Inkatha-police cooperation in killings aimed at UDF supporters in which the assailants attacked the wrong house, a dwelling accommodating Inkatha adherents. Police were also among those convicted for their part in murders at KwaShange near Pietermaritzburg in 1987: most of the killers belonged to UDF affiliates, and their victims were apparently Inkatha adherents.[100] In the cases investigated by the Truth and Reconciliation Commission (TRC), a large majority of killings were attributed to Inkatha as the 'perpetrator organization'.[101] The TRC's database, however, was incomplete and unlikely to have been reliably representative, as it was based on voluntary depositions. Inkatha withheld its cooperation from the TRC, and so its members were less likely to offer testimony. If they had done so, it is quite likely that they would have represented their actions as prompted by defensive concerns.

[99] Tom Lodge, 'Soldiers of the storm: a profile of the Azanian Liberation Army', in Cilliers and Reichardt (eds.), *About turn*, p. 114.
[100] Anthea Jeffries, *The Natal story: sixteen years of conflict* (Johannesburg: South African Institute of Race Relations, 1997), pp. 162–3.
[101] Truth and Reconciliation Commission of South Africa, *Report*, vol. 3 (Cape Town: Juta, 1998), p. 326.

Unlike most homeland-based organisations, Inkatha represented a significant force, its moral authority a consequence of its identity with the patrimonial political institutions of the Zulu kingdom. To its working-class adherents in the townships around Durban and in the hostel communities east of Johannesburg, it provided a source of 'moral rearmament' derived from its 'revival of ancestral rituals, traditional forms of justice . . . a reinvigoration of traditional familial relationships, and a belief in discipline'.[102] For the participants in this nostalgic movement, the generational iconoclasm of the comrades was a threatening affront, especially when it was directed at an idolised leader. Ironically, their struggles during the 1990s to maintain the moral order that Inkatha represented facilitated the ANC's political ascendancy, for widespread perceptions that the government was an accomplice in Inkatha's offensives or, alternatively, that it was incapable of preventing them, lost it public support and enhanced the ANC's stature. Even so, Inkatha's continuing capacity to mobilise a substantial independent African following enabled its leaders to exercise considerable leverage over deciding the details of the new dispensation, leverage that they failed to exploit to the full by withdrawing at an early stage of the constitutional negotiations.

The 1994 political settlement represented a compromise. National Party negotiators had to content themselves with interim power sharing and weak federalism while the ANC accepted the conventional restrictions on executive power that arise from entrenched constitutional rights in a procedural democracy, provisions that would ensure that any social reforms would have to be incrementally gradual rather than radically redistributive. Although the ANC succeeded in becoming the dominant force in the negotiations after 1992, it was also the case that its participation in a bargained transition deradicalised its leadership and demobilised its most volatile following. Residual traces of the emancipatory order envisaged by sections of the UDF's following were evident, though, in the participatory discourses of the ANC's election manifesto, the Reconstruction and Development Programme.

One condition for the successful implementation of the settlement was the ability of key leaders to exercise command over their armed followers. In general, the state could count on the loyalty of the security forces; the degree to which specialised covert military agencies were subject to central direction or were attempting to sabotage the prospects of settlement remains a contentious topic. The ANC exercised looser control over its forces, for despite the ending of military operations, uMkhonto continued

---

[102] Colleen McCaul, 'The wild card: Inkatha and contemporary black politics', in Frankel, Pines and Swilling (eds.), *State resistance and change*, p. 151.

its enlistment and many of the self-defence units it equipped remained poorly disciplined. Inkatha leadership's final eleventh-hour commitment to peace reined in the most significant armed group that might have opposed the transition. In general, ending violence in South Africa was easier because neither the 'national liberation struggle' nor white society was heavily militarised. In its guerrilla campaigning, the ANC became increasingly predisposed towards a militarised conception of struggle, but this conception remains qualified by both ethical and ideological considerations. Correspondingly, as we have noted, the apartheid state, even at a time when army commanders enjoyed most influence, remained subject to public opinion among white citizens. In 1994, the veterans of the insurgencies of the previous two decades could with justification claim credit for the settlement, for without their sacrifices, it is most unlikely that South Africa's transition to democracy would have happened when it did in the way it did. Those who defended the state could also believe that they had helped to shape the terms of transition. They, too, were correct, not least because as we have seen it was the state and its policies that created the setting and, as important, defined the limits of South Africa's great rebellions.

FURTHER READING

Adam, Heribert, *Modernizing racial domination: the dynamics of South African politics*, Berkeley: University of California Press, 1971

Alden, Chris, *Apartheid's last stand: the rise and fall of the South African security state*, Basingstoke, U.K.: Macmillan, 1996

Barrell, Howard, *MK: the ANC's armed struggle*, Johannesburg: Penguin, 1990

Bonner, Philip, 'Black trade unions in South Africa since World War II,' in Price and Rosberg (eds.), *The apartheid regime*, pp. 174–93

Bozzoli, Belinda, 'The taming of the illicit: bounded rebellion in South Africa, 1986', *Comparative Studies in Society and History* 46:2 (2004), 326–53

Braam, Conny, *Operation Vula*, Bellvue: Jacana, 2004

Brewer, John, 'Internal black protest', in Brewer (ed.), *Can South Africa survive to midnight?*, pp. 184–20

Brooks, Alan and Jeremy Brickhill, *Whirlwind before the storm*, London: International Defence and Aid, 1980

Carter, Charles, 'Community and conflict: the Alexandra rebellion of 1986', *Journal of Southern African Studies* 18:1 (March 1992), 115–42

Charney, Craig, 'Civil society and the state: identity, institutions and the Black Consciousness Movement of South Africa', unpublished D.Phil. thesis, Yale University (2000)

Chidester, David, *Shots in the streets: violence and religion in South Africa*, Boston: Beacon Books, 1991

Crocker, Chester, *High noon in southern Africa: making peace in a rough neighborhood*, Johannesburg: Jonathan Ball, 1992

Davis, Stephen M., *Apartheid's rebels: inside South Africa's hidden war*, New Haven, CT: Yale University Press, 1987

Delius, Peter, *A lion amongst the cattle: reconstruction and resistance in the Northern Transvaal*, Oxford: James Currey, 1997

Diseko, Nozipho, 'The origins and development of the South African Student's Movement (SASM): 1968–1976', *Journal of Southern African Studies* 18:1 (March 1992), 40–62

Du Toit, D., *Capital and labour in South Africa: class struggles in the 1970s*, London: Kegan Paul International, 1981

Ellis, Stephen and Tsepo Sechaba, *Comrades against apartheid: the ANC and the South African Communist Party in exile*, London: James Currey, 1992

Evans, Michael and Mark Phillips, 'Intensifying civil war: the role of the South African Defence Force,' in Frankel, Pines and Swilling (eds.), *State, resistance and change*, London: Croom Helm, 1988, pp. 117–45

Everatt, David, 'Alliance politics of a special type: the roots of the ANC/SACP alliance, 1950–1954', *Journal of Southern African Studies* 18:1 (1992), 19–39

Fieldhouse, Roger, *Anti-apartheid: a history of the movement in Britain*, London: Merlin Press, 2005

Fine, Alan and Eddie Webster, 'Transcending traditions: trade unions and political unity', in Moss and Obery (eds.), *South African Review V*, 1990, pp. 256–74

Frankel, Philip, *Pretoria's Praetorians: civil-military relations in South Africa*, Cambridge: Cambridge University Press, 1984

Frederikse, Julie, *South Africa: a different kind of war*, Johannesburg: Ravan Press, 1986

Friedman, Steven, *Building tomorrow today: African workers in trade unions, 1970–1984*, Johannesburg: Ravan Press, 1987

Geldenhuys, Deon, *The diplomacy of isolation: South African foreign policy making*, Johannesburg: Macmillan, 1984

Giliomee, Hermann, *The Afrikaners: biography of a people*, London: Hurst and Company; Cape Town: Tafelberg, 2003

Giliomee, Hermann, *The parting of the ways: South African politics, 1976–1982*, Cape Town: David Philip, 1982

Greenberg, Stanley, *Race and state in capitalist development*, New Haven, CT: Yale University Press, 1980

Grundy, Kenneth, *The militarization of South African politics*, Bloomington: Indiana University Press, 1986

Guelke, Adrian, *Rethinking the rise and fall of apartheid*, Basingstoke, U.K.: Macmillan, 2005

Halisi, C. R. D., *Black political thought in the making of South Africa*, Bloomington: Indiana University Press, 1999

Hanlon, Joseph, *Beggar your neighbours: apartheid power in southern Africa*, London: James Currey, 1986

Herbst, Jeffrey, 'Prospects for revolution in South Africa', *Political Science Quarterly* 103:4 (Winter 1988–1989), 665–85

Herbst, Jeffrey, 'Political and economic implications of South Africa's militarization', *Jerusalem Journal of International Relations* 8:1 (1986), 45–7

Herder, Carol, *The diary of Maria Tholo*, Johannesburg: Ravan Press, 1980

Heunis, Jan, *The inner circle: reflections on the last days of white rule*, Johannesburg: Jonathan Ball, 2007

Hirson, Baruch, *Year of fire, year of ash: the Soweto revolt: roots of a revolution*, London: Zed, 1979

Houston, Gregory, *The national liberation struggle in South Africa: a case study of the United Democratic Front, 1983–1987*, Aldershot, U.K.: Ashgate Publishing, 1999

Houston, Gregory, 'The post Rivonia ANC/SACP underground,' in South African Democracy Education Trust, *The road to democracy in South Africa*, vol. 1, 1960–1970, Cape Town: Zebra Press, 2004, pp. 601–60

Houston, Gregory and Bernard Magubane, 'The ANC political underground in the 1970s,' in South African Democracy Education Project, *The road to democracy in South Africa*, vol. 2, 1970–1980, Pretoria: University of South Africa Press, 2007, pp. 371–451

Hudson, Peter, 'The Freedom Charter and socialist strategy in South Africa', *Politikon* 13:1 (1986), 75–90

Institute of Industrial Education, *The Durban strikes, 1973: human beings with souls*, Durban: Ravan Press, 1976

Israel, Mark, *South African political exile in the United Kingdom*, Basingstoke, U.K.: Macmillan, 1999

Jeffries, Anthea, *The Natal story: sixteen years of conflict*, Johannesburg: South African Institute of Race Relations, 1997

Johnson, Phyllis and David Martin (eds.), *Frontline southern Africa: destructive engagement*, New York: Four Walls, Eight Windows, 1988

Johnson, R. W., *How long will South Africa survive?*, Johannesburg: Macmillan, 1977

Johnson, Shaun, 'Youth in the politics of resistance,' in Johnson (ed.), *South Africa: no turning back*, Bloomington: Indiana University Press, 1990, pp. 94–152

Kane-Berman, John, *Soweto: black revolt, white reaction*, Johannesburg: Ravan Press, 1979

Karis, Thomas G. and Gail M. Gerhart, *From protest to challenge*, vol. 5, *Nadir and resurgence, 1964–1979*, Bloomington: Indiana University Press, 1997

Kasrils, Ronnie, *Armed and dangerous: from undercover struggle to freedom*, Johannesburg: Jonathan Ball, 1998

Kondlo, Kwandile, *In the twilight of the revolution: the Pan-Africanist Congress of Azania, 1959–1994*, Basel: Basler Afrika Bibliographien, 2009

Legassick, Martin. 'South Africa: capital accumulation and violence', *Economy and Society* 3 (1974), 253–91

Leonard, Richard, *South Africa at war*, Craighall: Donker, 1983

Lodge, Tom, *Black politics in South Africa since 1945*, London: Longman, 1983

Lodge, Tom, 'Soldiers of the storm: a profile of the Azanian Liberation Army,' in Cilliers and Reichardt (eds.), *About turn*, Halfway House: Institute for Defence Policy, 1990, pp. 105–17

Mahlalela, L. N., 'Workerism and economism', *African Communist* 104 (1986), 77–88

Mare, Gerhard and Georgina Hamilton, *An appetite for power: Buthelezi's Inkatha and the politics of 'loyal resistance'*, Johannesburg: Ravan Press, 1987

Marks, Shula and Stanley Trapido, 'South Africa since 1976: an historical perspective', in Johnson (ed.), *South Africa: no turning back*, pp. 1–51

Marx, Anthony W., *Lessons of struggle*, New York: Oxford University Press, 1992

Mathabatha, Ngoanamadima Johannes Sello, *The struggle over education in the Northern Transvaal: the case of Catholic mission schools*, Amsterdam: Rozenburg Publishers, 2005

Mayer, Philip, 'Class, status and ethnicity among Johannesburg Africans,' in Thompson and Butler (eds.), *Change in contemporary South Africa*, Berkeley: University of California Press, 1975, pp. 138–67

Mayer, Philip, *Soweto people and their social universes*, Pretoria: Human Sciences Research Council, 1979

Mayer, Philip, *Urban Africans and the Bantustans*, Johannesburg: South African Institute of Race Relations, 1972

McCaul, Colleen, 'The wild card: Inkatha and contemporary black politics,' in Frankel, Pines and Swilling (eds.), *State resistance and change*, pp. 146–73

Meli, Francis, *South Africa belongs to us: a history of the ANC*, Harare: Zimbabwe Publishing House, 1988

Mitchell, Mark and Dave Russell, 'Black unions and political change in South Africa,' in Brewer (ed.), *Can South Africa survive?*, pp. 231–54

Murray, Martin, *South Africa: time of agony, time of destiny: the upsurge of popular protest*, London: Verso, 1987

Naidoo, Kumi, 'The politics of youth resistance in the 1980s: the dilemmas of a differentiated Durban', *Journal of Southern African Studies* 18:1 (March 1992), 143–65

Nolutshungu, Sam, *Changing South Africa: political considerations*, Manchester, U.K.: Manchester University Press, 1982

O'Malley, Padraig, *Shades of difference: Mac Maharaj and the struggle for South Africa*, New York: Viking, 2007

O'Meara, Dan, *Forty lost years: the apartheid state and the politics of the National Party, 1948–1994*, Athens: Ohio University Press, 1996

Plaatjie, Thami ka, 'The PAC in exile,' in South Africa Democracy Education Trust, *The road to democracy in South Africa*, vol. 2, 1970–1980, pp. 703–46

Price, Robert and Carl Rosberg (eds.), *The apartheid regime*, Cape Town: David Philip, 1980

Rantete, Johannes, *The third day of September: an eye-witness account of the Sebokeng Rebellion of 1984*, Johannesburg: Ravan Press, n.d.

Roberts, Ronald Suresh, *No cold kitchen: a biography of Nadine Gordimer*, Johannesburg: STE Publishers, 2006

Rosenthal, Richard, *Mission improbable: a piece of the South African story*, Cape Town: David Philip, 1998

Schleicher, Hans-Georg, 'GDR solidarity: the German Democratic Republic and the South African liberation struggle,' in South African Democracy Education Trust, *The road to democracy in South Africa*, vol. 3, Pretoria: University of South Africa Press, 2008, pp. 1069–1153

Seegers, Annette, 'Extending the security network to the local level,' in Heymans and Totemeyer (eds.), *Government by the people?* Cape Town: Juta, 1988, pp. 119–39

Seekings, Jeremy, *Heroes and villains: youth politics in the 1980s*, Johannesburg: Ravan Press, 1993

Seekings, Jeremy, 'Political mobilisation in the black townships of the Transvaal,' in Frankel, Pines and Swilling (eds.), *State, resistance and change*, pp. 197–228

Seekings, Jeremy, 'Trailing behind the masses: the United Democratic Front and township politics in the Pretoria-Witwatersrand-Vaal Region, 1983–1984,*Journal of Southern African Studies* 18:1 (March 1992), 93–114

Seekings, Jeremy, *The UDF: a history of the United Democratic Front*, Cape Town: David Philip, 2000

Shubin, Vladimir with Marina Traikova, 'There is no threat from the Eastern Bloc,' in South African Democracy Education Trust, *The road to democracy in South Africa*, vol. 3, pp. 985–1066

Sithole, Jabulani and Sifiso Ndlovu, 'The revival of the labour movement,' in South African Democracy Education Trust, *The road to democracy in South Africa*, vol. 2, 1970–1980, pp. 187–214

Slabbert, Frederick Van Zyl, *The other side of history*, Johannesburg: Jonathan Ball, 2006

Smith, Robin, 'The black trade unions: from economics to politics,' in Blumenfeld (ed.), *South Africa in crisis*, London: Croom Helm, 1987, pp. 90–106

Sono, Themba, *Reflections on the origins of Black Consciousness in South Africa*, Pretoria: Human Science Research Council, 1993

Spitz, Richard and Matthew Chaskalson, *The politics of transition: a hidden history of South Africa's negotiated settlement*, Oxford: Hart Publishing, 2000

Suttner, Raymond and Jeremy Cronin, *30 Years of the Freedom Charter*, Johannesburg: Ravan Press, 1986

Terreblanche, Sampie, *A history of inequality in South Africa*, Pietermaritzburg: University of Natal Press, 2002

Tom, Petrus, *My life struggle*, Braamfontein: Ravan Press, 1985

Trewelha. Paul, *Inside Quatro: uncovering the exile history of the ANC and SWAPO*, Cape Town: Jacana, 2009

Truth and Reconciliation Commission, *The Report of the Truth and Reconciliation Commission*, vol. 3, Cape Town: Juta, 1998

Van Kessel, Ineke, *Beyond our wildest dreams: the United Democratic Front and the transformation of South Africa*, Charlottesville: University of Virginia, 2000

Webster, Eddie, 'A profile of unregistered trade unions in Durban', *South African Labour Bulletin* 4:8 (January–February 1979), 43–74

Webster, Eddie, 'The rise of social-movement unionism: the two faces of the black trade union movement in South Africa', in Frankel, Pines, and Swilling, *State, resistance and change*, pp. 174–96

Welsh, David, *The rise and fall of apartheid*, Johannesburg: Jonathan Ball, 2009

10

THE EVOLUTION OF THE SOUTH AFRICAN
POPULATION IN THE TWENTIETH CENTURY

CHARLES SIMKINS

INTRODUCTION

Changes in core demographic variables – population size and composition, fertility, mortality and migration – can indicate a great deal about the development of a society. For a start, they indicate the status of the demographic transition, the move from a demographically wasteful regime of high fertility and high mortality rates to an efficient one of low fertility and mortality.[1] No society reaches developed status without passing through the demographic transition. To the core demographic variables, fertility and mortality, can be added marital status and household size, education, language most often spoken at home, religion, labour market status, urbanisation and inequality, and poverty. Each of these variables further illuminates social conditions.

The principal source of information on these variables is the population census. The first census of the century was taken simultaneously in all four of the colonies that would soon become the Union of South Africa on the night of 17 April 1904. Censuses covering the entire country and population after that were taken in 1911, 1936, 1951, 1960, 1970 and 1996. The 1904 census counted 5,175,824 people, and the 1996 census estimated the population at 40,583,573; for every 100 people in 1904 there were 784 in 1996, which implies an average annual growth rate over the ninety-two-year period of 2.25 per cent. For a society so poor in 1904 and only reaching the middle of the World Bank's 'middle income' category at the end of the twentieth century, and so racked by conflict, poverty and disease, the fact that it escaped a positive Malthusian check between the two

---

[1] See M. Livi-Bacci, *A concise history of world population*, 2nd ed. (Oxford: Blackwell, 1997), chap. 4. On an analogy with steam engines, wasteful regimes require a great deal of fuel (births) and consume a huge amount of energy (deaths).

I am grateful to Francis Antonie for helpful comments on an earlier draft.

census dates is remarkable, though not entirely unprecedented: Mexico's population increased, over the eighty years of its demographic transition, from an index of 100 in 1920 to 702 in 2000.[2]

Estimates of population drop in reliability before 1904. Whites were counted in the Cape and Natal in April 1891 and in the Transvaal and Orange Free State in March 1890. The 1911 census report estimated the 'normal European population' (i.e., excluding imperial military and naval forces) to have been 637,300 in 1891, 1,078,800 in 1904 and 1,246,000 in 1911. It had practically doubled in the twenty years before 1911. In 1911, 133,031 Indians lived in Natal, 89 per cent of all Indians in the Union. The 1891 Natal census returned an Indian population of 41,142 in 1891 so that in Natal at least the Indian population more than tripled in the twenty years before 1911. In 1878, the visiting British writer Anthony Trollope estimated the population of South Africa at 2,276,000,[3] but this is likely to have been a considerable underestimate. His estimate of 340,000 whites seems reasonable; coloureds and Asians would have accounted for more than 400,000 people; and Sadie puts the figure for Africans in 1878 at 2.2 million, giving a total of close to 3 million.

POPULATION SIZE AND COMPOSITION, AND VITAL STATISTICS

Table 1[4] presents midyear estimates of the population for each year from 1910 to 2000. The decade in which population growth was fastest was 1960–1970. The white share of the population peaked in 1920 at 21.0 per cent, the Asian share peaked at 2.9 per cent in 1976 and the Coloured share at 9.7 per cent in 1970. The African share has grown almost continuously from 68.4 per cent in 1910 to 78.0 per cent in 2000.

Table 2 sets out estimates of the total fertility rate and life expectancy at birth. From this table, one can date the onset of the fertility transitions. For whites, the fertility transition was well under way by the late 1920s (evidence of falling white fertility between 1891 and 1904 can be found in the Cape[5]); Asian fertility started to fall in the early 1950s; Coloured fertility, in the late 1960s; and African fertility, from the late 1970s. That there should have been such disparate dates for the four main population groups is not surprising. Detailed mapping of fertility levels in Europe from the middle of the nineteenth century often revealed marked ethnic

[2] Ibid., p. 116.
[3] A. Trollope, *South Africa* (London: Chapman and Hall, 1878), 1:52.
[4] Tables 1-9 are in the appendix of this book.
[5] See C. Simkins and E. van Heyningen, 'Fertility, mortality and migration in the Cape Colony, 1891–1904', *International Journal of Historical Studies* 22:1 (1989), 79–111.

variations in fertility levels, even within the boundaries of a single country.[6] The differences in the onset dates mean that the overall fertility transition in South African is spread out over more than a century, longer even than Mexico's eighty years.

INTERNATIONAL MIGRATION

Sadie estimated net white immigration into South Africa as follows:

TABLE 10.1. *White immigration*

1936–1946	11,560
1946–1951	53,780
1951–1960	38,820
1960–1970	259,000
1970–1980	196,750
1980–1985	122,680

Source: J. L. Sadie, *A reconstruction and projection of demographic movements in the RSA and TBVC countries*, Report 148 (Pretoria: University of South Africa, Bureau of Market Research, 1988), table 2.1.

Peak immigration post-1936, not surprisingly, was during the high-growth 1960s. Sadie estimated the contribution of immigration to the growth of the white population between 1936 and 1985 at 24 per cent. The 1996 census found that 8.3 per cent of whites were born outside South Africa, which is much higher than the 2.1 per cent of Asians, 1.4 per cent of Africans and 0.3 per cent of coloureds.

Sadie's estimate for 1980–1985 is probably too high, and his estimates and projections of net migration in later periods certainly were. His 1993 projections put the 1996 white population at 5,253,300, whereas the 1996 census estimate was only 4,248,179. What seems to have happened is that considerable numbers of foreign-born whites emigrated again in the late 1980s and early 1990s. The Statistics Council evaluations of the 1996 and 2001 censuses found official South African emigration statistics to be serious undercounts and relied instead on estimates of South African immigration into five main receiving countries: the United Kingdom, the United States, Canada, Australia and New Zealand.

Although immigration created the South African Asian (Indian) community in the fifty years after the first indentured labourers arrived in 1860, legislation in 1913 limited future immigration to the wives and children of

[6] See A. J. Coale and S. C. Watson, *The decline of fertility in Europe* (Princeton, NJ: Princeton University Press, 1986).

those already domiciled in South Africa. There was voluntary repatriation between 1911 and 1933, followed by limited immigration until 1956, when further legislation ended the practice of South African men marrying women in India and Pakistan as a means of acquiring immigration rights for them.[7] Sadie's view was that after 1956, Asian international migration was so low that it could be ignored when making population projections and that this was true for coloureds as well.

For Africans, Sadie's approach was to divide the population into South African born and foreign born; to assume that there was negligible migration for the South African born; and instead of producing cohort-component projections for the foreign born, to take merely the foreign-born population as enumerated in each census. On this basis, the estimates of the foreign born at census dates become:

TABLE 10.2. *Numbers of foreign born Africans*

1936	331,110
1946	535,840
1951	603,200
1960	585,830
1970	516,080
1980	342,900
1985	424,800
1996	503,189
2001	577,451

Note: All estimates are from the 1996 census, except the 2001 estimates, which are from the 2001 census.

The estimates are a far cry from very high estimates of illegal immigrants in South Africa produced in the mid-1990s, ranging up to 5 million or even 8 million,[8] which the statistical system has never recorded. It is impossible to refute such claims decisively, but the evidence for them is not strong.

MARITAL STATUS AND HOUSEHOLD COMPOSITION

Table 3 sets out the singulate mean age at marriage (SMAM) at various dates between 1911 and 1996. The table shows that the white SMAM was highest in 1911 and lowest in 1960. The proportion of whites never married

[7] J. L. Sadie, *A reconstruction and projection of demographic movements in the RSA and TBVC countries*, Report 148 (Pretoria: University of South Africa, Bureau of Market Research, 1988), pp. 21–2.
[8] South African Institute of Race Relations, *South African survey, 1995/96* (Johannesburg: South African Institute of Race Relations, 1996), p. 30.

at age 50 has decreased steadily and was less than 5 per cent in 1996. By contrast, the Asian SMAM has risen since 1936, and the proportion never married at age 50 has risen since 1946. By 1996, the Asian statistics were close to those for whites.

The coloured SMAM is trendless and in 1996 was somewhat higher than the Asian and white SMAMs. The proportions never married at age 50 have always been higher for whites and Asians. The African SMAM declined between 1911 and 1946, remained more or less constant to 1960, but has risen since then, reaching high levels in 1996. The proportion never married at age 50 rose sharply between 1960 and 1996. The 1994 October Household Survey data shows that the rise is a consequence of longer waiting times among men for their first job, reducing marriageability. The rise in the female SMAM is induced rather than directly caused by female unemployment. The 1911 census reported that 15 per cent of married African men had more than one wife; now the proportion is much lower.

Before the advent of census data sets in electronic format and modern high-speed statistical analysis packages, census tabulations do not reveal a great deal about household structure. Two anthropological studies of African households are very useful: Monica Wilson's study of kinship in the Keiskammahoek rural study of 1947–1951 and B. A. Pauw's urban study of East London in the late 1950s. Both are studies of the Xhosa, but they illustrate wider conditions and processes.

Monica Wilson found that, in two sections of the area studied, 56 per cent of households were headed by men (nearly all married); 39 per cent by widows; and 5 per cent by lineage daughters (i.e., unmarried women or women who have returned home with their children after being divorced or deserted).[9] She found that polygyny was very rare.[10] She divided households into three types: the primary (or nuclear) family with husband, wife and children; the residual family (in which the children have left home) and the rejuvenated family (when a husband remarries a woman who will bear him children, or when children of other parents live with them). Of the families, 41 per cent were primary, 41 per cent were residual and 18 per cent were rejuvenated.[11]

Wilson also found that the proportion of church and civil marriages had risen between the 1890s and the 1930s and that the average age at first marriage had risen from 24.3 years for men and 19.3 years for women in the 1890s to 30.1 years for men and 23.6 years for women in the 1940s. This she ascribed to the increasing tendency of young men to earn *lobola*

---

[9] M. Wilson, *Kinship in Keiskammahoek rural survey*, vol. 3, *Social structure* (Pietermaritzburg: Shuter and Shooter, 1952), p. 51.

[10] Ibid., p. 46.   [11] Ibid., pp. 55–6.

(bridewealth) rather than depend on their families, as well as the tendency of young women to work in the towns for a few years before marriage.[12]

B. A. Pauw found the urban households that he studied to be essentially a group of kin, with only 9 out of 613 persons not kinspeople or affines of the household head. The 109 households investigated were grouped as follows:

TABLE 10.3. *Household composition*

Male-headed multigeneration family	18
Father, mother and children	35
Father and children	5
Couples living together	4
Female-headed multigeneration family	21
Mother and children	17
Women plus other persons (e.g., grandchildren)	5
Single-person households	4

Women headed 42 per cent of households. The average household size was 5.8 people. On the basis of a detailed analysis of his results, Pauw concluded that the elementary (nuclear) family was the basic type but that it showed a strong tendency to lose the father at a relatively early stage and to develop a multigeneration span.[13]

Simkins reviewed surveys and estimates of household structure from the 1970s and early 1980s. The average family size was 3.7 for whites, 5.2 for coloureds and 5.0 for Asians. (The "family" is distinguished from the "household" by excluding single-person and non-related-person households on the one hand, and by dividing up extended or compound households into nuclear family units on the other hand). The distribution of family types was as follows:

TABLE 10.4. *Household structure, Whites, Coloureds and Asians*

	Whites	Coloureds	Asians
Husband and wife only	24.7%	10.7%	9.2%
Father, mother and children	68.2%	69.1%	77.4%
Father and children	1.0%	3.0%	2.4%
Mother and children	6.1%	17.2%	11.1%
	100.0%	100.0%	100.0%[14]

---

[12] Ibid., pp. 89–90.

[13] B. A. Pauw, *The second generation: a study of the family among urbanized Bantu in East London* (Cape Town: Oxford University Press, 1963), pp. 144–9.

[14] C. Simkins, 'Household composition and structure in South Africa', in Burman and Reynolds, *Growing up in a divided society*, p. 33.

On household structure, Simkins cited a Durban study in 1977, putting single and nonfamily households at 11 per cent, nuclear households at 67 per cent and extended or compound households at 22 per cent for whites. For coloureds in a Cape Town community, a 1976 study put nuclear households at 68 per cent, three-generation households or households with older kin present at 27 per cent and households with nonkin present at 5 per cent. For Indians in Durban in 1984, 1 per cent of households consisted of a single person, 79 per cent of the population were in nuclear or extended households and 19 per cent in multiple family households.[15] Finally, tabulations from the 1980 Current Population Survey for Africans revealed that 30 per cent of households in cities, 20 per cent in urban areas, 25 per cent on farms, 47 per cent in homeland urban areas and 59 per cent in homeland rural areas were female headed.

The distribution of African household types was as follows:

TABLE 10.5. *African household types*

	Male headed	Female headed
Single persons	2%	2%
Nuclear households not headed by a complete married couple	4%	46%
Nuclear households headed by a complete married couple	52%	
Extended households not headed by a complete married couple	7%	39%
Extended households headed by a complete married couple	25%	3%
Compound households (i.e. households containing two or more complete or incomplete married couples)	10%	10%[16]

Finally, Table 4 reports results from the 1996 census. The average sizes of African, coloured and Asian households were all in the range of 4–4.5, with average white household size much lower. Of white and Asian households close to 80 per cent were male headed. Coloured households were slightly more than 70 per cent male headed, and African households were less than 60 per cent male headed. Proportionally, more African households were headed by never-married women and married women than were households in other groups.

The proportion of households consisting of people living on their own was highest for Africans and whites. The proportion of households consisting just of a husband and wife was much higher among whites than among other groups, and the proportion of households with downward extension (grandchildren of the head present) was much lower. Complex households

[15] Ibid., pp. 22–4. [16] Ibid., p. 37.

(those containing a sibling of the head) were much less common among whites than among other groups.

EDUCATION AND HOME LANGUAGE

In examining the highest educational level achieved by population group, gender and age in the censuses from 1960 onward, one is able to open a window on the educational achievements of South Africans born from 1885 up to 1970. Successive censuses remeasure this achievement: for instance, the average educational level of the 35–45 age group in 1960 should be equal to the average level of the 45–55 age group in 1970, after allowing for the educationally selective effects of mortality and migration. Furthermore, there should be a stock-flow balance of the form:

Education-years embodied in the population in period n + 1 (E_{n+1})
equals education-years embodied in the population in period n (E_n)
plus education-years supplied by the education system between n and n + 1 (S_n)
minus education-years embodied in the people who have died between n and n + 1 (D_n)
plus net gain of education years through international migration between n and n + 1 (M_n):

$$\text{i.e.} \quad E_{n+1} = E_n + S_n - D_n + M_n$$

It turns out the stock-flow accounting is reasonably coherent over the 1960–1996 period.[17] The greatest defects of the educational statistics over the period are (a) that no distinction is made in the stock statistics between those who have attended grade 12 and passed the senior certificate and those who have attended grade 12 and not written or failed the senior certificate and (b) incomplete accounting of certificates and diplomas at the higher education level.

Figures 10.1A–10.4B display the average years of education by population group and gender for those born between 1885 and 1970. Whites born in 1885 achieved, on average, eight years of schooling. All others born in 1885 achieved less than two years of schooling. The twentieth century has been the era of catch-up. Africans born during the period 1965–1970 had achieved slightly more than eight years of schooling, coloureds nearly nine, Asians over eleven and whites over twelve. In 1960, 48 million education-years were embodied in the population, but by 1996, the number had reached 229 million.

[17] C. Simkins, 'The archaeology of South Africa's human capital', unpublished paper, p. 6.

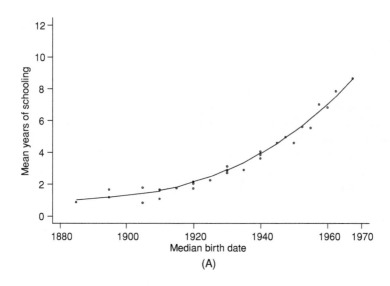

(A)

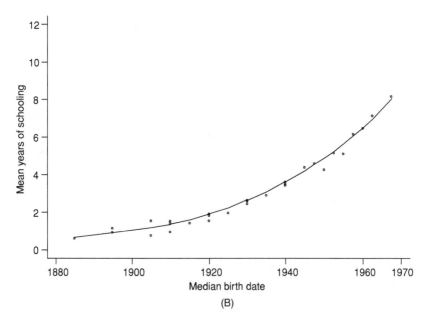

(B)

FIGURE 10.1. (A) Educational attainment – African males. (B) Educational attainment – African females.

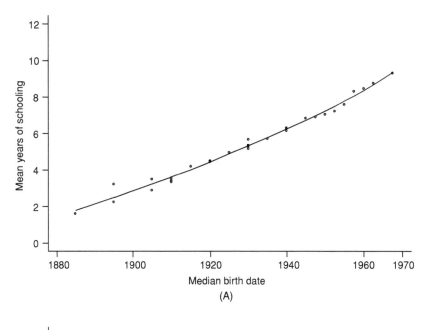

(A)

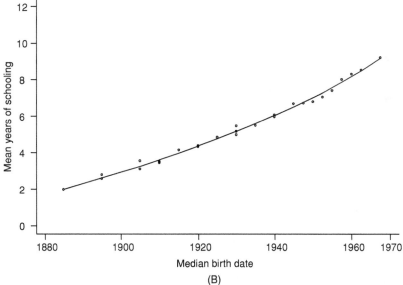

(B)

FIGURE 10.2. (A) Educational attainment – Coloured males. (B) Educational attainment – Coloured females.

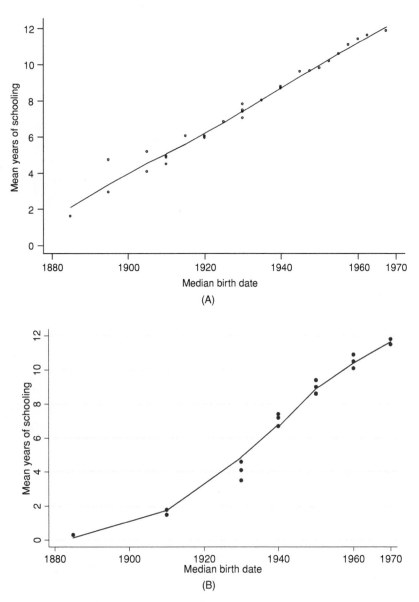

FIGURE 10.3. (A) Educational attainment – Asian males. (B) Educational attainment – Asian females.

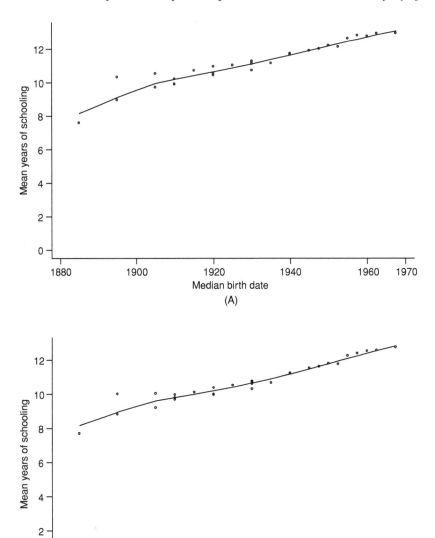

FIGURE 10.4. (A) Educational attainment – White males. (B) Educational attainment – White females.

The figures show that there has been little difference by gender in each population group except for Asians. Among Asians, the difference peaked in about 1920 and had been eliminated by 1970. The inequality of educational achievement (measured as the standard deviation) rose throughout the period for Africans, rose until about 1910 for coloureds then stabilised, rose until about 1910 then dropped for Asian men, rose until about 1930 then dropped for Asian women and dropped throughout the period for whites.[18]

Years of schooling are only one part of the story. Quality of schooling is another. In the 1930s, as a rule of thumb, Malherbe concluded that educational testing had shown that the abilities of African pupils in any given grade were equal to those of white pupils in the two grades below.[19] Much more recently, regression analysis of marks received in the senior certificate examination showed that, relative to a candidate with Afrikaans as a first language, an African-first-language student could expect to get 400 fewer marks in aggregate in 1998 and 341 fewer marks in 2000.[20] (To put these differences in perspective: 720 marks are required for a senior certificate without endorsement and 950 for a senior certificate with endorsement. Endorsement is required for university entrance).

Performance in mathematics is abysmal throughout the system. South Africa participated in the Third International Mathematics and Science Study and came last out of forty-five countries, some less developed than South Africa. Of 527 197 senior certificate candidates in 2000, only 19 327 passed at the higher grade.[21] It is not that mathematics classes are not being delivered – they are in huge number – but they are so often completely ineffective. Baseline grade-appropriate mathematics tests applied to grade 9 and grade 11 pupils in 102 Quality Learning Project schools in townships and rural areas in 2000 produced an average result of 8 per cent in both grades.[22]

Too many schools are unable or unwilling to deliver quality. If one sorts schools by a mathematics performance factor, the top decile produced a 98 per cent pass rate in the senior certificate, and 62 per cent of those passing achieved endorsement for university entrance. Of these candidates, 66 per cent entered for mathematics; of those who did, 97 per cent passed and 32 per cent of the passes were at the higher grade. There was a marked

---

[18] Ibid., p. 3.

[19] E. G. Malherbe, *Education in South Africa*, vol. 2 (Cape Town: Juta, 1977).

[20] C. Simkins, *Mathematics and physical science results in the Senior Certificate examinations of 1998 and 2000: report* (Johannesburg: Centre for Development and Enterprise, 2001), table 8.

[21] Ibid., table 1.

[22] C. Simkins and A. Paterson, *The social and economic determinants of performance in the language of instruction and mathematics in Quality Learning Project Schools* (Pretoria: HSRC Report to Joint Educational Trust, 2002).

difference in the performance of the second decile. The senior certificate pass rate dropped to 85 per cent, and 38 per cent of those passing achieved endorsement. Of these candidates, 53 per cent entered for mathematics; of those who did, 84 per cent passed, and 11 per cent of passes were at the higher grade. And things tail off from there: the bottom decile had a 24 per cent senior certificate pass rate and a 4 per cent mathematics pass rate. The percentage of non-Africans in the first decile of schools was 81 per cent, which indicates that this decile is largely drawn from suburban schools.[23] There are a few outstanding schools outside the suburbs that, with imagination and determination, produce remarkable results with the resources they have but they exist in a sea of mediocrity and worse.

Another factor affecting educational outcomes is educational-language policy in relation to home language. Language policy has followed a rather unsettled course during the twentieth century, veering from Milner's promotion of education in English to the South African Party's interest in dual-medium education and to National Party insistence on mother-tongue education throughout school for whites and mother-tongue education in the first years of primary school for Africans and dual-medium (English-Afrikaans) instruction in African secondary schools for a while before 1976. The adoption of eleven official languages in the 1996 Constitution changed the picture again, with the Department of Education largely ducking the issue by allowing individual schools to decide on their language policy. Most secondary schools with predominantly African pupils use English as the medium of instruction (76 per cent in 1997), with a small minority using Afrikaans (11 per cent in 1997).[24]

Table 5 sets out the distribution of home language by population group between 1936 and 1996. It shows that 60 per cent of Africans spoke at home the four Nguni languages, 31 per cent the three Sotho languages, 7 per cent Xitsonga and Tshivenda, 1.5 per cent other African languages and 0.5 per cent English or Afrikaans in 1960. In 1996, the picture was little different: 58 per cent spoke an Nguni language, 32 per cent Sesotho or Setswana, 8 per cent Xitsonga and Thsivenda, 0.3 per cent other African languages and 1.1 per cent English or Afrikaans. The disjunction between home language and secondary school language remains as sharp as ever for African pupils.

Nearly all coloureds have spoken English or Afrikaans at home since 1936, with English gaining a little ground at the expense for Afrikaans,

---

[23] C. Simkins, *School and community determinants of mathematics and physical science results in the Senior Certificate examination of 1998 and 2000: report* (Johannesburg: Centre for Development and Enterprise, 2001), table 6.

[24] South Africa, Department of Education, *Education statistics in 1997* (Pretoria: The Department, 1999), table 30.

which, however, remains the home language of more than 80 per cent of this group. By contrast, the language practices of the Asians have changed completely since 1936. In that year, 95 per cent of Asians spoke an Indian language and another 2 per cent Chinese or Japanese. In 1960, 83 per cent spoke an Indian language, 1 per cent Chinese and 14 per cent English. By 1970, the proportion who spoke English at home had risen to 32 per cent, and in 1996, it was reported as 94 per cent. Asians more than any other group would have found the 1996 census questionnaire a Procrustean bed in that there were no boxes for Indian languages, so Indian languages may still play a somewhat bigger role than the census indicated. All but a small minority (which has decreased over the years) of whites speak either English or Afrikaans, in proportions that have not changed much since 1936. In 1996, 39 per cent of whites spoke English at home, and 59 per cent spoke Afrikaans.

The general point is that South African pupils – like all those in multilingual countries – are obliged to spend much time learning languages, with a corresponding opportunity cost in other realms of knowledge. It may be that the ultimate language policy requires every learner to take two noncognate languages (i.e., one of English and Afrikaans and one African language), in which case Afrikaans speakers who want a working knowledge of English would have to take three languages. A more specific point is that success in mathematics requires a substantial degree of competence in the language of instruction. For instance, a higher-grade pass in mathematics in the senior certificate is associated with a mark of about 215 in the language of instruction. If the language of instruction is a first language, this represents a mark of about 54 per cent, as first-language papers are marked out of 400. If the language of instruction is a second language, it represents a mark of 72 per cent, as second-language papers are marked out of 300. An achievement this high in a second language is quite rare among African first language candidates.[25]

The third point is subtler. The concept of a language of instruction owes its origin to European nationalism in the phase of expansion in education. A correct French, a correct German, was established by means of dictionaries, grammars and manuals of usage, all depriviliging the position of dialects. The old Dutch term *Algemeen beschaafde Nederlands* encapsulated the process.[26] Nonstandard usage was penalised in written and spoken classroom performances. In its turn, Afrikaner nationalism devoted effort to dictionaries and grammars, not only for Afrikaans but also for the African languages it regarded as appropriate for Africans to speak. But the limited

[25] Simkins, *Mathematics and physical science results*, p. 27.
[26] *Beskaafde* came to be regarded as 'toffee nosed' and has been dropped.

evidence from classrooms suggests that, particularly in urban settings, instruction is not delivered uniformly in one language.[27]

RELIGION

Table 6 sets out the percentage distribution of people across major religious groups in census years from 1921 to 1996. Because most South Africans had returned themselves as Christian of some sort, the Christian category is divided into four subcategories:

1. Denominational
2. Apostolic, Full Gospel, Pentecostalist, or Seventh Day Adventist (Pentecostalist)
3. African
4. Other

Up to 1970, whites returned themselves as overwhelmingly Christian and largely denominational. Between 1970 and 1996, the proportion returning themselves as Christian dropped from 94 per cent to 81 per cent, and within Christianity, there was a marked shift toward Pentecostalism, though this remained a fairly small minority.

The position is broadly similar for coloureds, though the proportion of Christian is slightly lower (except in 1996) and the denominational percentages are lower. Pentecostalism has made particularly rapid inroads since 1970.

Among Asians, the proportion of Hindus was roughly constant between 1921 and 1970, but fell from 68 per cent to 50 per cent between 1970 and 1996. The proportion of Muslims moved up between 1921 and 1946 and has remained roughly constant since then. The proportion of Christians has risen, with the main gains among Pentecostalists and other Christians.

Figures for Africans were first collected in 1960 and show a slight rise in proportion of Christians, from 73.4 per cent in 1960 to 75.7 per cent in 1996. There has been a marked swing away from the denominations to the Pentecostalists and a much smaller swing to the African independent

---

[27] See, e.g., P. Vinjevold, 'Language issues in South African classrooms', in Taylor and Vinjevold (eds.), *Getting learning right*. For instance, suppose a mathematics teacher initially explains a concept in English to a class of African students. Some of the learners get it and some don't. So Zulu-speaking learner A who does might use isiZulu in helping Zulu-speaking learner B understand it. And Setswana speakers in another corner might be going through the same process. Moreover, the isiZulu spoken might be larded with English words and the Setswana with Afrikaans. The teacher might well join in as far as his or her linguistic competence allows. Once the lesson is complete, who can say what it has been 'in'?

churches. The recent trend in Christianity is akin to the rise of Pentecostalism in Latin America.

A countervailing trend is the increase between 1970 and 1996 in numbers reporting that they had no religion. Among whites, the number jumped from 69,541 to 244,135; among coloureds, from 25,689 to 79,894; and among Asians, from 11,318 to 71,432. In 1996, 4,293,161 Africans reported that they had no religion, up from around 2.5 million in 1970.

LABOUR-MARKET STATUS

Table 7 sets out labour-force participation rates as measured by censuses from 1946 for Africans, and from 1921 for minorities. There are some difficulties. Up to 1970, censuses did not differentiate clearly between the unemployed and those whose industrial classification was missing or impossible to determine. There has been variable coverage of the subsistence agricultural sector, which was strongest in 1946 and 1970 and weakest in 1996. Up to 1970, no distinction was made between the formal and the informal sector, and it is impossible to tell how much of the informal sector was captured then. The 1996 and 2001 censuses captured about half of the informal sector found by the Labour Force Surveys from February 2000, and the Labour Force Surveys have done better at capturing the informal sector than the October Household Surveys in the late 1990s.

Nonetheless, some trends are clear. One is increasing feminisation of the labour force. Among Africans, this increase in the 1960s was large, and the trend has continued. Female participation was greatest among coloureds in 1921, and there has been a further upward push since 1960. Female participation among Asian women was low until 1960 but has increased sharply since 1970. The process has taken longer among white women; it accelerated after 1960. By contrast, male labour-force participation has moved downward, partly as a result of lengthening periods spent in educational institutions.

Employment growth was slow between 1946 and 1951 but picked up during the 1950s and was fast in the 1960s. The slow growth in employment since the 1970s ushered in a period of rising unemployment.

The Labour Force Surveys since February 2000 have consistently estimated unemployment on the official definition (which requires active search in the previous four weeks and readiness to work within a week) at more than 4 million. Unemployment on the expanded definition, which includes discouraged workers, was close to 8 million in February 2002.[28]

---

[28] Statistics South Africa, *SA statistics, 2002* (Pretoria: Statistics South Africa, 2002), pp. 7.55 and 7.44.

Sixty per cent of the unemployed on the official definition had never worked before in September 2002. Women and, to a limited extent, the rural suffer disadvantage in absorption, and the poorly educated and Africans suffer a disadvantage that increases with age. At age 30, close to 20 per cent of the Africans continue to wait for the first job. Unemployment among people who have never worked stood close to 20 per cent for those in their mid-20s, drifting downward to about 15 per cent by the time people have reached their mid-40s. Nearly two-thirds of unemployed people said that they had been looking for work for a year or longer. The informal sector serves as a reserve sector, but entry is not free to the unemployed. It helps to have had a job, to be an older worker and to have relatively little education. The gap between an informal sector income and what might be earned by way of wage if a job is found to increase with education.[29]

It is clear that there was something of a golden age between the mid-1930s and the mid-1970s, when the nonagricultural sector was absorbing a great deal of the labour released by agriculture and of labour created as a result of a rapidly increasing population. The last quarter of the twentieth century saw a loss of that balance, with slower growth confronting a rapid rise in the number of people, particularly women, wanting to work. A major unemployment problem has been bequeathed to the twenty-first century; its solution will be the work of decades.

Finally, analysis of the occupational composition of employment is of interest. The Manpower Surveys, which started in the late 1960s and lasted until 1996, collected statistics of formal employment in more than 500 occupational categories. The categories were consistent enough over the entire period to yield the finding that the skill composition of employment increased steadily over the period.[30] Table 7 sets out the distribution of occupations over the entire employed population and for each population group.

URBANISATION

Table 8 sets out the percentages of each population group living in urban areas at census dates between 1904 and 1996. Throughout the period, the definition of *urban* was essentially an administrative one: an urban area is one that has known boundaries and an urban form of local government. This rule was applied strictly in 1936. The definition broadened in later censuses. In 1951, the definition of an urban area was changed to include all population concentration of an urban nature, without regard to legal boundaries and status. In 1970, *urban* referred to all cities or towns with some or other

---

[29] See Simkins, 'Employment and unemployment'.

[30] See, e.g., Human Sciences Research Council, *South African labour market trends and future work force needs, 1998–2003* (Pretoria: HSRC, 1999).

form of local management plus areas of an urban nature (i.e., areas with urban amenities but without some or other form of local management). The 1996 census distinguished urban areas (within municipal and local authority boundaries), semiurban areas (population concentrations adjacent to a municipal area) and rural areas.

Table 8 shows a conventional pattern of urbanisation for whites, coloureds and Asians. White and coloured urbanisation was more than 50 per cent as long ago as 1904. Although Asian urbanisation was lower in 1904, when many Asians were agricultural workers in Natal, it was highest of all population groups in 1996, at 97 per cent. White urbanisation stood at 91 per cent in 1996, with farming families accounting for much of the rural population. Coloured urbanisation stood at 83 per cent, with agricultural labour in the Western and Eastern Cape accounting for most of the rest.

The experience of the African population has been different. African urbanisation was a very low 10 per cent in 1904 and stood at only 43 per cent in 1996. The rate of increase was fastest between 1936 and 1960. Table 9 adds to the story. It creates three groups for the African population: those resident in African Reserves, those resident on farms not owned by Africans and those resident elsewhere (mainly, but not exclusively, in urban areas). From 1936 to 1951, the ratio of Africans living in reserves to those living on farms dropped slightly. The ratio rose considerably between 1951 and 1970 and astronomically between 1970 and 1996. The ratio of Africans living elsewhere rose from 1936 to 1951, dropped between 1951 and 1970 and then rose substantially between 1970 and 1996. Two processes, both associated with apartheid, explain these statistics. The first was tightened influx control in the early 1950s. A patchwork of influx control laws and regulations had existed before then, but as the urbanisation statistics suggest, they had little effect on African urbanisation. The tightened system was built around section 10 of the Urban Areas Act of 1945 as amended. Africans were categorized into four groups: (1) those who had resided in the same urban area since birth, (2) those who had worked continuously for 10 years or in spells for 15 years in the same urban area, (3) dependents of people in categories 1 and 2, and (4) those admitted to urban areas on contract work for defined periods of time. It was a system designed to keep urban unemployment low, to keep as many dependents of workers as possible out of the urban areas and to prevent category 4 workers from building up work experience to enable them to enter category 2. The tightened system had a marked effect on African migration to the cities for about 20 years from 1955 to 1975. After that, it became more difficult to enforce, and in 1986 the whole system was scrapped.[31]

---

[31] See Simkins, *Four essays on the past, present and possible future distribution of the black population of South Africa* (Cape Town: SALDRU, University of Cape Town, 1983) for more demographic detail.

The second process was the removal of 'black spots' (i.e., land in African ownership not destined for incorporation into the homelands), the removal of squatters especially from mission stations and informal settlements, the removal of 'surplus' Africans on white farms and the relocation of African townships across homeland boundaries. The process got under way at the beginning of the 1960s and continued well into the 1980s, and beyond in the case of farms. Group Areas relocations apart, the Surplus People's Project estimated that more than 2.5 million people were removed between 1960 and 1983.[32] Table 9 shows that the absolute number of Africans on commercial farms nearly halved between 1970 and 1996, whereas the number in the homelands more than doubled over the same period.

INEQUALITY AND POVERTY

The longest-running indicators of inequality are the racial shares in household income. First estimated by Lehfeldt for 1917, they have been reestimated at regular intervals. McGrath concludes that there was a remarkable constancy in the white share of income between 1917 and 1970. Whites received close to 70 per cent of the household income while comprising less than 20 per cent of the population. The constant racial share reflected a widening gap between the average income of whites and the average income of everyone else, as the white share of population fell over the period.

Since 1970, this constancy has been broken, as the following estimates by McGrath and others show:

TABLE 10.6. *Income inequality*

Year	Source	Percentage shares			
		Africans	Coloureds	Asians	Whites
1970	McGrath	19.8	6.7	2.4	71.2
1980	McGrath	24.9	7.2	3.0	65.0
1985	Simkins	28.8	8.2	4.3	58.7
1990	Simkins	32.5	8.7	4.7	54.0
1991	McGrath & Whiteford	28.2	7.3	3.9	60.5[a]
1995	Simkins	34.1	9.2	5.0	51.7[b]
1995	IES	41.1	6.6	4.6	47.7[c]

[a] A. Whiteford and M. McGrath, *Income inequality over the apartheid years* (Cape Town: South African Network for Economic Research, 1998), working paper 6, table 1.
[b] Urban Foundation, *Income distribution model*, 2nd ed. (Johannesburg: The Foundation, 1994).
[c] Statistics South Africa, *The income and expenditure survey, 1995* (Pretoria: Statistics South Africa, 1997).

[32] Platzky and Walker, *The surplus people*.

There are indications that the McGrath estimates of the movement away from the 1970 pattern are too conservative with respect to the African share. The Simkins estimates are higher and the 1995 Income and Expenditure Survey, as published, found the African share of household income to be 41 per cent.

McGrath found the Gini coefficient for the distribution of household income to be 0.68 in 1975 and 0.676 in 1991 and concluded that the overall distribution of household income was trendless. When per capita household income is considered (i.e., when one normalizes for household size), the 1991 Gini coefficient increased to 0.706, which suggests that poorer households are larger than wealthy ones.[33] The 1995 Income and Expenditure Survey, as published, yields a Gini coefficient of 0.591 for the distribution of household income and 0.629 for the distribution of per capita household income. These are considerably lower than the McGrath estimates for 1991 and raise the possibility that there was some equalisation of household incomes between the mid-1970s and the mid-1990s. McGrath expresses the general view that, since 1970, there has been some reduction in inequality between population groups, whereas inequality within population groups has risen.

If one uses the Bureau of Market Research's Minimum Living Level (which varies with household size) as a poverty line, then 49 per cent of households in South Africa were poor in 1991. In the then Ciskei and Venda, more than 70 per cent of households were poor and more than 90 per cent in Transkei. The poverty rates varied greatly among population groups: 67 per cent for Africans, 38 per cent for coloureds, 18 per cent for Asians and 7 per cent for whites.[34]

The literature on poverty and inequality is spotty and scattered. However, there are two fairly comprehensive sources that open a window on the mid-1940s and mid-1980s, respectively.

The Social and Economic Planning Council's report 'The Economic and Social Conditions of the Racial Groups in South Africa'[35] provided estimates that the average income per head of the white population in 1941–1942 was about £125 per annum; that of coloureds, £25 per annum; and that of Africans, £10. In 1938–1939, about 55 per cent of coloured households fell below the poverty datum line, compared with about 5 per cent of white households. In Durban, a survey found that 5 per cent of whites, 38 per cent of coloureds, 25 per cent of Asians and 71 per cent of Africans fell

---

[33] Whiteford and McGrath, *Income inequality*, pp. 10–11.

[34] Ibid., pp. 13–14.

[35] Union of South Africa, *The economic and social condition of the racial groups in South Africa* (Pretoria: Government Printer, UG53, 1948).

below the poverty datum line in 1943–1944. The low figure for Africans reflects the fact that a high proportion of those in Durban lived as single working households, some of whom were provided with food and housing. In Johannesburg, 87 per cent of African households fell below the poverty datum line in 1940.

The report ascribed the reasons for these differences in part to historical chance, in part to legal and customary barriers such as the colour bar (then largely conventional), restrictions on movement by Africans and Asians, job reservation on the mines under the Mines and Works Amendment Act of 1926, the minimum educational qualification for apprenticeship under the Apprenticeship Act of 1944, exclusion of Africans under the Industrial Conciliation Act of 1937 and the civilized labour policy, and in part to a low-level equilibrium trap of poor education, poor health and nutrition and poor earning capacity. It did, however, observe a tendency in manufacturing between 1937–1938 and 1943–1944 for white wages to rise more slowly than those for other groups.

The policies it recommended were the reconstruction of agriculture; the maintenance of a strong mining industry for as long as possible; a vigorous expansion of secondary industry, accompanied by cost cutting and the greater employment of people other than whites; the enlargement of the African Reserves; and the provision of greater opportunities for education for people other than whites in the civil service, railways and harbours and local authorities.

Forty years later, the summary volume from the Second Carnegie Inquiry into Poverty and Development was published with the title 'Uprooting Poverty'.[36] In many ways, the themes explored were similar to those in the 1948 report: poor farming conditions in the African Reserves, with lack of fuel and clean drinking water, the structure of wages in the various industrial sectors, hunger and disease, housing and education. A new theme was unemployment, far more of a concern in 1989 than in 1948.

But the tone and the explanations for poverty were very different. The 1948 report was produced from within the state, although its recommendations would be ignored and the commission disbanded after the National Party's accession to power. The 1989 book was a critical report from outside the state in a turbulent time. Apartheid was in its terminal crisis-ridden decade, as was white political dominance. How that dominance had been assembled over the centuries was much better understood than before; it was no longer possible to speak of historical chance. And the record of

---

[36] F. Wilson and M. Ramphele, *Uprooting poverty: the South African challenge* (Cape Town: David Philip, 1989).

apartheid's assault on the poor formed the central portion of the analytical account. This consisted of 'excorporation' of reserves, the prevention of black urbanisation, forced removals and the suppression of black political organisations.

CONCLUSION: THE TWENTIETH CENTURY'S INCOMPLETE AND DISFIGURED DEMOGRAPHIC MODERNISATION

In the movement from a wasteful to an efficient demographic regime, several transitions need to take place. Fertility declines, from natural to close to a replacement rate. Mortality declines. Average educational attainment rises, as does the proportion of people living in urban areas. The proportion of agricultural employment in total employment drops. Household size declines.

The evidence presented indicates that all these things have happened in South Africa. Ethnic diversity has meant that the demographic transition has been stretched out over more than a century (compared with about 20 years in Taiwan) with a correspondingly high ratio of posttransition to pretransition population. A country that had about 3 million people in 1880 had 44 million in 2000. Compared with European war mortality over this period, South African mortality from war and violence was light, totalling not more than the excess mortality in the first three months after the arrival of the influenza epidemic in October 1918. Life expectancies rose more or less continuously throughout the twentieth century, except for its final few years, when AIDS mortality started to appear. At the end of the century, the total fertility rate was about 2.7, much closer to replacement than to natural fertility.

Equally, the number of person-years of education in the population has moved up sharply, from 48 million in 1960 to 229 million in 1996. Urbanisation increased from 23 per cent in 1904 to 54 per cent in 1996. Table 7 shows, for all its limitations, the decline in the proportion of people working in agriculture. Household size dropped from 4.2 in the 1996 census to 3.8 in 2001 census. In part, this reflects dropping fertility. In part, it reflects the fact that living with relatives is an inferior good, which people consume less of as they become richer.[37]

But the transition is incomplete. Fertility has further to drop. We now face a period of rising mortality rather than a continuation of the twentieth century's downward trend. The relatively high levels of education achieved by the youngest cohorts of the South African adult population have yet to move through the system, thus displacing older and poorly educated

---

[37] Cf. Oscar Wilde (*The Happy Prince*) 'A ridiculous match', twittered the other swallows, 'she has no money and far too many relations'.

people. Urbanisation is far from complete. Movement of employed people from agriculture and mining to manufacturing, utilities and construction and to the service sectors has certainly happened, and average skill levels have moved up, but the economy is nowhere near full employment.

Moreover, the transition has been disfigured. The two most lasting effects of apartheid are to be found in education and in the spatial distribution of the population. Some of apartheid's unequal allocation of resources has already been undone; teachers are more evenly spread, schools in poor communities actually get more by way of nonpersonnel recurrent funds and, slowly, resources are being allocated to schools with below-par endowments of buildings and amenities. But the damage inflicted by Bantu education to the self-respect and sense of purpose in African education remains. The dilemmas of educational language policy have not been resolved; they have merely been decentralized down to the school level. Although the resources pumped into education are high in relation to Gross Domestic Product, the quality of the output remains poor – the American problem, but worse. This situation undermines one of the most powerful mechanisms producing greater equality in the distribution of income: the creation of more substantial stocks of human capital among the bulk of the population. Human capital is a function not only of the number of years a person spends in the educational system but also of the value that is added while he or she is there.

That apartheid failed should not blind one to the fact that it had a huge impact on the distribution of the African population. It slowed urbanisation for 20 years and it directly caused and induced a huge rural to rural migration. Both of these processes moved people away from sites of economic opportunity and contributed to unemployment and inequality. In so doing, apartheid created conundrums for postapartheid policy. Although there has been some restoration and compensation, most people either cannot or would not want to move to the places from which they came. Equally, the experience of apartheid industrial decentralisation efforts suggests that trying to move economic opportunities to where people now are would be largely ineffective. New sites will open up, for instance in the minerals belt north of Pretoria, and these will attract people, just as mining developments in the late nineteenth and early twentieth century did. So places with no economic hope are likely to empty gradually, depending on the rate of growth. Catering to the needs of people in such places will have to steer between the Scylla of doing very little and the Charybdis of creating assets that may be abandoned before the end of their useful lives.

Analysts often speak of poverty traps: processes that make the escape from poverty very difficult or impossible. Poorly designed social security systems can have this effect, for example, by imposing an effective tax rate of 100 per cent or more on a low level of earned income, which is sufficient to trigger the withdrawal of means-tested benefits. Disfigured modernisation has created peculiar traps of its own. High unemployment in cities discourages migration, for instance, and traps people in remote areas, where they have a few assets that it would be too risky to abandon. The difficulties of finding a first job delay marriage, thus exposing some to lengthy periods of risk of contracting HIV. High unemployment itself weakens the incentives of learners to apply themselves at school. The trap of low-level nutrition, health and human capital, identified in the 1940s, continues to exist. Identifying such traps and dismantling them will be a necessary part of the completion of South Africa's own demographic modernisation.

FURTHER READING

Coale, A. J. and S. C. Watkins, *The decline of fertility in Europe*, Princeton, NJ: Princeton University Press, 1986

Giliomee, H., *The Afrikaners: biography of a people*, Cape Town: Tafelberg, 2003

Human Sciences Research Council, *South African labour market trends and future work force needs, 1998–2003*, Pretoria, Human Sciences Research Council, 1999

Livi-Bacci, M., *A concise history of world population*, 2nd ed., Oxford: Blackwell, 1997

Malherbe, E. G., *Education in South Africa*, vol. 2, Cape Town: Juta, 1977

Pauw, B. A., *The second generation: a study of the family among urbanized Bantu in East London*, Cape Town: Oxford University Press, 1963

Platzky, L. and C. Walker, *The surplus people: forced removals in South Africa*, Johannesburg: Ravan Press, 1985

Sadie, J. L., 'Estimating the March 1991 population of the RSA', in Central Statistics Service, *1991 Population Census*, Vol. 03–01-26, Pretoria: Central Statistics Service, 1991

Sadie, J. L., *A projection of the South African population, 1991–2011*, report 196, Pretoria: University of South Africa, Bureau of Market Research, 1991

Sadie, J. L., *A reconstruction and projection of demographic movements in the RSA and TBVC countries*, report 148, Pretoria: University of South Africa, Bureau of Market Research, 1988

Simkins, C., *Four essays on the past, present and possible future distribution of the black population of South Africa*, Cape Town: Southern Africa Labour and Development Research Unit, University of Cape Town, 1983

Simkins, C., 'Household composition and structure on South Africa', in Burman and Reynolds (eds.), *Growing up in a divided society*, pp. 16–42

Simkins, C., *Mathematics and physical science results in the Senior Certificate examinations of 1998 and 2000*, Johannesburg: Report for the Centre for Development and Enterprise, 2001

Simkins, C., *School and community determinants of mathematics and physical science results in the Senior Certificate examination of 1998 and 2000*, Johannesburg: Report for the Centre for Development and Enterprise, 2001

Simkins, C. and Andrew Paterson, *The social and economic determinants of performance in the language of instruction and mathematics in Quality Learning Project Schools*, Pretoria: Human Sciences Research Council Report to the Joint Educational Trust, 2002

Simkins, C. and E. van Heyningen, 'Fertility, mortality and migration in the Cape Colony, 1891–1904', *International Journal of Historical Studies* 22:1 (1989), 79–111

South Africa, Department of Education, *Education statistics in 1997*, Pretoria: The Department, 1999

South Africa, Department of Statistics, *South African statistics 1978*, Pretoria: The Department, 1978

South Africa, Statistics South Africa, *The income and expenditure survey, 1995* (electronic version), Pretoria: Statistics South Africa, 1997

South Africa, Statistics South Africa, *South African statistics 2002*, Pretoria: Statistics South Africa, 2002

South African Institute of Race Relations, *South African survey, 1995/69*, Johannesburg: South African Institute of Race Relations, 1996

Trollope, A., *South Africa*, London: Chapman and Hall, 1878

Union of South Africa, *The economic and social condition of the racial groups in South Africa*, Social and Economic Planning Council, Report 13, Pretoria: Government Printer U.G. 53 of 1948

Union of South Africa, *Union statistics for fifty years*, Pretoria: Government Printer, 1960

Urban Foundation, *Income distribution model*, 2nd ed., Johannesburg: Urban Foundation, 1994

Vinjevold, P., 'Language issues in South African classrooms', in Taylor and Vinjevold (eds.), *Getting learning right*, pp. 205–26

Whiteford, A. and M. McGrath, *Income inequality over the apartheid years*, working paper 6, Cape Town: South African Network for Economic Research, 1998

Wilson, F. and M. Ramphele, *Uprooting poverty: the South African challenge*, Cape Town: David Philip, 1989

Wilson, M., et al., *Kinship in Keiskammahoek rural survey*, vol. 3, *Social structure*, Pietermaritzburg: Shuter and Shooter, 1952

11

THE ECONOMY AND POVERTY IN
THE TWENTIETH CENTURY

NICOLI NATTRASS AND JEREMY SEEKINGS

The South African economy experienced substantial growth and change over the twentieth century. By the time of Union in 1910, gold mining on the Witwatersrand had already and rapidly transformed what had been a peripheral agricultural economy into one that was industrialising around mineral exports. Gold attracted British capital and immigrants from Europe (as well as from across southern Africa), and made possible secondary industrialisation and four decades of sustained economic growth in the middle of the century. Between the early 1930s and early 1970s, the South African economy grew approximately tenfold in real terms. Even taking into account the steady increase in the population, real gross domestic product (GDP) per capita tripled (see Figure 11.1). Despite faltering growth in the 1980s, South Africa accounted for almost exactly one half of the total GDP of sub-Saharan Africa at the end of the apartheid period, in 1994.[1]

The South African growth path followed the typical development trajectory, with the leading sector shifting from agriculture, to minerals, manufacturing and then services. South Africa adopted many policies and built institutions not dissimilar to those in Australia and elsewhere in the industrialising world. A modern state intervened extensively in the economy, through both ownership and regulation. Labour-market institutions and an embryonic welfare state protected the incomes of some workers and other citizens identified as deserving. In other respects, however, South Africa was far from typical. First, South Africa had a set of unusually coercive and discriminatory policies and institutions that served both to constrain the economic opportunities open to African people and to depress the wages paid to the many African workers forced into unskilled employment. It was the combination of typical policies and institutions, on the one hand, and

---

[1] UN Development Programme, *Human development report 1997* (New York: UNDP, 1997), table 25, pp. 200–1.

Real GDP per capita (2000 prices)

FIGURE 11.1. Real GDP per capita, 1932–2001. *Source:* Statistics South Africa and the South African Reserve Bank (from 1932); data for 1911–1912, 1917–1918 and 1927–1928 from J. C. du Plessis, *Economic fluctuations in South Africa, 1910–1949*, Publication no. 2, University of Stellenbosch, Bureau for Market Research (1950), rescaled on data for 1937–1938.

distinctive ones, on the other hand, that ensured high inequality in terms of who gained in the short term and that shaped the economic growth path that ensured that high inequality persisted over time. Second, structural economic change was accompanied by a fundamental shift in the labour market, from chronic labour shortages to what was almost the highest measured unemployment rate in the world. Rising unemployment was a feature of most oil-importing countries following the oil price hikes of the early 1970s. In South Africa, however, unemployment was exacerbated by government policies and institutions that had destroyed the African peasantry, organised the labour market for the benefit of a small number of privileged insiders, and undermined employment growth. Under apartheid, the economy moved down an ever more capital- and skill-intensive growth path, with the result that at the end of the century, fewer than 50 per cent) of people of working age were actually working. Skilled labour shortages constrained economic growth and hence the demand for all kinds of labour. Despite the transition to democracy in the 1990s, many of the institutional and structural features that shaped the economic growth path under apartheid continued after apartheid, explaining the persistence of inequality and poverty into the twenty-first century.

Much of this simultaneous history of growth and failure can be traced to the patterns of state intervention in the economy. South Africa enjoyed obvious natural advantages, such as climate, minerals and harbours. But it also faced a set of severe challenges. First, industrialisation was driven by

gold, which was located deep underground and required massive investments of capital before mining could commence. Second, imperial South
Africa inherited a high-wage institutional and cultural framework from
Great Britain. Third, it faced a large indigenous (mostly African) population that had sufficient access to land to be able to exercise some choice over
whether to provide industrial labour. Finally, the state had to manage the
social and political tensions both within the white population and between
it and the much larger African majority. From the outset, the state played
a major and central role in almost every aspect of the economy in response
to these constraints. In crucial respects, public policy served to facilitate
profitability and economic growth, albeit often weakly. In broadly Marxist
terms, the state played a major role in ensuring 'an abundant supply of disenfranchised, low-wage, unskilled black labour', especially for farms and
mines, which in turn largely determined 'the particular path of industrialization in South Africa'.[2] 'Cheap' (African) labour was, however, only half
the story. The state also implemented policies and established institutions
designed to protect the 'civilised' standard of living of white workers. The
commitment to maintaining white citizens' standard of living at a level
commensurate with those in the much wealthier economies of Australia and
Britain shaped both the path and the pace of economic growth and change.
Racial discrimination and coercion largely excluded unskilled workers and
African people generally from the institutional framework that fostered
and protected privilege. When, in the later apartheid period, African workers pushed their way inside the edifice of wage-raising institutions, they
encouraged employers to shift toward more skill- and capital-intensive production, thereby limiting even further the growth of unskilled jobs and
contributing to the perpetuation of unemployment, poverty and inequality.

This chapter analyses three periods of South African economic history
in the twentieth century, pointing to crucial changes in the economy, the
roles played by the state and the consequences for poverty in each era. The
first period, from Union in 1910 until 1932, was characterised both by
economic stagnation and by an extraordinary building of state institutions
to intervene in the economy. In this phase, the foundations were laid for
the labour market and other institutions that shaped subsequent economic
development and the distribution of earnings. The second period, from
1933 to about 1945, saw rapid growth and structural change. Strong
growth continued into the third, 'apartheid' period, at least until the
1970s. But growth was slow relative to comparable economies as South

---

[2] Philip Bonner, Peter Delius and Deborah Posel, 'The shaping of apartheid: contradiction,
continuity and popular struggle', in Bonner, Delius and Posel (eds.), *Apartheid's genesis*,
p. 4.

Africa failed to take full advantage of either the benefits of gold mining or the postwar global boom. Export growth was lacklustre, production depended more and more on limited internal markets and the profit rate fell. Growth faltered in the 1970s and stagnated in the 1980s.

ECONOMIC STAGNATION, 1910–1932

At the time of Union, South Africa was a sparsely populated, predominantly arid country. Although it was a largely agrarian society, it possessed crucially important pockets of extraordinary industrial activity. Johannesburg and the Witwatersrand, and to a lesser extent Cape Town, appeared to be booming. But the entire Witwatersrand had a population of only half a million people in 1921; three quarters of the country's almost 6 million people lived in the countryside. Although deep poverty was probably generally limited to episodes of drought or disease, rural prosperity was limited to specific areas producing for lucrative export markets or the small but growing domestic urban and industrial markets. Indeed, 'poor whites' – unskilled and unable to compete even with African farmers disadvantaged by inferior access to capital and markets – constituted a substantial minority of the rural white population. Agricultural exports, including especially wool, ostrich feathers and maize, as well as sugar cane from the 1920s, resulted in pockets of rural affluence, but agriculture was unable to transform the South African economy. That was the historical task of gold mining.

In 1911, agriculture accounted for 22 per cent of South African national income, but this was already less than the 27 per cent accounted for by mining and barely more than gold mining alone.[3] The gold mines of the Witwatersrand spread out in a crescent across the southern Transvaal. Both the dollar price of gold and the exchange rate were fixed, which meant that the rand price of gold remained stable even while other commodity prices fluctuated erratically. In 1910, South Africa produced a third of world gold output, which rose to more than half by 1930.[4] Fewer workers were employed in mines than on farms, but the mines served to stimulate growth in many other sectors (notably coal, timber, food and transport), and gold accounted for more than half, by value, of all exports from the Union. The gold mines, producing a product for which demand was unlimited at its fixed price, were the powerhouse of economic development, enabling South

---

[3] Charles Feinstein, *An economic history of South Africa: conquest, discrimination and development* (Cambridge: Cambridge University Press, 2005), p. 129.

[4] Union of South Africa, *Official Year Book, 1934/5* (Pretoria: Government Printer), p. 519.

Africa 'to break free from the constraints which had for so long held back its economic development'.[5]

The economy had grown rapidly in the late nineteenth and early twentieth centuries, notwithstanding the disruption of the South African War, because of the combination of rapidly expanding gold production and a growing world economy. However, in terms of GDP per capita (taking into account purchasing power), South Africa remained poorer than Spain, Italy or Ireland (although its GDP per capita was higher than Portugal's), and it lagged far behind other settler societies such as Australia, New Zealand, Canada and Argentina.[6]

If gold mining was the engine of the economy, it was an engine that required constant assistance from the state. The depths from which gold was mined on the Witwatersrand meant that huge investments of capital were needed to drive mining ever more deeply underground and to extract the gold from the ore. Labour was needed to hack or blast underground and to bring the generally low-grade ore to the surface. Though a costly enterprise, the rate of return on investment in South African gold mining in the period up to 1932 was broadly commensurate with the rates earned on alternative investments elsewhere in the world.[7] Foreign and domestic investors would not have invested in South African gold mining if profitability had not been underpinned by the only cost component that could be controlled: unskilled, black labour (as was well known at the time[8]). Doubling the very low wages paid to African workers would have reduced dividends and taxes by almost two thirds. High wages for all workers were simply incompatible with profitability.[9]

The mines could have raised wages for African workers if they had been able to reduce the wage bill of their white workers. The ratio of the cash earnings of white workers to the value of payments in cash and kind to African workers peaked at about 12:1 in 1921 and was to remain at about 10:1 for the rest of the interwar period.[10] The minority of white workers consistently received, in total, more, and sometimes substantially more,

---

[5] Feinstein, *Economic history*, p. 109.

[6] Angus Maddison, *The world economy: a millennial perspective* (Paris: Organisation for Economic Co-operation and Development, 2001), pp. 185, 195, 224.

[7] S. Herbert Frankel, *Investment and the return to equity capital in the South African gold mining industry, 1887–1965: an international comparison* (Oxford: Basil Blackwell, 1967), p. 47.

[8] Union of South Africa, *Report of the Economic and Wage Commission* (Cape Town: Government Printer. U.G. 14 of 1926); Union of South Africa, *Official Year Book, 1934/5*, p. 245.

[9] Feinstein, *Economic history*, pp. 110–11; Jonathan Crush, A. Jeeves and D. Yudelman, *South Africa's labor empire: a history of black migrancy to the gold mines* (Boulder, CO: Westview; Cape Town: David Philip, 1991), p. 1.

[10] Francis Wilson, *Labour in the South African gold mines* (Cambridge: Cambridge University Press, 1972), p. 66.

than the large majority of African workers. The high wages paid to white workers reflected the influence of British wage rates (which were the highest in the world),[11] as well as local politics. Unsurprisingly, the mines sought to employ cheaper workers, including both Chinese labour (in 1906–1910) and African workers, provoking industrial protest, violent rebellion (in the 1922 Rand Revolt), and political intervention. Given their fiscal and general economic dependence on gold mining, successive governments were wary of raising further production costs on the mines and therefore looked to other sectors to employ increased numbers of white workers at appropriately high wages; but the state did not allow the mining industry to change significantly its cost structure by employing African workers in more skilled positions.

The distinctive economics of gold mining encouraged the emergence of large mining-finance houses that could raise the massive capital necessary for opening mines as well as for operating them thereafter. In 1887, Cecil John Rhodes and his partner Charles Rudd paved the way with the establishment of Gold Fields of South Africa (which later became Consolidated Gold Fields). Registered in London, the company served as a vehicle for raising British capital. Other houses were established by the Albu family (which later grew into General Mining), Eckstein (which became Rand Mines), Wernher and Beit (which grew into Central Mining), Goerz (which became the Union Corporation), and Barnato (Johannesburg Consolidated Investments, or JCI). These six mining and finance houses dominated the industry. Given the fixed price of gold, there was little reason for them to compete, and many reasons for them to collude – which they did, through the Chamber of Mines, established in 1889. The Chamber of Mines regulated wages paid to African workers while recruiting widely across Southern Africa ensuring sufficient labour despite depressed wages.

In the 1910s, gold mining expanded into the Far East Rand, which was the turf of Ernest Oppenheimer and the Anglo American Corporation, formed in 1917 with British and American funding. By 1919, the eleven mines on the Far East Rand were generating more than twice as much profit as the forty-odd mines along the rest of the Witwatersrand. Although Anglo American was the most profitable, Rand Mines remained the largest of the mining and finance houses in the mid-1930s in gold production, employment and number of mines. At much the same time as it emerged as a major force in gold, Anglo American began to expand aggressively in the diamond industry, in direct competition with De Beers. Using its political contacts inside the South African state and access to foreign funding, Anglo American bought massive diamond-mining companies in

---

[11] Robert C. Allen, *The British industrial revolution in global perspective* (Cambridge: Cambridge University Press, 2009), especially pp. 25–56, 135–55.

Namibia. In the 1920s, it expanded rapidly in Angola, the Congo, West Africa, British Guiana and – within South Africa – in Namaqualand and Lichtenburg. Finally, in 1929, Ernest Oppenheimer and Anglo American took over De Beers.[12]

Although this was a period of flux in the ownership and control of mines, it was not a period of growth for either the gold mining industry in particular or the economy as a whole. The volume and value of gold production and employment remained broadly stable through the 1910s and 1920s.[13] The South African economy grew in current prices, but there were large fluctuations in prices (and inconsistencies in how those were measured), and it is therefore difficult to calculate a reliable real growth rate. Indeed, the South African state began to collect systematic data on prices only in 1919. The prices of agricultural exports, such as wool,[14] were especially volatile. What is clear is that the South African economy experienced two sharp recessions, in the early 1920s and then during the first part of the Great Depression (approximately 1929–1932), with a short period of growth in the mid-1920s and sustained growth from 1933.[15] Depending on the choice of price data, real GDP per capita between 1911 and 1932 probably stagnated, perhaps rose marginally, but may even have declined. Figure 11.1 does not show a series for the period before 1932, but it shows estimates for three years.[16] This picture of slow, if any, growth is supported by data on wages.[17]

[12] Wilson, *Labour in the South African gold mines*, p. 24; D. Innes, *Anglo: Anglo American and the rise of modern South Africa* (Johannesburg: Ravan Press, 1984), pp. 97–117.

[13] Feinstein, *Economic history*, p. 105; Crush et al., *South Africa's labour empire*, pp. 234–5, table A.4.

[14] D. H. Houghton, 'Economic development, 1865–1965', in Wilson and Thompson (eds.), *The Oxford history of South Africa*, vol. 2, p. 24.

[15] J. C. du Plessis, *Economic fluctuations in South Africa, 1910–1949*, publication no. 2, (Stellenbosch: University of Stellenbosch, Bureau for Market Research, 1950), pp. 50–2.

[16] Calculations by Frankel (reported by Du Plessis, *Economic fluctuations*, p. 21). Du Plessis reports estimates for selected years between 1911–1912 and 1948–1949, for national income per capita, in 1938 prices. We have rescaled the pre-1932 estimates to fit the 1938 estimate from the Statistics South Africa and SARB series. Houghton ('Economic development') suggests that it was only in 1933 or 1934 that real GDP per capita reattained its 1920 level, before accelerating. Feinstein fudges his analysis of growth, probably because of this unacknowledged uncertainty over prices. Drawing on Maddison (*The world economy*), he discusses the 1913–1950 period as a whole (Feinstein, *Economic history*, pp. 5–7), even though it really comprised two distinct periods, of fluctuating stagnation (to 1932) followed by rapid growth (thereafter). Feinstein emphasises that South Africa 'escaped most of the adverse effects of the depression' (ibid., p. 7), but this does not mean it escaped adverse effects altogether. Uncertainty over prices might also mean that Maddison's estimates for real GDP per capita in 1913 exaggerate the extent of South Africa's relative prosperity.

[17] Union of South Africa, *Official Year Book 1934–35*, pp. 240, 243.

Economic growth may have been muted during the 1920s, but the economy did not suffer as adversely during the Great Depression as did most other major economies. The demand for most agricultural exports and diamonds fell sharply, but the demand for gold was unaffected. Most farmers and South African manufacturers were producing for the local rather than the export market and were therefore partly cushioned from the global crisis. Retrenchments in manufacturing were largely limited to African workers, so that the main effects of the Depression were felt in the reserves. Moreover, public works programmes were established to employ unemployed white men (and, to a much lesser extent, coloured men). By mid-1933, perhaps as many as one in twelve white male workers was employed on a public or subsidised works programme.

BUILDING A MODERN, ECONOMIC STATE

The 1910s and 1920s might have been a period of general economic stagnation, but they saw a remarkable process of state building as the South African state acquired a wide range of economic roles. In South Africa, as in Britain and its other empire dominions, the state moved away from the laissez-faire liberalism of the nineteenth century to the more interventionist and regulatory mode associated with the 'new liberalism' (or, in parts of Europe, fledgling social democracy). The state's concern with economic management was evident in that no fewer than nine out of thirteen Union government departments covered broadly economic topics: Finance, Agriculture, Lands, Mines, Commerce and Industries (merged with Mines as Mines and Industries from 1912 to 1933), Education, Posts and Telegraphs, Railways and Harbours, and Public Works.[18] Over the following twenty years, the state acquired the capacity to intervene in these and other areas of the economy. In its fiscal capability, its capacity to collect and to use statistics, its strategic interventions in industrial development and social welfare and perhaps, above all, in its interventions in wage determination and the regulation of employment, the South African state adopted the form of the modern economic state, empowering it in its dealings with the powerful capitalist elites in gold mining and other sectors.

The new state had an almost insatiable thirst for statistics, especially economic statistics. The 1914 Statistics Act gave statutory authority for collection to a central statistical office, accountable to the Minister of the Interior, who would be advised by the Statistical Council. The purpose, as spelt out in the act's subtitle, was 'to provide for the collection of statistics relating to agricultural and to industrial, commercial, shipping, fishing

---

[18] The other four departments were defence, interior, justice, and native affairs, the last of which, especially, had important economic functions.

and other business undertakings and other matters in the Union'. The state began counting just about everything that could be counted. By 1919, it had already conducted censuses of manufacturing industries, agricultural and pastoral production, rents, the cost of living, wages, working hours and conditions.

The obsession with expertise extended to the appointment of commissions of enquiry into economic matters (as the British state had long been doing). These included a series of commissions concerned primarily with the incomes of white South Africans, including the Economic and Wage Commission (1925–1926) and the Commission on Old Age Pensions and National Insurance (1927–1929). The onset of the Great Depression led to a further flurry of enquiries, including one – the Native Economic Commission (1932) – that examined the welfare of the African population. Each of these commissions collated information and statistics, held hearings and recommended new government programmes and initiatives.

The new state needed additional resources. Its initial concern was with the consolidation of the 'provincial' fiscal systems that relied on profits from the state-owned and operated railways, company taxation of gold mines (in the Transvaal) and general income taxes in the Cape Colony and Natal. The 1914 Income Tax Act introduced a Union-wide progressive income tax that soon became the state's most important source of revenue. By 1920, income taxes (excluding taxes on gold mining) and property taxes (i.e., transfer and estate duties) together amounted to about 2 per cent of GDP. The Land and Agricultural Bank was established in 1912 to provide medium- and long-term loans to farmers. The establishment in 1921 of the South African Reserve Bank – the first in the British Empire outside of London – added to the government's capacity to mobilise and manage financial resources. By the early 1920s, the South African state had become, fiscally and monetarily, very much a modern state.

One conspicuous absence from the set of Union government departments was a dedicated Department of Labour. The government declined to appoint a Minister of Labour despite being pressed to do so by Members of Parliament who invoked the New Zealand precedent.[19] Labour matters were run by – and labour legislation drafted by – other departments. This changed dramatically in 1924, when the Pact Government (comprising the Labour and Nationalist parties) came to power in the aftermath of the Rand Revolt. The government established the first Department of Labour. Within a year, its staff had grown to 154, including the former director of census (indicating the importance of statistics for the department's

---

[19] *Hansard*, House of Assembly, 15 November 1910, col. 89.

regulatory work) and notable trade unionists who were recruited to its inspectorate.[20]

The impetus to this dimension of state building was the militancy of immigrant – mostly English and Scottish – white workers on the Witwatersrand, but the context was the much more general shift in thinking about the state's role in the economy. As even the relatively pro-employer members of the Economic and Wages Commission recognised in 1926 with respect to the role of the state in regulating wages, there had been 'a great change in the attitude of the public' from liberal laissez-faire to direct state intervention: 'every English-speaking country, following the precedent of the Australasian States, has passed legislation providing in certain circumstances for the fixing of wages under Statute', with the objects of preventing strikes and lockouts and eliminating 'excessively low rates of wages'.[21] Strikes by white workers prompted successive governments to institutionalise 'white' trade unions and to incorporate the semiskilled and skilled working classes through recognition, material concessions and negotiated procedures for dealing with industrial disputes. The state regulated the hours and conditions of employment, the use of machinery, the employment of (white) women and adolescents and apprenticeships. The 1924 Industrial Conciliation Act provided for the registration and regulation of trade unions and employers' associations, and for collective bargaining between unions and employers' associations in industrial councils (renamed bargaining councils in the post-apartheid period). Industrial councils could determine wages, benefits, hours and other conditions of employment. The accession to power of the Union-backed Labour Party, through the Pact Government, led to the establishment of the Wage Board, which could determine wage rates and employment conditions for workers not covered by industrial council agreements, and the Industrial Conciliation Act was amended to allow the extension of centrally bargained agreements to apply to all employers and employees in specified industries or areas. In the course of little more than ten years, the state had built the industrial institutions that characterised the nascent social democracies of northern Europe and Australasia.

With regard to African workers, however, the state retained an essentially repressive approach. The 1923 Natives (Urban Areas) Act provided for the registration and control of employment contracts, and regulated migration into and residence in towns through the pass system. In addition, colonial-era Masters and Servants laws and the 1911 Native Labour Regulation

---

[20] Simons and Simons, *Class and colour in South Africa, 1850–1950* (Harmondsworth, U.K.: Penguin Books, 1969; repr., London: International Defence and Aid Fund, 1983), p. 328.

[21] Union of South Africa, *Report of the Economic and Wage Commission*, p. 35.

Act served, inter alia, to criminalise breaches of employment contracts by African workers (e.g., through desertion). Trade unions representing African workers were also not recognised and not allowed to participate in centralised bargaining.

In addition, the racialised character of industrial institutions was reflected in the welfare state built from the mid-1920s. Just as the state accepted that wage setting for white workers could not be left to the market alone, so it accepted that the incomes of poor, non-working white people needed to be supplemented or at least organised by the state. One pillar of the new welfare state comprised contributory social insurance. More skilled workers secured industry- or employer-specific insurance against disability or poor health and against provision for old age. Through the extension of industrial council agreements on pension schemes, the state ensured that white workers in entire sectors were covered by quasi-social insurance. The second welfare pillar entailed non-contributory social assistance. The 1928 Old Age Pensions Act provided means-tested, non-contributory old-age pensions for white and coloured people. This prompted a short-lived conservative backlash against welfare state building, but in the mid-1930s and early 1940s, the state's responsibilities were expanded to cover further categories of 'deserving' (white and coloured) poor: the blind, people suffering from other disabilities, poor families with children and even some unemployed workers. The improved public finances resulting from the higher gold price made it easier for the state to respond to the challenges of drought and depression, and party political competition provided some impetus. The government also organised the construction of housing and controlled rents for white workers. These measures led a professor of sociology at the University of the Witwatersrand to proclaim in 1937 that 'provision for [the] European population' in South Africa was 'scarcely less complete than that of Great Britain'.[22]

Intervention in the economy extended also to industrial policy. In sector after sector, the state stepped in when private investors appeared unable or unwilling to commit the necessary capital. Thus, the government inherited and extended responsibility for the railways, in contrast to the Americas, where private railway companies built and operated the railways.[23] Almost

---

[22] J. L. Gray, 'The comparative sociology of South Africa', *South African Journal of Economics* 5 (1937), 270.

[23] The lines from the Cape ports and Durban to the Witwatersrand were built and operated by the Cape and Natal colonial governments, respectively. The line from Delagoa Bay to the Witwatersrand was operated by a private company, but it was taken over by the state after the South African War. A few minor private railways continued to operate until the 1920s. V. E. Solomon, 'Transport', in Coleman (ed.), *Economic history of South Africa*, pp. 89–126.

eight thousand miles of railway were laid between 1890 and 1919,[24] providing the basis for the spectacular expansion of the Witwatersrand as the industrial hub of southern Africa. In the 1920s, South African Railways focused primarily on improving the existing track and then on electrification, enabling the railways to carry greatly increased traffic. One major beneficiary was the Natal coal industry, which was able to supply coal to new power stations and to ports. In the 1920s, the state established the Electricity Supply Commission (ESCOM) and the Iron and Steel Industrial Corporation (ISCOR), again in large part in response to the failure of private firms to raise sufficient capital. Although the state was willing to set up new parastatal industries, it did not nationalise the mining houses. Its preferred mode of intervention was through regulation, including of the mining industry.

Similarly, there was promotion of the growth of both manufacturing and commercial agriculture. Prior to the 1920s, manufacturing had been largely limited to light industry producing food and beverages, and to a lesser extent textiles, clothing and shoes, whereas a growing chemical industry supplied the mines. Subsequently, several factors pushed the state toward a more interventionist policy: the development of local industry would reduce dependence on Britain, demonstrate that South Africa was as modern as the other British dominions and promote and protect employment and high wages for white workers. The primary means of state support was tariff protection, introduced in 1925. This contributed to the tripling of manufacturing output between 1924–1925 and 1938–1939. Manufacturing overtook agriculture in terms of value added just before the outbreak of the Second World War (and overtook mining soon after). The state also sought to modernise agriculture through agricultural extension services, training and irrigation projects, though with little obvious effect on the consistently sluggish growth of agricultural output.

INSTITUTIONS AND WAGES

In the period of economic stagnation lasting from Union to the gold-fuelled growth of the mid-1930s, the state built its capacity to intervene in almost every facet of the economy. It operated the transport system, provided power, ran the steel industry and set tariffs to nurture other manufacturing. It collated statistics, raised new taxes and managed the currency. It intervened in the labour, housing and agricultural produce markets. It provided income support through a nascent welfare state. And, of course, it acted to maintain an adequate supply of African labour to mines and farms at controlled

[24] Houghton, 'Economic development', pp. 19–20; Solomon, 'Transport', pp. 100–11.

wages. The state's concern was not simply to promote economic growth, or to assist capitalists in earning profits. It sought also to structure the distribution of earnings and incomes to bolster a privileged and generally racially defined minority. In establishing institutions that maintained wages and incomes at 'civilised', 'fair' or 'European' levels, it constructed a high-wage institutional framework that would endure through the segregationist and apartheid era and beyond, with enormous consequences for poverty and inequality.

For various reasons in the early twentieth century, immigrant white workers, urbanising poor Afrikaans workers and those members of the political or economic elite who were either sympathetic or racist or both all sought to maintain the white South African standard of living at a level commensurate with those of Australia and New Zealand, and as high if not higher than in Britain. Granted, the cost of living for (white) working-class South Africans was much higher than in Australia, Britain and elsewhere. But this was in part because expenses such as a domestic worker and a large house were deemed necessities in South Africa but would have been considered luxuries in Australia or Britain. At the same time, in actual purchasing power, South African artisans were better paid than their British, European or American counterparts. Lower down, unskilled (African) workers were paid much the same as labourers in Italy and some other parts of Europe, which was less than in Britain. The result was that the ratio of skilled to unskilled workers' wages was about 5:1, compared to (at most) 1.5:1 in Britain.[25] Significantly, the wages paid to African workers were low relative to white workers' wages, but not by comparison with workers elsewhere in the global South. In the 1930s, unskilled workers on South African coal mines were paid twice as much as their counterparts in India.[26] South Africa was, in fact, a relatively high wage economy overall.

Such high local wage rates were an issue because, as a report to the 1925–1926 Economic and Wage Commission recognised, South Africa was not an affluent country, despite the value of its gold mining. Rather, as the commission observed, 'The aggregate capacity of industry to pay wages is of the same order of magnitude as that of Germany and Italy rather than of Australia or North America'. Skilled workers on the Witwatersrand could be paid high wages, the report argued, only because they constituted a small minority of the workforce and did so 'at the expense' of lower-paid

---

[25] South Africa, *Report of the Economic Commission* (Pretoria: Government Printer, U.G. 12 of 1914); South Africa, *Report of the Economic and Wage Commission*, pp. 19–25, 243; Feinstein, *Economic history*, p. 134.

[26] Peter Alexander, 'Women and coal mining in India and South Africa, c1900–1940', paper presented at the Worlds of Labour conference, University of the Witwatersrand (2006).

African workers, of consumers (in the case of the railways, who passed cost increases onto their customers) and of taxpayers (in the case of public-sector employees).[27]

The election of the Pact government, in the aftermath of the Rand Revolt, resulted in direct state interventions in the labour market that both protected the high wages paid to white workers and ensured their employment. In the 1924 elections, the National and Labour parties denounced the incumbent government for promoting 'big financial' interests and jeopardising the future of (white) South Africans 'as a civilised people'. National Party leader J. B. M. Hertzog emphasised the threat to South Africa remaining 'a white man's country' and called for a *skeidsmuur* (literally, a dividing wall) between 'civilised' (i.e., white, and perhaps coloured) and 'uncivilised' labour. After winning the election, Prime Minister Hertzog introduced the 'Civilised Labour Policy', under which the state, and later the private manufacturing sector (but not mining), would replace black with white labour, 'wherever practicable', at 'civilised' or 'fair' wages.[28] The case for high wages for white workers was set out more explicitly in the alternative report of the Economic and Wage Commission: skilled white workers' wages had not risen in relation to the growth of national income, nor were they sufficient to maintain a family of five (or more) at a 'civilised' standard of living. 'To maintain a white civilisation in South Africa the white workers must receive a civilised wage', the report maintained. Higher wages paid for unskilled work would also encourage immigration from Europe, which would in turn 'strengthen European civilisation in South Africa'. The implicit ideal was the creation of a new South Africa in the image of 'white' Australia, with low-wage African workers largely excluded from all urban and industrial occupations except domestic work.[29]

Wage determination through industrial councils and the extension of agreements to non-parties were important instruments for raising white workers' wages, but inevitably some employers responded by retrenching workers. In the first two sectors affected – printing and building – minimum wage setting for skilled workers led to dismissals. Apologists for the 'civilised labour' and 'fair wage' policies argued that only low-productivity workers would lose their jobs and that such workers were dispensable in the noble cause of paying 'civilised' wages to 'civilised' workers.[30] In practice, the institutional apparatus of wage determination established under the

[27] South Africa, *Report of the Economic and Wage Commission*, pp. 33, 86–7, 145–6.
[28] Prime Minister's Circular no. 5, quoted in *Official Year Book*, vol. 9, p. 203.
[29] South Africa, *Report of the Economic and Wage Commission*, pp. 352, 356.
[30] Ibid., pp. 57, 290–1.

Pact government was fundamentally racist, deepened inequalities in earnings, encouraged employers to acquiesce in the exclusion of African workers
from the institutions that ensured high wages for insiders, and, perversely,
deterred employers from labour-intensive, low-productivity production.

At the same time, the construction of a welfare state mirrored labour-
market institutions in deepening and perpetuating overall and interracial
inequality through the manner in which it addressed the 'problem' of
'poor whiteism'. The Pact government's strong commitment to old-age
pensions – for insider white and coloured men and women – was in large
measure due to a concern to restore the racial income hierarchy. Racial
segregation entailed both excluding and repressing Africans and elevating white people through land-settlement policies in the countryside and
welfare reform as well as 'civilised' labour policies. 'White civilisation',
according to one National Party Member of Parliament, required that
'not a single white person should be allowed to go under'.[31] Yet repli-
cating British and Australian levels of 'civilised' earnings and incomes for
white 'insiders' could be sustained only through systematic discrimination
against the majority of the population and resulted in long-term economic
inefficiencies.[32]

The racialised assumptions underpinning high levels of 'civilised' wages
or incomes were rendered explicit in Edward Batson's pioneering definition
of a poverty line in Cape Town in 1938–1940. The poverty line entailed
sufficient food to meet needs 'taking into account the established food
customs of the Western World' and sufficient clothing to meet the 'minimum compatible with health and conformity with Western customs'. This
was, Batson emphasised, 'the barest minimum upon which subsistence and
health can be achieved under Western conditions'. Housing posed a particular problem, given that racialised norms meant that poor white and even
coloured people did not live in areas where the cost of housing was lowest.
Batson's way around this problem was to compare each household's income
net of actual housing costs to a poverty line that was defined exclusive of
housing costs. Similar allowance was made for the actual expenses incurred
in transport to and from work. What this meant is that households might
be deemed poor in part because they chose to spend more money on housing

---

[31] *Hansard*, House of Assembly, 12 August 1924, cols. 429–32. See Jeremy Seekings, '"Not
a single white person should be allowed to go under": swartgevaar and the origins of
South Africa's welfare state, 1924–1929', *Journal of African History* 48:3 (November
2007), 375–94.

[32] Union of South Africa, *Report of the Industrial Legislation Commission* (Pretoria: Government
Printer, U.G. 37 of 1935); see also Union of South Africa, *Official Year Book*, vol. 17
(1934–35), p. 243; Feinstein, *Economic history*, pp. 132–5.

than they might have done in a less segregated setting. Pervasive racism thus inflated even the poverty line.[33]

Through all of this, the state – even under the Pact government – remained dependent on the gold mining companies and helped the mines to secure sufficient supplies of unskilled African men to work even at prevailing, regulated wages. The Pact government was also electorally and ideologically committed to the maintenance and improvement of white standards of living. The beneficiaries – skilled, white workers – were moreover sufficiently powerful to secure institutions through which they could advance or protect their interests, especially in the fast-growing manufacturing and service sectors. For white workers, this was a period of remarkable achievement. Not only did the Labour Party enter government (in 1924), but also union representatives participated in the deliberations over the global regulation of work at the International Labour Conferences in Geneva. The price of success, however, was the oppression of African workers. Although poverty declined fast among white people, it persisted or even worsened among African people.

POVERTY AMID STAGNATION

Through most of the twentieth century, poverty was regarded as a 'problem' only insofar as it involved white people. Poor whites had been identified as a 'problem' in the late nineteenth century, but their conditions – and the causes of their poverty – were more fully documented in the early twentieth century.[34] The subdivision of small farms into unsustainably smaller and uncompetitive units drove unskilled white workers to urban labour markets, where they were unable to compete with African workers. The erosion of support by kin for those who were unable to work on grounds of age, infirmity or ill health, as well as domestic workload or unemployment, deepened vulnerability. If too many sank into 'apathetic indigency', living with or even below the 'non-European majority', then white people could not maintain their position as a 'dominant race'.[35] The government responded primarily through racially discriminatory job

---

[33] Edward Batson, 'The poverty datum line' (Cape Town: University of Cape Town, Department of Social Science, 1941), pp. 1–2.

[34] See, e.g., Union of South Africa, *Report of the Economic and Wage Commission*, pp. 105–20, 334–50; and *The poor white problem in South Africa: Report of the Carnegie Commission: joint findings and recommendations* (Stellenbosch: Ecclesia, 1932).

[35] In the words of the Transvaal Indigency Commission of 1908, quoted in Jon Lewis, *Industrialisation and trade union organisation in South Africa: the rise and fall of the South African Trades and Labour Council* (Cambridge: Cambridge University Press, 1984), p. 25.

reservation and minimum-wage setting, aimed primarily at ensuring that white men of working age earned enough to support themselves and their dependents. During the Great Depression, which coincided with drought on the South African platteland, the state operated massive public works programmes to prevent mass unemployment among white working-age men. In addition, it provided direct financial assistance to people who were unable to work (because of age, disability or gender) and whose kin failed to support them.

In relation to the poverty line implicit in the concept of the 'civilised' standard of living that applied to white South Africans, almost all African people were poor, but poverty among the African majority (or the coloured and Indian minorities) was rarely acknowledged. As W. M. Macmillan noted in 1930, most white South Africans were 'amazingly ignorant of the true state of the Natives in their midst'.[36] Successive government commissions reported that African people in rural areas had few needs and that the 'communal system' ensured that everyone's needs were met.[37] Still, in the 1930s, commissions began to acknowledge that poverty was on the increase, because 'communal traditions' were breaking down.[38] Nonetheless, the exclusion of African people from benefits under new welfare legislation continued to be justified with reference to the redistributive informal welfare system.[39]

It was true that even droughts, pestilence and terrible losses of livestock through disease did not lead to widespread starvation. During a devastating famine in the Eastern Cape in 1945–1946, the Department of Public Health's officer in charge of nutrition reported that he 'saw no children dying of actual hunger or starvation', and concluded that 'it is more a question of chronic malnutrition or lack of proper and enough food than one of actual famine and starvation'.[40] Such assessments belittled the suffering that existed on a wide scale and excused the limited relief activities undertaken by the state. At the same time, they reflected an important truth: the consequences of natural disaster were mitigated by the integration of rural societies into a cash economy through labour migration. Put another way,

---

[36] Macmillan, *Complex South Africa*, p. 117.

[37] Union of South Africa, *Report of the Native Economic Commission* (Pretoria: Government Printer, U.G. 22 of 1932), p. 142.

[38] Ibid., p. 143; Union of South Africa, *Report of the Inter-Departmental Committee on Poor Relief and Charitable Institutions* (Pretoria: Government Printer, U.G. 61 of 1937), pp. 15–16.

[39] Union of South Africa, *Report of the Department of Social Welfare for the Financial Years 1937–1939* (Cape Town: Government Printer, U.G. 15 of 1940), p. 64.

[40] Quoted in Wylie, *Starving on a full stomach*, p. 84. See also ibid., pp. 64–73, and Beinart, *The political economy of Pondoland*, pp. 70–6.

the factors that propelled as many as one in three adult men of working age to migrate routinely to the mines or other employment served to ensure that a cash income flowed into rural areas even when drought or pestilence reduced production.

Severe poverty remained exceptional because most Africans either continued to have access to land or could take advantage of expanding opportunities for wage employment. Land was relatively plentiful given that the total population of South Africa at the beginning of the twentieth century was just one tenth of its level at the century's end. African people might have owned little of the land, but they had access to a lot more as insecure tenants or sharecroppers on land owned by white farmers, at least in the first half of the twentieth century. In the course of the century, this access was slowly but inexorably stifled through a combination of ecological denudation, population growth, punitive and racist legislation including forced removals and the changing economic interests of white landowners. Outside of the reserves, the 1913 Natives' Land Act prohibited the purchase of land by African people and criminalised sharecropping. Although exemptions enabled labour tenancy to continue in some areas, and continued illegal sharecropping was tolerated in others, the act marked an important tightening of the squeeze on successful African farmers, accelerating processes of de-agrarianisation and proletarianisation.

As access to or the productivity of land declined, so access to employment became more and more important. In the most denuded reserves, such as Herschel (in the Eastern Cape), the population was dependent on the earnings of migrant workers to purchase imported grain by the 1920s, and 'a huge proportion of the community' existed 'on the very lowest level of bare subsistence'.[41] Men migrated to work regardless of the weather and harvest – and despite low wages, dangerous working conditions (especially in mining) and separation from families – precisely because smallholder agricultural production was almost never and nowhere sufficient to meet the needs of growing rural populations.[42] At the same time, however, the strong demand for unskilled labour meant that, for most of the period, there was little severe poverty. The demand for unskilled labour chronically exceeded the domestic supply, such that the gold mines recruited a large part of their workforce in southern Mozambique (and even further afield), and farmers resorted to child labour in response to labour shortages. Indeed, one of the reasons farmers were often hostile to the state providing emergency relief in times of famine was their fear that aid would stiffen workers' resolve

---

[41] Macmillan, *Complex South Africa*, p. 185.

[42] Ibid.; Isaac Schapera, 'Present-day life in the native reserves', in Schapera (ed.), *Western civilisation and the natives of South Africa*, pp. 39–62.

not to work for low agricultural wages. In such circumstances, the very poor were generally not people with access to employment but people who were unable to work and who could no longer count on employed kin for support.

ECONOMIC BOOM, 1933–1945

Although South Africa was not immune to the Great Depression, its economy recovered very rapidly and entered a period of extraordinary growth, even after the outbreak of war in 1939. In only twelve years, between 1933 and the end of the Second World War, GDP per capita almost doubled in real terms (i.e., accounting for inflation). Manufacturing grew especially rapidly, in part a result of increased government expenditure and planning, and in part a result of the relaxation of some of the racial restrictions in the labour market. Rising wages for African workers and the expansion of the welfare state to cover some African people meant that racial inequalities diminished.

Gold exports pulled the economy out of the Depression with extraordinary speed in 1933. At the end of 1932, after costly prevarication, South Africa finally abandoned the gold standard, which led to the depreciation of the exchange rate. This, combined with an increase in the global dollar price of gold in 1934, raised the local proceeds of gold sales considerably. The sudden increase in the mines' revenues prompted the government to introduce a tax on the windfall gains, which resulted in a rapid increase in government expenditure. Between 1932 and 1939, total industrial employment (including on the railways) rose from 555,000 to 929,000.[43]

This boom continued through the Second World War. Unlike most countries, South Africa experienced little economic disruption in wartime. Gold production, which amounted to one-third of global production in 1939, was maintained and even expanded during the war, despite persistent labour shortages. Together with an increase in the price of gold over the period, this largely covered the costs of the war.[44] The strong supply of foreign exchange also enabled South Africa to repay foreign-owned debt. 'Our territory has been spared the ravages of war', declared Jan Hofmeyr, the Minister of Finance, in his budget speech in 1946. 'As a state, we have ceased to be a foreign borrower. Our foreign exchange reserves are soundly invested in a sufficient gold reserve. Our ability to buy from the world the goods which we do not produce at home is not limited, as is the case with so

---

[43] Houghton, 'Economic development', pp. 33–4.
[44] C. S. Richards, 'Some thoughts on the Union's economic outlook', *South African Journal of Economics* 17:2 (1949), 149.

many war-torn countries, by a lack of internationally acceptable money'.[45]
Moreover, war conditions allowed the government to increase taxes on
individuals and companies. Accordingly, government revenues grew by an
average of 11.1 per cent per year in real terms between 1939 and 1945.
But as its expenditures rose by only 10.6 per cent per year, Pretoria was
able to run a budget surplus in every war year and to use that to reduce
debt. Thus, while South Africa's allies (especially Britain) ran large deficits
and borrowed money during the war, South Africa accumulated substantial
gold reserves and repaid government and private debt.[46]

The war years also saw a major expansion of state economic planning in
South Africa, as in Britain and elsewhere. Thus, the Industrial and Agricultural Requirements Commission (IARC) was appointed in 1940 to facilitate
an efficient mobilisation of wartime resources. The Industrial Development
Corporation was established in the same year 'to facilitate, promote, guide
and assist in, the financing of: a) new industries and industrial undertakings;
and b) schemes for the expansion, better organisation and modernisation
of and the more efficient carrying out of operations in existing industries
and industrial undertakings'.[47] Prices and wages were closely regulated. In
1942, the Social and Economic Planning Council (SEPC) was established
to provide more informed advice on policy (although its actual role in the
formulation of policy was unclear).

Sustained state support combined with high wartime demand and the
lack of import competition to ensure that the manufacturing industry continued to grow strongly. At the start of the war, South Africa's engineering
industry had comprised little more than 'mine and Railway Administration
repair shops plus certain fabricating firms, chiefly on the Reef', with little
capacity for high specification fabrication.[48] Indeed, for some time, the only
factory that could manufacture rifle cartridges was the South African Mint
(which switched its production from coins to ammunition at the start of
the war). By the end of hostilities, South Africa had developed a domestic
machine tool industry and substantial manufacturing capacity. The manufacturing share of GDP rose from 12 to 19 per cent between 1939 and
1949.

---

[45] *Hansard*, House of Assembly, 28 February 1946, col. 2, p. 642.

[46] Evan Lieberman, *Race and regionalism in the politics of taxation in Brazil and South Africa* (Cambridge: Cambridge University Press, 2003), pp. 138–44; Nicoli Nattrass, 'Eco- nomic growth and transformation in the 1940s', in Dubow and Jeeves (eds.), *South Africa's 1940s*, p. 20.

[47] Quoted in C. S. Richards, 'Some aspects of South Africa's war effort', *South African Journal of Economics* 8:4 (1940), 340.

[48] Ibid., p. 344; see also S. Herbert Frankel, 'Whither South Africa? An economic approach', *South African Journal of Economics* 15:1 (1947), 27–39.

Foremost among the 'resources' that needed to be mobilised efficiently was labour. The IARC and subsequent SEPC adopted the arguments made in 1926 in one of the reports of the Economic and Wage Commission and largely endorsed in the 1934 Industrial Legislation Commission: the colour bar should be relaxed; coloured, Indian and African workers should be permitted to do more skilled work; and wage differentials between skilled and unskilled workers should be reduced. The costs of not doing these things would have been enormous, given that 200,000 white men out of a labour force of 790,000 volunteered for military service, and the available supplies of 'emergency workers' (women and unemployed artisans) were quickly exhausted.

The short-term consequences were dramatic. In manufacturing, the wage share rose at the expense of profits, and the racial wage gap shrank dramatically. The employment of African workers in manufacturing rose by almost 8 per cent per year during the war and their real wages increased, primarily because of reduced skill differentials but also because of upward occupational mobility. Wartime emergency regulations allowed employers to engage (and train) black workers for jobs normally occupied by whites. Employers took advantage of the situation to restructure the labour process through mechanisation and deskilling. In firms investigated by the Wage Board between 1937 and 1946, only one in three semi-skilled jobs was filled by a white worker. Furthermore, wage differentials declined through direct state intervention. The Wage Board, which until the mid-1930s had been concerned primarily with protecting white workers' standard of living through setting high ('civilised') minimum wages for semi-skilled and skilled workers, turned its attention to the wages paid to unskilled, African workers, which it reported were 'insufficient for the maintenance of a healthy existence'. Unskilled wages should rise even if it meant squeezing profits. African workers' protests also helped to raise wages. Responding to protests, in 1942, the state provided for compulsory arbitration of industrial disputes by the Wage Board. At the same time, it sought to 'stabilise' the wages of skilled white workers through prohibiting strike action, regulating industries to prevent the poaching of skilled labour, capping overtime pay and drawing white women into the labour force.[49]

Although racial discrimination continued, not least with respect to training, two facts indicate the scale of the shift in the utilisation of labour. First,

[49] Nattrass, 'Economic growth and transformation', 26–32; see also D. Duncan, *The mills of God: the state and African labour in South Africa, 1918–1948* (Johannesburg: Witwatersrand University Press, 1995), pp. 170–8, 194–204; Peter Alexander, *Workers, war and the origins of apartheid: labour and politics in South Africa, 1939–1984* (Oxford: James Currey, 2007).

total factor productivity grew more rapidly between 1939 and 1945 than in any other period in South Africa's economic history.[50] Second, there were bitter complaints by agricultural and mining employers, as well as tensions between the Departments of Labour (which managed industrial conciliation and wage setting) and Native Affairs (which was primarily concerned with defending the migrant labour system for the mines).[51]

The reformism of these boom years reflected the influence of a more progressive conception of social justice as well as a harder-hearted concern with economic efficiency. Efforts to raise unskilled wages or to assist poor, elderly people through old-age pensions were motivated by a strong sense that doing so was right as well as necessary, and they were inspired by social policy reforms elsewhere in the world, especially in New Zealand. A social security movement that included leading economists and sociologists lobbied for reforms along the lines of the 1942 British Beveridge Report. Caught up in this idealism, the governing United Party campaigned in the 1943 election on the promise of a 'better life for all' (although the party leader and Prime Minister, Jan Smuts, voiced scepticism in his private correspondence). In 1944, old-age pensions were extended to African men and women, albeit with racially discriminatory benefits, and restrictions were relaxed on public spending on schools for African children.[52]

The appeal of welfare reforms did not rely on idealism alone. The outcome of studies that sought to measure poverty fuelled concern among both state officials and employers (including in the Chamber of Mines). One set of findings suggested that malnutrition was stable or in decline in the white population but rising in the African population.[53] The Chamber of Mines, concerned over the poor health of the mine workers it was recruiting in rural areas, sponsored a study that revealed malnutrition in the Transkei.[54] The 1944 Lansdowne Commission found that overpopulation relative to production in the reserves had resulted in widespread malnutrition and deepened dependence on migrants' remittances. On average, families in the Transkei and Ciskei met only half of their minimal needs out of their own agricultural production. Subsistence was 'but a myth' for

---

[50] T. Moll, 'Output and productivity trends in South Africa: apartheid and economic growth', unpublished Ph.D. thesis, Cambridge University (1990), p. 165.

[51] Duncan, *The mills of God*, pp. 175–8.

[52] Jeremy Seekings, 'The origins of social citizenship in South Africa', *South African Journal of Philosophy* 19:4 (2000), 386–404; Seekings, '"Visions and Hopes,"' in Dubow and Jeeves (eds.), *South Africa's 1940s*, pp. 44–84.

[53] Wylie, *Starving on a full stomach*, pp. 127–62.

[54] F. Fox and D. Back, *A preliminary survey of the agricultural and nutritional problems of the Ciskei and Transkei: report for the Chamber of Mines* (Johannesburg: Chamber of Mines, 1937).

some households.[55] As the Social and Economic Planning Council concluded bluntly, '[I]n practically no areas do the Reserve inhabitants as a
whole produce sufficient food for the most elementary requirements of
health'.[56] Starvation may have been rare, but life was nonetheless precarious for many African people in rural areas, some African people in urban
areas and some coloured people. Poverty was reflected in infant mortality.
Although white infant mortality declined from less than one in ten in the
1920s to less than one in twenty in the 1940s, almost one in five African
babies countrywide was dying before the age of one in the latter decade,
and an even greater number in some urban areas.[57]

Meanwhile, the circumstances of war had strengthened reforming tech-
nocrats, whether with respect to wage determination, job reservation, influx
control or social policy. In contrast, as soon as the war was won, the conservatism of many white voters and interest groups became much more
significant politically, and many of the reforms of the previous years were
suspended or reversed. Having tolerated urbanisation and squatting during the war, in 1945, the government passed the Urban Areas Act, which
restored influx control. Pass-law prosecutions increased, and the Wage
Board adopted a much harder line on the wages paid to unskilled African
workers. When African mine workers, whose wages had fallen in real
terms during the war, resorted to strike action in 1946, they were severely
repressed by the state. The functional distribution of income (i.e., between
capital and labour) shifted back in favour of profits, with the share of profits
in value added rising from 38 per cent in 1945 to 47 per cent by 1950. The
racial wage gap began to widen again.[58] It was also made much harder for
African workers to claim unemployment insurance.

For its part, the reformist Social and Economic Planning Council sought
to resist the changing political tide. Its final report, before it was abolished
by the new National Party government, argued that limiting the incomes
and social conditions of African people would dampen economic growth

---

[55] Union of South Africa, *Report of the Witwatersrand Mine Natives' Wages Commission on
Remuneration and Conditions of Employment of Natives on Witwatersrand Gold Mines* (Pretoria:
Government Printer, U.G. 21 of 1944), p. 17.

[56] Union of South Africa, *The Native Reserves and their place in the economy of the Union of
South Africa*, Social and Economic Planning Council Report no. 9 (Pretoria: Government
Printer, U.G. 32 of 1946), p. 49.

[57] Union of South Africa, *Official Year Book, 1934–35*, p. 987; H. Sonnabend, 'Population',
in Hellman (ed.), *Handbook on race relations in South Africa*, p. 22; W. P. Mostert, J. S.
Oosthuizen and B. E. Hofmeyr, *Demography: textbook for the South African student* (Pretoria:
Human Sciences Research Council, 1998), tables 4–5, p. 77.

[58] Nattrass, 'Economic growth and transformation', pp. 34–6.

and encourage disease and crime. The Council spelt out its vision by summarising the recommendations made in its many previous reports. These included the need for improved statistics; the enlargement and development of the reserves; the 'proper settlement in planned townships of those Native families who form a permanent part of the urban population'; improvements to agriculture; the vigorous expansion of industry, including 'mechanisation and the employment of non-Europeans as operatives'; the 'provision of greater opportunities for educated Non-Europeans in the Public Service, the Railways and Harbours administration and local authorities'; compulsory education for all and 'greatly increased funds for non-European, especially Native education'; improved and subsidised housing for Africans; food subsidies; and the adoption of a comprehensive social security system.[59]

The National Party's electoral victory in 1948 ensured a return to the essential policies of the Pact government and a rejection of the more inclusive vision given some substance during the Second World War. Three years later, the new Commission of Enquiry on Industrial Legislation firmly rejected the SEPC's arguments for reducing inequalities. The (Botha) Commission argued not only that inequality was necessary for the survival of 'European civilisation in Southern Africa' but also that this was in the interests of the 'Native'.[60] This was the basis on which the apartheid economy was rebuilt.

GROWTH AND STAGNATION UNDER APARTHEID

Between 1948 and the early 1970s, the economy grew rapidly and steadily, with real GDP almost tripling between 1948 and 1970. Even taking into account population growth, real GDP per capita almost doubled over this period. The strong growth of the era since 1933 was sustained. Gold mining was boosted by an increased gold price as a result of devaluation (in 1949) and the subsequent opening up of the Orange Free State goldfields. Gold production, investment and revenues all rose dramatically. Massive investments in agriculture, heavily subsidised by the state, resulted in a steady increase in output. Still, despite their strong performances, the mining and agricultural sectors were overshadowed by growth in the manufacturing sector. The share of GDP accounted for by industry – including construction and electricity as well as manufacturing – overtook the combined

---

[59] Union of South Africa, *The economic and social conditions of the racial groups in South Africa*, Social and Economic Planning Council Report no. 13 (Pretoria: Government Printer, U.G. 53 of 1948), pp. 111–16.

[60] Union of South Africa, *Report of the Industrial Legislation Commission of Enquiry* (1951), p. 220.

share of agriculture and mining in the 1950s and reached 30 per cent by the mid-1960s. In that boom decade, investment in manufacturing grew by 12 per cent per year, and real output by almost 9 per cent per year.[61]

This period of growth coincided with the reversal of some of the policy shifts of the war years. The new government introduced a swath of racially discriminatory legislation and policies that further protected white workers from competition; limited the supply of skilled African, coloured and Indian labour; and favoured farming and the mines over manufacturing in terms of access to unskilled labour. It delivered inflated earnings and living standards for white South Africans, in part at the expense of black South Africans and in part at the expense of future growth, as the economy became less and less competitive internationally.

Strong growth rates in the 1950s and 1960s were widely but mistakenly identified by conservative, liberal and Marxist scholars alike as exceptional by global standards. Liberal commentators explained this in terms of strong entrepreneurship, despite restrictive government policy, whereas pro-government and Marxist scholars attributed growth to the 'success' of the same government policies. In fact, the South African economy grew less rapidly than most other similar countries during what was the 'golden age' of capitalist development globally.[62] The growth rate of GDP per capita in South Africa over the period 1950–1973 was only one-half of the average for a sample of thirty similar countries. South Africa's GDP per capita was at its highest relative to similar countries in 1950; thereafter, its relative position declined.[63] The exceptional phase of South African economic growth was the period prior to 1950, not the early apartheid era.

South Africa's relatively poor economic performance during this period of global growth is reflected in other indicators. First, even in the 1960s, gross capital formation was lower as a percentage of GDP in South Africa than the average for either lower or upper middle-income countries and for the world as a whole. Moreover, throughout the entire postwar period, government accounted for a substantial proportion of gross fixed capital formation.[64] Second, profit rates declined over the apartheid period (see Figure 11.2 and Figure 11.4). Third, productivity growth was very weak. Total factor productivity (i.e., that part of growth that cannot be explained by increased use of capital or labour) rose by a meagre 0.2 per cent per

---

[61] Feinstein, *Economic history*, pp. 144, 165–72, 193–9.

[62] See Moll, 'Did the apartheid economy "fail"?', pp. 271–2.

[63] Feinstein, *Economic history*, p. 145; S. Du Plessis and B. Smit, 'Accounting for South Africa's growth revival after 1994', in Aron, Kahn and Kingdon (eds.), *South African economic policy under democracy*, p. 34.

[64] J. Fedderke, 'Capital formation in South Africa', in Aron, Kahn and Kingdon (eds.), *South African economic policy*, pp. 183–4.

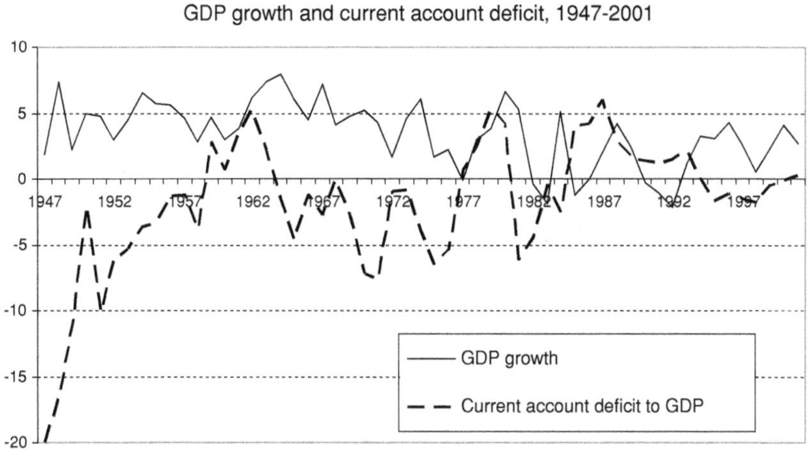

GDP growth and current account deficit, 1947-2001

FIGURE 11.2. GDP growth and current account deficit. *Source:* South African Reserve Bank (www.reservebank.co.za).

year in South Africa between 1950 and 1973. By contrast, in Korea and Taiwan, total factor productivity rose by about 3 per cent per year across the period, and even in Brazil, Chile and Mexico, it grew by about 2 per cent per year. If total factor productivity had grown at the same rate as in Brazil, the South African economy would have been 50 per cent larger by 1973.[65] Fourth, South Africa failed to increase its exports and accounted for a steadily declining share of world trade. The country's share of global manufactured exports fell from 0.8 percent in 1955 to 0.4 per cent in 1970, whereas its share of developing-country manufactured exports fell similarly by half, from more than 12 per cent to about 6 per cent.[66]

Economic growth declined from 5 per cent per year in the 1960s to 3 per cent per year in the 1970s and only 1.5 per cent per year in the 1980s – which was less than the population growth rate, meaning that GDP per capita actually declined. It is true that South Africa was not unique in experiencing economic difficulties in the 1970s or 1980s: most of Latin America also experienced similarly slow growth. Changing global conditions were unfavourable. But even during this period, and despite the crisis across Latin America, South Africa's relative performance deteriorated even further.[67] Its share of global manufactured exports fell to less than

[65] Moll, 'Did the apartheid economy "fail"?', pp. 287–8; see also T. Bell, 'Improving manufacturing performance in South Africa: a contrary view', *Transformation* 28:1 (1995), 3–4.

[66] Ibid., p. 282.

[67] Ibid., p. 278; Feinstein, *Economic history*, p. 145; Du Plessis and Smit, 'Accounting for South Africa's growth revival', p. 34.

0.3 per cent, and its share of developing-country manufactured exports fell to less than 2 per cent in 1985.[68]

One reason growth was relatively weak is that it led repeatedly to balance of payments crises, as exports failed to match imports and the current account moved into deficit (see Figure 11.2). Politics also affected both growth and the balance of payments in the 1980s. The townships' uprising and general political uncertainty discouraged investment, whereas sanctions inhibited trade. This political turbulence was itself in part due to the economic crisis. The township revolt in 1984 was initially concentrated primarily in the Vaal Triangle and the East Rand, where the downturn in manufacturing had resulted in deepened hardship, exacerbated by drought in the countryside.[69]

One approach to the interpretation of the apartheid economy has been to contrast the supposed health of the economy in the 1950s and 1960s with the crisis of the 1980s. In this view, apartheid was functional to economic growth in the earlier decades in that the supply of cheap labour through the coercive mechanisms of the pass laws (and other policies) had ensured high profits. In the 1970s and 1980s, however, the dynamics or contradictions of the apartheid growth model had become apparent: rising capital intensity and a restricted internal market (because of the meagre purchasing power of poorly paid African workers) led to the economic crisis.[70]

This interpretation, however, exaggerates the performance of the economy during the global postwar boom and underestimates its chronic economic weaknesses. Figures 11.3 and 11.4 show that profit rates in South Africa were declining from 1960, when good data are available. This trend probably began in the 1940s. Only in mining did the profit rate fit the story of strength to crisis: it rose (and then fell) dramatically with sharp increases in the gold price but declined steadily only in the 1980s. In commerce (i.e., wholesale and retail trade, catering and accommodation), the decline began in the late 1960s. In manufacturing, however, the profit rate fell steadily over the 1960s, 1970s and early 1980s.[71]

None of this is to suggest that apartheid was not without its short-term benefits to some employers, at some times, and in some sectors. Influx control and the colour bar served to protect the supply of unskilled labour to farms and mines, and profitability in mining actually rose in the 1950s.

---

[68] Ibid., p. 282.

[69] Jeremy Seekings, 'Quiescence and the transition to confrontation: South African townships, 1978–1984', unpublished D.Phil. thesis, Oxford University (1990), pp. 47–50, 226–7.

[70] E.g., John Saul and Stephen Gelb, *The crisis in South Africa* (London: Zed, 1981).

[71] Nicoli Nattrass, 'Wages, profits, and apartheid', unpublished D.Phil. thesis, Oxford University (1990), pp. 227–57.

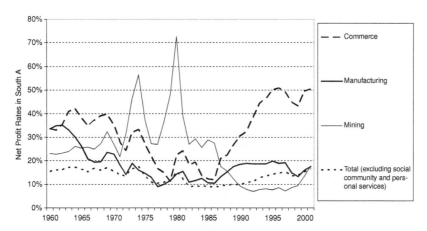

FIGURE 11.3. Net profit rates in South Africa by economic sector, 1960–2001. *Source:* Calculated from published and unpublished data from the South African Reserve Bank; see Nicoli Nattrass, 'Wages, profits, and apartheid', unpublished D.Phil. thesis, Oxford University (1990).

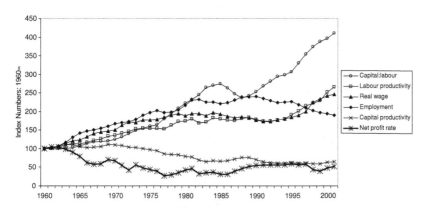

FIGURE 11.4. Key trends in South African manufacturing profitability, 1960–2001. *Source:* Published and unpublished data from the South African Reserve Bank.

This was not the case in manufacturing, however, given the combination of wages rising faster than labour productivity, on the one hand, and falling capital productivity, on the other hand (see Figure 11.4). In the early 1950s, wage increases for white manufacturing workers were compensated for by falling wages for non-white workers. But from 1955, rising wages for skilled and semi-skilled workers in all population groups put pressure on profitability. By the 1970s, competition between producers for the limited domestic market was a further factor. Another was the continuing pressure on costs

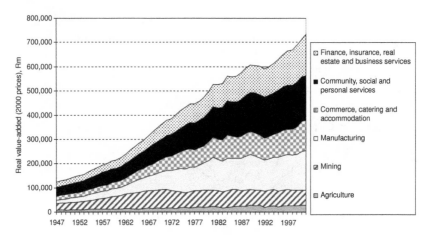

FIGURE 11.5. Structural transformation in the South African economy, 1947–2001.
Source: South African Reserve Bank.

from new restrictions on the employment of African workers (including the
1967 Physical Planning and Utilization of Resources Act, which limited
employment in certain industries and urban areas). Generous investment
subsidies and tax breaks as well as negative real interest rates encouraged
capital intensification but led to declining capital productivity. State investment in large-scale capital-intensive projects such as the South African Coal,
Oil and Gas Corporation (SASOL) energy parastatal exacerbated this trend.
Between the 1960s and early 1980s, the cost of capital relative to labour
fell by about one-half, due to rising wages and negative real interest rates.
Even when profit rates stabilised in the mid-1980s, employment did not
grow, perhaps because of high levels of industrial conflict. A 1991 survey
of manufacturing employers found that 'labour problems' were most often
cited as the cause of the continuing drift toward capital intensity. The net
result was that the South African industrial sector became steadily more
capital intensive over time, even as the productivity of capital fell.[72]

The performance of manufacturing was especially important because
of the rising share of this sector in overall production. Under apartheid,
the structure of the economy continued to change, from being a heavily
minerals-based economy into one more dependent on manufacturing and
services (see Figure 11.5). Between 1948 and 1989, mining's share of value

---

[72] Nattrass, 'Economic aspects of the construction of apartheid', in Bonner et al. (eds.),
Apartheid's genesis, pp. 42–64; Raphael Kaplinsky, 'Capital intensity in South African
manufacturing and unemployment, 1972–90', *World Development* 23:2 (1995), 179–92;
C. Meintjies, 'Impediments on the labour absorption capacity of the South African
economy', discussion paper no. 2, Development Bank of Southern Africa (1998), 11.

added fell from 19 per cent to 9 per cent, whereas manufacturing's share rose from 11 per cent to 21 per cent. Naturally, the distribution of employment between sectors changed accordingly.

The growth of manufacturing was the result of deliberate government policy. One aspect of this was the creation of massive public and parastatal sectors. Prior to 1948, the state already owned and operated the railways and harbours, electricity production and the iron and steel industry. In 1951, the South African Coal, Oil and Gas Corporation (SASOL) and Phosphate Development Corporation (Foskor) were established. The Armaments Corporation (Armscor) was established in 1963 following the imposition of an international arms embargo against South Africa. Parastatals were established also in the aluminium industry (Alusaf) and in merchant shipping (Safmarine). The state was also involved in various other manufacturing sectors through businesses established in whole or in part through its Industrial Development Corporation. By 1970, the South African state controlled the 'commanding heights' of the economy, with the very notable exception of the mining industry.[73] Furthermore, state intervention was not limited to the parastatal sector. It also played a crucial role in promoting Afrikaner ownership of private capital. In addition, low-wage, labour-intensive firms were given incentives to locate in or near to Bantustans. And security considerations led to the promotion of industries such as telecommunications and electronics.[74]

At a more general level, the state also fostered the private sector through tariffs on imports and, from 1948, through import licensing. In the motor industry, for example, Ford and General Motors first established small operations in South Africa in the 1920s because tariffs were lower on unassembled kits and components than on fully assembled cars. In the late 1940s, new controls on imports led to investments by British companies Morris and Austin, and a new wave of controls in the 1960s led to investments by companies including British Leyland, Renault, Chrysler, Datsun-Nissan and Volkswagen. The establishment of South African Pulp and Paper Industries (SAPPI) required massive initial capital investment. One of the mining houses took this 'risk' with state assurances that no import licenses would be granted until SAPPI could no longer supply the entire local market. A consequence of this protected operating environment was that much of the new manufacturing production was very inefficient. In the late 1960s and early 1970s, it cost 50 per cent more to produce a

---

[73] Clark, *Manufacturing apartheid*, p. 88.
[74] David Kaplan, *The crossed line: the South African telecommunications industry in transition* (Johannesburg: Witwatersrand University Press, 1990), pp. 27–37.

motor car in South Africa than in the United States.[75] 'Infant' industries failed to become internationally competitive and required continued protection. Granted, growth remained rapid during the 'easy' stage of import substitution, in light final and intermediate goods industries, which ended in the early 1960s. But the failure to begin to export light manufactures and to produce and export capital goods such as mining machinery meant that growth rates slowed and manufacturing remained inefficient.[76] When the state began to encourage manufacturing exports, South African firms were slow to respond. Thus, the real value of South African exports grew by only 34 per cent between 1960 and 2004, compared to growth of 169 per cent in Argentina, 238 per cent in Australia, 390 per cent in Chile, and 1,277 per cent in Mexico.[77]

At the same time, protected domestic markets and constraints on foreign investment encouraged the concentration of ownership in the private sector. Anglo American had begun to expand its activities beyond gold and diamonds prior to 1948 (acquiring chemicals manufacturer AECI through De Beers in 1929 and Union Steel in 1945), and continued such expansion under apartheid. In the 1960s, it established Highveld Steel to compete with ISCOR, took over Scaw Metals and established the Mondi paper business. The 1970s saw further diversification, including into automobile retailing and production, property and banking (acquiring a larger share in Barclays Bank, with which it had long cooperated). Through various intermediaries it also had a large stake in the massive Barlow Rand group.[78] In the 1980s, Anglo American took over the South African operations of Ford and Barclays Bank (which became First National Bank) when their parent companies divested. Other manufacturing interests included South

[75] David Duncan, 'Foreign and local investment in the South African motor industry, 1924–1992', *South African Journal of Economic History* 7:2 (1992), 53–81; David Duncan, *We are motor men: the making of the South African motor industry* (Caithness, U.K.: Whittles Publishing, 1997), pp. 16–30, 47–8; Feinstein, *Economic history*, pp. 181–3.

[76] Moll, 'Did the apartheid economy "fail"?', 283–4; Avril Joffe, David Kaplan, Raphael Kaplinsky and David Lewis, *Improving manufacturing performance in South Africa: report of the Industrial Strategy Project* (Cape Town: University of Cape Town Press, 1995), p. 12; see also Feinstein, *Economic history*, pp. 211–21; and Lawrence Edwards and R. Z. Lawrence, 'South African trade policy matters: trade performance and trade policy', *Economics of Transition* 16:4 (2008), 585–608. Bell queried whether South Africa was more inefficient than other, similar economies: T. Bell, 'Improving manufacturing performance', pp. 1–34; see also David Kaplan and David Lewis, 'Improving productivity performance in South Africa: a response to Trevor Bell', *Transformation* 30 (1996), 115–28; T. Bell, 'Improving manufacturing performance in South Africa: a rejoinder', *Transformation* 31 (1996), 43–56.

[77] Ricardo Hausmann, *Final recommendations of the International Panel on ASGISA*, CID working paper no. 161 (Cambridge, MA: Harvard University, 2008), p. 2.

[78] Innes, *Anglo*, pp. 175–84, 194–200, 215–9.

African Breweries, Premier Milling (co-owned with Liberty Life) and the sugar giant Tongaat-Hulett. By 1992, Anglo controlled 34 per cent of the entire Johannesburg Securities Exchange (JSE) capitalisation. The insurance giant Sanlam (16 per cent of the JSE) and Anton Rupert's Rembrandt Corporation (15 per cent) followed Anglo's lead in becoming massive conglomerates. Sanlam, for example, owned most of Gencor, whose interests included Genmin (mining), SAPPI (forestry), Engen (fuel distribution) and diverse manufacturing and financial firms. Six conglomerates – Anglo American, SANLAM and Rembrandt, together with insurance companies S.A. Mutual (14 per cent, including Barlow Rand) and Liberty Life (five per cent), and Anglovaal (three per cent) – together controlled a total of 86 per cent of the JSE.[79] This concentration of ownership, via complex cross-holdings and preferential shares, led Schneider to include South Africa in his list of 'hierarchical market economies', in which the locus of coordination is the conglomerate rather than either the market or corporatist institutions.[80]

In another respect, too, the country was not an orthodox case of import substitution industrialisation (ISI). Industrialisation did not proceed simply through the sequence of, first, the development of consumption goods industries and subsequently, backward linkages, intermediate and capital goods industries. Rather, it involved a mix of both this and of industrialisation through forward linkages from the 'core' mining-related sectors. Export-oriented mining remained central to the economy. The share of mining in value added might have declined steadily (see Figure 11.5), but its continuing importance was still evident in the early 1980s, when the high gold price helped to cushion South Africa from a still-deeper recession.[81]

That notwithstanding, the failure to diversify and to increase exports had two especially serious consequences. First, it contributed to the structural constraint that, whenever growth rates improved, the current account fell rapidly into deficit. This, coupled with skills shortages, fuelled inflation and led to restrictive economic policies. Second, employment growth was

---

[79] David Lewis, 'Markets, ownership and manufacturing performance', in Joffe et al. (eds.), *Improving manufacturing performance*, pp. 133–85.

[80] Schneider, Ben Ross, 'Comparing capitalisms: liberal, coordinated, network and hierarchical varieties', unpublished paper (2008).

[81] Ben Fine and Zaverah Rustomjee, *The political economy of South Africa: from minerals-energy complex to industrialisation* (Johannesburg: Witwatersrand University Press; London: C. Hurst, 1998). Fine and Rustomjee err in their estimation of the size of what they call the minerals-energy complex by including all related manufacturing in the 'complex': see T. Bell and G. Farrell, 'The minerals-energy complex and South African industrialisation', *Development Southern Africa* 14:4 (1997), 591–613; see also Fine and Rustomjee, 'Debating the South African minerals-energy complex: a response to Bell and Farrell', *Development Southern Africa* 15:4 (1998), 689–700; T. Bell, 'The minerals-energy complex and South African industrialisation: a rejoinder', *Development Southern Africa* 15:4 (1998), 701–14.

further inhibited. In the 1980s, manufacturing as well as mining and agriculture shed jobs. The parts of the economy whose growth came to propel the overall growth rate – notably, finance and business services – were the most skill intensive, whereas the relatively labour-intensive export sectors were disadvantaged.[82] In turn, that aggravated the skills constraint while placing further pressure on the balance of payments (as the growing service sectors used rather than generated foreign exchange).

THE TRANSFORMATION OF THE LABOUR MARKET

Economic growth during the apartheid period – especially in the industrial and service sectors – was accompanied by significant change in the structure of employment and, consequently, in patterns of inequality and poverty.[83] Just as tractors transformed the countryside, so new technology and ways of organising production transformed factories, building sites, mines and offices. Employers were keen to reorganise production through increased mechanisation not simply because the state provided strong incentives to mechanise and therefore to employ fewer African workers but also because they wanted to reduce their dependence on scarce, expensive and autonomous artisans or skilled workers. The high wages paid to skilled (white) workers and persistent skills shortages both provided strong incentives to employers to 'fragment' the skilled trades (occupied by white workers) into semi-skilled occupations (occupied by coloured, Indian or African workers). But white artisans were powerful, industrially (in the workplace, in part through their societies or trade unions), ideologically (as *white* workers) and electorally (through the ballot box), and employers had to move cautiously.

Although 'Fordist' production was first introduced in South African manufacturing in the 1930s, at the Durban Falkirk iron foundry, its wider introduction was delayed in many sectors until the 1970s or even later, to the 1990s. Production tended to change first and fastest in sectors free of well-organised and powerful constituencies of white artisans. For example, African workers moved into white-collar occupations in services far faster than into skilled work in manufacturing or mining. In sectors where white workers were well organised, deskilling could be implemented only with their consent, which meant that mass production was often delayed until

---

[82] Hausmann, 'Final recommendations', p. 4; see also Feinstein, *Economic history*, pp. 224–30; G. de Kock, 'The business cycle in South Africa: recent tendencies', *South African Journal of Economics*, 43:1 (1975), pp. 1–8.

[83] Seekings and Nattrass, *Class, race and inequality*, pp. 90–127.

employers could move white artisans into better-paid supervisory or managerial positions. At the level of the economy as a whole, the reorganisation of production in manufacturing thus depended in part on the growth of well-paid employment opportunities in services. Equally, given the continuing power of (white) skilled workers, mechanisation meant not so much replacing skilled with semiskilled work as replacing large quantities of unskilled labour with smaller quantities of semiskilled labour.[84]

For those with the skills, qualifications, racial classification or passlaw status to be able to secure employment in the expanding, better-paying classes, the period was one of rising prosperity. In contrast, for people competing for the stagnant number of unskilled jobs, the era was one of continuing or deepening hardship. The primary beneficiaries of economic growth and change were white. The white labour force became almost entirely urban and employed in white-collar rather than blue-collar occupations. Among Afrikaans-speaking white workers, employment in agriculture fell from 30 per cent in 1946 to 8 per cent in 1970, whereas white-collar employment rose from 29 to 65 per cent between 1946 and 1977.[85] Real per capita incomes among the white population more than doubled in one generation,[86] thus raising the demand for consumer goods.

As semi-skilled, skilled and white-collar employment grew in the economy as a whole, so coloured and Indian workers were also able to move into better-paying occupations (although this did not prevent their forced removal under the Group Areas Act). Upward occupational mobility among coloured and Indian people was based on improved public education, at both secondary and tertiary levels. Urbanisation, better schooling and rising incomes also led to improved health. Child survival rates improved faster among coloured people in South Africa, between 1970 and 1985, than in almost any other case worldwide for which data are available.[87]

The growing, changing economy also brought huge changes for the urban African population. Despite influx control, this population grew from about 2.2 million in 1950 to 5.6 million by 1980.[88] This growth was

[84] E. Webster, *Cast in a racial mould: labour process and trade unionism in the foundries* (Johannesburg: Ravan Press, 1985); Owen Crankshaw, *Race, class, and the changing division of labour under apartheid* (London: Routledge, 1997).

[85] Dan O'Meara, *Forty lost years: the apartheid state and politics of Afrikaner nationalism* (Johannesburg: Ravan Press; Athens: Ohio University Press, 1996), p. 138.

[86] Michael McGrath, 'Output and productivity trends in South Africa: apartheid and economic growth', unpublished Ph.D. thesis, Cambridge University (1990), p. 95.

[87] N. Eberstadt, *The tyranny of numbers: mismeasurement and misrule* (Lanham, MD: AEI, 1992), p. 160.

[88] C. Simkins, *Four essays on the past, present and possible future of the distribution of the Black population of South Africa* (Cape Town: Southern African Labour and Development Research Unit, 1983), pp. 53–6, table 1.

accompanied by change in just about every aspect of life: schooling, work, household structure, living conditions, culture and leisure activity, and politics. Urban African people also benefited from technological and economic change. When forklift trucks, cranes and other handling equipment were introduced into factories, the African workforce in manufacturing was reduced by 10 per cent, but the remaining jobs required more skill and were better paid.[89] Until 1960, almost all African workers were unskilled, but by 1980, unskilled labour accounted for less than half of African employment in the Johannesburg area and less than two-thirds in other areas of what would later become known as Gauteng. By 1994, a survey of its own members conducted by the Congress of South African Trade Unions found that only around one-third were classified by employers as unskilled; 30 per cent were unskilled, 21 per cent skilled, 9 per cent supervisory and 10 per cent clerical (with 5 per cent classified as 'other').[90] For better-educated, younger African men and women, opportunities steadily improved.

Even employment in gold mining was transformed. Across many decades, large numbers of men from rural areas had migrated to the mines, earned low wages (i.e., low relative to white workers) and remitted a share of their earnings to rural kin. Many of those had also taken breaks between successive employment contracts, so that there was de facto job sharing. In the late 1970s, however, the mines began to 'stabilise' their workforce by employing a smaller pool of better-paid, more highly skilled workers for the long term rather than a larger number of less skilled workers who might work one year but not the next. This stabilisation of mine labour removed the safety net of unskilled mine work for a whole generation of work seekers.[91]

Outside of mining, the new opportunities for African workers were mostly filled by newcomers to the labour force; that is, upward occupational mobility was inter- rather than intra-generational.[92] This reflected the massive expansion in primary and, later, secondary schooling for African people under apartheid (notwithstanding its poor quality relative to public education for white people). This expansion occurred in two distinct periods. First, from the mid-1950s onward there was a massive increase in the provision of primary schooling for African children, the effect of which was

[89] Crankshaw, *Race, class and the changing division of labour*, pp. 54–7.

[90] Sakhela Buhlungu, 'Introduction', in Buhlungu (ed.), *Trade unions and democracy*, p. 8.

[91] Jonathan Crush, 'Mine migrancy in the contemporary era', in Crush and James (eds.), *Crossing boundaries*, p. 25; see also Colin Murray, 'Structural unemployment, small towns, and agrarian change in South Africa', *African Affairs* 94:374 (1995), 5–22.

[92] Steffen Schneier, *Occupational mobility among blacks in South Africa*, working paper no. 58 (Cape Town: Southern African Labour and Development Research Unit, University of Cape Town, 1983), pp. 52–3, 67–8.

to raise dramatically urban adult literacy rates. Second, from the late 1960s (but later in urban areas), there began a massive expansion of secondary schooling. Secondary school enrolment rates rose from a mere 4 per cent in 1960 to 16 per cent in 1970 and 35 per cent in 1980.[93] In greater Soweto, for example, there were only eight secondary schools in 1972. Within the following five years there were twenty, with three times as many students as in 1972. By the end of 1984, there were fifty-five secondary schools. There was also a marked expansion of tertiary education. In 1960, there were fewer than eight hundred African students at residential universities. By 1983, there were about twenty thousand.

Equally, not all African people enjoyed the same opportunities with respect to education and thus to the newer, better-paying jobs. It was not merely that the children of the already better-off were advantaged relative to the children of the poor,[94] for the opening of new employment opportunities in the towns exacerbated emerging class inequalities in the African population. The large numbers of African people who had been removed from farms into sprawling slums in the homelands were for the most part denied good schooling and had no prospect of finding well-paid urban employment.[95]

Employers saw the promotion of African workers into semi-skilled and skilled work as a way of both overcoming the shortage of white skilled labour and reducing labour costs. Some employers favoured extending to African workers the rights enjoyed by white workers, crucially with respect to union representation and access to the wage- and benefit-setting industrial council system. The upsurge of strike action and the formation of new 'independent' trade unions (i.e., independent of the established unions dominated by white workers) representing mostly African workers in the 1970s encouraged reformist thinking. Reformers saw the incorporation of labour into the industrial relations system as preferable to chronic confrontation. Anglo American led the reformist wing of business, in the face of conservatism from the other members of the Chamber of Mines and other manufacturers (notably in the Barlow Rand group). In time, the Wiehahn Commission embraced much of the reformist agenda in its 1979 report, recommending that unions representing African workers be recognised.

The government's recognition of the independent unions opened up the possibility of their participation in the existing institutions of collective

---

[93] Pundy Pillay, 'The development and underdevelopment of education in South Africa', in Nasson and Samuel (eds.), *Education*, p. 34.

[94] Schneier, 'Occupational mobility', pp. 45–6.

[95] Murray, *Black mountain*, pp. 204–46; Seekings and Nattrass, *Class, race and inequality*, pp. 186–7.

bargaining, that is, the industrial councils and their counterparts in sectors such as mining. The industrial council system offered different benefits to different participants at different times. From the perspective of the new independent trade unions, organised white labour used the councils to negotiate wage increases for themselves at the expense of low-paid black workers.[96] The established unions certainly used the councils to defend the colour bar, but by the 1970s, the agreed minimum-wage rates seem to have been of marginal concern to most white workers, as the skills shortage meant that white artisans were generally paid much more than the stipulated minima.[97] It was more a case of the councils serving to protect white workers' pensions and other benefits. Minimum wages were, nonetheless, of value to large employers, which used the extension of negotiated minimum wages across entire sectors to remove the possibility of employers competing on the basis of lower wages. The extension of agreements to non-parties was perhaps the major reason employers continued to negotiate in the industrial councils.[98] Unionists themselves recognised the importance of this, especially in labour-intensive industries.[99]

Yet if minimum wages were of marginal interest to the established unions by the late 1980s, they were of great concern to the independent unions. The prospect of negotiating over minimum wages and improved benefits across entire sectors, rather than piecemeal at the plant level, was very attractive – as long as the unions could avoid being bureaucratised and could continue to use strike action. In 1981, for the first time, one of the smaller new unions joined the industrial council in the metals industry. Anglo American pushed employers' bodies such as the Steel and Engineering Industrial Federation of South Africa (SEIFSA) to open industrial councils to the new unions. In 1983, unions affiliated to the Federation of South African Trade Unions (FOSATU) joined industrial councils in the textiles and metals sectors, after employers made important procedural concessions to them and overrode opposition from the established unions. The FOSATU unions insisted on their right to organise and to negotiate at the plant level as well as the industrial level, and they backed the demands presented in the councils

---

[96] Jeremy Baskin, *Striking back: a history of COSATU* (Johannesburg: Ravan Press, 1991), p. 256.

[97] Steven Friedman, *Building tomorrow today: African workers in trade unions, 1970–1984* (Johannesburg: Ravan Press, 1987), p. 267.

[98] Quoted in Guy Standing, John Sender and John Weeks, *The South African challenge: restructuring the South African labour market* (Geneva: International Labour Organisation, 1996), p. 194.

[99] Devan Pillay, 'Pursuing centralized bargaining', *South African Labour Bulletin* 15:4 (November 1990), 8.

with strike action.[100] As long as an independent union was just one of several unions on an industrial council, the value of participation remained muted. But as the membership of the independent unions outgrew that of the established unions, they faced the prospect of being the majority unions on the councils – and of acquiring the power that came with that. The National Union of Mineworkers, which negotiated centrally with the Chamber of Mines (though without any need for an industrial council), provided an example. After the formation of the new union federation, the Congress of South African Trade Unions (COSATU), in 1985, several major unions in both manufacturing and services identified industrial councils as an opportunity to advance their campaigns for a 'living wage' through negotiating industrywide minima.[101] As the new unions entered into and made use of industrial councils, they reinvented the discourse of 'living' or 'civilised' wages that white workers had employed in the same institutional context half a century earlier.

The growing enthusiasm of COSATU for the industrial councils prompted mixed responses among employers. Some employers – especially those in the Barlow Rand group – became more hostile to centralised bargaining over wages, although they were more willing to negotiate centrally over issues such as provident funds, medical aid and training. Unions blamed the collapse in 1989 of the printing industrial council – one of the oldest in the country – on Barlow Rand's subsidiary Nampak. In an increasing number of sectors, however, including engineering and car manufacturing, COSATU unions reached agreement with employers over centralised bargaining.[102]

The new unions reinvigorated the industrial council system, using it just as white workers' unions had used it earlier in the century, to push up minimum wages and to secure improved benefits and working conditions in the face of economic pressures to depress wages and labour costs. Unions affiliated to COSATU rightly saw that the 'wage gap' between salaries and wages paid to better-paid (mostly white) employees and wages paid to unskilled workers was very wide and that most of their members (including semi-skilled and unskilled workers) were paid less than a living wage (which a union-linked service organisation calculated in 1989 at R1,140 per month (approximately US$430 per month at the time)). What made industrial councils especially attractive was that they enabled a union to neutralise the downward pressures on wages exerted by non-members. For most of the twentieth century, such pressure on unionised white workers'

[100] Friedman, *Building tomorrow today*, pp. 270, 326–31.
[101] Baskin, *Striking back*, pp. 256–9.
[102] Pillay, 'Pursuing centralized bargaining', 8–12; Baskin, *Striking back*, pp. 259–60.

wages came from coloured and African workers, and the solution, negotiated in part in the industrial councils, was the colour bar. At the end of the
century, the pressure on unionised African workers' wages came from the
growing numbers of unemployed African workers. The extension of minimum wages across whole sectors had the effect of preventing the survival or
emergence of smaller, low-wage, labour-intensive enterprises, and thereby
contributing to the rising capital intensity of production and, perversely,
the very unemployment that was threatening wages in the first place.

The increase in unemployment in the last decades of apartheid was rapid
and dramatic. In the 1940s and 1950s, the economy had been plagued by
chronic labour shortages, and workers sought to avoid poorly paid work.
Commercial farmers, unable to compete with the wages paid by urban
employers, successfully lobbied the apartheid state to extend and tighten
the pass laws to ensure their supply of cheap labour. In this context, the
only unemployment was among people in town who could afford and
were legally able to wait for better-paid jobs rather than take relatively
low-paid employment. By the end of the 1970s, however, the scale of
unemployment was evident in the crowds of men seeking employment
through rural labour bureaux or by queuing outside urban factories. When
scholars began to conduct local labour-market surveys in the 1970s, they
invariably found that open unemployment among African people was both
high and apparently recent.[103]

It is likely that widespread underemployment gave way to open unemployment in the early 1970s. There are, unfortunately, no good aggregate
statistics on unemployment over time. The official register of the unemployed excluded Africans, whereas the population census both misclassified
unemployed African people (including as 'peasant farmers' or 'housewives')
and excluded entirely those Bantustans that had become 'independent'.
This meant that the best proxy for unemployment data was estimates of
the gap between the total labour force and employment (including in peasant agriculture), that is, of the under-utilisation of labour through either
unemployment or underemployment. In the 1940s and 1950s, the under-
employed included 'idle' African men and women in town looking for
better-paying work as well as African families on white farms and in the
Bantustans who had some residual access to land. The aggregate employment gap seems to have widened primarily during the 1950s and increased
only a little during the 1960s and 1970s. The dramatic increase in the
visibility of open unemployment in the early 1970s probably resulted from
the shift from widespread underemployment (as many unskilled people

---

[103] Seekings and Nattrass, *Class, race and inequality*, pp. 167–77, 277–80.

worked for part but not all of each year) to a more dualistic labour market in which a smaller number of people were permanently employed, increasingly in semi-skilled, better-paid employment, whereas others were excluded entirely. The highest open unemployment rate recorded in the late 1970s was in a resettlement area in Limehill (in KwaZulu), at 42 per cent. Such resettlement villages were home to the most marginalised section of the population, removed from white farming areas and denied access to the towns.[104]

By 1994, more than one-third of the African labour force indicated that they wanted work but could not find it. Two surveys conducted forty years apart in Keiskammahoek (a poverty-stricken part of the Ciskei) reveal the extent of this dramatic shift from labour shortage to surplus in African areas: in 1949, many poor households were unable to farm all of their land because they lacked labour; four decades later, up to 50 per cent of the labour force in the area was unemployed.[105] Apartheid policies created an underclass of the landless, unskilled and unemployed, concentrated in places like Limehill and Keiskammahoek, unwanted by farmers or on the mines, poorly integrated into the networks through which people might find employment and without any safety net in subsistence agriculture.[106]

DE-AGRARIANISATION AND LANDLESSNESS

One of the causes of unemployment and inequality was the destruction of the African peasantry. This was rooted in the legal dispossession of most of the land by white settlers, in both the British colonies and the Boer republics, in the nineteenth century. Despite brief periods of buoyant production for markets and sustained struggles to retain access to land, the combination of racist legislation on land ownership (notably the 1913 Natives' Land Act) and the rise of capitalism in agriculture had marginalised the African peasantry in most – but not all – of South Africa by the 1940s.[107]

Yet the final destruction of the peasantry was completed only under apartheid. Sharecroppers continued to find niches in poorer corners of 'white' South Africa into midcentury, as Charles van Onselen shows in his biography of Kas Maine. Maine's best ever harvest was in 1948–1949:

---

[104] Ibid., pp. 177–87.

[105] D. Hobart Houghton and E. Walton, *The economy of a native reserve*, Keiskammahoek Rural Survey, vol. 2 (Pietermaritzburg: Shuter and Shooter, 1952); F. Sperber, 'Rural income, welfare, and migration: a study of three Ciskeian villages', unpublished M.Com. thesis, University of Cape Town (1993), p. 19.

[106] Seekings and Nattrass, *Class, race and inequality*, pp. 271–99.

[107] Bundy, *Rise and fall*; Mike Morris, 'The development of capitalism in South Africa: class struggle in the countryside', *Economy and Society* 5:4 (1976), 292–343.

after paying his landlord and the twenty-five labourers he had employed to supplement family labour during the harvest, Maine earned £300 after selling his produce, the equivalent of the annual salary of a teacher.[108] In many areas, the African workers employed by white farmers were also their labour tenants or retained rights to use some land for crops or cattle. In the African Reserves, households were dependent on both migrant remittances and agricultural production. Indeed, one-third of all cattle in South Africa in the 1940s were in the reserves. Taking into account the more successful African labour tenants, sharecroppers and farmers in the reserves, perhaps 15 per cent of the total population of South Africa in midcentury was sufficiently involved in independent farming to warrant the label 'peasant' (a similar or even larger proportion, in the towns as well as the countryside, still aspired to that status).

By 1970, however, the last vestiges of an independent African peasantry were all but eliminated, both on white-owned farms and in the reserves. Without access to land, African families were unable to preserve their cattle holdings. The loss of land and cattle led to massive social disruption, with the effect that even rural society bore little resemblance to the agrarian society of the first half of the twentieth century. This transformation began on white-owned farms. Buoyant demand for agricultural products meant that landowners sought to utilise more of their land themselves, whereas mechanisation enabled them to do so without relying on the oxen, ploughs or family labour of African households. In 1946, there were a mere 20,000 tractors in South Africa. By 1950, there were 48,000, and by 1960, almost 120,000. The introduction of combine harvesters in the 1960s as well as irrigation systems and chemical weed killers further reduced landowners' dependence on African labour. The state showed great determination in its assault on labour-intensive forms of production and a consequent dependence on African labour. Mechanisation was subsidised, and sharecropping, already notionally illegal, was stamped out, thus leaving labour tenancy to persist in only a few areas.[109]

---

[108] Charles van Onselen, *The seed is mine: the life of Kas Maine – a South African sharecropper, 1894–1985* (Cape Town: David Philip, 1996), pp. 306–7; see also Tim Keegan (ed.), *Facing the storm*, pp. 29–35, 58–61, 144.

[109] Michael de Klerk, ' "Seasons that will never return": the impact of farm mechanization on employment, incomes and population distribution in the Western Transvaal', *Journal of Southern African Studies* 11:1 (1984), 84–106; Tessa Marcus, *Modernising super-exploitation: restructuring South African agriculture* (London: Zed, 1989), pp. 58–69, 80–5; Stefan Schirmer, 'Reactions to the state: the impact of farm labour policies in the mid-eastern Transvaal, 1955–1960', *South African Historical Journal* 30 (1994), 61–84; Van Onselen, *The seed is mine*, pp. 331–431.

Farmers declared African families to be 'surplus' to their needs, and state officials removed the new surplus population to the African 'reserves'. More than 1 million people (i.e., about one-third of the resident African population) were removed from white-owned farms to the reserves, and the proportion of the total African population living in rural areas outside the reserves fell from around 35 per cent in 1950 to about 25 per cent in 1970.[110] Independent production declined steadily in its importance for African households on white-owned farmland after about 1953. Country-wide, independent agricultural production contributed about 20 per cent of the 'income' of African households on white farms in 1950 but less than 10 per cent by 1970.[111] That said, many Africans continued to live and work on the farms. Indeed, the absolute number of Africans on white-owned farms actually rose slightly in the 1950s, 1960s and 1970s: it was the 'surplus' population caused by natural demographic growth that was removed. The African households that remained on white farms were still dependent on agriculture but were fully proletarianised, entirely dependent on wages (and in-kind payments) from their employer and with little opportunity to keep the cattle that had been so central to social and cultural life.

The process of de-agrarianisation was most evident in the reserves, home to a rapidly growing proportion of the population. Forced farm removals combined with natural population growth and tightened controls on emigration to the cities, with the result that average population density in the reserves almost doubled between 1955 and 1969. The proportion of the total African population living there rose from 40 per cent through the 1950s to more than 50 per cent by the late 1970s. Rising populations meant growing numbers of effectively landless households. The total value of agricultural production remained steady, but the value per capita fell rapidly. By 1967, agricultural production accounted for only about one-quarter of the reserve population's food requirements and one-sixth of total subsistence requirements.[112] The proportion of household cattle owners declined, just as it did on white-owned farms. Lacking oxen and without the means to hire tractors, even families with access to land could rarely

---

[110] Platzky and Walker, *The surplus people*, pp. 10–11; Simkins, *Four essays*, pp. 53–7.

[111] Charles Simkins, 'African population, employment, and incomes on farms outside the reserves, 1923–1969', Carnegie Conference paper no. 25 (Cape Town: Southern African Labour and Development Research Unit, University of Cape Town, 1984).

[112] C. Simkins, 'Agricultural production in the African Reserves of South Africa, 1918–1969', *Journal of Southern African Studies* 7:2 (1981), 256–83; see also G. Lenta, 'Land shortage and land unused: the paradoxical patterns of KwaZulu', occasional paper no. 10 (Durban: Economic Research Unit, University of Natal, 1981), p. 23.

plough it. Many supposedly rural areas became, in practice, thoroughly urban, housing the dependents of urban workers.

Studies of the Transkei in 1982 showed that more than two-thirds of the income of poor and middle-income households came from remittances. With about one-sixth, on average, coming from old-age pensions and the remaining one-sixth from wages in local jobs, the contribution from agricultural production was insignificant.[113] Social and economic change further accentuated inequality in the reserves. In one Transkeian area, the average monthly income of the top 10 per cent of households was fifteen times that of the poorest 10 per cent; the poor could afford only simple mielie-meal, samp and porridge, and clothing was a luxury.[114] Income inequality in the reserves thus increased: a large majority of households actually had rising absolute incomes during this period, but the poor got poorer – even in absolute terms – because of increasing landlessness and unemployment.[115]

By the end of apartheid, subsistence agriculture was of negligible importance in the country as a whole. Household surveys suggest that, excluding large commercial farmers, the value of agricultural production amounted to only about 1 per cent of total income in 1993. Of course, these surveys might well under estimate the value of subsistence agriculture and natural resource harvesting. Still, even when taking such under estimation into account, the value of agriculture for poor households was very small compared to what poor households received from kin through remittances, wages and government grants.

POVERTY AND INEQUALITY UNDER APARTHEID

The lack of data on incomes prior to the 1970s makes it difficult to plot the changing level of poverty with precision. Around 1970, it is estimated that almost no white people, perhaps half of the coloured population, a somewhat lower proportion of the Indian population and between one-third and two-thirds of the urban African population were living in poverty.[116] Poverty

[113] F. Wilson and M. Ramphele, *Uprooting poverty: the South African challenge* (Cape Town: David Philip, 1989), pp. 62–3.

[114] T. Moll, 'A mixed and threadbare bag: employment, incomes, and poverty in Lower Roza, Qumbu, Transkei', 2nd Carnegie Inquiry into Poverty and Development in Southern Africa, 13–19 April 1984 (Cape Town: Southern African Labour and Development Research Unit University of Cape Town, 1984), 38.

[115] C. Simkins, 'What has been happening to income distribution and poverty in the homelands?' 2nd Carnegie Inquiry into Poverty and Development in Southern Africa, 13–19 April 1984 (Cape Town: Southern African Labour and Development Research Unit, University of Cape Town, 1984), p. 13.

[116] H. L. Watts, 'Poverty', in Randall (ed.), *Some implications of inequality*, pp. 40–57.

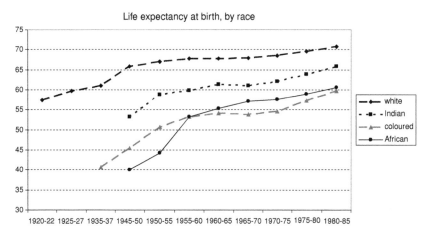

FIGURE 11.6. Life expectancy by race. *Source:* Union of South Africa, *Official Year Book 1934–35*, 987; South Africa, *South African Statistics 1994*, table 3.17.

rates among the rural population were clearly very high. Estimates of life expectancy and infant mortality supplement this vague picture. Although African people in rural areas were not required to register births and deaths under the 1923 Births, Marriages and Deaths Registration Act, and many municipalities were exempted from the general requirement that statistics be collected in urban areas, basic demographic data have been estimated (including by race) from the 1930s or 1940s. Life expectancy for both men and women rose sharply in the 1940s and 1950s, after which it grew at a slower pace (see Figure 11.6). By the 1980s, the life expectancy for African (and coloured) people had reached the level attained by white people about fifty years earlier. Infant mortality also improved, with a similar sharp improvement after the war, followed by a more gradual improvement thereafter. By the 1980s, infant mortality among African children nationally had fallen to about sixty deaths per thousand births (see Figure 11.7). The fact that the infant mortality rate had not dropped further reflected, in large measure, the persistence of poverty, especially in rural areas. Significantly, too, despite there being an overall improvement in child nutrition, as many as one in three African, coloured and Indian children were underweight, with stunted growth.[117]

The conduct of a countrywide poverty survey in 1993 allowed for the first comprehensive national analysis of impoverishment at the very end of the apartheid era. How many people were poor depended on the choice of poverty line. The incoming post-apartheid government's analysis of the data showed that more than half of the population was living in 'poverty'

[117] Wilson and Ramphele, *Uprooting poverty*, pp. 101–6.

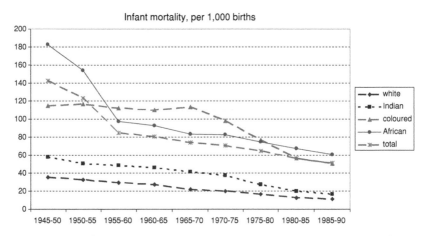

Infant mortality, per 1,000 births

FIGURE 11.7. Infant mortality, by race. *Source:* Union of South Africa, *Official Year Book 1934–35*, 987; South Africa, *South African Statistics 1994*, table 3.17.

and more than one-quarter in 'ultrapoverty', using its preferred poverty lines. By the international measure of the equivalent of US$1 per person per day, however, only 24 per cent of the population was poor. This was a higher poverty rate than in most other middle-income countries but was similar to that of Brazil and much lower than in most other countries in southern Africa. Even the South African 'ultra poor' category included a small number of households with incomes above the $1 line. In South Africa, however, 'even people having somewhat more than $1 a day are *considered* poor', because of the very evident wealth that existed alongside poverty.[118]

The 1993 survey showed not only that poverty – however defined – was extensive but also that there had already been considerable upward mobility within the African population. By 1993, two out of three households in the eighth income decile, one-third of the households in the ninth income decile and 11 per cent of households in the richest or tenth income decile were African. Although the Gini coefficient for income distribution in South Africa as a whole had not changed since the 1970s, the Gini coefficients for intraracial income distribution had risen sharply. The Gini coefficient for the African population had risen to greater than 0.6, not much less than for South Africa as a whole. The within-race component of total income distribution was larger than the between-race component,

---

[118] Stephan Klasen, 'Poverty, inequality and deprivation in South Africa: an analysis of the 1993 SALDRU Survey', *Social Indicators Research* 41 (1997), 54, emphasis added; UNDP, *Human Development Report 1999*, pp. 146–8.

according to decompositions using income inequality.[119] In other words, growing numbers of African people were benefiting substantially from economic growth and change – even though a small minority was suffering from debilitating poverty.

Survey data also showed very clearly who was poor at the end of the apartheid period. At the beginning of apartheid, households were poor if there was no one within them of working age and if they received no remittances from absent members. The ranks of the poor also included some households with members working in very low-wage occupations. By the end of the apartheid order, this picture had changed, especially because of the rise in unemployment. The poor constituted households where no one was working, including adults of working age who wanted to work. The generous level of the old-age pension meant that households that included a pensioner were lifted out of deep poverty.[120]

The typical poor household in 1994 lived in a mud house, without electricity and running water, in a supposedly 'rural' area. It was headed by a woman in her forties or fifties and therefore too young to receive an old-age pension, whose own parents had died and who was neither employed nor supported by a husband employed elsewhere. Such households were poor for a set of reasons. Fundamentally, they were landless, and their adult members were unemployed, usually because they lacked the skills and connections required to get a job in a labour market that offered few opportunities to the unskilled. Living in poor areas, and lacking financial and social capital as well as skill and experience, they would have been hard-pressed to start a small enterprise. Poor households were poor also because they were unable to make any significant claim on either kin (for whatever reason) or on the state (through ineligibility for government grants or pensions).

By the end of the apartheid period, government grants and pensions were considerably reducing the extent of poverty in South Africa. The National Party had inherited, in 1948, a rudimentary welfare state. It was distinctly unusual in the world at the time in that the state paid means-tested, noncontributory old-age pensions and disability grants to many inhabitants. These included payments to poor African people and grants for poor mothers with nonpresent fathers and dependent children to many poor coloured people. The apartheid state refused to raise the real, maximum value of the old-age pension paid to African people for almost twenty-five years (see the grey line in Figure 11.8), despite doubling the

---

[119] Murray Leibbrandt, Ingrid Woolard and Haroon Bhorat, 'Understanding contemporary household inequality in South Africa', in Bhorat et al., *Fighting poverty*, pp. 21–40.

[120] Klasen, 'Poverty, inequality and deprivation in South Africa'; Seekings and Nattrass, *Class, race and inequality*, pp. 188–235.

Old-age pensions in South Africa

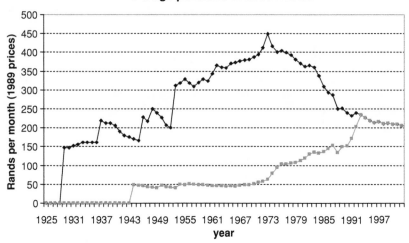

FIGURE 11.8. The real value of the maximum old-age pension benefits paid to white and African people, 1925–2000. *Source:* McGrath, 'The racial distribution of taxes and state expenditures', 1979.

real, maximum value of the pension paid to white people (see the black line in Figure 11.8). However, in the later apartheid years, the state slowly raised the real value of the old-age pension paid to African men and women, finally removing racial discrimination in benefits in 1993. In consequence, the real value of the old-age pension in 1993 was almost five times the real value of the pension paid to African people between 1948 and the early 1970s (see Figure 11.9).

Social assistance programmes such as state pensions, together with public health expenditure in African areas, were the reasons, even at the peak of apartheid, that there was some limited redistribution from whites to Africans through the budget. Although whites enjoyed a large share of the benefits of the government's social expenditure, they paid an even larger share of the taxes that financed those. The average per capita 'income' of African people was increased by about 10 per cent in 1960 and 1970, if account is taken of cash transfers and of the benefits in kind of public health and education spending, as well as taxes paid. The per capita income of white South Africans was reduced by about 5 per cent.[121] This redistribution was not unimportant to key beneficiaries – especially pensioners – but it was tiny in comparison with the inequality generated in the labour market and through unequal landownership. Indeed, the state could afford some

[121] M. D. McGrath, 'The racial distribution of taxes and state expenditures', Black/White Income Gap Project Final Research Report no. 2 (Durban: Department of Economics, University of Natal, 1979).

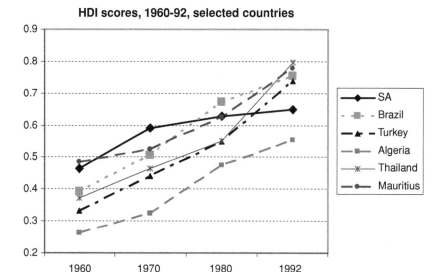

FIGURE 11.9. HDI data, 1960–1992, selected countries. *Source:* UNDP, *Human Development Report 1997.*

redistribution through the budget precisely because the budget was not the primary mechanism by which interracial distribution was shaped. One way of looking at this is to say that the apartheid state was so successful in steering the economy down a growth path that favoured and reserved places for a white racial minority that it could readily afford to tax high-earning white people and to redistribute small sums to the disadvantaged majority.

By the early 1990s, the old-age pension provision and other social assistance programmes were major vehicles for redistribution from rich to poor and had a substantial effect on the incidence of poverty. Overall, at the end of the apartheid era, about 1.7 times more money was redistributed through the public welfare system than between households through remittances. The consequence of this was that the very poor (i.e., people with incomes of less than approximately US$1 per day, or the poorest income quintile) were people living in households where no one was eligible for a pension or grant. The moderately poor (i.e., people who were poor in terms of South Africa's poverty line but were not very poor, or approximately the second income quintile) included many households that had been lifted out of deep poverty by a pension or grant.[122]

In another area, the role of public education in the mitigation or reproduction of inequality under apartheid was rather more complex than the

[122] Seekings and Nattrass, *Class, race and inequality*, pp. 201–6, 214–9.

role played by other kinds of social policy. Public education was central to the state's project of ensuring that all white people enjoyed advantaged positions in society. Through superior public education, white children would be given skills that privileged them in the labour market and that in time meant that they no longer had to rely on a job colour bar to get the better-paying jobs. Crucially, state investments in the education of children from poorer white families meant that the parents' disadvantages – and vulnerability to competition from low-cost coloured or African labour – were not passed onto the next generation. The importance of public education for white people was reflected in the fact that the state spent much more on the white minority than on the African majority, whereas the public health system spent more, in aggregate, on the latter. (One consequence of this was that the private health-care sector grew much faster than the private education sector). By 1968, average public expenditure on African schoolchildren was just 6 per cent of the value of such spending on white schoolchildren. At the beginning of that decade, the total number of white students passing the school-leaving matriculation examination was sixteen times higher than the combined total number of coloured, Indian and African students, despite the fact that fewer than one in five eighteen-year-olds was white. The educational gap remained enormous until late in the apartheid period, when rapidly rising numbers of African children began moving into and through secondary schooling. By 1991, two-thirds of the candidates writing the matric (including in the Bantustans) were African, and fewer than one-sixth were white. African students made up more than half of the successful candidates, with white students making up about one-third.[123]

Expenditure on the education of African children rose sixfold (in real terms) between the mid-1970s and early 1990s – both because of increasing expenditures per student and rising enrolment in school. There were good reasons for the reforms. Continued economic growth needed more semiskilled and skilled labour than was available in the white, coloured and Indian populations. Moreover, the maintenance of political stability required that the state both improve opportunities for upward occupational mobility and for rising incomes for some African inhabitants while at the same time mitigating the extremes of poverty. Just as important as the incentives to reform was the removal of political impediments. The

---

[123] F. Auerbach and D. Welsh, 'Education', in van der Horst and Reid (eds.), *Race discrimination in South Africa*, p. 70; J. Fedderke, R. de Kadt and J. Luiz, 'Uneducating South Africa: the failure to address the 1910–1993 legacy', *International Review of Education* 46:3–4 (2001), 257–81; Malherbe, *Education in South Africa*, vol. 2, p. 722; South African Institute of Race Relations, *Race Relations Survey 1992/1993* (Johannesburg: South African Institute of Race Relations, 1993), p. 606.

state's past investments in public education for white children had ensured that almost all white South Africans enjoyed the privileges of class and no longer needed overt racial discrimination to maintain those privileges. Although the expansion of educational and economic opportunities for some African people and the removal of the job colour bar exposed white South Africans to interracial competition, white men and women competed from positions of existing educational and economic advantage.

Fiscal incidence analysis reflects the scale of these changes. The value of social expenditure per capita on African people relative to that on white people rose from about 12 per cent in 1975 to 21 per cent by 1986 and 69 per cent by 1993. By 1993, the effects of taxation and social expenditure were to reduce the average income of whites by about one-sixth while raising the average income of Africans by one-third ('income' includes the estimated value of educational and health-care benefits in kind).[124] Compared to other middle-income countries (e.g., Brazil), there has been considerable redistribution through the budget in South Africa both because of the incidence of social expenditure and because of the fact that most taxes are paid by the rich. Standard fiscal incidence analysis does, however, value benefits in kind in terms of their cost, not their actual consequences. So, the value of education to poor children is calculated in terms of what the government spends on the education of poor children. Insofar as teachers in poor areas were paid by the state but provide low-quality education, then standard fiscal incidence analysis would overestimate the real value to the poor of public education. At the end of apartheid, children from poor families attended school, often into their late teens or even early twenties. But they left with few skills.

The UN Development Programme's (UNDP) Human Development Index (HDI) is a composite measure of well-being that takes into account life expectancy, measures of educational attainment and real GDP per capita (but not the distribution thereof). Figure 11.9 shows UNDP data for South Africa and selected other middle-income countries from 1960 until 1992.[125] South Africa – together with Mauritius – started off in the lead of this particular set of countries. Its HDI rose sharply in the 1960s, so that South Africa actually increased its lead. In the 1970s and 1980s, however, its growth rate slowed dramatically, and South Africa was overtaken by Brazil, Mauritius, Thailand and Turkey. Of the six countries shown in Figure 11.9, only Algeria continued to trail South Africa and the gap between them was narrowing. (In the course of the 1990s, the

---

[124] Servaas van der Berg, 'Trends in racial fiscal incidence in South Africa', *South African Journal of Economics* 69:2 (2001), 243–68.
[125] UNDP, *Human Development Report 1997*, pp. 158–60.

HIV/AIDS-driven decline in life expectancy in South Africa resulted in a plummeting HDI, but this had not begun to have any effect by 1992).

THE LEGACY OF APARTHEID

In 1994, Nelson Mandela and the African National Congress inherited an economy beset by problems. Over the previous decade, economic growth had been erratic and weak, with GDP per capita growing by an average of only 0.8 per cent per annum. Investment had all but dried up, and capital was steadily draining out of the economy. Exports were limited, but there was a strong demand for imports, thus posing severe pressure on the exchange rate. The budget deficit had widened to more than 7 per cent of GDP in 1993, and the prospect of a debt trap loomed large. As many as three of every ten adults who wanted work were unemployed. Although life expectancy was longer and income poverty was lower than ever before, poverty remained stubbornly high, even by the austere measures (e.g., $1 per person per day) used for global comparisons.

The challenges facing the new government were the product of deep-rooted patterns of economic activity. Most important, perhaps, was the inefficiency of much of South African business. Business had developed behind protective controls on imported competition, helping it to survive with what was, in important respects, a high-cost labour structure imposed for political reasons. Industrialisation had been based not on 'cheap' labour alone but on a distinctive combination of (somewhat) cheap and (very) expensive labour. Skilled labour was expensive, not least because the state had for most of the century systematically prevented or inhibited African workers from competing with white voters to maintain and raise the standard of living of the latter. Some employers favoured cost cutting, by replacing expensive white or skilled labour with cheaper African, unskilled or semiskilled labour. But employers in general could live with expensive white or skilled labour as long as they were protected from foreign competition, enjoyed rising demand from white consumers or the state and could secure an abundant supply of cheaper, unskilled African labour when necessary. Tariffs, the circumstances of the Second World War and postwar import controls helped to protect domestic producers, and thereby helped to protect the broader system of racial discrimination and inequality.

Ironically, when employers in the last decades of apartheid acquired more freedom to do away with the privileged status of skilled, white workers, they faced an ever more strongly organised African working class determined to acquire the privileges previously reserved for white workers. One of the mechanisms by which the standard of living of white South Africans was protected was the system of wage setting built around industrial councils (and the Wage Board for workers in unorganised sectors). By the late apartheid period, both of these had ceased to be necessary for the maintenance of white workers' standard of living, because discrimination in public education had given white South Africans the scarce skills and credentials that allowed them to command higher earnings without regard for negotiated minima. The wage-setting machinery became, instead, the mechanism through which white workers protected work-related benefits (e.g., pension funds) and employers prevented low-wage, labour-intensive competition. When in the 1980s independent unions emerged to represent mostly unskilled and semiskilled African workers, they came to recognise the value of controlling industrial councils and the Wage Board to raise the wages and benefits paid to their members. Preventing the emergence of low-wage, low-cost employers was as important to them as it was to the large firms that dominated the employers' side of the industrial council system. By the early 1990s, the consolidation of centralised bargaining through the industrial councils, the provision for the extension of bargained agreements across whole sectors, and the strengthening of minimum wage-setting in unorganised sectors and industries had become core demands of the trade union movement.

The new trade unions' interests gelled with arguments, put forward by union-friendly academics, that the way to make South African industry more competitive and promote economic growth was to raise productivity. Between 1995 and 1998, the new South African state reformed South African labour legislation, essentially extending to unionised African workers the rights won by white workers in the 1920s and, more important, strengthening the institutions that allowed for the realisation of those rights. The institutions of wage setting thus served as the mechanism by which the economic growth path was reproduced, with continuing capital intensification (despite unemployment). Put another way, the path dependence displayed by the South African economy was rooted in the new unions' taking over of existing labour market and related institutions.

Marxist scholars had long argued that South African capitalism was based on the low wages or exploitation of African workers. In the face of rising real wages paid to African workers in the 1960s and early 1970s, historians such as Martin Legassick defended the cheap-labour thesis by arguing that apartheid policies continued 'to "cheapen" labour, to make it cheaper than it would have been in their absence, whether or not the absolute magnitude of the wage of employed persons is rising or falling'.[126]

---

[126] Martin Legassick, 'Post-script to "Legislation, ideology and economy in post 1948 South Africa"', in Schlemmer and Webster (eds.), *Change, reform, and economic growth in South Africa*, pp. 73–4.

In the 1990s, formerly Marxist scholars switched to arguing that higher wages were appropriate because they would compel employers to manage more effectively and raise productivity.[127] Trade liberalisation certainly put inefficient producers under pressure, with substantial reductions in tariffs between 1994 and 2000.[128] (The relaxation of exchange controls also contributed to the 'unbundling' of the large conglomerates; Anglo American, most dramatically, more than reduced its share of the JSE to 17 per cent in 1998 and then shifted its primary listing to the London Stock Exchange and its head office to London.)[129] Rising wages for unskilled workers also pushed employers to invest in more skill- and capital-intensive technology, which had the effect of raising average productivity. In manufacturing, after 1994, the rise in average wages and labour productivity came at the cost of falling employment (see Figure 11.4). The rising profit share was good for those employers who remained in business, and higher wages were good for those workers who kept their jobs. The 'losers' were the predominantly unskilled workers who lost jobs, and the many more for whom the lack of job creation meant continuing unemployment.

Rising productivity would have been unambiguously good if resources were fully employed, but the economy failed to grow anywhere like fast enough to generate the required jobs. In the decade after 1994, South Africa's GDP per capita growth of 1.2 per cent per annum was comparable to that of sub-Saharan Africa (1.1 per cent per annum) and Latin America (0.8 per cent per annum) but substantially below that of East Asia (6.2 per cent per annum) and South Asia (3.7 per cent per annum).[130] Post-apartheid economic planners had hoped to develop a strong export sector. However, exchange-rate instability, skilled labour shortages and high unit labour costs and structural rigidities (notably specialisation in sectors with highly specific factors of production that could not easily be redeployed elsewhere) contributed to the decline of non-mineral exports rather than the hoped-for expansion.[131] Overall employment growth lagged behind real output in all sectors – which meant that ever-larger increases in output were

---

[127] Joffe et al. (eds.), *Improving manufacturing performance*, pp. 15–43.

[128] Lawrence Edwards, 'Has South Africa liberalised its trade?', *South African Journal of Economics* 74:4 (2005), 754–75; Lawrence Edwards, Rashad Cassim and Dirk van Seventer, 'Trade policy in South Africa', in Aron, Kahn and Kingdon (eds.), *South African economic policy*, pp. 151–81.

[129] Competition Commission, 'Review of changes in industrial structure and competition', paper prepared for South African government's fifteen-year review (Pretoria: Policy and Research Division, Competition Commission, 2008), 15.

[130] Dani Rodrik, 'Understanding South Africa's economic puzzles', *Economics of Transition* 16:4 (2008), 770.

[131] Ibid.; Hausmann, 'Final recommendations'; Ricardo Hausmann and B. Klinger, 'South Africa's export predicament', *Economics of Transition* 16:4 (2008), 609–37; Lawrence

necessary to facilitate new job creation. The failure to increase exports meant that, during economic upswings, South Africa experienced persistent and growing balance of payments deficits as import demand outstripped exports. Although this replicated an old pattern in its growth path, what differentiated the post-apartheid period was the reliance on increasingly erratic flows of foreign savings (notably portfolio investment) to finance the current account deficit. This left the country increasingly vulnerable to destabilising reversals in capital flows.

Growth was not entirely jobless, but rising participation rates meant that unemployment actually increased in the late 1990s. The consequence was that interracial inequality continued to decline, but intraracial inequality continued to grow and income poverty worsened in the late 1990s. Faced with a severe fiscal crisis, inherited from the National Party government but exacerbated by generous wage settlements in the public sector in the mid-1990s, the post-apartheid state adopted a cautious approach to new social expenditure, mitigating but not preventing immiserisation stemming from the labour market.

In some respects, the post-apartheid state faced the fundamental economic challenge and dilemma that had faced the South African state across the course of the twentieth century. On the one hand, a well-organised set of citizens demanded a certain minimum standard of living – a 'civilised' or 'living' wage, for 'decent' work, insisting on the justice of their claims. On the other hand, internal markets were too small and global markets too competitive for employers to be able to employ the entire labour force at those wage rates. This dilemma was resolved politically, in that the state intervened in the labour market to ensure that selected workers would be assured of higher incomes. For most of the twentieth century, employers were protected against imported competition in return for employing high-wage white workers. After apartheid, trade liberalisation exposed employers to much more intense competition, making it much harder to pay higher wages unless they were matched with increased productivity. As formal, unskilled work disappeared, unemployment worsened.

FURTHER READING

Aron, Janine, Brian Kahn and Geeta Kingdon (eds.), *South African economic policy under democracy*, Oxford: Oxford University Press, 2009

Bhorat, Haroon and Ravi Kanbur (eds.), *Poverty and policy in post-apartheid South Africa*, Pretoria: Human Sciences Research Council Press, 2006

Edwards and P. Alves, 'South Africa's export performance: determinants of export supply', *South African Journal of Economics* 74:3 (2006), 473–500.

Clark, Nancy, *Manufacturing apartheid: state corporations in South Africa*, New Haven, CT: Yale University Press, 1994

Crankshaw, Owen, *Race, class, and the changing division of labour under apartheid*, London: Routledge, 1997

Crush, Jonathan, Alan Jeeves and David Yudelman, *South Africa's labor empire: a history of black migrancy to the gold mines*, Boulder, CO: Westview; Cape Town: David Philip, 1991

Duncan, David, *We are motor men: the making of the South African motor industry*, Caithness, U.K.: Whittles Publishing, 1997

Feinstein, Charles, *An economic history of South Africa: conquest, discrimination and development*, Cambridge: Cambridge University Press, 2005

Fine, Ben and Zaverah Rustomjee, *The political economy of South Africa: from minerals-energy complex to industrialisation*, Johannesburg: Witwatersrand University Press; London: C. Hurst, 1996

Hofmeyr, Julian, 'An analysis of African wage movements in South Africa', Research Monograph no. 9, Economic Research Unit, University of Natal, Durban, 1994

Houghton, D. H., 'Economic development, 1865–1965', in Wilson and Thompson (eds.), *The Oxford History of South Africa*, vol. 2, *South Africa 1870–1966*, Oxford: Oxford University Press, 1971, pp. 1–48

Houghton, D. H., *The South African economy*, 4th ed., Cape Town: Oxford University Press, 1976

Innes, Duncan, *Anglo: Anglo American and the rise of modern South Africa*, Johannesburg: Ravan Press, 1981

Joffe, Avril, David Kaplan, Raphael Kaplinsky and David Lewis, *Improving manufacturing performance in South Africa: report of the Industrial Strategy Project*, Cape Town: University of Cape Town Press, 1995

Moll, Terence, 'Did the apartheid economy "fail"?', *Journal of Southern African Studies* 17:2 (1991), 271–91

Nattrass, Nicoli and Elizabeth Ardington (eds.), *The political economy of South Africa*, Cape Town: Oxford University Press, 1990

Schlemmer, L. and E. Webster (eds.), *Change, reform and economic growth in South Africa*, Johannesburg: Ravan Press, 1978

Seekings, Jeremy and Nicoli Nattrass, *Class, race and inequality in South Africa*, New Haven, CT: Yale University Press, 2005; Pietermaritzburg: University of KwaZulu-Natal Press, 2006

Wilson, Francis, *Labour in the South African gold mines*, Cambridge: Cambridge University Press, 1972

Wilson, Francis and Mamphela Ramphele, *Uprooting poverty: the South African challenge*, Cape Town: David Philip, 1989

Yudelman, David, *The emergence of modern South Africa: state, capital and the incorporation of organized labor on the South African gold fields, 1902–1939*, Westport, CT: Greenwood Press, 1983

MODERNITY, CULTURE, AND NATION

TLHALO RADITLHALO

As with identities, the arts in South Africa are characterised by diversity rather than a common set of concerns, styles, and approaches. Although the postcolonial state has sought to marshal the arts in the service of the notion of a new nation, major South African writers continue to insist that one cannot speak of a unique South African literature, for that literature rests on a paradox. Apart from vernacular texts, the greater readership of the work of South African writers exists outside the country. These readers' sense of aesthetics, derived from previously read texts, influences the way South African writing is received. Until the late twentieth century, the major divide in the arts was racial: black creative arts were not produced under the same conditions and experienced audiences and reception responses that were generally different from colonial writing, painting, and performance activities. Equally, both colonial and postcolonial contexts have been characterised by the contestation of meanings, literariness, and artistic value. Moreover, the political domain has tended to dominate in the arts, encroaching on the ways in which artistic works have been received, albeit in dynamic ways. The processes of reading and interpretation are constantly changing, and new readings make possible new interpretations. Selecting a finite set of themes, this chapter explores the links among modernity, culture and nation in the broad field of cultural production in South Africa over the long twentieth century.

COLONIALISM, TRANSLATION AND CULTURE

The emergence of a black literature was initially influenced by Christian missionaries who encouraged converts to write religious treatises and meditations, together with translations of the Bible, the Ten Commandments, and the Lord's Prayer. One of the most successful translations of a text in South Africa after the Bible was John Bunyan's *Pilgrim's Progress*. The

Reverend A. Mabille's Sesotho version of the text was the first literary work
published by Morija in 1872. This had been preceded by the Lovedale
Press translation into Xhosa by Tiyo Soga as *Uhambo Lomhambi* (1866).
Mabille's version was then followed by a Zulu translation by J. W. Colenso
as *Ukuhamba Kwesihambi* in 1883, with a Setswana version completed by
R. Moffat and A. Sandilands (1848/1909). A Tshivenda version, *Lwendo
la Muendi*, followed much later in 1960 and, thereafter, a Northern Sotho
translation, *Leeto la Mokriste*, by R. Ramaala in 1966.

David Attwell emphasises an important element in these translations in
his observation that such narratives are far more than a mere recapitulation
of missionary imperatives. Indeed, on the contrary, there is often a distinctly
secular subtext that underpins an overtly Christian reading. Such works
entail an attempt to resituate African experience through modernity, a
concept through which some of the formal and ideological resources that
buttressed colonial conquest could be recoded and appropriated. However,
for translation, the results were distinctly uneven, for that act in itself
influenced the writers who undertook this activity. As they negotiated the
crossings and recrossings of linguistic thresholds, they were themselves
actually translated and retranslated.

A clear line separates the initial colonial encounter and the stage at which
native writing by 'interpreters' began to appear. Influenced by colonial
teachings, literary works actually began as texts in African languages before
being translated into English – usually into imitative English, tied to the
conventions of a metropolitan English literature. The print medium thus
transformed the hitherto oral-based tradition of the cultural terrain in South
Africa. Church, school and the printing press became a three-pronged
excursion, and converts became the first translators and interpreters of
colonial literature. In this instance, and on the basis of a firm Christian
morality, early writing flourished in the Cape Colony, with missionaries
such as Tiyo Soga (c. 1829–1871) publishing Christian tracts in newspapers
such as *Ikwezi*. Through most of the eighteenth and nineteenth centuries,
black literature in African and English languages continued to grapple
with colonial challenges. Writers and intellectuals such as Walter Benson
Rubusana – who published *Zemk' Inkomo Magwalandini* (The Cattle Are
Gone, You Cowards) in 1906 in London – Pambani Mzimba, John Tengo
Jabavu, and others, struggled to reimagine a changing society in which
equality and justice would be respected within an increasingly racialising
world. Alongside them, Lydia Umkasetemba (1840–1915) wrote prose
pieces that could be read as folktales and historical narratives, and S. E. K.
Mqhayi's Xhosa novel *Ityala Lamawele* (The Lawsuit of the Twins) rendered
a profound reflection on cultural practices. Mqhayi composed Christian
hymns in African languages – the first African to do so on the subcontinent.
In doing so, he connected what the critic A. C. Jordan recognised as the

first literary composition ever assigned to individual formulation – therefore constituting a bridge between traditional and the post-traditional period.[1]

From the outset, politics was a central concern for black writers. Many of this generation of mission-educated writers sought to popularise the notion of the 'new' African, who embraced Christian beliefs and liberal principles. Their commitment to political awareness, modernity, reading and writing found expression in the establishment of the first black-owned and black-run newspaper, *Imvo Zabantsundu* (1884), which was preceded by journals such as *Isigidimi samaXhosa, Christian Express*, and *Indaba* and in Pixley ka Isaka Seme's seminal essay, 'The Regeneration of Africa'. Seme received the George William Curtis gold medal from Columbia University in 1906. There, his address to a Columbia audience developed a pan-African perspective, elaborating on how colonialism oppressed African people, denied their cultures and undermined their humanity. Earlier, as one of the first Africans to have received a European education, Tiyo Soga can be designated as a pioneering modern African intellectual who believed in the power of newspapers to nurture historical consciousness and to change cultural sensibility.

In the 1920s, a second generation of African intellectuals came under the influence of the 'new Negro consciousness' of the United States of America. R. V. Selope Thema was a leading figure in this intellectual movement, with *Umteteli wa Bantu* the key forum for the views of this generation. *Umteteli* published pieces by Thema, Sol Plaatje, H. I. E. Dhlomo, H. Selby Msimang, and Allan Kirkland Soga. Together these thinkers developed a notion of African modernity and encouraged modern forms of artistic expression. As Dhlomo summed up the new African: 'Put briefly and bluntly, he wants a social order where every South African will be free to express himself and his personality fully, live and breathe freely, and have a part in shaping the destiny of his country; a social order in which race, colour and creed will be a badge neither of privilege nor of discrimination'.[2]

To achieve this vision, the African (represented as male) would expose the 'contradictions' in South African society and assume the battle for democracy. Although the idea of the new African was coterminous with modernity, as Njabulo Ndebele observes, it also implied the subordination of the elite and its cultural expression to the language of political principle. Politically conscious cultural production often served as a mask that obscured the ordinary, the everyday, and the mundane in people's lives. Even so, there was no singular vision or uniformity of expression. For example, B. W. Vilakazi and H. I. E. Dhlomo adopted different approaches in deciding

---

[1] Eskia Mphahlele, 'Landmarks of Literary History: A Black Perspective', in Michael Chapman, Colin Gardner and Eskia Mphahlele (eds.), *Perspectives of South African Literature* (Parklands: AD Donker, 1992:40).

[2] Tim Couzens, *The new African: a study of the life and work of H. I. E. Dhlomo* (Johannesburg: Ravan Press, 1985), p. 34.

on an appropriate form for modern African poetry, with Vilakazi distancing himself from African stylistic forms and Dhlomo consciously adopting African traditional forms in his work.

Sol Tshekisho Plaatje epitomised the best of the new African movement, making an outstanding contribution in the field of literature, both in his native tongue, Setswana, and in English. His seminal *Native Life in South Africa: Before and since the European War and the Boer Rebellion* (1916) was a scathing eyewitness indictment of the Natives' Land Act of 1913. *Mhudi: An Epic of South African Native Life a Hundred Years Ago* (1930) was the first novel in English to be written by a black South African. Plaatje's political campaigning took him to London on two occasions in the early decades of the twentieth century, where he met the Colonial Secretary, Lewis Harcourt, and other leading British politicians. He quickly became disillusioned with the unwillingness of the imperial government to share what he considered the discourse of reason. Literary critics such as Attwell suggest that Plaatje's *Mhudi* was written as a lamenting reflection on the failure of the South African Native National Congress delegation to check the passing of the Land Act. He also visited the United States on his own, where he interacted with prominent black leaders such as Marcus Garvey, president of the Universal Negro Improvement Association, and W. E. B. Du Bois, the leader of the National Association for the Advancement of Colored People.

Earlier, while working as a court interpreter in the office of the Civil Commissioner and Magistrate during the siege of Mafikeng in the South African War, Plaatje wrote his *Boer War Diary of Sol T. Plaatje: An African at Mafeking* (1973), the manuscript of which was found only many years after his death. His diary is unique in its presentation of a firsthand African perspective on the position of blacks in the Anglo-Boer hostilities. Plaatje became part owner and editor of *Koranta ea Becoana* (*Bechuana Gazette*), and subsequently owned and edited two other newspapers in Kimberley, *Tsala ea Becoana* (*Bechuana Friend*) and *Tsala ea Batho* (*The Friend of the People*). Although he lost all three publishing and business ventures, they were important platforms in the campaign for African rights.

Plaatje was among the group of mission-educated African intelligentsia who in 1912 founded the South African Native National Congress, forerunner of the African National Congress. He was also an accomplished linguist, fluent in at least seven languages, and very much preoccupied with the preservation of the Setswana language. He compiled the first Setswana phonetic reader, titled *A Sechuana Reader in International Phonetic Orthography*, a bilingual collection of Tswana folklore in collaboration with a well-known linguist, Daniel Jones, during his first trip to England. He also collected Setswana proverbs, producing *Sechuana Proverbs with Literal Translations and Their European Equivalents* (1916) during the same period. His preoccupation with the writings of Shakespeare led to the translation of several plays into Setswana, of which only *Diphosho-Phosho* (*Comedy of Errors*) (1930) and *Dikhontsho tsa bo-Juliuse Kesara* (*Julius Caesar*) (1937) have survived.

Elsewhere, there were also other significant cultural developments by the early decades of the twentieth century. Several white writers broke with the imperial style of figures, such as Rudyard Kipling and John Buchan, to produce more distinctively South African–inspired novels and poetry. Olive Schreiner, radical thinker, feminist suffragist, pacifist, and advocate of greater rights for indigenous people, was clearly influenced by Western European thinkers. Yet her work demonstrated an ambivalent attitude to the metropolis. Thus, Schreiner's *Story of an African Farm* challenged British representations of colonial life in South Africa. The poet Roy Campbell, too, saw himself as breaking with Western traditions and becoming part of a modern literary movement that went beyond a simple imperial-colonial model. But for all these early traces of an independent voice, South Africa after Union in 1910 was not yet a nation emerging from empire, and its writing remained strongly influenced by educational and social documentary concerns. At the same time, though, the country's writers were stirring, with some extending their reach into new areas. They included Herman Charles Bosman, whose deft combination of humour and pathos provided striking vignettes of rural life. Although South African–born Pauline Smith and William Plomer were both educated in Britain, their 1920s stories were steeped in the particularities of a South African locality and evoked worlds stamped with social themes. Smith's *The Little Karoo* (1925) was a critique of the poverty and injustice of small town and rural life, whereas Plomer's first novel, *Turbott Wolfe* (1925), ventured a liberal vision of interracial love and marriage. Plomer was also associated with the short-lived but influential literary journal *Voorslag*, which advocated a common South African society.

In an accompanying cultural development, Afrikaans poets like Eugene Marais and C. Louis Leipoldt drew on rural landscapes in artistic works, which were influential in establishing Afrikaans as a written language. The staunchly nationalist Maria Elizabeth Rothmann (M. E. R.), the first editor of a women's page in a South African newspaper (*Die Burger*), filtered Afrikaner culture and history through her novels and poems, and established a commitment to the plight of 'poor whites' in the interwar era. A vividly romantic evocation of the African environment characterised the work of D. J. Opperman, one of the most prominent Afrikaans poets of the 1940s and later decades. Nelson Mandela was an admirer of his poetry, reading it during his years of imprisonment on Robben Island. Among other early Afrikaans writers, few had as internationalist a literary strategy as Uys Krige, who not only produced poems, novels, plays and travelogues but also translated Shakespeare into Afrikaans; the poetry of Lorca and Neruda from Spanish into Afrikaans; and works by Baudelaire and Villon from French into Afrikaans.

POLITICS AND THE PERFORMING ARTS

The evolving world of the colony was not a smooth one: the cultural, economic, and political interests of the dominated and the dominant collided regularly, and three streams of performance and music evolved along the divisions mapped out by disparate communities. Afrikaans theatre from the outset was tied to what became termed the *taalstryd* (language struggle), and its content became suffused by themes of patriotism and history. The first notable Afrikaans theatre group, the Afrikaans-Hollandse Toneelvereninging, was founded by Gustav Preller and Hart Oost in 1907 and displayed solidarity with the cause of promoting Afrikaner cultural and language interests.[3] Indeed, the nationalist Afrikaner was the early prototype of postcoloniality, as the fervour with which the South African War was fought was essentially to be rid of English imperial dominance. The group's first pageant before the opening of Parliament in May 1910 was a staging of colonial triumphalism through historical sketches recounting the European (Portuguese, Dutch, and British) 'discovery' of the native inhabitants and the appropriation of their lands by treaty or conquest. In so doing, it reenacted the familiar teleology of the 'progress of prosperity' over hordes of ignorance, cruelty, savagery, unbelief, war, pestilence, and famine. Interestingly, the pageant acknowledged the historical role of some blacks such as Moshoeshoe and Sheik Yusuf, a Muslim cleric credited with bringing Islam to the Cape while exiled there by the Dutch authorities.

Theatre also took root among Africans. Here, the missionary Bernard Huss based at St Francis College, Mariannhill, Natal, was one of the most influential pioneers of the social and pedagogical uses of theatre among Africans. The earliest recorded performances at St Francis took place in 1904 when African students staged *Joseph in Egypt*. The pedagogical appeal of performance for missionaries and liberal whites was that it seemed amenable to the transmission of Christian and 'civilising' ideals and values, eschewing boisterous dancing and other forms of unrefined expression.

In the early 1900s, *isicathamiya* male choirs and *isicathulo* boot dancers were popular forms of working-class entertainment, thriving alongside ethnically inspired Bhaca dancing and *isiRashiya* concertina style, 'Tipperary', bone clappers of minstrels, and the *amathambo* (bones) repertoire of traditional instrumentation. Middle-class musical entertainment centred on

---

[3] T. Hauptfleisch and Ian Steadman (eds.), *South African theatre: four plays and an introduction* (Pretoria: Hollandsch Afrikaansche Uitgevers Maatschappij, 1984), pp. 9; 237.

choral groups that specialised in *imusic*, English ballads, hymns, and classical songs. *Ingomabusuku* (night song) was a favourite for choral groups. Reuben Caluza's ragtime, a combination of traditional and American ragtime music, also became popular. By the 1920s, popular dance forms like *induduma* had become a craze in urban areas of Durban. *Nduduma* was connected to Johannesburg's *marabi*, with returning migrant workers acting as conduits for the importation of *marabi* elements. A typical *nduduma* programme consisted of a two-part format: first, *ingomabusuku* competition involving choirs dressed in suit jackets and, for the main part, piano-driven dance music that blended *ingomabusuku* with the pulsating syncopation of *marabi*. With such leisure pursuits involving not merely entertainment but also the consumption of alcohol, segregationist authorities set up committees to find ways of controlling black recreational time.[4]

Blacks became highly adept at making do with what they had, and groups such as the Mthetwa Lucky Stars, the Darktown Strutters, and the Bantu Dramatic Society came to the fore in the 1930s. The relationships forged between these groups and white patrons such as Bertha Slosberg, who adopted an ethnographic stance toward African artistic performance, reflect some of the obstacles faced by African performers who were attempting to make a living as independent artists. After watching the Lucky Stars rehearse, Slosberg commented that it was 'as though deep in my pagan self, I had become one with Africa. . . . I found myself chanting with them, my voice shrill, and the native words falling naturally from my tongue. I was . . . singing like a Zulu girl'.[5] Probably unbeknown to 'addicts' like Slosberg, the dramatic narratives of the Lucky Stars displayed a tension between town and countryside, pastoralism and industrialisation, that proved highly popular with urban audiences.[6]

In June 1932, H. I. E. Dhlomo – regarded as the pioneer of black drama in South Africa – established the Bantu Dramatic Society at the Bantu Men's Social Club in Johannesburg. The club was established by the American Mission Board as a place where christianised Africans could engage in wholesome recreation as an antidote to the degrading influences of slum yards and liquor dens, vice and drink. The primary aim of the Bantu Dramatic Society, while presenting European plays 'from time to time', was 'to encourage Bantu playwrights and to develop African dramatic and operatic art. Bantu life is full of great and glorious figures that would form the basis of first-class drama'.[7] The Society's first production in 1933,

---

[4] B. Peterson, *Monarchs, missionaries and African intellectuals: African theatre and the unmaking of colonial marginality* (Johannesburg: Witwatersrand University Press, 2000), p. 29.
[5] Ibid., p. 170.   [6] Ibid., p. 165.
[7] Ibid., pp. 112, 120–1.

Oliver Goldsmith's *She Stoops to Conquer*, was taken to Pretoria, where it was followed by a performance of the Merry Blackbirds Orchestra.[8] The Bantu Dramatic Society's internal wrangling led to its folding and reconstitution as the Bantu Dramatic and Operatic Society, producing *Nongqause: A Drama of the Cattle Killing of 1857* (*The Girl Who Killed to Save*, published in 1935) and *Dingane, Cetshwayo* and *Moshoeshoe*. These plays hinted at the need for African self-awareness and self-determination.[9] The society folded in the early 1940s, with Dhlomo returning to Natal to work on *Ilanga Lase Natale* (*The Natal Sun*) as assistant editor.

THE VISUAL ARTS

Pronounced European influences in the visual arts in South Africa were sustained by Jacobus Hendrik Pierneef, with other already-established artists such as Anton van Wouw, Hugo Naudé and Frans Oerder. Born of Dutch parents in Pretoria in 1886, Pierneef was taken back to the Netherlands in 1900 to avoid the South African War. There, he encountered the works of the 'Old Masters', an experience that led him to study part-time at the Rotterdamse Kunsakademie. Pierneef went on to research South African art and its influences intensively, and he often spoke on the subject. In due course, he became a prolific artist of multiple mediums – one major 1920 exhibition in Pretoria with more than three hundred works was followed by another one in Cape Town a year later. Pierneef set the trend for a unique colonial South African style, particularly with his haunting landscape paintings of the veld and his San paintings, which were well received in Europe. As a public artist he received government commissions, producing works for the Ficksburg High School (1924), the Johannesburg Railway Station panels (1929–1932), murals for South Africa House in London (1933–1935), a mural for SS *Pretoria Castle* (1937), large paintings for the Johannesburg Magistrate's Courts (1940), and a painting for Broadcast House in Johannesburg (1955).

A contemporary artist of another kind was Irma Stern, who studied painting not in Holland but in her native Germany. Well known for her portraits of people of colour, her painting was strongly influenced by German expressionism, and her perceptions of her subjects were often romanticised. As a woman who made her disdain for the establishment apparent, Stern was a radical figure in the art world, but her studies evoked criticism from critics who found her representation of Africans patronising.

---

[8] Ibid., p. 141.
[9] Peterson, B., 'Apartheid and the political imagination in black South African theatre', *Journal of Southern African Studies* 16:2 (1990), 230.

Yet for her adoption of a modernist visual language and conscious rejection of bourgeois social values and official art, she has come to be regarded as a pioneer of modern art in South Africa.

Unsurprisingly, black artists tended to be entirely local in background and influences. One notable example was Gerard Bhengu, born in the year of Union, a fine early artist from Natal who painted portraits and rural Natal landscapes. His work was exhibited nationally in the 1930s. Born in 1912 in Korsten village, Port Elizabeth, George Milwa Mnyaluza Pemba was only sixteen years old when two of his pencil portraits were shown at an exhibition at the Feathermarket Hall, Port Elizabeth. His father's death in 1928 following a motor accident is shown in his earliest watercolour painting, titled *Funeral Procession* (1930). A spell in hospital also saw him drawing nurses, doctors, and patients. After studying at Lovedale College, Pemba worked for the Lovedale Press as an illustrator in the 1930s. As did Bhengu, Pemba concentrated on his native landscape and its peoples. In 1944, he toured Lesotho and produced portraits of Basotho women in national dress. In the following year, he exhibited at the annual exhibition of the Society of Arts and Crafts in Port Elizabeth and through the Durban International Club exhibition for black artists. Following a major exhibition at the Everard Read Gallery in Johannesburg in the 1990s, Pemba sold 178 works to an art dealer for a paltry sum, noting subsequently that individual works were placed on sale in the gallery for more than he had received for the entire collection. Developing a vision that was more than rural, Pemba described himself aptly as a 'township artist'. His oeuvre encompassed portraits that reflected on the implications of acculturation and modernisation through urbanscapes and landscapes of Port Elizabeth's Korsten and New Brighton townships, and their social interiors of shebeens, churches, hospitals, and homes. Through these, over many decades, Pemba sought to convey universal human elements in the contexts of suffering, pain, and conflict brought on by apartheid police raids, poverty, homelessness, alcoholism, and urban gangsterism. In 1979, the University of Fort Hare awarded him an honorary degree, and in 2004, President Thabo Mbeki posthumously awarded George Pemba national honours for his pioneering and exceptional contribution to the development of the art of painting and literature.

Born in 1913, Pemba's renowned contemporary Jan Gerard Sekoto took the path of exile to realise his exceptional talent. Sekoto grew up in Wonderhoek in the Eastern Transvaal, where his father was an evangelist teacher. In 1930, Sekoto entered a Diocesan college near Pietersburg and qualified as a schoolteacher but, like Pemba, his teaching career gave way to his passion for painting. In 1938, he abandoned teaching and moved to Sophiatown, the mixed freehold working-class residential area near Johannesburg. A

year later, Brother Roger Castle of St Peter's Secondary School mounted the
'Exhibition of the paintings of Gerard Sekoto and the African Schoolboys
from Priory, Rosettenville', to considerable acclaim. Despite the growing
success of his exhibitions, Sekoto was frustrated by racist reviewers who
saw him as a kind of illustrative 'tribal' curiosity. In 1946, he painted *Soka
Majoka (Sixpence a Door)*, depicting a crowd of people who could not afford
the entrance fee to a performance. *Sixpence a Door* was taken on an international touring exhibition; featured later on the cover of *Time* magazine; and
in 2002, was sold by a Johannesburg art dealer for the sum of R1 million.
Sekoto's work demonstrated a mastery of colour and form, accentuating
his remarkable capacity to convey mood and movement. Ultimately, like
the characters in his paintings who frequently face away from the viewer,
Sekoto turned his back on the world he knew. In 1947, he left for Paris,
where, as an outsider to French life and culture, he agonised about his place
and identity. His eventual reconnection with an African tradition came not
through South Africa but Senegal when, in 1966, he was invited to the Festival of Negro Arts in Dakar. Slightly more than a decade later, he painted
a portrait of Stephen Bantu Biko, leader and founding member of the Black
Consciousness Movement. In 1988, in collaboration with Barbara Lindop,
a Johannesburg art enthusiast, he launched Project Sekoto, an art book
of his major paintings. A year later, the University of the Witwatersrand
awarded him an honorary doctorate.

Although few black artists received the recognition of Pemba and Sekoto,
several talented men and women emerged from art centres established from
the late 1940s by liberal white supporters. The best known of these was
the Polly Street Centre in Johannesburg, where gifted artists, like Ephraim
Ngatane and Durant Sihlali, and the sculptors Lucas Sithole, Sydney
Kumalo and Ezrom Legae, all born in the 1930s, were trained. Together
with Dumile Feni and Julian Motau of the post–Second World War era,
these figures moved away from depicting township scenes to exploring the
'emaciating effects of poverty and malnutrition on the human figure'.[10]

The reputation of Polly Street as a place of training for black artists
was enhanced by the appointment as its cultural officer of Cecil Skotnes,
a fine arts graduate who was associated with the centre for three decades.
In 1963, he and others formed the Amadlozi (Spirit of the Ancestors)
group of artists, who sought to work at the intersections of African and
European art. Skotnes, a printmaker, developed a trademark style of incised
and painted wood panels. His subjects encompassed nature, Christianity,

---

[10] Warren Siebrits (narrative) and Wayne Oosthuizen, *Art and urbanisation: South Africa,
   1940–1971* (Johannesburg: Warren Siebrits Modern and Contemporary Art, 8 May–29
   June 2003).

political turmoil and the more abstract emotions of good and evil, anguish and pain. He said of his work, 'as chronicler of the South African situation, I could not think in European terms. My approach had to originate here, otherwise my art would be of little importance'.[11] When Skotnes moved to Cape Town in 1978, he contributed to the development of the Nyanga Arts Centre and the Community Arts Project. The recipient of honorary degrees from the Universities of Cape Town, Rhodes and the Witwatersrand, in 2003 he was also awarded national honours for his significant contribution to the deracialisation of the arts.

Other endowed art centres, such as the Ndaleni Art School and the Rorke's Drift Art and Craft Centre at Msinga, all provided classes for aspirant African artists. Azaria Mbatha's linocuts and Michael Zondi's wooden sculptures received recognition through the South African Institute of Race Relations' biannual exhibition, held from 1963 to 1975. Mbatha, like Sekoto, eventually chose self-exile in preference to life under apartheid. At the same time, many black artists worked entirely outside of this philanthropic support network. One of the best known among these was the sculptor Jackson Hlungwani, a lay priest in the African Zionist Church. Hlungwani was 'discovered' by the white art establishment in the late 1970s. Inspired both by Christianity and by Tsonga divinity, his powerful wooden carvings featured animal and Christian symbols. Hlungwani's gallery, where his many larger-than-life wood carvings were displayed, was an Iron Age site on which he conducted Zionist religious services.

Naturally, professional photography became a powerful art form in the apartheid era for both white and black photographers who had a strong political and social gaze and skill with the lens. Inevitably, the ease with which searing images circulated attracted the attention of the authorities; for example, in 1967, Ernest Cole's book of photographs *House of Bondage* was banned. Representatives of critical photojournalism, such as Bernard Magubane and Guy Tillim, became well known for their images of resistance. At another level, Santu Mofokeng's exhibition of his family photographs in *Black photo album/Look at me, 1890–1950*, provided a narrative of South African history and an oblique critique of apartheid. Above all, it is undoubtedly in David Goldblatt's images of people and places that the social history of apartheid South Africa has come to be most comprehensively recorded as a visual chart. His range is unequalled in its depth and breadth and in his more distanced, searching stance – as in his earlier images of Afrikaner suburban life and African mine workers or later depictions of truck stops in his account of South Africa's battle with HIV/AIDS – Goldblatt's photographic canvas is powerfully evocative.

[11] Emile Maurice and Jo-Anne Duggan, 'Cecil Skotnes', *South African Art Times* (May 2009).

Away from the artistic space occupied by men, much of the creative work of black women has been obscured by the dichotomy between definitions of art and of craft or decorative utility. Since the 1970s, African women's beadwork – a marker of status and affiliation since the eighteenth century – and weaving have become sought after by international art collectors. In 1963, Swedish missionaries established the Rorke's Drift Art and Craft Centre in the Msinga area so that women might put their weaving skills to use in the production of marketable crafts. Weavers' thematic threads wove both abstract depictions of the local landscape and African accounts of the impact of colonialism, modernisation and Christianity into magnificent tapestries. Allina Ndebele and Jessie Dlamini became the first grand weavers at the centre, achieving international recognition for their tapestries and procuring prestigious commissions. A similar initiative established the Vukani Association in Natal in 1972 for the production and marketing of decorative basketry, a project that revived grass-weaving skills and facilitated the marketing of grass and *ilala* palm baskets.

Litema, the mural art of Southern Sotho women, was another art form 'discovered' by the international art establishment in the 1970s. In the Southern Sotho or Sotho-Tswana communities straddling the borders of Botswana and Lesotho, *litema* patterning on homestead walls was most often an expression of continuity between hearth and landscape, between the living in the homestead and the dead buried under the *lapa* floor. In its traditional form, *litema* (derived from the word *tema*, "the ploughed field"), highlighted the centrality of women's labour to the homestead, the field and reproduction. *Litema* patterns often extended the patterning of the ground itself, emphasising the sacredness of the earth where women are buried and the centrality of family and homestead to Sotho-Tswana identity.[12] Following the Sotho-Tswana, neighbouring Ndebele women also developed a more popular style of mural art. Ndebele designs were, however, more eclectic, incorporating Western images in their iconography. Images of electric pylons, lights, aeroplanes and motor cars were frequently inserted into the brightly coloured Ndebele murals, and commercial paint was used alongside natural pigments.

FLICKERS OF RENAISSANCE: SOPHIATOWN AND THE *DRUM* SET

Industrialisation during and after the Second World War led to increased urbanisation, and the popular media in this period began to cater to the growing number of urbanised black city dwellers. In this period, Peter

---

[12] G. van Wyk, 'Through the cosmic flower: secret resistance in the mural art of Sotho-Tswana women', in Nooter (ed.), *Secrecy*, pp. 80–7.

Abrahams's *Mine Boy* (1946) ushered in the age of black realist fiction. The text dealt as much with the dehumanising mining industry and the subsequent beginnings of trade unionism as it criticised black political and economic marginalisation. Abrahams's counterpart, H. I. E. Dhlomo, was influenced by Countee Cullen and Langston Hughes, and in that sense, they were both at the forefront of the quest to create African modernism in service of the political struggle.[13] Prolific fictional writing in English blossomed in this era, leading to what became known as the golden decade of the fifties. Writers of the time included Can Themba, Es'kia Mphahlele, Lewis Nkosi, Arthur Maimane, Bessie Head, Casey Motsisi and Bloke Modisane, all of whom worked for *Drum* magazine and related publications such as the *Golden City Press*. The racy, energetic prose evident in the flamboyant writings of this phase owed much to the self-confidence and exuberance of writers who were beginning to experiment with newer urban themes and social settings in a changing cultural milieu. Their short stories, autobiographies, essays and fast journalism constituted the fifth and last generation of new African intellectuals.

The *Drum* set was fiercely critical of Alan Paton's *Cry the Beloved Country: A Story of Comfort in Desolation*, which was first published in the United States in 1948 and serialised in *Drum* magazine in 1951. *Drum* writers recognised and objected to the paternalism of Paton's white trusteeship; his stereotyped black characters, largely shorn of individual characteristics; and his naive rural-urban, 'Jim goes to Jo'burg' plot. In contrast, the novel was well received in the United States as a moving novel of tragedy, a well-written work of social documentary art that resonated with American fears of the consequences of institutional racism in its South. Paton's novel was also acclaimed by many liberal white South Africans for its reformist sentiments, but not necessarily for its aesthetic qualities.

The racy journalism of *Drum*'s Sophiatown writers and the sophisticated lives they led in the city were the antithesis of the uniform bleakness of African life as represented in *Cry the Beloved Country*. Those writers told of street life and shebeens in Sophiatown and celebrated its multicultural community where stores were owned by Indian or white immigrants. They evoked a place where city workers, black radicals, bohemians of all colours and criminals rubbed shoulders, and where professionals such as Dr A. B. Xuma, political activists such as the communist J. B. Marks and writers such as William 'Bloke' Modisane enjoyed elite celebrity status.[14] Although

---

[13] Ntongela Masilela, *The cultural modernity of H. I. E. Dhlomo* (Trenton, NJ: Africa World; London: Turnaround, 2007).

[14] L. Kruger, *The drama of South Africa: plays, pageants and publics since 1910* (London: Routledge, 1999) p. 89.

Sophiatown has undoubtedly been mythologised through the nostalgia and memories of black life in this freehold suburb, it remains symbolic of the resilience of an independent urban culture despite apartheid harassment.[15]

Arts organisation took time to become established. Still, in 1955, under the stewardship of Ian Bernhardt and Harry Bloom, the Union of Southern Artists was formed. The Union sought, for the first time, to protect the professional rights of black performers so that they might rehearse, improvise and create without hindrance or interference.[16] *King Kong* (1959), the musical story of the life and death of boxing champion Ezekiel 'King Kong' Dlamini, was the outcome of cooperation between the Union Artists and the African Theatre Workshop. Its creators had intended it to become a model of fruitful cooperation between blacks and whites. With production, direction, script and musical direction by whites, but with the use of black musical actors and musicians and a score by Todd Matshikiza, the show sought to combine the polish and style of New York's Broadway with the cultural vitality and resources of the local townships. Its musical actors included members of groups such as the Manhattan Brothers and the Woody Woodpeckers. In the lead were Nathan Mdledle as King Kong and Miriam Makeba. Music was provided by the Jazz Dazzlers Orchestra and included members of the Shantytown Sextet, Harlem Swingsters and Huddleston Jazz Band. Although the play was not overtly political, its content did show something of the hardships, violence and frustration of township existence.

King Kong might have taken root as a watershed creation in the performing arts had the apartheid regime not begun removing Africans and Asians from the inner cities under the 1950 Group Areas Act. Thus, when *King Kong* went for an international run in London, a whole generation of displaced performers went with it and remained in exile. Its original Dorkay House survived as the remnants of the Union Artists financed the African Music and Drama Association and sponsored a theatre and drama school. Into the breach created by the departure of the *King Kong* contingent stepped Athol Fugard and Gibson Kente. At Dorkay House, Fugard presented his play *The Blood Knot* (1963), and Alan Paton and Krishna Shah did their musical *Sponono* (1964). Mhangwane's *Crime Does Not Pay* (1963) and *Unfaithful Woman* (1964), and Ben Masinga's *Back in Your Own Backyard* (1962), were also produced at Dorkay House in the early 1960s.[17]

The Sharpeville shootings of 21 March 1960 signalled the end of the restrained protest politics of the 1950s. With the state banning most extra-parliamentary political movements and jailing a number of their leaders,

---

[15] Ibid., pp. 96–9.   [16] Coplan, *In township tonight!*, p. 172.

[17] Hauptfleisch and Steadman (eds.), *South African theatre*, p. 143.

the environment for free cultural expression became more endangered. Having been proscribed politically as individuals, a number of black writers were increasingly liable to have their works banned. Some opted for exile, where they continued writing and made contact with fellow writers from other African countries. There, Nigerian literary modernism and its South African counterpart found shared expression in two key magazines, *Black Orpheus* and *Transition*. After Mphahlele went into exile, he published his classic autobiography *Down Second Avenue* (1959) and a major work of literary criticism, *The African Image* (1962). The Cape Town author Alex la Guma went into exile after his novel *A Walk in the Night* was banned. His works were then published overseas in the Heinemann African Writers' Series. Another dissenting coloured writer and poet, the high school teacher Richard Rive, who had written for *Drum* in the 1950s, avoided exile but travelled abroad to further his scholarly studies at Columbia University in the United States and at Oxford University, where in the 1970s he obtained a doctorate on Olive Schreiner.

At the same time, the country lost a number of its most noted musicians to exile, including members of the Jazz Maniacs and the Jazz Epistles, Dollar Brand (Abdullah Ibrahim, piano), Kippie Moeketsi (alto sax), Jonas Gwangwa (trombone), Hugh Masekela (trumpet), John Gertse (guitars) and Early Mabuza (drums), who had linked Johannesburg, Cape Town, Port Elizabeth and Durban into an interlocking matrix of sound and cultural innovation.[18] Many of these highly acclaimed musicians, including double bassist, Johnny Dyani, who became a sought-after session player in exile, were untutored. Dolly Rathebe, a leading singer of the era, once declared that as bad as things were for Africans, the government could not take away their music, even if as a business this was run in a highly exploitative manner.[19] Indeed, there were a good many talented black musicians who stayed put, such as the saxophonist Winston Mankunku Ngozi, whose style was very much inspired by the American John Coltrane. Continuing to live in Cape Town's Gugulethu Township under apartheid, in 1964 he even played at a concert in its city hall but was obliged to do so behind a curtain and under a pseudonym to avoid prosecution under legislation that prohibited racially mixed performances. A unique form of jazz expression combining African American, African and Cape minstrel sounds was developed by Cape Town artists at home and in exile. This style is perhaps best exemplified by the saxophonist Basil Manenberg Coetzee's evocative *Manenberg* and by the pianist Dollar Brand's album *African Marketplace*, and

---

[18] A fascinating reading of this period is by Hugh Masekela in his autobiography, *Still grazing: the musical journey of Hugh Masekela* (New York: Crown, 2004).

[19] As quoted in Masekela, *Still grazing*, p. 85.

it was developed further in the 1980s and 1990s by musicians like Paul Hamner, Jonathan Butler, Errol Dyers and Hilton Schilder.

Popular black performing arts in the 1960s were sustained largely by the musicals of Gibson Kente, whose depictions of the impoverished circumstances of township life provided an alternative to white theatre. Beginning with *No-Good Friday* (1958) and *Manana, the Jazz Prophet* (1963), respectively, these two plays were to serve as diverging cultural artefacts. Born in the 1930s and based in Soweto, Kente came to be known eventually as the father of black theatre in South Africa, and he was one of the first stage writers to deal with life in the South African black townships. He formed his own independent company in 1967 and created plays such as *Lifa* (1972) and *Zwi* (1970). In all, Kente produced twenty-three plays and television dramas between 1963 and 1992. He was also responsible for producing some of South Africa's leading musicians and actors, including Mary Mhlongo, Mbongeni Ngema and Darlington Michaels, all of whom owe their first opportunities on stage to him. Three of his plays produced between 1974 and 1976 drew criticism for being antiapartheid and were banned: *How Long, I Believe* and *Too Late!* (1975). Although Kente's work was seen as formulaic by critics and was questioned for its lack of political engagement, he was nonetheless jailed for a year in 1976 after filming his play *How Long*. It was never released and the film's master negative was given to the National Film Board in Pretoria.[20]

APARTHEID THEATRE

Meanwhile, the apartheid government's provincial councils poured funds into forty-eight new theatres in designated white areas. The Nico Malan, in Cape Town, and the Pretoria State Theatre, corresponded with the respective tenth and twentieth anniversary celebrations of the Republic. The Johannesburg Civic Theatre was a reminder of fifty years of Union, and the Etienne Rousseau Theatre was donated to Sasolburg by the Sasol petrochemicals parastatal to mark its twenty-fifth anniversary. Windybrow in Johannesburg was a product of Johannesburg's centenary celebrations, and the Johannesburg Art Gallery and the Market Theatre received face-lifts for the centenary celebrations. The history represented by these venues recorded the dominance of white minority culture. Needless to say, no theatres were built in black townships.[21]

---

[20] Hauptfleisch and Steadman, *South African theatre*, p. 144.
[21] Peterson, 'Apartheid and the political imagination', p. 232. At present, 2007, Soweto is to get its first theatre complex courtesy of Dutch initiatives.

In 1962, sectional Afrikaner interests were served further by the creation of four performing arts councils: the Performing Arts Council of the Transvaal (PACT), the Cape Performing Arts Board (CAPAB), the Performing Arts Council of the Orange Free State (PACOFS) and the Natal Performing Arts Council (NAPAC). Increasing censorship legislation crystallised in the Publications and Entertainment Act of 1963 and become embodied in its administrative body, the Publications Control Board. The government's promotion of the arts included an attempt to dislocate cultural practices from social struggles and to market them instead as universal and transhistorical 'civilising forces'. Patronage of the arts became a barometer by which to measure South Africa's 'level of civilisation' and the commitment of state and major business interests to their conception of social responsibility programmes.[22] In the first decade, the performing arts boards produced a dozen original Afrikaans plays – from N. P. van Wyk Louw's revisionist 1966 South African War drama *Die Pluimsaad Waai Ver* (*The Plumed Seed Blows Far*) to P. G. du Plessis's portrayal of poor whites in *Siener in die Suburbs* (*Seer in the Suburbs*, 1971) and Chris Barnard's play of a misfit Afrikaner clerk in *Die Rebellie van Lafras Verwy* (*The Rebellion of Lafras Verwy*, 1974) – and undertook revivals of 1930s plays. In their promotion of the plays and their artists, the performing arts boards constituted powerful cultural institutions of Afrikaner nationalism. Equally, not all work confirmed to this vision. Although some plays were deemed too provocative for arts board performance, such as *Die Verminktes* (*The Maimed*, 1960), *Putsonderwater* (*Well-without-water*, 1968) and *Christine* (1971), by Bartho Smit, they were still published by subsidised presses and performed in minority venues. Despite its intimate semantic and historical association with Africa, the identity of Afrikaner was reserved exclusively for members of the white *volk*, and thus conditioned theatrical practice and theatregoing. The coloured writer Adam Small had to wait seven years for his 1965 play *Kanna Hy Kô Huis Toe* (*Kanna's Coming Home*) to be performed by local actors at the designated coloured University College of the Western Cape. Two years later, the play was staged separately by an all-white PACT cast.[23]

At the same time, crass distortions of the image of African life emerged in efforts by the state and allied commercial interests to influence the direction of black performing arts. Productions considered of most value were those that possessed a degree of approved 'authenticity' because they drew on historically remote instances of black initiative, traditional themes and cultural forms. The most noteworthy of such productions were *Dingaka* in 1962 and *Meropa* (or *Kwazulu*), *King Africa*, *Ipi Tombi* and Welcome

---

[22] Ibid., p. 232.
[23] Kruger, *The drama of South Africa*, pp. 100–2.

Msomi's *Umabatha*, a Zulu version of Shakespeare's *Macbeth*, in the 1970s. A privileging of traditional African culture in these productions was meant to celebrate the notion of an organic tribal past, then either already lost or under threat from the evils of the city. The ahistorical narrative of many of the plays implicitly gestured toward the modern 'homelands' of apartheid as reincarnations of tribal society. For the most part, their illustrations of 'traditional' cultural practices were little more than an attempt to titillate Eurocentric minds with various forms of 'African exoticisms', whereas an emphasis on the depiction of great chiefs differed little from stock colonial representations of the noble savage.[24]

If anywhere, it was on the nonconformist margins of Afrikaner society that a fresh literature of dissent could be seen by the mid-1960s. During that decade, a self-consciously new generation of avant-garde Afrikaans writers, the Sestigers, began to produce both fiction and poetry that, in experimental form and content, went against the grain of a stultifying apartheid culture. Figures like Etienne le Roux, Jan Rabie, Uys Krige, Breyten Breytenbach and Ingrid Jonker were critical of the apartheid order and the values of white South African society. Some struggled to survive as writers, their more radical works banned, their views marginalised and themselves denied the establishment patronage of even more sympathetic artists. One novelist, Le Roux, found an outlet in English translation, with novels like *Sewe Dae by die Silbersteins* (*Seven Days at the Silbersteins*) published in Britain. Another emerging writer, Andre Brink, who was strongly influenced by this group, turned to writing in English in works reflecting a concern with multiracialism and social and political life under apartheid.

THE INFLUENCE OF BLACK CONSCIOUSNESS

By the end of the 1960s, Black Consciousness began to inspire creative expression. Its call for black initiative, self-definition, self-reliance, determination and liberation to restore the dignity of oppressed communities soon made an impact on the cultural terrain. The Black Consciousness Movement had a profound cultural effect at a time when a worldwide cultural boycott against South Africa was beginning to take shape, following the 1969 UN General Assembly recommendation of the suspension of cultural, educational, sports and other exchanges with the apartheid regime. The ideal of self-reliance as promoted by the Black Consciousness Movement was seen as self-destructive in some quarters but was part of a larger

---

[24] B. Peterson, 'A rain a fall but the dirt it tough: scholarship on African theatre in South Africa', *Journal of Southern African Studies* 21:4 (1995), 234–5.

and more general campaign to internally and externally eradicate the idea of normalcy in an abnormal society. Committed to forging a link between cultural expression and national and personal liberation, Black Consciousness poets sought to reach beyond an elite readership and to engage the masses. Mongane Serote and others – collectively called the Soweto Poets – were at the forefront of explorations in Black Consciousness poetry in the 1970s. Modikwe Dikobe published what can possibly be considered the first African working-class novel, *The Marabi Dance*, in 1973, and Miriam Tlali's politically conscious fictional works, *Muriel at Metropolitan* in the mid-1970s and her later *Amandla* in 1980, were banned on publication. Following the Soweto student uprisings of 1976, increasingly militarised police action provided the raw material for a literature that perused and dissected the extremities of apartheid oppression. Black literature captured those cruelties in graphic detail. Works such as Mthuthuzeli Matshoba's 1979 collection of short stories *Call Me Not a Man* and Zakes Mda's dramas, beginning with *The Hill*, also in 1979, and Mongane Wally Serote's *To Every Birth Its Blood*, exemplified some of the characteristic features of a prose fiction and drama that focused on the repressive horrors of later apartheid. Elsewhere in this period, black theatre groups that operated without any state subsidy came to the fore, as seen by the establishment of the Cape Flats Players; the Music, Drama, Arts and Literature Institute (MDALI); People's Experimental Theatre (PET), an Afro-Indian group from Lenasia; Theatre Council of Natal (TECON); and the South African Black Theatre Union (SABTU).

As a 'theatre of determination', Black Consciousness drama became increasingly radical. In 1972, Adam Small's play *Ode to a Blackman* was performed at a TECON festival in Natal, an event that aimed to narrow a politics of ethnic division among African, Indian and coloured communities. In 1973, PET was instrumental in the production of Mthuli Shezi's *Shanti*, a production based on the 1964 Lewis Nkosi play *The Rhythm of Violence*, which asserted the necessity for a violent overthrow of the state. Some TECON and PET members were tried for treason in 1975, but their theatre of determination continued to set the tone for much of the resistance theatre of the 1970s and 1980s.[25]

ALTERNATIVE THEATRE UNDER APARTHEID

In the late 1960s and early 1970s, minor apartheid legislative anomalies continued to leave a handful of small 'liberated spaces' that allowed for the performance of plays to integrated audiences. The Market Theatre

[25] Kruger, *The drama of South Africa*, p. 130.

in Johannesburg and the independent Space Theatre, and later People's Space/Volkruimte/Indawo Yezizwe in Cape Town, became arenas for staging left-wing European and radical American drama as well as venues to nurture black actors and to represent politically conscious renditions of forms and themes in township life. As liberal artistic ventures, the theatres were supported in part by the Anglo American Corporation and its philanthropic affiliate, the Urban Foundation. Plays such as *Woza Albert!* – a collaborative effort between Mbongeni Ngema, Percy Mtwa and Barney Simon – played at the Market Theatre in 1981; in 1972, the Space Theatre hosted the world premiere of *Sizwe Bansi Is Dead*, Athol Fugard's acclaimed play about the iniquities of apartheid pass laws. Throughout its short existence, the Space encouraged theatre that was not merely politically challenging but also provocative about sexual politics. This combination characterised the work of the leading satirist, Pieter-Dirk Uys, whose career was launched in 1975 with *Selle ou Storie*, a satire of gay and heterosexual whites.

By the time that *Sizwe Bansi Is Dead* was first performed at the Space Theatre, the Port Elizabeth dramatist Athol Fugard had been writing plays for well more than a decade and was emerging as the country's leading playwright. Fugard worked extensively with two African actors, John Kani and Winston Ntshona, improvising three major plays of the 1970s, *Sizwe Bansi Is Dead*, *The Island*, and *Statements after an Arrest under the Immorality Act*. The early plays crafted in workshops with Kani and Ntshona (known as the Serpent Players after their first performance took place in the abandoned snake pit of a zoo), were staged as rudimentary performances in townships in front of mainly migrant labourers, with the drama mirroring the frustrations of the lives of those in the audience. Although the implicit critique of apartheid in Fugard's plays brought him into conflict with the authorities, his works focused more on individual integrity and personal endurance than on political action.[26]

After Fugard's *Blood Knot* was produced in England at the beginning of the 1960s, his passport was withdrawn for four years. In 1963, he publicly supported an international boycott against segregated theatre audiences, which led to further restriction of his personal liberties. In 1971, however, the restraints on Fugard were eased, allowing him to travel to England to direct his *Boesman and Lena*. His later and more introspective *Master Harold and the Boys* was a semiautobiographical work of the 1980s. An overriding theme in all Fugard's plays is the suggestion of an essential redemptive human quality in the most abject of circumstances. On this basis, some critics have argued that the playwright's notion of universal redemption

[26] Ibid., pp. 88–9.

could be seen as tending to reduce the exploitation of apartheid to some unchanging existential fate.[27]

After the demise of the Space, alternative theatre in the 1980s was supported by the Johannesburg Market Theatre, which ran its own company's productions and hosted the productions of black-run institutions such as the Dhlomo Theatre, the Soyikwa Institute and the FUNDA Centre in Soweto, and the Stable Theatre in Durban. The Market Theatre also hosted independent black groups such as Bahumutsi (Maishe Maponya) and Committed Artists (Mbongeni Ngema) that were often the object of state surveillance. The Market acted both as a site for resistance to apartheid and as a bulwark of liberal capital against the threat of civic repression implied by such resistance.

Meanwhile, African playwrights continued to be active, reflected by Zakes Mda, who in 1979 won the country's prestigious Amstel Playwright of the Year award. His plays *The Hill* and *We Shall Sing for the Fatherland* exploited the growth of a deepening, evolving social awareness of the injustices of apartheid. In addition, Maishe Maponya and the Bahumutsi Drama Group produced *The Hungry Earth*, an account of daily life on the mines. At the same time, theatre was exploring new visions, with a new mood beginning to emerge as younger writers, including Paul Slabolepszy, attempted to imagine the beginnings of another South Africa in plays of the 1980s and early 1990s. These included *Cincinnati*, *Saturday Night at the Palace*, *Silent Movie*, *Mooi Street Moves*, *Born in RSA*, *Over the Hill*, and *Somewhere on the Border*; Pieter-Dirk Uys's *Just Like Home*; and Susan Pam-Grant's *Curl Up and Dye*. Seeking to capture the rise of new social realities, these works sought to develop an alternative to apartheid theatre. Elsewhere, on a didactic political front, the Congress of South African Trade Unions (COSATU) and the United Democratic Front (UDF) were, by the mid-1980s, establishing cultural secretariats that encouraged sketches and plays promoting the aims of shop-floor solidarity and worker communication. In an associated development, Mtwa's 1986 *Bopha!* (*Arrest!*) told a story of resistance politics, whereas Ngema came up with *Asinamali!* (*We have no money!*), a creative depiction of the context of township antiapartheid rent boycotts. Ngema's musical enactment of the Soweto students' uprising in *Sarafina!*, also in the 1980s, won an American-theatre Tony award. This work was followed by the financially costly postapartheid *Sarafina II* in 1996, a scandal-ridden, government-commissioned musical intended to advance the country's campaign against HIV/AIDS.

When the apartheid state began to lift many of its proscriptions of literary works after 1979, a handful of white artists – prominent writers such as

[27] Ibid., p. 107.

Etienne le Roux, Andre Brink and Nadine Gordimer – benefited most. This was not altogether surprising. The significant grounds for setting aside bannings were literary merit, difficult reading matter and the fact that a white liberal readership was not only relatively small but also fairly docile. Still, creative work that had earlier fallen foul of state censorship had conveyed trenchant criticism of the country's ruling order – to be seen in the novels and short stories of Nadine Gordimer. Arguably more than any other white writer, Nadine Gordimer was influenced by an understanding of the politics of Black Consciousness. From the late 1960s, her writings grappled with the tensions of radical engagement and liberal critique, leading her to declare in the mid-1980s that 'the white writer's task as cultural worker is to raise the consciousness of white people'.[28] As art of conscience, her work conveyed a wealth of information about conditions in South Africa and earned her the Nobel Prize in Literature.

The relationship between literature and the writer's immediate world remained always more oblique in the novels of J. M. Coetzee. Although all his fiction until the end of the first decade after apartheid is set in South Africa, Coetzee's works cannot be seen simply as a product of the country. Exploration of postmodernist concerns and efforts to leave open the possibility of multiple interpretations of his work contribute to continuing international interest in his work. An interest in postmodernism means that Coetzee rejects realism and the devices of 'linear plot, well-rounded characters, clear settings and close endings' and instead explores language in a manner that investigates 'the very act of story-telling[,] . . . creating self-reflexive narratives which question the nature of the text itself'.[29] Treated in this way, issues of power and violence, colonialism and racial discrimination quickly become bound up with interiority – the subjectivities of language, psyche and identity. Coetzee has come to be regarded increasingly as an international rather than only a South African creative writer, and the greater part of his work has been located in and inspired by South African contexts. His local and international honours far exceed those of any other writer.

A world away from J. M. Coetzee, the politically driven black literature of the 1980s, with its stark formulaic conventions of obvious symbols and narratives of good versus evil, came increasingly to irk writers and scholars such as Njabulo Ndebele and Lewis Nkosi, who exposed what they considered a naïveté in black writing. For instance, Ndebele argued

---

[28] Kathrin Wagner, *Rereading Nadine Gordimer* (Bloomington: Indiana University Press; Johannesburg: Witwatersrand University Press, 1994), p. 8.

[29] Michela Canepari-Labib, *Old myths – modern empires: power, language and Identity in J. M. Coetzee's work* (Bern: Peter Lang, 2005), pp. 15–16.

that black literature was mostly a literature of spectacle and exteriority that flattened the range and complexity of human experience. Excessive use of surface symbols dulled the power of characterisation. Too rooted in an agitational political agenda, such literature gave short shrift to classic human themes of interiority, ambiguity, doubt and resilience. Illuminating another angle of vision in his 1983 short stories *Fools and Other Stories* – irony, ambiguity and paradox, rather than the simplistic opposition between good and evil – formed the central literary motif.

POSTCOLONIAL WRITING, ART AND DEMOCRACY

As the apartheid crisis inched toward a final resolution in the early 1990s, the political crusade became less pressing for South African writers. Literature began to acquire qualities that it had lacked in the turbulent 1980s. Again, Ndebele's 1984 essay 'Turkish Tales and Some Thoughts on South African Fiction' and his *The Rediscovery of the Ordinary: Essays on South African Literature and Culture* (1991) anticipated an age of dawning maturity in a black literature becoming less preoccupied with public spheres of resistance. As confirmation, Mda's *Ways of Dying* in 1995 and his 2000 *Heart of Redness* were some of the first texts of their kind to move beyond a literary preoccupation with the external.

Political expression itself also took on new forms, with younger poets using the rap form to start interrogating what they perceived as sham change. Accordingly, Lesego Rampolokeng's 1990s collections of poetry, *Horns for Hondo* and *Talking Rain*, together with Kgafela oa Magogodi's *Thy Condom Come* in 2000, reexamined the transition to South African democracy in the light of unfulfilled promises. Although these poets explored the early premises of reconciliation as a national project, in subsequent literary works, there has been a growing emphasis on the sense of a loss of moral moorings and on the consequences of a downright ruthlessness fanned by the turbulence of the 1980s. Thus, in the dramatic arts, John Kani's 2003 *Nothing but the Truth* was acclaimed for its portrayal of the ambiguities of political liberation, and Phaswane Mpe's *Welcome to Our Hillbrow* sought to demonstrate that, though past experiences remain tenacious, they can be explored with a sense of sober detachment.

Visual artists, too, began to experiment with new forms of sociopolitical commentary and an engagement with history and humanity. Artistic expression ranged from Jonathan Shapiro's (Zapiro) searingly satirical cartoon images to Robert Hodgins's stream-of-consciousness critiques of power and William Kentridge's ironic *Casspirs Full of Love*, depicting heads pushed into a cupboard at awkward angles. Women artists also rose to new prominence in this period. Penny Siopis's deconstruction of patriarchal and racist representations of African women are powerful assertions of a new artistic confidence, and Jane Alexander's photomontages and sculptures probe the dark side of humanity in the context of 1980s political violence. Alexander's best-known piece, *The Butcher Boys*, is a sculpture of three male figures, half human and half beast, sitting on a bench. The faces are distorted into grimaces, their flattened noses are snouts and horns grow out of their skulls. The writer Mike Nicol has described them as blood-crazed 'malificents' without morality, unable to curb their frenzy of gratuitous killing.[30]

The formal ending of apartheid and the symbolic founding of a new nation of South Africans did not pass without penetrating artistic exploration. Kentridge's videos and theatrical productions continued to hold up a mirror to South African society through a profound layering of images. Ranging from literature to religion, family and everyday life experiences, his figurative character, Soho Eckstein, a 'property developer extraordinaire', provided, in the words of the artist Sue Williamson, a 'sustained and emblematic representation of contemporary South African art'.[31] Kentridge's collaboration with the Handspring Puppet Company and Jane Taylor to produce the pungent 1997 *Ubu and the Truth Commission*, an adaptation of French playwright Alfred Jarry's 1888 play, offered a potent critique of the terms and processes of the Truth and Reconciliation Commission (TRC). Inevitably, testimonies to the TRC inspired several other plays aside from Kani's *Nothing but the Truth*. These included Michael Lessac's 2006 *Truth in Translation*, a work that focussed on the difficulties of translating painful narratives. Fugard, too, in his postapartheid works *Valley Song* and *Playland* also turned to settings in a discourse of reconciliation.

All the while, whatever the sombre political mood of so much South African artistic production, sight should not be lost of the persistent and infectious presence of a lighter vein. This was represented partly but not exclusively by the country's visual satirists, such as the post–Second World War newspaper cartoonist David Marais, or a more recent Zapiro or by stage satirists like Pieter-Dirk Uys. It could also be seen in rich traditions of indigenous music and musicals, embodied in popular entertainers such as David Kramer and Taliep Petersen's rendition of *ghoemaliedjies* (songs of the Cape minstrels), which reflected the hybridisation of South African performance culture. The idea of a contagious cultural hybridity is also present in the music and dance spectacle *Umoja*, and in the Disney film production of the South African Lebo M.'s *The Lion King*, which recasts the ancient narrative of good and evil in an African setting.

---

[30] Sue Williamson, *Resistance art in South Africa* (Cape Town: David Philip, 1989), p. 92.
[31] Ibid.

CONCLUSION

Despite the continuing lack of a unified national culture, very many artists have been informed by widely disparate South African contexts. Many of these artists and their works were either ignored, consciously marginalised or proscribed at different times under apartheid. Even the majority who escaped censorship found the political a compelling and almost-unavoidable avenue of exploration. Although since the end of apartheid some artists have begun to move more towards the personal and the individual, political and social commentary and reflection have remained a preoccupation for many. That said, the question asked by the essayist Njabulo Ndebele in his collection *South African Literature and Culture* remains acute. In 1994, he remarked that as the demise of grand apartheid had become a certainty, what would South African writers be writing about thereafter?

FURTHER READING

Arnold, Marion, *Women and art in South Africa*, Cape Town: David Philip; New York: St Martins Press, 1996

Attwell, David, *Rewriting modernity: studies in black South Africa literary history*, Athens: Ohio University Press, 2005

Barnett, Ursula, *A vision of order: a study of black South African literature in English, 1914–1980*, Cape Town: Maskew Miller Longman, 1983

Boehmer, Elleke, Robert Eaglestone and Katy Idols, *J. M. Coetzee in context and theory*, London: Continuum International Publishing Group, 2009

Braam, Conny and Fons Geerlings, 'Towards new cultural relations: a reflection on the cultural boycott', in Campschreur and Divendal (eds.), *Culture in another South Africa*, pp. 170–81

Campschreur, William and Joost Divendal (eds.), *Culture in another South Africa*, London: Zed, 1989

Canepari-Labib, Michela, *Old myths – modern empires: power, language and identity in J. M. Coetzee's work*, Bern: Peter Lang, 2005

Chapman, Michael, Colin Gardner and Es'kia Mphahlele, *Perspectives on South African English Literature*, Johannesburg: Donker, 1992

Clegg, Johnny and Michael Drewett, 'Why don't you sing about leaves and the dreams? Reflecting on music censorship in apartheid South Africa', in Drewett and Cloonan (eds.), *Popular music censorship in Africa*, pp. 127–36

Coetzee, J. M., *White writing: on the culture of letters in South Africa*, New Haven, CT: Yale University Press, 1986

Coplan, David B., *In township tonight! South Africa's black city music and theatre*, Johannesburg: Ravan Press, 1985

Gikandi, Simon (ed.), *Encyclopedia of African literature*, London: Routledge, 2003

Gray, Stephen, *South Africa plays*, London: Nick Hern Books and Heinemann-Centaur, 1993

Grossberg, Lawrence, Cary Nelson and Paula Treichler (eds.), *Cultural studies*, New York: Routledge, 1992

Huddleston, Sarah, *George Pemba: against all odds*, Johannesburg: Jonathan Ball, 1996

Jordan, Zweledinga Pallo, 'Keynote address on behalf of the National Executive Committee of the ANC', in Campschreur & Divendal (eds.), *Culture in another South Africa*, pp. 259–65

Kruger, Loren, *The drama of South Africa: plays, pageants and publics since 1910*, London: Routledge, 1999

Lee, Donvé, *Dumile Feni: making art out of suffering*, Kelvin: Awareness Publishing Group, 2006

Lee, Donvé, *George Pemba: the painter of the people*, Kelvin: Awareness Publishing Group, 2006

Lee, Donvé, *Noria Mabasa: carving her name in history*, Kelvin: Awareness Publishing Group, 2006

Lee, Donvé, *Peter Clarke: following dreams and finding fame*, Kelvin: Awareness Publishing Group, 2006

Manganyi, N. Chabani, *A black man called Sekoto*, Johannesburg: Witwatersrand University Press, 1996

Masilela, Ntongela, *The cultural modernity of H. I. E. Dhlomo*, Trenton, NJ: Africa World; London: Turnaround, 2007

Mda, Zakes, 'The role of culture in the process of reconciliation in South Africa', seminar no. 9, Centre for the Study of Violence and Reconciliation Seminar, Johannesburg, 1994

Morris, J. and E. Preston-Whyte (eds.), *Speaking with beads: Zulu arts from southern Africa*, London: Thames and Hudson, 1994

Mphahlele, Es'kia, *Down Second Avenue*, London: Faber and Faber, 1959

Ndebele, Njabulo, 'Liberation and the crisis of culture,' in Boehmer, Chrisman and Parker (eds.), *Altered state?*, pp. 1–10

Ndebele, Njabulo, *Rediscovery of the ordinary: essays on South African literature and culture*, Johannesburg: Congress of South African Writers, 1991

Ndebele, Njabulo, *South African literature and culture: rediscovery of the ordinary*, Manchester, U.K.: Manchester University Press, 1994

Ndebele, Njabulo, 'Turkish tales and some thoughts on South African fiction', *Staffrider* 6:1 (1984), 24–5, 42–8

Ndlovu, Duma (ed.), *Woza Afrika! An anthology of South African plays*, New York: George Braziller, 1986

Nkosi, Lewis, *Tasks and masks: themes and styles of African literature*. Harlow, U.K.: Longman, 1985

Orkin, Martin, *Drama and the South African state*, Manchester, U.K.: Manchester University Press and Witwatersrand University Press, 1991

Peterson, Bhekizizwe, 'A rain a fall but the dirt it tough: scholarship on African theatre in South Africa', *Journal of Southern African Studies* 21:4 (1995), 573–84

Peterson, Bhekizizwe 'Apartheid and the political imagination in black South African theatre', *Journal of Southern African Studies* 16:2 (1990), 229–45

Peterson, Bhekizizwe, *Monarchs, missionaries and African intellectuals: African theatre and the unmaking of colonial marginality*, Johannesburg: Witwatersrand University Press, 2000

Raditlhalo, Sam, 'Forgotten son,' *Southern African Review of Books* (November–December 1996), 15–17

Sekoto, Gerard, *Gerard Sekoto: my life and work*, Johannesburg: Viva, 1995

Stevenson, M. and M. Graham-Stewart (eds.), *South East African beadwork, 1850–1910: from adornment to artefact to art*, Cape Town: Fernwood Press, 2000

Van Der Vlies, A., *South African textual cultures: white, black, read all over*, Manchester, U.K.: Manchester University Press, 2007

Van Wyk, G. 'Through the cosmic flower: secret resistance in the mural art of Sotho-Tswana women', in Nooter (ed.), *Secrecy*, pp. 80–7

Willan, Brian, *Sol Plaatje: a biography Solomon Tehekisho Plaatje (1876–1932)*, Johannesburg: Ravan Press, 1984

Williamson, Sue, *Resistance art in South Africa*, Cape Town: David Philip, 1989

Williamson, Sue, *South African art now*, New York: Collins Design, 2009

13

ENVIRONMENT, HERITAGE, RESISTANCE, AND HEALTH: NEWER HISTORIOGRAPHICAL DIRECTIONS

ALBERT GRUNDLINGH, CHRISTOPHER SAUNDERS,
SANDRA SWART AND HOWARD PHILLIPS

Through its preceding chapters, this book has sought to provide not only a sustained account of modern South Africa's historical development but also, as its contributors stress at various points, a conscious reflection of what has been a particularly fertile brand of national historiography. Naturally, the rethinking of approaches to the understanding of both pre-1994 and post-1994 South African society continues, and in this initial postapartheid phase, scholars have been inserting new explanatory perspectives or empirical information into a complex story. As the introduction to the volume has emphasised, more recent stories remain to be told. Equally, there are older or more established stories that may have been told but that can bear retelling through fresh analytical perspectives or on the basis of categories of evidence previously neglected or unavailable. Thus, in this concise concluding chapter, we consider four significant thematic areas with which South Africa's historians have been engaging particularly since the 1990s. These are the issues of the environment, of heritage and history, of later anti-apartheid resistance – or what has also come to be known as struggle history – and the history of health.

ENVIRONMENT

In this country's versions of national history, nature and landscape have long been a core part of what has come to be understood popularly as South Africa's heritage. Equally, conceptualised as the environment, nature has also come to constitute a newer framework of historical investigation. International in its reach, and on the rise in South African historiography, environmental history is simultaneously establishing its disciplinary status and exploring new themes. Taking as its subject the effect of humankind on nature and nature on humankind over time, it emerged in the United

States and in Europe in the 1960s and 1970s, in chorus with vigorous sociopolitical movements that were reacting to the external concerns of the ecology and the animal rights lobbies. Unsurprisingly, a growing sense of environmental crisis and the consequent environmental revolution had an impact on historical writing internationally.

Moreover, from within the history academy, there was reaction against the more extreme reifications of the 'textual turn' within the discipline, which made some trained historians yearn for the possibilities of solid corporeality offered by the environment as an arena of study. Nature – as plants, animals, landscapes, diseases, weather and so on – existed undeniably in a way that rested uneasily with a postmodern insistence on textual primacy. Although approaches have been, and remain, widely varied, they all granted a measure of significance to the environment as a shaping factor in human history. Perspectives, too, have varied. The first possible focus is on the environments of the past, incorporating human impact both on and from, for example, living organisms, climatic change and the land itself. A second approach analyses the political economy of the environment – the modes of production that humans have developed in ecologically circumscribed circumstances, with the material base resting on an environmental foundation. The third line of research draws on changing human ideas about the environment, including what might be loosely called ideology, myth, philosophy and science. Research seldom fits neatly into one category alone, mostly overlapping in at least two.

As a distinct trajectory of South African history, environmental history represents a recent development. Yet although research consciously calling itself environmental history has begun to proliferate only in the past decade or so, preceding scholarship demonstrates a tradition of regarding the environment as a subject and, indeed, even as an agent of historical change. Indeed, the environment has featured in writing from established historiographical perspectives – delineated roughly as settler, nationalist, liberal and social history or radical – and particularly in the current post-paradigmatic phase where such divisions are less defined. Of course, in earlier works, nature figured as a relatively deterministic historical factor. Thus, it appeared as an economic resource, chiefly a commercial resource for surplus food production or a vector of social determination in explaining differential class and racial divisions. For example, the role of nature in shaping some of the contours of South African history was deployed by Afrikaner historians such as P. J. van der Merwe in his 1930s *Trekboer* trilogy. Another pioneering intervention in the same decade was made by B. H. Dicke, writing on one of the first groups of Voortrekkers to be annihilated, purportedly by the Amatongas of the Makuleke and Mahlengwe clans. But Dicke made the radical environmental argument that what had overcome the trekkers was tsetse fly rather than the Amatongas.

A decade later, one of the most significant early historians of South Africa to really focus on people's relationship with their environment (and to insist on a measure of environmental determinism), was C. W de Kiewiet. And a generation later, also in the liberal tradition, Francis Wilson's section on farming in *The Oxford History of South Africa* explored how the environment, specifically agriculture, helped to mould racial relationships. Here, nature offered a stage set against which the drama of racial relationships was enacted.

The seductive but misguided simplicity of environmental determinism in earlier works may have rendered later historians uncomfortable with incorporating environmental issues. This was exacerbated by disciplinary insularity, by a lack of familiarity with science and by increasing local political isolation, which greatly diminished the impact of the international environmental revolution. Moreover, and perhaps much more significant, the central historiographic thrust was directed toward opposing (and, for some historians, defending) apartheid. Apartheid, as this volume underlines, was the enemy that animated the most vigorous of the historiographical schools – the radical and social history – and many of its most capable historians focused their research on the deconstruction of racial consciousness and on class formation. But democracy after 1994 has allowed for a growing historiographical diversity. With their old enemy defeated, what constitutes radical or progressive history has become both less cohesive and more on the prowl for new lines of critique.

A number of the newer approaches have been environmental, focusing on a specific group of people and on their relations with the nonhuman living world, and on how communities related to the environment as they interacted with one another, emphasising issues of social power and identity. Accordingly, the end of apartheid has helped to redirect the attention of some radical social historians toward fresher pastures, in a sense prompting a shift in orientation from red to green. More broadly, this momentum, coming largely from social historians and from some political historians, can be seen as reflecting an international trend in which, right from the beginning, environmental history has been influenced by a radical approach forged by social history. In other words, it shares the idea of exploring history from below, except that here the exploited element would be the biota and the land itself.[1] If for social historians the focus has been on the human oppressed, for environmental historians it is that which is literally

---

[1] R. Nash, 'American environmental history: a new teaching frontier', *Pacific History Review* 41 (1972), 362–72.

trampled underfoot – minute organisms, the soil, water and biophysical surroundings.

Furthermore, both schools seek examples not only of oppression but also of agency, exercised by ecological and social communities. In essence, therefore, the socioenvironmental approach seeks to underline fresh facets of power, their sources and the intentions behind their mobilization. Environmental history has also run in parallel with radical history because both approaches have wished to offer a corrective line that emphasises African agency in the face of European conquest and capitalist exploitation. For this reason, some scholars consciously designate their work as socioenvironmental history rather than as purely environmental.[2] Here, too, in the radical tradition, in recent decades, there has been some implicit use of the environment in explaining change over time, even though such writings in agrarian social history were not self-classified as works of environmental history.

Accordingly, one scholar has underscored the catholic nature of environmental historical writing in South Africa, as a 'broad church', whose catechism has thus far 'defied efforts at scholarly synthesis'.[3] Approaches run a gamut from nature as a backdrop to the unfolding of human drama and another extreme, which offers an analysis of the changing environment itself, with humans as merely players in the environment's story. Yet another approach is the subject of nature as part of human culture. Beyond this, South Africanists have been exploring the interaction of humans and their environments in a diversity of epochs and time frames. Thus, even the pre–*Homo sapiens* hominids, from the australopithecines, have received attention. Historians have also shown that contact between human communities and their natural environments offers a lens for the analysis of encounters between different societies. Therefore, the issue of relations between ecology and human lifeways has seen extensive research into both nomadic hunter-gatherer and pastoral societies. In like vein, the development of independent African states in the precolonial past has been studied, for example, in work on the ecological dynamics buttressing the rise of the nineteenth-century Zulu polity.

In that sense, research has generally reflected the role of the environment in shaping the country's social, political and economic history, and, vice versa, the manifestation of specific power struggles over land and the

[2] N. Jacobs, *Environment, power and injustice: a South African history* (Cambridge: Cambridge University Press, 2003); S. Swart, 'But where's the bloody horse? Textuality and corporeality in the "animal turn"', *Journal of Literary Studies* 23:3 (2007), 271–92.

[3] L. van Sittert, 'Writing and teaching the history of the land and environment in Africa in the twenty-first century', report on conference session, *South African Historical Journal* 50 (2004), 223–4.

alienation of water resources. For instance, taking the workings of the environment more seriously has offered a key to understanding the decline of the Khoesan, which has come to be seen as attributable less to smallpox epidemics than to their alienation from grazing land and water that accompanied white expansion in the course of the eighteenth century.

Natural phenomena have received glancing attention, in particular, drought. Here, local work on climate history has been stimulated largely by crises of food supply and perceptions of natural resource degradation. Alongside this, research on colonial contact has shown that at times conquest was accompanied by devastating environmental phenomena – drought, cattle disease and crop failures – as settlers sought to entrench their power. Historians have revealed that potent African resistance to colonial rule often emerged at environmental crisis points. Settler ideas and farming practices, particularly among white English-speaking 'progressive' farmers, have been comprehensively explored, as have attempts by white landowners to manipulate the landscape ideologically as part of an insistence on the natural right to belong. In this context, animal diseases and the development of veterinary science have both come under examination, and the ensuing ecological transformations wrought by human action have been delineated.

Through environmental studies, scholars have also been able to illuminate the ways in which human incursion was accompanied by other invaders. Just as in Europe, Asia and North Africa, animal and plant colonisers transformed their new habitats – both biophysical and social – in various ways. On this front, the animal turn is recent and still very small. Still, research that uses animals as a window into understanding human society has been developed on the dog in South Africa and on horses in southern Africa. Such animal history offers a way into the interstitial spaces of human societies and provides a means of crossing literal and figurative borders.

Subject matter such as animals and, indeed, nature itself are hard to contain within the boundaries of the nation-state. For environmental, ecological and biological processes work on transregional, transcontinental and global scales, defying 'a narrow view of political boundaries and nationality'.[4] Environmental history can thus offer a very useful avenue for escaping the overreliance on the nation-state paradigm in which South African historians are largely trained. Here, even though excellent comparative work exists, South Africanists have as yet not availed themselves fully of the potential to explore cross-regional terrain. Still, a start has been made with work comparing South Africa and the United States, with comparative studies of the impact on, and interaction with, the environment

---

[4] D. Worster (ed.), *The ends of the earth* (Cambridge: Cambridge University Press, 1988), p. 290.

by settler societies in Canada, Australia, New Zealand and South Africa, and with ideas on comparing southern Africa and South Asia.

As an intercontinental information and biotic exchange arose and became entrenched in imperial networks, environmental history has become a filament in studies of colonialism and empire. These, for instance, have examined the results of biological exchanges for both the human and the natural world, whereas environmental knowledge production and its dissemination have both received nuanced deconstruction. Environmental and social control have also been seen as inextricably linked, with writers demonstrating that scientific understanding has been embedded in broader political and cultural agendas in which interventions have seldom been socially neutral. At this level, environmental history has thus supplemented our understanding of state praxis: environmental management has been analysed as a strategy deployed by the colonial state and the national governments that followed. Colonial science has thus been seen to operate in interaction with a 'vernacular science', a hybrid of indigenous African, local settler and metropolitan knowledge systems.[5] There is a large body of writing on governmental environmental policy, particularly on the development of state conservation strategies and the political ecology of natural resource use. Not surprisingly, local wildlife policies have received considerable attention in the light of British imperialism and its hunting network. In the specific case of South Africa, key work has corrected public myths regarding wildlife protection. Both romantic myths about a pristine, presettler African conservation ethic cultivated by self-consciously Afrocentric scholars and the hagiographic treatment of conservation efforts of whites have been subject to critique and subtle evaluation.

Aside from wildlife conservation, in the study of natural resources, most historiographic energy has been directed towards soil erosion measures, forestry, fresh water and marine resources. Preliminary interest in soil conservation developed from work on rural black political movements. Hence, pioneering work on colonial conservation has inspired other studies that have focused on reactions to agricultural betterment planning. Here, studies of soil conservation have exposed it as a form of colonial control – like pest eradication and conservationist discourse – which veiled the real intent of colonial authorities. Some historians have investigated the exploitation of wood resources, and others have pioneered the analysis of marine water reserves. Yet other research has debunked simplistic declensionist

[5] See, e.g., Beinart, *The rise of conservation;* M. Draper, 'Zen and the art of garden province maintenance: the soft intimacy of hard men in the wilderness of KwaZulu-Natal, South Africa, 1952–1997', *Journal of Southern African Studies* 24:4 (1998), 801–28.

narratives of resource use, offering a complex understanding of the inter-leaving of social and environmental dynamics.

Given the nature of South Africa, it goes almost without saying that historians have also been tracing the interface between environmental and human action and human ideology through the rise of segregation and apartheid, leading into some tentative research on postapartheid South Africa. Through this, scholarship has exploded the notion of a lack of a con-servation ethic among black societies historically.[6] Other research has been initiated into the repressive responses of the South African state, the lim-ited environmental dimensions to African National Congress (ANC) policy and into the environmental movement itself. On this last element, study of developments in the South African environmental movement from the early 1970s, tracing its peculiar development under apartheid, shows that the environment was marginalised because of the state's agenda in pursu-ing unfettered economic growth coupled with isolation from international trends due to sanctions. In other considerations of broadly the same era, historians have also turned to the environmental impact of forced removals, the establishment of restrictive homelands with limited land holdings and inadequate water and sanitation and the concomitant overutilisation of resources. The picture that has been emerging suggests that in the shadow of the liberation struggle was the everyday struggle between Africans and their environment.

With its roots in ground long ploughed by historians, presently growing environmental history has explored the reciprocal influences of a changing nature and a changing society, shifting away from reductionist notions and permitting nature an acknowledged space on the flanks of the social and political institutions of local peoples and regional social formations. Of no little significance is that the very term *environmental* carries with it a wide suggestion of social relevance, with ample state and institutional funding helping to smooth its way in South Africa's increasingly corporate academia. There have been special journal editions devoted to environmen-tal history and journals of record regularly carry articles overtly or tacitly on South African environmental history. In the academy, there is a cohort of researchers defining themselves as environmental or socioenvironmen-tal historians – a positive indicator that interest in this subject matter will endure and is already sufficiently established for it to be considered a separate disciplinary trajectory.

[6] F. Khan, 'Rewriting South Africa's conservation history: the role of the Native Farmers' Association', *Journal of Southern African Studies* 20:4 (1994), 499–516; 'Soil wars: the role of the African National Soil Conservation Association in South Africa, 1953–1959', *Environmental History* 2:4 (1997), 439–59.

At the same time, it is nonetheless important to acknowledge that, so far, the bulk of historical writing on South Africa that takes the environment seriously has been by historians who do not identify themselves as 'environmental historians'. Indeed, some scholars shy away from the notion of a history subdiscipline, preferring the idea of an interdisciplinary arena, and here there has certainly been some useful collaboration with natural scientists and policy researchers.[7] That notwithstanding, research still tends toward firm social history, to which 'environment' has been added to the usual older analytical categories of 'class', 'race' and 'gender'.[8] So, whether a greater focus on the environment implies a distinct new branch of South African history or is a subdisciplinary area is, in a sense, unresolved. In any event, a rigid definition may well be unhelpful. Rather than as a separate subdiscipline, environmentalism could be described as a recent turn, or possibly even a minor paradigm shift, in which conventional historians simply write more environmentally. In that sense, including environmental factors in understanding the past just becomes another way of doing history. Historiographically, it amounts to a continuing process of inclusion and gradual mainstream acceptance of the environment as subject, object and even agent in the complex story of South Africa.

HERITAGE

If an awareness of the environment has something of a pedigree in twentieth-century South African historiography, a distinctively recent and immediately noticeable feature of the period since the 1990s is the degree to which it has witnessed increasing scholarly involvement in the understanding of heritage outside of the formal museums arena while, at the same time, notions of what constitutes heritage have informed some of the topics that historians have chosen to pursue. Moreover, in the final apartheid decade, most South African university history departments were developing courses that, in one way or another, engaged with heritage matters. In part, they were responding to an increasingly salient global trend in education. But more pertinently, this curriculum shift was also a pragmatic attempt to arrest falling student numbers as the notion of heritage study, especially if linked to tourism, appeared to have a marketable commercial edge.

---

[7] See, e.g., C. L. Griffiths et al., 'Impacts of human activities on marine animal life in the Benguela – an historical overview', *Oceanography and Marine Biology Annual Review* 42 (2004), 303–92; S. Stefano and L. van Sittert, 'Black Economic Empowerment (BEE) in industrial fisheries', *African Affairs* 106 (2007), 437–62.

[8] For a rare exception, see J. Guy, 'Gender oppression in southern Africa's precapitalist societies', in C. Walker (ed.), *Women and gender*, pp. 33–47.

This development also coincided with and mirrored wider trends in society. In a new postapartheid context, an earlier radical social history perspective with its emphasis on the fault lines in society and on class in particular, appeared increasingly inappropriate as the new South Africa slipped into a nation-building rhythm. The disaggregating imperatives of social history and the conforming impulses that underpin a nation-building project made for a tricky combination, or something that barely fitted together. For what the socially marginalised – such as the black underclasses and the poor whites who loomed large in social history analyses – had come to represent was a politically awkward element. Their presence was too jarring or too ideologically dissonant to be accommodated in the homogenising fold of a new nation eager to display a neatly rounded African unity rather than the messiness of a society with loose strands that were frayed at more than just its capitalist edges. Accordingly, the time for a 'socially responsible past' had come, and heritage studies were very much a part of the creation of that past.[9]

Equally, the broader cultural purchase of new legacy and associated heritage projects on the popular imagination cannot be assumed automatically, and its hold on a general audience appears also to be uneven. Thus, although the appeal of the great and the good of the postapartheid order may certainly have some resonance, heritage of this kind can also have its limits. This has been suggested by the experiences of one ex–history lecturer at the University of the North West in Mafikeng, at which most students are from rural areas and country towns. As he recalls of heritage studies students, their consciousness alerted him to

> the pitfalls of 'national' history . . . with its predictable focus on 'big' national events and figures. . . . [S]tudents have frequently expressed frustration at the tenuous connections between their own lives and the way in which the emerging national narrative (e.g. the Sharpeville massacre, the symbolism of Robben Island, Mandela-ism is commemorated). . . . I have tried . . . to [encourage them] to recall their own family and local stories of poverty, oppression and resistance . . . experienced mainly in the Bophuthatswana homeland.[10]

Yet heritage has become important for economic reasons. As one South African newspaper reflected without exaggeration in 2003, a national asset was a heritage worth millions. According to a former director of the Robben

---

[9] Cf. A. Cobley, 'Does social history have a future? The end of apartheid and recent trends in South African historiography', *Journal of Southern African Studies* 27:3 (2001), 618. See also P. Bonner, 'Keynote address to the "Life after Thirty" Colloquium', *African Studies* 69:1 (2010), 13–27; D. Posel, 'Social history and the Wits History Workshop', *African Studies* 69:1 (2010), 29–40.

[10] Quoted in J. Comaroff, 'The end of history, again? Pursuing the past in the postcolony', unpublished paper, Department of History, University of Basel (January 2003), p. 21.

Island Museum, with the heritage industry spending R200 million on the island itself and R350 million on Pretoria's Freedom Park, the enormous financial scale of the enterprise would have important and far-reaching consequences. He added that, 'while complaints about the decline of history abound, a whole new billion Rand heritage infrastructure is being put in place which will fundamentally reshape the heritage and public heritage environment in future, and create more opportunities for historians, educators and heritage practitioners'.[11]

At the same time, such developments, whatever their merits, ought not to be considered a displacement of history. A nuanced distinction is drawn by one influential study of the heritage industry,

the historian, however blinkered and presentist and self-deceived, seeks to convey a past consensually known, open to inspection and proof, continually revised and eroded as time and hindsight outdate its truths. The heritage fashioner, however historically scrupulous, seeks to design a past that will fix the identity and enhance the well-being of some chosen individual or folk. History cannot be wholly dispassionate, or it will not be felt worth learning or conveying; heritage cannot wholly disregard history, or it will seem too incredible to command fealty. But the aims that animate these two enterprises, and their modes of persuasion, are contrary to each other. . . . [I]t is vital to bear that opposition in mind.[12]

In short, and without labouring the point, memory is not the same as history. Nor is memorialisation the same as historical writing. Yet this is not necessarily a completely watertight division. For a particular framing of pastness can draw from a variety of historical dimensions that can, for example, be writing, visual imagery, oral traditions, memory and political perceptions of the past, or usually an amalgam of such elements. In turn, if deemed worthy of memorialisation, in a truncated form, these can feed into, and reinforce, a more general historical consciousness.

Furthermore, it is conceptually important to distinguish between the categories 'heritage and/or the production of heritage', on the one hand, and the 'study of the making of heritage', on the other hand. For these ought not to be used interchangeably, as they deal with divergent activities. 'Heritage' and its construction can be viewed as the product, whereas the 'study of the making of heritage' is the unpicking of that which is produced. This is, of course, not intended to imply that the production of heritage proceeds without substantial historical verification but to emphasise that

---

[11] A. Odendaal, 'Heritage and the arrival of post-colonial history in South Africa', unpublished paper, U.S. African Studies Association Conference, Washington, D.C. (2002), pp. 9–10.

[12] D. Lowenthal, *The heritage crusade and the spoils of history* (Cambridge: Cambridge University Press, 1998), p. xi.

its ultimate aim differs from the objective of those who seek to interrogate the making of heritage from a variety of angles.

Nor, to clarify matters conceptually, is it the intention to convey the impression of a hierarchy of knowledge and to assert that the writing of history is in any way superior to the unpacking of heritage. To the contrary, at times the latter may be more challenging analytically because several layers of understanding over time have to be unravelled. In South Africa, as much as anywhere else, if not more so, interpretative problems arise in relation to commemorative history, as the meaning of the past derives from elements of both the original event and the new context in which a commemorative event or episode occurs.

In this respect, a considerable amount of work has already been done by South African historians, most notably those from the University of the Western Cape. By focusing on public pasts and the complex and often-contradictory processes that impinge on the making of heritage, such scholarship has opened up a fruitful and multidimensional area of enquiry. Here, a popular topic of investigation has been historical festivals. Thus, the 1952 Van Riebeeck Festival, which marked the 1652 arrival of the Dutch under Jan van Riebeeck, has become the subject of a book, with the pageant of colonialism scrutinised in an attempt to 'name, frame, locate and historicize the "internal contents" of the land'.[13]

Public history was also conspicuously on display with the 1999 centenary commemorations of the South African War. Taking place in the wake of a major political transition, this opened up ample opportunities for historians to unravel the way in which the past was constituted in the context of a dramatically changed political present.

What emerged, then, was that several competing groups tried to reshape the war's significance from different perspectives. The new majoritarian state tried to graft its particular visions onto a body of previously congealed historical understanding by emphasising African participation and suffering. More purist Africanist groupings considered the centenary of a white man's squabble on African soil as irrelevant to the 'new' South Africa. Understandably, Afrikaners showed a lively interest in the commemoration but by and large steered clear of overt political interpretations linking the war to renewed calls for ethnic mobilisation. Last, commercial interests tried to market 'battlefield products' for purposes of tourism.

A more enduring and visible dimension of heritage is represented by historical monuments. Here, too, there has been no shortage of studies dealing

---

[13] L. Witz, *Apartheid's festival: contesting South Africa's national pasts* (Cape Town: David Philip, 2003), p. 27; 'Eventless history at the end of apartheid: the making of the Dias Festival', *Kronos* 32 (2006), 162–91.

with the contemporary processes of reimagining or repositioning monuments that have their origins in the apartheid or segregationist order. It has, in its way, been an inviting task. After all, in 'the wake of Marxism, deconstruction, postmodernism and other contemporary critical movements, it is all too easy to detect – the symbols of – Western cultural hegemony, male chauvinism, homophobia, and on and on – so many meanings multiplied by contemporary theory that these monuments are sitting ducks before modern critics'.[14]

Not surprisingly, the Voortrekker Monument, situated prominently on a Pretoria hillock and regarded as a prime symbolic embodiment of Afrikaner nationalism, has become one of those proverbial sitting ducks, drawing considerable attention. At the heart of critical discourse was the issue of how the monument was to be viewed in the light of post-1994 political changes. Largely absent was a crucial sense that by 1994 old-style Afrikaner nationalism had for a fair period of time been superseded by the pragmatic and entrepreneurial outlook of a relatively prosperous Afrikaner middle class. This was an influential stratum with an increasingly limited need for formal and imposing statements of ethnic consciousness. Thus, it was relatively easy for the monument to shed whatever remained of its former nationalistic remit. Despite occasional well-attended gatherings on 16 December on the annual Day of the Vow commemoration, with at least a fair number of those present being of right-wing persuasion, on the whole, the monument was no longer positioned as the exclusivist Afrikaner shrine of yore. Instead, it could become a more subdued place of heritage, not only reflecting soberly and cerebrally on the Afrikaner past but also marketing itself as a leading tourist site, as it draws more than 80 per cent of its visitors from abroad. Apart from occasional low-level friction, the Monument seems also to have reached a largely peaceable coexistence with the adjacent large-scale and ongoing Freedom Park project. Representing the post-1994 government's flagship interpretation of 'new' heritage, in scope and narrative it is, unsurprisingly, decidedly at odds with the Voortrekker Monument.

Unlike the Voortrekker Monument, the Freedom Park construction awaits a full critical dissection by scholars. There have, however, been probing studies of other heritage sites such as the Emlotheni Memorial in New Brighton, Port Elizabeth, where six ANC uMkhonto weSizwe soldiers were reburied. There, in the view of the local community, the Memorial was foisted on them with scant regard for cross-cutting political sensibilities and Xhosa burial rituals. Similarly, the much-publicised return from France in 2002 of the remains of the Khoesan woman Saartjie Baartman and their reinternment in the Eastern Cape have also been

---

[14] N. Glazer, 'Monuments in an age without heroes', *Public Interest* 123 (1996), 25.

subjected to investigation, particularly in relation to its genderised dimension and to neglectful conservation of the grave site.

On the sensitive issue of the return of South African bodily remains from Europe, heritage received another unexpected twist in 1996. From the old rural Transkei of the Eastern Cape province, Chief Nicholas Tilana Gcaleka embarked on a personal heritage expedition to find the skull of Hintsa, the Xhosa king between 1789 and 1835 who was killed by the British on the eastern frontier. Claiming that the skull was buried somewhere in Britain, Gcaleka declared that Hintsa's head had to be recovered to bring peace to South Africa. The fact that there was no evidence to substantiate his burial claims contributed to his public ridiculing. Scholars, however, were more sensitive in trying to explore the deeper cultural meanings of what on the face of it may appear to have been an idiosyncratic quest for heritage retrieval. In their analyses, questions are raised about the nature of historical knowledge and the multiplicity of imaginative ways in which the past can be represented and possessed.

In another turn, a far more recent form of overtly ideological heritage, the Freedom Charter, has been examined as a document of national heritage. Seeking to review its historical legacy in the broadest way possible, this has identified the question of 'unacknowledged knowledge, in some cases through people communing with ancestors',[15] as a dimension that ought to be reflected culturally in the notion of the charter as a people's document. Furthermore, analysis of this kind reflects a sensitivity to gender questions and takes issue with a slick application of the charter's heritage for a nation-building agenda.

In addition to unravelling political heritage, historians have also focused on other ways in which memories can be created, constructed and manipulated in the commercial world. One case study has investigated how South African Breweries (SAB) has manufactured and utilised heritage in its national beer-marketing campaigns. Through the reinvention and mythologising of a genial colonial brewmaster, Charles Glass, a point is reached in which both black and white men come to be seen in a shared sociability of drinking, lifting their glasses to the figure who supposedly made such mutual conviviality possible. The formal ending of apartheid enabled SAB advertising to add 'a new multiracial nationalism to the values of heritage and male bonding, obliterating past divisions and enabling the corporation's brands to reflect the emotional power of the post-apartheid moment'.[16]

---

[15] R. Suttner, 'Talking to the ancestors: national heritage, the Freedom Charter and nation-building in South Africa in 2005', *Development Southern Africa* 23:1 (2006), 4.

[16] A. Mager, 'One beer, one goal, one nation, one soul: South African Breweries, heritage, masculinity and nationalism, 1960–1999', *Past and Present* 188 (2005), 194.

A more conventional biographical heritage subject for another kind of academic scrutiny has been Cecil John Rhodes. Recent study has disaggregated the myriad ways in which memory of this arch-imperialist and mining magnate has lived on in the historical consciousness of many South Africans and of others further afield in Zimbabwe. Ultimately, despite his dark history, the controversial Rhodes has to some degree managed to retain a favourable heritage reception because, through the bequest of his legacy, he has been able to purchase his own 'immortality'.[17]

Although few South African historians have consciously aligned themselves with French scholars working on *lieux de mémoire* (translated loosely as "consciousnesses of historical memory"), it would not be inaccurate to see elements of this in their scholarship. *Lieux de mémoire* are 'moments of history torn away from the movement of history, then returned; no longer quite life, not yet death, like shells on the shore when the sea of living memory has receded'.[18] In reflecting this, some of the best practitioners have broadened the scope of the historical profession and have imbued it with greater awareness of the complexity and longevity of pastness in its various guises.

At the same time, while historians have been increasingly adept in engaging with aspects of memory, there remain some intriguing counterideas relating to ways of remembering or non-remembering. In this respect, questions raised by one scholar in the context of India may be equally relevant in current South Africa: '[C]an we at all remember without commemorating? Can we recollect without celebrating; or recall without avenging? Why are national histories invariably encrusted in a lapidary mode?'[19]

RESISTANCE

More recent scholarship on the history of the struggle against racial discrimination and domination has, unsurprisingly, come to inform popular notions of an antiapartheid struggle heritage. So, too, as in the opening example of environmental history, has earlier historical writing on twentieth-century black resistance politics helped to inspire and to shape recent studies. Such work would include Edward Roux's seminal 1948 *Time Longer Than Rope*, a general history of 'the black man's struggle for freedom', which was actually not read widely until its paperback appearance in 1964, a year

---

[17] P. Maylam, *The cult of Rhodes: remembering an imperialist in Africa* (Cape Town: David Philip, 2005), p. 159.

[18] P. Nora, 'Between memory and history: *les lieux de mémoire*', *Representations* 26 (1989), 12.

[19] S. Amin, *Alternative histories: a view from India* (Calcutta: Centre for Studies in Social Sciences and South-South Exchange Programme for Research on the History of Development, 2002), p. 36.

after the publication of Mary Benson's *The African Patriots*, the first general history of the ANC. The first major scholarly monograph, Peter Walshe's 1971 history of the ANC to 1952, was followed two years later by the first volume in the *From Protest to Challenge* series, with commentaries on African political activity from the late nineteenth century. By 1977, the third volume in that indispensable series had appeared, taking the story to the outcome of the Rivonia Treason Trial in 1964, with Gail Gerhart's major study of the Africanist strand in black politics following close on its heels. By the end of the 1970s, therefore, the groundwork had been laid for later work. No less significant, almost all of it had been undertaken outside the country.

From about then, however, notably in the aftermath of the Soweto uprising, scholars working in South Africa began to tackle aspects of earlier resistance, mostly in the years before 1960. Such writing was clearly influenced by open resistance in the present, just as those who had written about early resistance from a location outside the country often saw their writing as a contribution to the global solidarity movement against apartheid. Not surprisingly, then, in such writing and almost without exception, there was not only little criticism of the resistance movement but also considerable romanticisation in studies that set out to recover previously unknown history and tended mostly to be heavily descriptive. Furthermore, most of the writers were not professional historians but sociologists and political scientists, some of whom lacked a sure sense of historical context. The best of these studies of the history of black politics focused on the detail of particular cases in a broad overall synthesis. Thereafter, although the 1980s era of mass urban resistance witnessed considerable writing about urban and youth politics, such works, again, often lacked historical depth and were limited in terms of the range of their sources. All the while, general histories of the country continued to tend to ignore or to downplay the history of the struggle. Indeed, major work completed before 1994 on topics such as the ANC's armed struggle remained unpublished.

If, as a moment, 1994 may not have marked any major break in South African historical writing in general, it certainly represented a considerable turning point in writing on the history of the struggle against apartheid. This was partly because the new political dispensation meant that political censorship and apartheid restrictions fell away, and new archives became available at places like the University of Fort Hare and the University of the Western Cape. Newly available ANC papers were exploited not only by local researchers but also by foreign scholars, most notably one Russian writer who drew also on his personal involvement in the South African struggle. The Truth and Reconciliation Commission (TRC), which began its work in 1995, was much criticised in some quarters for the limitations of its mandate, but nonetheless still became a major new potential resource for scholars. Although the vast TRC archive is still not readily accessible, its five-volume 1998 report and subsequent volumes issued in 2003 provide much new information on human rights violations during the struggle.

The initial openness after the transition to democracy, along with fresh publication opportunities, meant that soon a large body of new writing began to emerge. This ranged from numerous memoirs by activists and biographies of leading resistance figures to alternative versions of general histories that gave the struggle a prominent place; brief essays on different aspects of the struggle theme; and heavier monographs, including a history of the Communist Party of South Africa, then published for the first time, decades after having being completed. And the fifth volume in the From Protest to Challenge series, covering the years 1964 to 1979, saw the light of day, along with volumes of documents on the country's radical tradition.

Probably the single most important post-1994 project in this field of scholarship to date was launched at the suggestion of Thabo Mbeki, soon after he assumed the presidency in 1999. Financed by the private sector and designed especially to draw on oral data, this presidential project, known as the South African Democracy Education Trust (SADET), produced a series of volumes that set out to tackle the 'hidden' history of the South African struggle, decade by decade from 1960. Drawing heavily on new oral interviews conducted with leading personalities as well as the rank and file, these volumes began to appear in 2004.

A distinctive feature of the SADET initiative was its recognition that the South African struggle could not be understood without taking into account a wider context of mobilisation, and thus a large volume in two parts was published on international solidarity with the antiapartheid cause, with another planned on the role of African countries, including the frontline states, in supporting the South African struggle. A set of studies of the role of the Nordic countries in aiding the antiapartheid cause had led the way in the study of the global struggle against apartheid, and in the early twenty-first century, those volumes were followed by significant works on the British Anti-Apartheid Movement (AAM) and the Africa Groups of Sweden as global social movements, and on the role of African Americans in the antiapartheid campaign in the United States.

As originally conceived, the SADET project was to focus primarily on the history of the ANC, and on its armed struggle in particular, to fit in with what had by then become the dominant national metanarrative, in which other competing political tendencies were either excluded or diminished in their antiapartheid role. In the event, however, the volumes produced turned out to be relatively comprehensive, with the first including chapters on the anticommunist African Resistance Movement of the early 1960s and on aboveground activity, including the contribution of church and student leaders. For its part, the second volume contained much material on the Black Consciousness Movement and incorporated different perspectives on the activities of whites in the 1970s trade union movement. An illustration of the usefulness of the SADET project material to analysis of the antiapartheid struggle can be glimpsed in this volume's Chapter 9, on resistance and reform.

Meanwhile, specialised monographs opened up new fields of enquiry in political history. These encompassed political imprisonment on Robben Island; knowledgeable, firsthand accounting of underground activity before 1976; and a history of the Liberal Party. Although aboveground activity of the 1980s continued to be treated lightly, several studies analysed the key internal organisation of that decade, the United Democratic Front, surveying its general history, exploring its ideology, and providing local case studies of its regional activities.

Most of the newer studies of the 1960–1994 period were preoccupied with organisational politics. Only gradually did research begin to consider, say, the culture of resistance politics and the exile experiences of South Africans, or to take the study of gender further than in earlier studies. Predictably, a fair portion of this historical writing was triumphalist, either ignoring or minimising more morally troubling issues in the past, such as the imprisonment and torture of activists in exile. Furthermore, the absence of balance in some writings reflected the fact that it was not the work of professional historians, few of whom engaged with struggle history in any event. In part, this was due to the difficulties of securing access to relevant resistance documentation, despite the legal efforts of the South African History Archive based at the University of the Witwatersrand, to obtain material under the Promotion of Access to Information Act through court challenges, and despite new digitisation initiatives to ease access to material, both inside and outside the country.

At the same time, much about the campaigning conducted by the liberation movement has remained difficult to probe and to document because of the deep secrecy with which it was surrounded, the basis on which it was conducted by both sides. A further reason South African historians have generally not engaged with struggle history has been, undoubtedly, the controversial nature of the topic, with controversies that have remained very much alive in contemporary political debate in the post-1994 era. Still, that notwithstanding, the sheer volume of recent publications in this area, inadequate though so much of it may be as critical scholarly history, suggests that professional historians may not be able to continue to ignore it. In time, they will surely need to grapple with such questions as the significance of the so-called period of quiescence from the mid-1960s, whether or not the armed struggle was a military failure, and the consequences for postapartheid political culture of the limitations on democratic practices in the ANC in exile.

What is required, of course, is an approach that is both critical and evenhanded, and, perhaps in the radical history tradition, sensitive to that which is local and specific. For, as with the historiography of the American civil rights movement, many of the early studies of the South African struggle have tended to be overly concerned with the national picture, glossing over regional and local differences, as well as top down in their approach. So, there remains much scope for work on particular themes (e.g., education), for more detailed local studies of grassroots struggles of a kind that has been produced on the Northern Transvaal and the Eastern Cape, and for assessments of the interaction between the national and the local. To which could be added the question of the commemoration of struggle as heritage, such as the construction, by the post-1994 state, of Freedom Park and the erection of local memorials to ANC guerrillas, initiatives considered earlier in this chapter. At the time of writing, there is as yet no major overarching study of how the struggle has come to be memorialised, whether as history or as heritage. No less crucially, South African history awaits scholarship that attempts to integrate the new corpus of struggle history work to provide a substantive overview that would encompass the story both of resistance in the country and that of the assistance given to it from outside.

As this closing historiographic overview has sought to show, the continuous maturing of South African history has come to be reflected in the ways in which it has begun recently to address new topics or to expand its categories of analysis when excavating the terrain of the past. As with other galvanising forces that have had an impact on historiography, such as the environment or the creation of heritage, so it is with the emergence of health as a distinctive area of focus.

HEALTH

Scholarship here has been coming from another group of historians committed to a more inclusive and democratic vision of South Africa's past and present. Since the late 1970s and 1980s, increasing attention has been directed by a small but growing circle of academic historians to the history of health, disease and medicine. An explanatory key has been provided by the terms epistemics, the study of how knowledge is acquired and moulded, and epidemics. Taking a lead from Kuhn's ideas on how and why new intellectual paradigms emerge, epistemics would trace this developing concentration, ultimately, to the international rise of the new social history in the 1960s and 1970s and its influence on historians of South Africa, at the expense of the established and then still-dominant paradigm of political history. What a focus on health, disease and medicine offered to some of the country's newly emerging social historians was rich insight into the past experience of ordinary people. In a confirmation of the potential of this perspective, one monograph opened with the words of the American social historian of medicine George Rosen, for whom disease 'related causally to the social and economic situation of the members of a given population . . . [and that] the health care received also reflects the structure of a society, particularly its stratification and class divisions'.[20]

For new social historians of medicine and health, such perspectives were especially appealing. The existing South African Whiggish brand of heroic medical history had concentrated on great doctors achieving great things, with dutiful nurses by their side. Far too narrowly conceived, unproblematised and one dimensional, it was well outmoded. For a new band of scholars, it was particularly deficient in its failure to explore the connection between the state's racial policies and ill health. Tellingly, therefore, the first extended survey of the country's modern medical history by two such writers in 1983 was titled, 'The Health Implications of Racial Discrimination and Social Inequality'.[21]

From the late 1980s, the belief in the need for a broadly conceived, socially informed South African medical history was strengthened by the emergence of the HIV/AIDS epidemic, which was, by then, beginning to gather pace in the country. As the full extent of its impact began to become increasingly apparent burial by burial, so did historians begin to recognise the dread, all-encompassing power of disease to ravage society, and therefore the need to study it so as to make better sense of its impact. Examining responses to premature death in South African history, in 2003 one young historian declared, '[T]en years after South Africa's transition from strife-torn apartheid to multiracial democracy, HIV/AIDS has superseded freedom struggles as the urgent matter of the day'.[22]

The historical work that the swing to social history and the AIDS epidemic has helped to spur during the past twenty years can be grouped usefully into three categories by, appropriately enough, using an amplified version of Hippocrates' ancient division of medicine. In his perception,

---

[20] G. Rosen, 'Health, history and the Social Sciences', *Social Science and Medicine* 7:4 (1973), 236.

[21] World Health Organisation, *Apartheid and health*, pt. 2 (Geneva: WHO, 1973). Its authors were Shula Marks and Neil Andersson.

[22] B. Carton, 'The forgotten compass of death: apocalypse then and now in the social history of South Africa', *Journal of Social History* 37:1 (2003), 199.

its three prime elements were the disease, the patient and the healer. As to the first, given South Africa's long, baleful and continuing encounters with epidemics, it is not surprising that the study of communicable diseases like tuberculosis, influenza, smallpox, polio, bubonic plague, sexually transmitted infections, leprosy and HIV/AIDS has come to attract particular study. This is not only because of their demographic, psychological, cultural, social and economic impact, but also because of their capacity to expose underlying features, relationships and attitudes in society, not least those pertaining to racial stereotyping, stigmatising and pathologising.

Epidemics, as an early social historian of disease put it over three decades ago, reveal 'the nerve system' of society.[23] Allied to this has been the emergence of local historical studies of industrial diseases such as miners' phthisis (silicosis) and asbestosis, which have driven home the dire impact on the health of mine labour of the long-enduring determination of mine owners to contain costs and maximise profits. Thus, for one historian of the Rand, it is through the history of silicosis that 'a tragic history of avarice and apathy [toward costly reforms]' can be traced.[24]

If the second explanatory Hippocratic category, the patient, has begun to attract study only recently, this is something not peculiar to South African medical historiography. In this respect, little but the surface of this component of the country's medical history has been scraped, with historical investigation limited to the issues of patients' selective choice of healers from different medical systems (the so-called hierarchy of patient resort), the interwar attitudes of women to birth control and the experience of patients at Cape Town's Groote Schuur Hospital since the end of the 1930s. In a lament on the undeveloped historiography of this particular topic, one of the few scholars to have written on it has remarked that 'patient history is generally elusive'.[25]

In contrast, historical writings directed toward the third classic Hippocratic category, healers and their institutions, has been comparatively plentiful. At this level, the focus has fallen largely on biomedical doctors, nurses and pharmacists through the lens of group studies of bodies of, for instance, women doctors or black nurses, individual biographies or histories of professional organisations. Yet, despite their continuing to be probably the first port of call for most South Africans in times of illness, to date very little that is historical rather than anthropological has been

---

[23] M. W. Dols, 'The comparative communal responses to the Black Death in Muslim and Christian societies', *Viator: Medieval and Renaissance Studies* 5 (1974), 275.

[24] E. Katz, *The white death: Silicosis on the Witwatersrand gold mines, 1886–1910* (Johannesburg: Witwatersrand University Press, 1994), p. 179.

[25] A. Digby, *Diversity and division in medicine: health care in South Africa from the 1800s* (Oxford: Lang, 2006), p. 373.

published on indigenous or alternative-to-biomedicine healers. There are, nonetheless, two recent pioneering studies that have begun to remedy this neglect. Anne Digby's *Diversity and Division in Medicine* and Karen Flint's *Healing Traditions* both explore the two-way exchange between indigenous healers and biomedical and other healing systems. Such examinations of this phenomenon in the past will lead other scholars to further perspectives that straddle the boundaries among healing systems in an historically informed way.

For their part, healing institutions have also begun belatedly to attract the critical gaze of historians. By virtue of the voluminous records they generated, hospitals, clinics and mental asylums are obvious subjects for searching historical analysis, for they are potentially revealing microcosms of biomedicine in operation as it interacts on a large scale with society. At the same time, the fact that historians have finally begun to probe these interactions is not necessarily a source of delight to the institutions themselves, which often have an uncritical sense of their own historical reputation. Yet causing a flutter in the medical dovecotes is not something that historians should avoid. After all, theirs is the approach of the eclectic outsider, whose historically informed contextualisation, comparative grasp and long perspectives allow the experience of disease, medicine and health to be viewed in fresh and novel ways. In a land in the midst of a deepening health crisis at the time of publication – HIV/AIDS, a failing public health service and declining medical provision as a result of the flight of health workers – these are not unhealthy perspectives to add to current debates about South Africa's development.

In its concluding words, the introduction to this second volume of *The Cambridge History of South Africa* pointed to the importance of new kinds of stories and themes that are continuing to unfold. Those touched on in this concise historiographic overview are not only representative of such newer interpretations of aspects of the national past. They also raise in another form a large point about historical understanding of South African society that the contributors to the present volume all, in one way or another, recognise. It is not merely that scholars of any stripe can no longer have the confidence of earlier liberal, nationalist or Marxist schools that they can write the story of South Africa's history in an entirely convincing way. In part, that is because of a heightened sensitivity to the complexities of historical factors, be they religion, gender or the environment. But it is partly also because of an awareness of the complications of multiple perspectives and of the resonance of an emerging range of new topics with their own explanatory power and expository techniques.

SELECT FURTHER READING AND BIBLIOGRAPHY

Environment

Bankoff, G. and S. Swart, *Breeds of empire: the 'invention' of the horse in the Philippines and Southern Africa, 1500–1950*, Copenhagen: Nordic Institute of African Studies Press, 2007

Beinart, W., *The rise of conservation in South Africa: settlers, livestock and the environment, 1770–1950*, Oxford: Oxford University Press, 2003

Beinart, W. and P. Coates, *Environment and history: the taming of nature in the USA and South Africa*, London: Routledge, 1995

Brown, K., 'Political entomology: the insectile challenge to agricultural development in the Cape Colony, 1895–1910', *Journal of Southern African Studies* 29:2 (2003), 529–49

Carruthers, J., *The Kruger National Park: a social and political history*, Pietermaritzburg: University of Natal Press, 1995

Crosby, A., 'The past and the present of environmental history', *American Historical Review* 100:4 (1995), 1177–89

Dicke, B. H., 'The tsetse-fly's influence on South African history', *South African Journal of Science* 29 (1932), 792–96

Dovers, S., R. Edgecombe and B. Guest, *South Africa's environmental history: cases and comparisons*, Athens: Ohio University Press, 2003

Dubow, S., *A commonwealth of knowledge: science, sensibility and white South Africa, 1820–2000*, Oxford: Oxford University Press, 2000

Griffiths, T. and L. Robin (eds.), *Ecology and empire: environmental history of settler societies*, Seattle: University of Washington Press, 1997

Guelke, L. and R. Shell, 'Landscape of conquest: frontier water alienation and Khoikhoi strategies of survival, 1652–1780', *Journal of Southern African Studies* 18:4 (1992), 803–23

Hoffman, T. and S. Todd, 'A national review of land degradation in South Africa: the influence of biophysical and socio-economic factors', *Journal of Southern African Studies* 26:4 (2000), 743–58

Phoofolo, P., 'Epidemics and revolutions: the rinderpest epidemic in late nineteenth century southern Africa', *Past and Present* 138 (1993), 112–43

Steyn, P., 'The lingering environmental impact of repressive governance: the environmental legacy of the apartheid-era for the new South Africa', *Globalizations* 2:3 (2005), 391–403

Van Der Merwe, P. J., *The migrant farmer in the history of the Cape Colony, 1657–1842*, trans. R. Beck, Athens: Ohio University Press, 1995

Van Sittert, L., 'The supernatural state: water divining and the Cape underground water rush, 1891–1910', *Journal of Social History* 37:4 (2004), 915–37

Van Sittert, L. and S. Swart (eds.), *Canis familiaris: a dog history of southern Africa*, Leiden: Brill, 2008

Heritage

Coombes, A., *History after apartheid: visual culture and public memory in a democratic South Africa*, Johannesburg: Witwatersrand University Press, 2004

Dubin, S., *Transforming museums: mounting Queen Victoria in a democratic South Africa*, London: Palgrave Macmillan, 2006

Grundlingh, A., 'A cultural conundrum? Old monuments and new regimes: the Voortrekker Monument as symbol of Afrikaner power in post-apartheid South Africa', *Radical History Review* 81 (2001), 95–112

Grundlingh, A., 'Reframing remembrance: the politics of the Centenary commemoration of the South African War of 1899–1902', *Journal of Southern African Studies* 30:2 (2004), 358–77

Hamilton, C., 'The poetics and politics of public history', *South African Historical Journal* 27:1 (1992), 234–7

Hansen, B. R., 'Public spaces for national commemoration: the case of Emlotheni Memorial, Port Elizabeth', *Anthropology and Humanism* 28:1 (2003), 43–60

Kerseboom, S., '"Our Khoi heroine": remembering and recreating Sara Baartman in post-apartheid South Africa, 1994–2007', unpublished M.A. thesis, University of Stellenbosch (2007)

Kros, C., 'Heritage vs. history: the end of a noble tradition?' *Historia* 48:1 (2003), 326–36

Kros, C., 'Public history/heritage: translation, transgression or more of the same', *African Studies* 69 (2010), 63–77

Lalu, P., *The deaths of Hintsa: postapartheid South Africa and the shape of recurring pasts*, Pretoria: HSRC Press, 2009

Nasson, W., 'Commemorating the Anglo-Boer War in post-apartheid South Africa', *Radical History Review* 78 (2000), 140–59

Rassool, C., 'Power, knowledge, and the politics of public pasts', *African Studies* 69:1 (2010), 79–101

Rassool, C., 'The rise of heritage and the reconstitution of history in South Africa', *Kronos* 26 (2000), 1–21

Rassool, C., L. Witz and G. Minkley, 'Repackaging the past for South African tourism', *Daedalus* 130:1 (2000), 277–96

Witz, L., *Apartheid's festival: contesting South Africa's national pasts*, Cape Town: David Philip, 2003

Witz, L., 'From Langa Market Hall and Rhodes Estate to the Grand Parade and the Foreshore: contesting Van Riebeeck's Cape Town', *Kronos* 25 (1999), 187–206

Resistance

Barrell, H., 'Conscripts to their age: African National Congress operational strategy, 1976–1986', unpublished D.Phil. thesis, Oxford University (1993)

Dubow, S., *The African National Congress*, Johannesburg: Jonathan Ball, 2000

Ellis, S. and T. Sechaba, *Comrades against apartheid: the ANC and the South African Communist Party in exile*, London: James Currey; Bloomington: Indiana University Press, 1992

Fieldhouse, R., *Anti-apartheid: a history of the movement in Britain*, London: Merlin Press, 2005

Gerhart, G., *Black power in South Africa: the evolution of an ideology*, Berkeley: University of California Press, 1978

Karis, T. and G. M. Carter (eds.), *From protest to challenge: a documentary history of African politics in South Africa, 1882–1964*, 4 vols., Stanford, CA: Hoover Institution Press, 1972–1977

Karis, T. and G. Gerhart (eds.), *From protest to challenge: a documentary history of African politics in South Africa*, vol. 5, *Nadir and resurgence, 1964–1979*, Pretoria: UNISA Press; Bloomington: Indiana University Press, 1997

Lodge, T., *Black politics in South Africa since 1945*, London: Longman, 1983

Lodge, T. and W. Nasson, *All, here, and now: black politics in South Africa in the 1980s*, London: Hurst, 1992

Minter, W., G. Hovey and Charles Cobb Jr. (eds.), *No easy victories: African liberation and American activists over half a century*, Trenton, NJ: Africa World Press, 2008

Roux, E., *Time longer than rope: a history of the black man's struggle for freedom in South Africa*, 2nd ed., Madison: University of Wisconsin Press, 1964

Sellstrom, T., *Sweden and national liberation in southern Africa*, 2 vols., Uppsala: Nordic Africa Institute, 2002

Shubin, V., *ANC: a view from Moscow*, Cape Town: Mayibuye Books, 1999; new ed., Cape Town: Jacana, 2008

South African Democracy Education Trust, *The road to democracy in South Africa, 1960–1980*, 3 vols., Cape Town: Zebra Press, 2004; Pretoria: UNISA Press, 2006–2008

Vigne, R., *Liberals against apartheid: a history of the Liberal Party of South Africa, 1953–68*, London: Macmillan, 1997

Walshe, P., *The rise of African nationalism in South Africa: the African National Congress, 1912–1952*, Berkeley: University of California Press, 1971

Health

Deacon, H., H. Phillips and E. van Heyningen (eds.), *The Cape doctor in the nineteenth century: a social history*, Amsterdam: Rodopi, 2004

Digby, A., *Diversity and division in medicine: health care in South Africa from the 1800s*, Oxford: Lang, 2006

Flint, K. E., *Healing traditions: African medicine, cultural exchange, and competition in South Africa, 1820–1948* (Athens: Ohio University Press; Scottsville: University of KwaZulu-Natal Press, 2008

Jochelson, K., *The colour of disease: syphilis and racism in South Africa, 1880–1950*, New York: Palgrave, in association with St Antony's College, 2001

Katz, E., *The white death: silicosis on the Witwatersrand gold mines, 1886–1910*, Johannesburg: Witwatersrand University Press, 1994

Klausen, S., *Race, maternity and the politics of birth control in South Africa, 1910–1939*, Basingstoke, U.K.: Palgrave Macmillan, 2004

Marks, S., *Divided sisterhood: race, class and gender in the South African nursing profession*, London: Macmillan; New York: St Martin's Press, 1994

McCulloch, J., *Asbestos blues: labour, capital, physicians and the state in South Africa*, Oxford: James Currey; Bloomington: Indiana University Press, 2002

Packard, R. M., *White plague, black labour: tuberculosis and the political economy of health and disease in South Africa*, Pietermaritzburg: University of Natal Press; London: James Currey, 1990

Parle, J., *States of mind: searching for mental health in Natal and Zululand, 1868–1918*, Scottsville: University of KwaZulu-Natal Press, 2007

Phillips, H., *'Black October': the impact of the Spanish Influenza epidemic of 1918 on South Africa*, Pretoria: Government Printer, 1990

STATISTICAL APPENDIX

TABLE IA. *Population, 1910–1950*

	Population (thousands)				Whites	Total	Growth rate (%per annum compound)		Shares by population group			
	Africans	Coloureds	Asians	Whites					Africans	Coloureds	Asians	Whites
1910	4156	517	148	1257	1257	6078			68.4%	8.5%	2.4%	20.7%
1911	4237	526	153	1280	1280	6196			68.4%	8.5%	2.5%	20.7%
1912	4322	530	154	1305	1305	6311			68.5%	8.4%	2.4%	20.7%
1913	4406	534	156	1330	1330	6426			68.6%	8.3%	2.4%	20.7%
1914	4491	538	157	1355	1355	6541			68.7%	8.2%	2.4%	20.7%
1915	4576	541	159	1380	1380	6656			68.7%	8.1%	2.4%	20.7%
1916	4660	545	161	1405	1405	6771			68.8%	8.0%	2.4%	20.8%
1917	4746	549	162	1429	1429	6886			68.9%	8.0%	2.4%	20.8%
1918	4830	553	164	1454	1454	7001			69.0%	7.9%	2.3%	20.8%
1919	4779	539	163	1476	1476	6957			68.7%	7.7%	2.3%	21.2%
1920	4865	542	164	1500	1500	7071	1910–20	1.52%	68.8%	7.7%	2.3%	21.2%
1921	4957	548	166	1524	1524	7195			68.9%	7.6%	2.3%	21.2%
1922	5090	563	170	1550	1550	7373			69.0%	7.6%	2.3%	21.0%
1923	5223	578	174	1586	1586	7561			69.1%	7.6%	2.3%	21.0%
1924	5356	593	177	1620	1620	7746			69.1%	7.7%	2.3%	20.9%
1925	5489	608	181	1650	1650	7928			69.2%	7.7%	2.3%	20.8%
1926	5622	623	184	1682	1682	8111			69.3%	7.7%	2.3%	20.7%
1927	5755	638	188	1710	1710	8291			69.4%	7.7%	2.3%	20.6%
1928	5888	653	191	1741	1741	8473			69.5%	7.7%	2.3%	20.5%

(continued)

TABLE 1A (*continued*)

	Population (thousands)							Growth rate (% per annum compound)		Shares by population group			
	Africans	Coloureds	Asians	Whites	Whites	Total				Africans	Coloureds	Asians	Whites
1929	6021	667	195	1770	1770	8653				69.6%	7.7%	2.3%	20.5%
1930	6154	682	199	1801	1801	8836	1920–30	2.25%		69.6%	7.7%	2.3%	20.4%
1931	6287	697	202	1833	1833	9019				69.7%	7.7%	2.2%	20.3%
1932	6420	713	206	1868	1868	9207				69.7%	7.7%	2.2%	20.3%
1933	6553	727	210	1899	1899	9389				69.8%	7.7%	2.2%	20.2%
1934	6686	742	213	1934	1934	9575				69.8%	7.7%	2.2%	20.2%
1935	6819	757	217	1970	1970	9763				69.8%	7.8%	2.2%	20.2%
1936	6950	772	221	2009	2009	9952				69.8%	7.8%	2.2%	20.2%
1937	7111	788	227	2041	2041	10167				69.9%	7.8%	2.2%	20.1%
1938	7272	804	234	2085	2085	10395				70.0%	7.7%	2.3%	20.1%
1939	7436	820	240	2123	2123	10619				70.0%	7.7%	2.3%	20.0%
1940	7671	836	247	2160	2160	10914	1930–40	2.13%		70.3%	7.7%	2.3%	19.8%
1941	7766	852	253	2197	2197	11068				70.2%	7.7%	2.3%	19.8%
1942	7933	868	260	2231	2231	11292				70.3%	7.7%	2.3%	19.8%
1943	8101	883	267	2268	2268	11519				70.3%	7.7%	2.3%	19.7%
1944	8270	899	273	2305	2305	11747				70.4%	7.7%	2.3%	19.6%
1945	8442	915	280	2342	2342	11979				70.5%	7.6%	2.3%	19.6%
1946	8618	931	286	2380	2380	12215				70.6%	7.6%	2.3%	19.5%
1947	8820	964	301	2432	2432	12517				70.5%	7.7%	2.4%	19.4%
1948	9024	999	317	2505	2505	12845				70.3%	7.8%	2.5%	19.5%
1949	9229	1034	336	2565	2565	13164				70.1%	7.9%	2.6%	19.5%
1950	9438	1070	353	2609	2609	13470	1940–50	2.13%		70.1%	7.9%	2.6%	19.4%

TABLE 1B. *Population, 1951–2000*

	Population (thousands)					Total	Growth rate (% per annum compound)		Shares by population group			
	Africans	Coloureds	Asians	Whites	Whites	Total			Africans	Coloureds	Asians	Whites
1951	9645	1108	368	2649	2649	13770			70.0%	8.0%	2.7%	19.2%
1952	9915	1138	378	2695	2695	14126			70.2%	8.1%	2.7%	19.1%
1953	10192	1171	389	2751	2751	14503			70.3%	8.1%	2.7%	19.0%
1954	10474	1207	400	2803	2803	14884			70.4%	8.1%	2.7%	18.8%
1955	10761	1242	410	2856	2856	15269			70.5%	8.1%	2.7%	18.7%
1956	11053	1281	421	2907	2907	15662			70.6%	8.2%	2.7%	18.6%
1957	11362	1319	431	2957	2957	16069			70.7%	8.2%	2.7%	18.4%
1958	11665	1360	441	3011	3011	16477			70.8%	8.3%	2.7%	18.3%
1959	11974	1405	450	3067	3067	16896			70.9%	8.3%	2.7%	18.2%
1960	12287	1450	459	3123	3123	17319	1950–60	2.55%	70.9%	8.4%	2.7%	18.0%
1961	12416	1554	488	3119	3119	17577			70.6%	8.8%	2.8%	17.7%
1962	12764	1607	503	3174	3174	18048			70.7%	8.9%	2.8%	17.6%
1963	13123	1663	517	3244	3244	18547			70.8%	9.0%	2.8%	17.5%
1964	13491	1723	531	3331	3331	19076			70.7%	9.0%	2.8%	17.5%
1965	13869	1782	548	3408	3408	19607			70.7%	9.1%	2.8%	17.4%
1966	14259	1844	566	3493	3493	20162			70.7%	9.1%	2.8%	17.3%
1967	14659	1905	584	3577	3577	20725			70.7%	9.2%	2.8%	17.3%
1968	15070	1966	601	3655	3655	21292			70.8%	9.2%	2.8%	17.2%
1969	15493	2020	622	3746	3746	21881			70.8%	9.2%	2.8%	17.1%
1970	15779	2170	652	3864	3864	22465	1960–70	2.64%	70.2%	9.7%	2.9%	17.2%
1971	16212	2217	668	3925	3917	23014			70.4%	9.6%	2.9%	17.1%
1972	16719	2266	683	3987	3970	23658			70.7%	9.6%	2.9%	16.9%
1973	17231	2315	699	4050	4025	24270			71.0%	9.5%	2.9%	16.7%
1974	17720	2366	715	4114	4080	24881			71.2%	9.5%	2.9%	16.5%

(continued)

TABLE 1B (continued)

	Population (thousands) Africans	Coloureds	Asians	Whites	Whites	Total	Growth rate (% per annum compound)		Shares by population group Africans	Coloureds	Asians	Whites
1975	18137	2418	732	4179	4136	25423			71.3%	9.5%	2.9%	16.4%
1976	18635	2470	749	4245	4192	26046			71.5%	9.5%	2.9%	16.3%
1977	19020	2524	768	4312	4249	26561			71.6%	9.5%	2.9%	16.2%
1978	19438	2579	786	4380	4307	27110			71.7%	9.5%	2.9%	16.2%
1979	19891	2636	803	4449	4366	27695			71.8%	9.5%	2.9%	16.1%
1980	20377	2695	819	4522	4428	28819	1970–80	2.34%	72.0%	9.5%	2.9%	16.0%
1981	20900	2757	836	4598	4502	28994			72.1%	9.5%	2.9%	15.9%
1982	21459	2816	851	4675	4577	29703			72.2%	9.5%	2.9%	15.7%
1983	22084	2872	869	4747	4647	30472			72.5%	9.4%	2.9%	15.6%
1984	22721	2929	886	4812	4711	31247			72.7%	9.4%	2.8%	15.4%
1985	23370	2986	902	4867	4761	32019			73.0%	9.3%	2.8%	15.2%
1986	24032	3042	918	4908	4787	32779			73.3%	9.3%	2.8%	15.0%
1987	24707	3095	932	4938	4813	33547			73.6%	9.2%	2.8%	14.7%
1988	25368	3146	947	4969	4839	34299			74.0%	9.2%	2.8%	14.5%
1989	26013	3199	961	5006	4865	35038			74.2%	9.1%	2.7%	14.3%
1990	26664	3251	976	5044	4891	35782	1980–90	2.37%	74.5%	9.1%	2.7%	14.1%
1991	27400	3254	960	4238	4841	36455			75.2%	8.9%	2.6%	11.6%
1992	28072	3317	976	4275	4792	37157			75.5%	8.9%	2.6%	11.5%
1993	28760	3381	992	4312	4744	37877			75.9%	8.9%	2.6%	11.4%
1994	29464	3447	1008	4349	4696	38615			76.3%	8.9%	2.6%	11.3%
1995	30184	3514	1024	4387	4648	39370			76.7%	8.9%	2.6%	11.1%
1996	30922	3582	1041	4424	4647	40192			76.9%	8.9%	2.6%	11.0%
1997	31677	3651	1058	4462	4646	41032			77.2%	8.9%	2.6%	10.9%
1998	32449	3721	1075	4500	4646	41891			77.5%	8.9%	2.6%	10.7%
1999	33240	3793	1092	4539	4645	42770			77.7%	8.9%	2.6%	10.6%
2000	33879	3797	1093	4522	4644	43413	1990–2000	1.95%	78.0%	8.7%	2.5%	10.4%

Source: The estimates are based on estimates from Union Statistics for Fifty Years, South African Statistics 1978, South African Statistics 2002 and Sadie (1988, 1991, 1993).

TABLE 2. *Vital statistics, 1911–1996*

Year	Life expectancy at birth								Total fertility rate			
	Africans		Coloureds		Asians		Whites		Africans	Coloureds	Asians	Whites
	Males	Females	Males	Females	Males	Females	Males	Females				
1911												
1921												
1924–28												3.49
1930–33												3.16
1936											7.30	
1935–37												3.01
1936–41	39.6	40.5	43.2	43.6	52.7	50.9	58.6	62.5	6.48	6.05		
1941											7.20	
1941–44												3.16
1941–46	38.2	38.5	42.2	44.7	51.3	49.9	61.0	65.0	6.59	5.87		
1946											6.70	
1945–50												3.38
1946–51	41.0	41.5	45.5	47.4	54.9	55.1	63.7	68.3	6.69	6.16		
1951											6.11	
1950–55												3.38
1951–55	44.9	46.6	49.1	52.3	58.3	59.9	64.1	69.4	6.75	6.42	5.45	
1955–60												3.50
1956–60	49.2	53.1	51.3	56.1	59.0	61.2	64.2	70.0	6.75	6.67	5.18	
1960												
1960–65	50.7	56.9	51.7	56.6	60.1	63.0	64.6	71.7	6.56	6.71	4.55	3.23
1965–70	51.1	57.9	50.6	56.9	59.8	63.9	64.5	72.6	6.28	6.29	4.01	3.03
1970												
1970–75	53.2	60.3	50.9	58.2	60.0	65.1	65.2	72.8	5.98	5.43	3.78	2.80
1975–80	54.1	61.6	53.8	61.4	61.4	67.2	65.9	73.5	5.64	3.88	2.94	2.15
1980–85	56.4	63.6	55.4	63.6	63.1	69.8	66.8	74.3	5.29	3.31	2.80	2.10
1985–90	57.8	64.8	57.6	65.7	64.5	71.2	69.4	75.8	4.34	2.80	2.45	1.81
1990–95	59.8	66.8	58.5	66.7	64.7	71.8	69.3	76.5	3.96	2.37	2.29	1.73

Source: Sadie (1988, 1991, 1993) for fertility and mortality.

TABLE 3A. *Marital status, 1911 census*

Numbers	All others		White	
	Male	Female	Male	Female
15–19 yrs				
Never married	237412	221522	63822	57747
Married	3935	18318	147	3919
Widower/widow	28	299	3	27
Divorced/separated	49	58	1	2
Unspecified	148	362	9	12
20–24 yrs				
Never married	188798	97583	59089	30930
Married	36528	108256	6543	26230
Widower/widow	316	3051	46	256
Divorced/separated	133	435	7	34
Unspecified	286	317	41	17
25–29 yrs				
Never married	127881	32168	36385	12779
Married	100158	146276	25957	37743
Widower/widow	1319	6779	292	625
Divorced/separated	168	683	51	114
Unspecified	204	129	31	9
30–34 yrs				
Never married	60325	14093	21614	6164
Married	121460	151013	39007	36861
Widower/widow	2340	11325	589	1115
Divorced/separated	202	848	109	119
Unspecified	195	84	29	8
35–39 yrs				
Never married	27592	6275	12856	4177
Married	111963	105761	40340	32483
Widower/widow	2844	11319	925	1647
Divorced/separated	232	568	155	117
Unspecified	112	38	15	6
40–44 yrs				
Never married	16177	4630	7080	2790
Married	96514	87174	32994	25008
Widower/widow	3468	15365	1149	2184
Divorced/separated	234	522	147	105
Unspecified	110	41	12	9
45–49 yrs				
Never married	7314	2644	4074	1978
Married	72047	55212	25701	18702
Widower/widow	3088	14603	1224	2506
Divorced/separated	154	353	116	58
Unspecified	40	30	19	5
50–54 yrs				
Never married	5343	2459	2724	1446
Married	54954	47348	19282	13282
Widower/widow	3495	23130	1422	3054
Divorced/separated	154	284	97	41
Unspecified	51	56	8	3

TABLE 3B. *1936 census numbers*

	Coloured		Asian		White	
	Male	Female	Male	Female	Male	Female
15–19 yrs						
Never married	36485	35196	11977	6806	97549	88678
Married	281	2403	753	4357	296	6459
Widower/widow	11	47	10	48	4	53
Divorced/separated	1	26	9	36	1	28
Unspecified	5	14	8	9	14	12
20–24 yrs						
Never married	27157	21485	6207	1640	81064	54382
Married	6288	15508	4438	7596	13283	39372
Widower/widow	103	317	78	152	72	272
Divorced/separated	26	145	42	78	67	311
Unspecified	71	55	45	10	184	125
25–29 yrs						
Never married	13727	9327	1826	420	44765	26990
Married	15955	20665	6345	6832	46281	62436
Widower/widow	318	600	125	233	306	803
Divorced/separated	102	211	48	49	367	764
Unspecified	53	45	70	8	220	117
30–34 yrs						
Never married	6963	4403	556	142	17993	12908
Married	16881	17848	5327	5043	55273	57612
Widower/widow	499	950	130	297	499	1332
Divorced/separated	119	209	25	33	608	890
Unspecified	58	30	46	7	126	62
35–39 yrs						
Never married	4570	2634	310	69	8643	8034
Married	16301	16217	5201	4024	50224	50796
Widower/widow	647	1235	180	399	656	2459
Divorced/separated	154	206	42	30	757	967
Unspecified	46	25	26	7	86	57
40–44 yrs						
Never married	2719	1631	202	57	5669	5537
Married	13360	12503	4043	2708	50232	47817
Widower/widow	743	1681	216	511	937	3929
Divorced/separated	132	169	28	16	638	857
Unspecified	32	20	25	4	64	60
45–49 yrs						
Never married	2077	1170	248	41	4528	4407
Married	12490	10758	4471	2143	45102	40605
Widower/widow	950	1991	341	669	1192	5473
Divorced/separated	136	149	49	23	629	707
Unspecified	26	15	20	5	73	38
50–54 yrs						
Never married	1581	881	273	40	3677	3437
Married	10227	10756	4110	1503	39498	31908
Widower/widow	1139	1991	464	744	1683	6783
Divorced/separated	103	149	43	23	512	549
Unspecified	29	15	16	8	54	40

TABLE 3C. *1946 and 1951 census numbers*

	African (1946)		Coloured (1946)		Asian (1946)		White (1951)	
	Male	Female	Male	Female	Male	Female	Male	Female
15–19 yrs								
Never married	406170	358594	47189	47094	15314	11558	107950	95513
Married	7315	31192	355	2497	327	3487	466	9504
Widower/widow	64	430	12	26	4	37	6	16
Divorced/separated	22	240	2	18	4	23	2	56
Unspecified	948	853	100	397	33	35	6	12
20–24 yrs								
Never married	263858	143918	32263	23912	8764	3474	80827	13754
Married	69123	180284	6676	15486	4114	8769	22929	8001
Widower/widow	595	4912	89	290	58	156	50	25
Divorced/separated	223	1666	62	201	30	91	201	74
Unspecified	2292	1309	877	1504	88	65	57	4
25–29 yrs								
Never married	175566	55686	15974	9668	2760	892	32099	28596
Married	191944	238719	16727	21669	7924	8984	65424	51910
Widower/widow	1836	11065	332	723	128	319	180	202
Divorced/separated	757	2819	176	346	58	103	942	706
Unspecified	1836	809	1392	1590	65	29	58	31
30–34 yrs								
Never married	74405	25110	7388	4986	836	313	14105	13750
Married	214924	223891	19916	21504	8137	7392	81053	83205
Widower/widow	3365	19045	552	1187	125	463	356	617
Divorced/separated	1185	3132	254	385	67	88	1444	1633
Unspecified	1192	507	1323	1284	44	19	37	19
35–39 yrs								
Never married	40934	12571	4618	3145	380	207	9235	8093
Married	218004	176661	19638	18898	7341	5621	84671	84935
Widower/widow	4410	21538	740	1522	152	625	582	1315
Divorced/separated	1369	2456	251	372	40	66	1852	2069
Unspecified	806	344	1135	1059	22	19	40	14
40–44 yrs								
Never married	21985	8060	3004	2059	180	118	7071	7518
Married	181079	153247	16620	15164	5344	3734	82275	83887
Widower/widow	5392	32095	863	2039	186	792	841	2367
Divorced/separated	1258	2031	235	288	34	28	1918	2577
Unspecified	602	319	1055	870	23	14	37	18
45–49 yrs								
Never married	13437	4895	2404	1475	137	48	4895	7776
Married	159022	106247	13863	11803	4646	2584	65327	76189
Widower/widow	6246	35621	1016	2356	232	934	1131	4184
Divorced/separated	1119	1384	179	215	29	29	1681	2632
Unspecified	387	199	716	615	20	14	39	26
50–54 yrs								
Never married	7276	3113	1543	1008	92	37	3583	6671
Married	100857	75885	9869	8049	3013	1490	48608	57055
Widower/widow	5700	41533	1051	2582	258	818	1386	5914
Divorced/separated	647	1007	139	136	21	21	1278	2277
Unspecified	240	181	568	420	7	12	36	17

TABLE 3D. *1960 census numbers*

	African		Coloured		Asian		White	
	Male	Female	Male	Female	Male	Female	Male	Female
15–19 yrs								
Never married	514534	459330	70624	67760	27548	24747	137170	123637
Married	7985	51611	663	4744	185	3379	679	10386
Widower/widow	30	358	5	20	3	8	5	28
Divorced/separated	16	378	1	34	0	16	3	69
Unspecified	52	51	0	3	2	1	1	1
20–24 yrs								
Never married	373256	208804	49144	38942	17362	10668	87619	45259
Married	99143	258960	15605	28824	4540	12189	29904	69218
Widower/widow	369	3754	55	213	12	97	37	234
Divorced/separated	389	2696	75	257	18	123	330	973
Unspecified	6761	4541	807	422	495	260	422	157
25–29 yrs								
Never married	201259	85590	20805	16006	6105	3624	28032	10709
Married	242191	322572	32456	38832	11126	13810	75221	89042
Widower/widow	1244	9291	184	580	32	252	134	535
Divorced/separated	1213	4882	211	619	48	188	1174	1859
Unspecified	5737	2905	526	275	223	152	227	70
30–34 yrs								
Never married	88832	42354	10746	8097	2016	1527	12232	6265
Married	277802	294295	34685	36394	13101	12769	88560	92503
Widower/widow	2332	16705	394	1084	70	501	263	1112
Divorced/separated	1926	5552	369	826	65	235	1814	2428
Unspecified	3501	1648	244	131	63	62	105	34
35–39 yrs								
Never married	50652	22572	6558	4624	791	649	7568	5175
Married	279665	247067	30499	30069	11551	10669	87860	88519
Widower/widow	3335	23189	577	1476	74	873	411	1995
Divorced/separated	2121	5054	412	781	82	168	2223	2796
Unspecified	2523	1044	164	91	28	26	67	31
40–44 yrs								
Never married	29420	14639	4425	3164	403	294	5592	4940
Married	253702	214715	26170	24865	10094	8194	84034	82182
Widower/widow	5254	37944	904	2502	132	1202	685	3740
Divorced/separated	2210	4772	418	741	90	150	2333	3076
Unspecified	1826	711	150	69	11	9	52	36
45–49 yrs								
Never married	18129	8267	3187	2352	246	161	5087	5585
Married	216798	147657	22986	20918	8591	5913	83949	77687
Widower/widow	5879	41852	1142	3417	209	1730	1112	6587
Divorced/separated	1955	3196	395	644	68	90	2346	3256
Unspecified	1283	538	99	58	5	7	52	49
50–54 yrs								
Never married	10712	5461	2316	1660	146	86	4648	6275
Married	153071	107630	18290	15183	6165	3400	75447	65252
Widower/widow	6652	51700	1433	4190	254	1836	1598	10233
Divorced/separated	1422	2073	343	447	41	57	2034	3035
Unspecified	873	476	92	54	16	4	45	57

TABLE 3E. *Singulate mean age at marriage and proportions never married at age 50,*
1911–1996

| | Singulate mean age at marriage | | | | | | | |
| | Africans | | Coloureds | | Asians | | Whites | |
	Male	Female	Male	Female	Male	Female	Male	Female
1911	28.8	22.9					29.3	23.6
1936			27.4	24.8	23.5	19.1	27.7	24.4
1946	27.6	23.1	27.2	24.5	24.9	20.8		
1951							25.8	24.1
1960	27.4	23.2	26.4	24.3	26.4	23.3	25.2	21.3
1996	31.1	28.1	27.1	26.7	26.7	23.5	26.7	24.4

| | Percentage never married at age 50 | | | | | | | |
| | Africans | | Coloureds | | Asians | | Whites | |
	Male	Female	Male	Female	Male	Female	Male	Female
1911	8.6	3.5					12.3	8.3
1936			12.7	7.4	5.2	1.6	8.5	8.3
1946	6.9	2.9	13.0	8.9	2.7	1.4		
1951							6.6	8.9
1960	6.9	3.7	10.9	8.2	2.5	1.8	5.5	6.7
1996	16.7	19.5	14.1	15.3	4.4	7.6	4.9	4.2

TABLE 4. *Household structure, 1996*

	Africans	Coloureds	Asians	Whites	Africans	Coloureds	Asians	Whites
Average household size	4.27	4.42	4.17	2.89				
Identity of head								
Male	56.7%	71.4%	81.9%	78.3%	3667804	522626	199040	1144049
Female never married	14.2%	8.7%	2.7%	4.7%	916015	63672	6447	69241
Female married	17.2%	5.9%	3.2%	2.6%	1114573	43501	7750	38064
Female widowed	8.9%	9.2%	9.1%	8.8%	578464	67570	22127	129298
Female divorced/separated	2.8%	4.7%	3.2%	5.5%	183883	34690	7686	80637
Female marital status not known	0.1%	0.0%	0.0%	0.0%	9554	361	94	529
Total	100.0%	100.0%	100.0%	100.0%	6470293	732420	243144	1461818
Structure of household								
Single person	17.21%	8.47%	5.59%	18.74%	1113661	62022	13596	273899
Unrelated persons	1.25%	1.28%	0.63%	2.77%	80570	9356	1536	40560
Husband and wife only	7.19%	8.01%	8.21%	24.11%	465396	58668	19961	352407
Husband and wife and children	20.08%	35.68%	45.80%	32.78%	1299009	261300	111358	479189
Father and children	2.25%	1.27%	1.24%	1.32%	145803	9325	3023	19345
Mother and children	12.58%	7.67%	6.37%	4.19%	813755	56208	15490	61218
Nuclear plus unrelated person(s)	1.10%	3.61%	3.14%	5.93%	70924	26404	7623	86664
Upward extension	2.50%	1.90%	4.87%	2.88%	161844	13880	11834	42140
Upward extension plus unrelated person(s)	0.08%	0.21%	0.37%	0.43%	5424	1503	891	6230
Downward extension	21.00%	17.63%	9.86%	1.89%	1358560	129109	23970	27598
Downward extension plus unrelated person(s)	0.70%	1.91%	0.49%	0.29%	45372	14005	1197	4260
Complex	13.45%	10.99%	12.55%	3.98%	870526	80465	30522	58233
Complex plus unrelated person(s)	0.61%	1.39%	0.88%	0.69%	39450	10176	2143	10073
Total	100.0%	100.0%	100.0%	100.0%	6470294	732421	243144	1461816

TABLE 5. *Language spoken at home, 1936–1996*

Africans	1960	1996
IsiXhosa	28.0%	23.1%
IsiZulu	26.2%	29.5%
IsiNdebele	2.7%	1.9%
SiSwati	3.1%	3.3%
Sesotho	11.8%	10.0%
Setswana	10.5%	10.6%
Sepedi	8.8%	11.9%
Xitsonga	4.6%	5.6%
Tshivenda	2.2%	2.8%
Other African languages	1.5%	0.3%
Afrikaans	0.5%	0.7%
English	0.0%	0.4%
Unspecified	–	–
Total	100.0%	100.0%

Coloureds	1936	1951	1960	1970	1996
English	7.6%	9.8%	10.1%	11.0%	16.4%
Afrikaans	89.9%	89.2%	88.7%	88.0%	82.1%
English and Afrikaans	1.0%	0.8%	0.9%	0.8%	
Dutch	0.1%			0.0%	
Other European languages	0.0%		0.0%	0.0%	
Arabic	0.0%				
Indian languages	0.1%				
African languages	0.7%				1.3%
Khoi or San	0.5%				
Other	0.1%	0.3%	0.2%	0.2%	0.2%
Unspecified	–	–	–	–	–
Total	100.0%	100.0%	100.0%	100.0%	100.0%

Asians	1936	1951	1960	1970	1996
Tamil	38.3%	32.8%	29.7%	24.4%	
Hindi	27.5%	24.3%	26.4%	18.5%	
Telegu	11.5%	8.2%	7.2%	4.9%	
Gujarati	11.6%	10.8%	11.3%	7.3%	
Urdu	6.3%	6.9%	7.5%		
Other Indian	2.0%	7.1%	0.4%		
Chinese	1.1%	1.3%	1.0%		
Japanese	0.1%				
European languages	1.6%				
English		6.0%	14.4%	31.8%	94.4%
Afrikaans		2.0%	1.7%	1.5%	1.5%
English and Afrikaans		0.2%	0.3%	0.4%	
African languages					0.4%
Other	0.1%	0.3%	0.1%	11.3%	3.8%
Unspecified	–	–	–	–	–
Total	100.0%	100.0%	100.0%	100.0%	100.0%

TABLE 5 *(continued)*

Whites	1936	1951	1960	1970	1996
English	39.1%	39.4%	37.1%	37.2%	39.1%
Afrikaans	55.9%	56.9%	58.1%	56.9%	58.5%
English and Afrikaans	2.5%	1.4%	1.6%	1.0%	0.0%
African languages					0.4%
Dutch	0.2%	0.4%	0.7%	0.6%	
German	0.9%	0.7%	1.0%	1.4%	
Yiddish	0.9%	0.4%	0.2%		
Greek	0.1%	0.2%	0.3%		
Italian	0.1%	0.2%	0.4%		
Portuguese	0.1%	0.1%	0.3%		
French	0.1%	0.1%	0.1%		
Other	0.1%	0.2%	0.2%	2.9%	2.0%
Unspecified	–	–	–	–	–
Total	100.0%	100.0%	100.0%	100.0%	100.0%

TABLE 6. *Distribution of religious affiliation by population group, 1921–1996*

	1921	1936	1951	1960	1970	1996
Whites						
African traditional belief						
Buddhist or Confucian						202
Christian	1427715	1854970	2503591	2899756	3540272	3431792
Anglican	294026	345130	416472	384448	404024	237522
Baptist	15414	20152	26717	33929	46427	68068
Catholic	61246	92453	141330	192234	309572	292290
Christian Scientist	2326	7250	6612			
Congregational	10598	11504	13915	15487	21373	11191
Dutch Reformed	838982	1087723	1402703	1615344	1847626	1421089
Other reformed churches						234205
Lutheran	19098	25817	26262	34080	41972	26692
Methodist	102771	141747	219021	267122	361727	310373
Orthodox churches			7347		24389	17002
Presbyterian	74999	82344	100739	111267	118782	73899
Apostolic Faith Mission	7742	31765	50765	60691	72904	211341
Other Apostolic churches			26175		81708	161729
Full Gospel	513	9085	14821		35421	
Pentecostal/charismatic churches						194932
Seventh Day Adventist			618			
Bandla lamaNazaretha			10033	11401	14582	838
Ethiopian-type churches						3865
Zion Christian Church						4006
Other Zionist churches						11841
Other African Independent Churches						4930

(continued)

	1921	1936	1946	1960	1970	1996
African churches						
Other Christian			40061	173753	159765	145979
Hindu			33			1697
Jewish	62103	90645	108497	114762	118200	55734
Muslim			200			3741
All other and unspecified	29670	58242	29317	63181	114810	755012
Other			1978		10617	24580
No religion			14176		69541	224135
Refused, other, not stated			13163		34652	506297
Total	1519488	2003857	2641689	3077699	3773282	4448178
Coloureds						
African traditional belief						188
Buddhist or Confucian	25	1	9			
Christian	498899	709100	847878	1371702	1854734	2867654
Anglican	129182	163423	185827	260849	322790	326080
Baptist	1377	3145	5372		19001	33476
Catholic	13410	36093	56157	118900	197628	340183
Christian Scientist			23			
Congregational	60674	86649	99771	139873	156846	144275
Dutch Reformed	166536	225271	292465	450475	591080	629684
Other reformed churches						32298
Lutheran	46449	59485	48111	73918	95499	109084
Methodist	67917	81475	90056	117123	116131	117058
Orthodox churches			268			716
Presbyterian	7059	6188	4675	6191	7953	9443
Apostolic Faith Mission				17245	20746	111158
Other Apostolic churches			23753	129756	129756	473455

TABLE 6 (continued)

	1921	1936	1946	1960	1970	1996
Full Gospel			1742		11917	284280
Pentecostal/charismatic churches			248			
Seventh Day Adventist			4471		9521	2812
Bandla lamaNazaretha						59986
Ethiopian-type churches						16676
Zion Christian Church						23528
Other Zionist churches						6064
Other African Independent Churches						
African churches			2528			
Other Christian	6295	47371	32411	187128	175866	147398
Hindu	90	291	841			2285
Jewish			86			1058
Muslim	22566	35058	43890	92130	134087	246433
All other and unspecified	23968	25211	35780	46494	61878	398558
Other	1931	403	5362		14501	15004
No religion	6741	19661	17597		25689	79894
Refused, other, not stated	15296	5147	12821		21688	303660
Total	545548	769661	928484	1510326	2050699	3516176
	1921	1936	1946	1960	1970	1996
Asians						
African traditional belief						190
Buddhist or Confucian	12472	1771	2329	1073	874	
Christian	8716	10718	16212	35962	53851	191458
Anglican	1304	2246	2759	6007	7282	5035
Baptist	467	978	1216		2922	3671
Catholic	5419	4775	5249	10316	14755	23219

			1951	1960	1970	1996
Christian Scientist	51					220
Congregational	62	77	266			2159
Dutch Reformed		90				410
Other reformed churches						492
Lutheran	45	50				2357
Methodist	749	1025	1263	2482	2570	1766
Orthodox churches						928
Presbyterian	19	9	61			8062
Apostolic Faith Mission			305			4895
Other Apostolic churches						
Full Gospel			1051		8028	55846
Pentecostal/charismatic churches						
Seventh Day Adventist						219
Bandla lamaNazaretha						1313
Ethiopian-type churches						1977
Zion Christian Church						1980
Other Zionist churches						338
Other African Independent Churches						
African churches						
Other Christian	600	1468	4042	17157	18294	76571
Hindu	109163	159823	180051	327783	430318	516227
Jewish						359
Muslim	26917	42590	61405	99068	125987	236315
All other and unspecified	8463	4789	25263	14088	19342	90813
Other	2289	3174	16748		1920	6040
No religion	3645	716			6104	13341
Refused, other, not stated	2529	899	8515		11318	71432
Total	165731	219691	285260	477974	630372	1035362

(continued)

TABLE 6 (continued)

	1921	1936	1946	1960	1970	1996
Africans						
African traditional belief						16402
Buddhist or Confucian						
Christian			5078910	7420059	10977538	23357231
Anglican			579647	752095	982093	1012157
Baptist			76780	103700	178673	331276
Catholic			462130	755073	1375456	2743200
Christian Scientist						
Congregational			121053	136330	216627	270329
Dutch Reformed			326290	564383	979349	1450447
Other reformed churches						117210
Lutheran			415548	542668	811669	907712
Methodist			1041656	1320566	1825862	2363735
Orthodox churches						13977
Presbyterian			172415	203929	451186	639325
Apostolic Faith Mission			149789	119960	125181	786585
Other Apostolic churches					500025	2852204
Full Gospel					47356	
Pentecostal/charismatic churches					41660	1652829
Seventh Day Adventist			28900	22604	40732	
Bandla lamaNazaretha						448910
Ethiopian-type churches						729435
Zion Christian Church						3826449
Other Zionist churches						2111394
Other African Independent Churches						216680
African churches			1593939	2313365	2716019	
Other Christian			110763	585386	685650	883377
Hindu						12872

		1960	1970	1996
Jewish				10449
Muslim				43253
All other and unspecified	3481173	3501572	4364437	7211129
Other				146757
No religion				4293161
Refused, other, not stated				2771211
Total	8560083	10921631	15339975	30651336
All				
African traditional belief		1073	874	16982
Buddhist or Confucian				0
Christian		11727479	16426395	29848135
Anglican		1403399	1716189	1580794
Baptist		137629	247023	436491
Catholic		1076523	1897411	3398892
Christian Scientist				
Congregational		291690	394846	426015
Dutch Reformed		2630202	3418055	3503379
Other reformed churches				384123
Lutheran		650666	949140	1043980
Methodist		1707293	2306290	2793523
Orthodox churches			24389	3346
Presbyterian		321387	577921	723595
Apostolic Faith Mission		197896	218831	1117146
Other Apostolic churches			711489	3492283
Full Gospel			102722	
Pentecostal/charismatic churches			41660	2187887
Seventh Day Adventist		34005	64835	

(continued)

643

TABLE 6 (continued)

	1921	1936	1946	1951	1960	1970	1996
Bandla lamaNazaretha							452779
Ethiopian-type churches							794599
Zion Christian Church							3849108
Other Zionist churches							2148743
Other African Independent Churches							228012
African churches					2487118	2875784	145979
Other Christian					963424	1039575	1253325
Hindu					327783	430318	533081
Jewish					114762	118200	67600
Muslim					191198	260074	529742
All other and unspecified					3625335	4558467	8455512
Other						27038	192381
No religion						101334	4610531
Refused, other, not stated						67658	3652600
Total					15987630	21794328	39451052
Per cent							
Whites							
African traditional	0.0%	0.0%		0.0%	0.0%	0.0%	0.0%
Buddhist or Confucian	0.0%	0.0%		0.0%	0.0%	0.0%	0.0%
Christian	94.0%	92.6%		94.8%	94.2%	93.8%	80.8%
Denominational	93.4%	90.5%		89.4%	86.2%	84.2%	63.4%
Apostolic/Full Gospel/Pentecostal/Seventh Day Adventist	0.5%	2.0%		3.9%	2.3%	5.4%	13.4%
African	0.0%	0.0%		0.0%	0.0%	0.0%	0.6%
Other	0.0%	0.0%		1.5%	5.6%	4.2%	3.4%

644

Hindu	0.0%	0.0%	0.0%	0.0%	0.0%	0.0%
Jewish	1.3%	3.1%	3.7%	4.1%	4.5%	4.1%
Muslim	0.1%	0.0%	0.0%	0.0%	0.0%	0.0%
All other and unspecified	17.8%	3.0%	2.1%	1.1%	2.9%	2.0%
Total	100.0%	100.0%	100.0%	100.0%	100.0%	100.0%

Coloureds

African traditional	0.0%	0.0%	0.0%	0.0%	0.0%	0.0%
Buddhist or Confucian	0.0%	0.0%	0.0%	0.0%	0.0%	0.0%
Christian	81.6%	90.4%	90.8%	91.3%	92.1%	91.4%
Denominational	49.6%	73.5%	77.3%	84.3%	86.0%	90.3%
Apostolic/Full Gospel/Pentecostal/Seventh Day Adventist	24.7%	8.4%	1.1%	3.3%	0.0%	0.0%
African	3.1%	0.0%	0.0%	0.3%	0.0%	0.0%
Other	4.2%	8.6%	12.4%	3.5%	6.2%	1.2%
Hindu	0.1%	0.0%	0.0%	0.1%	0.0%	0.0%
Jewish	0.0%	0.0%	0.0%	0.0%	0.0%	0.0%
Muslim	7.0%	6.5%	6.1%	4.7%	4.6%	4.1%
All other and unspecified	11.3%	3.0%	3.1%	3.9%	3.3%	4.4%
Total	100.0%	100.0%	100.0%	100.0%	100.0%	100.0%

Asians

African traditional	0.0%	0.0%	0.0%	0.0%	0.0%	0.0%
Buddhist or Confucian	0.0%	0.1%	0.2%	0.8%	0.8%	7.5%
Christian	18.5%	8.5%	7.5%	5.7%	4.9%	5.3%
Denominational	3.9%	4.4%	3.9%	3.8%	4.2%	4.9%
Apostolic/Full Gospel/Pentecostal/Seventh Day Adventist	6.6%	1.3%	0.0%	0.5%	0.0%	0.0%
African	0.6%	0.0%	0.0%	0.0%	0.0%	0.0%
Other	7.4%	2.9%	3.6%	1.4%	0.7%	0.4%
Hindu	49.9%	68.3%	68.6%	63.1%	72.7%	65.9%
Jewish	0.0%	0.0%	0.0%	0.0%	0.0%	0.0%
Muslim	22.8%	20.0%	20.7%	21.5%	19.4%	16.2%

(continued)

TABLE 6 (continued)

	1921	1936	1946	1951	1960	1970	1996
All other and unspecified	5.1%	2.2%	8.9%		2.9%	3.1%	8.8%
Total	100.0%	100.0%	100.0%		100.0%	100.0%	100.0%
Africans							
African traditional					0.0%	0.0%	0.1%
Buddhist or Confucian					0.0%	0.0%	0.0%
Christian					67.9%	71.6%	76.2%
Denominational					40.1%	44.5%	32.1%
Apostolic/Full Gospel/Pentecostal/Seventh Day Adventist					1.3%	4.9%	18.7%
African					21.2%	17.7%	23.9%
Other					5.4%	4.5%	2.9%
Hindu					0.0%	0.0%	0.0%
Jewish					0.0%	0.0%	0.0%
Muslim					0.0%	0.0%	0.1%
All other and unspecified					32.1%	28.4%	23.5%
Total					100.0%	100.0%	100.0%
All							
African traditional					0.0%	0.0%	0.0%
Buddhist or Confucian					0.0%	0.0%	0.0%
Christian					73.4%	75.4%	75.7%
Denominational					51.4%	52.9%	36.3%
Apostolic/Full Gospel/Pentecostal/Seventh Day Adventist					1.5%	5.2%	18.4%
African					15.6%	13.2%	19.3%
Other					6.0%	4.8%	3.2%
Hindu					2.1%	2.0%	1.4%
Jewish					0.7%	0.5%	0.2%
Muslim					1.2%	1.2%	1.3%
All other and unspecified					22.7%	20.9%	21.4%
Total					100.0%	100.0%	100.0%

TABLE 7. *Labour-force statistics*

	Africans		Coloureds		Asians		Whites	
	Male	Female	Male	Female	Male	Female	Male	Female
			Economically active as a percentage of population 15+					
1921			95.8	37.4	93.6	12.6	91.2	19.2
1936			93.1	33.0	90.7	7.3	87.0	19.4
1946	94.9		91.9	38.3	88.4	8.7	84.7	22.7
1951	94.2	22.5	91.1	37.5	86.0	7.3	85.8	23.6
1960	88.9	25.2	80.9	39.7	81.1	8.6	81.5	27.4
1970	74.0	42.5	80.9	41.8	77.7	18.2	81.7	33.7
1996[a]	63.0	48.0	74.5	56.2	76.8	41.1	77.4	56.3

Employed

	1946	1951	1960	1970	1996
Numbers					
Agriculture	1912939	1508642	1687486	2482452	814350
Mining	498326	510091	614852	680384	541546
Manufacturing	359745	502100	643520	1026082	1119973
Utilities	12646	25380	28332	46761	109334
Construction	153000	240139	275920	475595	555129
Trade and finance	248976	327659	642592	897835	1778171
Transport etc.	207216	202866	204981	338249	483652
Services	961632	1073665	1137038	1595840	2653787
Unspecified	232406	202125	485976	571050	1077868
Total	4586886	4592587	5720697	8114248	9113810
Percentages					
Agriculture	41.7%	32.8%	29.5%	30.6%	8.9%
Mining	10.9%	11.1%	10.7%	8.4%	5.9%
Manufacturing	7.8%	10.9%	11.2%	12.6%	12.3%
Utilities	0.3%	0.6%	0.5%	0.6%	1.2%
Construction	3.3%	5.2%	4.8%	5.9%	6.1%
Trade and finance	5.4%	7.1%	11.2%	11.1%	19.5%

(continued)

TABLE 7 (continued)

	Africans	Coloureds	Asians	Whites	Total
Transport etc.	4.5%	4.4%	3.6%	4.2%	5.3%
Services	21.0%	23.4%	19.9%	19.7%	28.9%
Unspecified[b]	5.1%	4.4%	8.5%	7.0%	11.8%
Total	100.0%	100.0%	100.0%	100.0%	100.0%

Occupational distribution by population group, 1996

	Africans	Coloureds	Asians	Whites	Total
Legislators, senior officials and managers	1.9%	3.0%	9.3%	12.8%	4.5%
Professionals	8.3%	7.3%	14.2%	19.7%	10.7%
Technicians and associate professionals	3.5%	5.4%	12.4%	16.6%	6.7%
Clerks	4.8%	10.2%	18.3%	18.3%	8.7%
Service workers, shop and market sales workers	10.0%	9.1%	12.2%	10.7%	10.1%
Skilled agricultural and fishery workers	5.2%	3.5%	0.6%	3.2%	4.4%
Crafts and related trade workers	17.4%	15.6%	14.5%	12.2%	16.0%
Plant and machine operators and assemblers	11.4%	9.7%	12.1%	3.2%	9.6%
Elementary occupations	37.4%	36.3%	6.4%	3.4%	29.3%
Total	100.0%	100.0%	100.0%	100.0%	100.0%

[a] In 1996, the percentages are for people between the ages of 15 and 65.
[b] Up to 1970, the unspecified included the unemployed. In 1996, the unemployed were separately identified.

TABLE 8. *Percentages of population urban, 1904–1996*

	Africans	Coloureds	Asians	Whites	Total
1904	10.1	50.5	36.6	52.7	23.4
1911	12.6	46.7	43.2	51.6	24.7
1936	17.3	53.9	66.3	65.2	31.4
1951	27.2	64.7	77.5	78.4	42.6
1960	31.8	68.3	83.2	83.6	46.7
1970	33.1	74.1	86.7	86.8	47.8
1996	43.3	83.4	97.3	90.6	53.7

Source: South Africa Statistics 2002, table 1.4.

	1936	1946	1951
Urban	390395	588318	821599
Urban location	355167	746346	915633
Suburban areas		57964	79926
Quasi-urban townships		14268	47982
Rural suburb	11305		
Rural township	35845	5740	13458
Native township	31749		
Farms owned by Europeans	2053440	2188757	2336785
Farms owned by coloureds or Asians	26946	35442	37501
Farms owned by companies	101417		
Farms owned by governments	13932		
Farms and agricultural holdings not occupied by whites, Asians or coloureds	167782	203784	
Crown reserves or locations	2420348	2595648	2612816
Other trust-vested land		36999	68258
Trust-purchased land		125496	160518
Mission reserves or stations	114135	70299	67573
Tribally owned farms	134424	189174	196347
Native-owned farms	143110	178704	145661
Crown lands	150379	70865	56061
Alluvial diggings	24632	13755	7700
Mine compound	386858	437560	474060
Industrial compound	113736	122179	146271
Municipal compound	36050	39911	29019
Construction gangs	43195	44908	51065
Government areas		67578	54960
Other areas	9626	32866	33106
Total	6596689	7830559	8560083

TABLE 9. *Distribution of African population, 1936–1996*

	1936	1946	1951	1970	1996
Other than farms and African reserves	1438558	2171393	2674779	4475356	14469369
Farms	2195735	2391981	2578070	3726422	1952085
African reserves	2962396	3267185	3307234	7138197	14667883
Ratio: African reserves to farms (per hundred)	135	137	128	192	751
Ratio: Other to farms and African reserves (per hundred)	28	38	45	41	87

BIBLIOGRAPHY

MANUSCRIPT SOURCES

Duncan, Sir Patrick, papers, Cape Town, Manuscripts and Archives Department, University of Cape Town Libraries

Fitzpatrick Papers, Grahamstown, National English Literary Museum

Lodge Papers, Johannesburg, William Cullen Library, University of the Witwatersrand

Milner Papers, Oxford, Bodleian Library

Rand Mines Archive, Johannesburg

Simons Collection, Cape Town, Manuscripts and Archives Department, University of Cape Town

Stow Papers, Cape Town, National Library of South Africa

Stuart Papers, Durban, Killie Campbell Africana Library

Oliver Tambo Papers, Alice, University of Fort Hare

Trial Records

State v Mewa Ramgobin, Pietermaritzberg, 1984, schedule A in respect of Accused no. 1, Indictment: transcript of speeches, Tom Lodge Papers, University of the Witwatersrand

State v Mncube MZ and Nondula ME, Messina, 1988, Lodge Collection, E25 A3104, Historical Papers, Cullen Library, University of the Witwatersrand

State v Wilfred Mapumula, Estcourt Circuit Court, October–December 1955, Exhibit BB, typescript, pp. 16–22, Tom Lodge Papers, University of the Witwatersrand

National Archives, Kew

Colonial Office

CO 417/259 Despatches: South African Republic, 1899

CO 179/229 Natal correspondence, January–July 1904

OFFICIAL PUBLICATIONS

United Kingdom

'Copy of a despatch from Lieutenant Governor Keate to His Grace the Duke of Buckingham and Chandos,' in Cape of Good Hope and Natal, Despatches from the Governor of the Cape of Good Hope and the Lieutenant Governor of Natal on the Subject of the Recognition of Moshesh, Chief of the Basutos, and of His Tribe, as British Subjects, command paper 4140, London: Her Majesty's Stationery Office, 1869

South Africa

Union of South Africa, *Commission on Remuneration and Conditions of Employment of Natives on Witwatersrand Gold Mines*, Pretoria: Government Printer, U.G. 21 of 1944

Union of South Africa, *The economic and social conditions of the racial groups in South Africa*, Social and Economic Planning Council Report no. 13, Pretoria: Government Printer, U.G. 53 of 1948

Union of South Africa, *Interim report of the Drought Investigating Commission, April 1922*, Cape Town: Government Printer, U.G. 29 of 1922

Union of South Africa, *The native reserves and their place in the economy of the Union of South Africa*, Social and Economic Planning Council report no. 9, Pretoria: Government Printer, U.G. 32 of 1946

Union of South Africa, *Official Year Books, 1924, 1934/5*, Pretoria: Government Printer

Union of South Africa, *Report of the Department of Social Welfare for the financial years 1937–1939*, Cape Town: Government Printer, U.G. 15 of 1940

Union of South Africa, *Report of the Economic and Wage Commission*, Cape Town: Government Printer, U.G. 14 of 1926

Union of South Africa, *Report of the Economic Commission*, Pretoria: Government Printer, U.G. 12 of 1914

Union of South Africa, *Report of the Industrial Legislation Commission*, Pretoria: Government Printer, U.G. 37 of 1935

Union of South Africa, *Report of the Industrial Legislation Commission of Enquiry*, Pretoria: Government Printer, 1951

Union of South Africa, *Report of the Inter-Departmental Committee on Poor Relief and Charitable Institutions*, Pretoria: Government Printer, U.G. 61 of 1937

Union of South Africa, *Report of the Native Economic Commission*, Pretoria: Government Printer, U.G. 22 of 1932

Union of South Africa, *Report of the Smallholdings Commission, Transvaal*, Cape Town: Government Printer, U.G. 51 of 1913

Union of South Africa, *Report of the Witwatersrand Mine Natives' Wages*

Union of South Africa, *Summary of the report of the Commission for the Socio-Economic Development of the Bantu areas within the Union of South Africa*, Pretoria: Government Printer, U.G. 61 of 1955

Union of South Africa, *Union statistics for fifty years*, Pretoria: Government Printer, 1960

South Africa, *South Africa 1984: official year book of the Republic of South Africa*, Johannesburg: Chris van Rensburg, 1984

South Africa, Department of Education, *Education statistics in 1997*, Pretoria: The Department, 1999

South Africa, Department of Statistics, *South African statistics 1978*, Pretoria: The Department, 1978

South Africa, Statistics South Africa, *The income and expenditure survey, 1995* (electronic version), Pretoria: Statistics South Africa, 1997

South Africa, Statistics South Africa, *South African statistics 2002*, Pretoria: Statistics South Africa, 2002

BOOKS AND ARTICLES

Abrams, P., 'Notes on the difficulty of studying the state', *Journal of Historical Sociology* 1:1 (1988), 58–89

Adam, Heribert, *Modernizing racial domination: the dynamics of South African politics*, Berkeley: University of California Press, 1971

Adam, Heribert and Hermann Giliomee, *Ethnic power mobilized: can South Africa change?*, New Haven, CT: Yale University Press, 1979

Adhikari, M., *Not white enough, not black enough: racial identity in the South African coloured community*, Cape Town: Double Storey; Athens: Ohio University Press, 2005

African National Congress, 'Political report of the National Executive Committee,' in African National Congress, *Documentation of the Second National Consultative Conference*, Lusaka, ANC, 1985

African National Congress, *1987: What is to be done?*, document distributed by the African National Congress Politico-Military Council to regional command centres, October 1986

African National Congress, *Statement of the National Executive Committee of the African National Congress on the question of Negotiations*, 9 October 1987

Akita, S. (ed.), *Gentlemanly capitalism, imperialism and global history*, Basingstoke, U.K.: Palgrave Macmillan, 2002

Alden, Chris, *Apartheid's last stand: the rise and fall of the South African security state*, Basingstoke, U.K.: Macmillan, 1996

Alegi, P., *'Laduma': soccer, politics and society in South Africa*, Pietermaritzburg: University of KwaZulu-Natal Press, 2002

Alexander, Peter, *Workers, war and the origins of apartheid: labour and politics in South Africa, 1939–1984*, Oxford: James Currey, 2007

Allen, Robert C., *The British industrial revolution in global perspective*, Cambridge: Cambridge University Press, 2009

Ally, Russell, *Gold and empire; the Bank of England and South Africa's gold producers*, Johannesburg: Witwatersrand University Press, 1994

Amin, S., *Alternative histories: a view from India*, Calcutta: Centre for Studies in Social Sciences and South-South Exchange Programme for Research on the History of Development, 2002

Anonymous, 'Errors of workerism', *Isizwe: The Nation: Journal of the United Democratic Front* 1:3 (November 1986)

Anonymous, 'Jhb gets into gear on UDF', *SASPU Focus* (June 1983), 5

Anonymous, 'Sowing confusion', *New Era* (March 1986), 38

Anonymous, 'Tactical differences', *Work in Progress* (October 1985), 23

Anonymous, 'UDF message', *Grassroots* (February 1986)

Anonymous, '*Ya, the community is the main source of power*' (interviews), *Isizwe: The Nation: Journal of the United Democratic Front* (March 1986), 40–1

Arnold, Marion, *Women and art in South Africa*, Cape Town: David Philip; New York: St Martin's Press, 1996

Aron, J., B. Kahn and G. Kingdon (eds.), *South African economic policy under democracy*, Oxford: Oxford University Press, 2009

Attwell, David, *Rewriting modernity: studies in black South Africa literary history*, Athens: Ohio University Press, 2005

Auerbach, F. and D. Welsh, 'Education', in Van der Horst and Reid (eds.), *Race discrimination*, pp. 66–89

Baker, Pauline, *The United States and South Africa: the Reagan years*, South Africa Update Series, New York: Ford Foundation and Foreign Policy Association, 1989

Ballantyne, R. M., *Settler and the savage: a tale of peace and war in South Africa*, London: Nisbet, 1877

Bankoff, G. and S. Swart, *Breeds of empire: the 'invention' of the horse in the Philippines and southern Africa, 1500–1950*, Copenhagen: Nordic Institute of African Studies Press, 2007

Barnett, Ursula, *A vision of order: a study of black South African literature in English, 1914–1980*, Cape Town: Maskew Miller Longman, 1983

Barrell, Howard, *MK: the ANC's armed struggle*, Johannesburg: Penguin, 1990

Baskin, Jeremy, *Striking back: a history of COSATU*, Johannesburg: Ravan Press, 1991

Batson, Edward, *The poverty datum line*, Cape Town: University of Cape Town, Department of Social Science, 1941

Beinart, W., *The political economy of Pondoland*, Cambridge: Cambridge University Press, 1982

Beinart, W., *The rise of conservation in South Africa: settlers, livestock, and the environment, 1770–1950*, Oxford: Oxford University Press, 2003

Beinart, W., *Twentieth century South Africa*, Oxford: Oxford University Press, 1994

Beinart, W., and C. Bundy, *Hidden struggles in rural South Africa: politics and popular movements in the Transkei and Eastern Cape, 1890–1930*, London: James

Currey; Berkeley: University of California Press; Johannesburg: Ravan Press, 1987

Beinart, W. and P. Coates, *Environment and history: the taming of nature in the USA and South Africa*, London: Routledge, 1995

Beinart, W., P. Delius and S. Trapido (eds.), *Putting a plough to the ground: accumulation and dispossession in rural South Africa, 1850–1930*, Johannesburg: Ravan Press, 1986

Bekker, S. and R. Humphreys, *From control to confusion: the changing role of administration boards in South Africa*, Pietermaritzburg: Shuter and Shooter, 1985

Belich, James, *Replenishing the earth: the settler revolution and the rise of the Anglo-world, 1783–1939*, Oxford: Oxford University Press, 2009

Bell, T., 'Improving manufacturing performance in South Africa: a contrary view', *Transformation* 28:1 (1995), 1–34

Bell, T., 'Improving manufacturing performance in South Africa: a rejoinder', *Transformation* 31 (1996), 43–56

Bell, T., 'The minerals-energy complex and South African industrialisation: a rejoinder', *Development Southern Africa* 15:4 (1998), 701–14

Bell, T. and G. Farrell, 'The minerals-energy complex and South African industrialisation', *Development Southern Africa* 14:4 (1997), 591–613

Benson, Mary, *The African patriots: the story of the African National Congress of South Africa*, London: Faber and Faber, 1963

Benson, Mary, *Nelson Mandela*, London: Panaf, 1980

Benyon, J., '"Intermediate" imperialism and the test of empire: Milner's "eccentric" high commission in South Africa', in Lowry (ed.), *The South African War reappraised*, pp. 84–103

Berger, Iris, *Threads of solidarity: women in South African industry*, London: James Currey, 1982

Berman, B., 'Structure and process in bureaucratic states', *Development and Change*, 15:2 (1984), 161–202

Bhana, Surendra, *Gandhi's legacy: the Natal Indian Congress, 1894–1994*, Pietermaritzburg: University of Natal Press, 1997

Bhana, Surendra and Bridglal Pachai (eds.), *A documentary history of Indian South Africans*, Cape Town: David Philip, 1984

Bhorat, Haroon, Murray Leibbrandt, Muzi Maziya, Servaas Van Der Berg and Ingrid Woolard, *Fighting poverty: labour markets and inequality in South Africa*, Cape Town: University of Cape Town Press, 2001

Bhorat, Haroon and Ravi Kanbur (eds.), *Poverty and policy in post-apartheid South Africa*, Pretoria: HSRC Press, 2006

Bickford-Smith, Vivian, *Ethnic pride and racial prejudice in Victorian Cape Town*, Cambridge: Cambridge University Press, 1995

Bickford-Smith, Vivian, 'Protest, organization and ethnicity among Cape Town workers, 1891–1902', in van Heyningen, *Studies in the history of Cape Town*, vol. 8, pp. 84–108

Bickford-Smith, Vivian, E. van Heyningen and N. Worden, *Cape Town in the twentieth century*, Cape Town: David Philip, 1999

Bleek, W. H. I., *Comparative grammar of South African languages*, London: Trübner, 1862–1869

Blom, Ida, Karen Hagerman and Catherine Hall (eds.), *Gendered nations: nationalisms and gender order in the late nineteenth century*, Oxford: Berg Publishers, 2000

Blumenfeld, Jesmond (ed.), *South Africa in crisis*, London: Croom Helm, 1987

Boehmer, Elleke, Laura Chrisman and Kenneth Parker (eds.), *Altered state? Writing and South Africa*, Sydney: Dangaroo Press, 1994

Boehmer, Elleke, Robert Eaglestone and Katy Idols, *J. M. Coetzee in context and theory*, London: Continuum International Publishing Group, 2009

Bonner, Philip, 'Black trade unions in South Africa since World War II', in Price and Rosberg (eds.), *The apartheid regime*, pp. 174–93

Bonner, Philip, 'Keynote address to the "Life after Thirty" colloquium', *African Studies* 69:1 (2010), 13–27

Bonner, Philip, 'The Transvaal Native Congress, 1917–20: the radicalization of the black petty bourgeoisie on the Rand', in Marks and Rathbone, (eds.), *Industrialisation and social change*, pp. 270–313

Bonner, Philip, P. Delius and D. Posel (eds.), *Apartheid's genesis, 1935–1962*, Johannesburg: Ravan Press and Witwatersrand University Press, 1993

Bonner, Philip, P. Delius and D. Posel, 'The shaping of apartheid: contradiction, continuity and popular struggle', in Bonner, Delius and Posel (eds.), *Apartheid's genesis*, pp. 1–41

Bonner, P., I. Hofmeyr, D. James and T. Lodge (eds.), *Holding their ground: class, locality and culture in 19th and 20th century South Africa*, Johannesburg: Witwatersrand University Press and Ravan Press, 1989

Bottomley, J., 'The Orange Free State and the Rebellion of 1914: the influence of industrialisation, poverty and poor whiteism', in Morrell (ed.), *White but poor*, pp. 29–39

Boyce, D. George (ed.), *The crisis of British power: the imperial and naval papers of the second Earl of Selborne, 1895–1910*, London: Historians' Press, 1990

Bozzoli, Belinda, 'Marxism, feminism and South African studies', *Journal of Southern African Studies* 9 (1982), 99, 131–72

Bozzoli, Belinda, *The political nature of a ruling class*, London: Routledge, 1981

Bozzoli, Belinda, 'The taming of the illicit: bounded rebellion in South Africa, 1986,' *Comparative Studies in Society and History* 46:2 (2004), 326–53

Bozzoli, Belinda, (ed.), *Town and countryside in the Transvaal: capitalist penetration and popular response*, Johannesburg: Ravan Press, 1983

Bozzoli, Belinda, with Mmantho Nkotsoe, *Women of Phokeng: consciousness, life strategy, and migrancy in South Africa, 1900–1983*, Johannesburg: Ravan Press, 1991

Braam, Conny, *Operation Vula*, Bellevue: Jacana, 2004

Braam, Conny and Fons Geerlings, 'Towards new cultural relations: a reflection on the cultural boycott', in Campschreur and Divendal (eds.), *Culture in another South Africa*, pp. 170–81

Bradford, Helen, 'Gentlemen and Boers: Afrikaner nationalism, gender and colonial warfare', in Cuthbertson, Grundlingh and Suttie (eds.), *Writing a wider war*, pp. 37–66

Bradford, Helen, 'Regendering Afrikanerdom: Afrikanerdom, the 1899–1902 Anglo-Boer War', in Blom, Hagerman and Hall (eds.), *Gendered nations*, pp. 207–25

Bradford, Helen, *A taste of freedom: the ICU in rural South Africa, 1924–30*, New Haven, CT: Yale University Press, 1987

Brandel-Syrier, M., *Reeftown elite: a study of social mobility in a modern African community on the Reef*, London: Routledge and Kegan Paul, 1971

Brewer, John, *Black and blue: policing in South Africa*, Oxford: Clarendon Press, 1994

Brewer, John (ed.), *Can South Africa survive: five minutes to midnight*, Basingstoke, U.K.: Macmillan, 1989

Brewer, John, 'Internal black protest,' in Brewer (ed.), *Can South Africa survive?*, pp. 184–205

Breytenbach, B., *A season in paradise*, London: Jonathan Cape, 1980

Brookes, E. H., (ed.), *Coming of age: studies in South African citizenship and politics*, Cape Town: Maskew Miller, 1930

Brooks, Alan and Jeremy Brickhill, *Whirlwind before the storm*, London: International Defence and Aid, 1980

Brown, Douglas, *Against the world: attitudes of white South Africans*, London: Collins, 1966

Brown, K., 'Political entomology: the insectile challenge to agricultural development in the Cape Colony, 1895–1910', *Journal of Southern African Studies* 29:2 (2003), 529–49

Buhlungu, Sakhela (ed.), *Trade unions and democracy: COSATU workers' political attitudes in South Africa*, Pretoria: HSRC Press, 2006

Bunche, R. J., *An African American in South Africa: the travel notes of Ralph J. Bunche, 28 September 1937–1 January 1938*, Johannesburg: Witwatersrand University Press, 1992

Bundy, Colin, 'New nation. New history? Constructing the past in post-apartheid South Africa', in Stolten (ed.), *History making*, pp. 73–97

Bundy, Colin, *The rise and fall of the South African peasantry*, London: Heinemann, 1979

Burger, John {Leo Marquard}, *The black man's burden*, London: Gollancz, 1943

Burke, Gillian and Peter Richardson, 'The profits of death: a comparative study of miners' phthisis in Cornwall and the Transvaal, 1876–1918', *Journal of Southern African Studies* 4:2 (April 1978), 147–71

Burman, Sandra and P. Reynolds, *Growing up in a divided society: the contexts of childhood in South Africa*, Johannesburg: Ravan Press, 1986

Burman, Sandra and P. van der Spuy, 'The illegitimate and the illegal in a South African city: the effects of apartheid on births out of wedlock', *Journal of Social History* 29 (March 1996), 613–36

Calpin, G. H., *There are no South Africans*, London: Nelson, 1941

Cammack, D., *The Rand at war, 1899–1902: the Witwatersrand and the Anglo-Boer War*, London: James Currey; Berkeley: University of California Press; Pietermaritzburg: University of Natal Press, 1990

Campbell, James, *Songs of Zion: the African Methodist Episcopal Church in the USA and South Africa*, New York: Oxford University Press, 1995

Campschreur, William and Joost Divendal (eds.), *Culture in another South Africa*, London: Zed, 1989

Canepari-Labib, Michela, *Old myths – modern empires: power, language and identity in J. M. Coetzee's work*, Bern: Peter Lang, 2005

Carnegie Commission, *The poor white problem in South Africa: report of the Carnegie Commission: joint findings and recommendations*, Stellenbosch: Ecclesia, 1931

Carruthers, J., *The Kruger National Park: a social and political history*, Pietermaritzburg: University of Natal Press, 1995

Carter, Charles, 'Community and conflict: the Alexandra rebellion of 1986', *Journal of Southern African Studies* 18:1 (March 1992), 115–42

Carton, B., 'The forgotten compass of death: apocalypse then and now in the social history of South Africa', *Journal of Social History* 37:1 (2003), 199–218

Chanock, M., *The making of South African legal culture, 1902–1936: fear, favour and prejudice*, Cambridge: Cambridge University Press, 2001

Chapman, Michael, Colin Gardner and Es'kia Mphahlele, *Perspectives on South African English literature*, Johannesburg: Donker, 1992

Chidester, David, *Shots in the streets: violence and religion in South Africa*, Boston: Beacon Books, 1991

The Christian citizen in a multiracial society, Strand [Cape]: Christian Council of South Africa, 1949

Christie, Renfrew, *Electricity, industry and class in South Africa*, London: Macmillan, 1984

Cilliers, Jackie and Markus Reichardt (eds.), *About turn: the transformation of the South African military and intelligence*, Halfway House, Midrand: Institute for Defence Policy, 1995

Clark, Nancy, *Manufacturing apartheid: state corporations in South Africa*, New Haven, CT: Yale University Press, 1994

Clegg, Johnny and Michael Drewett, 'Why don't you sing about leaves and the dreams? Reflecting on music censorship in apartheid South

Africa', in Drewett and Cloonan (eds.), *Popular music censorship in Africa*, pp. 127–36

Coale, A. J. and S. C. Watkins, *The decline of fertility in Europe*, Princeton, NJ: Princeton University Press, 1986

Cobley, A., 'Does social history have a future? The end of apartheid and recent trends in South African historiography', *Journal of Southern African Studies* 27:3 (2001), 613–25

Coetzee, J. M., *White writing: on the culture of letters in South Africa*, New Haven, CT: Yale University, 1986

Coillard, F., *On the threshold of Central Africa*, London: Hodder and Stoughton, 1897

Cole, Ernest, *House of bondage*, New York: Random House, 1967

Coleman, F. L. (ed.), *Economic history of South Africa*, Pretoria: Hollandsch Afrikaansche Uitgevers Maatschappij, 1983

Comaroff, Jean, *Body of power, spirit of resistance: the culture and history of a South African people*, Chicago: University of Chicago Press, 1985

Comaroff, Jean and John Comaroff, (eds.), *Modernity and its malcontents: ritual and power in postcolonial Africa*, Chicago: University of Chicago Press, 1993

Comaroff, Jean and John Comaroff, *Of revelation and revolution*, vol. 2, *The dialectics of modernity on a South African frontier*, Chicago: University of Chicago Press, 1997

Competition Commission, *Review of changes in industrial structure and competition, paper prepared for South African government's 15-year review*, Pretoria: Policy and Research Division, Competition Commission, 2008

Coombes, A., *History after apartheid: visual culture and public memory in a democratic South Africa*, Johannesburg: Witwatersrand University Press, 2004

Cooper, F., *Colonialism in question: theory, knowledge and history*, Berkeley: University of California Press, 2005

Cope, Nicholas, *To bind a nation: Solomon ka Dinizulu and Zulu nationalism, 1913–33*, Pietermaritzburg: University of Natal Press, 1993

Cope, R. L., *Ploughshare of war: the origins of the Anglo-Zulu War of 1879*, Pietermaritzburg: University of Natal Press, c. 1999

Cope, R. L., 'Strategic and socio-economic explanations for Carnarvon's South African confederation policy', *History in Africa* 13 (1986), 13–34

Coplan, D. B., *In township tonight: South Africa's black city music and theatre*, London: Longman; Johannesburg: Ravan Press, 1985

Couzens, Tim, *The new African: a study of the life and work of H. I. E. Dhlomo*, Johannesburg: Ravan Press, 1985

Couzens, Tim and Essop Patel (eds.), *The return of the Amasi bird: Black South African poetry, 1891–1981*, Johannesburg: Ravan Press, 1982

Crais, Clifton, *The politics of evil: magic, state power and the political imagination in South Africa*, Cambridge: Cambridge University Press, 2002

Crankshaw, Owen, *Race, class and the changing division of labour under apartheid*, London: Routledge, 1997

Crocker, Chester, *High noon in southern Africa: making peace in a rough neighborhood*, Johannesburg: Jonathan Ball, 1992

Crosby, A., 'The past and the present of environmental history', *American Historical Review* 100:4 (1995), 1177–89

Crush, Jonathan, 'Mine migrancy in the contemporary era', in Crush and James (eds.), *Crossing boundaries*, pp. 14–32

Crush, Jonathan and Wilmot James (eds.), *Crossing boundaries: mine migrancy in a democratic South Africa*, Cape Town: Institute for Democracy in South Africa, 1995

Crush, Jonathan, A. Jeeves and D. Yudelman, *South Africa's labor empire: a history of black migrancy to the gold mines*, Boulder, CO: Westview; Cape Town: David Philip, 1991

Cuthbertson, Greg, Albert Grundlingh and Mary-Lynn Suttie (eds.), *Writing a wider war: rethinking gender, race, and identity in the South African War, 1899–1902*, Athens: Ohio University Press; Cape Town: David Philip, 2002

Darley-Hartley, W. H., 'The beginnings of the South African League being some personal reminiscences,' pamphlet based on extracts from *New Era* (May–June 1904)

Darwin, John, 'Afterword', in Omissi and Thompson (eds.), *The impact of the South African War*, pp. 289–302

Darwin, John, *The empire project: the rise and fall of the British world system, 1830–1970*, Cambridge: Cambridge University Press, 2009

Das, V., A. Kleinman, M. Ramphele and P. Reynolds (eds.), *Violence and subjectivity*, Berkeley: University of California Press, 2000

Davenport, T. R. H., *The Afrikaner Bond: the history of a South African political party, 1880–1911*, Cape Town: Oxford University Press, 1966

Davis, Stephen M., *Apartheid's rebels: inside South Africa's hidden war*, New Haven, CT: Yale University Press, 1987

Deacon, H., H. Phillips and E. van Heyningen (eds.), *The Cape doctor in the nineteenth century: a social history*, Amsterdam: Rodopi, 2004

De Kiewiet, C. W., *British colonial policy and the South African republics, 1848–1872*, New York: Longmans, Green, 1929

De Kiewiet, C. W., *A history of South Africa: social and economic*, Oxford: Clarendon Press; London: Oxford University Press, 1941

De Kiewiet, C. W., *The imperial factor in South Africa: a study in politics and economics*, London: Cass, 1965

De Klerk, Michael, 'The business cycle in South Africa: recent tendencies', *South African Journal of Economics* 43:1 (1975), 1–8

De Klerk, Michael, *History of the South African Reserve Bank, 1920–52*, Pretoria: Van Schaik, 1954

De Klerk, Michael, '"Seasons that will never return": the impact of farm mechanization on employment, incomes and population distribution in the Western Transvaal', *Journal of Southern African Studies* 11:1 (1984), 84–106

Delius, Peter, *The land belongs to us: the Pedi polity, the Boers and the British in the nineteenth century Transvaal*, Johannesburg: Ravan Press, 1983; Berkeley: University of California Press, 1984

Delius, Peter, *A lion amongst the cattle: reconstruction and resistance in the Northern Transvaal*, Johannesburg: Ravan Press; Portsmouth, NH: Heinemann, 1996; Oxford: James Currey, 1997

Delius, Peter, 'Witches and missionaries in nineteenth century Transvaal', *Journal of Southern African Studies* 27:3 (2001), 429–43

Delius, Peter and S. Schirmer, 'Soil conservation in a racially ordered society: South Africa, 1930–1970', *Journal of Southern African Studies* 26:4 (2000), 719–42

Denoon, Donald, *The grand illusion: the failure of imperial policy in the Transvaal colony during the period of reconstruction, 1900–1905*, London: Longman, 1973

Deutsch, J.-G., P. Probst and H. Schmidt (eds.), *African modernities*, Oxford: Greenwood Press, 2002

De Villiers, A. (ed.), *English-speaking South Africa today*, Cape Town: Oxford University Press, 1976

Dhlomo, H. I. E., *Collected works*, ed. N. Visser and T. Couzens, Johannesburg: Ravan Press, 1985

Dicke, B. H., 'The tsetse-fly's influence on South African history', *South African Journal of Science* 29 (1932), 792–96

Digby, A., *Diversity and division in medicine: health care in South Africa from the 1800s*, Oxford: Lang, 2006

Dikobe, Modikwe, *The Marabi dance*, London: Heinemann, 1973

Diseko, Nozipho, 'The origins and development of the South African Student's Movement (SASM), 1968–1976', *Journal of Southern African Studies* 18:1 (March 1992), 40–62

Dols, M. W., 'The comparative communal responses to the Black Death in Muslim and Christian societies', *Viator: Medieval and Renaissance Studies* 5 (1974), 269–88

Dovers, S., R. Edgecombe and B. Guest, *South Africa's environmental history: cases and comparisons*, Athens: Ohio University Press, 2003

Draper, M., 'Zen and the art of garden province maintenance: the soft intimacy of hard men in the wilderness of Kwa-Zulu-Natal, South Africa, 1952–1997', *Journal of Southern African Studies* 24:4 (1998), 801–28

Drew, A. (ed.), *South Africa's radical tradition: a documentary history*, 2 vols. Cape Town: Mayibuye, 1996

Drewett, Michael and Martin Cloonan (eds.), *Popular music censorship in Africa*, Hampshire, U.K.: Ashgate, 2006

Drus, E., 'Select documents from the Chamberlain papers concerning Anglo-Transvaal relations, 1896–1899', *Bulletin of the Institute of Historical Research* 27 (1954), 156–89

Dubin, S., *Transforming museums: mounting Queen Victoria in a democratic South Africa*, London: Palgrave Macmillan, 2006

Dubow, Saul, *The African National Congress*, Johannesburg: Jonathan Ball, 2000

Dubow, Saul, 'Colonial nationalism, the Milner Kindergarten and the rise of "South Africanism", 1902–1910', *History Workshop Journal* 43 (1997), 53–86

Dubow, Saul, *A commonwealth of knowledge: science, sensibility and white South Africa, 1820–2000*, Oxford: Oxford University Press, 2000

Dubow, Saul, *Illicit union: scientific racism in modern South Africa*, Johannesburg: Witwatersrand University Press, 1997

Dubow, Saul, *Racial segregation and the origins of apartheid in South Africa, 1919–1936*, Basingstoke, U.K.: Macmillan in association with St Antony's College, Oxford, 1989

Dubow, Saul (ed.), *Science and society in southern Africa*, Manchester, U.K.: Manchester University Press, 2000

Dubow, S. and A. Jeeves (eds.), *South Africa's 1940s: worlds of possibilities*, Cape Town: Double Storey, 2005

Dugard, J., *Human rights and the South African legal order*, Princeton, NJ: Princeton University Press, 1987

Duka, N., *From shanty town to forest: life histories from the revolution, South Africa, ANC 1*, Richmond: LSM Information Centre, 1974

Duminy, A. H. and Guest, W. R. (eds.), *Fitzpatrick: South African politician: selected papers, 1888–1906*, Johannesburg: McGraw-Hill, 1976

Duncan, David, 'Foreign and local investment in the South African motor industry, 1924–1992', *South African Journal of Economic History* 7:2 (1992), 53–81

Duncan, David, *The mills of God: the state and African labour in South Africa, 1918–1948*, Johannesburg: Witwatersrand University Press, 1995

Duncan, David, *We are motor men: the making of the South African motor industry*, Caithness, U.K.: Whittles Publishing, 1997

Du Pisani, Andre, *What do we think? A survey of white opinion on foreign policy issues*, Braamfontein: South African Institute of International Affairs, 1990

Du Plessis, J. C., *Economic fluctuations in South Africa, 1910–1949*, publication no. 2, Stellenbosch: Bureau for Market Research, University of Stellenbosch, 1950

Du Plessis, S. and B. Smit, 'Accounting for South Africa's growth revival after 1994', in Aron, Kahn and Kingdon (eds.), *South African economic policy*, pp. 28–57

Du Toit, D., *Capital and labour in South Africa: class struggles in the 1970s*, London: Kegan Paul International, 1981

Du Toit, Marijke, '"Dangerous motherhood": maternity care and engendered construction of Afrikaner identity, 1904–1939', in Fildes, Marks and Marland (eds.), *Women and children first*, pp. 203–29

Du Toit, Marijke, 'The domesticity of Afrikaner nationalism: *volksmoeders* and the ACVV, 1904–1929', *Journal of Southern African Studies* 29:1 (2003), 155–76

Du Toit, S. J., *Die geskiedenis van ons land in die taal van ons volk*, Cape Town: Smuts and Hofmeyr, 1877

Dyzenhaus, D. *Truth, reconciliation and the apartheid legal order*, Cape Town: Juta, 1998

Eberstadt, N., *The tyranny of numbers: mismeasurement and misrule*, Lanham, MD: American Enterprise Institute, 1992

Edwards, Lawrence, 'Has South Africa liberalised its trade?', *South African Journal of Economics* 74:4 (2005), 754–75

Edwards, Lawrence and P. Alves, 'South Africa's export performance: determinants of export supply', *South African Journal of Economics* 74:3 (2006), 473–500

Edwards, Lawrence, Rashad Cassim and Dirk van Seventer, 'Trade policy in South Africa', in Aron, Kahn and Kingdon (eds.), *South African economic policy*, pp. 151–81

Edwards, Lawrence and R. Z. Lawrence, 'South African trade policy matters: trade performance and trade policy', *Economics of Transition* 16:4 (2008), 585–608

Elder, G., *Hostels, sexuality and the apartheid legacy*, Athens: Ohio University Press, 2003

Ellis, S. and T. Sechaba, *Comrades against apartheid: the ANC and the South African Communist Party in exile*, London: James Currey; Bloomington: Indiana University Press, 1992

Elphick, R. and R. Davenport (eds.), *Christianity in South Africa: a political, social and cultural history*, Oxford: James Currey, 1997

Erasmus, Z. (ed.), *Coloured by history, shaped by place*, Cape Town: Kwela, 2001

Erlank, Natasha, 'Gendering ethnicity: African men and the 1883 Commission on Native Law and Custom', *Journal of Southern African Studies* 29:3 (December 2003), 937–53

Erlman, V., 'But hope does not kill: black popular music in Durban', in Maylam and Edwards (eds.), *The people's city*, pp. 67–101

Etherington, N. A., 'Labour supply and the genesis of South African confederation in the 1870s', *Journal of African History* 20 (1979), 235–53

Etherington, N. A., *Preachers, peasants and politics in southeast Africa, 1835–1880: African Christian communities in Natal, Pondoland and Zululand*, London: Royal Historical Society, 1978

Evans, Ivan, *Bureaucracy and race: native administration in South Africa*, Berkeley: University of California Press, 1997

Evans, Michael and Mark Phillips, 'Intensifying civil war: the role of the South African Defence Force,' in Frankel, Pines and Swilling (eds.), *State, resistance and change*, pp. 117–45

Evans, Peter, Dietrich Rueschemeyer and Theda Skocpol (eds.), *Bringing the state back in*, Cambridge: Cambridge University Press, 1985

Everatt, David, 'Alliance politics of a special type: the roots of the ANC/SACP alliance, 1950–1954', *Journal of Southern African Studies* 18:1 (1992), 19–39

Fedderke, J., 'Capital formation in South Africa', in Aron, Kahn and Kingdon (eds.), *South African economic policy*, pp. 183–4

Fedderke, J., R. de Kadt and J. Luiz, 'Uneducating South Africa: the failure to address the 1910–1993 legacy', *International Review of Education* 46:3–4 (2001), 257–81

Feinburg, H. M., 'The Natives Land Act of 1913 in South Africa: politics, race and segregation in the early 20th century', *International Journal of African Historical Studies* 26:1 (1993), 65–109

Feinstein, Charles, *An economic history of South Africa: conquest, discrimination and development*, Cambridge: Cambridge University Press, 2005

Ferguson, James, *Expectations of modernity: myths and meanings of urban life on the Zambian Copperbelt*, Berkeley: University of California Press, 1999

Fieldhouse, R., *Anti-apartheid: a history of the movement in Britain*, London: Merlin Press, 2005

Fildes, Valerie, Lara Marks and Hilary Marland (eds.), *Women and children first: international maternal and infant welfare, 1870–1945*, London: Routledge, 1992

Fine, Alan and Eddie Webster, 'Transcending traditions: trade unions and political unity', in Moss and Obery (eds.), *South African Review V*, pp. 256–74

Fine, Ben and Z. Rustomjee, 'Debating the South African minerals-energy complex: a response to Bell and Farrell', *Development Southern Africa* 15:4 (1998), 689–700

Fine, Ben and Z. Rustomjee, *The political economy of South Africa: from minerals-energy complex to industrialisation*, Johannesburg: Witwatersrand University Press; London: C. Hurst, 1998

Fitzpatrick, P., *The Transvaal from within: a private record of public affairs*, London: Heinemann, 1900

Flint, K. E., *Healing traditions: African medicine, cultural exchange, and competition in South Africa, 1820–1948*, Athens: Ohio University Press; Scottsville: University of KwaZulu-Natal Press, 2008

Foucault, M., *Society must be defended*, London: Penguin, 2004

Fox, F. and D. Back, *A preliminary survey of the agricultural and nutritional problems of the Ciskei and Transkei: report for the Chamber of Mines*, Johannesburg: Chamber of Mines, 1937

Frankel, Philip, *Pretoria's Praetorians: civil-military relations in South Africa*, Cambridge: Cambridge University Press, 1984

Frankel, Philip, Noam Pines and Mark Swilling (eds.), *State resistance and change in South Africa*, Johannesburg: Southern Book Publishers, 1988

Frankel, S. Herbert, *Investment and the return to equity capital in the South African gold mining industry, 1887–1965: an international comparison*, Oxford: Basil Blackwell, 1967

Frankel, S. Herbert, 'Whither South Africa? An economic approach', *South African Journal of Economics* 15:1 (1947), 27–39

Frederikse, Julie, *South Africa: a different kind of war*, Johannesburg: Ravan Press, 1986

Frere, Bartle, 'Native races of South Africa', *Transactions of the South African Philosophical Society*, 1:2 (1877–1888)

Freund, Bill, *Insiders and outsiders: the Indian working class of Durban, 1910–1990*, Portsmouth, NH: Heinemann; Pietermaritzburg: University of Natal Press; London: James Currey, 1995

Freund, Bill, 'The social character of secondary industry in South Africa, 1915–45', in Mabin (ed.), *Organisation and social change*, pp. 78–119

Friedman, Steven, *Building tomorrow today: African workers in trade unions, 1970–1984*, Johannesburg: Ravan Press, 1987

Froude, J. A., 'Leaves from a South African journal', in *Short studies on great subjects*, vol. 3, London: Longmans, 1898

Furlong, Patrick, *Between crown and swastika: the impact of the radical right on the Afrikaner Nationalist movement in the Fascist era*, Johannesburg: Witwatersrand University Press, 1991

Fuze, M., *The black people and whence they came*, Pietermaritzburg: Killie Campbell Africana Library, 1979

Garson, N. G., 'English-speaking South Africans and the British connection, 1820–1961', in De Villiers (ed.), *English-speaking South Africa today*, pp. 17–39

Gelb, Stephen, 'The origins of the South African Reserve Bank', in Mabin (ed.), *Organisation and social change*, pp. 48–77

Geldenhuys, Deon, *The diplomacy of isolation: South African foreign policy making*, Johannesburg: Macmillan, 1984

Gerhart, G., *Black power in South Africa: the evolution of an ideology*, Berkeley: University of California Press, 1978

Gikandi, Simon (ed.), *Encyclopedia of African literature*, London: Routledge, 2003

Giliomee, Hermann, 'The Afrikaner economic advance', in Adam and Giliomee, *Ethnic power mobilised*, pp. 145–76

Giliomee, Hermann, *The Afrikaners: biography of a people*, Cape Town: Tafelberg; London: Hurst, 2003

Giliomee, Hermann, *The parting of the ways: South African politics, 1976–1982*, Cape Town: David Philip, 1982

Glazer, N., 'Monuments in an age without heroes', *Public Interest* 123 (1996), 22–39

Goedhals, Mandy, 'African nationalism and indigenous Christianity: a study in the life of James Calata (1895–1983)', *Journal of Religion in Africa* 33:1 (February 2003), 63–82

Goldin, I., *Making race: the politics and economics of coloured identity in South Africa*, Cape Town: Maskew Miller Longman, 1987

Goodfellow, C. F., *Great Britain and the South African federation, 1870–1881*, Cape Town: Oxford University Press, 1966

Gordon, C. T., *The growth of Boer opposition to Kruger, 1890–1895*, Cape Town: Oxford University Press; Charlottesville, University of Virginia Press, 1970

Gray, J. L., 'The comparative sociology of South Africa', *South African Journal of Economics* 5:3 (1937), 269–84

Gray, Stephen, *South Africa plays*, London: Nick Hern Books and Heinemann-Centaur, 1993

Green, Reginald and Carol Thompson, 'Political economies in conflict: SADCC, South Africa and sanctions', in Johnson and Martin, *Frontline southern Africa*, pp. 339–86

Greenberg, Stanley, *Race and state in capitalist development*, New Haven, CT: Yale University Press, 1980

Griffiths, C. L., et al., 'Impacts of human activities on marine animal life in the Benguela – an historical overview', *Oceanography and Marine Biology Annual Review* 42 (2004), 303–92

Griffiths, T. and L. Robin (eds.), *Ecology and empire: environmental history of settler societies*, Seattle: University of Washington Press, 1997

Grossberg, Lawrence, Cary Nelson and Paula Treichler (eds.), *Cultural studies*, New York: Routledge, 1992

Grundlingh, Albert, 'Collaborators in Boer society', in Warwick (ed.), *The South African War*, pp. 258–78

Grundlingh, Albert, 'A cultural conundrum? Old monuments and new regimes: the Voortrekker Monument as symbol of Afrikaner power in post-apartheid South Africa', *Radical History Review* 81 (2001), 95–112

Grundlingh, Albert, *Die 'Hensoppers' en 'Joiners': die rasional en verskinsel van verraad*, Pretoria: Hollansch Afrikaansche Uitgevers Maatschappij, 1979

Grundlingh, Albert, 'Reframing remembrance: the politics of the Centenary commemoration of the South African War of 1899–1902', *Journal of Southern African Studies* 30:2 (2004), 358–77

Grundy, Kenneth, *The militarization of South African politics*, Bloomington: Indiana University Press, 1986

Guelke, Adrian, *Rethinking the rise and fall of apartheid*, Basingstoke, U.K.: Macmillan, 2005

Guelke, L. and R. Shell, 'Landscape of conquest: frontier water alienation and Khoikhoi strategies of survival, 1652–1780', *Journal of Southern African Studies* 18:4 (1992), 803–23

Guest, Bill and John Sellars (eds.), *Receded tides of empire: aspects of the social and economic history of Natal and Zululand since 1910*, Pietermaritzburg: University of Natal Press, 1994

Gunner, Elizabeth, 'Power house, prison house: and oral genre and its use in Isaiah Shembe's Nazareth Baptist Church', *Journal of Southern African Studies* 14 (1987–8), 204–27

Gunner, L., *The man of heaven and the beautiful one*, Leiden: Brill, 2002

Guy, Jeff, 'Gender oppression in southern Africa's precapitalist societies', in Walker (ed.), *Women and gender*, pp. 33–47

Guy, Jeff, *The Maphumulo uprising: war, law and ritual in the Zulu Rebellion*, Scottsville: University of Natal Press, 2005

Habib, A. and K. Bentley (eds.), *Racial redress and citizenship in South Africa*, Pretoria: Human Sciences Research Council, 2008

Haggard, Henry Rider, *Cetywayo and his white neighbours; or remarks on recent events in Zululand, Natal and the Transvaal*, London: Trübner, 1882

Halisi, C. R. D., *Black political thought in the making of South Africa*, Bloomington: Indiana University Press, 1999

Hamilton, C., 'The poetics and politics of public history', *South African Historical Journal* 27:1 (1992), 234–7

Hamilton, C., *Terrific majesty: the powers of Shaka Zulu and the limits of historical invention*, Cambridge, MA: Harvard University Press, 1998

Hancock, W. K., *Smuts*, 2 vols., Cambridge: Cambridge University Press, 1962–1968.

Hancock, W. K. and Jean Van Der Poel (eds.), *Selections from the Smuts papers. Vol. 1, June 1886–May 1902*, Cambridge: Cambridge University Press, 1962

Hancock W. K. and Jean Van Der Poel (eds.), *Selections from the Smuts Papers. Vol. 2, June 1902–May 1910*, Cambridge: Cambridge University Press, 1966.

Hanlon, Joseph, *Beggar your neighbours: apartheid power in southern Africa*, London: James Currey, 1986

Hansen, B. R., 'Public spaces for national commemoration: the case of Emlotheni Memorial, Port Elizabeth', *Anthropology and Humanism* 28:1 (2003), 43–60

Harries, Patrick, 'Histories old and new', *South African Historical Journal* 30:1 (May 1994), 121–34

Harries, Patrick, *Work, culture and identity: migrant laborers in Mozambique and South Africa, c. 1860–1910*, Portsmouth, NH: Heinemann; London: James Currey; Johannesburg: Witwatersrand University Press, 1994

Hart, K. and V. Padayachee, 'Indian business in South Africa after apartheid: new and old trajectories', *Comparative Studies in Society and History* 42:2 (2000), 683–712

Hattersley, A. F., *The convict crisis and the growth of unity: resistance to transportation in South Africa and Australia, 1848–1853*, Pietermaritzburg: University of Natal Press, 1965

Hauptfleisch, Temple and Ian Steadman (eds.), *South African theatre: four plays and an introduction*, Pretoria: Hollandsch Afrikaansche Uitgevers Maarschappij, 1984

Hausmann, Ricardo, *Final recommendations of the International panel on ASGISA*, CID working paper no. 161, Cambridge MA: Harvard University, 2008

Hausmann, Ricardo and B. Klinger, 'South Africa's export predicament', *Economics of Transition* 16 (2008), 609–37

Headlam, C. (ed.), *The Milner papers*, 2 vols., Toronto: Cassell, 1931–1933

Hellmann, Ellen (ed.), *Handbook on race relations in South Africa*, Cape Town: Oxford University Press, 1949

Herbst, Jeffrey, 'Political and economic implications of South Africa's militarization', *Jerusalem Journal of International Relations* 8:1 (1986), 45–7

Herbst, Jeffrey, 'Prospects for revolution in South Africa', *Political Science Quarterly* 103:4 (Winter 1988–1989), 665–85

Herder, Carol, *The diary of Maria Tholo*, Johannesburg: Ravan Press, 1980

Heunis, Jan, *The inner circle: reflections on the last days of white rule*, Johannesburg: Jonathan Ball, 2007

Heymans, Chris and Gerhard Totemeyer (eds.), *Government by the people? The politics of local government in South Africa*, Cape Town: Juta, 1988

Hexham, I., *The irony of apartheid: the struggle for national independence of Afrikaner Calvinism against British imperialism*, New York: Mellen Press, 1981

Higginson, John, 'Upending the century of wrong: the American South: agrarian elites, collective violence, and the transformation of state power in the American South and South Africa, 1865–1914', *Social Identities* 4:3 (1998), 399–415

Hindson, Doug, *Pass control and the urban African proletariat*, Johannesburg: Ravan Press, 1987

Hirson, Baruch, *A history of the left in South Africa: writings*, London: Tauris, 2005

Hirson, Baruch, *Year of fire, year of ash: the Soweto revolt: roots of a revolution*, London, Zed, 1979

Hirson, Baruch, *Yours for the union: class and community struggles in South Africa, 1930–1947*, London: Zed, 1989

Hirson, Denis, *White scars: on reading and rites of passage*, Johannesburg: Jacana, 2006

Hobson, J. A., *The war in South Africa: its causes and effects*, London: Nisbet, 1900

Hoffman, T. and S. Todd, 'A national review of land degradation in South Africa: the influence of biophysical and socio-economic factors', *Journal of Southern African Studies* 26:4 (2000), 743–58

Hofmeyr, Isabel, 'Building a nation from words: Afrikaans language, literature and identity, 1902–1924', in Marks and Trapido (eds.), *The politics of race, class and nationalism*, pp. 95–123

Hofmeyr, Isabel, 'Popularising history – the case of Gustav Prellar', *Journal of African History* 29:3 (1988), 521–35

Hofmeyr, Isabel, *'We spend our years as a tale that is told': oral historical narratives in a South African chiefdom*, Portsmouth, NH; London; Johannesburg: Heinemann, James Currey and Witwatersrand University Press, 1993–1994

Hofmeyr, J. H., with F. W. Reitz, *The Life of Jan Hendrik Hofmeyr (Onze Jan)*, Cape Town: van de Sandt de Villiers, 1913

Hofmeyr, Julian, 'An analysis of African wage movements in South Africa', Research Monograph No. 9, Economic Research Unit, University of Natal, Durban, 1994

Hooper, C., *Brief authority*, London: Collins, 1960

Horrell, Muriel, *Legislation and race relations*, Johannesburg: South African Institute of Race Relations, 1971

Horrell, Muriel, Tony Hodgeson, Suzanne Blignaut and Sean Moroney, *A survey of race relations in South Africa, 1976*, Johannesburg: South African Institute of Race Relations, 1977

Houghton, D. Hobart, 'Economic development, 1865–1965', in Wilson and Thompson (eds.), *The Oxford history of South Africa*, vol. 2, *South Africa 1870–1966*, pp. 1–48

Houghton, D. Hobart, *The South African economy*, 4th ed., London: Oxford University Press, 1976

Houghton, D. Hobart and E. Walton, *The economy of a native reserve*, Keiskammahoek Rural Survey, vol. 2, Pietermaritzburg: Shuter and Shooter, 1952

Houston, Gregory, *The national liberation struggle in South Africa: a case study of the United Democratic Front, 1983–1987*, Aldershot, U.K.: Ashgate Publishing, 1999

Houston, Gregory, 'The post Rivonia ANC/SACP underground,' in South African Democracy Education Trust, *The road to democracy*, vol. 1, pp. 601–60

Houston, Gregory and Bernard Magubane, 'The ANC political underground in the 1970s,' in South African Democracy Education Project, *The road to democracy in South Africa*, vol. 2, pp. 371–451

Huddleston, Sarah, *George Pemba: against all odds*, Johannesburg: Jonathan Ball, 1996

Hudson, Peter, 'The Freedom Charter and socialist strategy in South Africa', *Politikon* 13:1 (1986), 75–90

Human Sciences Research Council, *South African labour market trends and future work force needs, 1998–2003*, Pretoria, Human Sciences Research Council, 1999

Hyslop, Jonathan, *The classroom struggle: policy and resistance in South Africa, 1940–1990*, Pietermaritzburg: University of Natal Press, 1999

Hyslop, Jonathan, 'The imperial working class makes itself "white": white labourism in Britain, Australia and SA before the First World War', *Journal of Historical Sociology* 12:4 (1999), 398–421

Hyslop, Jonathan, *The notorious syndicalist. J. T. Bain, a Scottish rebel in colonial South Africa*, Johannesburg: Jacana, 2004

Hyslop, Jonathan, 'Why did apartheid supporter capitulate? "Whiteness", class and consumerism in urban South Africa, 1985–1995', *Society in Transition* 31:1 (2000), 36–44

Iliffe, John, *The African AIDS epidemic: a history*, Oxford: James Currey; Athens: Ohio University Press; Cape Town: Double Storey, 2006

Innes, Duncan, *Anglo: Anglo American and the rise of modern South Africa*, Johannesburg: Ravan Press, 1984

Institute of Industrial Education, *The Durban strikes, 1973: human beings with souls*, Durban: Ravan Press, 1976

Israel, Mark, *South African political exile in the United Kingdom*, Basingstoke, U.K.: Macmillan, 1999

Jabavu, D. D. T., *The Black problem*, Lovedale: Lovedale Press, 1920

Jabavu, N., *The ochre people: scenes from a South African life*, London: John Murray, 1963

Jacobs, N., *Environment, power and injustice: a South African history*, Cambridge: Cambridge University Press, 2003

Jaffe, Hosea, *Three hundred years: a history of South Africa*, Cape Town: New Era Fellowship, 1952

Jeeves, Alan H., *Migrant labour in South Africa's mining economy: the struggle for the gold mines' labour supply, 1890–1920*, Kingston: McGill-Queens's University Press; Johannesburg: Witwatersrand University Press, 1985

Jeffries, Anthea, *The Natal story: sixteen years of conflict*, Johannesburg: South African Institute of Race Relations, 1997

Jeppie, Shamil, 'Re-classifications: Coloured, Malay, Muslim', in Erasmus (ed.), *Coloured by history*, pp. 80–96

Jochelson, K., *The colour of disease: syphilis and racism in South Africa, 1880–1950*, New York: Palgrave, in association with St Antony's College, 2001

Joffe, Avril, D. Kaplan, R. Kaplinsky and D. Lewis, *Improving manufacturing performance in South Africa: report of the Industrial Strategy Project*, Cape Town: University of Cape Town Press, 1995

Johnson, Phyllis and David Martin (eds.), *Frontline southern Africa: destructive engagement*, New York: Four Walls, Eight Windows, 1988

Johnson, R. W., *How long will South Africa survive?*, Johannesburg: Macmillan, 1977

Johnson, Shaun, *South Africa: no turning back*, Bloomington: Indiana University Press, 1989

Johnson, Shaun, 'Youth in the politics of resistance,' in S. Johnson, *South Africa*, pp. 94–152

Johnstone, Frederick, *Class, race and gold: a study of class relations and racial discrimination in South Africa*, London: Routledge and Kegan Paul and University Press of America, 1976

Jones, S., '"To come together for progress": modernisation and nation-building in South Africa's Bantustan periphery', *Journal of Southern African Studies* 25:4 (1999), 579–605

Jones, Stuart and Andre Muller, *The South African economy, 1910–90*, London: Macmillan, 1992

Jordan, Zweledinga Pallo, 'Keynote address on behalf of the National Executive Committee of the ANC', in Campschreur and Divendal (eds.), *Culture*, pp. 259–65

Judd, D. and K. Surridge, *The Boer War*, London: John Murray, 2002

Junod, H.-A., *Life of a South African tribe*, London: Macmillan, 1912–13

Kallaway, P. (ed.), *The history of education under apartheid, 1948–1994*, New York: Peter Lang Publishing, 2002

Kane-Berman, John, *Soweto: black revolt, white reaction*, Johannesburg: Ravan Press, 1979

Kaplan, David, *The crossed line: the South African telecommunications industry in transition*, Johannesburg: Witwatersrand University Press, 1990

Kaplan, David and David Lewis, 'Improving productivity performance in South Africa: a response to Trevor Bell', *Transformation* 30 (1996), 115–28

Kaplinsky, Raphael, 'Capital intensity in South African manufacturing and unemployment, 1972–90', *World Development* 23:2 (1995), 179–92

Karis, T. and G. M. Carter (eds.), *From protest to challenge: a documentary history of African politics in South Africa, 1882–1964*, 4 vols., Stanford, CA: Stanford University Press, 1972–1977

Karis, T. and G. Gerhart (eds.), *From protest to challenge: a documentary history of African politics in South Africa*, vol. 5, *Nadir and resurgence, 1964–1979*, Pretoria: UNISA Press; Bloomington: Indiana University Press, 1997

Kasrils, Ronnie, *Armed and dangerous: from undercover struggle to freedom*, Johannesburg: Jonathan Ball, 1998

Katz, Elaine, *A trade union aristocracy: a history of white workers in the Transvaal and the General Strike of 1913*, Johannesburg: African Studies Institute, 1976

Katz, Elaine, *The white death: silicosis on the Witwatersrand gold mines, 1886–1910*, Johannesburg: Witwatersrand University Press, 1994

Bibliography

Katzen, Kit, 'Mysteries and unanswered questions in the CCB trial', *Star* (22 September 1990)

Katzenellenbogen, Simon, *South Africa and southern Mozambique: labour, railways and trade in the making of a relationship*, Manchester, U.K.: Manchester University Press, 1982

Keegan, Tim (ed.), *Facing the storm: portraits of black lives in rural South Africa*, Cape Town: David Philip; London: Zed, 1988

Keegan, Tim, 'The making of the rural economy: from 1850 to the present', in Konczaki, Parpart and Shaw (eds.), *Studies in the economic history of southern Africa*, vol. 2, pp. 36–63

Keegan, Tim, *Rural transformations in industrializing South Africa: the southern highveld to 1914*, Johannesburg: Ravan Press, 1986

Keppel-Jones, A., *Friends or foes?*, Pietermaritzburg: Shuter and Shooter, 1949

Kershaw, Ian, *The Nazi dictatorship: problems and perspectives of interpretation*, London: Edward Arnold, 1991

Khan, F., 'Rewriting South Africa's conservation history: the role of the Native Farmers' Association', *Journal of Southern African Studies* 20:4 (1994), 499–516

Khan, F., 'Soil wars: the role of the African National Soil Conservation Association in South Africa, 1953–1959', *Environmental History* 2:4 (1997), 439–59

Kidd, Dudley, *The essential Kafir*, London: Adam and Charles Black, 1904

Kidd, Dudley, *Kafir socialism and the dawn of individualism*, London: Adam and Charles Black, 1908

Kidd, Dudley, *Savage childhood*, London: Adam and Charles Black, 1906

Kiloh, M. and A. Sibeko (Zola Zembe), *A fighting union: an oral history of the South African Railways and Harbour Workers' Union, 1936–1998*, Johannesburg: Ravan Press, 2000

Klasen, Stephan, 'Poverty, inequality and deprivation in South Africa: an analysis of the 1993 SALDRU Survey', *Social Indicators Research* 41:1–3 (1997), 51–94

Klausen, S., *Race, maternity and the politics of birth control in South Africa, 1910–1939*, Basingstoke, U.K.: Palgrave Macmillan, 2004

Klug, H., *Constituting democracy: law, globalism and South Africa's political reconstruction*, Cambridge: Cambridge University Press, 2000

Koch, E., '"Without visible means of subsistence": slumyard culture in Johannesburg, 1918–1940', in Bozzoli (ed.), *Town and countryside in the Transvaal*, pp. 151–75

Konczaki, Z. A., Jane Parpart and Timothy Shaw (eds.), *Studies in the economic history of southern Africa*, vol. 1, London: Frank Cass, 1991

Kondlo, Kwandile, *In the twilight of the revolution: the Pan-Africanist Congress of Azania, 1959–1994*, Basel: Basler Afrika Bibliographien, 2009

Kopytoff, I. (ed.), *The African frontier: the reproduction of traditional African societies*, Bloomington: Indiana University Press, 1987

Krikler, Jeremy, *The Rand Revolt: the 1922 insurrection and racial killing in South Africa*, Johannesburg: Jonathan Ball, 2005

Krikler, Jeremy, *Revolution from above, rebellion from below: the agrarian Transvaal at the turn of the century*, Oxford: Clarendon University Press, 1993

Krikler, Jeremy, *White rising: the 1922 insurrection and racial killing in South Africa*, Manchester, U.K.: Manchester University Press, 2005

Kros, C., 'Heritage vs. history: the end of a noble tradition?', *Historia* 48:1 (2003), 326–36

Kros, C., 'Public history/heritage: translation, transgression or more of the same', *African Studies* 69 (2010), 63–77

Kruger, Franz, 'Flirting with the Residents' Committees', *Work in Progress* 54 (June 1988), 23–6

Kruger, Loren, *The drama of South Africa: plays, pageants and publics since 1910*, London: Routledge, 1999

Kuper, L., *An African bourgeoisie*, New Haven, CT: Yale University Press, 1965

Kuzwayo, Ellen, *Call me woman*, London: Women's Press; Johannesburg: Ravan Press, 1985

Kynaston, David, *The city of London*, vol. 2, *Golden years, 1890–1914*, London: Pimlico Press, 1995

Kynoch, G., *We are fighting the world: a history of the MaRashea gangs in South Africa, 1947–1999*, Athens: Ohio University Press; Pietermaritzburg: University of KwaZulu Natal Press, 2005

Laband, John, *The Transvaal rebellion: the First Boer War, 1880–1*, Harlow, U.K.: Longman-Pearson, 2005

Lacey, Marian, *Working for Boroko: origins of a coercive labour system in South Africa*, Johannesburg: Ravan Press, 1981

La Guma, Alex, *A walk in the night and other stories*, London: Heinemann, 1968

La Hausse de Lalouvière, P., 'The message of the warriors: the ICU, the labouring poor and the making of popular culture in Durban, 1925–30', in Bonner et al. (eds.), *Holding their ground*, pp. 19–57

La Hausse de Lalouvière, P., *Restless identities: signatures of nationalism, Zulu ethnicity and history in the lives of Petros Lamula (c. 1881–1948) and Lymon Maling (1889–c. 1936)*, Pietermaritzburg: University of Natal Press, 2000

Lalu, P., *The deaths of Hintsa: postapartheid South Africa and the shape of recurring pasts*, Pretoria: HSRC Press, 2009

Lambert, John, *Betrayed trust: Africans and the state in colonial Natal*, Scottsville: University of Natal Press, 1995

Landman, C., *The piety of Afrikaner women*, Pretoria: UNISA Press, 1994

Langenhoven, C. J., 'The problem of dual language in South Africa', *State* (March 1910)

Lavin, Deborah, *From empire to international commonwealth: a biography of Lionel Curtis*, New York: Clarendon Press, 1995

Lee, Donvé, *Dumile Feni: making art out of suffering*, Kelvin: Awareness Publishing Group, 2006

Lee, Donvé, *George Pemba: the painter of the people*, Kelvin: Awareness Publishing Group, 2006

Lee, Donvé, *Noria Mabasa: carving her name in history*, Kelvin: Awareness Publishing Group, 2006

Lee, Donvé, *Peter Clarke: following dreams and finding fame*, Kelvin: Awareness Publishing Group, 2006

Legassick, Martin, 'Post-script to "Legislation, ideology and economy in post 1948 South Africa"', in Schlemmer and Webster (eds.), *Change, reform and economic growth*, pp. 73–4

Legassick, Martin, 'South Africa: capital accumulation and violence', *Economy and Society* 3 (1974), 253–91

Leibbrandt, Murray, Ingrid Woolard and Haroon Bhorat, 'Understanding contemporary household inequality in South Africa', in Bhorat et al., *Fighting poverty*, pp. 21–40

Le May, G. H. L., *British supremacy in South Africa, 1899–1907*, Oxford: Clarendon Press, 1965

Lembede, A. M., 'Policy of the Congress Youth League', *Inkundla ya Bantu* (May 1946), in Karis and Carter (eds.), *From protest to challenge*, vol. 2, no 53.

Lenta, G., *Land shortage and land unused: the paradoxical patterns of KwaZulu*, occasional paper no. 10, Durban: Economic Research Unit, University of Natal, 1981

Leonard, Richard, *South Africa at war*, Craighall: Donker, 1983

Lewis, David, 'Markets, ownership and manufacturing performance', in Joffe et al., *Improving manufacturing performance*, pp. 133–85

Lewis, Desiree, 'Black women and biography in South Africa', in Yousaf (ed.), *Apartheid narratives*, pp. 163–89

Lewis, Gavin, *Between the wire and the wall: a history of 'Coloured' politics*, Cape Town: David Philip; New York: St Martin's Press, 1987

Lewis, Jon, *Industrialisation and trade union organisation in South Africa: the rise and fall of the South African Trades and Labour Council*, Cambridge: Cambridge University Press, 1984

Lewson, P., *John X. Merriman: paradoxical South African statesman*, Cape Town: Donker, 1982

Lewson, P. (ed.), *Selections from the correspondence of John X. Merriman, 1870–1890*, Cape Town: Van Riebeeck Society, 1960

Lieberman, Evan, *Race and regionalism in the politics of taxation in Brazil and South Africa*, Cambridge: Cambridge University Press, 2003

Livi-Bacci, M., *A concise history of world population*, 2nd ed., Oxford: Blackwell, 1997

Lodge, Tom, *Black politics in South Africa since 1945*, London: Longman, 1983

Lodge, Tom (ed.), *Resistance and ideology in settler societies*, Southern African Studies 4, Johannesburg: Ravan Press, 1986

Lodge, Tom, 'Soldiers of the storm: a profile of the Azanian Liberation Army,' in Cilliers and Reichardt (eds.), *About turn*, pp. 105–17

Lodge, Tom and W. Nasson, *All, here, and now: black politics in South Africa in the 1980s*, London: Hurst, 1992

Longmore, L., *The dispossessed: a study of sex-life of Bantu women in urban areas in and around Johannesburg*, London: Cape, 1959

Lowenthal, D., *The heritage crusade and the spoils of history*, Cambridge: Cambridge University Press, 1998

Lowry, D. (ed.), *The South African War reappraised*, Manchester, U.K.: Manchester University Press, 2000

Luckhardt, Ken and Brenda Wall, *Organize or starve! The history of the South African Congress of Trade Unions*, London: Lawrence and Wishart, 1980

Luthuli, A., 'The Christian and political issues', in *The Christian citizen in a multi-racial society*, pp. 70–7

Mabin, A., 'Comprehensive segregation: the origins of the Group Areas Act and its planning apparatuses', *Journal of Southern African Studies* 18:2 (1992), 405–29

Mabin, Alan (ed.), *Organisation and social change*, Southern African Studies 5, Johannesburg: Ravan Press, 1989

Macmillan, W. M., *Complex South Africa: an economic footnote to history*, London: Faber and Faber, 1930

Macmillan, W. M., *My South African years*, Cape Town: David Philip, 1975

Maddison, Angus, *The world economy: a millennial perspective*, Paris: Organisation of Economic Co-operation and Development, 2001

Mager, A. K., *Gender and the making of a South African Bantustan: a social history of the Ciskei, 1945–1959*, Portsmouth, NH: Heinemann; Oxford: James Currey; Cape Town: David Philip, 1999

Mager, A. K., 'One beer, one goal, one nation, one soul: South African Breweries, heritage, masculinity and nationalism, 1960–1999', *Past and Present* 188 (2005), 163–94

Magubane, B. M., 'Whose memory – whose history? The illusion of liberal and radical historical debates', in Stolten (ed.), *History making*, pp. 251–79

Mahlalela, L. N., 'Workerism and economism', *African Communist* 104 (1986), 77–88

Maimane A., *Hate no more*, Cape Town: Kwela Books, 2000

Malherbe, E., *Education in South Africa*, vol. 2, *1923–1975*, Cape Town: Juta, 1977

Mamdani, Mahmood, *Citizen and subject: contemporary Africa and the late colonialism*, Kampala: Fountain, David Philip and James Currey, 1996

Manganyi, N. Chabani, *A black man called Sekoto*, Johannesburg: Witwatersrand University Press, 1996

Mangena, Mosibudi, *On your own: evolution of Black Consciousness in South Africa/Azania*, Johannesburg: Skotaville, 1989

Marais, J. S., *The Cape coloured people*, London: Longmans, 1939

Marais, J. S., *The fall of Kruger's republic*, Oxford: Oxford University Press, 1961

Marcus, Tessa, *Modernising super-exploitation: restructuring South African agriculture*, London: Zed, 1989

Mare, G. and G. Hamilton, *An appetite for power: Buthelezi's Inkatha and the politics of 'loyal resistance'*, Johannesburg: Ravan Press, 1987

Markham, Violet, *The new era in South Africa: with an examination of the Chinese labour question*, London: Smith Elder, 1904

Marks, Shula, 'Afterword: worlds of impossibilities', in Dubow and Jeeves (eds.), *South Africa's 1940s*, pp. 267–82

Marks, Shula, *The ambiguities of dependence in South Africa: class, nationalism and the state in twentieth-century Natal*, Johannesburg: Ravan Press, 1986

Marks, Shula, *Divided sisterhood: race, class and gender in the South African nursing profession*, Basingstoke, U.K.: Macmillan, 1994

Marks, Shula, *Reluctant rebellion: the 1906–8 disturbances in Natal*, Oxford: Clarendon Press, 1970

Marks, Shula and A. Atmore (eds.), *Economy and society in pre-industrial South Africa*, London: Longman, 1980

Marks, Shula and Richard Rathbone (eds.), *Industrialisation and social change in South Africa: African class formation, culture and consciousness, 1870–1930*, London: Longman, 1982

Marks, Shula and Stanley Trapido, 'Lord Milner and the South African state', *History Workshop* 8 (Autumn 1979), 50–80

Marks, Shula and Stanley Trapido, 'Lord Milner and the South African state', in Twaddle (ed.), *Imperialism, the state and the third world*, pp. 80–94

Marks, Shula and Stanley Trapido (eds.), *The politics of race, class and nationalism*, Harlow, U.K.: Longman, 1987

Marks, Shula and Stanley Trapido, 'South Africa since 1976: an historical perspective', in Johnson (ed.), *South Africa: no turning back*, pp. 1–51

Marx, Anthony W., *Lessons of struggle*, New York: Oxford University Press, 1992

Masekela, Hugh, *Still grazing: the musical journey of Hugh Masekela*, New York: Crown, 2004

Mashinini, Emma, *Strikes have followed me all my life: a South African autobiography*, New York: Routledge, 1991

Masilela, Ntongela, *The cultural modernity of H. I. E. Dhlomo*, Trenton, NJ: Africa World; London: Turnaround, 2007

Mathabatha, Ngoanamadima Johannes Sello, *The struggle over education in the Northern Transvaal: the case of Catholic mission schools*, Amsterdam: Rozenburg Publishers, 2005

Matshoba, Mthuthuzeli, *Call me not a man*, Johannesburg: Ravan Press, 1979

Maurice, Emile and Jo-Anne Duggan, 'Cecil Skotnes', *South African Art Times* (May 2009)

Mayer, Philip, 'Class, status and ethnicity among Johannesburg Africans', in Thompson and Butler (eds.), *Change in contemporary South Africa*, pp. 138–67

Mayer, Philip, *Soweto people and their social universes*, Pretoria: Human Sciences Research Council, 1979

Mayer, Philip, *Urban Africans and the Bantustans*, Johannesburg: South African Institute of Race Relations, 1972

Mayer, Philip and I. Mayer, *Townsmen or tribesmen: conservatism and the process of urbanization in a South African city*, Cape Town: Oxford University Press, 1971

Maylam, Paul, *The cult of Rhodes: remembering an imperialist in Africa*, Cape Town: David Philip, 2005

Maylam, Paul, *A history of the African people of South Africa: from the early Iron Age to the 1970s*, London: Croom Helm, 1986

Maylam, Paul and I. Edwards (eds.), *The people's city: African life in twentieth-century Durban*, Pietermaritzburg: University of Natal Press; Portsmouth, NH: Heinemann, 1996

Mazower, M., *Dark continent: Europe's twentieth century*, New York: Vintage Books, 2003

McCaul, Colleen, 'The wild card: Inkatha and contemporary black politics', in Frankel, Pines and Swilling (eds.), *State resistance and change*, pp. 146–73

McClandon, T. V., *Genders and generations apart: labor tenants and customary law in segregation-era South Africa, 1920s to 1940s*, Cape Town: David Philip, 2002

McCulloch, J., *Asbestos blues: labour, capital, physicians and the state in South Africa*, Oxford: James Currey; Bloomington: Indiana University Press, 2002

McGrath, M. D., 'The racial distribution of taxes and state expenditures', Black/White Income Gap Project Final Research Report no. 2, Durban: Department of Economics, University of Natal, 1979

McLennan, B., *Apartheid: the lighter side*, Cape Town: Chameleon Press, 1990

Mda, Zakes, 'The role of culture in the process of reconciliation in South Africa', Centre for the Study of Violence and Reconciliation (Johannesburg) seminar no. 9, 1994

Meer, Ismail, *A fortunate man*, Cape Town: Zebra, 2002

Meintjies, C., 'Impediments on the labour absorption capacity of the South African economy', discussion paper no. 2, Development Bank of Southern Africa (1998)

Meli, Francis, *South Africa belongs to us: a history of the ANC*, London: James Currey, 1989

Millin, S. G., *The South Africans*, London: Constable, 1926

Minkley, Gary and Ciraj Rassool, 'Orality, memory and social history in South Africa', in Nuttall and Coetzee (eds.), *Negotiating the past*, pp. 89–99

Minter, W., G. Hovey and C. Cobb Jr. (eds.), *No easy victories: African liberation and American activists over half a century*, Trenton, NJ: Africa World Press, 2008

Minty, Abdul, 'South Africa's military build-up', in Johnson and Martin (eds.), *Frontline southern Africa*, pp. 233–80

Mitchell, Mark and Dave Russell, 'Black unions and political change in South Africa', in Brewer (ed.), *Can South Africa survive?*, pp. 231–54

Mitchell, T., *Rule of experts: Egypt, techno-politics, modernity*, Los Angeles: University of California Press, 2002

Modisane, Bloke, *Blame me on history*, Cape Town: Donker, 1986 (originally published 1963)

Mofolo, T., *Shaka*, Morija: Sesuto Book Depot, 1925; London: Heinemann, 1981 (trans. D. P. Kunene)

Molema, S. M., *The Bantu: past and present*, Edinburgh: Green, 1920

Moll, Terence, 'A mixed and threadbare bag: employment, incomes and poverty in Lower Roza, Qumbu, Transkei', 2nd Carnegie Inquiry into Poverty and Development in Southern Africa, Cape Town, 13–19 April 1984, Cape Town: Southern African Labour and Development Research Unit, 1984

Moll, Terence, 'Did the apartheid economy "fail"?', *Journal of Southern African Studies* 17:2 (1991), 271–91

Moloi, Godfrey, *My life: the godfather of Soweto*, Johannesburg: Jonathan Ball, 1991

Moodie, T. Dunbar, *The rise of Afrikanerdom: power, apartheid and the Afrikaner civil religion*, Berkeley: University of California Press; Johannesburg: Witwatersrand University Press, 1975

Moodie, T. Dunbar, 'The South African state and labour conflict in the 1940s', *International Journal of African Historical Studies* 21 (1988), 21–61

Moodie, T. Dunbar with Vivienne Ndatshe, *Going for gold: men, mines and migration*, Berkeley: University of California Press; Johannesburg: Witwatersrand University Press, 1994

Morrell, Robert, 'The poor whites of Middelburg Transvaal, 1912–1930: resistance, accommodation and class struggle', in Morrell (ed.), *White but poor*, pp. 1–28

Morrell, Robert (ed.), *White but poor: essays on the history of poor whites in southern Africa, 1880–1940*, Pretoria: UNISA Press, 1992

Morris, J. and E. Preston-Whyte (eds.), *Speaking with beads: Zulu arts from southern Africa*, London: Thames and Hudson, 1994

Morris, Mike, 'The development of capitalism in South Africa: class struggle in the countryside', *Economy and Society* 5:4 (1976), 292–343

Moss, Glen and Ingrid Obery (eds.), *South African Review 4*, Johannesburg: Ravan Press, 1987

Moss, Glenn and Ingrid Obery (eds.), *South African Review 5*, Johannesburg: Ravan Press, 1989

Mostert, W. P., J. S. Oosthuizen and B. E. Hofmeyr, *Demography: textbook for the South African student*, Pretoria: Human Sciences Research Council, 1998

Mphahlele, E., *The African image*, London: Faber and Faber, 1962

Mphahlele, E., *Down Second Avenue*, London: Faber and Faber, 1959

Muller, C. F. J., *500 years: a history of South Africa*, Pretoria: Academica, 1969

Murray, Colin, *Black mountain: land, class and power in the eastern Orange Free State, 1880s–1980s*, Johannesburg: Witwatersrand University Press for International African Institute, 1992

Murray, Colin, 'Structural unemployment, small towns and agrarian change in South Africa', *African Affairs* 94:374 (1995), 5–22

Murray, Martin, *South Africa: time of agony, time of destiny: the upsurge of popular protest*, London: Verso, 1987

Mzala, 'Building people's power, *Sechaba* (September 1986)

Naidoo, Kumi, 'Internal resistance in South Africa: the political movements', in Johnson (ed.), *South Africa: no turning back*, pp. 172–205

Naidoo, Kumi, 'The politics of youth resistance in the 1980s: the dilemmas of a differentiated Durban', *Journal of Southern African Studies* 18:1 (March 1992), 143–65

Nash, R., 'American environmental history: a new teaching frontier', *Pacific History Review* 41 (1972), 362–72

Nasson, W., *Abraham Esau's War: a black South African war in the Cape, 1899–1902*, Cambridge: Cambridge University Press, 1991

Nasson, W., 'Commemorating the Anglo-Boer War in post-apartheid South Africa', *Radical History Review* 78 (2000), 140–59

Nasson, W. and J. Samuel (eds.), *Education: from poverty to liberty*, Cape Town: David Philip, 1990

Nasson, W., *The South African War, 1899–1910*, London: Arnold, 1999

Nathan, Laurie, 'Resistance to militarisation: three years of the End Conscription Campaign', in Moss and Obery, *South African Review 4*, pp. 104–16

Nattrass, Nicoli, 'Economic aspects of the construction of apartheid', in Bonner et al. (eds.), *Apartheid's genesis*, pp. 42–64

Nattrass, Nicoli, 'Economic growth and transformation in the 1940s', in Dubow and Jeeves (eds.), *South Africa's 1940s*, pp. 26–32

Nattrass, Nicoli, and Elizabeth Ardington (eds.), *The political economy of South Africa*, Cape Town: Oxford University Press, 1990

Ndebele, Njabulo, 'I hid my love in a sewage', in Couzens and Patel (eds.), *The return of the Amasi bird*, pp. 213–14

Ndebele, Njabulo, 'Liberation and the crisis of culture', in Boehmer, Chrisman and Parker (eds.), *Altered state*, pp. 1–10

Ndebele, Njabulo, *Rediscovery of the ordinary: essays on South African literature and culture*, Johannesburg: Congress of South African Writers, 1991

Ndebele, Njabulo, *South African literature and culture: rediscovery of the ordinary*, Manchester, U.K.: Manchester University Press, 1994

Ndebele, Njabulo, 'Turkish tales and some thoughts on South African fiction', *Staffrider* 6:1 (1984), 24–5 and 42–8

Ndlovu, Duma (ed.), *Woza Afrika! An anthology of South African plays*, New York: George Braziller, 1986

Newton, A. P. (ed.), *Select documents relating to the unification of South Africa*, vol. 2, London: Frank Cass, 1968

Newton-King, S. 'The labour market of the Cape Colony, 1807–1828', in Marks and Atmore (eds.), *Economy and society*, pp. 171–207

Nkosi, Lewis, *The rhythm of violence*, London: Oxford University Press, 1964

Nkosi, Lewis, *Tasks and masks: themes and styles of African literature*. Harlow, U.K.: Longman, 1981

Noble, John, *South Africa past and present*, London: Longmans, 1877

Nolutshungu, Sam, *Changing South Africa: political considerations*, Manchester, U.K.: Manchester University Press, 1982

Nooter, Mary H. (ed.), *Secrecy: African art that conceals and reveals*, New York: Museum of African Art, 1993

Nora, P., 'Between memory and history: *les lieux de mémoire*', *Representations* 26 (1989), 7–25

Norval, A., *Deconstructing apartheid discourse*, London: Verso, 1996

Ntantala, P., *A life's mosaic*, Cape Town: David Philip and Mayibuye Centre, University of the Western Cape, 1988

Ntsebeza, Lungisile, *Democracy compromised: chiefs and the politics of land in South Africa*, Leiden: Brill, 2005

Nuttall, Sarah and Carli Coetzee (eds.), *Negotiating the past: the making of memory in South Africa*, Cape Town: Oxford University Press, 1998

Odendaal, Andre, *Vukani Bantu! The beginnings of black protest politics in South Africa to 1912*, Cape Town: David Philip, 1984

O'Malley, Padraig, *Shades of difference: Mac Maharaj and the struggle for South Africa*, New York: Viking, 2007

O'Meara, Dan, *Forty lost years: the apartheid state and politics of Afrikaner nationalism*, Johannesburg: Ravan Press; Athens: Ohio University Press, 1996

O'Meara, Dan, *Volkskapitalisme: class, capital and ideology in the development of Afrikaner Nationalism, 1934–48*, Cambridge: Cambridge University Press, 1983

Omissi, D. and A. Thompson (eds.), *The impact of the South African War*, Basingstoke, U.K.: Palgrave Macmillan, 2002

Orkin, Martin, *Drama and the South African state*, Manchester: Manchester University Press; Johannesburg: Witwatersrand University Press, 1991

Packard, Randall M., *White plague, black labor: tuberculosis and the political economy of health and disease in South Africa*, Berkeley: University of California Press, 1989; Pietermaritzburg: University of Natal Press; London: James Currey, 1990

Palmer, Mabel, *The history of Indians in Natal*, Cape Town: Oxford University Press, 1957

Pampallis, J., *Foundation of the new South Africa*, Cape Town: Maskew Miller Longman, 1971

Parle, J., *States of mind: searching for mental health in Natal and Zululand, 1868–1918*, Scottsville: University of KwaZulu-Natal Press, 2007

Parnell, Susan, 'Creating racial privilege: the origins of South African public health and planning legislation', *Journal of Southern African Studies* 19 (1993), 471–88

Parnell, Susan and A. Mabin, 'Rethinking urban South Africa', *Journal of Southern African Studies* 21:1 (1995), 39–61

Paton, Alan, *Cry the beloved country: a story of comfort in desolation*, New York: Charles Scribner's Sons, 1948

Paton, Alan, *South African tragedy: the life and times of Jan Hofmeyr*, New York: Charles Scribner's Sons, 1965

Pauw, B. A., *The second generation: a study of the family among urbanized Bantu in East London*, Cape Town: Oxford University Press, 1963

Pauw, S., *Beroepsarbeid van die Afrikaner in die stad*, Stellenbosch: Pro Ecclesia, 1946

Pelzer, A. N. (ed.), *Verwoerd speaks: speeches, 1948–1966*, Johannesburg: APB Publishers, 1966

Peterson, B., 'Apartheid and political imagination in black South African theatre', *Journal of Southern African Studies* 16:2 (1995), 229–45

Peterson, B., 'A rain a fall but the dirt it tough: scholarship on African theatre in South Africa', *Journal of Southern African Studies* 21:4 (1995), 573–84

Peterson, B., 'Liberation and the crisis of culture,' in Boehmer, Chrisman and Parker (eds.), *Altered state?*, pp. 1–10

Peterson, B., *Monarchs, missionaries and African intellectuals: African theatre and the unmaking of colonial marginality*, Johannesburg: Witwatersrand University Press, 2000

Phillips, L., *All that glittered: selected correspondence of Lionel Phillips, 1890–1924*, Cape Town: Oxford University Press, 1977

Phillips, L., *Some reminiscences*, London: Hutchinson, 1924

Phimister, I., 'Empire, imperialism and the partition of Africa', in Akita (ed.), *Gentlemanly capitalism*, pp. 65–82

Phoofolo, Pule, 'Epidemics and revolution: the rinderpest epidemic in late nineteenth-century southern Africa', *Past and Present* 138:1 (February 1993), 112–43

Phoofolo, Pule, 'Face to face with famine: the Basotho and the rinderpest, 1897–1899', *Journal of Southern African Studies* 29:2 (2003), 503–27

Pillay, Devan, 'Pursuing centralized bargaining', *South African Labour Bulletin* 15:4 (November 1990), 8–13

Pillay, G., *Voices of liberation*, vol. 1, *Albert Lutuli*, Pretoria: Human Sciences Research Council, 1993

Pillay, Pundy, 'The development and underdevelopment of education in South Africa', in Nasson and Samuel (eds.), *Education*, pp. 30–47

Pityana, B., M. Mpumlwana and L. Wilson (eds.), *Bounds of possibility: the legacy of Steve Biko and Black Consciousness*, Cape Town: David Philip, 1991

Plaatje, S. T., *The Boer War diary of Sol T. Plaatje: an African at Mafeking*, Johannesburg: Macmillan, 1973

Plaatje, S. T., *Mhudi: an epic of South African native life a hundred years ago*, Lovedale: Lovedale Press, 1930

Plaatje, S. T., *Native life in South Africa, before and since the European war and the Boer rebellion*, London: P. S. King, 1916

Plaatje, S. T., *Sechuana proverbs with literal translations and their European equivalents*, London: University of London Press, 1916

Plaatje, S. T. and D. Jones, *A Sechuana reader in international phonetic orthography*, London: University of London Press, 1916

Plaatjie, Thami ka, 'The PAC in exile,' in South Africa Democracy Education Trust, *The Road to Democracy*, vol. 2, pp. 703–46

Platsky, Laurine and Cherryl Walker, *The surplus people: forced removals in South Africa*, Johannesburg: Ravan Press, 1985

Plaut, Martin, 'Debates in a shark tank – the politics of South Africa's non-racial trade unions', *African Affairs* 91 (1992), 389–403

Porter, A., 'Lord Salisbury, Mr Chamberlain and South Africa, 1895–1899', *Journal of Imperial and Commonwealth History* 1:1 (1972), 3–26

Posel, D., 'The case for a welfare state: poverty and the politics of the urban African family in the 1930s and 40s', in Dubow and Jeeves (eds.), *South Africa's 1940s*, pp. 64–86

Posel, D., 'A mania for measurement: statistics and statecraft in the transition to apartheid', in Dubow (ed.), *Science and society*, pp. 116–42

Posel, D., *The making of apartheid, 1948–1961*, Oxford: Clarendon Press, 1991 and 1997

Posel, D., 'Marriage at the drop of a hat: housing and partnership in South Africa's urban African townships', *History Workshop* 61 (2006), 57–76

Posel, D., 'Race as common sense', *African Studies Review* 44:2 (2001), 87–114

Posel, D., 'Social history and the Wits History Workshop', *African Studies* 69:1 (2010), 29–40

Posel, D., 'Whiteness and power in the South African civil service: paradoxes of the apartheid state', *Journal of Southern African Studies* 25:4 (1999), 99–119

Pretorius, Fransjohan, 'Boer attitudes to Africans in wartime', in Lowry (ed.), *The South African War reappraised*, pp. 104–20

Price, Robert M. and Carl G. Rosberg (eds.), *The apartheid regime: political power and racial domination*, Berkeley: Institute of International Studies, University of California; Cape Town: David Philip, 1980

Raditlhalo, Sam, 'Forgotten son', *Southern African Review of Books* (November–December 1996), 15–17

Randall, Peter (ed.), *Some implications of inequality*, Johannesburg: Spro-Cas, 1971

Rantete, Johannes, *The third day of September: an eye-witness account of the Sebokeng Rebellion of 1984*, Johannesburg: Ravan Press, n.d.

Rassool, C., 'Power, knowledge, and the politics of public pasts', *African Studies* 69:1 (2010), 79–101

Rassool, C., 'The rise of heritage and the reconstitution of history in South Africa', *Kronos* 26 (2000), 1–21

Rassool, C., L. Witz and G. Minkley, 'Repackaging the past for South African tourism', *Daedalus* 130:1 (2001), 277–96

Reader, D. H., *The black man's portion*, Cape Town: Oxford University Press, 1961

Reitz, F. W., *Een eeuw van onrecht*, Dordrecht: Morks and Gueuze, 1899

Richards, C. S., 'Some aspects of South Africa's war effort', *South African Journal of Economics* 8:4 (1940), 325–63

Richards, C. S., 'Some thoughts on the Union's economic outlook', *South African Journal of Economics* 17:2 (1949), 142–54

Rive, Richard, *'Buckingham Palace', District Six*, Cape Town: David Philip, 1986

Roberts, Ronald Suresh, *No cold kitchen: a biography of Nadine Gordimer*, Johannesburg: STE Publishers, 2006

Robertson, H. M., '150 years of economic contact between black and white', 2 pts., *South African Journal of Economics* 2 (1934), 381–425; 3 (1935), 3–25

Robinson, J., *The power of apartheid: state, power and space in South African cities*, Oxford: Butterworth-Heinemann, 1996

Robinson, Ronald and J. Gallagher, *Africa and the Victorians: the official mind of imperialism*, New York: William Blackwood, 1961

Rodrik, Dani, 'Understanding South Africa's economic puzzles', *Economics of Transition* 16:4 (2008), 769–97

Rosen, G., 'Health, history and the Social Sciences', *Social Science and Medicine* 7:4 (1973), 233–48

Rosenthal, Richard, *Mission improbable: a piece of the South African story*, Cape Town: David Philip, 1998

Ross, R., *A concise history of South Africa*, Cambridge: Cambridge University Press, 1999

Roth, Mirjana, 'Domination by consent: elections under the Representation of Natives Act, 1937–48', in Lodge (ed.), *Resistance and ideology*, pp. 144–67

Rotberg, Robert I., *The founder: Cecil Rhodes and the pursuit of power*, New York: Oxford University Press, 1988

Roux, Eddie, *Time longer than rope: a history of the black man's struggle for freedom in South Africa*, London: Gollancz, 1948

Roux, E., *Time longer than rope: a history of the black man's struggle for freedom in South Africa*, 2nd ed., Madison: University of Wisconsin Press, 1964

Sadie, J. L., 'Estimating the March 1991 population of the RSA', in Central Statistics Service, *1991 Population Census*, vol. 03-01-26, Pretoria: Central Statistics Service, 1991

Sadie, J. L., 'The political arithmetic of the South African population', *Journal of Racial Affairs* 1:4 (1950), 3–8

Sadie, J. L., *A projection of the South African population, 1991–2011*, report 196, Pretoria: University of South Africa, Bureau of Market Research, 1991

Sadie, J. L., *A reconstruction and projection of demographic movements in the RSA and TBVC countries*, report 148, Pretoria: University of South Africa, Bureau of Market Research, 1988

Sanders, J., *Apartheid's friends: the rise and fall of the South African Secret Services*, London: John Murray, 2006

Sarakinsky, Ivor, 'The state of the state and the state of resistance', *Work in Progress* 52 (March 1988), 47–51

Sarakinsky, Ivor, 'A web of national manipulation', *Work in Progress* 55 (August 1988), 38–41

Saul, John and Stephen Gelb, *The crisis in South Africa*, London: Zed, 1981

Schapera, Isaac, 'Present-day life in the native reserves', in Schapera (ed.), *Western civilization*, pp. 39–62

Schapera, Isaac (ed.), *Western civilization and the natives of South Africa: studies in culture contact*, London: George Routledge and Sons, 1934

Schirmer, Stefan, 'Reactions to the state: the impact of farm labour policies in the mid-eastern Transvaal, 1955–1960', *South African Historical Journal* 30 (1994), 61–84

Schleicher, Hans-Georg, 'GDR solidarity: the German Democratic Republic and the South African liberation struggle', in South African Democracy Education Trust, *The Road to Democracy*, vol. 3, pp. 1069–153

Schlemmer, Lawrence and Edward Webster (eds.), *Change, reform and economic growth in South Africa*, Johannesburg: Ravan Press, 1978

Schneier, Steffen, *Occupational mobility among blacks in South Africa*, working paper no. 58, Cape Town: Southern African Labour and Development Research Unit, 1983

Schreiner, Olive, *Story of an African farm*, London: Collins, [1924?]

Schreiner, Olive, *Thoughts on South Africa*, London: Unwin, 1923

Scott, Gordon R., 'The murrain now known as rinderpest', *Newsletter of the Tropical Agriculture Society* 20:4 (2000), 14–16

Scott, J., *Seeing like a state: how certain schemes to improve human condition have failed*, New Haven, CT: Yale University Press, 1999

Scully, Pam, *The bouquet of freedom: social and economic relations at Stellenbosch, c. 1870–1900*, Cape Town: Centre for African Studies, University of Cape Town, 1990

Scully, W. C., *Sir J. H. Meiring Beck: a memoir*, Cape Town: Maskew Miller, n.d.

Seegers, Annette, 'Extending the security network to the local level', in Heymans and Totemeyer (eds.), *Government by the people?*, pp. 119–39

Seekings, Jeremy, *Heroes and villains: youth politics in the 1980s*, Johannesburg: Ravan Press, 1993

Seekings, Jeremy, '"Not a single white person should be allowed to go under": swartgevaar and the origins of South Africa's welfare state', *Journal of African History* 48:3 (November 2007), 375–94

Seekings, Jeremy, 'The origins of social citizenship in South Africa', *South African Journal of Philosophy* 19:4 (2000), 386–404

Seekings, Jeremy, 'Political mobilisation in the black townships of the Transvaal,' in Frankel, Pines and Swilling (eds.), *State, resistance and change*, pp. 197–228

Seekings, Jeremy, 'Trailing behind the masses: the United Democratic Front and township politics in the Pretoria-Witwatersrand-Vaal Region, 1983–1984, *Journal of Southern African Studies* 18:1 (March 1992), 93–114

Seekings, Jeremy, *The UDF: a history of the United Democratic Front*, Cape Town: David Philip, 2000

Seekings, Jeremy, '"Visions and hopes and views about the future": the radical moment of South African welfare reform', in Dubow and Jeeves (eds.), *South Africa's 1940s*, pp. 44–84

Seekings, Jeremy and Nicoli Nattrass, *Class, race and inequality in South Africa*, New Haven, CT: Yale University Press, 2005; Pietermaritzburg: University of KwaZulu-Natal Press, 2006

Sekoto, Gerard, *Gerard Sekoto: my life and work*, Johannesburg: Viva, 1995

Selborne, Lord, *The crisis of British power: the imperial and naval papers of the second Earl of Selborne, 1895–1910*, ed. G. D. Boyce, London: Historians' Press, 1990

Sellstrom, T., *Sweden and national liberation in southern Africa*, 2 vols., Uppsala: Nordic Africa Institute, 2002

Serote, Mongane Wally, *To every birth its blood*, Johannesburg: Ravan Press, 1981

Shain, M., *The roots of antisemitism in South Africa*, Johannesburg: Witwatersrand University Press, 1994

Shepherd, R. H. W., *Lovedale South Africa: the story of a century, 1841–1941*, Lovedale: Lovedale Press, [1941]

Shubin, V., *ANC: a view from Moscow*, Cape Town: Mayibuye Books, 1999; new ed., Johannesburg: Jacana, 2008

Shubin, Vladimir with Marina Traikova, 'There is no threat from the Eastern Bloc', in South African Democracy Education Trust, *The Road to Democracy*, vol. 3, pp. 985–1066

Sibeko, A. (Zola Zembe), with J. Leeson, *Freedom in our lifetime*, Durban: Indicator Press, 1996

Siebrits, Warren and Wayne Oosthuizen, *Art and urbanization: South Africa, 1940–1971*, Johannesburg: Warren Siebrits Modern and Contemporary Art, 2003

Simkins, Charles, *African population, employment and incomes on farms outside the reserves, 1923–1969*, Carnegie conference paper no. 25, Cape Town: Southern African Labour and Development Research Unit, 1984

Simkins, Charles, 'Agricultural production in the African reserves of South Africa, 1918–1969', *Journal of Southern African Studies* 7:2 (1981), 256–83)

Simkins, Charles, *Four essays on the past, present and possible future of the distribution of the Black population of South Africa*, Cape Town: Southern African Labour and Development Research Unit, 1983

Simkins, Charles, 'Household composition and structure on South Africa', in Burman and Reynolds (eds.), *Growing up in a divided society,* pp. 16–42

Simkins, Charles, *Mathematics and physical science results in the Senior Certificate examinations of 1998 and 2000*, Johannesburg: Report for the Centre for Development and Enterprise, 2001

Simkins, Charles, *School and community determinants of mathematics and physical science results in the Senior Certificate examination of 1998 and 2000*, Johannesburg: Report for the Centre for Development and Enterprise, 2001

Simkins, Charles, 'What has been happening to income distribution and poverty in the homelands?' 2nd Carnegie Inquiry into Poverty and Development in Southern Africa, Cape Town: Southern African Labour and Development Research Unit, University of Cape Town, 1984

Simkins, Charles and Andrew Paterson, *The social and economic determinants of performance in the language of instruction and mathematics in Quality Learning Project Schools*, Pretoria: Human Sciences Research Council Report to the Joint Educational Trust, 2002

Simkins, Charles and E. van Heyningen, 'Fertility, mortality and migration in the Cape Colony, 1891–1904', *International Journal of African Historical Studies* 22:1 (1989), 79–111

Simons, H. J., *African women: their legal status in South Africa*, London: C. Hurst and Company, 1968

Simons, H. J. and R. E. Simons, *Class and colour in South Africa, 1850–1950*, Harmondsworth, U.K.: Penguin Books, 1969; repr., London: International Defence and Aid Fund, 1983

Sithole, Jabulani and Sifiso Ndlovu, 'The revival of the labour movement', in South African Democracy Education Trust, *The road to democracy in South Africa*, vol. 2, pp. 187–214

Skocpol, Theda, 'Bringing the state back in: strategies of analysis in current research', in Evans, Rueschemeyer and Skocpol (eds.), *Bringing the state back in*, pp. 3–43

Skota, T. D. Mweli (ed.), *The African yearly register: being an illustrated national biographical dictionary (who's who) of Black folks in Africa*, Johannesburg: [Esson, 1930]

Slabbert, Frederick van Zyl, *The other side of history*, Johannesburg: Jonathan Ball, 2006

Smith, I. R., *The origins of the South African War, 1899–1902*, London: Longman, 1996

Smith, Robin, 'The black trade unions: from economics to politics', in Blumenfeld (ed.), *South Africa in crisis*, pp. 90–106

Smuts, J. C., *Memorandum on government natives and coloured bills*, Pretoria: South African Party, 1926

Sole, Sam, 'Top team to reopen probe into arms project's missing millions', *Sunday Independent* (19 May 1996)

Solomon, V. E., 'Transport', in Coleman (ed.), *Economic history of South Africa*, pp. 89–126

Sonnebend, H., 'Population', in Hellman (ed.), *Handbook on race relations*, pp. 4–26

Sono, Themba, *Reflections on the origins of Black Consciousness in South Africa*, Pretoria: Human Sciences Research Council, 1993

South African Democracy Education Trust, *The road to democracy in South Africa, 1960–1980*, 3 vols., Cape Town: Zebra Press, 2004; Pretoria: UNISA Press, 2006–2008

South African Institute of Race Relations, *Race relations survey, 1992/1993*, Johannesburg: South African Institute of Race Relations, 1993

South African Institute of Race Relations, *South African survey, 1995/96*, Johannesburg: South African Institute of Race Relations, 1996

Spitz, Richard and Matthew Chaskalson, *The politics of transition: a hidden history of South Africa's negotiated settlement*, Oxford: Hart Publishing, 2000

Standing, Guy, John Sender and John Weeks, *The South African challenge: restructuring the South African labour market*, Geneva: International Labour Organisation, 1996

Statham, F. R., *Blacks, Boers and British: a three-cornered problem*, London: Macmillan, 1881

Stefano, S. and L. van Sittert, 'Black Economic Empowerment (BEE) in industrial fisheries', *African Affairs* 106 (2007), 437–62

Stein, Mark, 'Max Gordon and African trade unionism on the Witwatersrand, 1935–40', in Webster (ed.), *Essays in southern African labour history*, pp. 143–60

Stevenson, M. and M. Graham-Stewart (eds.), *South East African beadwork, 1850–1910: from adornment to artefact to art*, Cape Town: Fernwood Press, 2000

Steyn, J. C., *Tuiste in eie taal: die behoud en bestaan van Afrikaans*, Cape Town, Tafelberg, 1980

Steyn, P., 'The lingering environmental impact of repressive governance: the environmental legacy of the apartheid-era for the new South Africa', *Globalizations* 2:3 (2005), 391–403

Stolten, Hans Erik (ed.), *History making and present day politics: the meaning of collective memory in South Africa*, Uppsala, Sweden: Afrikainstitutet, 2007

Stow, G. W. *The native races of South Africa: A history of the intrusion of the Hottentots and Bantu into the hunting grounds of the Bushmen, the aborigines of the country*, London: Swan Sonnenschein, 1905

Stultz, N., 'The politics of security: South Africa under Verwoerd, 1961–6', *Journal of Modern African Studies* 7:1 (1969), 3–20

Suttner, R., 'Talking to the ancestors: national heritage, the Freedom Charter and nation-building in South Africa in 2005', *Development Southern Africa* 23:1 (2006), 3–27

Suttner, Raymond and Jeremy Cronin, *30 years of the Freedom Charter*, Johannesburg: Ravan Press, 1986

Swan, Maureen, *Gandhi: the South African experience*, Johannesburg: Ravan Press, 1985

Swart, S., 'But where's the bloody horse? Textuality and corporeality in the "animal turn"', *Journal of Literary Studies* 23:3 (2007), 271–92

Swilling, Mark, 'The politics of negotiation', *Work in Progress* 50 (October 1987), 17–22

Swilling, Mark and Mark Phillips, 'The emergency state; its power and limits', in Moss and Obery (eds.), *South African Review* 5, pp. 68–90

Tamarkin, Mordechai, 'The Cape Afrikaners and the British Empire from the Jameson Raid to the South African War', in Lowry (ed.), *The South African War reappraised*, pp. 121–39

Tamarkin, Mordechai, *Cecil Rhodes and the Cape Afrikaners: the imperial colossus and the colonial parish pump*, London: Frank Cass, 1996

Tamarkin, Mordechai, *Volk and flock: ecology, culture, identity and politics among Cape Afrikaner sheep farmers in the late nineteenth century*, Pretoria: UNISA Press, 2009

Tatz, Colin, *Shadow and substance in South Africa: a study of land and franchise policies affecting Africans*, Pietermaritzburg: University of Natal Press, 1962

Taylor, Dora, *The role of the missionaries in conquest*, Johannesburg: Society of Young Africa, 1952

Taylor, Nick and Penny Vinjevold (eds.), *Getting learning right: report of the President's Education Initiative Project*, Johannesburg: Joint Education Trust, 1999

Terreblanche, Sampie, *A history of inequality in South Africa*, Pietermaritzburg: University of Natal Press, 2002

Theal, G. M., *Compendium of South African history and geography*, Lovedale: Lovedale Press, 1873

Theal, G. M., *History of South Africa*, London: Swan Sonnenschein, 1892–1919

Theal, G. M., *South Africa: the Cape Colony, Natal, Orange Free State, South African Republic and all the other territories south of the Zambesi*, London: T. Fisher Unwin, 1994

Theal, G. M., *Yellow and dark-skinned people of Africa south of the Zambesi*, London: Swan Sonnenschein, 1910

Thema, Selope, 'The race problem, 1922', in Karis and Carter, *From protest to challenge*, vol. 1, p. 214

Thompson, Leonard, *A history of South Africa*, New Haven, CT: Yale University Press, 1990

Thompson, Leonard, *The unification of South Africa*, Oxford: Clarendon Press, 1960

Thompson, Leonard and Jeffrey Butler (eds.), *Change in contemporary South Africa*, Berkeley: University of California Press, 1975

Tlali, Muriel, *Amandla: a novel*, Soweto: M. Tlali, 1986

Tlali, Muriel, *Muriel at Metropolitan*, Johannesburg: Ravan Press, 1975

Tom, Petrus, *My life struggle*, Johannesburg: Ravan Press, 1985

Torrance, David R., *The strange death of the Liberal empire: Lord Selborne in South Africa*, Liverpool: University of Liverpool Press; Montreal: McGill University Press, 1996

Trapido, Stanley, 'Africa in a comparative study of industrialization', *Journal of Development Studies* 7:3 (1971), 309–20

Trapido, Stanley, 'Putting a plough to the ground: a history of tenant production on the Vereeniging Estates, 1896–1920', in Beinart et al. (eds.), *Putting a plough to the ground*, pp. 336–72.

Trapido, S., 'Reflections on land, office and wealth in the South African Republic, 1850–1900', in Marks and Atmore, *Economy and society*, pp. 350–368

Trewelha, Paul, *Inside Quatro: uncovering the exile history of the ANC and SWAPO*, Cape Town: Jacana, 2009

Trollope, Anthony, *South Africa*, London: Chapman and Hall, 1878

Trollope, Anthony, *South Africa*, new ed., Cape Town: Balkema, 1973

Truth and Reconciliation Commission, *The Report of the Truth and Reconciliation Commission*, 7 vols., Cape Town: Truth and Reconciliation Commission, 1998–2003

Turner, R., *The eye of the needle: an essay on participatory democracy*, Johannesburg: Sprocas, 1972

Turrell, R., *Capital and labour on the Kimberley diamond fields, 1871–90*, Cambridge: Cambridge University Press, 1987

Turrell, R., 'Kimberley: labour and compounds, 1871–1888', in Marks and Rathbone (eds.), *Industrialisation and social change*, pp. 45–76

Twaddle, M. (ed.), *Imperialism, the state and the third world*, London: British Academic Press, 1992

United Democratic Front, *National launch*, Cape Town: University of Cape Town Students' Representative Council, 1983

UN Development Programme, *Human development report, 1997*, New York: UN Development Programme, 1997

UN Development Programme, *Human development report, 1999*, New York: UN Development Programme, 1999

Urban Foundation, *Income distribution model*, 2nd ed., Johannesburg: Urban Foundation, 1994

Vahed, G., 'Uprooting and rerooting: culture, religion and community among indentured Muslim migrants in colonial Natal, 1860–1911', *South African Historical Journal* 45 (2001), 191–222

Vail, L. (ed.), *The creation of tribalism in southern Africa*, London: James Currey, 1989

Van Der Berg, Servaas, 'Trends in racial fiscal incidence in South Africa', *South African Journal of Economics* 69:2 (2001), 243–68

Van Der Horst, S. and J. Reid (eds.), *Race discrimination in South Africa: a review*, Cape Town: David Philip, 1981

Van Der Merwe, P. J., *The migrant farmer in the history of the Cape Colony, 1657–1842*, trans. R. Beck, Athens: Ohio University Press, 1995

Van Der Vlies, A., *South African textual cultures: white, black, read all over*, Manchester, U.K.: Manchester University Press, 2007

Van Heyningen, E. (ed.), *Studies in the history of Cape Town*, vol. 8, Cape Town: University of Cape Town Press, 1994

Van Jaarsveld, F. A., *The awakening of Afrikaner nationalism, 1868–1881*, Cape Town: Human and Rousseau, 1961

Van Kessel, Ineke, *Beyond our wildest dreams: the United Democratic Front and the transformation of South Africa*, Charlottesville: University of Virginia Press, 2000

Van Onselen, Charles, 'The reconstruction of a rural life from oral testimony: critical notes on the methodology employed in the study of a Black South African sharecropper', *Journal of Peasant Studies* 20:3 (1993), 494–514

Van Onselen, Charles, *The seed is mine: the life of Kas Maine, a South African sharecropper 1894–1985*, Cape Town: David Philip, 1996

Van Onselen, Charles, *Studies in the social and economic history of the Witwatersrand, 1886–1914*, 2 vols., Johannesburg: Ravan Press, 1982

Van Rensburg, Thariza (ed.), *Camp diary of Henrietta Armstrong: experiences of a Boer nurse in the Irene Concentration Camp, 6 April–11 October 1901*, Pretoria: Human Sciences Research Council, 1980

Van Sittert, L. and S. Swart (eds.), *Canis familiaris: a dog history of southern Africa*, Leiden: Brill, 2008

Van Sittert, L., 'The supernatural state: water divining and the Cape underground water rush, 1891–1910', *Journal of Social History* 37:4 (2004), 915–37

Van Sittert, L., 'Writing and teaching the history of the land and environment in Africa in the twenty-first century', report on conference session, *South African Historical Journal* 50 (2004), 223–4

Van Wyk, G. 'Through the cosmic flower: secret resistance in the mural art of Sotho-Tswana women', in Nooter (ed.), *Secrecy*, pp. 80–7

Verschoyle, F., *Cecil Rhodes: his political life and speeches, 1881–1900*, London: Bell, 1900

Vigne, R., *Liberals against apartheid: a history of the Liberal Party of South Africa, 1953–68*, London: Macmillan, 1997

Vinjevold, P., 'Language issues in South African classrooms', in Taylor and Vinjevold (eds.), *Getting learning right*, pp. 205–26

Wagner, Kathrin, *Rereading Nadine Gordimer*, Bloomington: Indiana University Press; Johannesburg: Witwatersrand University Press, 1994

Walker, Cherryl, *Women and gender in southern Africa to 1945*, Cape Town: David Philip; London: James Currey, 1990

Walker, Cherryl, *Women and resistance in South Africa*, London: Onyx Press, 1982

Walker, Eric (ed.), *Cambridge history of the British Empire*, vol. 8, *South Africa, Rhodesia and the Protectorates*, Cambridge: Cambridge University Press, 1936

Walker, Eric, *History of South Africa*, London: Longmans, Green, 1928

Walshe, P., *The rise of African nationalism in South Africa: the African National Congress, 1912–1952*, London: C. Hurst, 1970; Berkeley: University of California Press, 1971; Johannesburg: Ravan Press, 1973

Walton, E. H., *The inner history of the National Convention of South Africa*, Cape Town: Maskew Miller, 1912; Westport, CT: Negro Universities Press, 1970

Warwick, Peter (ed.), *The South African War; the Anglo-Boer War, 1899–1902*, Harlow, U.K.: Longmans, 1980

Watts, H. L., 'Poverty', in Randall (ed.), *Some implications of inequality*, pp. 40–57

Webster, Eddie, *Cast in a racial mould: labour process and trade unionism in the foundries*, Johannesburg: Ravan Press, 1985

Webster, Eddie (ed.), *Essays in southern African labour history*, Johannesburg: Ravan Press, 1978

Webster, Eddie, 'A profile of unregistered trade unions in Durban', *South African Labour Bulletin* 4:8 (January–February 1979), 43–74

Webster, Eddie, 'The rise of social-movement unionism: the two faces of the black trade union movement in South Africa', in Frankel, Pines and Swilling (eds.), *State, resistance and change*, pp. 174–96

Welsh, David, *The rise and fall of apartheid*, Johannesburg: Jonathan Ball, 2009

Western, John, *Outcast Cape Town*, Minneapolis: University of Minnesota Press, 1981

Whiteford, A. and M. McGrath, *Income inequality over the apartheid years*, South African Network for Economic Research, working paper no. 6, Cape Town: South African Network for Economic Research, 1998

Wieder, Alan, *Teacher and comrade: Richard Dudley and the fight for democracy in South Africa*, Albany: State University of New York Press, 2008

Wilkins, I. and H. Strydom, *The super-Afrikaners*, London: Corgi Books, 1980

Willan, Brian, 'An African in Kimberley,' in Marks and Rathbone (eds.), *Industrialisation and social change*, pp. 238–58

Willan, Brian, *Sol Plaatje: a biography. Solomon Tehekisho Plaatje (1876–1932)*, Johannesburg: Ravan Press, 1984

Williamson, Sue, *Resistance art in South Africa*, Cape Town: David Philip, 1989

Williamson, Sue, *South African art now*, New York: Collins Design, 2009

Wilmot, A., *A history of the Zulu War*, London: Richardson and Best, 1880

Wilmot, A. and J. C. Chase, *History of the Colony of the Cape of Good Hope*, Cape Town: Juta, 1869

Wilson, Francis, *Labour in the South African gold mines*, Cambridge: Cambridge University Press, 1972

Wilson, Francis and Mamphela Ramphele, *Uprooting poverty: the South African challenge*, Cape Town: David Philip, 1989

Wilson, Monica, 'Kinship', Keiskammahoek rural survey, vol. 3, *Social structure*, Pietermaritzburg: Shuter and Shooter, 1952

Wilson, Monica and Leonard Thompson (eds.), *Oxford history of South Africa*, 2 vols., Oxford: Oxford University Press, 1968, 1971

Witz, L., *Apartheid's festival: contesting South Africa's national pasts*, Cape Town: David Philip, 2003

Witz, L., 'Eventless history at the end of apartheid: the making of the Dias Festival', *Kronos* 32 (2006), 162–91

Witz, L., 'From Langa Market Hall and Rhodes Estate to the Grand Parade and the Foreshore: contesting Van Riebeeck's Cape Town', *Kronos* 25 (1999), 187–206

Wolpe, Anne Marie, *The long way home*, London: Virago, 1994

Wolpe, H., 'Capitalism and cheap labour-power in South Africa: from segregation to apartheid', *Economy and Society* 1:4 (1972), 425–56

Worger, Willam H., *South Africa's city of diamonds: mine workers and monopoly capitalism, 1867–95*, New Haven, CT: Yale University Press; Johannesburg: Ravan Press, 1987

Worster, D. (ed.), *The ends of the earth*, Cambridge: Cambridge University Press, 1988

Wylie, Diana, *Starving on a full stomach: hunger and the triumph of cultural racism in modern South Africa*, Charlottesville: University Press of Virginia, 2001

Yousaf, Nahem (ed.), *Apartheid narratives*, Amsterdam: Rodopi, 2001

Yudelman, David, *The emergence of modern South Africa: state, capital and the incorporation of organized labor on the South African gold fields, 1902–1939*, Westport, CT: Greenwood Press, 1983

THESES AND UNPUBLISHED PAPERS

Theses

Baines, G. F., 'New Brighton, Port Elizabeth, c. 1903–1955: a history of an urban African community', unpublished Ph.D. thesis, University of Cape Town (1994)

Barrell, H., 'Conscripts to their age: African National Congress operational strategy, 1976–1986', unpublished D.Phil. thesis, Oxford University (1993)

Berger, D., 'White poverty and government policy in South Africa, 1892–1934', unpublished Ph.D. thesis, Temple University (1982)

Bitensky, Maybelle F., 'The South African League British Imperialist Organisation in South Africa, 1896 to 1899', unpublished M.A. thesis, University of the Witwatersrand (1950)

Brown, Karen, 'Progressivism, agriculture and conservation in the Cape Colony, c. 1902–1908', unpublished D.Phil. thesis, Oxford University (2002)

Charney, Craig, 'Civil society and the state: identity, institutions and the Black Consciousness Movement of South Africa', unpublished D.Phil. thesis, Yale University (2000)

Clynick, T., 'Afrikaner political mobilisation in the Western Transvaal, 1920–1930', unpublished Ph.D. thesis, Queens University (1996)

Drus, E., 'The political career of Saul Solomon, member of the Cape Legislative Assembly from 1854 to 1883', unpublished M.A. thesis, University of Cape Town (1939)

Du Toit, M., 'Women, welfare and the nurturing of Afrikaner nationalism: a social history of the Afrikaans Christelike Vroue Vereeniging, c. 1879–1936', unpublished Ph.D. thesis, University of Cape Town (1996)

Harris, Karen L., 'A history of the Chinese in South Africa to 1912', unpublished Ph.D. thesis, University of South Africa (1998)

Kerseboom, S., '"Our Khoi heroine": remembering and recreating Sara Baart-man in post-apartheid South Africa, 1994–2007', unpublished M.A. thesis, University of Stellenbosch (2007)

Klaaren, J., 'Migrating to citizenship: mobility, law and nationality in South Africa, 1897–1937', unpublished Ph.D. thesis, Yale University (2004)

Khumalo, Cyrius Vukile, 'Epistolary networks and the politics of cultural pro-duction in KwaZulu-Natal, 1860–1910', unpublished Ph.D. thesis, Uni-versity of Michigan (2004)

La Hausse, P., 'The struggle for the city: alcohol, the Ematsheni and popular culture in Durban, 1902–1936', unpublished M.A. thesis, University of Cape Town (1984)

Lange, M. L., 'The making of the white working class: class experience and class identity in Johannesburg, 1890–1922', unpublished Ph.D. thesis, Univer-sity of the Witwatersrand (1998)

Lazar, J., 'Conformity and conflict: Afrikaner Nationalist politics, 1948–1961', unpublished D.Phil. thesis, Oxford University (1987)

Lekgoathi, S. P., 'Ethnicity and identity: struggle and contestation in the making of the Northern Transvaal Ndebele, c. 1860–2005', unpublished Ph.D. thesis, University of Minnesota (2006)

Mbenga, B. K., 'The Bakgatla-Baga-Kgafela in the Pilansberg district of the Western Transvaal from 1899–1931', unpublished Ph.D. thesis, University of South Africa (1996)

McGrath, Michael, 'Output and productivity trends in South Africa: apartheid and economic growth', unpublished Ph.D. thesis, Cambridge University (1990)

Minkley, G., 'Border dialogues: race, class and space in the industrialisation of East London, c. 1902–1936', unpublished Ph.D. thesis, University of Cape Town (1994)

Mokoena, H., 'The making of a *kholwa* intellectual: a discursive biography of Magema Magwaza Fuze', unpublished D.Phil. thesis, University of Cape Town (2005)

Moll, T., 'Output and productivity trends in South Africa: apartheid and eco-nomic growth', unpublished Ph.D. thesis, University of Cambridge (1990)

Nattrass, Nicoli, 'Wages, profits and apartheid', unpublished D.Phil. thesis, Oxford University (1990)

Nieftagodien, N., 'The implementation of urban apartheid on the East Rand, 1948–1973: the role of local government and local resistance', unpublished Ph.D. thesis, University of the Witwatersrand (2001)

Odendaal, André, 'African political mobilisation in the Eastern Cape, 1880–1910', unpublished Ph.D. thesis, University of Cambridge (1983)

Parnell, S. M., 'Johannesburg slums and racial segregation in South African cities, 1910–1937', unpublished Ph.D. thesis, University of the Witwater-srand (1993)

Raman, Parvathi, 'Being an Indian communist the South African way: the influence of Indians in the South African Communist Party, 1934–1952', unpublished Ph.D. thesis, London University (2002)

Seekings, Jeremy, 'Quiescence and transition to confrontation: South African townships, 1978–1984', unpublished D.Phil. thesis, Oxford University (1990)

Simpson, G. N., 'Peasants and politics in the Western Transvaal', unpublished M.A. thesis, University of the Witwatersrand (1986)

Sperber, F., 'Rural income, welfare and migration: a study of three Ciskeian villages', unpublished M.Com. thesis, University of Cape Town (1993)

Suttner, Raymond, 'Rendering visible: the underground organisational experience of the ANC-led Alliance until 1976', unpublished Ph.D. thesis, University of the Witwatersrand (2005)

UNPUBLISHED PAPERS

Alexander, Peter, 'Women and coal mining in India and South Africa, c. 1900–1940', paper presented at the Worlds of Labour Conference, Johannesburg: University of the Witwatersrand (2006)

Comaroff, J., 'The end of history, again? Pursuing the past in postcolony', unpublished paper, Department of History, University of Basel (January 2003)

Guy, Jeff, 'An accommodation of patriarchs: Theophilus Shepstone and the foundations of the system of native administration in Natal', unpublished paper presented at Conference on Masculinities in Southern Africa, University of Natal Durban (July 1997)

Odendaal, André, 'Heritage and the arrival of post-colonial history in South Africa', unpublished paper, U.S. African Studies Association Conference, Washington, D.C. (2002)

Schneider, Ben Ross, 'Comparing capitalisms: liberal, coordinated, network and hierarchical varieties', unpublished paper (2008)

Simkins, Charles, 'The archaeology of South Africa's human capital', unpublished paper

South African Communist Party, *Politburo discussion document on negotiations*, May 1986

Suttner, Raymond, 'Popular justice in South Africa', paper delivered at Sociology Department seminar, University of the Witwatersrand, 5 May 1986

INTERVIEWS AND WEBSITES

Battersby, John, Transcript of an unpublished interview with Chris Hani and Steve Tshwete, Lusaka, 3 June 1988

http://post.queensu.ca~forsdyke/rindpsto.htm

http://www.anc.org.za/ancdocs/history/mbeki/1996/sp960508.html

http://www.anc.org.za/ancdocs/policy/manifesto.html

http://www.anc.org.za/ancdocs/speeches/1950s/lutuli58.html

INDEX

Abdurahman, Abdullah, 203, 204
Abrahams, Peter, 584–585
absentee landowners, in ZAR, 71
Act of Union of 1909, 192
Act of Union of 1910, 152–153, 254
Active Citizens Force, 48
activist autobiographies, 6
Adhikari, Mohamed, 405
administration, professionalisation of, 344–345
African Americans, and Council on African
Affairs, 52
African Food and Canning Workers Union, 377
African Methodist Episcopal Church (AMEC),
45, 146–148, 197
African National Congress (ANC): in Alexandra,
427, 450–451; alliance with NIC and TIC,
371–372; armed wing of, 391–392, 396;
banning of, 346, 396; Defiance Campaign of,
5; and environment, 606; failure of, 303–304;
and guerilla warfare, 433–435; insularity of in
Cape, 296; insurgent training in Angola,
435–436; internal reconstruction of,
426–437; and Johannesburg squatter
movement, 317; in Lebowa homeland, 449;
on need for armed struggle, 431; and
non-racialism, 7; passive resistance to unjust
laws, 372–373; and People's War, 461–466;
resurgence of, 426; under Seme presidency,
303–304; and South African Students
Movement, 432; strategy of, 430–431; trade
union affiliate of, 453; and transition to
democracy, 482, 483–486; youth league, 45,
52–53, 372, 382
African nationalism, 29–30
African People's Organisation (APO), 296, 297
African Political (People's) Organisation, 147
African Renaissance, 63–64

African Renaissance Holdings, 64
Africander League, 105–106
African-Indian relations, in late nineteenth
century, 140
Africanist historiography, 11
Africans' Claims in South Africa, 52
Africans: and clientism, 351; and ethnic
settlements, 350–351; increase in secondary
enrollment, 416, 424, 449; increase of
workers in manufacturing, 398, 413–414; old
age pensions extended to, 539; and
performing arts, 578–579; political exclusion
of, 348–351; public spending on schools for,
539; representation in parliament, 238;
responses to denial of citizenship, 44–46; and
self-government, 349–350; and state
interventions, 527–528; and unemployment
insurance, 540; urban elites at Kimberly, 142;
urban working class in nineteenth century,
135; Westernised in Eastern Cape, 141–142
Afrikaans language: dissent literature, 590;
instruction mandate, 419; lyric poetry, 271;
movement for, 271–272; and nationalism,
230; Pact government, 230; use in schools,
419–420; writers, 577–578
Afrikaansche Beskermings Vereeniging, 111
Afrikaanse Christelike Vroue Vereniging (Afrikaans
Christian Women's Society; ACVV), 183
Afrikaans-Hollandse Toneelvereninging, 578
Afrikaner Bond, 29–30, 110, 111, 150–151,
152–153
Afrikaner Broederbond, 231, 233
Afrikaner nationalism, 29–30, 216, 230–233,
270, 271–274; and Afrikaans language, 230;
and Afrikaner business elite, 231–232; and
Nazism, 232; and South African flag, 230;
and unions, 230–231; and whites, 230

697

Afrikaner nationalist historiography, 3

Afrikaner Party, 216

Afrikaner women, 174–175; and franchise, 178; and Garment Workers Union, 229; literature for, 187; and urbanisation, 291–292

Afrikaners, 70–72; before British occupation, 67–68; colonial identity of, 68; independence of settler groups, 70; intermarriage with English speakers, 264, 290–291; language movement by, 271–272; and moral economy, 68, 70; nationalism of, 29–30, 230; and poverty, 227; theatre of, 589; and urbanisation, 261, 262. *See also* Afrikaner nationalism; National Party; Oranje Vrystaat (OVS); Zuid-Afrikaansche Republiek (ZAR)

Aggett, Neil, 454

Aggrey, J.E.G., 294

agriculture, 66, 68; agrarian expansion in Natal, 120; agrarian reform in Cape Colony, 177; under apartheid, 541; in Cape Colony, 73; and cheap labour, 249; commercial, 529; and cooperatives, 249; and drought, 284; and economic stagnation, 521; and Foreign Farm Labour Scheme of 1944–48, 249–250; labour issues, 220–221, 240; and Marketing Act of 1937, 249; ostrich feather exports, 221; self-sufficiency in food, 221; specialisation, 221; state intervention in, 249, 250, 529, 541; subsistence, 293; and Sugar Act of 1936, 249; tractorisation, 221; unevenness of material conditions in, 217, 220–221; in Western Cape, 120; wheat, 283–284; wool exports, 221; in Zuid-Afrikaansche Republiek, 71. *See also* cattle; de-agrarianisation and landlessness; land issues

Albany (Cape Colony), 69

Alexander, Jane, 596

Alexander, Ray, 377. *See* Simons, R.E. (Ray)

Alexandra Action Committee (AAC), 451–452

Alexandra Civic Association, 450–451

Alexandra Residents' Association (ARA), 451

Alexandra Youth Congress, 451, 452

Alexandra: African National Congress in, 427, 450–451; bus boycott in, 316, 317; union support of rebellion in, 452–453

Aliens Act of 1937, 232

All-African Convention (AAC), 382

alternative theatre under apartheid, 591–595

Alusaf, 547

amakholwa (Christian believers), 35, 116, 131, 298

amalaita (youth gangs), 278, 302

amaNazaretha, 14

Amatongaland, British annexation of, 108

American Methodist Episcopal Church, 292, 311

Amery, L.S., 243

Andrews, Bill, 267

Anglican Church, 14; and South African citizenship, 311

Anglo-American, 219; expansion during apartheid, 548–549; expansion into diamond industry, 523–524; reforms during apartheid, 553, 554

Anglo-Zulu War, 106

Angola, 479–480

anthropology: early studies, 40–42; functionalist, 41; South Africanist, 11

anti-convict transportation association, 28

anti-modernist movement, Dutch, 30

anti-Semitism, 34–35

anti-slavery movement, and Cape Colony, 69

Anti-Squatting legislation, 173

apartheid: and Afrikaner nationalism, 324–325, 326; and Betterment and Rehabilitation schemes, 382–383; and bio-politics, 323; and Christian nationalism, 325–326, 335; and coloured franchise, 385–386; and coloured workers, 363; and communism, 346–347; contradictions/tensions of, 319–320; and Defiance Campaign, 372–373; defining features of, 331–351; and domestic workers, 357; dread of insurgency during, 322–323; and economic engineering, 336–343, 360–363; and education, 339–340, 383–385, 404–405; efficacy of, 352–355; and emergence of Black Consciousness Movement, 405–406; family, gender, sexuality regulation, 334–335; genealogy of, 328–331; and Indians, 363; and labour issues, 322, 336, 337–338, 340–341, 361–362; and law-violence interconnection, 345–348; and modernising project, 343–345; and national economy notion, 330; and National Party election of 1948, 327; and need for racial overhaul, 328–329; and non-racialism, 376–378; opposition in cities, 395–396; and pass laws, 364–365, 373; petty apartheid measures, 356–357; and political exclusion of blacks, 348–351; and political power, 364; and population removals, 342, 360; primary imperatives of, 321–328; and revised influx control laws, 373–374; spatial issues in, 329, 385–387; stages of, 320, 365–366; and state capitalism, 365; and statecraft, 330–331; and state intervention, 330, 336–337; and state/local balance, 352–354; success/failure mix of, 366; and theatre, 588–590; and trade unions, 378; and tribalism, 334, 341–342; ubiquity of race, 331–334; and upward mobility, 383; and urbanisation, 323–324, 325, 336, 340–341, 359–360, 370–371, 398–399; and welfarism, 330–331; and white supremacy, 321, 322; and white voters, 327–328; and women, 357–358, 377–378, 379–382, 388–389. *See also* ethnic identity; homelands; race/racism

apartheid theatre, 588–590; and Afrikaners, 589; and traditional Afrikaner culture, 589–590

Appleyard, J.W., 23

Apprenticeship Act of 1944, 260

Apprenticeship and Vocational Guidance system, 260–261

apprenticeships, 260–261, 288–289

Armaments Corporation (Armscor), 547

arms industry, 474

artisans: undermining of, 297; and urbanisation, 292

Asian Indians. *See* Indians, Asian

Asiatic Land Tenure and Indian Representation Bill, 1946, 242, 371

Asquith, Henry, 153

Attwell, David, 574, 576

Azania, 62

Azanian People's Liberation Army (APLA), 484

Azanian People's Organisation (AZAPO), 426

Baartman, Saartjie, 611–612

BaHurutse resistance, 390–391

Bain, James, 265, 266, 267

Balfour Declaration, 301

Ballinger, William, 300

Bank of England, 247

banking, 526

banning: of photographic images, 583; of texts, 54, 587, 591

Bantu and Bantu-speakers: classification of, 42; coining of *Bantu*, 24; origins of, 38–39

Bantu Authorities Act, 55, 389–395

Bantu Dramatic Society, 579–580

Bantu Education Act of 1953, 339–340, 383–384, 385

Bantu education policy, 339–340

Bantu Homelands Citizenship Act of 1970, 59

Bantu Labour (Settlements of Disputes) Act of 1953, 377

Bantu Laws Amendment Act of 1963, 398

Bantustans: defining, 389. *See also* homelands (Bantustans)

Barnard, Chris, 589

Barnard, Neil, 465

Barrell, Howard, 428

basketry, 387, 584

Basutoland: agrarian expansion in, 120; British annexation of, 28; geopolitical boundaries of, 193; move toward segregation in, 34; Pentecostal churches in, 310; Phuti uprising in, 114

Batson, Edward, 532–533

Battle of Majuba, 107

beadwork, 584

Beaufre, Andre, 467–468

Beaumont Commission, 235–236

Bechuanaland: British annexation of, 28, 113; geopolitical boundaries of, 193; as provisioning source for mines, 113

Beck, Meiring, 33, 34

beer brewing: in Port Elizabeth, 305–306; in Pretoria, 305–306; use of heritage in marketing, 612–613

beer hall: boycott in Durban, 302–303; boycott in Natal, 388–389

Beinart, W., 281

Benoni, New Kleinfontein mine in, 265

Benson, Mary, 5, 613–614

Berlin Mission Society, 145–146

Bernhardt, Ian, 586

Betterment Areas, 382–383

Beveridge Report, 539

Beyers, Christiaan, 214

Bhambatha, 124, 201–202

Bhana, Surendra, 371

Bhengu, Gerard, 581

Bhulose, W.F., 279

Biko, Steve, 62, 405, 406, 418, 424–425

bio-politics, 323

bio-power, 335

Bismarck, Otto, 113

Black Allied Workers' Union (BAWU), 405, 414, 415, 426

Black Community Development Bill, 437

Black Community Programmes (BCP), 405

Black Consciousness Black Allied Workers' Union, 453

Black Consciousness Movement (BCM), 7, 11, 61–62, 409, 590–591, 594; demise of, 425–426; emergence of, 405–406; influence on schoolchildren's movement, 417–419

Black Flag Rebellion, 125

black literature, criticism of in 1980s, 594–595
Black Local Authorities Act, 437, 439
Black Parents' Association (BPA), 421, 424
black protest and politics, 1921–1937,
    294–306; beer hall boycott in Durban,
    302–303; Communist Party role in, 301–302,
    303; and ethnic identities, 305; failure of
    black national political organisations,
    303–306; Industrial and Commercial
    Workers' Union role in, 296–300; *Inkatha*
    movement, 298–299; local politics, 305–306;
    marabi culture in Johannesburg, 294–295;
    pass protest of 1929, 301–302. *See also*
    Africans
black theatre, 591
Black Workers' Project (BWP), 405
Black, Wally, 473
Bleek, Wilhelm, 24, 26
Bloemfontein, politics reduced to local in,
    305–306
Bloom, Harry, 586
Board of Reference system, 268
Boers: annexation of portion of Zululand,
    108–109; commando system of, 48; Froude
    on, 19; resettlement after South African War,
    173–174; social Darwinism on, 26; success
    against British in Transvaal, 110
Boesak, Allen, 437–438, 458
Bokwe, John K., 142
Bond van Afrikaanse Moeders, 184
Bondelswarts Rebellion, 294
Bophutatswana, 395
Boshielo, Flag, 391–392
Bosman, Herman C., 577
Botha Commission, 541
Botha, Annie, 184
Botha, Louis, 33, 424; and militarisation, 467,
    476; and mine labour, 266; on multiracism,
    482; and raids on African National Congress
    facilities, 470; and segregation, 471; and
    South African War, 161, 163
Botha, Pik, 470, 478
bo-tsotsi, 401
Botswana: basket makers deported to, 387; raids
    on African National Congress facilities in,
    470
boycott: beer hall in Natal, 388–389; bus in
    Alexandra, 316, 317; bus in Eastern Cape,
    387; bus in Transvaal, 387–388; consumer
    and UDF, 446–447; consumer in Cape Town,
    453; consumer in East London, 453; consumer
    in Transvaal, 388; rent boycott, 456

Bozzoli, Belinda, 380, 451–452
Brand, J.H., 76
Breytenbach, Breyten, 332
bridewealth (*lobola*), 276, 397, 496–497
Brink, Andre, 590, 593–594
Britain: Afrikaner Nationalists and
    independence from, 243; annexation of
    Amatongaland, 108; annexation of
    Basutoland, 28; annexation of Bechuanaland,
    28, 113; annexation of diamond fields, 73–76;
    annexation of Griqualand West, 28;
    annexation of Transkei, 28; annexation of
    Transvaal, 28, 30, 106; Boer success against in
    Transvaal, 110; cultural ideology and Cape
    Colony, 69, 75; early settlers in Cape Colony,
    68–70; economic policy in Zuid-Afrikaansche
    Republiek, 70–71; as export market, 247;
    land distribution favoring British merchants,
    66; objectives of occupation of Cape Colony,
    66, 67, 68; resistance to frontier policy in
    Cape Colony, 69–70; seizure of territories in
    Cape Colony from Xhosa, 69; transfer of
    Zululand to Natal, 109; Tswana as
    protectorate of, 108. *See also* South African
    War (1899–1902)
British Kaffraria, local self-government in, 104
British South Africa Company, 245
Broederbond, 326
Bryce, James, 32
Buchanan, James, 28
Building Workers Act, 376
Bundy, C., 281
Bunga system, 394
Burger, J.F., 109, 307
Burgers, Thomas S., 76–78
burial societies: formed by women, 380; in Pedi
    homeland, 391
burials, Khoesan, 611–612
bus boycott: in Alexandra, 316, 317; in Eastern
    Cape, 387; in Transvaal, 387–388
Bushmen, 26–27
Buthelezi, Mangosutho, 393–394
Buthelezi, Wellington, 45, 281, 422, 484
bywoners, 121, 182, 257, 259–261, 262–263

Calata, James, 384, 403
Callaway, Henry, 23
Calpin, G.H., 51
Caluza, Reuban, 579
Campaign for Right and Justice, 234
Campbell, Roy, 577
Campbell, William, 237

Campbell-Bannerman, Henry, 160
canning industry, 377–378
Cape African Teachers' Association (CATA), 384, 394
Cape colonial nationalism, 29–30
Cape Colony (Cape Town): African Methodist Episcopal Church in, 147; African National Congress in, 427; Afrikaner Bond and 1898 election, 152–153; agrarian reform in, 177; agricultural economy in, 73; anti-slavery movement in, 69; British cultural ideology and, 69, 75; Cape Dutch nationalism in, 68; cattle in, 68; coloured franchise in, 385–386; diamond economy in, 72; early British settlers in, 68–70; early European settlement in, 67–68; forced removals from, 385; franchise in, 192–193, 237; Industrial and Commercial Workers' Union in, 296–297; joins Union, 193–194; labour segmentation in, 376; land issues in, 69, 259; language policy in, 185–186, 187; objectives of British occupation, 66, 67, 68; politics of African identity in, 305; population removals in, 385; poverty in, 532–533; provisioning role of, 68, 71; representative government acquired by, 28; resistance to British frontier policy, 69–70; responsible government acquired by, 28; slums in, 261; Space Theatre in, 591–593; urbanisation in, 288–289; wool trade in, 72; working conditions in, 69
Cape Dutch nationalism, 68
Cape Federation Professional League, 402
Cape midlands, pastoralism in, 120
capitalism: Marxism/liberalism on apartheid and, 4–5; monopoly by De Beers Company, 128; racial, 336; state, 365
capital, location of new, 192
Carmichael, Stokely, 418
Carnarvon (Lord), 79, 110; and confederation, 23, 106, 190
Casalis, J.E., 23
Catholic Church, 14
Cato Manor, 371, 385
cattle: in Cape Colony, 68; and drought, 280, 284; and East Coast Fever, 280; protest at culling of, 383; on Reserves, 558; and rinderpest epizootic, 133, 134–135
Celliers, Jan, 271
censorship, in recording industry, 400
central statistical office, 525–526
Cesaire, Aime, 417
Cetshwayo, 108, 141

Chamber of Mines, 132, 135; and cost of white labour, 268; and de-skilling of miners, 265; and labour recruitment, 255; and labour shortage, 169–170; and miners' strikes, 269, 270; and mining-finance houses, 523; and value of gold, 219
Chamberlain, Joseph, 149
Champion, George, 299, 302
Charney, Craig, 416
Charterists, 56, 426, 442, 451, 460, 483
Chase, J.C., 21, 22
cheap labour thesis, 569–570
chiefdoms and chiefs: chiefdom in Zululand, 393–394; denouncement of Chief Buthelezi by UDF, 484; Griqua chiefdom, 112–113; indirect rule by chiefs in Zululand, 275; Lovedu chiefdom, 112; Msutu (Chief), 382; paramount chiefs, 279; Poto (Chief), 392; power of chiefs and segregation, 237–238; power of chiefs in Transkei, 237–238; rule by chiefs in Natal, 275, 276; rule by chiefs in Transvaal, 275, 276; Tswana chiefdom, 112–113; Venda chiefdom, 112
Chikane, Frank, 438
child labour, 535
Chinese indentured labourers, 133, 169–170, 176, 178
Christian Catholic Church in Zion, 198
Christian National schools, 185
Christianity: *amakholwa* (believers), 35, 116, 131, 298; Catholic Church, 14; conversion to, 309–311; increase in African church membership, 416; Lutheran Bapedi Church, 145–146; Methodist Church, 14; nationalism of, 325–326, 335; Pentecostal churches, 272, 310; radical separatists in Transkei, 148. *See also* Anglican Church; Dutch Reformed Church (DRC)
circumcision, 398
Ciskei: centralized control of Bantu authorities in, 389–390; dismantling of *Bunga* system in, 394; rural resistance in, 382; Spanish flu in, 280
citizenship: African responses to denial of, 44–46; Anglican Church and South African, 311; colonial, 27–28; common, 59; definitions of South African, 34–35; dual-pronged claim for, 38; and homelands, 59; Indians, 34–35, 49–50; social citizenship, 50
civilised labour, 227, 288; displacement of blacks through, 297–298; policy at Iron & Steel Corporation, 227–228; and women, 291

Civilised Labour Policy, 531
clientism, 351
closed compounds, for African mine workers, 130–131
Closer Union Societies, 192
coal industry, 529
Code of Native Law (1878), 104
Coetzee, J.M., 594
Coillard, François, 134
Cole, Ernest, 583
Colenso, J.W., 574
Collins, William, 147
Colonial Born and Settler Indian Association, 308
Colonial Born Indian Association, 206
Colonial Born South African Indian Association, 49
Colour Bar, 178, 193, 376
Coloured Labour Preference policy, 336, 376
Coloured Labour Importation Ordinance of 1904, 170
Coloured People's Congress (CPC), 385–386, 396
coloured persons: and education, 404–405; factory work by coloured women, 136; and franchise, 192–193, 385–386; as garment industry workers, 229; labour policy in Western Cape, 336; political control over own affairs, 403–404; upward mobility of, 551; workers under apartheid, 363
Coloured Persons Education Act, 404
Coloured Persons Representative Council, 404
Coloured Persons Rights Bill of 1926, 49
Coloured Representative Council, 348
Comaroff, Jean, 403
commando system, 48
Commission of Enquiry on Industrial Legislation, 541
Commission on Native Laws and Customs (1883), 104
commissions of enquiry, 526
Committee of Ten, 424
Commonwealth membership, 243
communism: and apartheid, 346–347; statutory, 372–373; suppression of, 346
Communist Party of South Africa, 45, 53, 301–302; failure of, 304; and urbanisation, 316; in Witwatersrand, 301
Community Resource Information Centre (CRIC), 459–460
concentration camps, 158–159, 160, 161
conceptualisation, of South Africa, 18–19

confederation, 23, 106, 190
Congo (organisation), 392–393
Congress Alliance of 1950s, 440
Congress of South African Students (COSAS), 442
Congress of South African Trade Unions (COSATU), 454–455, 456, 555, 593
Congress of the People (1955), 55, 56, 57
'congress of the people', 378–379
Congress of Traditional Leaders, 483
consciousness: in South African historiography, 10. *See also* Black Consciousness Movement
consociational model of governance, 58
Consolidated Gold Fields, 523
Constitution Act of 1983, 437
constitution, draft, 192–194; colour bar in, 193; female suffrage in, 193
consumer boycott: in Cape Town, 453; in East London, 453; in Transvaal, 388; by United Democratic Front, 446–447, 457–458
consumer goods, 399
containment and subjugation of blacks, legislation concerning, 254–255
control and coercion, 13–14
Convention of Pretoria, 110
Cooperative Societies Act of 1939, 249
cooperatives, 304
Coplan, David, 399–400
Cornish, in South Africa, 152
Council for Scientific and Industrial Research, 248
Council of Industrial Workers, 415
Council of Non-European Trade Unions (CNETU), 315–316
cricket, 402
crime, and violence-law interconnection, 345–348
Cronje, Piet, 81
cultural hybridity, 596
cultural transformations, 306–311; by Afrikaner community, 307–308; conversion to Christianity, 309–311; by coloured persons, 308; by Indian community, 308–309
'cultural turn', 10–11
Curtis, Lionel, 34, 166–167, 191
customary law, 104, 276

Dadoo, Yusuf, 49–50, 309
Dalindyebo, Sabata, 197, 395
dam construction, 249
Darley-Hartley, William, 152
Dart, Raymond, 42

Darwinism, 150, 311
Davidson, J.H., 18
Davis, Steve, 433
De Beers Company, 75; closed compounds for
African workers at, 129; evolution of, 74–75;
monopoly by, 128; takeover of, 524; white
worker hostility toward, 128–129. *See also*
diamond economy, in Cape Colony
de Kiewiet, C.W., 3, 43–44, 61, 78, 602
de Klerk, F.W., 478, 480–482
de la Ray, Jacobus, 214
de Wet (General), 263
de-agrarianisation and landlessness, 557–560;
Africans on white-owned farms, 559; labour
tenants, 558; mechanisation effect on, 558;
Reserves, 558, 559–560; sharecroppers,
557–558
Dealers' Licences Act, 206
debt bondage, 284–285
Defiance Campaign of African National
Congress, 5, 372
Delius, Peter, 391–392
democracy: national, 456; parliamentary, 346
democratic transition, 481–486; and ANC, 483,
485–486; compromised settlement, 485;
implementation of, 485–486; and National
Party, 485; political leadership, 483; and
UDF, 483; violence during, 483–485; white
support for, 482–483
demographic transition: census data for,
492–493; disfigured transition, 515–516;
education, 499–505, 515; efficient transition,
514; fertility rates, 359, 493–494, 514, 629t;
growth/shares, 1951–2000, 627–628t;
household structure, 496–498, 514, 635t;
incomplete transition, 514–515; inequality
and poverty, 511–514; international
migration, 494–495; labour market status,
508–509, 514, 515, 647–648t; language of
instruction, 506–507; language spoken at
home, 1936–1996, 505–506, 636–637t; life
expectancy, 514; life expectancy at birth,
629t; marital status, 495–496, 630t;
mortality, 514; population distribution, 515;
population statistics, 493, 625–626t; religion,
507–508, 638–646t; size and composition,
493–494; urbanisation, 509–511, 514, 515;
vital statistics, 1911–1996, 629t
Department of Bantu Affairs (BAD), 390
Department of Coloured Affairs, 404
Department of Labour, 526–527
Department of Native Affairs, 355

development trajectory, 518–519
Dhlamini, Ma, 302
Dhlomo, Herbert I.E., 52, 306–307, 575–576,
579–580, 585
Dhlomo, R.R.R., 312
Dhlomo, Rolfes, 38, 306–307
Diale, Nelson, 391–392
diamond economy, in Cape Colony, 72; creation
of artificial scarcity of diamonds, 74; evolution
of diamond cartel, 74–75; geological
considerations in ownership, 74; racism
against diggers, 73–74; Rhodes' role in,
75–76. *See also* De Beers Company; diamond
industry
diamond industry: British annexation of fields,
73–76; exclusion of Zuid-Afrikaansche
Republiek, 70; joint stock companies in, 125;
unevenness of material conditions, 219
Dicke, B.H., 601–602
Diederichs, Nico, 233
Digby, Anne, 620
diggers, racism toward, 73–75
Dikobe, Modikwe, 591
Dinkwanyane, Johannes, 145–146
Dinuzulu, 108–109, 141, 200–201
disarmament, of Africans after South African
War, 173
diversity, internal, of South Africa, 2
Dlamini, Jessie, 584
Dlamini, Kuzwayo, 441
Doctors Pact, 49–50
Dollar Brand, 400
domestic animals. *See* cattle; sheep
domestic workers, 136, 357, 379
Dominion Party, 215
Dowie, Alexander, 198
drought, 260, 280, 291, 534
du Bois, W.E.B., 576
du Plessis, Barend, 478
du Plessis, L.J., 232, 279, 311
du Plessis, P.G., 589
du Toit, S.J., 21, 30, 110
Dube, John, 38, 197, 200, 298, 305, 311
Dudley, R.O., 404–405
Durban: beer hall boycott in, 302–303; causes of
strikes in, 412, 413–414; Indian businessmen
at, 363; Indian property ownership at, 242;
Indians and urbanisation in, 287; Industrial
and Commercial Workers' Union branch in,
297; and inter-racial rioting, 371; labour
segmentation in, 376; leadership in strike
movement, 412–413; liaison committees in

Durban (*cont.*)
aftermath, 414; population removals in, 385; shift in attitudes to black trade unionism, 414–415; spread of, 413; strike movement, 411–415; textile industry, 410; workers' rebellion, 411–414; Zionist church at, 309–310

Durban system (segregation), 236, 287–288

Dutch Reformed Church (DRC), 14, 77; on Bantu marriage, 358; and poor whites, 227; rejection of apartheid by, 482–483; resurge in interest in, 310–311; and urbanisation, 261

Dwane, James, 148

dynamite concessions, 83, 84

East Coast Fever, 280

East London: politics reduced to local in, 306; unrest in, 372, 373; and urbanisation, 289–290

East Rand: African National Congress on, 427; union organisation on, 454

Eastern Cape: African National Congress in, 427, 429; bus boycott in, 387; famine in, 534; mine labour from, 220; pastoralism in, 120; population removals in, 387; racial populism in, 148; rugby in, 402; Westernised blacks in, 141–142

Eastern European Jews, 49

Economic and Wage Commission, 527, 530, 531

economic boom, 1933–1945, 520, 536–541; gold mining industry, 536; labour issues, 538–539; racial wage gap, shrinkage of, 538; rise in industrial employment, 536; social security movement, 539; social welfare needs after World War II, 540–541; social welfare reform, 539–540; social welfare reform, reversal after World War II, 540; during World War II, 536–537

economic engineering, 336–343, 360–363

economic growth, 410; during twentieth century, 518

economic growth and stagnation, under apartheid, 520–521, 541–550; agriculture, 541; capital formation, 542; discriminatory labour legislation, 541; economic stagnation, 542–544; exports, 543, 548; GDP per capita, 541, 542, 543; gold production, 541; industrialisation process, 549; inflation, 542; manufacturing sector, 541–542, 545–547; mining sector, 544, 546–547; parastatal sector, 547; private sector, 547–548; private sector, concentration of ownership in,

548–549; profit rates, 542, 544; total factor productivity growth, 542–543. *See also* economic stagnation, 1910–1932

economic stagnation, 1910–1932, 520, 521–525; agriculture, 521; GDP per capita, 522, 536; and gold mining industry, 521–522; and Great Depression, 525; recessions, 524

economic state, modern, 525–529; and African workers, 527–528; banking, 526; central statistical office, 525–526; commercial agriculture, 529; commissions of enquiry, 526; income tax, 526; industrial policy, 528–529; labour department, 526–527; labour policy, 527–528; manufacturing, 529; taxes, 526; welfare state pillars, 528; white workers, 527

economics, after apartheid, 568–571; decline of non-mineral exports, 570–571; deficits, 571; independent unions, 569; labour issues, 568, 569–570; per-capita GDP, 570; tariffs, 568; unemployment, 571; wage-setting, 568–569

economy: colonial nature of, 222–223; development trajectory, 518–519. *See also* economy, state intervention in

economy, state intervention in, 245–250; and agriculture, 249, 250; under apartheid, 330, 336–337; banking industry, 247; and communications, 248; and electric power, 248; under Fusion government, 246, 249, 250; and gold standard, 247; infrastructure, 248; under Pact government, 246, 247–248; under Smuts government, 248; and tariffs, 247–248; and textile industry, 248–249; in twentieth century, 519–520

education, 499–505, 515; African secondary enrolment increase, 416, 424, 449; and apartheid, 404–405; Bantu Education Act of 1953, 339–340, 383–385; Bantu Education Act of 1953, resistance to, 384; Bantu education policy, 339–340; for coloured persons, 404–405; educating women as mothers of the nation, 184; expansion of higher and secondary, 409; language policy in relation to home language, 505–507; mathematics, 504; mission schools, 292, 339–340; public spending on schools for Africans, 539; quality of schooling, 504–505; teaching jobs for educated Africans, 298; veldt schools, 475; years of schooling, 499–504, 514–515

Eiselen, W., 339–340
Electricity Supply Commission (ESCOM), 248, 529
Eminent Persons' Group, 470
Emlotheni Memorial, 611
English liberal historiography, 3–4
environmental history, 600–607; animal turn in, 604; changing ideas about environment, 601; and colonialism and empire, 605; comparative work in, 604–605; environment of past, 601; and natural resources, 605–606; political economy of environment, 601; and radical social history, 602–603; and scientific determinism, 602; and segregation and apartheid, 606; as socio-environmental history, 603; as sub-discipline/new branch of history, 607
Essack, Faried, 447–448
Ethiopian movement, 45
Ethiopianism, 199
ethnic identity: African diamond workers, 131; Afrikaner colonial, 68; Asian Indian, 308–309; ethnic in Transvaal, 305; politics of African in Cape Town, 305; reworking in 1930s, 305; in Transvaal, 305; white after South African War, 174; white South Africanism, 270–271; Xhosa, 305; Zulu, 298, 299, 305
ethnic pluralism, 58
ethnic settlements, 350–351
ethnographic research: in early twentieth century, 39; in nineteenth century, 23, 24–25, 26–27
eugenics, 40
Eustace, J.T., 28
Evangelical "Saints," 69
evangelical movement, 69
evolution, 26, 311
exceptionalism, South African, 15–16, 20–21
exile-based histories, 6
exports: under apartheid, 543, 548; decline of non-mineral, 570–571; dependence on Britain as market, 247; ostrich feather, 221; wool, 221

Fabian Society, 84
faction fights, over land, 124
factory work: in Mozambique, 448; by poor white and coloured women, 136. *See also* industrialisation; manufacturing
Fagan Commission, 240
Fairbairn, John, 27, 28

farm labour, 283–285; and labour tenancy, 283–285; and racial violence, 285
Federasie van Afrikaanse Kultuurvereenigings (FAK), 231, 307, 326
Federation of South African Trade Unions (FOSATU), 452–454
Federation of South African Women (FSAW), 380–381
feminist historiography, 9
fertility rates, 359, 493–494, 514, 629t
Fiddes, George, 166
First Anglo-Transvaal War, 107
First, Ruth, 54
Fisher, Percy, 269
Fitzpatrick, Percy, 84, 166–167
foco theory, 427
Food and Canning Workers' Union (FCWU), 377, 453
food processing, 222
Foreign Affairs department, 478
Forest and Veld Conservation Act of 1941, 249
Forman, Lionel, 54
Fortnightly Club, 39
Foucault, M., 323, 335
France, return of Khoesan remains from, 611–612
franchise, 177–178, 238; and adult white males, 192, 327–328; and Africans, 192–193, 237; and Afrikaner women, 178; and coloured persons, 192–193, 385–386; and draft constitution, 193; in Natal, 153; non-racial, qualified male, 192; and segregation, 238; and women, 178, 193, 238
Franchise Action Committee (FAC), 372, 385–386
Freedom Charter (1955), 55–56, 58–59, 63, 64, 378–379, 455, 612
Freedom Park, 611
Frere, Bartle, 24–25, 106, 108, 114, 115
Freund, William, 386
frontier, resistance to policy in Cape Colony, 69–70
Froude, James A., 19–20
Fugard, Athol, 592–593, 596
Fuller, Arthur, 152
functionalist anthropology, 41
Furnivall, J.S., 58
Fusion government, 215; and agriculture, 249; state intervention into economy, 246
Fuze, Magema, 38–39

Gabriel, Lazarus, 206

Gaitskell, Deborah, 379
Gandhi, Mohandas K., 139–140, 204, 205
gangs: *amalaita* (youth gangs), 278, 302; *Isitoshozi*, 278; in Reserves, 278; in townships, 401
garment industry: Afrikaner women workers in, 229; coloured and Indian workers in, 229; unionisation of, 228–230
Garment Workers Union, 229
Garvey, Marcus, 576
Garveyism, 45, 280–281
Gaza kingdom, conquest of, 133
Gcaleka kingdom, 106, 114
Gcaleka, Nicolas T., 612
GDP per capita: after apartheid, 570; under apartheid, 541, 542, 543
Gebennewini (Chief), 284
gender: Afrikaner relations during South African War, 160–161; and customary law, 104; difference in state classification, 14; regulation under apartheid, 334–335. *See also* women
geopolitical boundaries of state, 193–194
Gerhart, Gail, 614
German South-West Africa, 212
Germany, colonisation of Africa, 107, 113
Giliomee, Hermann, 476
Gladstone, William E., 80–81
Glass, Charles, 612
Glen Grey, 382
Glen Grey Act, 32, 116
Glen Grey Voters' Association, 394
Godley Commission, 236
gold discovery: implications for South Africa, 216–217; in Orange Free State, 541; on Witwatersrand, 13, 75–76, 83, 85, 131–132. *See also* gold mining industry; Witwatersrand
Gold Fields of South Africa, 523
gold mining industry: during economic stagnation, 521–522; expansion into Far East Rand, 523–524; during Great Depression, 219; mining-finance houses, 523–524; price of gold, 268; revenues from, 246; stagnation of, 524; state intervention, 522; unevenness of material conditions, 216–217, 218–219; worker wages, 522–523. *See also* Witwatersrand
gold standard, 215, 247
Goldblatt, David, 583
Golden Decade of the Fifties, 585
Gomas, John, 303
Good Areas Act, 438
Gordham, Pravin, 459

Gordimer, Nadine, 425, 593–594
Goshen Republic, 112–113
government: consociational model of, 58; direct personal administration, 275–276; and militarisation, 472; representative, in Cape, 28; responsible, in Cape, 28; tricameral parliament, 437. *See also* chiefdoms and chiefs; self-government
Gqabi, Joe, 428
grammars: in nineteenth century, 23, 24; produced by missionaries, 23
Great Depression: agriculture during, 283–284; economic stagnation during, 525; gold mining industry during, 219; public works programmes for white workers during, 525, 534; Witwatersrand during, 219
Great Trek: reenactment of, 307; Second Great Trek, 307–308
Grey, Sir George, 23, 24, 190
Griffith, Arthur, 152
Griqua chiefdom, 112–113
Griqualand West, 72, 73, 85; British annexation of, 28
Group Areas Act of 1950, 335, 363, 372, 373, 385–386
Group Areas, spatial segregation in, 471
Gumede, Josiah, 45, 46, 257, 298; and beer hall boycott, 302; labour union founding by, 299; as land agent, 305; and mobilisation of Zulu ethnicity, 298; ousted from ANC presidency, 302; radical stance of, 301

Haddon, Alfred, 39
Hahn, Theophilus, 23
Hamilton, Georgina, 393
Hamitic myth, 38–39
Hani, Chris, 428, 429, 462
Harare Declaration, 465
Harcourt, Lewis, 576
Harmel, Michael, 54
health, 617–620; epidemics, 619; healers and institutions, 619–620; HIV/AIDS epidemic, 567–568, 593, 618; malaria, 280, 294; malnutrition, 534–535, 539–540, 561; miners' phthisis (silicosis), 151, 171–172, 224–225, 264, 619; patient studies, 619; public health, 385; Spanish flu in Transkei, 280; tuberculosis, 294
hegemony, threats to, 211–214; Afrikaner working class, 212–213; coloured and Indian militancy, 213–214; failure to integrate surrounding territories, 212; racial

segregation, 213; uneven economic growth, 211; white labour unrest, 212

heritage history, 607–613; biographical heritage, 612–613; conceptual caveats, 609–610; difference from memoralisation, 609; economic value of, 607, 608–609, 610; Freedom Charter, 612; heritage sites, 611–612; historical festival studies, 610; *lieux de memoire*, 613; political heritage, 610–612; public history on significance of South African War, 610; return of human remains, 611–612

Herstigte Nasionale Party (HNP), 328

Hertzog, Albert, 230

Hertzog Bills of 1926, 301

Hertzog, James B.M., 42–43, 48–49, 214; and black representation in parliament, 238; and gold standard, 247; and importance of Commonwealth membership, 243; labour policy of, 531; and segregation, 237; and South African independence of British imperial sphere, 246–247; support of colour bar by, 226

Het Eerste Fabrieken (HEF), 83

Het Volk (The People), 176, 180; and Africa-wide constitution, 192; and reconciliation, 188–189

Heunis, Chris, 465, 470, 478

Heunis, Jan, 478

High Commission Territories, 244. *See also* Basutoland; Bechuanaland; Swaziland

High Commissioner of South Africa, office of, 28–29

Hirson, Baruch, 5

historical festival studies, 610

historiography: Africanist, 11; Afrikaner nationalist, 3; consciousness in, 10; English liberal, 3–4; and environment, 602–603; feminist, 9; radical, 5, 7–11, 369–370; radical social, 8–9

history: archival, 12–13; festival studies, 610; labour, 6–7; oral, 12–13; political heritage, 610–612; public, 610; socio-environmental, 603. *See also* environmental history; heritage history; resistance history

HIV/AIDS, 567–568, 593, 618

Hlungwani, Jackson, 583

Hodgins, Robert, 595

Hoernlé, Alfred, 51, 57

Hofmeyr, Jan H., 43, 111, 195, 234, 241–242, 536–537

homelands (Bantustans): accorded self-government, 397; and Bantu Authorities Act, 55, 389–395; consolidation of, 389–395; gender relations in, 397–398; increased social stratification in, 397; increase in population in, 397; and National States Citizenship Act, 396–397; and National States Constitution Act. *See also* Reserves

Hooper, Charles, 390

Hosannas, 387

'Hottentots', 26. *See* Khoesan peoples

Houghton, Hobart, 4

house marriage, 358–359

household structure, 496–498, 514, 635t

housing: closed compounds, 127–128, 129, 130–131; and poverty level, 532–533; residential rights under apartheid, 341–342, 362; slums, 261; sub-letting, 306

Huddleston, Trevor, 387

human agency, 9–10

hunter-gatherers, 603

hunting rights, in Zuid-Afrikaansche Republiek, 71

Huss, Bernard, 578

identity. *See* ethnic identity

ideology of South Africanism, 33

Imbumba Yama Nyama, 29–30, 145, 203

Immigration Quota Act of 1930, 34–35

Immorality Act of 1949, 335, 357

Imvo Zabantsundu, 145

income: comparison among agriculture/mining/ industry, 223; functional distribution after World War II, 540; racial income hierarchy, 531–532, 533

income tax, 526

Income Tax Act of 1914,

indentured labour: from China, 133, 169–170; from India, 122, 137, 138–139

Indians, Asian: as aliens, 49; and apartheid, 363; businessmen at Durban, 363; and citizenship, 34–35, 49–50; colonial born in Natal, 204, 205–206; emigration to South Africa, 34–35; as garment industry workers, 229; identity issues, 308–309; and inter-racial rioting, 371; political control over own affairs, 403–404; and property ownership, 242; registration in Transvaal, 204–206; relations with Africans in late nineteenth century, 140; repatriation of, 242, 495; and separatist legislation, 386; upward mobility of, 551; and urbanisation, 286, 287

Industrial and Agricultural Requirements Commission (IARC), 537, 538

Industrial and Commercial Workers' Union (ICU), 45, 273, 276, 296–298, 300; and African People's Organisation, 297; in Cape Town, 296–297; collapse of rural, 300; expansion of, 299; failure of, 304; and farm workers, 296, 299–300; in Natal, 298, 300; national organising campaign, 297–298; in Reserves, 300; in Transvaal, 299–300; and Western Cape African Congress, 296–297; and women, 296, 302

Industrial Conciliation Act of 1924, 226, 527

Industrial Conciliation Act of 1937, 513

Industrial Conciliation Act of 1956, 376, 377

Industrial Conciliation Amendment Act of 1979, 437

Industrial Conciliation (Natives) Bill of 1947, 240

industrial decentralisation, 342–343

Industrial Development Corporation, 248, 537, 547

industrial disease, 151, 172, 224–225, 619

industrial schools, 262

industrial unionisation, 267

industrialisation, 13; food processing, 222; mining and, 221; policy in modern state, 528–529; textile industry, 221–222; and unevenness of material conditions, 217, 221–222; during World War II, 216

industrialisation through import-substitution (ISI), 549

industry: increase in wages in, 398; rise in employment, 536; secondary industry on the Rand, 291

inequality and poverty, 511–514; distribution of household/per capita income, 511–512t; poverty, explanations for, 512–514; racial shares in household income, 511

infant mortality, 540

inflation, 232, 443, 542; as cause for strikes, 256, 315, 412; and Wage Act, 239

Inkatha movement, 298–299, 483–485

Inkatha yaKwaZulu, 393–394

Inkatha Youth Brigade, 422

Innes, Rose, 152

institutional wage setting, 529–533; white worker wages, 530–532

institutionalised migrant labour, 256

Intaba, 392

international migration, 494–495; African, 495; Asian Indian, 494; illegal, 495; white, 494

internment camps, 159

inter-racial rioting, 371

Inter-State College, 197–198

Irish, in South Africa, 152

Iron & Steel Corporation (ISCOR): civilised labour policy at, 227–228; founding of, 248, 529

irrigation schemes, 249

Isitoshozi gangs, 278

Israelite sect, 280–281, 294

Izwi Labantu, 148

Jabavu, D.D.T., 37–38, 203, 383–384

Jabavu, John T., 31, 145, 148, 304–305, 574

Jabavu, Noni, 379

Jameson, Leander S., 148–149, 177

Jameson Raid, 148–149

jazz bands, 399–400

Jews: and anti-Semitism, 34–35; Eastern European Jews, 49; immigration to South Africa blocked, 232

jingoism, 186

job reservation policy, 339, 354, 361, 376

Johannesburg: art centre in, 582–583; *bywoners* in, 291; forced removals from, 385; implications of gold discovery for, 216–217; justification for segregation in, 167; *marabi* culture in, 294–295; Market Theatre in, 593; mining properties within, 166–167; pass protest in, 301–302; service-oriented employment in, 292; slums in, 261; squatter movement in, 317

joiners, 181–182

Joint Management Centres, 468

Joint Management Committees, 468

joint stock companies, in diamond industry, 125

Jones, Daniel, 576

Jordaan, Kenny, 54

Jordaan, Kobus, 465

Jordan, A.C., 54

Jorissen, E.J.P., 80

Joseph, Helen, 381

Joubert, Piet, 80, 81, 83–84, 110, 112

Junod, Henri-Alexandre, 40

Juvenile Affairs Boards, 260

Kadalie, Clements, 296, 299, 300, 305

kaffir-farming, 121

Kani, John, 595, 596

Keate, R.W., 78

Keegan, Tim, 237

Kente, Gibson, 400, 588

Kentridge, William, 595, 596

Keppel-Jones, Arthur, 57

Kerkorrel, Johannes, 476
Khaki Election, 216
Khoesan peoples, 26; burials, 611–612; decline
    of, 604; land seized from, 69; military role of,
    67; working conditions in Cape Colony, 69
kholwa, 117
Khuduthamaga, 391
Kidd, Dudley, 40
Kies, Ben, 54
Kimberly: black urban elite at, 142; black urban
    elite women at, 142; closed compounds for
    African workers at, 127–128, 129; discovery
    of diamonds at, 13; industrial revolution at,
    124–125; institutional control of labour at,
    126; racial division of labour at, 126–127;
    white/black worker cooperation during strikes
    at, 127; working conditions at, 133
"kindergarten," 191–192; on Indians in
    Transvaal, 205; role in bringing about union,
    194–195
King Kong (film), 586
King Willimastown, African National Congress
    in, 427
kinship, 41, 104; quasi-, 285
Kitchener, Horatio (Lord), 163
Kolbe, F.W., 23
Koornhof Bills, 437, 438
Kora, 112
Korsten, 287
Kramer, David, 596
Krige, Uys, 577–578
Kruger, Paul, 48, 82, 110, 111, 113, 177
Kruger, S.J.P., 80
Kuper, Leo, 58
Kuzwayo, Ellen, 6
Kwa Ndebele, 483
KwaShange, 484
KwaZakele, 387

la Guma, Alex, 587
labour history, 6–7
labour issues, 66; during 1920s on
    Witwatersrand, 218; after apartheid, 568,
    569–570; black labour, 322, 336, 337–338,
    340–341, 361–362; cheap labour thesis,
    569–570; child labour, 535; Chinese
    indentured labourers, 133, 169–170, 176,
    178; and confederation strategy, 23; cost of
    white labour, 268; and de-skilling of miners,
    265; discriminatory labour legislation, 541;
    institutional control at Kimberly, 126;
    institutionalised migrant labour, 256; and job

colour bar, 178, 193, 376; and labour
    shortage, 169–170; labour shortage after
    South African War, 168–170; mine labour
    from Mozambique, 168, 220, 255, 535; mine
    labour from Transkei, 255; racial division of at
    Kimberly, 126–127; recruitment control,
    255; segmentation in Cape Town, 376;
    segmentation in Durban, 376; in
    Zuid-Afrikaansche Republiek, 72. *See also*
    labour market transformation, during
    apartheid; strikes
labour market status, 508–509, 514, 515;
    statistics on, 647–648t
labour market transformation, during apartheid,
    550–557; African worker rights, 553; class
    differences among Africans, 553; coloured
    upward mobility, 551; education for African
    children, 552–553; and established trade
    unions, 554; and Fordist production, 550;
    gold mining, 552; increase in white-collar
    employment, 551; and independent trade
    unions, 553–555; Indian upward mobility,
    551; technology effect on, 550–551;
    unemployment, 556–557; urban African
    employment, 551–552
labour tenancy, 283; and Industrial and
    Commercial Workers' Union, 296, 299–300;
    on Reserves, 339; and urbanisation, 286
Labour Party, 214, 215, 226, 228; founding of,
    404; at Labour Conference, 533; wage board
    under, 527
Ladysmith Black Mambazo, 400
Lagden, Godfrey, 168, 171
Lamula, Alfred, 298, 299, 302, 306–307
Lamula, Petros, 39
Land Act of 1910, 256–259
Land Act of 1913. *See* Natives' Land Act of 1913
Land Claims Commission, 7
land issues: African access to, 535; Afrikaner,
    before British occupation, 67–68; buy backs
    in Transvaal, 281–282, 305; distribution
    favoring British merchants, 66; faction fights,
    over land, 124; legislation on purchase,
    257–259; in Natal, 124, 257; ownership and
    policy in Zuid-Afrikaansche Republiek, 71;
    ownership by Asian Indians, 242; ownership
    by women, 381–382; shortage in Natal, 124;
    territory seizures in Cape Colony, 69. *See also*
    de-agrarianisation and landlessness
land purchase legislation, 257–259
Land Settlement Act of 1912, 227
landless whites. *See bywoners*

Langalibalele, 141
Langenhoven, C.J., 65, 273
Language Act of 1925, 230
language of instruction, 506–507
language policy: in Cape Colony, 185–186, 187; in Orange Free State, 185, 186–187; in Transvaal, 187–188
language spoken at home, 1936–1996, 505–506, 636–637t
Lanyon, Owen, 81
Laundering Cleaning and Dyeing Workers' Union, 377
Lawrence, Harry, 240
law-violence interconnection, 345–348; and power of police and military, 347; and township crime, 348
le Grange, Louis, 478
le Roux, Etienne, 590, 593–594
le Roux, P.L., 310
League of African Rights (LAR), 301–302
Leballo, Potlake, 57, 436
legal system: containment/subjugation of blacks, 254–255; customary law, 104, 276; People's Courts, 447, 450, 451; vagrancy law in Cape Colony, 69. *See also* pass laws
Legassick, Martin, 60, 569, 570
Leipoldt, C. Louis, 271, 577
leisure: activities in cities, 399; aimed at black working class, 416
Lembede, Anton, 45, 52–53
Lessac, Michael, 596
Letanka, J.S., 311
liberal historiography, 3–4
liberalism, *vs.* Marxism on apartheid and capitalism, 4–5
Libya, 447–448
life expectancy, 514; AIDS effect on, 567–568; at birth, 629t; of white miners, 264
linguistic research, in nineteenth century, 23, 24
linguistic revolution, 30
liquor brewing: in slums, 295. *See also* beer brewing
liquor laws, 168
litema (mural art), 584
literacy, 416, 417; grammars, 23, 24. *See also* translations and culture
literature: and Afrikaner women, 187; criticism of black, 594–595
living standards: for Africans on white-owned farms, 339; under apartheid, 387–388
living wage, 555
lobola (bridewealth), 276, 397, 496–497

location stands, 295, 306
Locke, Alain, 52
Louw, Eric, 233
Lovedu chiefdom, 112
Loyal Colonial League, 152
Luckhardt, Ken, 5
Lutheran Bapedi Church, 145–146
Luthuli, Albert, 57, 388

Mabhida, Moses, 389
Mabille, A., 573–574
MacBride, John, 152
Macdonald, Ramsay, 174–175
Mackenzie, John, 112, 165
Macmillan, W.M., 3, 42, 61, 534
Madikizela, Solomon, 392
Madzunya, Josias, 57
Magogodi, Kgafela oa, 595
Magubane, Bernard, 583
Maharaj, Mac, 429, 459
Maine, Kas, 397, 557–558
maize, 283–284
Majeke, Nosipho (Dora Taylor), 53–54
Makeba, Miriam, 400
Makgatho, S.M., 298, 299–300, 305, 311
Malan, Daniel F., 49; Purified National Party of, 215, 216, 232–233; and Second Great Trek, 307–308
Malan, F.S., 176, 191
Malan, Magnus, 478
malaria, 280, 294
Malawi, mine labour from, 220
Malherbe, E.G., 51, 273
Malinowski, Bronislaw, 41
Malivhe, Alpheus, 283
malnutrition, 293–294, 534–535, 539–540, 561
Mamdani, Mahmood, 213
Mampuru, 109
Mandela, Nelson, 58, 63, 432, 577; arrest/imprisonment of, 396; call for release of, 439; convicted of statutory communism, 372–373; leaves prison, 481; and National Intelligence Service, 478; and People's War, 465; and transition to democracy, 483
Mandela, Winnie, 421, 427–428, 460, 481
Mangope, Lucas, 391
Mankunku, Winston, 587
manufacturing: under apartheid, 541–542, 546–547; expansion during World War II, 314; factory workers in Mozambique, 448; increased employment in Transvaal, 301;

increase of African workers in, 398, 413–414; in modern economic state, 529; tariff protection in, 529

manyanos (African women's prayer groups), 14

Maponya, Maishe, 593

marabi culture, 294–295, 312

Marais, David, 596

Marais, Eugene, 577

Marais, J.S., 43–44, 85

Mare, Gerhard, 393

marital status, 495–496; 1911 Census, 630t; 1936 Census, 631t; 1946/1951 Census, 632t; 1960 Census, 633t; married at age 50, 1911–1996, 634t; singulate mean age at marriage, 1911–1996, 634t. *See also* marriage

Market Theatre, 593

Marketing Act of 1937, 249

Marks, J.B., 585

Marks, Shula, 7, 60

Marquard, Leo, 51, 54

Marquard, Nell, 51

marriage: under apartheid, 357–358; mine marriages, 376; mixed, 264, 290–291, 335, 357. *See also* marital status

Marshall, T.H., 50

Marxism: on non-racialism, 7; on South African capitalism, 569–570; *vs.* liberalism on apartheid and capitalism, 4–5

Mashanini, Emma, 6

Mashiyane, Spokes, 400

Mass Democratic Movement, 483

Masters and Servants Act, 377

Masters and Servants laws, 173, 240, 527–528

Matanzima, George, 394–395

Matatiele, African National Congress in, 426–427

material conditions, unevenness of, 216–224

mathematics, 504

matrifocalism, 380

Matthews, Joe, 54

Matthews, Z.K., 46

Maxeke, Charlotte, 311

Maxeke, Marshall, 197

Mayekiso, Moses, 451, 452

Mayer, Philip, 416–417, 419

Mayne, Charlotte, 196–197

Mbatha, Azaria, 583

Mbeki, Govan, 394

Mbeki, Thabo, 63–64, 429, 464, 478, 615

McGrath, M., 511–512t

Mda, Peter, 52–53

Mda, Zakes, 593, 595

Meer, Ismail, 36

Meli, Francis, 5

memoralisation, 609

merchant-traders, in Zuid-Afrikaansche Republiek, 70–71

Merriman, John X., 28, 150–151, 152, 176, 177, 188–189

metal workers' union, 231

Methodist Church, 14

Mfengu, 47, 305

Mgijima, Enoch, 280–281

migrant labour: institutionalised, 256; and Reserves, 535

migration, international, 494–495

migration thesis of Stow, 26

militarisation: air/commando raids on African National Congress facilities, 470; Angolan military setbacks, 478–479; arms industry, 474; decrease in government intervention, 472; economic and fiscal effects of, 474–475, 476, 477, 479–480; June 1986 State of Emergency, 470–471; and policy making, 469–470; restoration of local authority, 472–473; and sanctions, 479; and shifts in government policy, 472; sociological effects of, 475–478; and Soviet Union, 479; and State Security Council, 467; and total national strategy, 466–467; and total onslaught doctrine, 467–468, 479; and township Upliftment, 471, 479

Military Intelligence Department for Renamo (MNR), 469

Millin, Sarah G., 43

Milner, Alfred: and agricultural settlement in Transvaal, 177; and deportations to Europe, 166; and imperial supremacy, 86, 153; language and education policy of, 184–185; and mining labour, 169–170, 171, 176; and Rand mining post–South African War, 167, 168; and taxes, 166–167; and *Uitlander* dominance, 166; and unification, 190–191; on white rule, 175

mine marriages, 376

Mine Workers' Union, 230

miners' phthisis (silicosis), 151, 171–172, 224–225, 264, 619

mines/mining: under apartheid, 544, 546–547; deserting workers, 254–255; labour costs, reducing, 85, 88–89; provisioning, 68, 71. *See also* diamond industry; gold mining industry

Mines and Works Amendment Act of 1926,

mini-JMCs, 471

minimum wage, 226, 388, 411, 531–532, 533–534, 538, 554–555, 556–557

mining capitalism, 66

Mining Industry Commission, 179

mining labour sources, 219–220

Ministry of Economic Development, 248

miscegenation fears, 325–326, 332

mission schools, 292, 339–340

missionaries: and closed compounds, 130, 131; grammars produced by, 23; translations by, 573–574

mixed marriage, 264, 290–291, 335, 357

Mixed Marriages Act of 1950, 335, 357

Mji, Diliza, 425

Mnguni (Hosea Jaffe), 53–54

modernising project, during apartheid, 343–345

Modisane, William 'Bloke', 386–387, 403, 585

Moeketsi, Kippie, 400

Moffat, R., 574

Mofokeng, Santu, 583

Mofolo, Thomas, 38, 39

Mokgatle, August, 281

Mokoena, Aubrey, 460

Molefe, Popo, 458

Molema, Silas M., 37

Molepo, Matthews, 283

monopoly: diamond, 124, 126; dynamite, 83, 96

monopoly capital, 464

Moodie, Dunbar, 255–256, 376

Mopeli, Paulus, 383

moral economy, 68, 70, 255–256

Moroka, James S., 372, 395

mortality, 514; infant, 540

Mosenthal, Adolph, 71

Mosenthal, Joseph, 71

Moss, Joseph, 105–106, 405

Motlana, Nthatho, 424

Motsoaledi, Elias M., 391–392

Mozambique: conquest of Gaza kingdom in, 133; mine labour from, 168, 220, 255, 535; port in, 212; Portuguese rights and South Africa, 243–244; Renamo insurgency, 469–470, 479–480; views of factory workers in, 448

Mpanza, James S., 316, 317, 371

Mpe, Phaswane, 595

Mpetha, Oscar, 460

Mphahlele, Es'kia, 406

Mphahlele, Moses, 311, 587

Mpondoland: and Betterment schemes, 382; paramountcies in, 279; youth in, 278

Mqayi, S.E.K., 574

Msimang, H. Selby, 575

Msomi, Hamilton, 302

Msutu (Chief), 382

Mtwa, Percy, 592, 593

Mulder, Connie, 59

Muller, C.F.J., 60

mural art, 584

Murray, Colin, 395

music, 311–312; exiled musicians, 587–588; jazz bands, 399–400

Mzimba, Pambani, 574

Naicker, G.M., 49–50, 309

Nambia, 212

Natal, 70–71, 78, 79–80; African National Congress in, 428; African population living on white-owned lands in, 121; agrarian expansion in, 120; beer hall boycotts in, 388–389; coal industry in, 529; Code of Native Law (1878), 104; colonial-born Indians in, 204, 205–206; extent of franchise in, 153; female suffrage proposed in, 193; indentured Indian workers in, 122; Industrial and Commercial Workers' Union in, 298, 300; joins Union, 193–194; labour tenancy in, 283; land issues in, 257; land shortage in, 124; Poll Tax rebellion in, 188; relative lack of school protests in, 422; religious independence in, 146; resentment toward powers of High Commissioner, 29; rule by chiefs in, 275, 276; and separatist legislation, 386; soccer in, 402; youth gangs in, 278

Natal African Congress, 299

Natal Indian Congress, 139–140, 204, 371–372, 438, 439, 459

Natal Indian Patriotic Union, 205–206

Natal Native Congress, 299

national democracy, 456

national economy notion, 330

National Education Union of South Africa, 442

National Indian Council, 404

National Intelligence Service, 478

National Land and Agricultural Bank, 249

National Parks, 271

National Party, 214, 215, 216, 226; and Afrikaner business elite, 231; and changing composition of state institutions, 353–354; factors in 1948 victory, 327; inequality policy of, 541; and territorial segregation, 240;

verkrampte (more conservative) faction of, 328; *verligte* (more pragmatic) faction of, 328; and white electorate, 327–328. *See also* apartheid
National Professional Soccer League (NPSL), 402
National Question, 17–18
National Roads Act, 248
National Security Management System (NSMS), 468
National States Citizenship Act of 1970, 396–397
National States Constitution Act of 1971, 397
National Union of Mineworkers, 555
National Union of South African Students (NUSAS), 62, 405
nationalism: African, 29–30; Afrikaner (*See* Afrikaner nationalism, 29–30); Cape colonial 29–30; Cape Dutch, 68; Christian, 325–326, 335
Native Administration Act of 1927, 237, 276–277
Native Affairs Department (NAD), 168, 240, 285, 377, 382–383
Native Affairs Society, 39
Native Bills, 234, 237
Native Commissioners, 173–174
Native Economic Commission, 282
Native Educational Association, 197
Native Farm Labour Committee, 285
Native Labour Regulation Act (NLRA) of 1911, 254–255, 256
Native Land and Trust Act of 1926, 281
Native Laws Amendment Act, 337
"native question," 20, 23, 24, 32
Native Recruiting Corporation, 255
Native Representative Council (NRC), 238–239, 242, 389
Native Service Contract Act, 240, 284
Native Trust and Land Act of 1936, 239, 282–283, 285
Natives' Land Act of 1913, 37, 220, 254, 256–259, 275, 535; literature on, 576
Natives' (Urban Areas Amendment) Act of 1923, 236, 288, 374, 527
Nchabeleng, Peter, 391–392
Ndebele, 350; campaign against Ndzundza, 112; mural art by, 584
Ndebele, Allina, 584
Ndebele, Njabulo, 406, 575, 594–595, 597
Ndobe, Bransby, 303
Nederduits Gereformeerde Kerk (NGK), 311
Nellmapius, Alois H., 83
Nembula, Mzvuma, 197

New Brighton, Port Elizabeth, 286–287; heritage site in, 611; politics reduced to local in, 305–306
New Kleinfontein mine, 265
newspapers, black-owned and black-run, 575, 576
Ngema, Mbongeni, 592, 593
Ngidi, Mbiana, 146
Ngoyi, Lilian, 381
Ngubane, Jordan, 52
Nguni-speaking Africans, 27; origins of, 38–39
Ngwenya, Thomas, 54
Nicholls, George H., 41
Nicholls, Heaton, 237
Nicol, Mike, 596
Nkadimeng, John, 391–392
Nkomati Accord, 469–470
Nkomo, Nkwenkwe, 406
Nkondo, Curtis, 460
Nkosi, Johannes, 303
Nkosi, Lewis, 594
Nkosi, Mandlesilo, 299
Nkwenkwe, Nontetha, 280
Noble, John, 21, 22
Non European Unity Movement (NEUM), 379, 382, 396, 402, 404
non-racialism, 7, 55, 61, 143, 153
North Basotho, 350
Ntantala, Templeton, 436
Ntonjeni, Elliot, 303
Ntsebeza, Lungisile, 394, 395
Nursing Amendment Act, 384
Nyanda, Siphiwe, 428
Nyasaland Protectorate, mine labour from, 220
Nyerere, Julius, 417–418
Nyquist, Thomas, 399
Nzo, Alfred, 464

old age pensions: under apartheid, 563–564; extended to African men and women, 539
Old Age Pensions Act, 528
O'Meara, D., 480
Oost, Hart, 578
Oppenheimer, Ernest, 219, 524
Opperman, D.J., 577
oral history, 12–13
oral-based tradition, 379, 574
Orange Free State: administration in, 275; African Methodist Episcopal Church in, 147–148; all adult white male franchise in, 192; gold discovery in, 541; labour tenancy in, 283; language policy in, 185, 186–187; and

Orange Free State (*cont.*)
Natives' Land Act of 1913, 256–259; Oranje
Vrystaat (OVS), 70; pastoral economy in, 120;
Pentecostal churches in, 310; politics reduced
to local in, 305–306; Reserves in, 121; soccer
in, 402
Orange River Colony: schools in, 185;
self-government in, 180–181
Oranje Vrystaat (OVS), 70
Orderly Movement and Settlement of Black
Persons Bill, 437
orthography, African, 61
Ossewabrandwag, 233
Oxford History of South Africa (Wilson &
Thompson), 59–60

Paarl, 67–68
Pact Government, 215, 224, 226; and Afrikaans
language, 230; and racial income hierarchy,
531–532, 533; and Wage Act of 1925, 226;
and Wage Board, 527
Pam-Grant, Susan, 593
Pan Africanist Congress (PAC), 395–396, 436;
banning of, 346, 396; military wing of, 396
pan-Africanism, in nineteenth century, 23–24
parastatal sector, under apartheid, 547
parliamentary democracy, 346
Parliamentary Registration Act of 1887, 145
Parnell, Susan, 241
pass laws, 168, 173, 236, 240; under apartheid,
364–365, 373; number of convictions under,
373–374; in Port Elizabeth, 305–306;
prosecutions after World War II, 540; protest
in 1929 in Johannesburg, 301–302
pastoralism, 603; in Cape midlands, 120; in
Eastern Cape, 120; in Orange Free State, 120.
See also cattle
Paton, Alan, 585
patriarchy, 325
Pauw, B.A., 496, 497
Peace Preservation Act, 114
Peace of Vereeniging, 163, 164–165
Pedi: institutionalized migrant labour, 256;
thwarted invasion of Zuid-Afrikaansche
Republiek, 80
Pedi homeland: burial societies in, 391;
Sekhukhuneland rebellion in, 391–392
Pedi kingdom, 106; and Betterment schemes,
382; conquest of, 107, 109; land issues after
South African War, 173–174; paramountcies
in, 279
Pegging Act of 1943, 242

Pemba, George Milwa Mnyaluza, 581
Pentecostal churches, 272, 310
People's Courts, 447, 450, 451
People's War, 461–466; attacks, 462; settlement
negotiations, 464–466; *uMkhonto weSizwe* role
in, 461–464
Peregrino, F.Z.S., 147
performing arts, and politics, 578–580; African
dance, 578–579; African theatre, 578–580;
Afrikaans theatre, 578
Petersen, Taliep, 596
Phala, John, 391–392
Phaphama Africa (Wake up Africa!) Commercial
Enterprises, 405
Phetoe, Molefe, 400
Phillips, Lionel, 84, 190
Phooko, H.L., 189–190
Phosphate Development Corporation (Foskor),
547
phthisis, miners' (silicosis), 151, 171–172,
224–225, 264, 619
Phungula, Johannes, 316, 428
Pierneff, Jacobus H., 580
Pietersburg, 283
Pim, Howard, 39–40
Plaatje, Solomon, 36–37, 142, 236, 575,
576–577
Plaatjie, Thama ka, 436
Plomer, William, 577
poetry, Afrikaans lyric, 271
political economy of environment, 601
political heritage history, 610–612
political overview, of South Africa, 214–216
poll tax, 284
Poll Tax rebellion, 124, 188, 201–202
Polly Street Centre, 582–583
polygamy, 277, 496
polygyny, 496
Pondoland: African National Congress in,
426–427; militancy in, 392–393; paramounts
in, 279
poor whites: under apartheid, 362; and Dutch
Reformed Church, 227; employed by
railways, 263–264; factory work by, 136; in
Johannesburg, 291; and Pact government,
227, 228; poverty amidst, 533–536; problem
of, 225, 249; racism among, 273–274;
recruited into armed services in World War II,
314; in Transvaal, 261–262; and urbanisation,
261; in Witwatersrand, 261–262
population: distribution, 515; distribution of
African, 1936–1996, 650t; growth/shares,

1910–1950, 493, 625–626t; growth/shares, 1951–2000, 627–628t; statistics, 217–218; urban, 1904–1996, 649t

Population Registration Act of 1950, 55, 333, 356, 372, 385

population removals: and apartheid, 342, 360; in Durban, 385; in Eastern Cape, 387; in Port Elizabeth, 385

populism, rural, 272–273

Poqo (Pure/Alone), 396

Port Elizabeth: African National Congress in, 427; establishment of *Imbumba Yama Nyama* in, 145; ethnic identities in, 305; forced removals from, 385; politics reduced to local in, 305–306; slums in, 261; unrest in, 372, 373; urbanised population in, 286–287; Westernised blacks in, 141–142

Portuguese rights, in South Africa, 243–244

postcolonial visual arts, 595–596

postcolonial writing, 595

postmodernism and arts, 594

Poto (Chief), 392

poverty: amidst poor whites, 533–536; and inequality in Cape Town, 532–533. *See also* poverty and inequality under apartheid

poverty and inequality under apartheid, 363, 560–568; household composition of poor persons at beginning/end of, 563; infant mortality, 561; life expectancy, 561; poverty rate, 561–562; and public education, 565–567; redistribution from rich to poor, 564–565, 567; and social programs, 563–564; typical poor household, 1994, 563; upward mobility of Africans, 562–563

preaching jobs, for educated Africans, 298

Precious Stones Act of 1927, 227

Preller, Gustav, 183, 271–272, 274, 578

Preller, Johanna, 184

Pretoria: Indian traders removal from, 385; politics reduced to local in, 305–306

Pretorius, M.W., 76

Prevention of Illegal Squatting Act, 335

Pringle, Thomas, 27

Prisons and Reformatories Act, 262

private schools, 185

private sector, under apartheid, 547–549

productivity, worker, 570

Progressive Federal Party, 58

Progressive Party: and Africa-wide constitution, 192; on multiracialism, 57

Promotion of Bantu Self-Government Act of 1959, 55, 341, 389

public health, 385

public history, on significance of South African War, 610

Public Utility Transport Corporation (PUTCO), 387–388

public works programmes, for white workers, 525, 534

publishing rights, in nineteenth century, 27

Purified National Party, 215, 216, 232–233

quasi-kinship, 285

Queen Victoria Memorial, 197–198

Race Classification Act, 385–386

Race Classification Appeal Boards, 356

race/racism: and changing composition of state institutions, 354–355; inter-racial rioting, 371; non-racialism, 7, 55, 61, 143, 153; racial income hierarchy, 531–532, 533; racially separatist electioneering, 403–404; racial purity, 332; racial shares in household income, 511; scientific racism, 26, 150; urban racial separation, 398–399

racial capitalism, 336

racial classification, 42; under apartheid, 332–334, 355–356; and Population Registration Act, 55

racial mixing, 38, 332

racial populism, in Eastern Cape, 148

racial purity, 332

Radcliffe-Brown, A.R., 40–41

Radebe, Jabu, 451

radical historiography, 5, 7–11, 369–370

radical social historiography, 8–9; and environment, 602–603; environmental history, 602–603

railway workers' union, 231

railways, 70, 77, 83; civilised labour policy, 227; expansion of, 528–529; poor whites employed by, 263–264; in South Africa, 216

rainbow nation, 58, 63

Ramala, R., 574

Ramgobin, Mewa, 439

Ramokgadi, Martin, 391–392

Rampolokeng, Lesego, 595

Rand. *See* Witwatersrand

Rand Revolt of 1922, 45–46

Randlords, 85–86

Rebellie, 214

recessions, 260, 294, 524

reconciliation, represented in arts, 596

Reconstruction and Development Programme of African National Congress, 485
recording industry, censorship in, 400
Reddingshuis (Rescue Home), 183–184
reformatories, 262
reformist public policy, 409–410
relations, in region and world, 243–245
Release Mandela Organisation, 460
relief works, for poor whites, 262
religion, 507–508; affiliation by population group, 1921–1996, 638–646t; apartheid, 402–403; during apartheid, 402–403; Christianity, 14; Israelite sect, 280–281, 294; radical separatist Christianity in Transkei, 148; religious independence in Natal, 146
remittances, migrant, 558, 560
removals. *See* population removals
renaissance, Sophiatown and Drum Set, 584–588
Renamo insurgency, 469–470, 479–480
rent boycott, 456
repatriation, of Asian Indians, 242, 495
Repatriation Department, 173
Report of the South African Native Affairs Commission, 39
Representation of Natives Act of 1936, 239
republicanism, 272
Reservation of Separate Amenities Act of 1953, 356
Reserves: administration modes, 275–276; African women's rights, erosion of, 277; black Americans as saviors, 280–281; customary law, 276; de-agrarianisation on, 558, 559–560; economic dependency of, 338–339; effects of labour tenancy on, 339; gangs, 278; land buy back, 281–282; life under apartheid, 338–339; malnutrition on, 535; migrant labour, 280; and migrant workers, 535; Native Administration Act of 1927, 276–277; natural disasters, 280; natural disasters, reaction to, 280; in Orange Free State, 121; paramountcies, 279; reclaiming, 282–283; reconfiguring, 275–282; sexuality, 278–279; youth culture, 278. *See also* homelands
residential rights, under apartheid, 341–342, 362
resistance history, 5–6, 613–617; further research needs, 616–617; lack of professionalism, 614, 616; openness after transition to democracy, 614–615; pre-1960s studies, 614; recent studies, 613–614; SADET project, 615–616; urban studies, 614
respiratory disease, at mines, 171

retribalisation, 55
revolving credit associations, formed by women, 380
Rhodes, Cecil, 75–76, 85–86; becomes Prime Minister of the Cape, 125–126; biography of, 613; and Commonwealth membership, 243; introduces proto-segregationist legislation, 32; mining-finance house of, 523; and unification, 190
Rhodesias, and annexation, 245
Riekert Commission, 423–424
Riley, James, 179
rinderpest epizootic, 133, 134–135
Rive, Richard, 587
Robertson, H.M., 3
Robeson, Paul, 52
Robinson, Hercules, 22–23
Robinson, William, 77
Rolong, 112
Roos, Jacob de Villiers, 262
Roos, Tielman, 215
Rosen, George, 618
Roth, M., 242
Rothmann, Maria E., 577
Roux, Edward, 5, 44, 54, 613
Roux, J.L., 198
Rubusana, Walter B., 574
Rudd, Charles, 523
rugby, 402
rural populism, 272–273

Sachs, Solly, 229
Sadie, J.L., 359, 493, 494
Safmarine, 547
Saint Ntsikana Memorial Association, 403
Saloojee, Cas, 438
sanctions, 479
Sandilands, A., 574
Sandile, Archibald, 394
Sandile, Velile, 394
Sanlam, 549
Sargant, E.B., 184–185
satire, 596
Sauer Commission, 240
Sauer, J.W., 150, 176
Schapera, Isaac, 42
schoolchildren's movement, 416–426; American Black Power movement influence on, 418; Black Consciousness influence on, 417–419; social influences on, 416–417, 419, 424; and South African Students Movement (SASM), 418, 419–420, 422; and Soweto Students

Representative Council (SSRC), 420, 421. *See also* schoolchildren's movement, and instruction in Afrikaans mandate

schoolchildren's movement, and instruction in Afrikaans mandate, 419; under Botha administration, 425–426; casualties, 421–422; consequences of, 422–424; first phase of revolt, 419–422; government reaction to, 420; mandate rescinded, 421; parental control loss, 422–423; rebellion in Natal, 422; reforms, 423–424; second phase of revolt, 420–421; South African optimism, 423; third phase of revolt, 421–422; white emigration, 423

Schreiner, Olive, 31–32, 34, 84, 150, 193, 203, 238

Schreiner, W.P., 31, 150–151

scientific determinism, 602

scientific racism, 26, 150

scorched earth policy, during South African War, 158–159, 160

Scots, in South Africa, 151–152

scramble for Africa, 107

Sebatakgomo, 391

Second Great Trek, 307–308

secondary industry, on Rand, 291

security, and confederation strategy, 23. *See also* inflation

Seekings, Jeremy, 440, 460

segregation: Durban system, 236, 287–288; justification in Johannesburg, 167; and law, 143–144; under Pact government, 240; policy after South African war, 174; proto-segregationist legislation, 32; provisions of early, 35; racial, 229–230; under Smuts government, 237, 240, 241–242. *See also* segregation, construction of

segregation, construction of, 213, 233–242; black labour rights, 239–240; elements of legislation, 235; female franchise, 238; Fusion Period, 238; and Indians, 242; Land Act of 1913, 236–237; land settlement, 239; male franchise, 238; Natives (Urban Areas) Act of 1923, 236; and Pact Party, 234–235, 238; power of chiefs, 237–238; Slums Act of 1934, 241; and Unionist Party, 234; and urbanisation of blacks, 235, 240–242; white representation of blacks, 238–239

Sekhukhune, 109

Sekhukhune III, 279

Sekhukhuneland, 382, 391–392, 448–450

Sekoto, Gerard, 581–582

Selborne (Lord): and mine labour, 149; on rights of coloured men, 203–204; and unification, 190–191

Selborne Memorandum of 1907, 34, 152, 191, 202

Self Defence Units, 485–486

Self Help Labour Union and Organisation of Non-European Races of South Africa, 299

self-government, 349–350; and Africans, 349–350; in British Kaffraria, 104; and homelands, 397; in Orange River Colony, 180–181; in Transkei, 104; in Transvaal, 180–181

Seme, Pixley ka Isaka, 45, 302, 303–304, 305, 575

Senghor, Leopold, 417

Senne, Pegge, 399

Separate Amenities Act of 1953, 373, 385–386

separate development, 349–350

Separate Representation of Voters Act of 1956, 348, 385–386

Separate Universities bill, 384

Serote, Mongane, 406, 591

service-oriented employment, in Johannesburg, 292

Setswana orthography, 576–577

sexual violence towards women, 279

sexuality: under apartheid, 334–335; house marriage, 358–359; venereal disease, 262, 294

Sexwale, Mosima "Tokyo," 428

Shabalala, Joseph, 400

Shabangu, Elliot, 428

Shaka fallacy, 276

Shaka Zulu, 38

Shangane people, institutionalised migrant labour, 256

Shapiro, Jonathan, 595

sharecropping, 123–124; banning of, 237, 339; and de-agrarianisation, 557–558; in Transvaal, 121

Sharpeville, unrest in, 395–396, 586

Shaw, George B., 84

shebeeners, 401

sheep, 72, 283–284

Shembe, Isaiah, 14, 309–310

Shepstone, Theophilus, 79–80, 106, 108

Sigcau, Botha, 392

silicosis (miners' phthisis), 151, 171–172, 224–225, 264, 619

Simelane, Samuel, 298

Simkins, Charles, 221, 498

Simon, Barney, 592
Simons, H.J. (Jack), 54, 85
Simons, R.E. (Ray), 54, 85, 432
singulate mean age at marriage (SMAM),
  1911–1996, 634t
Siopis, Penny, 595–596
Sisulu, Walter, 372–373; arrest/imprisonment
  of, 396
Skocpol, Theda, 477
Skota, T.D. Mweli, 44
Skotnes, Cecil, 582–583
Slabolepszy, Paul, 593
slavery and slave trade, 69
Slosberg, Bertha, 579
Slovo, Joe, 431
slums: in Cape Town, 261; in Johannesburg,
  261
Slums Act of 1934, 241, 292
Small, Adam, 589, 591
Smit Commission, 240
Smith, Andrew, 47
Smith, M.G., 58
Smith, Pauline, 577
Smuts, Jan, 32, 33, 41, 149, 157; and
  Commonwealth membership, 243, 247; and
  developmentalism, 248; and gold standard,
  247; and government intervention in
  industrial disputes, 226; and immigration,
  328; and mine labour, 189, 265–266, 270;
  and rail labour, 267; and reconciliation,
  188–189; and registration of Indians in
  Transvaal, 205; and segregation, 237, 240,
  241–242; and South African War, 161, 163;
  on wartime suffering, 183
Sobhuza (Swazi king), 244
soccer, 401–402
Social and Economic Planning Commission
  (SEPC) of 1942, 241, 537, 538, 540–541
social anthropology, 41, 42
social citizenship, 50
social class, 224–230; craft unions, 228–230;
  differences among Africans, 553; in gold
  mining industry, 225, 226; poor-white
  problem, 226–228; ratio of white to black
  workers, 225–226; reasons for militancy of
  white miners, 224–225; and status in
  townships, 363–364
social Darwinism, 144
social insurance, contributory,
  528
social security movement, 539
social welfare, needs after World War II,
  540–541

social welfare reform, 539–540; reversal after
  World War II, 540
'Societies of Southern Africa' seminar (1969),
  60–61
socio-environmental history, 603
Soga, Allan Kirkland, 31, 575
Soga, Tiyo, 574, 575
Soil Conservation Act of 1946, 249
Solomon ka Dinizulu in Zululand: and
  Industrial and Commercial Workers' Union,
  300; as paramount chief, 279
Solomon, Georgina, 184
Solomon, Richard, 150–151, 152
Solomon, Saul, 28–29
Sons of Young Africa (SOYA), 384
Sophiatown, 386–387
Sotho kingdom, 106
South Africa: early use of term, 18; withdrawal
  from British Commonwealth, 326
South African Allied Workers' Union
  (SAAWU), 453–454
South African Breweries, 612–613
South African Broadcasting Corporation, 248
South African Bureau of Racial Affairs (SABRA),
  326
South African Coal, Oil and Gas Corporation
  (SASOL), 546, 547
South African Coloured People's Congress
  (CPC), 385–386
South African Coloured People's Organisation
  (SACPO), 317, 378–379, 385–386
South African Communist Party: and African
  National Congress, 430, 432–434; support of
  Rand Revolt, 226
South African Congress of Trade Unions
  (SACTU), 378, 388, 412–413, 453
South African Constabulary, 168
South African Constitution, on common
  citizenship, 59
South African Council of Sport (SACOS), 402
South African Defence Force (SADF), 467–468
South African Democracy Education Trust
  (SADET), 615–616
South African Federation of Native Trade
  Unions, 301
South African Indian Council (SAIC), 348, 372,
  378–379, 404
South African Industrial Federation (SAIF), 268,
  270
South African Labour Party (SALP), 179, 267
South African League, 149
South African Native Affairs Commission, 35,
  174

South African Native Commission, 197–198
South African Native Congress (*Ingqungqutela*) (SANC), 148, 196–198, 202, 430, 432–434
South African Native National Congress (SANNC), 36, 576
South African Party, 177, 214–215
South African Pulp and Paper Industries (SAPPI), 547
South African Republic (ZAR), 106
South African Reserve Bank, 247
South African Soccer League (SASL), 401–402
South African Students Movement (SASM), 405, 418, 419–420, 422
South African Students Organisation (SASO), 405, 417
South African Textile Workers Industrial Union, 415
South African Trade & Labour Congress, 228
South African War (1899–1902): African deserters, 162; African subversion of hierarchy and obedience, 162–163; Afrikaner gender relations during, 160–161; and Afrikaner women, 183; Afrikaner women's attitude toward British forces, 160; civilian fatalities, 159, 161; concentration camp conditions, 158–159, 160, 161; deportations, 165–166; initial British offensive, 158; initial republican offensive, 158; internment camp conditions, 159; as lengthy conflict, 157–158; outcomes of, 164–165; and Peace of Vereeniging, 163, 164–165; peace proposal of Kitchener rejected, 163; reconstruction of former Republics after, 166–167; republican deserters, 161–162; republican guerilla tactics and British response, 158–159; republican losses, 161; results of, 32–33; scorched earth policy, 158–159, 160; significance of, 157; surrender of republican forces, 163
South African Women's Federation (*Vroue Federasie*), 184
South Africanism, ideology of, 33
South Basotho, 350
South-West Africa, 244; Bondelswarts Rebellion in, 294
Southern Africa Labour and Development Research Unit (SALDRU), 4
Southern Rhodesia, remains outside Union, 193, 212
Southey, Richard, 73–74
Soviet Union, and militarisation, 479
Soweto: African National Congress in, 427–428; Black Consciousness in, 418; Committee of

Ten, 424; cost of living in, 420; demonstrations concerning evictions in, 456; deterioration of local government in, 420; education in, 340, 416; housing in, 420; instruction in Afrikaans mandate, 419; unemployment in, 420; urban sprawl in, 398
Soweto Poets, 591
Soweto Students Representative Council (SSRC), 420, 421
Soya, Tiyo, 23–24
Space Theatre, 591–593
Spanish flu, 280
Spoorbond (railway workers' union), 231
sports, 271, 312–314; cricket, 312–313; rugby, 313; soccer, 313–314; social control through, 314
squatters, 121, 182, 257, 259–261, 262–263; banning of, 257; movement in Johannesburg, 317
Stallard, C.F., 238
stand-holders, 295–296; women, 295, 306
Stanford, Walter, 114
starvation, 294, 534–535
state capitalism, 365
State of Emergency, June 1986, 470–471
State Security Council (SSC), 467, 468
Statham, F.R., 21, 22
statistical office, central, 525–526
Statistics Act of 1914, 525–526
statutory communism, 372–373
Stead, W.T., 163
Steel and Engineering Industrial Federation of South Africa (SEIFSA), 554
Stellaland, 112–113
Stellenbosch, 67–68
Stern, Irma, 580–581
stock raising, 66. *See also* cattle
Stockenström, Andries, 69
Stow, George, 26–27
strikes: causes of in Durban, 412, 413–414; in diamond mines, 125; in gold mining industry, 225, 226, 269, 270; inflation as cause, 256, 315, 412; labour strike of 1913, 265–266; labour strike of 1920, 255–256; leadership of strike movement in Durban, 412–413; liaison committees in aftermath of strike movement in Durban, 414; repression after World War II, 540; spread of strike movement in Durban, 413; strike movement in Durban, 411–415; white/black worker cooperation at Kimberly, 127; by white working-class mineworkers, 265–266, 268–270; by white working-class

strikes (*cont.*)
railworkers, 266–267; and women, 296; workers' rebellion in Durban, 411–414; during World War II, 315
structuralism-functionalism, 40–41
struggle history. *See* resistance history
Stuart, James, 200
Study Project on Christianity in an Apartheid Society (SPROCAS), 4
Stultz, Newell, 327
sub-imperialisms, 66
sub-letting: in East London, 306; in Pretoria, 306
subsistence agriculture, 293
Sugar Act of 1936, 249
Suppression of Communism Act of 1950, 346, 372
Surplus People's Project, 511
Swart Gevaar (Black Threat), 215
Swati, 350
Swaziland: and annexation, 244; geopolitical boundaries of, 193

Taalbond, 186
Tabata, I.B., 382, 392
Tambo, Oliver, 429, 431, 437
Tariff Acts of 1925, 301
tariffs: after apartheid, 568; protection in manufacturing sector, 529, 547–548
taxes, 526; income tax, 526
Teachers' Action Committee, 424
Teachers' League of South Africa (TLSA), 384, 404–405
teaching jobs, for educated Africans, 298
technology, 339; in diamond industry, 125; effect on Africans living on white-owned farms, 339; effect on mining on Witwatersrand, 218–219; effect on worker productivity, 570
tenancy rights, 237
territorial segregation, 256–259
territorial separation, labour leaders on, 179
textile industry, 221–222
Textile Workers Industrial Union, 377
Thabane, Philip, 400
Thaele, James, 296–297, 303
The Atlantic Charter from the Standpoint of Africans, 52
Theal, G.M., 18, 21, 27
Thema, Selope, 38, 575
Thembu Church, 145

Thompson, E.P., 9
Thompson, Leonard, 4, 59–60
Tile, Nehemiah, 145
Tillim, Guy, 583
Tlali, Lefifi, 406
Tlali, Miriam, 406, 591
togt system, 287
Tom, Petrus, 415
tot system, 122
total factor productivity growth, 542–543
total national strategy, 466–467
total onslaught doctrine, 467–468, 479
Totius, 271, 273
tourism industry, 289
towns, 261–263
township Upliftment, 471, 479
townships: gang activity in, 401; jazz music in, 399–400; leisure in, 401–402; liquor consumption in, 400–401. *See also* urbanisation
trade liberalisation, 570, 571
Trade Union Advisory and Coordinating Council (TUACC), 415
trade unions: black movement, 315–317; collapse of black movement, 315–316; effects of black movement on urbanisation, 316; federation of, 454; founding by Gumede, 299; garment industry, 228–230; independent, 553–555; independent unions, 569; industrial, 267; metal workers' union, 231; national coordinated political protest by, 454; organisation on East Rand, 454; shift in attitudes to black unionism in Durban, 414–415; support of rebellion in Alexandra, 452–453; unionisation of mine workers, 220. *See also* strikes
Transkei, 118; African National Congress in, 426–427; agrarian reform in, 177; British annexation of, 28; centralized control of Bantu authorities in, 389–390; direct personal administration in, 275–276; dismantling of *Bunga* system in, 394; income sources, 560; institutionalised migrant labour in, 256; local self-government in, 104; mine labour from, 255; opposition to Bantu Authorities in, 395; PAC in, 436; power of chiefs in, 237–238; radical separatist Christianity in, 148; Spanish flu in, 280
translations and culture, 573–578; African language works translated into English, 574; break with Western tradition, 577; Christian missionary translations, 573–574; and

mission-educated black writers, 575, 576; and New African Movement, 575–576; subtexts and modernity, 574

Transvaal: agricultural settlement in, 177; all adult white male franchise in, 192; Boer-English dualism in, 149–150; British annexation of, 28, 30, 106; bus boycott in, 387–388; consumer boycott in, 388; ethnic identities in, 305; franchise in, 177–178; Industrial and Commercial Workers' Union in, 299–300; job colour bar in, 178; labour tenancy in, 283; land buy back in, 281–282, 305; language policy in, 187–188; manufacturing employment, increase in, 301; and Natives' Land Act of 1913; Pentecostal churches in, 310; poor whites in, 261–262; reclaimed/lost by Africans, 164; registration of Indians in, 204–206; rule by chiefs in, 275, 276; self-government in, 180–181; sharecroppers in, 121; Trust control of lands in, 283; youth gangs in, 278

Transvaal Anti-South African Indian Congress, 438

Transvaal Indian Congress (TIC), 309, 371–372, 438

Trapido, Stanley, 7, 60

Treason Trial, 316

Treaty of Vereeniging, 196

trekboers, 262–263

Treurnicht, Andries, 419, 421, 472

tribalism, 53; under apartheid, 334, 341–342

tricameral parliament, 437

Trollope, Anthony, 20–21, 43, 493

"tropicals" (mining labourers), 219–220

Trust Feed Massacre, 484

Truth and Reconciliation Commission (TRC), 7, 63, 420, 484, 596, 614–615

Tshwete, Steve, 462

Tsiki, Naledi, 428

Tsonga, 350

Tsonga people, study on, 40

Tsotsi, W.M., 382

Tswana: as British protectorate, 108; chiefdom in, 112–113

tuberculosis, 294

TUCSA, 414

Turner, Rick, 62

Tutu, Desmond, 58, 63

Uitlanders, 98, 99; and franchise, 151–152; and South African War, 165, 166

Umkasetemba, Lydia, 574

uMkhonto weSizwe (Spear of the Nation), 391–392, 396, 410, 428, 433–434, 436, 444, 461–464, 485–486

Umtata, African National Congress in, 427

UNDP Human Development Index, 567–568

unemployment, after apartheid, 571

unemployment insurance, and Africans, 540

Union Defence Act of 1912, 48

Union of Southern Artists, 586

Unionist Party, 214–215

unions. *See* trade unions

United Democratic Front (UDF), 59, 409–410, 437–461, 593; activists, 442–443, 445–446, 449, 450–451; attraction for youth, 444–445; consumer boycotts by, 446–447, 457–458; democratic ideology of, 447–448; and denouncement of Chief Buthelezi, 484; disintegration of, 456–457; and federation of unions, 454; finance sources, 443–444; Friends of the UDF, 457–458; ideology of, 444, 449–450; impact of, 441–442; judicial functions of, 447, 450; leadership factions, 458–461; leadership of, 445; organisation and functions of, 442; police view on, 471; prosecution of leaders, 458; regional committee structure of, 441; relationship with African National Congress, 445; structural developments leading to action, 443, 448–449

United Party, 215, 216; 'better life for all' rhetoric, 539

United Transkeian Territories General Council, 237–238

Unity Movement, 5–6, 53–54

University Christian Movement, 417, 418

University of Natal National Union of Students Wages Commission, 412

Upliftment, 471, 479

upward mobility, under apartheid, 383

Urban Areas Act of 1923, 306

Urban Areas Act of 1945, 510, 540

Urban Training Project, 414–415

urbanisation, 13, 217–218, 286–293; and Afrikaners, 261, 262; and Afrikaner women, 291–292; under apartheid, 323–324, 325, 336, 340–341, 359–360, 370–371; and artisans, 292; in Cape Town, 288–289; and Communist Party of South Africa, 316; and consumer goods, 400–401; and demographic transition, 509–511, 514, 515, 649t; in Durban, 287; and Dutch Reformed Church, 261; in East London, 289–290; and gang

urbanisation (*cont.*)
    activity in townships, 401; and Indians, 286,
    287; and jazz music in townships, 399–400;
    and labour tenants, 286; and leisure in
    townships, 401–402; and liquor consumption
    in townships, 400–401; and mission-educated
    men, 292; and poor whites, 261; in Port
    Elizabeth, 286–287; on the Rand, 261,
    290–292; and resistance and reform,
    1973–1994, 410; and segregation, 235,
    240–242; and social stratification, 398–399;
    trade union movement effect on, 316; and
    Witwatersrand, 261, 290–292; and women,
    288, 290–292, 379, 380; during World
    War II, 314
urbanised/tribal African distinction, 337–338
Uys, Pieter-Dirk, 592, 593, 596

Vaal Civic Organisation, 440–441
vagrancy law, in Cape Colony, 69
van den Berghe, Pierre, 58
van der Bijl, H.J., 248
van der Merwe, P.J., 601
van der Ross, Richard, 404
Van der Westhuizen (General), 469
van Heerden, Auret, 459
van Onselen, Charles, 10, 85, 397, 557–558
van Rensburg, Niklaas, 272
Van Riebeeck Festival, 610
van Riebeeck, Jan, 610
van Warmelo, N.J., 42
van Wyk Louw, N.P., 307, 589
veldt schools, 475
Venda, 350
Venda chiefdom, 112
venereal disease, 262, 294
verkrampte (more conservative) faction of
    National Party, 328
verligte (more pragmatic) faction of National
    Party, 328
Verwoerd, Hendrik, 56, 337–338, 339–340,
    379
Vilakazi, B.W., 38, 575–576
Viljoen, Constand, 470
violence-law interconnection, 345–348; and
    power of police and military, 347; and
    township crime, 348
visual arts, 580–584; artists, 580–582;
    photographers, 583; postcolonial, 595–596;
    white-supported art centres for training,
    582–583; women artists, 584, 595–596
vital statistics, 1911–1996, 629t

Voortrekker Monument, 611
Vorster, John, 467

Wage Act of 1925, 226, 239
Wage Board, 538, 540
wages: gold mining, during economic
    stagnation, 522–523; increase in industrial,
    398; institutional wage setting, 529–533;
    living wage, 555; minimum wage, 226, 388,
    411, 531–532, 533–534, 538, 554–555,
    556–557; racial gap, 540; racial gap,
    shrinkage of, 538; wage-setting after
    apartheid, 568–569. *See also* civilised labour
Walker, Eric, 43
Wall, Brenda, 5
Walshe, Peter, 296, 614
Walvis Bay, 113
weaving, 584
welfare: under apartheid, 330–331; exclusion of
    African people from benefits, 534; pillars of in
    modern state, 528
Western Cape: African Methodist Episcopal
    Church in, 147; agriculture in, 120; black
    wage labourers in, 122; coloured franchise in,
    385–386; coloured labour policy in, 336;
    illicit liquor brewing in, 303; soccer in, 402
Western Cape African Congress, 297
wheat, 283–284
White Labourism, 151
white South Africanism, 270–271
white working class, 263–270; mineworkers,
    aboveground, 264–265; mineworkers,
    Africans as semi-skilled workers, 267–268;
    mineworkers, *bywoners*, 264; mineworkers,
    militancy of Afrikaner workers, 268;
    mineworkers, strikes by, 265–266, 268–270;
    mineworkers, underground, 264; railworkers,
    poor white, 263–264; railworkers, strikes by,
    266–267
white-collar employment, increase in, 551
whites: and Afrikaner nationalism, 230; *bywoners*,
    121, 182, 257, 259–261; ethnic identity after
    South African War, 174; and franchise,
    327–328; prosperity under apartheid,
    321–322; public works programmes for, 525,
    534; and state intervention, 527; support for
    democratic transition, 482–483; supremacy
    under apartheid, 321. *See also* poor whites;
    white working class
Wiehahn Commission, 423, 553
Williams, Henry S., 147
Wilmot, A., 21, 22

Wilson, Francis, 602
Wilson, Monica, 59–60, 496–497
witch burnings, 450
witchcraft, 281
Witwatersrand: African National Congress on,
316; and black labour, 132; black spot
clearance in, 386–387; Communist Party on,
301; during Depression, 219; gold discovery
on, 13, 75–76, 83, 85, 131–132; health of
miners at, 170–172; intermarriage on, 264,
290–291; labour issues during 1920s, 218;
labour shortage after South African War,
168–170; and labour strike of 1913,
265–266; and labour strike of 1920,
255–256; and labour strikes during World
War II, 315; and life in mining compound,
374–376; poor whites in, 261–262;
reconstruction after South African War,
167–172; soccer on, 402; technology effect on
mining, 218–219; unfree labour on, 217; and
urbanisation, 261, 290–292; use of Chinese
indentured labourers, 169–170; and white
labour, 132–133; working conditions at, 133
Witwatersrand Mine Employees and Mechanics
Union, 132
Witwatersrand Native Labour Association
(WNLA), 255
Witwatersrand Trades and Labour Council, 179
Witzieshoek, rural rebellion in, 382–383
Witzieshoek Vigilance Association, 383
Wodehouse, Philip E., 29, 78
Wolmarans, A.D.W., 186
Wolpe, Ann Marie, 6
Wolseley, Garnet, 109
women: Afrikaner, 174–175; as artists, 584,
595–596; as beer brewers, 288, 295, 296;
black urban elite at Kimberly, 142; burial
societies formed by, 380; in canning industry,
377–378; and civilised labour, 291; as
domestic workers, 136, 357, 379; educating
as mothers of the nation, 184; and franchise,
178, 193, 238; and Garment Workers' Union,
229; in labour strikes, 296; as landlords, 306;
and land ownership, 381–382; literature for,
187; and non-racial trade movement,
377–378; and politics, 380–381; prayer
meetings of, 379–380; revolving credit
associations formed by, 380; sexual violence
towards, 279; as stand-holders, 295, 306; and
urban family life, 380; and urbanisation, 288,
290–292, 379
Women's Enfranchisement Act, 238

Women's Enfranchisement Association, 238
Women's Enfranchisement League, 193
wool, 72, 283–284
World War I: politics and economics during,
243; relations in region and world, 243; white
South Africans in, 270–271
World War II: economic boom during,
536–537; industrialisation during, 216;
labour strikes on Witwatersrand during, 315;
manufacturing expansion during, 314;
manufacturing sector expansion, 314; politics
and economics during, 244; poor-white
problem during, 314; relations in region and
world, 244; society and culture during,
314–315; and strikes, 315; and urbanisation,
314
writers: Afrikaans, 577–578; exiled, 587;
mission-educated black, 575, 576
Wybergh, Wilfred, 179

Xhalanga, resistance to Rehabilitation in,
394–395
Xhosa, 350; attempt at tribal separation, 394;
British seize territories in Cape Colony from,
69; defeat of, 114; ethnic identity of, 305;
household structure of, 496–497; return of
human remains to, 611, 612
Xuma, A.B., 49–50, 52, 316, 372, 585

Yergan, Max, 52
Youth League (African National Congress), 45,
52–53, 372

Zambia, raids on African National Congress
facilities in, 470
Zibhebhu, 108–109
Zimbabwe, raids on African National Congress
facilities in, 470
Zionist Christian Church (ZCC), 14, 402–403
Zionists, 272, 309–310
Zoutpansberg, 283
Zuid-Afrikaansche Republiek (ZAR), 70, 71;
absentee landowners and, 71; agriculture in,
71; annexation by Britain, 78–80; British
Afrikaners in, 81–82; dynamite concessions,
83, 84; economic policy of British, 70–71;
economic policy of Kruger, 82–84; exclusion
from oversight of diamond fields, 70; failed
insurrection in, 86; hunting rights in, 71;
labour issues in, 72; land ownership and
policy in, 71; merchant-traders in, 70–71;
modernising program of Burgers in, 77–78;

Zuid-Afrikaansche Republiek (ZAR) (*cont.*)
political policy of Kruger in, 84, 85; politics
and policy in, 76–87; return to independence,
80–82; transportation issues in, 70, 76, 77,
83. *See also* Oranje Vrystaat (OVS)

Zuid-Afrikaansche Zustersvereniging (South
African Union of Sisters), 183–184

Zulu, 350

Zulu ethnicity, 298, 299, 305

Zulu kingdom: conquest of, 107; thwarted
invasion of Zuid-Afrikaansche Republiek, 80

Zululand: and Betterment schemes, 382;
chiefdom in, 393–394; and Code of Native
Law of 1878, 104; conquest of, 108–109;
drought in, 280; indirect rule by chiefs in,
275; malaria in, 280; paramountcies in, 279;
transferred by British to Natal, 109

Zuurveld, 69